THE HISTORY OF THE

RHODES TRUST

1902–1999

THE HISTORY
OF THE
RHODES TRUST
1902–1999

EDITED BY

Anthony Kenny

OXFORD
UNIVERSITY PRESS

OXFORD

UNIVERSITY PRESS

Great Clarendon Street, Oxford OX2 6DP

Oxford University Press is a department of the University of Oxford.
It furthers the University's objective of excellence in research, scholarship,
and education by publishing worldwide in

Oxford New York

Athens Auckland Bangkok Bogotá Buenos Aires Cape Town
Chennai Dar es Salaam Delhi Florence Hong Kong Istanbul Karachi
Kolkata Kuala Lumpur Madrid Melbourne Mexico City Mumbai Nairobi
Paris São Paulo Shanghai Singapore Taipei Tokyo Toronto Warsaw
and associated companies in Berlin Ibadan

Oxford is a registered trade mark of Oxford University Press
in the UK and certain other countries

Published in the United States
by Oxford University Press Inc., New York

British Library Cataloguing in Publication Data
Data available

Library of Congress Cataloging in Publication Data

The history of the Rhodes Trust, 1902–1999 / edited by Anthony Kenny.
p. cm.
Includes bibliographical references and index.
1. Rhodes scholarships. 2. University of Oxford—Funds and scholarships.
I. Kenny, Anthony John Patrick. II. Rhodes Trust (Oxford, England)
LF503.F8 H57 2001
378.425′74—dc21 2001016284

ISBN 0–19–920191–9

1 3 5 7 9 10 8 6 4 2

Typeset by Best-set Typesetter Ltd., Hong Kong
Printed and bound in Great Britain by Biddles Ltd
www.biddles.co.uk

Preface

Cecil Rhodes died on 26 March 1902. In 1997 the Rhodes Trustees decided that they wished to commemorate the centenary of their Founder's death by commissioning a history of his Trust during the twentieth century, and they asked me, then Secretary of the Trust, to assemble a team of contributors and to edit the volume. The most important and best known of the Trust's activities is the maintenance of the scholarship scheme described in Rhodes's will, which each year brings students from many different parts of the world to Oxford University. The major part of the present volume tells the story of those scholarships from the viewpoint of the countries to which they are assigned. However, as the reader will discover, Rhodes's Trustees, particularly in the first half of the century, kept alive a number of his other projects, of a political rather than an educational kind, and that story too deserves telling. The history of the scholarships in the two major English-speaking constituencies is told here by academics who, having been themselves Rhodes scholars, went on to be the national representatives of the Trust in their home countries: David Alexander (Tennessee and Christ Church 1954),[1] who for many years combined the presidency of Pomona College with the American secretaryship of the Trust, and John Poynter (Victoria and Magdalen 1951), who while Australian Secretary was a professor of history and a senior administrator in the University of Melbourne. The narrative of the scholarships in Canada and South Africa, both bilingual constituencies for much of their history, is told by two Rhodes scholars who now hold professorships of history in their home country: Doug McCalla (Alberta and Oriel 1965), of Trent University in Ontario, and Tim Nuttall (St Andrew's, Grahamstown, and Pembroke 1982), of the University of Natal. The history of the Rhodes scholarships in Germany has a unique character, and it is narrated here, largely on the basis of original research in German archives, by Richard Sheppard, fellow of Magdalen College and professor of German at Oxford University. Rhodesia, naturally, had a special place of its own in the provisions of Rhodes's will, and the story of what are now the Zimbabwean scholarships is told by David Morgan (Rhodesia and Worcester 1958), the Trust's current representative in Harare. All these accounts have been based on documentation in the relevant constituences as well as on the archives of the Rhodes Trust. I have myself written an account of the smaller constituencies (i.e. those which for some or all of their history elected only a single annual scholar), basing my account on the archives of the Rhodes Trust in Oxford.

The introductory chapter describes the history of the Trust from the point of view of its central administration; in writing it I have drawn not only on the Rhodes House

[1] This is the customary method of identifying Rhodes scholars among the Rhodes community, by giving the name of the constituency from which they were elected, the college which they entered at Oxford, and the year of their taking up their scholarship.

archives but on my experience of ten years as chief executive of the Trust. John Darwin, in a chapter on the Trust in the Age of Empire, singles out a number of the more significant non-scholarship activities of the Trust and evaluates them within a wider context. Finally, Caroline Brown, who, on the advice of the Royal Commission on Historical Manuscripts, was employed by the Trustees from 1998 to 2000 to catalogue their archives, provides for scholars who may be interested in the present history a guide to the material which the Trustees have made available to scholars for research.

I am indebted to all the contributors to this volume who kept close to the demanding schedule I imposed and who tolerated with remarkable patience my dictatorial method of editing. All the contributors are indebted to Caroline Brown for her erudite and imaginative guidance through the mysteries of the Rhodes archives, and to Ralph Evans, the editor of the *Register of Rhodes Scholars 1903–1995*, published by the Trust in 1996, from which we have all drawn information about the biographies of particular scholars. I am also personally greatly indebted to Professor Brian Harrison, Dr Colin Lucas, Mr Richard Symonds, Lord Blake, and Lady Williams for valuable suggestions for the improvement of the text.

A. K.

1 May 2000

Contents

Notes on Contributors

PROFESSOR DAVID ALEXANDER was educated at Southwestern at Memphis (now Rhodes College) 1950–3; Rhodes Scholar, Christ Church, Oxford, 1954–6, D.Phil 1957. Taught Old Testament languages and literature; President of Southwestern at Memphis 1965–9; President of Pomona College, Claremont, California 1969–91. U. S. Secretary for the Rhodes Scholarships 1981–99.

CAROLINE BROWN was from 1997–2000 archivist of the Rhodes Trust.

DR JOHN DARWIN is a contributor to *The History of Oxford University*, Volume VIII. He is a Fellow of Nuffield College, Oxford, and his publications include *Britain and Decolonization* (1988).

SIR ANTHONY KENNY, FBA is Pro-Vice Chancellor of Oxford University. He was a Fellow of Balliol College from 1964–78 and Master from 1978–9. He was Secretary of the Rhodes Trust and Warden of Rhodes House, Oxford 1989–99.

PROFESSOR DOUGLAS McCALLA was educated at Queen's University, Kingston 1960–4, BA 1964; University of Toronto, 1964–5, MA 1965; Rhodes Scholar, Oriel College, Oxford 1965–8, D.Phil 1972. Assistant Professor, Trent University, Ontario, Canada 1968; Associate Professor, 1973; Professor 1981; Departmental Chairman, 1988–92. Author of *The Upper Canada Trade 1934–72* (1979); *Planting the Province: The Economic History of Upper Canada* 1784–1870 (1993).

DAVID MORGAN was educated at the University of Cape Town, 1953–7, LLB 1957; Rhodes Scholar, Worcester College, Oxford 1958–60, BA 1960. He has practised law in Salisbury/Harare since 1964, and has been Secretary for the Rhodes Scholarships in Rhodesia/Zimbabwe since 1976.

PROFESSOR TIM NUTTALL was educated at the University of Natal, 1979–82, BA 1980; Rhodes Scholar, Pembroke College, Oxford 1982–5, BA 1984; D.Phil 1992. Tutor, and later Senior Tutor, in historical studies at the University of Natal from 1985.

PROFESSOR EMERITUS JOHN POYNTER, AO, OBE is Honorary Professorial Fellow, Australian Centre, University of Melbourne. He was educated at Trinity College, University of Melbourne, 1948–50, BA 1950; Rhodes Scholar, Magdalen College, Oxford 1951–3, BA 1953; Dean, Trinity College, University of Melbourne 1953–64, PhD 1962; Senior Lecturer, Reader, then Scott Professor of History 1963–75; Dean of the Faculty of Arts, 1971–2; Vice-Chancellor 1975–90. Australian Secretary for the Rhodes Scholarship, 1974–98. His publications include *Russell Grimwade* (1967); *Society and Pauperism* (1969); *Alfred Felton* (1974).

PROFESSOR RICHARD SHEPPARD is a Fellow of Magdalen College and Professor of German in the University of Oxford.

Abbreviations

AAU	Association of American Universities
AO	*American Oxonian*
BSAC	British South Africa Company
CARS	Canadian Association of Rhodes Scholars
HEW	US Department of Health, Education, and Welfare
MIT	Massachusetts Institute of Technology
NAC	National Archives of Canada
RH	Rhodes House, Oxford
RT	Rhodes Trust Archives
RTA	Rhodes Trust Archives, American Files
RTC	Rhodes Trust Archives, Canadian Files
RTF	Rhodes Trust, Numbered Files
RTM	Rhodes Trust Minutes
RTPF	Rhodes Trust Personal Files
RTR	Rhodes Trust, Numbered Reports to Trustees
RTSA	Rhodes Trust South Africa
SCRF	Scholarship Capital Reserve Fund
SF	Scholarship Fund
UCT	University of Cape Town

Abbreviations for German archives will be found at the beginning of Chapter 6.

I

The Rhodes Trust and its Administration

ANTHONY KENNY

The Founder's Estate

The will of Cecil Rhodes is principally remembered for the scheme which it established to bring scholars from the British Empire and the United States to study in England. Candidates for Rhodes scholarships, he laid down, were to be selected on the basis of qualities of character as well as of intellect. His aim was to provide future leaders of the English-speaking world with an education which would broaden their views and develop their abilities. He chose to endow these scholarships at Oxford University rather than elsewhere in the United Kingdom because he believed that its residential colleges provided an environment specially conducive to personal development. The Rhodes scholarships thus established have provided Cecil Rhodes's most enduring monument.[1]

However, there is much in Rhodes's will besides the scholarship scheme, and in the early years the Trustees he appointed spent most of their time considering these other matters: bequests to individuals, the management of various estates and enterprises in South Africa and in England, and the pursuit of the political causes with which he had been identified.

The first meeting of the Trustees was held on 5 May 1902, at 38 Berkeley Square, the London residence of Lord Rosebery, the liberal imperialist who, when Prime Minister, had made Rhodes a Privy Counsellor. Rosebery was the senior of the seven Trustees named by Rhodes in his will. Five of the others were present. There was Dr Leander Starr Jameson, Rhodes's friend and physician who had administered Mashonaland and Matabeleland in the 1890s until his illegal invasion of the Transvaal had led to his imprisonment in Holloway, but who was now, on the rebound, MP for Kimberley in the Cape Parliament, and Rhodes's successor as leader of the Progressive Party. There was also Earl Grey, who had been on the board of Rhodes's chartered British South Africa Company since 1889 and who had succeeded Jameson in the administration of Rhodesia. There were two Trustees with close links to De Beers, Rhodes's diamond company: Alfred Beit, who had been, like Rhodes, a life governor of the company, and Sir Lewis Michell, its

---

[1] The will was published in *The Last Will and Testament of Cecil John Rhodes, with Elucidatory Notes*, ed. W. T. Stead (London: *Review of Reviews* Office 1902). It was republished by the Rhodes Trust in 1928, printed by Oxford University Press.

present chairman, who had until recently been Rhodes's banker in Cape Town. Both of these men were also directors of the British South Africa Company. Finally, there was Bouchier Hawksley, solicitor to Rhodes and Jameson, who had come into the public eye during the Westminster inquiry into the Raid. The one missing Trustee was Alfred Milner, High Commissioner in South Africa, who in that very month signed the Treaty of Vereeniging which brought to an end the Anglo-Boer War.[2]

In the first decade of the Trust's existence it was to be very rare for such a full quorum to meet. Michell and Jameson were resident in South Africa, and so, for much of the time, was Beit. From 1904 to 1911 Grey, initially a regular attender, resided in Canada as Governor General. It was left to Rosebery and Hawksley to provide continuity for the Trustees' meetings. By 1908 attendance had become so sparse that it was decided that routine business of the Trust could be done even if only a single Trustee was present (RTM 859).

An office of the Trust was established in London, first in Temple Chambers (RTM 44, 57, 152), then, from 1905, on the second floor of Seymour House, 17 Waterloo Place (RTM 243, 261).[3] The office was run by Charles Boyd, assisted until 1905 by Douglas Brodie (RTM 15, 44, 291). Coopers were appointed as the Trust's accountants, and they and their successors have audited the accounts ever since; as solicitors the Trustees appointed Hawksley's firm—the ancestor of Clifford Chance, which still acts for the Trust (RTM 11–12).

The estate which the Trustees were to manage was vast. Farmland at Inyanga (north of Salisbury) and in the Matopos mountains (near Bulawayo) had been left for the Trustees to 'cultivate for the instruction of the people of Rhodesia'. In South Africa too, in addition to shareholdings in De Beers and other mining companies, there were substantial interests in experimental agricultural ventures, notably the R.B. and B. farming syndicate and the Rhodes Fruit Farms around Boschendal. More important was the Smartt Syndicate, which owned great tracts of farmland in Bechuanaland and near Britstown in the Northern Cape.[4] The finest of Rhodes's estates was his own residence at Groote Schuur, in a magnificent mountain setting outside Cape Town. This, according to the will, was to be retained as a residence for the Prime Minister of South Africa once the several states had been federated.

[2] There are entries in the *DNB* for all the original Trustees except Hawksley. Milner had been named in a codicil to the will, but did not take up his trusteeship until his return from South Africa. W. T. Stead, the former editor of the *Pall Mall Gazette*, was named as a Trustee in the original will, but struck out in a codicil on the grounds of his 'extraordinary eccentricity'. This may have had something to do with Stead's interest in psychical research. Some time after 1903 the secretaries of the Trust were taken by him to a seance in which the medium announced, on behalf of the dead Rhodes, that his one regret was that he had not followed the advice of his greatest friend Stead. (Lady Butterworth to Lord Elton, 1 Jan. 1959, RTF 1451.) Stead died on the *Titanic* in 1912.

[3] One of the secretaries of the Trust used to boast that his office was at the centre of the Empire 'in sight alike of Big Ben and the National Gallery'. (Kerr, cited in J. R. M. Butler, *Lord Lothian* (London: Macmillan, 1960), 127.)

[4] The R.B. and B. syndicate had been set up by Rhodes, Beit, and Sir Abe Bailey, a mining financier and racehorse breeder; the Smartt Syndicate was again a project of Rhodes and Beit, which had been originally promoted in 1895 by Dr Thomas Smartt, an Irish surgeon who was a substantial stockfarmer in the Britstown district and became Colonial Secretary of the Cape in 1896–8 (RTF 1854).

The Rhodesian estates were managed by James McDonald, who had been Rhodes's comrade at the great Matabele Indaba, assisted by F. E. Weinholt who managed the Inyanga farms (RTM 272). McDonald was an energetic and independent administrator, who often paid little attention to the Trustees' attempts to keep his expenditure within the annual budget of £6,000 authorized by the will (RTM 305, 422). From time to time he attended meetings in London to report to the Trustees and be rebuked for over-spending on breeding stock or giving too favourable leases (RTM 499). In accordance with clause 8 of the will, the Trustees built a railway line from Bulawayo to Westacre, 'in order that the people of Bulawayo may enjoy the glory of the Matoppos from Saturday to Monday' (RTM 460).

The South African estates rarely produced any income for the Trust; they had been acquired by Rhodes for research and training purposes rather than as investments. The Rhodes Fruit Farms eventually led to substantial exports of citrus fruits and wine, and they won medals at the Royal Horticultural Show in London in 1906, but owing to inef-ficient marketing they showed little return. The Smartt Syndicate over the years sucked in substantial sums of the Trust's capital, beginning with an investment of £20,000 in 1902 (RTM, 46).[5] Reports monitoring the South African ventures were sent regularly to London, at first monthly by Michell or his assistant Bertram Woods (RTM 65, 82, 273) and later by E. R. Syfret (RTM 381).

Besides the African holdings, there was substantial real property in England to be managed: many streets of suburban houses in Hackney, known as the Dalston estate (RTM 54), and ample acres in Suffolk at Dalham whose purchase was still incomplete at Rhodes's death.[6] The Trustees left it to Hawksley to manage these assets from his office in Mincing Lane. He was, in the words of a colleague, 'the working Trustee of that time'.[7]

Rhodes had spoken to more than one of his Trustees of the importance he attached to bringing British settlers to Southern Africa, particularly women. (RTM 19–20, 42, 48).[8] From the outset the Trustees carried out his wishes loyally. Beit, Jameson, and Michell were given £10,000 to make loans to immigrants. The Trustees made grants to the Rhodesian committee of the South African Colonization Society, for whom they purchased a hostel (RTM 98, 107). They also supported a grant to a women's hostel in Kimberley, and in Cape Town built and partly maintained the hostel in Mowbray, which was named after the Society's patron Princess Christian (RTM 99, 902). In 1906 £1,000 was granted towards the building of another hostel in Port Elizabeth (RTM 524). The Trustees also raised with the Colonial Secretary, Joseph Chamberlain, and with Dr Barnardo, the possibility of encouraging emigration by children (RTM 50, 64, 67, 77, 166).

[5] Other largely unprofitable South African holdings were in the Turffontein estates (RTM 337, 536), the Klippoortje estates and tramway company (RTM 386, 437, 580), and the La Rochelle syndicate (RTM 724).
[6] In both of these estates members of Rhodes's family held life interests (RTM 24, 54–5, 1363). The Dalston estate was mortaged for £80,000.
[7] Lady Butterworth to Lord Elton, 1 Jan. 1959, RTF 1451.
[8] Hawksley to Michell, 9 Jan. 1904; Rhodes to Grey, 25 July 1901.

In 1904 Rosebery got his fellow Trustees to minute that while Rhodes benefactions were available for the Empire at large, 'after the scholarships, the strong intention and wish of Mr Rhodes was to further the settlement of people of British race in south Africa' (RTM 216). As the decade progressed the Trust made grants and guarantees to British settlers in the Orange River Colony and the Transvaal (RTM 736). A major purpose of the Smartt Syndicate irrigation scheme was to encourage English settlement into a pre-dominantly Dutch area. Settlement schemes of various kinds continued to be a preoc-cupation of the Trust right up until the 1950s.

In South Africa the Trustees were also active in party politics. Jameson was authorized to arrange payments for political purposes 'in continuance and on the same scale as hith-erto made by Mr Rhodes'. In 1903, in the run-up to the Cape elections, the Trust under-wrote £20,000 for the expenses of the Progressive Party.[9] They must have been gratified when the party was victorious and Jameson became Prime Minister of the Colony.[10] He moved into Groote Schuur as the Trust's tenant, at a rent of £800 a year.[11]

There were other ideas which the Founder had put forward for spending the will funds which the Trustees wisely left unfulfilled. They did not, as Rhodes had suggested to Grey and Hawksley, found an imperial party in the House of Commons; and they did not fund selected former scholars to travel as celibate imperial missionaries to different parts of the world.[12]

The Rhodes Scholarships

Despite the preoccupations of the estate, the Trustees lost no time in setting up the schol-arships. At their first meeting they resolved to arrange for the students from the USA, the colonies, and Germany to go into residence in October 1903. In summer 1902 they appointed G. P. Parkin, the Principal of Upper Canada College, Toronto, an apostle of imperial federation, to set up the scholarship system (RTM 41, 45, 58, 66).[13]

Rhodes's will provided for fifty-two scholarships each year. Twenty scholarships ('the Colonial Scholarships') were for countries then forming part of the British Empire: two for Canada (one each for Ontario and Quebec), six for Australia (one for each colony or state), five for South Africa (one each for Natal and for four named schools in the Cape), three for Rhodesia, and one each for New Zealand, Newfoundland, Bermuda, and Jamaica. Thirty-two scholarships were for the United States: two every three years for each of the then States of the Union. In a codicil to his will, added in the belief that the

---

[9] Hawksley to Michell, 17 Oct. 1903. The Trust maintained an ample political account in Cape Town, from which payments were made on Jameson's instructions, half of each political contribution being matched by Beit (RTF 1038).

[10] Michell became minister without portfolio.

[11] RTM 171. The upkeep of Groote Schuur cost £4,624 annually. Lady Salisbury remarked to Boyd that it was much more expensive than Hatfield; £1,500 per annum should have been enough.

[12] Rhodes to Grey, 25 Aug. 1901; Rhodes to Hawksley, July 1899. The missionaries, Rhodes said, 'would be better unmarried as the consideration of babies and other domestic agenda generally destroys higher thought. Please understand I am in no sense a woman hater but this particular business is better untram-melled with material thought.'

[13] For Parkin's previous career, see McCalla, below p. 204. He was paid £2,000 per annum (RTM 169).

Kaiser had made instruction in English compulsory in German schools, Rhodes added five annual German scholarships. 'The object', he said, 'is that an understanding between the three great powers will render war impossible and educational relations make the strongest tie.'

Parkin set about his task with enthusiasm, touring the USA and Canada in 1902–3, and South Africa later in 1903, but he was unable to meet the Trustees' ambitious timetable. Only twelve scholars (all from Germany and Southern Africa) were able to come into residence in 1903; it was not until 1904 that a full complement of seventy-two arrived.[14] The system of selection set up by Parkin was approved by the Trustees in 1903; one of his principal achievements was to persuade them to increase the number of scholarships for Canada from two to eight (RTM 80). In most constituencies, in these first years, selection was closely tied to educational institutions in the countries of origin. In Rhodesia, however, whose scholarships were given pride of place in the will, and where there were no universities, the scholars were for many years chosen by the Trustees themselves, after consulting the Director of Education (RTM 78). There was often difficulty in assessing the merits of candidates pressed upon them by Rhodesian administrators anxious to be relieved of the cost of their sons' education (RTM 235, 298, 675, 1184). Some who were declared ineligible as scholars, on grounds of inadequate domicile, were given grants to be educated at Oxford outside the scholarship scheme.[15] The German scholarships, which lasted two years instead of three, were allotted to candidates by the Kaiser himself (RTM 228).[16] In many parts of the world candidates had to pass a qualifying examination, issued from Oxford by the examination Delegacy (RTM 163). This exempted them from the first of the three examinations required for an Oxford BA, known as Responsions.[17]

Early in 1903, Francis Wylie, a fellow of Brasenose currently serving as proctor, was appointed as the Trust's resident agent in Oxford 'for all purposes connected with the scholarships' (RTM 92, 97, 101). He was in post in time to welcome the first scholars in 1903 and in 1904 he was given a residence in South Parks Road (RTM 175).[18] For the next decade routine issues concerning the scholarships were dealt with by a triumvirate consisting of Parkin, who dealt with the countries of origin, Wylie, who dealt with matters

[14] Details of Parkin's visits to individual constituencies are found below, in Alexander, pp. 105–10, McCalla, pp. 204–10, Nuttall, p. 259, and Kenny, p. 419. Parkin describes the setting up of the international system in his book *The Rhodes Scholarships* (Boston: Houghton Mifflin, 1912) and the story is told again in *The First Fifty Years of the Rhodes Trust and the Rhodes Scholarships, 1903–1953* (Oxford: Basil Blackwell, 1955), the commemorative history edited by Lord Elton.

[15] See Morgan, below p. 410.

[16] See Sheppard, below pp. 357–9.

[17] Responsions consisted of an elementary test in Greek, Latin, and mathematics. The Rhodes examination was modelled on it; a special examination 'in lieu of Responsions' had been available for British schoolboys to take in the September before their first term since 1881. Many schoolboys coming up to Oxford were exempted from Responsions in virtue of having passed school examinations of higher standard. M. G. Brock and M. C. Curthoys (eds.), *The History of the University of Oxford*, vi (Oxford: Clarendon Press, 1997), 356. Schoolboys from the Cape often found it difficult to pass Responsions when they reached Oxford.

[18] His salary was fixed at £1,000 per annum, with an entertainment allowance of £250 (RTM 233); in 1910 he was given a full-time secretary (RTM 1322).

in Oxford, and the London Secretary of the Trust reporting in practice to Hawksley.[19]
Each scholar was paid £75 per term in advance, out of which he had to pay his own
battels and fees (RTM 126).

The progress of scholars was carefully monitored. From time to time individuals mis-
behaved and complaints were received from their colleges: the Trustees debated in each
case whether to terminate or suspend a scholarship, or merely to impose a fine (RTM
311, 430, 544, 517, 700, 1169). In 1908 two early German scholars were reported for idle-
ness to the Kaiser; this was regarded as sufficient punishment without any diminution
of stipend (RTM 916). Each university distinction won by a scholar was recorded with
satisfaction by the Trustees, one of the first of a long series being the Vinerian and Eldon
prizes won in 1906 by John Behan (Victoria and Hertford 1904) (RTM 531)—honours
which he was to follow up, in 1909, by becoming the first scholar elected to an Oxford
fellowship.[20]

Several issues which were to be matters of concern throughout the century were already
raised in these early years. What were the age limits for candidates? Commonly 19 to 24,
with some regional variation (RTM 264). Did candidates need to know Greek to be
elected? Not necessarily, but scholars once elected must get it up before coming to Oxford
(RTM 451).[21] Could scholars incapacitated for athletics be elected? Yes (RTM 852).
Could scholarships be extended for a fourth year? No (RTM 368, 570). Were women to
be eligible for scholarships? No: a petition from Lady Margaret Hall was turned down
in May 1903 (RTM 116). Could there be scholarships outside the USA and the Commonwealth? In 1907 proposals for Hawaiian and Japanese scholarships were negatived
(RTM 566).

Most difficult of all was the question whether scholarships could be awarded to blacks.
This was first addressed by Parkin during his tour of the USA. His initial attitude, as he
reported to the Trustees, was that 'The terms of the will, as well as my own inclination,
make me anxious to give every possible opportunity that the white man has to the
black.'[22] He was soon made aware, however, of the strength of feeling in the South. President Venables of the University of North Carolina claimed that if blacks were admitted
to the examination, white candidates would refuse to appear and the system would collapse. The Trustees discussed the issue several times in the first year of the scholarship
(RTM 188, 194, 224); they declined to regard the issue as one of principle. 'While recognizing with you', they told Parkin, 'that the attitude of President Venables is scarcely
consistent with the strict terms of the will the Trustees feel that the Question is one which
the selective committees must be left to fight out with the Negro colleges.'[23]

In 1907 the first black scholar was elected in the USA, Alain Le Roy Locke of
Pennsylvania. Parkin professed himself delighted, but Wylie was aghast: the new scholar

---

[19] One of the secretaries of the Trust remembered that Hawksley 'was at work from eight in the
morning till late at night and the one Trustee of my day who spared enough time to Scholarship matters
to even satisfy Dr Parkin'. Lady Butterworth to Elton, 1 Jan. 1959.

[20] On Behan, see Poynter, below pp. 320–1.

[21] See Alexander, below pp. 114–5.

[22] Memo of June 1903, RTF 1122.

[23] Boyd to Parkin, 21 Nov. 1904, RTF 1122. See Alexander, below pp. 108 ff.

would be difficult to place in a college, particularly if there were white southerners in residence.[24] American scholars in Oxford sent a delegation to wait on the Trustees to protest. They were sympathetically received by Milner and Hawksley, but the Trustees refused to interfere with the choice of the Pennsylvania committee, and confirmed Locke's election.[25] Parkin was told, however, to see what could be done to prevent selection committees making appointments in conflict with feeling in the southern states (RTM 630).

Rosebery, who had declined to meet the scholars' delegation, wrote as follows.

1. I do *not* rejoice at the election of the negro scholar. We do not realise here the strength of the feeling in America against black blood. 2. But I do not think that the terms of Rhodes' will give us a leg to stand on in refusing him. The word 'race' seems conclusive. Moreover, our general policy of strictly respecting local arrangements tends in the same direction.[26]

Other Trustees, who knew Rhodes better, took a different view of the intention of the word 'race' in clause 24 of the Will. But henceforth Rosebery's interpretation was applied in every official decision of the Trust.[27]

No constituency in the USA again elected a black until 1963. But in 1910 Jamaica elected a coloured scholar, and in 1908 a scholar was elected in Queensland who had one parent from Tobago. Once again, the Trustees confirmed the elections (RTM 1256).[28]

Oxford and the Trust

In his will Rhodes had left £100,000 to his old college Oriel, partly for new buildings, and partly to subsidize fellows' income and 'to maintain the dignity and comfort of the High Table'.[29] Others in Oxford spotted the opportunity for benefactions. President Warren of Magdalen asked the Trust to establish a number of professorships (RTM 102). He was turned down by the Trustees, Lord Grey in particular being firmly of the opinion that the Trust should not endow the University. However it was agreed towards the end of 1904 to give £200 for five years to subsidize a University lecturer in pathology, a grant which continued into the 1920s (RTM 217, 1732). This exceptional contribution was perhaps influenced by clause 16 of Rhodes's will which suggested that Oxford should 'try and extend its scope so as if possible to make its medical

[24] Wylie to Boyd, 14 Mar. 1907, RTF 1122. See Alexander, below p. 110.

[25] Locke had a difficult time in Oxford: see Alexander, below p. 112.

[26] Rhodes to Boyd, 22 Mar. 1907, RTF 1122.

[27] Boyd wrote to Hawksley, on receipt of Rosebery's letter (20 Mar. 1907), 'In section 24 of the Will, did the Testator mean no distinction of race, to mean no distinction of colour? had he not Dutch, English, Jew, and the rest in his mind?' To Wylie, Boyd reported (6 Apr. 1907), 'Jameson, in disagreement with Hawksley, is quite clear that Mr Rhodes did not mean to include black men. "He would turn in his grave to think of it"' (RT 1122). Lady Butterworth later remembered Hawksley as being of the same mind as Jameson (Butterworth to Elton, 1 Jan. 1959, RTF 1451).

[28] See Kenny and Poynter, below, pp. 437 and 323–4. Wylie reported in 1911 that these two scholars were having a better time in Oxford than Locke had, partly because they were good athletes (RTF 1122).

[29] He added, 'As the College authorities live secluded from the world and so are like children as to commercial matters I would advise them to consult my Trustees as to the investment of these various funds.'

school at least as good as that at the University of Edinburgh'.[30] It was not only to Oxford, however, that medical grants were made: in 1905 the same sum was given for five years to the London School of Tropical Medicine (RTM 238). In 1908 for the first time the Trustees moved beyond the medical sphere: a grant of £200 for five years, later renewed, was made in support of a readership in English law at Oxford (RTM 945, 2059). From 1910 to 1920 grants were made for lectures in Oxford by American professors on topics in American history and politics (RTM 1265, 1985).[31] The first grant to Oxford sport was in 1911 when £50 was voted towards the erection of kennels for the University drag hounds (RTM 23 Jan. 1911).

In 1907 a memorial tablet to Rhodes was unveiled in the examination schools, at which Rosebery gave an address which was long remembered (RTM 765).

For Union and Empire

Alfred Beit often matched from his own funds benefactions to which he was a party as a Rhodes Trustee. In the last year of his life he founded the professorship in colonial history at Oxford which still bears his name. His death in 1906 was much mourned by his fellow Trustees (RTM 457), but the vast estate which he left for charitable purposes in Rhodesia freed the Rhodes Trust to concentrate on the support of causes in South Africa. More than £16,000 was paid in death duties by the Rhodes Trust, on the grounds that the deceased's seventh share in the residuary estate accrued to the other joint tenants (RTM 707). But the death simultaneously brought a much larger sum within the Trustees' control: 26,667 deferred De Beers shares were handed to the Trust in virtue of an agreement reached between Beit and Rhodes in 1898.[32] By agreement with Beit's executors the shares were handed over to a distinct but overlapping group, consisting of Milner, Michell, and Hawksley, plus Sir Julius Wernher, a close colleague of both Rhodes and Beit in the diamond business. The Rhodes Trustees believed that they were setting up a separate trust to administer this 'Rhodes–Beit Share Fund' for public and political purposes in South Africa. From the papers of Milner, who was one of the Trustees of this sub-trust, it appears that most of the income on these shares went to Progressive Party politicians in the Cape and Transvaal, in particular for election expenses in 1910.[33] However, because the Rhodes Trustees believed themselves to have no

---

[30] From 1914 the readership in pharmacology also was subsidized (RTM 1963).

[31] Between 1913 and 1916 grants were made to London University for lectureships in colonial law and the promotion of imperial studies (RTM 1830, 1890).

[32] Rhodes and Beit had been life governors of De Beers Consolidated Mines Ltd., and in 1898 they bought out the other governors' rights, which were commuted in 1901 for 160,000 deferred shares of £2 10s. The agreement was that if Rhodes died during Beit's lifetime, one-third would be held by Rhodes's executors for public purposes, one-third by Rhodes's residuary estate, and one-third by Beit. A single non-transferable share certificate was issued in the name of Beit. When Rhodes died no British estate duty was paid, and the shares were listed in the books 1903–6 as an asset reversionary on the death of Beit. When Beit died, his executors, for reasons which remain mysterious, handed over not two-thirds, but one-sixth of the shares (Lothian memorandum of 1933, RTF 2709).

[33] See F. Madden and D. K. Fieldhouse (eds.), *Oxford and the Idea of Commonwealth* (London: Croom Helm, 1982), 87.

interest in the fund, its activities were not reported to them; and by the time the Rhodes–Beit Share Fund began to be reincorporated in the Rhodes Trust in the 1920s the then Trustees themselves seem to have been in the dark about the creation and history of the fund.

During his lifetime, Beit had played a leading part in the management of the Rhodes Trust's South African assets. After his death the Trust's affairs were handled by a financial committee consisting of Milner, Hawksley, and Michell, in whose names the Trust's portfolio was now registered (RTM 549). One of the first acts of the new committee was to commence a series of substantial reductions in De Beers holdings (RTM 491, 989). Milner, since his return in 1905, had been the dominant Trustee, though Rosebery continued as chairman until 1917.

In 1907 the Trustees funded the first of a number of initiatives designed to strengthen the attachment of colonies and dominions to the mother country. At the suggestion of Lord Grey an award of £1,000 a year for three years was made to the Canadian humorist Stephen Leacock, a professor of politics at McGill, to 'secure his exclusive services for Imperial missionary work' (RTM 606, 647). Whatever the Trustees' precise expectations, Leacock's lecture tour did not come up to them, and their minutes make clear that they did not feel they had received value for money (RTM 952).

Southern African Ventures

South Africa continued to be the focus of the Trust's attention. Throughout the decade appeals for ecclesiastical and educational causes poured in, strongly supported by Michell. The one most warmly received was for the foundation of Rhodes University College in Grahamstown, a pet project of Jameson's. An endowment of £60,000 was necessary; the Trustees gave £10,000 outright, and earmarked the income of £50,000 worth of De Beers shares to support chairs in Latin, Greek, and mathematics.[34] In the years before the setting up of the Union, libraries and clubs in Umtali, Bulawayo, Livingstone, Kimberley, and Cape Town were more successful than schools in attracting grants from the Trust.

In Rhodesia the Trustees assisted several experimental ventures. A loan was made to start up a cheese factory (RTM 905); £7,000 was lent to the Matabele Central Estates Committee, on the recommendation of Milner and Hawksley (RTM 715).[35] McDonald continued his intrepid overspending at Inyanga, buying bulls and transport mules, building cottages, and constructing bridges and weirs (RTM 839, 1004). The Trust's two hotels in the Matopos never seemed profitable. However, when Michell visited Inyanga and the Matopos in 1908 he reported back favourably on the condition of the estates (RTM 896). With the Trustees' approval, McDonald wrote a book of *Hints to South African Farmers* which was widely distributed and went into several editions (RTM 1040, 1083, 1796).

[34] Michell to Boyd, 13 Sept., 1 Dec. 1903; Jameson to Boyd, undated, 1903; RTF 2009.
[35] Rosebery thought this imprudent, and minuted his dissent. But the loan was in the end repaid (RTM 1228).

Correspondence continued between Salisbury and London about candidates for the Rhodesian scholarship. In 1908 the secretary of the British South Africa Company inquired about the eligibility of C. N. Lobengula, the son of the Matabele King pursued to death by the Company's armies. Certainly the young man was eligible, the Trustees said, provided he could pass Responsions—which he did not, in the event, attempt (RTM 857).

In South Africa, the Trustees became restive about some of Rhodes's experimental ventures. In 1908 they took the first steps towards selling to Abe Bailey their interest in the RB and B. syndicate, steps which did not reach fruition until 1914 (RTM 890). The history of the Smartt Syndicate was one of repeated qualms about its viability, followed by further spasms of investment (RTM 1859). Between 1907 and 1912 a further £67,500 was poured into it, towards the construction of a dam to improve the Britstown estates.[36] The Fruit Farms at last began to show a profit: in the financial year ending in 1909, after an initial deficit of £3,000 in three months, they showed an overall profit of £2,187 (RTM 1034). In 1913 it was resolved to sell the substantial holdings in the La Rochelle syndicate and the Turffontein estates (RTM 1754). New investment in South Africa was very rare. In 1909 Rhodes's former agent, Dr Rutherfoord Harris, secured the involvement of the Trustees in the flotation of a mining company on the Klippoortje estate in Johannesburg, but these holdings were soon sold (RTM 966, 1112). The Trustees began to diversify their holdings, investing outside South Africa not only in consols, as instructed in Rhodes's will, but in firms around the world such as Bombay Electric Supply; Chicago, Milwaukee, and St Paul Railways; Canadian Northern Railways; and Utah Gas and Coke (RTM 1078, 1262).

On the political front the Trustees began to take an interest in the prospect of South African federation. They were encouraged to do so by Lionel Curtis, Patrick Duncan, and Geoffrey Robinson, all of whom had worked for Milner in South Africa as members of his 'Kindergarten' of brilliant young Oxford graduates. In 1906, in great secrecy, the Trustees agreed to give £1,000 to support Curtis as the full-time organizing secretary of a group to examine the problems involved in South African federation and the preparation of a draft constitution. The blueprint for federation which was the outcome of this was handed over to the High Commissioner in South Africa, who published it under his own name so that it is known to history as the 'Selborne Memorandum'. 'It is of course very important', Milner wrote, 'that the act of the Rhodes Trustees having subventioned the enterprise should, if possible, never become public.'[37] A further grant of £1,000 was approved in February 1908 'for a purpose recommended strongly by Lord Milner and Dr Jameson, and referred to in Mr Lionel Curtis's letter to the Secretary of the 22nd of November 1907' (RTM 818). The project thus obliquely described was the subsidizing of a journal to promote federation.[38]

---

[36] Michell was a director of the syndicate, but often talked of resignation (RTM 1839). In 1916 Milner wrote, 'I have always *hated* that enterprise' (Milner to Gilmour, RTF 1854).

[37] Milner to Boyd, 21 Sept. 1906; RTF 1210.

[38] See Curtis to Duncan, 15 Nov. 1907, Jameson to Milner, 30 Dec. 1907, and Rosebery to Boyd, 18 Nov. 1908; RTF 1210.

The Union of South Africa

By 1909 a Union of South Africa was obviously close, but it was clear that the Union would not include Rhodesia. The Trustees, visited briefly by Jameson who was playing a large part in the National Convention to set up the Union, discussed what should happen to Groote Schuur under the new dispensation. Would the creation of the Union of South Africa count as the federation mentioned in the will?[39] They decided that the estate should indeed be transferred to the new government, but not until 'the position had been regularised by the passing of an act of the Union Government, relieving them of their trust and safeguarding their conditions' (RTM 1000, 1114).

Union was achieved in 1910, and General Botha became the first Prime Minister of the Union, with Jameson as leader of the opposition. A draft bill on Groote Schuur was sent to the Trustees in July 1910, and they added a provision permitting the erection of university buildings (RTM 1279). At the end of the year the new Prime Minister took over Groote Schuur, and the Union Parliament passed the Rhodes Estate Devolution Act, indemnifying the Trustees and relieving them of all responsibility for the estate in return for a grant of £23,000 (1331, 1348).[40]

In the years after Union the Trustees offered considerable support to education in South Africa, whether by grant, loan, or guarantee. Between 1911 and 1913 Bishops school in Cape Town and St Andrew's in Grahamstown, two of the schools assigned scholarships in Rhodes's will, received loans and grants of over £10,000 (RTM 1353), and in 1914 £1,000 was given to St John's College, Johannesburg (RTM 1353, 1911). In 1911 £1,000 was offered to a scheme for a 'South African Native College'.[41]

The Scholarship Fund

In the new decade the Trustees took a keen interest in details of the international scholarship programme, such as the constitution of selection committees and the wording of the annual memoranda setting out conditions of eligibility. They dealt with complaints made against the choices of particular selection committees, whether on grounds of linguistic bias in Quebec (RTM 1203) or religious bias in Prince Edward Island (RTM 1042, 1173).[42] They encouraged selection committees to treat Greekless candidates on equal terms with classicists (RTM 980, 1232). They gave rulings on age limits in different constituencies, and spelt out the interpretation of the requirement that scholars should be fond of and successful in manly outdoor sports. They considered, and usually

[39] When Union was achieved, Milner deprecated the idea that it was the realization of Rhodes's aims. 'In so far as South Africa is one country under the British Flag, that is no doubt true. But that is pretty nearly all, in my opinion, which Rhodes, or at least *Rhodes as I knew him*, would find to rejoice at in the actual turn which things have taken in South Africa at the present time.' Milner to Parkin, 21 June 1912; RTF 2109.

[40] The Trustees for some years continued to pay for the upkeep of the Woolsack, the house on the estate which Rhodes had assigned for life to Rudyard Kipling (RTM 1646, 1693).

[41] Bursaries, prizes, and trophies were also offered to schools in Rhodesia (RTM 1805).

[42] See McCalla, below p. 206.

refused, proposals for special grants, outside the normal system, to enable study at Oxford.[43]

Decisions about the postponement, suspension, and termination of scholarships were initiated by Wylie and confirmed by the Trustees.[44] Residence in Oxford by scholars was very strictly enforced: it took a special resolution of the body of Trustees for a scholar to be paid a full stipend if he had missed one day of term (RTM 1269). A proposal was made, but never carried out, that the Trustees should assemble a library of all books written by scholars.[45]

As the will had prescribed, the Trustees gave an annual dinner for scholars, usually at Oxford in the Randolph Hotel, or the Town Hall, or the new Masonic Centre. Grandees were invited and, in addition to the toast to the Founder and the three loyal toasts (to the King, the President, and the Kaiser), there might be as many as seven speeches. In 1914, for instance, the US Ambassador was then to propose 'Prosperity to the Rhodes Scholars', and a Liberal peer responded with a toast to 'The Hundred Years of Peace' between the USA and the UK. Rosebery used to engage a special train to return the guests to London at a late hour.[46]

The Trustees had been instructed by clause 35 of the will to set apart a scholarship fund sufficient to pay the scholarships and leave £1,000 a year over. The foundation of the scholarships was obviously a charitable purpose in English law, but the Rhodes Trust itself was not a charity. Many of the purposes of the will were not charitable, and the individual Trustees were not only Trustees but also residuary legatees. The Trustees from the outset treated the entire gift as a trust, but they would have been within their legal rights in diverting substantial sums to their individual benefit.[47] Accordingly death duties were payable, not only on Rhodes's own estate[48] but also on the death of each successive Trustee. It was early resolved that the Trust would pay these duties out of the residuary estate (RTM 33). However, during the first decade of the Trust Beit was the only Trustee to die, and it was not until 1910 that the Trustees began to consider setting up separate charitable funds

[43] Thus in 1911 a Cingalese and an Iroquois were refused such grants (RTM 1392, 1403) though in 1912 an Iroquois was given a grant to complete a course at McGill (RTM 1807).

[44] In 1914, Wylie was authorized to allow Wilder Penfield to postpone coming up to Oxford in order to coach the Princeton football team. 'At Princeton', the Trustees minuted, 'coaching a football team appears to be an honour much thought of' (RTM 1931).

[45] The Secretary started the collection with a circular of 4 Oct. 1910. Such books as were collected in Seymour House were transferred to the Warden's Lodgings in 1938, and were dispersed among the general collections in Rhodes House Library in 1950 (RTF 1717).

[46] Lady Butterworth to Lord Elton, 1 Jan. 1959. She reports that 'many scholars from far distances had no experience of the potency of champagne and other wines and liqueurs thereafter, with the resulting failure of attention to Speeches and most obvious illness'. RTF 1451.

[47] Michell once complained that everyone believed that the will had made each Trustee very rich. 'Although we are the legal possessors of the residuary funds we have never yet touched a penny of the money. For my part my trusteeship has been a sheer & serious loss to me.' Michell to Parkin, 25 Dec. 1916; RTM 1682.

[48] As late as 1910 death duties were still being claimed by the British Inland Revenue on the transfer of De Beers shares at Rhodes's death. The Trustees resisted this, but agreed to pay nearly £10,000 on Rhodes's English investments, particularly the Dalham estate (RTM 1246).

which would not attract estate duty (RTM 1276).[49] But Hawksley was reluctant to set up such a fund and it was not until after he died himself in 1916, at a time when the war had taken death duties to a punitive level, that the scholarship trust came into being.[50]

The Founder's Memory

In 1910 Michell produced a two-volume life of Rhodes. The Trustees minuted that it was not to be taken as an official publication of the Trust (RTM 1277). Two of Rhodes's secretaries also had ambitions as biographers. Gordon Le Sueur was not regarded by the Trustees as reliable, and his notes for Rhodes's life were bought up for £500 in 1907 (RTM 664, 714). He went ahead with his plans, and in 1913 Lord Grey suggested that in order to stop publication the rights should be purchased. But the Trustees declined to pay twice for the same work, and *Cecil Rhodes: The Man and his Work* appeared (RTM 1868). Le Sueur, however, had been beaten to the post by another secretary, Philip Jourdan, whose *Cecil Rhodes: His Private Life* appeared in 1911. In 1913 Parkin's book *The Rhodes Scholarships* was distributed by the Trust to shareholders of the British South Africa Company and to the heads of Oxford colleges. The Trustees did their best to place it in the libraries of the steamers of the main shipping lines.

The Matopos railway built in accordance with the will was a constant source of concern (RTM 525, 538). It did not pay its way, and various devices were proposed to make it profitable. Should it be extended (RTM 1710, 1761)? Should it be given a petrol engine (RTM 1501, 1538, 1848)? How should the Trust insure against accidents (RTM 1248, 1285)? Should natives travel on it? (In 1913 they were allowed to do so, at an exorbitant fare of one penny per mile (RTM, 1887).) In 1914 it was offered for sale to the Rhodesia Railway Company; but the company would only accept it when, in 1917, it was handed over gratis (RTM 2004).

In May 1912 the Trustees resolved, on Jameson's recommendation, that the fruit industry in the Cape was sufficiently established for them to be able to sell the Fruit Farms (RTM 1617). Michell was given a directorship, plans were made for regular dividend payments, and the farms were offered for sale to De Beers (RTM 1840, 1955, 1981). Farms were sold from time to time, but it was not until 1925 that the sale was completed, after

---

[49] The Trustees were criticized in Parliament in 1916 for not setting up a scholarship fund. In their defence it was said that Rhodes's investments had been speculative, that it took a long time to convert them into gilt-edged stock, and that until that was done a scholarship fund could not be set up with any advantage to the public. (Halford MacKinder MP in the Commons; see below p. 15.)

[50] Hawksley, though a hard worker, was not a fast one and he was many years in arrears even in sending in bills for the professional services of his own firm (RTM 1465, 1717). But his failure to set up a trust was not inadvertent. He told Michell in 1904, 'Rhodes advisedly left us unfettered by any trust relying as he often said upon our using the funds put at our disposal as we knew he wished them to be used in preference to declaring any trust that would have exposed us to interference by the Courts or the Charity Commissioners' (Hawksley to Michell, 9 Jan. 1904). Thomas Pakenham has pointed out to me that it is ironic that a trust dominated by Milner should have been so insouciant about estate tax, since it was he who, as chairman of the Board of Inland Revenue, had been largely responsible for the budget of 1894 in which the modern system of death duties was introduced.

the failure of an alternative scheme to merge with Crosse and Blackwell (RTM 2002; RTM 9 June 1925).[51] In 1913 the Trustees decided that no more capital should be invested in the Smartt Syndicate, but the farms it owned should be sold. This decision took even longer to implement than the sale of the Fruit Farms, and indeed in October 1914 the Trustees were willing to agree to a further (and of course 'final') outlay of nearly £30,000 on the Ongers River Dam project (RTM 2026). In Rhodesia, the Trustees decided to close one of the unprofitable Matopos hotels, the Dam, and to threaten to close the other, the Terminus, if it could not be made profitable (RTM 1987). Like many a similar decision of the Trust, this ultimatum was not enforced (RTM 2064).

In 1914 the Trust's portfolio was valued at £3.4 million, of which about a third was still in De Beers shares, a third in gilts in various countries, and a third in the Southern African properties.

The War with Germany

The world war came out of a blue sky. At the July meeting of 1914 the Trustees confirmed the Kaiser's nomination of a batch of German scholars (RTM 2022). By August they were inspecting a list of scholars in the army and discussing the provision of free newspapers for the navy (RTM 2038, 2042). It was agreed that battels left unpaid by German scholars were to be paid by the Trust (RTM 2055), and that US scholars could suspend their scholarships to serve with the Belgian relief fund (RTM 2068).

In the United States, elections to scholarships continued until the autumn of 1915, and as late as 1916 there were seventeen scholarships confirmed. In the Trustees' papers a prominent place was soon taken by lists of colonial scholars who had obtained military distinctions or who had been killed on active service. The Trust funded a number of organizations concerned with the welfare of overseas servicemen, such as Colonel Lascelles's scheme for dominion soldiers' scholarships. Towards the war's end part of the Trust's London offices became a club room for scholars on active service.

Soon after the war began some in South Africa and elsewhere began to clamour for the Kaiser's scholarships to be redistributed to other countries.[52] Parkin thought this would be petty and unbecoming, and the pressure was at first resisted. In 1916, however, the Trustees gave in and Hawksley drew up a private bill for the revocation of the German codicil to the will (RTM 7 Feb. 1916). Michell, from South Africa, protested against the bill, which he thought was untrue to Rhodes's ideals and set a dangerous precedent for parliamentary interference.[53] Milner cabled:

Rosebery and I both most unwilling to act in absence of Colleagues, but Jameson and Grey are agreed and public feeling on the subject here is so strong that delay might injure Trust. Parliamentary interference is to be feared unless we do something.

[51] In 1918 the Trust received a dividend of £5,000, largely the result of farm sales.
[52] Wylie to Parkin, 24 Feb. 1915. RTF 1682; RTM 7 June 1915.
[53] In RT 1682 there is a series of bitter letters from Michell of 16 May 1916, 26 June 1916, culminating in a threat of resignation on 16 Aug. Wylie and Parkin also regretted the Trustees' decision; see correspondence of 11 Feb. 1916; RTF 1682.

Originally it had been intended that the bill should provide for specific reallocation of the scholarships.[54] Wylie suggested to Milner that one scholarship might be transferred to the West Indies. 'No doubt we must expect an occasional "coloured man" from Barbados or Trinidad, as we already do from Jamaica; but that can't be helped.' From the India Office, Austen Chamberlain proposed that the German scholarships might be allocated to Indians. Other people suggested scholarships for the Bahamas, Hong Kong, France, Belgium, Serbia, Switzerland, Ceylon, China, Japan, Argentina, and Scandinavia.

Most of the Trustees felt that the Transvaal and the Orange Free State should have a preferential claim on the ex-German scholarships.[55] But Michell, complaining about 'cutting up the hide before killing the bear', opposed earmarking any scholarship for the Transvaal, since Afrikaners might be no better friends to the British Empire than Germans had been.[56] Milner and Jameson pressed ahead with the bill, but they modified it in such a way as to leave the detailed allocation of the ex-German scholarships to the discretion of the Trustees.[57]

The bill recalled the hope expressed in Rhodes's codicil that 'an understanding between the three great powers will render war impossible' and stated that this object of the testator's had failed to be realized. Accordingly, it revoked the codicil with effect from 4 August 1914, and instructed the Trustees to replace the fifteen two-year German scholarships of £250 a year with twelve three-year scholarships of £300 for students from places within the British Empire.

The bill's passage through the Commons was not altogether easy. Joseph King MP set down a motion of opposition, to instruct the Trustees to set up a scholarship fund as directed in the will and to consult Oxford's Hebdomadal Council before abolishing any scholarships.[58] King implied that the Trust had been running short of funds and that the abolition was a device for the Trustees to line their own pockets. Describing the bill as 'the meanest Bill ever introduced by big men' he went on to say: 'Every year of the war robs a public educational trust of £3,750 and adds that sum to the residuary legatees.' The former Solicitor General H. J. Mackinder was briefed on behalf of the Trust. He had no difficulty in showing that King, who believed that Rhodes had left £6 million, had got his figures wrong and that the reorganization of the scholarships would not save the Trust any money.[59] The Attorney General, F. E. Smith, said that the only serious point at issue was whether the new scholarships should be restricted to the Empire or, as Lord Hugh Cecil had proposed, be available, at the Trustees' discretion,

---

[54] Milner to Wylie, 19 Mar. 1916; RTF 1682.

[55] Milner to Wylie, 19 Mar. 1916; RTF 1682; RTM 5 July 1915.

[56] Michell to Trustees, 19 Dec. 1916, in RTF 150.

[57] The eventual form of the bill was partly due to pressure from Lord Bryce, the recently returned Ambassador to Washington. RTF 1682.

[58] There was some opposition in Oxford to the abolition of the scholarships, and the Warden of Keble wrote an anonymous letter to *The Times* urging that the scholarships be suspended rather than abolished. (The editor, Dawson, refused to publish it but sent it on to the Trustees.) In the Commons debate one of the MPs for Oxford University said that the University authorities did not wish to be consulted.

[59] The debate is recorded in Hansard and described in Gilmour to Lewis, 20 Oct. 1916; RTF 1682.

anywhere in the world. The matter was referred to the private bill committee, which supported the Trustees, and the bill in the end was passed unamended, with the restriction to the Empire intact. The Rhodes Estate Act 1916 received the Royal Assent on 18 December.[60]

It was not easy to assemble a quorum of Trustees to decide on the reallocation of the scholarships. Hawksley had died before the Act was passed, and Milner was now a member of Lloyd George's war cabinet. Only Jameson could attend the first meeting of the Trust after the passing of the Act. At that meeting a long overdue step was taken: £7,500 was placed on deposit as the nucleus of the Scholarship Fund, and the Inland Revenue was approached in order to ensure its tax exemption (RTM 12 Feb. 1917). Subsequently a list of securities was drawn up for transfer to the Scholarship Fund, and the fund was formally constituted on 2 July 1917 with an initial capital of £65,000, quickly built up into a fund yielding an annual income of £8,500 (RTM 2 July 1917). Some £21,000 of tax was eventually recovered in respect of expenditure on scholarships between 1913 and 1917 (RTM 6 May 1918, 8 July 1918).

In 1917 the Trustees took steps to renew their own depleted body. Parkin had suggested in 1915 that because of the poor health of a number of Trustees, funds for the scholarship might be transferred to the authorities at Oxford. Milner was horrified.

I am quite sure that we could not render greater disservice to Oxford itself than by giving up our independent position as regards the scholarships. The last thing we want to happen is to have them run by Dons with donnish ideas. . . . The thing will never work as it ought to work, or produce the effect which Rhodes intended it to produce, if you get a lot of crusted old Dons at Oxford to run it.[61]

However, Milner agreed that a turnover of Trustees was necessary. Rosebery resigned in July 1917, on his seventieth birthday, having been the chairman of the Trust for fourteen years. Lord Grey resigned in September, 'endeared to his colleagues' according to the minutes 'by a charm of disposition'. At the same time Michell, whose resignation had already once been offered and refused, ceased to be a Trustee, though he remained an executor until 1925.[62] Three new Trustees were appointed: Otto Beit, the younger brother and trustee of Alfred Beit, a director of the BSAC; Lord Lovat, the Sudanese cotton-planter who had raised and commanded the Lovat Scouts in the Boer War; and Rudyard Kipling (RTM 26 Mar., 2 July, 10 Sept. 1917). Now only Milner and Jameson were left of the original Trustees. The Trust's securities were transferred into the names of Milner and Otto Beit, who now joined the Trust's finance committee (RTM 2 July 1917).

At the end of 1916 the Trustees agreed in principle to hand over their estates in Rhodesia to the Rhodesian government, and the details were settled in discussion between

---

[60] The costs of the Act, £456, were born by the Trust.

[61] Milner to Michell, 31 Dec. 1915, quoted by Colin Newbury in Madden and Fieldhouse (eds.), *Oxford and the Idea of Commonwealth*, 90.

[62] He was asked to continue to represent the Trust as a director of the Smartt Syndicate and the Fruit Farms, and to act in scholarship matters in Southern Africa. The Cape Town office of the Trust was closed and the management of their South African business was handed over to Syfret (RTM 2 July 1917).

Michell and Drummond Chaplin. The £6,000 per annum provided in the will for the upkeep of the estates was to be redeemed by payment of a capital sum of £120,000 (RTM 26 Mar. 1917). The Trust's transfer agreement was signed on 30 June 1917 and the properties in future were administered under the Rhodes Estate, Matopo and Inyanga, Transfer Ordinance 1918. McDonald remained for a while as administrator, responsible to the BSAC; he was given a set of plate by the Trustees and made their honorary representative in Rhodesia.[63] His sheep farming had not been a success, but the government inspector declared his cattle to be the finest herd in the country.

On 10 September 1917 the new scholarships were allocated, on the recommendation of Jameson and Beit. For only the second time in the history of the Trust the full board of Trustees was present at the meeting. One scholarship each year was to go to the Transvaal, one to the Orange Free State, one to the Prairie provinces in Canada, and one in alternate years to Kimberley and Port Elizabeth. A proposal for scholarships for 'the domiciled community of India' was not carried further. A few weeks later Jameson died: the Trustees minuted their grief at the loss of the man 'who in their work and in their hearts stands second only to the Founder' (RTM 13 Dec. 1917). Grey too had now died: an era had ended.

Africa at the War's End

As the Trustees had hoped, a site on the Groote Schuur estate was dedicated to the foundation of a University of Cape Town. In 1918 the Trustees paid £10,000 for a hall on the centre of campus to be a memorial to Jameson.[64] Educational subsidies continued to Bishops and St Andrew's, and £1,000 grants were made to Michaelhouse in Natal and St John's in Johannesburg (RTM 1681–2, 1776). The support of emigration continued, with a gift in 1919 to new hostels in Pretoria and Bulawayo and regular grants to Princess Christian's hostel in Mowbray.[65]

In England the Trustees were called on to make arrangements for the support of the families of Rhodes's brothers. In South Africa it was not so much Founder's kin as Founder's kith who sought assistance. Grootboom, 'a native who is reported to have done most valuable work for Mr Rhodes during the Rebellion of 1896', claimed a plot of land, a wagon, and a span of oxen (RTM 8 July 1918). J. Norris, a servant mentioned in the will, was given £1,500 as a capitalization of his annuity (RTM 10 Mar. 1919). In 1919 Michell and Syfret were authorized to make donations of up to £50 without reference to the Trustees, within a total of £500 per annum.[66]

---

[63] RTM 2 July 1917. He was also awarded an OBE for his services to the Rhodesia Munitions Committee during the war; he was later knighted and died in 1943.

[64] They refused, however, to give further funds for a Rhodes Hall of Residence (RTM 2 Sept. 1918, 3 Apr. 1919).

[65] This was now linked with the Society for the Overseas Settlement of British Women, which had resulted from the amalgamation of three previous emigration societies.

[66] It was for them, for instance, to decide whether to make a grant to the Salt River Moslem School. RTM 10 Mar. 1919.

Post-war Scholarships

When, in Europe, the war came to an end the Trustees issued a press release: '240 Rhodes scholars from the Dominions and the Colonies of the British Empire have taken part in the war. Of these 83 or nearly 35% have gained honours and distinctions, and 46 or nearly 20% have died in action' (RTM 4 Nov. 1918). By the time a memorial was erected to fallen Rhodes scholars in 1928, no less than seventy fallen had been identified.[67]

Elections had not been held for Rhodes scholarships for 1918 or 1919. It was decided to hold elections in October 1919 for the 1918 and 1919 cohorts, to come into residence in 1920, and in October 1920 for the 1920 and 1921 cohorts, to come into residence in 1921. Scholars who had married during the war might if they so wished resume their scholarships, though no scholar who was not already married would be permitted to marry.[68] These rules were not easy to apply in practice, and the Trustees were asked to rule in disputed cases until as late as 1925 (RTM 4 Oct. 1920, 7 Mar. 1921, 14 Apr. 1923, 28 Apr. 1925). Since the value of a 1920 pound was only about half that of a 1915 pound, Parkin and Wylie pressed for the scholarship to be increased from £300 per annum; but all the Trustees would grant was a war bonus of £50 to those in residence.[69]

To preside over the election system in the United States the Trustees had appointed Frank Aydelotte (Indiana and Brasenose 1905), professor of English at the Massachusetts Institute of Technology.[70] Aydelotte was the first of the Trust's overseas secretaries. Shortly after his appointment the Trustees rescinded the rule that American candidates had to pass a qualifying examination (RTM 9 Jan. 1919). At the same time, a new degree of Doctor of Philosophy, or D.Phil., was created by Oxford University; it was believed that this would be particularly attractive to Americans. Parkin, who had spent part of the war in the USA, reported to the Trustees in March 1919 that the election procedures in the US scholarships needed overhaul. Aydelotte was given leave from MIT and paid full-time by the Trust to reorganize the system, and Wylie was dispatched across the Atlantic to help him.

Parkin's report to the Trustees in 1919 contained a number of suggestions for improving the standard of scholars not only in America, but worldwide, particularly in Bermuda, Jamaica, and Southern Africa.[71] Wherever possible, returned Rhodes scholars should be brought onto selection committees in place of ex officio and institutional members: they could contribute knowledge of Oxford, and reduce the possibility of local bias. When

[67] For the war records of the individual constituencies, see below, Poynter, pp. 325–6, McCalla, p. 211, Kenny, pp. 420, 429, 437.

[68] RTM 9 Jan. 1919. Kipling had strong views on the marriage of scholars. He agreed with the exemption for the wartime returners, but he insisted that no one else should be allowed to marry while a Rhodes scholar. 'Scholars should benefit above all by actual contact with the Oxford college atmosphere, precisely as Oxford was to benefit by their intimate association with her life. If scholars are allowed to marry they will inevitably lose this advantage and they will also direct more or less of their allowances towards domestic housekeeping.' Kipling to Beit, 6 Dec. 1918; RTF 1432.

[69] RTM 1 Dec. 1919. The Trustees were reluctant to confirm scholarships of conscientious objectors such as Ordean Rockey.

[70] RTM 6 May 1918. On Aydelotte's previous career, see Alexander, below pp. 119–21.

[71] See pp. 262–3 below. Parkin suggested Smuts and Botha be consulted about selection in Transvaal and the Orange Free State. RTF 1256.

scholars reached Oxford, their colleges should be required to provide annual reports on their progress, and scholars who got bad reports should be disciplined (RTM 10 Mar. 1919).

The year 1919 ended with an expansion of the scholarship scheme, funded by wartime savings.[72] Open or 'at-large' scholarships were offered in Canada, Australia, and New Zealand. The Orange Free State and Transvaal scholarships were established; and a decision was taken in principle to offer a scholarship to Malta.[73] In the following year the Trustees received a proposal from Colonel Lascelles for the setting up of Indian scholarships; they considered it seriously, but on Wylie's advice they turned it down.[74]

In 1920 the Trustees were called on to settle a number of issues referred by Aydelotte. New York state had elected an alternative or runner-up; the Trustees confirmed the election, but said that in future if any state did not have a suitable candidate, a USA-at-large scholarship should be allotted (RTM 28 May, 28 June 1920). In response to a query about athletics, they ruled that 'Proficiency and interest in open air and athletic pursuits form an essential qualification for a Rhodes Scholar; but exceptional athletic distinction is not to be treated as of equal importance with the other requirements' (RTM 28 June 1920).[75] In general, they decided a few meetings later, after a dispute about a New Jersey election, committees were to be left 'with a free hand to decide the relative weight of intellectual and moral qualifications'. They reaffirmed several times that 'it would be contrary to the principles of the Trustees to allow a Rhodes scholarship to be held elsewhere than at Oxford' (RTM 4 Oct. 1920). But they sometimes made exceptions to this principle for short periods, especially for scholars pursuing medical work in London and Edinburgh. They even allowed a scholar to remain on stipend while apprenticed to an engineering firm, but they declared all these dispensations to be purely wartime measures (RTM 26 Aug. 1920, 7 Mar. 1921). (The war, for these purposes, continued well into the 1920s.)

In the post-war period the Trustees made grants in England to academic causes with an imperial aspect. Thus they gave £20,000 to establish an Oxford readership or professorship in Roman Dutch law at Oxford, and for several years they gave modest support to the teaching of elementary Dutch in Oxford.[76] They helped with the setting up of a Rhodes Chair of Imperial History at King's College London which they supported up to 1933, and they gave £5,000 to Imperial College in South Kensington (RTM 1 Dec. 1919).

[72] Lord Curzon, supported by Beit and Kipling, proposed that the son of the commander-in-chief of the Serbian army should be given the equivalent of a scholarship. The Trustees agreed, but the offer was never taken up (RTM 5 Jan. 1920).

[73] On Malta, see Kenny, below p. 442.

[74] See below, p. 447. They also declined to set up scholarships for Switzerland, as proposed by John Murray MP (RTM 1 Mar. 1920).

[75] L. S. Amery's view was that any love of open air life should be regarded as meeting Rhodes's athletic criterion. 'You will remember', he wrote to Elton, when the latter was preparing his history in 1955, 'that "the playing fields at Eton" where Waterloo was won were not the scene of organized games so much as wandering about bird nesting etc.' RTF 3121.

[76] RTM 8 Nov. 1920, 10 July 1923. Few students attended the classes and they were terminated in 1927.

The General Secretaryship

In 1919 Parkin began to talk of retirement. This led to a reorganization of the Trust's management. Hitherto, the secretaries of the Trust—Brodie and Boyd, and then Mrs Mavor (later Lady Butterworth) 1908–16 and T. L. Gilmour from 1916—had been little more than amanuenses, with hardly any power to make or even recommend decisions. Now the Trustees decided to appoint in Parkin's place a London-based chief executive. Milner offered the post of General Secretary to E. W. M. Grigg, a New College graduate and *Times* journalist much decorated as a lieutenant colonel in the Guards (RTM 7 July 1919). L. S. Amery MP, once a fellow of All Souls, later a member of Lloyd George's wartime secretariat, and now a junior minister in the Colonial Office, was invited to join the Trust, on which he was to remain for thirty-six years.[77]

In June 1921, the new General Secretary, after consultation with Parkin, proposed a number of changes to the scholarship system with the object of improving the standard of scholars, which he thought was not as high as it should be. Scholarships were allotted to constituencies with very disproportionate populations: to remedy this, he suggested, a federal system of election should be introduced into Canada, Australia, and South Africa. Salaried secretaries should be appointed in the dominions with duties similar to those of Aydelotte in the USA.[78] Places for Rhodes scholars should be reserved in the civil services of the dominions, paid at a higher rate than normal; for this purpose they should be encouraged to study the humanities rather than the sciences, and should be given an extra period of scholarship for vocational training. If the Trustees accepted his other proposals, Grigg was prepared to approach the dominion prime ministers, who were due to visit England in the same month (RTF 2524).

Nothing came of Grigg's final proposal, but the organization of elections in the countries of origin was, in accordance with his recommendation, devolved to local ex-Rhodes scholar secretaries, with John Behan in Australia, J. M. McDonnell in Canada, and P. T. Lewis in South Africa joining Aydelotte in 1922.[79] Behan's appointment as dominion Secretary in Melbourne was seen in some parts of Australia as a federal intrusion on states' rights. It was a year or more before sentiment had cooled enough for him to undertake a tour of the Australian state capitals.[80]

Apart from the institution of regional secretaries, it was some time before the creation of the office of General Secretary began to have a serious impact. This was because it was not until 1925 that any single individual held the office long enough to get a grip on the

---

[77] RTM 5 May 1919. Amery, who had edited the seven-volume *Times* history of the Boer War, was a regular attender at Trust meetings during his years as a Trustee. He kept a very full diary, which is now with his papers at Churchill College, Cambridge, but is not yet generally available to researchers. The extracts printed in the published diaries do not cover Trust meetings. A disciple of Milner, Amery was an ardent supporter of imperial preference against free traders, and has been described as the 'theorist par excellence of British Imperialism'. (W. R. Louis, *In the Name of God, Go!* (New York: Norton, 1992).)

[78] Grigg wrote: 'Professor Aydelotte is a rather expensive institution: he costs the Trust about £3,000 a year. I do not suggest that the Trustees should appoint Professor Aydelotte in all the Dominions.' Memorandum of 3 June 1931; RTF 2524.

[79] See Poynter, McCalla, and Nuttall, below pp. 327, 212, and 264.

[80] See Poynter, below p. 328.

management of the Trust. At the beginning of 1920 Grigg was called away to accompany the Prince of Wales as his military secretary on a tour of the dominions. In his absence his duties to the Trust were performed by Geoffrey Dawson, a fellow of All Souls who had recently stepped down as editor of *The Times*, assisted by T. L. Gilmour, the last of the non-executive secretaries. When Grigg returned from his tour, he took over from Dawson, but shortly afterwards he was appointed private secretary to the Prime Minister, Lloyd George. Dawson obliged again until Lloyd George's government fell in 1923, when Grigg, now National Liberal MP for Oldham, returned to the Trust for a further two years (RTM 2 Feb. 1920, 11 July 1921, 19 Dec. 1922, 23 Jan. 1923).

At the beginning of the decade the Trustees began to consider setting up an establishment in Oxford. Wylie lived in a private house at the east end of South Parks Rd, with a secretary, a salary of £1,500 per annum, and an entertainment allowance of £500. At the last meeting of 1919 it was resolved to offer £7,500 to the Warden and fellows of Wadham for a piece of garden on South Parks Rd 'on which they would ultimately erect a house to be the Oxford Home of the Trust' (RTM 1 Dec. 1919). An initial approach was made, but without success. A meeting of the Trustees on 1 March 1920, presided over by Kipling, was told that negotiations had fallen through.[81]

The Public Purposes Trust

The Scholarship Fund of 1917 was exempt from tax, but the Inland Revenue was unwilling to refund tax on other grants for educational and charitable purposes since the general funds were not held in trust for charity only. While there were personal and political commitments of the Founder to be satisfied, and while there were speculative ventures to be managed in Africa, the Trustees had been unwilling to tie up the residual legacy in a trust. However, by the time of Jameson's death their desire to keep their hands free in this way had cost the Trust £158,000 in death duties.

Accordingly, in February 1920 the Trustees, at the suggestion of Otto Beit, who was now their chairman, decided to set up a charitable fund with a founding capital of £100,000, held in Nigerian government stock (RTM 5 Jan., 2 Feb. 1920). In the next months a sum of £1.7 million had been put into the fund, and on 15 June 1921 it was established by deed poll as the Public Purposes Trust.[82] In the Rhodes Trust there was retained the sum of £200,000, half of it to meet future claims for death duties on the estates of the original Trustees.[83]

One of the first grants from the new PPT was a sum of £5,000 to the 1820 Memorial Settlers' Association to assist British emigration into South Africa; further grants of £20,000 followed in later years (RTM 8 Nov. 1920, 6 Dec. 1921, 22 Nov. 1922). Regular

---

[81] At this time the Trustees were thinking only of a dwelling for their Oxford Secretary. Later they added the idea of a library of books on the British Empire as a memorial to Parkin. See Elton, *The First Fifty Years*, 116–17.

[82] Separate minute books were now opened for the Rhodes Trust (non-charitable) and the Scholarship and Public Purposes Trusts.

[83] In fact, when the claims came in for Grey and Jameson they amounted to over £113,000, and the Trustees had to borrow from Hoares to pay them off (RTM 8 July 1924).

grants were also made to a scheme for child emigration devised by Kingsley Fairbridge, a Rhodesian Rhodes scholar of 1908, who had in 1913 opened a school near Perth to teach farming to young emigrants from Britain.[84] His idea caught the Trustees' imagination, and besides making grants to his Child Emigration Society they underwrote the activity of the Balliol Boys' Club, which managed the London end of the scheme, at the rate of £16 per boy.[85]

In spring 1920 Otto Beit went to represent the Trustees at the reinterment of Jameson near Rhodes in the Matopos. While in Africa he laid the foundation stone of an arts block at Rhodes University College and the cornerstone of a new block at St Andrew's. He also visited the Smartt estates, and persuaded the Trustees to allow the transfer of some of their farms to settlers. As a result a further £20,000 of Trust money was poured into the syndicate (RTM 28 June 1920, 7 June, 11 July 1921).

Wylie followed Beit to South Africa, and returned with a number of recommendations about the scholarships. A new Cape scholarship was to be set up, and the new scholarships were so far as possible to come into line with scholarships elsewhere. It was impossible, however, to avoid special treatment for the schools scholarships: a post-matriculation period at St Andrew's or Bishops could qualify in lieu of the two years of university residence that was a requirement elsewhere. Rhodesia was at long last to get its own selection committee (RTM 8 Nov. 1920).

As a result of the visits of Beit and Wylie generous educational grants were approved by the Trustees: £5,000 in total to three girls' schools, and £16,000 to four boys' schools. A grant of £5,000 was given to the University of the Witwatersrand. A grant of £10,000, plus four further annual instalments of £5,000, was made to Rhodes University College. This brought the Trust's contributions to the College to more than £100,000; at this point the Trustees called a halt, feeling it was time for the South African government to take more responsibility for the funding of the College.[86]

From time to time critics complained that while the Trustees were willing to spend a lot of money on the education of British children in South Africa, they spent almost nothing on black education. In 1905 a convention had been held at Lovedale in the Western Cape, attended by many chiefs, which drew up a petition for an Interstate Native College in memory of a recently deceased associate of Dr Livingstone. The Trustees were asked for their support, but Michell was unenthusiastic, and the scheme languished until the Union was created.[87] In 1910 it was proposed to build a college at Fort Hare near Lovedale, and Jameson was one of those who pressed the South African government to support the scheme. In all £50,000 was needed; £40,000 had been promised by local donors, and the Rhodes Trust was asked for support. Parkin was in

---

[84] See Poynter, below p. 324.

[85] RTM 1 Dec. 1919, 12 Apr. 1920. After Fairbridge's death in 1924 grants were made to his wife and family for the upbringing of his children; later, when Rhodes House was built, his name was the sole one to be inscribed (temporarily) on a roll of honour in the rotunda.

[86] RTM 7 Dec. 1920. Many smaller grants were made, including £500 towards a Schreiner memorial hostel in Cape Town, and £623 for a bell for City Hall, Cape Town.

[87] The correspondence is in RTF 1156.

favour of the idea,[88] but the Trustees' response was hardly handsome. They offered £1,000 provided that the remaining £49,000 had been raised. In 1916, when £20,000 had come in, the college was opened by Prime Minister Botha, but in spite of requests the Trustees did not pay over their contribution until April 1923.[89] In the same year a committee at the Higher Mission School at Paarl asked for £5,000 to set up a 'Rhodes Memorial Training College' for coloured teachers. In spite of support from Michell and Smartt the Trustees turned down the request. On their behalf Grigg replied, 'while they appreciate the importance of adequate arrangements for training coloured teachers, they consider the responsibility for providing them rests with the public authorities'.[90]

Very occasionally, the Trustees made educational grants in other parts of the Empire. In 1922 Milner (who, in the Colonial Office, had shown a special interest in Egypt in 1919–20) was given discretion to give £5,000 to Victoria College, Alexandria, and this was followed by a grant of £2,000 towards the endowment of a Kitchener memorial school in Khartoum (RTM 16 Oct. 1923). In 1923 the Trustees agreed to another proposal of Milner's and made a grant of £5,000 to a school of tropical agriculture in Trinidad; they suggested that it should be renamed 'The Imperial School of Tropical Agriculture'.[91] However, a request for a Rhodes scholarship for Kenya was turned down.

Problems with the Scholarships

The Trustees' dinner of 1923 was attended by Stanley Baldwin, who had just formed his first cabinet. His cousin Kipling reported to his colleagues that the Prime Minister had much enjoyed the dinner, and the Trustees were able to minute their satisfaction at 'the quieter behaviour of the scholars'.[92]

Later in the year Grigg toured Canada and the USA. In Canada, he found, French Canadians felt they were virtually excluded from scholarships. It was difficult to make special provision for them without contravening the provisions of the will about 'race', but in the event an extra scholarship was offered to Quebec.[93] In the USA Aydelotte had proposals for raising the profile of the scholarships. An annual scholars' dinner should

[88] He told the Trustees that many blacks went to the USA for higher education and came back to be disturbing influences; it would be far better if they were educated in their own country by teachers who understood the environment. Parkin to Trustees, 11 Jan. 1911, RTF 1156.

[89] RTM 25 Jan. 1911, 4 Oct. 1916, 24 Apr. 1923; RTF 1156. In 1919 the Trustees bought 100 copies of a work on Bantu languages, by Sir Harry Johnson, for free distribution 'to further the study of those languages'. RTM 6 Oct. 1919.

[90] RTR 198, 13–17.

[91] RTM 10 July 1923. But a proposal from Basil Williams for a chair of colonial and American history at McGill was rebuffed in 1922.

[92] In the previous year there had been complaints of rowdyism, with champagne corks being fired at Milner and Lord Grey of Fallodon. In the following year, the occasion was marred by an ungracious speech made by an American Rhodes scholar in response to a toast by Kipling; see Alexander, below pp. 181–2.

[93] See McCalla, below p. 216.

be held in New York, Rhodes scholars should be invited into government offices in their final year in Oxford, and the Prince of Wales should be made a Trustee.[94]

Aydelotte, now President of Swarthmore College in Pennsylvania as well as American Secretary, attended the Trustees' meeting in April 1924. He explained the problems caused by the inequality of population between the different states of the USA. Each year many were rejected in populous states who would make better scholars than those selected for other states. He proposed to introduce a system of regionalization, grouping the states into districts for purposes of election. The Trustees told him that this would need 'overwhelming support from body of old Rhodes Scholars and from educational authorities in the U.S.'.[95]

By July 1924 the Trustees had paid off the claims on the Jameson estate, and they felt confident enough to revive the prospect of a Rhodes House in Oxford. Wadham, which was in financial straits, was now willing to offer 1.5 acres of college garden for £15,000; Grigg was told to offer £20,000 for 2 acres, at the corner of Parks Rd and South Parks Rd (RTF 2637). Sir Herbert Baker, who had worked for Rhodes and Milner in South Africa, and designed the Union Building in Pretoria, and the memorial to Rhodes on Table Mountain, was chosen as architect. He was to be asked to submit plans 'consisting as to one wing, of a Library, Offices for the Secretary, and a Common Room for Scholars; and as to the other wing, of a dwelling house for the Secretary—a central building between the two wings to be a Rhodes Hall capable of seating 200 persons at dinner, with a gallery'. Agreement was reached with Wadham, despite problems about a copper beech, in December 1924. The Trustees agreed, if ever they disposed of the land, to give the College first refusal to repurchase it at £10,000 an acre for unimproved value.[96] Discussions were opened with the University about a proposal for a library at Rhodes House 'which would for the first time make a complete collection of official records and documents from all parts of the Empire and which would, at the same time, relieve Bodley's library by taking over the care of new books dealing with Imperial subjects'.

Oxford University was at this time in a state of alarm. It was rumoured that the city was about to sell a block of land bounded by Broad St, Turl St, and Ship St for the construction of a printing works. Many said that the Rhodes Trustees should be buying this site rather than building on the green fields of Wadham. Wylie reported that the site was quite unsuitable; but the Trustees offered to buy the Broad St site immediately on condition that the University took it off their hands at the same price, with a mortgage provided by the Trust. New arcades, it was suggested, might be designed by Baker with shops at ground level, and student accommodation for Balliol, Exeter, and Jesus above. At the west end of the Broad there might be a grand edifice to bear the name of Rhodes, to match the splendours of the Sheldonian at the east. But the University authorities were unable to organize themselves to give the scheme serious

[94] RTM 16 Oct. 1923. The only response to this was an offer by Lovat to invite finalists to tea on the terraces at Westminster.
[95] See Alexander, below p. 131.
[96] The contract was signed on 16 Oct. 1925 (RTF 2637 (1)).

consideration.[97] The only effect of the Trustees' generous offer was to call their critics' bluff.

Early in 1925 the Trustees, at Grigg's suggestion, dispatched Montague Rendall (the newly retired headmaster of Winchester, Grigg's old school) to travel round the world in their behalf and report on the state of the scholarships in the various constituencies. The trip had no very clear purpose, achieved little, and proved in the end something of an embarrassment to the Trustees.[98]

In spring 1925 Milner died, the last of the original Trustees. Because of his death, the annual dinner for scholars was cancelled. Baker was asked to modify the plans for Rhodes House so as to incorporate a room which would be a fitting memorial to Milner.[99] Kipling reported that Baldwin, since the previous November Prime Minister for the second time, would be willing to take his place as a Trustee, and the offer was accepted with alacrity.[100]

A New Regime

The Trustees already included a member of Baldwin's cabinet. Amery had been Colonial Secretary since 1924[101] and in that capacity in June 1925 he appointed Grigg Governor of Kenya. In his place as General Secretary, the Trustees appointed Philip Kerr, a former member of Milner's Kindergarten, and a founder and editor of the imperialist journal the *Round Table*, who had been Lloyd George's private secretary 1916–21, attending the Peace Conference as his confidential lieutenant.[102] Two weeks later, at the first Trustees' meeting attended by Baldwin, it was announced that in protest at Kerr's appointment Kipling had resigned from the Trust.[103] During his seven years as a Trustee he had been

[97] The file (RTF 2641) contains plaintive notes from the Vice-Chancellor (Warden Wells of Wadham) about the difficulty of reaching decisions during the vacation.

[98] RTM 13 Oct. 1925; Kipling to Otto Beit, 22 June 1925, unpublished text at the University of Sussex, kindly communicated to me by Prof. T. Pinney. See also Poynter, McCalla, and Kenny, below pp. 330, 217, 421, 430, and 438.

[99] See G. Tyack, *Oxford, an Architectural Guide* (Oxford: OUP, 1998) 291. A classical rotunda facing South Parks Rd, envisioned by Baker as a hall of fame for statesmen, was added to the manor-like H-block which formed the main part of Rhodes House.

[100] Baldwin, it must be said, was never very active as a Trustee. Amery in 1941 suggested that his portrait should be painted. 'He has not done very much as a trustee but he has an interesting face.' Amery to Elton, 10 Nov. 1941, RTF 3000.

[101] In June 1925 he was appointed also Dominions Secretary.

[102] Kerr obtained a first class in history from New College in 1904; educated as a Roman Catholic, he became a Christian Scientist in 1912 under the influence of Nancy Astor, with whom he maintained an intense, though Platonic, relationship until his death. See J. Fox, *The Langhorne Sisters* (London: Granta, 1998).

[103] The precise reasons for his objection remain unclear to this day. In his letter of resignation, Kipling said that Kerr was 'a brilliantly clever man, but he did not fight in the war' and complained that he was too much associated with the policies of the *Round Table* 'which were not parallel with those of the Trust' (Kipling to Beit, 22 June 1925). Amery noted in his diary for 30 June: 'Rhodes Trust meeting to accept Kipling's resignation based on the fact that he does not like Philip Kerr's smile or the fact that he did not serve in the war' (*The Leo Amery Diaries*, i: *1896–1929*, ed. John Barnes and David Nicholson (London, 1980), 415). Much later Amery told Elton, who repeated it in *The First Fifty Years*, 17, that Kipling's objection was that Kerr 'was a liberal and associated with Lloyd George'. This is most unconvincing, since

a regular attender, and he was in demand at annual dinners to propose the toast of 'prosperity to the scholars'.[104] The Trustees were embarrassed by his abrupt departure; but privately some were not sorry to see him go.[105]

Before the appointment of Kerr and the departure of Kipling, the Trustees had already decided to expand their number.[106] Four new Trustees were appointed on 6 July. The first was Dawson, the former secretary. Edward Peacock, once a school colleague of Parkin's, recently a governor of the Bank of England, and now on the board of Baring Brothers, was appointed at the age of 54 to a trusteeship which he held until his death at the age of 91.[107] The third new Trustee was Douglas Hogg MP, the Attorney General. Finally, there was H. A. L. Fisher MP, former President of the Board of Education and author of the 1918 Education Act. Now Warden-elect of New College, he became the first Oxford-based Trustee.

Kerr brought to the secretaryship a broad vision which combined imperialism with Atlanticism. The UK and the USA, he believed, should combine to preserve international peace through the mastery of the seas, now that the Royal Navy was no longer strong enough to enforce a Pax Britannica. Kerr had a very personal interpretation of the Founder's intentions. His primary idea, he maintained, was 'of leaving his fortune to promote the Unity of the Empire, the union of the English-speaking races and the prevention of war'. To this end the scholarship was only a means.[108]

But Kerr was not just a visionary, he also proved a capable administrator. He made it his first task, in conjunction with Peacock, to take a grip on the Trust's finances. At the end of 1924 the Trust's assets were valued at £2.271 million (£1.350 million being in the Scholarship Trust, £655,000 in the Public Purposes Trust, and £266,000 in the residual Rhodes Trust on which death duties were still payable). Peacock wished to know how the Trust's assets had shrunk by some £1.462 million since they had been valued in 1903 as worth £3.732 million. Kerr discovered that half a million had been lost on the realization of Rhodes's investments (particularly shares in De Beers) and more than a quarter of a million on the endowment of properties, such as Groote Schuur and the Inyanga estates, which had been handed over to Southern African governments. Nearly £350,000

Kipling had happily worked with Grigg, Lloyd George's uncritically adoring private secretary. Perhaps the key is given by an earlier remark of Kipling's to the effect that he found Kerr's mixture of Catholicism and Christian Science nauseating (*Letters of Rudyard Kipling*, ed. T. Pinney (Iowa city: University of Iowa Press, 1999), iv. 509). At all events, it appears likely from Amery's diaries (20 June 1925) that Kipling initially acquiesced in the appointment, but was got at by Milner's widow who disapproved of Kerr's 'internationalism', and who alleged that he had been a conscientious objector.

[104] Also, at the Trustees' request, he had revised, and found a publisher for, Ian Colvin's subsidized life of Jameson, who had been the model for his poem 'If'. RTM 7 June 1921, 14 Feb. 1922.

[105] Amery confided to his diary, 'Poor old Beit has been very much worried and distressed about it . . . I cannot say that it has worried me much because Kipling has not really contributed anything really material.'

[106] Amery records that after Milner's funeral he and Grigg drove to Kipling's house, Bateman's, to discuss possible future Trustees. In addition to the four who were eventually chosen they discussed Herbert Baker, Rendall, and Violet Milner.

[107] Except for a brief gap in the 1960s, the entire century is straddled by three Trustees: Milner 1903–25; Peacock 1925–62; John Baring, later Lord Ashburton, 1970–99.

[108] Lothian spelt out his vision in 1928 in preparation for the Rhodes Trust Act. RTF 2524.

had been paid in death duties. The remaining loss was due to the depreciation of estates and investments.[109]

In July Aydelotte returned to England to explain to the Trustees his new District Plan for scholarship elections. Supported by Wylie, he also proposed that the scholarship should be raised from £350 per annum to £400.[110] Having completed his financial review, Kerr decided that an increase could be afforded provided that the cost of building Rhodes House (estimated at £100,000) was spread over ten years, and the level of other donations was reduced.[111] The Trustees agreed to increase the scholarship to £400 per annum, a figure at which it remained until 1946.

When Aydelotte proposed his reorganization of the system of election in the USA Hogg pointed out that it would not be legal in terms of Rhodes's will. Either the Board of Education would have to vary the terms of the will, or a private Act of Parliament would be needed. The Trustees were not difficult to convince of the merits of Aydelotte's scheme, but they insisted that university associations in the USA should be consulted. If they agreed, then an application would be made to the Board of Education.[112]

Kerr worked hard to reduce the Trust's tax burden. At his insistence the Trustees transferred many assets, including in due course the site of Rhodes House, from the Rhodes Trust to the Public Purposes Fund, and they assured the charitable nature of that fund by charging all personal grants against the residuary Rhodes Trust (RTM 9 Mar. 1926). From the Public Purposes Fund a new Scholarship Capital Reserve Fund was set up, whose first purpose was to make up any shortfall on the funds available annually for scholarship expenditure. Remaining unexpended balances in the Public Purposes Trust were earmarked for the building of Rhodes House; otherwise expenditure from that fund was to be kept to a minimum. Finally, Baring Brothers were asked to oversee the Trustees' investments, under the guidance of a finance committee consisting of Beit and Peacock which was to report to the Trustees twice a year. From the low point in 1924 the Trust's assets now began to show a steady growth.

During the General Strike of 1926 a number of dominions Rhodes scholars volunteered for work; some Americans wished to be enrolled as special constables, but they could not do so without passing themselves off as Canadians. Wylie was careful not to urge them to serve; but with the Trustees' approval he gave scholars permission to leave Oxford without forfeiting their stipends. Not all the scholars

---

[109] In 1925 £1.234 M of the Trust's assets were in gilts, £557,000 in 'first-class' investments (foreign government and municipal bonds, and overseas railways prefence shares and debentures), and £531,000 in less reliable investments (such as De Beers and other mining shares). Kerr's financial memorandum is in RTF 2709.

[110] Wylie in fact thought £450 would be necessary to make scholars as well off as before the war. By 1925 the pound had recovered only about half the value it had lost between 1915 and 1920. Protests about the inadequacy of the stipend had come in from many quarters, including the Governor of South Australia.

[111] Gifts out of the annual surplus of £20,000, Kerr suggested, should be divided among four purposes: (1) expenditure in Oxford to maintain its pre-eminence as a world university; (2) maintenance of higher education in South Africa; (3) general 'Imperial Purposes' such as the promotion of emigration; (4) personal grants arising out of the scholarships and the will.

[112] RTM 20 July 1925. See Alexander, below p. 131.

approved of strike-breaking, and one Australian distributed communist propaganda. Despite protests from the British Association of Loyalists, he was allowed to remain on stipend.[113]

Rhodes House

The project for Rhodes House had been taking shape. In October 1925 the secretary was authorized to sign the contract with Wadham to purchase the two acres, and the conveyance was completed in January 1926. Baker's plans for the building were approved, and a tender of £84,000 for the building works accepted in May 1926 (RTF 2637 (3)). An article setting out the project was published in *The Times*. The Trustees wanted Rhodes House to be of value to the University, and consulted widely about possible uses. Four proposals emerged: that it should contain a library and work rooms for the study of the literature and history of the English-speaking world; that learned and other societies should use it as a meeting place; that world figures should be invited to reside in Oxford and give lectures; and that travelling fellowships should be set up for Oxford dons to travel to the USA and to the dominions.[114] All these proposals were acted upon, two of them even before the completion of Rhodes House. In 1926 Sir Robert Borden, a former Canadian Prime Minister, was appointed the first Rhodes Memorial Lecturer, and in 1927 M. R. Ridley of Balliol became the first Rhodes travelling fellow. A short list was drawn up for future Rhodes Memorial Lecturers, including Einstein, Bergson, Croce, and Clemenceau. All these plans were announced at the annual dinner in June 1926.

Planning and construction of Rhodes House took from 1926 to 1929. There was a brief hiccup in the planning when it was rumoured that the Bodleian was to be rebuilt in the Parks, on a scale which would make the Rhodes House library superfluous. Otherwise, there was a steady development of the architect's plans: besides the entrance rotunda inspired by Milner's death, a caretaker's block and a double garage were added to the building, and Wylie, prompted by Aydelotte, insisted that the number of bathrooms in his lodgings was increased from five to seven. The architect was allowed to design and order the furniture; he was full of fresh inspirations for the rotunda, such as a text of Aristotle around the inner dome, a slab of Matopos stone within the floor, and a Zimbabwe bird to top the building off. The rooms of the principal building were to be named after the original Trustees, so that the main hall—first proposed as Rhodes Hall—became Milner Hall.[115] Agreement was reached with the Bodleian about the new library, an initial £5,000 was set aside for book purchases, and a joint committee was set up to appoint a

---

[113] See Wylie to Kerr, 15 May 1926; RTM 26 Jan., 8 June 1926. On the Australian, see Poynter, below p. 329.

[114] See Kerr's memorandum of 26 Apr. 1926; RTF 2709.

[115] The architecture of Rhodes House was much criticized by writers such as Sharp and Pevsner; but in the recent *Oxford, an Architectural Guide* by G. Tyack it is described as 'one of Oxford's most successful inter-war buildings'. Elsewhere Tyack has remarked, of the entrance from South Parks Rd into the baronial Milner Hall, 'there are few more impressive sequences of internal spaces in Oxford' ('Baker and Lutyens in Oxford', *Oxoniensia*, 62 (1997), 295).

librarian, and to 'organise higher studies in history, government, and economics' (RTM 14 Oct. 1926, 18 Jan., 1 Mar., 26 May 1927).

When Wylie moved into Rhodes House his house at 9 Parks Rd was sold. The building was opened officially on 10 May 1929, and on 5 July 1929—the twenty-fifth anniversary of the foundation of the scholarships—a reunion of all Rhodes scholars was held there, in the presence of the Prince of Wales. A staff of eight servants was installed, and Wylie, now newly knighted, began to dispense hospitality on a grand scale; his entertainment allowance was increased to £1,050 per annum. The routine now was that instead of a single dinner for all the scholars, the Trustees hosted two dinners a year in Milner Hall, one in autumn for freshers, and one in June for the departing scholars. Individual Trustees henceforth took it in turn to preside in rotation over these dinners.[116]

The Rhodes Trust Act 1929

One day after the grand opening of Rhodes House a new Rhodes Trust Act was passed. This had been made necessary by Aydelotte's plan to reorganize the American system so that districts, rather than individual states, had the final say in the election of scholars. The Board of Education, approached on Hogg's advice in 1925, did not feel able to authorize the scheme itself, but the President of the Board, Lord Eustace Percy, was willing to introduce an Act to amend the will as a public bill (RTM 5 Apr. 1927). The Trustees had hoped to have the bill passed in the autumn session of 1927; but they were unable to secure civil service agreement to its introduction as a public bill, and they had to bear the costs, some £1,800, of promoting a private bill (RTM 27 Sept. 1927, 13 Jan. 1928).

Aydelotte, who had travelled from coast to coast in the USA canvassing his district scheme, placed an announcement of the bill in the major US papers. Sir Esmé Howard, the British Ambassador in Washington, was assured by Secretary of State Kellogg that the US government had no objection to the proposed changes. No opposition was at first heard, but by May complaints about the bill had been received from Chicago.

In the end the major complications in passing the bill came not from the American reorganization but from other constituencies. The Trustees were warned by Grigg from Kenya that a bill giving power to reallocate scholarships would be bound to raise the issue of the German scholarships; there was a considerable body of public opinon, he said, in favour of their restoration, which would now probably find expression in Parliament (RTM 17 May 1927). The Trustees were still reluctant to reintroduce scholarships for Germans, but in July 1926 they had agreed to make a grant of £500 for three years for exchanges of students between British and German universities. When the bill was introduced they announced that there was no question of reversing the Rhodes Estate Act of 1916, and that the restoration of German Rhodes

---

[116] In describing the purpose of Rhodes House the Trustees were always anxious to squash any idea that it would deflect men from their colleges. 'Rhodes House is not intended to be in any way a meeting place for Rhodes Scholars still in residence,' Kerr wrote in the press release announcing the plans for Rhodes House. See correspondence between Kerr and Dawson, 29 Feb. 1928; RTF 2637.

scholarships was therefore dependent on fresh financial resources being available (RTM 4 Dec. 1928).

The Trustees intended to use the new powers they sought in order to reduce the frequency of the Bermudan and Jamaican scholarships, and they notified the governors of those colonies to that effect. In response each colony lobbied the West India committee and the Colonial Office, and when the bill came before the Lords in March 1929 it was amended in such a way as to prevent the Trustees tampering with these provisions of the will.[117]

The bill received the Royal Assent on 11 May. The new Act provided that the Trustees could vary 'the value, number, duration and administration of the Scholarships' provided that the total number of scholarships allotted by the will to each of the constituencies was not reduced, and that the distribution of scholarships to parts of, and schools and colleges in, South Africa, Australia, and Canada should not be affected.[118]

The Act contained three other important provisions. The Trustees could henceforth place scholars elsewhere if suitable places could not be found in Oxford. They could also use the scholarship income in promoting postgraduate studies, in such places as they felt would promote the Founder's main purposes. Finally, the Act gave statutory standing to Kerr's Scholarship Capital Reserve Fund.

At the reunion of Rhodes scholars in the new Rhodes House it was announced that the Trustees had decided to make Rhodes scholarships once more available to German students at an early date. Hogg, now ennobled as Lord Hailsham and holding office as Lord Chancellor, had decided in May that he did not wish to be party to the decision. However, he did not wish to embarrass the Trustees, so he gave as his reason for resigning the pressure of his new responsibilities (RTM 15 May 1929). Peacock, too, disapproved of the decision, but he did not push his disapproval to the point of resigning.[119]

Duncan in South Africa

Until the completion of Rhodes House, Kerr had consistently advised the Trustees to limit their benevolence in South Africa. After the series of grants triggered by Milner's final tour, they had turned down many requests from schools, stating that their general policy was to assist education in the outlying parts of South Africa rather than in the wealthier centres of population. At the end of 1926 Kerr went on tour in South Africa, and inspected the Trust's projects there. While impressed by the Ongers River Dam, he

---

[117] See Kenny, below p. 431.

[118] Even after the passing of the Act, Aydelotte's reforms met considerable opposition; see Alexander, below p. 134.

[119] It is not clear whence the Trustees derived the power in 1929 to create the German scholarships. In 1945 a lawyer at Coward Chance opined that the creation was *ultra vires*. '[T]he then Trustees read the 1929 Act as conferring upon them the power to establish German Scholarships if they thought fit to do so. In my opinion, which has been confirmed by Counsel, there is nothing in the 1929 Act which conferred upon the Trustees power to establish German scholarships.' Tylor to Elton, 13 July 1945; RTF 3016.

was critical of the Smartt Syndicate.[120] He reported back that the Trustees were being criticized for spending so much on Rhodes House while ignoring the claims of African institutions of higher education. In July 1928 the Trustees agreed that after the completion of Rhodes House South African education should have the first claim upon its benefactions.[121]

Henceforth the Trustees' policy in South Africa was guided largely by Patrick Duncan, once a colleague of Kerr's in Milner's Kindergarten, and now a South African opposition MP in Smuts's party. He had in effect taken Michell's place as the Trustees' main adviser in South Africa.[122] On his advice the Trustees in 1928 and 1929 made a series of grants to educational institutions in South Africa.[123] The Trust also took a substantial holding of shares in the Argus Printing and Publishing Company to encourage the Cape Town *Argus*, 'to uphold British views in South Africa' (RTF 1184).

The Trustees, hitherto reluctant to contribute to the University of Cape Town beyond the original donation of the Groote Schuur site, now made a grant to its library. But they continued much more sympathetic to the claims of Rhodes University College in Grahamstown, which they could claim to have founded, and which they regarded as a more solid incarnation of English ideals.[124] To it they promised £1,000 for three years in 1929, and a matching grant of £10,000 for the library in 1930; two scholarships were offered to British graduates to take teaching diplomas there (RTM 23 July 1929).

The Trustees also began to take an interest in the education of Africans. A grant was made to the college at Fort Hare, and £4,000 was given to a school at Modderpoort founded by the Bishop of Bloemfontein; £500 went to Clarkebury Mission School, where Nelson Mandela was shortly to begin his schooling (RTM 7 Oct. 1930). In the years 1929–34, an annual grant of £100 was made to the International Institute of African Languages and Cultures, in response to a request from its chairman, Lord Lugard (RTM 5 Mar. 1934, 25 June 1929).

The Trust's holdings of real estate in South Africa had now been much reduced. In October 1925 a renewed bid was accepted from De Beers for the Trust's shares in the Rhodes Fruit Farms. The Smartt Syndicate remained. Smartt himself died in 1929 and the Trustees recorded their grief at the departure of a man 'who was one of Mr Rhodes

[120] 'While the old-fashioned type of Dutch farmer who was accustomed to the loneliness of karoo life and who did not want to make money out of his farm because he was content with a simple life provided his flocks and herds increased, might do well as a settler, the British type of settler, especially the 1820 settler type, whose object in farming was to make a certain amount of cash, which he could spend on motor cars and gramophones and books and clothes and holidays, was unlikely, except in exceptional cases, to settle down on the karoo or to be content with what the Smartt syndicate could offer it.' On Kerr's trip see Butler, *Lothian*, 132.

[121] At this time officers of the Trust regularly affirmed that the scholarship programme was now complete: Oxford had as many scholars as it could absorb. See, for instance, Kerr's memorandum of Dec. 1928; RTF 2709.

[122] For some years after Michell's death the Trustees also turned for advice to Sir Charles Crewe, the secretary of the 1820 Memorial Settlers' Association.

[123] Among the beneficiaries were St Andrew's, Bloemfontein; St Mark's, Mbabane; Bishops; St Andrew's, Grahamstown; Kingswood College, Grahamstown; Pietersberg school; and the agricultural college for women at Harrismith. RTM 11 Dec. 1928, 19 Feb. 1929.

[124] By the time of his visit, Kerr estimated that they had invested £105,437 in the University.

most loyal and devoted supporters and who rendered unstinted services throughout a
long life to South Africa and the Empire'.[125] A contribution was made to a Smartt memorial scholarship and a £30,000 loan was cancelled 'in view of the fact that there was some
uncertainty as to how far the loan was a personal loan to Sir Thomas Smartt' (RTM 8
Oct. 1929, 16 Dec. 1930). The Trustees would have been happy to dispose of their interest in the Smartt Syndicate, but they were forced to retain, and indeed increase, their
holdings throughout the 1930s.

In 1929 Kerr made a gallant attempt to grasp another South African nettle. It was
unclear to what extent the Rhodes Trust retained responsibility for the Rhodes–Beit Share
Fund, which had been handed over to separate management in 1907. Sir Otto Beit was
now the only Rhodes Trustee who was also on the board of the Rhodes–Beit Share Fund.
It was his view that the fund was a quite separate trust, and that it should be kept in
being to be used for political purposes in South Africa. Kerr, on the contrary, maintained
that the entire fund should be handed back to the Rhodes Trustees: there could be no
justification for keeping alive a political fund long after the Union of South Africa had
been achieved and when political circumstances were so different from what they had
been at Rhodes's death. At all events, the present Rhodes Trustees could not take responsibility for political activity.[126]

Much of the fund was spent on payments to South African individuals associated with
Rhodes.[127] But in 1929 an annual payment of £3,000 was promised for ten years to the
South African Party of General Smuts.[128] Kerr was indignant and thought the money
could be much better used for African studies, or for a school of political science, in
Rhodes House. Against him, Beit invoked the memory of Milner, who would have
approved of the continuation of a party fund.[129]

Kerr obtained counsel's opinion to the effect that the Rhodes–Beit Share Fund had
never really been a trust, and that its 'Trustees' were acting on a revocable mandate from
the Rhodes Trustees. Beit was willing to agree that a large part of the Rhodes–Beit Share
Fund was no longer required for their purposes and that £80,000 could be retransferred
to the Rhodes Trust. He insisted, however, on retaining the remainder, which he estimated might be worth £360,000, as a separate fund for ten years.

The legal position of the fund was never finally determined. The Trustees feared that
if it was correct that the sub-trust was no real trust, then the Rhodes Trust might be

---

[125] RTM 30 Apr. 1929. The encomium contrasts interestingly with the cold terms in which they had
recorded the passing of Michell in the previous November.
[126] See the history of the fund in Kerr's memorandum of 1933, vetted by the Trust's lawyers, in RTF
2773.
[127] Beneficiaries included the Smartt family, Lady Michell, and several of Rhodes's political agents. A
special £100,000 fund was set aside for the 1820 Memorial Settlers' Association. The recipient of a £3,000
grant was long identified to the Rhodes Trustees only as 'X'. Only after Otto Beit's death was it revealed
that 'X' was Sir Percy Fitzpatrick, a former Jameson raider and Cape and Union MP, best known as the
author of *Jock of the Bushveld*. On his death a farm and a substantial sum passed from the Rhodes–Beit
Share Fund to his sons. The Rhodes Trustees were so anxious that the Inland Revenue should not be put
on the trail of the share fund that they paid the estate duties themselves. RTF 2773.
[128] Holland to Kerr, 12 June 1929; Kerr to Beit, 30 May 1929; RTF 2773.
[129] Kerr to Beit, 30 May 1929.

made liable for death duties on the deaths of all the Rhodes–Beit Trustees since 1907. In 1933, however, Peacock and Kerr (who had now succeeded to the title of Marquess of Lothian) made a clean breast of the long story to the Inland Revenue. The legal position was so complicated and uncertain that both sides were happy to agree to a compromise rather than test the matter in court. The Rhodes–Beit 'Trustees' handed over a further £28,000 to the Public Purposes Fund in 1935 and a final payment of £167,000 was made in 1938–9.

In 1931, at Duncan's suggestion, a private Act of the South African Parliament was passed, registering the Trust as a body corporate, and enabling it to hold real estate in the Union. The purpose of the Trust was stated in the Act in the most general terms: 'for the promotion of education and other public purposes'. Initially the Hertzog government was reluctant to agree to the legislation: it was suspicious of possible political motives behind the bill, and sought power to investigate the Trust's affairs. Ministers seem to have been reassured, however, when told that for many years the Trustees' activities had been confined to educational and a few personal grants only.[130]

At this time the Trustees made a number of significant grants for African purposes north of the Limpopo. Already in 1904, at Michell's suggestion, they had spent money on archaeological exploration of Great Zimbabwe; now the anthropologist Leakey was asked to make further investigations there, and support was given to his research on the Kikuyu in Kenya.[131] Margery Perham was funded for two successive years to study the British treatment of African populations. The Trustees were proud of the work she produced, and when Sir Edward Grigg protested to the Trustees about some of her statements about East Africa they rebuffed his choleric complaints. Rhodes travelling fellows were responsible for their own views, which were not necessarily those of the Trustees (RTM 29 Sept. 1931).

Kerr was anxious to set up, in connection with Rhodes House, an institute of government which would study 'the great imperial experiment' with special emphasis on Africa. His plans went through several drafts,[132] and after a 1929 conference on Africa chaired by Fisher and attended by Smuts it was proposed that the institute should take the form of a centre for African studies. A committee under Fisher wrote a constitution for the institute, with half a dozen research professors under a director, and prepared to launch an appeal.[133] The Trustees agreed to pay for an extension to Rhodes House if £100,000 could be found elsewere. The Rockefeller Foundation was asked, by Smuts and others, to provide this funding. However, the proposal was turned down as too British and insufficiently international. Julian Huxley then sought the Trust's support for a

---

[130] In view of the purchase of *Argus* shares and the activities of the Rhodes–Beit Fund, this assurance was economical with the truth.

[131] See RTF 2653 and 2911.

[132] RTF 2792; see also R. Symonds, *Oxford and Empire* (Oxford: OUP, 1986), 173–4. At one time Kerr thought that the main thing Oxford lacked was 'adequate contact with the higher direction of large-scale industry', and he looked to Rhodes House to remedy this. Memorandum of 26 Apr. 1926; RTF 2709.

[133] Among suggestions for professors were: Reginald Coupland for history, Julian Huxley for ecology, Malinowski for anthropology. As director, Smuts proposed Grigg, but Kerr thought he was too identified with the settlers, and proposed instead Richard Feetham or Sir Arnold Wilson (RTR 2792).

bureau of African ecology, but by this time the financial situation had worsened and the Trustees declined to help.[134]

Rhodes House in the 1930s

After moving into Rhodes House Wylie had only two further years in post. During this time the Trustees took advantage of the new powers which the 1929 Act gave them in respect of the scholarships. The district system in the United States was introduced in December 1930, in spite of a further spate of protests from Chicago and some state governors.[135] A selection committee was set up to appoint the German scholars.[136] After a period of hesitation a scholarship for East Africa was introduced.[137]

By now most Rhodes scholars came to Oxford with senior standing, which meant that they were enabled to take a BA at the end of their second year. In consequence, the third year was henceforth treated, under the terms of the new Act, as a prize to be awarded only to scholars who had obtained a first or second class (or an advanced degree). For the next decade these optional third years were awarded on liberal terms, with scholars allowed to spend them in postgraduate studies anywhere in Britain, Europe, the dominions, or the USA, provided they did not return to their home country (RTM 23 July 1929). Indeed, some scholars were allowed to take third years as far away as China (RTM 10 Jan. 1937).

Scholarships were not extended into the fourth year, but specially deserving scholars (such as the future Trustee Kenneth Wheare) were given loans to complete their doctorates, loans which were often quickly written off (RTM 6 Dec. 1932). A new and generous rule was introduced whereby a scholar who obtained a degree at the end of his second year and pursued an academic career could apply within the next ten years to take the third year of his scholarship as a sabbatical at Oxford. For scholars on stipend the ban on marriage was still enforced, but with a degree of clemency. One American Rhodes scholar was allowed to return for a third year on stipend, having married during the vacation owing, it was said, to a misunderstanding of a speech by President Aydelotte.[138]

In March 1931 Wylie was succeeded by C. K. Allen, who was given the new title 'Warden of Rhodes House'.[139] An Australian graduate of New College, Allen had been a fellow of University College since 1920 and professor of jurisprudence since 1931; as

---

[134] The African Survey which Smuts had proposed as part of the Oxford centre's programme was eventually carried out by Lord Hailey on behalf of the Royal Institute of International Affairs. See Symonds, *Oxford and Empire*, 177.

[135] See Alexander, below p. 140. The system was supposed to be reviewed after five years, but in fact it operated unaltered until 1997.

[136] See Sheppard, below p. 374.

[137] See Kenny, below p. 457.

[138] RTM 22 Dec. 1931. The rule against marriage was not to apply in the case of returners on sabbatical.

[139] There were objections, which went unheard, from some colleges whose wardens had a more ancient title.

Warden he continued a career of distinguished legal scholarship, which led to his becoming a fellow of the British Academy in 1944 and taking silk in 1945.

It fell to Allen to establish the pattern of usage of Rhodes House. A series of Rhodes Memorial Lectures was held in Milner Hall; in the 1930s the lecturers included Élie Halévy, General Smuts, Albert Einstein, and Edwin Hubble. In 1930 the Trustees had agreed that the house could be used 'for charitable meetings of general interest to the University at which in special circumstances collections or the sale of literature for the benefit of the charity should be permitted, but that the sale of tickets by agencies in the town beforehand should not be allowed' (RTM 27 May 1930). Outside bodies organized lecture courses on many different topics, including one on Russia in which, the Trustees insisted, 'the Russian situation must be exposed both from the Soviet and anti-Soviet point of view' (RTM 12 Jan. 1932). The Congress of Empire Universities made it their headquarters while in Oxford. An Oxford Association promoted by Lionel Curtis, later to become the Oxford Society, was given a temporary office there in 1932. A piano was purchased in 1932, and from time to time the Trustees paid for bands to play at Rhodes scholar dances. In 1934 the Trustees gave instructions for the laying down of a wine cellar (RTM 18 Dec. 1934). This was principally for the annual dinners for the scholars; but from time to time entertainment was provided for Commonwealth visitors, such as a group of Canadian writers sponsored by John Buchan in 1933, or the Rhodesian guests at the coronation in 1937 (RTM 13 Mar. 1933, 3 May 1937).

The Trustees' dinners for scholars in Rhodes House were attended by many Oxford luminaries and addressed by speakers of international renown. The 1933 dinner, for instance, presided over by L. S. Amery, had as principal speakers two who had fought on opposite sides in the Boer War, Sir Abe Bailey and General Smuts. Abe Bailey, once a crony of the Founder's, proposed the toast to him with a wealth of earthy reminiscence. Smuts, in proposing the toast to the scholars, told them that he had just flown from the Cape to Cairo on his way to the world economic conference, on an airline which fulfilled, in a way Rhodes could never have dreamed of, his idea of a great transport line across Africa from south to north. In Oxford, Smuts told the scholars, they had picked up wisdom, experience, and learning, but the most important thing they had learnt was the code of a gentleman and sportsman. 'If everything else fails you I think you will find that is sufficient to help you over the rough places.'[140]

Recession and Recovery

The appointment of Allen as Warden coincided with the financial crisis of 1931. In the national government formed by Ramsey MacDonald in August of the year, Lothian became Chancellor of the Duchy of Lancaster, and later Under-Secretary for India.[141] In the crisis year the Trust's investments lost 12.5 per cent of their value (RTM 22 Dec. 1931).

---

[140] The speeches were printed by the Trustees in a pamphlet for private distribution.

[141] He visited India in the winter of 1931–2, but resigned from the government shortly afterwards in protest at the Ottawa agreements which offended his free trade principles. On Lothian's Indian involvement, see A. Bosco, *Lord Lothian* (Milan: Jaca, 1989), 175–217.

For several years to come there were deficits in the Scholarship Fund; the Trustees were able to weather the slump because of the Capital Reserve Fund, but it was no longer possible to contribute £10,000 per annum to that fund as originally planned.

There was disagreement over how best to respond to the crisis. Peacock argued that investments should be restricted to UK and better-class colonial gilts, security taking priority over yield. He was supported by the newly appointed financial Trustee, Reginald Sothern Holland.[142] Lothian, on the other hand, believed that too much of the Trust's money was invested in fixed interest; he favoured investment in land, and expansion in equities, in the USA as well as at home.

Kerr won the argument, and the Trustees agreed in July 1932 that they should buy good urban property to the value of £100,000.[143] At the same time it was resolved to cut down on donations and to warn some previously favoured beneficiaries that financial circumstances might force their support to be cut.[144]

By mid-1933, things had improved. Persuaded by Duncan, the Trustees resumed their benefactions to South Africa, commencing with £1,000 for the library at Rhodes University College. Encouraged also by Smuts, the Trustees made annual grants to the South African Institute of Race Relations (RTM 5 Mar. 1934). In 1934 £1,000 was given to Fort Hare, in 1936 a grant was made for the training of native teachers in Basutoland, and in 1937 grants were made to native schools in Sophiatown and Orlando (RTM 6 Nov. 1934, 21 July 1936, 15 Nov. 1937). In the same year Duncan's close links with the Trust were terminated because of his appointment as Governor General of South Africa.[145]

When Otto Beit died in 1930 the Trustees had minuted their regret at the passing of one who had been 'the last survivor of the personal friends of the Founder'. During the 1930s they had several problems about keeping the Founder's memory green. From Rhodesia, where the Inyanga estate had been handed over to the government, they received frequent complaints of neglect from its former administrator McDonald (22 June 1937). Kipling, who had been given permission by Rhodes to live in the Woolsack in Groote Schuur, neither made use of the house nor relinquished his claim. The Trustees, who had long wished it to be used as a residence for a senior politician, were relieved when in 1936 they could inform the South African government that Kipling's life interest had expired.[146] They were happy to agree to an arrangement whereby J. H. Hofmeyr

---

[142] Appointed in 1932, Holland had been an associate of Jameson and had long been a manager of the Rhodes–Beit Share Fund. He is one of the few Rhodes Trustees not to figure in the *DNB*.

[143] RTM 19 July 1932. At the same meeting there was considerable discussion whether it was proper for an educational trust to invest in liquor shares.

[144] More than once in these years the Trustees resolved to be strict in the approval of third year funding, in order to save expense (RTF 2709). Allen believed that 60% of scholars benefited from a third year, but Lothian wanted it to be reserved for exceptional cases. A Third Year committee of Trustees was formed in 1935; it behaved generously, allowing 47 cases in 1936 and 59 in 1938.

[145] At his request the Trustees discontinued the grant which they had hitherto made in support of the education of his children (RTM 10 Jan. 1937).

[146] RTM 18 Feb. 1936. In 1932 Sir Herbert Baker suggested to Kipling that he might give up the Woolsack so that it could be used as a residence for an artist, writer, or musician. Kipling refused. 'Translated,' he wrote, 'this means some sort of soft billet for some pet of the Trustees—probably a pink Bolshie.' Kipling to Elsie Bambridge, 23 Dec. 1932; unpublished letter kindly communicated by Prof. Tom Pinney.

(SACS and Balliol 1910), now a government minister, should take up residence there (RTM 19 May 1936). Muizenberg, the cottage in which Rhodes had died, still belonged to the Trust: during the decade they made attempts to get rid of it, first, unsuccessfully, to the government of Northern Rhodesia, and later, successfully, to the city council of Cape Town (RTM 14 Apr. 1931, 16 Nov. 1936).

Many people in the 1930s were anxious to celebrate the memory of Rhodes: most of them received scant support from the Trust. McDonald was anxious that every school in Rhodesia should have a portrait of the nation's founder; he was turned down in 1933, though in 1937 the Trustees did agree to present a portrait to Government House in Salisbury.[147] In 1933 a proposal that Kipling should be asked to write a life of Rhodes was very coldly received (RTM 18 July 1933). In the same year the Trustees, who had earlier turned down a request from John Buchan that they should put up a £5,000 guarantee for the making of a film of Rhodes's life, turned down a further proposal for a subsidy to a similar Gaumont British project (RTM 11 Dec. 1928, 5 Mar. 1934).

The legal and fiscal position of the Trust still needed attention. The Public Purpose Trust had been set up by deed poll in 1921. The Scholarship and Scholarship Capital Reserve Funds were entrenched in the 1929 Act. But there were still substantial funds held by the Trustees as residuary legatees, not as charity trustees, which were therefore subject to tax and death duties. In 1937 the Trustees decided to convert the bulk of the residuary estate into a charitable trust, to be known as 'The Rhodes Trust'. To avoid the payment of death duties whatever funds were necessary to preserve for non-charitable purposes were put into a company to be known as 'The Rhodes Estate Co. Ltd.'.[148] At last in September 1938 the Estate Duty Office was able to assure the Trustees that no death duty claims would arise in connection with the death of any existing Trustee (RTM 29 Sept. 1938).

Though the Rhodes Trust had made frequent contributions to the Oxford Preservation Trust (formed on the initiative of Fisher and Kerr in 1927),[149] it was not until 1936 that the Trustees made their first really substantial benefaction to Oxford University. Vice-Chancellor Lindsay planned an appeal for £500,000, half for the new Bodleian Library and half for research in science and social studies. There were now about 200 research students a year in Oxford, of whom 64 were Rhodes scholars. The appeal had been suggested in a memorandum of Lionel Curtis, and Fisher and Lothian commended it enthusiastically to the Trustees. If Oxford was to continue to attract good students as Rhodes scholars it must be distinguished in research as well as in teaching, he insisted. When the appeal went public in 1937 it was launched with a gift of £100,000 from the Trustees and a matching one from Lord Nuffield.[150] The Trustees expressed the wish that their gift

---

[147] RTM 22 Dec. 1931, 10 Jan. 1937. The Trustees did allow copies to be made of portraits to be distributed to Rhodesian schools and Fairbridge schools.

[148] The company remained in existence only for a year; it was liquidated on 14 Nov. 1938, and its assets transferred to the Rhodes Trust. RTF 2891.

[149] Kerr wrote the Oxford Preservation Trust's first circular and the Rhodes Trust initially provided office space.

[150] Money was collected, with reluctance, by Allen from scholars in residence. Aydelotte raised more than $75,000 in the USA, and something was raised in Canada, but Behan and Lewis refused to collect in their constituencies. RTF 2935.

should be used to support research into social studies with special reference to 'the problems of modern government in the British Commonwealth and the American Republic'.[151]

No new scholarships were founded in the 1930s. Lothian, after his term as Under-Secretary of State for India, retained a keen interest in that country; but in 1933 when the Trustees considered establishing scholarships for India they did not feel able to proceed.[152] Proposals for scholarships in Hawaii and in the Leeward Islands were rejected (RTM 27 May, 1 July 1930). In 1934 a schoolmistress in Pietermaritzburg asked the Trustees to introduce scholarships for women; but the Trustees took no action (RTM 16 Apr. 1934).

Of the original constituencies the one which gave the Trustees most concern was Germany.[153] The restoration of the scholarships in 1930 had not been well timed, and it took quite an effort to preserve the selection procedure from contamination by Nazi infiltration. Allen attended a selection committee in 1932 and was impressed by the judgement and independence of the chairman, Schmidt-Ott, who had been the scholarship adviser to the Kaiser before the war. Lothian paid more than one visit to Germany on Rhodes business. He was indignant at Nazi outrages, but he had long been a critic of the Treaty of Versailles, and he was sympathetic to German grievances.[154] He was courted by the German government, and on 29 January 1935 he had a long interview with Hitler. In the course of the interview he quoted the codicil to Rhodes's will to the effect that Britain, the USA, and Germany would together preserve the peace of the world.[155] In May 1937 he saw the Führer again and repeated Rhodes's ideal.

As a close associate of the Astors, who consorted at Cliveden with members of the Chamberlain government, Lothian was deeply involved in the politics of appeasement.[156] But he was always anxious to preserve the independence of the German Rhodes scholarships. His position here was quite precisely thought out. 'It would', he wrote,

be quite impossible for the Trustees to veto [an] election on the grounds of the political opinions of the candidate. The Trustees cannot differentiate between candidates on the grounds of race, religion, or political opinion. Our objection to Nazism is precisely that they do these things. I told the committee that the Trustees were indifferent to whether the candidate was a Nazi or not. What they were concerned with was that Non-Nazis should have an equal chance of application with

---

[151] Some of the Trustees felt that too much of the appeal money was earmarked for the Bodleian and for the natural sciences. From 1936 onwards the Trustees administered a fund set up by the Carnegie Corporation for research purposes in Oxford; the first grant was made to an Idaho Rhodes scholar, H. S. Arms. Grants were made at intervals until the fund was wound up after the war's end. RTF 2935B.

[152] See Kenny, below p. 448.

[153] See Sheppard, below pp. 380 ff.

[154] After the Night of the Long Knives, Lothian told A. L. Rowse, 'we can't have any dealings with these people, they are a lot of gunmen'. But he was, Rowse avers, unstable and later 'hobnobbed with Hitler' (*All Souls and Appeasement* (London, 1961), 31).

[155] A record of the interview is published as an appendix to Butler, *Lothian*. Lothian was the first British establishment figure to have a serious meeting with Hitler.

[156] Bosco, *Lothian*, 225 describes him as 'maggior teorico dell' *appeasement* mediante i due organi di informazione controllati dagli Astor, conferenze a Chatham House e soppratutto mediante una serie di articoli di ampio respiro su "Round Table"'.

Nazis and that the Committee should elect that man who in the independent opinon of a Committee constituted by themselves most nearly conformed to Mr Rhodes's ideal.[157]

Once Hitler's true designs became clear, in the year of Munich, Lothian's position was little different from that of L. S. Amery, the chairman of the Trustees since 1933. Amery, as is well known, was the most eloquent of the MPs who in 1940 called for the replacement of the Chamberlain government by that of Winston Churchill.[158]

From Munich to Dunkirk

Early in 1939 Lothian resigned as Secretary of the Trust to take up the post of Ambassador to Washington. His last months in office were overcast by the shadow of war. Meeting in London on 29 September 1938, the day Chamberlain flew to Munich, the Trustees learnt that the American scholars had been held temporarily at Swarthmore because of the fear that war was imminent.[159] Provision was made for scholars in residence to be paid off and sent home, with permission to resume their scholarships after the war. In the event the Munich agreement gave an extension of peace, and a full quota of scholars came on stipend for the year 1938–9. But early in Hilary term it was agreed to offer Rhodes House as a hospital, if war broke out, and the Allens were given permission to take in refugee children (RTM 7 Feb. 1939). The Lodge was to become an air raid post (RTM 1 May 1939).

As successor to Lothian the Trustees appointed Lord Elton, a former don at Queen's, who had twice stood for Parliament in the Labour interest, and had been made a peer by Ramsay MacDonald, whom he much admired.[160] Almost as soon as Elton took up his post in July 1939 the Trust evacuated its offices in Waterloo Place, never to return, though it was not until 1944 that it was decided to move permanently to Oxford. With a reduced staff Elton occupied some rooms in Rhodes House, where he remained until 1947.

In the last year of peacetime, cash came into the Trust from a number of sources. F. W. Rhodes, the Founder's nephew, died in July 1938 and the Dalham estate passed to the Trust. Its assets, worth £55 million, were consigned to the Scholarship Capital Reserve

---

[157] Lothian to F. C. Scott, 1 Feb. 1935—a correspondence triggered by the election of a candidate who was alleged to be a Nazi.

[158] See Louis, *In the Name of God, Go!*, 116–22.

[159] See Alexander, below p. 142.

[160] Elton's appointment was not uncontroversial. The Provost of Queen's advised H. A. L. Fisher against the choice. 'He is the son of a Wellington master who was left a fortune by an aunt', Fisher told Lothian, 'was head of the school at Rugby and a scholar of Balliol where he was clearly much disliked by the Smith family . . . for his affected and superior manners. Returning to Oxford after the war he stood for Labour seats, and, as is only to be expected, attracted criticism from his political opponents, the more so since he wore a monocle, walked about with a bloodhound and generally affected the air of the youthful Dizzy.' The left-wing members of Queen's, Fisher was told, regarded him as a rigid conservative who had used Labour politics to get into the House of Lords. Not a good man of business, the Provost thought, and unsound in judgement about college matters; unlikely to go down well with Australians, but a fluent and articulate speaker. Fisher to Lothian, 29 Nov. 1938, National Archives of Scotland, GD 40/17/371 fos. 295[r]–296[r].

Fund (RTM 18 July 1939). The Trustees had long wished to dispose of their interest in the Smartt Syndicate, attempting to sell it to the Imperial Cold Storage Company and the Union government. At length in July 1939 they disposed of their shares and debentures to Hirschorn, the administrator of the property. The sale realized something over £75,000, which was invested in Rhodes Trust South Africa (RTM 18 July, 13 Dec. 1939). In November 1939 the residue of the Rhodes–Beit Share Fund was at last handed over to the Rhodes Trustees, a sum of £164,000. In the following July the fund was closed and its assets taken into the main trusts. A sum of £500,000 was paid into each of the scholarship funds, and the residue was held in the Rhodes Trust for pensions and other purposes. The separate £100,000 fund for the benefit of the 1820 Settlers was taken into the Public Purposes Fund (RTM 29 July 1940).

Scholars had been elected in the normal way to come into residence in October 1939. On the outbreak of war it was decided that no scholar or scholar-elect in the USA was to be allowed to travel to England. US scholars in Oxford might reside and retain their scholarships, but only if the Warden obtained the written consent of their parents. Scholars from the dominions were given the choice of continuing their scholarships, volunteering for military service, or returning home. Those who had left Oxford, or who had not yet arrived, were allowed to come to Oxford but should be warned that their scholarships might be suspended. Scholars whose scholarships were suspended would not necessarily forfeit them if they married before resuming (RTM 26 Sept. 1939). Eighty scholars, scattered throughout Europe, returned to Oxford in October, often after adventurous journeys, to join conscripts who were doing 'war degrees' under a depleted staff of dons. The Beit room in Rhodes House was turned into a common room for scholars during the vacations (RTM 13 Dec. 1939).

No scholars had been elected from Germany in 1939. With regard to those elected in 1938 it was decided that they could not stay in Oxford but would be funded to continue their studies, if they wished, in a neutral country.[161] All over the world, elections of scholars for 1940 were initially suspended; but after the immediate shock of the declaration of war the Trustees did allow elections to be made, for 1940 and 1941, in the Commonwealth countries. However, most of the scholars elected did not take up their scholarships until the war was over.

Throughout the war Oxford continued to function as a university, with up to 2,000 students in residence; but once the phoney war was over hardly any Rhodes scholars remained. In May 1940 the first Rhodes scholar was killed in action, Major Cecil Bowen of the Irish Guards (Rhodesia and Brasenose 1913). The US government threatened to deprive of citizenship any of its nationals who remained in belligerent countries. Thirteen American Rhodes scholars left from Ireland on 14 June 1940 on the *President Roosevelt*, the last ship to carry expatriates home across the Atlantic. Some of the scholars had been on the verge of taking finals. Special arrangements were made for them to sit their Oxford papers in Swarthmore.[162] By the end of the 1939–40 academic year only

---

[161] See Sheppard, below p. 396.   [162] See Alexander, below p. 143.

seventeen scholars were in residence, and from 1941 to 1945 only Bermuda and Malta went on making regular elections.

In July 1940 the Rhodes Trustees assisted with the evacuation of 125 children of Oxford dons to safety across the Atlantic, at the invitation of Swarthmore College and the Universities of Yale and Toronto.[163] Much of the burden of organization and the expense of the evacuation was borne by the Warden and the Trust (RTM 24 June 1940). Between June and September survivors from the Dunkirk evacuation used Rhodes House as a centre for rest and recreation. During the invasion fears of September 1940 a hundred women and children were evacuated from Kent to Oxford, and were accommodated for ten days on palliasses in Milner Hall while awaiting their permanent billets. One family, which could not find a billet, stayed on the top floor of the house throughout the war years, as did a number of evacuees from a London girls' high school.

In December 1940 Lothian died in Washington. Winston Churchill paid him a handsome obituary tribute: 'In all the years I had known him he had given me the impression of high intellectual & aristocratic detachment from public affairs. Airy, viewy, aloof, dignified, censorious, yet in a light and gay manner, he had always been good company. Now, under the same hammer that smote upon us all, I found an earnest deeply-stirred man.'[164]

Rhodes House in Wartime

During the war Rhodes House served a number of uses. Air raids were a constant fear, particularly after German planes had flown over Oxford to devastate Coventry. The basement of the house was made an air raid shelter (RTM 24 June 1940). A regular fire picket was maintained, sometimes by evacuated sixth-formers, sometimes by Oxford medical students; they were given accommodation and paid 3 guineas a week (RTM 15 Feb., 16 Dec. 1941). At one time the Oxford City Council planned to move to Rhodes House in the event of any damage to its own offices; the Trustees agreed reluctantly, but the move was never necessary.[165] The west lawn was planted with vegetables; on the south lawn a static water tank was erected for firefighting. Milner Hall was used for Red Cross training (RTM 14 Mar. 1942).

Warden Allen travelled frequently to London to sit on an appellate tribunal for conscientious objectors. Lady Allen, whose staff of eight had departed for war work, showed herself a capable and motherly organizer.[166] In the later years of the war, with a subsidy

---

[163] The Allens' daughter Rosemary was evacuated to live with Michener, the Canadian Secretary.

[164] Butler, *Lothian,* 305. Lothian had been a successful Ambassador in Washington. As a lifelong friend to the USA and a converted appeaser, he was particularly convincing as an advocate of British war aims. In view of his long-held belief that the UK and the USA should combine to maintain the freedom of the seas, it was fitting that his last achievement was securing the handover of fifty US destroyers to the Royal Navy.

[165] However, the city did set up in the basement a control centre for air raid precautions (RTM 14 June 1941).

[166] She left a vivid account of her work in Rhodes House during the war in ch. VIII of her memoir *Sunlight and Shadow* (Oxford: OUP, 1960).

from the Trustees, she set up an information office in Oxford for American soldiers. She made Rhodes House available for dances and other entertainments for Allied soldiers, and for service students at A. D. Lindsay's educational courses in Balliol. This direct hospitality to overseas Allies supplemented grants made by the Trust to the YMCA, the YWCA, the Church Army, and the Salvation Army for comforts for soldiers and prisoners of war.[167]

In April 1940 H. A. L. Fisher was killed in a street accident; he was replaced, as an Oxford Trustee, by Dean Lowe of Christ Church, an Ontario Rhodes scholar of 1922. Lowe was the first Rhodes scholar to become head of a house in Oxford, and the first to become a Trustee. The Dean was joined as a Trustee by his treasurer, G. T. Hutchinson, a friend of the Rhodes family who had been considered as a possible General Secretary at the time of Lothian's appointment.[168] In 1941 the Trustees co-opted Lord Hailey, a former Indian Governor and editor of the magisterial *African Survey* of 1938.

During the war the Trustees continued grants to South African schools: £5,000 was given to Bishops for its centenary fund, and £3,000 to St Andrew's, Grahamstown, including special scholarships for Afrikaner boys. Regular payments were made to the 1820 Settlers' Association and £1,000 per annum was given to support its London office. The Association administered training farms for British settlers in South Africa which had come into the Trust's possession along with the Rhodes–Beit Fund.[169] A two-year grant was given to a student of the psychologist F. C. Bartlett at Cambridge to research into 'the backward races of the Union' (RTM 2 Nov. 1940). Towards the end of the war a grant of £5,000 was made to the college at Fort Hare (RTM 28 July 1945).

At this time two seventeenth-century Flemish tapestries were offered for sale by the Countess of Londesburgh which matched a pair hung by Rhodes in Groote Schuur. The Trustees purchased them for £900, and sent them as a present to General Smuts. He hung them not in Groote Schuur but in the South African Prime Minister's other official residence in Libertas, Pretoria.[170]

During the war Elton ensured that the Trustees were active in promoting the memory of the Founder. Arthur Bryant, the popular historian whose patriotic volumes on the Napoleonic era were regarded as a significant contribution to the British war effort, was invited in 1943 to write the authorized biography (RTM 17 July 1943). He accepted, but took his time over getting down to work. In the meantime Hutchinson wrote a 5,000-word pamphlet, of which 3,000 copies were bought by the Trust for distribution to former scholars (RTM 12 Nov. 1943, 14 Mar. 1944).

Having long ago handed over to the British South Africa Company responsibility for Rhodes's burial site in the Matopos, the Trustees often suspected that the Company's successor, the government of Southern Rhodesia, was neglecting the site, and was diverting

---

[167] Hospitality to Allied forces is documented in RT 2987.

[168] RTM 27 Sept. 1940; see Amery's diary for 26 May 1925.

[169] The Trustees were divided about the utility of these farms. One farm, Robian, was sold in 1942; the other, Tarka, was retained until 1951. Another farm had been left to the Trust in 1937 by Charles Crewe; when this was sold the proceeds were given to the Settlers (RTF 2478, 2672).

[170] RTM 17 May 1941, 4 Dec. 1945. The tapestries were eventually reunited in Groote Schuur by Mrs Vorster.

to other purposes the funds the Trust had provided for its upkeep. In 1943 Sir James McDonald was drowned at sea, and the Trustees appointed Robert Tredgold (Rhodesia and Hertford 1919) as their representative in the country. He persuaded the Prime Minister of Southern Rhodesia to set up a new board for the administration of the Matopos and Inyanga estates.

Elton also persuaded the Trustees to hang portraits of their predecessors and their officers on the walls of Milner Hall which hitherto, in deference to architectural purists, had remained bare. The first commission was a posthumous painting of Lothian. The proposal for a portrait gallery was surprisingly controversial. Sothern Holland strongly objected to such a use of Trust funds, and threatened resignation, but his objection was overruled.[171]

During the years of war the Trustees made a number of grants to promote popular education in Empire history, in order, as Elton put it, to repair the disrepute into which the Empire had fallen during the years of cynicism before the war. A proposal was made that when the war was over the Trustees should make 'residential additions to Rhodes House to enable it to go further towards becoming a social and cultural centre of the Empire' (RTM 11 Oct. 1941). Like other proposals to extend Rhodes House, this was never carried out. However, grants to organizations such as the Imperial Institute continued until well after the war (RTM 13 Dec. 1944, 4 Feb. 1947).

While the ordinary scholarships were suspended, several suggestions were made for replacements. A. D. Lindsay proposed that a scholarship should be offered to Czech, German, and other refugee students (RTM 9 Apr. 1940). The philosopher Donald Mackinnon suggested that scholarships should be offered to members of the British community in the Argentine (RTM 10 June 1944). The Colonial Office proposed a scholarship for Hong Kong Chinese (RTM 29 July 1940).

All these proposals were rejected: the one new constituency which interested the Trustees was India. In February 1940 they voted in principle to set up an Indian scholarship; but it was not until after the war that the decision was put into execution.[172] In June 1940, Amery, the senior Trustee, joined Churchill's cabinet as Secretary of State for India, and from time to time the Trustees held their meetings in the India Office. In 1942 a grant of £2,500 was made to Delhi University; several grants were made to the Student Christian Movement of India, and a scholar was given a subsidy for work on Bengali literature (RTM 13 June 1942, 26 Apr. 1945).

By July 1944 the Trustees were sufficiently confident that the war was nearly over to discuss the resumption of scholarships. They were willing to offer 200 additional scholarships to men of the war years, and to raise the stipend to £450 (an increase which they optimistically hoped would be only temporary). They agreed

that while it is not the business of selection committees to pronounce upon the political opinions of candidates it would be well at the appropriate moment to remind committees that Mr Rhodes clearly expressed his desire that his scholars should make the rendering of public service their highest aim and that he would undoubtedly have regarded the rendering of public service at such a time

---

[171] Holland to Elton, 30 Dec. 1942; RTF 3000.   [172] See Kenny, below p. 449.

as this as one of the clearest ways in which a candidate could exhibit his qualifications for a Rhodes scholarship. (RTM 7 Oct. 1944)

This was not, in the event, interpreted either by the Trustees or by the selection committees as excluding from the scholarships those who had been conscientious objectors. The rule against marriage was to be relaxed for those who had served in the war, though the Trustees insisted that scholars should themselves be responsible for the upkeep of wives and families, and advised scholars to come alone at first to prepare the way in Oxford (RTM 26 Apr. 1945).[173]

In 1945, while elections were held in most constituencies, Rhodes House prepared to return to its normal uses. The fireguards had been disbanded at the end of 1944 (RTM 13 Dec. 1944). New stacks for the library, designed by Sir Herbert Baker, were ordered for the basement at a cost of £15,000 (RTM 28 July 1945). The garden was restored and improved. It took a year or two before the static water tanks were removed and the wine cellar was restocked (RTM 28 Apr. 1947, 24 Feb. 1949).[174]

The Rhodes Trust Act 1948

During the war the Trust's assets increased substantially. The market value of their investments at the end of 1939 was £2.364 million; at the end of 1944 it was £3.312 million. During the same period their properties were estimated to have appreciated by about 30 per cent. However, during the closing years of the war the Trustees began to worry whether their governing instruments were adequate to meet their investment and other needs. In 1943 Coward Chance raised questions about the limits of the Trustees' entitlement. In the early 1940s, in addition to the will, the UK Acts of Parliament of 1916 and 1929, and the South African Act of 1931, the Trustees' activities were based on the deed poll of June 1921 which had set up the Public Purposes Trust, and the deed poll of 1937 which had set up the Rhodes Trust. In July 1944 the Trustees were advised that the language of these trust instruments was too narrow for their purposes. The 1921 deed poll contained no reference to charitable purposes 'in any part of the world', and on a strict interpretation the Trust was only allowed to support purposes within the jurisdiction of the English courts. Secondly, the deeds refer to the application of the funds *by the Trustees*, and accordingly it was perhaps improper for the Trustees to hand sums over to other organizations. This would mean that many of the Trust's regular grants were *ultra vires*. There was a further doubt whether the Trustees had any power to invest in land. It was suggested that only a new private bill would suffice to remove these doubts and set the Trustees' activities on a secure legal footing (RTM 2 Oct., 12 Nov. 1943).

[173] A South African scholar elected in 1946 presented an unusual problem on return. He had married and been divorced since taking up his scholarship. The Warden was instructed to advise him to wait before attempting the experiment of a second marriage with his former wife. If, however, he should prove determined to marry her again, he might bring her to Oxford. RTM 4 Dec. 1945.

[174] In 1944 the library and offices of the *Round Table* were given temporary accommodation (RTM 13 Dec. 1944).

This news was greeted with irritation. Elton thought it ridiculous that on a strict interpretation the Trustees, instead of making grants to the Fairbridge Farm Schools, the YMCA, or the Red Cross, ought themselves to be supervising the emigration and training of children overseas, running canteens for the forces, or dispatching books to prisoners of war. On the issue of making grants outside Britain, he wrote to the Trustees:

The Deed in question was drawn up (in 1921) by legal advisers, who were of course well aware that the Rhodes Trust was an imperial trust, primarily concerned with objects overseas, and since they nevertheless contrived to produce a Deed which, the Trustees are now told, may perhaps not entitle them to make grants outside these islands, it is difficult to avoid the disquieting reflections that whatever Deed or Act may now be framed, twenty years hence some fatal flaw in it may well be discovered by a future generation of lawyers.

However, there was nothing for it but for the Trustees to do their best to put things right 'as advised in their own day and generation'.[175]

The Attorney General and the Charity Commissioners had to be approached, and the Ministry of Education and the Treasury Solicitor had to be consulted. Once their approval was secured a bill was drafted and lodged early in 1945. Amery, as chairman, gave evidence to the private bill committee on behalf of the Trust.[176] It was not until July 1946 that it passed into law.

The principal effect of the Act was to constitute the Trustees a body corporate, and to draw up regulations for their conduct of business. The 1921 and 1937 deeds were revoked and the assets of the Public Purposes Trust and the Rhodes Trust of 1937 were aggregated into a fund of the new incorporated Rhodes Trust under the title 'Public Purposes Fund'. The trusts of the scholarship fund remained as before, but the trusts of the Public Purposes Fund were defined as 'the promotion or advancement in any part of the British Commonwealth of Nations or in the United States of America of any educational or other charitable purpose'. Very wide powers of investment were specified. It was made explicit that grants could be made to other institutions: indeed the Trust was empowered to transfer any part of the income or capital of the Public Purposes Fund to any particular educational or other charitable organization in any part of the world. Finally, the Trustees were authorized to make provision for pensioners such as the Founder's nieces and Lady Smartt.

When he came to write a history of these years Elton said of the Act: 'As I glance through its fourteen mostly quite intelligible clauses today I find it difficult to believe that it will give our successors much further trouble.'[177] But in fact the Act contained ambiguities which came to light later. For instance, further advice was needed to ascertain whether the Act permitted the support of causes in countries which left the

---

[175] RTM 22 July 1944, with Elton's report to the Trustees.
[176] RTM 26 June 1945. In response to a question from Lord Hailsham he gave assurances that there was no intention to use the Act to revive the German scholarships.
[177] Elton, *The First Fifty Years*, 42.

Commonwealth. Again, how was the restriction of the purposes of the fund to the Commonwealth and the USA to be reconciled with the power to transfer funds to charitable organizations in any part of the world?

Scholars Demobilized

The Rhodes scholars who took up residence in Oxford at the end of the war were a very unusual group. In 1945 thirty-two arrived to take up postponed or interrupted scholarships; altogether there were fifty in residence in 1945–6. Most of these had been elected in the early years of the war and had been unable to take up their scholarships: they were now well over the normal age limit, and many had married. Most of them had to support their wives and families from demobilization grants. Australian scholars, who did not receive ex-service grants from their government, were given an extra £60 a year by the Trust (RTM 10 Feb. 1946).

In the USA elections were first held in 1946: in that year and in the next the Trustees allowed forty-eight scholars to be elected, to make up for the lost years. After 1946 no more scholars were allowed to return who had interrupted their course (RTM 3 Dec. 1946). Even so, by 1948 there were 220 scholars in residence, a record number. Eighty-four of these were accompanied by their wives, and there were, according to Allen's count, some fifty children in residence. Life was far from easy for the scholars and their families in the post-war England of rationing and austerity, especially in the exceptionally severe winter of 1946–7. Rhodes House served as creche and playgroup and centre for wives battered by the English climate.[178]

Gradually life returned to normal. Marriage after arrival was allowed only to ex-servicemen, and non-servicemen who married forfeited their scholarships. In 1949 the Trustees decided henceforth to refuse permission to marry, 'except to those who on election might have legitimate expectations' (RTM 14 Dec. 1949). There continued to be married scholars on stipend until the early 1950s. Thereafter, the pre-war regime was reimposed for a decade. Normal age limits were reimposed, though an exception was made in the early 1950s for those who had served in the Korean War.

The savings of the war years enabled the Trust to support the unprecedented number of scholars. However, the Trustees instructed their Third Year committee that on both academic and financial grounds it was desirable to restrict numbers, and a strong case was needed for the grant of a third year. It was, they were told, 'not desirable to extend special indulgence in the matter of third years to ex-service men, some of whom may be unduly reluctant to enter competitive civil life' (RTM 3 Dec. 1946). Henceforth it was much less usual than it had been for a third year to be granted at another university, or for a third year to be postponed and taken later in Oxford. While no strict quota was set, the target was that no more than 50 per cent of those completing their second year should be allowed to stay on.

---

[178] Again, the most vivid account is given by Dorothy Allen in *Sunlight and Shadow*, ch. IX.

Indian Summer in South Africa

In the decade after the war the Trustees continued to take a great interest in education at all levels and in all parts of South Africa.[179] Rhodes University College now became a university, and the Trust paid the stipend of its chaplain. It also supported student hostels at the Universities of Cape Town and Witwatersrand. The Trustees continued to see it as their duty to foster emigration to South Africa and in addition to their annual grant to the 1820 Settlers' Association they made substantial gifts to the Society for the Overseas Settlement of British Women.

The Trustees began to take more interest than hitherto in the education and welfare of the non-British population of South Africa, making grants for these purposes to the Salvation Army and to church groups such as the Community of the Resurrection in Johannesburg and the Good Shepherd nuns at Grahamstown (RTM 20 May 1950). A further grant was made to the college at Fort Hare (RTM 26 Feb. 1952). In 1948 and 1950 grants were made to the African Music Society in Johannesburg. In 1950 the Trustees voted a grant of £5,000 to the Bantu Press, a venture which owned most of the mother-tongue newspapers in South Africa. The Trustees believed that it was doing useful work in relief of racial tension, and they supported it for several years with grants and loans.[180]

The Rhodes Estate Devolution Act of 1911 had released the Trustees from any responsibility for the Groote Schuur estate, a large part of which was now the campus of the University of Cape Town.[181] In 1948 Elton paid a visit to South Africa on behalf of the Trust. He was affronted by some unsightly prefabricated buildings which had been erected by the University. He tried, in vain, to get Field Marshal Smuts to effect their removal. At the same time, the owners of the Rosebank Showground (not part of the Groote Schuur estate, but once the property of Cecil Rhodes) wished to sell their land to the government for development by UCT. Under the terms of the original transfer, the agreement of the Rhodes Trustees was required, and at Elton's prompting they made it the price of their consent that they should be given a degree of general control over the building plans of the University of Cape Town. This control was formalized in 1956 in a deed of servitude between the Trust, the University, and the provincial administration of the Cape of Good Hope. This conferred upon the Trustees powers and responsibilities which they were in no real position to exercise, and which for the next fifty years were to prove both burdensome and ineffective.[182] The buildings to which Lord Elton

---

[179] Grants or loans were made to Bishops and St George's in Cape Town; to St Andrew's, Bloemfontein; to St John's and St Benedict's in Johannesburg; to St Mark's, Mbabane; to Michaelhouse, Hilton College, and Kearsney College in Natal. RTM 4 Feb. 1947, 27 Apr. 1948, 30 Apr. 1949.

[180] RTM 29 July, 15 Dec. 1950. The Trustees had been worried that such a grant might bring them into bad odour with the South African government, but the High Commissioner, Sir Evelyn Baring, reported that Prime Minister Malan viewed the press favourably. Rather to the Trustees' embarassment, Syfret arranged for the managing director of the press to see the Prime Minister in person and obtain his blessing for their benefaction.

[181] See above, p. 11.

[182] Decisions of the Trustees about the erection of buildings and the widening of roads on the estate are to be found in RTM 22 Mar. 1950, 13 Aug. 1959, 25 May 1968, and elsewhere.

objected are still in place, and in spite of the assistance of the Cape Institute of Architects from time to time, several buildings have been erected on the campus, nominally
with the approval of the Trustees, which are widely regarded as eyesores.[183]

The Trust at Half-Century

In 1952 C. K. Allen retired as Warden and withdrew, with a knighthood, to the Banbury
Rd.[184] He was succeeded by Brigadier Edgar Trevor ('Bill') Williams, then senior
tutor of Balliol, who had had a remarkable military career as chief of intelligence to
General Montgomery during the war.[185] In the same year Frank Aydelotte, the first US
Secretary of the Trust, who had held office since 1918, stepped down and made way for
his successor as President of Swarthmore College, Courtney Smith (Iowa and Merton
1938).[186]

After taking up office as Warden, Williams persuaded the Trustees to redesign the lodgings in Rhodes House, moving the Warden's office on the ground floor into what had
been the drawing room, and moving the dining room and kitchen up to the first floor
so as to make room for a new ground floor drawing room (RTM 8 May 1954).[187]

The fiftieth anniversary of the scholarships fell in 1953, and a reunion of scholars was
held in Oxford. In a ceremony in the Sheldonian distinguished Rhodes scholars from
several continents—including Wilder Penfield and Senator Fulbright—received honorary
degrees,[188] and Vice-Chancellor Bowra conferred BAs and MAs on those who had not
hitherto troubled to take them. Individual colleges gave Gaudies for their members. A
history of the first fifty years of the Trust and the scholarships was commissioned, with
a retrospect on the Trust by Lord Elton, a history of the scholars at Oxford in two parts
by Wardens Wylie and Allen, and an essay on the American scholarships by Frank
Aydelotte.[189] The jubilee history was presented to all Rhodes scholars, and 500 additional copies were printed for sale to the public (RTM 21 Oct. 1954).

At Elton's instigation, the Trustees exhibited new concern not only with their own
history but with the memory of the Founder.[190] Already in 1948 it had been had agreed
that all Rhodes's non-financial papers should be made accessible to bona fide scholars.[191]
In 1955 C. H. Wilson of Cambridge, described as 'a highly qualified accountant', was

---

[183] After repeated attempts, the Trustees had by 1999 still not been able to disencumber themselves of
the powers and obligations imposed by the deed of servitude.

[184] He lived on until 1966 and published books on legal theory during his retirement.

[185] By academic profession, Williams was a historian and became editor of the *Dictionary of National
Biography*.

[186] See Alexander, below p. 146.

[187] The old Warden's office became available for secretarial staff, which was useful when the Beaumont
St. office was closed.

[188] These included Senator William Fulbright (Arkansas and Pembroke 1925) and the neurophysiolo-
gist Wilder Penfield (New Jersey and Merton 1914).

[189] He had already, in 1946, published with Princeton University Press a book-length review of the first
forty years of the American scholarships, entitled *The Vision of Cecil Rhodes*.

[190] In 1954 Elton visited Southern Rhodesia to urge the Prime Minister there to take proper care of
the Matopos estate and the Rhodes monument. RTM 17 July 1954.

[191] RTM 19 June 1948. An exception was made for any papers connected with Princess Radziwill.

asked to examine Rhodes's business papers, and report on their contents, with a view to the destruction of anything disedifying (RTM 26 Oct. 1955, 21 July 1956).[192] Meanwhile, Arthur Bryant was making heavy weather of his promised biography. In 1953 he announced that it would take until 1960 to complete, and it soon became clear that he had no real intention of finishing the job. In 1956 the Trustees commissioned J. G. Lockhart to write a biography, giving him access to all the Rhodes papers.[193]

An iconography of Rhodes was commissioned, and additions were made to the embryo portrait gallery in Milner Hall.[194] Portraits of previous Trustees were a natural choice: but there was now also a portrait of Kingsley Fairbridge. Originally Fairbridge's name had been inscribed in the rotunda, the first on a projected roll of honour for Rhodes scholars. After the war, the Trustees recoiled from the prospect of a series of invidious decisions, and decided that the roll of honour should include only those who had lost their lives in war. They deleted Fairbridge's name, and as a compensation prize placed a posthumous portrait in the hall (RTM 24 Feb. 1949).

In 1955 L. S. Amery died. He had been a Trustee for thirty-six years and had been a very regular attender at meetings.[195] He had been chairman since the 1930s; he was now succeeded by Sir Edward Peacock. Three new members joined the board: Lieutenant General Sir Archibald Nye, who after distinguished service in two wars had been High Commmissioner in Delhi and Ottawa; Sir Oliver (later Lord) Franks, the Provost of Queen's; and Lord Harcourt, a merchant banker recently returned from a tour as director of the IMF in Washington.[196]

Though the post-war years saw a temporary large increase in the number of scholars from the established constituencies, there was not, until the late 1950s, any expansion of the area from which Rhodes scholars were drawn. The first Indian scholars came into residence in 1948, only after the subcontinent had been partitioned. Henceforth one of the two Indian scholarships was given to Pakistan, from which the first scholar arrived in 1950.[197] In the same year, the Trustees suspended the East African scholarship. Grigg, now Lord Altrincham, protested, and elections were held in 1952 and 1956.[198] Throughout the 1950s appeals were made to the Trustees to restore the German scholarships, but these were firmly rejected.[199]

By 1957, Elton, under pressure from the Colonial Office, came to the view that the Trust should make some provision for the rapidly emerging self-governing

---

[192] Sir T. Gregory, however, was allowed to study the papers with a view to writing the history of the diamond industry. RTM 13 Dec. 1956.

[193] Some of Rhodes's associates and retainers at this time were still alive and receiving pensions from the Trust, such as 'Matabele' Wilson, Sheppy, who was with Rhodes during the Kimberley siege, the widow of his valet, and Mary M'Lamla, who had been a servant at the time of his death (RTM 9 Oct. 1951, 26 Feb. 1952, 16 Feb. 1954).

[194] See above, p. 43.

[195] However, his diary does not confirm the legend that in all his years he missed only a single meeting.

[196] (RTM 27 July 1957). In the same year Malcolm MacDonald retired. Once a pupil of Elton's, he had become a Trustee in 1948 but had never attended a meeting.

[197] See Kenny, below p. 451.

[198] See Kenny, below p. 457.

[199] See Sheppard, below pp. 402–4.

Commonwealth. 'The civilisation which we are handing on', he told the Trustees (RTR 429, 27), 'may collapse before it has been able to take root.' After long deliberation it was decided to create one triennial scholarship for each of six constituencies: Ceylon, Ghana, Nigeria, Kenya, Malaya, and the British Caribbean. The new scholarships began in 1959 when one was offered in Ceylon: others followed in subsequent years. The creation of these new Commonwealth scholarships was Elton's last achievement as Secretary.[200]

Plans for Rhodes House

Lord Elton retired on 30 September 1959. No General Secretary was appointed to replace him. Instead, 'Bill' Williams, Warden of Rhodes House since 1952, took over in addition the duties of Secretary of the Trust.[201] He was the first Secretary to be an Oxford don, and was already a respected figure in the University hierarchy.[202] During his secretaryship he prompted the Trustees to turn their attention away from the Trust's imperial past, and to devote themselves to the needs of the University of Oxford. He was unenthusiastic about expanding the scope of the scholarship scheme; he often expressed the opinion that the current intake of seventy scholars a year was the maximum Oxford could absorb. He preferred to focus, not on bringing more scholars to Oxford, but on ensuring that Oxford was a place fit for the scholars. 'Bluntly', he put it in a report in 1966 (RTR 459, 16), 'Oxford has got to remain good enough for Harvard men to want to come to it'.[203]

On taking over, Williams amalgamated under one roof the two offices hitherto separate in 36 Beaumont St and Rhodes House. He brought Miss Bain, Elton's secretary, to Rhodes House, and overall reduced the office staff from ten to five. He took his time about appointing an assistant secretary. 'My own work has not increased', he wrote, 'since the additional duties of looking over Miss Bain's shoulder are compensated for by not having to keep the Secretary informed and by dealing with all sorts of things concerning Selection Committees direct, instead of via Beaumont Street.' He interviewed a number of distinguished ex-colonial civil servants, but he was uncertain whether there would be enough work for them. 'I am most unwilling', he added, characteristically, 'to have a really able man my frustrated junior. Even in wartime it was difficult.'[204] Eventually R. G. Feltham was appointed, but when he left, six years later, to direct the Institute of Commonwealth Studies at Queen Elizabeth House, he was not replaced. Henceforth the Warden-and-Secretary was to be the single executive officer of the Trust.

---

[200] The story of the creation of the new Commonwealth scholarships is told in detail in Ch. 8 below.

[201] Already, as Warden, he had attended Trustees' meetings: the first Warden to do so rather than to be notified by the Secretary of those decisions which directly concerned the scholarships.

[202] Since 1951 he had been a member of its governing Hebdomadal Council and a curator of the University Chest (i.e. a member of its finance committee).

[203] The focus on Oxford was reflected in the composition of the Trust. Since the appointment of Sir Oliver Franks in 1957 no less than three of the younger Trustees were heads of Oxford colleges, and this was henceforth to be the pattern.

[204] RTR 440.

In his early years, Williams liked Rhodes House better as an office than as a residence. In a memorandum to the Trustees in May 1960 he dwelt on the difficulties of running the lodgings with only two morning cleaners and the prospect of a cook ('the sheer distances to be covered and on different floors are exhausting'). He proposed that both main floors of the Warden's wing should be used for offices, and a new compact house built next door for the Warden and his wife. But he also floated a more radical alternative.

Rhodes House was planned as a memorial to Mr Rhodes and as a thank-you gift to Oxford for its kindness to Rhodes Scholars. It was not built as their headquarters and successive Wardens have tried never to let any allegiance grow up there contrary to that to the College.

There had been many changes since Rhodes House had been built: with the development of Oxford science the centre of gravity of the University had moved north, and the Old Clarendon Building had become too small for the central administration. The Trustees should consider offering Rhodes House to the University as its headquarters. 'It would be no less (and in many ways more remarkable) a memorial to Mr Rhodes to make the building named after him the central University building' (RTR 439, 9–10).

The Trustees referred the matter to a committee chaired by Sir Oliver Franks (RTM 7 May 1960). In May 1961 Williams made his proposal more specific: Rhodes House should be offered to the University as an administrative centre on condition that the University provided an alternative site for a new set of offices and a Warden's residence. A possibility, he suggested, would be the site in Holywell belonging to Merton, occupied by the abandoned vicarage and school of St Cross church. Franks and his committee discussed the proposal with the Warden of Merton and the Vice-Chancellor, President Norrington of Trinity. The Holywell proposal was held to be impractical, but there was an alternative site, also belonging to Merton, at the east end of South Parks Rd. In September 1961, Sir Edward Peacock, the chairman, wrote to the Vice-Chancellor, surrendering the Beaumont St. premises to the University, and making a formal, but conditional, offer to hand over Rhodes House as well.[205]

The Rhodes Trustees understand that the University is finding difficulty in providing itself with a modern headquarters large enough for the Vice-Chancellor and the administrative staff of the University. We are therefore contemplating the gift of Rhodes House for this purpose. Rhodes House was built as a memorial to Cecil Rhodes in the Oxford he loved and in gratitude for its many kindnesses to the Rhodes Scholars. We should like, in token of our continuing gratitude, to see his memorial become the headquarters of the University.

The letter set out the conditions attached to the offer: the assent of Wadham, as required under the 1925 conveyance of the Rhodes House site, the provision of the alternative site on South Parks Rd, the retention of the name of Rhodes House, and its continued availability for the Trustees' dinners for scholars.

Wadham stood on its rights: backed by counsel's opinion, the Warden, Maurice Bowra, asked for compensation equivalent to the difference between the current market value of

---

[205] Peacock to Norrington, 29 Sept. 1961, RTM 21 Nov. 1961; RTM 13 May 1961.

the land and the £25,000 originally paid for it.[206] The Trustees secured their own legal advice that they could achieve their object, without breaching the covenants with Wadham, by allowing the University to use and occupy Rhodes House under a revocable licence. Meanwhile it was discovered that if Rhodes House was to accommodate the University Chest as well as the Registry, it would have to be extended into the garden at the north-west corner of the site. A deal still had to be done with Merton if the Warden's lodgings and offices were to be housed at the far end of South Parks Rd.

The tortuous bargaining was brought to a halt when Oxford City Planning Committee informed the University that the Merton playing field site, including 9 and 10 South Parks Rd, was the ideal location for the University to erect new scientific buildings. The architect Sir William Holford was called in to give the University advice on its forward planning.

In December 1962 Williams reported these frustrations to the Trustees, and added:

A committee under Mr A. R. W. Harrison (Warden-elect of Merton) has reported *inter multa alia* in favour of the establishment of more graduate Colleges in Oxford and was dissuaded from including in its final draft the suggestion that Rhodes House (as Rhodes College) would be just the place.

Benefactors must be used to offering a gift for one specific purpose and finding it readily accepted for quite another. So far this suggestion of a quite different use of Rhodes House is still unbaked pie in the sky. (RTR 446, 12)

So, too, it turned out, was the Trustees' own plan. This became clear when Sir William Holford backed the recommendation that the area north of the Merton playing fields should be developed for science, especially zoology. His report included the following paragraph:

From an architect's point of view and from my own sense of fitness, I cannot help feeling that the Vice-Chancellor should not have to vacate the Clarendon Building: that Rhodes House should retain something of its collegiate character; and that it is much less suitable for offices. (RTR 448, 10)

It was now three years since Williams had first floated his plan to the Trustees. In the meantime, Peacock had been succeeded as chairman of the Trustees by Kenneth Wheare, the Rector of Exeter, while Merton had changed wardens and the University had acquired a new Vice-Chancellor, Walter Oakeshott of Lincoln.[207] Merton's new Warden was the Harrison who had chaired the committee on the needs of graduates. His college now offered to make the St Cross vicarage available for Rhodes purposes, but only on condition that Rhodes House became a new graduate college. Oakeshott, who had been advised independently that Rhodes House was unsuitable for conversion into offices, let it be known that he had in mind to approach the Trustees to turn the building into a college. It would not be a residential institution, but it would afford accommodation for

---

[206] Wadham's real ambition was to secure two houses in Holywell which it hoped the University would persuade Merton to surrender as part of a quadripartite package.

[207] Peacock died in Dec. 1962 at the age of 91, having handed over the chair in the previous March to Wheare, who had been a Trustee since 1948 (RTM 30 Mar. 1962).

meals, common room facilities, and if possible some teaching and seminar rooms (RTR 450).

Williams was outraged by the new proposals, and the Trustees clearly resented being told the form their benefactions to the University should take. On 23 January 1964 they minuted:

The Trustees instructed the Secretary to inform the Vice-Chancellor that they did not wish to be invited to present Rhodes House to the University as the site of a new graduate College; moreover, that they did not believe that the purposes of the Trust could be carried out as effectively in the alternative site suggested for the Trust in St Cross Road; and, by the same token, they did not wish the University to return to the Trustees' original and conditional offer of Rhodes House as the head-quarters for the Vice-Chancellor since one of the conditions upon which that offer had rested, the agreed purchase of 9 and 10 South Parks Road, had been put out of the reckoning by the University's own decision to build on that site.[208]

At this distance of time it is difficult to dissent from the judgement that the architecture and structure of Rhodes House is more suited for collegiate purposes than for the housing of administrative offices. However, the episode illustrates the difficulties experienced by would-be benefactors in dealing with a collegiate university. It was neither the first nor the last time that the Rhodes Trust was to have benevolent plans for Oxford frustrated by the intended beneficiaries.

The Memory of the Founder

In 1959 J. G. Lockhart, after working for three years on his life of Cecil Rhodes, died, having completed only eighteen out of twenty-one proposed chapters. After considering the possibility of asking Robert Blake to write a completely new biography (RTM 11 Feb. 1960), the Trustees commissioned the former director of Chatham House, the Hon. C. M. Woodhouse, then MP for Oxford, to complete the task (RTM 18 Nov. 1960). He did so with great skill, and the book which resulted is still, in the opinion of many, the most balanced biography to have appeared; though written with sympathy, it is very candid about Rhodes's faults.[209]

The Trustees continued to be concerned that sites in Africa associated with Rhodes should be well looked after. They corresponded with the government of Southern Rhodesia about the burial site at 'the View of the World', and a proposed park in the Matopos estate (RTM 11 Feb. 1960, 19 Dec. 1962, 19 Mar. 1964). In South Africa they asked the Cape Society of Architects to see that buildings erected on the Groote Schuur estate should be in accord with the spirit of Rhodes's will (RTSA 487). In 1960 they made a grant to the Rhodes Livingstone Museum near the Victoria Falls (RTM 7 May 1960; RTR 439, 16). In the 1960s death removed the last of the Trust's pensioners who had been personally associated with Rhodes: Benjamin 'Matabele' Wilson, once involved in the

[208] The withdrawal of the offer was announced in the *Oxford University Gazette* of 13 Feb. 1964.
[209] J. G. Lockhart and C. M. Woodhouse, *Rhodes* (London, 1963). The book was read through by Williams before publication.

negotiations with Lobengula, died at 98, shortly to be followed by the widow of Rhodes's valet W. J. Young, by Mary M'Lamla, a servant of Rhodes in Kimberley, and by Philip Jourdan, one of the last of his secretaries.

Once the Lockhart/Woodhouse biography of Rhodes was published, the Rhodes papers were made freely available to scholars in Rhodes House Library, and permission was given to microfilm them for South African archives. The question now arose of access to the Trust's own papers. Many had already been microfilmed to build up a Parkin archive in Canada; others were available among Milner's papers in New College. Williams, himself a historian, questioned the secrecy which had been maintained over the earlier papers of the Trust—e.g. those in connection with the *Round Table*—and he asked the Trustees to adopt the fifty-year rule then applicable to government papers. The Trustees, less tender to researchers, declined to allow any access at all to the Trust's papers (RTM 23 Jan. 1964).

The Withdrawal from South Africa

In the early 1960s benefactions in Oxford continued, despite the Trustees' irritation with the University authorities over the negotiations about Rhodes House. Though the annual grant to the Bodleian Library ceased in 1962 (RTM 23 July 1960), £10,000 a year was given to the Oxford Historic Buildings appeal, reaching a total of £100,000 by 1965 (RTM 13 Dec. 1965). In 1964 the Trustees offered to spend up to £75,000 on a University gymnasium beside Iffley Rd, and followed this up in 1966 with £5,000 for sporting facilities for women (RTM 19 Mar. 1964, 11 June 1966). Small grants were made from time to time to minor Oxford causes, such as the Playhouse, Vincent's club, and the Roman Catholic Chaplaincy (RTM 11 June 1966).

The Trustees also began to make grants to individual colleges. Rhodes had left £100,000 in his will to his own Oriel, and the first college grant made by the Trustees was to the Oriel endowment fund in 1956. In 1959 £5,000 was given to the Exeter College building appeal, and in 1964 the Trustees contributed £10,000 to the St Antony's endowment fund.[210] But other colleges who were running appeals, including Williams's own two colleges Balliol and Merton, were made to wait.

Money was available for generous gifts to Oxford partly because the flow of Trust benefaction to South Africa was coming to an end.[211] In 1961 Hendrik Verwoerd, Nationalist Prime Minister since 1958, and chief architect of apartheid, turned South Africa into a republic and led his country out of the Commonwealth in anticipation of its expulsion by the other members. Once South Africa was outside the Commonwealth, the Trust's lawyers advised, it was no longer lawful to apply any of the Public Purposes Fund to South African causes, since the purpose of the fund, according to section 12 (1)

---

[210] The Rector of Exeter was a Trustee and another Trustee, Lord Harcourt, was an honorary fellow of St Antony's.

[211] In 1960 £1,000 had been given to the Smuts Memorial Trust and £500 to St George's School, Windhoek, and in 1960 and 1961 the usual annual £1,000 was given to the 1820 Memorial Settlers' Association.

of the Act of 1946, was 'to promote and advance educational and other charitable purposes in any part of the Commonwealth or the United States of America', and the Act had expressly defined the 'The British Commonwealth of Nations' as including only those countries '*for the time being* forming part of the British Commonwealth of Nations'. The South African scholarships, however, were not to be affected, because they were defined by reference to South Africa and its institutions by name and not as part of the Commonwealth (RTR 444, 19).[212]

The biggest impact of the change was on the South African 1820 Settlers' Association. Since 1938 the Rhodes Trustees had paid over to the association the annual income on a special fund ('the £100,000 fund') inherited by the Public Purposes Fund from the Rhodes–Beit Trustees, and in addition had made an annual donation of £1,000 to the Association's London office. In the year of grace before South Africa's departure from the Commonwealth took effect, the Trustees made a one-off payment of £6,800 to the Association. Thereafter they made no further grants.[213]

Quite apart from legal constraints the Trustees were reluctant to spend money in South Africa in the heyday of apartheid. For some time they had adopted a policy of refusing grants to any educational institution which—however reluctantly—excluded any candidates on grounds of race (RTR 459, 31). In time the apartheid legislation came to affect the Cape schools which had been assigned scholarships in Rhodes's will; but these scholarships were not paid out of the Public Purposes Trust and for the moment they were left undisturbed. In 1967 the Trustees appointed as their South African Secretary Rex Welsh (Transvaal and Oriel 1941), the leader of the Johannesburg Bar, who had been Nelson Mandela's counsel at the 1958 treason trial.[214]

Meanwhile the wind of change reached Rhodes House with the arrival of the first black African scholars. They were elected to the triennial new Commonwealth scholarships approved in Elton's last years. Williams had been lukewarm about this scheme from the start, and its operation in its early years did little to allay his misgivings. True, Ceylon had no difficulty in electing, every three years from 1959, scholars who found places in a college and successfully completed graduate courses. But the committee in Ghana failed to make an election in 1962 and of the two scholars it did elect in the 1960s, one obtained a third in PPE and the other was sent home without a degree. The first Nigerian scholar found life in Oxford very difficult, but overcame the difficulties to obtain a doctorate; his successor, elected after a year in which no suitable candidate could be found, had to leave Oxford to complete his degree elsewhere. From 1961 the Malaysian region sent a series of solid scholars, though there too the committee was unable to make an election in 1965. None of the first three scholars elected in the new

---

[212] It was true that section 12 2 (c) of the 1946 Act empowered the Trust 'to pay or transfer any part of the income or capital of the public purposes fund to any particular educational or other charitable institution in any part of the world'. However, counsel advised that this clause gave merely auxiliary powers, to be used only in furtherance of educational and charitable purposes within the Commonwealth and the USA.

[213] The final grant to Southern Africa from the Public Purposes Fund was £1,000 to St George's, Windhoek, in Mar. 1962.

[214] See Nuttall, below p. 276.

Caribbean constituency obtained Oxford degrees, though they went on to distinguished careers with qualifications from elsewhere. By the end of the decade only a dozen scholars had been elected to any of the new Commonwealth scholarships. It was very different from Elton's vision of a generation of Oxford-trained leaders of the multiracial Commonwealth.

Williams consistently opposed any increase in the number of scholarships.[215] In 1966 a suggestion that the Trust was not spending enough on scholarships was made by Lord Amory, a comparatively new Trustee.[216] In response Williams expounded the difficulties he had in placing candidates from weaker constituencies (which he identified as 'Bermuda, Stellenbosch, South African College School, the third Rhodesian or a Scholar from a not very outstanding university in the Southern States') (RTR 458, 18). He concluded:

It is not recommended that there is an increase of Rhodes scholarships at Oxford. Other overseas awards might be contemplated—in Oxford itself in the women's or the graduate colleges; or in the graduate colleges at Cambridge perhaps. But it is suggested that straight grants to such institutions would obviously be more welcome. (RTR 459, 19)

If there were to be any more scholarships, he said in conclusion, the country with the greatest claim to them was Germany.

The German Scholarships

The revival of the German scholarships abolished in 1939 had often been discussed by the Trustees.[217] During his secretaryship, Elton was strongly opposed to the revival; in his view the German scholarships abolished at the time of the Second World War had been replaced by the scholarships created at the same time for the Indian subcontinent. The creation of the new Commonwealth scholarships naturally tended to increase resentment at Germany's continued exclusion; but Elton urged the Trustees to ignore these susceptibilities, and at one of his last meetings the Trustees minuted, 'these Scholarships cannot at present be revived, since the first obligation of the Rhodes Trust is to the British Commonwealth' (RTM 5 Feb. 1959).

Williams did not share Elton's implacable attitude to Germany, and before becoming secretary, in 1955, he had surreptitiously lent assistance to an approach to the Trustees by Robert Birley, but he had warned, 'With three Trustees over eighty I doubt if they are going to change their views in their lifetime now.'[218] In July 1960 he reported to the

---

[215] He was unenthusiastic about the decision to give a second scholarship to India in 1961 (RTR 442, 17).

[216] Derick Heathcoat Amory had been a Trustee since 1961, having resigned from Westminster in 1960 after two successful terms as Chancellor of the Exchequer.

[217] Appeals for their reinstatement came from many quarters during the 1950s, as narrated by Sheppard, below p. 404.

[218] The three Trustees were L. S. Amery, Sir Edward Peacock, and Lord Hailey. After Amery's death in 1955, three new Trustees were appointed in 1957, but one of them, Sir Archibald Nye, was equally firmly opposed to German scholarships.

Trustees that feelers were being put out by the British Ambassador in Bonn. Quoting the minute of February 1959 he said:

This is a Minute with which I have never felt quite at ease: we know that Mr Rhodes wanted German Rhodes Scholarships, because he said so, whereas we can but guess that he would have wanted a scholarship for e.g. Ghana (or indeed, that he would still have wanted Germans . . .) For myself, I would have contemplated one German Scholarship's being revived or created when the five new Commonwealth Scholarships were announced: perhaps, however, but to relieve one's own uneasiness in the matter since, personally, I can manage well enough without Germans. (RTR 440, 20)

The pressure was soon increased. Later in the same year the Prime Minister, Harold Macmillan, became Chancellor of Oxford University. Informally, he sounded out Vice-Chancellor Norrington and three other heads of houses about German scholarships, and found all of them in favour of renewal. For the Trustees' meeting in November Williams rehearsed the arguments for and against, laying particular stress on the claim that Oxford colleges were short of spare places. Against the susceptibilities of the pre-war German Rhodes scholars, he suggested, should be set the susceptibilities of the many Jewish Rhodes scholars from other constituencies. The Trustees maintained their refusal to renew the scholarships and issued the following statement

The Rhodes Trustees respect the record of the German Rhodes scholars and a proper anxiety for the revival once more of Rhodes Scholarships for Germans; but after careful consideration the Trustees are convinced that the growing needs of the developing Commonwealth have the prior claim upon the resources of the Rhodes Trust.

The exclusion of the Germans became even more pointed when the second Indian scholarship was created in 1961. In 1963, Edward Heath, then Lord Privy Seal, renewed the Foreign Office assault, but the Trustees, unmoved, repeated their earlier refusals in identical terms (3 Oct. 1963).[219]

There the matter rested until 1969,[220] by which time there had been a number of

---

[219] They were in fact irritated by the tone of Heath's letter, which they regarded as 'maladroit'. The ideas behind Rhodes's will, the Trustees decided, made it virtually certain he would reject the German claim. The decision was formally unanimous, but Abell voted for it only to preserve unanimity. (Note by Williams on meeting of 3 Oct. 1963.)

[220] In Dec. 1963, however, counsel's opinion was sought from John Brunyate and J. G. Foster 'as to whether the Rhodes Trust is empowered under the 1946 Act to re-establish the German Scholarships, or to establish new German Scholarships, either out of the Scholarship Fund or out of the Public Purposes Fund', and in general whether the Trustees were bound or entitled to continue a scholarship established (whether by the will or by the Trustees) for places which cease to be part of the Commonwealth. Their joint opinion said that no legislation subsequent to the 1916 Act had granted the Trustees any power to re-establish the German scholarships. To use the Scholarship Fund would be a breach of trust; so too, very likely, if the Capital Reserve Fund was used. However, the clause in the PPF allowing the Trustees to spend money for the promotion of educational purposes in the Commonwealth did 'give the Rhodes Trust a power to establish scholarships for foreigners at Oxford University . . . for to do so is the promotion of education at Oxford'. If the Trust decided to establish scholarships for Germans at Oxford University out of the PPF 'it would not in our opinion be committing a breach of Trust'. The same presumably went for countries leaving the Commonwealth, though the question was not addressed. This opinion seems to have been forgotten in 1986 when the Trustees, on the advice of their lawyers at Coward

changes among the Trustees since the 1959 rejection. Lord Amory and John Phillimore had joined the Trust in 1961. Sir Edward Peacock had died in 1962, and Lord Hailey had resigned in 1964 at the age of 92. Sir Archibald Nye died in 1967.[221] Wheare, who had succeeded Peacock as chairman, stepped down in 1969 in favour of Sir George Abell.[222] Abell had all along been sympathetic to the German scholarships, and under his chairmanship they were at last revived.[223] Williams placed the item on the agenda for the meeting of February 1969, and after two successive meetings the Trustees at last reached a positive decision (RTM 6 Mar. 1969). Williams went to Hamburg to attend the first selection meeting, and reported that he was impressed with both the procedures and the candidates.[224]

The Marriage Bar

In 1959, for the first time in peacetime, scholars were allowed to marry without forfeiting their stipend, but only in their third year (RTM 5 Feb. 1959).[225] Many in the United States pressed for further relaxation; the rule was believed to put off many excellent candidates. Each year a number of scholars, in order to marry, resigned after their first year: in 1963, for instance, there were four such resignations (RTM 3 Oct. 1963). One man, when leaving Oxford, confessed to having been married, to a wife in the States, all the time he was a Rhodes scholar; he promised to repay his stipend (RTM 13 June 1964). By June 1964 Williams had come to believe that the rule needed review. In a long paper he put the case for and against change (RTR 452, 3–9).

Would colleges object to a change? That depended on what they expected from scholars.

The Rhodes Scholar is surely a man of some maturity who is prepared to pitch into everything, since he is an all-round man, and somebody who adds at once yeast and ballast. Now if this paragon is going to be available in College for one year only—for I think we must admit that marriage even in the most remarkable cases does tend to withdraw a man from his College a bit—will it make a

Chance, shifted the funding of the German scholarships from the PPF to the SCRF (Fletcher to Holmes, 8 July 1986; Holmes to Fletcher, 11 July 1986; RTF 1682).

[221] At this point the remaining Trustees decided to put a limit on tenure: they decided in 1965 that Trustees should retire at 75 and that a chairman should hold office for not more than five years at a time (RTM 12 June 1965).

[222] Wheare remained an influential Trustee for another eight years; though senior to Abell as a Trustee, he was three years his junior in age. Williams noted, 'since George Abell has got five more years to serve before he retires under the new dispensation, he will have them as Chairman. He has moved from London and is living at Ramsbury, half way between Oxford & Marlborough and so he is readily available, but being George he is not bossily available' (Williams to Haslam, 11 Sept. 1969; RTF 1628).

[223] The initiative came from Lord Amory, who wrote to Abell in Nov. 1968: 'I should like to have a chat to you some time about the possible restoration of the German scholarships. The American Minister over here, Kaiser . . . pressed this on me the other day.' Amory to Abell, Nov. 1968; RTF 1682.

[224] For the record of the German scholars elected since 1970 see Sheppard, below p. 406.

[225] Williams had been in favour of repealing the ban on matrimony since early in his wardenship, but had bided his time until the retirement of elderly Trustees. 'Godfrey [Elton] too will be retiring in the next few years', he wrote, 'and, I suppose, his mythical Rhodes Scholar with him.' Williams to Courtney Smith, 12 Dec. 1957.

difference to Colleges over the years? So often it is the Rhodes Scholar who becomes Secretary or Treasurer of the Junior Common Room, and then perhaps later President, who is so obviously the man in College that the undergraduates come to rely on as their spokesman and elected leader. This is not likely to happen if he marries.[226]

But the new middle common rooms would offer less opportunity for Rhodes scholars to be senior statesmen among their peers, so changing the rule would make little difference. The decisive issues were these:

The first point is this: every year there are some broken engagements and most years there is a res-ignation of Scholarship to go off to marry in the States. The broken engagements sometimes turn out, I suppose, to be rather a good thing, for it is not long before the man who left a damp patch on one's shoulder reappears, beaming all over, with an entirely different girl. In fact, two Rhodes Scholars have told me that looking back they were glad that the rule was as it was. I don't think, however, that one year would make much difference in this case.

Secondly, I think it is very remarkable what extremely nice girls Rhodes Scholars marry and I am quite certain that if they, the wives, have an experience of Oxford which they enormously enjoy—and not all of them do of course—then they become the most tremendous recruiting sergeants in the years to come. I have noticed this particularly in the States. If a girl doesn't share any of Oxford with her husband, often she remains jealous of it for life.

Marriage had not had a bad effect on academic performance: on the contrary, many self-sacrificing wives had got their husbands down to work and improved their results in Schools. With two years of marriage, it was true there was more likelihood of scholars being distracted from their studies by having to look after babies. On balance, however, he favoured allowing marriage without loss of stipend in the second year. 'I have no doubt', he concluded, 'that we must stick very hard to the bachelor rule in the first year if we are going really to stress, as was the Founder's intention, the residential nature of the opportunity.'

The Trustees, by a majority, accepted Williams's arguments and with effect from the academic year 1965–6 scholars in their second year could marry and keep their stipends.[227] They were obliged to certify that they would not be supporting their wife out of their stipend. Those who had resigned in order to marry in the year 1964–5 were now allowed back onto stipend.

The new rule continued in force for over thirty years. When, in 1973, a majority of scholars petitioned for the total abolition of the marriage bar, Williams argued vigorously

[226] The memorandum to selection committees of this period, which had been rewritten by Williams in 1961, contained the following passage: 'Quality of both character and intellect is the most important requirement for a Rhodes scholarship and this is what the Selection Committee will seek. The Rhodes Scholar should not be a one-sided man; or a selfish man. Intellectual ability should be founded upon sound character and integrity of character upon sound intellect. Success in being elected to office in student organisations may or may not be evidence of leadership in the true sense of the word. Cecil Rhodes evidently regarded leadership as consisting of moral courage and interest in one's fellow men quite as much as in the more aggressive qualities. . . . Physical vigour is an essential qualification for a Rhodes scholar, but athletic prowess is less important than the moral qualities which can be developed in sports.'

[227] General Nye, absent from the meeting, wrote in to argue that a man married in his second year, unless he was prepared to neglect his wife, could not really contribute to college and university life as the Founder had intended (RTR 452).

for its retention. If scholars arrived married, it would be hard to find them places to live, and if they did not spend their first year in college they would never get much out of their college membership. 'I welcome the wives,' he said in conclusion, 'I think they play a great part here and later in the successful development of the Rhodes scholarships throughout the world; I don't welcome them until their husbands have made Oxford ready to welcome them' (RTR 485, 10).

In several other ways during the 1960s the Trustees, at Williams's prompting, took measures to make the tenure of the scholarships more attractive. In 1959 the scholarship stipend had been £750 a year, to cover fees as well as living expenses; transportation costs in general were not paid, nor any allowances made for clothing, books, or research. By 1963 the scholarships had ceased to be competitive, in financial terms, with Marshall, Fulbright, and Commonwealth awards, all of which paid fees separately from stipend, and gave generous allowances including a marriage allowance. It was true that there was no known instance in which a Marshall winner had turned down a Rhodes scholarship; but this was not because of its emoluments but because of its prestige, recently enhanced in the USA by President Kennedy's inclusion of a large number of Rhodes scholars in his administration. Moreover, within Oxford the financial burdens were unequally distributed among the scholars, since well-endowed colleges charged less than others, and arts students had less to pay in fees than laboratory scientists. A scholar reading English at Merton, Williams reckoned, had much more spare cash than a research scientist at Balliol. More and more scholars from North America, he reported, now went home in their first long vacation to earn a nest-egg to carry them through their scholarship (RTR 448, 3–7).

In 1963, in response to Williams's arguments, the Trustees raised the stipend to £900, but they were not yet willing to pay any allowances, or meet transportation costs, or make research grants. For a while they continued to pay a straight stipend out of which scholars had to meet all fees, which Williams claimed was preferred by the scholars as 'a more adult way of going about matters'. But after a few years he changed his mind. British students were publicly funded by their local authorities, who paid fees to colleges direct. Because of this, the custom had grown up in colleges to place cost increases against fees rather than charges, and the inequalities between the burden on the Merton humanist and the Balliol scientist had now increased intolerably. So in 1966 the Trustees agreed to follow the example of the Marshall scholarships and pay approved fees plus a living allowance, now fixed at £720 per annum (RTM 11 June 1966).[228]

The Overseas Fees Crisis

The fee bills thus picked up by the Trustees soon increased unexpectedly. At the end of 1966 the Labour Education Secretary, Antony Crosland, announced that universities were expected to charge higher fees to foreign than to home students. From the block grant

---

[228] At the same time it was agreed to make a grant of £25 towards the preparation of a research dissertation.

which the government made to each university, £250 would be deducted for each foreign student enrolled. It would be for the individual university to decide whether to charge higher fees or to forgo the income. At their next meeting the Trustees minuted 'with exasperation' that it was likely that the cost to the Trust of increased fees would be some £18,000 in 1967–8, £27,000 in 1968–9, and from 1969 £33,000 a year (RTM 16 Mar. 1967).

Oxford University did not, however, increase its fees as expected. Hebdomadal Council proposed to charge discriminatory fees, but its motion was defeated in summer 1967 by an overwhelming vote of Congregation, much angered by the government's stance. Senior members were asked to contribute £5 a head to an Independence Fund, to offset the loss of income to the University.[229] Again in November 1968 Congregation repeated its opposition to differential fees, this time by 147 votes to 108. By this time Cambridge, which had hitherto joined with Oxford in opposition to what Williams called 'the Crosland tax on knowledge', had given up the fight and raised its fees to the level anticipated by the government. Oxford's quixotic stance had, by March 1969, saved the Trust some £28,500; but it had cost the University about five times as much. The Trustees rejected Williams's invitation to them to plug this deficit, but they did make a grant of £28,500 for the University's general purposes (RTM 6 Mar. 1969). In 1970, while those who attended Congregation in person were all for showing the Dunkirk spirit, their vote was overturned by two successive postal votes, and thenceforth the University charged differential fees to overseas students.[230]

During the 1960s a fundamental change took place in the nature of the scholarship which was not the result of any decision by the Trustees. Hitherto, the great majority of Rhodes scholars had come to Oxford to obtain second BAs. During the 1950s, for instance, undergraduates were usually twice as numerous as those reading for graduate degrees. In 1960 104 scholars were reading for honour schools, while 72 were working for higher degrees. In 1966, for the first time, the BA students were outnumbered by those doing research or attending taught master's courses; and this henceforth was to be the pattern. This change was not unnoticed by Williams, and not unregretted; when he revised his memorandum to selection committees in 1968, he included this advice:

It is notoriously more difficult for the researcher, particularly if he is a scientist, to take as full a part in college life as do those reading for final Honour Schools. Instead of mingling freely with the other members of his College, the advanced student may find himself associating too exclusively with a smaller number of older men. . . .

When Mr Rhodes said, in his Will, that he attached 'very great importance' to the residential character of the University, without which 'students are left without any supervision', we believe that he had in mind not only the social life of the Colleges but the tutorial system and the Final Honour Schools which usually provide a closer and more regular contact between teacher and

[229] The fund was chaired by Lord Franks, a Rhodes Trustee, and in January 1968 the Trustees made a contribution to the fund of £2,500 (RTM 11 Jan. 1968). Soon afterwards, however, the fund stalled.

[230] B. Harrison (ed.), *The History of the University of Oxford*, viii (Oxford: Clarendon Press, 1994), 651. The extra cost to the Trustees of the new fees was an eventual £35,000 a year.

taught than is always experienced by those working for an advanced degree. It is natural and proper that as Oxford, in common with all Universities worth the name, develops increasing emphasis on research, a growing proportion of Rhodes Scholars should avail themselves of the new opportunities. Nevertheless, it remains true that for some Rhodes Scholars, once they are reconciled to taking a second B.A. degree, a final honour school may provide a more unusual and fruitful educational experience than they might have obtained from reading for an advanced degree at Oxford.

Like Congregation in its opposition to discriminatory fees, Williams was defending a cause which was already lost. In almost every year since his memorandum was issued, the number of students working for advanced degrees has been greater than those taking a second BA. Few, today, would seek to reverse the change.[231]

Southern African Scholarships

In 1963 the federation of Rhodesia and Nyasaland came to an end. A year later Northern Rhodesia became the independent republic of Zambia. Ian Smith, the Prime Minister of (Southern) Rhodesia, unilaterally declared independence from Britain in November 1965. Britain denounced his government as rebellious, and imposed economic sanctions. For a while the flow of Rhodesian scholars continued uninterrupted, selected in Salisbury from candidates from 'the geographical area known as Rhodesia in 1899'. But in 1969 the Zambian education department suggested that the scholarships should be split between the territories (RTR 469, 12). The Trustees were advised by counsel that they did not have the power to reapportion these awards, the most entrenched of all in the will, without a new Act of Parliament. Selection for Rhodesian scholarships became difficult to organize because Zambians would not go to Salisbury, and the Salisbury committee was not allowed to travel to Lusaka.[232]

The difficulties with the Rhodesian scholarships were soon absorbed in the much larger problems of the South African scholarships. In the academic year 1970–1 a group of black American scholars at Balliol and University organized a protest against the lack of black scholars from Rhodesia and South Africa and the existence of closed scholarships for the all-white schools in the Cape. Williams described the events to the Trustees in March 1971.

A few days before the last Trustees' meeting, three freshmen Rhodes Scholars at Balliol came to see me to tell me that they were getting together a round-robin among Rhodes Scholars about the South African Scholarships and that they wished to keep the matter 'in the family'. The Trustees agreed to consider it at their next meeting. However, the three emissaries arrived with the Press and Radio Oxford. The Warden was not in and after full benefit of photography on the steps of Rhodes House, the manifesto was handed to him eventually in the buttery at Balliol.

---

[231] Williams also worried that selection committees, particularly in the USA, were paying too little attention to the athletic criterion. 'I have a terrible sort of suspicion at times that when Committees are faced with a straight A record they then look round a little despairingly and find in one of the testimonials that a man once opened a window and this is taken as clear evidence of his interest in the outdoors, and then over here he comes.' On the other hand he was disturbed by the election of blind or physically disabled scholars, on the grounds that 'they cannot take a full part in the life of the place' (Williams to Stott, 29 Dec. 1965).

[232] The legal opinions are in RTF 2308.

Eighty-five Rhodes scholars in residence signed the petition, which described the operation of the scholarship as 'an intolerable example of the most extreme form of racial prejudice' and insisted that unless the current South African and Rhodesian policies were altered immediately 'the Rhodes Scholarships program in those countries must be discontinued altogether, by Act of Parliament if such be necessary'. Many scholars who had not signed the petition informed Williams that they supported it. He advised South African scholars to give him their opinion in private 'for if signatures reached the Press they would have passport troubles at home'. One hundred and twenty senior members signed letters of support, including the Master of Balliol, the President of Corpus, and Professors A. J. Ayer and H. L. A. Hart.

Some of the senior members appealed to clause 24 of Rhodes's will which laid down that 'no student shall be qualified or disqualified for election to a Scholarship on account of his race or religious opinions'. In reporting this to the Trustees Williams commented that

since [Rhodes] was referring to 'the education of young Colonists' (Clause 16) he was probably not thinking of young 'natives' and he used the word 'race' to differentiate between Afrikaans and British stocks. However, today—(and yesterday—but probably not in his day) the clause has been used widespread to emphasise the liberality of the benefaction and those who have done so (as the Secretary has frequently) are now hoist with their own petard. (RTR 475, 10)

Williams was clearly wounded by the behaviour of the scholars, in particular by what he regarded as violations of confidence beyond 'the family'. 'The present generation of "students"', he wrote, 'have found South Africa the cushiest "demo" available.' But he ended his account of the troubles thus:

The Secretary must state to the Trustees at once that, however tiresome the Term has been, however distasteful some of the ways of going about the matter, in short, however old fashioned he is, he shares with the petitioners their very real disquiet about the question. (RTR 475, 14)

Rex Welsh, the South African Secretary, was invited to attend the Trustees' meeting of 25 March 1971. The outcome of their deliberations was set out in a statement published in the press and sent to the four Cape schools.

The Rhodes Trustees, after careful consideration, have decided that it is their duty to seek powers enabling them to broaden the basis of eligibility of the Scholarships in South Africa to come into line with the clause in the Founder's Will enjoining that 'no students shall be qualified or disqual-ified for election to a Scholarship on account of his race or religious opinions'. Their aim is to restructure the nine annual Scholarships in the light of this requirement and, therefore, to replace those awards specifically restricted in the Will to four Schools in Cape Province. This decision may require legislative sanction before it can be implemented. Meanwhile, the Trustees propose at once, as a pattern of their intentions in relation to Rhodes Scholarships from South Africa, to institute a Scholarship for South-Africa-at-Large. (RTR 476, 21)

Sir George Abell and two of the Oxford Trustees met the three Balliol petitioners and explained the Trust's intentions. The meeting was tense but remained polite. 'The three young men', Williams noted, 'were evidently surprised to find themselves dealing with such wise and nice men. Until then, they had only met the Warden.'

Welsh, with the assistance of Sir Robert Birley, set up a multiracial selection committee for the new scholarship. The outcome, however, was a disappointment to the reformers: the first holder of the new scholarship was a white Transvaaler and it was not until 1978 that the first black South African was elected.

The restructuring of the existing scholarships was not going to be easy. The Trustees were informed by Michael Fox QC that they had no power under the Trust instruments to alter the South African scholarships. The High Court could not vary the terms of the will since it had been incorporated in Acts of Parliament. The Minister of Education could not properly intervene unless the spirit of Rhodes's gift was being trangressed; but Rhodes must surely have contemplated that only whites would benefit. None the less, the Trustees were advised, they should make application to the Minister. 'Apart from any other consideration, it would be a necessary preliminary to any attempt to promote legislation.'

An attempt to change the law, however, would itself need the consent of the court or the Minister. The Minister was likely to agree only if convinced that the scholarship scheme might break down in Oxford, or in other constituencies worldwide, if the closed scholarships were not removed. The Cape schools themselves made clear that they would fight any application to the courts for reallocation of the scholarships. The Trustees, so their counsel told them, 'had got themselves onto a political limb beyond his legal ingenuity'. On the other hand Rhodes's niece Georgia, at the age of 80, strongly supported the changes and claimed that they were 'what Uncle Cecil would have proposed' (RTR 476, 20).

The Balliol petitioners now published a further manifesto denouncing the inadequacy of the Trustees' attempts at reform and calling for more effective affirmative action. They had now been joined as leaders by a white American, Grant Crandall (Iowa and University 1969), who in 1972 wrote to the Trustees resigning his scholarship in protest at their alleged racism. In the same year the first black scholar from sub-Saharan Africa was elected: O. D. Ncube from Rhodesia, already in residence at St Catherine's College.

At the meeting of June 1972, which was attended by both the South African and the American secretaries, the Trustees had to fight on two fronts. Current Rhodes scholars were demanding the abolition of the schools scholarships and the suspension of all other Southern African awards. On the other hand, Sir Richard Luyt, Vice-Chancellor of the University of Cape Town, had travelled to the meeting to express the schools' determination to fight in the courts the Trustees' interpretation of clause 24.[233]

Despite Luyt's protest, the Trustees persevered with their attempt to annul the schools scholarships. Their petition to the Department laid stress on clause 24 of the will and an opinion from Sidney Kentridge SC that at the time of Rhodes's death there was no discriminatory legislation in force in the Cape in respect of education. Under present South

[233] See Nuttall, below p. 283.

African legislation both Paul Roos and SACS had no right to admit any other than white pupils. The Diocesan College and St Andrew's, being private schools, were not subject to the provisions of the legislation; but it would be virtually impossible for an African pupil to attend them in the light of the Group Areas Act.

The Trustees stated that Rhodes's expressed views about the indigenous peoples in Southern Africa were 'that while they might not at that time have been fitted to take part in the direction and leadership of their country, such participation should in due time be accorded equally with men of European origin, to those who through the civilizing influence of education and their own energies had demonstrated that they deserved equal status with white men'. The Trustees also urged that in the light of the English Race Relations Act scholarships excluding non-whites were contrary to the public good. The Minister was invited to make a scheme abolishing the twelve schools scholarships and substitute for them South Africa-at-large scholarships. The scheme should also replace the Rhodesian scholarships with an alternation of scholarships between Zambia and Zimbabwe.[234]

The Secretary of State for Education in 1972 was Margaret Thatcher. Unimpressed by the Trustees' arguments, she refused to make a scheme for the South African scholarships. However, she stated that the Trustees had powers to reallocate the Rhodesian scholarships as they wished.[235]

Rebuffed in their approach to the Department of Education for a reallocation of the scholarships, the Trustees decided, in the spring of May 1973, to promote a private Act of Parliament. But to do this they once again needed the Secretary of State's permission, at least if they were to use Trust money to promote the bill.[236] If she refused again, then the only remaining option was to seek the Attorney General's approval of an approach to the courts to review her refusal (RTM 3 May, 9 June 1973). But by August it was clear that the Attorney General was no more favourable to the Trustees' plans than was the Secretary of State.

Don Price (Tennessee and Merton 1932), an American Trustee who had recently joined the board, wrote to Williams:

I assume that this ends the possibility of pursuing the matter at Rhodes Trust expense. But I wonder whether we should consider the possibility—if it is not ruled out by law—of using other funds that might be contributed for this purpose. I will find it much harder to explain our decision to people here if we simply give up at this point than if I could say, in effect, if you are so interested in this, suppose you raise the money to enable us to submit a private bill. (RTR 486, 4)

At the Trust's October meeting of 1973 Williams was asked to find out from some unimpeachable source the legal status of such a suggestion (RTM 4 Oct. 1973). Meanwhile, the Trustees turned their attention to promoting the education of black South Africans by means other than Rhodes scholarships. They proposed that Welsh and his assistant

[234] The proposal was that each nation should have two scholars in one year and one scholar in the next.
[235] This latter decision took the Trust's lawyers by surprise; they thought it was almost certainly incorrect. See above p. 62.
[236] The likely cost of the bill would be £10,000.

Kinghorn might, during the next seven years, spend £15,000 from the income of the Rhodes Trust South Africa, on the secondary or university education of gifted black Africans. At a meeting in December Kinghorn presented a system whereby bursaries of 500 rand per annum would be offered to non-whites in their last two years at school, or in order to take a first university degree. The fund, it was proposed, was to be administered by the South African Institute of Race Relations, which was already administering 120 bursaries for other charities (RTM 13 Dec. 1973).

Kinghorn's scheme was approved by the Trustees, and the first elections were made early in 1974. It has continued up to the present day, administered by the Trust's assistant secretary in South Africa.

At the same meeting, having received the opinion of Michael Fox QC that the Price proposal was impracticable,[237] the Trustees informed the Cape schools that they did not propose to press the issue further themselves. However, should other people seek a legislative change the Trust would not oppose them. Each of the schools was later paid 500 rand towards their legal costs (RTM 8 June 1974). In the light of Fox's advice no action was taken on the proposal to set up a private fund to promote an Act of Parliament.

Women Rhodes Scholars

Among present and past Rhodes scholars the issue of discrimination against blacks had by 1972 taken second place to the issue of discrimination against women. When the Trustees had considered, in the 1960s, how best they could help Oxford, they had minuted 'benefactions for the education of women at Oxford were not to be regarded as beyond their purview'. The possibility of opening the scholarships to women surfaced at the Trustees' meeting of June 1968. Williams's advice was that 'it would be a mistake to have women Rhodes Scholars with all the muscular jokes which they would have to endure'.[238] Instead, he proposed that from each Rhodes scholarship territory in turn the five women's colleges, again in turn, might receive a Rhodes visiting fellow for a year or two years, preferably a postdoctoral candidate under 30 (RTR 464, 8).

The proposal was received favourably by the Trustees, and by Lucy Sutherland, the South African Principal of Lady Margaret Hall. The first experimental visiting fellowship was established at her college. The Trustees agreed to leave the selection to the college, and to pay £1,500 with a room rent, plus transportation; the Trust should pay to bring over shortlisted candidates for interview. The first Rhodes fellow elected at LMH, an Australian psychologist, distinguished herself within half an hour of her interview by rescuing a drowning man from the Cherwell. Other colleges were included in the scheme

---

[237] Though it would not be illegal for the Trust to promote a bill without spending Trust money, a third party would not be able to give money to the Trust itself for this purpose, and if a new fund were to be set up to pay the expenses, it might be difficult to secure charitable status for it. Without such status, there would be problems with regard to estate duty.

[238] Reporting the meeting to the American Secretary, Williams wrote, 'I certainly don't think Rhodes Scholarships for women are necessary or, I believe, even apt in terms of Oxford undergraduate education.' Williams to Courtney Smith, 2 Dec. 1968.

in later years: Somerville and St Hugh's in 1970, St Hilda's and St Anne's in 1971. For the first time round, Americans were excluded from the competition. Soon after establishing the system, the Trustees were called upon to give substantial sums to the colleges to provide the visiting fellows with residential sets (RTM 8 June 1968, 9 June 1973).

At the beginning of the 1970s, two new Trustees were elected: John Baring, of the family of the Trust's bankers, who soon succeeded Phillimore as chairman of the finance committee, and Robert Blake, the Provost of Queen's College, a distinguished historian. Henceforth the pattern was established of matching four Oxford Trustees with four London Trustees. All Trustees were soon heavily involved in the discussions about discrimination in its various forms. In 1971, when considering their application for a reallocation of South African and Rhodesian scholarships, the Trustees considered whether to seek powers to make women eligible for the scholarships. They decided not to do so, in spite of American pressures of which Price, and the American Secretary Barber, had made them well aware.[239] In 1972 a woman from the University of Minnesota applied for a scholarship and was disqualified. The President of Minnesota told the Trustees that in order to comply with recent federal and state equal opportunity policies his University might be forced to withdraw from participation in the Rhodes scholarship programme. The Minnesota selection committee gave its support to his request that women be allowed to compete. The Trustees told him that under the Act of Parliament which governed their activities women remained ineligible (RTM 14 Dec. 1972).[240]

In 1973—a year which saw the death of Elton and a knighthood for Williams—the pressure on the Trustees increased. The Women's Equity Action League in the USA urged the leader of the anti-discrimination group in the British House of Commons to urge the Trustees to seek a change in the will. Lord Cromer, the British Ambassador in Washington, wrote to the Trustees. Complaints in the USA against discrimination, he pointed out, especially on grounds of sex, 'tend nowadays to assume great stridency'. Moreover, because the Trust was governed by an Act of Parliament restricting scholarships to males, many Americans laid the responsibility for the discrimination at the door of the British government (RTR 483–4; RTM 3 May 1973).

Rhodes scholars in residence organized a petition calling for the admission of women and the abolition of the rule against marriage. Of the 180 circulated, 106 responded, of whom 88 thought women should be eligible, 12 were opposed, and 6 undecided (RTM 9 June 1973). The issue was taken up by the presidents of Harvard and Radcliffe: the latter, at least, had some sympathy with the Trustees' position. 'We can't ask a group to behave illegally,' she told the Harvard Crimson in November 1973.

However, British law was changing. In 1973 a White Paper on equal opportunity was published, proposing to outlaw various forms of discrimination. Williams, reporting a proposal that there should be special scholarships for women, opined that the Trustees would not find second-class citizenship of this kind attractive.

---

[239] See Alexander, below p. 151.

[240] The University of Minnesota was threatened with a lawsuit by the Minnesota Civil Liberties Union: see Alexander, below p. 152.

I imagine that they would prefer some legal way of making women eligible rather than even a temporary parallel award (with its inevitably second eleven flavour). Do they hope that Parliamentary legislation in this matter of 'equal opportunity' might be influenced in some way, and, if so, how, since it would appear from the White Paper that both charities and universities are to be excluded from the legislation proposed? One supposes that they would welcome a clause which would *inter alia* override the Rhodes Trust Act of 1946 with its restriction to 'male students'? (RTR 487)

Sir George Abell sought an audience with the Secretary of State for Education. She was able to point out that jurisdiction over educational trusts was to be transferred to the Charity Commissioners, to whom application should now be made.

American pressure tightened. Early in 1974 the HEW drafted a guideline which prohibited colleges and universities from assisting private fellowship or scholarship programmes limited to members of one sex.[241] Under this a university which distributed on its campus information about Rhodes scholarships might endanger its federal funding. The Trust's new American Secretary, William Barber, operated the scholarship scheme from Wesleyan University: under the new guidelines his activities might put Wesleyan in peril. Disagreeable as this news was, it did give the Trustees plausible grounds to seek from the Charity Commissioners a change in the terms of the Trust on the grounds that it had become unworkable (RTR 488, 5).[242]

So, in June 1974 the Trustees drafted a request to the Charity Commissioners for a scheme to allow women to compete on equal terms for the scholarships. The wording of their request owed much to the petition of the resident Rhodes scholars (RTM 8 June 1974). The petition was submitted and argued before the Commissioners in the following December and January. But despite the appearance in September of a White Paper on sex discrimination, the Charity Commissioners were not easily convinced. 'The intention to provide scholarships for men appears to be paramount, and as yet the evidence submitted to the Commissioners is not sufficient to convince them that this purpose cannot be carried out' (RTR 491).

Meanwhile, however, the Trust's lawyers had written to the Home Secretary requesting him to consider including in the proposed anti-discrimination legislation provisions which would enable, but not compel, trustees of educational charities voluntarily to amend their trusts so as to give effect to the principle of equality of opportunity for women (RTM 6 Mar. 1975).

This approach was more successful. The government inserted into the bill an amendment providing that educational charities which heretofore were legally bound by single-sex restrictions in their awards might petition the Secretary of State for Education and Science requesting authority to lift such limitations. In the House of Lords Lord Blake, on the Trust's behalf, welcomed the amendment. 'Ever since I have been a Trustee, and long before that, the Trustees have been endeavouring to make Rhodes Scholarships open to women as well as men. But after taking the best legal advice we could, we came to

---

[241] See Alexander, below p. 153.

[242] In fact, when the guidelines were published in June, they contained a clause which removed the threat to the Rhodes scholarships. See Alexander, below p. 157.

the conclusion that it was impossible, as the law now stands or stood hitherto, to do anything about it at all.' The new bill, he said, 'was an excellent solution to a difficult problem'.

The Trustees prepared an application to be sent to the Secretary of State at the Department of Education as soon as the bill became law. All selection committees were told to add a woman to their membership.[243]

It was December when the Equal Opportunities Bill became law, and the Rhodes Trust was the first educational trust to avail itself of the exempting clause, applying immediately to make women eligible for the scholarships. There was now a Labour government, and the Secretary of State was Shirley Williams. It was she who, at the end of 1976, made the appropriate order striking out the words 'manly' from the provisions of the will and opening the competition to women. Constituencies in Australia, New Zealand, Germany, and South Africa anticipated the Order in Council and elected women for 1977. The first South African woman was elected at the same time as the first non-white South African, an Indian from Natal. In the USA the number of candidates for the award reached a record of 1,184. The total number of women elected worldwide was 24. Williams was at first afraid that it might be difficult to place all the women in Oxford, at a time when only five of its colleges were open to both sexes. But his fears proved unfounded.

Founder's Kin

When F. W. Rhodes, the son of the Founder's brother Ernest, died in 1938 the Dalham estate in Suffolk passed to the Trust. A life interest in the estate passed to his sisters Georgia and Violet. The Trustees invited them to live, with their mother, in Hildersham Hall, a Georgian manor house in Cambridgeshire which had come into the Trust's possession in 1931. They were to retain, during their lifetime, the chattels or 'heirlooms' at Dalham which Cecil Rhodes in his will had destined ultimately for the Trust. After the death of their mother, the two sisters conceived the idea of leaving their fortunes to each other and thereafter to the Trust. From the time of the reunion of 1953 they were regular visitors to Trustees' dinners. In 1966 Georgia, by now the only survivor, made a will leaving all her possessions to the Trust, and in 1970 she renounced the income from her brother's estate.[244]

Miss Rhodes had few friends, other than some distant cousins in Lincolnshire, and the Bishop of Woolwich, whom she had come to know when he was the Vicar of All Saints, Margaret St. She continued to live at Hildersham Hall until 1977, when, at the age of 86, she surrendered her lease to move to sheltered accommodation in Hedingham

[243] RTM 27 Nov. 1975. The instruction was much resented by the Governor of South Australia, who chaired the local committee.

[244] RTR 502. Williams was made executor, later to be joined by Marmaduke Hussey who had become a Trustee in 1972. 'Neither executor', Williams later recalled, 'could persuade her to give the capital to the Trust in her life-time to save the tax she hated giving to a Government of which she increasingly disapproved.'

Castle. The furniture was dispersed, and the more precious items sent to Rhodes House.[245]

In a report to the Trustees, Williams described Georgia's last days:

Hildersham at last almost empty the Warden proceeded to authorise its sale, as the trustees had agreed, and this decision upset Miss Rhodes who still nursed the hope of returning there, her sojourn at Hedingham to be temporary . . . [S]he decided to change her will and Mr Hanby Holmes of Coward Chance visited her for that purpose. The cousins were clear that all the furniture and pictures would come to them, the Bishop hoped that there would be mention of him—he had already received £27,000 in cash and some lesser gifts including the episcopal ring—and the Warden made it clear that the Trust could not leave Hildersham to rot empty since it had already been broken into although hitherto without loss. He also made it clear that she was of course entirely free to leave everything she possessed to whomever she wanted but that it would be a help if she would leave instructions about what was to go where. Mr Hanby Holmes, himself, indicated to her that if she were to change her will leaving all her possessions away from the Trust, she could hardly expect Mr Hussey and the Warden to continue to be her executors. Meanwhile she enjoyed creating tenterhooks for them, the cousins and the Bishop. The Christmas of 1977 was to be a Eucharistic celebration as the Bishop's guest after which she would go from Hedingham to stay with the cousins in Lincolnshire. The visit to the Bishop was evidently most unsuccessful and she was too unwell to set off after her return to the Castle, miserable and lonely after a Christmas in which she didn't eat. She became increasingly weak and died, without pain, her will unchanged, after a few days' illness on the 18 February 1978, not long before her eighty-eighth birthday. (RTR 503, 12)

Miss Rhodes's estate was worth about £500,000; after duty and costs had been paid, the sum which eventually found its way to the Scholarship Fund was £250,000. On the basis of a letter subsequent to the will, the Trustees felt morally obliged to give the silver and the furniture to the Lincolnshire cousins. No more was heard from the Bishop. Hildersham Hall was sold for £142,000 (RTM 2 Mar. 1978).

Georgia Rhodes was the last descendant of Cecil Rhodes's parents, and she had inherited, over her lifetime, all the property of her many uncles and aunts. Her bequest was the last great addition to the capital of the Trust, and since that time the growth of the funds has been due simply to the income and appreciation of investment property and portfolio holdings.

During Williams's secretaryship the real value of the Trust's assets grew by some 12 per cent. At the end of the financial year 1958–9 the market value of the funds managed by Barings had been £4,655,000, and the real property (including the Dalston estate, then being sold) was worth £867,000, making a total, for the English funds, of £5,552,000. With the still separate F. W. Rhodes estate of £22,000 the total value of the Trust's assets was £5,554,000. At the end of the financial year 1977–8 the Trust (excluding, as before, the Rhodes Trust South Africa) was worth £24,605,000 plus the still unrealized £250,000 from Miss Rhodes's estate, making a total of £24,855,000 (RTR 504, financial appendix).

---

[245] 'They include', said Williams, 'the alleged Angelica Kaufmann portrait said to be a Reynolds; a mirror said to be a Grinling Gibbons, but not by the Ashmolean people; a Second Empire (but third rate) table; and a remarkable marquetry cabinet' (RTR 501, 9).

Throughout most of his stewardship, Williams felt complacent about the Trust's financial position. In his Christmas letter for 1969 he had paid tribute to the members of the Trustees' finance committee—Sir Edward Peacock, who had joined it in 1924 when the assets were worth just over £2.25 million, Howard Millis, John Phillimore of Barings, Lord Harcourt of Morgan, Grenfell, and Sir George Abell of the Bank of England. 'Today', he wrote, 'as a result of inflation, devaluation, but good husbandry, the committee controls, on the Trust's behalf, the investment of funds of, expressed in sterling, some £13 million.' The increase from £2.25 million to £13 million represented, in real terms, an increase of about 50 per cent. The income of the Trust throughout the 1960s and 1970s was always ample to carry out its purposes. True, the Scholarship Fund rarely provided enough income to support the increased number of more expensive scholarships which the Trust now provided; but the shortfall was made good in most years by the Scholarship Capital Reserve Fund. Only occasionally, as in 1977–8, was the deficit on the Scholarship Fund greater than the surplus on the SCRF, so that the Public Purposes Fund had to bear some of the cost of the scholarships. From time to time, e.g. in 1979–80, transfers were made into the Scholarship Fund capital from the Public Purposes Fund. Even so in every year there was a surplus in that fund adequate to finance a generous series of benefactions. During the later 1970s the total income from all funds income was around £1.5 million, and expenditure prior to benefactions about £1 million.[246]

In the 1970s the pattern of benefactions was each year to support one major national appeal and to spend the bulk of the remaining surplus in Oxford. Among national causes which benefited were Westminster Abbey, Canterbury Cathedral, York Minster, Wells Cathedral, and the Royal Opera House (RTM 9 Mar. 1972, 8 June 1974, 12 June 1976, 9 June 1979). Generous assistance was given to the editing of Gladstone's diaries and Burke's speeches. A house was given to accommodate students at the new private University of Buckingham (RTM 5 Oct. 1978) Every year from 1972 onwards grants were made to one or more Oxford colleges. St Antony's, Linacre, Oriel, Lincoln, Green, Worcester, Magdalen, Wadham, St Peter's, and each of the five women's colleges received grants of between £10,000 and £110,000. The size of grants to colleges was usually in inverse proportion to the size of the recipient's own endowment. Grants were made to the University for squash courts and women's sports facilities, and the cricket club received £25,000.[247]

In some benefactions it was still possible to discern the ghost of the Trust's past. Gifts were made to schools in Swaziland and Botswana (then known as 'front-line states'), and to the rehabilitation of the library of Makerere University (RTM 21 Mar. 1980). A sum of £5,000 was given to the University of the West Indies. And in the early 1970s £1,000 per annum was given to assist in the publication of the *Round Table* (RTM 25 Mar. 1971).

---

[246] Details can be found in the financial statements which were regularly submitted to the Trustees with the report to their autumn meeting.

[247] There was also a donation for the gymnasium, which was welcomed by Rhodes scholars for its basketball facilities (RTM 12 June 1965).

Overseas Fees Once More

In 1979, however, the finances of the Trust suffered a severe shock. One of the first acts of the Conservative government which took office under Mrs Thatcher in that year was to announce a massive increase in overseas fees. For the year 1980–1 fees for foreigners were increased from £940 a year to some £2,000 for arts students, £3,000 for science students, and £5,000 for medical students. These increases were far more damaging than the 'tax on knowledge' earlier imposed by a Labour government. When the scale of the proposed increases became apparent in October 1979, Williams prepared a paper advising the Trustees how far they could cut down the number of scholarships if the funds proved insufficient to support them all (RTR 508, 8).

In Rhodes's will priority had been given to the Rhodesian scholarships, then to the Cape schools scholarships, then to the colonial scholarships, and fourthly to the American scholarships. If there was not sufficient income to pay all the scholarships, the colonial and American scholarships were to 'abate proportionately'.

Williams advised the Trustees not to try to alter the dispositions of the entrenched Southern African scholarships, even though since Zambia had been independent 'we have had a run of charming Zambians who are all without exception very ill prepared for Oxford'. The Rhodesians, he noted, had alternated between choosing a black and a white scholar, the latter 'often the only incoming Rhodes Scholar with a decent hair cut because he has just emerged from anti-guerilla duties'. In South Africa, unlike the schools scholarships, the at-large scholarships were at the Trust's discretion, and their number could be reduced.

In Australia the Trustees had added a seventh scholarship to the six in the will, and this could be cut. But 'the Australian Scholars by and large have been the best Rhodes Scholars. The educational and University system is so much more in step with Oxford's that the transfer is easy.' The single New Zealand scholarship in the will had been doubled in 1926; the second one could be abolished if necessary. In Canada the situation was complicated, but one scholarship could be taken away from the Maritimes and another from the Prairies. Jamaica and Bermuda were entrenched will scholarships. Bermuda 'remains our rotten borough but like many rotten boroughs it has produced some very good candidates'.

In the United States it would be administratively simple to reduce the number of scholars, because of the District Plan introduced by Aydelotte. The total elected annually could be reduced from 32 to 24 by alllowing each district to elect 3 instead of 4 scholars. 'The American Rhodes Scholars have been increasingly disappointing over the last few years and it has been for a long time an anomaly that, despite the Founder's declared preference for the "Colonial" scholarships, the Americans have bulked so large by comparison with them.'

Among the scholarships not mentioned in the will, the Maltese and Pakistan scholarships should be wound up, and the Indian awards, though very successful, should be reduced from two to one a year. The new Commonwealth scholarships had not been an entirely successful experiment.[248] Overseas secretaries had been warned that reductions were likely: but Williams concluded, 'the only immediate reductions one would like to commend to the Trustees' attention are one Maritimer fewer from Canada and one fewer South-African-at-Large from South Africa'. Despite the sweeping cuts paraded for their contemplation the Trustees decided not to make even the modest reductions eventually recommended. In the coming year the normal number of awards should be advertised (RTM 5 Oct. 1979).

In the following March the Trustees returned to the topic. Expenditure on scholarships was estimated to rise to £1.55 million, and the estimated income of both scholarship funds would be no more than £1.1 million, leaving £450,000 to be taken out of the £600,000 surplus in the PPF. The Trust's solicitors had advised that the Trustees could not reduce the number of American awards except when the scholarship funds could not afford them.[249] Unconvinced, Williams persuaded the Trustees to take counsel's opinon, but received the same answer. The Trustees once again declined to make any change in the number to be advertised for election for Michaelmas term 1981.[250] By June 1980 Williams was estimating that the expenditure on scholarships would rise by 1982 to a level of £1.775 million, which might be very difficult to meet from the Trust's income.

The meeting of the Trust in June 1980 was the last while Williams was Secretary. The overseas secretaries of the major constituencies were present. The fee crisis was again a major item of discussion, and the possibility was canvassed of making the scholarship subject to a means test. The overseas secretaries were opposed, but they were equally reluctant to face any reduction in the number of their constituency scholarships. The issue, unresolved, was passed on to Williams's successor.[251]

Sir Edgar and Lady Williams were warmly thanked for their twenty-nine years of service to the Trust. The Trustees joined with the Rhodes scholars in establishing a memorial fund, which totalled £22,000, to enable the curators of the University Parks to plant trees to acknowledge their achievement. After an occasionally stormy period in Rhodes House, the Williamses went into retirement on a great swell of gratitude and goodwill.

From Contraction to Expansion

The new Warden was Robin Fletcher, Bursar of Trinity, University Lecturer in Modern Greek, and Olympic medallist for hockey. He took over at a difficult time. However, the

---

[248] 'The Warden has for a long time felt', Williams said, 'that we have just a few too many Rhodes Scholars to place in Oxford each year: and in recent years we have had to look elsewhere, outside Oxford which is never entirely satisfactory.'

[249] See Hanby Holmes to Williams, 11 Oct. 1979, RTF 2567.

[250] RTM 21 Mar. 1980. Holmes to Williams, 3 Apr. 1980 with instructions to counsel and opinion of Michael Miller QC; RTF 1233.

[251] There was an irony in the fact that while Elton had spent his last years in office persuading the Trustees to increase the number of awards, his successor's last years were spent in a vain attempt to reduce it. The burden of administering the scholarships had weighed particularly heavily on Williams after he suffered a coronary in early 1978.

end of the first financial year of the new wardenship showed that the note of panic in previous discussions had been uncalled for. Even with the increased scale of fees, expenditure on scholarships was more than covered by the income on the two scholarship funds, recently refreshed by transfers from the Public Purposes Fund.[252] But the Trustees resolved on a more cautious policy with regard to benefactions, waiting until the end of each financial year before making grants, and putting to capital two-thirds of the budgeted surplus on the combined funds, giving away only one-third (RTM 20 Nov. 1981). In 1981–2 expenditure on scholarships exceeded income on the scholarship funds by some £26,000, but this was not alarming since the PPF showed a healthy surplus of nearly £600,000 after benefactions. Henceforth the Trustees did not make any transfer to the scholarship funds, since retention in the Public Purposes Fund gave them greater discretion in future use of the funds.

No more was heard of proposals to reduce the number of scholarships. By June 1982 Fletcher felt confident enough of the financial position to suggest that further scholarships might be given to African and Far Eastern countries (RTR 517). The Trustees gave his paper a cautious welcome; some of them were anxious to include the Middle East among the scholarship constituencies.

Having taken advice from the British Council, Fletcher submitted a further report in November. Middle Eastern scholarships were excluded by the terms of the 1946 Act.[253] Hong Kong was adequately provided for by Jardines, and India was catered for by the Inlaks Foundation. The triennial scholarship shared between Malaysia and Singapore was unsatisfactory and should be replaced by separate scholarships for each constituency. The Pakistan scholarship should become annual instead of triennial, but nothing should be offered to Bangladesh or Sri Lanka. In Africa, only Nigeria and Kenya looked like providing qualified Rhodes scholars on a regular basis. The Malta scholarship should not be renewed, but Cyprus might be considered.

But instead of an addition to the existing quota of scholarships, Fletcher himself preferred a scheme of postdoctoral awards for Third World countries, to be created on the same lines as the women's visiting fellowships. Such fellowships might with profit replace the existing Nigerian, Malayan, and Caribbean scholarships (RTR 518, 27).

The Trustees took several meetings to digest these proposals. By 1984 there were about 1,500 overseas students present in Oxford, numbers having climbed back, after the drop due to full-cost fees, to the peak reached at the end of the 1970s. The Trustees were inclined to favour an increase in the normal scholarship programme as being more in line with the Founder's wishes than postdoctoral fellowships. They doubted in any case whether colleges would welcome postdoctoral fellowships restricted to underdeveloped countries (RTM 16 Mar. 1984; RTR 524, 30).

At the June meeting, Fletcher argued that a traditional Rhodes scholarship programme aiming to make an appreciable impact in Third World Africa would be very expensive,

---

[252] At the beginning of the year, £700,000 was transferred from the Public Purposes Fund to the Scholarship Fund, and at its end it was possible to make a further transfer of £500,000 after benefactions to colleges and the Bodleian of £150,000 (RTM 14 June 1980, 20 Nov. 1981).

[253] In the light of counsel's opinion of 1963, this was incorrect; see above p. 57.

and even if the funds were available he doubted if it would be possible to make a success of such a scheme in traditional terms at Oxford.[254] British Council advice was that the best way to assist black Africans was by the provision of postdoctoral fellowships. Indeed, rather than set up more Rhodes scholarships, it might be preferable to fund a large scheme of a different kind, focusing on professional and technical education elsewhere than in Oxford (RTR 524).

The Trustees were unconvinced and in June 1984 decided instead on a substantial increase in the traditional Rhodes scholarship scheme. It was decided to offer an annual scholarship to Kenya (in place of the old East African scholarship abolished in the 1950s); to turn the triennial scholarships for Nigeria, Pakistan, and the British Caribbean into annual scholarships; to offer annual scholarships for Malaysia and Singapore in place of the triennial Malay region scholarship; and to set up a new annual scholarship in Hong Kong. In addition, a third annual scholarship was added for India.

Williams had always objected to proposals for additional scholarships, on the grounds that colleges would refuse to absorb them. Whether or not this was true in his time, it was unlikely to be true in the 1980s when Rhodes scholars were less than 15 per cent of the overseas students in Oxford. But Fletcher in July 1984 took the precaution of notifying all the colleges of the Trust's intention to create the new scholarships. The conference of colleges raised no objection to the increase, but merely made a plea for a more even distribution of Rhodes scholars among the Oxford colleges. Fletcher had not waited for its response before authorizing elections in Nigeria, Singapore, Malaysia, and the British Caribbean for November 1984, and making arrangements in Kenya and Hong Kong for elections in 1985. With rising rents and dividends in a buoyant market, the Trustees accepted the extra expenditure without a tremor. What the Thatcher government had taken from the Trust with one hand in increased expenditure, it had given back with the other hand in increased income.

The Reunion of 1983

At the twenty-fifth and fiftieth anniversaries of the foundation of the Trust, reunions of Rhodes scholars had been held in Oxford. The seventy-fifth anniversary, which had occurred in 1978 when Warden Williams, in poor health, was on the point of retiring, had been allowed to pass unnoticed. Fletcher now proposed that the eightieth birthday should be celebrated in 1983. Each college was to house its own alumni, charging £35 a head for residence and meals; other costs were to be met by the Trust, at an estimated expense of £150,000.[255]

The main events proposed were an interdenominational service in Christ Church, a dinner at Rhodes House, a reception at Oriel, a degree ceremony in the Sheldonian, a

---

[254] His opinion was based partly on the record of Zambia, the one black African country with a succession of Rhodes scholars. Of the thirteen elected since 1974, three had failed to find places in Oxford and two others obtained places only after studying first at another British university.

[255] RTM 20 Nov. 1981, 19 Mar. 1982. Basil Stubbings (Natal and Corpus 1935), resident in Oxford, was appointed conference organizer.

garden party at Christ Church, a general conference in the Sheldonian, and a final Gaudy at each college. The degree ceremony would be an opportunity for those who had not taken a degree to do so. A slate of honorary degrees was sent up for consideration by the Vice-Chancellor.

By November 1982 1,500 acceptances had been received, from 850 scholars and 650 spouses. A group of this size was too large to dine in Rhodes House, so arrangements were made for marquees to be set up in the gardens of Trinity. Rhodes House would be used for the garden party, but it would not be large enough unless Wadham lent its fellows' garden. Roman Catholic and Presbyterian Rhodes scholar clerics were secured to assist the Dean at the service in Christ Church. The Cathedral held 1,000; the Trustees alternated between alarm about the potential overflow and worry that the pews might be embarrassingly empty (RTM 19 Nov. 1982; RTR 518).

At the beginning of 1983 a special reunion committee was set up, consisting of Lord Blake (who had now become chairman), Lady Blake, the Warden and his wife, and two Trustees. By now the Queen had been invited to be the guest of honour at the garden party. It was decided to punch a temporary hole in the wall between Wadham and Rhodes House to allow the 2,000 party guests to move freely between the two gardens. This decision, which cost the trust £10,000, was the subject of much amused, and some outraged, press comment around the world, but especially in the USA.

Months of extremely detailed planning paid off. The 850 scholars and their families enjoyed a lively holiday. The Oxford colleges, which were just getting into their stride in the art of fund-raising, welcomed the opportunity to bring their needs to the attention of some of their wealthier alumni. John Templeton (Connecticut and Balliol 1934) announced a benefaction of £3 million for the Oxford Centre for Management Studies. Honorary degrees were given to Sir Zelman Cowen, the former Governor General of Australia, the novelist and poet Robert Penn Warren, General Bernard Rogers, the supreme Allied commander, and Gordon Robertson, a former Cabinet Secretary in Canada. Bob Hawke (Western Australia and University 1953), the Prime Minister of Australia, sent a congratulatory telegram. The highlight of the gathering was a characteristically moving after-dinner speech by the Chancellor, Harold Macmillan. It was recorded and long treasured on tape by many of those present.

The Sheldonian conference, however, was not merely celebratory. Several speakers drew attention to the fact that only two non-whites had won scholarships from South Africa in the last eleven years. George Keys, one of the Balliol protesters of the 1970s, now an attorney in Washington, said that little had come of his manifesto, and that he proposed to relaunch a campaign. Bremer Hofmeyr (Transvaal and University 1930) proposed that the Trust should set up twenty to thirty scholarships for blacks at private schools, to bring them up to the standard where they could compete on equal terms for scholarships. Warden Fletcher pointed out that the Trust was already spending £15,000 a year on scholarships for blacks. As Lord Blake was summing up, he was interrupted by another white South African, Michael Smuts, who protested against any change in the tradition of Rhodes scholarships.[256]

---

[256] RTR 521. See Alexander, below p. 174, on the involvement of the AARS.

South African Schools Again

As a result of the Sheldonian meeting, South Africa came back onto the Trustees' agenda. Edwin Cameron, the new assistant secretary in South Africa, began raising funds to add to the annual 45,000 rand voted by the Trust for black education. This grant, Fletcher noted sagely, should be looked on as 'a gesture to improve the lot of Black South Africans rather than as a likely breeder of Rhodes Scholarship candidates' (RTR 522; RTM 13 Jan. 1984).

Shortly before retiring Williams had suggested that the Trust's assets held in South Africa, worth some £2 million, should be sold and replaced by an English portfolio managed by Barings. In November 1983 the Trustees agreed to do so: the move was justified on financial grounds, and there was also the possibility of confiscatory measures by present or future South African governments (RTM 1 Nov. 1985).[257] Legal advice was that neither the relevant Act nor South African exchange controls presented an obstacle to the assets of Rhodes Trust South Africa being invested in the UK. However, the accounts of the RTSA should be kept separate and its operation would remain subject to South African law (RTR 321, 30).

Once again the Trustees had to address the issue of the Cape schools. To a special meeting in January 1984 Fletcher presented a copy of the submission which had been made ten years previously to the Department of Education. In the meantime nothing had changed except that Bishops and St Andrew's had begun to admit a small number of non-whites. It seemed unlikely that a fresh submission to the Department would meet with any more favourable response. At the reunion it had been suggested that these school scholarships should be matched by scholarships closed to black universities; but the Trustees thought that this would set an undesirable precedent. The South Africa-at-large scholarships had been academically successful, and even though in 1983 all shortlisted candidates had been white, they did provide the one chance for black South Africans to acquire Rhodes scholarships. The Trustees minuted:

In the particular circumstances in South Africa the disparity of educational background between the privileged whites and underprivileged non-whites did seem to impose a special responsibility on the South African selection committees to take account of potential rather than achievement.

But, having had their fingers burnt once, they decided against making any further attempt to reallocate the schools scholarships.[258]

Fletcher set off on a trip to South Africa, principally to arrange for the transfer of the RTSA assets, but also to explore ways of increasing the number of black applicants for the scholarships, whether by setting up of pre-selection panels in black universities

---

[257] The Trustees were anxious that no political interpretation should be put on their decision; but it proved tactically advantageous when, later in the 1980s, anti-apartheid campaigners argued for disinvestment as part of the economic boycott of South Africa.

[258] Quite apart from the racial issue, the Cape schools scholarships were an anachronism, long after closed awards for English schools had been abolished as a method of entry to Oxford. In a paper written before the reunion Fletcher had complained of difficulties in finding places for scholars from the schools. 'The only proper solution to the health of the South African scholarships', he wrote, 'will be to get rid of the "closed" awards' (RTR 519, 15).

or the canvassing of black academics by members of the scholarship selection committees. In South Africa Fletcher found that other foundations were also having difficulty
in recruiting blacks to prestigious scholarships.[259] He did not receive the impression that
the Rhodes scholarships were there perceived as discriminating against non-whites (RTR
523).

At home, and in the USA, however, protest grew louder against the schools scholarships. A series of articles appeared in the *American Oxonian*.[260] A meeting of fifty resident scholars in Oxford in March 1984 proposed the setting up of a joint committee of
Trustees and past and present scholars to discuss a number of South African issues (RTR
523, 14). Two South African scholars produced a carefully researched and well-reasoned
memorandum which took account of such facts as that the proportion of black to white
graduates in South Africa was 1 to 6, that Afrikaners as well as blacks were underrepresented in the scholarships, and that the ideology of the black consciousness movement
made blacks reluctant to apply. None the less they were critical of the operation of the
scholarships and made a number of proposals for reform, including a restructuring of
the constituencies and an advertising campaign to create a new image of the scholarships
(RTR 524, 21–4).

The reasoned moderation of the 1984 memorandum was far removed from the strident rhetoric of the 1970s. The Trustees immediately agreed to one of its proposals, the
raising of the age limit to 27 for South Africa-at-large candidates.[261] But they did not
agree to the proposal for a joint committee, and Lord Blake reiterated that because the
Cape schools could still provide Rhodes scholars a convincing case could not be made
for the abolition of their awards.[262]

In March 1985 a petition was signed by 171 resident Rhodes scholars (some 94 per cent
of the total) calling on the Trustees to seek legislation to amend the will. Of the eight
Trustees under the chairmanship of Lord Blake, only four recalled the troubles of the
1970s; four had joined since 1975.[263] It was now resolved to take another initiative,
however unhopefully, to remove the schools scholarships. It was decided that the best
first step would be to try to secure the cooperation of the schools themselves (RTM 16
Nov. 1984).

Senator Lugar (Indiana and Pembroke 1954), now chairman of the US Senate
Committee on Foreign Relations, expressed the hope in a letter to Lord Blake 'that the
trustees will adopt one of a number of potential courses of action to ensure that black
South Africans are not excluded for reasons of race from full participation in the Rhodes

---

[259] In the last three years, for instance, all but two of ten Cambridge Livingstone scholars had been
white.

[260] See Alexander, below p. 176.

[261] This proposal, which had earlier been rejected by the Trustees, was supported by a conference of
the selection committees in South Africa itself.

[262] RTM 9 June 1984. In lieu of the joint committee Fletcher organized a series of seminars for concerned scholars in Michaelmas term 1984; he described the discussions as 'reasonable and amicable'. RTR
525.

[263] Sir Robert Armstrong, the Cabinet Secretary, and Greig Barr, the Rector of Exeter, had joined in
1975; Sir John Sainsbury, chairman of the supermarket chain, and Mary Moore, the Principal of St Hilda's,
joined in 1984.

Scholarship program'. In his response Blake mentioned the increase of the age limit, and the annual sums set aside each year for the support of black children in mixed schools, but emphasized the Trustees' reluctance to 'earmark scholarships for persons of particular race' (RTR 527).

In June Fletcher warned that there was likely to be an explosion of protest in Oxford beyond the Rhodes community; a debate in Congregation could not be ruled out. The schools themselves had been uncooperative, so it was decided to make an application to the Charity Commissioners to remove the scholarships from the two schools— SACS and Paul Roos—which still did not admit blacks. But first counsel's opinion was to be taken, and Fletcher should go to South Africa to inform the schools (RTM 8 June 1985; RTR 527, 27).

Counsel's opinion, which arrived just in time for the November meeting of the Trustees, was very discouraging. The Race Relations Act of 1976 had not changed the situation and the Charity Commissioners would be very likely to reject the Trust's request. None the less, the Trustees agreed unanimously that an approach should be made, and at their following meeting, in March, a draft of the submission was approved.[264]

Members of the American Association continued to take a keen interest in the affair. They invited the South African Secretary, Welsh, to attend the quadrennial meeting of October 1986; initially he accepted, but the Trustees, fearing adverse publicity, made him withdrew his acceptance. When the meeting was held, feeling ran so high that all other business was abandoned. Members were annoyed that they had not been allowed to see the Trust's submission to the Charity Commissioners, and they felt the Trustees were being inactive and evasive. Fletcher reported his impression that members of the board 'see Mr Welsh as the blue-eyed boy, the Secretary as a suspicious character and the Trustees as definitely bad eggs'. In the discussion Strobe Talbott was particularly eloquent in drawing a contrast between the transparency of American society and the closed nature of the British establishment. The board of the Association clamoured for a meeting with the Trustees. In November Fletcher was authorized to meet Jack Justice, the new president of the AARS, and in the following October Sir John Baring, now chairman, attended the meeting of the Association's board of direction (RTR 532, 28–31).[265]

In South Africa, Welsh had now retired. He was succeeded as Secretary by Judge Laurie Ackermann, while Arthur Chaskalson was appointed chair of the South Africa-at-large selection committee.[266] The South Africa-at-large committee elected, from time to time, non-white scholars. One, Kumaran Naidoo, arrived prematurely in Oxford while being pursued by the South African police on charges of subversion: he was allowed by the Trustees to anticipate his stipend (RTR 533, 3).

[264] RTM 23 Mar. 1986. Earlier, the Trust's solicitor had suggested the possibility that the schools scholarships could be removed on the ground of sexual, rather than racial, discrimination. 'There is a very small chance that the Secretary of State for Education might be willing to use his powers under S.78 of the Sex Discrimination Act to break the tie and thus the de facto discrimination.' Fletcher thought this 'an underhand manoeuvre unworthy of the Trustees' (RTR 527).

[265] See Alexander, below p. 177.

[266] Both these men were to become members of the post-apartheid Constitutional Court of South Africa.

Meanwhile, the Charity Commissioners had sidestepped the request for a scheme. They drew attention to a clause which said, in effect, that if a case was too difficult to be adjudicated by the Commission it could be referred to a court to make a scheme. If counsel's opinion could be obtained favourable to the Trust's proposals, they would allow proceedings before the High Court (RTR 523, 22–7).[267]

Since the only counsel's opinion so far received had been negative, Sir John Sainsbury urged the Trustees to press immediately for a private bill (RTM 28 Nov. 1986). But at the next meeting, at which Sir John Baring took over from Lord Blake as chairman, a majority were in favour of attempting to secure a favourable opinion, and they approached Sidney Kentridge QC, who had been defence counsel for Steve Biko (RTM 6 Mar. 1987).

In Kentridge's opinion, delivered in June, though it was not impossible to recruit scholars from the schools it was now impractical given Rhodes's basic intention of assisting the unity and cooperation of English-speaking peoples throughout the world, and of excluding differentiation on grounds of race.[268] On the basis of this opinion the Commissioners in September authorized charity proceedings, and in November the Trustees decided to make an application to the chancery court. Kentridge agreed to be senior counsel.

During the winter Fletcher prepared a long historical affidavit. It was modified by the Trustees at their meeting in March 1988. They summed up their reasons for seeking relief in three points: (1) the Trustees themselves regarded the obligation to award scholarships to schools obliged to refuse non-whites as distasteful, unreasonable, and inconsistent with clause 24 of the will. (2) The continuation of the Cape school scholarships was damaging to the reputation of the scholarship programme both worldwide and in Oxford. (3) Rhodes scholars disenchanted with the programme might refuse to help in selection (RTM 4 Mar. 1988).

There followed a long delay while material was awaited from South Africa, and while junior counsel delved in the Trust's archives for supporting material for the revision of the affidavit. The only progress which had been made by March 1989 was that the Trustees had agreed to bear the costs of the schools' defence up to the point when proceedings began. At the time of Fletcher's last Trustees' meeting, in June 1989, he had still not been able to sign the affidavit, now in its fourth draft. He did so at last in July, shortly before handing on the conduct of the case to his successor. There then followed a further delay while waiting for the affidavit of the schools in response.

In the interim, a hint was received that the schools might be willing to drop their opposition to the Trust's action if that had as its goal not the extinction but the suspension of the scholarships. The Trustees—advised by their lawyers that their

---

[267] The Trustees had always previously been advised that as the Trust was a statutory charity the most a court could do was to permit an approach to Parliament for a private bill. In response to a query, the Commissioners now ruled that the Trust was not a statutory charity after all (RTR 533; RTM 6 Mar. 1987).

[268] He rejected the schools' interpretation of the word 'race' in Rhodes's will on the grounds that the will was meant to apply throughout the world and not just in South Africa.

chance of success in the litigation, on which they had already spend nearly £60,000, was less than 50 per cent—agreed to explore the possibility of suspending the scholarships for a period of five years. The suspension was to be followed by permanent abolition if conditions for equal opportunity in education did not by that time exist in South Africa. The Attorney General and the Charity Commissioners welcomed this approach. But in February 1990 the schools refused the offer of compromise and in March submitted their counter-affidavit. After a brief response was submitted on behalf of the Trust, the action was set down in the Chancery List to be heard on 4 March 1991.[269]

Meanwhile, change was afoot in South Africa. The government of F. W. de Klerk began, slowly and painfully, to dismantle the apartheid legislation. One new law permitted state schools to open their doors to all races, provided that several conditions were fulfilled, one being that a quorum of parents voted by a substantial majority in favour. Before the Trust's action came on, SACS had gone through all the necessary procedures for desegregation, and Paul Roos was in process of doing the same. This cut the ground from under the Trustees' action, and in an emergency meeting on 1 February 1991 they decided to instruct their lawyers to adjourn *sine die* the action against SACS, and to suspend that against Paul Roos until the outcome of their desegregation proceedings. Shortly afterwards the parents of the Paul Roos schoolboys voted by a convincing majority to make the school open. At a brief hearing on 1 March the Master made the order requested with regard to discontinuance and adjournment. The chairman was instructed by the Trustees to write to the headmasters of the two schools to congratulate them on opening their doors to all races.

It was in 1985 that the Trustees had decided to make a second attempt to go to law to abolish the closed school scholarships. Now, after the lapse of five years and the expenditure of some £250,000 in the lawyers' fees of both sides, their legal case had collapsed. They had to console themselves that they had won a moral victory. Henceforth, no Rhodes scholars would be elected from a segregated constituency. Their own activities had been one small part of the worldwide pressure which had made the continuance of apartheid an impossibility for the South African government.

A Period of Prosperity

When Fletcher handed over to his successor in 1989 the Trust was in much better financial shape than when he had inherited it from his predecessor at a time of crisis. In the year ending June 1989 the Trust's income was £5,422,000; with expenditure of £3,213,000 this left a surplus of £1.777 million after £1 million had been given away in benefactions. Even the Scholarship Fund was in surplus and needed no topping up. The total value of the four funds on 30 June was just below £67 million. Nine years earlier it had been worth £22 million. Its real value had increased by some 60 per cent, despite a temporary drop in 1987 (RTR 541).

---

[269] The trial was expected to last six days.

Nearly a quarter of the Trust's assets were in real estate. The dozen properties owned in London, Bromley, Brighton, Warwickshire, and elsewhere had all been bought as investments; they had no historical connections with Cecil Rhodes or the early days of the Trust. The largest single item was an office block in Old Jewry. This was a constant subject of concern, and the Trustees gave a sigh of relief when it was disposed of for £10 million in 1989. On being appointed a Trustee, Sir John Sainsbury had questioned whether the Trust's funds were large enough to support an appropriately balanced property portfolio. A gradual reduction of the proportion held in property began in Fletcher's time and was continued afterwards, as the Trust followed the general fashion of charitable foundations (other than Oxbridge colleges) of moving away from direct investment in real estate. However, while held, property made a healthy contribution to the income of the Trust even if it did not share in the growth of the equity portfolio during the long bull market of the 1990s.[270]

The Trustees could afford to be generous. Research grants were now awarded frequently to Rhodes scholars, by an academic committee of the Trustees which had inherited the role of the Third Year committee. The stipend was increased regularly to match inflation, and transportation costs were now paid both ways, plus a settling-in allowance. The Trustees were, however, unwilling to fund research travel to scholars' home countries during their time on stipend. The scholarship was intended to broaden the experience of scholars; in addition, it was not always easy for the academic committee to distinguish between deserving and spurious applications for home-based research.[271]

An extra annual scholarship awarded to Australia in the bicentennial year of 1986 brought the total offered annually to eighty-one (RTM 7 June 1986). Despite the expansion in scholarship numbers the Trustees were able to make handsome benefactions during the second half of the 1980s—to Oxford colleges above all, but also to a number of causes redolent of the Trust's earlier concerns, such as the English Speaking Union, the Royal Commonwealth Society, and the British Commonwealth ex-services league (RTM 8 June 1985).

Despite the benefactions, surpluses built up in the Trust's funds.[272] In his 1986 Budget speech the Chancellor hinted that charities which did not spend the major portion of their annual income might not get tax relief on income unspent, and in March 1987 the Charity Commissioners queried the surplus of over £1 million in the income account of the Public Purposes Fund. Were the Trustees keeping this sum for a specific purpose? In reply Fletcher argued that the four funds should be considered together. Because of full-cost fees and the increased number of scholarships, the balance in the Scholarship Fund had been reduced to nil during the period 1982–6. In this broader context the

---

[270] In 1986 the management of the Trust's properties was transferred from St Quintin to Richard Ellis. RTM 28 Nov. 1986.

[271] This policy drew an ineffective round robin of protest from resident scholars in 1988, and at regular subsequent intervals (RTR 536, 10).

[272] In 1984 the Trustees relaxed their policy of putting two-thirds of surplus income to capital, and agreed to a 50/50 split between saving and benefaction.

retention of funds in the PPF was only prudent stewardship. In the four years in question, 86 per cent of Trust's total income had been spent, even though in the PPF taken by itself 52 per cent had remained unspent. The Commissioners seemed content with this reply.

Oxford University would have been only too happy to mop up the surplus. Vice-Chancellor Neill had decided to launch a substantial capital campaign. In spring 1987 he approached Lord Blake to invite a large contribution from the Trust. At a preliminary discussion in March the Trustees agreed that £5 million might be an appropriate sum. However, during the academic year 1986–7 no definite decision was reached though donations were made to the University as well as to colleges in the normal course. These included £30,000 for sports facilities and £10,000 to the Bodleian Library to assist with the purchase of the Opie collection of children's literature.[273]

It was in November 1987 that the first formal appeal for Campaign for Oxford was received from the Vice-Chancellor. The Trustees hesitated about their response. They were unhappy that no definite target had been fixed, and uncertain whether the structure of the campaign management was sufficiently robust. They worried about the danger of competition between the University and its constituent colleges. They were reluctant to make donations for unspecified purposes, and concerned that some of their previous endowments now seemed to need supplementation.[274]

Neill tried to reassure the Trustees in a long letter to their March meeting. On the basis of *pro bono* advice from McKinsey's, he had fixed the campaign target as between £100 million and £200 million, and planned to continue it for five years from October 1988. He promised to review the position of the frozen chair, and set out the steps that were being taken to coordinate college appeals with the University campaign. He asked the Trustees to contribute specifically to the setting up of a Development Office.[275]

The Trustees were impressed by Neill's letter and, despite an unenthusiastic memorandum from Fletcher, agreed to make an immediate gift of £0.5 million for the office expenses. At their June meeting they agreed to make a further pledge of £2.5 million, to be spread over the next five years. The first priority for the use of the gift should be the topping up of the endowments of four posts created by the Trust in the past. At several meetings the Trustees discussed the merits of other items on the Vice-Chancellor's shopping list. The list changed from time to time as other benefactors stepped in to support particular causes, and the Trustees' deliberations were accordingly prolonged. In the end the Trustees' contribution substantially exceeded the sum originally pledged, and in addition to the Development Office and an increase in the endowment of the existing Rhodes posts, they supported chairs in archaeology, lecturerships in management studies, the Ashmolean and Pitt Rivers Museums, and the projected Institute for American Studies. Gifts were also made for the provision of child care and the construction of an all-weather running track (RTM 3 Mar. 1989).

[273] RTM 6 June 1987. At the same time £20,000 was given to the Southern African Advanced Education project; see p. 95.
[274] The post of Rhodes professorship of American history had been frozen because of shortage of funds.
[275] The letter is in RTR 536.

As will be seen, this list reflected the particular needs and priorities of the University campaign in the course of its progress towards its successful conclusion. Only the re-endowment of the Rhodes chairs and the Institute of American Studies fell clearly within the traditional concerns of the Rhodes Trustees, while the contribution to the running track followed the pattern of sporting subventions initiated by Warden Williams. But once again, as in the appeal for the Higher Studies Fund, and in the Oxford Historic Buildings Appeal, the Trust had shown itself to be one of the most generous and flexible of the University's benefactors.

Prosperity and Extension

To succeed Robin Fletcher the Trustees in 1987 appointed Anthony Kenny, who was shortly to retire as Master of Balliol. He took up office as Secretary and Warden in 1989 and remained in post until retiring, at the age of 68, in 1999.[276]

During the 1990s the Rhodes Trust benefited from the succession of long bull markets. The total value of its funds at the end of the financial year 1988–9 was £105 million. After a brief drop early in 1990 to £91 million it began a steady climb, which became sharper as the decade progressed. The upward trend survived the shock, in 1995, of the collapse of Barings' Bank. Baring Asset Management, which managed the Trust's portfolio, was not involved; but when the crash occurred, more than £2 million of the Trust's liquid cash was held in the firm's custodian bank. In order to pay the current instalment of scholars' stipends £0.25 million had to be borrowed from a high street bank. In the end the Dutch bank IMG, which bought Barings, repaid every penny of the Trust's losses. The Trustees, however, had independently decided that with the growth in the size of their assets it was time to split the management of their portfolio. Accordingly, in 1996 the Public Purposes Fund and the funds of Rhodes Trust South Africa were handed over to Gartmore, with the scholarship funds remaining with Baring Asset Management (RTM 1 Mar. 1996).

In 1997 the combined funds passed the £150 million mark, in 1998 the £175 million mark, and at the end of the financial year 1999 the value of the fund was within touching distance of the £200 million mark. One reason for this rapid growth was that the Trust, like most endowed charities of a similar size, gradually moved out of the property market. Having disposed of the Old Jewry property for £10 million in 1989 (RTR 541), the Trustees sold a block of shops in Queensway for a similar sum in 1995 and completed the disposal of the remainder of their properties by 1998.[277] Towards the end of the decade, in the published league tables of UK charities deriving their income principally from endowment, the Rhodes Trust was just below the top twenty.

---

[276] His previous career is narrated in two memoirs, *A Path from Rome* (London: Sidgwick and Jackson, 1985), and *A Life in Oxford* (London: John Murray, 1997).

[277] The sale of real estate led to a diminution in the Trust's income in real terms, but the Trustees had adopted a policy of maximizing total return. Throughout the decade the Trust's income fluctuated between £5.5 m and £6.5 m.

Because of the prosperity of the 1990s, the Trustees felt able to expand the scholarship scheme. Early in 1991 a third at-large scholarship was given to Australia, and a second discretionary scholarship to the Caribbean region (RTM 1 Feb. 1991). Later in the same year a second scholarship was awarded to Kenya, and a third to New Zealand (RTM 1 Nov. 1991). Though from 1993 the Nigerian scholarship had to be suspended, after a series of difficulties with selection procedures, a new scholarship was founded for Uganda in 1994 (RTM 5 Mar. 1993, 3 June 1994). The states neighbouring South Africa—known during the apartheid era as 'front-line states'—namely Botswana, Lesotho, Namibia, and Swaziland, were given a scholarship of their own in 1996, administered initially by the South Africa-at-large committee (RTM 7 June 1996). A second Pakistan scholarship was created in 1966 and at the same time the number of scholarships offered anually in India was raised to six (RTM 1 Nov. 1996). Finally, at the end of 1997, for the first time a scholar was chosen from Bangladesh. During the 1990s more new scholarships for Commonwealth countries were created than in any previous decade of the Trust's history.[278]

The decade was a period when Britain was concerned to define its relation not only to its partners in the Commonwealth, but more importantly to fellow members of the European Community. When, at the end of 1991, the Maastricht Treaty brought the member states into a new and closer European union, a majority of the Rhodes Trustees felt that it would be appropriate to mark this by the introduction of an experimental scheme of European scholarships. Had Cecil Rhodes been alive in 1991, it was argued, he would have seen that if Oxford was to train an elite of leaders to fight the world's fight, it was as important to draw scholars from the continent of Europe as from the Commonwealth and the United States.

Accordingly, it was agreed to offer, for each of the three years beginning in 1992, eight scholarships open to nationals of any of the member states of the European Union other than the UK and Germany. It was not possible to set up selection committees parallel to those in the traditional constituencies. Instead, all postgraduate applicants to Oxford from the EU were invited to apply for Rhodes scholarships in accordance with the normal criteria, providing the normal documentation and personal statement. Only when they had secured admission to Oxford were applicants considered by the Trust for scholarships. The papers of successful applicants were sent by the University to Rhodes House, where a shortlist of sixteen was drawn up. The shortlisted candidates were then interviewd by a panel of Trustees, and eight were offered scholarships. Because these scholars were chosen by a special procedure, they were known not as 'Rhodes scholars' but as 'Rhodes European scholars'. In other respects they enjoyed in Oxford the same privileges as Rhodes scholars.[279]

---

[278] At various times the Trustees also gave consideration to proposals for the creation of scholarships in Malawi and Tanzania, and for the restoration of the scholarships in Ghana and Sri Lanka (RTM 7 Mar., 7 Nov. 1997).

[279] European scholars were less expensive to support than other scholars, since the University charged them fees at the domestic rate rather than the 'full-cost' overseas rate.

At the same time as creating the European scholarships the Trustees increased the number of German scholarships to four. Thus, during the years of the experiment, twelve scholarships were available annually for citizens of the European Community. The German scholars continued to be chosen in the normal way.[280]

The first Rhodes European scholars were chosen by the Trustees after interview in June 1992. Eight were elected from forty-six applicants. Three were from Greece, two from Ireland, one from France, one from Italy, and one from Denmark. Panels of Trustees met in Rhodes House in the spring of successive years, electing eight more scholars in 1993 and six in 1994. Though this completed the experimental cycle originally planned, it was agreed to continue the experiment for a further year, and in 1995 eight scholars were elected from fifty-four applicants. The European scholarships brought the number of scholars supported by the Trust to a record level. In 1995–6 there were 247 scholars resident on stipend, a number surpassed only in the post-war years 1920–2.

At this point the Trustees decided to terminate the European experiment. Some of them had felt from the start that European scholarships did not fit well with the traditional Rhodes emphasis on the English-speaking world. Others, who had initially been enthusiastic about the scheme, had to admit that it had not turned out quite as expected. The distribution of candidates had not reflected the size or importance of the different countries of the European Union. In the three years of the scheme's operation seven of the successful candidates came from Ireland and six from Greece; three came from France and two from Italy; Denmark, Spain, and the Netherlands contributed one each. While the European scholars had performed with great credit academically, only a few of them had taken the full part in sporting and other extra-curricular activities which is characteristic of most other Rhodes scholars. Finally, while the scheme was very popular with the European scholars themselves—who petitioned the Trustees eloquently for its continuation—it had proved unpopular with former Rhodes scholars worldwide, many of whom complained that if the Trust had money to spare for extra scholarships they should be given to Third World countries in the Commonwealth rather than to the countries of the European Union.

When the Trustees suspended the experiment, they gave consideration to setting up a new European scheme, initially in France and Italy, to be administered in the normal way by local selection committees (on which, of course, returned Rhodes European scholars could play an important part). But after a generous bequest from elsewhere enabled Oxford University to award a number of scholarships to citizens of the Community, the Trustees decided to take no further action with regard to Rhodes scholarships in Europe (RTM 1 Nov. 1996). Instead, for several years, they made a substantial contribution to the Entente Cordiale scholarships scheme, founded by Sir Christopher Mallaby, to enable postgraduate students from Britain and France to spend a year at universities on the other side of the channel (RTM 1 Mar. 1996, 1 Nov. 1996).

---

[280] Before 1989 two scholars were elected annually from West Germany. In that year the Trustees agreed to offer a scholarship also in East Germany, and a selection committee was chosen (RTR 541, 32). But before a scholar could be elected by that committee the nation was reunited. Henceforth there were three German scholarships, and the first scholar from the former DDR, Christian Ganz, was elected by the national committee in 1991.

The Scholarship Evaluated

In 1991 the Trustees commissioned General Technology Systems Limited to undertake an evaluation of the scholarship programme by submitting a questionnaire to all living scholars whose addresses were known. In all, 1887 responses were received, a response rate of some 55 per cent. The main results of the survey were known in time to be circulated to scholars with the Rhodes House Christmas Letter in 1992.

Respondents were asked which elements were regarded as important or very important in their decision to apply for a Rhodes scholarship. Answers were as follows:

To become a Rhodes scholar (RS) (71 per cent)
To go to Oxford (83 per cent)
To do further study (82 per cent)
To follow a particular course (45 per cent)
To study with a particular don (8 per cent)
To take part in university sport (11 per cent)
To live in the UK or Europe (55 per cent)
To acquire international experience (67 per cent)
To improve job prospects on return (33 per cent)
To improve long-term career (54 per cent)

The survey showed that 12 per cent of all RS had gone to Balliol, and 11 per cent to Magdalen. The next three most frequented colleges were New College (8 per cent), University (6.5 per cent), and St John's (5.5 per cent). During their first year, 23 per cent had changed the course for which they were enrolled. While on stipend 35 per cent of scholars had studied social sciences (including PPE); 23 per cent science or maths; 14 per cent law; 13 per cent language-based humanities; 8 per cent history; and 7 per cent medicine.

Fifty-seven per cent of scholars had read for a BA; of those who took classified examinations, 21 per cent obtained a first, 45 per cent an undivided second, 12 per cent a 2.1, and 2 per cent a 2.2. Of those who worked for a thesis degree, 15 per cent had failed to submit a thesis, 3 per cent had submitted but were failed, 15 per cent had received an M.Litt. or M.St., and 67 per cent had received the D.Phil. Sixty per cent of Rhodes scholars had applied for a third year of tenure, and all but 2 per cent had their application granted. Twenty-two per cent of scholars had stayed on in Oxford after coming off stipend.

Respondents were asked to grade aspects of their Oxford experience on a scale from 1 (very good) to 5 (very bad). Seventy-nine per cent rated their academic study good or very good; only 7 per cent rated it bad or worse. In terms of personal development, 91 per cent rated their experience good and only 2 per cent bad.

Thirty per cent of Rhodes scholars had a full or half-blue, and another 12 per cent had a full or half-blue for a second sport. Thirty-four per cent had played regularly for a college first team in their favourite sport, and 27 per cent had played on a recreational basis. Rowing was the most popular sport (26 per cent took part) with rugby second (17 per cent) and tennis and cricket roughly equal third with 10 per cent.

Eighteen per cent of scholars were elected to JCR/MCR office, and 15 per cent to office in sporting clubs. Political clubs were the most popular among other associations, with 65 per cent of scholars describing themselves as active or occasional participants (by comparison with only 34 per cent in religious groups).[281]

Scholars were asked what problems they had encountered in Oxford. The most serious were with accommodation (32 per cent reported problems here, of whom 5 per cent regarded the problems as serious). Only 68 per cent felt they had had enough money while in Oxford, and 5 per cent reported serious financial problems. Twenty-five per cent had problems with the course they had chosen; in 81 per cent of cases these problems were resolved satisfactorily. Only 1 per cent felt a serious need to change college, and 97 per cent had no problem with their college.[282]

RS were asked to rate the stipend they received on a scale from 1 (very generous) to 5 (inadequate). While 90 per cent rated it adequate or better, 61 per cent reported that it had covered less than 90 per cent of their expenditure in Oxford.

Scholars were asked whether, at the end of their scholarship, they felt they had achieved what they had set out to do. Fifty-nine per cent felt that their academic achievement had been above their expectation, and 72 per cent found their social and cultural experience had surpassed their hopes.

Sixty-five per cent returned to their home countries immediately after their tenure; 20 per cent never returned home to live and work, and the remainder returned home after some years. Forty-two per cent reported that the scholarship had altered their career plans, and 65 per cent claimed that the scholarship had helped them to get the job they really wanted after leaving Oxford.

On taking up a job after the scholarship, a scholar was most likely to have gone into higher education (39 per cent of first employment). The next most likely first employer was national government (18 per cent). When scholars who had reached the twenty-fifth year after their scholarship were asked how far they had progressed up their career ladder, about 13 per cent of respondents claimed to have reached a level equivalent to that of four- or five-star general, and a further 29 per cent to have reached the level of lieutenant or major general.[283]

Respondents were asked whether, with hindsight, they would make again the same choices, to accept a scholarship, to go to a college, and to follow a course. Ninety-eight per cent said they would accept a scholarship, 76 per cent would attend the same college, and 71 per cent would follow the same course.

Finally, respondents were asked how positive or negative they felt the effect of the Rhodes experience had been on their overall career and outlook, on a scale from 1 for

---

[281] 47% sampled the Oxford Union, but only 5% described themselves as active participants and only 1% became officers.

[282] 67% of scholars had found Rhodes House helpful in dealing with their problems, and 15% found it unhelpful.

[283] Such, according to the designers of the survey, was the level of an academic dean.

'very positive' to 5 for 'very negative'. Ninety-four per cent ranked as positive or very positive both having been at Oxford and having been a Rhodes scholar.[284]

A Rhodes Society?

When Rhodes House was built, South Parks Rd on which it stands was the southern boundary of the University Parks. In succeeding years the road became lined with university laboratories. The professors and senior academic staff of these science departments were, like their colleagues in arts, fellows of colleges. Towards the end of the century, however, many of the academics in the laboratories were employed on fixed-term contracts which did not carry entitlement to a fellowship. Though they were no less academically distinguished than their non-scientific colleagues, they had no senior common room membership, and had to depend for social facilities on a small club on South Parks Rd called Halifax House, whose site was now coveted for laboratory expansion.

The lack of collegiate provision for such a large and important section of the academic staff was regarded as a scandal by many in the University,[285] and in particular by Sir Richard Southwood who, having been a Rhodes Trustee since 1986, became Vice-Chancellor in 1989. He brought the University's needs to the attention of the Trust, and the Trustees resolved that they would offer to provide social facilities for non-collegiate members of the academic staff, academic visitors, and postdoctoral students.

The plan was to modify the kitchens and basements of Rhodes House so that university staff from the science area could take their meals in Milner Hall and enjoy common room facilities in the Beit and Jameson rooms. Rhodes House would thus take over, on a much enhanced scale, the functions hitherto performed by Halifax House, whose staff it would absorb. The Trustees were also willing to build a new wing which would provide twenty bedrooms, some equipped for long-stay visitors such as the holders of University visiting lecturerships.[286]

In December 1992 the University set up a working group to discuss with the Trust the details of such a development. The structural boundary between the library and the new facilities needed defining; so too did the legal relationship between the Trust and the University, and in particular, the division of financial responsibility for running costs. The working group, having visited Rhodes House and Halifax House and interviewed the relevant staff members, reported favourably to Council in March 1993 (RTR 551, 16–25).

At their meeting in that March the Trustees asked Lords Ashburton and Sainsbury to commission a number of architects to prepare outline drawings of modifications to Rhodes House and of a possible new building on the Rhodes House site. Wadham was

---

[284] These overall figures, of course, mask some regional and temporal differences.

[285] A report to Hebdomadal Council in 1991 stated: 'There are already some 1,600 research staff on outside grants and contracts and the University cannot continue indefinitely the present low level of provision for the needs of those of its staff and associates who are outside the college system' (RTR 556).

[286] RTM 4 June, 30 Oct. 1992. The Trustees resolved that any development on the Rhodes House site should not involve significant loss of amenity to the Warden and his successors.

to be informed about the plans, in view of its rights under the covenants on Rhodes House.[287]

Over the summer of 1993 several practices presented attractive plans to the Trustees.[288] The preferred design was that of Robert Adam, of Winchester Design. Two small pavilions were to be added to the main building, in place of the garages and caretaker's flat, to provide accommodation for academic guests and returning Rhodes scholars. The scheme, which was estimated to cost £2,672,000, was given a favourable initial reception from the planning officers and from the fire officer and highway department. The Trustees spent some time deliberating on the title of the development. 'University Hospitality Centre' was rejected in favour of 'The Rhodes Society'. A subcommittee was set up to work out the details of the brief. It was hoped that the building could be completed, and Halifax House vacated, in 1995.

The Trustees were willing to take responsibility for the maintenance, heating, and lighting of the new building and of the modified Rhodes House. The responsibility for providing catering would rest with the University, which would also reimburse the Trust for the extra expenses involved in the maintenance of the new structure. The Trust's lawyers drew up a document incorporating these terms in due form (RTM 5 Nov. 1993; RTR 554, 65–86; RTM 4 Mar. 1994).

The agreement, however, was never signed, because of a number of adverse developments on the University side, subsequent to Sir Richard Southwood's retirement as Vice-Chancellor in October 1993. Some on the University side believed that the new Rhodes Society should include not only academic and academic-related staff, but also postgraduate students. They also wished to offer membership to the technical scientific staff currently provided for in a clubhouse with sporting facilities on Mansfield Rd. The Trustees were unwilling to agree to this change, which would have overburdened the projected facilities. Postgraduate students already had membership of colleges, and the whole intention of the project had been to offer a senior common room to those senior members who lacked one (RTM 4 Mar. 1994).

The future of the technicians on the Mansfield Rd site now became tied up with a project of which, for some years to come, neither the Trust nor the University at large was informed. Mr Wafic Saïd, a Syrian-born financier and philanthropist, offered the University a sum of £20 million in support of its new Business School. A 10,000-square-foot building was planned, and the site which Mr Saïd was offered was the Mansfield Rd sportsground. During the negotiations concerning this offer, plans for the Rhodes Society assumed a certain unreality, but discussions about the terms of the legal agreement and the appropriate draft statute continued during summer 1994.

In July Hebdomadal Council decided to amalgamate Halifax House with the Mansfield Rd facilities into a University Club. The Trustees, believing that this was merely

---

[287] RTM 5 Mar. 1993. In response, the bursar maintained that the Trustees' proposals amounted to 'parting with' the land on which Rhodes House was built, and therefore would trigger Wadham's right to repurchase. Clifford Chance assured the Trustees that this claim was without merit (RTR 552, 32–3).

[288] They included Edward Jones and Jeremy Dixon, and Michael Hopkins. The outline plans are in RT.

an interim measure, raised no objection. They went ahead with plans for the Rhodes Society, appointing project managers, and structural, electrical, and mechanical engineers. But in October 1994 Rhodes House was informed by the Registrar that it was intended to keep Halifax House in operation for a long period after the proposed Rhodes Society had opened.

This called in question the assumptions on which the Trustees had made their original offer. It now appeared that the university no longer felt the need to demolish the Victorian buildings in which Halifax House was situated. It was, apparently, no longer thought urgent to provide senior common room facilities for the 1,600 academic and academic-related staff. Moreover it would no longer be possible to operate the Rhodes Society with the staff of Halifax House: an entire new establishment would have to be hired.

The Trustees, at their meeting in November 1994, were disquieted by these developments. They informed the Vice-Chancellor that until the University committed itself to a date for leaving the Halifax House site, approved a realistic budget for the running costs of the Rhodes Society and the University Club in parallel, and made suitable arrangements to provide staff for the Rhodes Society, they did not feel able to undertake any construction work on the project.[289]

When the Trustees next met, in March 1995, none of this had happened. The chairman wrote to the Vice-Chancellor stressing that no further design expenditure would be incurred, and no building contracts let, until the University had fulfilled the conditions laid down in the previous November. But as a pledge of good faith, the Trustees went ahead and presented the development for local authority approval (RTM 3 Mar. 1995). Planning permission and listed building consent for the proposed alterations and extensions in Rhodes House was received at the end of the year (RTR 560).

In July 1996 the University at last announced Mr Wafic Saïd's benefaction for a school of business studies to be built on Mansfield Rd. Since this would displace the present premises of the University Club, the announcement explained, but did not resolve, the ambiguities of the University's response to the Trustees' offer. Since it now seemed unlikely that the ambiguities would be resolved in time for the Rhodes Society to be set up during the current wardenship, the Trustees felt the time had come to withdraw the offer made to the University four years earlier (RTM 1 Nov. 1996).

Ironically, the project for a business school on Mansfield Rd in the end came to nothing. The scheme needed the approval of Congregation, and opposition to it built up. The University scientific and technical staff did not wish to be deprived of their sportsground. Environmentalists resented the disappearance of a vital green space in central Oxford. Most importantly, many recalled that when the University acquired the sportsground from Merton thirty years earlier, it had pledged that the land would remain green in perpetuity. When the motion to assign the site to the Saïd School came before Congregation it was defeated, after a vigorous debate, by 259 votes to 214. Mr Saïd

---

[289] RTM 4 Nov. 94. At the same meeting the Trustees learnt that Wadham had withdrawn all objection to their plans.

generously kept his offer open while an alternative was sought. After an extensive search during the first part of 1997, a suitable site was identified near the railway station, and in June Congregation voted by 342 to 55 to approve the building of the school on this new site.

While waiting for a decision on the Rhodes Society, the Trustees had built up, to meet its costs, a substantial surplus in the Public Purposes Fund. This fund enabled them, in 1997, to make a gift for a different University purpose, the proposed Institute of American Studies. Fund-raising had been proceeding for this project for some years, and a building in contemporary style, between Rhodes House and Mansfield College, had been designed by the architects Kohn Pederson Fox. The Rhodes Trustees had already made a challenge gift of £1 million for this purpose, to be matched by contributions from the Rhodes scholar community. They now committed themselves to a further benefaction of £4 million, conditional on the University beginning construction within twelve months from the announcement of the gift.

The new building was to contain a substantial library. On its completion it was planned to move the Bodleian's American holdings from the heavily overcrowded Rhodes House Library, which would then become the University's Commonwealth Library. Besides a library, the new Institute was to house undergraduate and postgraduate teaching activities, and to contain seminar and conference rooms as a research base for resident and visiting scholars.

Changes in the Scholarship

During the 1990s the status of married scholars was once again an issue. Early in 1990 it was decided that married scholars whose spouses were accompanying them should receive a marriage allowance of £1,500 (RTM 2 Mar. 1990). This continued until 1992, but there were frequent complaints from scholars that it was an unfair award which discriminated against those cohabiting without being married, whether heterosexual or homosexual. In 1992 the allowance was abolished, and the funds released were distributed among the scholars in general as an enhancement of their stipend (RTM 5 June 1992). The stipend itself continued to be increased each year in line with inflation, but by the end of the decade it was clear that the system of paying an annual award (in six equal instalments) was unfair to certain classes of scholar whose studies required them to reside in Oxford for longer periods than their colleagues. The University now offered a variety of degree courses of different lengths (nine months, twelve months, twenty-one months, twenty-four months, and so on), and those completing a doctorate, unlike those taking courses leading to examinations, had to continue working during the vacation after their last term on stipend. Accordingly, in 1998 stipends began to be paid monthly, for as long as scholars were working for a degree, up to a limit of thirty-six months.[290]

In 1994 the Trustees reviewed once again the rule prohibiting marriage during a scholar's first year. Since the relaxation of the ban on marriage in a second year in 1964,

[290] For 1998–9 the stipend was fixed at £700 per month.

many changes had taken place. In 1964, all Rhodes scholars were male; in 1994 many were female, and scholars' potential spouses, of both sexes, might have independent careers. Married accommodation for graduates had become much more plentiful, and all colleges now aimed to provide overseas graduates, married or not, with accommodation in college at least for their first year. It was accordingly easier to combine the maintenance of a marital household with participation in college activities.[291] In several of the countries which provided scholars, the average age at marriage had risen in recent years. During the same time, cohabitation outside marriage had become more common.

Having taken all these considerations into account, the Trustees in June decided to abolish all restrictions on marriage for Rhodes scholars and candidates. The news was promulgated sufficiently swiftly for two of the 1995 intake of scholars—one male and one female—to arrive in Oxford accompanied by their newly married spouses. (One of them was the first ever Ugandan Rhodes scholar, John Mary Matovu.)

Washington, London, and Oxford

In 1992 the presidential campaign of Bill Clinton (Arkansas and University 1968) excited Rhodes scholars past and present. The Trust's staff were also involved, because journalists and others unfriendly to the campaign would telephone, and sometimes visit, Rhodes House in pursuit of imaginary material to support various calumnies about Clinton's Oxford days. The Trustees upheld their usual policy of refusing to release material from the dossiers of living scholars without the permission of the scholar in question and of the authors of confidential reports.[292] On the day of the election all US Rhodes scholars were invited to Rhodes House to toast the first Rhodes scholar President. A toast was also drunk to the second Rhodes scholar President who might, for all we knew, be among those present at the party.[293]

In June 1993 the Association of American Rhodes Scholars and its Canadian counterpart held a reunion of North American Rhodes scholars at Georgetown University. Many hundreds of North American scholars and their spouses attended, and seven of the eight Rhodes Trustees flew over for the occasion, met many of those attending, and empanelled themselves to answer questions from the gathering. The British Embassy hosted a reception for the conference at which President Clinton met the Trustees and chatted with the assembled scholars.

In the following year, the President came to Oxford to receive a degree by diploma. At luncheon in Merton the place of honour facing Clinton was given to Sir Edgar

---

[291] According to the 1995–6 Graduate Prospectus the University provided 36 houses and 180 flats for married graduates. In addition twenty colleges advertised the provision of married accommodation, sometimes on a lavish scale.

[292] While Clinton was seeking nomination as the Democrat presidential candidate in the USA Bryan Gould (New Zealand and Balliol 1962) stood for election as leader of the UK Labour Party. For a moment it looked as if the leftward party on each side of the Atlantic might be led by a Rhodes scholar.

[293] A portrait of President Clinton by Mr Michael Noakes now hangs in Milner Hall. It was unveiled by Lord Ashburton at the Trustees' summer dinner in 1996.

Williams. In the afternoon an academic procession led the honorary graduand up the High, past demonstrators on every conceivable issue, into the Sheldonian for the conferment of the degree. Afterwards he was welcomed to Rhodes House to take tea in Milner Hall with the scholars and to mingle in the garden with the other US students in Oxford.[294]

During this period President Clinton was not the only Rhodes scholar to have served as a head of state. During 1993, on the resignation of the President of Pakistan, Wasim Sajjad (Pakistan and Wadham 1964), the Chairman of the Senate, took over the presidential duties during the period leading up to elections. He combined this office with his tenure as secretary of the Rhodes selection committee for Pakistan.

Throughout the 1990s the tradition was continued that the board of the Trust should consist of four Oxford Trustees and four 'London' Trustees. Throughout the decade the Trust was chaired by the senior of the 'London' Trustees, Sir John Baring, who in 1991 succeeded his father as Lord Ashburton. Marmaduke Hussey, the former chairman of the BBC, retired in 1992 and was succeeded by the Rt. Hon. William Waldegrave, a former fellow of All Souls who held a succession of cabinet posts in Conservative governments between 1990 and 1997. In 1995 Dr John Roberts, having retired as Warden of Merton, resigned from the Trust. He was succeeded by Dr Colin Lucas, for many years a history don at Balliol, who had returned to the College in 1994 to become Master, after a period as professor of history and dean of social sciences at the University of Chicago. The Trustees' judgement in asking him to join them was swiftly confirmed when, a few weeks later, the University elected him to be Vice-Chancellor from 1997 to 2001. Professor Robert O'Neill (Victoria and Brasenose 1961), the Chichele Professor of the History of War at All Souls, was appointed to the Trust at the same time, continuing the tradition that at least one of the Trustees should be a former scholar. In that capacity he replaced Duncan Stewart (New Zealand and Queen's 1953), the Principal of Lady Margaret Hall, who resigned shortly before his death in 1996. In that year Mary Moore resigned and was replaced by Ruth Deech, the Principal of St Anne's College.

In 1995 the Trustees were informed that a spectacular television film about Cecil Rhodes was in preparation, narrating the life of 'a man consumed by ambition, blessed with unique charisma, tortured by love and destroyed at the pinnacle of his power by an exotic princess'. They were invited to invest £3 million in the project, or offer it sponsorship (RTR 229). They declined the invitation, and when the film was shown by the BBC in 1998, to very mixed reviews, they were glad to be able to disown it.

They were proud, however, to be among the sponsors of a six-year project to produce an *Oxford History of the British Empire*. In 1994 they made a grant of £150,000 to the editor-in-chief, Professor Roger Louis of the University of Texas at Austin. The five volumes of the *History* had all appeared, and been received with acclaim, by the end of 1999.

---

[294] The President's brief visit put a strain on the Trust's staff for some weeks beforehand. At one time some sixteen members of the White House security and protocol staff had twenty-four-hour passes giving them access to Rhodes House.

The Trust was also concerned with its own history and that of the scholarships. In 1996 it published a *Register of Rhodes Scholars 1903–1995*. This was the eighth in a series which began in 1910; it replaced the seventh edition of 1981. It listed 5,910 scholars, though it contained no more than the names of those scholars already deceased in 1981. It contained comprehensive entries for all scholars still alive, and it was distributed free to them all by Rhodes House.[295]

In December 1978 two experts from the Royal Commission visited Rhodes House by invitation to inspect the archives of the Trust and to advise on their preservation and access. They produced a summary report, briefly detailing the contents of the archives, which was published by the Commission. On their advice, the Trustees appointed a temporary archivist, Caroline Brown, to catalogue the archives and ensure that they were appropriately stored.[296]

In the last years of the decade there was a changing of the guard in many of the Trust's overseas constituencies. John Poynter, Australian Secretary since 1974, retired in 1997, and was replaced by Dr Graham Hutchinson of Melbourne University (Victoria and Magdalen 1971). In India Ranjit Bhatia (India and Jesus 1957) had administered the Indian Rhodes scholarships since 1962, and in recent years had added to his portfolio the administration of a number of other scholarships which bring Indians to the UK. He too resigned in 1997 and was succeeded by Dr Vir Chauhan (India and St Catherine's 1974). In Jamaica, Delroy Chuck stepped down to pursue a political career, and his place was taken by Peter Goldson (Jamaica and St John's 1985).[297]

As the century drew to its close two Trustees, both born in 1927, reached their seventieth birthday and retired, Lord Sainsbury after thirteen years of service and Lord Armstrong of Ilminster after twenty-two. They were replaced, as 'London' Trustees, by Sir John Kerr, recently returned from the British Embassy in Washington to preside over the foreign civil service, and by Rosalind Hedley Miller of Dresdner Kleinwort Benson.

The Return to South Africa

At the beginning of the 1990s the lawsuit between the Trust and the Cape schools was dragging out its dismal length. The unexpectedly rapid decay of apartheid and the progress to democratic rule meant that in the course of the decade the Trust could take on a much more productive involvement in South Africa and resume its tradition of benefaction to the land in which the Founder's wealth originated.

During the last years of apartheid, before the ban on the ANC was lifted, the Trustees took an interest in an imaginative venture, the Southern African Advanced Education

---

[295] The volume was the fruit of several years' labour by its editor, Ralph Evans; it was based on entries submitted by the scholars themselves.

[296] Her guide to the contents of the archives appears as Appendix I below.

[297] In South Africa Charles Carter, who had administered for many years the Trust's educational programme of support at high school level, retired as assistant secretary of the Trust. His work with schools was taken over by Isaac Shongwe (South Africa-at-large and Christ Church 1989).

Project, which was created in 1986 as a result of discussions between Oliver Tambo, Thabo Mbeki, David Astor, and Antony Sampson. Its purpose was to enable members of the ANC, whether in South Africa or in exile, to obtain hands-on experience in the running of businesses and public organizations. In supporting it the Trust joined the Ford Foundation, the Cummins Engine Foundation, and a number of other charitable trusts and foundations. Many of the several hundred fellows who were supported on its tailor-made training and work experience programmes in various countries of the Commonwealth later went on to positions of responsibility in the new South Africa (RTM 3 June 1990).

At the same time the Trust supported a number of health and health-education projects directed by Rhodes scholars: examples were the Alexandra Health Centre in Johannesburg, run by Tim Wilson (Bishop's and Lincoln 1963), the Valley Trust in Natal, run by Christopher Mann (Bishop's and St Edmund Hall, 1971), and the Witwatersrand University Health Unit run by Steven Tollman (RTM 1 Nov. 1991). Some of these causes were supported not only by the Trustees, but by the invididual contribution of current scholars who were members of a group initally called Rhodes Scholars against Apartheid which, after the abolition of apartheid in 1991, became the Rhodes Scholars Southern Africa Forum. At the suggestion of this group the Trustees, every year from 1992 onward, funded the travel and accommodation expenses of half a dozen current scholars to work during vacations as interns for various progressive Southern African associations. This scheme allowed current Rhodes scholars to offer their skills to contribute to the building of a new South Africa (RTM 6 Mar. 1992).

The South African Secretary of the Trust, Laurie Ackermann, had been professor of human rights at Stellenbosch, and a member of the Supreme Court in Lesotho and Namibia after resigning as a judge in South Africa rather than administer apartheid legislation. After the release of Nelson Mandela, he took part in the framing of the new constitution for South Africa and became one of the first members of its Constitutional Court.[298] He continued to act as South African Secretary, assisted, until 1993, by Edwin Cameron, and then by Charles Carter, each of whom administered the scheme of Rhodes bursaries for schoolchildren founded in 1973.[299]

In the course of the decade, in addition to this annual programme of scholarships, the Trustees gave over £4 million to South African causes. A principal beneficiary was the University of Cape Town where the Trustees funded a programme of bursaries for disadvantaged students.[300] Others have been Rhodes University, the University of the Western Cape, the Institute of Natural Resources of the University of Natal, All Saints College in Bisho, and Tiger Kloof Educational Institution (RTM 3 Mar., 3 Nov. 1995). The Trust also funded a research programme devised by the Royal Society in

[298] In 1995 the Trust underwrote the expenses of the secondment of a librarian from the British Library to South Africa to assist in setting up the library of the new Constitutional Court (RTM 3 Mar. 1995).
[299] In 1993–4 122 schoolchildren held bursaries in twelve different schools.
[300] RTM 4 June 1993. In 1995 there were 79 bursars attending UCT. Taking all levels of education together, there were in 1995–6 and subsequent years more blacks being educated in South Africa through the Trust's support than there were Rhodes scholars on stipend in Oxford.

conjunction with the Universities of Zululand, Durban-Westville, and Fort Hare (RTR 563).

In 1996 the archives of the anti-apartheid movement, from its inception in 1959 to 1995, were deposited in Rhodes House Library, which already held the archives of the anti-slavery society, the Africa bureau, and the Fabian colonial bureau. The Rhodes Trustees paid for the support of an archivist to catalogue these collections.

In 1996 the largest of the Trust's South African benefactions was made public at the installation of Dr Mamphela Ramphele as Vice-Chancellor of the University of Cape Town. In the presence of President Mandela, Dr Ramphele, the first black woman to preside over a South African university, announced that the Rhodes Trust had earmarked 7 million rand for the construction of an All Africa House at UCT.[301] This was to be the focal point of UCT's growing academic contact with faculty members and graduate students from universities throughout Africa. The building was formally opened in 1999 by Lord Ashburton.

The Warden and the Scholars

From the time when the posts of Secretary of the Trust and Warden of Rhodes House were combined in the person of Sir Edgar Williams, the tasks facing him and his successors have remained constant in nature, but have grown steadily in quantity. They fell into four categories.

As Secretary of the Trust, a Warden had to prepare business for the meetings of the Trustees, to give appropriate advice and information on matters affecting the Trust, to ensure that the Trustees' policy and decisions were carried out, and to prepare regular reports on the Trust's activities. As the executive responsible for the Trust's finances, he had, with the assistance of an accountant, to oversee the activities of the Trust's professional agents. In the 1990s the Trust's assets and the volume of transactions grew considerably, and a number of complications were introduced into charity accounting practice. These challenges were met by the automation of bookkeeping procedures.

As international Secretary of the Rhodes scholarship scheme, a Warden had to keep in regular contact with national secretaries in other countries, and monitor the activities of selection committees throughout the world.[302] In the 1990s the number of countries grew from eighteen to twenty, and the number of selection committees came to total ninety-two. The Trustees' contemporary interpretation of the characteristics sought in Rhodes scholars by the Founder was communicated from Rhodes House in annual

---

[301] 'We are here this evening', she said in her address, ' to lay to rest the ghosts of the past; the ghosts of Cecil John Rhodes, Jan Smuts, and their peers, whose vision and foresight contributed to the founding of this illustrious institution. It is sad that their vision failed to acknowledge the inhumanity of racism and sexism. They must, however, find peace . . . This installation ceremony presents us with an opportunity for ritual cleansing of the UCT community to enable us to tackle the future with greater confidence.'

[302] Throughout the history of the Trust, this had involved wardens travelling around the world to meet selection committees and sitting, from time to time, as observers during elections of scholars.

memoranda to these committees.[303] For many years it had been customary for the Warden to report annually to selection committees on the performance of each of their candidates.[304]

The Warden's responsibilities to Rhodes scholars fell into three categories: before coming to Oxford, while at Oxford, and after leaving Oxford. Once scholars were chosen by their home committees, it was the Warden's task to find places for them in the colleges and departments and faculties of Oxford. This task became more demanding towards the end of the century as more scholars opted for postgraduate degrees—and therefore needed acceptance by departments as well as colleges—and as the University's admissions procedures became more regimented. Responsibilities to current scholars involved ensuring that those in residence received their stipends and college and University fees were paid on their behalf. A Warden had to monitor the scholars' progress and offer advice, if needed, on how to make the best use of their time in Oxford.[305] Finally, wardens have always kept in contact with Rhodes scholar associations in the larger constituencies, and provided links with individual former scholars through communications such as Christmas letters.

The fourth task of a Warden was the maintenance and management of Rhodes House. Throughout its existence, in addition to providing a residence for the Warden, it contained a portion of the Bodleian Library and monumental rooms which were frequently used for meetings and social purposes by academic and charitable bodies. The Warden had responsibility for the maintenance of the fabric, furnishings, and fittings, the employment of the janitorial staff, liaison with the Rhodes House librarian, and the issue of permission to outside bodies for the use of the building. Successive wardens and their wives, ever since 1928, had their own individual patterns of entertainment of present and past scholars in Rhodes House.

In the 1990s two new activities were added to the tasks of the Warden, one voluntarily and one by compulsion.

The new task forced on the Warden arose from the obligation imposed on the Trust by recent legislation to register as a charity and send annual reports to the Charity Commissioners. This meant that the Trust's benefactions found their way into published registers of grant-making bodies, and this in turn led to a large number of begging letters

---

[303] At the end of the century these were interpreted to mean that a good Rhodes scholar is someone who is able to get at least an upper second in Schools, or a pass in an M.Phil., or to complete a solid dissertation; who competes in at least one sport at least at college level; who takes part in University societies of some social value (e.g. concerned with the welfare of the Third World); and who takes some part in MCR government or the leadership of other Oxford organizations. From time to time complaints were received that selection committees were paying insufficient attention to sporting ability. But—to take one example—the number of those elected to scholarships in the USA who had won athletic letters before being elected rose from an average of 3.8 in the 1950s to an average of 6 by the mid-1990s. In all the Olympic and Commonwealth Games of the 1990s current Rhodes scholars were represented.

[304] Even a brief report on each candidate could amount to over 20,000 words of prose to be composed each summer.

[305] In addition to this traditional role, a Warden in the 1990s had to administer, under the guidance of the Trustees' academic committee, a scheme whereby some £120,000 per annum was allotted to scholars for specific research purposes.

reaching Rhodes House seeking support for worthy causes most of which had very little connection with the historic purposes of the Trust. In a typical year about 140 of these appeals would arrive, about one-half of which would be passed on, with a positive or negative recommendation, to the Trustees, who liked to consider all requests, unless there was some special urgency, in June, at the third of their three annual meetings. Their general policy, to which there were occasional exceptions, was to restrict their benefactions to Oxford University and its colleges and to educational causes in Southern Africa (RTM 3 June 1995).

The other new task was self-imposed. There is a chalet on a spur of Mont Blanc above Saint-Gervais, originally the property of F. F. Urquhart, a well-known Balliol don of the inter-war era, which has for many years been used for long vacation reading parties by three Oxford colleges. In 1992 the Warden, who with his wife had in the past taken many parties of Balliol students to this chalet, persuaded the trustees who now own the chalet to provide an annual slot for reading parties of Rhodes scholars. A reading party is half way between a seminar and a holiday. On a typical day at the chalet the morning is devoted to private study, the afternoon to hiking on the mountainside, and the evening to the reading and discussion of papers prepared by the participants on a chosen topic. Topics were chosen for discussion to which Rhodes scholars from different countries and from different disciplines could be expected to make a characteristic contribution. Thus, in 1993 the topic for discussion was bioethics, including both medical and environmental ethics; in 1995 it was the moral and legal issues of humanitarian intervention in civil wars. These reading parties proved a welcome innovation in the Rhodes curriculum.[306]

One feature has remained constant in the wardenship throughout its history: it is a job which all those who have held it have valued and enjoyed, not least the fifth Warden who with his wife said goodbye to their scholars on 1 July 1999, 100 years to the day after Cecil Rhodes signed his final will.

---

[306] An account of the 1992 party was published in the *AO* by G. Cardinale, one of the scholars present. In some years the reading party was conducted not by the Warden but by Dr Ngaire Woods, a tutor of University College (New Zealand and Balliol 1987).

2

The American Scholarships

DAVID ALEXANDER

The Rhodes Scholarships have achieved a unique place in American life. This purely educational programme not only has exercised transformative power over education in the United States, but also has influenced the political and social life of the nation. The American public has conferred iconic significance upon the Rhodes scholarship and its holders, ranging from the respect paid the scholars, admittedly sometimes grudgingly, to the ubiquitous use of the jocular homophone 'Road scholar'. In this chapter we shall consider reasons why the Rhodes scholarship has been invested with the high regard with which many persons in the United States view it.

The first reason is Cecil Rhodes himself. Unusual among the powerful men of the nineteenth century, he was an entrepreneur, a politician of national stature, and a philanthropist. One can recall nineteenth-century titans in the United States who may be placed in two of these three categories, but it is hard to think of another, with the possible exception of Governor Leland Stanford, who falls with such distinction within all three. Rhodes's imaginative exercise of his benevolence incorporated all three: 'the best men for the world's fight'.

The second reason is the luck of timing. Rhodes's benefaction came to the United States at the time when the modernization of American higher education was in its early stages. The old denominational colleges were giving way to the idea of the modern liberal arts college, with its broadened curriculum and its more ecumenical, even rationalist, outlook. Similarly the universities, both public and private, were beginning their transformation into research universities, with increased emphasis on graduate education and advanced research. Oxford University was itself a factor in the reach and success of the Rhodes scholarships. Oxford's international reputation had entered American consciousness long before; villages of learning, for example, in Ohio and Mississippi, called themselves 'Oxford' to invite comparison with the ancient university; no fewer than twenty states have their 'Oxford', while half as many have their 'Cambridge'—one of which is a paramount seat of learning.

The third reason is the national dispersion of the scholarships. Rhodes gave each state a scholarship, thus assuring a national distribution from the beginning. The colleges and universities in each state became vectors of information about Rhodes and his scholarships, and by working assiduously to promote their best students for these awards, they enhanced the value and prestige of holding a scholarship. The prestige of the young

Rhodes scholar would then be claimed by home towns in remote places, as well as large cities, in turn spreading knowledge and respect for the scholarships themselves. The Organizing Secretary, Dr George Parkin, shrewdly enlisted the leaders of American higher education, including the presidents of the most prestigious private universities and the presidents of the state universities, as well as high national officials, including the President of the United States. By engaging these men of great distinction in the process, he ensured that soon the colleges and universities themselves would be vying for the honour which their scholars contributed to their institutional renown. To this day, colleges and universities use the numbers of their scholars as an index of their reputation.

The fourth reason is the sense of self-consciousness election conferred upon the Rhodes scholar. Rhodes himself made certain that such self-consciousness would be the outcome of election; his criteria transcended the purely academic, and the winner was expected to be public spirited, eager, compassionate, vigorous, and bright. This self-consciousness promoted strong bonds among the scholars, although it could also lead to rebarbative arrogance and tragic self-destructiveness. The bonds among the scholars were carefully cultivated through the extension of the years in Oxford into a lifelong association with classmates and other Rhodes scholars. This alumni feeling helped consolidate the national reputation of Rhodes scholars. Because the Rhodes scholars were in the main highly talented young men and later young women, their achievements would be noticed by the public and celebrated by their alumni association.

Finally, the manner in which the scholarships were structured and promoted by the American scholars greatly assisted in their public recognition. In these areas one man deserves most of the credit. Frank Aydelotte, the first American Secretary, had a keen understanding of how to achieve public notice. His idea of a national election, simultaneously reported over the wire services and carried in all the home-town newspapers, might not seem such a fresh idea in an age when every campus has its army of professional publicists, but at the time such publicity was unprecedented. Here the name of Cecil Rhodes undoubtedly helped, just as it had opened doors for Dr Parkin earlier. Aydelotte, however, persistently worked to great effect to keep the name and idea of the Rhodes scholarships before the general American public, not content to let the scholarships languish in isolated academic splendour on the campuses.

In short, two men set the stage for the current reputation of the American Rhodes scholarships. Parkin's shrewd assessment of the factors required for establishing the scholarships and his insistence on institutional integrity in electing scholars and Aydelotte's promotion of the scholarships and his administrative skills offered priceless advantages to the introduction and development of Rhodes's scheme. The generally high qualities of the scholars confirmed the reputation for which these two men laid the groundwork.

This chapter will endeavour to explore these reasons in describing the origins and development of the American scholarships.

I. THE EARLY YEARS

Cecil Rhodes and the American Scholarships

Rhodes had the United States on his mind. He deplored the political blunders that led to the War of American Independence, and he longed to find a way for the Empire to regain the American states. In his first will, written in 1874, he left his estate for the establishment of a secret society among the purposes of which was the return of the United States to the Empire. He put these ideas into a 'Confession of Faith', in which he envisioned this recovery as neither a conquest nor a reversal of the outcome of the American Revolution, but rather as the incorporation of the United States in a new kind of international federation based upon the British Empire. Subsequent wills tied to the Confession of Faith were superseded in 1893 by his sixth will, which established the colonial scholarships. These colonial scholarships incorporated the provision that the scholars should not be mere bookworms—that is, not merely scholars in any traditional sense—but bright young men of character and physical stamina. These ideas persisted in the final will which he signed on 1 July 1899. In this will, however, Rhodes surprised Oxford and the world by appropriating one of these new-style scholarships to each of the states and territories of the United States. Rhodes put the matter precisely in clause 16; what better means was available to him to advance his goal of a closer union between Britain and its colonies and the United States than to devise a perpetual scheme for the education in England of young Americans from throughout the United States?

The contemporary surprise at Rhodes's extension of the scholarships beyond the Empire to the United States was compounded by the large numbers of American scholarships he provided. Three clauses in this will establish the 'American Scholarships', as he called them to distinguish them from the 'Colonial Scholarships'. Although he appropriated twenty colonial scholarships annually, he appropriated two American scholarships to each state and territory, one to be elected each year but limiting the number to two at any one time. Because the number of states and territories was understood to be forty-eight when the scheme was settled in 1904, ninety-six American Rhodes scholars were expected to be in residence. Such a generous provision was controversial and difficult to administer from the beginning.

At the time of Rhodes's death in 1902, the states were forty-five in number, and Oklahoma, Arizona, and New Mexico were territories within the contiguous area of the United States. Dr George R. Parkin dealt with the definition of 'states and territories' in his report to the Trustees in May 1903, following his first visit to the United States to organize the administration of the scholarships.[1] Under the heading 'Doubtful Territories', he listed the District of Columbia, 'Indian Territory' (then a separate part of what became the state of Oklahoma), Hawaii, and Alaska. The District of Columbia—neither state nor territory—was a special case, Hawaii was a territory at the time, 'Indian Territory' became part of Oklahoma when it was granted statehood, but Alaska did not achieve territorial status until 1912. Hawaii presented a puzzling case. The Hawaiian Islands, annexed by

---

[1] RTR 1903, 14 f.

the United States on 7 July 1898, were granted territorial status as the Territory of Hawaii in 1900. As early as 1903 Hawaii's territorial status was adduced as grounds for its inclusion, but the Trustees steadfastly declined to incorporate it into the scheme. The Trustees accepted only the territories lying within the traditional boundaries of the United States, while refusing those outside. In any event, Oklahoma became a state in 1907, Arizona and New Mexico in 1912.[2]

The most obvious question is why Rhodes was so generous with the United States and its territories. The colonial scholarships had been appropriated to the specific colonies and provinces of Australia, Tasmania, New Zealand, Canada, Newfoundland, Bermuda, and Jamaica. He could have decided upon a national competition, leaving his Trustees to work out the details.[3] He could have given scholarships to regions. One could imagine a decision to allocate scholarships to a smaller number of states, say three scholarships to New England and three to the middle Atlantic states, where the great universities and colleges were concentrated, or some other allocation to some other combination of states—as, in fact, he strangely did in the case of Canada. Rhodes must have realized that the fundamental political subdivision of the United States is the state or territory, and is thus the analogue to a province or colony. Under such consideration, one can readily see how difficult choosing a limited combination of states or universities would have been, and, trying to see the matter from Rhodes's strategic perspective, one can sense the risk in attempting to guess which parts of the United States might in future be the most vital to the realization of his goals. While a national competition might have been contemplated, the analogy of his specific bequests of scholarships to individual colonies seems to argue that he saw national dispersal by states and territories as a valuable factor.

Rhodes must also have considered that the vast geographical expanse and growing potential of the United States as a major world power would demand a sufficient investment to accomplish his ends. He would have recognized that the sheer size of the United States and its expanding population required a number large enough to ensure the effectiveness of the scholarships as a force in international relations. In creating the German scholarships in his 1901 codicil he alluded to his larger strategy of uniting the Anglo-Saxon and German powers to establish a twentieth-century Pax Britannica. Such a decision having been taken, the practical problem of assuring a sufficient distribution to make the American scholarships work effectively required a national distribution by an allocation of scholarships to the individual states and territories. His evident attachment to the American scholarships suggests that he saw how any limited plan might frustrate his vision; nothing less than spreading the scholarships throughout the states would do.

[2] Beginning in 1906 several unsuccessful efforts to secure Hawaii's inclusion were mounted. In 1930 a formal claim was made by the Governor of Hawaii. Lothian, recognizing the potential for an 'awkward political controversy', asked Aydelotte to handle the matter as well as he could. The enquiry was dropped. Lothian's anxiety was well founded, because the Trustees' position was of doubtful legality. Hawaii's status as a territory was as valid as that of Oklahoma, Arizona, or New Mexico. Residents of Hawaii did not become eligible until 1959, after statehood was granted (RTF 1244).

[3] Parkin commented in his 1903 Report, 'The circumstances that the bequest of Mr. Rhodes was made to each individual state, and not to the states as a whole, was constantly dwelt upon in the discussions,' p. 9.

A beguiling speculation about an additional aspect of Rhodes's vision arises in the close friendship he enjoyed with Rudyard Kipling and his American wife Carrie Balestier Kipling. The Kiplings were in Cape Town from January to April 1898; Carrie wrote in her diary that they had lunch with Rhodes on 26 January, and frequently thereafter. Kipling was well acquainted with the United States, having travelled widely throughout the country, and Carrie Balestier Kipling would have been able to advise Rhodes on the intricacies and value of including American students in his plan. In his regular conversations with the Kiplings, Rhodes might have discussed the place of the United States in his vision of international influence through his scholarships. In fact, Carrie Kipling wrote in her diary for 1 February 1901, 'Lunch with Mr Rhodes to meet the Archbishop. We discuss in conclave the interesting conditions of Mr Rhodes' "Oxford Scholarships." ' Mr and Mrs Kipling had ample opportunities to advise and encourage Rhodes in his idea of widening the influence of his international scholarships by incorporating the burgeoning American nation in a hitherto imperial programme.[4]

The American scholarships were vital to Rhodes's purpose of cementing an Anglo-American relationship through the agency of his scholars. Rhodes fully recognized how large his investment in the United States would have to be, if he were to realize his dream.[5]

Organizing the Competition

The difficulties inherent in setting up these scholarships in the United States were formidable. The Trustees needed to seek advice without losing control of the administration of the scholarships, a need compounded by the sheer complexity of the American system of higher education—public and private, accredited and not, small and large, prestigious and unknown—and its geographical diversity. In order to implement the terms of the will, the Trustees resolved at their first meeting on 5 May 1902 'to communicate with the United States Minister here with reference to the American Scholarships',[6] and prepared a circular letter in 1902, which they sent to the American Ambassador, Joseph Choate. He in turn communicated with the American Secretary of State John Hay to set up appropriate channels for responding to the Trustees' intention to establish the American scholarships. Letters were then sent to 'the chief officials having control of education in the various states and territories of the union', those officials whose positions most nearly matched the October 1901 codicil's assignment of responsibility to 'the Min-

---

[4] Extract from the transcript of Carrie Balestier Kipling's diary in the Kipling Papers at the University of Sussex. I am grateful to Prof. Thomas Pinney for originally suggesting the possibility of the Kiplings' conversations with Rhodes at Groote Schuur on the subject of the American scholarships and for furnishing me with this extract.

[5] Many years later in an article entitled 'Did Rhodes Know How Many "States and Territories" There Were?', Sir Francis Wylie, by using budget figures Rhodes sent in a letter to Earl Grey in Aug. 1901, demonstrated that Rhodes had a clear idea of appropriating forty-eight scholarships annually. Wylie was pleased 'to assist at the funeral' of the misguided story that Rhodes thought there were only thirteen states which succeeded to the original colonies. *AO* 31 (1944), 68–9.

[6] RTM 5 May 1902, § 27.

ister having the control of education'. These letters went to university presidents and other educational officials in the various states, and the aid of the US Bureau of Education was also enlisted.

In late 1902 the Trustees sent Dr Parkin to canvass American opinion, to discuss the requirements for the scholarships, and to lay the basis for the process of selection by setting up committees for that purpose. To describe Parkin as indefatigable is to indulge in bewildering understatement. On his first trip to the United States in early 1903 he held conferences and attended meetings in Cambridge and Boston, New York, Philadelphia, Washington, Atlanta, Kansas City, Chicago, Minneapolis, Spokane, Portland, San Francisco, and Denver, a journey, as he reported in May 1903, of about 17,000 miles of railway travel. His biographer, Sir John Willison, added that Parkin covered 140,000 miles in his first two years of service.[7]

In May 1903 Parkin reported to the Trustees that he had been in contact with nearly all the most prominent educational men in America. He also met with other notables. On 5 January 1903, Parkin held a 'profoundly interesting talk with the President [Theodore Roosevelt] . . . he is a very striking personality and the American people will have plenty to think about while he is in the White House.'[8] In what Parkin called the President's 'emphatic advice', Roosevelt warned him against political interference in the administration of the scholarships. According to Willison, Parkin asked the President about including governors on the state selection committees, and Roosevelt said that he '"wouldn't trust one of them—not one of them"; and then, turning to one who sat near by, "Take my friend . . . here, for instance; if he were on the committee he would be thinking all the time how he could use it for the next election."'[9] Roosevelt's shrewd observation came true all too soon for Parkin's peace of mind. Parkin, in a widely quoted conversation, also heard from Andrew Carnegie that the scholarships would not succeed because the best young American men would not go to Oxford, 'because what Oxford has to give is not what they are after'. Parkin asked what Carnegie meant, and he said, 'Dollars.' In another encounter with American grandees, Parkin had lunch in Philadelphia, and he reported that

a distinguished American thinker and writer, known wherever the English language is spoken, entered a vehement protest against the desecration of Oxford by an irruption of young barbarians from Kalamazoo and Wallamaroo, from Auckland, Arizona, and Africa, not even forgetting the descendants of those Teutonic tribes of whose barbaric virtues Tacitus gives such a glowing account.

Parkin responded with equal fervour, although he did not know at the time who this opinionated gentleman was. Later he learned that his antagonist was Henry James.[10]

The agenda of the conferences included six subjects for discussion: the method of selecting scholars and the body to whom selection should be entrusted; age limits;

---

[7] Report to the Trustees, on Tour through Canada and the United States, May 1903. RTR archives. Sir John Willison, *Sir George Parkin: A Biography* (London: Macmillan, 1929), 162.

[8] Parkin to Hawksley, 6 Jan. 1903, RTF.   [9] Willison, *Parkin*, 162.

[10] The incident is described ibid. 164–5 n.

academic standing; domicile for eligibility; the criteria for selection; and the course of study to be recommended.[11] These questions were freely discussed. At its meeting in Washington on 5 January 1903, the National Association of State Universities adopted a set of five resolutions dealing with the issues posed by Parkin's agenda, and these resolutions became the national norm. First, candidates should have at least junior standing and not be more than two years beyond the bachelor's degree; not exceed 24 years in age; be unmarried; and be advised 'as a rule' to read for an undergraduate honours degree rather than undertake research. Second, examinations sent from Oxford should be used to ascertain the fitness of the candidate to enter Oxford. Third, the state committees might decide on other examinations, but always subject to the rules of the Trust's agent. (All states used the same examinations, which were based on Responsions, the qualifying examination for the University.) Fourth, the president of the state university was to establish, in consultation with other authorities in the state, the method of rotation or competition among the institutions in the state. Fifth, all expenses of this selection process 'shall be met without cost to the Trustees of the Rhodes Will', this provision being prompted by the widespread sense of appreciation and obligation among the American educators for Rhodes's generous gift of the scholarships to the United States.[12]

A controverted principle involved residency. Should a candidate apply at home or from college? Rhodes appropriated scholarships to the states, making no definitions of residency. Perhaps Parkin's paramount intervention in the organization of the American scholarships was his successful recommendation to the Trustees that a candidate could apply either as legal resident in a state or as a student in a university or college in the state. Parkin from the beginning noted the mobility of American students across state lines, and he noted that many of America's most distinguished colleges and universities drew their students from both their regions and the nation as a whole. 'In the East,' he wrote in his 1903 Report, 'where groups of universities or colleges lie within a narrow radius—for instance, Yale, Harvard, and Columbia, or Princeton, Pennsylvania, and Johns Hopkins—State boundaries or State considerations have little influence in deciding the choice of the place of education.' He went on to point out that the same practices could be found throughout the United States, and that students from the east go west and vice versa. Under a domiciliary limitation, students going out of state would only be allowed to apply where they lived.

Parkin saw that limiting eligibility to legal residency would weaken the competition, although some educators in the states held firmly to a more chauvinistic view that would have limited applications to students educated within the state. Arguing that 'often it is the most enterprising and energetic students who thus diverge from the ordinary local routine of education', he urged that these students should not be penalized. While

---

[11] RTR 1903, 2.

[12] Ibid. 44–5. One exception to the first rule was the concession Parkin reluctantly made at the insistence of President Charles William Eliot of Harvard, who had successfully insisted that the 'highly organized' secondary schools in Massachusetts should qualify schoolboys for the scholarship. This provision, unsupported by anyone else, including the Principal of the Boston Latin School, was never availed of and was finally dropped in 1914.

Parkin was firm in his advocacy of the option, he was willing to compromise somewhat. He recommended that the Trustees instruct local selection committees in those states where the educational system was strong enough to prefer, other things being equal, the locally educated candidate. The Trustees finally decided that a student might apply either in the state of collegiate education or in the state of legal residence.

Clause 21 of the will severely complicated the administration of the American scholarships. In this clause, Rhodes directed 'that of the two Scholarships appropriated to a State or Territory not more than one shall be filled up in any year so that at no time shall more than two Scholarships be held for the same State or Territory'. He placed no such limitation on any other constituency, allocating three scholarships with one to be appointed each year, the will precisely stating that the scholarships 'be tenable at any College in the University of Oxford for three consecutive academical years' (clause 16). Indeed, the German codicil could not be more specific on this point: five yearly scholarships to students of German birth, '[e]ach scholarship to continue for three years so that each year after the first three there will be fifteen scholars' (codicil 1901). Perhaps he felt a need to limit the Americans, because under an annual election in each state the full number of Americans in residence after three years would reach 144. While a concern about such a large number may be a sufficient reason for the limitation, it is nevertheless administratively mischievous.[13] With scholarships tenable for three 'academical years' the two American scholars elected in the same state would therefore overlap with a new election in the third year. Thus, for example, the 1904 scholar from a state and the 1905 scholar from the same state would both be in residence in 1906, so that, under clause 21, no election of a scholar from that state could be held in 1906. Is it possible that this miscalculation was not an oversight and that Rhodes thought the completion of a degree programme would be optional for Americans, or that Americans, unlike his other scholars, would be considered to have fulfilled the terms of the scholarship in only two years, or would be permitted to complete their work on their own?

Whatever prompted Rhodes to stipulate the limitation of two Americans in simultaneous residence in a three-year academic programme, the clause forced an adjustment to the yearly election of one scholar in each state. The Trustees decided to hold elections throughout the United States two years out of three: 1904 and 1905; 1907 and 1908; 1910 and 1911; and so on. This plan proved to be quite unsatisfactory. On the one hand, the Oxford college authorities were confronted by an irruption of possibly forty-eight Americans each year for two years with none in the third. On the other hand, a strong candidate in a state with a fallow year had to wait, and this was thought to make the scholarships less attractive in some cases. Mitigating the effects of the limitation was the principal cause for the realignment of the states in 1914, which will be discussed later. This awkwardness, having plagued the operation of the scholarships from the beginning, provided a powerful argument for the adoption of the District Plan in 1930.

---

[13] The problem was discussed as early as 26 Mar. 1903, at the New York conference. Minutes of the New York Committee of Selection, 9–12. RTA 32.

Clause 24

Rhodes had stipulated in clause 24 of his will that 'No student shall be qualified or disqualified for election to a Scholarship on account of his race or religious opinions.' Very likely, Rhodes used the word 'race' in the sense of 'nationality', as in the English race, the Dutch race, the American race.[14] Parkin took the view, however, that black American candidates were eligible, and he tried to discuss the matter openly on his earliest visit to the United States. As an indication of his conclusion that eligibility of blacks was the most vexing social issue in organizing the scholarships in the United States, he devoted a section of his 1903 Report to the Trustees to the subject. He visited Atlanta University and the Tuskegee Institute in Alabama, both all-black institutions. He met with W. E. B. Du Bois at Atlanta and with Booker T. Washington at Tuskegee, 'where he is carrying on a very remarkable educational work'. Parkin told the Trustees, 'They both recognized the difficulty a Negro applicant would meet with in coming before a Southern Committee.'[15]

The state of Georgia thrust Parkin directly into a controversy. Having decided to hold one of the regional conferences in Atlanta, he had instructed the organizing host, the Chancellor of the University of Georgia, to invite all institutions with a matriculation standard equivalent to the state university and an enrolment of at least 300 students to send representatives. Parkin had already received requests from traditionally black colleges to be represented, but he was surprised to find no representatives from these colleges at the conference. On his own authority the Chancellor had excluded Atlanta University, the leading black institution in the region, on the technical grounds that its requirements in algebra were somewhat lower than the University's. Parkin declared himself 'inclined to think that this exclusion, which at first sight seems opposed to the spirit of Mr Rhodes' bequest, may possibly have been judicious, and at any rate is not a thing with which the Trustees should feel called upon to deal.'[16] Bitter letters in 1903 and 1904 from the Dean of Atlanta University, the Revd M. W. Adams, and Professor Du Bois, protested the decision and the discriminatory manner of administering the scholarships in Georgia.[17]

Going north Parkin encountered more recalcitrance. The North Carolina selection committee took an action to inform the Trustees that they could not function if blacks were admitted to the qualifying examinations. Francis P. Venables, President of the University of North Carolina, in November 1904 wrote to the Trust in his capacity as chair of the North Carolina committee, expressing the members' interpretation of Rhodes's benefaction and their conclusions about its implementation. Venables wrote that, in order to fulfil Rhodes's purpose, which was 'to bind more closely together the English

[14] See Kenny, above p. 7.
[15] RTR 1903. In his 1918 Report (Georgia) Parkin reflected again on this early visit, recalling that at his meeting at Tuskegee, the faculty were anxious for their students to be able to compete for the scholarships, 'but admitted that in the present stage of Southern feeling it would be impossible for a Negro to be appointed in a Southern State. Some bitterness on the point was shown by one member of the staff, but the others took very moderate views.' RTR 1918, (Alabama).
[16] RTR 1903, 19.   [17] Adams to Parkin. Du Bois to Parkin, 7 Apr. 1904; RTF 1122.

speaking peoples', men were carefully chosen to go to England and return as 'leaders of influence and prominence among their own people and serve as powerful cementing links between the peoples of the English speaking race'. He continued, 'We feel that a man of the colored race would be of little or no value for such a purpose and that to appoint such a one to a Rhodes Scholarship would be simply a wasted opportunity and a failure to carry out the original plan of the testator.'[18] While other southerners like Brown Ayres, President of the University of Tennessee, disagreed with this interpretation of Rhodes's 'original plan', one cannot doubt that many Americans shared the North Carolina committee's opinion.[19] In an angry cablegram to the Trustees on 17 November 1904 Parkin accused the committee of violating the Atlanta agreement 'where I was told negroes [*sic*] would have fair play', and he mentioned a letter from a black university 'indicating that both sides are watching the case'. He doubted that any compromise could be reached without a 'consultation on the spot', and he concluded by saying, 'exclusion seems most dangerous both on account of clause 24 & also northern opinion'.[20]

Clearly, if the Trust wished the scholarships to succeed in the South, they would have to accept the committee's ultimatum; the Trustees, obviously unconvinced by Parkin's advice about northern opinion, worried that the American scholarships as a whole might well be at risk. At their meeting of 19 July 1904, the Trustees had adopted what would be their firm policy with respect to black American and coloured scholars: they determined not to interfere with the actions of the local committee of selection. Now in response to Parkin's telegram, the Trustees reiterated this policy 'strongly and unanimously' at their meeting on 17 November.[21]

Parkin's attitude was one of disappointed pragmatism; strong racial biases seem entirely absent from his writings about the American scholarships. Keenly concerned about the success of the new scholarships in the United States, no matter what his own views might have been, Parkin believed that the scholarships stood hostage to pervasive American racial prejudice. As he wrote in 1903,

I pointed out to Mr Booker Washington . . . [and others] that while the Trustees were perfectly ready to receive an American citizen of any class sent to them, it was no part of their business to solve the race problem, or enter into the race conflicts of the south, and that the negro [*sic*] people must rely for justice upon public opinion in their own country. I think the more thoughtful among the negroes whom I met recognised that the Trustees might easily defeat the purpose of the bequest if they tried to run counter to the dominant race feeling in the south.[22]

Another solution to the brutal conundrum of the eligibility of black Americans was proposed. Parkin was asked if the Trustees would consider assigning 'a proportion of the

[18] Venables to Trust, 4 Nov. 1904; RTF 1122.
[19] Ayres wrote to Parkin on 8 Nov. 1904: 'While I do not anticipate there will be applications in the immediate future from young colored men, I think that in all fairness they should be given an equal opportunity to compete if they do apply. To do anything else than this would be to substitute our own desire for that of Mr Rhodes and I do not think we have any right to do that. Whatever may be our own feeling on the color question, that feeling is entirely irrelevant to the matter of the Rhodes Scholarships.' RTF 1122.
[20] Parkin to Trust, 17 Nov. 1904; RTF 1122.
[21] RTM 19 July, 17 Nov. 1904.   [22] RTR 1903, 20.

scholarships' to black American candidates exclusively; that, Parkin asserted, would contravene clause 24. Parkin declared that 'If a preliminary qualifying examination is held,
negro students will be as free as others to present themselves for it. When this examination is successfully passed, any subsequent chance of election will depend upon the impartiality of the selecting committees.' Parkin continued, 'Some negroes expressed their
conviction that the same means would be used to prevent their getting scholarships as
are sometimes used to prevent them from voting.' Yet he optimistically concluded, 'The
constitutions of the committees of selection should be a sufficient guarantee upon this
point.'[23]

The election of Alain Locke (Pennsylvania and Hertford 1907), a black American
graduate of Harvard, precipitated an early and serious crisis for the Trustees. As soon as
word of Locke's election was received in Oxford, the American scholars began their agitation. Wylie wrote to Boyd in London with evident alarm that 'the Americans are all
horrified at the reported Negro Scholar from Pennsylvania. They say that the Southerners will tend to boycott the Scholarships.' His report went on, 'The Americans here seem
agreed that that is a most unfortunate election, which will prejudice the interests of the
Rhodes scheme. They might at least have waited until the thing had established itself
firmly in the States.'[24] Parkin had already expressed to the Trustees in his 1903 Report
the concern raised in him by a southern professor who assured him 'that if negro competitors were admitted, the white student would not present himself'. Wylie echoed this
concern in his letter of 20 March to Boyd.[25] In Oxford American scholars protested and
some threatened resignation. The newly elected scholar from Mississippi, Richard C.
Beckett (Mississippi and Pembroke), wrote to Wylie requesting not to be placed in the
same college with Locke. Six days later Wylie reported that another southerner requested
that 'under no circumstances' should he be placed in a college 'to which the Pennsyl-
vanian should be admitted'.[26] Parkin wrote to Michell on 26 April that Wylie had
reported Magdalen's refusal to admit Locke 'on the ground that the South Carolina
Scholar [Eugene Sumter Towles] there was so irate at his election that it is probable that
difficulties might arise if they were members of the same College'. He added, 'I do not
feel that a coloured man from Jamaica would raise quite so much difficulty.'[27]

The protests were not confined to demands by southern Rhodes scholars that Locke
not be admitted to their college. Unwilling to let Locke's election stand without protest,
some of the American Rhodes scholars in residence decided to seek an audience of the
Trustees to express their views; Wylie said that, while they felt strongly about the election, they were 'quite reasonable'. Wylie reported to Boyd on 17 March that the scholars had held a meeting and had selected three delegates, James H. Winston (North
Carolina and Christ Church 1904), C. F. Tucker Brooke (West Virginia and St John's
1904), and Edward McPherson Armstrong (Maryland and Oriel 1905).[28]

---

[23] RTR 1903, 20–1.
[24] Extract from Wylie's letters nos. 3491 and 3492, 14 and 15 Mar. 1907; RTF 1122.
[25] RTR 1903, 21. Wylie to Boyd, 20 Mar. 1907; RTF 1122.
[26] Extract from Wylie's letter of 4 Apr. 190[7]; RTF 1122.
[27] Parkin to Michell; RTF 1122.   [28] Wylie to Boyd, 17 and 20 Mar. 1907; RTF 1122.

The scholars met the Trustees in London on Friday, 22 March 1907, and on 25 March Boyd sent Wylie a report on the meeting. He said that the deputation made an 'excellent appearance', and that Milner and Rosebery were in sympathy with them. While Rosebery and Milner felt 'that that the addition of a solitary native will not hurt the Confraternity', the risk to the scholarships was great: 'If anything occurs to keep away our Southern Scholars, the whole Scholarship system will be a heavy loser.'[29] From Oxford Wylie on 25 March reported to Boyd that Winston had told him about the meeting. Wylie was 'sure that the sympathetic way in which Lord Milner and Mr. Hawksley met the men will do good', and he hoped that threatened resignations might be avoided. 'If they are,' he wrote, 'it will be because the men are anxious not to do anything to prejudice the success of the Scholarship Scheme.'[30]

While the Rhodes Trustees were administratively ill disposed to annulling the Pennsylvania election, they were surely not pleased by it because of their own objections to the election of men of colour.[31] Lord Rosebery wrote a pencilled note outlining his view of Locke's election, revealing an internal tension in the administration: 'I am astonished that Parkin & Wylie should rejoice in his election; especially the former who knows the US. The idea that the loathing of black blood is confined to the Southern states is, I think, entirely fallacious. It is so strong as to be entirely beyond the comprehension of Englishmen. The Rhodes trustees and their agents may rest assured of that.'[32] Parkin had telephoned Wylie to say that 'he is delighted by the choice made in Pennsylvania, but at the same time is greatly in favour of the Scholars being allowed to meet the trustees'. He had drawn sharp criticism from the Trustees for his acceptance of the action by the Pennsylvania committee and for his insistence that Americans were not unanimous in their opinion on this matter. Boyd disagreed with Parkin's assessment of American feeling, and Lord Rosebery's confident assertions of American opinion were at odds with Parkin's goodwill effort to put the question into a national framework. Of course, Parkin may, in fact, have been less correct in his views about American feeling than Boyd and the Trustees. He was not deterred, and he later firmly reminded the Trustees in his Report for 1908 that Locke had been properly deemed a worthy candidate by the Pennsylvania committee.[33] He wrote to Earl Grey, then governor-general of Canada, several months after the shock of Locke's election had struck Oxford: 'It is a curious thing that any boycotting of colour at Oxford should come from the citizens of the great republic.'[34]

From a position of humanitarian enlightenment, we may ask ourselves why the Trustees did not take a firm stand against the palpable racism of some of the American Rhodes scholars, but at the time the matter was not seen as we see it. Moreover, the

---

[29] Boyd to Wylie, 25 Mar. 1907; RTF 1122.
[30] Extract from letter no. 3542; Wylie to Trust, 25 Mar. 1907, RTF 1122.
[31] See Kenny, above, p. 7.   [32] RTF 1122.
[33] '[Locke's] testimonials were so strong that members of the Committee had pretty well made up their minds before seeing the candidates, and did not think it right to reconsider this judgment when it was found that the one to whom their attention was so strongly directed was a negro.' He went on to say, however, that the chairman of the committee 'did not think it likely that the case would occur again'. Report on Qualifying Examinations 1908.
[34] Parkin to Grey, 20 Nov. 1907; RTF 1122.

Trustees felt—wrongly we might say and curiously inconsistently with what soon happened in Bermuda—that they had to consider the attitudes of other constituencies. As Boyd emphasized in a letter to Hawksley on 21 March 1907, 'Americans will readily understand that African feeling must mean something to Mr. Rhodes' Executors.' Moreover, to say that anti-black feelings were a particularly American phenomenon seems specious; behind the hauteur and annoyance of the Trustees and officers their feelings toward persons of colour were at best ambiguous. Whatever else, their greatest fear was damage to the fledgling programme, as Wylie wrote to Boyd: 'I feel strongly that the first consideration for the Trustees is the success of the Scheme, and that they are not concerned to preach any particular doctrine, or press any particular prejudice, but simply to take into account any factor in the situation in the States which may have a bearing on the success or failure of the Scholarships.'[35]

Anxieties about the future of the scholarships were the ineluctable consequences of the action by the Pennsylvania committee. Widespread acceptance of so novel an idea as an international scholarship was not a foregone conclusion in the United States, as we have seen in the efforts to introduce the scholarships and in Wylie's wish that the premature decision 'might at least have waited until the thing had established itself firmly in the states'. Equally relevant to a better understanding of the issue, however, is the effect of Rhodes's allocation of the scholarships to individual states. This allocation had come to be regarded as conferring a testamentary right to each state, and thus, some argued, the laws and practices of a state would be dispositive; we will see later how the testamentary right argument was also used to oppose the District Plan. The southern states had strict rules of segregation which applied to all schools. By analogy, the scholarships as administered by the states with their testamentary right, as they saw it, should be subject to the laws and customs of the states.[36] The Trustees could worry that if several states boycotted the scholarships both public and legal embarrassment might ensue. Several advisers had argued that the threat of boycott had a subtler dimension: would the best men in these states, or in all the states, be disinclined—or under some far-fetched theory be legally impeded from doing so under the segregation statutes—to apply if blacks were eligible? One can be certain that the 'disappointed' Americans would have stressed, if not exaggerated, these questions.[37]

What about the Pennsylvania election himself? Alain Locke must have been miserable at Oxford. The first black Rhodes scholar from any constituency, he was a source of

---

[35] Quoted in a letter from Boyd to Hawksley, 21 Mar. 1907; RTF 1122.

[36] Elmer Ellsworth Brown, in the Bureau of Education in Washington, wrote to Parkin on 4 June 1907, offering an explanation: 'It is not surprising that the white students from states in which the law requires separate schooling for the two races, will find it extremely difficult to adjust themselves to an arrangement which would assign them to the same college to which colored students are assigned, with the close association which such an arrangement would involve at Oxford.' RTF 1122.

[37] In an exchange of correspondence in the spring of 1907 W. T. Harris, the United States Commissioner of Education, supported Parkin's view about national opinion, and he noted that white southerners who were attending northern universities must have experienced at least some form of racial integration. He went on to declare his astonishment at the protest, especially in the light of clause 24: 'Such a delegation and such a protest I should have thought impossible.' Harris to Parkin, 22 May 1907; RTF 1122.

embarrassment to scholarship officials, shunned by his fellow Americans, and the cause of social boycotts. In May 1908 fifteen American scholars from southern states refused to attend the fifth dinner given the scholars by the Trustees. Mrs Mavor in the office in London commented, 'all giving no reason for their refusal. Mr Alain Le Roy Locke has accepted.'[38] When the American Ambassador invited the Rhodes scholars to London, some scholars refused to attend because Locke had accepted the invitation. Parkin reported this incident to the Provost of the University of Pennsylvania: 'A short time ago there was some little anxiety about the attitude that would be taken towards him when he was included in a luncheon given by the American Ambassador, but by a little tactful management the difficulty was got over.'[39] Locke had enjoyed a brilliant career at Harvard, so that this ostracism must have been corrosive and dispiriting. Wylie reported on his career there: 'Not very successful. Had a good deal of intellectual interest and ambition. But superficial and wanting in solid character.'[40] Locke was not an athlete, and Wylie later speculated that participation in sports might have eased his entry to Oxford and improved his lot there. In 1911 Wylie reported to the Trustees that the two coloured Rhodes scholars who had come into residence from Jamaica and Queensland were doing better than Locke had done, because, Wylie believed, they were athletes and because 'they have more balance and more grit'. Perhaps because they were not Americans, they were thought less threatening: 'the Scholars from the Southern American States have shown themselves, this time, less uncompromising than they did when their own country sent a negro.' [41]

No other black American was elected a Rhodes scholar until 1963.[42]

Finding Candidates

If Rhodes's appropriation of a scholarship to each state and territory was controversially generous, it was educationally naive and administratively impractical. States and territories varied widely in population, geographical extent, and educational provision. Each state had its scholarship, but did it have applicants who were qualified for admission to Oxford University? Oklahoma, Arizona, and New Mexico were frontier territories when the scholarships were set up, and the mountain states were vast underpopulated areas. Several of the southern states suffered from neglected school systems and a dearth of strong institutions of higher education, while the more urban eastern states could already boast a number of distinguished universities and adequate public schools. Furthermore, the quality of universities and colleges scattered throughout the Union did not always meet international educational standards. This shortage of potential candidates in many

---

[38] RTF 1384.   [39] Parkin to C. C. Harrison, 19 Apr. 1909; RTF 1365.

[40] RTPF Locke, A. (Pennsylvania and Hertford 1907). The gentleness of Locke's spirit shines through his continuing friendly correspondence with the Wylies after he left Oxford.

[41] RTR Oct. 1910–11; RTF 1122.

[42] 'It is ironic that in the whole history of the Trust there were only two occasions when US Scholars waited on the Trustees in person. The first time, in 1907, was to protest against the election of a Black from Pennsylvania. The second time, in the 1970s, was to protest about the non-election of Blacks from Cape Town.' Kenny to Alexander, 4 Dec. 1998. Personal correspondence.

states and these wide disparities in the numbers of eligible candidates have continued to impose difficulties upon the administration of the scholarships, and virtually all efforts at reforming the system have been directed toward mitigating the effects of the unequal distribution of candidates among the states.

The early conferences had decided that a qualifying examination would be required to ascertain admissibility to Oxford and that passage of this examination must be a prerequisite for application. Discussions centred on the nature of such an examination, which must offer a standard equivalent to Oxford's. The prevailing opinion was that these examinations should be controlled from Oxford and administered in the states with the results certified by the University. The Trustees decided to base the qualifying examination on Responsions, the first of the public examinations required by the University for a degree. Passage of these examinations would therefore exempt American Rhodes scholars from Responsions.

Under the standard of Responsions, a candidate had to be qualified in arithmetic and either algebra or geometry, and he had to be able to read from a specified list of Greek and Latin authors. Results of the first qualifying examination were bleak. Of 236 who took the examination, only 120 passed; in five states no one passed. In 36 states three or fewer candidates qualified to appear before the selection committees. In only twelve states did four or more candidates qualify, thus producing a more convincing level of competition, while in twelve other states only one candidate passed, whom the committees proceeded to elect to a scholarship. Parkin was deeply disturbed by these results. In his circular letter to the chairs of the state selection committees he pointed out that the action of these twelve states in electing the one candidate qualified by the examination effectively meant that 'all comparison of moral and physical qualifications, on which Mr. Rhodes laid such stress, is excluded'. Because Responsions actually represented the lowest level of academic progress at Oxford, 'there is obviously danger lest the aims of the Testator should under these circumstances be defeated'. He urged these committees not to elect unless the qualified candidate reached 'a high, all-round standard of excellence'.[43]

Greek was the highest hurdle. Latin was taught widely enough, and at a standard reasonable enough, to make this part of the requirement passable for most American students. Elementary competence in Greek, however, was for many who considered applying a formidable, if not impossible, qualification. Because so few Americans took Greek, potential candidates had to take crash courses to prepare themselves merely to apply for the scholarships. This powerful hindrance to applications from the beginning of the scholarships did not entirely disappear until the University dropped Greek as a requirement for admission at the time of the First World War. So much chronic trouble was caused by requiring even such an elementary knowledge of Greek in order to apply that as early as 1908 Parkin and Wylie were discussing allowing candidates to apply and

---

[43] Parkin, RTR 1904 16–18. Aydelotte gave figures of the rate of success—or failure, which seems a better term—of candidates from 1904 to 1913: of 1,654 candidates who took the examination, 649 passed in all subjects. Aydelotte, 'The America Scholarships,' in Lord Elton (ed.) *The First Fifty Years of the Rhodes Trust and the Rhodes Scholarships, 1903–1953* (Oxford: Basil Blackwell, 1955), 186–7.

otherwise qualify and then satisfy the condition of Greek after election.[44] In 1909 the Trustees arranged an accommodation to the University's requirement so that henceforward a man who had passed the qualifying examination in Latin and mathematics was eligible to present himself before the selection committees. If elected to a scholarship, he still had to qualify himself in Greek to be admitted to Oxford.

Once the candidate had passed this examination, his papers were submitted to a selection committee. The qualified applicant had to provide a certificate of age and a statement of his academic and athletic record. The candidate had to be between 19 and 25 years old, unmarried, a citizen of the United States, and had to have completed his sophomore year of college. If he was deemed to have met the criteria, the state selection committee would summon him to an interview. These selection committees, so carefully organized by Parkin across the United States, would then have the privilege of electing the young men who best fitted the criteria.

The Selection Committees

To Parkin fell the duty of turning Rhodes's optimistic belief about each state's ability to produce a scholar annually into a practical and successful programme. He had to make recommendations to the Trustees about the composition of selection committees. He stated in May 1903 at the conclusion of his first visit that he had originally favoured the creation of a central committee to serve 'as a superintending body and as a board of reference'. The committee would have to be composed of men of highest prominence and national visibility. Distances were too great for a national committee to function well, and such busy men 'would be compelled to relegate the essential part of their work to a secretary, who would himself be compelled to depend chiefly upon the judgment of the academic authorities in each state'. Nevertheless, the New York conference, under the leadership of Nicholas Murray Butler, President of Columbia University, felt that the country needed a national administrator and recommended the appointment of an 'active and sympathetic agent' to promote the scholarships by visiting universities and colleges from time to time, and to oversee the operations of the committees. The seed for the appointment of an American Secretary was thus planted as early as 1903.[45] On the basis of these conferences and Parkin's recommendations the Trustees decided to appoint state committees, with the power of electing Rhodes scholars from the pool of qualified young men. Parkin's May 1903 report appended lists of chairs and committee members, and the first memorandum, published in June 1903, announced the names of the chairs along with the conditions for application for the first election of scholars in the United States to be held between February and May 1904.

In spite of the self-evident need for fairness, politics, both public and academic, obtruded. The natural pride of states and institutions in the election of Rhodes scholars pushed them at times to excesses that destroyed all impartiality in choosing the best young

[44] Parkin to Aydelotte, 27 Nov. 1908. RTA 3. 'Many a man who would not learn Greek on the chance of getting a Scholarship, might be glad to do so after it is secured.'
[45] Report to the Trustees, May 1903, 7–8. RH.

men. Although Parkin's unwavering object was to minimize political influence in all of the states and among the institutions, his 1917 history of the early elections is replete with accounts of institutional politics and charges of outright mistrust, rivalry, and blatant favouritism. Parkin's history specifically cited political problems in Alabama, Arkansas, Colorado, Delaware, Oklahoma, and Tennessee. He had encountered difficulties of blatant political interference by the Governor of Colorado. Delaware's public politics were thought to be so corrupt that Parkin was advised by the educators at the New York conference to create a selection committee of three outsiders, the presidents of Princeton, Johns Hopkins, and the University of Pennsylvania. This committee served for four years before an indigenous committee could be appointed. In varying degrees in other states, political interests influenced educational matters with the consequent threat to the fairness and soundness of the selection process. A Tennessee Rhodes scholar responding to Parkin's request for advice declared that it was 'utterly impossible to devise any Committee of Selection [in Tennessee] . . . which would not be influenced by either political or denominational feelings in making appointments'. Each year 'denominational feelings' and institutional rivalry plagued Parkin.[46] Oklahoma presented Parkin with the greatest political difficulties in the country. Immediately after Oklahoma became a state in 1907, the 1908 elections swept away 'all the educational authorities who then constituted the Committee of Selection'. Parkin feared that the political situation threatened the fairness of the selection of Rhodes scholars, and he was constrained to place the choice of Oklahoma's scholars in the hands of the Trustees. As late as 1917, Parkin was unsure when 'changes in local conditions [in Oklahoma] would allow a local committee'.

A number of states fell into the improper practice of passing the scholarships around in a case of 'Buggin's turn', to which Parkin unremittingly objected. Although rotation among institutions was formally established in five states according to Parkin's 1903 Report to the Trustees, he felt that merely passing the scholarships around in order would seriously reduce competition. Under no illusions about the power of institutional rivalry, Parkin wrote, 'I once asked a Scholar at Oxford what the feeling of the [Louisiana] State University towards Tulane was and he summed it up in the one word "Hate."' In a number of states taking turns was clearly the preferred solvent of institutional rivalry, but whenever Parkin encountered signs of this practice, he would take steps to acquaint committees with the impropriety of their actions.[47]

The Scheme Does Not Work

From 1904 to 1914 many states frustrated Rhodes's intention of a full national distribution. In none of these years was the full number elected, so that 33 scholarships went begging in this earliest period of the scholarships. Of the 8 scholarships allocated to each state during this period, only 31 states elected their full entitlement. Eight states failed to

---

[46] RTR 1918 Tennessee.   [47] RTR 1918 described these difficulties in detail.

elect one of their allocated scholars. Montana was able to elect only 2, Arizona 5, Wyoming 5, New Mexico 5, Nevada 6, North Dakota 6, South Dakota 6, Utah 6, and, rather surprisingly, Florida 6. Perhaps equally surprisingly Idaho, with its small population, elected its full quota. The possibilities of strengthening the competition through combining states were early considered, but the will stood as an unyielding obstacle. The states had been allocated their scholarships, and legal opinion persisted in holding that the will would not permit any plan that combined states so that one state would have to compete with another state for its scholarship. Parkin had noted from the beginning in his 1903 Report to the Trustees, 'The strength of state feeling was one of the facts brought out most strongly during my conferences throughout the Union.'

Even while these lost opportunities concerned the states and the Rhodes Trust authorities, a major administrative concern within the University demanded immediate attention. Francis Wylie, the Oxford Secretary, was faced with the placement of potentially forty-eight Americans per year—the number he had to contend with actually never exceeded forty-three—but only in two years out of three. Thus, admissions planning under the irregularity of the American election cycle on Oxford colleges asserted itself as a powerful motivation for change. In his memorandum to the Trustees on 28 March 1914, Parkin quoted Wylie's letter in which he expressed the worry that this biennial feast with its third-year famine might one day present him with such obstacles as to cause him to fail to be able to place a scholar in a college. He added, 'already I have had, more than once, to make something like an appeal to Colleges to take more Rhodes Scholars than they were first inclined to'.

Someone must have begun to factor the combinations of the number 48. The elementary observation is that 96, the maximum number of American scholars in residence, divided by 'three academical years', equals 32. Rather than electing all 48 scholars in two years out of three, two groups of 16 states each could elect each year, with a rotation among the three groups in a fixed cycle. This pattern would provide a steady stream of 32 Americans every year, and this manageable number would not contravene Rhodes's limitation of more than two Americans from each state in simultaneous residence for the three years of the scholarship. Parkin's memorandum to the Trustees, in which he recommended the change, pointed out that such a plan would mean that 'thereafter we should always have in residence the nominal maximum of 96 Americans as at present'.[48] In connection with this proposal, Wylie had a presciently brilliant idea. In a letter dated 21 March 1914, he set forth a scheme whereby the Trustees would arrange to elect 32 American scholars every year by giving one scholarship each to 16 states, and one scholarship each to pairings of 16 states.[49]

Although Wylie's imaginative plan was not adopted, his arithmetic was. The American scholarships were factored by 32, by dividing the states into two-thirds of 48 and applying the result to the two years out of three plan to which the United States had

[48] Parkin memorandum, RTR 130, 28 Mar. 1914, 33. RT.
[49] Wylie 21 Mar. 1914 Quoted by Parkin in RTR 130 memorandum. Wylie's plan paired the District of Columbia with Maryland, thus anticipating the later solution to the question of the eligibility of the residents of the District by almost ten years.

become accustomed. Rhodes's 48 scholarships appropriated to the states and territories over two years out of three became 32 scholarships to be divided among the states listed in three groups. Thirty-two states from groups A and B were eligible to elect scholars for 1916, 32 from groups A and C in 1917, and so forth. The 1914 memorandum announced the change. Offering as the reason the 'problem of allocating the Scholars among the various colleges', the states were assigned to these three groups. States in Group C, being postponed by the plan, lost their normal opportunity for the 1916 election. The Trustees anticipated their possible complaints by stating, 'The group C, in which no election will be held for 1916, consists of those States which have furnished the least competition since the organisation of the Scholarship System.' In his memorandum to the Trustees on 26 March 1914 Parkin also recognized the problem facing a candidate whose state was not on the list for a particular year. He further proposed that the qualifying examinations be administered in all forty-eight states every year, 'in order that Scholars should have the opportunity of passing the Qualifying Examination at the time when they are best pre-pared for it'. Thus in a year when a state was not on the list to elect a scholar these annual examinations would generate 'a waiting list of candidates for the year in which its turn comes, while candidates who have failed in the qualifying test will have a second chance to take the examination in the year of selection. My impression', he continued, 'is that in operation this system will tend to increase competition.'[50]

The plan was an immediate success in one sense. In 1914, for the first time in the history of the American scholarships, every eligible state elected a Rhodes scholar. Although the First World War interrupted the regularity of the new scheme when all elections were placed in abeyance, the tripartite list of states became the basis of the elec-tion of American Rhodes scholars until 1929. The allocation of one scholarship to each state remained intact for the present.

Parkin made six trips to the United States between 1902 and 1918, visiting every state in the Union. From having to deal with gross political interference to complaints about a father sitting on a committee before which his son appeared, from concern about suffi-cient numbers of qualified candidates to broken communications with the states as in the case of Montana in 1917, he kept his hands tightly on the process, taking full advan-tage of his prodigious energy and vast knowledge of American education and its edu-cators. He knew better than anyone that a London-based administrator was at a geographical disadvantage. He was an old man, in spite of the vitality which he tirelessly displayed in his management of the scholarships, and he knew that his retirement would bring inevitable changes. In the earliest conferences in the United States, the appoint-ment of a national coordinator for the scholarships was brought up, and the Trustees had again discussed appointing a representative in the United States in April 1910. Sometime around 1916 Parkin decided that the time had come to recommend the appointment of a national coordinator for the American scholarships.

---

[50] Memorandum by Dr Parkin, RTR 130.

2. WAR AND REFORM

Frank Aydelotte (Indiana and Brasenose 1907)

If the Muses to whom Cecil Rhodes listened throughout his life had designed his vicegerent, Frank Aydelotte could have been the result. Superbly able, thorough and industrious, committed to 'esteeming public duties as his highest aim', influential to an extent scarcely credible, well liked and fiercely loyal to his friends, faithful to the causes in which he believed, and tough, this man with famously big ears earned a knighthood and a portrait on the cover of *Time Magazine* (a rare honour for the president of an educational institution, especially of a small college). After graduating from high school in Sullivan, Indiana, in 1896, he went to Indiana University in Bloomington where he played football, being chosen for the All-Indiana team in 1899. Attracted by the allure of an academic life, he became a teacher of English at the Southwestern Normal School at California, Pennsylvania (now California University of Pennsylvania). In 1900 he took a job as a reporter on the newspaper in Vincennes, Indiana, but soon decided he would return to teaching. He went to graduate school at Harvard and received the AM degree in 1903. He then taught high school in Louisville, Kentucky, for two years until his election as a Rhodes scholar. Aydelotte had actually thought about applying for a place in the first class of Rhodes scholars, but he waited until the examination for the class of 1905. Frances Blanshard in her biography captured the agonies of having to pass the qualifying examination for the scholarship, a prospect viewed by all candidates with anxiety, even by so bright, well educated, and mature a man as Aydelotte. Abraham Flexner, then in Louisville and already his friend, offered Aydelotte advice on cramming for the examinations in Greek and Latin. We will hear of Flexner later. Thus, although older than his fellows and with a breadth of experience already behind him, Aydelotte was elected the Rhodes scholar from Indiana in the class of 1905. Born on 16 October 1880, he was the third oldest man in the class of 1907 Rhodes scholars.[51]

Aydelotte was admitted to Brasenose College, and he took an active part in collegiate life. A man from the farmland of Indiana for whom canoes or rowboats were the accustomed river vessels, he took up rowing with his characteristic keenness, and he was photographed with the Brasenose eight in 1907.[52] He ran track, played rugby, and was invited to membership in the Ingoldsby, a literary club in college whose membership was limited to eleven. Having already received a graduate degree in English from Harvard, he decided to read for a second BA in English and simultaneously to work for the University's highest research degree in the humanities then available, the Bachelor of Letters. In March 1907 he decided not to take the examinations for the BA, but rather to submit a thesis in Elizabethan studies for the B.Litt. In the meantime he was clearly seen to be an unusually responsible young man by the Rhodes scholarship authorities, who asked him to accompany the body of Amasa K. Reed (Louisiana and Christ Church 1904) back to Louisiana.

---

[51] Frances Blanshard, *Frank Aydelotte of Swarthmore*, ed. Brand Blanshard (Michigan and Merton 1913) (Middletown, Conn.: Wesleyan University Press, 1970).
[52] Ibid., facing p. 75.

Reed had died of acute meningitis on 21 March 1906, and Aydelotte returned to Oxford a month later. Frances Blanshard reported that Wylie called Aydelotte 'his favourite Rhodes Scholar'.[53]

Aydelotte created many precedents in his life. Although he was not the first American Rhodes scholar to marry while in residence, he was the first to be given a grant to return to Oxford after marriage.[54] After he had completed his second year, he married Marie Osgood in Abingdon on 23 June 1907, and they lived in Oxford until December. Having submitted his thesis on Elizabethan rogues and vagabonds,[55] he was successfully examined in November. The Aydelottes sailed for home in December 1907, and he joined the faculty of Indiana University in January. He was awarded the B.Litt. degree *in absentia* in March 1908. Although he had forfeited his third year by his marriage, he felt his research had not been completed, and before leaving Oxford he raised the question of claiming that year to return to continue his research at some later time. Parkin wrote to Aydelotte on 30 September 1907 that the Trustees had just dealt with his case 'in a way that I hope will meet your wishes', and that the Trustees would consider making a 'special grant' when the time came.[56] Five years later, when Aydelotte was able to obtain leave from Indiana, on 5 February 1912 the Trust voted him a special grant, and the Aydelottes, now including a son and a friend to help Marie, spent the academic year 1912–13 in Oxford.

Aydelotte became active in the affairs of the newly organized Rhodes scholar alumni, becoming founding editor of the *American Oxonian*, the defunct *Alumni Magazine*'s successor, in 1914. He continued teaching at Indiana, but in 1915 he accepted a full professorship at the Massachusetts Institute of Technology. At MIT he was to intensify his quest for the best method of teaching the liberal arts by developing English courses for engineers, a field of pedagogy in which he became nationally recognized; indeed, his interest in the methods of teaching English bore fruit in three books he published between 1913 and 1917. His eye was on a larger goal: how to remake the American college curriculum in order to capture some of the essential features of Oxford's approach to undergraduate education, which he had come to value so highly. He had used his platform as editor of the *American Oxonian* to promote his admiration for Oxford's way, and in 1921 he gained an even more visible platform when he became president of Swarthmore College. His retrospective book, *Breaking the Academic Lockstep*, which he published in 1944, not only described his vision for undergraduate education, but also gave a practical account of the widely admired reform of the curriculum at Swarthmore and the national movement toward honours courses among American liberal arts colleges. In 1939 he became Director of the Institute for Advanced Study in Princeton, a position he held until his retirement in 1947. He was deeply involved in the organization of the John Simon Guggenheim Memorial Foundation from 1925 on, and, as chairman of its

---

[53] Frances Blanshard, 92.

[54] Warren Schutt (New York and Brasenose 1904) was married on 15 Jan. 1907, and he resigned his scholarship, according to the *Register*, in Apr. 1907. Also the *Alumni Magazine*, 1/2 (Apr. 1908), 20.

[55] Published as *Elizabethan Rogues and Vagabonds* (Oxford: Oxford University Press, 1913).

[56] Parkin to Aydelotte at Brasenose College, 30 Sept. 1907; RTA.

Educational Advisory Board, he played a decisive role in the creation of the Guggenheim fellowships. He kept three separate offices, each with its own staff: the office of the President of Swarthmore, the American Secretary's office across the hall, and, in New York, an office at the Guggenheim Foundation. He also served as a trustee of the Carnegie Foundation, and was a director and trustee of many educational boards. In 1937 Oxford University awarded him the honorary degree of Doctor of Civil Law, and he was elected to an honorary fellowship of Brasenose.[57] Aydelotte also took part in government service in both the First and Second World Wars. Perhaps his most significant government assignment was his membership of the Anglo-American Committee of Inquiry on Palestine in 1945 and 1946.[58] In June 1952 Marie Aydelotte, who had accompanied him to the Friends' World Conference held in Oxford, died in her sleep at Rhodes House, virtually their home from home. On 21 October 1953 at Buckingham Palace Queen Elizabeth invested Frank Aydelotte with the insignia of a Knight Commander of the Order of the British Empire. Tragically the joys of this last triumph were denied to his companion who had shared in all the activities which this honour celebrated. He never recovered from Marie's death, and, after a period of failing health and strength, he died on 17 December 1956.

Parkin's close oversight of the selection procedures required him to come to the United States as often as possible. The war forced him to abandon his trip planned for 1915, but he was able to come to Canada and the United States in the spring of 1917. Parkin and Aydelotte had corresponded extensively since 1907, and in this correspondence Parkin demonstrated a warm regard for Aydelotte. On 2 July he wrote to Aydelotte that he 'was full of a new idea this morning'. He needed a secretary to travel with him, and 'the thought of getting you to go with me for a while has suddenly occurred to me. I fear that it will not be possible. But if it could be managed it would be a splendid introduction to the kind of work we are thinking of for the future.'[59] Aydelotte immediately telegraphed his acceptance, and they travelled together in August and September. Evidently satisfied with his close association with Aydelotte, Parkin recommended that he become the American administrator of the scholarships under the title of American Secretary. The Trustees agreed to this recommendation and made the appointment at their meeting on 6 May. In his letter of 15 May confirming the appointment T. L. Gilmour, Secretary to the Rhodes Trust, gave Aydelotte his first assignment, namely to 'take necessary steps' to inform the selection committees that the 1918 elections were to be postponed.[60]

Parkin set out the 'outline for work', in which he listed eight duties, including obvious responsibilities such as publicizing and managing elections, communicating with the

[57] Blanshard, *Aydelotte*, 291.

[58] Ibid. 150. Her account of Aydelotte's activities portrayed what she called 'a man of action', a description no one can gainsay.

[59] Parkin to Aydelotte, 2 July 1917, from Toronto. Parkin wrote to Sir Lewis Michell from Chicago on 6 Sept. 1917, 'I am having Professor Aydelotte, one of the best and most successful of our Rhodes Scholars, along with me. He is the man whom Wylie and I think can be worked in to best advantage as our representative here in the States when any appointment of the kind has to be made.' RTA.

[60] Quin to Parkin, 2 Apr. 1918. Gilmour to Aydelotte, 15 May 1918. RTA. RTM 6 May 1918.

authorities in England, 'arranging Committees of Selection . . . where it is decided to apply the new plans', and 'considering the methods of election, including further examinations outside Responsions'. His other four duties were the 'formation of local organizations of ex-Rhodes Scholars to look after the interests of the scholarships'; keeping 'lists of Canadians in the hope of getting co-operative work'; 'forwarding co-operation between American and British universities in regard to graduate work and degrees'; and 'promoting a determination in the United States that the country shall be well and worthily represented at Oxford'.[61] Parkin recognized the value of the interest of Rhodes scholar alumni in securing the prestige of the American scholarships. By making this a particular duty of the American Secretary, Parkin would also assist the development of the Alumni Association by having a permanent officer paid by the Trust detailed to keep an eye on their affairs. Mandating alumni activities in support of the scholarships by asking the American Secretary to form organizations of ex-Rhodes scholars gave rise to an overlap between the work of the Association and the Trust. As secretary of the Association and editor of the *American Oxonian* Aydelotte had specific responsibilities remarkably similar to those of a university officer of alumni relations. As American Secretary he was placed in charge of the scholarships with a different set of interests and responsibilities. The overlap became even more pronounced when in 1930 he was elected president of the Association of American Rhodes Scholars, a position he kept until his retirement as American Secretary. This aggregation of duties had a highly beneficial effect in that the reins of both organizations were tightly and expertly held by a man of Aydelotte's acumen and energy, and he can surely be given much of the credit for developing a loyal and engaged alumni group similar to those found in every well-established college and university.

From evidence of the behaviour of other groups of alumni winners of fellowships that are unaffiliated with universities, some commentators have expressed wonder at the strength of the alumni feeling of Rhodes scholars. Some critics attribute it to an imagined persistence of Rhodes's abandoned idea of a secret society, but other less fanciful explanations may be adduced. The idea of winning a graduate fellowship like the Rhodes scholarship does not prima facie predict that winners will remain as close as graduates of universities typically do. Other fellowship programmes unaffiliated with universities have not been as successful as the Rhodes scholarships in creating strong bonds among their alumni. Nor does an appeal to the status of being an 'alumnus' or 'alumna' of Oxford University fully explain the solidarity of the Rhodes alumni organization in the United States. The alumni of Oxford who are Rhodes scholars have exhibited an additional dimension to their loyalty, because, from the beginning, a large number of Rhodes scholars have recognized themselves as beneficiaries of the Founder and have found in that relationship a common bond which they wish to preserve. The perpetuation and strengthening of those feelings of friendship and obligation was a consequence of the determination of members of the first class of 1904 who wished to nurture their bonds of experience and friendship even as they scattered. Their successors were also zealous to

---

[61] 'Outline of work for Aydelotte', undated memorandum; RTA.

remain in contact with one another. This alumni feeling has persisted to the present day and is a factor in the public prominence of the Rhodes scholarships. One must also not overlook the tireless efforts of the office of the American Secretary and the Association of American Rhodes Scholars in promoting the scholarships and in turn nurturing the idea of a continuing community of Rhodes scholars, as the salutation of the second class letter in the *Alumni Magazine* foreshadowed, 'The American Colony at Oxford to the Rhodes Scholars of the Dispersion, Greeting.'[62]

War's End, Regularity, and a New Plan

Aydelotte was about to enter on a decade of important and lasting changes, which he himself had to guide and to secure. The early part of the decade began routinely enough, with enough administrative spice to keep him on his toes. The health of the competition and the quality of the candidates were still troubling, however, even after the new system of grouping the states had come into practice. In a long letter to Aydelotte dated 6 November 1916, Parkin reported that the former British Ambassador, Lord Bryce, at lunch two days before had expressed his view that the scholarships were not attracting the 'right men' and he expressed disappointment 'that the Trustees did not ask for fuller powers to modify their distribution and election'. Parkin was deeply troubled by the poor results in the qualifying examination, an examination which he in his frustration noted that his 17-year-old son had passed easily. The greater mischief, though, was the loss of genuine competition: 'State after State will only have a single candidate to choose from if choice that can be called.'[63] Aydelotte immediately replied, arguing that the war had certainly reduced the number of candidates: 'I am only surprised that the number is not less.' He propounded two reasons for the inadequate competition: lack of knowledge about the requirements of the scholarships and the opportunities they offer, and lack of knowledge within the selection committees and their failure to spend 'enough time and trouble and thought in making their choice'. He could have added the perceptible educational handicaps of so many Americans, which thwarted their success in passing Oxford-style examinations for which they had no experience. He offered 'remedies': more publicity through the *American Oxonian*, and more involvement of Rhodes scholars together with some responsibility for the elections. He recommended the appointment of Rhodes scholars to the committees, as Parkin had already mentioned. With great acumen, he recommended holding the elections on the same day throughout the country, and using the elections as an occasion to invite Rhodes scholars and other Oxonians to come as non-voting advisers to an annual dinner and reunion in each state. In a remarkable paragraph, Aydelotte proposed that the results of the national elections be assembled from reports of the states and that a press release be given to the wire services for national distribution. When he became American Secretary sixteen months later he made the proposed procedure standard practice, and it is still followed by the American Secretary.[64] He was right. It can be argued that

---

[62] *Alumni Magazine*, 1/2 (1908), 4. [63] Parkin to Aydelotte, 6 Nov. 1916.
[64] Aydelotte to Parkin, 29 Nov. 1916; RTA.

this simultaneous national election with aggressive publicity, so typical of Aydelotte, has been a primary contributor to the growing prestige of the American scholarships through the century.

The problem of catching up with the classes postponed by the war occupied Parkin and Wylie, and they devised a system for doubling up the classes of 1918, 1919, 1920, and 1921 by having scholars enter in both October and January. The class of 1922 resumed the normal pattern and went into residence in Michaelmas term 1922. Not only were the numbers swollen by the war, but also several of the returning veterans were married. The Trust had not relaxed the basic prohibition against marriage, but they conceded that already married Rhodes scholars could resume or take up their scholarships.[65]

In the summer of 1919 Wylie made a visit to the United States for the purpose of becoming better acquainted with the American scholarships; plans for catching up the suspended scholarships needed to be formulated. Oxford University itself provided welcome changes, including the creation of a new degree, the *philosophiae doctor*, the D.Phil., which was seen as a great new advantage for the scholarships in the United States. Indeed, the impulse for its creation was reported to have been a desire to 'divert the stream' of Americans in pursuit of graduate degrees from Germany.[66] The happiest news, however, was broadcast to a relieved American constituency under the heading 'Qualifying Examination Withdrawn' in the 1919 memorandum.[67] Under the new regulations the credentials of American universities or colleges on the Association of American Universities' list of 'approved' institutions would qualify their graduates for senior standing, thus exempting them from both Responsions and Moderations.

On 9 January 1919 the new American Secretary wrote to Wylie of his great optimism for the scholarships: 'I think conditions are in our favor now: the dropping of the qualifying examination, the new Ph.D., the visit of the [British Universities] Mission, the experience of our men overseas and our close relations with England.'[68] Aydelotte editorialized in the April 1919 issue of the *American Oxonian* that Oxford showed evidence 'of a very decided movement' to remove the requirements which had 'deterred so many candidates from applying', and that further changes would allow an American student to be admitted on his record 'without being forced to "get up" a little Latin and Greek especially for that purpose'.[69] On 2 March 1920 the examination in Greek was dropped as well.

Aydelotte then decided that the new position and the post-war organization of the scholarships required more time than he could give the tasks if he were to continue to teach at the Institute, so that after negotiations between the Trust and MIT he was given

---

[65] See Kenny, above p. 18.

[66] *Oxford Magazine*, quoted by Robert Currie, 'The Arts and Social Studies, 1914–1939', in Brian Harrison (ed.), *History of the University of Oxford*, viii: *The Twentieth Century* (Oxford: Clarendon Press, 1994), 125.

[67] Wylie, in Elton, *The First Fifty Years*, 112. This legislation was a result of the visit in 1918 of the British Universities Mission to American universities. Aydelotte was deeply involved in working with the Mission.

[68] Aydelotte to Wylie, 9 Jan. 1919; RTA.   [69] *AO* 6 (1919), 52.

a leave of absence for the academic year 1919–20. The Trustees on 19 May 1919 voted to confirm this arrangement and to pay him $7,500.[70]

Wylie's conferences with Aydelotte offered an opportunity to make a dramatic change in the system of elections, indeed a change which became a defining characteristic of the election of Rhodes scholars to the present day. Henceforth members of the selection committees would be Rhodes scholars, as far as possible. Several advantages were seen in such a change. Rhodes scholars had direct personal knowledge of Oxford, its programmes, and its ethos. The principle of Rhodes scholars electing Rhodes scholars should ease the problem of potential bias, because *arguendo* they were less likely to be institutionally biased. They would provide a significant source of information about Oxford and the scholarships, and be able to promote the scholarships energetically and responsibly. Because Wylie and Aydelotte felt some worry about the reaction of the current members of the committees, they sought to avoid protests by taking advantage of the war-caused suspension of the elections to start with a virtually clean slate in the membership of the committees. Nevertheless, with committees of Rhodes scholars it would still seem desirable 'to give Committees weight by securing for Chairman in each state some person of more position than can, as yet, be claimed for our Rhodes Scholars'.[71]

Through the summer Wylie and Aydelotte set about organizing these committees and establishing the procedures under which they were to operate. Serious questions remained. What if an insufficient number of Rhodes scholars resided in the state? Would the committees in such cases still have local members, mainly drawn from the university faculty, as before the war? Such a held-over practice would seriously compromise, and possibly defeat, the principle of Rhodes scholars electing Rhodes scholars. As a solution, Wylie's recommendation to the Trustees was to bring in Rhodes scholars from neighbouring states as 'peripatetics', using a classical term that still amuses onlookers. In spite of the difficulties of finding Rhodes scholars for all committees, Wylie wanted as clean a break as possible with past practices, so he and Aydelotte held firmly to the principle that the primary goal was to establish the precedent that committees would be composed principally of Rhodes scholars. He and Aydelotte feared that difficulties would be exacerbated if the new system 'were adopted half-heartedly—that is, if Rhodes Scholars formed the committees in some states, and College Presidents in others'. After the principle had been accepted, exceptions could then be made, and non-Rhodes scholars might be appointed.[72] Simple as the process may seem, Wylie reported difficulties from the beginning, because some states and even certain districts lacked a sufficient number of Rhodes scholars to bring selection committees to full strength. Finding peripatetic

---

[70] RTM 6 Oct. 1919. This was a generous stipend. In fact, throughout his professional life Aydelotte was one of the highest paid academic administrators in the United States. Blanshard wrote in her biography that 'Beginning in 1925 he had three salaries: $6,000 from the Rhodes Trust, $10,000 and sometimes more from Senator Guggenheim, and from Swarthmore a salary which had been $10,000 in 1921, rising in 1935–1936 to $18,000.' For comparison, she noted that the salaries of the presidents of 51 land-grant (state) universities ranged from $7,125 to $10,600. Blanshard, *Aydelotte*, 285.

[71] Wylie, RTR 1919, 2. Also Wylie to Gilmour, 7 June 1919; RTA.

[72] Wylie, RTR 1919, 3–4.

members of committees for a number of states remains an annually daunting task for the American Secretary.

The new policy was announced in a letter from Parkin to college and university presidents dated from London 18 May 1919. He reported that 'we are making the bold experiment' of abandoning the qualifying examination, 'and we are leaving the primary nomination of candidates to the Universities and Colleges of each State. The standard of qualification thus becomes entirely American.' He concluded with an expression of thanks and the comment that 'The sole object in view is to make the American representation at Oxford as strong as possible.'[73] Not every one approved, but protests at the time were muted. Aydelotte wrote to Parkin expressing characteristic confidence that the new plan would be accepted; the approval of Presidents Lowell of Harvard and Hadley of Yale 'will prevent college presidents in backward states from resenting changes which are necessary there'.[74] He also gained the support of the 'overwhelming majority' of presidents attending the meeting of the Association of American Colleges in 1920.[75]

After the postponed elections had been resolved through the accelerated intake of American scholars, the system seemed ready to settle into the normal pre-war pattern of the states electing by groups two years out of three. Aydelotte noted with regret that from 1904 to 1917 thirty-seven American scholarships were not filled, and he revived the old discussions about transferring an unused scholarship to another state. In 1917, because of the war, only twenty-eight scholars were elected. Aydelotte wrote to Parkin on 12 November 1919 a letter adumbrating policies for the administration of these potential scholarships-at-large. After discussion and Aydelotte's persistent urging of the remedy of utilizing vacancies among the thirty-two authorized scholarships by appointing scholars-at-large, the Trustees decided to take the extraordinary step of creating 'Open' or 'Loose' scholarships at their meeting on 1 December 1919. The legal justification was that when a state failed to fill its allocated scholarship the vacated scholarship was available for allocation elsewhere. These scholarships were to be filled by those whom state committees had recommended as strong runners-up from the state competition in a national competition adjudicated by a national committee. At the same time, the age limit for these scholarships was also raised to 27.[76]

Three vacancies were declared open, and the meeting of the first committee of selection of scholars-at-large was held in Washington on 31 January 1920. The committee had sixty-eight nominations to consider, and they selected Paul Coleman-Norton of Princeton University, Robert Hamilton, Jr., of the University of Virginia, and Theodore S. Wilder of Oberlin College.[77] The committee was seriously divided at the end of its

---

[73] Parkin to presidents, 18 May 1919; RTA. In a document attached to this letter described in Parkin's handwriting as 'First draft' the Instructions to Committees of Selection are set forth. A fascinating advisory note told committees: 'It has been found that the specialisation of Athletics in American institutions limits unduly the field from which candidates can be drawn if distinction in Athletics is made an essential qualification. While full value should be given to records of Athletic success or interests allowance should also be made for virile qualities acquired in other ways.'

[74] Aydelotte to Parkin, 28 Feb. 1919; RTA.

[75] Aydelotte to Parkin, 13 Jan. 1920, and Aydelotte to Secretary of the Trust, 20 Jan. 1920; RTA.

[76] Aydelotte to Parkin, 12 Nov. 1919; RTA. RTM 1 Dec. 1919.

[77] Official report of the committee, 4 Feb. 1920; RTA.

deliberations. A fourth candidate, Henry Allen Moe of Hamline University, was eliminated by a vote of two to two with the chair casting the deciding vote. Moe was in naval
hospital at the time having suffered severe injuries in a fall while performing 'a duty so
dangerous [to repair his ship] that he was unwilling to order any of his men undertake
it'. The minority prevailed at least to the extent of allowing Moe's credentials to be sent
to London, 'if under any circumstances another appointment became available, Moe
should have it',[78] and two members of the committee who had not voted for Moe were
moved to write letters in his support. The Trustees agreed to award him an extra
scholarship-at-large at their meeting on 1 March, warning Aydelotte at the same time
that, in Parkin's words, Moe's was 'an exceptional case, not to be considered a precedent,
and in fact not to be repeated'. Thus began the career of one of the most influential
American Rhodes scholars in the history of the scholarships; if any single decision in the
administration of the American scholarships has paid higher dividends, it is hard to find.[79]

Aydelotte wrote to the Secretary of the Trust, T. L. Gilmour, expressing satisfaction
with the results of the first national competition. He believed that the four scholars-at-
large were stronger candidates than 'several men who were elected in the first instance
from our weaker states. The situation brings out very clearly the inherent difficulty which
we face in trying to get as many good Scholars from states with populations running
from one hundred to five hundred thousand as from states with a population of from
five to ten millions.' The essential unfairness of the testamentary allocation of one scholarship to each state was the issue which would occupy Aydelotte and the Trust for the
next decade.[80]

Reorganization

The scholarships in general were now going well. After lengthy negotiations, the District
of Columbia was combined with Maryland in 1922, making its residents eligible to
apply.[81] A major change in the class of 1925 was the admission of cadets from the United
States Military Academy who had not previously been eligible. The service academies
had not been included on the AAU list because of their technical curricula; the Naval
Academy was not admitted to the list until 1930.[82]

Although applications were up on a group-to-group comparison at this time, reaching a peak in 1924 with 507 from the eligible states, the imbalances in applications among

[78] Aydelotte to Parkin, 4 Feb. 1920; RTA.
[79] RTM 1 Mar. 1920. Parkin to Aydelotte, 2 Mar. 1920; RTA.
[80] Aydelotte to Gilmour, 12 Mar. 1920; RTA.
[81] Aydelotte to Dawson, 26 Oct. 1920; Dawson to Aydelotte, 15 Nov. 1920. Also Dawson to Aydelotte,
11 Nov. 1920. Aydelotte to Wylie, 29 Sept. 1922; Wylie to Aydelotte, 9 Jan. 1923. RTA.
[82] As early as 1916 the question of eligibility of West Point cadets had been raised. Henry Bradshaw to
Wylie, 23 Feb. 1916. Extensive correspondence may be found in RTF 1233. Also see Wylie to Aydelotte,
29 Sept. 1925; RTA. Three cadets were elected in the class of 1925. When the Naval Academy was admitted to the list in 1930, phenomenally six Rhodes scholars of the class of 1930 were elected from the Naval
Academy and another in the class of 1932. After these successes the Navy Department shut off applications from candidates from the Academy, and the midshipmen were not allowed to apply again until
1946. RTA.

the states, disparities in academic populations, and underachievement of some American Rhodes scholars at Oxford continued to worry Aydelotte and the scholarship authorities in London and Oxford. In the autumn of 1923 Aydelotte began in earnest his campaign to reform the election system. The idea of an electing committee or committees superior to the state committees had been considered, and the manner of organizing this two-tier election by regions or even nationally was being quietly discussed. Wylie had written to Aydelotte in October 1923 that the Trustees, who had been opposed to any such plan, were now more favourably inclined 'to some kind of pooling'.[83]

The effectiveness of the central committee system, as had been implemented for the election of scholars-at-large in the classes of 1919 and 1921, had convinced Aydelotte that a more centralized selection process was preferable to the will's enforced reliance upon election by each state. These scholars-at-large, nominated as runners-up by the state committees, had been elected by the central committee without interview on the recommendations of the state committees, and they had proved to be exceptional scholars. By the autumn of 1923 the results were already impressive: among the four scholars elected at-large in the class of 1919, two had been awarded first-class honours, one had received the B.Sc., and one had received his D.Phil. Aydelotte was confident that the two 1922 scholars-at-large would do equally well. He referred repeatedly to the success of the scholars-at-large. For example, he wrote to Stanley Hornbeck (Colorado and Christ Church 1904) on 20 February 1924 that, while the current system had brought 'remarkable' improvement, 'on the other hand we have been a hundred per cent successful with Scholars-at-large. . . . If all our Rhodes Scholars were as good as are the Scholars-at-large at present, it would give the Scholarships simply enormous prestige on this side of the ocean and in England.'[84]

Aydelotte decided to propose a national committee of review, to which the state committees would forward their selections. Membership of the committee of review would be drawn from Rhodes scholars who had not served on any state committee, and these men would 'advise the Trustees as to which appointments should be confirmed and which should not'. To approximate the legal requirements of the will, unsatisfactory nominations would be rejected on the authority of the Trustees and the vacancies thus created would be replaced by scholars-at-large, on the basis of the precedent of the action taken in 1919 by the Trustees in their own discretion. Aydelotte wrote, 'By this means it should be possible to give the different States such representation at Oxford as the merits of their

[83] Wylie to Aydelotte, 25 Oct 1923; Aydelotte to Wylie, 3 Nov. 1923; RTA.

[84] Aydelotte to Hornbeck, 20 Feb. 1924; RTA Committee of Review. R. P. Hamilton (at-large and Christ Church 1919) was awarded a Boulter Exhibition at Christ Church; Henry Moe later went on to receive a second in the BCL, was admitted to the English Bar, and was elected to a tutorial fellowship at Brasenose. Of the two scholars-at-large in the class of 1921 one was awarded a second in jurisprudence in 1923, and the other who did not take Schools until 1924 was awarded a second. On the other hand, perhaps for the sake of argument, Aydelotte seems to have ignored the achievement of scholars elected by the states in the class of 1919: of the thirty-two scholars elected by the states one was awarded firsts in both jurisprudence and the BCL, seven were awarded D.Phil. degrees in addition to Coleman-Norton, and five were awarded BCL degrees in addition to Hamilton and Moe. Of the thirty-two scholars elected by the states only one went home without a degree, four took thirds, one a fourth, and two finished the BA degree later 'overstanding for honours'. J. G. Madden (Missouri and Wadham 1919), who took firsts in both jurisprudence and the BCL, was also called to the English Bar, with a first class in the finals.

candidates deserve and at the same time to make sure that the group of Scholars sent from the United States in any one year will be substantially the best thirty-two young men from among all the applicants for that year.' Finally, the current plan of dividing the states into three groups with elections for each group held two years out of three would be replaced by a system that would permit applications to be received in every state every year. Again, the existing loophole of electing candidates-at-large would be used so that states not having a regular election in a given year could send up candidates 'for appointments-at-large in case there are vacancies'. An important provision of Aydelotte's plan was the election of candidates by the central committee without interviews; the states' recommendations would be full enough to obviate the need for further interview, in keeping with the practice followed in the election of scholars-at-large.[85]

Aydelotte sent out a confidential draft of his plan for a national 'Committee of Review' for discussion by approximately fifty Rhodes scholars in the winter of 1923 and 1924. These Rhodes scholars were located throughout the United States, and obviously were not selected for their likely acquiescence to the plan. Aydelotte received thoughtful comments from almost all of those to whom he wrote; forty-six replies have been preserved.[86] Their objections were quite similar. Many doubted that the plan was legal under the will, a doubt which Aydelotte admitted that he shared.[87] The loss of geographical diversity would harm the scholarships; Frank E. Holman (Utah and Exeter 1908) wrote, 'It seems to me that it was by design and not by accident that Rhodes scattered his scholarships territorially.'[88] This recurring point implied that the better men came from more advanced states, so that the weaker states would be chronically deprived of scholars; regional paranoia about the hegemony of the north-east or, to a lesser degree, of both coasts reinforces this political and psychological concern to this day. A national committee of review would not, in fact, be less likely to be prejudiced and it would certainly be less knowledgeable about universities in remoter states. No one put this point more acutely than C. F. Tucker Brooke (West Virginia and St John's 1904). Writing on the letterhead of the *American Oxonian* Tucker Brooke, its editor and professor at Yale, admitted that 'If I were on the central Committee . . . I should be likely to discount pretty heavily testimonials concerning candidates in Arizona and Arkansas, as against candidates in Massachusetts or Pennsylvania. . . . I should be sanguine that your modification would improve the individual Rhodes Scholar average, but perhaps at the expense of the representative character of the scholarships, and with bad political consequences.'[89] A

[85] Undated memorandum 'Strictly Confidential: Committee of Review' sent with cover letters dated 28 Nov. 1923; RTA Committee of Review.

[86] RTA Committee of Review.

[87] Aydelotte to Jacob Van der Zee, 21 Feb. 1923; RTA Committee of Review.

[88] Holman to Aydelotte, 3 Mar. 1924; RTA Committee of Review.

[89] Brooke to Aydelotte, 27 Feb. 1924; RTA Committee of Review. Aydelotte bluntly admitted that the opportunity to improve the competitiveness of the scholarships was more important to him than the loss of representation. Among other concerns, he was certain that the argument about spreading Oxonian and English influence throughout the United States was illusory at best; the scholars did not go home. Nor was he interested in the argument that geographical diversity contributed to Oxford's understanding of the United States. What gain would Oxford realize in getting to know a New Mexican or an Arizonan as against a New Yorker or North Carolinian? RTA Committee of Review.

corollary of the loss of representation was the potential loss of interest on the part of scholars around the country and the likely sense of resentment among state committee members whose careful choices were rejected by the central committee. Under such perceptions, candidates, especially those from the less populated states, would thus be discouraged from applying in a national competition.

The respondents argued that, without interviews, in spite of Aydelotte's confidence in the success of the new scheme of electing scholars-at-large, the central committee of review would tend to rely more on the written record, in which the academic record would preponderate. What was called the 'character' dimension of the criteria would be lost, because academic records are more tangible and measurable; the 'character' of the candidates, so the argument ran, was best drawn out in interview. R. M. Scoon (New York and Merton 1907) wrote from Princeton that the plan placed too much reliance on the scholarly record, perhaps at the expense of the other qualifications. 'The fact that Mr. Wylie was a don, you are a college president, and many of us State secretaries are engaged in education ought not to lead us to overemphasize scholarly attainment in working the Rhodes Scholarship. I sometimes wonder if that has not happened in the appointment of Scholars-at-large.'[90]

In several of his replies, Aydelotte expressed another kind of anxiety about the scholarships. He was afraid that some new scholarship programme, similar to the Rhodes scholarships but based entirely on merit without regard to geographical representation, would supplant the Rhodes scholarships in the hard-won prestige they enjoyed. What this threat was he did not reveal, but he clearly had an inkling that a philanthropist might be moved to create such a scheme. He wrote to E. R. Lloyd (West Virginia and Wadham 1905), 'The Rhodes Scholarships are proving a great success, but a more flexible system of selection would give them a much greater prestige than they have at present. If some philanthropist who was impressed with the difficulty of the Rhodes Scholarships should establish a more flexible system to England, they could without difficulty eclipse the Rhodes Scholarships in public estimation. This contingency is not so remote as one might think.' He also wrote to F. D. Metzger (Washington and Wadham 1908) in the same vein, suggesting that if such a more flexible system were started by another philanthropist 'as might easily happen any day' it would have 'a certain advantage over ours in quality and prestige'.[91]

The threat of a rival scholarship on the scale of the Rhodes scholarships but based entirely on merit never materialized, nor did the central committee. Aydelotte had stated repeatedly that he was not prepared to recommend any change which diminished the support of the Rhodes scholars and others. He asserted that he did not wish to recommend a plan without an overwhelming majority in support, and that he would be fair in presenting the matter to the Trustees: 'I realize there are two sides and I am concerned

[90] Scoon to Aydelotte, 19 Feb. 1924. Scoon further reported that he had discussed the matter with President Hibben of Princeton University, who expressed the same objections. Aydelotte in his reply admitted that one of the at-large scholars had proved to be more academic, referring to Paul Coleman-Norton, who had completed his D.Phil. Aydelotte to Scoon, 20 Feb. 1924; RTA Committee of Review.
[91] Aydelotte to Lloyd, 25 Feb. 1924. Aydelotte to Metzger, 25 Feb. 1924. RTA Committee of Review.

to present them both to the Trustees.'[92] He wrote to Addison White (Alabama and Christ Church 1907): 'I think at present the majority of the men are inclined to take your attitude [of opposition], and it may be that we should sacrifice by the change more than we should gain.'[93]

One can argue that the failure of the proposal for a central committee was not seen by Aydelotte as a defeat. It was the first major skirmish in the long battle to achieve a full district plan. The committee of review, one might cynically conclude, was his stalking horse for the establishment of regional committees which would elect Rhodes scholarships from the states' nominees under a 'pooling' system that had been discussed for many years.[94] In the summer of 1924 Aydelotte wrote to Sir Edward Grigg, Secretary of the Trust, proposing a scheme of eight districts from which a variable number of scholars (based on population) would be chosen. Grigg calculated that over a twelve-year period, the effect on each state would be, 'a very small reduction, hardly more, I should think, than is automatically created by failure to find suitable candidates'. Aydelotte replied that he was delighted with Grigg's views of a centralized electoral procedure, and furthermore, he declared that 'One beauty of the scheme [the central committee] which need not be mentioned now is this: once the principle is accepted, it will be possible to re-district the country at any time with no particular difficulties either with the law in England or public sentiment in the United States.'[95]

Years later Aydelotte, recalling these and other discussions about reorganization, also told of 'many long conversations' with Lord Milner:

In 1924 I told him that I had brought over two plans, one of which I thought was probably legal under the terms of the Will, while the other, I was pretty sure, was not. 'Doubtless,' he replied, 'the illegal plan is the better.' I admitted that it was. 'I think,' he said, 'we must have the illegal one.'[96]

Aydelotte appeared before the Trustees at their meeting in London on 20 July 1925 to present a plan for reorganization. At the meeting Douglas Hogg stated that the plan was not legal under the terms of the will, and that the Trustees must ask the Board of Education to vary the will's terms or secure a private bill in Parliament. Aydelotte was instructed to get further opinions on reorganization from American universities and colleges through their several associations.[97]

[92] Aydelotte to Clason, 20 Nov. 1926; RTA Committee of Review.
[93] Aydelotte to White, 18 Feb. 1924; RTA Committee of Review.
[94] See above p. 117. In the discussions of the committee of review, Carroll Wilson (Massachusetts and Worcester 1908) referred to a district plan which Aydelotte and he had discussed in June 1923; Wilson actually developed a plan with eight 'regions' of six states each, which, except for the details of state alignments in districts, was similar to the plan finally adopted. Wilson to Aydelotte, 8 Dec. 1923. R. P. Brooks (Georgia and Brasenose 1904) also suggested a district plan with sixteen districts of approximately equal population. Brooks to Aydelotte, 16 Feb. 1924; RTA Committee of Review.
[95] Grigg to Aydelotte, 3 July 1924. Aydelotte to Grigg, 14 July 1924. RTA Committee of Review.
[96] F. Aydelotte, *The American Rhodes Scholarships: A Review of the First Forty Years* (Princeton: Princeton University Press, 1946), 30. The plan for a committee of review, i.e. of rejection and replacement, was evidently thought legal on the analogy of the committee to fill up the allotted number of scholarships by scholarships-at-large. See below p. 135.
[97] RTM 20 July 1925. See Kenny, above p. 27.

Emboldened by these instructions and expressions of support from England, Aydelotte now began a more widespread and vigorous campaign first to find alternatives and then to secure the approval of American Rhodes scholars and educators. The national committee of review was dropped, and Aydelotte now concentrated on two district schemes, which were similar in their fundamental division of the United States into eight districts each electing four scholars. One plan was a simple division of the United States into eight districts of six states; the other was based on the assumption that the districts could have differing numbers of states, which were equalized as far as possible on the basis of general population or university enrolments. The former had the potential political advantage of being less disturbing to the right of a state directly to elect a scholar two years out of three; the latter offered more promise of equality of competition throughout the country. Both plans, however, compromised a state's testamentary right to elect its own Rhodes scholar directly. Under the plan which provided for districts with varying numbers of states, the direct testamentary right was virtually abandoned. Under the six-state plan each state would have the right to nominate as many as two candidates every year as against the existing plan which allotted two direct appointments in each three-year period, but the district committee could elect only four scholars. The less populated states were certain that the stronger states in each district would dominate so that their opportunity to nominate a winner would be essentially nil.

Aydelotte's campaign took him across the United States in 1925. Taking maps with him, he held meetings with Rhodes scholars in major cities, at which those present were asked to sign the maps with their votes yea or nay.[98] On 12 January 1926, Aydelotte sent a confidential circular to all Rhodes scholars, enclosing a postcard for their response. He began the letter by noting that appointing Rhodes scholars to selection committees since 1918 has resulted in 'a decided increase of interest in the Scholarships and much keener competition'. Applications were annually averaging 500. While this increased competition had produced some improvement in the quality of the scholars, he claimed that the 'very great inequalities in population and educational facilities' among the states impeded greater improvement. In five years one state produced 157 candidates while another had only 12. Aydelotte's remedy was a plan that incorporated three major features. First, the plan would combine the states into eight regions 'approximately equal as to population and educational advantage', each region selecting four scholars each year; second, it provided that a competition be held every year in each state to select two nominees, or possibly three in some cases; and finally that the states' nominees would be interviewed by the regional committees, with their expenses of appearing before the regional committees reimbursed. These regional committees—later to be called 'district committees'— would be composed of Rhodes scholars with a non-Rhodes scholar in the chair, as in the states, but no man would serve on both state and regional committees. Unlike the plan finally adopted, the 1926 plan created regions which varied in numbers of states in an effort to move toward an equalization of populations. Even so the ratio of the general

[98] In the extensive files formerly kept in the office of the American Secretary, maps abound with different groupings of states.

population of the smallest region to the largest was 1 to 3.2, and the ratio of total university population was 1 to 2.5. The ratio of numbers of students in 'approved' universities was 1 to 6.8.

In supporting this proposal, Aydelotte had to persuade the Rhodes scholars that the present defects were so serious as to imperil the future success of the scholarships and that the best remedy was to abandon direct election by the states. He summarized the justification for the change by saying, 'If the Rhodes Scholarships are to advance in prestige as we should all like to see them, we must devise some means of ensuring that a larger proportion of our Scholars will be up to the level of the best.' It was thus not lost on many scholars that their assent was being sought to a plan that implied that they had not been up to standard. The circular letter concluded with a page of statistics showing general population, university population, and 'resident ex-Rhodes Scholars'. The last page was the map showing the new plan. The proposal with its reply cards was sent out, and responses started pouring in.[99]

Aydelotte also presented the proposal to educators in the meetings of their several associations. He later reported that the plan was endorsed by overwhelming majorities, or by unanimous vote, of the Association of American Universities, the Association of Urban Universities, and the Association of American Colleges. The National Association of State Universities, however, decided not to take a formal vote in 1925, because of opposing arguments that had been advanced at the meeting. In the debate that would erupt in 1930, this negative reaction, and Aydelotte's dismissive interpretation of it, sparked a searing controversy, about which we shall hear later.[100]

Critics were quick to repeat the refrain that such a change violated the terms of the will: Rhodes had allocated the scholarships to the states, without regard to their population or educational strength. The arguments which had been advanced against the 1923–4 committee of review proposal re-emerged. Testamentary rights with consequent geographical spread and diversity of the scholars were the focal points of opposition. Rhodes had intended for the widest possible distribution of the scholarships *throughout* the United States. Diversity of type of scholar was guaranteed by western and eastern, southern and northern states electing. Diversity of institutions, public and private, small and large, college and university, was guaranteed by the allocation of scholarships to the states. The states' power to elect inhibited domination by students from elite eastern institutions.

As might be expected, one proposal begot many. Respondents offered countless suggestions for improvement or change to the plan. Five districts. Seven districts with four scholars elected at-large. Nine districts. Ten districts. Twelve districts with four supercommittees selecting candidates-at-large! Sixteen districts. One district (i.e. a single national competition). One respondent offered an ingenious proposal that would somehow group universities in competition without reference to state lines, not unlike, one assumes, regional athletic conferences. An elaborate scheme would transfer a scholarship

[99] 'Confidential: To the Rhodes Scholars', 12 Jan. 1926, signed by Frank Aydelotte; RTA Reorganization.
[100] Aydelotte, *American Rhodes Scholarships*, 31–2.

from a smaller state every six years; thus, Rhode Island would transfer a scholarship to Massachusetts one year, Vermont to Massachusetts in another year, and Maine to Massachusetts in still another year. One proposal would require, for the sake of fairness, that these new regional committees make certain every state has a scholar at Oxford at all times.

Close friends of Aydelotte were unable to agree with the plan. Emory Niles (New Hampshire and Christ Church 1917), who, although opposed to the idea in principle, had tried to help in considering variations in district lines, wondered why it was necessary 'to divide the country into groups which uniformly have four scholarships'. Charles Clason (Maine and Christ Church 1914) objected to the plan, the possible necessity of which he was willing to concede. He thought greater fairness on the committees' part could be attained merely by prohibiting the appointment of any member who had any connection with an institution from which a candidate had been nominated. Clason somewhat sarcastically suggested that, if the administration of the scholarships is 'too complicated', it would be fairer simply to appoint four scholars from Harvard and four from Yale to save 'the feelings of the smaller colleges'. Gilchrist B. Stockton (Florida and Christ Church 1914) wrote rather painfully that, although the votes favoured the plan, he remained opposed. He urged Aydelotte to go slowly, perhaps putting the plan into effect experimentally in those districts where the majority wished to do so, say in New England, but not in those areas with states like Florida where Stockton lived: a case, one fears, of 'Not in my Backyard'. In a concluding paragraph, which may well have stung Aydelotte, Stockton accused him of presenting the case for reorganization to a large extent *ex parte*: 'Do you think it would do any harm to present the other side of the case?' This accusation was to be repeated.[101]

The real work of opposition was taken in hand by James H. Winston, who had, one recalls, been a member of the delegation protesting the election of Alain Locke in 1907. Winston, with whom Aydelotte evidently had and continued to have cordial relations, was his implacable foe in the matter of reorganization. To Aydelotte he wrote on 16 January 1926,

I vote 'No': reasons are both legal and from policy, i.e. the welfare of the Trust. After all it was *his* [i.e. Rhodes's; emphases Winston's] scheme and *his* money. Maybe there are *many* better plans, but *we* ought not to change *his* plan after he is gone. 2nd the more benighted a state is, the greater need for a Rhodes Scholar.[102]

Winston proceeded then to write a long letter to Wylie, outlining his objections. This was the first salvo in a public campaign conducted by Winston for the next four years. He was unalterably against changing 'a dead man's will' and he argued persistently that the parties in England should not do so absent 'overpowering' necessity. Second, Rhodes must have known what he was doing; he knew of the states, their political significance, their disparities in population, and that he wanted the best man from each state, 'even though a better man could be found in another state'. If Rhodes had wished to settle his

---

[101] Clason to Aydelotte, 24 Feb. 1926, and Aydelotte to Clason, 3 Mar. 1926. Stockton to Aydelotte, 10 Sept. 1926. RTA Reorganization.
[102] RTA Reorganization.

scholarships otherwise, 'I dare say that he knew he could have obtained a better class of men by providing that all of the appointees each year were to be made at large from the entire United States, without regard to residence or place of education.'[103]

For several months Aydelotte gathered the responses and answered many of the objectors, often with lengthy, firm, but patient replies. To Wylie he reported that he was in the midst of 'an immense correspondence', that he was anxious to give objectors 'every opportunity of expressing their opinion', but that, after going into all their arguments with care, he remained convinced of the rightness of the new plan.[104] Aydelotte reconsidered the January proposal in the light of the objections, and in September submitted to the Trustees a revised plan which had eight districts of six states each. He wrote Wylie that 'a good many men' felt that the equal number of states offered 'distinct advantages', adding his hope that 'there will be some of the fifty-eight Rhodes Scholars who were opposed to the plan who will change their vote when they see this arrangement'.[105] The final tally of the votes of the Rhodes scholars in response to the January memorandum was 369 in favour, 58 opposed, 17 doubtful, and 92 not voting.[106]

In order to respond to the legal objections the Americans had made, Henry Moe, who had become the chief administrator of the Guggenheim Foundation, and Carroll A. Wilson, who was general counsel for the investment firm Guggenheim Brothers and other Guggenheim interests, prepared a twelve-page legal brief with another fifty-eight pages of authorities and exhibits, which Moe sent to the Trustees on 28 September 1926. The principal argument was that the Trustees needed only to get approval for 'the practice of refusing to appoint in one State whenever in an adjoining State of the same district better candidates present themselves', which Moe and Aydelotte saw merely as an extension of the Trustees' prior approval of the practice of appointing scholars-at-large. The brief relied upon the doctrine of *cy-pres*, arguing that the failure of one state to produce a satisfactory candidate generated a surplus under the terms of Rhodes's appropriation of a scholarship to each state. The use of that surplus for the appointment of a candidate from another state lay within the existing powers of the Trustees, and the existing authority to elect scholars-at-large could be applied to the District Plan: 'under the plan which has hitherto been followed a vacancy due to non-appointment in Nevada might be filled by a scholar from New York; under this plan [the proposed District Plan] the vacancy from Nevada could only be filled by a Scholar from a state contiguous thereto.'[107]

---

[103] Copy of letter from Winston to Wylie, 6 Mar. 1926; RTA Reorganization. Wylie sent Aydelotte a copy of his reply of 25 Mar. 1926 in which he tried reasonably to deal with Winston's objections, for example, asking if Winston had not made 'an unnecessary assumption' that the 'less progressive states' will no longer elect Rhodes scholars. 'The representation you have in mind would be reduced, not extinguished. We should all regret the extinction of such representation.' In this letter, Wylie quoted Sir Lewis Michell as saying, 'Were I still a Trustee, I should not hesitate to make the change he suggests, unless Counsel pronounces it to be beyond the authority of the Trustees.' RTA Reorganization.

[104] Aydelotte to Wylie, 17 Feb. 1926; RTA.

[105] Aydelotte to Wylie, 9 Sept. 1926; RTA. Wylie's reply revealed that Kerr had been 'very doubtful about it' before he visited the United States in the summer. Wylie to Aydelotte, 15 Sept. 1926.

[106] Memorandum to Rhodes Scholars, 15 Jan. 1930; RTA Reorganization. Aydelotte again quoted these numbers in *American Rhodes Scholarships*, 31.

[107] Aydelotte to Wylie, 29 Sept. 1926. Moe to Kerr, 28 Sept. 1926. RTA Reorganization.

The matter was now in the hands of the Trustees for their action. Philip Kerr sent Aydelotte a discouraging letter stating that the Law Officers' opinion was the Trustees did not have the power to authorize the reorganization plan on their own account, and further that the Minister under the Charitable Purposes Act did not have the power either to 'authorise or instruct' the Trustees to do so. He listed four methods of dealing with the problem, the fourth of which did fall within the existing powers of the Trustees, namely constituting either for the eight districts or for the United States as a whole a committee of review 'with instructions ruthlessly to eliminate any candidate whom it did not consider to be up to Rhodes Scholar standard, the vacancies so created being immediately filled by scholars-at-large chosen by it from the rejected candidates in other States'. Aydelotte immediately replied with a complicated proposal for the consideration of the Trustees, which, simply put, would create district committees of review with the responsibility of confirming the states' nominees and recommending others for scholarships-at-large.[108] Nothing came of this plan, because the Trustees decided to seek parliamentary relief, another of the options described by Kerr in his letter to Aydelotte. During the discussions it was reported that the American Secretary of State, Frank B. Kellogg, had offered no objections to the Trustees' proposal. The Rhodes Trust Act 1929, which received the Royal Assent on 10 May, extended the powers of the Trustees, providing *inter alia* that they may 'make such changes in the number distribution tenure duration and administration of the Scholarships provided for by the Will as will in their judgment best fulfill the purposes and intention of the Testator'.[109]

In March 1929 the Trustees, 'anxious that there should be a thorough stocktaking of the present working of the Rhodes Scholarship System at the old Scholar Reunion at Rhodes House next July', sent a questionnaire asking for opinions around the world. As Aydelotte reported later, the Americans continued the discussions on shipboard going over and at two meetings at the reunion, at which Trustees were present. The Trustees, meeting on 23 July, authorized Aydelotte to proceed to implement the District Plan beginning with the elections in December 1930;[110] the campaign of opposition, however, had only just begun.

After informing the directors of the Association of American Rhodes Scholars on 14 December 1929, Aydelotte sent out a circular letter to all American Rhodes scholars. This circular letter dated 15 January 1930 rehearsed the steps taken, recorded the votes in the referendum of 1926, and reported the actions of the associations of universities and colleges. The letter announced the final plan that established eight districts of six states each. Aydelotte declared that, 'while there was a certain amount of opposition, the weight of opinion in the United States among Rhodes Scholars and in educational circles generally was in favor of the change'. Such a muted statement of triumph was drowned in a deluge of objection and public controversy. Winston, whose opposition had never flagged and who was now confronted by the *fait accompli*, became more strident by going public

---

[108] Kerr to Aydelotte, 15 Feb. 1927. Aydelotte to Kerr 7 March 1927. RTA Reorganization. One is reminded of the aborted proposal of a committee of review of 1923. See above p. 129.

[109] Rhodes Trust Act 1929 (19 & 20 George V, session 1928–9). See Kenny, above pp. 29–30.

[110] RTM 23 July 1929.

with his battle and by personalizing the campaign by alleging Aydelotte to be the scheme's sole originator. Winston early solicited support from the former American Secretary of State Frank B. Kellogg, who had seen no objection when consulted in 1928; he now wrote to Kerr saying, 'I think this is a great mistake.'[111] Others joined Winston. Newspapers were enlisted; Winston wrote a letter to the editor of *The Times* of London, 'knowing as we do from association, the Englishman's love of fair play, we will appreciate your giving the matter an adequate presentation in your great paper'.[112] The *Chicago Tribune*, no friend to the Rhodes scholarships, ran several articles denouncing the plan. The *Christian Science Monitor* published an extensive article 'Rhodes Scholarship Changes: Pro and Con' on 10 April 1930. What had been a debate within higher education and the community of the Rhodes scholars erupted into what Aydelotte mildly called 'a flare-up' in public for all to see.[113]

Winston wrote to governors of the states and to United State Senators, believing that the loss of the testamentary right their states had under the will would galvanize them into effective protest. He was correct in a number of cases. According to the records in the American Secretary's office, governors of twenty states registered their opposition, claiming 'inalienable' rights, and the Governor of Arizona, John C. Phillips, propounded the unfortunate argument that 'since the educational advantages are not equal in all of our forty-eight states it is a great injustice to deprive the weaker states of the privilege of sending their representatives to Oxford'.[114] Franklin D. Roosevelt, Governor of New York, however, wrote to Winston to say that he agreed with the plan. Winston wrote to Roosevelt again, who replied briefly, 'It still seems to me, however, that where a situation has been highly unsatisfactory for a term of years and we have a chance to improve it, it would be better to try out some new plan and not settle the merit of such a proposal upon any *a priori* basis.' This letter generated a strong rejoinder from Winston, who wondered where he got the notion that the existing procedure was unsatisfactory, but Roosevelt shut down the correspondence with a terse reply.[115] Winston mounted his campaign in the Senate in a letter addressed to eleven Senators on 13 February. Winston correctly calculated the political advantage of bringing senatorial opposition to bear, because two Senators are elected from each state, as were Rhodes scholars. His campaign bore fruit when on 20 February 1930 Senator Duncan U. Fletcher of Florida rose in the United States Senate to discuss the scholarships, obtaining unanimous consent to print Winston's letter and attached clippings in the *Congressional Record*. Winston wrote to fifteen Senators on 27 February urging them to pass a resolution against the

---

[111] Kellogg to Kerr, 20 Feb. 1930; RTA Reorganization.

[112] Winston to the Editor, 3 Mar. 1930; RTA Reorganization.

[113] Aydelotte to Kerr, 13 Mar. 1930; RTA Reorganization. Even the Union League Club of Chicago was enlisted to protest the 'perversion of the worthy purposes of Cecil Rhodes' to the Trustees. Public Committee of the Union League Club to the Trustees, 20 Mar. 1930; RTA Reorganization.

[114] John C. Phillips to Kerr, 4 Apr. 1930; RTA Reorganization.

[115] Copies of these letters dated 6 Mar. Roosevelt to Winston, Winston to Roosevelt 13 Mar., Roosevelt to Winston 24 Mar., Winston to Roosevelt 28 Mar., and a draft reply to the third letter; RTA Reorganization. Actually these copies were sent to Aydelotte on a confidential basis by Frank P. Graves, President of the University of the State of New York and Commissioner of Education, who had drafted the replies for Roosevelt's use.

change and offered points to be incorporated in such a resolution. Nothing came of the effort.[116]

Aydelotte also encountered opposition among educators, although his optimistic view of the support of the associations embroiled him in a controversy with one of his close friends, John J. Tigert (Tennessee and Pembroke 1904), President of the University of Florida.[117] Tigert was opposed, and he and Aydelotte publicly disagreed over the position taken by the National Association of State Universities. In spite of the formal letter sent to Aydelotte on 27 November 1928 by the president of the National Association of State Universities informing him of the unanimous vote to communicate the Association's opposition to the administrators of the scholarships and the Trustees, Aydelotte boldly asserted that the vote merely reflected the fact that 'an actual majority of those present passed a resolution opposing the plan'.[118] Tigert sent out a questionnaire to confirm the earlier negative vote and wrote to Wylie that the questionnaire's results were seriously at odds with Aydelotte's claim. Tigert wrote to Wylie that 'The idea of changing the wishes of a man's will after his death is abhorrent to the American people.' Adopting conciliatory language in a letter to Aydelotte, he urged him to delay implementation of the plan, or at least to recommend that the Trustees put the new plan into effect in only half the states, leaving the other half undisturbed.[119]

Aydelotte was not idle. Besides canvassing university and college presidents for their opinions, he wrote to men of distinction in public life and the foundation world. He received favourable replies, or at least abstentions, from them all.[120] Aydelotte went to Chicago on 18 March to attend a meeting set up by Winston. Fourteen Rhodes scholars, including a Canadian Rhodes scholar and Aydelotte, were present. The vote after discussion was seven against and five for. (The Canadian, William H. Irving (New Brunswick and Exeter 1914), was in favour, but his and Aydelotte's votes were not included in the twelve.) Aydelotte wrote to Kerr reporting the outcome of this meeting and providing a précis of the opinions expressed there. Aydelotte, who never whined in his letters, unburdened himself in this letter to a degree rarely seen in what was ordinarily a patient and dispassionate correspondence:

---

[116] Winston to Fletcher; RTF. On 5 Mar. 1930 Fletcher inserted another article against the plan in the *Record*.

[117] Tigert, one of the most distinguished Rhodes scholars, was the first to be appointed to a major position in the US government. He wrote an article for the Apr. 1930 issue of *Banta's Greek Exchange*, a national magazine devoted to the interests of national social fraternities, which, because of their Greek letter names, were known as 'The Greeks'. The article was entitled 'Why Change Rhodes scholar Plan?' and was illustrated with pictures of notable Rhodes scholars who were members of these college fraternities. RTA Reorganization.

[118] A. H. Upham, president of the NASU, to Aydelotte, 27 Nov. 1928. Aydelotte repeated this misleading report verbatim in *American Rhodes Scholarships*, 32. In Aydelotte's defence, however, he could argue that not all these presidents had voted carefully: the President of the University of New Hampshire, for example, confessed that while he may have voted for the old plan, 'I did it without any *real* [his emphasis] conviction and in a "don't care attitude."' Edward Lewis to Aydelotte, 1 Apr. 1930; RTA Reorganization.

[119] Tigert to Wylie, 11 Apr. 1930. Tigert to Aydelotte, 19 Mar. 1930. RTA Reorganization.

[120] Aydelotte listed the names of ten foundation executives who supported the plan in *American Rhodes Scholarships*, 32.

In practically all of his pronouncements on the subject, he [Winston] saddles the whole blame on me, accusing me of having deceived the Rhodes Scholars and educational authorities in this country as to the illegality of the plan, and having deceived the Rhodes Trustees by overemphasizing the sentiment in its favor. Some of the newspaper editorials, written under his inspiration, intimate that if we play fast and loose with Rhodes's Will in this way, rich men will undoubtedly hesitate to leave money to institutions in the future, all of which I think is intended to have its effect on the Swarthmore Endowment campaign.[121]

The *American Oxonian* now became the platform for the debate. The heart of the April 1930 issue[122] was devoted to 'Mr. Winston's Protest', 'Mr. Moe's Rejoinder', and 'A Statement from Lord Lothian'. Winston repeated the arguments he had made earlier. Henry Moe followed with eleven pages of legal argument, using English case-law, exhibits, references to the practice of law in the United States, and comments about Rhodes himself. Moe defended Aydelotte against allegations that he had acted *ex parte*, describing in detail, and as an eyewitness to some of Aydelotte's presentations, how assiduously Aydelotte had sought advice, collected opinions, and then tallied the 'votes', a term to which Winston objected and which Moe explained. Moe quoted Winston's version of Rhodes's intentions to bring representatives of each of the states for association with Englishmen for the purpose of a better understanding; with a deft thrust he quoted Winston's statement that Rhodes 'was looking for representatives—not prodigies'. Moe concluded that after clearing away 'the debris of "changing a dead man's will" and of "legalizing a wrong", and the charges of railroading the reorganization plan through', the issue resolved itself into the following dispute: Winston stressed 'the representation of the States', while Aydelotte stressed 'the quality of the Scholars'. Moe stood with Aydelotte. He ended by offering a practical observation, 'Under the new plan the Scholars will come from eight districts covering all parts of the United States, and does anyone think that there are more than eight kinds of Americans?'[123]

Lord Lothian's statement presented a summary of legal arguments from the charitable exemption from the rule against perpetuity to Mr Rhodes's own repeatedly expressed fear of the 'dead hand'. He referred to the effects of clause 21, which in its mischief had caused the Trustees to compel the election of American scholars 'in only two years out of three'. He asserted that

It is almost certain that the American clauses were drafted in their present form in order to reduce the total number of American Scholarships from 96 to 64 per annum, and that Mr. Rhodes expected in this matter, as in most others, that his Trustees would be free to make such modifications as experience showed them to be necessary in order to realise his major intentions.[124]

---

[121] Aydelotte to Kerr, 25 Mar. 1930; RTA. (Actually Kerr was now the Marquess of Lothian, having succeeded his cousin in the title on 16 Mar.) Aydelotte evidently reconsidered this last point after the letter was typed. In the office copy he has recovered his old spirit enough to have added in his own hand, 'That does not disturb me. I hope to get opinions from Julius Rosenwald, J. D. Rockefeller, Jr., & Ed Harkness in favor of the reorganization.' The Swarthmore endowment campaign had been under way since 1928 and had only recently doubled its goal to $4,000,000, with its deadline set as 30 June 1930. Blanshard, *Aydelotte*, 229–30.

[122] *AO* 17 (1930), Apr. issue.   [123] Ibid. 92.   [124] Ibid. 94.

The novelty of this argument is astonishing. One may readily accept the conclusion that Rhodes expected his Trustees to have general discretion in fulfilling the terms of his will, to alter the structure of the Trust for reasons of taxability, to increase stipends, to meet expenses of administration as circumstances required, and the like, but evidence for this specific assertion that it was Rhodes's intention in the American clauses to limit his bene-faction to sixty-four Americans per annum is at best obscure. Like other claims in this debate, Lothian's argument seems overbroad. Lothian further described the process that had been followed to secure American support for the reorganization, and reported the care taken by the Trustees in deciding to seek a private bill in Parliament. He concluded, 'Thus every precaution is taken to avoid the possibility of Parliament disregarding legal principles and practice or acting unjustly to private rights.'[125]

At their meeting on 8 April 1930 'The Trustees decided that no considerations had been urged in this correspondence which would justify them in departing from the decision to introduce the new system as an experiment as contained in Minute 781.'[126] Here the matter ended, although some controversy lingered. The elections in December were held under the new plan, and the experiment lasted essentially unchanged until 1996.

Thirty-three Rhodes scholars in the class of 1931 were elected on 6 December 1930 from an applicant pool of 529. They were elected from 29 states; under the old plan 32 states would have been eligible to elect scholars. During the years from 1931 to 1939, when the scholarships were suspended because of the war, 25 states elected both of their nom-inees, including the smallest states like Montana and Oklahoma. Every state elected at least one Rhodes scholar during the period, so that national dispersion, though attenu-ated, was maintained. Aydelotte's office monitored the operation of the new plan by the academic results obtained by the scholars elected under the plan. The results showed a marked improvement: 107 Rhodes scholars elected between 1931 and 1934 had taken first-or second-class honours or 78.68 per cent of the total; that percentage compared to 61.97 per cent of the earlier American scholars or to 74.23 per cent of holders of open scholar-ships at Oxford. A more complete comparison can be made by analysing the records of the 1931–8 scholars with those of the preceding eight years (1923–30). Scholars elected from 1923 to 1930 took 27 firsts and 83 seconds in final honour schools, and 7 firsts and 16 seconds in the examinations for the Bachelor of Civil Law degree, representing 51.91 per cent. Scholars elected from 1931 to 1938 took 30 firsts and 102 seconds in final honour schools, and 7 firsts (including three in the class of 1933) and 19 seconds in the BCL, rep-resenting 61.24 per cent. And from the bottom up? From the earlier classes 43, or 16.4 per cent, did not take any degree, and from the 1931–8 group, excluding the class of 1938 whose studies were interrupted by the war, 22 or 9.7 per cent left without degrees. (In the badly affected class of 1938 only 10 completed degrees, 2 of whom went back to finish after the war ended.) On the basis of these academic comparisons Aydelotte could justly claim significant improvement in the Rhodes scholars. Whether he could make the same claim for their personal qualities and ability to become leaders or not was harder to prove.

---

[125] *AO* 17 (1930), 97.   [126] RTM 8 Apr. 1930.

Retirement?

In the early 1930s Aydelotte threw in the spanner of his possible retirement. Evidently he had spoken of retiring from the American secretaryship as long ago as 1926, because Kerr at that time mentioned his need during his visit to the United States to make certain that the scheme of reorganization would survive Aydelotte. Kerr wanted to satisfy himself that the scheme would continue working 'year in and year out when there is a less dynamic figure at the centre than Aydelotte himself'.[127] Aydelotte brought up the matter of retirement in conversations with Lothian in late 1933, and Lothian wrote to Aydelotte that he had reported to the Trustees their conversations about Aydelotte's plan to resign 'in a few years'.[128] After receiving Lothian's letter on 1 February Aydelotte wrote to him regretfully stating that 'the time for decision had arrived and that I should retire as soon as the Trustees find it convenient to name my successor'. Having become American Secretary in 1918, he believed that his length of service made him senior to all the Rhodes Trustees and to all the active officers of the Trust. He concluded the letter with an offer to send a list of possible successors and the hope that he might take his part in the discussion 'of everything relating to the future of the Scholarships . . . even more effectively when I have been relieved of the actual details of administration'.[129] Lothian's reply stated that 'the Trustees were very disturbed to read your letter of resignation at their last meeting and hope it may not be quite so conclusive as you say'.[130] The Warden of New College and Rhodes Trustee H. A. L. Fisher wrote of his gratitude for what Aydelotte and Marie Aydelotte had done together to promote and safeguard 'the interests of the Trust'. Sir Francis and Lady Wylie both wrote warm notes of appreciation for his work. Wylie said, 'It is almost frightening to try to think what might have been the fortunes of the Scholarships if they had not found you to inspire and direct them.' C. K. Allen wrote a cordial letter.[131]

Aydelotte prepared a memorandum for the Trustees, and attended their meeting on 16 July 1934. His memorandum reflected his experiences as American Secretary, on the basis of which he offered observations on the structure of the office and recommendations for its future: the job should be half-time; the Secretary should travel extensively as Aydelotte had done; the half-time job would best be matched by an academic position which would allow the Secretary to maintain academic connections and 'to make himself a figure of importance in the academic world'; he should be a younger man; he should be an academic man. Finally, he gave the names of six Rhodes scholars whom he felt the Trustees should consider, pointing out the significance and prestige of the office

[127] RTF 2567. Lothian asserted that Aydelotte could make the reorganization work, because he was the 'oldest American Rhodes Scholar' and knew everyone. He was not mistaken about Aydelotte's knowledge of American Rhodes scholars, but he was mistaken in saying that at the time Aydelotte was the oldest Rhodes scholar. That honour belonged to William L. Kendall (Oklahoma and Brasenose 1904) who was born in 1879.
[128] Lothian to Aydelotte, 20 Dec. 1933; RTA.
[129] Aydelotte to Lothian, 1 Feb. 1934; RTA. Recorder in RTR 285, 2 Mar. 1934.
[130] Lothian to Aydelotte, 7 Mar. 1934; RTF 1233.
[131] Fisher to Aydelotte, 7 Mar. 1934. Francis Wylie to Aydelotte, 22 Mar. 1934. Lady Wylie to Aydelotte, 22 Mar. 1934. RTA.

of American Secretary. Lothian appended a note recommending that the Trustees authorize Aydelotte to enter into informal discussions with these men, about none of whom either Allen or Lothian had recent knowledge. Someone should go over to see them, but Lothian was not immediately available.[132] Correspondence about succession continued for the next few years.

Aydelotte decided after all not to retire. Perhaps he found that giving the job up would be too much of a wrench and that he had now fulfilled the additional responsibilities Swarthmore's capital campaign and ambitious construction programme had imposed upon him.[133] The agitation over the District Plan had subsided, and, at least according to the analyses the office was continuously making, the elections under the plan were meeting expectations. Furthermore, the creation of the Eastman professorship brought a fascinating new dimension to the work of the American Secretary by giving him the responsibility of working with the Oxford University Board of Electors in nominating the professors. In addition, Oxford awarded him the honorary degree of Doctor of Civil Law in 1937, and he was elected an honorary fellow of Brasenose, the first Rhodes scholar to be so recognized by an Oxford college. Aydelotte remained American Secretary even after his resignation from the presidency of Swarthmore in 1939 when he succeeded his old friend and colleague Abraham Flexner as Director of the Institute of Advanced Study in Princeton, New Jersey. The turmoil of the war, the suspension of the scholarships, and their resumption after the war kept him in office until 1952.

Another War Begins

The class of 1936 was the last class of American Rhodes scholars to enjoy a relatively normal programme at Oxford before the Second World War broke out. The majority of the class completed their work in 1938 and 1939, indeed with three firsts and a first in the BCL; three others completed graduate degrees in 1940. Only four members of this class left without taking degrees. The class of 1937 began to feel the force of the growing international conflict, and seven did not complete their work at Oxford, although two returned after the war to finish. Three members of the class received firsts. The class of 1938 was badly affected. Because of the threat of war they were not permitted to sail from the United States as planned, and they were put up instead at Swarthmore to await a later sailing. Aydelotte wrote to Allen that the group had slept in dormitories, doubling with Swarthmore students, had played games, and had attended lectures, giving the Aydelottes the idea that they might in future arrange for such a weekend for the sailing parties.[134]

On 1 September 1939 Aydelotte wrote to American Rhodes scholars about the strong possibility that the members of the class of 1939, who had not yet sailed for England, would not be permitted to sail and that Rhodes scholars in residence would be required to leave. Urgent cables passed back and forth between Rhodes House and Swarthmore

[132] RTR 288, 13 July 1934.
[133] Frances Blanshard has a chapter devoted to this period of Aydelotte's presidency. The academic reputation of Swarthmore was soaring. Blanshard, *Aydelotte*, 255–94.
[134] Aydelotte to Allen, 1 Oct. 1938; RTF 1233A.

about the safety and whereabouts of scholars. Nason, in an article he published in the *American Oxonian*, reported that thirty-five American Rhodes scholars were in England and fourteen were scattered throughout Europe when war was declared on 3 September 1939.[135] The Warden, he wrote, 'worked night and day' to keep in touch with all the Rhodes scholars and keep their parents informed. Lord Elton, who had succeeded Lothian as Secretary to the Trust, cabled Aydelotte on 3 September not to allow the 1939 class to sail and to cancel the 1940 elections. One member of the class, Charles Colling-wood (Maryland and New College 1939),[136] was already in Europe, and he spent part of the year in residence before becoming a full-time war correspondent, undertaking a career which brought him international fame. Special arrangements had to be made for the neutral Americans to remain in Britain after September 1939. Members of the class of 1938 still in residence, who had been expecting to take examinations that term, were nevertheless forced to leave before taking them. An extraordinary effort by A. D. Lindsay, the Master of Balliol, and Allen persuaded the University, under an obscure provision of the University Statutes, to allow four members of the class to take their examinations at Swarthmore. This they did in subfusc and under strict invigilation in June 1940.[137] The American Rhodes scholarships were suspended until after the war's end, not to resume until the elections on 14 December 1946.[138]

Taking advantage of the lull in the work of the American Secretary which the war imposed, Aydelotte wrote a book on the history of the American scholarships. The book was published in 1946 in the United States under the title *The American Rhodes Scholar-ships: A Review of the First Forty Years* by Princeton University Press and in England by Oxford University Press as *The Vision of Cecil Rhodes*. In its six chapters Aydelotte gave an account of Rhodes's life and discussed the selection of Rhodes scholars, the American record at Oxford, what the American Rhodes scholar gets from Oxford (this chapter was based on Aydelotte's 1923 article in *Scribner's Magazine*), careers of American Rhodes scholars, and he concluded with a chapter on 'American Rhodes Scholars and the Vision of Cecil Rhodes'. A handy set of tables and a directory were appended. Aydelotte's unabashed internationalism was summed up in the last sentence of the book: 'If all the far-flung nations of the English-speaking world remain united in support of a new international order in which force will be the servant of the law, they will bring to reality, in ways which he could not have foreseen, the Vision of Cecil Rhodes.'[139] Such a sentiment as this would shortly be used by the detractors of the scholarships in the United States as proof of the secret and subversive goals which Rhodes had in mind.

---

[135] *AO* 27 (1940), 1–4.

[136] Collingwood holds the distinction of being the only member of the class of 1939 to have attended the University before the war.

[137] RTF 1233. Gilmore Stott (Ohio and Balliol 1938) published his eyewitness account of the events leading up to the evacuation in his 'Letter from Oxford' in *AO* 27 (1940) 96 f. In *AO* 86 (1999), 16 ff., Stott published further reminiscences of the return voyage and the examinations.

[138] In Sept. 1939 Aydelotte had written to Allen that the Association of American Rhodes scholars was asking the Carnegie Corporation for a grant to assist Rhodes scholars whose Oxford careers had been interrupted by the war to continue their studies in the United States. The grant, in the amount of $25,000, was made available to thirty-two scholars displaced by the war. RTF 1233A. Nason, *AO* 27 (1940), 2–3.

[139] *American Rhodes Scholarships*, 120–1.

3 · POST-WAR AMERICA

The suspended American scholarships were resumed in the election held on 14 December 1946. Scholars whose studies had been interrupted by the war were permitted to return, married or not. Once again the Trustees had to make some adjustment to the number of scholarships to make up for the war-enforced hiatus, and they decided to add sixteen scholarships each to the classes of 1947 and 1948. They also altered the age limit for applicants with war service, which was defined to include both 'membership in the Armed Forces' and any work 'for which Draft Boards have granted deferment',[140] so that any man born between 1 October 1915 and 1 October 1928 was deemed eligible if his war service qualified. Thus, the class of 1947 had a scholar who was born in December 1915 and another who was born in April 1927. This range of years, compared with the normal age of eligibility from 18 to 25, was the greatest in the history of the American scholarships, and contributed to the special character of the experiences of the first post-war class.[141]

Normal practices for the scholarships were resumed in the elections for the class of 1949, but a new challenge quickly emerged. On 25 June 1950 the North Koreans crossed the 38th parallel into South Korea, and on 27 June President Harry S. Truman ordered United States forces to engage in a 'police action' under the aegis of the United Nations. After the brief respite of peace, the United States was again in an armed conflict, and its demobilized armed forces had to be quickly re-equipped with men and matériel on an emergency basis. To do so required an expansion of the draft, and young men of college age were subject to being called up, with deferments under certain circumstances at the discretion of the local draft boards. The Trustees agreed in principle at their meeting on 29 July 1950 to permit scholars-elect who might be drafted or otherwise sent into the conflict 'to take up their Scholarships at a later date'.[142] From this time forward, the office of the American Secretary was to be occupied for the next few years with working with local draft boards for deferments from military service, and not always successfully. In order to be fair to men who had served and who faced a problem with the age limit, after much consultation, an exception to the age limit that allowed veterans to deduct the length of time in military service from their actual age was adopted. Although the Korean War formally ended with the armistice which was signed on 27 July 1953, conscription continued, and this provision was not terminated until 1960.[143]

Although the time for Frank Aydelotte's retirement as American Secretary was inexorably approaching, he stood firmly in the centre of the administration of the

---

[140] Annual memorandum Apr. 1946.

[141] The class of 1947, with its unique mix of age and experience, performed well academically and athletically at Oxford. Members of the class took thirteen D.Phil. degrees, one first-class BCL, four research degrees (B.Sc., B.Phil., or B.Litt.), one first class in final honour school, fourteen seconds, seven thirds, one fourth, and seven left without taking degrees (five resigned in order to get married), and five members of the class remained or returned to complete work for second degrees. In sport, the class with an average age greater than normal performed notably well.

[142] RTM 29 July 1950.   [143] Annual Memoranda and file 'Korean Veterans' RTA.

scholarships, and, as president of the Association of American Rhodes Scholars, he oversaw its continued smooth operations. The office of the American Secretary seemed to be up to any challenge, from managing the catch-up elections of 1946 and 1947 to the planning of a reunion which was held in Princeton in June 1947 to the delight of all who attended. Aydelotte had retired as Director of the Institute for Advanced Study in 1947 at age 67, but he continued his work as American Secretary from his office in Princeton. After the war, Aydelotte renewed the office of assistant American secretary, and appointed Gilmore Stott (Ohio and Balliol 1938) in 1946.[144]

Under cover of coming to look over the operations of the American Secretary's office to justify its expenses, Lord Hailey, Rhodes Trustee, came to Princeton in early April 1949; his other mission was to talk with Aydelotte about succession. Hailey found Aydelotte 'not only ready but anxious to discuss this matter. He does not see (and I do not see) why he should not carry on for a number of years to come; but he would be glad to feel secure about the future, and would meanwhile be glad also to have someone on whom he could devolve part of his work.'[145] When in 1950 Stott left Princeton for an appointment at Swarthmore, Aydelotte asked James N. Hester (California and Pembroke 1947) to replace Stott as assistant American secretary. Hester was able to serve only a few months before returning to active duty in the US Marine Corps in 1951. Aydelotte then turned to a young member of Princeton University's faculty, Courtney Craig Smith (Iowa and Merton 1938). Smith, who had been forced by the war to leave England before completing his work for the B.Litt., received his Ph.D. from Harvard in 1943 and was commissioned as a lieutenant (junior grade) in the US Naval Reserve. After he was demobilized from the US Naval Reserve in 1946, he joined Princeton's faculty as a member of the English Department. He had attracted Aydelotte's attention, as well as

[144] Stott had been one of the last Rhodes scholars who remained at Oxford until their last-minute evacuation in June 1940. See p. 143. Stott also served as deputy secretary from 1962 to 1970; he was the only person to hold this office. The position of assistant to the American Secretary has been held by four-teen Rhodes scholars: Alan Valentine (Pennsylvania and Balliol 1922) 1928–32, John W. Nason (Minnesota and Oriel 1928) 1932–40, Stott 1946–50, James N. Hester (California and Pembroke 1947) Sept.–Dec. 1950, Courtney Smith Jan. 1951–Jan. 1953, Prosser Gifford (Connecticut and Merton 1951) 1956–8, Aldon D. Bell (Oklahoma and Hertford 1951) 1958–60, Richard W. Pfaff (Kansas and Magdalen 1957) 1960–2, Alan J. Gayer (Massachusetts and Balliol 1965) 1971–3, John H. Churchill (Arkansas and New College 1971) 1974–7, Elliot F. Gerson (Connecticut and Magdalen 1974) 1977–9, William J. Cronon (Wisconsin and Jesus 1976) 1980, Clay S. Jenkinson (North Dakota and Hertford 1977) 1981–3, and Steven A. Crown (Washington and Queen's 1980) 1983–4. The position of Assistant American Secretary has been in abeyance since 1984. Successive American Secretaries have been assisted by extraordinarily able and committed secretaries and associates. Emma Abbett was Aydelotte's secretary first in Washington, then at MIT, and she remained with him in the American Secretary's office until 1929 when she gave up work for the scholarships in order to be full-time in the President's office. Janet Middleton succeeded her, and in 1937 Elsa Jenkins succeeded Middleton. Jenkins was indispensable to the administration of the American scholarships, remaining in office during Courtney Smith's tenure and after his death. Her work for the scholarships and her encyclopedic knowledge of the scholarships and the scholars was recognized by election to honorary membership in the Association of American Rhodes Scholars in 1970. Her successors were equally devoted and effective. Marian Haagen served as secretary to William Barber throughout his tenure as American Secretary from 1970 to 1981. In 1982 Alexander appointed Sherrill Pinney, who served the Trust until her retirement in June 1998. Both Haagen and Pinney were also made honorary members of the AARS in appreciation for their service at their retirement.

[145] Hailey to Elton; RTF 2567.

that of the administrators at Princeton, and Aydelotte appointed him assistant American secretary in January 1951 in succession to Hester.

In preparation for his new duties as Sir Carleton Allen's successor as Warden of Rhodes House, E. T. Williams had come to the United States and Canada in the autumn of 1951 on his world tour of the scholarship's constituencies. One of his tasks was to clarify the American Secretary's succession. The Trustees had decided to invite Smith to be the next American Secretary at their meeting on 21 July 1951, but the terms of the transition between Aydelotte and Smith were not fully settled. Williams recommended 'a firm and business-like offer' to Smith, adding the point that 'the right job to combine with the American secretaryship may not crop up as conveniently (in point of time) as one hopes. He [Smith] should be a College President as well—but it must be the right college (or university) both from his own point of view, as to career, and from the Trust's point of view, as to strategic positioning.' Williams found Aydelotte to be 'a very old man (much older than I expected) but his indomitability—plus Marie's Christian Science—makes him try to ignore the fact that, but for Elsa Jenkins and Courtney, he couldn't really do the job any more.'[146] The fell blow of Marie Aydelotte's death in Oxford in the summer of 1952 brought it all to a head. Frances Blanshard described Aydelotte's condition at the time: 'Frank was in a daze. The vagueness from which he was suffering deepened; it was as if he did not quite realize the tragedy that had overtaken him or know how to cope with it.'[147] The Trustees minuted Aydelotte's retirement at their meeting on 2 December 1952.

Courtney Smith Succeeds Aydelotte

In the meantime, Princeton University had inaugurated the Woodrow Wilson graduate fellowship programme, the appeal of which was so great that it was decided to expand it into a national scheme. Smith wrote to Aydelotte on 20 January 1952 about 'one new, and interesting, and in the long run quite beneficial change in my status at Princeton this coming term', and he outlined his new responsibilities as the first national director of the Woodrow Wilson National Fellowship Foundation. Smith continued by noting the 'advantages of this "mission" to my eventual role as your successor'. He would be thrust into national prominence as the administrator of an exciting national educational initiative, and his travels would bring him into contact with the leaders of major American universities.[148]

Williams's hoped-for opportunity timed itself quite conveniently. John Nason had resigned the Presidency of Swarthmore College to become president of the Foreign Policy Association, and on 17 October 1953 Courtney Smith was inaugurated as President of Swarthmore College at the age of 36. During his presidential career Smith held a number

---

[146] Williams to Elton, 27 Oct. 1951; RTF 3076. Aydelotte was only 71 years old; his seventy-first birthday was 16 Oct.

[147] Blanshard, *Aydelotte*, 387.

[148] Smith to Aydelotte, 20 Jan. 1952; RTA 14. Smith resigned as national director of the Woodrow Wilson National Fellowship Foundation when he became President of Swarthmore.

of responsible positions in national foundations and educational associations. He was made an honorary Officer of the Order of the British Empire in 1960. He sent a memorandum to the American Rhodes scholars on 17 July 1968, informing them that he intended to relinquish the American secretaryship at the end of his presidency of Swarthmore. The Rhodes Trustees accepted his resignation as American Secretary at their meeting on 17 October, and the search for his successor as American Secretary was begun, although without great urgency.[149]

Soon after assuming office, Smith began to look at the possibilities of recruitment of black Americans. His staff analysed the list of colleges and universities which had institutional representatives, and they found that none of the historically black colleges was represented on campus by a specifically appointed member of the faculty or administration. In the summer of 1954 Smith wrote to these institutions and invited them to appoint campus representatives; the action produced surprising results. Fisk University in Nashville announced that it had been invited to make such an appointment. *Jet Magazine* in Chicago and *Time Magazine* reported this action as a newsworthy change in policy. The *Christian Science Monitor* wrote, 'Heretofore, Negroes have been limited in competition for the scholarships, since such awards were made only at outstanding white or interracial institutions. This policy had excluded Negroes studying in the South, since southern white colleges have only recently begun to admit them.' This initiative was important, but the opening of American colleges to more minority students was the primary factor in the gradual appearance of more ethnic minorities among the Rhodes scholars. In response to an enquiry about the eligibility of black Americans to apply Smith wrote in December 1956 expressing his hope that 'top standing Negro students in both the integrated and the Negro colleges and universities . . . will enter the competition for [the scholarship]. I have made special efforts in the leading Negro colleges and universities to encourage them to do so.'[150] J. Stanley Sanders (California and Magdalen 1963) and John Edgar Wideman (Pennsylvania and New College 1963), the second and third black American Rhodes scholars after Alain Locke (Pennsylvania and Hertford 1907), were elected in 1962. Recalling clause 24 of the will, Smith wrote to Williams immediately after their election, 'Cecil Rhodes was so very far ahead not only of his own time ("disqualified") but of our own ("qualified").'[151]

The most significant change in the administration of the scholarships during the decade of the 1950s was the admission of Alaska and Hawaii as states, and their subsequent incorporation into the scholarships in 1959. After consultation with state secretaries, it was decided to add Alaska to the north-western district (Washington, Oregon, Idaho, Montana, Wyoming, and North Dakota), and to add Hawaii to the south-western district (California, Nevada, Utah, Arizona, Colorado, and New Mexico).[152] By this

[149] RTM 17 Oct. 1968.
[150] *Christian Science Monitor*, 21 Aug. 1954; Smith to Carl Murphy, 2 Jan. 1957; RTA 15.
[151] Smith to Williams, 16 Dec. 1962; RTA 120.
[152] RTM 5 Feb., 2 May 1959. Annual memorandum Sept. 1959. Although scarcely noted, adding these two states violated the politically valuable principle of all districts having equal numbers of states, so much a part of the compromises that permitted the District Plan's hard-won adoption.

action, Hawaii, a territory since 1902, at long last was allowed to participate. The class of 1961 was the first with competition in fifty states, but the first scholar from Alaska was not elected until 1963 and from Hawaii not until 1967.

The war in Vietnam had begun severely to torment the American body politic by 1966. The war's unpopularity and the mood of disaffection on American campuses, the complex roots of which were twisted by widespread anomie among the young and by their elders' suspicion of them as cannabis-sated libertines, not unsurprisingly galvanized the feelings of American Rhodes scholars in Oxford. Williams cabled Smith on 24 January 1967 that

some forty American Rhodes Scholars in residence propose writing to President Johnson protesting about Vietnam STOP Have stressed to them that they must make it clear that some of their contemporary Scholars disagree with them and views expressed neither represent Rhodes Trust nor Scholars of other vintages STOP Am unhappy about use of term Rhodes Scholar in political protest but consider they must make up their own minds about this STOP Understand their protest likely to appear in American press this week STOP.

He went on to urge Smith to warn the service academies because serving officers at Oxford would 'naturally be among those not wishing to be involved'.[153]

A press release stated that fifty American Rhodes scholars in residence on 26 January 1967 presented a letter addressed to President Lyndon Johnson to Philip Kaiser (Wisconsin and Balliol 1936), minister in the American Embassy in London, whom they described in the release as the Deputy American Ambassador to Great Britain. The press release carefully identified the fifty signatories' states (29) and American universities (25), and noted that they were fifty of the sixty-eight American Rhodes scholars in residence. They offered the disclaimer that 'the letter does not necessarily reflect the views of the five American Rhodes Scholars now at Oxford who are on active duty, or of other Rhodes Scholars past or present, or of the Rhodes Trust'.[154] The reaction was immediate. On Friday 27 January the *New York Times* had a news article about the letter, and published excerpts and the list of signatories, complete with the traditional style followed by the Rhodes scholarships of name, state, Oxford college, and year (although the press release had not provided these identifications). Other newspapers and *Newsweek* magazine reported the letter. The *New York Post* in an editorial entitled 'Serious Voices' pointed out that this letter followed a similar statement signed by 100 student leaders on campuses across the country. The *Post*'s position was that 'The knownothings will dismiss their declaration as new proof of the perils of higher education. We view it as another sign of the unease that afflicts large areas of the thoughtful American community.'[155]

The letter was a conventional conspectus of anti-war arguments in which a series of questions about American foreign policy was put to the President, but its identification with the Rhodes scholars in residence created a stir. Some older Rhodes scholars were outraged by what they saw as a cynical ploy to capture public attention. These objectors pointed out that it was 'American Rhodes scholars' and not 'American students' in

[153] RTF 2567. Williams to Smith, 24 Jan. 1967.   [154] RTF 2567.
[155] *New York Post*, 28 Jan. 1967; *Newsweek*, 6 Feb. 1967. RTA.

residence at Oxford who drafted and signed the letter, and they claimed that the name 'Rhodes scholar' was used to guarantee journalistic attention. What right, these critics went on, did this group of Rhodes scholars have to claim the banner of the scholarship for themselves? Although Williams had earlier counselled the scholars against writing the letter in this form, the controversy swept up both Rhodes House and the office of the American Secretary in its brief tempest. Both Williams and Smith refused to issue formal statements, but the American office prepared a statement to be used in response to reporters' enquiries: 'they speak as individuals . . . We know that in referring to themselves as Rhodes Scholars their purpose is simply to identify themselves; and they disclaim any suggestion that they speak for all of the American Rhodes Scholars in residence at Oxford, or for the older American Rhodes Scholars as a total group.'[156] The war ground on, and the corrosive effects of its conscription spread ever more widely.

In 1967 the new draft law limited deferments for graduate students. Student deferments were available only to undergraduates in good academic standing, and graduate students, except in designated fields like medicine, were subject to call-up. The regulations essentially permitted a graduate student to complete the academic year in which the induction notice came. Going abroad to study required that local draft boards be informed, and in their discretion they could deny permission to leave the country. Smith published an annual memorandum to the Rhodes scholars in residence and the Rhodes scholars-elect on the effects of the draft on the conditions for taking up or maintaining a scholarship. Both Rhodes House and Smith's office tried to keep tabs on the constantly changing draft status of scholars in residence and scholars-elect. Williams in a letter to Smith caught the mood of the American Rhodes scholars who 'are terribly unsettled because of the threat of the draft and watch their mailboxes with a disquieting anxiety. You must know from [your] own experience at Swarthmore how muddled they are about both the question of the draft itself and the particular war concerned, and I think this may be to some extent intensified here by the men being away from their own country.'[157] The turmoil took its toll, and thirty-nine scholars in the five classes of 1966 to 1970 either did not take up their scholarships or left Oxford before completing their degrees, among them President Bill Clinton (Arkansas and University 1968).[158] Not all of these cases were directly related to the Vietnam War, because in normal times some students have left Oxford before taking degrees for legitimate academic reasons, for example, enrolment in

[156] Smith's office prepared a statement pointing out that the signers were speaking for themselves as individuals and not for the different views of 1,434 Rhodes scholars. 'Statement to be made available to reporters if desired,' 27 Jan. 1967; RTA. Both Smith and Williams expressed their personal dismay over the form of the letter. Williams wrote to Smith, 'I also remain worried that men whom I like don't have the instinctive understanding to know that using a label which has been made honourable by other people is something which in essence they should abjure. In short, the Rhodes Scholar who tells you he is one maybe shouldn't be one.' Smith to Williams, 2 Feb. 1967; Williams to Smith, 7 Feb. 1967. Actually Smith's office only received twenty-one letters of protest. RTA.

[157] Williams added a handwritten note, 'I mean that they muddle the two together.' Williams to Smith, 31 Jan. 1968; RTA.

[158] The question of Clinton's draft status became a campaign issue when he was running for President in 1992. Contrary to the widely published reports, Clinton was in good standing in his work for his degree at Oxford when he chose to go to Yale Law School rather than return to Oxford.

medical school. The dramatic impact on Rhodes scholars as well as on other American students, however, cannot be ignored. In the years from 1968 to 1972, the years of the maximum impact of the Vietnam War, the number of drop-outs soared to an average of more than eight per year. For comparison, one may note that in the period from 1947 to 1961 the average number of scholars who did not complete degrees was four per year, including five who did not take up their scholarships.

The American campus of the 1960s roiled with unprecedented turbulence. Colleges and universities were caught up in the maelstrom of national rage over the war in Vietnam and national outrage over the slow pace of the extension of full civil rights to minorities, particularly to black Americans. Many Americans who were genuinely concerned for racial equity and equality fomented confrontations in the streets and on the campuses across the country. The passage of the Civil Rights Act in 1964 did not alleviate these concerns, and local and specific actions to implement the Act were demanded throughout the United States. The crescendo of American involvement in South-East Asia was echoed in the deafening shouts of chanting students, who violently made known their opposition to the war and to the draft by burning draft cards and the American flag. The anti-war movement and the civil rights movement had collided on the steps of Old Main, Campus USA. Swarthmore College, in spite of its Quaker heritage, was not immune to these confrontational forces. Courtney Smith, who had embraced the Quaker standard of always seeking the consensus, was bitterly disappointed to find that reasonable discussion had been supplanted by the brute force of physical intimidation on Swarthmore's campus. In early January 1969 students had occupied the College's admissions office in a dispute over minority admissions and financial aid. Smith's duty was to minimize the disruption caused by the occupation while maximizing the effectiveness of the College's own goals in increasing educational opportunity for minority students. Elsa Jenkins wrote to Williams that 'Courtney, Gil and all of the College administration has been involved with an internal college problem literally morning, noon, and night (sometimes into the small hours of the morning).'[159] The strain was too much. On his way to a college meeting on 16 January Courtney Smith collapsed and died in his office at 9.58 a.m. Because of the circumstances of his death, Smith was regarded as a martyr to the forces racking American campuses, and news of his death was spread almost instantly throughout the country by the national news services. The occupation at Swarthmore ended soon afterwards. Williams attended Smith's memorial service, and Rhodes scholars sent a profusion of letters in an outpouring of sympathy for Betty Smith and their three children. Gilmore Stott and Elsa Jenkins in the aftermath of this tragedy competently managed the operations of the office of American Secretary *sede vacante.*

William Barber Appointed American Secretary

The Trustees had accepted Courtney Smith's resignation on 17 October 1968. Williams had canvassed the possibilities and recommended Professor William J. Barber (Kansas and Balliol 1949), professor of economics at Wesleyan University. The Trustees appointed

[159] Jenkins to Williams, 13 Jan. 1969; RTA.

Barber as the third American Secretary on 16 October 1969.[160] Barber had gone to Harvard in 1942 and had joined the US Army in 1943 when he was only 18, and served in Europe until 1946 when he returned to Harvard. He graduated from Harvard in 1949 and went to Balliol College. At Oxford he took first-class honours in the shortened final honour school of philosophy, politics, and economics. He taught at Kansas State College in 1951 and 1952, and during the Korean War he served in the Central Intelligence Agency from 1952 to 1954. He returned to Oxford in 1955 as a student at Nuffield College, and took a D.Phil. in economics in 1958. In 1957 he was appointed to the faculty of Wesleyan University in Middletown, Connecticut, where he has remained. His field is economic history, and he has written and edited a number of books. In 1981 he was made an Officer of the Order of the British Empire. He and Alan Gayer (Massachusetts and Balliol 1965), whom he had appointed to be his assistant, began their work by taking part in the activities in the Swarthmore office at the time of the elections in December. The Swarthmore office closed down, and the library and files were moved to Middletown in the early summer of 1970.

The files had scarcely been unpacked when William Barber was thrust into the most dangerous controversy ever faced by an American Secretary.[161] Quite early in the history of the American scholarships Rhodes's limitation of the scholarships to 'male students' had been questioned. In 1921 the secretary of Smith College, a college for women, wrote asking why women might not be considered, in view of the recent changes in the status of women at Oxford. Again an enquiry was made by the President of Wilson College, also a women's college, in 1926.[162] The era of the 1960s in the United States had seen unprecedented changes in public policy affecting discrimination in employment, education, and access to public facilities, and major policy changes in the early 1970s made it impossible for the scholarships to continue to exclude women. The Civil Rights Act of 1964 had outlawed all forms of race discrimination, and the national movement for equal rights for women had a significant impact on higher education. Any programme that was limited to a single sex was a target, and a number of previously single-sex institutions had begun to admit women for the first time in their long histories.

As early as November 1971 Barber had sent a memorandum to the secretaries of state and district committees of selection, pointing out that the conditions of eligibility were governed by the terms of the will and that, whatever their wishes might be with respect to opening the scholarships to women, neither the Trustees nor their officials had any discretion to alter the will.[163] He went on to describe the Trustees' effort to expand

---

[160] RTM 16 Oct. 1969.

[161] In 2000 Barber published an article in *AO* in which he recounted the events in the United States relating to the extension of eligibility to the scholarships to women: 'A Footnote to the Social History of the 1970s: The Opening of the Rhodes Scholarships to Women', *AO* 87 (2000), 135 ff. I am indebted to him for allowing me to see a pre-publication version of this article.

[162] Robert Withington, Secretary of Smith College, to Aydelotte, 10 Dec. 1921. E. D. Warfield, Wilson College, to Aydelotte, 27 Jan. 1926. RTA.

[163] Barber, Memorandum, 24 Mar. 1971. Stephen B. Hitchner (Maryland-DC and New College 1967) had visited Don K. Price, in his capacity as Rhodes Trustee, to report that nine of his classmates in the vicinity of Harvard had met and had voted unanimously to urge the Trustees to open the scholarships to women. Price to Williams, 29 Oct. 1971; RTA.

educational opportunities by establishing the Rhodes fellowships for women and by giving financial support to the five women's colleges at Oxford.[164] Nor could the limited facilities of the women's colleges at Oxford be ignored: 'Oxford is thus not now in a position to offer hospitality to women from overseas on the same generous terms it can offer to men from overseas.'[165] At the end of December Harvard University's Graduate and Career Plans Office announced that it would ask permission of the office of the American Secretary to allow its women students to apply, publicizing its announcement widely. The Women's Equity Action League issued a press release on 1 February 1972 announcing that it was challenging the legality of the scholarships and that it supported the students of Radcliffe College, the women's college affiliated with Harvard, who were petitioning Harvard to nominate women. Rhodes scholars themselves were writing letters to Barber and to the *American Oxonian*. Congressman John Brademas (Indiana and Brasenose 1950) wrote to Barber to say that a member of his staff had looked into the matter and had reached a negative conclusion about the legality of continuing American institutional involvement with the scholarships.

Rhodes scholars in residence, who organized major protests against the selection procedures in South Africa and Rhodesia, castigated the Trustees for practising racial discrimination in the administration of these scholarships. Grant Crandall (Iowa and University 1969) resigned his scholarship in 1972 'on conscientious grounds' in protest against the racist and discriminatory nature of the scholarships.[166] Crandall made public his letter to the Trustees, and his action was widely reported in the press. He charged that the Trust was more concerned 'with bolstering its public image than with ending the racial discrimination it acknowledges having practiced' in its administration of the scholarships in South Africa and Rhodesia, and he also accused the Trustees of having taken no action to end the 'gross injustice' of excluding women from the scholarships; 'on the contrary, Rhodes Trust representatives have indicated that to them this is not even a deficiency in the Scholarship.'[167]

The most comprehensive legal challenge came in Minnesota. The University of Minnesota had endorsed a woman student in October 1972, stating that the University's anti-discrimination policies required University endorsement of its 'otherwise qualified male and female candidates'. When her application was declined, the Minnesota Civil Liberties Union intervened, and subsequently filed a lawsuit to enjoin the University of Minnesota and all other higher educational institutions in Minnesota from participating in the Rhodes scholarship programme. The complaint named University officials and the Rhodes scholar members of the University's selection committee as defendants.[168]

[164] For an account of the Rhodes fellowships for women, see Kenny, above p. 66.
[165] Memorandum, 29 Nov. 1971. RTA.
[166] The 1981 edition of the *Register* recorded that he had resigned for reasons of conscience. The 1996 edition omitted this comment. See also Kenny, above p. 64, for a more extended account of the protests.
[167] RT Crandall, G. (Iowa and University 1969). Crandall's protest over the ineligibility of women was later cited by the Women's Equity Action League in a report on Women and Fellowships which was published in Apr. 1974, 22. RTA. For a fuller account of the Trustees' action see Kenny, above p. 68.
[168] The suit, which was not actually filed until June 1974, was dismissed on 27 June 1977, after women had become eligible to apply. File *Lach* v. *University of Minnesota*. RTA.

In the autumn of 1973 women from Yale, LaSalle College in Pennsylvania, and the University of Oklahoma had applied for the scholarships in spite of the will's specific language, and another woman at the University of Oklahoma filed a complaint against the University to force it to stop participating in the competition for the scholarships. Harvard University, with full knowledge that a candidate must apply only in the state of either education or of residence, sent nominations of three women to every state secretary in the United States. This action was obviously contrived to increase pressure on the American Secretary and the Trustees by bringing maximum publicity to the issue. The *Harvard Crimson* in an editorial on 10 October 1973 unfairly castigated Harvard alumnus Barber for his 'timid stand'. Professor Don K. Price (Tennessee and Merton 1932), Dean of Harvard's Kennedy School of Government and the only American Rhodes Trustee, wrote to the editors in Barber's defence, calling attention to the conditions established in the will: 'if Mr. Barber tried to break this law, the Rhodes Trustees would have to get another American Secretary.'[169] Price and Barber were in close consultation throughout this period.

In 1972 the United States Congress passed the Education Amendments of 1972, a series of amendments to prior legislation such as the Higher Education Act of 1965. One section of these Amendments, Title IX, decreed that 'No person in the United States shall, on the basis of sex, be excluded from participation in, be denied the benefits of, or subjected to discrimination under any education program or activity receiving Federal financial assistance,' allowing certain quite specific exceptions.[170] The Act did not cover the Rhodes scholarships, as a foreign programme of fellowship grants to study at a foreign university. What it did affect was institutional involvement with any discriminatory programme and whether or not such involvement might imperil all federal support. The Department of Health, Education, and Welfare was charged with the preparation of regulations under Title IX and their implementation and enforcement. Final regulations implementing Title IX were not issued until 1975. In the interim, public discussion was extensive, and university and college administrations were keenly aware of the risks of non-compliance. Even before final regulations had been promulgated, the widespread feeling in the colleges and universities, both public and private, was that on penalty of forfeiting all federal support the permanent regulations would certainly prohibit the cooperation of almost all American educational institutions in any discriminatory programme, and that such a prohibition was morally right. The loss of such support, especially of the federally supported student aid programmes, would be disastrous for them and their students.

Although the Rhodes scholarships were not subject to American legislation, the institutional nexus of the scholarships was pervasive. The policies of the scholarships required a formal institutional endorsement of every candidate. The institutions cooperated in other ways, including publicity about the scholarships on campus, coordination through

---

[169] Price to Editors, of the *Harvard Crimson* 10 Oct. 1973. RTA.

[170] Public Law 92–318 92nd Congress, s. 659, 23 June 1972. The exceptions applied to private colleges, newly co-educational colleges, religious institutions, military schools, and public institutions that were historically single-sex.

an office or a faculty representative, facilities for production of letters of recommendation and other secretarial support, interviews conducted by campus committees in many
cases, and the services of presidents and faculty members on state and district committees of selection. Because of this linkage the taint of the Rhodes scholarships now threatened the institutions themselves.

Barber during this time was considering contingency plans, from the most benign to
the executioner's blindfold. He prepared a memorandum on 'The Pros and Cons of Operations Independent of Formal Contact with U. S. Universities Vs. Suspension.'[171] The
losses of 'going underground', that is, severing all ties with American universities, would
certainly compromise the essence of the scholarships. Abandonment of the institutional
endorsement would deprive the process of a valuable screening device, since the
institutional endorsement helped assure the quality and sense of purpose of the applicants.[172] On the other hand, sustaining modified operations would have the benefits of
denying the opponents a complete victory, and, more significantly, some continuity of
operations would help maintain morale among Rhodes scholars and keep selection committees' skills honed. Even so, an underground strategy would probably result in a greater
concentration of candidates from institutions where the scholarships were well known,
making 'our enterprise less national and less comprehensive'. Barber wondered if an
underground strategy would end HEW's oversight, because such necessities as academic
recommendations, especially on university letterhead, might be defined as institutional
involvement with all the attendant risks. Finally, the underground strategy would be
interpreted as a 'rather sleazy maneuver', beneath the perceived dignity of the Trust and
its operations. It would be wrong to be seen as obstructing the movement toward
equality of opportunity.

The director of the Department's Higher Education Division's Office for Civil Rights
sent Barber a letter at the end of November, stating that two complaints had been received
from women who had been denied Rhodes scholarships on the basis of sex. Although
the regulations implementing Title IX had not been issued, the director warned Barber
of the Office's view that, because 'many institutions of higher education apparently have
a direct role in the administration of the Rhodes Scholars program', their participation
was likely to be subject to Title IX's prohibition against discrimination on the basis
of sex. The letter requested that Barber supply information about the number of
institutions with which the 'Rhodes Scholar Committee' was affiliated, about the
nature of the role played by these institutions, about the process by which the restriction
against women might be removed and if any such action was contemplated, and that he
provide an estimate 'of the consequences for the Rhodes Scholars Committee of eliminating institutions of higher education from direct participation in the awarding of the
scholarship'.[173]

Barber, troubled by the breadth of the interpretation of the Title by the Office for
Civil Rights, consulted with Williams, Price, and three Rhodes scholars who were lawyers.

---

[171] Undated memorandum; RTA.
[172] The institutional endorsement, which was dropped in 1975, was not reinstated until 1995.
[173] Mary M. Lepper to Barber, 28 Nov. 1973; RTA.

To what extent did a finding of non-compliance affect *all* federally funded programmes? Barber's position was that the Department's interpretation went far beyond the plain language of section 902: 'such termination or refusal shall be limited to the particular entity, or part thereof, or other recipient as to whom such a finding [of non-compliance] has been made, and shall be limited in its effect to the particular program, or part thereof, in which such noncompliance has been so found.'[174] Before responding to this enquiry, Barber tried to get clarification of the Department's interpretation of section 902, but he was told by telephone that the draft regulations would place all federal financial assistance to a non-complying institution in jeopardy. The Department's written reply to his enquiries was harsh: 'As agreed, rather than discuss further the legal basis under Title IX . . . you will furnish the information requested in my letter to you dated November 28, 1973, upon receipt of this letter.' The Department was in the process of attempting 'to ascertain whether involvement with the Rhodes Scholarship Trust by institutions . . . is sufficient for such activities to be subject to the nondiscrimination requirements of Title IX'. If their conclusion were affirmative, the American Secretary would be so advised 'prior to contacting these institutions in an effort to resolve this matter on a voluntary basis'.[175]

Barber's position was that the involvement of the colleges and universities, although historical and significant, did not make them administrators of the scholarships. Therefore neither American law nor regulation could affect the conditions laid down in a foreign will which had been embodied in legislation of a foreign government. He rehearsed the legal position in the United Kingdom, and expressed the view that legislation affecting opportunities for women was in the early stages of consideration by the British government.[176] The issue was clearly joined. The Trustees could not change the impermissible limitation of the scholarships to 'male students' without British governmental intervention. If the limited formal participation of American institutions in the procedures of nomination and election to the Rhodes scholarships thrust them into a condition of non-compliance with Title IX, and if that non-compliance jeopardized *all* federally assisted programmes, the Rhodes scholarships would have to become somehow divorced from the institutions of its applicants.

Barber wrote to the Secretary of the Department of Health, Education, and Welfare, Caspar W. Weinberger, and he called the Secretary's attention to the communications he had received from the Office for Civil Rights which declared that *all* federal financial assistance would be jeopardized. Barber asked Weinberger if this was the 'well-considered position of the United States Government', averring that the matter of governmental obstruction of 'the free flow of information between the University of Oxford [on the availability of the scholarships and the method of acquiring them] and the American academic community is not a trivial matter'. Barber focused his argument on the nature of the institutions' participation as conduits of information, rather than as administrators of the programme, and he called attention to the fact that any mitigation of the

---

[174] Barber to Lepper, 21 Dec. 1973; RTA.   [175] Lepper to Barber, 13 Feb. 1974; RTA.
[176] Barber to Lepper, 12 Feb. 1974; RTA.

difficulty lay beyond the discretion of the Trustees. In a pointed attack upon the position taken by the Office of Civil Rights, he argued that 'our English academic hosts' would have difficulty in understanding 'why American students should be denied funds linked to the University of Oxford when analogous non-discriminatory tests were not applied to endowed scholarships administered by private undergraduate colleges in the United States'. These 'single-sex' scholarships, because they were linked to admissions to private institutions, were not affected by the proposed regulations, and Barber argued that the Rhodes scholarships were similarly related to the scholars' admission to 'private undergraduate colleges in the University of Oxford'. Such fine distinctions that the Office might be able to draw between the practices permitted in the United States and the allegedly impermissible practices of the Rhodes scholarships would be difficult to explain in England.[177]

Barber's deadline was at hand. He had concluded that he must recommend that the Trustees suspend the American scholarships in the light of the Department's broad application of Title IX. Two hours before he was to leave Middletown for the flight to London to attend a meeting of the Trustees on 14 March, he received a telephone call from an aide to Secretary Weinberger. The aide told Barber that a letter signed by the Secretary was being sent. In the letter the Secretary would express his belief that, when the regulations were made final, the results would be satisfactory. Barber appeared before the Trustees on 14 March, and gave them a full report, calling their attention to the possible peril Wesleyan University itself faced because of the presence of the office of the American Secretary on its campus.[178] On 26 March Williams had written Barber a formal statement for publication that 'the Rhodes Trustees reaffirm their hope that women should become eligible to compete for Rhodes Scholarships equally with men', and that the Trustees were seeking the legal powers necessary to effectuate 'this fundamental change in the benefaction bequeathed by Mr. Rhodes which is now embodied in an Act of the British Parliament: The Rhodes Trust Act of 1946.'[179] Good intentions and asseverations thereof were fair enough, but what really mattered was the final regulations.

The Secretary of HEW replied on 16 April, first apologizing for the delay in his answer, and then saying that he understood Barber's concern 'that a provision of the regulation might jeopardize the Rhodes Scholarship program and force you to tell the Rhodes Trustees that their hospitality to American students would no longer be welcome. I assure

---

[177] Barber to Weinberger, 25 Feb. 1974; RTA. Also Barber, 'A Footnote to Social History', 141–2. Barber felt that he could not call on Rhodes scholars in Congress for specific support, fearing, because of the Watergate atmosphere in Washington, that any advocacy by the Rhodes scholars might be leaked with a potentially negative fallout that might affect the delicate negotiations in which the Trustees were then engaged, and also because he did not wish to place them 'in a position that could be awkward in their constituencies. Instead I merely asked them for assistance in facilitating the flow of my message to Weinberger.' Barber made contact with the office of the Speaker of the House, Carl Albert (Oklahoma and St Peter's 1931), expressing 'hope that a way might be found to insure that our case could be brought to the Secretary's personal attention'. Barber, 'A Footnote to Social History', 142.

[178] RTM 14 Mar. 1974.

[179] Williams to Barber, 26 Mar. 1974; RTA. The letter was published at Barber's request in AO 61 (1974), 17.

you that I am fully aware of the great importance of the Rhodes Scholarship program, and I expect that a reasonable solution will be outlined in the proposed regulation.'[180] On 18 June 1974 in the *Federal Register* the Department issued proposed regulations for comment, and the time for public comment extended to 15 October. The newly proposed regulations, to Barber's credit, provided that 'the general prohibition does not apply to administration by a recipient of a scholarship or similar financial assistance program which is restricted to one sex *and* [emphasis theirs] is established under a foreign will, trust, or similar legal instrument or by a foreign government.'[181] Thus ended the American legal skirmishes. The larger issue of women's eligibility remained. Barber, the Trustees, and the Rhodes scholars had to hope for a victory in the only legal system that mattered, the British. Such a victory was gained. In 1976 women became eligible to apply, and in the class of 1977 thirteen women were elected.

Barber's tenure was again disturbed by a major threat to the American scholarships. The British government had imposed additional fees on overseas students for a number of years. At their meeting on 16 March 1967 the Trustees 'noted with exasperation' the fact that the increase would cost the Trust an additional £33,000 per year. Williams reported this to Smith in an unrestrained explosion of fury: 'My anger about all this is unbridled.'[182] His anger perdured, for these increases were but the start of an escalation that eventually reached crisis proportions for the Trust. Williams warned Barber that he and the other overseas secretaries should be prepared to recommend cuts in the next round of elections. Harking back to the order of abatement of the scholarships in Rhodes's will, he wrote, 'It will be simplest to cut your 4 per District to 3 and make a similar deduction in other constituencies when possible: back to the Will with a vengeance.'[183] Because announcements and materials for the 1979 elections had been printed and were already being distributed, Barber urged at least a year's delay in any retrenchment to avoid embarrassment. Such a delay would permit further discussion with the British government, gaining time for legal consideration of the ticklish issue of the order of abatement, and for a search for a better solution than simply reducing each district's allocation by one. Barber argued that reducing the scholarships from four to three in each district was 'mechanically tidy', but in the longer term 'a superior arrangement' might emerge from a reconsideration of the District Plan in the light of population shifts that had occurred since 1930. While he was not filled 'with glee' at the daunting prospect of realigning districts, additional time would offer a chance 'to come closer to an optimal solution'.[184] In November he nevertheless drafted a memorandum,

---

[180] Weinberger to Barber, 16 Apr. 1974. RTA.   [181] HEW News, 18 June 1974. RTA.

[182] RTR 460. Williams to Smith 28 March 1967. RTA.

[183] Williams to Barber, 31 July 1979; RTA. Clause 22 (iv) established that the American scholarships would be first to be abated if income was insufficient, but because the Trustees in their discretion had created other scholarships, abatement was a matter of legal complexity, according to the Trust's lawyers.

[184] Barber to Williams, 17 Aug. 1979; RTA. In a letter written the following month, Barber raised the possibility of raising additional funds from American Rhodes scholars to maintain the thirty-two scholarships. In this letter Barber also raised the question of a thorough review of the District Plan, with an eye toward realignment along more up-to-date population factors. 'If, for example, we could divide some states in two and allocate halves to different districts, it might make life much easier.' Barber to Williams, 20 Sept. 1979; RTA.

to be used only if needed, which announced that the Rhodes Trustees, 'with great reluctance', had been forced to reduce the number of American scholarships from thirty-two to twenty-four, but that the forthcoming elections in December 1979 would proceed normally.[185] In the event, however, a reprieve was granted because the Trust's reserves could be availed of; but Williams instructed Barber to plan for the contingency in 1980. Fortunately for all the constituencies the assets of the Trust rose to the occasion, and the danger passed.

David Alexander Appointed American Secretary

Dr Robin Fletcher succeeded Sir Edgar Williams in 1980, and William Barber had expressed his intentions to resign as American Secretary in 1980 in order to return to scholarship and teaching. John David Alexander (Tennessee and Christ Church 1954) was appointed fourth American Secretary with effect from 1 January 1981. He had graduated from Southwestern at Memphis (now Rhodes College) in 1953, attended Louisville Presbyterian Theological Seminary for one year, and had taken a D.Phil. in church history and biblical languages in 1957. He taught biblical studies at San Francisco Theological Seminary in San Anselmo, California, from 1957 to 1964. He was inaugurated President of Southwestern at Memphis in 1965 at age 32, and resigned to become President of Pomona College in 1969. He retired from the presidency of Pomona College in 1991. In 1998 he was made an honorary Commander of the Order of the British Empire. He retired as American Secretary at the end of January 1998, and was succeeded by Elliot F. Gerson (Connecticut and Balliol 1974).

David Alexander was spared the impact of protracted wars and threats of termination or retrenchment of the American scholarships. With the exception of an unaccustomed involvement by the board of direction of the Association of American Rhodes Scholars in the affairs of the Rhodes Trustees in the controversy over the four testamentary schools in South Africa, he enjoyed a period of routine administration, not unlike those relatively rare times in the 1920s and in the 1930s after the District Plan was adopted or in the years between the mid-1950s and the beginning of student unrest in the mid-1960s. Using this period of routine management of the operations of the scholarships as an opportunity to return to the perennial quest for greater equity under the District Plan of 1930, he and his assistant Sherrill Pinney reopened this issue.

At a meeting of district secretaries in Chicago in 1985 Fletcher and Alexander discussed a number of issues relating to the organization of the elections, including the lack of equity among the districts. When Anthony Kenny came to the United States on his orientation tour of the constituencies, he discussed the possibility of realigning districts with Alexander, and on his return to Oxford he drafted a drastically altered district plan, which incorporated combinations of states in sub-districts that would nominate candidates to the districts, as the larger states did.[186] This scheme pulled together several themes then

---

[185] 'Draft Announcement of a Modification in Rhodes Scholarship Competition in the United States for 1979.' Undated, but sent under covering letter Barber to Williams, 7 Nov. 1979; RTA.
[186] Kenny to Alexander, 14 Apr. 1989; RTA.

under discussion: first, and most obvious, abandonment of the rigid division of the country into six or seven states per district; second, abandonment of the absolute principle of each state as an autonomous nominating unit; and third, permitting states to nominate more than two applicants to the districts. Underlying these themes was the desire to equalize to the greatest extent possible the populations of the states, whether their general population or, as a refinement, their undergraduate populations, in order to take cognizance of the educational prowess of each state. By considering differences in population this scheme would no longer grant the smaller states the same absolute number of nominations as the largest states, thus further weakening the states' control over the elections.

Alexander and Pinney consulted with Kenny, and they all worked with maps, population tables, and application numbers in a profusion of permutation and combination.[187] The binary calculations of two, four, eight, and finally thirty-two for these purposes reconciled ill with fifty nominating states. Indeed, the files in the office of the American Secretary contain doodles and drafts of new plans from almost every era since Frank Aydelotte and his contemporaries began drawing their maps in the 1920s. The simplest solution would be to use the standard technique followed by many national fellowship programmes: let the United States be divided into a fixed number of districts, each with a population optimized for equity. This was the plan utilized by the Marshall scholarships. Alexander felt, however, that a simple district plan would both exacerbate the danger of losing the national dispersion of Rhodes scholars which Rhodes's will had successfully guaranteed and increase the probability of an even greater concentration of winners from those 'conspicuously successful' institutions about which Courtney Smith had written.[188] The goal was to find a *via media* which preserved the nominating role of the states within more equitably arranged districts.

A wide array of possible changes was considered: simple shifts of states within the eight districts; variable nominations among the states; varying the number of scholars to be elected by the districts on the basis of population; establishing districts with unequal numbers of states; increasing the number of districts; making the largest states, e.g. California and New York, self-contained districts; creating sub-districts which were unrelated to state boundaries. Another line of enquiry emerged. A hybrid plan would combine smaller states into electoral units, while the larger states would elect Rhodes scholars autonomously as they had originally done. This scheme would involve only a single tier

[187] While discussions and analyses continued, two intermediate modifications were adopted: in 1989 larger states were permitted to nominate three candidates, a practice first mentioned in the 1926 District Plan; and Colorado and North Dakota were moved to different districts in an effort to approach a greater equality of population in the western districts in 1991. Alexander to State Secretaries, 27 June 1988, and Annual Memoranda 1991 and 1994; RTA.

[188] Courtney Smith described the major national institutions as 'conspicuously successful' in responding to criticism about the concentration of scholars from a relatively small number of universities and colleges. *AO* 47 (1960), 169–80. He later published an expanded version, with a table of numbers of scholars by endorsing institutions, in *Graduate Journal*, 5/2 (1963), 361–74. These comprehensive institutional statistics have not been published since. Since the election of the class of 1977, when women first became eligible, up to the class of 2000, graduates of only thirteen institutions have won 45.6% of the scholarships.

of election committees in fourteen districts. Under this plan a committee made up of representatives of the states in the district would consider applications which had been received by a secretary, and, on the basis of these applications, they would invite the most promising applicants to an interview, after which the committee would elect the assigned number of Rhodes scholars. The process of reading the dossiers and deciding whom they would interview would thus merge current state and district procedures. The members of these committees would be Rhodes scholars resident in the states, peripatetic Rhodes scholars, and non-Rhodes scholars, following current practice. Furthermore, the districts themselves were restructured. They were smaller and the number of scholarships varied among them.

Planning for a single tier began in tandem with a gradually emerging realignment of the states. This hybrid plan and a revised version of the expanded District Plan (twenty-one districts) were offered for discussion at a meeting of state secretaries held in New York in the autumn of 1994. On 1 November Alexander sent a memorandum outlining the single-tier plan to American Rhodes scholars for their comment, and their response was requested by 15 February 1995. Alexander also set up an advisory committee with ten members, their consultations being conducted by telephone and correspondence, and the committee met in New York City on 8 May. Between 31 March and 9 April Sir Anthony Kenny and Lady Kenny held meetings with Rhodes scholars in Washington, DC, Los Angeles, and Chicago.[189] Both supporters and opponents attended these meetings. One hundred and sixty-nine Rhodes scholars responded in writing to the November memorandum, and only sixty-three expressed opposition.[190]

The opposition was essentially that encountered by all previous proposals for reform beginning with the old claim that the national dispersion of scholarships was better served by the District Plan on the analogy of the US Senate with its fixed number of Senators for each state. The responses this time, however, raised questions about basing the allocation of scholarships on historical application statistics or on population, either university population or general population. In an argument reminiscent of the controversy engendered by the 1923–4 proposal for a committee of review, several respondents argued that replacing the state interviews with a committee's screening of the files of applicants to decide whom to interview removed a personal encounter deemed highly valuable to the process. Moreover, although it was pointed out that the numbers of applications in each of the smaller districts would probably not exceed the numbers already being considered in the larger states, respondents argued that the amount of reading imposed on the new single-tier committees was daunting and would lead to faulty decisions. Both Kenny and Alexander tried to answer these objections, but, although the need for reform was voiced by many, the elimination of the state interviews was regarded as too drastic.

[189] RTR 4 May 1995. A meeting scheduled for New York was cancelled because only two Rhodes scholars accepted the invitation to attend. Kenny commented that 'New York is one of the states which most stands to gain by the proposed reforms.' RTA.

[190] Alexander to Advisory Committee, 5 Apr. 1995; RTA. The opposition was strongest among the youngest Rhodes scholars: 28 of 43 respondents from the classes of 1977 to 1994 were against the plan. Overall, with the exception of the opposition of the younger scholars, it is difficult to discern any clear pattern by category, undoubtedly because of the small numbers involved.

Alexander and Pinney began to see administrative defects in the single-tier system. A major factor in the opposition's view was the increased burden of reading applications. The single-tier scheme, however, suffered from a much more fundamental weakness. It reintroduced the American scholarships' original risk that a state, or a small constituency, would be unable to produce truly competitive candidates year after year. Alexander's confidence in the plan was shaken, for example, when Connecticut's applications dropped from a five-year average of thirty-one to fifteen in 1995, while the plan was being promoted.[191] At least in the arbitrary world of the eight districts, committees would always be able to look to other states in their six- or seven-state supply.

Suffering from these deficiencies, the single-tier plan did not fully recompense its supporters by a sweeping improvement over the old District Plan. Whatever equalization of applicant pools it brought, it was unable to promise full equity among the states and districts. Its most glaring fault, however, was that it was not inherently persuasive as a change. It was too subtle in its reform, so that, unlike Aydelotte's District Plan, it dealt in second-order improvements based on disputable statistics. As a hybrid approach, the single-tier system was at once too timid and too radical. It eliminated the role of the states, in the minds of its opponents, while in the minds of its supporters it did not go far enough in tackling such issues as breaking up the largest states, or making them districts by themselves, or pairing more of the smaller states into single electoral units. However hard Alexander might work to present the plan as preserving the dispositive powers of state representatives as the determining actors in the process, many among the most thoughtful and experienced participants in past procedures remained unconvinced.

Alexander reached the conclusion that difficulties in structuring well-balanced committees with full regard to state representation and the risks inherent in having smaller pools of applicants were severe enough to compromise the attractiveness of the plan. In February 1996 Alexander abandoned his recommendation of the single-tier scheme in favour of a drastic realignment of the eight districts. He recommended to Kenny an eight-district plan with districts ranging in size from four states to eight states. The Trustees approved this realignment at their meeting on 1 March 1996, and the plan was announced to the American Rhodes scholars on 4 April 1996.[192]

On 31 January 1998, Alexander retired as American Secretary. His successor, Elliot F. Gerson (Connecticut and Magdalen 1974), opened his office in Washington, DC, in early 1998, and the files of the American Secretary were shipped from Claremont, California, in the summer of 1998. Gerson graduated from Harvard University in 1974 *summa cum laude* and was elected to a Rhodes scholarship. At Oxford he was awarded an Underhill exhibition at Magdalen College, and he took first-class honours in philosophy, politics, and economics in 1976. After graduating from Yale Law School in 1979, he served as a law clerk in the United States Court of Appeals in 1979. He was awarded the Meritorious Civilian Service Medal for his work as staff assistant to the Secretary of Defense from 1979 to 1980. He served as a clerk to Associate Justice Potter Stewart of the Supreme

---

[191] Alexander to Kenny, 16 Feb. 1996; RTA.   [192] Kenny to Alexander 4 Mar. 1996; RTA.

Court of the United States from 1980 to 1981. He entered the private practice of law, and in 1983 was appointed deputy Attorney General of the state of Connecticut. Gerson joined the Travelers Corporation in 1986, becoming president of its health and life insurance company in 1993. When the company was merged with the health insurance subsidiary of the Metropolitan Life Insurance Company, he became successively executive vice-president and president of the new entity. In 1997 he became chief executive officer of ETC, a holding company that invests in and operates education, training, and technology businesses, and in 1999 he founded a new health-advisory company. When he became Secretary, he immediately created a web site for the office of the American Secretary on the Internet. A new age had dawned.

4. AN ALUMNI ASSOCIATION

Gregarious Americans in Oxford

The first class of American Rhodes scholars had entered Oxford in Michaelmas term 1904. Facing the uncertainties of being pioneers they sought mutual support by organizing a club for themselves. Not only did they imagine themselves less familiar with English education and customs than the colonial scholars, but also they found themselves the objects of a paradoxical curiosity and indifference. They delighted in recounting their adventures with Oxford men who asked about their firearms and their chewing gum.[193] In preparation for their arrival, members of the class of 1904 had organized themselves into a 'temporary organization' on board the SS *Ivernia*, and, as the American Club with a full array of officers, they acquired rooms in the High St. in 1905. They eventually set themselves up in club rooms at 167 St Giles, opposite St John's College. Finding these rooms cramped, they first planned to move to rooms over the Old Bank in the High St., but when that did not work out, they remained in St Giles until they moved in 1909 to 49 Cornmarket, near the entrance to the Oxford Union.[194] The Club offered a lively programme of debate, distinguished visitors, and libations. 'Jolly-ups' opened and closed each term, between which debates and visiting speakers provided intellectual stimulation. The Club also sponsored an annual American Thanksgiving Day service, with a distinguished preacher, and a Thanksgiving feast in the evening with English approximations of harvest foods: 'mock turkey', vegetables 'sent over from Brussels', and 'American ices' served '*a l'Anglaise* in thimbles'.[195] The Thanksgiving Day festivals were important occasions. At the feast in 1907, at which 130 were present, W. T. Stead, as the honoured guest, proposed the toast to the King and the President. Through

---

[193] See, for example, Oxford Letter by Beverly D. Tucker (Virginia and Christ Church 1905), 29 Nov. 1907, *Alumni Magazine*, 1/1 (1907), 12–15.

[194] The earliest history of the Club was already lost by 1922, when a plea for information was published in *AO* 9 (1922), 112–13. The early locations of the Club, however, were reported in the *Alumni Magazine*, 1/1 (1907), 12 ff.; 1/2 (1908), 6; 2/1 (1909), 5; and *AO* 2 (1915), 192.

[195] Tucker, Oxford Letter, 29 Nov. 1907, *Alumni Magazine*, 1/1 (1907), 12. Also R. M. Scoon (New York and Merton 1907), Oxford Letter, *Alumni Magazine*, 2/1 (1909), 5.

the years the American Club heard, among others, Mark Twain in 1907,[196] William Jennings Bryan in 1910, President A. T. Hadley of Yale, Josiah Royce, Lord Birkenhead, Lady Astor,[197] H. A. L. Fisher, Rebecca West, Bertrand Russell, G. K. Chesterton, and from the Rhodes Trust, Parkin, Wylie, and Kerr.[198] When Theodore Roosevelt gave the Romanes Lecture in 1910, the American Club entertained him and Mrs Roosevelt, their daughter Alice, and their son Kermit at lunch on 7 June.[199] Their debates were spirited affairs, with subjects ranging from Prohibition to 'Resolved: that residence in Oxford involves a subtle deterioration of the moral fibre.'[200]

The Club was not without criticism. W. T. Harris, United States Commissioner of Education, was fervent in his attack in 1906 on 'allowing clanship to be cultivated by our contingent at Oxford if they formed an American Club or were brought together in one College'.[201] Others concurred. W. W. Thayer (New Hampshire and Magdalen 1905), commenting on allegations of American 'insularity', quoted the *Daily Mail* which had sniffed that while 'Englishmen go out of their way to make an American feel at home, the latter "retires into his shell—the club—where he reads American papers, discusses American politics, sings American songs, and might, indeed just as well be back in America for all the good he does to himself or to Oxford."' Thayer, president of the Alumni Association, objected, claiming that the Club only gave Americans 'an occasional common meeting place without interfering with their loyalty to Oxford or their participation in its undergraduate life'.[202] Some Americans did not join, because they apparently shared the opinions of the critics. Other clubs were founded; George Parkin, Jr., who was involved in the founding of the British-American Club, wrote to Aydelotte asking him to be a patron of the new club.[203] The possibility of the Rhodes scholars joining in a

[196] The meeting at which Twain was present was chaired by Ralph Blodgett (Missouri and Wadham 1904), who was also from Hannibal, Mo. One of the most gregarious of Rhodes scholars, he was the source of the often quoted story of the self-introducing American. On his first night in hall he walked up to the undergraduates standing there and said, 'My name is Blodgett, I hail from Missouri.' Paul Kieffer, *AO* 27 (1940), 106.

[197] Lord and Lady Astor invited American Rhodes scholars to Cliveden for outings. One such occasion on 23 May 1925 was described with great verve by William Blackburn (South Carolina and Hertford 1923) as 'a good old-fashioned "spend the day" invitation'. *AO* 12 (1925), 83 She held a ball for American and dominion Rhodes scholars on 15 March 1926, which was attended by the Prince of Wales. *AO* 13 (1926), 40 and 89. Crane Brinton wryly noted in 1936 that Lord Astor's horse Rhodes Scholar, although the favourite for the St Leger, was unplaced. *AO* 23 (1936), 286. In 1938 the Astors invited the Rhodes scholars to tea at Cliveden, and Lothian was present. *AO* 25 (1938), 166. Penn Kimball (Connecticut and Balliol 1937) recalled teaching George Bernard Shaw the Lambeth Walk at one of these parties. *AO* 80 (1993), 143.

[198] *Alumni Magazine passim* and *AO passim*.

[199] H. G. Cochran (Delaware and St. John's 1908), Oxford Letter, *Alumni Magazine*, 3/3 (1910), 5–6. More than 160 persons were present. Also *AO* 68 (1981), 159 ff.

[200] A debate on Prohibition was held as early as 1908. *Alumni Magazine*, 1/2 (1908), 6. The debate on the deterioration of moral fibre was recalled by E. H. Eckel (Missouri and Wadham 1910) in his class letter almost thirty years later. *AO* 26 (1939), 299.

[201] W. T. Harris, United States Commissioner of Education, to Parkin, 5 Nov. 1906; RTF 1233.

[202] *AO* 2 (1915), 40. London *Daily Mail*, 11 Oct. 1910.

[203] G. R. Parkin, Jr., to Aydelotte, 28 June 1919, and Aydelotte to Parkin, 23 July 1919; RTA. In typical fashion, Aydelotte in accepting went one step further and suggested the formation of 'a chain of British-American clubs in various universities over here'.

federation of the Colonial Club, the Anglo-German Society, and the American Club was considered. While nothing seems to have come of this plan at that time, nothing prevented the Americans from holding 'a joint binge' with the Colonials.[204] Toward the end of its life the Club was forced to move several times 'on account of the Club's two chronic troubles—the lack of funds and the superfluity of beer'. In a speech in New York Kerr reported in 1927 that the American Club had died.[205]

A natural response to the logistics of bringing the American Rhodes scholars to Oxford was the practice of having them travel together from a single port of embarkation. The pleasure of one another's company on the sea voyage made Rhodes scholars eager to travel together, and, since they had to pay their own passage, the practical advantage of group fares provided an economic incentive.[206] The class of 1904 had sailed on the SS *Ivernia*, and subsequent classes were able to thrill to the romance of transatlantic voyages on, among other ships, the *Mauretania*, the *Albania*, the *Aquitania*, the *Leviathan*, the *America*, the *Queen Mary*, the *Queen Elizabeth*, the *United States*, and the *QE II*. Group travel provided other opportunities for social bonding.[207] Gatherings in New York, however, offered them and members of the AARS resident in the New York area the chance of arranging social events that would bring old and new Rhodes scholars into contact with one another. Because many of the Rhodes scholars had never been to New York before, arrangements for sightseeing excursions and dinners before the sailings became common. The *American Oxonian* annually announced these arrangements, inviting older Rhodes scholars to attend.[208]

[204] F. C. Light (New Mexico and Hertford 1908), Oxford Letter, *Alumni Magazine*, 4/1 (1911), 5. The American and Colonial Clubs enjoyed friendly relations, holding reciprocal smokers. *Alumni Magazine*, 3/1 (1910), 8.

[205] William Blackburn reported Michaelmas term 1925 to have been 'a trying term' for the Club, because the presence of one of its speakers, Shapurji Saklatvala, Communist MP for Battersea, precipitated a small riot to which the police had to be summoned. *AO* 13 (1926), 3–4. The 'Oxford Letters' in the *American Oxonian* described the collapse of the American Club in successive issues: *AO* 11 (1924), 51 and 76; 12 (1925), 16; 13 (1926), 3–4, 40. The actual end was reported by Dexter Bennett (Wyoming and Oriel 1924), *AO* 14 (1927), 2. Kerr referred to the demise of the American Club in a speech he gave on 22 Dec. 1927 at a meeting of the English-Speaking Union in New York City. He attributed its death to lack of attendance, which gave evidence that Americans were taking 'a normal part in the life of Oxford'. *AO* 15 (1928), 58–9. The American Club was revived after the Second World War.

[206] The Rhodes Trust did not reimburse scholars' travel expenses to and from Oxford until 1973.

[207] On board they were entertained at dinners and they entertained their fellow passengers. Such occasions could be quite grand, like the tea on board the *Adriatic* in 1918 at which Viscount Grey of Fallodon spoke. *AO* 7 (1920), 101, RTF 1233 A photograph of a programme of entertainment aboard the *Franconia* in 1913 was published in *AO* 26 (1939), at 208.

[208] *AO passim*. The Munich crisis thwarted the plans of the class of 1939 to sail on the brand new *Nieuw Amsterdam*. The war broke the pattern of the New York gatherings, and in the early 1950s Courtney Smith's practice was to invite the new Rhodes scholars to come to Swarthmore for tea. John Nason, *AO* 26 (1939), 59. In 1963 the dinners in New York were resumed. Since then Barber, Alexander, and Gerson have invited members of the board of direction to lunch with the new scholars, and until 1998 the Canadian Rhodes scholars with the Canadian Secretary, A. R. A. Scace (Ontario and Corpus Christi College 1961), joined them. The sailings themselves ended in 1981. The elaborate weekend in New York or Washington was reintroduced under the sponsorship of the AARS by its president, Robert G. Edge (Georgia and Oriel 1960), in 1996.

Gregarious Americans Go Home

The time had come for the members of the class of 1904 to go home. Before departing, however, they realized the need for an organization to keep alive the bonds they had formed over the past three years. This decision, based on nostalgia and personal loyalty, would have important consequences for the Rhodes scholarships in the United States. In December 1907 the newly formed Alumni Association published the first issue of the *Alumni Magazine*, which printed the constitution and 'A Programme' by the president, Richard F. Scholz (Wisconsin and Worcester 1904), in which he set forth the aims and mission of the Association. Certain features which were to be permanent were introduced: a Letter from Oxford, written by a Rhodes scholar in residence, and an address list. This issue, however, did not carry the other permanent feature, the 'Personals', which later became the annual class letters. Earle W. Murray (Kansas and St John's 1904) was elected general secretary and treasurer of the Association, offices which carried the duties of editing the magazine. One of the objects of the new Association was to try to keep alive the old camaraderie through regular printed and personal communications and by holding periodic reunions, the first of which was a two-week cruise on the Great Lakes in 1911. The members present voted to hold these reunions quadrennially with the next one to be held in San Francisco.[209] Other reunions, on a less than national scale, were held from time to time, and class reunions and periodic dinners across the nation sustained the fraternal spirit.[210] The Alumni Association of Rhodes Scholars remained in existence until it was reorganized as the Association of American Rhodes Scholars in 1928.

The most important instrumentality for maintaining the sense of sodality among the returned scholars was the publication of a magazine, first the *Alumni Magazine*, and then the *American Oxonian*. These publications quickly assumed the character of a university alumni newsletter, a fraternity magazine aimed at keeping brotherly bonds alive, and a journal of general and scholarly interest. Their greatest value lay in the annual class letters, which through the years have generated an archive of collective biography of unusual value. Because of the dispersion of the scholars, the variety of their professions, the disparities in their views, all against a backdrop of the shared experience of application and interview, of matriculation and academic work and play in Oxford, the Rhodes scholars kept themselves together by the simple means of ritualized communication. Even if they did not all go back to their home states and even if their occupations tended to cluster in a relatively narrow range of professions, their differences and similarities could all be celebrated in a regular exchange of triumph and envy. The honours that came to one were noted, and the disappointments of another at not having been all that successful were ruefully recorded as well. 'The best men for the world's fight' had a vehicle for preening themselves while assuring the continuity of their network with one another.

---

[209] In all fourteen attended, but only seven were able to stay for the entire fortnight. *Alumni Magazine*, 4/2 (1911), 2 ff., and 4/3 (1911), 1–4. The San Francisco reunion was not held.

[210] Two important dinners were held in Boston and New York in Sept. 1914, at which the scholars present discussed the newly launched *American Oxonian*. *AO* 1 (1914), 106. Rhodes scholars in the New York area, for example, were reminded in 1934 that a weekly luncheon was held on Wednesdays at the British Luncheon Club. *AO* 21 (1934), 207.

When women became Rhodes scholars, they joined in, bringing their sororal touch to this previously masculine club. From election list to obituary a Rhodes scholar can expect the span of his or her life to be encapsulated in the pages of the *American Oxonian*.

The *Alumni Magazine* was a brave, but poorly supported, founding effort. Its doughty editor, Earle 'Pat' Murray, stressed in the first issue the value of personal communications: 'We must all realize that it is only by concerted action along these lines that we can hope to continue our existence.'[211] Its existence was destined to be hand-to-mouth. To help defray expenses the magazine accepted advertising from book publishers and business card advertisements from Rhodes scholars, or what it could get. Volume 6 was published in only two numbers. Lack of finances, ever the magazine's nemesis, then claimed victory. Murray plaintively reported in August 1912 that he 'had paid more than there is in the treasury'. Two-fifths of the subscriptions were unpaid, and Murray had been forced to advance between $40 and $70 'all the time'.[212]

Having offered his resignation eight months before, Murray was able to announce in April 1913 that he had been succeeded as secretary and treasurer of the Alumni Association by Grover Cleveland Huckaby (Louisiana and Wadham 1908). When the *Alumni Magazine* had quietly sputtered out, Huckaby tried to light a rocket. With the best of intentions, Huckaby let his ambition far exceed his grasp, causing great embarrassment to Parkin, Wylie, and the Trustees. His idea was to produce an international magazine under the title 'The Colossus' (of Rhodes!). He prepared a prospectus which was sent in eye-catching envelopes boldly seeking subscriptions. He wrote to Parkin on 18 March 1913 outlining his plans for the magazine. Parkin, ill at the time, did not immediately reply, but Huckaby proceeded. The three issues of 'The Colossus' each year were to be comprehensive in their coverage of Oxford, the Rhodes scholars, and their homelands. The first issue in each volume would be a statistical yearbook giving information about Oxford and detailed information about all scholars, including their annual income. The second issue would provide attractive information about the scholarships, including travel articles from all over. The third issue would be devoted to articles of general educational interest. Huckaby had begun the design for its cover: Rhodes as Apollo Belvedere holding a globe in one hand and a dove in the other, with a banderole bearing the words 'I direct my Trustees to establish certain scholarships,' with the drapery of the 'English', German, and American flags above.[213]

Parkin and Wylie were aghast at what they saw as an unauthorized and ill-advised American takeover. Wylie wrote to Parkin on 10 May to report that he had 'only just received the enclosed horror of an envelope' with an advertisement, a covering letter, and 'blanks to fill up'. Wylie fumed that Huckaby had gone off on his own, without seeking

---

[211] *Alumni Magazine*, 1/1 (Dec. 1907), 3. Also see Murray's reminiscences about the *Magazine*'s beginnings in a note in the class letter in 1938. *AO* 25 (1938), 244–5.

[212] *Alumni Magazine*, 5/3 (Aug. 1912), 1, and 6/1–2 (Apr. 1913), 1–2. For a brief history of the *Alumni Magazine* see Alexander, 'The Ninetieth Anniversary of *The Alumni Magazine* of the Alumni Association of American Rhodes Scholars', *AO* 85 (1998), 3 ff.

[213] Huckaby to Parkin, 18 Mar. 1913; RTF 2120. Huckaby felt justified in putting Rhodes in the guise of Apollo, because, as he claimed, the original Colossus of Rhodes was a statue of Apollo. The Apollo Belvedere, one surmises, was artistic licence.

any advice, and he had transformed the 'Alumni Magazine of the <u>American</u> [Wylie's underlining] Rhodes Scholars' into this unwarranted plan for an international magazine. Wylie wrote, 'It is extraordinary that Huckaby should have no feeling as to the inappropriateness in suddenly assuming that the Magazine represents *all* [his emphasis] Rhodes Scholars.' His choler rising, Wylie acknowledged that the American Alumni Association was independent, but 'it seems . . . hardly decent to launch a thing like this upon the world as representing the Rhodes Scholarships'. Wylie ended the letter, 'The notion that this envelope has been going out, as he [Huckaby] says, "all over the world to educational institutions and libraries", to say nothing of "publishing houses, banks, hotels and art dealers" is simply terrible. I should be alarmed for the consequences if one of these were found by Lord Rosebery on his breakfast table!' Parkin and Wylie decided to send cables forthwith to Huckaby and the president of the Alumni Association, W. W. Thayer. In their joint cable on 14 May to Thayer, which came as close to an order to cease and desist as they had in their power to issue, they expressed their anxiety over the 'objectionable' change 'from American Alumni Magazine to General Scholarship organ not justified without consulting Scholars of other communities'.[214]

Parkin wrote to Huckaby in patient and kindly language chiding him for moving so precipitately in changing the American publication into an international journal 'without a great deal of consultation'. Although Parkin had thought of such a publication earlier, the time was not ripe. Huckaby had made a 'fundamental mistake' in trying to convert the *Alumni Magazine* into a colossus. He was particularly annoyed with the envelope: the shock given recipients of the envelope would 'seem to them like an effort to work out a great educational idea of world-wide interest on lines somewhat similar to those used in connection with local agricultural Shows'. Parkin, seriously ill, did not need a colossus at that time, yet his humane spirit shone through this episode. Tough, angry, and personally annoyed at a time of physical stress, he nevertheless showed a touching concern for Huckaby, and offered to help with the expenses the latter had incurred.[215] Huckaby withdrew from the editorship of the magazine that never appeared.

The need to replace the defunct and editor-less *Alumni Magazine* remained. Aydelotte, in a brief history of the *American Oxonian*, recalled how he had issued a prospectus 'toward the end of 1913, or early in 1914', laying out the plans for the publication. Parkin urged Aydelotte, then a professor at Indiana University, to assume the editorship. After alluding to Huckaby, who had acted 'in the most honorable way about the whole thing', Parkin expressed his confidence that Aydelotte could make the American magazine 'something useful', and after some years have elapsed 'we may develop something on more general lines that will serve all the countries interested'.[216] The first issue of the

---

[214] Wylie to Parkin, 10 May 1913; RTF 2120. Parkin and Wylie to Thayer, 14 May 1913; RTF 2120.

[215] Parkin to Huckaby, 5 May 1913 and continued on 14 May 1913; RTF 2120. No trace has been found of the infamous original materials announcing 'The Colossus'.

[216] Aydelotte, 'Pioneer Days of the *American Oxonian*', AO 26 (1939), 85 ff. Parkin to Aydelotte from New York, 14 Nov. 1913; RTA 3. Aydelotte said that he had been in contact with Talbot M. Papineau (Quebec and Brasenose 1905), his close friend, who wanted the Canadian Rhodes scholars to participate. Tragically Papineau was killed in the war, and no other Canadian came forward. Had such collaboration occurred the magazine would have been named The 'North American Oxonian'.

American Oxonian, Frank Aydelotte, editor, appeared in April 1914. Intended to be published semi-annually, until support and material warranted its anticipated enlargement to a quarterly, one of the announced aims of the *American Oxonian* was to publicize the scholarships by expanding its subscription list to include high school and college libraries. Aydelotte, uncertain about the value of personal news, invited readers' comments on the subject. His notion was to print only a few pages of such news, but he was willing to print more if so desired. Seven pages, not arranged as class letters, carried brief notices of the activities and whereabouts of the scholars.[217] Notices of prizes at Oxford and the list of newly elected Rhodes scholars were printed. The lead article in the October issue was a symposium on the lack of competition for the Rhodes scholarships. Parkin provided an article on the new tripartite schedule of elections, and Aydelotte published the first of many accounts of the involvement of neutral American Rhodes scholars in the war. The main lines of the magazine were fully formed by now, and the second issue had a touching obituary of Paul Williams (Iowa and Lincoln 1913), who at age 20 had died in a fall while climbing in Switzerland. In addition, five books were reviewed. Volume 2, which marked the beginning of quarterly publication, opened with a statement of purpose and several highly favourable press comments.[218] The *American Oxonian* was off to a sound start. The Trustees gave it an annual subsidy of £20 in 1917, which was increased in 1921 to £50 and ceased in 1928. Sir Lewis Michell declared the magazine 'to be a sane one & always an interesting one . . . The magazine deserves our support.'[219] By carrying general articles, news about Oxford and Rhodes scholars, information about the scholarships, memorials to beloved professors, and appeals for funds by colleges and the University itself, the *American Oxonian* thus systematically performed a service typical of an alumni publication of an American college or university.

After Aydelotte assumed the presidency of Swarthmore College, he was succeeded as editor of the *American Oxonian* in 1921 by C. F. Tucker Brooke (West Virginia and St John's 1904). Tucker Brooke as editor brought literary sensibilities while consolidating the features of the magazine. The editors after Brooke, with their terms of office, were:

Alan Valentine (Pennsylvania and Balliol 1922), then assistant professor of English and dean of men, Swarthmore College, and assistant American secretary, 1930–6

Crane Brinton (Massachusetts and New College 1919), professor of ancient and modern history, Harvard University, 1936–43

B. Harvie Branscomb (Alabama and Wadham 1914), then professor of New Testament and dean of the Duke University Divinity School, 1943–6

Gordon K. Chalmers (Rhode Island and Wadham 1926), President of Kenyon College, 1946–9

Paul S. Havens (New Jersey and University 1925), President of Wilson College, 1949–56

---

[217] Vol. 1, no. 2, printed more news notes reverting to the arrangement by classes.

[218] The Manchester *Guardian* compared *AO* with other periodicals published by Oxford undergraduates, none of them 'of quite this purposeful and mature sobriety'. The *Dial* and the *Oxford Magazine* commended it to the attention of others, not just the Rhodes scholars. *AO* 2 (1915) inside front cover.

[219] Aydelotte, 'The American Scholarships', in Eldon (ed.), *The First Fifty Years*, 192. Lewis Michell to Parkin, 5 Oct. 1916; RTF 2120.

E. Wilson Lyon (Mississippi and St John's 1925), President of Pomona College, 1956–63

Carleton B. Chapman (Alabama and St John's 1936), professor of internal medicine, University of Texas, 1963–5

Deric O'Bryan (New Mexico and New College 1936), US Geological Survey, 1965–70

Aldon D. Bell (Oklahoma and Hertford 1951), professor of history, University of Washington, 1970–7

Charles G. Bolté (New Hampshire and New College 1947), freelance writer, formerly with the Carnegie Endowment for World Peace, 1977–88

John H. Funari (Virginia and Queen's 1951), formerly dean of the Graduate School of Public and International Affairs, University of Pittsburgh, 1988–95

James J. O'Toole (California and Hertford 1966), then senior fellow of the Aspen Institute, 1996–97

David Alexander (Tennessee and Christ Church 1954), formerly President of Pomona College and formerly American Secretary, 1998–2000

Todd R. Breyfogle (Colorado and Corpus Christi College 1988), fellow and program officer of the Liberty Fund, 2001–

Like any enterprise the quality and character of the *Oxonian* varied with the energy, commitment, ambition, and philosophy of its editors. Under Aydelotte the magazine was fiercely pro-Allies; articles about the voluntary participation of American Rhodes scholars, in spite of American neutrality, kept readers abreast of these patriotic activities. The next editor, Crane Brinton, was a fierce controversialist. He set out his platform in his first issue: 'THE OXONIAN ought to be something more than just another alumni bulletin. In this country it would not be feasible to imitate the Australians, who have produced in their *Australian Rhodes Review* a periodical in the grand manner of the *Yale Review*.' He intended to make the *Oxonian* 'a pretty complete account of [Rhodes's] experiment', and 'distinctions' and 'disgraces' were to be recorded—'jail sentences as well as Nobel Prizes'.[220] Brinton's assertive editorship did not set well with all his readers. Two highly critical letters were published in January 1938.[221] By any standard, Brinton was an excellent editor, whose personality and sense of style lifted the *American Oxonian* well above the ruck of alumni publications.

Of the recent editors, both Charles Bolté and John Funari also evinced a taste for controversy. Under Bolté the *Oxonian* twice changed its format, and he announced his objective 'to produce a magazine at least half as distinguished as its readership'.[222] He started a series about Rhodes scholars and their careers under the title 'The World's Fight'. Funari's tenure covered the years of the controversy over the testamentary schools, about which he published a number of pieces. Both Bolté and Funari were also ready to insert

---

[220] *AO* 23 (1936), 31.

[221] Neil Carothers (Arkansas and Pembroke 1904) expressed the feelings of those who objected to the intrusion of controversy into the pages of the *Oxonian*: 'I don't want to see THE OXONIAN become the vehicle of petty and partisan discussion irrelevant to those matters with which Rhodes men are concerned. But if its columns are to be open to the ventilation of personal spleen, I should like to be so informed, as I have a number of contributions to make.' *AO* 25 (1938), 42.

[222] *AO* 64 (1977), 200.

their own comments as full editorials or as smaller editorial comments. On balance, however, anyone who studies the full sweep of the *American Oxonian* will conclude that the magazine has remained at heart little more than an alumni bulletin, in Crane Brinton's locution. Carleton Chapman in 1963 in a half-century history of the *Oxonian* asked if it should be content to be the annual directory and the repository of class letters; 'on the other hand,' he wrote, 'it *could* proceed to develop its potential as a forum for [Rhodes scholars] and as such *could* perform a function the importance of which would be all out of proportion to the size of its circulation.' That ambition is yet to be realized.[223]

The Association of American Rhodes Scholars, the American Trust for Oxford University, and the Eastman Professorship

While alumni associations are virtually universal in American universities and colleges, an association of Rhodes scholars differed from institutional alumni organizations in two important respects: first, it was not sponsored by the University or by the Rhodes Trust, but was the spontaneous creation of its founding members; and further, its loyalties to Oxford University and its colleges were mediated through a sense of fraternity that came from the shared experiences of winning a Rhodes scholarship and attending Oxford. These differences meant that the Alumni Association of Rhodes Scholars, and its successor, had the additional responsibility of promoting the scholarships and enhancing their reputation.

What the Alumni Association did not have was a legal status, because it was not formally affiliated with any corporate institution. In 1928 a committee of lawyers had drafted a constitution and by-laws. The new organization was to be called the Association of American Rhodes Scholars,[224] and it was to be legally organized as a voluntary association. In addition to holding meetings and reunions[225] and publishing the *American Oxonian*, its purposes were to encourage and promote among Americans 'an appreciation of the advantages' of educational and cultural exchanges among English-speaking peoples of the world, to receive gifts and to hold property, and 'to cause some return to be made to the University of Oxford or to any or all of the colleges or halls therein, for

---

[223] *AO* 50 (1963), 26. The verdict of T. J. and K. Schaeper in *Cowboys into Gentlemen* (New York: Berghahn Books, 1998) is that 'it continues to be a relatively tame publication and not the product of a close-knit band of revolutionaries', p. 339. In a survey conducted by the AARS in 1998, a majority of Rhodes scholars who responded admitted that their primary interest lay in the class letters of those classes who were up at Oxford with them. Relatively few read the entire magazine.

[224] Elmer Davis objected to the 'phonetically unhappy combination' of its initials, AARS. *AO* 26 (1939), 44.

[225] In addition to smaller reunions held by individual classes, the Alumni Association held its reunion in 1911, and the AARS has sponsored four national reunions, in June 1933 at Swarthmore (197 were present; 114 Rhodes scholars and 83 wives), in June 1947 at Princeton (365 were present; 222 Rhodes scholars and 143 wives and children), in June 1965 at Swarthmore (497 present; 315 Rhodes scholars and 182 wives and children), and in June 1993 in Washington, DC, at which almost 1,300 were present. President Bill Clinton invited his classmates to the White House, and he attended a garden party given by the British Ambassador at the Ambassador's residence.

the benefit from that University which American Rhodes Scholars have enjoyed'.[226] With forty-nine Rhodes scholars present at the Harvard Club in New York City on 18 June, the constitution was approved subject to the receipt of a majority of postal votes of the Rhodes scholars. The secretary, F. F. Russell (New York and Brasenose 1911), issued a press release announcing the formation of the Association of American Rhodes Scholars and the American Trust for Oxford University, a tax-exempt endowment fund for the benefit of Oxford and its entities. Russell's announcement continued, 'The scheme for an international university endowment is said to be unique in educational history.' The goal for the endowment had not been definitely set, but by the fiftieth anniversary of the scholarships in 1953 they hoped to have raised a 'substantial sum' for the University.[227] Oxford had never seen anything like this before, nor had Cambridge; it remained for the universities to create their own fund-raising bodies well in the future.[228]

Dr Abraham Flexner, formerly Secretary of the General Education Board and one of Aydelotte's oldest friends, had persuaded George Eastman, founder of the Eastman Kodak Company and philanthropist, that endowing a professorship in American studies at Oxford would be intellectually valuable to the University and, like the Rhodes scholarships, it would become an instrument for furthering closer political and cultural ties between Great Britain and the United States. In a letter written to Aydelotte on 13 September 1928 Eastman offered to give the AARS the sum of $200,000 for the endowment of a professorship of American studies at Oxford. He cited Rhodes's example and expressed the hope that others from other countries would be moved to do the same. He proposed four conditions: (1) that the incumbent be an eminent American selected by a board composed of members from Oxford University and the AARS; (2) that the term of the professorship should be not less than one year, 'preferably two to five years or even more'; (3) that the holders of the chair should 'represent different subjects' and come from different parts of the country; and (4) 'that the incumbent should regard it as his special duty to come into contact, formal and informal, with the groups of students—British, Colonial and American—who are likely to be engaged in significant activities'.[229] Aydelotte formally communicated the offer in a letter 23 October 1928 to the Vice-Chancellor, Francis Pember, and asked for the University's acceptance.[230]

---

[226] *AO* 15 (1928), 79 ff. The 'Call to Meeting' issued by the president Leonard W. Cronkhite (Rhode Island and Worcester 1905) was inserted into the issue.

[227] *AO* 15 (1928), 132.

[228] *The Times* of London published a leading article on 24 May 1928: 'There can be no day more appropriate than Empire day for making grateful acknowledgment' of the creation of the Trust. Crediting Aydelotte by name as one of the originators of 'this movement which has begun spontaneously and most auspiciously', *The Times* declared, 'There could be no better evidence of the vitality of RHODES's benefaction or of the fundamental soundness of his view when he established it' than the new Trust. Reprinted in *AO* 15 (1928), 167–8. Donald Rivkin (Iowa and Merton 1948), administrator of the American Trust from 1974 to 1998, reported that in the quarter of a century during which he was administrator more than $15,000,000 had been contributed to Oxford University and its entities and that the annual rate of contributions had reached $1,000,000. *AO* 86 (1999), 23 ff.

[229] Eastman to Aydelotte, 13 Sept. 1928; RTA.

[230] Aydelotte to the Vice-Chancellor, 23 Oct. 1928; RTA.

The authorities in Oxford, while grateful, were somewhat puzzled about this benefaction and troubled by some of its terms. Flexner, Rhodes Memorial Professor at Oxford in 1928, wrote that Kerr, whom he had seen in London, had expressed a concern that 'Oxford people are a little touchy on the subject of both Rhodes things and America. They are beginning to ask themselves whether the Rhodes folks aren't a little too prominent and a little too active.' Any gesture by American Rhodes scholars must not appear to be either interference or 'even doing something for the old place, but rather as a warm-hearted expression of gratitude for what Oxford has done for the Rhodes Scholars and for America—that—rather than an attempt to remedy defects or improve conditions'.[231] The substantive issue was the proposed designation of the chair as a professorship of American studies. Wylie wrote a series of letters, pointing out that the existing professorships of Spanish and Italian studies were intended to cover the history and literature of these countries. He asked if that was not too narrow a limitation for the systematic and comprehensive exposition of American contributions to 'the many problems of modern civilization'. Kerr shared this view, and Flexner reported his concern that the professorship of American studies 'might just be another professorship of American history', an outcome Flexner knew was not Eastman's intention. After much discussion the Vice-Chancellor decided to recommend that it simply be called the Eastman visiting professorship and that the terms of reference of the professorship be as broad as possible, so that it might be held by a person 'eminent in teaching or research in any branch of University study'.[232]

Wylie and Kerr reminded Aydelotte of the political complexity that had affected the University's response. The University was struggling to raise money for its own priorities, in particular, a project for the expansion of the Ashmolean Museum and the extension of the Taylor Institution. The University also urgently needed help to improve the Bodleian Library. In the face of these pressing University needs, Eastman's gift of an unwanted professorship rankled some Oxonian sensibilities, and the basic idea of creating a chair in American studies was seen as otiose at best.[233] Kerr wrote to Aydelotte his frank assessment of these sensitivities, and he urged that, if at all possible, the first announcement of the activities of the AARS be 'that it had placed a sum at the disposal of the Vice-Chancellor for some purpose for which Oxford is trying to raise money'. Kerr recommended that if the AARS were to 'show recognition of what Rhodes and Oxford have done for them' by contributing 'quite a small sum like £10,000' as a contribution to the 'Taylorian-Ashmolean problem', the Foundation 'would go off to the best possible start'. Kerr, after declaring his belief in the usefulness of the Eastman professorship, wrote that in the circumstances, 'I am sure that from the point of view of Oxford it will make all the difference if your first act is to meet a need which Oxford recognises, rather

---

[231] Flexner to Aydelotte, 25 Oct. 1928; RTA.

[232] Wylie to Aydelotte, 5 Oct. 9 Oct., and 9 Nov. 1928. Pember, Vice-Chancellor, to Aydelotte, 26 Nov. 1928. RTA. Pember concluded with a cautious comment: 'One cannot of course predict with absolute certainty what a body like the University will decide . . . I personally should very much like to see these first-fruits of the activities of the Association of American Rhodes Scholars accepted by the University.'

[233] The Harmsworth professorship in American history had been established in 1922.

than to supply a need which you recognise that Oxford lacks!'[234] While the Taylor Institution had to await other support, the Hebdomadal Council agreed after further negotiations to submit the decree establishing the professorship to Congregation. On 4 June 1929 Congregation voted to accept the offer and establish the George Eastman visiting professorship for an American citizen 'eminent in teaching or research in any branch of University study' and to 'record its gratitude to Mr. Eastman and to the association for their munificence'.[235]

Aydelotte's discussions with A. D. Lindsay, Master of Balliol (they had lunch together with Eastman in January 1929), led to the attachment of the professorship to Balliol College. Lindsay, after consulting his colleagues at Balliol, reported that they were 'very keen' to have the professorship attached to the college.[236] This collegiate affiliation was of crucial importance; so was housing. Eastman, the practical man of business, had definite ideas about the kind of house to be sought. He suggested that the house be selected 'for its suitability of the plumbing and heating arrangements and that these be installed after purchase'.[237] A house at 18 Norham Gardens came into the market, and Aydelotte wrote to Eastman about it. One big hindrance stood in the way: income from the $200,000 endowment would not be sufficient to pay an adequate stipend to attract the 'best American professors' and cover the other expenses, including mortgage payments. An undesirable expedient would be appointing professors only two years out of three. 'If we had another $100,000 of endowment', the expenses of stipend, mortgage payments on the house, and reimbursement for British income tax could all be met. By return mail, Eastman simply wrote: 'I have no doubt but that the extra $100,000 which you suggest will be necessary to properly finance the Professorship undertaking; therefore I enclose herewith check on the Bankers Trust Company for this amount. I am also enclosing copies of specifications for the heating and plumbing installations.'[238] A commodious house at 18 Norham Gardens was acquired. Eventually the house, which was too large for its purpose, was sold, and after a period of renting property, in the mid-1950s the AARS decided to proceed with the construction of a house. With Balliol's offer of a site near its sports grounds on a lease for sixty years and for as long as the professorship was to be attached to Balliol, the AARS began construction of Eastman House in Jowett Walk in August 1959.[239]

The first Eastman Professor was John Livingston Lowes, professor of English at Harvard. Following a general cycle of humanities, natural science, and social science, the

[234] Kerr to Aydelotte, 4 Dec. 1928; RTA.   [235] Decree 4 June 1929; RTA.
[236] Aydelotte to Wylie, 18 Jan. 1929; RTA.
[237] Eastman to Aydelotte, 5 Feb. 1930. He did not believe Oxford plumbing and heating arrangements would 'be wholly satisfactory to an American occupant'. He thought a crude oil system for heating and hot water would provide 'a plenteous supply of hot water', and he helpfully added, 'I have had considerable experience in this line and would be glad to suggest, or scrutinize any plans proposed.' RTA.
[238] Aydelotte to Eastman, 13 May 1930. Eastman to Aydelotte, 20 May 1930. RTA. A brief article describing 18 Norham Gardens and Eastman's additional donation was published in AO 17 (1930), 113–14.
[239] The construction of Eastman House cost $110,165, a sum which was paid from the income reserves accumulated by the AARS during the war-imposed hiatus in the professorship. An account of the building of the house may be found in AO 48 (1961), 54–6 with a photograph. This article by Emory H. Niles was reprinted in AO's Eastman professorship anniversary issue in 1980. AO 67/2 (1980).

electors have selected professors 'eminent in teaching or research in any branch of University study' including literature, ancient and modern history, the natural sciences, medicine, mathematics, social sciences, anthropology, political science, law, philosophy, and music. The third Eastman Professor was Felix Frankfurter, then professor of law at Harvard, but soon after appointed to the Supreme Court of the United States. Six Rhodes scholars have been appointed Eastman Professors.[240] Professor Natalie Zemon Davis, professor of history, Princeton University, was the first woman Eastman Professor in 1994–5, the fifty-fifth holder of the chair; Renee C. Fox, professor of the social sciences at the University of Pennsylvania, was the second in 1996–7. The influence of the chair on intellectual life at Oxford is hard to judge, but, without doubt, several of the professors have more than amply fulfilled Eastman's wishes. George W. Beadle of the California Institute of Technology was awarded the Nobel Prize while in residence at Oxford. Baruch Blumberg of the Institute for Cancer Research, Philadelphia, was invited to return to Oxford as Master of Balliol. Norman F. Ramsay, professor of physics at Harvard, collaborated with Dr Patrick Sandars on experiments in fundamental physics with widespread implications for the field. The visit of Willard V. Quine, professor of philosophy at Harvard, was credited by Anthony Kenny, when Master of Balliol, with being 'a turning point in the history of English philosophy since the War'.[241]

Although the Eastman gifts were called 'munificent' at the time, income from the Eastman donation was stretched to meet all the obligations entailed by the professorship. The donation had suffered badly during the Depression, and even with the wartime hiatus in the professorship, it had barely regained its value in absolute terms in the years after the war; its valuation in 1951 was only $308,000. In 1980 gloomy analyses of the endowment's financial future prompted the board of direction to establish a fund-raising committee with twenty-two members to be chaired by Charles F. Barber (Illinois and Balliol 1939).[242] The Eastman Kodak Company offered a challenge grant of $100,000, the matching to be $1 for each $4 raised. At the Eightieth Anniversary Reunion in Oxford in 1983, at a presentation at Eastman House on 28 June the president of the AARS, Bruce McClellan (Massachusetts and New College 1947), announced that the sum of $200,000 had been added to the Eastman donation. At the conclusion of the campaign in 1983 the principal had reached $702,411.[243]

The AARS Becomes Interventionist

In March 1971, originally led by black American Rhodes scholars, a protest against the administration of the South African scholarships erupted and was to continue for the

---

[240] Donald A. Stauffer (Colorado and Merton 1924), professor of English, Princeton University, 1951–2; Roger S. Loomis (Massachusetts and New College 1910), professor of English, Columbia University, 1955–6; Don K. Price (Tennessee and Merton 1932), professor of government, Harvard University, 1985–6; Robert Darnton (Massachusetts and St John's 1960), professor of history, Princeton University, 1986–7; A. Walton Litz (Arkansas and Merton 1951), professor of English, Princeton University 1989–90; Richard H. Ullman (Texas and New College 1955), professor of international affairs, Princeton University 1991–2.

[241] Kenny, 'The View from Oxford', *AO* 67 (1980), 84–5.

[242] *AO* 67 (1980), 245.   [243] *AO* 71 (1984), 187.

next fifteen years.[244] The issue was a tangled one of fiduciary duty and incendiary politics. Rhodes's specific bequests to the four schools in South Africa were seemingly impregnable, although the Trustees were able to take other actions which brought more blacks into the programme in spite of apartheid. During this time, however, the protests took another turn. In the United States and in other countries, a movement against investments in South Africa spread and intensified, and, because their investments in South African business through their endowment portfolios were regarded as making them complicit with the government of South Africa, universities and colleges found themselves embroiled in the controversy. Few academic communities in the United States escaped this controversy, and on some American campuses the level of protest reached beyond polarization to physical violence and vandalism.

At the international reunion of Rhodes scholars held in Oxford in June 1983, a convocation was held at the Sheldonian Theatre; it was here that the discussion about the South African scholarships again erupted. One of the speakers was George R. Keys (Maryland-DC and Balliol 1970), who had, in fact, been one of the Balliol petitioners in 1971. He spoke eloquently about what he saw as an unacceptable lack of progress since the petitions had been submitted.[245] Nicholas D. Kristof (Oregon and Magdalen 1981) in a lead article in the fall 1984 issue of the *American Oxonian* reported on developments since the reunion in 1983, and recounted the history of the Trust's efforts to convert the scholarships assigned by the will to the four schools into scholarships-at-large. He also reported on other developments, such as the efforts in South Africa to establish scholarship programmes for South African blacks and the American South African Scholarship Association, which had been founded by Daniel Bloomfield (New Jersey and St John's 1982). Kristof concluded with a plea for support of these philanthropic efforts and requested that letters be sent to Fletcher and the Trustees.[246] The board of direction of the Association of American Rhodes Scholars became involved and voted at its meeting in April to address a number of questions to the Trustees. Its president, Bruce Mc-Clellan, entered into a correspondence with Fletcher and Lord Blake, chairman of the Rhodes Trustees, in which he reflected the mood of the board.[247] The board also authorized the appointment of a committee to make recommendations on the basis of their study of Lord Blake's reply.

The grounds upon which the board based its intervention were, obviously, concern of its members and American Rhodes scholars about general conditions in South Africa and in particular a concern that the scholarships themselves might be subjected to an American boycott, or at least, adverse publicity in the United States. Indeed, under the headline 'Rhodes Scholars Quietly Protest Founder's Rules', the *Wall Street Journal*, in an article which it reprinted in its overseas editions, reported that, 'While cities and campuses around the world erupt in protests against South African policy, a quieter

---

[244] For an account of these events from the point of view of the Rhodes Trust see Kenny, above p. 62.
[245] For a full account of the controversy over the South African schools see Kenny, above p. 77.
[246] *AO* 71 (1984), 173–7.
[247] The board voted at its October meeting to publish McClellan's letter and Blake's reply in *American Oxonian. AO* 72 (1985), 157–63.

demonstration of anti-apartheid feeling is taking place among Rhodes Scholars.' According to the article, not only did some of the scholars feel guilty about accepting 'blood money', but also they were agitating to change the will's provision of scholarships to the four schools. The article went on to report that the *American Oxonian*, an alumni magazine 'that usually sticks to travelogues, reminiscences and scholarly articles', had begun to publish 'strongly worded stories', and further reported that the AARS had begun to write to the Trustees urging them 'to resolve the controversy'. Nevertheless, 'It's unlikely that the South African controversy will diminish the prestige or popularity of Rhodes scholarships', because of the confinement of the debate to Rhodes scholars and the Trustees' refusal to make public comments, and because 'today's success-oriented students covet graduate fellowships, and the name Rhodes still carries a lot of weight'.[248]

Correspondence between Fletcher and McClellan ensued. The Americans expressed a concern over potential damage to the scholarships, perhaps even causing a boycott. Alexander was closely monitoring the level of applications, which did not significantly decline.[249] McClellan and Charles Barber of the board of direction discussed these issues with Lord Blake and Fletcher in Oxford in November. Fletcher was pessimistic about the legal position. On their return, the emissaries of the board of direction were unable to convince the other directors that the Trustees' efforts were sufficiently energetic. Members of the board of direction wondered if they might provide funds to assist the Trustees in pursuing legal remedies. The board of direction invited Rex Welsh to come to the United States to its quadrennial meeting 6 October 1986, but, in the event, Welsh and the Trustees decided against such a visit.[250] The *American Oxonian* published a statement by McClellan on behalf of the board of direction and other articles on the subject, including an article by Douglas Jehl (California and St John's 1984) which brought up the point that the four schools did not admit women.[251] The board's special committee addressed a series of questions to the Trustees, including a request to see the Trust's legal submissions, and Fletcher responded in a lengthy letter to Donald Rivkin, who chaired the board's special committee. In this letter Fletcher presented an account of the actions of the Trustees, but declined to send the actual documents which had been laid before the Charity Commissioners.[252]

At the quadrennial meeting of the AARS on 6 October 1986 in New York City, Jack B. Justice (West Virginia and Merton 1952) succeeded Bruce McClellan as president and

---

[248] *Wall Street Journal*, 31 July 1985, Europe edition 6 Aug., and *Asian Wall Street Journal*, 6 Aug. 1985. The *New York Times* published a follow-up article, 'Change is Urged in Rhodes Awards', 5 Jan. 1986.

[249] Alexander wrote to Fletcher in 1986 that he was perforce 'alert and watchful', about any adverse effect on applications. Alexander to Fletcher, 21 Sept. 1986; RTA. The annual average for the decade from 1984 to 1993 was 1,165, including the all-time record year 1992, when 1,292 applications were received. That was the year of Bill Clinton's successful campaign for the US presidency. Statistics: files of American Secretary.

[250] McClellan to Welsh, 19 May 1986. Fletcher to Alexander, 29 July 1986. RTA.

[251] *AO* 73 (1986), 153. This argument against single-sex schools persisted until the discussion of the four schools vanished from the agenda of the board of direction. Alexander had to point out to members of the board of direction that candidates from American colleges for women would be rendered ineligible on these grounds.

[252] Fletcher to Rivkin, 25 July 1986; RTA.

inherited the responsibility of pursuing these enquiries on behalf of the Association. A report, which was printed in the *American Oxonian*, was given at the meeting by Donald Rivkin. He summarized the developments and ended by saying that he was satisfied that there was full and 'uninhibited communication between the Association and the Warden'. It was agreed that the matter of these scholarships would remain on the agenda of the board of direction.[253] At the next meeting in April the board resolved to ask one or more Trustees to come to a special meeting for a further discussion, and Sir John Baring, now chairman of the Trustees, attended the regular meeting of the board on 5 October in New York. Alexander in a letter to Welsh expressed his opinion that Baring explained matters in the meeting 'in so sincere a manner that the members of the Board of Direction appear to be thoroughly convinced about both the difficulties and the actions taken by the Trustees'.[254] In the next issue of the *American Oxonian* Justice reported that the Charity Commission had given the Trustees leave to pursue the matter of the testamentary schools and he explained the procedures to come.[255] With this report the intervention of the Association of American Rhodes scholars ended.

Opinions will differ about the appropriateness of the actions taken by American Rhodes scholars in respect of the administration of the scholarships in another country. Their standing as quasi-litigant was dubious, a point emphasized by McClellan. Their readiness to intervene was disliked by persons of other nationalities who were ready to see these actions as another example of American moral imperialism. The American Rhodes scholars' public actions evidently alarmed the Trustees, who were discomfited by this zealotry and embarrassed by the offers of help. On the other hand, one may conclude that persons of goodwill were moved by their consciences to seek change in a faraway country so that the Rhodes scholarships, from which they had gratefully benefited, might be purged of the taint of inhumanity, as they saw it.

5. REPUTATION AND IMPACT

The Best Men—and Women—for the World's Fight

In the self-conscious atmosphere generated by an international talent search to find exceptional young men and women with superlative qualities of academic achievement, physical vigour, convincing compassion, and demonstrated capacities to lead others, expectations will run high. Those who look upon the winners may display admiration or doubt, while the winners may exhibit self-admiration or self-doubt. Because Rhodes willed that his philanthropy would change the world, those who attained the legacy of his scholarships were to be held to a high standard of public performance. From the beginning, then, the winners of the Rhodes scholarships were put under severe scrutiny, both by the world at large and by themselves. Both unalloyed arrogance and hopeless depression have afflicted Rhodes scholars who have spent too much time looking in

---

[253] *AO* 74 (1987), 28–9.   [254] Alexander to Welsh, 23 Oct. 1987; RTA.
[255] *AO* 75 (1988), 36–7.

Narcissus' pool. A fair question presents itself: what assessment can one make of the American scholarships?

The first criticism of the American scholarships did not wait long to appear. 'A scathing article' about the American Rhodes scholars in the *Brooklyn Eagle* was read to the merriment of members of the American Club on 7 March 1908. Evidently W. E. Schutt (New York and Brasenose 1904) was accused of being the returned Rhodes scholar who had made the critical remarks; he vehemently denied either having been interviewed or ever having held the views expressed in the article. This episode provided an early example of the artful misquotations about the American scholarships which were to dog Parkin and others, through the years.[256] Stanley Hornbeck (Colorado and Christ Church 1904) in 1909 was moved to respond in the *Alumni Magazine* to several articles which had denigrated the performance of the Americans, and he sought to correct their errors by recording the academic results of the earliest classes,[257] which included 10 firsts, 19 seconds, 20 thirds, and 4 fourths. Murray, in an editorial in the Jan. 1909 issue of the *Alumni Magazine,* thanked Wylie for his response in the 17 November 1908 issue of the *Nation* to 'those who have condemned the record of Americans at Oxford without mercy and without knowledge'. In 1910 the *Alumni Magazine* again reported adverse comments about American Rhodes scholars in the *Oxford Magazine*: 'We expected more from the picked men of young America. . . . But it must be admitted that we look in vain among our Rhodes Scholars for those qualities which make American politics and business so vivid and picturesque. The United States have not given us of their best.'[258] In October and November 1910 the *Daily Mail* ran a series of seven articles, beginning with a mean-spirited attack on the Americans as stand-offish, unsportsmanlike, and selfish: 'He has taken from Oxford everything she has to give, and withholds from her anything that may be in his power to give in return.' This article by 'An Oxford Man' unleashed responses from other unnamed correspondents who knew and liked Americans. The series ended with a signed column favourably comparing Americans with the German Rhodes scholars, arguing that the aristocratic Germans might more fairly be said to represent the traits so extensively deplored by 'An Oxford Man'.[259] Aydelotte asked Sidney Ball, fellow of New College, to write the first article in the first issue of the *American Oxonian* in 1914. Ball had known Rhodes as an undergraduate at Oriel College. Ball's article, 'Oxford's Opinion of the Rhodes Scholars', was a balanced account of Oxford's opinion of Rhodes scholars, and it was followed by W. W. Thayer's *tour d'horizon* of published comments on the scholarships, the first of many such articles through the years.[260] Editorials and

---

[256] *Alumni Magazine*, 1/2 (1908), 6–8.   [257] *Alumni Magazine*, 2/2 (1909), 28 ff.
[258] *Alumni Magazine*, 2/1 (1909), 3–4, and 3/3 (1910), 11–12.
[259] *Daily Mail*, 11, 12, 13, 14, 18, 20 Oct. and 18 Nov. 1910.
[260] Ball, *AO* 1 (1914), 3–20, Thayer, *AO* 2 (1915), 34–44. Ball wrote from the tentative stance of a witness to a fledgling programme. He disclaimed the value of his generalizations of Oxford's opinion—'*quot homines*—and I may add *quot Collegia—tot sententiae*', and he strove to write in the good tutor's manner of judging the scholars' 'conduct, industry and progress'. He felt that the Rhodes scholars gave less trouble than other students and were for the most part 'serious-minded' and 'keen'. He wrote, 'They are good at book work, but they are better at getting up things than at getting inside them. They are not very teachable, are little accustomed to criticize their textbooks, and in particular have been quite unused to working

statistical reports on the quality of American Rhodes scholars appeared with such regularity in the *Oxonian* that one could conclude that the magazine's editors felt obliged to
disprove the criticisms.

Criticisms also came from within. That unidentified Rhodes scholar who gave the
interview to the *Brooklyn Eagle* in 1908 was matched by others. The *Yale Daily News* published an article by Donald G. Herring (New Jersey and Merton 1907) in which he was
highly critical of the selection committees and their failure to send enough 'all-round
men' to Oxford.[261] Parkin himself provoked criticism of the American scholars in his zeal
to improve the election procedures. He summed up these efforts in a lengthy article he
published in the *Atlantic Monthly* in September 1919. He wrote of the poor academic
preparation of some American scholars which led to their failure in large numbers on
the qualifying examination—roughly one-half of those taking them. On the other hand,
he deplored the practice in some states of appointing the surviving candidates merely
because they had passed this simple examination. He did not want, however, to leave the
reader with an impression of widespread failure of the scheme; to the contrary, 'the Trust
has every reason to congratulate itself on the quality and spirit of a large proportion of
the American Scholars drawn to Oxford by its first and tentative methods of selection'.[262]
F. F. Beirne (Virginia and Merton 1911) took issue with Parkin in the next issue of the
Atlantic Monthly in a reply entitled 'The Inadequate Rhodes Scholar: A Defense', and
Aydelotte rejoined with a 'Defensio contra Defensionem'. Beirne's argument had
advanced the excuse that the American was forced to play the Englishman on his own
ground and according to his own rules, and that lower academic performance should be
expected of 'all round men'. Aydelotte wrote to Parkin that he feared Beirne's assumption that the American scholars were on the whole intellectual failures would do more
harm than any other criticism. Hence, his 'Defensio' defiantly declared, 'American
Rhodes Scholars have proved that they can meet the Englishman on his own ground,
whether that ground be the playing field or the Examination School, and our best have
been able to do it in both.'[263]

The American press kept up its vigilant interest in the Rhodes scholarships, furnishing them valuable publicity while eagerly pointing out the scholars' shortcomings or outright failures. Goaded by an article in the *American Mercury,* Tucker Brooke devoted a
long editorial in the *Oxonian* in 1927 to taking issue with the author's arraignment of
'the Rhodes prodigy'. According to the article, this prodigy, as 'our cultural champion',
arrogantly strove to convert the English to Middle-Western ways, consorted with fellow
Americans who constantly preached patriotism, hastened to the Continent to indulge 'a
premeditated profanity for worshipful delight', which led him to great wickedness in

with original authorities. Generally speaking, they are "goodish" rather than first-rate' (p. 11). The
scholars came off reasonably well, in his judgement, in mixing with the English and in sportsmanship,
if a bit more 'professional' in their attitudes toward athletic training. He did point out, however, that
they had a reputation for being mean. They were 'an influence tending to economy', scrutinizing their
expenditure closely, 'and in some respects indeed much too closely' (p. 8).

[261] *Yale Daily News*, 1 Mar. 1913.
[262] *Atlantic Monthly*, Sept. 1919, 365–75. This passage is found on p. 370.
[263] Aydelotte to Parkin, 7 Oct. 1919; RTA. Also Aydelotte to Wylie, 24 Sept. 1919; RTA.

Paris, only to return to Oxford, where, having realized his time was up, he fell into a wistful sense of loss of the charms and beauties of Oxford, and finally was repatriated to begin his destruction of America's national idols. Brooke rebutted the charge of arrogance by calling attention to the 'scared, serious, diffident' qualities of scholars both at Oxford and after their return; 'the very best of them probably was not so sure as, for the sake of his *amour propre*, he would have liked to be that *his* selection was not a fluke.' Brooke noted that these Rhodes scholars were barely established in their careers—the first had only returned twenty years before—yet they were already making their way into the professions and were working at 'something which rather particularly needs to be done'. He concluded, 'Prodigy is the last word to apply to a typical Rhodes Scholar, either in scorn or earnest.'[264]

Scribner's Magazine, whose editor was Harlan Logan (Indiana and Lincoln 1928), published an extensive article by Milton Mackaye in January 1938. The article, 'What Happens to our Rhodes Scholars', was based on research and a survey sent to 100 randomly selected Rhodes scholars. Mackaye examined the history of the scholarships and described Oxford. He entertainingly repeated some of the lore, including the arrival in England of the scholar whom the Associated Press called the 'Perfect Man'. Lionized at Oxford, this scholar later discovered that the Englishmen were charging a shilling admission to see him in various social settings.[265] Mackaye analysed the careers of the scholars, and he gave the names of a number of scholars who had risen to prominence in education, law, government service, journalism, and writing. Yet 'after thirty-odd years . . . in America the Scholarships have failed to produce national political leaders'; by 1938 one Rhodes scholar had been elected to Congress, Charles R. Clason of Maine. Noting sarcastically that an agrarian fraternal organization, the Modern Woodmen of the World, enjoyed greater influence on policy than American Rhodes scholars *en masse*, Mackaye offered a thesis to explain this 'political sterility', as he called it. He argued that the Rhodes scholars' lack of political influence as a group was less their fault than Rhodes's fault. Rhodes, not fully understanding the United States, had wrongly assumed that his scholars would be drawn from the ruling class in the United States and that as in Britain they in turn would naturally succeed their fathers in positions of political influence. Moreover, Mackaye declared that the preponderance of 'schoolmen' among the American scholars demonstrated the failure of the scheme. Citing Rhodes's 'contempt for the professorial mind', using the language in clause 12 of the will about the dons at Oriel, he declared that the founder had not intended to establish a fund for 'training of schoolteachers'. Mackaye attributed the large percentage of academics both to the promotion of the scholarships by professors who wanted to reproduce their own kind and to his own theory that the lack of specialized training unfitted the liberally educated scholar to get a commercial or scientific job. 'Teaching offers him a small salary, but it offers it to him immediately, and teaching jobs are easy to find. So— one more schoolman is made.' Mackaye ended with a lament for Rhodes, noting that in

---

[264] *AO* 14 (1927), 29–36.
[265] The story line was remarkably similar to that employed by John Monk Saunders (Washington and Magdalen 1918) in his screenplay for *A Yank at Oxford*.

1935 some of the Rhodes scholars had formed an organization for the promotion of social-ism in the United States.[266]

Nightmares under the Dreaming Spires

After-dinner remarks made by William Chace Greene (Rhode Island and Merton 1922), in his response to a witty toast to the Rhodes scholars by Rudyard Kipling at the Trustees' dinner in the Town Hall on 6 June 1924, created a *cause célèbre*. The severe and unamused Trustees heard Greene say that 'romance has died in us, and the gray and beautiful buildings of Oxford have become just old buildings'. Not content with this acceptable albeit ungracious assertion of growing maturity, Greene continued:

We have come to see the need of the new attitude towards peoples and people, towards the State and the running of the State, of which the little group of the Fabian Society is for many of us the chief spiritual example. . . . We do not go home with regret. Whatever may have been the unex-pressed desires of Cecil Rhodes in laying the foundations of these scholarships, if he meant us to love another nation, if he meant us to become apostles of that great creed for which the proposer of this toast has laboured so long and so finely, we must deny his hopes. Oxford and England and Europe have only made us love America more. . . . sick of handshaking across the sea . . . we go home gladly, eagerly, to a nation which we know and love and understand, if often we cannot admire.[267]

This speech stunned its audience. Francis H. Herrick (Ohio and Balliol 1923) later described the scene: 'The faces of the Rhodes Trustees froze; this may have been the sort of vigorous young man that Cecil Rhodes had wanted, but the effect of Oxford on him was not. The dark, brooding face of Rudyard Kipling was a study.' Herrick recalled that the London press featured Greene's remarks 'as a typically American affront to England'. The speech was, he thought, 'the culmination of the political direction taken by the American Club in the past two years'.[268] Two issues of the *Oxonian* referred to the event. The Oxford Letter in the October issue reported on 'that much misquoted and mis-understood speech', and, rather immaturely stressing Greene's theme of *dolce far niente*, rhapsodized that the best part of the Rhodes scholar's education was that to be gained on continental vacations from 'the blue and gold of Italian pictures, and the human warmth of Parisian Cafés'.[269]

---

[266] *Scribner's Magazine*, Jan. 1938, 9–15 and continued p. 84. Other articles of this sort have appeared. For example, in 1932 *AO* published 'The Rhodes scholarship System: An English Point of View', *AO* 19 (1932), 177–84, which provoked a strong reaction from Geoffrey Dawson and Allen. Dawson to Millar, 29 Apr. 1932. Allen to Millar, 2 May 1932. RTF 2120. A recent and widely noted critical account of the American scholarships is Andrew Sullivan's 'All Rhodes Lead Nowhere in Particular', *Spy Magazine*, Oct. 1988, 108 ff. The title summarized the article.

[267] RTF 666.

[268] Francis H. Herrick, 'The American Club in the '20's: Some Oxford Memories, 1923–1926', *AO* 65 (1978), 124. Herrick incorrectly gave the date as 1925.

[269] Fitzgerald Flournoy (Virginia and Exeter 1922), 'Oxford Letter', *AO* 11 (1924), 98. Brooke noted the speech in an editorial later in the issue, in which he quoted a letter from an unnamed American who sided with Greene declaring that 'parts of [the speech] were certainly in bad taste as an after-dinner address, but the heart of it was sound'. Brooke offered an exculpation of Greene: 'What one remembers most

One would be amazed if all American scholars were happy at Oxford, or even if the alleged prestige of the scholarships impresses everyone. In an extraordinary case, the mother of a newly elected Rhodes scholar tried to get his election annulled. The mother of John Ocheltree (Nevada and Exeter 1926) had written to the scholarship authorities denouncing him as being dishonest and unworthy, after which she announced his resignation to the press. Wylie then received a telegram tendering Ocheltree's 'resignation of great honour to care for my aged mother who needs my help more than any Oxford honour'.[270] In each generation a squeal of pain or a scream of anger may be heard. Persisting to the current day such expressions of disillusionment may result in confessions of bitter regret at having received a scholarship; such regret, real or feigned, has made some of the scholars Rhodes's 'laughing heirs', as Thomas Hughes (Minnesota and Balliol 1947) described them.[271] In a sour 'Letter from Oxford' John Cloud (Arkansas and Brasenose 1993) claimed to speak for his contemporaries, who 'none of us would have chosen to be here if we hadn't won scholarships. That's as much true for Marshall and Rotary Scholars, and other funded students as it is for Rhodes Scholars.' He continued, 'And I know many Americans—including myself—who wouldn't even have pursued graduate work if we hadn't won.'[272] Those who were not successful in the competition for these scholarships might be bewildered by Cloud's desipient arrogance.

The Great Conspiracy?

Fanciers of conspiracies have savoured Cecil Rhodes's secret society for a century. By never ceasing to refer to it, they kept alive his idea of the international brotherhood, vaguely constituted like the Society of Jesus, that would carry forward his ideas of the Anglo-Saxon domination of the world that would lead finally to an international comity of peace and commerce. Although the secret society entirely vanished from his later wills, these delvers into the mind of Rhodes regularly pointed out that he had never explicitly disavowed the idea. John Corbin wrote in the *Saturday Evening Post* on 13 July 1912, '[Rhodes's] idea of organizing a religious and patriotic brotherhood fell into abeyance toward the end—but he never said a word or wrote a syllable indicating that he had abandoned it; and it must be clearly held in mind by any one who wishes to grasp the

sympathetically in thinking of Mr. Greene's speech is that he was in the dire predicament of having to reply to a toast proposed by Mr. Kipling and to "be not too tame neither." Passion has often been torn to tatters for less than this.' *AO* 11 (1924), 182–3. Also *AO* 12 (1925), 21–3. Grigg wrote to Aydelotte on 3 July 1924 about 'how much protest and displeasure were evoked amongst the American Rhodes Scholars' by the speech, and he added his regret that Wylie had dissuaded them from expressing 'their disfavour' to the press. Aydelotte replied that he had been disgusted by Greene's speech but that he thought 'the effect over here is negligible'. Aydelotte to Grigg, 14 July 1924; RTA.

[270] In July 1926 Wylie wrote to Aydelotte, 'the wording of the telegram, in its second half, is also suggestive of the mother, rather than the son'. Her letter to the Riverside (California) *Daily Press*, 15 July 1926, stated that he had decided to remain in America to look after his mother's interests: 'He has a splendid position with the main office of the Southern Pacific' in San Francisco. RTA Aydelotte to Wylie, 12 Jan. 1926; RTA.

[271] *AO* 85 (1998), 305.   [272] *AO* 81 (1994), 270–1.

full meaning of the course which he chose as most likely to further his large purposes.'[273] In the time of American neutrality in the First World War this alleged conspiracy was never more evident. In *The Fatherland: Fair Play for Germany and Austria-Hungary*, edited by George Sylvester Viereck, Frederic Schrader stated that Rhodes in his secret will of 1877 set as his goal 'the ultimate recovery of the United States of America as an integral part of the British empire'. Schrader quoted a letter from Rhodes to Stead in which Rhodes had suggested that the federal parliament could be held in Washington for five years and for five years in London. Schrader's discovery that the 'virus of high treason under the mask of serving civilization has penetrated the whole political system of our country' impelled him to appeal for a congressional investigation.[274]

As editor of *the Oxonian*, Aydelotte vigorously supported the Allied cause before the United States entered the war. Furthermore, Parkin used the communication system already in place to send copies of six official British documents for distribution among American Rhodes scholars. His covering note read, 'Dr. Parkin thinks that ex-Rhodes scholars in America will be interested in having the official documents and statements which furnish a narrative of the events leading up to the present war.'[275] Parkin, of course, never shrank from proclaiming the Rhodes scholarships as a means for accomplishing the imperial vision he shared with Rhodes. Aydelotte wrote in the *Oxonian* in 1915 that if complaints were lodged about the magazine's lack of neutrality, 'we must frankly plead guilty to the charge'. Again in 1917 his editorial position was powerfully stated in connection with the appeal for financial support of Mrs Wylie's fund for soldiers in the Oxford Military Hospital. 'We have our "bit" to do in this war as well as the countries that are fighting, and one of the most obvious duties which falls upon us is relief work of this kind. It is not merely a duty; it is an opportunity to express that warm sympathy with the cause of the Allies which we all feel and which our government has expressed so inadequately thus far.'[276]

As one would expect, however, not all Rhodes scholars had imbibed so deeply at the imperial spring. In the years after war had broken out in Europe in 1938, Americans once again were badly divided between interventionism and isolationism. John W. Bodine (Connecticut and Balliol 1933) polled his classmates for the 1941 class letter, and on the basis of their replies wrote a thoughtful essay. One of the non-interventionists among his classmates wrote, 'People like me, the Irish, German, anti-snob core of the country, consider Anglicanism bankrupt and a dangerous *mortmain.*' Another classmate wrote negatively about Britain which 'only fought when her own imperial interests were threatened . . . This doesn't mean I am not immensely pro-England and anti-Hitler.

[273] *Saturday Evening Post*, 13 July 1912, 8; RTA.   [274] *Fatherland*, 4/7, 22 Mar. 1916, 99; RTA.
[275] RTA. Jacob van der Zee (Iowa and Merton 1905) in a letter to the editor of the *Oxonian* called attention to Harold D. Lasswell's comments about Rhodes scholars in his article on propaganda in the *Encyclopaedia of the Social Sciences*. AO 27 (1940), 111–12. Lasswell wrote: 'In 1914 the United States became the seat of one of the most famous propaganda battles in history, with the British working through native sympathizers, Rhodes Scholars and other cultural and business affiliates and the Germans rather through German nationals . . .' E. R. A. Seligman (ed.), *Encyclopaedia of the Social Sciences* (New York: Macmillan, 1934), xii. 523.
[276] AO 2 (1915), 135–8; 2 (1915), 202; 4 (1917), inside front cover.

It just means I can't see any great light coming into the world when suddenly the bombers quit flying. I don't want to carp at a very brave country conducting a dreadful war, to a great extent a war made by its own majestic ineptitude.'[277]

Still another manifestation of the cordial relations between Britain and the United States has been the 'special relationship', as Winston Churchill termed it. In his presidential campaign in 1992 Bill Clinton was accused of having abandoned support of this historic kinship. The alleged intervention in the campaign on behalf of the Republican candidate by the Conservative Prime Minister, John Major, was pointed to as the proximate cause. Yet in a powerful essay written four years before, Robert B. Reich (New Hampshire and University 1968) had already declared his opinion that the relationship was dead. He averred that the relationship had been killed by both partners. The Americans, having seen British power waning, found Britain increasingly 'just a pestering voice'. The anti-Americanism of the British and Britain's 'shift towards Europe' did the relationship in from that side. Reich concluded ruefully, 'Thus as Britain moves away from America in response to America's having moved away from Britain and her allies, she will be leaving America more alone than she has been at any time over the last half-century. It is a solitude which is at once poignant and dangerous.'[278] Commentators, taking their cue from the high Victorian purposes celebrated by Cecil Rhodes in the creation of the scholarships, have tended to use the special relationship as evidence of Rhodes's ideals. On this basis they assess the influence of the scholarships on American life as negligible, if not an outright failure in achieving Rhodes's intentions of ever closer links between his nation and ours. Thomas Hughes (Minnesota and Balliol 1947) argued that 'As backgrounds, affiliations, and aspirations grow ever more diverse, the disposition toward acculturation declines on the American side. On the British side, the unspoken purpose of turning American naifs into professional Anglophiles also has disappeared. The Anglo-American cultural embrace is steadily receding.'[279]

No one was more certain that the Rhodes scholars were the vector of the malign British virus into the United States than the owner and publisher of the *Chicago Tribune*, Col. Robert McCormick. From time to time he remembered to warn his fellow Americans of this disease, putting his journalistic resources at the disposal of the microbe hunters. A major campaign was mounted by the *Chicago Tribune* in 1943, including rehashed material that Aydelotte was able to show came from the *Fatherland* of 1916, whose editor George Sylvester Viereck had by then been convicted for failing to register as a foreign agent while spreading Nazi propaganda. Harvie Branscomb, the editor of the *Oxonian*, indulged himself and his readers in a careful examination of press reaction to the *Tribune*'s attacks. He ended the article with a lengthy essay from the *Christian Science Monitor* which soberly catalogued the service of the Rhodes scholars throughout American society,

---

[277] *AO* 28 (1941), 296. The mention of the Irish in this context calls attention to an editorial in the *Irish Echo*, 4 Sept. 1954: '[Rhodes devised] a scholarship system at Oxford University for American college students with the avowed purpose of impressing them with the idea of bringing the United States within the British Empire. The Oxford scholars have always lived up to that idea. They are, in fact, Britain's first line of defense, or shall we say, offense in the United States.' RTA.

[278] *AO* 74 (1987), 149–55.   [279] *AO* 85 (1998), 305.

not least in their war service.[280] Eight years later, the *Chicago Tribune* returned to battle with a series entitled 'Rhodes' Goal: Return U.S. to British Empire'. Beginning with a photograph of Senator J. William Fulbright (Arkansas and Pembroke 1925), the articles appeared over a two-week period. The series culminated in a report on Stanley Hornbeck's testimony on behalf of Alger Hiss, and, as a coda, an attack on Elmer Davis (Indiana and Queen's 1910) who ran the Office of War Information, 'the biggest propaganda set-up'. Davis, it was charged, had become one of the 'most violent critics' of Senator McCarthy the year before. Once again, the tactic was to link names, organizations, and ideas in order to expose the conspiracy that was aimed at placing in positions of responsibility persons who 'have pushed the British concept of policing the world with American soldiers and economic aid and have fought for a world federation under which the United States would surrender its sovereignty'.[281] Charges like these linger, and now may be found on the Internet.

If the Rhodes scholars were dangerous Anglophiles in the minds of some, in the minds of others they were even more dangerous because of their left-wing politics. The long-running theory held that American scholars had become enamoured of socialist politics and were greatly influenced by the Fabian Society, as Greene had declared to the Trustees and their guests in 1924. This theory taught that these scholars brought their views back to imperil the American capitalist economy, even while they were infiltrating positions of influence in order to spread their imperial ideas throughout American political thought.[282] A truly serious threat to the Rhodes scholars emerged along these lines in the fierce campaigns against communists in the early 1950s. The well-known McCarthy hearings in the Senate were matched in the House of Representatives by the Velde Committee. Representative Harold H. Velde, Republican of Illinois, announced in November 1952 that the House Committee on Un-American Activities, when reconstituted after the opening of the new Congress under his chairmanship, would begin an investigation into 'communist influence in Rhodes scholarship matters'.[283] Velde, incidentally, had just defeated John T. McNaughton (Indiana and Oriel 1948) for the House seat by 15,000 votes out of 150,000 cast.[284]

In the climate of the time, nothing could be more alarming than to fall under the scrutiny of the Senate or the House accused of subversive activity, however the Senators or the Congressmen chose to define it. Daniel Boorstin (Oklahoma and Balliol 1934),

[280] *AO* 31 (1944), 32–9.
[281] *Chicago Tribune*, 15 to 31 July 1951. Courtney Smith, in fact, was asked if Alger Hiss had ever applied for a Rhodes scholarship. According to the records, he had not, but his brother Donald had applied. Smith to M. N. Fulton (Rhode Island and Merton 1919), 6 Apr. 1953; RTA. *Cowboys into Gentlemen* incorrectly repeated the assertion that Alger Hiss had been an applicant, p. 153.
[282] One of the most extensive studies of the subversive influence of communists, socialists, and fellow travellers is Rose Martin, *Fabian Freeway: High Road to Socialism in the U.S.A. 1884–1966* (Chicago: Heritage Foundation, 1966). Martin, ever certain of her facts, nevertheless had to confess that no statistics on the number of Rhodes scholars who were members of the London Fabian Society 'have been released' (p. 358).
[283] Chicago *Sunday Tribune*, 30 Nov. 1952; RTA.
[284] McNaughton enjoyed a brilliant career that was tragically cut short by his death with his wife and son in an aeroplane crash in 1967.

Richard M. Goodwin (Indiana and St John's 1934), and Richard Schlatter (Massachusetts and Merton 1934), were three Harvard graduates who remained friends at Oxford. While there they and others like Donald N. Wheeler (Oregon and Pembroke 1935) became interested in Marxism and the communist opposition to fascism. Schlatter and Goodwin had travelled to Germany before going up to Oxford, and with Boorstin, Wheeler, and a Harvard friend who was at Cambridge University they went to Italy in 1936. These facts later haunted them. In February 1953 Boorstin testified before the Committee that he had belonged to Marxist study groups at Oxford and later at Harvard, but that he was no longer involved. Indeed, he testified that if he were a college president, he would not hire a communist, because a communist professor could not be 'intellectually free'. Richard Schlatter testified before the Committee about his membership of communist groups at Oxford and Harvard, and he testified that he had left the Harvard group after the signing of the Nazi–Soviet pact of 1939. Rutgers University did not fire Schlatter because of these admitted communist affiliations. Goodwin and Wheeler, however, both suffered reverses in their careers, which Wheeler blamed on their former affiliations and beliefs. Goodwin, who had been teaching at Harvard since 1938, was denied tenure in 1950. A cynical axiom of American academic politics is that universities always have many reasons for denying tenure, but Goodwin's friends, like Wheeler, felt that the charges of his having been a communist in the 1930s during the congressional hearings were the major deciding factor. Goodwin's subsequent career at Cambridge amply confirmed his earlier academic promise, and, according to his friends, he never referred again to the Harvard incident. Wheeler declared that he too had suffered for his views, because he was fired from the Office of Strategic Services in 1946 because of his open dissent from the official government position as the war was drawing to its end.[285]

Courtney Smith, barely installed as American Secretary, found himself on point for the next several weeks. After the testimony of Boorstin, Schlatter, and others, Courtney Smith sought advice from Rhodes scholars, including Senator Fulbright, Congressman Robert Hale (Maine and Trinity 1910), and from Owen Roberts, former Associate Justice of the Supreme Court. Keeping Elton informed, he wrote that if the Committee was so disposed, he and Aydelotte might be called to testify.[286] The threat passed. Not finding many big fish in these waters—that is, newsworthy ones—Velde announced that he would expand the Committee's remit to investigate communist infiltration into the churches and that the Committee would renew its investigations into the entertainment

[285] *New York Times*, 27 Feb. 1953. Statement by Professor Schlatter, Rutgers University, 26 Feb. 1953. RTA. Wheeler wrote Goodwin's obituary, *AO* 84 (1997), 213–15, with an addendum by Walter Chudson (Pennsylvania and Balliol 1934).

[286] Smith to Elton, 26 Feb. 1953. Notes from telephone calls and informal communications also may be found in the file. RTA. One Rhodes scholar who got into serious trouble with the Congress was Conrad E. Snow (New Hampshire and Magdalen 1913), who, as legal counsel to the State Department, made a speech in which he accused Senator McCarthy of trying to smear the Department with 'rumor, half-truths, invention or no truths at all'. He was subpoenaed to testify before the McCarran subcommittee to explain what right he had to attack a member of the Senate. He defiantly replied, 'I am a citizen of the United States and I am engaged in public office.' Many others in Washington were less courageous at the time. *AO* 63 (1976), 342.

industry. His interest in the churches proved to be his undoing; he had gone too far. The excesses of the efforts to exorcize the Red menace brought an end to the movement, but not until after many lives had been blighted by its fanaticism.

The Influence of the American Scholarships

Only two book-length studies of the American Rhodes scholarships have so far appeared, and both of them endeavour to ascertain the degree of the influence of the scholarships on American life. Frank Aydelotte's *The American Rhodes Scholarships: A Review of the First Forty Years* was published in 1946, and he also wrote a section on the American scholarships in *The First Fifty Years*. In 1998 Thomas J. Schaeper and Kathleen Schaeper published a study under the title *Cowboys into Gentlemen: Rhodes Scholars, Oxford, and the Creation of an American Elite*.[287] In sixteen chapters to which they appended a complete roster of Rhodes scholars elected up to 1998, they wrote a friendly sociological account of the history, development, and influence of the scholarships. Its catchy title, *Cowboys into Gentlemen*, made it sound as if it belonged to the genre of sociological studies of elites and their networks. To the contrary, much of its material suggested that the American scholarships had been not able to produce an elite with any significant influence on American life. Moreover, the cowboy image, though colourful, really was left unsupported by evidence from the history. *Cowboys* offered much information about individual Rhodes scholars, including two chapters on what the Schaepers called 'New Voices, New Faces'. In these chapters they discussed the election of black and other minority candidates, calling attention to the long delay in the election of blacks between 1907 and 1963. Their analysis suggested that two factors created this situation: the taint of Rhodes's 'racist' legacy and the relatively small number of blacks who attended the 'better' universities. They noted in this connection that until mid-century most blacks attended historically black universities[288] and that once those barriers were broken more blacks were elected. Similarly they described the opening of the scholarships to women. The Schaepers faulted American Rhodes scholars both for their slowness in joining the civil rights movement and for their passive acceptance of the injustice to women. While their careful analysis of the scholars' network of communications and ideology might have exposed an unending conspiracy, the Schaepers finally dismissed the notion of the American scholars as an influential and cohesive elite with the observation that Rhodes 'might be disappointed that they had not acted more in union'.[289] They discussed what John Funari had called 'the impostor complex', from which many scholars allegedly suffer, and their discussion of the psychology of Rhodes scholars relied heavily on this syndrome, especially in their treatment of suicides. Their interest in the homosexuality of Rhodes scholars might have been less gossipy. The most important section, to judge by its length, was the chapter on President Bill Clinton, about whom the Schaepers wrote sympathetically. One may conclude that the book is a useful

---

[287] (New York: Berghahn Books, 1998).
[288] *Cowboys into Gentlemen*, 223.   [289] Ibid. 358.

compendium of information about the American scholarships, written unfortunately without a steady voice. The book veers between the extremes of tabloid-style journalism and serious and balanced history.[290]

One is still faced by a need to explain the inescapable phenomenon of the fame of the scholarships. The early efforts to make them well known, their longevity, and especially the prominence of some Rhodes scholars all might be adduced to explain the reputation of the scholarships in the United States. Moreover, the annual elections and the assiduous publication of names and information about newly elected scholars has kept the programme in the public eye. Also adding to the weight of the reputation of the scholarships is the institutional pride, and rivalry, in the success of their candidates. Colleges and universities regularly cite the number of their graduates who are Rhodes scholars as one of the indicia of their quality.

The influence of the Rhodes scholarships on education has been profound. Through the agency of the Rhodes scholars American undergraduate education has been broadly affected by the introduction of strictly Oxonian (and Cantabrigian) elements into American academic life. The purest form of the importation was to be found at Swarthmore College, where Frank Aydelotte was able to refashion the curriculum; and, because of his tireless advocacy and his use of his bully pulpit as American Secretary of the Rhodes Trust, elements of the Swarthmore reform were adopted by many colleges across the United States. The three principal features that differentiate the educational structure utilized by Oxford and Cambridge from that which is typical of American higher education are a primary reliance on tutorials for instruction, a division between honours and pass degrees, and the use of external examiners.[291] The American pattern is classroom lectures, degree programmes with majors and any honorific distinctions limited to Latin honours at graduation (*cum laude*, *magna cum laude*, and *summa cum laude*), and examinations graded by the teacher. Aydelotte was able to introduce all three elements of the Oxbridge pattern into the curriculum at Swarthmore. The honours degree at Swarthmore, inaugurated in 1922, was completely separated from the pass degree, which reflected traditional American curricular practice. Students for the honours degree followed an academic programme with tutorials and seminars, a required thesis, and comprehensive written and oral examinations conducted by outside examiners. The prominence of Swarthmore's innovation was assured by a series of large grants made by the General

---

[290] Thomas Hughes (Minnesota and Balliol 1947) wrote an extended review of *Cowboys into Gentlemen* in the fall 1998 issue of *AO*. He questioned the authors' judgement in writing for the two audiences of Rhodes scholars and 'outsiders', arguing that their 'awareness of two audiences leads [them] to write with one eye on each, leading to some double vision'. *AO* 85 (1998), 303. He also objected to the attention given to newer generations with less emphasis given to the accomplishments of older Rhodes scholars. He especially criticized the absence of commentary on the actions of Nicholas Katzenbach (New Jersey and Balliol 1947) as Deputy Attorney General enforcing the desegregation of the University of Mississippi in 1962 and the influence of this incident on the subsequent election of black Rhodes scholars (pp. 310–11). He lamented the 'missing chapters' on the involvement of Rhodes scholars in the New Deal, the Second World War, European post-war recovery, Third World development, the Cold War, and the short shrift given the Rhodes scholars' engagement in the 'fratricidal conflict' of Vietnam (p. 315). *AO* 85 (1998), 301–19.

[291] Oxford no longer admits students for pass degrees.

Education Board under Abraham Flexner.[292] Frederick Rudolph, in his history of the American collegiate curriculum, counted at least ninety-three honours programmes that had adopted Oxbridge features in emulation of Swarthmore.[293] For example, Reed College, under the presidency of Richard F. Scholz (Wisconsin and Worcester 1904), undertook in the early 1920s major curricular reform which offered the students a programme of comprehensive general education taught in the smaller settings of discussion sections in the first two years with specialization reserved for the final two years, in a programme somewhat reflective of the Moderations and final honour schools of Oxford.[294] Charles E. Diehl, President of Southwestern at Memphis, embarked upon a deliberate programme of appointing Rhodes scholars to the faculty, appointing seven to a faculty of slightly more than thirty in 1935; with them and other Oxonians whom he appointed he introduced tutorial instruction and an honours degree.[295] The curriculum of St John's College was drastically reformed by two Rhodes scholars, Stringfellow Barr (Virginia and Balliol 1917) and Scott M. Buchanan (Massachusetts and Balliol 1917). They went further than others, founding the curriculum upon a canon of 120 Great Books, in the manner of Robert Hutchins's reforms at the University of Chicago. Abolishing majors and electives, they instituted a pedagogy of thrusting faculty and students into a constant intellectual discussion. Rudolph paid tribute to the reformed St John's College by saying that it may have been 'the first, and only, intellectual community in the history of American higher education'.[296] James A. Blaisdell, President of Pomona College, hit upon the novel idea of importing the collegiate structure of Oxford University (or Cambridge, although it was Oxford of which he spoke most often) when the explosive growth of Southern California in the early 1920s forced the College's administration and trustees to consider expansion. Instead he was able to keep Pomona College small by creating an educational consortium of small adjacent but legally autonomous colleges, the Claremont Colleges, which now comprise five undergraduate colleges and two graduate schools.

On the other hand, two other collegiate experiments that were affected by Rhodes scholars bore little resemblance to the staid elegance of Oxbridge's ancient reverence for text. The famous Black Mountain College, an experiment in bringing creative artists and

---

[292] Flexner described his admiration for Aydelotte and his work in his autobiography, *I Remember* (New York: Simon & Schuster, 1940), 322–3. Also Blanshard, *Aydelotte*, 230.

[293] Rudolph, *Curriculum: A History of the American Undergraduate Course of Study since 1636* (San Francisco: Jossey-Bass, 1977), 231. Rudolph discussed Swarthmore's influence extensively in this chapter.

[294] Ibid. 241. Also Wilson D. Wallis (Maryland and Wadham 1907), 'The Educational Ideals of Richard Frederick Scholz', *AO* 13 (1926), 91–7.

[295] *AO* 22 (1935), 11. Two German Rhodes scholars in exile in the United States, Alexander Böker (Germany and Corpus Christi 1934) and Fritz Caspari (Germany and St John's 1933), also taught at Southwestern from 1937 to 1939 and in 1936–7 respectively after they had been exiled. *AO* 24 (1937), 286.

[296] *Curriculum*, 280. Barr wasted no time. His educational programme was announced at the time he became President in July 1937 as 'The New Program at St John's College'. *AO* 24 (1937), 232. The programme attracted wide attention, and Walter Lippman, the famous columnist, devoted a column to its praise, venturing to believe that in future it would be regarded as 'the seedbed of the American Renaissance'. *AO* 26 (1939), 167–8. *Life Magazine* ran a feature article on St John's in its 5 Feb. 1940 issue. The College has retained its distinctive programme, and it later opened a second campus at Santa Fe, N.M.

academics together, was begun by several persons, including John Andrew Rice (Louisiana and Queen's 1911), Aydelotte's brother-in-law. The short-lived Commonwealth College in Mena, Arkansas, led by Haven Perkins (Massachusetts and Queen's 1923), was a utopian institution founded upon the principal of cooperative work, both physical and academic. Because of its espousal of organizing farmers into unions, workers' rights, and labour unions in general, the College was attacked in Arkansas as a communist enclave.[297] It did not survive.

The *Oxonian*, from Aydelotte's editorship forward, regularly printed articles or notes about the introduction of Oxford-style courses or tutorials. Oberlin College introduced pass and honours courses in 1915 on the basis of the dean's experiences during a year-long residence in Oxford. The *Oxonian*, having noted that it had printed seven articles on 'English Methods in American Universities' from 1915 to 1918, stated, 'This change in university methods is by no means the sole work of Rhodes Scholars, but in most cases Rhodes Scholars will be found helping in the administration of the new system.'[298] In 1936 the *Oxonian* issued an invitation to all American Rhodes scholars to attend a luncheon conference to be held in conjunction with the annual meeting of the Association of American Colleges in Washington in January 1937, for the purpose of discussing the changes in American higher education: 'It is recognized that since the establishment of the Rhodes Fund the old English universities have had a most marked influence upon the development of the American college, and for the first time a nation-wide opportunity will be given at this meeting of the Association of American Colleges to evaluate this influence.'[299]

Rhodes invented organized study abroad on a large scale. Most American educational institutions, including secondary schools, now feature junior years abroad, academic terms of travel and study in other countries, and, in some cases, entire campuses exported with all the accoutrements of home. International exchanges at high schools and colleges are now to be found everywhere, but at the time of Rhodes's death study abroad was a personal and specialized journey to a foreign university for work not ordinarily available at home. American graduate students in the latter part of the nineteenth century attended European universities, especially German ones, in order to acquire higher credentials than were available in the United States. Although Yale University had offered a doctorate as early as 1861, American higher education did not generally provide the opportunities for scientific research and pure scholarship to be found in Europe and particularly in Germany.[300] Rhodes's innovation may not be the singular source for the current popularity of study overseas, but it must be given credit for making the attractiveness of such

---

[297] *AO* 24 (1937), 127–32. Black Mountain College was a worthy, if frustrated, attempt to make the creative arts part of what Rice called a 'democratic' education.

[298] *AO* 5 (1918), 21.

[299] *AO* 23 (1936), 288. Aydelotte's article which emerged from this conference again cited the influence of Rhodes scholars on American education. *AO* 22 (1935), 79–80 and reprinted *AO* 24 (1937), 33–6. Also, Articles on higher education regularly appeared in *AO* from 1916 to 1939. After the war these articles no longer appeared with any regularity; the changes had by then become commonplace.

[300] Frederick Rudolph, *The American College and University: A History* (New York: Vintage Books, 1962), 269.

opportunities known to a wider public. Moreover, Aydelotte cared as much about the influence the scholarships exercised as an exemplar of international exchange programmes as about the curricular influences of Rhodes scholars. Using his position as American Secretary, he worked tirelessly for the creation of scholarships for British students to come to the United States. In his book *American Rhodes Scholarships* he described how he began in 1918 to encourage foundations and individuals to establish 'reciprocating fellowships'. When the Commonwealth fellowships were announced in 1925 he was given public credit for his advice. Recipients of the Commonwealth fellowships were listed annually in the *Oxonian*. His involvement in the creation of the Guggenheim fellowships was equally noteworthy. He was deeply involved in the appointment of Henry Moe as organizing administrator of the John Simon Guggenheim Memorial Foundation, and when the Guggenheim fellowships were announced on 23 February 1925, he was appointed educational adviser to the programme. In *American Rhodes Scholarships*, Aydelotte proudly enumerated five programmes that had been introduced by 1945 that performed the function of the reciprocating fellowships he had so earnestly desired; he claimed that normally the number of Englishmen who came to the United States for study exceeded the number of American Rhodes scholars. He also pointed out that several Rhodes scholars were administering these programmes.[301]

Two other international fellowship programmes can trace their origins to Rhodes and his scholarships. The Fulbright scholarships, while different in programme, shared a common purpose with the Rhodes scholarships in striving to improve international relations through international study. Senator J. William Fulbright (Arkansas and Pembroke 1925) credited his Rhodes scholarship and his experiences in Oxford with the idea of an international educational exchange using counterpart funds frozen in other countries to send American scholars abroad and to bring scholars from abroad to the United States. The success of this programme is one of the important features of higher education in the United States since the end of the Second World War. In his obituary of Fulbright, President Bill Clinton reported that more than 120,000 persons had come from 130 countries to study in the United States while more than 90,000 Americans had gone overseas under the auspices of the Fulbright programme.[302] The British government, in turn, established a programme which it named in appreciation for the post-war recovery plan first proposed by General George C. Marshall. In the early 1950s the British government decided as a gesture of thanks for American support during and after the war to establish scholarships to be based upon selection criteria similar to those of the Rhodes scholarships. The Marshall scholarships permit American students to undertake degree programmes at any university in the United Kingdom. Members of the staff of the Foreign Office consulted authorities in the Rhodes scholarships. Frank Aydelotte was among those who were consulted, and he had three interviews at the Foreign Office in that fateful summer of 1952 when his wife Marie died.[303] The Marshall scholarships

---

[301] *American Rhodes Scholarships*, 108. Blanshard, *Aydelotte*, 206, 244–5. The *Oxonian* regularly reported news of other international fellowships. *AO* 11 (1924), 23 and 19 (1932), 191.
[302] *AO* 82 (1995), 221.   [303] RTF 3096.

celebrated their fortieth anniversary in 1994 and a commemorative article describing the achievements of the Marshall scholars was published in the *Oxonian*.[304]

The Careers of American Rhodes Scholars

American Rhodes scholars have engaged in a wide variety of careers, from the presidency of the United States to unemployment. The majority of them, exhibiting a general worthiness, have lived in the vast middle of achievement between these extremes.[305] The academic and legal professions lead in numbers overall, but shifts in the patterns of employment can be observed from decade to decade. The numbers of Rhodes scholars entering academic life have declined, and especially noteworthy is the decline in the numbers of clergy. In the early days, a significant proportion of them went into the clergy, foreign missions, and YMCA work, but those numbers in recent years have dwindled to a handful in every decade.[306]

Rhodes's own life and his language about esteeming public duty as one's highest aim suggest that an appropriate arena for his scholars' activities would be in politics. Certainly early and later critics of the scheme dwelt on the absence of Rhodes scholars in the highest reaches of American government, as Milton Mackaye noted in *Scribner's Magazine* in 1938 that only Charles Clason (Maine and Christ Church 1914) had been elected to national office. Subsequently other Rhodes scholars have attained national office, culminating in the election of William Clinton (Arkansas and University 1968) as President of the United States in 1992. Moreover, two other Rhodes scholars have been candidates for the presidency: Richard Lugar (Indiana and Pembroke 1954) and Bill Bradley (Missouri and Worcester 1965). Since Clason's election to the House of Representatives from Maine in 1936, seven Rhodes scholars have been elected to the United States Senate: J. William Fulbright (Arkansas and Pembroke 1925) from Arkansas in 1945, Paul Sarbanes (Maryland-DC and Balliol 1954) from Maryland in 1976; Lugar from Indiana in 1976; Bradley from New Jersey in 1978; David Boren (Oklahoma and Balliol 1963) from Oklahoma in 1979; Larry Pressler (South Dakota and St Edmund Hall 1964) from South Dakota in 1978; and Russell Feingold (Wisconsin and Magdalen 1975) from Wisconsin in 1994. Fourteen Rhodes scholars have been elected to the House: Clason from Maine, 1936; Robert Hale (Maine and Trinity 1914), Maine 1942; Fulbright, Arkansas 1943; Carl Albert (Oklahoma and St Peter's 1931), Oklahoma 1947, who as Speaker of the House was third in the constitutional succession to the presidency; John Brademas (Indiana and Brasenose 1950), Indiana 1958; Sarbanes, Maryland 1970; Pressler, South Dakota 1974; Elliott Levitas (Georgia and University 1952), Georgia 1975; James

[304] Robert Ratcliffe, 'The Marshall Scholarships Forty Years on', *AO* 81 (1994), 13 ff.

[305] Elton wrote an entertaining account of the careers of American Rhodes scholars in the May 1964 issue of *Harper's Magazine*, 98–106. The article, entitled 'An Englishman's Audit of Rhodes scholars', bore the secondary heading, 'They haven't turned out exactly as The Founder (or his American critics) expected—but they have contributed some extraordinary people "to the world's fight" . . . ranging from a Secretary of State to a lumberjack.' RTA.

[306] Beverly D. Tucker (Virginia and Christ Church 1905) was Bishop of Ohio from 1938 to 1952. Other clergy have served a number of churches and in ecclesiastical organizations and the military chaplaincy.

Cooper (Tennessee and Oriel 1975), Tennessee 1983; Thomas McMillen (Maryland-DC and University 1974), Maryland 1987; Melvin Reynolds (Illinois and Lincoln 1975), Illinois 1993; Thomas Allen (Maine and Wadham 1967), Maine 1996; Heather Wilson (New Hampshire and Jesus 1982), New Mexico 1997; and David Vitter (Louisiana and Magdalen 1983), Louisiana 1999.

At the state and local levels of American government Rhodes scholars have won elective office. Clinton was Governor of Arkansas from 1983 to 1992, Boren Governor of Oklahoma from 1975 to 1979, and Richard Celeste (Ohio and Exeter 1960) Governor of Ohio from 1983 to 1991. Rhodes scholars have been lieutenant governors, speakers of state assemblies, members of state senates and assemblies, state attorneys general, and have held other state-wide elective offices. Two major American cities have elected Rhodes scholars as their mayors: Richard Lugar served as mayor of Indianapolis from 1968 to 1975, and Kurt Schmoke (Maryland-DC and Balliol 1971) was mayor of Baltimore from 1988 to 1999. Other civic offices, elected and appointed, have been filled by Rhodes scholars across the United States, from town councils and planning commissions to school boards. Two Rhodes scholars had notable careers in law enforcement, one of whom was killed in the line of duty. Arthur L. St Clair (Nevada and Wadham 1907), who had returned to Nevada to farm and practise law, acting as a deputy sheriff was killed in a gun battle with car thieves in 1919. W. H. Drane Lester (Mississippi and St John's 1922) left the practice of law and joined the US Department of Justice, becoming a special assistant to J. Edgar Hoover of the Federal Bureau of Investigation.[307]

With the large number of Rhodes scholars in the legal profession, finding them at all levels of legal practice is unsurprising. The first Rhodes scholar to be appointed to the United States Supreme Court was John Marshall Harlan (New Jersey and Balliol 1920), who after a distinguished career as both a government attorney and a highly successful lawyer in private practice in New York was appointed to the Court in 1954. One of the truly spectacular American Rhodes scholars, Byron White (Colorado and Hertford 1938), a nationally renowned football player, had his career at Oxford ended by the war. After serving as Deputy Attorney General of the United States he was appointed to the Supreme Court in 1962. David Souter (New Hampshire and Magdalen 1961) practised law in his home state, entering public service as Assistant Attorney General in 1968, rising to the post of Attorney General in 1976. He was appointed to the Superior Court of New Hampshire in 1978 and in 1983 to the Supreme Court of New Hampshire. He was named to the United States Court of Appeals for the First Circuit in 1990, and in the same year he was appointed to the United States Supreme Court. On the international scene, one of the most unusual careers on the bench was that of Robert L. Henry (Illinois and Worcester 1904). Henry taught and practised law, including additional years he spent at Oxford from 1921 to 1924. He was awarded a Doctor of Civil Law by Oxford in 1926. He was appointed judge of the Tribunaux Mixtes in Alexandria in the Kingdom of Egypt in 1924, and, after serving as presiding judge of the Mixed Courts from 1939 to 1941, he

---

[307] Lester resigned in 1940 to undertake a career as a lecturer on law enforcement and counter-espionage. He was killed in a motor accident at age 42. St Clair's obituary was published in *AO* 7 (1920), 96, and Lester's in *AO* 28 (1941), 202 ff.

became a justice of the Court of Appeals of the Mixed Courts, from which he retired in 1949. In the federal judiciary, Rhodes scholars have served on the Circuit Courts of Appeal and the District Courts. At the state level, Rhodes scholars have served on courts from local courts of first jurisdiction to the states' highest courts. John C. Sherburne (Vermont and Wadham 1904) was Chief Justice of the Supreme Court of Vermont from 1949 to 1959. Other Rhodes scholars have been in private and corporate practice, as well as practising as public interest lawyers.

In the executive branch of the federal government, John J. Tigert (Tennessee and Pembroke 1904) was the first American Rhodes scholar to be appointed to a nationally prominent position. Tigert was precociously elected a college president when he was only 27 years old. In 1921 he was appointed United States Commissioner of Education, a position which later evolved into a cabinet-level appointment, and he served as Commissioner until 1928. Dean Rusk (North Carolina and St John's 1931) attained the highest appointed position in the executive branch when he became Secretary of State in 1961. Elvis J. Stahr (Kentucky and Merton 1936) was Secretary of the Army in 1961 and 1962. Nicholas de B. Katzenbach (New Jersey and Balliol 1947) was Attorney General from 1965 to 1966. John T. McNaughton (Indiana and Oriel 1948) was Secretary of the Navy-designate when he was killed in 1967. Robert Reich (New Hampshire and University 1968) served as Secretary of Labor from 1993 to 1996. Richard J. Danzig (Oregon and Magdalen 1965) became Secretary of the Navy in 1998. Other Rhodes scholars have served as deputy and assistant secretaries, as heads of administrative agencies, and as advisers to presidents on the White House staff. The first woman Rhodes scholar to head a federal agency is Nancy-Ann Min DeParle (Tennessee and Balliol 1979), who in 1998 was appointed head of the Health Care Financing Administration, which administers Medicare. Perhaps the most famous service performed by a sub-cabinet-level officer was the physical intervention of Katzenbach as Deputy Attorney General of the United States in the stand-off at the University of Mississippi over the admission of a black student in 1962; in the civil rights campaign of the time Byron White also played an important role when he was Deputy Attorney General. Clifford J. Durr (Alabama and Queen's 1918), after holding a number of significant assignments in the federal government, including serving on the Federal Communications Commission at the time when the public broadcasting system was developed, achieved national notice for his defence of the landmark civil rights case in Montgomery, Alabama, involving Rosa Parks who had been arrested for refusing to sit in the back of the bus.[308] Two Rhodes scholars have been Librarians of Congress: Daniel Boorstin (Oklahoma and Balliol 1934), 1974 to 1987, was succeeded by James H. Billington (New Jersey and Balliol 1950).

In the diplomatic service Rhodes scholars have played a significant role. Stanley K. Hornbeck (Colorado and Christ Church 1904) spent much of his career in the State

---

[308] He took part in a major freedom of speech decision before the FCC, and the right of an atheist to express his opinion over the air was upheld. Durr's remarkable career was celebrated in a memorial service on 12 June 1975. He did not allow President Truman to reappoint him to the FCC when his term ended in 1948, because of the strong anti-communist fervour that eventually led to the Loyalty Oath controversy.

Department, and because of his early experiences in China after leaving Oxford, he became chief of the Division of Far Eastern Affairs in 1928. Once described in the press as 'the Roosevelt–Hull [Cordell Hull, Secretary of State] confidant on far-eastern problems', he later served as Director of the Department of Far Eastern Affairs and as special assistant to the Secretary of State.[309] He was Ambassador to the Netherlands from 1944 to 1947. Others reached ambassadorial rank, and several held more than one ambassadorship. The first Rhodes scholar to reach the highest ranks of the foreign service was Gilchrist Stockton (Florida and Christ Church 1914), who was named Envoy Extraordinary and Minister Plenipotentiary to Austria by President Hoover in 1930. Perhaps the record is held by Philip M. Kaiser (Wisconsin and Balliol 1936), who, having learned diplomacy as president of the junior common room of Balliol, served as Ambassador to Senegal and Mauritania from 1961 to 1964, minister in the Embassy in London 1964 to 1969 (it was he who accepted the anti-war petition signed by the American Rhodes scholars), Ambassador to Hungary from 1977 to 1980, and Ambassador to Austria from 1980 to 1981. In addition to duties in the State Department including service as special assistant to the Under-Secretary of State for Political Affairs, George C. McGhee (Oklahoma and Queen's 1934) later served as Ambassador to Turkey from 1951 to 1953, Ambassador to the Federal Republic of Germany from 1963 to 1968, and Ambassador-at-large from 1968 to 1969. Carl W. Strom (Iowa and Queen's 1924) was Ambassador to Cambodia from 1956 to 1959 and Ambassador to Bolivia from 1959 to 1961, after which he was appointed Director of the Foreign Service Institute.

The first Rhodes scholars were swept up into the events that led to the First World War, and a number of them were cited for bravery and gallantry. The United States entered the war in 1917, but scholars in residence volunteered before then for non-combatant duty. The *Oxonian* devoted a special issue to the work of nineteen of them in Belgian relief in April 1915, and a number had volunteered for service as ambulance drivers in France.[310] The first American to die in the war was Robert H. Warren (South Dakota and Queen's 1914), who died on service in 1916 after contracting tuberculosis as an ambulance driver in France. A member of the first class of Rhodes scholars, William A. Fleet (Virginia and Magdalen 1904), who had enlisted in the Grenadier Guards in 1916 and was commissioned second lieutenant in 1917, was killed in Flanders in May 1918. In the years immediately after the war extensive records of the war service of all Rhodes scholars were published by the Trust.[311] The Second World War also found a large number of American Rhodes scholars in military service, and subsequent wars and conflicts up to Vietnam have claimed the service, the health, and the lives of Rhodes scholars.

Rhodes scholars have risen to the highest ranks of the military. The first to reach the rank of full general was Charles H. Bonesteel (New York and Exeter 1931), who served as commander-in-chief of the UN Forces in Korea. Bernard W. Rogers (Kansas and

---

[309] *AO* 25 (1938), 49.
[310] *AO* 2/2. Aydelotte devoted the main articles in vol. 3/2 (1916), to preparedness.
[311] The first American Rhodes scholar to be decorated in the war was Everett Jackson (Colorado and Brasenose 1914) who was awarded the Croix de Guerre for bravery as an ambulance driver in France on 18 July 1916. *AO* 3 (1916), 163.

University 1947) served as Supreme Allied Commander Europe from 1979 to 1987, and was awarded an honorary doctorate by the University of Oxford at a ceremony during the Rhodes scholars' reunion in 1983. Wesley K. Clark (Arkansas and Magdalen 1966) was commander of the NATO forces during the conflict in Kosovo in 1999. Stansfield Turner (Illinois and Exeter 1947) was promoted to the rank of admiral and served as commander-in-chief of the NATO Southern Command from 1975 to 1977. He was then appointed Director of the Central Intelligence Agency, joining an agency which from its earliest days as the Office of Strategic Services in the Second World War has attracted a number of American Rhodes scholars to its service. R. James Woolsey (Oklahoma and St John's 1963) was Director of the CIA from 1992 to 1996. Duncan Lee (Virginia and Christ Church 1935), who had been in the highest ranks of the OSS, was accused of being a Russian spy after the war; these charges which he denied under oath troubled his reputation until his death in 1988.[312]

The academic profession naturally attracted a substantial number of Rhodes scholars. Perhaps the most distinguished is Robert Penn Warren (Kentucky and New College 1928). Literary critic, professor, and poet, he attained great honours in all aspects of his work. He won two Pulitzer Prizes for his poetry and one for fiction, along with many other prizes including the MacArthur prize fellowship. He was awarded the Presidential Medal of Freedom in 1980 and an honorary doctorate by Oxford University at the reunion of Rhodes scholars in 1983. Perhaps the largest work of scholarship undertaken by an American Rhodes scholar was the seven-volume work *The British Empire before the American Revolution*, published between 1936 and 1948 by Lawrence H. Gipson (Idaho and Lincoln 1904). Gipson was awarded the Pulitzer Prize for history in 1962, and was Harmsworth Professor of American History in 1946–7. Other professors who have won Pulitzer Prizes include Bernadotte Schmitt (Tennessee and Merton 1905) for history in 1931; Robert P. T. Coffin (Maine and Trinity 1916) for poetry in 1936; Daniel Boorstin for history in 1975; and Robert K. Massie (Tennessee and Oriel 1950) for history in 1981. Besides Warren, six other Rhodes scholars have been awarded MacArthur prize fellowships, which recognize extraordinary achievement and promise: Guy Davenport (North Carolina and Merton 1948), professor of English at the University of Kentucky and a highly acclaimed poet and writer; Frank von Hippel (Massachusetts and Magdalen 1959), research physicist at Princeton University; Robert Darnton (Massachusetts and St John's and Nuffield 1960), professor of history at Princeton and Eastman Professor in 1986–7; John E. Wideman (Pennsylvania and New College 1963), professor of English at the University of Massachusetts and winner of the PEN/Faulkner Award for Fiction; John Gaventa (Tennessee and Balliol and Nuffield 1971), Director of the Highlanders Research and

---

[312] Sir Arnold Cantwell Smith CH (Ontario and Christ Church 1935) and Armistead Lee (Virginia and Pembroke 1938), Duncan Lee's brother, wrote letters in Nov. 1990 challenging the accuracy of an account of Duncan Lee's alleged espionage activities which *Time Magazine* (22 Oct. 1990, 74) published in an extensive excerpt from Christopher Andrew and Oleg Gordievsky, *KGB: The Inside Story of its Foreign Operations from Lenin to Gorbachev* (New York: HarperCollins, 1990). *Time* did not publish the letters, but John Funari published them in *AO* 78 (1991), 52–4. Lee's name resurfaced in Christopher Andrew and Vasili Mitrokhin, *The Sword and the Shield: The Mitrokhin Archive and the Secret History of the KGB* (New York: Basic Books, 1999).

Education Center and professor of sociology at the University of Tennessee; and William J. Cronon (Wisconsin and Jesus 1976), professor of history at the University of Wisconsin and winner of both the Parkman Prize and the Bancroft Prize for history. As of 2000, the colleges of Oxford University have recognized the achievements of forty-eight American Rhodes scholars by electing them to honorary fellowships; in 1937 Frank Aydelotte was the first of all Rhodes scholars to be so honoured.

Academic administration beckoned a number of Rhodes scholars into its service. The first college president was John J. Tigert in 1909, and since then more than fifty American Rhodes scholars have held the position of president or chancellor of large state universities like California and New York, private universities and colleges, and theological seminaries. Neil Rudenstine (Connecticut and New College 1956), who became President of Harvard University in 1991, was awarded an honorary doctorate by Oxford in 1998. Several colleges and universities have had appointed more than one Rhodes scholar as president or chancellor. Swarthmore had three in succession: Aydelotte, John Nason, and Courtney Smith. Johns Hopkins University, New York University, the Universities of Alabama, West Virginia, and Oregon, Vanderbilt University, and Pomona College have had two presidents who were Rhodes scholars. Rhodes scholars are to be found in profusion among the ranks of deans and provosts as well. George van Santvoord (Connecticut and Oriel 1913), who had taken first-class honours in English and a B.Litt. in 1917, taught at Winchester College before going to war, and he became the first headmaster among the Rhodes scholars when he was named headmaster of the Hotchkiss School in 1926, a position he held until 1956. Others have served as heads of secondary private schools and as superintendents of public school systems.

Although large numbers of returning Rhodes scholars in the past found the academic profession attractive, the trend latterly has been away from such careers. In a national study of the academic profession it was found that in each five-year period from 1904 to 1959 the proportion of Rhodes scholars entering the academic profession ranged from one-third to almost half. These percentages continued until the 1960s when they dropped to around 31 per cent, and in the period 1975–7 the proportion dropped to 18.2 per cent. As the study showed, almost twice as many Rhodes scholars chose academic careers as those who went into law, medicine, or business during the period from 1945 to 1959. Since then, however, 2.3 times as many have entered these other fields.[313] The new sirens beckoning the Rhodes scholars are the management consulting firms.

In the related field of non-profit cultural and educational organizations and foundations, a number of Rhodes scholars have taken positions of leadership. Henry Moe was the head of the Guggenheim Foundation from 1924 until his retirement in 1963. Oliver C. Carmichael (Alabama and Wadham 1913) was president of the Carnegie Foundation for the Advancement of Teaching, and he was also chairman of the board of trustees of the State University of New York. Clarence Streit (Montana and University 1918) was the indefatigable president and promoter of Federal Union, Incorporated, and the

---

[313] Howard R. Bowen and Jack H. Schuster, *American Professors: A National Resource Imperiled* (New York: Oxford University Press, 1986), 224–6.

International Movement for Atlantic Union. Francis Pickens Miller (New York and Trinity 1919) served as officer and finally from 1928 to 1938 as chairman of the World Student Christian Federation. Dean Rusk was president of the Rockefeller Foundation from 1952 to 1961. Thomas L. Hughes (Minnesota and Balliol 1947) was president of the Carnegie Endowment for World Peace from 1971 until his retirement. Two Rhodes scholars were active in administering the Commonwealth Fund: Richard H. Simpson (Indiana and Brasenose 1913) was secretary of the Commonwealth Fund fellowships in London from 1925 to 1949, and Howland H. Sargeant (New Hampshire and Balliol 1932) became director of the Commonwealth Fund's Harkness fellowships in 1980. Stanley Pargellis (Nevada and Exeter 1918) served as the librarian of the Newberry Library in Chicago. Frank E. Taplin (Ohio and Queen's 1937) served as president of both the Cleveland Orchestra and the Cleveland Institute of Music, and he was president and chief executive officer of the Metropolitan Opera Association in New York from 1977 to 1984. Stephen Stamas (Massachusetts and Balliol 1953), after a successful career in business, became chairman of the New York Philharmonic Society.

In business as in law and the academic profession, Rhodes scholars have taken positions throughout the range of responsibility. Major international corporations have had Rhodes scholars as chief executive officers, and many lawyers have joined these firms as legal counsel. Banks, a railroad, an airline, movie and entertainment corporations, oil and gas companies, an international food conglomerate, aerospace enterprises, mining companies, and investment firms, among others, have had Rhodes scholars as their principal officers. One of the most extraordinary careers was that of Thomas Ellis Robins (Pennsylvania and Christ Church 1904). Ellis Robins briefly returned to the United States from Oxford, but he went back to England in 1909 to be an assistant editor of the *World*. He became a naturalized British subject in 1912, and served with distinction in the British Army. In 1928 he joined Cecil Rhodes's old company, the British South Africa Company, becoming president in 1957. He was created baron in 1958. John M. Templeton (Connecticut and Balliol 1934), whose investment firm successfully pioneered global mutual funds, endowed Templeton College at Oxford as a memorial to his parents in 1984 and created the Templeton Prizes for Progress in Religion in 1972. He was knighted in recognition of his philanthropy.[314]

The first Rhodes scholar to achieve prominence in the world of letters was Harry P. Steger (Texas and Balliol 1904) who left Balliol, where he had been president of the Arnold Society, to go into publishing in New York. He became literary executor of the short-story writer O. Henry, but his early death at age 30 in 1913 ended a promising career. Christopher Morley (Maryland and New College 1910), one of three Rhodes scholar brothers, took Steger's job at Doubleday, Page, and went on to become a celebrated writer himself.[315] Robert P. T. Coffin, Robert Penn Warren, W. S. Campbell (Oklahoma and Merton 1908), who wrote as Stanley Vestal, all became well-known

---

[314] Other American Rhodes scholars who have been knighted include Frank Aydelotte KBE 1953, Thomas Ellis Robins KBE 1954, J. William Fulbright KBE 1975, Dean Rusk KBE 1976, Wesley Clark KBE 2000.

[315] *Alumni Magazine*, 3/3 (1910), 18; 6/1–2 (1913), 2, and 8–10.

writers. In more recent times, John Wideman, Reynolds Price (North Carolina and Merton 1955), Willie Morris (Texas and New College 1956), and Caroline Alexander (Florida and Somerville 1977) are writers who have achieved international fame. Naomi Wolf (Connecticut and New College 1985) has been widely recognized as a social critic. Two literary magazines owed much to the contributions of Rhodes scholars. The now defunct but still remembered *Southern Review* had several Rhodes scholars on its staff: Charles W. Pipkin (Arkansas and Exeter 1922), Robert Penn Warren, and Cleanth Brooks (Louisiana and Exeter 1929), who served as cultural attaché at the embassy in London from 1964 to 1966, and J. J. E. Palmer (Louisiana and Exeter 1937). While the *Southern Review*'s life was brief, the *Kenyon Review* has continued to exercise an extensive literary influence. John Crowe Ransom (Tennessee and Christ Church 1910), who won the Bollingen Prize for poetry in 1950, and other Rhodes scholars were closely identified with the magazine. Paul Engle (Iowa and Merton 1933) was the head of the Writers' Workshop and the International Writing Program of the University of Iowa from 1940 until his retirement in 1967. William Jay Smith (Missouri and Wadham 1947) was named Consultant in Poetry to the Library of Congress in 1967, a position which was then the equivalent of Poet Laureate of the United States; Robert Penn Warren was the first to occupy that position when it was created in 1986.[316] In the world of movies, John Monk Saunders (Washington and Magdalen 1918) gained international fame for his screenplays, especially for the seminal films *Wings* and *The Dawn Patrol*, which won an Academy Award. Others who have become renowned for their work in films include Terence Malick (Oklahoma and Magdalen 1966) and Michael Hoffman (Idaho and Oriel 1979). Perhaps the Rhodes scholar who has achieved the greatest fame in popular entertainment is Kris Kristofferson (California and Merton 1958).

In science four American Rhodes scholars have made contributions of paramount importance. The modern telephone owes its early success to the technological breakthrough provided by an oscillator invented by Ralph V. L. Hartley (Utah and St John's 1910), who left a large endowment to the AARS from his royalties. Wilder Penfield (New Jersey and Merton 1914) moved to Canada where his neurosurgical innovations brought him worldwide fame, an honorary doctorate from Oxford, and the Order of Merit in 1953. The researches of Robert J. van de Graaff (Alabama and Queen's 1925) into electricity led to the invention of the van de Graaff generator from which high electron voltages permitted great advances in high-energy physics. Arguably the most significant Rhodes scholar scientist, and perhaps one of the major contributors to knowledge in the twentieth century, was Edwin P. Hubble (Illinois and Queen's 1910), who read law at Oxford before becoming an astronomer. His studies of the origin of the universe led to the discovery of what became the eponymous constant. Hubble enjoyed a vast array of honours during his lifetime, including an honorary Doctor of Science degree from Oxford, and his contributions were commemorated in the naming of the Hubble space telescope after him.

Newspapers that have had Rhodes scholars in editorial management include the *Christian Science Monitor*, whose executive editor for many years was Erwin D. Canham

---

[316] *AO* 55 (1968), 35 and 73 (1986), 96.

(Maine and Oriel 1926). James S. Childers (Alabama and Worcester 1921) was editor of the *Atlanta Journal*. Other major papers on which Rhodes scholars held editorial or reportorial positions include the Baltimore *Sun*, the Cincinnati *Times-Star*, the New York *Herald-Tribune*, the *New York Times*, the *Omaha World Herald*, the *St Louis Post-Dispatch*, the *Seattle Post Intelligencer*, and the *Washington Post*. Rhodes scholars who have received Pulitzer Prizes for journalism are: Felix Morley (Maryland and New College 1917), the second of three Morley brothers;[317] Robert Lasch (Nebraska and Oriel 1917), who also won a Nieman fellowship in 1941; Edwin Yoder (North Carolina and Jesus 1955); and Nicholas Kristof (Oregon and Magdalen 1981). Among the broadcast journalists, certain names stand out: Elmer Davis (Indiana and Queen's 1910); Charles Collingwood (Maryland-DC and New College 1939), who went directly from Oxford to report the war; and Howard K. Smith (Louisiana and Merton 1937). Elmer Davis was director of the Office of War Information from 1942 to 1945, and after the war his national radio news broadcast was famous for his flat Midwestern nasal delivery. *Time Magazine* and its corporate parents have had three Rhodes scholars as managing editors: Hedley Donovan (Minnesota and Hertford 1934), Jason McManus (North Carolina and New College 1958), and Walter Isaacson (Louisiana and Pembroke 1974). Harlan Logan (Indiana and Lincoln 1928) was editor of *Scribner's Magazine* from 1936 to 1939, when he became editor of *Look Magazine* from 1940 to 1946. *Harper's Magazine* has had two editors-in-chief who were Rhodes scholars: John Fischer (Ohio and Lincoln 1933), who was succeeded by Willie Morris. In a move to the cutting edge, Michael Kinsley (Michigan and Magdalen 1972), who also edited the *New Republic*, has edited the virtual magazine *Slate* on the Internet. A number of other Rhodes scholars have been reporters and editorial writers for national magazines like *Time* and *Newsweek*. Charles William Maynes (Utah and Merton 1960) edited *Foreign Policy* after working in the Foreign Service and on the staff of the Carnegie Endowment for World Peace. Peter Beinart (Massachusetts and University College 1993) was named editor of the *New Republic* in 1999.

Athletics, not surprisingly, figure among the careers of Rhodes scholars, although perhaps not to the extent one might expect from the language of the will. Olympian Rhodes scholars are led by Ray Loomis Lange (Oklahoma and St John's 1910) who ran the 100 yard dash in the 1912 Olympics. The class of 1922 holds the record of Olympic athletes with four. Edward P. F. Eagan (Colorado and New College) was one of very few Americans to win gold medals in two entirely different sports: in boxing in 1920 and in the four-man bobsled in 1932. He also went to the 1924 Olympics as a boxer. John P. Carleton (New Hampshire and Magdalen) was a member of the US ski team at Chamonix in 1924. William E. Stevenson (New Jersey and Balliol) was a member of the 1600 metre relay team which set the world record of 3 minutes 16 seconds in Paris in 1924. Alan Valentine was a member of the US rugby team which won a gold medal in 1924. More recently Thomas McMillen (Maryland and University 1974) was a member of the basketball team which won a gold medal in 1972. Annette Salmeen (California

---

[317] The third brother Frank (Maryland and New College 1919) was a director of Faber & Faber from 1929 to 1939 in London, and after the war returned to England to join the firm of Eyre & Spottiswoode.

and St John's 1997) was a member of the women's swimming relay team which won a gold medal in 1996. Peter Dawkins (Michigan and Brasenose 1959) won the Heisman Trophy, the highest award for collegiate football. John Misha Petkevich (Montana and Magdalen 1973) competed as a figure-skater in the 1968 and 1972 Olympics, and he was North American champion in 1971 and World Games champion in 1972. Professional athletes include Byron White (Colorado and Hertford 1938), whose prowess in football earned him the nickname 'Whizzer'. Pat Haden (California and Worcester 1975) combined quarterbacking for the Los Angeles Rams with work at Oxford. In basketball, Bill Bradley (Missouri and Worcester 1965) enjoyed a highly successful career with the New York Knickerbockers. Thomas McMillen played professional basketball in Bologna on leave from Oxford during his scholarship and afterwards with the Washington Bullets.

Not all Rhodes scholars achieved public recognition. Several suffered mental breakdowns and spent their lives in custodial care. Scholars in every generation have committed suicide. A particularly poignant case of failure was that of one of the most promising early Rhodes scholars. Millard F. Woodrow (Kentucky and Christ Church 1907) took first-class honours in 1909 and a second class in the BCL in 1910. He was the first American Rhodes scholar to win the Vinerian scholarship. He began practising law in New York City after taking an LLB at Harvard Law School. A fall down an elevator shaft in New York City severely injured him and ended his law career. Returning to his family farm in Kentucky he adopted a reclusive way of life, and he was trapped by fire and killed when his house burned down in 1941.[318]

Rhodes scholars have been indicted of crimes, and some have been convicted. On conscientious grounds Carl Haessler (Wisconsin and Balliol 1911) refused to serve in the First World War and was imprisoned at Fort Leavenworth. After his involvement in a prisoners' rebellion there, he was transferred to the maximum security of Alcatraz federal prison in San Francisco Bay where he remained until 1920. He later became a writer and editor for the United Auto Workers and the CIO. He was a lecturer at the Commonwealth College in Arkansas, and from 1943 to 1946 he was a lecturer at the Highland Folk School in Tennessee. Congressman Melvin Reynolds was sent to prison in 1998 for various crimes; his sentence was commuted by President Clinton in 2001.

Conclusion

Could the American Rhodes scholarships have failed? Without doubt, they could have been far less successful with early administrators less able than the redoubtable Parkin and the talented Aydelotte. Failure in the twentieth century, however, probably was never likely because of the originality and idealism of Cecil Rhodes's plan. Could they have enjoyed greater success? One suspects that Rhodes might have thought so, because relatively few of his scholars have followed the pattern of his life in its strenuous pursuit of economic and political power. In one of the best summaries of the meaning of the American scholarships, in a time of crisis for the scholarships, Henry Allen Moe wrote:

[318] *AO* 28 (1941), 214–15; 29 (1942), 35.

To me, the unique significance of the Rhodes Will is due to the exceptional qualities which he demands for appointment to the Scholarships which he founded. Upon these qualities he lays more stress than on anything else in the entire document. He wished his Scholars to excel in literary and scholastic ability, in character and personality, in manly outdoor sports, and he wished in addition that they should be the kind of men who would be fitted to occupy positions of leadership after their return. That quality of man he wanted to assist and only that quality of man, he thought, would be of importance to English-speaking friendship.[319]

Now that women have entered into this legacy, Moe's words can be amended to read 'the kind of men and women' and 'that quality of person'. One hundred years after the Founder's death the record shows that American Rhodes scholars have taken their places in positions great and small, of large influence and of quiet personal example. Perhaps that is sufficient.

---

[319] 'The Reorganization Plan: Mr. Moe's Rejoinder', *AO* 17 (1930), 92.

3

The Rhodes Scholarships in Canada and Newfoundland

DOUGLAS McCALLA

Establishing the Scholarships in Canada

'The Death of Cecil Rhodes, Most Remarkable Figure in South African History' head-lined Toronto's Liberal newspaper the *Globe* on 27 March 1902. Rhodes, it is clear, was well known to readers—and so were some of the central ideas of the will. Already English Canadians had strongly supported imperialists' call to send a large Canadian contingent to the South African War; and education, leadership, and manliness were all essential in the missionary campaign to 'evangelize the world in a generation' in which Canadian churches were so deeply engaged.[1] One prominent imperialist, Principal George M. Grant of Queen's University, was 'not an admirer of Cecil Rhodes', but the *Globe* other-wise found much enthusiasm when, on 8 April, it turned to 'Canadian Educationists and Cecil Rhodes' Will'.

Of course the *Globe* had consulted George Parkin, since 1895 Principal of Canada's

I have benefited from help of many kinds, which it is a pleasure to acknowledge here. Throughout the project, Arthur Scace's confidence and cooperation have been essential. He and Sir Anthony Kenny encouraged the widest exploration of the files and barred no topics; if by any chance I have been guilty of sins of omission, it is not their fault. Caroline Brown, archivist at Rhodes House, brought an imagin-ative understanding of the scope of this project to the material and was indispensable to the success of my research there. The Warden's secretary, Pam King, made it possible for me to submit drafts electroni-cally. And my research trip to Oxford was made possible by a grant from the Rhodes Trust. At McCarthy Tétrault in Toronto, Marjorie Koren's interest went far beyond the call of duty; she readily accepted the additional work this project generated and made an interloper in a busy law office feel welcome. Dr James A. Gibson and Dr David Stager read successive drafts as the work took shape, sharing their knowledge generously, advising wisely, and criticizing constructively. Knowing I could rely on them has been immensely reassuring. I want also to thank Michael Howarth, for valuable information and perspective, David Horsley, for his careful reading of the final draft; and my research assistant, Erin Stewart, who helped in organizing data from the *Register*. Finally, it is essential to note that this project was completed during the term of a Killam research fellowship, awarded by the Canada Council. Although for another project, it also made this one better by allowing me to focus exclusively on research and permitting me to make the most of the limited time I could devote to this project. Deficiencies in the final product are, of course, my responsibility.

[1] See A. B. McKillop, *Matters of Mind: The University in Ontario 1791–1951* (Toronto: University of Toronto Press, 1994), 204–52; and Carman Miller, *Painting the Map Red: Canada and the South African War 1899–1902* (Montreal: Canadian War Museum and McGill-Queen's University Press, 1993), ch. 1.

leading private boys' school, Upper Canada College in Toronto. Born in rural New Brunswick in 1846, Parkin was by 1871 the headmaster of the Collegiate School at Fredericton, New Brunswick, where he 'cast a powerful spell over his students, especially the ablest'.[2] He was granted leave to spend 1873–4 as a non-degree student at Oxford. He never met Cecil Rhodes, who matriculated in the same year, but a speech by Parkin on the imperial question at the Oxford Union (of which he had been elected secretary) led to friendship with Alfred Milner. Fifteen years later, Milner, by now a leading liberal imperialist, persuaded Parkin to become a full-time lecturer for the Imperial Federation League, initially to tour Australia and New Zealand on its behalf. Also in the League's inner circle were two future Rhodes Trustees, Grey and Rosebery. In Parkin's view of empire, Carl Berger writes, 'there ran the burning sense of religious mission . . . He was oblivious to personal wealth and when he embarked upon his tour he abandoned comfort, a secure income, and a settled home life.'[3] Perhaps there was some truth in the later comment by his son-in-law, W. L. Grant, that 'I don't think that he got God and Oxford and the British Empire wholly separated.'[4] Even so, Parkin's ideals and experience were excellent qualifications for the Organizing Secretary for the Rhodes scholarships.

Rhodes had provided for scholarships only for Ontario and Quebec. It was not hard to argue that Canada deserved more. As Parkin recalled, 'I attacked the Trustees vigorously upon the subject from the very first, and . . . I got Peterson [William Peterson, Principal of McGill University] to go with me to a Meeting of the Trustees to lay the whole matter before them. I must say that I think they dealt with the matter very generously.'[5] Even in Ontario, Canada's largest province, Parkin found 'a consensus of opinion that we would best meet the views of Mr Rhodes by giving a scholarship to each province'.[6] Doing so required six additional scholarships, including one for the North-West Territories, the vast lands between Manitoba and the Rocky Mountains.

Parkin arrived in New York on 30 November 1902 to begin a three-month, 17,000-mile organizing tour of Canada and the United States. Almost his first stop was on home ground, in Sackville, New Brunswick, on 19 December; by the end of the month, he had also held meetings of education and university officials in Montreal and Toronto. Everywhere, he found 'some who rather clung to the idea of arranging a system of competition which took in all the colleges each year. The difficulty felt by the majority is the impossibility of establishing a standard of comparison in moral and physical qualities between men coming out of widely separated institutions.'[7] In that the scholarships were assigned to provinces, that separation was less geographic than intellectual and cultural, and was reflected in the variety of post-secondary education in Canada.

[2] David R. Murray and Robert A. Murray, *The Prairie Builder: Walter Murray of Saskatchewan* (Edmonton: NeWest Press, 1984), 16.
[3] Carl Berger, *The Sense of Power: Studies in the Ideas of Canadian Imperialism 1867–1914* (Toronto: University of Toronto Press, 1970), 36.
[4] Grant to E. Robertson, 2 Dec. 1929, quoted in Claude Bissell, *The Young Vincent Massey* (Toronto: University of Toronto Press, 1981), 162.
[5] NAC, A621 (RTF 1202), Parkin to Maurice Hutton, 31 Jan. 1906.
[6] NAC, A621 (RTF 1202), extract from letter from Dr Parkin, 1 Jan. 1903.   [7] Ibid.

In four provinces, appointments would, essentially, alternate between denominational and non-denominational institutions. The latter were the University of Toronto, the country's largest university, with an enrolment of almost 2,000 men (and about 300 women) in 1901–2 (including students at its affiliated denominational colleges); McGill University in Montreal, which had over 900 men enrolled; Dalhousie University in Halifax, with almost 300 men; and the University of New Brunswick in Fredericton, with just 100.[8] In Ontario, Queen's, the Presbyterian university in Kingston, had three appointments every ten years, and the Roman Catholic University of Ottawa and McMaster (a Baptist university in Toronto) each had one award in ten years. In Nova Scotia, Acadia, a Baptist institution in Wolfville, had an appointment every four years; St Francis Xavier, a Roman Catholic college in Antigonish, one every six years; and King's, an Anglican college in Windsor, one in twelve years. In New Brunswick, Mount Allison, the Methodist university at Sackville, had three appointments in seven years. One year in seven the appointment would go to St Joseph's, a bilingual, Roman Catholic college in Memramcook. Although small (it awarded only six bachelor's degrees in 1904), it had, Parkin noted, 'a large proportion of Acadian French students, and a useful national purpose is served by bringing them under the influence of the system'.[9] Ironically, its first scholar, Rupert Rive, was not Acadian, which provoked extensive controversy in *L'Évangeline*, the Acadian newspaper.[10]

French Canadian participation in the scholarships was in fact a vital element in liberal imperialists' dreams for Canada.[11] Hence, half the appointments in Quebec were allocated to the French-speaking, Roman Catholic Université Laval, despite 'a very odd letter from the Superior . . . making it doubtful whether Laval will take any interest in the Scholarships'.[12] When its first turn arrived, however, Laval's Rector, the Reverend O. E. Mathieu, had a candidate. 'Malheureusement je ne l'ai pas sous la main; il est actuellement en Europe. C'est un beau jeune homme, qui appartient à une de nos meilleures familles canadiennes de Québec. . . . Le jeune homme parle cinq ou six langues couramment; il a fait un brillant cours d'études classiques; il veut entrer dans la carrière diplomatique anglaise.' After visiting Oxford, the candidate, Joseph Belleau, decided not to apply. Parkin, then in New York, rushed to Montreal. As he explained to Hawksley, 'the matter was a delicate one to handle as it is a very distinct object for us not to touch French Canadian sensibilities'.[13] Still, no Laval scholar could be found in 1905.

The 1905 Quebec selection was left to Peterson at McGill. Parkin was delighted at the choice of Talbot Papineau. 'They have evidently succeeded in finding a French Canadian

---

[8] Enrolments from Robin S. Harris, *A History of Higher Education in Canada 1663–1960* (Toronto: University of Toronto Press, 1976), 626–7. Note that the Anglican College, Trinity, which federated with the University of Toronto in 1904, would otherwise have had its own scholarship once every ten years.

[9] NAC, A728 (RTF 1216), undated memo [*c.*1915].

[10] NAC, A728 (RTF 1216), Revd L. Guertin to Parkin, 15 May 1908.

[11] See, e.g., H. V. Nelles, *The Art of Nation-Building: Pageantry and Spectacle at Quebec's Tercentenary* (Toronto: University of Toronto Press, 1999), 102–21.

[12] NAC, A728 (RTF 1272), extract from letter of Parkin [to Trustees], 22 Dec. 1902.

[13] NAC, A621 (RTF 1269), O. E. Mathieu to Parkin, 5 Sept. 1904; extract from Parkin to Hawksley, 24 Jan. 1905.

for the nomination. . . . [I]t will be interesting to find out if he is a descendant of the Papineau who led the Rebellion of 1837. Nothing could be more satisfactory.' Alas, as Grey (since 1904 Governor General of Canada) wrote later, 'the Mother of young Papineau is an American woman. . . . The Rhodes Scholar is the son of his Mother, and in temperament, they tell me, an American and not a French Canadian. Up to now he has taken no pride in his possession of his family name, and before he went to Oxford could hardly speak a word of French.'[14]

On Laval's next turn, in 1907, there was a serious competition, between Marius Barbeau, who would become perhaps 'the most eminent figure in Canadian anthropology', and the historian Gustave Lanctôt.[15] Barbeau having studied at Quebec, Laval ceded its 1909 choice to its Montreal branch. It still favoured Lanctôt, but as he was now two years beyond the age limit, Laurent Beaudry was nominated instead. This left Parkin regretful because 'the Beaudry family have a good deal of English mixture in them, and . . . probably the Laval people . . . have simply found someone who was willing to take the Scholarship'.[16] Whatever his background, years later, as a senior member of the Department of External Affairs, Beaudry angered Prime Minister Mackenzie King by trying to make French a working language there.[17]

With elections in the hands of a single institution, application numbers could be misleading. For example, there was only one from Queen's University in 1905; as the Principal informed Parkin, 'I fancy that [our fellows] thought it might be vain for them to compete.' In any case, the applicant, J. M. Macdonnell, would 'prove an admirable Rhodes Scholar, as he is a young fellow of splendid character, a member of our champion football and hockey teams, an excellent Classical scholar, and a good all-round student. You will not have many from Canada who stand higher, for he is 6 ft., 4 in.!'[18] On the other hand, as the first turn for King's College approached, its President gloomily reported that 'I see very small chance of our having a really worthy candidate in 1907.' Allowed to postpone until 1909, it then selected M. K. Parlee, described by the college's new President as 'not brilliant but a fairly good all round man—not of great polish— but a sound, good, man of excellent character—a typical Canadian'.[19]

In 1911, the Dalhousie senate decided not to allow the candidacy of a man who, according to its secretary, Howard Murray, was 'our ablest man by far from the intellectual point of view . . . [but] physically a cripple'. When this man was again a candidate on Dalhousie's next turn, Parkin consulted the Trustees. 'I do not like to say that a man of marked intellectual power should be excluded entirely. On the other hand, I

[14] NAC, A621 (RTF 1269), Parkin to Hawksley, 18 May 1905; Grey to Parkin, 13 Mar. 1906.
[15] The quotation is from the cover of Laurence Nowry, *Man of Mana: Marius Barbeau* (Toronto: NC Press, 1995). Laval had initially offered the scholarship to Barbeau's friend Louis St Laurent, the future Prime Minister, who declined.
[16] NAC, A621 (RTF 1269), Parkin to Hawksley, 17 Sept. 1909.
[17] See J. L. Granatstein, *The Ottawa Men: The Civil Service Mandarins 1935–1957* (Toronto: Oxford University Press, 1982), 5–6.
[18] NAC, A621 (RTF 1202), Daniel Gordon to Parkin, 17 Jan. and 18 Mar. 1905. Similarly, Alfred Ewert was the only applicant in Manitoba in 1912.
[19] NAC, A729 (RTF 1250), Ian Hannah to Parkin, 21 Oct. 1905; Revd C. J. Boulden to 'Dr Parkyn', 29 Jan. 1909.

wonder whether the appearance at Oxford of a Rhodes Scholar on crutches would cause undue surprise.' A decision followed quickly: 'Undesirable elect Dalhousie cripple.'[20]

Another question was what constituted a Canadian. After Bishop's College, a small Anglican institution in Quebec's Eastern Townships, gained the right to an appointment every seventh year, it selected Albert Sturley, whose parents still lived in Banbury, not far from Oxford. The result was a petition from students 'to express their regret that the generally known intention of the Bequest should . . . have not been conserved . . . [and to wish] that the choice had not fallen upon an Englishman'.[21] Here, as in most public controversies, the objections could be traced to the family of an unsuccessful applicant.

That students joined the debate was not surprising—indeed, universities were expected to consult them in choosing a scholar. Thus, Walter Murray, professor of philosophy (and a former student of Parkin), explained Dalhousie's first appointment:[22]

The scholar selected [Gilbert Stairs, who was by now at Harvard] is excellent but we narrowly escaped disaster. . . . One only of the candidates was attending classes. He made it his business to appear very popular. He tried to get into prominent positions on the foot ball [sic] team and in the students' societies. He and his friends tried to secure the election of representatives from the societies favorable to him and he partly succeeded. He canvassed every representative chosen. He got men of influence throughout the province to write to the Senate in his behalf . . .

The first inkling that we got of the darker side of his character was from first the estimates of a few fellow students; later their statements reinforced by the estimates of former teachers. The appeal to the students opened the door to this base intriguing yet the students saved the situation.

In Manitoba, Parkin created a selection committee to represent the four denominational colleges that constituted the provincial university. In the North-West Territories, British Columbia, and Prince Edward Island, there were no universities, and selection committees were created, initially chaired by the Lieutenant Governor and including the Chief Justice, and with a senior educational official as secretary. Almost as soon as two new provinces, Alberta and Saskatchewan, were created in the west, they sought to alternate the NWT appointment, to Parkin's regret. 'As a compromise between the two provinces it seems satisfactory. On the other hand, the object we always have to keep in view is to get the very best man obtainable . . . Hitherto the competition from the two provinces together has been very slight, more so, I think, than from any other place to which a Scholarship is given.'[23] In British Columbia, the selection committee 'asked for special leave to select their Scholar some time in May. They say that it is practically impossible for them to pick the best candidate until the men return from the Eastern Colleges . . . and they are quite prepared to take whatever chance [of a college place] is left for

[20] NAC, A730 (RTF 1250), Howard Murray to Parkin, 18 Feb. 1911; Memorandum by Parkin, Washington, 22 Nov. 1912; Cable, Trust to Parkin, 14 Dec. 1912.
[21] NAC, A727 (RTF 1247), enclosure in Arthur N. Whalley to Parkin, 7 Feb. 1910.
[22] NAC, A729 (RTF 1250), Murray to Parkin, 12 May 1904.
[23] NAC, A727 (RTF 2357), Parkin to D. P. McColl, 12 Jan. 1909. In 1905, there had been only one candidate, who failed the qualifying examination, and there were only two in 1908.

them when he is finally selected.'[24] Often they were later: in 1910 and 1912 selections were not made until August.

Unlike the fast-growing west, the population in Prince Edward Island (103,000 in 1901) was actually falling. Nor did the colleges, St Dunstan's and Prince of Wales, grant degrees (students at the former wrote Laval examinations). Here the province's Chief Superintendent of Education, Alexander Anderson, a participant in the initial Sackville Conference, became secretary of a selection committee chaired by the Lieutenant Governor and also including the Chief Justice and the heads of the two colleges. The first scholar, W. E. Cameron (b. 1879), was over-age and his appointment controversial, as Walter Murray reported from Halifax. 'Private opinion, and even the newspapers . . . attacked the Committee, more particularly the Governor . . . for the way he talked before the Committee met. He evidently considered the scholarship a gift to be given to his religious friends.'[25] Anderson's reports of subsequent committee proceedings confirmed such gossip. In 1909, for example, 'the Rector of St D [said] that this was their year' and was supported by the Principal of Prince of Wales, whose man had won the previous year. The decision was made on the casting vote of the chairman. The news prompted Parkin to recall his visit the previous summer—and to recommend that the Trustees take the election into their own hands, keeping Anderson as local secretary.[26]

[T]he Governor . . . evidently did not attach the same importance to the question that Dr Anderson and I did. I suspect that only drastic action will deal adequately with such cases.

. . . Mr Wylie tells me that Leitch, who was selected from Prince Edward Island last year, under circumstances mentioned by Dr Anderson, is a distinctly disappointing man. . . . [H]e also agrees that . . . the inferior man has been chosen this year. Prince Edward Island has long been celebrated in Canada for turning out men of ability, and it would be a great pity if we should allow local jealousies or compromises to interfere with the most successful working of our system.

The Scholarships in Newfoundland

Newfoundland, of course, was a separate British colony, explicitly provided for in the will. Here Parkin's prior contacts had been with men like Alfred B. Morine, whose son attended Upper Canada College; Morine represented the Reid Newfoundland Company, the largest business and one of the central political issues in Newfoundland.[27] By the time Parkin visited Newfoundland, in May 1904, there had already been much controversy. After his first day of meetings, he sent a report to Hawksley.[28]

I left New York on Wed. the 18th and travelled directly through to New Brunswick. . . . I then came through to this point—nearly three days' rail and a night on board ship crossing from Cape Breton to Newfoundland . . .

[24] NAC, A727 (RTF 2016), minute, 24 Apr. 1907, to Mr Wylie [probably by Charles Boyd].
[25] NAC, A729 (RTF 1250), Murray to Parkin, 28 July 1904.
[26] NAC, A730 (RTF 1381), Anderson to Parkin, 22 Mar. 1909; Parkin memorandum, 28 Apr. 1909; also Parkin to Anderson, 11 Sept. 1909. At his death, Leitch was living in a tarpaper shack on the Halifax waterfront. See the obituary in the *Rhodes Scholar News Letter*, Oxford, Oct. 1957, 58.
[27] See NAC, A729 (RTF 1049), Alfred B. Morine to Parkin, 19 Apr. 1902 and J. S. Winter to Hawksley, 7 July 1902. One of Winter's sons would be the fourth Newfoundland scholar.
[28] NAC, A729 (RTF 1049), Parkin to Hawksley, 24 May 1904.

I have now spent one day in St John's, and I am already beginning to understand the inscrutable wisdom of Providence in preventing me from coming when I tried to do so a year and a half ago. Had I come then, I fear it would have discouraged me for all the rest of my course. Now the gathered experience gained from dealing with about seventy other communities is not more than I need in managing this seventy-first.

A large deputation of the Council of Higher Education met me at the Station, and were most civil.[29] Yesterday we spent the whole day—three sessions—from 11.30 a.m. till after midnight in constant discussion, save when we stopped for meals. At our opening meeting, the Chairman, Canon Pilot, gravely said that while the Railway policy and what is known as the Reid deal had upset Newfoundland a good deal, this was nothing to the perturbation caused by the Rhodes Scholarship. I thought at the moment it was a dry jest, but now I think he was quite in earnest. It seems that for more than a year it has been discussed by the Press and by the Council at numerous meetings with the greatest acrimony. Certainly I never saw a more Machiavellian astuteness and Jesuitical subtlety in argument developed in any gathering of men than in the thirty or thereabouts with whom I spent the day yesterday. The dialectic ability shown is wonderful. After listening to it all for about six hours I at last proposed a compromise and at first I thought it would be carried, but some time after midnight they broke up to give time for reflection, which I suspect will only consolidate opposition.

. . . The whole education system of the island is on a denominational basis. . . . This breaks all the higher school into fragments. Under these circumstances some of the more independent people send their boys away to be educated in a larger atmosphere. This the schoolmasters and others resent, and they were bent on excluding all of these outsiders from any share in the Scholarship. They claim that opinion would be 500 to one in favour of this throughout the island.

The outcome was to restrict competition in alternate years to 'regular attendant pupils or teachers in one of the public schools of the Colony for the three scholastic years immediately previous to the [Trust's qualifying] examination'. All applicants (or their parents) had to have resided in Newfoundland 'for the five years immediately preceding the examination' and 'not be under 18 . . . [or] over 20 years of age on the first of October in the year of the examination'.[30]

From the beginning, Parkin thought the age restriction deprived Newfoundland scholars of a 'fair chance' at Oxford. Thus, in 1911 he gave notice that 'there does not seem to be any sufficient reason why we should not exact from your men something like what we require from students in the remoter parts of Canada . . . [who] come all the way to Toronto, Queen's, or McGill University—much further than your students would have to go to get advanced education in the Colleges of Nova Scotia or New Brunswick'. Newfoundland's premier, Sir Edward Morris, took strong exception: 'our people would regard as objectionable any proposal to send our young men out of the Colony for any preparatory course, in order to qualify for Oxford. I think that our three Colleges here can, by a little reorganization, create quite as high an educational standard as would be reasonably expected.' When no 'reorganization' followed, Parkin returned to St John's in

[29] The Council included principals of the colleges, superintendents of education, 'and prominent lay gentlemen who are recognized as taking a special interest in the work of Education'. NAC, A729 (RTF 1049), Sir Robert Bond to Parkin, 17 Feb. 1903.
[30] NAC, A729 (RTF 1049), 'Minutes of the Conference held at St John's Newfoundland . . . May 24th and 25th 1904'.

November 1912. To give the Council of Higher Education time, he agreed to postpone requiring two years of university, but only until 1915.[31]

The First Scholars

As Parkin was journeying to Newfoundland in 1904, the first scholars were being selected in Canada. When McGill had difficulty choosing between two outstanding classicists, the Trustees agreed to accept both, a precedent that they subsequently had often to deny.[32] Herbert J. Rose and John Gordon Archibald fully justified the exception by taking firsts in Literae Humaniores and securing fellowships, at Exeter and All Souls respectively. When Rose won the Ireland Prize and first Craven scholarship, the Governor General at once cabled 'to congratulate him on having won honour for Canada'.[33] By 1914, six more Canadians had taken firsts. Another of the original scholars, Chester Martin, won several awards, including the first Beit essay prize.[34] Of course that was not the only measure of success, as Parkin noted to Grey. 'I am very much pleased with our team of Canadian boys especially. . . . Some of those who have not distinguished themselves as Scholars, have gained quite as much in breadth of thought and finish of manner—things which often count quite as much in life as mere scholastic superiority.'[35]

At one extreme in reactions to Oxford was 'a Rhodes Scholar from Alberta, named Fife', about whom Edward Peacock, formerly a teacher on Parkin's staff at Upper Canada College, wrote in 1911.[36]

This chap returned last summer, after two years at Oxford, to visit his parents. They found that his head had been completely turned by his success, with the result that he attempted to ape all the peculiarities—which he conceived to be those of the Oxford man—as to dress, accent, and mannerisms, to such an extent as to make himself quite ridiculous in a small Canadian town. His attitude towards everything with which he had been formerly connected was so completely changed that his parents were terribly wounded and disappointed, and the feeling in the community has been very strong over the matter.

Rather different reactions were possible. For example, in June 1907, Parkin warned the British Columbia secretary that 'we have not been particularly happy about your last two appointments. Both have been fined; the last one has lately been rusticated for a time. . . . [A]ny new Scholar whom you send over should have it made clear to him

---

[31] NAC, A729 (RTF 1049), Parkin to R. R. Woods, 10 May 1909; Parkin to A. Wilson, 6 Apr. 1911; Morris to 'Mr Parker', 26 Apr. 1911; and memorandum by Dr Parkin, Washington, DC, 22 Nov. 1912.
[32] NAC, A621 (RTF 1269), William Peterson to Parkin, 29 Apr. 1904.
[33] NAC, A621 (RTF 1202), Grey to Parkin, 27 Dec. 1905.
[34] The other firsts were Arthur Moxon, John Read, and J. B. McNair in jurisprudence; Thorleif Larsen in English; Sidney C. Dyke in physiology; and Alfred Ewert in French and German. Read and McNair also took firsts in the BCL. On Martin, see Frederick Madden, 'The Commonwealth, Commonwealth History, and Oxford, 1905–1971', in Frederick Madden and D. K. Fieldhouse (eds.), *Oxford and the Idea of Commonwealth: Essays Presented to Sir Edgar Williams* (London: Croom Helm, 1982), 10.
[35] NAC, A620 (RTF 1985), Parkin to Grey, 30 Oct. 1906.
[36] NAC, A727 (RTF 2357), Peacock to Parkin, 18 Apr. 1911. Although Fife was elected from Alberta, his family lived in (and he had attended school in) Peterborough, Ontario.

that he has the character of the Province to maintain in every particular of his life at Oxford.'[37]

When war broke out in August 1914, there was no doubt of its necessity, as Parkin made clear in a letter to the registrar of the University of Manitoba in September.[38]

A large proportion of our Colonial Rhodes Scholars are preparing to go to the front . . . and we have allowed the Scholarships of all such men to be suspended for the time to be taken up again when the War or their period of service is at an end. I hear that your Scholar Mr Nason is serving in the Colonial Corps, and that Mr Ewert is doing Red Cross work in France. It will be a great addition to their experience to have taken part in this great struggle.

Fifteen of the 1912 and 1913 scholars joined up immediately, most in British regiments; almost all the 1914–16 Canadian and Newfoundland scholars would also volunteer for military service; and most of those who had gone down by 1914 also served in the forces or in some civilian capacity. Many served as officers in the infantry or artillery on the western front. At least sixteen reached the rank of major, and eighteen won the Military Cross.

The first Canadian scholar to be killed in action was A. N. King, in May 1916; Fife was next, early in June. In the next seventeen months another nine scholars from Canada and Newfoundland would die in battle. The last, in October 1917, was Talbot Papineau; by then he was proudly claiming French Canadian heritage, having engaged in a widely publicized debate with his cousin Henri Bourassa on the meaning of the war for French Canadians.[39] Many more were wounded, such as Malcolm Hollett, who was left 'but a wreck of what he used to be'; E. W. Berry, who died in Oxford in January 1920; and Louis Brehaut, invalided home in 1915 (but who lived to 1933).[40] Even those not so visibly affected were deeply marked. Percy Corbett, for example, was in the 1930s determined that Canada not be drawn into the next European war, a viewpoint that generated much public controversy.[41] Conscious that an era had ended, Parkin struggled in a letter written to a friend in British Columbia on 11 November 1918 'to find words to express all that this means. It is simply the climax of all human history so far. And the mind is only paralyzed in the attempt to grasp its whole meaning. . . . At the instant I am thinking more of the boys who will never come back and the parents who will never see them again, as much as anything else.'[42]

Involving the Scholars: The Selection Process Revisited

By the end of the war it had been decided to replace institutional rotations by provincial selection committees. As Parkin explained, 'we have had instances under our old

---

[37] NAC, A728 (RTF 2016), Parkin to A. Robinson, 27 June 1907.

[38] NAC, A728 (RTF 1221), Parkin to W. J. Spence, 30 Sept. 1914.

[39] Sandra Gwyn, *Tapestry of War: A Private View of Canadians in the Great War* (Toronto: HarperCollins, 1992), 90–8, 313–28.

[40] NAC, A729 (RTF 1049), A. Wilson to Parkin, 30 Apr. 1919; RTC 150339 (Nova Scotia selection committee, 1922–35), S. W. Robertson to J. W. Godfrey, 26 Oct. 1933.

[41] See Michiel Horn, *Academic Freedom in Canada: A History* (Toronto: University of Toronto Press, 1999), 117–18.

[42] NAC, A728 (RTF 2016), Parkin to Dr Alexander Robinson, 11 Nov. 1918.

system where a quite inferior candidate was the only one a college had to offer . . . and when I knew that other colleges had far better men to compete had the election been open'.[43] Some still worried about Canadian partisanship, such as Dalhousie's President, A. Stanley Mackenzie, who 'doubt[ed] whether there are enough men within this province having [the] qualifications, and who are in a position to give the time to the business of selection, to make it wise to try to restrict the Committee to Nova Scotians'.[44] To overcome these concerns, it was essential, as Parkin told Mr Justice Lyman Poore Duff of the Supreme Court of Canada, to secure committee chairmen who 'would absolutely command public confidence and give weight to the decision of the Committee'.[45] Duff agreed to chair the Ontario committee; in Nova Scotia and New Brunswick, chief justices Robert Harris and Sir Douglas Hazen would be chairmen; and Edward W. Beatty, president of the Canadian Pacific Railway, accepted Parkin's invitation to chair the Quebec committee. The interest of such busy, prominent men (and, eventually, women) testified to their sense of duty. But they also welcomed the challenge of applying Rhodes's demanding criteria, found it a privilege and pleasure to meet the applicants, and enjoyed working intensively with other selection committee members. Many of the latter, especially the committee secretaries, would now be Rhodes scholars. As Parkin explained to Hazen,[46]

We are making it a settled policy to use our ex-Scholars as far as possible in making up the Committees. We want to train them up to responsibility, and their knowledge of Oxford and its requirements is no slight compensation for their youth. But primarily we want to create a body with the *esprit de corps* which will make them anxious to insist on a high standard among the applicants.

Now 74 years old, Parkin formally retired at the end of 1920. To mark his retirement, a worldwide campaign collected funds for a portrait by Frederick Varley (now in the National Gallery of Canada).[47] The obvious choice to become the Trust's representative in Canada was J. M. Macdonnell;[48] the secretary of the Ontario selection committee, he was also a member of the Parkin family, since his marriage in 1915 to Marjorie, the youngest of the three Parkin sisters. After reading Literae Humaniores at Balliol, he had articled with N. W. Rowell, one of Toronto's leading lawyers. He then joined the National Trust Company in 1911; it was a component of Toronto's most important cluster of businesses, centred on George Cox, which actively recruited men of educational distinction as future leaders.[49] Having volunteered for war service in August 1914, he served overseas

[43] NAC, A728 (RTF 1216), Parkin to Sir Douglas Hazen, 13 Feb. 1920. The change was already being discussed in 1914; see NAC, A727 (RTF 1247), Parkin to Walter Murray, 2 Apr. 1914.

[44] NAC, A730 (RTF 1250), Mackenzie to Parkin, 25 June 1919.

[45] NAC, A621 (RTF 1202), Parkin to Duff, 26 Aug. 1919. On Duff, see David Ricardo Williams, *Duff: A Life in the Law* (Vancouver: University of British Columbia Press, 1984).

[46] NAC, A728 (RTF 1216), Parkin to Sir Douglas Hazen, 14 Nov. 1919.

[47] NAC, A620 (RTF 1985), Frank Aydelotte to Grigg, 19 May 1921. The choice of Varley was apparently on Vincent Massey's advice.

[48] RTF 2524, Wylie to Grigg, 15 June 1921.

[49] See Michael Bliss, *A Canadian Millionaire: The Life and Times of Sir Joseph Flavelle, Bart. 1858–1939* (Toronto: Macmillan of Canada, 1978), 60–2, 122, 193–4, 247, 419. The future Trustee Edward Peacock, who had been gold medallist in English and political science from Queen's University in his graduating year, was recruited to another of these companies, Dominion Securities.

throughout the war in the Canadian Field Artillery and later as a staff officer, winning the Military Cross and the Croix de Guerre, and rising to the rank of major.[50] Like his brother-in-law William Grant, writes Claude Bissell, 'Macdonnell was a Presbyterian, with the same combination of idealism and moral integrity. Tall, spare, his expression verging on the severe, he gave an impression of austerity that was not entirely misleading. He had uncompromising ideas about responsibility and duty. . . . But the severity concealed a relaxed, light touch.'[51] Macdonnell declined payment for his Trust work; he wanted it to be clear that his first loyalty was to his employer.[52]

Almost immediately, National Trust promoted him, transferring him to Montreal as branch manager. When it became apparent that he did not have time to attend to details, he and Philip Kerr agreed in 1925 to engage Terry MacDermot, currently teaching history at Lower Canada College and McGill University, as an assistant. Together, Kerr hoped, they might 'develop a corporate spirit among Canadian Rhodes Scholars somewhat similar to that which is rapidly growing among American Rhodes Scholars'.[53] MacDermot's energy and enthusiasm were immediately evident, for example in the organization of Canada's first sailing dinner, hosted by Montreal Rhodes scholars for some of the 1926 scholars before the latter sailed to England, and in the appearance of a brief newsletter, dated Montreal, January 1927.[54]

During the 1920s, there was talk of more extensive change. '[T]o raise the prestige of the Scholarships and the standard of the men whom we get, . . . it is, I think, essential to abandon the allocation of Scholarships by States and Provinces and Towns in Canada, Australia, and South Africa,' Grigg wrote in 1921.[55] 'I mean this.' But already Canadian jurisdictions were strongly entrenched, as Macdonnell argued after a tour of the west in 1924.[56]

The feeling . . . was that the considerations of distance, etc. would make it almost impossible for all candidates to assemble at one place, and further that even if they could the difficulties of having a Committee which could compare with any degree of satisfaction the qualifications of the various people would be very great indeed—so great that they feel that even if the perfection of human wisdom could be secured for the personnel of the Committee, even then the dissatisfaction of the unsuccessful Provinces would be very great.

Local feeling won out. 'Conditions differ a good deal in the different provinces,' Wylie reminded the Trustees a few years later. 'It would, I think, be unwise to press for a uniformity which the conditions scarcely suggest.'[57]

[50] See Queen's University Archives, Kingston, 2119, J. M. Macdonnell Papers, Box 58, Additional MSS, for Macdonnell's letters home during this period.

[51] Bissell, *The Young Vincent Massey*, 164.

[52] RTF 2555, Macdonnell to Dawson, 19 July, 11 Aug., 24 Oct. 1921. His official title would be Canadian Representative of the Rhodes Trust.

[53] RTF 2555, extract from Secretary's Report on Tour in Canada & United States, 6 Oct. 1926, 14–15; see also RTC 150344, Kerr to Macdonnell, 20 Oct. 1925.

[54] See copy in RTC 150344.

[55] RTF 2524, Edward Grigg, Memorandum on Suggested Reorganization of Scholarship System, 3 June 1921, 5.

[56] RTC 150344, Macdonnell to Grigg, 29 Nov. 1924; for similar views from the Maritimes, see Macdonnell to Grigg, 20 Jan. 1925.

[57] RTF 1247, Report by the late Oxford Secretary on his visit to Canada, July 1932, 10.

In Alberta, which had been assigned one of the forfeited German scholarships, the dominant figure until 1928 was the founding university President, Henry Marshall Tory, another of the Maritimers who were so vital a force in Canadian education. His departure to assume the presidency of the National Research Council was the occasion for reconstructing the committees in both Alberta and Saskatchewan to remove ex officio members.[58] The new chairman in Alberta, L. R. Sherman, Anglican Bishop of Calgary, was the first scholar to chair a selection committee in Canada. He met the test of public reputation, although 'the Bish' had considerable ability to annoy Macdonnell privately. 'Incidentally', the latter asked MacDermot, 'in writing a personal letter do you think you should sign yourself "L. R. Calgary"?'[59]

In Saskatchewan, the founding university President was Walter Murray, who remained central despite a change in the form of the committee. Here the limited number of resident scholars helped to create a core of very long-term committee members, including Arthur Moxon, a member from 1920 until 1962. 'Our Committee has not generally written to the referees,' Moxon told Macdonnell. 'In most cases we knew the boys pretty well and our experience has been that referees outside the Colleges seldom give us any useful information.'[60] Interviews here, held at the Bessborough Hotel in Saskatoon, took less than a morning. Sometimes, when the choice was obvious, there was no interview at all, as when Francis Leddy was selected for 1933.[61] This style did not pass without dissent, notably from people in Regina.[62] However things worked, Oxford had reason to be satisfied; seven of the fifteen Saskatchewan scholars elected between 1927 and 1941 would take firsts.

'You will see that I am ready to sacrifice members of my own family,' Parkin commented to Macdonnell in writing of the original Ontario selection committee. 'You are such a band of brothers that I know you will understand this.'[63] Indeed, W. L. Grant, who had been the initial Beit Lecturer at Oxford and was from 1917 the Principal of Upper Canada College, was often consulted, and Parkin's other son-in-law, Vincent Massey, then heading his family's agricultural implement business, was also on the committee. Besides Duff, Macdonnell, and Massey, the other members of the first Ontario committee were Sherman, at the time Rector of Holy Trinity Church in Toronto, and George Smith, Massey's closest friend and godfather to his son Hart. J. M. Macdonnell's successor as Ontario secretary was his cousin Norman, a Toronto lawyer. Later, Will Rundle, general manager of National Trust, and Hugh Macdonnell, J. M.'s brother, also served; indeed, the first outsider was Roland Michener, recruited by Norman Macdonnell as committee secretary in 1926.[64]

When province-wide competitions were created, the interview became central. Most

[58] RTC 150339, Tory to Macdonnell, 19 Sept. 1927; A. L. Burt to Macdonnell, 17 Apr. 1928.
[59] RTC 150344, Macdonnell to MacDermot, 18 Feb. 1935.
[60] RTC 150339, Moxon to Macdonnell, 25 Jan. 1928.
[61] RTC 150344, MacDermot to Macdonnell, 3 Apr. 1933; for another example, see RTC 150343, Elton to Michener, 23 Feb. 1950.
[62] RTC 150339, Douglas Fraser to Macdonnell, 11 Oct. 1929.
[63] NAC, A621 (RTF 1202), Parkin to Macdonnell, 26 Aug. 1919.
[64] RTC 150339, J. M. Macdonnell to N. S. Macdonnell, 7 Sept. 1926.

provinces also required an essay, written just before the interview. The Ontario procedure was described in 1930 by Michener.[65] The other members of the committee this year were Mr Justice W. E. Middleton of the Ontario Court of Appeal as chair (Duff being unavailable), George Smith, Hugh Macdonnell, and Norman M. Rogers, recently appointed as professor of political science at Queen's University. J. M. Macdonnell also sat in. The meeting, held at Hart House, the men's student centre given to the University of Toronto by Vincent Massey, was later than usual, Saturday, 20 December. There were sixteen candidates, 'the largest number in my experience', including nine from the University of Toronto (one from Trinity College, three from University College, and five from Victoria College, including both winners, H. S. Day and E. B. Jolliffe). The applicants met at 9 o'clock and were given three hours to write an essay. The list of eleven topics ran from 'why I am making application for a Rhodes Scholarship' and 'the future of humane studies in our Canadian universities' to 'wheat' and 'has Plato a message for the modern world?' The applicants lunched with the committee, then each had an interview of about 25 minutes. With a break for dinner, this required until 11.30 p.m. On Sunday, the committee sat from 11 a.m. to 6 p.m., re-interviewing five applicants for an hour each. By the end of the day, the list had been narrowed to three; a further meeting on Monday morning was needed to make the final decision. 'I recite all this to show the time and care which the committee took in making the selection,' Michener explained. Not mentioned, but almost certainly present at some point, was Burgon Bickersteth, Warden of Hart House. So many Toronto applicants used him as a reference that he did not write letters but instead met with the committee to discuss the candidates.[66]

'[The Quebec] Committee follows neither the will of Rhodes nor the voice of Oxford, but is guided by its own instincts,' one Montrealer said to a 1925 visitor, who found the scholars there to be 'vigorous young men with views of their own'.[67] Interviews usually were held in the CPR boardroom at Windsor Station. Beatty was the central figure. His virtues were spelled out by Macdonnell, in the course of seeking advice on someone proposed as a chairman elsewhere.[68]

I should like to have your frank opinion . . . as to . . . his inaccessibility to any influence and his openness of mind. I am inclined to think that this last is as important as anything else, particularly as he will be sitting on a Committee with younger men and it is very undesirable that we should place on the Committee someone who will hastily form definite opinions and who will be quite unwilling to change. In this connection . . . I have been greatly struck, in my observation of the Quebec Committee, with the attitude of E. W. Beatty who, as Chairman, gives weight to the views of other people and on occasion comes round to them.

In its first year, the Quebec committee selected Ariste Brossard, but after anglophones won the next four competitions there began to be anxious discussion about the very

[65] NAC, 621 (RTF 1202), Michener to Macdonnell, 29 Dec. 1930; Macdonnell to Kerr, 31 Dec. 1930.
[66] RTC 150339, Henry Borden to MacDermot, 18 Dec. 1933; 150344, Michener to MacDermot, 13 Jan. 1931.
[67] RTF 1247, Report by Dr Rendall on the Rhodes Scholarships in Canada, 20 Jan. 1926, 8.
[68] RTC 150339, Macdonnell to W. S. Fisher, 22 Aug. 1927; see also RTC 150339, Arnold Heeney to Macdonnell, 27 Sept. 1935.

different backgrounds of French- and English-speaking applicants; this led ultimately to the allocation of a second scholarship to Quebec. Grigg summarized the issues in June 1923.[69]

Mr Beatty has just been in to see me and spoke upon . . . the difficulty experienced by French Canadian candidates in securing Scholarships. . . . So far as Rhodes's own wishes are concerned, he would certainly have desired to have French Canadians at Oxford amongst his Scholars. The fact that French Canadian candidates are always, or nearly always, rejected, would inevitably end in creating a general feeling that 'no French Canadian need apply'; at the same time, the Dominion would lose the broadening and moderating influence which French Canadians with Oxford experience would undoubtedly have upon French Canadian views and French Canadian politics.

Under terms of the will, the new scholarship could not be explicitly allocated, but as Lothian later summarized the decision, the Trustees gave the committee discretion to achieve their

object in creating the Scholarship [which] was to remove the disability in which French Canadians felt themselves when competing for the Scholarship . . . [T]hey were prepared to accept the view . . . put forward by the members of the Committee at that time that they should feel themselves free to allow one of the Scholarships to the British Canadians and one to the French Canadians provided always that an adequate candidate was forthcoming in each case.[70]

By the 1930s, the second scholarship had begun to create a larger group of French-speaking scholars resident in Quebec and to give the Trust access to voices from within French Canadian society. An example was a thoughtful 1934 review by Jean Casgrain, based on wide consultation, of issues posed for the scholarships by Quebec's system of classical colleges.[71] Later in the 1930s Ariste Brossard became the first francophone secretary; since 1953, when Paul Gérin-Lajoie became secretary, the position has always been filled by a francophone. The Quebec secretary has always had the additional responsibility of preparing French-language materials, which were used in all provinces for applicants whose first language was French.

Giving Canada one additional scholarship could be justified, but giving it to Quebec when Ontario was larger would have been hard to defend. The solution was to end altogether the Prince Edward Island scholarship, which had been biennial since 1921,[72] and award a second scholarship to Ontario beginning in 1926. The decision was protested by Prince Edward Island's Chief Superintendent of Education, who spoke of the province's scholarship as 'an inherent right'. He assigned the blame to the usual Canadian villain: 'This loss added to our loss of population can only add another grievance at the Federal relationship which has produced these results.'[73]

Of course no jurisdiction wanted to give up a scholarship. To encourage committees

[69] RTC 150344, Grigg to Macdonnell, 27 June 1923.

[70] RTF 1269, Lothian to Heeney, 25 May 1937.

[71] See RTC 84659, Jean, Casgrain, 'Rhodes Scholarships at Oxford and Candidates from Quebec Classical Colleges', Apr. 1934.

[72] NAC, A731 (RTF 1381), Memorandum on PEI by Parkin, 21 June 1920.

[73] RTC 150344, H. H. Shaw to Macdonnell, 8 Dec. 1925; and see Macdonnell's reply, 11 Dec. 1925.

not to make weak appointments, the Trust was briefly willing to guarantee an additional appointment in the subsequent year. The only Canadian jurisdiction to benefit was British Columbia, which made no award for 1930 and was allowed to make two appointments for 1931.[74] The committee chose Frederick Kergin (a medical student interviewed in Toronto by J. M. Macdonnell) and James Gibson. The latter, one of the youngest Canadian scholars ever appointed, had given much thought to the scholarship, as the BC secretary, D. N. Hossie, reported later.[75]

Gibson's father in Victoria . . . tells me incidentally that ten years ago the boy enquired of him regarding the Rhodes Scholarship . . . and that while he has never mentioned it since until his application was made this year, . . . he feels quite satisfied that the boy has endeavoured steadily ever since to develop along the lines that so appealed to Rhodes. The boy is a bit young but . . . he does not seem likely to let his head be turned.

In these years, the Trust sometimes provided grants to other Canadians, taking care to distinguish them from the scholarship. The most notable, made after strong recommendations by George Smith and others in Toronto, went to D. J. McDougall, later a major figure in the University of Toronto History Department, to support him for three years at Balliol. Blinded in the war, McDougall had nevertheless done outstanding undergraduate work, supporting his studies and his dependent mother on a Canadian pension and by working as a masseur.[76] When a tie in the 1923 Alberta competition forced the Trustees to make the decision, they awarded the scholarship to Robert Lamb, but made a special grant to the runner-up, K. H. Broadus.[77] A tie was highly unusual, but difficult decisions were not. The runner-up could, of course, apply again, and repeat applicants often won. In 1937, for example, two Canadian winners had applied twice before, five won on their second application, and just two won on their first try.[78] Arnold Heeney, although only 21 when he went up to Oxford, had likewise won on his third application.

One reflection of the rethinking during the 1920s was a tour of the dominions by Dr Montague Rendall, formerly headmaster at Winchester, who favoured recruiting scholars directly from independent schools.[79] Grigg in fact suggested that Rendall's forthcoming trip made it unnecessary for Macdonnell to make a long-planned visit to western Canada in 1924, prompting Macdonnell to complain to W. L. Grant: 'I cannot see any earthly reason why they should be so ready to send people from London across the Ocean and a Continent and not ready to send me across a continent.' Grant's reply emphasized the need 'to assert your own self-respecting position to the somewhat high-flying Grigg'.[80] By the time Rendall reached North America in September 1925,

---

[74] See RTM 23 July 1929.   [75] RTC 150339, Hossie to Macdonnell, 9 Dec. 1930.

[76] RTF 2638, extract from Report 212, 16 Dec. 1924; also Wylie to Kerr, 24 Nov. 1925.

[77] RTF 2357, Charles Stuart and H. M. Tory to Geoffrey Dawson, 29 Nov. 1922; see also Wylie to Dawson, 27 Dec. 1922 and Grigg to Macdonnell, 24 Jan. 1923.

[78] RTF 1247B, summary of Canadian scholars to be in residence, 1937–8.

[79] See J. A. Mangan, *The Games Ethic and Imperialism: Aspects of the Diffusion of an Ideal* (Harmondsworth: Viking, 1986), 28–33.

[80] RTC 150344, Macdonnell to Grant, 9 July 1924, and Grant to Macdonnell, 10 July 1924.

Kerr had taken over; Macdonnell asked for a meeting with him and Rendall at Swarthmore. This confirmed that the tour would continue, but with 'no official significance' in Canada.[81] Later in the autumn, Rendall reported to Kerr from Toronto that 'every one in Canada is most pleasant & our time passes happily. They sing out cheerily at intervals "Remember, we have to develop our own nationality on our own lines!" I try to remember it steadfastly.'[82]

Reorganization in Newfoundland

Rendall resumed his official role in Newfoundland. His visit at Christmas 1925 was the only one on behalf of the Trust between 1912 and 1951—except for a private visit in 1929 by Dr Albert Mansbridge, who was asked to speak to a few individuals 'about the possibility of improving the calibre of the Newfoundland Rhodes Scholars'.[83] Much of the solution to that problem was, in fact, being achieved as Rendall arrived: Memorial University College had just opened in St John's to provide the equivalent of the first two years of university. Its founding President, J. L. Paton, formerly headmaster of Manchester Grammar School, gave the college immediate authority in England.[84] Its value in Newfoundland is indicated by the fact that almost every Newfoundland scholar from 1928 until well into the 1980s had attended Memorial.

Rendall's extensive report was the occasion of renewed effort to align Newfoundland with practices elsewhere. One concern was to add Rhodes scholars to the selection committee. Another was to ensure that the committee secretary was formally the Trust's agent. The secretary at committee meetings had been Vincent P. Burke, Roman Catholic school superintendent (a member of the selection committee since 1904, who remained a member until 1950), while Andrew Wilson, secretary of the Council of Higher Education, handled other secretarial duties. Beginning in 1926, J. G. Higgins became the Trust's representative in Newfoundland. Born in May 1891, Higgins was, by a few months, the youngest Newfoundland scholar ever. He had taken a second in jurisprudence, been president of the ice hockey club, and, he delightedly underlined thirty years later, been president of the Canadian Club.[85] He was less in the public eye than H. A. Winter, his law partner at the time, or W. J. Browne, both of whom were appointed in 1932 to Frederick Alderdice's cabinet, the last one in Newfoundland before the suspension of responsible government in 1934.[86] To avoid offending Burke, he called himself assistant secretary and did not vote.

---

[81] RTC 150339, Macdonnell to Smith, 30 Sept. 1925.

[82] RTF 2611, Rendall to 'Secretary' [i.e. Kerr], 23 Nov. 1925.

[83] RTF 1049, Kerr to Mansbridge, 17 Sept. 1929, and to J. G. Higgins, 17 Feb. 1930. Of the five elected for 1920–4, for example, only Ralph Le Messurier gained a degree. See also Lothian to Wylie, 14 Jan. 1931.

[84] RTF 2611, Report by Dr Rendall on the Rhodes scholarships in Newfoundland, 12 Jan. 1926, 7–8. And see Malcolm MacLeod, 'Students Abroad: Preconfederation Educational Links between Newfoundland and the Mainland of Canada', Canadian Historical Association, *Historical Papers* (1985), 172–92.

[85] RTF 1049A, Higgins to E. T. Williams, 30 May 1956.

[86] RTF 1049, Vincent Burke to Lothian, 6 Sept. 1932; evidently they were the first scholars anywhere to be government ministers.

Despite a persistent mythology, the Newfoundland scholarship did not rotate among denominations.[87] To avoid the politics that might have produced a rotation, the committee had developed procedures that Higgins described in 1930.[88]

The procedure adopted in the election of a Rhodes Scholar in this country is as follows. The Committee meet and either elect the scholar at the first meeting or at a later meeting. A copy of the credentials of each candidate is given to each member of the Committee previous to the meeting. There is no discussion over the various candidates at the meeting or meetings. Voting is taken secretly and the candidate receiving the majority of votes is elected. Candidates never appear before the Committee at a meeting. They usually visit the Committee individually before the meeting.

Except that he recognized that applicants were away at university during the winter, Lothian (as Kerr had become in 1930) found this procedure very unsatisfactory.[89]

In no other Selection Committee in any part of the world—and there are over 60 such Committees—is the selection of a Rhodes Scholar made without a personal interview and without discussion by members of the Committee of their own estimate of the candidate and the opinions of those whose names he has given as references. . . . The Trustees . . . feel it difficult to understand how the Selection Committee can meet and not pool their knowledge of the candidates and discuss their qualifications before coming to a decision. They also understand that it is elsewhere the universal practice for members to cast their votes openly in the Committee.

There is no evidence that the committee changed its ways.[90]

Oxford and Beyond

'Do Rhodes Scholars Make Good?' asked *Maclean's Magazine* in 1928.[91] It was a question frequently asked by the Trust as well. In the autumn of 1927, for example, Macdonnell remarked that 'the Academic record is much better than formerly. At the same time one cannot be at all sure that we are getting the best people.'[92] Between 1904 and 1926, 212 scholars were selected in Canada and Newfoundland. Five did not come up at all; seven of those killed in the First World War had not had time to take a degree; and twenty-seven others earned no degree or diploma. At the other extreme, eighteen had

---

[87] See, e.g., Malcolm MacLeod, 'Parade Street Parade: The Student Body at Memorial University College, 1925–49', in Paul Axelrod and John Reid (eds.), *Youth University and Canadian Society: Essays in the Social History of Higher Education* (Kingston: McGill-Queen's University Press, 1989), 61–2. The religion of every Newfoundland scholar until 1976 is in the manuscript copy of Augustus Lilly's 'The Rhodes Scholarships in Newfoundland' (in Rhodes Trust archives), but not in the published version, A. G. Lilly, 'Rhodes Scholarships', in *Encyclopedia of Newfoundland and Labrador*, iv (St John's: Harry Cuff Publishers, 1993), 591–2.

[88] RTF 1049A, Higgins to Kerr, 18 Mar. 1930.

[89] RTF 1049, Lothian to Higgins, 23 May 1930.

[90] e.g. RTF 1049, Higgins to Lothian, 13 Dec. 1930.

[91] This was the title of an article in the issue of 1 Apr. 1928, by J. A. Stevenson.

[92] RTF 150344, Macdonnell to E. R. Peacock, 22 Nov. 1927.

achieved firsts in Schools and/or in the BCL, nine of them in law—five actually took two firsts.[93] When compared to Australians and New Zealanders, these were unimpressive results.

Many Canadians discovered quickly that they were unlikely to reach the standard of an Oxford first. Thus, Norman Robertson wrote home early in 1924 that his tutors in PPE found him 'solid and satisfactory, rather heavy and ponderous, too serious, and . . . likely [to] earn only a good second'.[94] Travelling in Canada some years later, Allen met similar views. When he asked for 'opinions on the comparative dearth of first class men, in the purely academic sense[,] the most interesting comments . . . were that the system in most Canadian universities tends to encourage mere absorption and reproduction of knowledge, at the expense of originality and imagination; and that insufficient attention is paid to form and clarity of writing.'[95]

Academic preparation was only one of the issues. Selection committees were reminded that 'study in another country under strange and exacting conditions often involves great intellectual, moral, and physical strain'.[96] Oxford culture—the structure of Schools, the return to freshman status, college curfews, proctorial discipline, etc.—had many 'peculiarities', George Estabrooks noted in reflecting on his own experience. 'No pains should be spared to point out . . . that the numerous restrictions of the English system are to be taken as part of the game. If that can be drilled in . . . much that would otherwise incite bitterness will only cause humor or something akin to it.'[97] There could be stress also in others' expectations; as Roland Michener told scholars in 1938, 'you will never live it down'.[98]

The biographies and memoirs of scholars of this period all remind us that the scholarship was much more than a course of study, and that the experience of Oxford varied according to one's background, expectations, schooling, personality, college, subject, tutors, and friends.[99] For men like Arnold Heeney and James M. Minifie, rowing was a key connection with undergraduate life. Hugh MacLennan played rugby and tennis; a championship tennis player in the Maritimes, he finally attained his ambition to play

[93] In addition to Alfred Ewert, John Read, and J. B. McNair, mentioned above, the others were Herbert Rose in classical Moderations and Literae Humaniores and John Lowe in Literae Humaniores and theology. For published academic statistics, I have used RTF 2696, Memorandum to selection committees, 1932. These data are for scholars elected to 1928. They show 16% of Canadians obtained firsts and 58% seconds. For Newfoundland the rate was 5.6% firsts, 50% seconds. Because these statistics were based on examinations taken, one scholar could be counted twice. That the Trust data included scholars for 1927–8 improved the Canadian rate, because five of this group took firsts in Schools, and two (Ronald Martland and George Curtis) also won firsts in the BCL.

[94] J. L. Granatstein, *A Man of Influence: Norman A. Robertson and Canadian Statecraft 1929–68* (Toronto: Deneau, 1981), 16.

[95] RTF 1247, Report of Oxford Secretary on Tour in Canada, Aug. and Sept. 1937, 8.

[96] RTF 2696, 'Memorandum to Selection Committees', 1932.

[97] RTC 150344, G. H. Estabrooks to Macdonnell, 20 Jan. 1927. A sophisticated essay on this theme is Michael Hornyansky, 'So You're Coming to Oxford', *AO* 40 (1953).

[98] RTC 84657, handwritten notes, on Rhodes House stationery.

[99] See, e.g., Elspeth Cameron, *Hugh MacLennan: A Writer's Life* (Toronto: University of Toronto Press, 1981), 23–62; and Eugene Forsey, *A Life on the Fringe: The Memoirs of Eugene Forsey* (Toronto: Oxford University Press, 1990), 35–48. Some other works are quoted below.

tennis for Oxford against Cambridge in his fourth year (a year financed by his father). Eugene Forsey, a non-drinker, tried to avoid the alcohol-steeped aspects of undergraduate life. For the socialists, Oxford included engagement in the Labour Party, visits to the home of Sir Stafford Cripps, and perhaps a reading party with G. D. H. Cole.

Outside Oxford experiences varied as well. Heeney, the son of an Anglican cleric, had a standing invitation from the Dean of Winchester, and the Cathedral Close became for him 'a serene and familiar sanctuary' from Oxford.[100] For Minifie, later a Paris-based correspondent for the New York *Herald-Tribune*, 'it was to the pleasant ambience of Pension Mollet [in Paris's Latin Quarter] that I always returned when feelings of homesickness overcame me'.[101] Most Canadians got to France, Germany, and Italy, and some travelled further. Many joined the Christmas ice hockey tour to Switzerland, where the match against Cambridge took place. 'The friends of my more sedentary years find it hard to conceal their surprise when I tell them I played on a team that won the championship in Europe,' J. A. Corry recalled. 'The main reason for our reaching that pinnacle was that everybody else was worse at the game than we were!'[102] Forsey, emphatically not an athlete, went to Switzerland for Quaker gatherings and to view sessions of the League of Nations Assembly. Although Canadians prided themselves on not clustering together, the closest friends and travelling companions were often other foreigners.[103]

'I am not one of those who thinks of his Oxford period as "the days of wine and roses",' Corry recalled, 'and I do not speak of it in reverential tones.'[104] As he left Oxford, W. L. Morton wrote an essay for the *Oxford Mail* entitled 'No Wish to be an Oxonian'.[105] 'Several times I heard the view that the Rhodes Scholar returns to Canada alienated both from his own country and from England,' Allen commented after his first tour in 1931. But, he went on, 'for the most part the accusation probably arises from a misunderstanding. With some Rhodes Scholars, a slightly cynical depreciatory attitude towards Oxford and England is the most Oxonian and the most English characteristic which they bring back with them. . . . [This] is sometimes mistaken in their own country for Anglophobia.'[106] Indeed, years later, as they reflected on university governance, men like Corry and Morton appealed strongly to the Oxford tradition of a self-governing community of scholars.[107] Certainly they appreciated what they had received—a chance for a liberal education; if they had to make it for themselves, that was fundamental to the process. Thus, Norman Robertson's biographer, J. L. Granatstein, summarizes the importance of Oxford to Robertson.[108]

[100] Arnold, Heeney, *The Things that are Caesar's: Memoirs of a Canadian Public Servant*, ed. Brian Heeney (Toronto: University of Toronto Press, 1972), 15.

[101] James M. Minifie, *Expatriate* (Toronto: Macmillan of Canada, 1976), 19–20.

[102] James A. Corry, *My Life and Work: A Happy Partnership* (Kingston: Queen's University, 1981), 50.

[103] e.g. Escott Reid, *Radical Mandarin: The Memoirs of Escott Reid* (Toronto: University of Toronto Press, 1989), 48–9.

[104] Corry, *My Life and Work*, 49.   [105] RTC 150339, clipping from *Oxford Mail*, 19 June 1935.

[106] RTF 1247, extract from Mr Allen's Report on Tour of Canada and USA 1931, 21 Aug. 1931.

[107] George Whalley (ed.), *A Place of Liberty: Essays on the Government of Canadian Universities* (Toronto: Clarke, Irwin, 1964) includes essays by W. L. Morton and F. R. Scott. See also Horn, *Academic Freedom in Canada*, 246–79.

[108] Granatstein, *A Man of Influence*, 18.

He had been unhappy with the training he had received at Oxford, but the university had nonetheless shaped and polished him. Oxford had confirmed the eclectic quality of his mind and had strengthened his humanism; it had also given him that special assuredness that only Balliol men seemed to possess . . . In addition, his time at Balliol had forced him to make up his mind on a wide range of questions on morals, religion, politics, and the Empire.

Writing in 1928 of 'the performance of old Rhodes Scholars in after life', Kerr reflected that

a percentage of the early Rhodes Scholars . . . did not get a great deal out of their experience at Oxford and . . . are not going to do very much in after life. On the other hand there is a considerable number who are doing extremely well. Moreover, three-quarters of the returned Rhodes Scholars are under 40 and few of them return to their own countries before they are 26 or 27. They have not therefore had a great deal of time in which to make their mark.[109]

Where they might make that mark is suggested by scholars' locations and careers in 1929. About two-thirds of those who had gone down were again in Canada or Newfoundland (see Table 1). Some had stayed in Britain, but more now lived in the United States. Ten were lost from view, and nineteen had died. A majority of the almost seventy who had returned to the jurisdiction that selected them were practising law.[110] So were another twenty elsewhere in Canada, Britain, or the United States. Several more were employed as lawyers by businesses, and six were teaching law. The latter were among the thirty-seven scholars who held university posts in Canada, mainly at three universities, Toronto (with 9), McGill (with 8), and Alberta (with 6). About twenty (i.e., more than in all other Canadian universities combined) were teaching at universities in the United States. Three were teaching in Britain, all by 1930 at professorial rank.[111] Two of those at McGill were Americans, W. L. G. Williams and Wilder Penfield. The latter was a particular coup; indeed, Allen remarked a few years later, 'no Rhodes Scholar whom I have met has struck me as more remarkable than Penfield'.[112]

Corporate Spirit and Canadian Spirit

In 1932, the Wylies spent two months crossing Canada on their farewell tour. As on other visits by Trust representatives, they met both scholars and other public figures. For example, in Ottawa they dined at the Barbeaus' home, lunched at the home of the former Prime Minister, Sir Robert Borden, and attended a lunch 'given by the Rhodes Scholars and their wives' which also included the Prime Minister (R. B. Bennett), the Bordens, the British High Commissioner and his wife, and O. D. Skelton, Under-Secretary of the Department

[109] RTF 1247, Report to the Trustees on Visit to Canada and the United States in 1927, P. Kerr, 27 Jan. 1928, 8.

[110] More than a third of scholars from Canada and Newfoundland had read law, for either or both the final honours school and the BCL. The only other widely popular schools were modern history and classics, each read by twenty-seven scholars.

[111] H. J. Rose and E. V. Gordon already held chairs, and Alfred Ewert would in 1930 be elected professor of Romance languages at Oxford.

[112] RTF 1247, Report by the Oxford Secretary on his visit to the United States and Canada, Apr. 1935, 18. Two other non-Canadians, K. G. Blaikie and A. O. Ponder, were also in Quebec, both in business.

TABLE I. *Location of Rhodes scholars from Canada and Newfoundland*

(1929, 1959, 1989)

(scholars elected to 1926, 1956, and 1986 only)

	1929	1959	1989
Total living	193	428	552
In Canada and Newfoundland	126	332	430
St John's	4	13	21
Halifax	5	12	19
Saint John	5	6	0
Fredericton	2	6	4
Quebec	2	9	9
Montreal	18	49	49
Ottawa	7	75	75
Kingston	2	10	14
Toronto	17	49	97
London	3	4	11
Winnipeg	15	13	15
Regina	2	4	5
Saskatoon	2	7	3
Edmonton	10	13	13
Calgary	4	4	11
Vancouver	9	27	38
Total, these cities	107	301	384
Percentage of Canadian residents	85%	91%	89%
In USA	34	48	52
In UK	18	38	29
Elsewhere	5	5	16
Location unknown	10	5	25

Note: Because scholars moved and because there are ambiguities, gaps, and lags in information in the *Register*, figures are slightly approximate. Suburban addresses are included in metropolitan centre. See text for additional discussion.

of External Affairs.[113] One of Wylie's purposes was to encourage a more active association among scholars, something Macdonnell thought unlikely, as he told Lothian.[114]

I think it is desirable to let you know exactly what I feel about Sir Francis's suggestion that Rhodes Scholars should have a corporate sense . . . The phrase was used to me some ten or eleven years ago by Sir George Parkin also . . .

I think I may say that most Rhodes Scholars feel that having been at Oxford is not in itself a sufficient bond of union to bring them naturally together except on special occasions—such, for example, as the visit of Wylie or yourself . . .

I mention this because I think . . . that Sir Francis expected something in the way of organizations which, in my opinion, simply will not come to pass. Rhodes Scholars are infinitely various, and . . . [i]t does not seem to me necessary, or for that matter desirable, that they should attempt to have a corporate sense as such, yet I think there is no doubt that that is what Wylie hoped for and the absence of which he somewhat deplored, and I think the same was true with the late Sir George Parkin. In the case of Parkin I felt that the Rhodes Scholars appeared in his mind, mutatis mutandis, as a kind of huge imperial federation league not necessarily devoted to the same end but necessarily capable of being banded together for certain common objectives.

Wylie continued to disagree.[115]

I felt in Canada that there was more individualism about among Rhodes Scholars than in the other Dominions—& this was, not unnaturally, especially noticeable in . . . Toronto & Montreal. . . . Perhaps this led me to press the idea more than I otherwise should have done . . . I explained that I realized that Rhodes Scholars wandered along many different paths in life, professionally & politically; but that I thought, & the Trustees thought, that there was enough of a common tie in the fact of having all been Rhodes Scholars at Oxford to make an occasional meeting of them, *as* Rhodes Scholars, possible, and desirable.

I believe that, when they get local Associations started, . . . they will feel that the thing is worth while . . . Not, probably, so much for those who, like Jim Macdonnell himself, are doing a great deal of public work of the kind that Rhodes had in mind, as for others who might drop out and do nothing for themselves or others. To be kept in touch, even slightly, with a body of men including a good number of the Macdonnell type, may be a healthy stimulus.

However, I needn't preach this to you. But I realize that there is in Canada among our Rhodes Scholars a tendency to react *against* any 'high-falutin' stuff.

Following his visit, a number of provincial or local organizations were in fact created. Allen was much encouraged, for example, to hear from H. A. Dyde of an 'informal gathering' in Edmonton and a subsequent meeting in Calgary at which eleven of sixteen scholars in Alberta had been present.[116] Such a small group, located mainly in one or two cities, hardly needed a formal organization, however.

More significant than any organization specifically of scholars was their participation in networks of English Canadians that sought both to build a Canadian national spirit

---

[113] RTF 1247, Report by the late Oxford Secretary on his visit to Canada, July 1932, 23.
[114] RTF 1247, Macdonnell to Lothian, 4 Oct. 1932.
[115] RTF 1247, Wylie to Lothian, 30 Oct. 1932.
[116] RTF 1247, Allen to Lothian, 6 June 1933. For another example, see, e.g., RTC 150343, Memorandum on Association of Rhodes Scholars of the Province of Quebec, 26 May 1933.

and to understand and reshape the international order. In Montreal, for example, a quite self-conscious group included Terry MacDermot, F. R. Scott, John Farthing, and Arnold Heeney along with Brooke Claxton (MacDermot's brother-in-law), Raleigh Parkin (son of Sir George) and G. R. McCall. In Winnipeg, John W. Dafoe, editor of the Winnipeg *Free Press*, the most influential nationalist voice in Canada, was a central figure; his closest associate was the fiercely anti-imperialist George Ferguson. Such local clusters were essential to national organizations such as the Canadian Clubs (of which Graham Spry was national secretary from 1926 to 1932), the Canadian Institute of International Affairs (established in 1926, of which Escott Reid became first national secretary in 1932), the League of Nations Society (established in 1921, of which Terry MacDermot became national secretary in 1934), and the Canadian Radio League (established in 1930, in which Spry was also a principal figure).[117]

By the 1930s, the tone of Canadian discussions had been deeply affected by the Depression. Contrasting that reality with the 'delightful comfort' of an American reunion he had just attended at Swarthmore, Terry MacDermot reported to Macdonnell in 1933: 'In such surroundings it was difficult to break away from unreality. Yet that was exactly what would have been so interesting and what a minority there hoped would happen. Ideas everywhere are boiling over and people are freely scrapping their mental furniture, and any serious discussion which cloaks this fact is simply not serious.'[118] MacDermot's political efforts were within the Liberal Party. In its transition toward more progressive ideas a key figure was Norman Rogers, who ran for Kingston in the 1935 federal election and was immediately appointed Minister of Labour in Mackenzie King's new government.[119] Other active Liberals included Thane Campbell, elected to the Prince Edward Island legislature in 1931, who became provincial premier in 1936, and J. B. McNair who became Attorney General of New Brunswick in 1935 and provincial premier five years later.

Other scholars sought to bring a Fabian approach to Canada. They aimed at a fundamental restructuring of Canadian politics by creating a socialist party that would challenge the capitalism that had evidently produced such economic devastation. Especially notable in the intellectual and organizational work that produced the Cooperative Commonwealth Federation (or CCF) were F. R. Scott (who, with the historian Frank Underhill, launched the League for Social Reconstruction), Graham Spry (who became the League's national secretary), King Gordon, Eugene Forsey, and Escott Reid.[120] Forsey and

---

[117] See, e.g., David Jay Bercuson, *True Patriot: The Life of Brooke Claxton 1898–1960* (Toronto: University of Toronto Press, 1993), 6, 55–7, 60–4; and Patrick H. Brennan, *Reporting the Nation's Business: Press–Government Relations during the Liberal Years, 1935–1957* (Toronto: University of Toronto Press, 1994), 14–16.

[118] RTC 150344, MacDermot to Macdonnell, 12 June 1933.

[119] Two other scholars, W. G. Ernst at the federal level and Edgar Rochette in Quebec, achieved ministerial rank in the mid-1930s, but very briefly, as the governments they joined were on the brink of defeat.

[120] See *Social Planning for Canada*, reprint edition, with introduction by F. R. Scott, Leonard Marsh, Graham Spry, J. King Gordon, Eugene Forsey, and J. S. Parkinson (Toronto: University of Toronto Press, 1975); and Michiel Horn, *The League for Social Reconstruction: Intellectual Origins of the Democratic Left in Canada, 1930–1942* (Toronto: University of Toronto Press, 1980). Underhill had recently moved from Saskatchewan to the University of Toronto; he was not a Rhodes scholar but had read history at Balliol and been on the selection committee in Saskatchewan.

Scott had not only been selected by the Quebec committee, under Beatty's chairmanship, but taught at McGill, of which he was Chancellor. As Wylie noted in 1932, their activities had alarmed McGill's Principal, Sir Arthur Currie, who worried that they were 'rather "wild"—in social theory, not in conduct: he was [also] a little anxious with regard to the latest Quebec election.' Others, Wylie found, 'did not share his anxiety, either as to the two Rhodes Scholars in question or as to the newly elected Scholar'.[121]

The new scholar was David Lewis. The son of a labour activist who had moved from Poland to Montreal in 1921, he was encouraged to apply by Wilfred Bovey, a friend of the scholarship at McGill, where his titles, which included Assistant to the Principal, hardly conveyed his importance. Lewis's interview, in which he pledged to nationalize the Canadian Pacific Railway if ever he became Prime Minister, has become part of scholarship lore in Canada. In his memoirs, Lewis also stresses his essay, which he wrote not on politics but on the topic 'Modern Culture Is Ugly', and his ability to convince the committee that he was not a communist.[122] His selection reflected the times and his exceptional quality—and reflected credit on the committee that chose him. Besides Beatty, its members were Gilbert Stairs (its secretary since 1919), Edgar Rochette, Alexandre Gérin-Lajoie, Ariste Brossard, Wilder Penfield, Lester Pearson (a young diplomat from Ottawa who actually would become Prime Minister; Oxford educated but not a Rhodes scholar, he was replacing Percy Corbett for the year), and Arnold Heeney.

At Oxford, Lewis was the first Canadian scholar to be elected president of the Union—and attracted much attention. Thus, Eric Millar wrote from London that 'Grigg is very upset about a speech which a Rhodes Scholar named Lewis made at the Union in the debate on the British Empire. . . . I wonder if you would mind me showing Grigg your note about Lewis in your Report to the Trustees?' Allen declined.[123]

If you do not mind, I would rather not show Grigg my remarks about D. Lewis. I do not think he would understand: indeed I am sure he would think that the whole of the Rhodes Foundation was going to the dogs! I don't know exactly what Lewis said at the Union, but I can imagine that it would be very startling to Grigg. I am not, myself, in sympathy at all with Lewis's views, but nowadays we must expect this type of opinion . . . This is specially true of Canada, where I find that most of the intelligent young men lean towards socialism, or kindred doctrines, such as the so-called C.C.F.

. . . To my mind, it is most important that Rhodes Scholars should feel that Oxford is a place of tolerance, free thought and free expression, always provided that they are not being merely silly or noisy or insubordinate, none of which terms I think can be applied to Lewis.

Allen surely knew it would be controversial to ask Lewis to speak at the farewell dinner in 1935. Lewis felt honoured, though as he recalled, 'I could not see myself ready to pay

[121] RTF 1247, Wylie's report, July 1932, 19–20. On this story, see Stanley Brice Frost, *McGill University: For the Advancement of Learning*, ii: *1895–1971* (Kingston: McGill-Queen's University Press, 1984), 187–210; Marlene Shore, *The Science of Social Redemption: McGill, the Chicago School, and the Origins of Social Research in Canada* (Toronto: University of Toronto Press, 1987), 264; Horn, *Academic Freedom in Canada*, 128–44; and McKillop, *Matters of Mind*, 395, 449, 643–4 n. 100.
[122] David Lewis, *The Good Fight: Political Memoirs 1909–1958* (Toronto: Macmillan of Canada, 1981), 33.
[123] RTF 2153, Millar to Allen, 23 Oct. 1934, and Allen to Millar, 24 Oct. 1934.

unqualified tribute to Cecil Rhodes.' All, he thought, went well, until, after his speech, in an incident with anti-Semitic overtones, he was confronted by Cecil J. Sibbett, a South African who took offence at 'a real Bolshie speech'.[124]

It was perhaps ironic in these years that a capitalist, J. M. Macdonnell, was 'easily the leading' Canadian scholar.[125] Though deeply conservative, he received, as Doug Owram notes, 'almost universal respect within the intellectual community' because of his commitment to learning and to ideas.[126] Among his many other commitments was Queen's University, of which he became chairman of the Board of Trustees in 1930.[127] He had returned to Toronto in 1930, becoming general manager of National Trust in 1931. Four years later, Terry MacDermot also moved to Toronto to succeed W. L. Grant as Principal of Upper Canada College.[128] In this position he could not continue his work for the Trust, and this necessitated a search for a new Trust representative in Canada.

Sir Edward Peacock was going to Canada on business and agreed to negotiate new arrangements there. There was evident consensus that the ideal successor to both Macdonnell and MacDermot was Arnold Heeney, a member of the Quebec committee since 1930, and its secretary since 1933. But because he seemed too busy, it was necessary to look more widely; Allen provided Peacock with confidential briefing notes.[129]

(1) The Secretary must be in Toronto or Montreal. Winnipeg might just be possible, but anywhere in the Maritimes or the West would be too far from the centre of things.

(2) He must be in such an occupation that he will be able to get time to travel about as often as possible. It is most important that the more distant Committees be kept in touch by periodical visits . . .

(3) *Personnel.* MacDermot and I discussed a good many names and reluctantly came to the conclusion that there was nobody very obvious for the job . . . There are people in the West whose names suggest themselves, e.g. Sherwood Lett in Vancouver, but it is no use considering them. . . .

(4) . . . The great need in Canada at present is some strong personal influence and enthusiasm, which can do for the Rhodes Scholarships something of the same kind that Aydelotte has done in America. The Scholarships do not stand as high as they ought to in Canada, not sufficient notice is take[n] of them, and not sufficient value is attached to them.

[124] Lewis, *The Good Fight*, 76–7. Lewis also recalls Dorothy Allen's interest in and kindness to his fiancée Sophie, who was in London during the first two years of his scholarship and in Oxford for the third year. RTF 2153, Sibbett to Elton, 22 May 1944.

[125] RTF 1247, Lothian to Wylie, 11 Jan. 1932.

[126] Doug Owram, *The Government Generation: Canadian Intellectuals and the State 1900–1945* (Toronto: University of Toronto Press, 1986), 169. His defence, later, of Frank Underhill probably saved Underhill's job at Toronto.

[127] He held the post from 1930 to 1957. See Frederick W. Gibson, *Queen's University*, ii: *1917–1961: To Serve and Yet be Free* (Kingston: McGill-Queen's University Press, 1983). Edward Peacock was another active Trustee.

[128] RTF 1247, extract from Vincent Massey to Sir Edward Peacock, 16 Feb. 1935; Massey chaired the selection committee.

[129] RTF 1247, 'Merely hasty notes, which read rather roughly, for discussion with Sir Edward Peacock. (C.K.A.)', 11 Sept. 1935. Other names included Corbett, Henry Borden, and Graham Spry, but the latter was unsuitable because of his politics. It is not clear from the files if Heeney was himself asked, or whether this was simply understood from others' comments, notably those of Gilbert Stairs.

One of those not 'obvious' was Roland Michener: 'I know him very well as he was a pupil of mine. He is an extremely good fellow with a charming wife, but I do not think that he has the drive for this job.' Even so, Peacock decided to recommend Michener, who was strongly endorsed by Macdonnell for his 'reliability and energy'.[130] The son of Senator Edward Michener, a prominent Alberta Conservative, Michener was the first Canadian scholar born in the twentieth century. Like his friend Alan Harvey, Michener had hoped to be admitted to Balliol, but his papers, sent by the Alberta secretary to London rather than Oxford, arrived so late that the best Wylie could do was Hertford.[131]

Perhaps to reassure Allen, Russell Hopkins, who had just been appointed to a sessional position in the faculty of law at the University of Toronto, was to act as Michener's assistant, with the office being located at the University of Toronto.[132] 'Hopkins and I shall have to experiment a bit with the division of work,' Michener wrote. 'At present he . . . is gathering information about available positions for returning scholars. We hope to give assistance to every returning Canadian scholar who has no position.'[133] Employment had in fact become a profound concern. As Hugh MacLennan recalled, 'I stress this aspect of the Thirties . . . because I went down from Oxford in 1932, when only about 5% of graduating Rhodes Scholars had even the prospect of a job. Three years later, with a Princeton Ph.D. I was unemployed for five months before I got a school-teacher's job at $25 a week.'[134] Others affected included George Stanley and James Gibson, who relied on fellowships and short-term positions for several years, and Lionel Gelber.[135]

Following a visit to Frank Aydelotte in April 1936, 'to discover, if we can, something of his magic', Michener and Hopkins toured the west.[136] Then Hopkins was unexpectedly offered a permanent job at the University of Saskatchewan, and the experiment in dual administration quickly ended.[137] Allen's 1937 Canadian tour and Michener's visit to Oxford in 1938 erased Allen's fears; their relationship deepened when the Allens' daughter Rosemary spent three of the war years with the Micheners in Toronto.

[130] RTF 1247B, Macdonnell to Lothian, 16 July 1935.
[131] NAC, A727 (RTF 2357), Wylie to B. Quin, 28 Apr. 1920.
[132] The space had been offered by W. P. M. Kennedy, the professor of law, who saw Hopkins's appointment by the Trust as 'a distinct compliment . . . to law in the University'. University of Toronto Archives, A82-41-3, 35-6 A-L, Kennedy to President H. J. Cody, 17 Jan. 1936. I am grateful to Prof. R. C. B. Risk for drawing my attention to this material, and for very helpful discussion of Hopkins and of J. A. Corry as Canadian legal scholars.
[133] RTC 150343, Michener to Lothian, 9 Mar. 1936.
[134] Hugh MacLennan, 'What it was Like to be in your Twenties in the Thirties', in Victor Hoar (ed.), *The Great Depression: Essays and Memoirs from Canada and the United States* (Vancouver: Copp Clark, 1969), 151.
[135] RTC 150342, Allen to Michener, 26 Jan. 1938.
[136] RTC 150342, Hopkins to Allen, 7 Apr. 1936; RTF 2555, Report no. 304, 2-10-36, Canadian Secretary's Report, 14 Aug. 1936.
[137] RTC 150343, Michener to Lothian, 14 Aug. 1936 (2nd letter of same date), Lothian to Michener, 30 Nov. 1936. Hopkins was to replace J. A. Corry, who was leaving for Queen's to replace Norman Rogers.

A Different War

Despite the return of war in September 1939, four new scholars got to Oxford, and four-teen of the twenty-one Canadian and Newfoundland scholars at Oxford continued their studies—five of them taking firsts in 1940. Competitions also went ahead for 1940 and 1941 (except for Newfoundland in 1941), but winners were not to come up until after the war.[138] Nine of the 1939–41 scholars never did go to Oxford (and another three spent no more than a year there after the war). Thirty years later, Neil German commented with tongue in cheek that 'he had never taken up his Rhodes, . . . but that he still hoped to do so when he had more time at his disposal'.[139]

In this war, some Canadian scholars were at the heart of government, and collectively their engagement was much more diverse than in 1914–18. Prime Minister King's imme-diate choice as Minister of Defence in September 1939 was Norman Rogers. And when Rogers died in June 1940 in the crash of a military aircraft taking him to Toronto, King reacted as if he had lost a member of his close family. King's principal secretary since 1938 had been Arnold Heeney. Indeed, within fifteen years of hearing Maurice Hankey speak at the Ralegh Club, Heeney by 1940 had become 'the Canadian Hankey' as Clerk of the Privy Council and secretary of the Cabinet War Committee.[140] Also in the Prime Minister's office were H. R. L. Henry, King's long-serving private secretary, and James A. Gibson, the liaison officer from the Department of External Affairs and one of a half-dozen scholars to join the Department between 1937 and 1940. At External Affairs itself, Norman Robertson, the youngest of the senior staff, became Under-Secretary after O. D. Skelton's sudden death in January 1941.[141] Later in the war, half the members of an 'extraordinarily high-powered' subcommittee responsible for reconstruction planning were Rhodes scholars: Alex Skelton from the Bank of Canada; J. R. Baldwin, Heeney's assistant in the Privy Council Office; and Jean Chapdelaine from External Affairs.[142] Else-where in Ottawa, H. A. Dyde, Rogers's friend since their days at University College, was military secretary to the Defence Minister; Henry Borden was counsel to and later chair-man of the Wartime Industries Control Board; C. H. Little was Director of Naval Intel-ligence; and P. D. McTaggart-Cowan was in charge of the meteorological office, RAF Ferry Command Headquarters.[143]

[138] See RTC 150342, Allen to Michener, 3 Oct. 1939 and 7 Nov. 1940; 150343, Michener to Scholars-elect, 15 Sept. 1939; and 84657, Michener to Crane Brinton, 11 Mar. 1940. Alberta, with only one application, decided not to elect a scholar in 1941.

[139] RTF 3140, Howarth to Williams, 16 Oct. 1971.

[140] Granatstein, *The Ottawa Men*, 193; Heeney, *The Things that are Caesar's*, 44–5.

[141] See John Hilliker, *Canada's Department of External Affairs*, i: *The Early Years, 1909–1946* (Montreal: McGill-Queen's University Press, 1990), 191, 195, 259, 278; RTF 3084, John E. Read, 'Rhodes Scholars in the Canadian Department of External Affairs' [n.d., c.1960].

[142] Granatstein, *The Ottawa Men*, 164.

[143] Others, including three of the 1941 scholars, did scientific work. See RTC 150343, Michener to Elton, 11 June 1941. J. R. E. Smith, who remained in Oxford doing war-related science after completing his D.Phil., drowned accidentally in 1944. Ralph James had to wait to serve in Germany until after the war; as Rolf Jessen, a 'strongly anti-Nazi' German scholar, he had been transferred to Canada as a wartime internee. RTC 150342, Allen to Michener, 17 Mar. 1941.

At least ninety pre-war Canadian and Newfoundland scholars served in uniform, most in Canadian forces. The most senior was Brigadier Sherwood Lett. Wounded in the Dieppe Raid in 1942, he subsequently became deputy chief of the General Staff in Ottawa; returning to command the 4th Canadian Infantry Brigade in 1944, he was again wounded in France.[144] Many used their civilian skills directly, such as Col. H. G. Nolan as Deputy Judge Advocate General in Ottawa, Lt. Col. George Stanley as a senior military historian, and Col. K. E. Taylor as principal Protestant chaplain in the 1st Canadian Army in 1944–5. At least twenty physicians and surgeons joined Canadian, British, and American medical services. One, Major Roy Clarke of the Royal Army Medical Corps, was lost at sea in December 1942. A few weeks earlier, P/O G. S. Cartwright had been killed returning from an 'operational flight'. John Kenneth Macalister, rejected for military service because of his weak eyesight, was accepted in the Intelligence Corps and parachuted into France as radio officer with Frank Pickersgill in June 1943. The Germans had penetrated the network they were to join, however, and both were tortured and, finally, executed at Buchenwald on 14 September 1944. How this brilliant young man came to this death is the subject of Douglas LePan's extended meditation on courage, *Macalister, or Dying in the Dark* (1995).[145]

It is striking that George Grant was not included on the Trust's record of war service.[146] The son of W. L. and Maude Grant, he bore the heavy expectations of the Parkin and Grant families—even his godfather (Sir Edward Peacock) was a Rhodes Trustee. Already a pacifist at Upper Canada College, he was a conscientious objector to the war; after volunteering as an air raid precautions warden, he served in Bermondsey through the worst of the Blitz.[147]

A very different response to the war was that of Paul Bouchard, editor of *La Nation*, a nationalist Quebec periodical. At a rally in Montreal on 4 September 1939, he declared himself 'resolutely, energetically, and squarely opposed to Canadian participation in the European war, because I don't want thousands of young Canadians going across the seas to die to save international Jewish finance'.[148] He ran against King's Quebec lieutenant, Ernest Lapointe, in Quebec East in the 1940 election and against Louis St Laurent, Lapointe's successor as Minister of Justice, in 1942. With the federal government retreating from its promise not to impose conscription, he won 10,000 votes. Michener reported that he hoped to be 'the De Valera of Canada'.[149]

In English Canada, polls by 1942 showed that the CCF had become the most popular

---

[144] Reginald H. Roy, *Sherwood Lett: His Life and Times* (Vancouver: Alumni Association, UBC, 1991), 110–17.

[145] *Macalister, or Dying in the Dark*, subtitled *A Fiction Based on What is Known of his Life and Fate* (Kingston: Quarry Press, 1995). Macalister's file at Rhodes House is one of LePan's main sources.

[146] RTC 84657, Michener, 'Notes on Rhodes Scholars from Canada', Aug. 1944; 84659, 'Dominion and Colonial Rhodes Scholars on Service, List No. 2, The Rhodes Trust, Oxford, 31 Aug 1943'.

[147] See William Christian, *George Grant: A Biography* (Toronto: University of Toronto Press, 1993), esp. 69–86.

[148] Conrad Black, *Duplessis* (Toronto: McClelland & Stewart, 1977), 201–2 (Black's translation). On the prevalence of such views among right-wing Quebec nationalists, see Esther Delisle, *Le Traître et le Juif* (Outremont: L'Étincelle, 1992).

[149] RTF 1247, Michener to Elton, 4 Apr. 1942.

party. Since 1937, David Lewis had been its national secretary, and Frank Scott became chairman in 1942. In 1944, the CCF captured power in Saskatchewan. In Ontario, Michener's junior partner, E. B. Jolliffe, became party leader in 1942 and leader of the opposition 1943–5 and again 1948–51. Unlike Britain, where Labour went on to capture power, the CCF could not hold its wartime popularity, as established parties reacted to its ideas and as it was denounced in an extra-party campaign that made no distinction between democratic socialism and Soviet communism.[150] A leader in the vilification was Gladstone Murray. Ousted from his post as general manager of the Canadian Broadcasting Corporation at the end of 1942, he turned, as Michener put it, 'his not inconsiderable powers of expression to an appraisal of political issues in Canada, giving particular attention to his fellow Rhodes scholars who are "shaped in the Marxian mold of thought"'.[151] A leader in the Conservative Party's reaction was J. M. Macdonnell; worried that socialism was becoming the only credible alternative to the Liberals, he set out in 1941 'to assist the Party to resume the important part it has played in the maintenance of constitutional government in Canada'.[152] In September 1942 he organized a conference at Port Hope to develop more progressive policies. After retiring from National Trust in 1944, he was elected to the House of Commons in the 1945 general election.

Roland Michener was also a keen participant in this movement to transform the party.[153] He ran unsuccessfully for the provincial legislature in 1943, but was elected from Toronto in 1945 and became Provincial Secretary in the administration of George Drew in 1946. In 1948, however, 'the Socialists, backed by Labour Unions and Communists, made unexpected inroads on us in . . . Toronto and Hamilton', as he reported to Wylie, and he and Drew lost their seats.[154] He now followed Drew into federal politics, losing in Toronto St Paul's in 1949, but winning in 1953.

Michener visited Oxford early in 1945, while attending a Chatham House conference, then toured throughout Canada to get competitions restarted. In addition to regular provincial competitions, there were five Canada-at-large scholarships, for which provincial committees could nominate runners-up with suitable records of war service, and five overseas scholarships for military applicants not yet back in Canada. For the latter, a special selection committee was constituted, chaired by Vincent Massey, High Commissioner in London. In the first four post-war competitions, rules were adjusted for service candidates. Veterans won the majority of scholarships in each of the four years. Among them were Marcel Lambert and Erskine Carter, who had been prisoners of war (the former captured at Dieppe, the latter at Arnhem), and men as senior as Lt. Col. J. C. Clunie OBE, who had served since 1939 and been awarded the Croix de Guerre. Clunie was one of five in 1946 who did not have a university degree, and, like half the 1946 scholars, he was over 25. Several were married. That year's sailing party, on the CPR's

---

[150] See Walter D. Young, *The Anatomy of a Party: The National CCF 1932–61* (Toronto: University of Toronto Press, 1969), 202–4.

[151] RTC 84657, 'Notes on Rhodes Scholars from Canada', Aug. 1944.

[152] Macdonnell to 'guests', 13 Jan. 1941, quoted in J. L. Granatstein, *The Politics of Survival: The Conservative Party of Canada, 1939–1945* (Toronto: University of Toronto Press, 1967), 70.

[153] See RTC 150343, Michener to Elton, 16 Sept. 1943.

[154] RTC 150343, Michener to Wylie, 23 Apr. 1949.

Beaverford, included twenty scholars (some of them pre-war winners), six wives—and one baby.[155]

Newfoundland and Canada

In Newfoundland, Higgins called a meeting of 'some Oxford men' early in 1945 to discuss the resumption of the scholarships. 'I note', he wrote to Allen, 'that I was entitled to go to any expense. The whole expense consisted of a couple of cigars, about a half bottle of whiskey and a half bottle of rum!' With regret, the meeting decided not to hold a competition for 1946. Later the same group requested a reduced standard of one year of university (or Grade 12) for 1947 and suggested that the Chief Justice replace the Governor as chairman of the committee.[156] Context for the latter, but not mentioned, was the Governor's role in the political process driving the colony towards union with Canada. John Higgins was on the other side, as he wrote to Elton.[157]

If a vote were taken at the National Convention a large majority would favour Responsible Government. Everything possible seems to be done to stop such a vote. If the English authorities interfere with the Convention in these days of small nations and ideas of democracy I shall be deeply sorry for I am deeply convinced . . . that we should remain with England . . .

Why is not a man like yourself sent out here? I am sure we would have supreme confidence in you.

Higgins was one of a delegation to London in 1948. A consolation for its failure was a visit to Oxford. 'It was a pleasure', he said, 'to feel that I had come back to my alma mater after many years of wandering and was not a stranger.'[158] For Allen it was a chance at last to meet Higgins. As he wrote later to Michener, Higgins had 'had a somewhat thankless job, but he has never relaxed his enthusiasm, even if his administrative methods have not always been of the most orthodox . . . I expect you found him, as we did, a real "character" and a most fascinating one. If you succeeded in ever getting him to introduce a pause into his conversation, I congratulate you.'[159] Higgins took his campaign to Newfoundland voters in the first provincial election, running as a Progressive Conservative. As one of the few anti-Confederates to win election, he became leader of the opposition in the Assembly, the first of three Newfoundland scholars to hold that post during the long reign of Premier Joseph Smallwood (Malcolm Hollett was the second and James J. Greene the third).

Encouraged by the Trust, Higgins visited Toronto in June 1950. 'Michener did me proudly' was his succinct summary of his visit, during which he met many scholars—and Progressive Conservatives.[160] Canadian procedures were now to apply in New-

---

[155] RTC 150342; (Rhodes Scholars Elect 1946); and Michener to Allen, 5 Oct. 1946.
[156] RTF 1049, Higgins to Allen, 23 Mar. 1945; 1049A, Higgins to Allen, 19 Feb. 1946. In fact, the standard was not reduced; Herbert Morgan (Newfoundland and Pembroke 1947) had a BA.
[157] RTF 1049, Higgins to Elton, 12 Jan. 1948.   [158] RTF 1049A, Higgins to Allen, 28 Dec. 1948.
[159] RTC 150342, Allen to Michener, 21 June 1950.
[160] RTF 1049A, Higgins to Allen, 14 June 1950; Allen to Elton, 21 Mar. 1949; and RTC 150343, Michener to Elton, 26 June 1950. The Micheners returned the visit a few years later. Note also that E. T. Williams included Newfoundland on his global itinerary in 1951.

foundland, except that the scholarship there would continue to be open only to New-foundland residents. Other practices continued informally; for another decade, for example, the committee did not interview applicants. Asked one year for an explanation, Fabian O'Dea, who succeeded Higgins as secretary in 1956, replied that all but one member of the committee already knew the only applicant actually in St John's in Decem-ber.[161] The community was intimate enough also that a scholar's mother might telephone Higgins to ask him for news about her son: 'He writes to her very rarely and she is wor-rying about him. Did he get through his exams? Do you know if he owes any money at Oxford?'

The Canadian Association

The evident ideological differences among Canadian scholars had not diminished the Trust's hope that Canadians would form an association. Elton was much encouraged by a 1949 discussion with Harry Logan, who 'thought it would not be difficult . . . He thinks (in contra-distinction to the view of Michener) that Canadians are very ready to be organised in fraternal societies. He instances the Fraternity at . . . Canadian Universi-ties . . . [and] points out that the Rhodes Scholarship is in a sense a "fraternity" idea itself.'[162] But fraternities were not universally supported—and sometimes strongly opposed—in Canadian universities. To some scholars an association, even a voluntary one they were under no obligation to join, carried unfortunate implications of exclusiv-ity and elitism.[163]

Michener put out a newsletter in 1950[164] and was among the planners of a banquet in honour of Lord and Lady Elton on 10 June 1951. Held at the Ritz-Carlton Hotel in Mon-treal, it was attended by eighty-five scholars and fifty wives, many from Montreal, Ottawa, and vicinity.[165] Next morning, a smaller group gathered at McGill to consider creating an association. Careful preparation, apparently the work of J. L. Stewart, had gone into the meeting. Even so, a later account reports, 'when an unsuspecting committee pre-sented the draft of a proposed constitution, it was promptly discovered that nearly half of those present were lawyers! At once the program fell behind schedule! . . . [T]he draft was relentlessly subjected to close scrutiny, brisk debate, deft amendment and finally, indulgent approval.'[166] The purposes of the Association were '(a) to further higher edu-cation; (b) to advise and assist in the administration of the Rhodes Scholarships in Canada; [and] (c) to assist Rhodes Scholars and to promote social intercourse among

[161] RTF 1247, O'Dea to Michener, 6 Jan. 1960; see also RTC 208604, Higgins to Michener, 7 Jan. 1955.

[162] RTF 1247, Elton to Allen, 27 June 1949.

[163] Paul Axelrod, *Making a Middle Class: Student Life in English Canada during the Thirties* (Montreal: McGill-Queen's University Press, 1990), 105–8; James A. Gibson, *The Canadian Association of Rhodes Scholars, 1951–1995* (Ottawa: Canadian Association of Rhodes Scholars, 1996), 9.

[164] RTF 1247, Elton to Trustees, 8 Nov. 1950. See RTC 84659 (Newsletters, CARS, 1 [1950–64]), 'Rhodes Scholarships in Canada: News and Notes', 13 Sept. 1950.

[165] RTF 3084, has a list of those attending the dinner and agenda for meeting, 11 June 1951.

[166] RTC 84659, Report of the Board of Directors, CARS, 10 June 1961, appended to *Newsletter*, 19 (July 1961).

them.'[167] J. M. Macdonnell, who was not at the meeting, was asked to be the first president. The secretary-treasurer was Clarence Campbell. 'When all is going smoothly in the National Hockey League [of which he was president],' Michener reported, 'it will be one of his duties to produce and distribute a periodic bulletin, something like the class letters in the American Oxonian.'[168]

Because of the 1953 reunion in Oxford, the next general meeting was not until 1955. By now there were over 260 paid-up members, and the Association had assumed responsibility for the annual sailing dinners, hitherto organized by Quebec Rhodes scholars, and production of a directory, hitherto Michener's responsibility.[169] The third meeting was held in Ottawa on 15 June 1957. The Eltons were again on hand, following a quick visit to Vancouver, Victoria, and Winnipeg. Air travel was beginning to change the possibilities for such visits—but still had not reached its modern state, as Michener's account of reuniting Elton with a missing suitcase, through Montreal traffic, suggests.[170]

We had a most exciting chase . . . When we . . . found the BOAC office, your plane was already on the runway. However, the BOAC officials were most obliging, they knew all about your bag and called the control tower and the captain of your ship, both of whom were ready to help. A red fire wagon, with wireless equipment, dashed across the airport to your plane and heaved the bag into a small upper hold. It was like the end of a thriller for all who were in the know.

The Association now had two substantial new projects. One was the publication of a book entitled *Oxford Today and the Canadian Rhodes Scholarships* (Toronto: W. J. Gage for the CARS, 1958), which responded to lower application numbers in the 1950s and to a sense that Oxford's attractions were no longer self-evident to potential applicants. Its author, Hugh W. Morrison, sought 'to make the work, as far as feasible, lively and even a bit "piquant"'.[171] Some 1,200 copies were distributed to Canadian schools, universities, and libraries. The other was a scholarship for an Oxford graduate to study at a Canadian university. This was initiated by Ralph Henson, as 'recognition and reciprocal acknowledgement' of his own Oxford experience. Wanting to address 'Britain's lack of leadership in the total business field', he believed the criteria for the award should be the 'same as for Rhodes Scholars [but] with greater emphasis on individuality and toughness of character'.[172] The directors of the Association enthusiastically adopted Henson's plan, but for tax reasons, a separate Canadian Rhodes Scholars Foundation was created. Henson was its first president, Michael Howarth was secretary-treasurer, and J. L. Stewart, Roland Michener, and Ian Wahn were also directors.[173]

---

[167] RTC 150343, draft constitution of the Canadian Association of Rhodes Scholars.

[168] RTC 84657, 'First Reunion of Canadian Rhodes Scholars'. In fact, the first edition produced by the association seems to have been no. 3, Jan. 1956.

[169] RTC 150343, Report of the President and Executive to the Second Meeting of the Canadian Association of Rhodes Scholars, 11 June 1955.

[170] RTC 150343, Michener to Elton, 1 July 1957. It is not clear why the suitcase was not at the airport, however.

[171] RTF 3084, Morrison to Elton, 15 Aug. 1957.

[172] E. M. Howarth, 'The Canadian Rhodes Scholars Foundation Scholarships: A Review of the First 37 Years 1957–93' (May 1993), not paginated (copy kindly supplied to me by Michael Howarth); RTF 3084, Henson to Howarth, 16 May 1957.

[173] RTC 84659, George Nowlan, Revenue Minister, to Foundation, 30 Dec. 1957.

On his return to Oxford, Elton found 'just the sort of man you want'. Joseph Youll was 'a good athlete and a vigorous and intelligent chap, much liked in his College, Worcester . . . [who] had already planned to spend a year in Canada . . . digging ditches, or otherwise supporting himself by manual labour, just to see what Canada is like'. He arrived in August 1957 at Halifax, where he was welcomed by Henry Hicks, until recently premier of Nova Scotia, and other scholars. In Montreal his host was Clarence Campbell. Henson then arranged a week of appointments in Toronto 'to give him as varied experience in business as I could', including an introduction at the Toronto Stock Exchange to 'a tough promoter, who regards a salaried person as the modern equivalent of the medieval serf'.[174] Youll spent a year in the business school at the University of Western Ontario, where he 'distinguished himself by leading the graduate class'.[175] As had been envisaged, he then transferred into the second year of the MBA programme at Harvard.

By the summer of 1958, over 120 donors had contributed enough money to ensure several years of an award set at $2,000 per year, and the directors had given more thought to criteria. They quickly dropped the explicit orientation to business, but only extended eligibility to women in 1971 (and did not appoint a woman until 1977).[176] In 1965, the Foundation made two awards; that eventually became the standard, meaning that four scholars at a time would be on stipend. Once every four years an appeal for funds was sent out, to which many scholars responded (at least 130, for example, after the 1982 call for contributions).[177] When Henson died, his will provided for a donation of shares that proved to be worth $330,000 and became the basis of a separate endowment trust. Until 1993, Michael Howarth, as secretary of the Foundation, took care of the administration of the scholarship in Canada. By then, there had been 55 Foundation scholars.[178]

The files in Rhodes House include copies of many reports to the Foundation from Canadian universities on reverse Rhodes winners; they testify to the commitment of successive wardens to the Oxford selection process and to the quality of the scholars and their impact within their programmes in Canada. The scholars' own reports of their encounters with Canada touched on some standard themes as well. Thus, Youll found 'the average student [at Western] . . . not so well-informed about matters outside his own field' as at Oxford. He appreciated the warmth of the welcome he received from students, and they had helped him 'to appreciate a little of the rather self-conscious desire for a truly Canadian national identity and culture'.[179] James K. Hiller had worked in Labrador before going up to Oxford, but still 'both St. John's and Memorial have taken a bit of getting used to', he told Williams in December 1965.[180] He found St John's

---

[174] RTF 3140, Elton to Henson, 27 June 1957; Henson to Elton, 10 Sept. 1957. Youll's name was suggested by the Oxford University Appointments Committee.

[175] RTF 3140, W. W. P. Jones to Howarth, 9 Oct. 1958. See also *Newsletter*, 11 (July 1958).

[176] RTF 3140, notice from *Oxford University Gazette*, no. 2963, 24 Apr. 1958; RTF 3084, Howarth to Williams, 16 Oct. 1971.

[177] RTF 3140, Philip Slayton to Canadian Rhodes Scholars, Dec. 1983.

[178] See Howarth, 'The Canadian Rhodes Scholars Foundation Scholarships: A Review of the First 37 Years 1957–93'.

[179] Youll to Michael Howarth, 27 Jan. 1958, printed in *Newsletter*, 9 (Jan. 1958), 5.

[180] RTF 3140, Hiller to Williams, 8 Dec. 1965.

somewhat provincial, and, compared to Oxford, the University seemed 'like a glorified high school, complete with long bare corridors, jangling bells, and a ban on alcohol.' Fortunately, he added, 'the history faculty seems pretty good'. After a doctorate at Cambridge, Hiller joined that faculty, and his writings are essential sources for this chapter's understanding of twentieth-century Newfoundland history.[181]

Scholars in Canada, 1957–1960

The Ottawa meeting took place just days after a federal election; to the surprise of many, the Liberals had lost. Five of the six scholars elected were on the winning Progressive Conservative side.[182] E. D. Fulton, member for Kamloops since 1945 and a candidate for the party leadership in 1956, became Justice Minister, and W. J. Browne and J. M. Macdonnell became ministers without portfolio. The latter, now 72, was distrusted by the new Prime Minister, John Diefenbaker, as one of 'the party establishment' that had tried to deny him the party leadership in 1956.[183] There was speculation in the English press that Roland Michener would become Minister of External Affairs, but he was offered a lesser post, Speaker of the House of Commons. The fifth Conservative was Marcel Lambert, who had defeated H. A. Dyde in Edmonton West.

As he was not to be a minister, Michener was most willing to continue as the Trust's representative. But he would need more assistance than just his secretary, Mrs M. E. P. Budd.[184] He and Elton agreed that the best person was Michael Howarth, currently executive secretary of the Canadian Institute of Chartered Accountants, who was already secretary-treasurer of the Association and incoming secretary of the Ontario selection committee.[185] Because Michener would now have help, the Trustees decided to reduce his honorarium by $300. They then rescinded the motion, recognizing that it would seem ungrateful. Elton may also have had second thoughts at facing Norah Michener— anything but a minor figure in her husband's life, she was both able and determined (she had, for example, recently earned a Ph.D. in medieval philosophy).[186] Not long before, she had 'confided to Allen, though with the obvious intention that he should pass on what she said, that she thought Roly's honorarium should be increased'.[187]

Just over 500 scholars had been elected from Newfoundland and Canada by 1956. About three-quarters of the 428 who were alive in 1959 lived in Canada; as in 1929, most

[181] See, e.g., his notable 2,000-page edition, with M. F. Harrington, of *The Newfoundland National Convention, 1946–1948*, 2 vols. (Montreal: McGill-Queen's University Press, 1995).

[182] The only Liberal was James Sinclair, outgoing Minister of Fisheries.

[183] See J. L. Granatstein, *Canada 1957–1967: The Years of Uncertainty and Innovation* (Toronto: McClelland & Stewart, 1986), 14, 18, 27–9.

[184] Routines were now well established; see, e.g., list of twenty different forms needed for committee secretaries, in RTC 208604, ending with '20—List of forms'.

[185] RTF 2555, Report no. 428, Extract from Secretary's Report on Canadian Tour, 27 July 1957; RTC 150343, Michener to Elton, 1 July 1957; Elton to Michener, 21 June 1957.

[186] A revised version had recently been published; see Norah Willis Michener, *Maritain on the Nature of Man in a Christian Democracy* (Hull: Éditions L'Éclair, 1955).

[187] RTF 2555, Elton to Sir Edward Peacock, 24 Jan. 1955. See also Elton to Peacock, 15 Apr. 1957; and Report no. 429, 31 Oct. 1957, Canadian Secretary.

of the others were in the United States or the United Kingdom (see Table 1).[188] In addition, about ten scholars from other jurisdictions lived in Canada. Ottawa, with 75 resident scholars in 1959, had become by far the leading centre for Canadian scholars. Nineteen Manitoba scholars lived there, for example, twice as many as in Winnipeg.[189] These figures do not include members of Parliament or John Higgins, who in 1959 was named to the Senate, the first scholar to be so honoured.

At least 40 per cent of the scholars counted in Ottawa worked in the Department of External Affairs (although at any time a number were in fact posted elsewhere). Thirty years earlier there had been only Laurent Beaudry, then in Washington, and John Read and Norman Robertson, who both joined the Department in 1929. Now scholars held the posts of Under-Secretary and Assistant Under-Secretary and were heads of Canadian missions in the United States, West Germany, the USSR, Brazil, Egypt, and Australia (where the High Commissioner was Terry MacDermot, who had joined the Department after the war). H. B. O. Robinson, the Department's representative in the Prime Minister's Office, had a particularly sensitive post, because John Diefenbaker was suspicious of the departmental establishment's ties to its former minister, Lester Pearson, now leader of the opposition.[190] The many scholars in more junior posts reflected the Department's systematic recruitment in Oxford in the 1950s; indeed, when Trade and Commerce began to visit, it urged scholars to consider its trade commissioner service, 'where there were not so many Rhodes Scholars in the way'.[191]

Outside External Affairs, scholars in Ottawa held a variety of other positions in 1959, some of them highly visible.[192] Thus, four others were deputy ministers; the governor, deputy governor, and chief of research at the Bank of Canada were all Manitoba scholars; and the director of the National Gallery of Canada was Alan Jarvis. J. T. Thorson had been President of the Exchequer Court since 1942, and Ronald Martland had recently been named to the Supreme Court of Canada. Beyond the government, there were three scholars at the law firm of Herridge, Tolmie, and four on faculty at Carleton University. Eugene Forsey was research director of the Canadian Labour Congress. An intimation of Ottawa's future was A. W. Duguid's position as manager of research and development at Computing Devices of Canada.

If the federal government had become an important destination, career patterns of scholars in Canada in 1959 otherwise resembled those of 1929. Law continued to lead: in

---

[188] Data are from the *Register* (1981), as of 1959, with some adjustments based on the 1959 *Directory*. Lists in the files offer slightly varying numbers, but very similar proportions.

[189] RTC 84659, Douglas G. Anglin, 'Manitoba's First Fifty Rhodes Scholars' [n.d., *c*.1957]; Anglin himself soon joined the exodus to Ottawa.

[190] Robinson played a crucial part, for example, when Diefenbaker was working through his position on whether a republican South Africa could remain in the Commonwealth. See Granatstein, *Canada 1957–1967*, 56–9; and H. B. O. Robinson, *Diefenbaker's World: A Populist in Foreign Affairs* (Toronto: University of Toronto Press, 1989).

[191] RTF 3189, Williams to Lord Amory, 16 Jan. 1962. Amory was currently British High Commissioner in Ottawa.

[192] There were also at least four scientists at the National Research Council or in defence research laboratories. Other scholars worked with the Colombo Plan, in the Prime Minister's Office, in the Cabinet Secretariat, and in other departments. There was one military officer, at RCAF Headquarters.

1959, about 70 scholars were in practice (including 8 holding political office), 13 were judges (including the chief justices of Prince Edward Island, New Brunswick, and British Columbia), about 15 were primarily teachers and scholars, and several worked as lawyers in business or government. As well, some who had trained in law were not at the time working in law, such as Alan Gotlieb in External Affairs, who had won the Vinerian scholarship and been elected to a fellowship in law at Wadham. About 30 scholars in Canada were physicians and surgeons, at least 20 of whom held research and faculty appointments. Including them and the law professors, about 100 scholars were teaching at 23 Canadian universities. As in 1929, the three leading employers were Toronto (with 17 Canadian scholars on faculty), McGill, and Alberta; Queen's, British Columbia, Saskatchewan, and Dalhousie now also had a number of scholars on faculty. At Bishop's, A. R. Jewitt, the first scholar to head a Canadian university, was nearing the end of his term as Principal.

Almost 40 scholars were in business, most in corporate enterprises. At least a dozen were now at very senior levels, such as A. E. Grauer, president of the giant British Columbia Power Corporation and lately a member of the Royal Commission on Canada's Economic Prospects. Before joining the company, he had briefly practised law and then taught social science at the University of Toronto for a decade. Among those in business, about one-third had science-based positions; in their careers, the branch-plant nature of many sectors of the Canadian economy tended to lead to the United States. Smaller numbers of scholars taught at schools and colleges, were ordained clergymen with congregations of their own (rather than being on a university faculty or working elsewhere), or worked in media or journalism. Jean Gérin-Lajoie was a labour organizer. Hugh MacLennan gave his main occupation as a writer.

To many, no scholar in Canada better represented the ideal Rhodes scholar than Wilder Penfield.[193] Now world famous for his bold work and for his ideas on the brain itself, he had become a Canadian citizen in 1934, the year his long-dreamt-of Montreal Neurological Institute opened. It drew students (and patients) from English- and French-speaking Quebec and far beyond; among those who trained there were Claude Bertrand and William H. Feindel (who in the 1970s would become the Institute's director). Penfield had been awarded the Order of Merit in 1952, only the second Canadian to be so honoured; and he and Marius Barbeau had been among the five scholars given honorary degrees by Oxford in 1953.

Speaking in 1957 on 'what the Founder may have hoped of his Scholars', J. A. Corry claimed there were 'no all-conquering men of action with a pathological lust for power [or] half-crazy geniuses capable of revolutionizing science or society—only a high proportion of capable and public-spirited citizens in responsible positions'.[194] A legal scholar who taught government and politics at Queen's and regularly advised governments and royal commissions, Corry could have been describing himself, as Jeffrey Simpson noted in an obituary in 1985: 'Great teachers and scholars are rare, and rarer still when found

---

[193] RTC 150343, Elton to Michener, 6 Aug 1953. See also 84659 re the portrait of Penfield, by Montreal artist Robin Watt, which now hangs at Rhodes House.

[194] RTF 1247, Report no. 428, Secretary's Canadian Journey, 27 July 1957, 20–1.

combined in a man of action. Nations possess only a few such people at any point in their history.'[195] In 1958, Corry was offered the presidency of his old university, Saskatchewan, but Queen's persuaded him to stay by designating him as Principal, with effect from 1961.

Another such figure was F. R. Scott, whose socialist politics had so far kept him from being dean of law at McGill (and from the Quebec selection committee, on which he never served). A man of extraordinary breadth (he was also a leading Canadian poet), he had been deeply engaged in challenging Quebec's authoritarian government in the courts, and in 1957 had won a famous victory when the Supreme Court of Canada overturned Quebec's Padlock Act.[196] Writing later, James Gibson recalled the Plaunt Memorial Lectures that Scott gave at Carleton University in 1959, on *Civil Liberties and Canadian Federalism*, at which one evening's audience included six of the nine justices of the Supreme Court of Canada. 'These lectures always represented to me a sense of heightened awareness of the centrality of civil liberties and human rights in a democratic society; I suppose in our lifetimes there has been no more persuasive champion.'[197]

In 1959, the Padlock Act's author, Maurice Duplessis, died. A year later, the provincial Liberals began what soon was called the Quiet Revolution. One of those at its heart was Paul Gérin-Lajoie. As Minister of Youth in the new government, he led its battle on education, which had been ceded to the Church almost a century before. It was fitting that in 1964 he became the province's first Minister of Education. Roger Gaudry's departure from industry in 1965 to become the first lay Rector of the Université de Montréal and Jean Chapdelaine's departure from External Affairs in 1965 to become Quebec's Delegate-General in Paris were other signs of the change of climate and direction in Quebec society.[198]

The ferment in Quebec was not the only force that John Diefenbaker was ill equipped to handle, and the 1962 general election left him at the head of a minority government. This election brought David Lewis into Parliament at last, representing the New Democratic Party (which had recently replaced the CCF). Other victors included three Liberals, John Turner, a young bilingual lawyer, elected from Montreal, Jack Davis, an engineer and economist, from British Columbia, and Ian Wahn, a lawyer, who defeated Roland Michener.[199] Michener's work as Speaker, however, and his exclusion from Diefenbaker's inner circle made him one of the few prominent Conservatives to have enhanced his

[195] Jeffrey Simpson, 'James A. Corry', *Toronto Globe and Mail*, 28 Dec 1985, A6; Gibson, *Queen's University*, ii. 417–26.

[196] The law, passed in 1937, gave the province power to lock up a building used to spread 'communism'.

[197] Obituary of F. R. Scott by James A. Gibson, *Newsletter*, 35/1 (Apr. 1985); the lectures were published by the University of Toronto Press in 1961. See also Sandra Djwa and R. St J. Macdonald (eds.), *On F. R. Scott: Essays on his Contributions to Law, Literature, and Politics* (Kingston: McGill-Queen's University Press, 1983); and Sandra Djwa, *The Politics of the Imagination: A Life of F. R. Scott* (Toronto: McClelland & Stewart, 1987).

[198] See Paul Gérin-Lajoie, *Combats d'un révolutionnaire tranquille: propos et confidences* (Montreal: CEC, 1989). On Gaudry, see, e.g., Lysiane Gagnon, 'Qui est le nouveau recteur de l'Université de Montréal?' *La Presse*, 10 Apr. 1965, suppl., 4–6.

[199] Another Conservative casualty in Toronto was J. M. Macdonnell.

public reputation since 1957. A year after the Liberals returned to office in 1963, Prime Minister Lester Pearson, a friend since Oxford, invited him to become Canadian High Commissioner to India; three years later, amid the celebrations of Canada's Centennial Year, he would return as a very popular Governor General.

Michener formally submitted his resignation on 6 July 1964. 'I will have to put my thinking cap on over this one,' Williams wrote to Sir Archibald Nye. 'One has got so used to Roly's being there that one has taken all his solid and friendly work all too much for granted.'[200] Meanwhile, Williams could rely on Howarth, who assumed full responsibility in August. Thus, he represented the Trust at events such as the installation of Francis Leddy as President of the University of Windsor, which Williams acknowledged in characteristic style: 'I'm glad you got to Leddy's installation. It would not lack splendour if I know my Francis. I wonder if the Pope had time to drop in.'[201]

Change and Challenge, 1965–1972

'Rhodes scholarships are "foreign" and associated with the age of colonialism,' Elmer Sopha, a member of the Liberal opposition, told the Ontario legislature in June 1965. He wanted Ontario to create 'Canada Scholars' to 'displace the Rhodes Scholarship as Canada's highest academic honor'.[202] The often outspoken Sopha could be ignored, but in emphasizing universities, criticizing an established institution, and loudly voicing his Canadian nationalism, he reflected the spirit of the period. A more influential voice in 1965 was George Grant, whose pessimistic *Lament for a Nation: The Defeat of Canadian Nationalism* quickly became a key nationalist document, despite its argument that Diefenbaker's defeat revealed the impossibility of a Canadian nationality in the context of modern capitalism, technology, and American power.[203]

'[A] lot of Canadian Rhodes Scholars . . . like having the Speaker of the House as Secretary,' Elton had noted in 1958.[204] So, it seems, did Williams and the Trustees. As they thought about a successor to Michener, the first names that came to mind were Arnold Heeney and Henry Borden, both of whom had been seriously considered in 1935.[205] But someone younger was needed, and attention soon turned primarily to J. L. Stewart. Amory was much reassured by 'a friend of mine who lives in Toronto and is knowledgeable in financial circles there . . . [who] gave an excellent opinion of [Stewart] and said he was steadily rising in status. He thought he would be of first-rate calibre for the job.'[206] Williams agreed, and in February 1965 wrote to ask Stewart to become the Trust's representative. After consulting Howarth about the work, Stewart accepted.[207]

A graduate of the University of Toronto Schools, source of numerous Ontario Rhodes scholars, and the University of Toronto, Stewart had had a distinguished war, serving in

[200] RTF 3150, Williams to Nye, 22 July 1964.   [201] RTC 84657, Williams to Howarth, 1 Oct. 1964.
[202] RTC 96311, clipping from *Toronto Star*, 5 June 1965.
[203] *Lament for a Nation: The Defeat of Canadian Nationalism* (Toronto: McClelland & Stewart, 1965).
[204] RTF 1247, Note for the Canadian Selection Committee File [*sic*], 18 June 1958.
[205] RTF 1247, Nye to Williams, 4 Oct. 1964.   [206] RTF 2555, Amory to the Warden, 27 Jan. 1965.
[207] RTC 145353, Williams to Stewart, 2 Feb. 1965; 96311 (General Correspondence 1, 1965–9), copy of press release.

north-west Europe, rising to the rank of lieutenant colonel in the Queen's Own Rifles, and being awarded the MBE. Now a senior partner in a leading Toronto law firm,[208] he was counsel to the Royal Commission on Taxation, a massive, path-breaking review of the Canadian tax system. He had been the second president of the Association and was a director of the Foundation, but had had no connection with the selection process. Much of that work would fall to the assistant that, it was clear, his workload made necessary. David Horsley, who took on this work, was a New Zealand scholar; he had recently joined Stewart's firm after working as managing editor of Carswell Legal Publications.[209] Stewart did not have Michener's range of connections and was much more reserved in personal style. It is striking, for example, that he knew only seven among the seventy or more members of selection committees for the 1965 competition well enough to address the standard letter of thanks to them by their first name.[210]

As the participation rate of young people doubled and total enrolments tripled in Canada during the 1960s, the university world in Canada changed radically. The sharp rise in enrolments was not immediately reflected in applications. In five different jurisdictions between 1965 and 1970 there was a year when only two or three applications were received.[211] And even with more applications, the British Columbia committee concluded that 'the time seems to have come . . . when the Scholarship has to "sell" itself to a degree'.[212] The New Brunswick committee agreed. After deciding not to make an appointment for 1970, it launched what its secretary, Fred Drummie, called 'Operation THIRST (To Heighten Interest in Rhodes Scholarship Trust)'.[213] Visiting the province's universities, the committee discovered that 'knowledge and understanding of the Rhodes was low on the part of both faculty and students [but that] there is a lively interest in the Scholarship once it is explained'.[214] One senior faculty member told them 'that until he heard our description, Rhodes Scholars, to him, were apparently magically selected through some almost secret process'. Whether through better information or from some other cause entirely, applications rose quickly in the 1970s, and most committees had to devise systematic shortlisting procedures.[215]

At Oxford, Williams was increasingly concerned in the mid-1960s at the difficulty of finding places. Obtaining faculty approval for graduate work could be problematic, and scholars might not be well advised in Canada—listing more than one of the most popular colleges, which filled up first, was a common error. Nor were traditional links of varying strength between a few provinces and colleges reliable; even the strongest, between Saskatchewan and Exeter, which had been inaugurated by Francis Leddy in 1933, faded quickly after he moved to Ontario. Explicitly rejecting the idea that weak selections were

[208] The firm was Fraser, Beatty, Tucker, McIntosh & Stewart.
[209] RTC 145353, Stewart to Williams, 22 Feb. 1965.
[210] RTC 96311, Stewart Memorandum for Mr Horsley, 20 May 1965. Howarth had, of course, been responsible for administration of this competition.
[211] RTF 2555, table summarizing applications, 1964–9.
[212] RTC 145352, M. J. Brown to Williams, 2 Dec. 1969.
[213] RTC 145352, Drummie to Stewart, 27 Feb. 1970.
[214] RTC 96311, summary of Information Program, attached to Drummie to Stewart, 2 Apr. 1970.
[215] See, e.g., RTC 96311, Scace to Williams, 13 Dec. 1979.

an issue, Willliams emphasized rather that 'we have got to realise that at this moment of the world's history certain constituencies have less to "sell" than others as a type'.[216] In particular, as he reminded Stewart a year later, 'it is the same old story of Maritimes and Prairies not being as quickly received as t'others'.[217]

Stewart's response was to wonder if 'it would not be logical for us to take a leaf out of the American book and divide the country . . . into four regions: the Atlantic provinces, Quebec, Ontario and the western provinces'. If the Atlantic and the west each lost one scholarship and Quebec and Ontario each gained one, he added, the result 'would be a more equitable distribution'.[218] He stressed the informality of the proposition, but it was substantial enough that Williams was proposing in January 1970 'to float it gingerly with the Trustees at our meeting this week'.[219]

Beginning with Saskatchewan's 1964 selection of Robin Boadway, a cadet at the Royal Military College, Scholars began to be selected with some regularity from their province of residence without having attended university there.[220] Since then, an average of about one scholarship per year has gone to someone who had studied elsewhere in Canada, two-thirds of them at either McGill (which produced winners in five other provinces, but not Ontario) or Queen's (whose graduates won in six other provinces, but not Quebec). About as many awards have gone to Canadians who studied outside Canada. The first went to Michael Spence, a Princeton student, who wrote to Stewart in September 1965 to point out his double ineligibility: as a Canadian he could not apply in the United States, but never having attended a Canadian university, he was also ineligible in Canada.[221] This, Stewart thought, was unfair. 'Incidentally,' he told Williams, 'I happen to know Spence's parents well. The boy was Captain of the school at my old school and may very well be a strong candidate if he could be worked in.'[222] The rule was changed immediately. A year later, Quebec chose John C. Tait, also from Princeton, and Nova Scotia selected G. J. Burchill, from the University of Nebraska. Between 1971, when the next such appointment was made, and 1993 there were 14 winners from Harvard (in 6 provinces), 3 more from Princeton, 3 from Stanford, and 7 from 5 other American universities. One scholar, Heidi Hauffe (Ontario and New College 1989), was already at Oxford. She, like Spence, has made her career outside Canada, as did about half of those from American universities. Tait, on the other hand, returned to a distinguished career in the Canadian public service.

In total, awards to those studying outside Canada represented less than 10 per cent of

---

[216] RTC 145353, Williams to Stewart, 25 Mar. 1966.

[217] RTC 96311, Williams to Stewart, 11 Feb. 1967.

[218] RTF 2555, Stewart to Williams, 25 Oct. 1966.

[219] RTC 96311, Williams to Stewart, 19 Jan. 1970.

[220] This does not apply, of course, to early years in provinces that did not yet have a university. It was not uncommon earlier to have attended a local university followed by an outside university. Also in 1964, New Brunswick chose Colin McMillan; having attended St Dunstan's, he was from within the jurisdiction, but no one educated entirely within PEI had previously been selected by one of the other Maritime provinces.

[221] J. J. Greene had graduated from Notre Dame; the last pre-Confederation scholar from Newfoundland, he had not been subject to Canadian rules.

[222] RTC 96311, Stewart to Williams, 5 Oct. 1965.

all Canadian scholarships between 1964 and 1993. In fact, close to three-quarters of Canadian scholars during the period had attended either universities in the original rotation or the first university established in a province. Another 11 per cent had attended the University of Western Ontario (whose graduates had first won scholarships in the 1930s), the Royal Military College (whose graduates became eligible when it began to grant degrees in 1959), Concordia in Montreal (or its predecessor, Loyola), or three new universities in the west, Regina, Calgary, and Victoria. Together, all the other new universities accounted for only twenty scholarships (or 6 per cent) in thirty years. About half of these went to students from universities in Ontario (including four to Trent and three to York) and four to students from new French-language universities, the Université du Québec à Montréal and Moncton.[223]

Stewart worked under intense stress, and his doctor ordered him to take three months away from work in the summer of 1968. 'Write me by return, will you,' Williams asked Horsley in July, 'and tell me how Jack Stewart is. I am worried that we, like many others, are overburdening him.' Horsley was reassuring. 'We are keeping things going quite smoothly and I know that he very much enjoys his association with the Trust and would be unhappy to have to relinquish it.'[224] Indeed, Stewart was now ready to involve himself more closely in the selection process, for example by attending selection committee meetings in British Columbia and Manitoba in 1970, something he had not previously done.[225] A year later, he collapsed and died, at the age of 60. If some in the Canadian Rhodes community had found him remote, all could appreciate his seriousness and his dedication. To Yves Fortier, who as a lawyer (and Quebec secretary) was well placed to understand Stewart's milieu, he was 'an outstanding man and . . . an effective and eloquent representative of the Rhodes Trust in Canada'.[226]

The Modern Era

Thanks to Horsley, Williams felt no need to rush to find a replacement. Writing to John Evans, who was about to become President of the University of Toronto, he noted that the successor had 'better be in Toronto or Montreal or maybe Ottawa: and preferably I think have had some experience of post war Oxford. . . . I regard you as ineligible in your new role (which will be a waste of a good doctor, anyway).'[227] Regretfully Horsley wondered if Evans was ruled out 'because you would not wish to have the president of a University as General Secretary (the American position may be different) or because with his new responsibilities he would not be in a position to undertake the additional assignment'. Williams arranged to meet a number of scholars in Toronto, Ottawa, and Montreal during a brief visit in September 1972. Afterwards, he wrote to tell Horsley that

---

[223] There were no winners at all from other parts of the Université du Québec system or from six Ontario universities, including Guelph (although there had earlier been two from its forerunner, the Ontario Agricultural College). Ryerson graduates first became eligible in 1973.

[224] RTC 96311, Williams to Horsley, 19 July 1968, and Horsley to Williams, 23 Aug. 1968.

[225] RTC 96311, Stewart to Williams, 3 Dec. 1970.

[226] RTC 145352, Fortier to Horsley, 14 Dec. 1971.

[227] RTF 2555, Williams to Evans, 14 June 1972.

he would recommend Arthur Scace to the Trustees. 'If that is agreed, I must then write to him because of course none of the people I saw could I ask about their own willingness if drafted.'[228]

Scace had been the secretary of the Ontario selection committee since 1970. Like Stewart, he was a graduate of UTS and an expert in tax law; although only 34, he was already a partner in a leading Toronto law firm, and the lead author of the standard textbook on income tax law.[229] His characteristic entry in the *Register* scarcely suggests the eminence he was quickly achieving in his profession. He became a bencher, then Treasurer, of the Law Society of Upper Canada and was a key figure in creating one of Canada's first and largest national law firms, McCarthy Tétrault, of which he ultimately was national chairman. His wife Susan was an important contributor to his Rhodes work. 'Please give my regards to your wife,' one grateful scholar later wrote,[230] '[her] friendliness on the night of the pre-interview cocktail party I still am thankful for.' The Scaces' subsequent practice of hosting a reception in Oxford for Canadian scholars each year made both familiar faces to Canadian scholars of all years.

Soon after taking over, Scace received a letter from Sholto Hebenton on behalf of the BC committee. Denying that it had 'been packed by unruly leftists', Hebenton stressed that it was time to rethink the issue of women's eligibility.[231] A year later, a formal complaint was made to Alberta's Human Rights Commission alleging that in discriminating against women the scholarship violated Alberta law.[232] Pressures such as these are the context for Scace's 1974 comments to one scholar at Oxford: '[T]here is a strong feeling in all quarters that women should be admitted. I suspect that the law suits will start fairly shortly and we will be in a comparable position to our counterparts in the U.S. . . . I hope the Trustees do something before we all end up in jail.'[233]

When the Trustees did at last 'do something', women were, evidently, ready to apply, and committees to accept them. 'You are not going to be very happy with we Canadians,' Scace wrote to Williams in December 1976 of the first competitions for which women were eligible. '[T]he total number of women is up to four . . . As a result of my participation in the Western Committee and fairly close cross-examination of everyone concerned, I am convinced that no tokenism was involved. Rather, each of the elections is of outstanding merit.'[234] One of these scholars, Eileen Gillese, became 'the first woman Rhodes Scholar first', in the BCL examinations of 1980.[235]

Other forms of discrimination remained, as human rights commissions and universities sometimes reminded Scace and committee secretaries.[236] These posed special prob-

---

[228] RTC 96311, Horsley to Williams, 5 May 1972; and Williams to Horsley, 18 Sept. 1972. For the visit schedule, see Williams to Horsley, 28 July 1972, Horsley to Williams, 16 Aug. 1972.

[229] Arthur R. A. Scace, et al., *The Income Tax Law of Canada* (Toronto: Law Society of Upper Canada, 1972).

[230] RTC 96311, Alan Morinis to Scace, 26 Nov. 1973.

[231] RTC 145352, Hebenton to Scace, 30 Mar. 1973.

[232] RTC 96311, Sheldon Chumir to Scace, 22 Apr. 1974; 145352, K. C. Henders (Alberta Human Rights Commission) to The Rhodes Trust, 1 Aug. 1974.

[233] RTC 96311, Scace to Owen Hughes, 9 Sept. 1974.

[234] RTC 96311, Scace to Williams, 7 Dec. 1976.

[235] RTC 145353, telegram, Williams to Scace, 9 July 1980.

[236] See RTF 2555, Scace to Kenny, 25 Mar. 1991.

lems for Saskatchewan's long-time secretary, Ken Norman, who became the province's chief human rights commissioner in the late 1970s. 'You can certainly validly want to know what the hell is Norman doing associating himself with something that discrimin- ates . . . on the basis of age and marital status,' he told a reporter in Saskatoon.[237] 'And I suppose my only answer to that is there's no way of correcting it. It's a scholarship that's established by a will . . . in England.'

Scace soon returned to the issue of restructuring competitions, at least in the Maritimes and on the Prairies. For political reasons, he told Williams, 'it would be preferable if you could give the impression that the decision was taken by the Trustees on their own initiative'.[238] This was the context for a letter he received in May 1975.[239]

The Trustees believe that it might at once ease secretarial and selection committee problems and make for greater competition if we offered three Scholarships for the Prairies instead of one each from Alberta, Manitoba and Saskatchewan; and two Scholarships from the Maritimes including P.E.I. instead of one each from Nova Scotia and New Brunswick . . .

The Trustees have already passed a minute authorizing this proposal . . . but you will doubtless wish to discuss matters at Edmonton [where the 1975 meeting of the Canadian Association was to be held] and sound out opinion.

That opinion included some very strong objections—none of which would have been unfamiliar to George Parkin. Ultimately, as the minutes of the Association's 1975 meeting record, the 'lively but very temperate discussion' produced unanimous approval of a care- fully phrased resolution expressing willingness 'to cooperate fully' in improving the selec- tion procedure but regret 'that there was no previous consultation about the intention to "regionalize" certain of the Scholarships'.[240]

As was obvious from the sequence of events, Williams and Scace had a clear sense of the relationship of the Association to the Trust. 'The Scholarships could not, of course, operate successfully without the wholesale cooperation of old Rhodes Scholars but the ultimate responsibility lies with the Trustees; and it rests with me as Secretary to try and remedy defects,' Williams wrote bluntly to one critic, Francis Leddy. 'Beginning with the Maritimes (one of which the Senator [Henry Hicks] fancies is his nomination borough, I suspect) it is time for a shake up or shake out.'[241]

For the 1976 competition, a single committee and jurisdiction would cover the three Maritime provinces.[242] On the Prairies, student numbers were larger and distances greater. There, on the American model and beginning with the competition for 1977, provincial

---

[237] RTC 145352, Paul Morgan, 'Norman Faces Awkward Conflict of Interest', *Saskatoon Star-Phoenix*, 8 Oct. 1981; clipping attached to Henry Kloppenburg to Scace, 9 Oct. 1981. Norman had studied in England on another award. When 'an exodus from Saskatchewan' left few potential scholar secretaries, scholars in Saskatoon put Norman's name forward with warm enthusiasm. See RTC 145352, Horsley to Williams, 2 Apr. 1970; Otto Lang to Stewart, 3 May 1971.

[238] RTF 2555, Scace to Williams, 4 Apr. 1975.   [239] RTC 96311, Williams to Scace, 14 May 1975.

[240] RTC 96311, Copy of minutes of CARS meeting, Edmonton, 7 June 1975.

[241] RTC 96311, Williams to Leddy, 30 Sept. 1975. Hicks had been president of Dalhousie University since 1963 and a Canadian Senator since 1972. See P. B. Waite, *The Lives of Dalhousie University*, ii: *1925–1980: The Old College Transformed* (Montreal: McGill-Queen's University Press, 1998), 244–403.

[242] For the role of provincial subcommittees, see RTC 145352, Dr John P. Finley to Scace, 16 Dec 1982; RTF 3311, minutes of meeting of Maritime Selection Committee, 28–9 Nov. 1986.

committees would interview applicants and select up to three for another interview a week later before a region-wide committee with members from each province.[243] Scholars from the new regions continued to be recorded by provincial names in Association publications, as was done in the United States. Robin Fletcher was willing to adopt the same policy, but the *Register* has, on the whole, not done so.[244]

The next major organizational challenge for Scace arose as the British government raised fees drastically for international students and Williams began to speak of deep retrenchment: Canada, he reminded Scace, was allocated only three scholarships in the will.[245] This crisis passed, but higher education in Britain continued to change rapidly—as was reflected in multiplying programmes at Oxford and in deep changes at many of the colleges. 'I find the hardest aspect of this job is advising candidates on Oxford's academic programmes and particularly opportunities for graduate study', wrote Trevor Anderson, secretary of the Manitoba Committee, in 1981. 'We have no very recent Scholars in the vicinity, and the Oxford official literature seems usually to be obsolete or unreadable.'[246] Most secretaries could have said the same thing. Scace was more up to date, thanks to the meetings of overseas secretaries now held annually in Oxford. Robin Fletcher also sought to connect overseas constituencies more closely to Oxford. For example, he sat in on the Ontario and Quebec selection committees during a visit in December 1984 and in July 1985 held a meeting of American regional and Canadian provincial secretaries in Chicago. After the latter, Scace wrote, 'the Canadian Secretaries returned with renewed enthusiasm and most importantly, strength. For the most part, they operate in a vacuum and association with you and the Trustees is extremely beneficial.'[247]

Whatever the reasons, there seemed in the 1980s to be fewer problems for Rhodes House in placing Canadian scholars. In 1982, a high point, ten of eleven Canadians gained admission to the college they had listed first.[248] And almost all scholars in most years were placed at the college of their first or second choice. Committees still might pick candidates for a programme with very limited space, or select someone with an unusual record who did not exactly meet the preferences of modern Oxford—but as of 1999, no Canadian scholar had yet failed to be admitted to an Oxford college.

Scholars and the World

One of Rhodes's hopes was that Scholars might 'in afterlife . . . esteem the performance of public duties as [their] highest aim'. The meaning of 'public duties' can always be

---

[243] RTC 145352, Scace to K. E. Norman, 18 Nov. 1975. Meetings would rotate among the provinces. Subsequent suggestions that the Prairies follow the Maritimes to a single tier of competition were strongly resisted. See RTC 222007, D. P. Jones to Scace, 9 Dec. 1987; RTF 2555, Report of the Warden on his and Lady Kenny's visit to Germany and Canada, Dec. 1995.

[244] See RTC 207161, James A. Gibson to Scace, 25 Oct. 1983; and RTF 3084, Fletcher to Gibson, 12 Sept. 1983.

[245] RTC 96311, Williams to Scace, 26 July 1979, and Scace to Williams, 3 Aug. 1979.

[246] RTC 145352, D. T. Anderson to Scace, 23 Aug. 1981.

[247] RTC 207161, Scace to Fletcher, 2 Aug. 1985.

[248] RTC 207161, Fletcher to Scace, 25 Feb. 1982.

debated, but if they are measured in terms of prominent public offices, Canadian scholars probably reached a pinnacle in the 1970s. Twenty years later, few scholars held equivalent positions. From 1967 to 1974, Roland Michener was a very popular Governor General. Three or four scholars were members of Pierre Trudeau's cabinet at any time between 1968 and 1979. From 1974, there were two scholars (and three for several years after 1979) among the nine justices of the Supreme Court of Canada. W. R. Jackett was Chief Justice of the Federal Court of Canada until 1979. David Lewis was national leader of the NDP until 1975 (and the NDP's influence was substantial, notably during the minority government of Pierre Trudeau between 1972 and 1974). Marcel Lambert had succeeded Michener as Speaker in 1962 and was a Conservative front bencher throughout the Trudeau years. Allan Blakeney of the NDP was premier of Saskatchewan from 1971 to 1982 and much respected on the national scene. In the 1960s and early 1970s, up to four or five scholars at a time were provincial chief justices, and scholars headed as many as eight or nine universities at a time.[249] Throughout the 1970s, scholars held the senior post in External Affairs, under-secretary. Gordon Robertson held the leading position in the entire public service, Clerk of the Privy Council and Cabinet Secretary, from 1963 to 1975. Arnold Smith was the first Secretary General of the Commonwealth, from 1965 to 1975. And men like F. R. Scott and Eugene Forsey were important national figures—and mentors and friends of Trudeau as well, as Forsey's appointment to the Canadian Senate in 1970 also suggested.

'We are without a federal Cabinet Minister for the first time in many years,' Scace wrote to Williams following the 1979 federal election.[250] Pierre Trudeau regained power in 1980 (bringing one scholar, Francis Fox, back to the cabinet table). On Trudeau's eventual retirement in 1984, the Liberal leadership went to John Turner. Long a leader-in-waiting, he had resigned as Finance Minister in the mid-1970s and moved to Toronto to practise law. His tenure as Prime Minister was brief, however, as there was little time to rebuild the party before he had to call an election.

Turner achieved the country's highest elective office at a time of deep change in postwar understandings of the state and of politics. These surely contributed to the diminishing engagement of scholars in electoral politics. One exception was Wilson Parasiuk. He was actually at a meeting of the Manitoba selection committee in December 1981 when he 'had to be excused temporarily to rush off to the Legislature . . . to be told of his position in the new [NDP] Government . . . Minister for Energy—and about everything else!'[251] Another was the 1960s student radical Bob Rae, who left federal politics and in 1990 led the NDP to power in Ontario.[252] After his government's defeat in 1995, the only scholar in an elected office, except perhaps at the municipal level, was Marcel Massé, a career public servant until he ran for the Liberals in the 1993 federal election. In the autumn of 1999, he resigned from the cabinet and Parliament.

[249] See, e.g., RTC 96311, Brian Dickson to Stewart, 10 Oct. 1967.
[250] RTC 96311, Scace to Williams, 28 May 1979.
[251] RTC 145352, D. T. Anderson to Scace, 2 Dec. 1981.
[252] See Rae's account in *From Protest to Power: Personal Reflections on a Life in Politics* (Toronto: Viking, 1996).

These and other changes in the lives of Canadian scholars were chronicled in the Association's *Newsletter*. In 1975, not long after retiring from his position as founding President of Brock University, James Gibson became its editor, presenting 'news of interest'
in his clear and distinctive voice.[253] 'What can one say that does justice to the interest
and quality of the Association Newsletter?' wrote Michael Howarth in 1987. 'Jim's . . .
meticulous attention to our comings and goings, together with his own thoughts . . . [on]
matters of interest to Rhodes Scholars, . . . result in a publication informed with a style
and grace we can only admire.'[254] As secretary-treasurer of the Association 1977–87,
Gibson was also responsible for its other publication, the *Directory*.

The Association itself remained, in the words of Sholto Hebenton, the president from
1983–5, 'a vehicle by which scholars keep in touch with themselves and with current developments in Oxford'. Resisting a call for it to take a stand on South Africa, he argued
that 'it would lose its usefulness as a linking organization if it became active in any particular political issue'.[255] Nor did the Association feel it appropriate to adopt a suggestion made by Stephen Clarkson, following a discussion with Roy McMurtry, Canadian
High Commissioner in London, on 'the dramatic decline in the intensity of the
relationship between Canada and Britain in the post war decades', that the Association
(and the Foundation) seek 'to encourag[e] the study of Canadian issues in England',
including in Oxford.[256]

By the end of the 1980s almost 100 Canadian scholars, twice as many as in 1959, lived
in Toronto (see Table 1). Numbers had also grown in St John's, Halifax, Calgary, and
Vancouver, but not in Ottawa, Montreal, and other Prairie cities. Kingston and London
now had about as many resident Rhodes scholars as any western city except Vancouver.
Indeed, almost half of those living in Canada were now in Ontario, as were a majority
of the thirty scholars elected from elsewhere who now lived in Canada and contributed
substantially both there and beyond.[257] Fifteen of these scholars were originally from
Rhodesia or South Africa; the remainder included four from the USA, two from Jamaica,
and one each from nine other jurisdictions.[258] Several had married Canadian scholars
(offsetting, as it were, Canadians who married scholars from elsewhere and now lived
outside Canada). The number of Canadian scholars living outside Canada had hardly
changed since 1959. Most lived in the United States and Britain, but the number in other
countries had grown from five to sixteen. Now, however, it was the more recent scholars who were most likely to live abroad. About a third of those elected from 1977–86
were outside Canada in 1989. And this was not a short-term pattern.

[253] RTF 3084, Gibson to the Warden, 1 Sept. 1989.
[254] RTC 222007, Howarth to Scace, 1 Apr. 1987. Gibson continued to edit the *Newsletter* until 1994.
[255] RTC 207161, Hebenton to James Gibson, 15 Dec. 1986.
[256] RTC 207161, Clarkson to Gibson, Howarth, and Scace, 2 May 1986, Waite, and Gibson to
Clarkson, 14 May 1986. See also RTF 3084, Gibson to Fletcher, 23 Nov. 1987.
[257] For example, the research of David Schindler in Ontario, Manitoba, and Alberta brought him global
recognition as 'the world's most distinguished freshwater ecologist'. Andrew Nikiforuk, 'Schindler's
Warning: Will it be Heard?', *Globe and Mail*, 24 Feb. 2000, R9.
[258] These were Australia, New Zealand, Pakistan, Sri Lanka, the Commonwealth Caribbean, Germany,
Malta, Zambia, and Bermuda.

As it had always been, law was the single most prominent career path for Canadian scholars in 1989.[239] Although universities and government were important, there were fewer scholars from the twenty years 1967–86 teaching in universities than from the ten years 1957–66, and the disproportion was even greater in government service. Indeed, 80 per cent of the scholars in Ottawa had been elected before 1967. If the trend is not surprising, the absolute numbers may be. For example, the Department of Foreign Affairs, which once recruited as many as three or four scholars per year, now hired fewer than that in a decade and was unable to retain some of them. On the other hand, the number of scholars pursuing careers in medicine grew rapidly, and it rivalled law in terms of the careers of the 1977–86 scholars.[260] For Canadians as for others, the principal recruiter of scholars at Oxford was, it seems, the management consulting firm McKinsey and Company.[261] But the proportion of scholars whose careers were somewhere (besides law) in the business world did not greatly increase. The fastest growing employment category was actually a very diverse 'all other' group: occupations in media and culture (radio, writing, broadcasting, editing, theatre, film), agencies and institutions of various sorts (foundations, international agencies, professional organizations), science in various non-university contexts, teaching outside the post-secondary sector, and the clergy.

In this chapter, I have tried to trace, without focusing exclusively upon, the main lines of the scholarship's administration in Canada. Because homogeneous stereotypes of Rhodes scholars and of Oxford are common, it has seemed important at least to suggest (without overemphasizing) some of the variation among scholars in Canada. In summarizing selectively the place of scholars in Canadian politics, I hope I do not seem to underestimate the importance and scope of leadership and service in the other settings in which scholars have worked in and beyond Canada. Nor can these qualities be measured only in public reputation. As Williams wrote of one Canadian, 'You chose well: and we here are very grateful. I reckon we shall all have cause to be so one fine day, but we may never know about it all because he will eschew those headlines from which misleading statistics may sometimes be compiled. None of us will be worrying about that.'

Almost everything about the context of the scholarships in Canada has changed in a century. It would be easy to cast this story in terms of a rise, to c.1960–80, followed by a fading in the significance of the scholarships in Canada. That does not, however, seem right for a history that continues. The selection process itself retains its character and distinguishes the Rhodes scholarship from most others. An increasingly demanding Oxford continues to attract Canadians and to admit the scholars who are sent from Canada. If the criteria in Rhodes's will are as open to debate and interpretation as ever, their vitality has not diminished, nor (as committee minutes clearly indicate) has the appeal of the scholarship to some young men and women of remarkable ability. The tragically short

---

[259] See David A. A. Stager with Harry W. Arthurs, *Lawyers in Canada* (Toronto: University of Toronto Press, 1990). Almost one-third of 1967–76 scholars and over one-fifth of the 1977–86 group went into law.

[260] See, e.g., RTC 222007, 'Medicine's Rhodes Scholars: A Common Bond, a Rare Coincidence', Memorial University *Gazette*, 12 Mar. 1987, 6–8.

[261] See Nicholas Lemann, 'The Kids in the Conference Room: How McKinsey & Company Became the Next Big Step', *New Yorker*, 18, 25 Oct. 1999, 209–16.

career of one 1985 scholar, Katherine Fleming, offers a perspective on the scholarships and leadership today—and brings us back to Africa, where we began. A graduate of St Francis Xavier University, she was deputy representative of UNICEF in Tanzania when she died suddenly in 1999. Her husband's tribute captures something of where the scholarship might lead a Canadian and of what 'public duties' might be in the modern world.[262]

'I think that this can be sorted out,' she would say of some complex matter before writing a few pages that would help to change the direction of a global, political and deeply bureaucratic corporation. . . . [I]nstead of worrying about [Africa's] risks, Katie took inspiration from the ability of most Africans to live lives of decency and humility even in the midst of poverty.

---

[262] Johannes Zutt, 'Life Story: Out of Africa: One Rhodent's Vision', *Toronto Globe and Mail*, 13 Aug 1999, A15.

4

A Century of South African Rhodes Scholarships

TIM NUTTALL

Introduction

The historical legacy of Cecil Rhodes has loomed large in twentieth-century Southern Africa. A symbolic icon to be vilified or praised, depending on one's perspective, the life of Rhodes has attracted widespread attention and controversy. This has been so amongst serious academic researchers, and within various media, school curricula, and annals of popular memory. This chapter concentrates on one aspect of the complex inheritance bequeathed by Rhodes, namely the scholarships which took his name. South Africa occupies a 'special place' as the umbilical locale for the origins of this worldwide scheme. During the first quarter-century of the life of the Rhodes Trust, a majority of the Trustees retained close personal connections with South Africa. If this sense of closeness waned during succeeding decades, it never disappeared. The controversies of the last quarter of the twentieth century thrust the South African constituency with fresh vigour into a different kind of special relationship with the Trust. When George Parkin, the founding organizer of the worldwide scholarships, predicted in 1912 that future Rhodes scholars would 'be drawn from remote generations, which cannot be expected to know much about Rhodes', this was certainly not to be the case in South Africa.[1]

Rhodes made his fortune from the mining revolution which transformed Southern Africa at the end of the nineteenth century. A mining metaphor can aptly be applied to the Rhodes scholarships. Leaders are a valuable resource embedded in the fabric of society. The exacting criteria of the Rhodes scholarships were designed to unearth and then nurture leaders of high quality. The implementation of the scholarships occurred, and still occurs, within a sociopolitical context; the history of the scholarships is one of changing patterns of social 'mining'. For most of the century the leadership seams considered worthy for prospecting were populated by white men; the discovery of new gold fields is a relatively recent development. The central actors in the long centennial narrative belonged to particular segments of a racial elite within a society emerging from colonial conquest, then consolidating into segregation and apartheid, and then negotiating the transitions towards a post-apartheid order. The scholarships offer a window onto these

---

[1] G. R. Parkin, *The Rhodes Scholarships* (Boston: Houghton Mifflin, 1912), p. vii.

changing permutations, from vantage points within both South Africa and the Rhodes Trust in England.

In many ways, the most interesting parts of the history of the South African scholarships belong to the first thirty years and the last thirty years of the century. It is a story of intriguing origins followed by mid-century consolidation and then the onset, from the 1970s, of crisis, reaction, creativity, and reorganization. The bulk of the portrayal which follows is concentrated on the first and last thirds of the century. The unique inclusion in the South African constituency of 'college schools', the profound educational, cultural, and political dimensions of the scholarships in the founding decades, and the persistence of widely varying styles of scholarship administration are the main themes addressed during the first thirty or so years. Bram Gie was South African Secretary from 1940 to 1967, and his admirable legacy was to 'get the house in order'. This was no small feat of consolidation in a context devoid of systematic administration.

It was this solid platform onto which Rex Welsh stepped as the new South African Secretary in 1967. But change was in the air, induced partly by Welsh and partly by international developments which put new pressure on the organization of the South African scholarships. Embroiled in two political and administrative 'storms', one in the 1970s and the other in the 1980s, Welsh reorganized the provincial scholarships and entered the fray on the future of the four 'schools' scholarships. These were tense times, moderated by the close friendship between Welsh and Bill Williams at Rhodes House. Welsh and his fellow selectors and administrators made a substantial contribution to the continuing legitimization of the scholarships during a period of deep systemic crisis in South African history. They paved the way for the steps taken by Welsh's successor, Laurie Ackermann, during the tumultuous 1990s and the move towards a post-apartheid order.

This chapter concentrates on personalities and issues in the history of scholarship administration.[2] It does so in a manner which draws connections between this administration and South Africa's complex and controversial history during the twentieth century. The unique combination of selection criteria infused the administration of the scholarships with varying conceptions of leadership. C. K. Allen, the Warden at Rhodes House during the 1930s and 1940s, coined the phrase 'intelligent muscularity' in describing South African scholars.[3] This was a particularly apt designation of the quintessential Rhodes scholar selected in South Africa, at least until the 1970s when selectors began progressively to uncouple notions of muscularity from assessments of 'character'. There were, of course, many variables in the combination of the two poles of intelligence and muscularity, and there were exceptions for whom the joint appellation was inappropriate.

The conceptions of leadership which informed the selection of Rhodes scholars naturally give rise to the question: what mark have Rhodes scholars made in their lives

---

[2] I am grateful to Caroline Brown in Oxford and Annette Gibson in Johannesburg, as well as to a number of past and present selection committee secretaries, for assisting me in the collection of archival material.

[3] RTF 2009, Allen to Elton, 30 Jan. 1951.

after Oxford? That question has been posed in many different times and places during the past century; and it forms a thread of this chapter.

Origins, Ties, and Particularities: Dimensions of South Africa's Special Status

In his book *The Rhodes Scholarships*, published in 1912, George Parkin wrote that the creation of the Union of South Africa in 1910 represented a fulfilment of one of Rhodes's political ideals.[4] English- and Dutch-speaking South Africans had negotiated a constitution that united the subcontinent under a single government, forging a new state within the British Empire. Alfred Milner questioned Parkin's view: Rhodes 'would find little to rejoice about' because 'the Dutch have gained far more influence than [he] would have liked'.[5] After all, a Boer War commander was the Union's first Prime Minister.

Milner had written his comments on a draft of Parkin's manuscript. To no avail, for Parkin's views prevailed in the published text. Elsewhere in this book readers can learn of the Trustees' support for political interventions and settler immigration schemes which sought to maintain and widen British influences in South Africa's polity and society. This was also a major intent of the scholarship scheme which forms the main focus of this chapter. But there were other intriguing aspects of this scheme as it developed in South Africa, lending themselves to a complex and varied story of 'special status'.

The scholarship scheme, conceived in the South African periphery of a worldwide empire, flowed from a bold international vision. Scholars from the colonies and the United States would imbibe the refinements, ethos, and culture of a university at the heart of the British Empire, while Oxford would be invigorated by fresh energy and new insights brought by students from 'new societies'.[6] The main loci of the scheme were to be Oxford and the Trust office in London, and the largest single block of scholars was to come from the United States. But at least for the first two decades of the Trust's life, and setting a pattern for the future, South Africa looms large.

The will laid out an exceptional arrangement for the South African scholarships: four out of an original five were allocated to specified schools in the Cape Colony. This became an early defining characteristic of the scholarships in South Africa, one which provoked a considerable array of responses among the Trustees, the Trust's officials, at Oxford, and in South Africa. Perceived from the start as both 'problem' and 'opportunity', the schools scholarships placed an intriguing imprint on both administrative practice and fluctuating discourses of 'quality' and 'leadership'.

When the Trustees added additional provincial scholarships after the first World War, this did not substantially alter a view commonly expressed during the first half-century

[4] Parkin, *The Rhodes Scholarships*, 10–11.
[5] RTF 2109, Milner to Parkin, 21 June 1912.
[6] Parkin, *The Rhodes Scholarships*, 92–3. For an important discussion of how the scholarships first made their way into Rhodes's will of 1893, see C. Newbury, 'Cecil Rhodes and the South African Connection: "A Great Imperial University"', in F. Madden and D. K. Fieldhouse (eds.), *Oxford and the Idea of Commonwealth* (London: Croom Helm, 1982).

by the Trust Secretary or the Oxford Warden: South Africa had the highest concentration of scholarships per capita of all the major constituencies. From this flowed the common expectation that Oxford could not normally expect South African scholars of high quality. In South Africa or, more accurately, among certain sectors of the elite, the scholarships became revered as a sign of high achievement and prestige, a resource to be cherished, promoted, and, if necessary, defended. Using different sets of reference points for success, South African scholars and their selectors tended to rate themselves more highly than did Trust officials.

If there were wide differences of perspective on the South African scholarships and scholars there was, however, one strikingly common assumption between 1902 and the late 1960s: the pool of potential scholars did not extend beyond white South Africans. The 'per capita' calculation was refracted through a prism of race that was unquestioned both on the periphery and in the imperial metropole. In the fascinating quest to unearth leaders who met the exacting criteria of Rhodes's will, only certain seams and pipes of South African society were identified and mined.

The World of the Will

Rhodes's final will of 1899 cannot be understood without a sense of the political geography of Southern Africa at that time. The term 'South Africa' was but a geographical expression for a cluster of settler-dominated territories. Under British authority, but ruled by settler governments, were the colonies of the Cape and Natal. The Cape had been ruled by the Dutch for the first 150 years of its life as a colony of European conquest and settlement. The British took it over early in the nineteenth century, and grafted new layers of administration, culture, economy, and territorial expansion on Dutch foundations. Natal, too, began as a colony of predominantly Dutch settlers in the 1830s and 1840s, but was then taken over by the British with the strategic intention of preventing the Boers from securing coastal territory on the sea route to the east. In developments which echoed the imperial partitioning of Africa during the 1880s and 1890s, both the Cape and Natal had, with the assistance of British troops, extended their control over land formerly ruled by Africans.

In the meantime, during the second half of the century, Boer settlers migrated into the interior and carved out two independent republics, which coexisted uneasily with resilient African polities. The Boer republics' cultural and international links were with Holland and Germany. From the late 1860s the political economy of the interior was dramatically transformed through impressive mineral discoveries, first diamonds and then gold. The subcontinent would never be the same again, for these discoveries brought in their wake new wars of conquest of African societies, greater imperial intervention, the strengthening of settler domination, economic integration of the colonies and republics, and a bitter conflict between the British and the Boers over who would ultimately control the direction of these developments.

Rhodes was a central and controversial actor in these seismic developments. His name, along with figures such as Alfred Beit and Barney Banato, became synonymous with the

tumultuous world of diamonds and gold. Propelled to become Prime Minister of the
Cape Colony in the 1890s, Rhodes sponsored the British South Africa Company's invasion of Matabeleland, laying the basis for the colony which would bear his name. *Punch*
magazine produced a cartoon of Rhodes straddling Africa, one foot at the Cape and the
other at Cairo: the quintessential colonial statesman who beckoned the British Empire
to rule Africa. He was intricately involved in the spectacle of intrigue and fiasco of 1895
which came to be known as the Jameson Raid. This bungled attempt to spark an English
revolt against Paul Kruger's Transvaal administration precipitated Rhodes's political
downfall as head of the Cape government. His rise as a leading Cape politician had
occurred in part through an alliance with Jan Hofmeyr's Afrikaner Bond, his fall through
the machinations that led to the outbreak of the Boer War in 1899.

This, in brief outline, was the political context in which Rhodes allocated his South
African scholarships. The will spelt out an order of priority. At the top of the list were
three scholarships annually for the embryonic colony of Rhodesia, a territory commonly
enveloped within the term 'South Africa'. Next were four 'college schools' in the Cape,
each with a scholarship, followed by one for the colony of Natal. After the South African
scholarships came the Australian, Canadian, and other colonial allocations, followed by
those for the United States. The Rhodesian awards can easily be understood. So too can
the Natal one, for this was a British colony and the place where Rhodes had initially
lived and worked on arrival from England. Rhodesia and Natal were geographic units,
as was the Cape Colony. But instead of earmarking scholarships for that colony, Rhodes
selected four 'college schools' and wrote these into his will. It was a unique stipulation
in the whole scheme. Why he did so is an intriguing question.

Seeking Precision for a Norm: Rhodes's Choice of 'College Schools'

One way to understand Rhodes's action is to argue that he needed a precise, tangible
focus for his broad, untested vision. His vision embraced an ideal type of student who
would be selected to go to Oxford from diverse constituencies worldwide. The mix of
personal qualities outlined in clause 23 of the will was to become the challenging hall-
mark of the Rhodes scholarship: intellect, athleticism, character and service, and leadership. In seeking to define a scholar as a man who would 'esteem the performance of
public duties as his highest aim', Rhodes was giving expression to ideals of the patrician
elite in classical Greece. He was also describing the manifestation of those ideals within
Britain's Victorian aristocracy, among whom Rhodes circulated with increasing frequency
during the 1890s. Rhodes's lawyer in London, Bourchier Hawksley, apparently penned
the wordy, overlapping phrases of clause 23 in expressing Rhodes's idealism. It was remembered that Rhodes summarized the criteria more brusquely to a friend as 'smugness, brutality, unctuous rectitude and tact'.[7]

Rhodes could have left things there: a broad statement of intent for his Trustees to put
into practice. But he wanted to be more precise, specifying the weighting of personal

[7] RTSA 12, R. Gibson to R. Welsh, 26 Jan. 1982, enclosing a draft article on Rhodes and Rhodes
scholars.

qualities. Even though he called them 'mere suggestions', the will spelt out that his 'ideal qualified student' should be ranked in the following manner: 40 per cent for intellect, 20 per cent for athleticism, 20 per cent for character and service, and 20 per cent for leadership. In a codicil dated 11 October 1901 he adjusted the weighting as follows: 30, 20, 30, 20. The test of intellect would be by examination, qualities of athleticism, character, and service would be voted on by a ballot of 'fellow students', and the headmaster of the candidate's school would assess leadership. In addition to making these specifications Rhode's will identified the institutions at which they should be applied. He had been considering investing his fortune in the founding of South Africa's first independent teaching university. The University of the Cape of Good Hope, established in the 1870s, did not have independent status; it was merely an examining authority for matriculation and the BA degree, a system based on the University of London. A handful of 'colleges' and 'college schools' in the Cape, and one at Bloemfontein, offered post-matriculation classes which prepared students for the examinations of the Cape University, as it was called. The 'school' taught up to matriculation; the 'college' taught for the university examination. When Rhodes decided in favour of his global scholarship scheme, and against funding an independent teaching university at the Cape, this caused great disappointment at Cape Town's premier educational institution, the South African College.[8] Founded in 1829, the South African College initially offered elementary and secondary schooling as well as post-matriculation classes to both Dutch and English students, educating many who became influential in colonial affairs.[9] The College was non-denominational and was supported by government grants from the 1830s. It underwent rapid expansion during the 1880s and 1890s, benefiting from the benefactions of Rhodes and other Cape luminaries. The three constituent parts of the College were established as distinctive entities: an elementary school, a 'college school' up to matriculation (SACS), and a post-matriculation 'college'. In 1897, the College's Jubilee Year, a Victoria scholarship was established, winning for two high achievers annually free tuition as they proceeded from school to college. It was to this growing college school that Rhodes decided to allocate one of his scholarships to Oxford.

According to Lewis Michell, his banker and fellow director of the British South Africa Company, Rhodes's first intention was to allocate just two scholarships in the Cape, one to SACS and the other to the Stellenbosch College School.[10] Founded as a pre-university gymnasium by public subscription of Stellenbosch residents in the 1860s, this institution developed into a constituent 'college' and 'college school' in 1879. In 1886 the Stellenbosch College was renamed Victoria College (an ambiguous political move in an Afrikaner-dominated town) and in 1899, when the 'college school' began to teach a senior matriculation class, it was renamed Stellenbosch Boys' High School. Like SACS, the

---

[8] W. Ritchie, *The History of the South African College* (Cape Town: Maskew Miller, 1918), 456.

[9] Details are from Ritchie, *History of the South African College*; J. Linnegar, *SACS: 150 Years* (Cape Town: SACS Committee, 1979).

[10] Details for this paragraph are drawn from RTF 3576, R. Luyt's speaking brief for meeting with Rhodes Trustees, 3 June 1972, and affidavit of J. H. Galloway in the High Court of Justice, Chancery division, 1990.

Stellenbosch College School was non-denominational (although it had Dutch Reformed leanings) and supported by government grants; its dominant medium of instruction was English but it was a multilingual school with English-, Dutch-, and German-speaking pupils. Interestingly, both had been influenced by Scottish educationalists. On one occasion Rhodes had written in the visitors' book at Victoria College: 'My visit here has made me think.'[11] His choice of these two schools for a scholarship award made sense politically: both were leading representatives of an emerging South Africanism with which Rhodes had been associated, alongside his wider imperial designs.[12] And the choice made educational sense, too, for in 1918 the South African College was to become the University of Cape Town and Victoria College was to become the University of Stellenbosch: South Africa's first two autonomous teaching universities.

Michell prevailed on Rhodes to add to his list two college schools quite different from the first two.[13] Michell punted two Anglican church schools, modelled on English public schools, and representing vital vanguards of British culture on South African soil. Their senior staff commonly hailed from an Oxbridge tradition, and were recruited directly from England. The first school, Diocesan College, was in Rondebosch, Cape Town, and the other, St Andrew's College, was in faraway Grahamstown, the former military garrison turned into a centre of the Eastern Cape separatist movement. Michell had personal connections with both schools. He sat on the council of Diocesan College, which had been founded by Bishop Gray, the first Anglican Bishop of Cape Town, in 1849. Michell was also a friend of Frances Armstrong, wife of the Bishop of Grahamstown, John Armstrong, who founded St Andrew's in 1855.

Diocesan College, nicknamed 'Bishops', was the more established of the two schools, nurturing an influential segment of Cape Town's elite. St Andrew's pupils were more commonly drawn from far-flung farming families in the Eastern Cape and beyond. Both institutions had 'college departments' with professors who taught post-matriculation classes for examination by the Cape University, but on a smaller scale than the South African College and Victoria College. Rhodes's heightened sense of mortality, due to his heart disease, helped to raise his interest in matters religious; and this may have been a factor influencing his inclusion of these two schools in his will.[14] In choosing St Andrew's there were assuredly political motives, for Rhodes assumed leadership of

[11] RTF 1654, T. Walker to Parkin, 6 Aug. 1903, recalling this incident.

[12] As late as the 1940s it was still remembered in Bloemfontein that Rhodes, after a dinner at Grey College School, was first inspired to found his scholarships. See RTF 2009, Report on Lord Elton's Visit to South Africa and Rhodesia, Feb.–Mar. 1948. As with SACS and the Stellenbosch College School, Grey enrolled both English- and Dutch-speaking boys. The increasing hostility between the British colonies and the Boer republics in the late 1890s made it impossible for Rhodes to consider including the Bloemfontein school in his scholarship provision.

[13] RTF 3576, R. Luyt's speaking brief for meeting with Rhodes Trustees, 3 June 1972; T. Stevens, *The Time of our Lives: St Andrew's College, 1855–1990* (Grahamstown: St Andrew's, n.d. [1990?]), 141; J. Gardener et al., *Bishops 150: A History of the Diocesan College, Rondebosch* (Cape Town: Juta, 1997), 240. See also the opening chapters of P. Randall, *Little England on the Veld: The English Private School System in South Africa* (Johannesburg: Ravan, 1982).

[14] D. McIntyre, *The Diocesan College, Rondebosch and a Century of 'Bishops'* (Juta: Cape Town, 1950), 36–41.

the Progressive Party in 1898. Grahamstown was at the heart of '1820 settler country' and had developed as an important centre of British heritage. Hawksley, too, may have influenced Rhodes, for it was surely more than coincidence that the newly appointed headmaster of St Andrew's in 1902, the Reverend W. S. MacGowan, was his personal friend.

If this saga of 'college schools' had taken a number of interesting turns, there was to be a final twist in Rhodes's attempt to specify how his scholarship ideal might work out in practice. It is part of the privileged story of origins that Rhodes sat one day on a bench on the mountainside above Groote Schuur; his eyes set upon the green fields and white buildings of Diocesan College far below him, and inspiration struck.[15] He would choose that school for his first Rhodes scholar experiment. Early in 1901 discussions ensued between Rhodes, the Anglican Archbishop West Jones, and the headmaster, Canon Jenkins, who, interestingly, had formerly been a teacher at St Andrew's. Rhodes offered the school £250 for an Oxford scholarship to be awarded according to the criteria laid out in his will. Jenkins, knowing the tough entry requirements of Oxford, tried to persuade Rhodes that the award should be made to an older boy in the post-matriculation 'college' class.[16] The benefactor insisted that his scholar should be selected from the 'school', that is, should not be older than 17. It was an insistence that was to spawn a complicated legacy for the future. Rhodes's only concession to Jenkins's concerns was to agree to a slightly heavier weighting of the academic criteria in the allocation of marks to candidates.[17]

A school ballot was held in the last term of 1901, and the Bishops headmaster informed Rhodes that there were two candidates between whom he could not easily choose. Canon Jenkins had experienced, baptismally, the agony of choice that was later to become an annual experience for Rhodes selection committees the world over. It was an agony amplified by the breadth of the will's selection criteria. Luckily for Jenkins, though, both the Archbishop and Rhodes lived near to the school and Rhodes could be persuaded to find the additional money. And so it was that, at the age of 16, Frank Reid and Farquhar Yeoman were confirmed as the first Rhodes scholars, in February 1902. In the event, they were not to be the first scholars to go up to Oxford; they were too young and they had to wait until October 1904.

Nowhere else in his scholarship scheme did Rhodes allocate scholarships to specific institutions, let alone schools. Would he have done so if he had known the other constituencies as well as he knew the Cape Colony? It remains an interesting anomaly that the four Cape 'college schools' were, from the start, an exception in a worldwide scheme, but they provided the normative context, in the mind of Rhodes, Michell, and Hawksley, for the language and intent of the will's selection criteria.

---

[15] Author's interview with John Gardener, Cape Town, 4 Dec. 1998; McIntyre, *A Century of 'Bishops'*, 36–41.
[16] RTF 1489, Jenkins to Parkin, 3 Aug. 1906.
[17] McIntyre, *A Century of 'Bishops'*, 39. It is interesting to note that in the codicil to his will, which was added after the discussions with Bishops, Rhodes reduced the academic criteria from 40% to 30%.

Mixed Patterns and Profound Impacts, 1903–1918

The only scholars to be selected in the first year after Rhodes's death were from South Africa, Rhodesia, and Germany. The first two constituencies were able to respond quickly to the new scheme because four of the Trustees had strong South African links and because the beneficiaries had advance warning, due to the local publicity which had surrounded Rhodes's will. Without much fuss the headmasters of the four 'college schools' applied the system of marks and the school ballot outlined in the will. Cyprian Brooke was selected for Diocesan College, Charles Gardner for St Andrew's, Percy Lewis for the South African College, and William MacMillan for Stellenbosch Boys' High School. The Cambridge-educated headmaster at Stellenbosch, W. Hofmeyr, reported that in the computing of the marks MacMillan had come second. The Afrikaans-speaking boy who had gained the highest score had turned the offer down; he did not want to be associated with Rhodes the British imperialist. This response by an Afrikaner candidate was to be a feature in the years ahead at Stellenbosch.

In the case of Rhodesia, ruled by the British South Africa Company which had offices in Bulawayo, Cape Town, and London, there was a simple, direct selection mechanism in the form of one man, the Director of Education. In 1903, he could fill only two of the three awards: Albert Bissett, a pupil at St George's in Bulawayo, and Cyril Blakeway, who had been to school at St Andrew's College, Grahamstown. A third candidate was selected, but did not take up the scholarship. The Roman Catholic St George's was the only high school in Southern Rhodesia capable of producing graduates able to pass Responsions.[18] The settler elite of Rhodesia was tiny and the paucity of good schools meant that, at least until the 1920s, a high proportion of Rhodesian scholars were not educated there.

In Natal, alone among the founding constituencies in South Africa, a selection committee was set up in the first year.[19] The Superintendent General of Education wrote to Hawksley proposing a committee consisting of the Minister of Education, the Chief Justice, and the Governor General. It seems that a similar committee already selected Natal exhibition scholars for Oxford, Cambridge, and Edinburgh. Using the system of 'marks' outlined in Rhodes's will, the committee chose the Mauritian-born resident of Stanger, Louis de Charmoy, as the first Natal scholar.

George Parkin toured South Africa in 1903 and again in 1910.[20] His overriding interest was in the scholarships of North America, but his reports from South Africa yield a fascination with its political and educational situation. His first visit occurred in the immediate aftermath of the Anglo-Boer War. His second coincided with the end of the rocky and surprising process through which the four colonies had embarked on the creation of the settler-governed Union of South Africa. An educationalist himself, Parkin devoted much attention to the question of the lack of universities in South Africa and

[18] R. J. Challiss, *Vicarious Rhodesians: Problems Affecting the Selection of Rhodesian Rhodes Scholars, 1904–1923* (Salisbury: Central Africa Historical Association, 1977), 1.

[19] See the correspondence in RTF 1000.

[20] For the details which follow, see RTF 2009, Parkin to Michell, 7 Aug. 1903 (a report of his 1903 tour); Dr Parkin's Report on his visit to South Africa, Feb. to June 1910.

to the quality of the scholars who were being selected. Together with Wylie, he stressed that South Africans were poorly equipped for Oxford's taxing entry examinations in Greek and Latin. Parkin worried that the predominance of South Africans in the first cohorts of Rhodes scholars carried the danger of tarnishing the academic image of the incipient scholarship scheme amongst Oxford dons.

As Bill Williams put it many years later, Oxford spoke disdainfully of the 'vulgarity of Empire' that was embodied in the new scholarships from 1903.[21] The early South African and Rhodesian scholars no doubt helped to reinforce this telling prejudice. A central theme of Parkin's report on his visit to South Africa in 1910 revolves around the question of why the South African scholars were, with 'honourable exceptions', intellectually unimpressive at Oxford. South African boys matriculated too early and the 'speculative, adventurous, or highly practical atmosphere . . . does not greatly encourage intellectual ambition'. South African boys were pushed into employment too early, and they relied too heavily on black people who served them from childhood. Parkin went so far as to venture the view that 'the stimulating air of the high veldt and plateau country tends to nervous exhaustion, and boys brought up there may not be constitutionally fitted to endure as much prolonged mental effort than others'. He reported that the SACS and Stellenbosch scholars, who had been required to complete at least two years of study for the Cape University, had done better academically than the St Andrew's and Diocesan College scholars who went straight from school. The scholars from Natal 'have almost all been very nice fellows, gentlemanly, industrious and anxious to do their best. They were probably the best that could be selected from those who offered. But they were all poorly prepared, and several not of special ability.' Parkin put this more positively to an education official in Cape Town a few years later: 'We do not receive a finer lot of fellows from any country than from South Africa, and yet many of them spend unusually anxious years at the University, apparently because they have not had the preparation that other men have enjoyed.'[22]

The burden of Parkin's argument was to insist that South African scholars should complete three years of post-matriculation study before going to Oxford. But it was not only Oxford which found the South Africans unsuited; Michell reported to Parkin that returning Rhodes scholars felt that they were 'receiving an education which unfits them for any career likely to be open to them on their return to their country'.[23] Some of the early scholars, however, adapted and thrived in the strange and exacting world of Oxford. For example, T. B. Horwood, who had arrived at Oxford from Natal 'poorly educated', in Parkin's view, had, two years later, come fifth in the 'stiff test' of the Indian civil service examination.[24]

In a number of ways, Parkin and the Rhodes Trustees had a profound impact on tertiary education in South Africa during the first two decades of the twentieth century. The most dramatic instance of this was Starr Jameson's offer of £50,000 to a small group

---

[21] Sir Edgar Williams, 'The Rhodes Scholarships: The First Dozen Years', *AO* 81/1 (1994), 3.

[22] RTF 2509, Parkin to W. A. Russell, 10 Sept. 1913.

[23] RTF 2009, 12 Jan. 1909.

[24] RTF 2009, Parkin to Michell, 28 Sept. 1910.

of Grahamstown lobbyists who wanted to found a university college.[25] This story of opportunities seized, and overlaid with Jameson's new career as a politician of the eastern Cape, is delightfully told by Ronald Currey (St Andrew's College and Trinity 1912).[26] Jameson's rash offer, not previously discussed among the Trustees but subsequently ratified, meant that Rhodes's name was now attached to the fledgling university college, founded in 1904 around the nucleus of the 'college department' at St Andrew's. Currey's account does not place enough emphasis on Parkin's role in this development. Specially commissioned by Michell to visit Grahamstown in 1903, Parkin wrote glowingly of the prospects there for a university. Grahamstown was already a growing educational centre, he said, and the foundation of a teaching university 'under very strong British influence' would benefit both the Eastern Province and South Africa.[27] While High Commissioner in South Africa immediately after the Boer War, Lord Milner had campaigned for a university at Johannesburg on similar lines to Parkin's advocacy of Grahamstown; there was always the possibility of other outcomes in these moments of birth in the new South African nation.[28]

As early as 1891 Rhodes had proposed the formation of a teaching university on his estate at Groote Schuur. In the ferment of higher education planning which accompanied the creation of the Union of South Africa, this idea was kept alive. When the University of Cape Town was legislated into existence in 1916, absorbing the South African College, the estate of Alfred Beit, Rhodes's colleague and his Trustee until Beit died in 1906, put up £500,000 for the construction of the new university.[29]

In addition to these large monetary investments, Parkin played an active networking role during his tours of 1903 and 1910. Wherever he went, he was able to secure meetings at leading schools, with university college senates, and with prominent officials and politicians, including General Smuts. Everywhere his message was the same: South Africa needed a better organized and higher-level university system, in which Rhodes scholars should do at least two years of study before going to Oxford. That he was able to secure the attention and interest of such a wide range of educationists speaks of the influence of the Rhodes Trust and its scholarships in the founding moments of South Africa's fledgling university system.

During the first two decades of the administration of the scholarships in South Africa, the Trustees relied on Lewis Michell as their main 'man on the spot'. Michell was an active politician at the Cape, and his correspondence yields fascinating insights into the context and imperatives of the scholarships. Supported by Parkin, Michell was a crucial figure in lobbying for Trust grants for South African causes, especially for Diocesan College and St Andrew's as the two best examples of 'British schools' in the Cape. Michell

[25] The other major founding contributor, investing £25,000, was Alfred Beit.
[26] R. F. Currey, *Rhodes University, 1904–1970: A Chronicle* (Grahamstown: Rhodes University, 1970).
[27] RTF 2009, Parkin to Michell, 7 Aug. 1903.
[28] B. K. Murray, *Wits: The Early Years* (Johannesburg: University of the Witwatersrand Press, 1982), ch. 1.
[29] H. Phillips, *The University of Cape Town 1918–1948: The Formative Years* (Cape Town: UCT Press, 1993), chs. 1 and 7.

kept a particularly beady eye on developments at Stellenbosch.[30] One senses that right from the start he disagreed with Rhodes's allocation of a scholarship there. In Michell's view, Stellenbosch was a dangerous hotbed of Afrikaner nationalism and not a suitable venue for a Rhodes scholarship. He had a keen ear for the hostility towards Rhodes and empire that circulated at Stellenbosch. When G. J. Maritz (Stellenbosch Boys' High and Trinity 1909) was arrested in the Transvaal in 1915 for participating in the Afrikaner anti-war rebellion, this confirmed his worst fears.[31]

Two other interesting matters involved Michell during the Great War. The first was a selection dispute in Natal.[32] Durban, a fervent outpost of empire where German families were hounded and their businesses burnt down, was the scene of an emotional exchange within the local city elite. In 1914 the selectors chose a scholar who had not offered to 'go to the Front'. For the detractors, this showed scandalous disregard for the criteria of manhood and moral courage laid down in Rhodes's will. Among the vociferous critics of the selection were fathers whose sons had 'joined up' and so denied themselves the chance of applying for the Natal scholarship. Michell visited Durban and found no irregularities in the selection, even though his sentiments no doubt lay with the critics.

The second matter was the prospect of South Africa gaining some of the annulled German scholarships. Michell was lobbied by a number of schools, each seeking to have a scholarship attached to itself. The most insistent proponent, whom Michell supported, was the headmaster of the Grey Institute in Port Elizabeth, W. A. Way, but forceful proposals came also from Grey College in Bloemfontein and from Potchefstroom High School where the headmaster was an Oxford graduate and ex-teacher at St Andrew's in Grahamstown. Michell and Jameson were also pressed by leading citizens of Kimberley, headquarters of De Beers mining company, that the town should have one or more scholarships.

Adding the Provinces, Retaining Diverse Particularities, 1918–1940

It was a continuing indication of South Africa's special status in the eyes of the Trustees that three of the five German scholarships came to it after 1916. The allocation did not come in quite the way Michell and the school lobbyists might have preferred. By then Parkin had established the principle that scholarships should not be attached to specific institutions, but rather to districts and regions. One scholarship was created for the Orange Free State and another for the Transvaal. Michell nevertheless secured a partial victory in persuading the Trustees to award an annually alternating scholarship to Kimberley and Port Elizabeth. When the Trustees created an additional scholarship for the Cape Province in 1922 this meant that six scholarships were contained within its boundaries, a density of endowment found in no other constituency.

Faced with the prospect of creating four new selection committees after 1916, Parkin relied heavily on the network of educationalists he had met with in 1910. He also corre-

---

[30] See correspondence in RTF 1654.
[31] RTF 2509, Michell to Parkin, 31 May 1915.
[32] See correspondence in RTF 1000.

sponded with the mining magnate Percy Fitzpatrick, Patrick Duncan, Jan Hofmeyr (SACS and Balliol 1910), who had become principal of the School of Mines in Johannesburg, the Bishop of Kimberley, and C. J. Gardner (St Andrew's College and Trinity 1903), his main contact in Port Elizabeth.[33] Parkin planned to visit South Africa in 1919 to cement the new arrangements, and to host a national conference on university education, but he fell ill, and the baton was handed to Francis Wylie, who toured in 1920.[34] Drawing on what already happened in Natal, Wylie established a similar structure in the two new provincial committees. The provincial administrator would chair them. A senior judge, usually the judge president, was invited to become a member, as was the provincial director of education, whose staff would handle the administration. The remainder of the committee members consisted of prominent academics and business people, among them, for the first time, Rhodes scholars. When the Cape provincial committee was created in 1920, it followed a similar pattern. In the case of Rhodesia, Wylie's visit led to the creation of that constituency's first selection committee, based on the provincial committees in South Africa. In Kimberley and Port Elizabeth the Trustees had to rely on local notables in education, politics, and business to staff the selection committees.[35]

Right from the start, the scholarship for the Orange Free State echoed the Afrikaner–English tensions which had characterized the Stellenbosch Boys' High award. Peter Dixon, elected to the first scholarship in 1919, had been interned as a young child in the British concentration camps of the Angle-Boer War; his Afrikaans-speaking mother had prevailed on him not to fight on the British side in the First World War. The Bloemfontein selection committee unanimously chose him, but his 'disloyalty' tempted Rudyard Kipling to resign as a Trustee when his selection was confirmed. In 1920, James Lyle, the principal of Bloemfontein's Grey School, informed Parkin that the 'political atmosphere' of Oxford had a negative effect on applications for the Rhodes scholarship. Furthermore, he wrote, 'many of our young professors have German degrees and they rather run down the British degrees'.[36] By the early 1930s, every British university except Oxford had recognized Afrikaans as a 'European language' for student admission purposes. Oxford's continuing refusal to do so sent ripples of discontent through the bilingual universities and professional communities of Bloemfontein, Stellenbosch, and Cape Town.[37]

The creation of the three provincial scholarships and their selection committees raised the profile of the Rhodes scholarships in the political establishment. Jan Hofmeyr became administrator of the Transvaal in the 1920s and he did a great deal for adding substance to the selections there. Elsewhere, the administrators were more symbolic figures, but their continuing involvement throughout this period signalled the endorsement of the

---

[33] See correspondence in RTF 2009A, 2365.

[34] RTF 2009, Report to the Rhodes Trustees on his South African trip, by the Oxford Secretary, Oct. 1920.

[35] See correspondence in RTF 2362.

[36] RTF 2009, A. Lyle to Parkin, 12 Jan. 1920.

[37] Interestingly, the Rhodes Trustees had in 1920 given £20,000 to Oxford to establish a chair in Roman Dutch law, motivated by the desire to attract South Africans, especially Afrikaners.

scholarships by both English- and Afrikaans-speaking members of the political elite. Patrick Duncan, who had been a member with Philip Kerr of Milner's Kindergarten, and who later became an MP, cabinet minister, and then South Africa's Governor General, was a Transvaal selector in the 1920s as well as a financial and political adviser to the Rhodes Trust. Judge Paul Fischer, Afrikaner nationalist and father of Bram Fischer (Orange Free State and New College 1931), was a stalwart member of the Orange Free State committee during the 1930s. When Trust officials visited South Africa in 1927, 1931, and 1932, they were entertained in the highest political circles, with Jan Smuts taking a particular interest in the scholarships.

By 1922, a scholarship pattern had been established that was to last until 1972: three for Rhodesia, four for the Cape schools, and one each for the four provinces. Alongside similar initiatives of local consolidation in the United States, Canada, and Australia, the Trustees appointed P. T. Lewis (SACS and Balliol 1903) in 1921 to act as South African General Secretary. An advocate in Cape Town, Lewis was asked to initiate contact with selection committees around the country, to standardize selection memoranda, and to act as a conduit for South African correspondence with the Trust. His oversight was to extend to Rhodesia, which the Trustees clearly still regarded as within a South African ambit. Until Lewis's appointment, each selection committee operated independently of the others and interacted directly with the Trust Secretary and the Oxford Warden.

The expectations which the Trustees had of Lewis were largely disappointed during his long tenure which lasted until 1940.[38] While he made periodic attempts to involve himself in the affairs of the four selection committees in the Western Cape, he did not travel beyond Cape Town. Both his legs had been injured in the Great War, and he found travel difficult. His correspondence with the Trust was sporadic; and he did not attend the first international Rhodes scholar reunion at Oxford in 1929. It was only in 1935, after repeated requests from Philip Kerr, that Lewis began to procure and forward to London some of the selection committees' minutes.

The dominant image of scholarship administration in South Africa during the 1920s and 1930s is of local autonomy. A constituency with distinctive peculiarities continued to exhibit these despite the Trustees' attempts to ensure greater uniformity of practice. The Trustees often knew little of the internal workings of selection committees, and visits by Trust officials were infrequent during these two decades. While Philip Kerr showed an initial enthusiasm of interest in South Africa during the late 1920s, his preoccupations were elsewhere in the 1930s. The decision of the Trustees to convert the Port Elizabeth scholarship into an Eastern Province one in 1932 was one of their few decisive acts; the accompanying resolution to close down the scholarship for the declining diamond town of Kimberley dragged on to 1938. Philip Kerr was masterfully polite in concealing frustrations with South African correspondents. C. K. Allen was wont to be blunt in internal memoranda within the Trust. To take one example: the Trustees had decided by the early 1930s, largely influenced by the Americans, to move away from the practice of

---

[38] For details see RTF 2556, 2009B.

appointing senior politicians to chair selection committees. Lewis was asked to take steps to prise the provincial administrators off the South African committees. When he dragged his feet on this, Allen wrote: 'I am inclined to think that South Africans of all political parties are some of the most conservative people I know, and I am not sure whether their dislike of change is due to this natural conservatism, or to an equally temperamental inertia.'[39]

There were many manifestations of autonomous particularities. On his tour of 1920 Wylie carried the message that all South African scholars were required to have done a minimum of two years' study at university before admission to Oxford. The St Andrew's headmaster, P. W. H. Kettlewell, secured approval that the St Andrew's scholar should rather stay on for eighteen months in the school's special 'Oxford and Cambridge class' than go to a South African university. None of the four will schools had regular selection committees and different headmasters approached the practice of the schoolboy ballot variously. In 1939, for example, when Ronald Currey arrived from Michaelhouse as the new headmaster of St Andrew's, he minimized the schoolboy ballot in selection deliberations because it gave the impression that the scholarship was about 'awarding a prize, rather than electing a scholar'.[40] At both SACS and Stellenbosch Boys' High it became obligatory for the scholar-elect, chosen in his final year at school, to go on to the Universities of Cape Town and Stellenbosch, respectively. The SACS election was then confirmed by the University senate at the completion of the candidate's undergraduate degree. The Stellenbosch Boys' High selection was confirmed once the headmaster had received a satisfactory report on the candidate's conduct from the University of Stellenbosch. On a number of occasions during the 1930s, in the case of both provincial and school committees, the Trustees agreed to hold over an unallocated scholarship to the subsequent year. In 1933 they agreed to create a special scholarship for Gideon Roos whose father Paul had ruled him out of contention for the Stellenbosch scholarship. The son of the charismatic headmaster had a highly successful sojourn at Oxford.

It was only after Allen's visit in 1932—a Warden with a new broom—that the four schools were required to constitute regular selection committees. SACS and Stellenbosch Boys' High agreed to select their scholars as undergraduates, not matriculants, and to accept applications from students at any university. But idiosyncrasies continued. Paul Roos habitually submitted scholars' dossiers late and incomplete, but Allen found him a likeable rogue and made allowances.[41] St Andrew's had established a tradition of sending its scholars to Trinity and habitually bypassed the Warden in making the arrangements. In Natal, the Rhodes scholar members of the selection committees began the practice in the early 1920s of inviting the candidates to have tea with them, or to play a game of tennis. This activity was, in effect, the 'interview', for the Rhodes scholar selectors would then make a recommendation of selection to the full committee.

[39] RTF 2009, Lewis to Lothian, 9 Mar. 1934, Allen to Lothian, 3 Apr. 1934.
[40] RTF 2009B, Currey to Gie, 21 Oct. 1949.
[41] See RTF 1654.

It was not surprising, with this variety of practices, that selection results were sometimes disputed. The exacting mix of criteria for the scholarship also brought forth periodic newspaper articles which assessed, often with forked tongue, the impact of Rhodes scholars in South Africa. The most dramatic example of a selection dispute found its way into the Cape Town newspapers in November 1929. The dispute grew out of a fascinating correspondence between Philip Kerr and Professor F. Clark of the UCT Education Department during 1928–9 on the question of 'brains and character' in the selection of Rhodes scholars.[42] Kerr had been influenced by the reorganization of the American scholarship system and the attempts there to improve the chances of 'picking the winners'. He also knew that of the South African Rhodes scholars up to 1926, 14 per cent had failed honour schools, 37 per cent had third- or fourth-class passes, 39 per cent gained seconds, and 9 per cent firsts. Although the South Africa results had improved significantly in the 1920s, the record of the South Africans was far behind scholars from Australia, New Zealand, and Canada.[43] Kerr was interested in raising the quality of Rhodes scholars generally, but he was also concerned with crises of leadership in the societies of Europe where fascism and communism were taking root. Clarke, an academic from Britain, was interested in the benefits of combining elements of Britain's aristocratic traditions of leadership with invigorated, less class-ridden patterns of leadership generated in the 'new societies' of the dominions. Kerr agreed eloquently:

Most Rhodes Scholars dislike the social gradation at Oxford, and have great practical and executive ability. But they are too often slovenly in their thinking and intellectually uninterested and uninteresting. What we want is to combine the advantages of the British and the overseas ideas but to do this each side has both to learn and unlearn. We want the thoroughness and calm and poise which comes from real intellectual interests and standards (and freed from the pride and inertia and negation with which they too often degenerate) coupled with the zest for life, the interest in action, the personal and social equality which are natural to new countries mainly engaged in the conquest not of thought but of nature.[44]

Clarke's view was that there were signs of a 'quasi-patrician, planter culture' in the Western Cape which made some South Africans 'less crude and Philistine than Canadians and Australasians', but this tendency was overshadowed by the debilitating reliance of white South Africans on the 'ample black cushion' under them, encouraging 'the reign of mediocrity'. The only solution for raising the calibre of leadership in South Africa was to increase the competition by 'giving a free run to the coloured peoples'.[45] Another part of Clarke's remedy was to stimulate private schools such as Bishops. He urged the Trustees to support this school financially for it offered the optimal chance 'of planting the real English school in fruitful adjustment to African needs'.

[42] See RTF 2009.

[43] F. J. Wylie, 'History of the Operation of the Rhodes Scholarships in the Dominions', in L. A. Crosby, F. Aydelotte, and A. Valentine, *From Oxford of Today*, 2nd edn. (New York: Oxford University Press, 1927), 243–4.

[44] RTF 2009, Kerr to Clarke, 30 Aug. 1928.

[45] For the quotations in this paragraph, RTF 2009, Clarke to Kerr, 22 June 1928 and 26 Sept. 1928.

It was with a shrill tone, no doubt influenced by common room discussions at the University of Cape Town, that Professor Lancelot Hogben—like Clarke an expatriate—wrote letters of protest in the *Cape Times* and the *Cape Argus* at the end of November 1929.[46] He criticized the Cape and Bishops selection committees for choosing sporting-type scholars over intellectually outstanding candidates. The selection committees were not 'nurtured in a tradition of learning' and they gave too much weight to 'manly outdoor sports'. He offered a cryptic alternative definition of this criterion: 'Chess is a sport for kings. Kings are human beings. Therefore, chess is a manly sport. Chess can be played out of doors in South Africa for several months in the year. It is, therefore, a manly outdoor sport.'[47] In Hogben's view, the 1929 selections expressed a 'policy which can only make the mention of a South African Rhodes Scholar a signal for merriment in educated English society'.[48]

This spat certainly reflected a personal gripe, but it was one that generated a number of newspaper editorials and comment from a wide range of people across the country. Jan Hofmeyr expressed the private view that a number of the early Rhodes scholars were a 'joke' academically, but in public he stated that selections since the war had been competitive and that it was too early to assess the impact of Rhodes scholars in South Africa.[49] Others wrote that Rhodes did not want 'bookworm' scholars; it was preferable to choose an all-rounder with 'character', even if the academic results were not brilliant. The incident attracted a full gamut of opinion about leadership attributes and their manifestation in the Rhodes scholarships.

The *Cape Times* of 27 November 1929 carried a cartoon titled 'According to Professor Hogben'. The drawing consists of an oversize young white man dressed in rugby kit, with powerful arms resting on his hips. The circumference of his calf is being measured by an Oxford don. Seated at a table, three of his fellows ask: 'Is he up to our standard of scholarship?' The don with the measuring tape replies: 'Yes, in fact I think his calves are a couple of inches over.' Each of the dons has an oversize forehead, a sign of erudition.

This cartoon epitomizes public perceptions, in Cape Town at least, of the quintessential Rhodes scholar at that time (and, indeed, one that was to persist until the 1970s).[50] In a country where rugby assumed high religious and cultural proportions in the making of manhood within a white settler elite,[51] and where great emphasis was put on 'the outdoors', the 'sport' category in Rhodes's will carried considerable weight. This was reinforced by the ballot system in the schools scholarships, requiring boys to vote on the sporting achievements of their peers. The cartoon illustrates that the Rhodes scholarships were readily part of Cape Town's public domain. The cartoonist could make assumptions about the general knowledge which readers had about the scholarships and about Rhodes

---

[46] Clippings can be found in RTF 2009.
[47] *Cape Times*, 27 Nov. 1929.
[48] *Cape Times*, 26 Nov. 1929.
[49] RTF 2009, Hofmeyr to Clarke, 17 June 1928.
[50] Author's interview with Wieland Gevers, Cape Town, 4 Dec. 1998.
[51] R. Morrell, 'Forging a Ruling Race: Rugby and White Masculinity in Colonial Natal, c.1870–1910', in J. Nauright and T. J. L. Chandler, *Making Men: Rugby and Masculine Identity* (London: Cass, 1996).

scholars. In a city where Cecil Rhodes had left a highly visible legacy, not least three annual scholarships to Oxford, this was not surprising. Finally, the four dons in the cartoon invite comment. Their oversize, egg-shaped heads are attached to effete bodies. The cartoonist's caricature expresses an ambiguous view of Oxford from a physically robust frontier outpost in the southern hemisphere.

There were more politically determined dimensions to the leadership debates. Kerr put this succinctly to Kettlewell in 1929–30, amidst an interesting discussion about the desirable combinations of 'brains' and 'character' in Rhodes scholars.[52] Why, he asked, had Afrikaner leaders become so prominent in national politics and where were the English-speaking leaders? Kerr was aware of the rise of Afrikaner nationalism as a potent force during the 1920s: two imperatives pressed on the Rhodes scholarships. The Stellenbosch and Orange Free State scholarships were vital conduits for Afrikaners to be influenced by an Oxford education. Secondly, the Trustees should deepen their support for Diocesan College and St Andrew's as laboratories for English-speaking leaders of the furture.[53] He could say this knowing that the Trust had already made substantial contributions to selected initiatives in South African education.

Investing in South African Education: Trust Benefactions up to the Second World War

Between 1903 and the mid-1940s the Trust made grants to South African universities, schools, and training colleges totalling £217,200, and low-interest loans totalling £56,350. In a number of cases, loans were written off after a period and so they became grants. These amounts signalled a substantial investment in a sector that was considered vital, both politically and culturally, by the Trustees as they sought to sustain 'British' interests during the first half of the twentieth century. The major beneficiaries were Rhodes University College and the University of Cape Town, and a group of private, particularly Anglican, schools which the Trustees called 'British South African schools'. Heading the group were the two will schools, Diocesan College and St Andrew's. The Trust's financial support was essential to the survival and expansion of certain private schools. Once it became clear, after 1906, that the Beit estate was to invest heavily in Rhodesian education, South Africa became the main focus of the Trustees' financial support.

Rhodes University College was the single biggest beneficiary. By 1930, the Trust had laid out £108,000 towards the cost of professorships, buildings, and bursaries at Rhodes.[54] During the 1930s another £12,000 was granted. The University of Cape Town, built on the Groote Schuur estate, gained £10,000 for the building of Jameson Hall and £5,000 for its library. Transvaal University College was granted £3,000 in 1921. In the same year, the School of Mines (forerunner of the University of the Witwatersrand) was allocated £5,000 and in the 1930s that university also received a number of small grants for its

---

[52] See correspondence in RTF 1378.
[53] RTF 2009, Report by the Secretary on his visit to South Africa, 18 Feb. 1927.
[54] RTF 3106, Elton to W. G. Adams, 1 Dec. 1952.

School of Bantu Studies. The University College of Fort Hare—South Africa's only university for black students—was funded £7,000.

In the first few years of the Trust there were few school grants, despite the urgings of Michell and Milner. In 1907, at a time when St Andrew's College in Grahamstown was in serious financial trouble, Milner urged that it had 'done more than any other [school] in South Africa to keep up a healthy British tone, morally and politically'.[55] This view underpinned the grant-making to selected church schools during the next three decades, with particularly heavy spending in 1919–21 and 1925–6. The allocation of grants often reflected the special urgings or rejections of individual Trustees, the Trust Secretary, and the Oxford Secretary. Otto Beit was especially influential during 1919–20, and on his last tour of South Africa, in 1924–5, Milner returned to the Trustees with a 'modest little list' that totalled £36,350.[56] It was the biggest single cluster of school grants ever to be awarded by the Trustees. Milner was no doubt motivated by Hertzog's election victory in 1924; the schools he wanted to support offered an important cultural counter to this electoral trend. During the 1930s, the Trustees were involved with the Jagger bequests which injected another £80,000 into roughly the same schools that had been supported by the Rhodes Trust.

Leaving aside the Jagger bequests, St Andrew's in Grahamstown was the largest beneficiary of grants and loans from the Rhodes Trust. It was followed by Diocesan College. Benefactions of notable size also went to Michaelhouse, near Pietermaritzburg; the Diocesan School for Girls, Grahamstown; St John's College, Johannesburg; St Winifred's, George; St Andrew's, Bloemfontein; and Kingswood College, Grahamstown.

Philip Kerr persuaded the Trustees in the late 1920s that they should pay attention to 'native education', a field they had hitherto ignored, with the exception of a £1,000 grant to the incipient South African Native College at Fort Hare in 1923.[57] In 1926 the Trustees gave £250 cautiously to John Dube's Ohlange Institute near Durban, having rejected appeals in 1914 and 1922. The Ohlange appeal was backed by Lord Buxton who pointed out that Rhodes could not have made his fortune without the labour of Africans, and urged that some of this fortune should be invested in African education. Kerr was persuaded not so much by this point, but by the need to nurture a cadre of moderate, constitutional African leaders at a time of radicalized black politics in South Africa during the late 1920s. Here was another interesting strand in Kerr's preoccupations with questions of leadership. It is noteworthy that the possible links between African leaders and the Rhodes scholarship were never discussed: the gulf of race was too wide to bridge. An influential correspondent with Kerr was Bishop Carey of Bloemfontein, who secured a grant of £4,000 in 1930 for the Modderpoort Native Training College. Over the next five years, another £4,000 or so was granted to various 'native education' institutions, including Fort Hare, and the Lovedale and Clarkebury missions. In the late 1930s, Modderpoort was loaned a further £4,000, and smaller grants went to a handful of African

---

[55] RTF 1426.
[56] RTF 2009, Milner to Grigg, 20 Nov. 1924.
[57] Details for this paragraph are drawn from correspondence in RTF 1156, 2552, 2077, 2817, 2957, 3094, extract from Elton's Report to the Trustees, 26 Feb. 1952.

schools, mainly in Johannesburg and Bloemfontein. In 1951 Adams College near Durban was added to the list of beneficiaries; and by 1952 the Trust had granted a total of £18,050 towards various causes in African education.

Godfrey Elton toured Southern Africa in 1948, the year the Afrikaner nationalists won the general election. His report to the Trustees dwelt at some length on the 'independent Church schools', singling out six of them for special mention. Echoing earlier views of his predecessors, he praised these schools for their character-building, their 'humane rather than utilitarian learning', and he concluded that they were 'just about the most promising product of South African civilisation to date'. He outlined his plan for the Trustees to set aside £100,000 for the founding of a new independent school in South Africa to complement those already well established.[58] While this scheme did not come to fruition, the schools which the Trust had traditionally funded received a further round of grants and loans in the late 1940s and early 1950s. Furthermore, Rhodes University gained an injection of £20,000.

The educational benefactions which followed Elton's tour were to be the last sizeable ones until the early 1990s. During the 1950s the focus of the Trust's charitable spending largely moved away from apartheid South Africa. When South Africa became a republic in 1961 and withdrew from the Commonwealth, a clause in the 1946 Trust legislation made South African benefactions illegal, unless they were granted from Trust moneys still invested in the country. The half-century of significant funding of educational initiatives in South Africa had run its course.

To mention the 1950s and the 1960s is to move ahead of the main narrative of the Rhodes scholarships. We pick up that story with the onset of the Second World War, which was to bring important changes to scholarship administration.

The Gie Years, 1940–1967: Getting the House in Order

The Second World War ruptured the mid-twentieth century, and its impact affected the administration of the Rhodes scholarships in South Africa. Within months of the outbreak of war in Europe, P. T. Lewis was summoned to military headquarters in Pretoria. Thinking that his role there might be short-term, he arranged for Bram Gie to stand in for him as General Secretary. Lewis did not return to Cape Town, however. His distinguished military work took him to East Africa, Egypt, and then London. In 1945 he decided to stay in England, turning his hand to farming. The Trustees confirmed that Bram Gie, who had been acting General Secretary between 1940 and 1945, should be appointed to the post.

Who was Bram Gie? Belonging to a family of Huguenot descent, he studied law at the South African College, winning the SACS Rhodes scholarship in 1915. A soldier with the Cape Province Rifles and the South African Horse in German South-West Africa and in East Africa during the First World War, he went up to University College, Oxford, where he read law between 1919 and 1921. He entered legal practice in Cape Town in

---

[58] RTF 2662, extract from the Secretary's Report on his visit to South Africa, 27 Apr. 1948.

1922, working as an attorney for the next forty-five years. Gie was active in a number of charity organizations, and he also became director of a number of businesses. The voluminous correspondence in the Trust's archives yields little else of Gie's life and interests; his style was strictly businesslike. Every now and then there is a glimpse of his views. In 1943 he wrote to Allen: 'I myself find it difficult to become greatly interested in politics in South Africa. There is so much bitterness of feeling and I have members of my own family and clients and friends on both sides.' He was writing of the bitter tensions which the war had brought between Afrikaner nationalists and those, both English and Afrikaner, who supported the Allied war effort.[59]

Gie was to prove to be a very different kind of General Secretary from Lewis; he was far more active and interventionist. Gie took to heart Elton's critique of the academic mediocrity of the South African scholars, and the dishevelled nature of scholarship administration. During the 1920s and 1930s the academic results of South African scholars had picked up, but they were still way behind those of the other dominions.[60] The 1930s had seen a fair share of unawarded scholarships in each of the provincial committees, and a few cases of resigned scholarships. Gie gained publicity in Cape Town's newspapers during 1945 for his view that the academic and leadership criteria should gain more weight in South African selections, as against sport and character.[61] Gie developed as a prolific writer of letters and memoranda. Gie badgered selection committees for their minutes, pushed for a turnover of selectors (finding that some had sat for periods of ten or even twenty years), and scrutinized the selection memoranda of each committee. Gie wrote periodically to the newspapers about the activities of Rhodes scholars, and he launched a brief annual newsletter for Rhodes scholars. He built up a scholars' mailing list, and began to compile selection statistics. He was no longer responsible for the Rhodesian committee which was officially separated from the South African ambit in 1946. While Lewis had corresponded mostly by hand (and none of his files survive in South Africa), Gie used a secretary in his law firm, Eve Bourke-Wright, to type for him, to keep carbon copies, and to file correspondence.[62] In short, Gie and his secretarial assistant put the South African scholarship administration on a sound, nationally organized footing for the first time. He did so with considerable energy, earning Elton's praise.

Gie revered Frank Aydelotte, his American counterpart whose books on the Rhodes scholarships he read avidly. Establishing a Rhodes scholars' association became one of Gie's main ambitions during the 1950s. This intention was reinforced by Elton during his tour of South Africa in 1948, the first visit by the Trust Secretary since Kerr's in 1926–7. The desirability of strong Rhodes scholar associations around the world was high on

[59] RTF 2009B, Gie to Allen, 24 June 1943.
[60] F. Aydelotte, *The American Rhodes Scholarships: A Review of the First Forty Years* (Princeton: Princeton University Press, 1946), 132.
[61] For example, 'Choice of Rhodes Scholars: Academic Ability Essential', *Cape Times*, 7 Dec. 1945; 'Selection of Rhodes Scholars', *Cape Times*, 21 Sept. 1946, in which he stressed that 'neither spineless laureates nor unintelligent he-men were required'.
[62] Eve Bourke-Wright worked unpaid by the Trust. She retired with Gie in 1967, with a farewell gift from the Trust of £100.

Elton's agenda, and was emphasized again when the new Oxford Warden, Bill Williams, toured Southern Africa in 1952. Gie had been a member of the small group which had tried, but failed, to start a Rhodes scholars' association in Cape Town in the 1920s. Gie had some success three decades later, instituting an annual dinner amongst Cape Town Rhodes scholars and, with the assistance of David Bean (SACS and Corpus Christi 1924) and Colin Hatherley (Transvaal and Brasenose 1950), creating a founding constitution for a national Association. The core membership was in Johannesburg and more particularly in the Anglo American Corporation.[63] A flamboyant character, Bean had proposed that South African Rhodes scholars charter an aeroplane to fly to the 1953 reunion. Between 1953 and 1956 the Association seems to have sustained a number of dinners and circulated a newsletter among Rhodes scholars, but this initiative soon spluttered. Annual dinners, often with other Cambridge and Oxford graduates, were held intermittently through the 1950s and 1960s, but the Association was not revived in any formal sense. In Cape Town, Gie involved Rhodes scholars in two local commemorative projects: an annual service at the Rhodes memorial on the slopes of Table Mountain, and a campaign to have Rhodes's cottage at Muizenberg established as a local museum.

Gie's most challenging tasks of a political nature were to remove provincial administrators from the chairs of selection committees, and to install Rhodes scholars as honorary secretaries in place of the provincial secretary of education. Lothian had argued for the removal of the ex officio administrators in the early 1930s, but by the end of that decade only the Transvaal committee had implemented this, with J. H. Hofmeyr—no longer administrator, but a cabinet minister—taking over the chair. At Elton's prompting Gie took action in 1946–7, securing relatively smooth transitions in the Orange Free State and the Cape. In the Free State, the new chairperson, Dr A. J. van Rhyn, was a Nationalist MP, former editor of *Die Volksblad*, and a personal friend of Gie. In the Cape, the administrator was replaced in the chair by Judge J. E. de Villiers (SACS and University 1914). In Natal the provincial administrator, Denis Shepstone, resisted what he saw as an attempt to 'oust' him; he was clearly attached to the scholarship. Finally, in 1948, Shepstone agreed to go and he was succeeded by Judge F. N. Broome (Natal and Oriel 1909), who had been a selector intermittently since 1920. After 1948 it was the Nationalist Party government which appointed provincial administrators; Gie's actions had been timely, for these appointees were on balance likely to be indifferent towards, or hostile to, the Rhodes scholarships. There were, indeed, signs of this in the cases of the secretaries of education, whose staff handled the administration of provincial selection committees.

Excising the provincial secretaries of education (called directors in some cases) from the committees was to be a more protracted task than removing the provincial administrators, partly because of the administrative service they provided. Once again, Gie had mixed success in implementing the proposal that Rhodes scholars should take over as honorary secretaries. In the late 1940s Gie established a collection of regional Rhodes scholar secretaries whose initial task was not to administer the selections but to organize

---

[63] See details in RTSA 15.

regional associations of scholars and to provide news to the General Secretary for the annual newsletter. In the Orange Free State there was a smooth changeover from provincial secretary to Rhodes scholar secretary, with David Marquard (Orange Free State and New College 1925) taking up the reins in 1949. In the Cape, Michael Smuts (Diocesan College and Magdalen 1935) became the first Rhodes scholar secretary in 1955. In the Transvaal the selection committee gained a Rhodes scholar secretary, O. G. Backeberg (Transvaal and Queens 1919), only in 1959, as did Natal where Colin Gardner (Natal and Wadham 1956) became secretary after a flurry of correspondence in opposition to the Trustees' wishes. In Natal, the Rhodes scholar members of the selection committee had, since the 1920s, interviewed candidates individually, and there had been no committee interview. In the 1950s the Natal selectors finally gave way to Elton's insistence that there should be a committee interview as well.

It was one thing to change the way selection committees organized their membership and administration, another to subject the existence of certain scholarships to special scrutiny.[64] In the period up the Second World War, the only South African scholarship which had been abolished was the Kimberley one. Trust officials had criticized the quality of South African Rhodes scholars, but they had not proposed any fundamental changes in scholarship allocation. In the four decades before the war, the schools scholarships had been accepted as ones privileged in the will, and the two 'British South African' private schools gained the active support of Parkin, Lothian, and a majority of Trustees. But in the late 1940s and early 1950s there were unprecedented discussions in the Trust's correspondence about the future of four of the South African scholarships.

The four scholarships were those for the Eastern Cape, the Orange Free State, SACS, and Paul Roos (Stellenbosch Boys' High School was renamed in 1946, in honour of its illustrious prewar headmaster). The reasons for scrutiny were many. Elton was concerned, after 1948, about the financial security of the Trust's account in South Africa which paid for the South African scholarships. He also wondered about the strong Afrikaner nationalist influences which he saw during his 1948 tour in the Orange Free State and Paul Roos committees. The move towards apartheid was at odds with the changing international order after the Second World War. Gie criticized the SACS and Paul Roos committees for failing to attract good candidates. His special concern was for his alma mater which was run by an ageing headmaster and which was being overtaken by dramatic changes in Cape Town's social landscape. The suburbanization of the city accelerated during the 1940s, and the dispersal of middle-class families from the city bowl had profound consequences for this once-proud school in the city centre. By contrast, Diocesan College impressed Gie, both in the way it organized its selection committee and through its string of prominent post-war Rhodes scholars. Similarly St Andrew's, with Ronald Currey at the helm, was for Gie on a sound footing, although he found that Currey had done away with committee interviews and had to persuade him to

---

[64] Details for the following four paragraphs are drawn from correspondence in RTF 1005; 2009B especially Allen to Elton, 5 Feb. 1951, and Allen to Gardner, 9 Feb. 1951; 2009 especially Allen to Elton, 30 Jan. 1951; 1654 especially Allen to Gie, 20 Dec. 1946; RTSA 1 General Report, South African Rhodes scholarships, 30 Dec. 1950.

bring them back. Things had turned full circle since Parkin's assessment of 1910, which had commended SACS and Stellenbosch Boys' High but criticized Diocesan College and St Andrew's.

At Elton's urging the Trustees decided to abolish the biennial Eastern Province scholarship, and Elton took legal opinion on the status of the schools scholarships. The lawyer's reply was that the school scholarships were inviolate, for they were explicitly listed in the will. Allen blamed Hawksley for creating a will which tied the Trust's hands, 'apparently in perpetuity', to the specified schools. But Allen did not extend his criticism of the rigidities of the will to advocate that the scholarships for SACS and Paul Roos should be 'suppressed'. He urged Gie to persuade the schools that they were not 'separate little kingdoms' but 'part of a large system'. Allen persuaded Elton that the overall record of the Paul Roos scholars justified that scholarship. He made the same point even more forcefully for the Orange Free State, stressing that scholars from there had fulfilled ably the requirements of 'intelligent muscularity' laid down in the will. From his many conversations with Afrikaans-speaking scholars at Oxford, Allen had gained a keen sense of the importance of these two scholarships in strategically significant centres of Afrikanerdom. Gie, too, while critical of the organization of the two schools scholarships, urged against talk of abolition. At Paul Roos, abolition would be heavily exploited by Afrikaner nationalists; at SACS, there was hope that the new headmaster, appointed in 1950, and the proposed move to a new site at Newlands would regenerate the school. Gie mounted a strong defence of the Eastern Province scholarship, joined in vehement protest by the chair of the Eastern Province committee, Judge C. J. Gardner, who had been involved in selections there since 1919.

During 1951 the Trustees reversed their decision to abolish the Eastern Province scholarship. Similar intentions for the Orange Free State were quietly dropped. Gie's reports on Paul Roos signalled evolving satisfaction, punctuated by breakdown in 1954. He disagreed with the Paul Roos choice of scholar that year, prompting him to fulminate to Elton that 'the granting of a scholarship to this school was an unfortunate mistake in Mr Rhodes' Will'. But by 1956 Gie reported that the Paul Roos committee was working in a businesslike manner. SACS continued to limp into the new decade, failing to elect a scholar in 1950 and 1951, and the weak run, with a few exceptions, continued into the late 1950s.

With the regularization of selection procedures at the schools by the mid-1950s, and with the installation of Rhodes scholar secretaries in all the provincial committees by the end of that decade, Gie's main contributions to scholarship administration had borne their fruit. He turned 65 in 1960 and his work during the following decade was one of less energetic consolidation, of keeping the ship on course. There was by then less of a preoccupation in Trust correspondence with the academic mediocrity of South African scholars, although there continued to be periodic exceptions. Indeed, in 1963, Bill Williams was able to write to Gie: 'I think the South African results are excellent.'[65] From as early as 1959 Gie initiated the idea that he retire, and this set the tone of his last eight

[65] RTSA 1, Williams to Gie, 30 Aug. 1963.

years in office. In 1964, Gie's proposed retirement was put off with the appointment of William Pietersen (Eastern Province and University 1961) as his assistant general secretary. Pietersen, however, does not seem to have brought new energy to Gie's work. The tone of administrative consolidation was accompanied by a political conservatism which characterized Gie's approach from the mid-1950s.

In brief, Gie's preoccupation was with how not to alienate conservative white South Africans, Afrikaners especially, from the scholarships. It was a preoccupation shaped by the increasingly isolationist laager white South Africans built for themselves during the fast-changing rearrangement of international relations and world politics during the 1950s and 1960s. From within the laager the Western world 'out there' was a source of growing criticism of apartheid, a place of threat and challenge. Oxford, too, was 'out there'. Although Gie defined himself as a critic of apartheid, he proved sensitive to the perceived alienation of white South Africans.[66] When David Bean wrote to the *American Oxonian* in 1953 lambasting the ruling Afrikaner nationalists for their apartheid policies, he received a sharp rebuke from Gie.[67] When Elton's new Commonwealth scholarships were introduced in 1957, Gie criticized them, urging that their multiracial emphasis would cause negative publicity for the scholarships in South Africa.

In his preoccupation with conservative white South African viewpoints, Gie did not once mention in his correspondence the absence of black scholars. It is striking how little discussion of this matter there is in the Trust's archive generally for the first sixty-five years. Way back in 1908 certain directors of the British South African Company had mooted the award of a Rhodes scholarship to Nguboyena Lobengula, son of the Ndebele chief, but this proposal came to nothing.[68] Between that date and the late 1940s there appears to be no discussion of the question of black African scholars. It was Elton who first raised the matter cursorily in 1949, wondering whether the new South African Citizenship Act would legally bar 'Natives and coloured persons' from eligibility for the Rhodes scholarship: 'In a sense, of course, this is an academic point, since at present, whether the regulations permit this or not, it is inconceivable that a Native should be elected to a Rhodes Scholarship by a selection committee in South Africa.'[69] In 1953, Jim Bailey, proprietor of the famous *Drum* magazine, wrote from South Africa to Lionel Curtis proposing that the Trustees should 'open the scholarships to all races in South Africa' and 'make a gesture by appointing a non-white scholar when a chap of the suitable class was available'.[70] This letter was forwarded to the Trust, but was simply filed, it seems. There remained broad agreement, more or less tacit, that prospectors for Rhodes scholars in South Africa should mine only in 'white' soil. That prospective candidates could only be found among white men was another unquestioned tenet. The fundamental assumptions underlying this approach were to be subject to intense scrutiny

---

[66] RTSA 1, General Report, South African Rhodes scholarships, 30 Dec. 1950, and General Report on election of Rhodes scholars, 1966.
[67] See details in RTSA 15.
[68] Challiss, *Vicarious Rhodesians*, 22.
[69] RTF 2009, extract from Report for Trustees, no. 390, 18 Oct. 1949.
[70] RTF 2009B, copy of Bailey to Curtis, 17 Apr. 1953.

during the 1970s and 1980s. These changes were to be the defining feature of the tenure of Gie's successor as General Secretary, Rex Welsh.

New Shafts, Tremors, and Heat at the Rockface: The Welsh Years, 1967–1987

When Bill Williams visited South Africa in late 1966 one of his primary tasks was to find a successor to Bram Gie. From the vantage point of Rhodes House, South Africa's position in the world order had worsened substantially. From being at the heart of the Empire under Smuts (a member of Britain's war cabinet) South Africa had become an apartheid deviant. It was no longer a member of the British Commonwealth and it was regularly subjected to strident critique in post-war bodies such as the United Nations Organization. And yet, because of the historical link through Cecil Rhodes and Oxford's long-standing relationship with South Africa, this constituency demanded careful attention from the Trust's Secretary.

The timing of Williams's visit to South Africa was influenced by the invitation he had received to attend the wedding in Cape Town of Tony Ardington (Eastern Province and Corpus Christi 1963) and Libby Robb, whose father owned the Table Mountain cable car company. The wedding festivities included a ride to the top of one of the world's most famous landmarks, an event perhaps unique amongst South African Rhodes scholars.

A couple of possible names for the position of South African General Secretary had been discussed prior to Williams's trip. The one which had received most attention was that of Clive van Ryneveld in Cape Town. Clive and his brother Tony were both Bishops Rhodes scholars in the 1940s, and had been stalwart members of Rhodes selection committees in the Western Cape for a number of years. Tony had recently become secretary of the Cape Province committee. Just before Williams left Oxford for South Africa, Clive van Ryneveld wrote saying that the workload of his law practice precluded him, reluctantly, from taking on the job of General Secretary. Another possibility was someone who was rising in the ranks of the Anglo-American Corporation, but Williams felt that, with considerations of 'public image' in mind, 'the Rhodes Scholarships should be kept quite distinct from the Oppenheimer empire as a concept, especially as so many Rhodes Scholars are serving in Anglo-American in one way or another'.[71]

Williams came to South Africa 'looking for a man who is an old Rhodes Scholar held in great respect in the world around him, with a clear head, an unwillingness to fuss, a liberal approach to racial problems, and a willingness to apply his mind to the question of the South African Rhodes Scholarships'.[72] He chose Rex Welsh, a prominent Johannesburg advocate. Williams's approach to Welsh came right at the end of his South African tour, and it was conducted in dramatic fashion. Before his departure for London

---

[71] RTF 2556, Williams to Gie, 8 Feb. 1967.
[72] RTF 2556, Williams to Welsh, 5 Jan. 1967, and Welsh to Williams, 6 Jan. 1967. By 'old' he did not mean so in a physical sense, but someone who had won a scholarship. For other details in this paragraph see RTSA 1 (1986–9): Welsh to Fletcher, 27 Aug. 1986.

by ship from Cape Town, Williams visited Johannesburg. He attended a dinner of Rhodes scholars; the guest list read like a 'who's who' of Johannesburg's big business and professional world. Perhaps it was at this event that Welsh's name was mentioned. Tommy Stratten (Kimberley and Balliol 1924), who was chairman of Union Corporation, one of Welsh's legal clients, arranged for Williams to meet Welsh over lunch at the Rand Club. The meal over, Williams asked Welsh to do the job. Their conversation continued in the car as they travelled to the airport for Williams's plane to Cape Town. Williams completed the dialogue in the form of a letter posted from the Mount Nelson Hotel in Cape Town, apologizing for the unorthodox manner of his invitation to Welsh to take up the job. Welsh's one-line reply was crisp: 'Thank you for your long letter of the 5th. Yes: I am persuaded.'

It had been a brief, rushed first encounter. So began a close and deepening friendship over the next fifteen years of working together in trying times. Williams and Welsh were forthright, passionate, acerbic, humorous, and hard-working correspondents, each with a sharp eye for human detail. At the end of 1969, Welsh wrote: 'I have so much enjoyed corresponding with you this year. It doesn't often happen that one happens to get on to quite such a satisfactory wave-length. I have a certain amount of gossip stored up for my next letter, but nothing of importance.'[73] And three years later Welsh wrote: 'I've just received my copy of the new *Fowler*, I prowl about it at random and become more and more convinced that I am not only illiterate but, what is worse, *vulgar*. The practice of my profession brings about a fatal prolixity and preponderosity and preposterosity in the use of the English tongue.'[74] Welsh experienced a difficult divorce in 1970–1, and discovered through it that Williams, too, had been divorced; this became another bond between the two men. When Williams returned home from a bout in hospital in the late 1970s, Welsh was the first person he wrote to as he resumed his Rhodes correspondence.

Who was Rex Welsh? He had a keen sense of his ancestry. His grandfather was a Scottish missionary in the Eastern Cape from the 1880s. His father grew up speaking Xhosa and his mother, too, was raised in the Eastern Cape in a family with a Dutch father and a mother whose ancestors were 1820 settlers. Welsh's father became Attorney General for the Transvaal and Rex attended Pretoria Boys' High School, where he matriculated brilliantly at the age of 14.[75] Welsh studied classics at the University of Pretoria in the 1930s, followed by a law degree at the University of the Witwatersrand. He was selected for the Transvaal Rhodes scholarship in 1941, but went up to Oriel only in 1945, having fought in the Middle East and Italy in South Africa's 6th Armoured Division. During the war, he married Anne Feetham, daughter of Judge Richard Feetham who had come to South Africa at the turn of the century as one of Milner's Kindergarten. In 1947, Welsh gained a first in the BCL and won the Prestigious Vinerian scholarship which, in an exceptional arrangement that year, was awarded to two people: Welsh and Zelman Cowen, later to

[73] RTF 2556, Welsh to Williams, 31 Dec. 1969.
[74] RTF 2556, Welsh to Williams, 24 May 1972. Emphasis in original.
[75] Interestingly, Welsh's future assistant general secretary, Edwin Cameron, and his successor as General Secretary, Laurie Ackermann, also attended the same school.

become Governor General of Australia. In 1966, when Williams first met him, Welsh was a Queen's Counsel, chair of the Johannesburg Bar Council, and Chancellor of the Anglican Diocese of Johannesburg. He had been part of the legal defence team in the famous Treason Trial of Congress leaders during the late 1950s, but made his name more as a commercial lawyer. Many years later a close colleague wrote that Welsh was widely regarded as 'the leading South African lawyer since World War Two', and that in a different political dispensation he would 'have been a very distinguished Chief Justice'.[76]

Of great significance for the future of the South African scholarships was Welsh's location in Johannesburg. His two predecessors as General Secretary, P. T. Lewis and Bram Gie, had lived in Cape Town. In a way still common for born-and-bred Capetonians, they had a Cape-centred view of the world from the vantage point of Africa's distinctive southern tip. One of Welsh's first moves as the new General Secretary was to highlight the anomaly of just a single scholarship for the Transvaal, South Africa's economic and demographic heartland. Reflecting his own regionalism, Welsh tended to see Cape Town and Durban as rather distant outposts of the 'city of gold'. During 1967 and 1968 either he or his new assistant secretary, Colin Kinghorn, attended all nine selection proceedings to familiarize themselves with a geographically and culturally diverse constituency. Welsh was keenly conscious that the lion's share—six of South Africa's nine Rhodes scholarships—were located in the Cape province, and he was the first General Secretary to question this as the natural order of things. The preponderance of the Cape scholarships took little cognizance of the substantial economic shifts in South Africa's political geography since the early twentieth century. Unlike Lewis and Gie, both SACS scholars, Welsh had no personal links with the schools scholarships and this, too, influenced his views.

Like Gie at the start of his term, Welsh wanted to enliven and regularize selection committees which had grown 'wooden'. At least until the early 1960s, Gie had been very good at standardizing selection committees' memoranda, ensuring that committees submitted reports on their meetings, and issuing periodic reminders that selectors be rotated every five years. But even the indefatigable Gie had found it difficult to sustain his vigour into the last five or six years of his secretaryship. A list of the selection committees of 1967 indicates that many selectors had been members since the early to mid-1950s. In the case of Paul Roos, there were two whose terms went back to the early 1940s. At Williams's request, Welsh tackled the thorny issue of trying to suggest that the headmasters of the four schools should not chair their selection committees, so as to 'open them up'. He got an early taste of rebuff as the schools defended established practice, prompting Welsh to muse about 'closed corporations'. In another move Welsh was more successful: he worked behind the scenes to prevent a 'Broederbonder of the deepest dye' from becoming chair of the Transvaal selection committee.

Welsh made two proposals during the course of 1967–8: replace the Eastern Cape scholarship with a South Africa-at-large one, and create a second scholarship

---

[76] 'Rex Welsh, giant of the South African Bar', *Star*, 19 Apr. 1994. An obituary written anonymously by a 'close colleague', probably Judge Michael Corbett.

for the Transvaal. The idea was to allocate the South Africa-at-large Scholarship to the strongest runner-up of all the provincial selection committees. The Trustees were persuaded that this would not easily be workable; and they resisted creating a tenth South African scholarship. The outcome was a compromise: the biennial Eastern Cape scholarship would be transferred as an annual one to the Transvaal. Welsh had taken one step in shifting the centre of gravity northwards. A second aspect of the compromise was that two of the Eastern Cape selectors, Ronald Currey and Judge Gie Kotze (who, in Welsh's view, was 'a member of that small but valiant band of "liberal" Afrikaners'), were drafted onto the Cape Province committee in Cape Town.[77] In this way, Welsh went some way to mollifying those who resented the removal of the Eastern Cape scholarship.

During his first two years of office, Welsh mooted another idea about the organization of the scholarships, proposing that candidates from the University of Botswana, Lesotho, and Swaziland should become eligible for the South African scholarships. Welsh was possibly influenced by a letter he had received in mid-1969 from Pax Theron (St Andrew's and Trinity 1921) saying that it was 'long overdue' that the Rhodes scholarships should be given to applicants from the universities of Fort Hare, Turfloop, Zululand, Lesotho, Botswana, Swaziland, Malawi, Zambia, and to 'South African Coloureds'. In Theron's view, black people were 'striving to take their place in the world of nations'. At the time that he wrote to Welsh, Theron was manager of the main labour recruiting organization for South Africa's mines. His work reached deep into Southern and central Africa, and would have exposed him to the successes of nationalism in securing decolonization there.

Very soon after his appointment, Welsh proposed to the Trustees that he should have an assistant general secretary, formally appointed. Welsh intended 'beefing up' the central office, gaining the capacity to be more interventive and proactive in the running of the scholarships. He told Williams that he had just the right person: a young advocate in Johannesburg, Colin Kinghorn (Transvaal and Lincoln 1953). From 1967 until his sudden death from cancer in February 1980, Kinghorn played a vital role during the troubled 1970s. Welsh and many other were devastated by his early death. In replacement, Welsh chose yet another lawyer, Edwin Cameron (South Africa-at-large and Keble 1976), who, like Welsh, won a Vinerian, and was to make a substantial impact on South Africa's legal profession during the 1980s and 1990s. Both Kinghorn and Cameron, through their ideas and their networks of influence, were to be central actors in the political repositioning of the Rhodes scholarships during Welsh's tenure as General Secretary. Furthermore, they maintained the strong grip of lawyers on the South African administration, a tradition reaching back to P. T. Lewis's assumption of the general secretaryship in 1923.

The First Storm: The Schools and South Africa-at-Large Scholarships, 1970–1973

The internationalist dimensions of Rhodes's original vision turned on the founding core of the scheme, namely Rhodesia and the four schools in the Cape. The main impulses

---

[77] RTSA 1, Welsh to Williams, 7 Nov. 1969.

for a radical critique of the Southern African scholarships emanated from a small group of American Rhodes scholars. These impulses found wide support amongst dons and Rhodes scholars resident in Oxford; and it was this reality which pushed the Rhodes Trustees into action and many South Africans into reaction.

By allocating thirty-two of the original fifty-seven scholarships annually to the United States, Rhodes ensured that American scholars would weigh heavily in his scheme; and twentieth-century international developments multiplied this weight exponentially. By the late 1960s, the world was a very different place from that at the turn of the century. The Second World War and its aftermath had altered profoundly the international order; and the United States had risen to a position of pre-eminence that few would have imagined just thirty years earlier. Britain's international influence and stature had shrunk with the rise of the Cold War superpowers and with decolonization in Asia and Africa. Oxford, the university of empire, was grinding through gears of change. It was at this juncture that the Southern African Rhodes scholarships controversy broke, and American Rhodes scholars were in the vanguard.

Before examining this controversy, we need to take note of the transformations in the domestic economies and societies of western Europe and North America which accompanied this changing international order. The unparalleled prosperity of these societies in the 1950s and 1960s was, in Eric Hobsbawm's view, revolutionary, ensuring radical changes in patterns of work, family, culture, and politics.[78] Any remaining vestiges of nineteenth-century America and Europe were swept away or fundamentally altered by this social revolution. Only with this idea in mind can we understand how it was that Oxford's array of 'closed' places and scholarships for Britain's famous public schools was progressively whittled away; and how, from the mid-1970s, women gained access to the hallowed halls of all-male colleges.

In entrenching apartheid, in violently suppressing the anti-apartheid resistance movements, the Afrikaner nationalist government of South African moved against the changing times, not with them. South Africa's position had worsened substantially in the dominant family of Western nations. From being one of the favoured dominions at the heart of the British Empire, earning pride of place with Australia and Canada (the only three embassies on Trafalgar Square), South Africa's embrace of apartheid from the 1940s onwards ensured a narrowing isolation. While many Western companies continued to do business with South Africa, anti-apartheid politicians in the West succeeded in building up public hostility to wards apartheid. In the case of Britain, the South African Springbok rugby tour there in 1969 was heavily disrupted by crowd protests.

If anti-apartheid demonstrators invaded the rugby fields of England, the Oxford campaigners against the South African Rhodes scholarships petitioned, lobbied, and gained press publicity. The organizers of the campaign—a word they themselves used—made their first move in December 1970 and January 1971 by circulating a petition amongst Rhodes scholars in residence. The petition spoke of the 'stark evil' of racial discrimination in the South African and Rhodesian scholarships, and urged that this made the

---

[78] E. Hobsbawm, *Age of Extremes: The Short Twentieth Century, 1914–1991* (London: Abacus, 1994), chs. 9–11.

scholarships 'unworkable under the precepts of the Will left by Cecil Rhodes'. Unless this situation changed immediately, and a 'fair and not token' number of black Rhodes scholars were elected in these two countries, the scholarship schemes there should be discontinued.[79] Of the 145 scholars in residence, 85 signed, including a handful of South Africans. The campaigners had their petition debated in student forums; and they secured 120 signatures of support from Oxford dons, including the Master of Balliol and the President of Corpus Christi.

It was no coincidence that two of the leading campaign organizers were African-American Rhodes scholars, Wentworth Miller and George Keys, influenced no doubt by the US civil rights movement. They were joined by Louis Grech from Malta and, later, by a third American, Grant Crandall, who had worked with the peace corps in Lesotho before going to Oxford. If there were broad political reasons inspiring the campaign leaders, there was also a personal dimension: Keys had become friendly with a black South African law student, Simon Mrwetyana, who was at Balliol on a JCR scholarship. When Keys asked Mrwetyana if he had applied for a Rhodes scholarship, Mrwetyana simply laughed. The tone of that laugh galvanized Keys to act.[80]

How did South African Rhodes scholars in residence at Oxford respond to the campaign? Many spoke to Williams personally; he seems to have made a special effort to keep the lines of communication open. A few of South Africans signed the petition, believing they were making a public protest about racial discrimination in South Africa. It was a common experience for young white South Africans during the apartheid period to become more sensitized about their country's plight while studying or travelling abroad. It was hard, nevertheless, to arrive in Oxford knowing that one had played a role in fighting apartheid through student politics and then to come under attack as a white South African.[81] Perhaps alone among scholars in residence, Herman Perold (Paul Roos and University 1968) publicly defended apartheid and 'the Afrikaner way of life'.[82]

Charles Simkins (Transvaal and Balliol 1970) and John Kane Berman (Transvaal and Pembroke 1969) wrote a detailed and thoughtful letter to Welsh, exploring the reasons why there had been no black Rhodes scholars from South Africa.[83] These reasons ranged from racial discrimination and educational disadvantage in South African society, to common perceptions amongst South African students that only white people ever won Rhodes scholarships. Perhaps their most telling point was the observation that anti-apartheid political activism by white student leaders was a common attribute of successful Rhodes scholars. This activism was broadly supported by the administrations of the white, liberal, English-medium universities such as Cape Town, Natal, the Witwatersrand, and Rhodes. For black student leaders attending the new 'tribal' universities,

---

[79] RTF 3576, copy of petition.
[80] RTSA 1 (1983), Fletcher to Welsh, 27 Sept. 1983, enclosing transcripts of the 1983 reunion 'general conference'.
[81] Personal communication, Andrew Burnett, 15 Sept. 1999.
[82] *Sunday Times News Magazine*, 25 July 1971.
[83] RTSA 1, J. Kane-Berman and C. Simkins to Welsh, 21 Jan. 1971.

political activism commonly resulted in expulsion and harassment by conservative university administrators. The consequences of disrupted academic studies, and the inability to secure favourable referees in support of scholarship applications, added immensely to the other obstacles facing potential black applicants for Rhodes scholarships. In the view of Gavin Williams (Cape Province and Trinity 1964), it was possible to find black Rhodes scholars from South Africa, but they would have to be carefully chosen and schooled for Oxford's tough academic environment.[84]

The Warden at Rhodes House was the focal point of the storm. He was the recipient of the petitions, the public face of the Trustees, the target of South African correspondents, and the confidant of Rhodes scholars in residence. He felt the tensions keenly. In July 1971 he wrote to Welsh: 'I expect your mail bag is pretty lousy. I find I dread the South African stamp except on your envelopes.'[85] He had, of necessity, to adjust the emphasis of his views for different audiences, and it is difficult to pin down precisely how he felt. The fullest expression of his views, in the heat of the moment, can be found in the long memorandum that he drafted for the Trustees' meeting in March 1971. He wrote about his disquiet at the 'built-in white privilege' in the South African scholarships, and of the distinctive history of the schools scholarships:

We always knew about the anomaly in the general theme, of the four Schools' Scholarships. We just popped it behind the overall arras. The whole thing started with two Scholarships from Bishop's in Cecil Rhodes's lifetime—and they got built, like all the rest of the phrasing about 'schooldays' into the Will. What began as two Scholarships for white schoolboys from a Cape Town Anglican Public School on Cecil Rhodes's doorstep, has grown into a worldwide graduate programme: and the 'sore thumbs' remain imbedded, and until now ignored in the general eclat.

Further in the same document, Williams outlines his view that

the whole Rhodes Scholarship idea . . . is one of permeation, of quiet, unexplosive, patient yeast; a dated, perhaps an arrogant gospel but it has provided its deep satisfactions. Good bets are chosen, (by good Committees), come to Oxford and return home to make their several societies nicer. *Festina lente*. Good South Africans, good Rhodesians, have done this in their day and way. But Americans, as is their nature, have been speedier. And they have been winning—and the South Africans, the Rhodesians losing, this aspect of the 'world's fight' which Mr Rhodes in using the phrase did not himself envisage.[86]

The Trustees invited Welsh and the American General Secretary, W. J. Barber, to their March 1971 meeting, where the South African scholarships issue was the main item of business. Under pressure from the Oxford petitioners to take concrete steps, the Trustees decided to institute legal actions to 'broaden the basis of eligibility of the Scholarships in South Africa' and to restructure the schools scholarships. The minutes record that they

---

[84] RTF 3576, G. Williams to E. T. Williams, 8 Mar. 1972, enclosing copy of his letter to the editor, *The Times*, 8 Mar. 1972. By this time, Williams was based at Sussex University, and had for a number of years been active in administering bursary schemes for black South Africans studying in Britain.

[85] RTSA 1, Williams to Welsh, 12 July 1971.

[86] All quotes from RTSA 1, 'The South African and Rhodesian Scholarships', [Feb.?] 1971.

did so 'reluctantly'.[87] They intended to convert the schools scholarships into South Africa-at-large ones; and, as a first step, Welsh agreed that the recently allocated second Transvaal scholarship should become an at-large one. The main reason given for the decision to abolish the schools scholarships was that they contravened clause 24 of the will which stipulated that 'no student shall be qualified or disqualified for election to a Scholarship on account of his race or religious opinion'. No black children attended to four schools; the only eligible scholarship applicants were therefore white men. The Trust's lawyers would set out to show that this racial restriction made the operation of the scholarships 'unworkable'.[88]

Welsh was open to these changes, both because he had been interested in reorganizing the South African scholarships and because he occupied a self-consciously 'liberal' position on the spectrum of white politics in South Africa. In June 1970 he had written to Williams: 'I wonder whether you can conceive how *lonely* the situation in this country is for me and people who think likewise. We are, most of us, leftish Tories or rightish Radicals; but in the local context we are, on the most charitable view, eccentric and heterodox and, on the official plane, "communistic".'[89] Interestingly, Welsh defined his position in relation to the government and its underpinning Afrikaner nationalism, rather than to black political organizations and ideas, at a time when the rise of 'black consciousness' posed new critiques of white liberals.

Understandably, the schools rallied to protect their scholarships. They formed a joint committee, with Tony Mallett of Bishops as secretary and Clive van Ryneveld (Diocesan College and University 1947) in the chair.[90] Bram Gie added his support. Stunned by the speed of the Trustees' decision, the schools' representatives protested that they had not been consulted. They hoped to persuade the Trustees to reconsider the matter, urging a meeting. They would oppose the Trust in court, if need be, and 'fight as far and as hard as we have to'.

The Trustees agreed to meet a schools' representative in June 1972. The schools sent Sir Richard Luyt (Diocesan College and Trinity 1936) to put their case and, once again, Rex Welsh attended. Luyt was a distinguished Rhodes scholar, having been a senior colonial administrator in East and central Africa, and then Governor General of Guyana before becoming Vice-Chancellor of the University of Cape Town. He was a member of the Bishops and Cape Province Rhodes selection committees. On the South African political spectrum Luyt was a liberal, but in his presentation to the Trustees he was obliged to defend the status of the four schools. He presented three main points of argument.[91] (1) Rhodes had not been known as a liberal politician; if he had wanted to choose racially mixed schools for his will scholarships he could have, but did not. (2) The word 'race' in clause 24 referred not to black and white but to English and Dutch at a time of rising tensions within South Africa's colonial

[87] RTM 25 Mar. 1971.
[88] RTF 3576 (1), Coward Chance to Williams, 10 Feb. 1971.
[89] RTSA 1, Welsh to Williams, 28 June 1970. Emphasis in original.
[90] For example, RTF 3576, Mallett to Williams, 21 Apr. 1972.
[91] RTF 3576, R. Luyt's speaking brief for meeting with Rhodes Trustees, 3 June 1972.

politics.[92] (3) The inclusion of the four schools by name in the will made them inviolate and not subject to the changing seasons of contemporary politics.

Rather than abolish the treasured school scholarships, Luyt urged, the Trustees should allocate five new scholarships to South Africa's new black universities and so ensure black Rhodes scholars. Luyt's address to the Trustees was punctuated by a phone call from Cape Town, reporting violent clashes between the police and anti-apartheid student demonstrations. These demonstrations were, in part, against the government policy of racially segregated universities. South African universities, too, were experiencing their own forms of turmoil.

Luyt's appeals for 'realism' in reforming the Rhodes scholarships system in South Africa did not persuade the Trustees to change their mind. One of the Trustees commented at a dinner party that evening that he had found Luyt's presentation 'interesting, but irrelevant'. Pressure for change was building on the Trustees. In the month before the June meeting with Luyt, Rhodes scholar campaigners in Oxford had circulated a 'fact sheet' and a revised programme of demands and proposals relating to the South African scholarships. Amidst practical suggestions for reform, the campaigners pressed the point that these scholarships were 'unworkable' under clause 24; they should be abolished and transferred to African countries neighbouring South Africa.[93] In April 1972, the Australian General Secretary reported that students in Melbourne had discussed boycotting the Rhodes scholarships because of their association with South Africa. In that month, too, Grant Crandall resigned his scholarship in protest against the Rhodes Trust's refusal to abolish the South African scholarships and to admit women as scholars.[94] Welsh, clearly in a different political place from Luyt, continued to side with Williams and the Trustees.

Defenders of the schools scholarships tried various tacks to ward off their impending excision. In a moment of exasperation, but indicating just how deeply race-based thinking permeated South African lives, one prominent Rhodes scholar wrote from Cape Town asking Williams for statistics of how many people of colour had been selected as Rhodes scholars from the United States, Canada, Australia, and New Zealand. Another South African Rhodes scholar, who had long been a selector, wrote that in his experience no appropriate black candidate had ever made it through to the final interviews, but this did not mean that there were racial restrictions.

Perhaps the fullest and most publicized defence of the schools scholarships was the second Rhodes Memorial Lecture, delivered by Ronald Currey (St Andrew's and Trinity 1912) at Rhodes University in September 1972.[95] Currey had the right pedigree to speak:

[92] In response to this point, Welsh agreed that it could have applied in a South Africa on the brink of the Anglo-Boer War, but how should the word 'race' be interpreted in other constituencies around the world? See RTSA 1, Welsh to Williams, 20 July 1972.

[93] RTF 3576, 'The Rhodes Campaign—December 1970 to May 1972', document signed by Wentworth Miller and 7 others.

[94] RTF 3576, G. Crandall to Rhodes Trustees, 28 Apr. 1972.

[95] See a copy of 'The Rhodes Heritage: 70 Years After', in RTF 3576. The first Lecture had been given by Harry Oppenheimer in 1970, at which he said that one of the aims of the Lecture was to 'bring Rhodes Scholars together to pay tribute to their benefactor'. See H. Oppenheimer, *The First Cecil Rhodes Commemoration Lecture*, delivered at Rhodes University, Grahamstown, 12 Aug. 1970 (Johannesburg: Frier & Munro, n.d.).

his grandmother had befriended the young Cecil Rhodes in Kimberley, and his father had been Rhodes's personal secretary from 1884 to 1892. Having been headmaster of St Andrew's College during the 1940s and 1950s, he was currently writing a history of Rhodes University. Currey's advancing years did not dull the passion of his views about the 'threats' he envisaged. The Rhodes scholarships emanated from South Africa and should not be cut off from their source; Rhodes had given special place to the schools in his will; the Rhodes Trust had invested heavily in the schools during the course of the century and should not now abandon them. Currey went on to argue that three of the schools were important centres of English-speaking liberalism in a South Africa dominated by apartheid and Afrikaner nationalism. The fourth school, Paul Roos at Stellenbosch, was located in the territory of *verligte* Afrikanerdom, a ray of hope in an otherwise gloomy sky. The Paul Roos selection committee added weight to this view: they minuted their protest that the Trustees were undermining Rhodes's specific intention to send Afrikaners to Oxford in order to broaden their horizons.[96]

Currey wrote often to both Welsh and Williams during 1971–2. He urged that one of the Trustees should be a South African (he contrasted the absence of any South Africans with the strong South African links of the original Trustees). Currey told Williams that many Rhodes scholars in South Africa had been 'wounded in the house of friends'.[97] In ways similar to other correspondents, he appealed to Oxford's sense of history, tradition, and obligation, as against the brash righteousness of Americans. In the following year, 1973, Lord Blake, historian of Rhodesia and by now a Rhodes Trustee, was invited to give the Rhodes Memorial Lecture. He was hosted by Rhodes scholars in the Eastern Cape, and met with St Andrew's selectors. In the meantime, in Britain, the proceedings against the schools had run into a dead end, the details of which are explained elsewhere in this volume.

Welsh had concentrated his efforts on setting up the South Africa-at-large initiative. As agreed at the Trustee's meeting of March 1971, he was to create a new, multiracial committee for a single South Africa-at-large scholarship to be awarded at the end of that year. Welsh's intention, spelt out in correspondence with Williams but not yet talked about in South Africa, was to convert the abolished schools scholarships and the provincial scholarships into South Africa-at-large ones. He envisaged that Natal would lose its will scholarship in the process of creating nine at-large awards. Williams persuaded him that Natal, which had a racially open constituency in principle (unlike the schools), should retain its scholarship. As well as awarding its own scholarship, Natal should join the other three provincial committees—Cape, Orange Free State, and Transvaal—in shortlisting candidates for the at-large selections.

Welsh's first task was to create a South Africa-at-large committee for the single new award at the end of 1971.[98] He had to draw on various white people for advice about who might be approached to become South Africa's first black selectors. He wrote to Leo Marquard in Cape Town, a Rhodes scholar who had been a prominent member of the

---

[96] RTF 3576 (1), Minutes, special meeting of the Paul Roos selection committee, 12 June 1971.
[97] RTF 3576, Currey to Williams, 21 May 1971.
[98] Unless specified, the details which follow about this committee are drawn from RTSA 9.

Liberal Party in the 1960s. Williams put Welsh in contact with Robert Birley, who stated that 'the best Africans in South Africa are mostly either in prison or at least under a banning order'. With this proviso, Birley provided a helpful list of contacts inside South Africa. The Vice-Chancellor of the University of Lesotho, Botswana, and Swaziland, added his suggestions. Kinghorn's contacts at the South African Institute of Race Relations provided further names.

Keen to have two black selectors on the committee, Welsh invited Alpheus Zulu, Anglican Bishop of Zululand, and Professor S. M. Guma, the pro-Vice-chancellor at the University of Botswana, Lesotho, and Swaziland. Both were flattered but declined on grounds of work pressure. Zulu, who knew Welsh from Anglican church circles, replied: 'It is good to believe there is a great future for South Africa. Only a few years ago none of us could have imagined this thinking possible. I rejoice that you have such a part to play. Good wishes.'[99]

The black selectors who agreed to join the committee were T. W. Kambule, headmaster of Orlando High School in Soweto, and W. M. Kgware, the professor of education at the University of the North. Both were highly conscious of the historic significance of their joining the committee as the first black selectors. Kambule wrote to Welsh in ways which signalled common perceptions amongst black people of the Rhodes scholarships: 'Earlier, I saw an advertisement for Rhodes Scholars in our dailies, and I never thought for once that things may turn in this direction. Let's hope that this will materialize. . . . so that our people may also avail themselves of this opportunity.'[100]

Welsh selected Gie Kotze, who was a Supreme Court judge in Grahamstown, to be chair and 'kingpin of the new dispensation'. The rest of the committee was made up of Issy Maisels, an influential Johannesburg advocate, and four Rhodes scholars: Jack de Wet, former fellow of Balliol and now dean of science at the University of Cape Town; Anthony Evans, a Free State farmer and recently returned from Oxford; Colin Kinghorn; and Sid Newman, managing director of Lonrho, South Africa. This committee's composition represented careful intersections of interest, race, and region, with Natal the only area left out. (In 1972, Dr Herby Govinden of Durban was brought onto the committee, closing this regional gap and adding an Indian person to the racial mix.) The committee met at one of just a few public venues where a government permit was not required for an interracial business meeting: the newly constructed Holiday Inn hotel at Jan Smuts airport.[101]

The Oxford petitioners wanted quick results—black Rhodes scholars—from these reforms, but Welsh recognized that his initiatives would take time to root in South Africa's rigid and conservative society. Besides, there were limits in the extent to which he was prepared to go in effecting social engineering. He wrote to Williams just before the first

---

[99] RTSA 9, A. Zulu to R. S. Welsh, 18 June 1971.

[100] RTSA 9, T. W. Kambule to Welsh, 14 July 1971.

[101] From 1973, Welsh moved the at-large selection meetings to the Carlton Hotel, Johannesburg's smartest, and the race laws required him to submit an annual application to the Secretary of Justice to entertain black selectors there. The permits were issued, allowing black and white people to dine together, but not to dance together. These 'odious' permits—Welsh's words—provided a point of uneasy jocularity within the selection committee.

South Africa-at-large selection, when he knew that only two black people, both Indian students, had applied for the new scholarship and both were too old and therefore ineligible:

The first Scholar for South Africa-at-Large will be white. . . . This situation is no doubt regrettable, but I think it would be completely wrong to describe it, in the words of one of the petitions which were presented to the Trustees earlier this year, as 'an intolerable example of the most extreme form of racial prejudice'. In my view this situation simply reflects the difficulties which 'non-white' people in this country have in obtaining the basic educational qualifications which are required (and which in my opinion must continue to be required) of candidates for the Scholarships. We simply have to face the fact that miracles cannot be wrought overnight in the racial situation which prevails in this country.[102]

The important point, form Welsh's perspective, was that possibilities were being created through his reforms for the net of potential Rhodes applicants to be cast wider than before, both racially and geographically.

Welsh's next step was to broaden the South Africa-at-large initiative. In March 1972 he met with Williams and Bill Barber in Oxford, and drew ideas from the American system in which state selection committees forwarded shortlisted applicants to district committees. Welsh put his case persuasively to a meeting of provincial secretaries in April—the first time ever that Rhodes officials from around the country had gathered in this way—and they agreed that the provincial committees should no longer award a scholarships but should shortlist finalists for a South Africa-at-large committee to award four scholarships. Natal was to retain its will scholarship, while the other three provincial scholarships were to come under Welsh's administrative hand, with Colin Kinghorn acting as secretary to the South Africa-at-large committee. That Welsh managed to effect this agreement was nothing short of remarkable, given the long history of prized provincial autonomy in the administration of the scholarships. The second important decision which flowed from this meeting was that shortlisted candidates for the provincial and the at-large interviews should have their travel expenses paid, so as to remove the obstacle of expense facing applicants.[103]

In addition to securing provincial participation in this way, Welsh blurred the lines of 'South Africa' by establishing a new umbrella selection committee for the neighbouring countries of Botswana, Lesotho, Swaziland, and South-West Africa. This committee was to shortlist for the South Africa-at-large selections. Welsh invited Professor Guma to chair the 'neighbouring' committee, and he asked John Kane Berman, recently returned from Oxford to a job with the South African Institute of Race Relations, to act as secretary. Ironically, this committee was not as multiracial as the new South Africa-at-large one, but the intention was clearly to increase the number of potential black finalists for the Rhodes scholarships.

What were the fruits of these significant and far-reaching initiatives taken by Welsh? They secured a new political legitimacy for the South African scholarships that went some

---

[102] RTSA 1, Welsh to Williams, 22 Oct. 1971.
[103] RTSA 1, Welsh to Williams, 22 Apr. 1972.

way to meet the criticism of the Oxford detractors. Welsh's original intention was to recreate nine at-large scholarships, absorbing the schools. By December 1973 the Trustees decided that they had exhausted all possible options for converting the schools scholarships. South Africa was to have a two-system operation: the schools and South Africa-at-large. During the course of 1971–3, each of the provincial committees recruited one or two black selectors. Welsh had created the possibilities for Rhodes scholars to come from a wider net, but it was to be a while yet before the first black scholar was elected.

The Rhodes Trust Scholarship Scheme

In April 1973, Colin Kinghorn lunched with the Rhodes Trustees at Balliol. Here germinated the idea of the Trust re-establishing its contributions to black education causes in South Africa. During mid-1973 Kinghorn investigated how a Rhodes Trust grant might be implemented. He and Welsh proposed that the Trust should set up scholarships for promising black students in the last two years of schooling and in their undergraduate studies. The central idea of the scholarships was to increase the number of eligible black candidates for Rhodes scholarships in the years ahead. Some of the scholarships could be attached to good black or multiracial schools such as St Barnabas College in Johannesburg, Maru a Pula in Botswana, or Waterford in Swaziland. Welsh and Kinghorn did not have the administrative capacity to run the scholarship scheme; they would rely on the well-established bursary office of the South African Institute of Race Relations. The Institute received hundreds of bursary requests annually from black applicants; it would provide a shortlist to a multiracial Rhodes Trust scholarships committee that Kinghorn would establish.[104]

At the end of 1973 the Trustees allocated the first funds to the scheme. They decided that the scholarships should primarily be for university study at any South African institution as well as the University of Botswana, Lesotho, and Swaziland. The Institute calculated that 500 rand would cover a year's fees; the Trustees specified scholarships ranging from 200 rand to 500 rand. They allocated 8,500 rand for 1974, 17,000 rand for 1975, and 25,000 rand in 1976.[105] The funds would come from the Rhodes Trust South Africa account inside the country, and so would not contravene the clause which restricted the Public Purpose Funds to charitable causes within the Commonwealth.

Measured against the Trust's spending on other benefactions, the amounts allocated to the Rhodes Trust scholarships were small. For the ten to fifteen annual scholarship recipients, though, these awards opened doors to university education. The lion's share of awards went to students at the University of Natal's Medical School (where Barry Adams (Natal and St John's 1939) was a professor) and to the University of Durban-Westville. In 1979, twenty-one of the twenty-five Rhodes Trust scholars were medical students.

---

[104] RTSA 1, Kinghorn to Williams, 9 May 1973; Welsh to Williams, 29 Oct. 1973.
[105] RTSA 10, Kinghorn to J. Kane Berman, 8 Feb. 1974.

This cornering of the scheme by medics prompted a major rethink during 1978–9.[106] Kinghorn and the Principal of St Barnabas, Michael Corke, argued that the scholarships should be concentrated at school level. One of the guiding ideas in the founding of the scholarships had been to nurture potential black Rhodes scholars. It was best that this nurturing began at school. On completion of their medical studies, most graduates were too old to apply for a Rhodes scholarship. Indeed, during the 1970s only two Rhodes Trust scholars had gone on to apply for a Rhodes scholarship. Furthermore, medical students tied up Trust scholarship funds for six years at time.

Due to the acute crises of state schooling for black children, Kinghorn and Corke argued, the Rhodes Trust scholarships should be tenable at private schools.[107] During 1979, the Trustees agreed to this change of focus, and to the proposal that St Barnabas should be used for piloting the new idea. After Kinghorn's sudden death in February 1980 it fell to Edwin Cameron to oversee and expand the new policy. From small beginnings the scheme grew to a sizeable operation by the late 1980s. Initially, the Trustees allocated 30,000 rand; by 1986 this had increased to 58,000 rand, and by 1988 totalled 139,000 rand.[108] The bulk of the funding went to St Barnabas College, but by 1986 the list of schools included PACE and Immacula Convent in Soweto and Promat College in Mamelodi and Thembisa. To this was added St Mark's in rural Lebowa, Trinity High School in Port Elizabeth, and Sacred Heart in Johannesburg. In the early 1980s, five or six scholarships were granted; by 1988, forty awards were made.

So far as I am aware, no Rhodes Trust scholar of the 1980s went on to apply for a Rhodes scholarship. In this sense the scheme did not bear one of its intended fruits. But for the schools and pupils who benefited, the scholarships made an important contribution to new developments in multiracial education and to alternative township schools during the crisisridden 1980s. For the Rhodes scholars involved—Edwin Cameron, Graham Craig (South Africa-at-large and Brasenose 1974), and David Pitman (South Africa-at-large and Merton 1976)—here was an opportunity for worthwhile social investment. Indeed, in 1983, Cameron, Pitman, and Steve Tollman (South Africa-at-large and Balliol 1980) created the South African Rhodes scholars scholarship (SARSS). This second scheme, financed by contributions from Rhodes scholars, ran parallel to that of the Rhodes Trust scholarships, albeit on a smaller and less formalized scale.

To talk of these two scholarship schemes of the 1980s is to jump ahead in the main narrative. We need to return to two highly significant events of 1976.

Two Milestones: The First Woman, the First Black Rhodes Scholar

The year 1976 saw two firsts in the history of the South African scholarships: the selection of Sheila Niven as the first woman scholar and Ramachandran Govender as the first black scholar. It was a significant moment, offering the first glimpses of new shafts to

---

[106] RTSA RT scholarships, Memoranda on Rhodes Trust scholarships, 29 May 1978 and 19 Nov. 1978.
[107] RTSA RT scholarships, Memorandum for R. S. Welsh by M. Corke, 1 Apr. 1980.
[108] RTSA RT scholarships, Minutes of meeting of the selection committee, 23 Feb. 1986; Report to the Trustees for 1989.

mine in South African society. The path-breaking selections were broadcast on national radio and television (the latter had just started in South Africa that year), and attracted wide newspaper coverage.

Both scholars hailed from Pietermaritzburg, an unlikely coincidence. Niven was an excellent all-rounder from a white middle-class family, well connected to the university world. Govender's social situation was quite different; he came from a working-class family living in an Indian township. He had enrolled at the University of Durban-Westville for a degree in maths and physics, and had caught the eye of Herby Govinden, a professor of chemistry who sat on the South Africa-at-large committee and on the Rhodes Trust scholarship committee. Govinden encouraged Govender to apply first for a Rhodes Trust scholarship and then for the Rhodes scholarship after he had obtained a string of distinctions in his courses.

Govender's selection represented three 'first': the first Trust scholar, the first black South African, and the first person to be selected from one of the country's historically black universities. Attending the segregated 'Indian' university of Durban-Westville, he came from a campus where conditions were far from conducive for the development of the multiple attributes of a Rhodes scholar. Durban-Westville had been established in the late 1960s as one of apartheid's ethnic universities for black South Africans. Its entrance was guarded by a sentry post, visitors' details were recorded, sports facilities were poor, and there were running tensions between a frustrated student body and a politically conservative university administration. The spaces for creative student leadership were slim.

The predominance of the 'race question' in the South African controversy of the early 1970s made Govender's selection especially noteworthy. But this should not distract us from the significance of Niven's selection. South Africa's social structure, both black and white, was firmly patriarchal. The redefinition of women's roles in society had not developed the momentum that was gathering in the post-war West.[109]

During 1975, Welsh invited Thelma Henderson to become the first woman selector. Active in university life and local politics in Johannesburg, she had recently moved to Grahamstown where her husband Derek (Eastern Province and Lincoln 1949) had been appointed Vice-Chancellor of Rhodes University. So began a long, energetic participation in the administration of the Rhodes scholarships by members of the Henderson family.[110]

Govender's application forced into the open the stark tension—perhaps more dramatically highlighted in the South African constituency than among others—between 'potential' and open competition. If all candidates hail from a broadly similar socio-economic background, the relationship between potential and achievement is often easier to assess. If there are strong discrepancies, this task is far harder. The paucity of black finalists for the Rhodes scholarship in its long history to the mid-1970s meant that this

---

[109] It was only in 1975, for instance, that women were allowed to compete in the Comrades Marathon.
[110] Over the next twenty years Thelma, Derek, and their daughter Margie (South Africa-at-large and Lincoln 1981) clocked up between them thirty-five years of service on the Transvaal, Eastern Cape and Orange Free State, St Andrew's, and South Africa-at-large selection committees.

tendentious question brooded over the selection process, without forcing direct engagement by selectors. From the mid-1970s onwards this issue began to move squarely into
the committee room where, to the present day, it continues to exercise the minds, emo-
tions, and judgements of selectors living in one of the world's most unequal societies,
where race and inequality have been linked so potently.

In the decade before Govender's selection, a handful of black applicants had been
shortlisted but none had crossed the threshold to a Rhodes scholarship. The Natal committee shortlisted an Indian medical student in 1967 and an African medical student in
1970. In 1971, an African candidate was shortlisted alongside a white one for the Orange
Free State committee. Welsh attended the meeting and heard David Marquard (Orange
Free State and New College 1925) say: 'I have always been regarded as a *kaffirboetie*
[negrophile] and I would dearly have liked to be the chairman of the first South African
committee to elect an African to a Rhodes Scholarship.' In the event, and a brave move
it was, considering the international pressure on the South African committees, the OFS
committee decided that neither of the two final candidates was of the academic standing required by Oxford: they made no election that year after what Welsh perceived as
a 'lengthy, intelligent and sympathetic discussion'. Welsh believed the decision was a
correct one and that 'no element of racial discrimination entered the proceedings'.[111] In
the same year, the Cape selection committee shortlisted a coloured person. He was a
musician and 'a most attractive candidate', in Welsh's view. But, against the demanding
criteria of Rhodes's will, Welsh continued, he was not the best of the candidates interviewed. After the selection proceedings, the Cape committee—among whom was Richard
Luyt—worked hard to ensure that this unsuccessful applicant got to Oxford by means
other than a Rhodes scholarship.[112]

In 1972, the selection committee for Botswana, Lesotho, Swaziland, and South-West
Africa sent through Ernest Twala to the new South Africa-at-large committee. Twala was
clearly a colourful character, a political refugee from Swaziland who learnt Portuguese
and went to Mozambique to study medicine. The at-large committee deliberated long
and hard about Twala's academic chances at Oxford; and it eventually decided that he
would battle to succeed. Richard Rive, later a prominent black author, attended the at-
large meeting as an invited observer. He was currently studying at Oxford, and was soon
to return to Magdalen for his doctorate. The minutes of that meeting recorded that Rive
agreed with the decision not to select Twala, adding that 'the first black Rhodes Scholar
from South Africa would have to be an exceptional person who would be able to withstand the pressures imposed upon him at Oxford'.[113] Twala subsequently made his way
to study in Canada and the United States, benefiting at least in part from the financial
support and connections of Rhodes scholarship officials in South Africa.

In 1976, the selection committee was persuaded that they had found the right kind
of 'exceptional' person in Govender. The following year Loyiso Nongxa made a similar
impression. Nongxa had been encouraged to apply by Thelma Henderson, who had met

---

[111] RTSA 1, Welsh to Williams, 18 Nov. 1971.
[112] RTSA 1, Welsh to Williams, 7 Dec. 1971 and 3 Jan. 1972.
[113] For the details in this paragraph see RTSA 1, Welsh to Williams, 30 Oct. 1972, and RTSA 10.

this bright mathematics student during a visit to Fort Hare University in Alice.[114] Nongxa's election as a South Africa-at-large scholar in 1977 marked another important moment: the first black African Rhodes scholar, and the first from Fort Hare, the university attended by a prominent array of Southern African black political figures during the twentieth century.

During 1978 and 1979 Colin Kinghorn and Thelma Henderson spearheaded a number of attempts to publicize the scholarships at South African universities. During the early 1980s the secretary and chair of the Natal committee, Tommy Bedford and Libby Ardington, held meetings on all four university campuses in the province, and organized 'schools meetings' in Durban and Pietermaritzburg for black teachers and potential candidates.[115] In the Cape, the secretary Peter Sauerman and Wieland Gevers had written to each head of department at the University of the Western Cape asking them to encourage potential applicants.

Despite these efforts at publicity by selection committee members, working voluntarily, there was not a significant increase in the numbers of quality black applicants. In the Cape Province, for example, the committee received only ten applications from black people between 1972 and 1984. Between 1978 and 1983, just two more black scholars were selected, Anthony Staak (South Africa-at-large and Balliol 1979) and Sean Naidoo (South Africa-at-large and Brasenose 1981). Six women scholars, all of them white candidates, were selected nationally during the six-year period from 1977 to 1982, out of a possible total of thirty scholarships (Natal and South Africa-at-Large). Both in race and sex terms, then, the scholarship winners remained heavily skewed in favour of white men, and this pattern is reinforced if one adds the four schools scholarships to the annual total.

The selection committee for Botswana, Lesotho, Swaziland, and Namibia failed to deliver a supply of black applicants to the South Africa-at-Large committee. The neighbouring committee attracted few candidates in some years and none at all in others, despite drafting prominent figures such as Desmond Tutu, Bishop of Lesotho at the time, onto the committee during the mid-1970s. Professor Guma, the first chair, wrote in 1973 about the Rhodes scholarships presenting 'icy winds of competition' in circumstances where other overseas scholarships were considered easier to obtain by black applicants from Botswana, Lesotho, Swaziland, and Namibia.[116] In 1982, Welsh decided that there was insufficient justification for a separate 'neighbouring territories' committee; and the various countries were attached to the provincial committees: Namibia to the Cape, Botswana to the Transvaal, Lesotho to the Orange Free State, Swaziland to Natal.[117] This signalled the ending of Welsh's bold experiment of direct Southern African involvement in the Republic's scholarship scheme.

---

[114] Author's interview with Loyiso Nongxa, Cape Town, 3 Dec. 1998.
[115] Details for the rest of this paragraph are drawn from RTSA 1 (1984–5), Memorandum on the meeting of representatives of the South African selection committees held on 28 Apr. 1984, Johannesburg.
[116] RTSA 10, S. M. Guma to J. Kane Berman, 22 Oct. 1973.
[117] RTSA 10, Welsh to Members of the Selection Committee, 15 Mar. 1982.

The Second Storm: Decade of Thunder, Spotlight on Apartheid, and the Scholarships of the 1980s

It is clear in retrospect that the 1976 uprisings, which began in Soweto and erupted elsewhere in the country, marked a seismic turning point in South Africa's political history. This was so in the drama of the marching crowds of young black South Africans, the police shootings, and in the social forces which those events expressed. The 'grand apartheid' of the 1960s—associated pre-eminently with the political repression and social engineering of the Verwoerd regime—was beginning to produce deep systemic instabilities. This was most evident in the large urban centres, where a rapidly growing number of young black people were disaffected by the potent mix of poverty, overcrowded and neglected schools, thwarted expectations, and the winning of independence by the Portuguese colonies of Mozambique and Angola.

The events of 1976 set in train government responses which combined repression with reform. Amidst government reforms of apartheid education, urban policy, and labour law, the 1983 tricameral constitution became a critical node of instability. It did so in conditions of economic recession. The 1983 constitution included Indians and coloureds as voters for a racially organized central parliament; but the African majority remained excluded from South African citizenship and central state power. The limits of reform were clear, and this provoked a massive upsurge of civil unrest and state suppression across the country, what some commentators have called the 'township revolt' of 1984–6.[118]

Until the government declared a nationwide state of emergency in June 1986, and clamped down heavily on the media's reporting of the conflict, the gripping South African tragedy was beamed to television networks around the world. In many quarters of the world, looking on, South Africa stood for a stark moral tussle between good and evil. Anti-apartheid movements blossomed, and fed into the domestic politics of Western democracies. Supported by the exiled and strengthening African National Congress, and by civic and trade union organizations in South Africa, Western anti-apartheid movements pushed for policies of economic disinvestment and cultural boycotts. Disinvestment became both a crusade and a business decision to reduce risk amidst political instability.[119]

It was not surprising, in the context just outlined, that the South African Rhodes scholarships became, once again, the focus of critical attention in Oxford, developing into a second, more protracted controversy than that of the early 1970s. By the early 1980s, the majority of South African Rhodes scholars remained white men. While the sex

---

[118] See, e.g., W. Beinart, *Twentieth-Century South Africa* (Cape Town: Oxford University Press, 1994), chs. 9–10.

[119] The Rhodes Trust itself disinvested in 1984, withdrawing its £2 million held by Syfrets in Cape Town and transferring the funds to Barings in London. The Trust did not want to have such a large chunk of its assets tied up in South Africa. RTSA 1 (1984–5), Fletcher to Welsh, 19 Jan. 1984. The timing of the withdrawal made it look like a response to the South African scholarships controversy, but the Trust had been discussing this matter since 1980. See RTF, Report of the Warden-elect to the Trustees on his and Mrs Fletcher's visit to the constituencies, Aug. 1980.

imbalance was commonly raised during the 1980s controversy, especially with reference to the four boys-only schools, this matter was overshadowed by preoccupations with questions of race. The racial pattern reflected not the prejudices of selection committees but the wider racial inequalities in South Africa society which skewed the pool of scholarship applicants so profoundly. The South Africa-at-Large reforms had brought in black selectors and had certainly widened the potential net of applicants; but for those critics who saw in the at-large selection patterns a continuing mirror of apartheid this was not enough. In the face of criticisms in Oxford, or the United States, it was not sufficient to point out that many of the white scholars had been active in anti-apartheid student politics, as had been the case in the 1970s.

By contrast with the 1970s campaign against the South Africa scholarships, that of the 1980s was wider and deeper in the scope of opposition mobilized in the anti-apartheid cause. Ironically, though, the target of the Trustees' actions in response to this mobilization was narrower than it had been in the 1970s. In the 1970s, the Trustees had agreed with Rex Welsh's plans for a far-reaching restructuring of the South African scholarships into an at-large scheme, and had taken steps to abolish the four schools scholarships as part of this process. In the 1980s, the Trustees stood by the at-large scheme, which still had Welsh at its helm, and they instituted legal action against just two of the four schools. These two were the government schools of SACS and Paul Roos which, by law, could not admit black children. By the 1980s, as part of South Africa's uneasy political reform, both St Andrew's and Bishops had joined other private schools in de-racializing their intake; they could not therefore be criticized for being racially exclusive and so contravening clause 24 of the will.

The trigger for what developed into the second storm of controversy over the South African scholarships was the 1983 reunion. The gathering in Oxford of Rhodes scholars from around the world for the eightieth anniversary coincided with the vexed introduction of the tricameral constitution in South Africa. This reform package was accompanied by a cluster of local government bills which were associated with the Minister of Cooperation and Development, Piet Koornhof (Paul Roos Gymnasium and Hertford 1948). This legislation was regarded with suspicion in South Africa's townships and it was widely resisted. The impact of the legislation, and Koornhof's association with it, reached all the way to Rhodes House, for the Warden did not include Piet Koornhof in his list of special invitations sent to those Rhodes scholars whose children or parents were also Rhodes scholars. Koornhof's son Johann (South Africa-at-large and Hertford 1980) was in residence at the time.[120] This private piece of boycott politics was accompanied by two public airings of South African issues. The first occurred at the reunion dinner in the gardens of Trinity. For reasons that entice speculation, the Trustees decided on a South African to reply to the speech by the University Chancellor, Harold Macmillan. They chose Julian Ogilvie-Thompson, the most prominent figure in a long list of Rhodes scholars who headed South Africa's vast mining companies. At the time, Ogilvie-Thompson

---

[120] Author's interview with Johann Koornhof, Belville, 7 Dec. 1998. Derek Henderson (Eastern Province and Lincoln 1949) and Margie Henderson (South Africa-at-large and Lincoln 1981) were a unique instance of father–daughter Rhodes scholars.

was deputy chairman of both Anglo-American and De Beers, and chairman of Minorco South Africa. He had been a Bishops Rhodes scholar at Worcester in the mid-1950s and ever since then had worked in the mining houses. In a business sense, Ogilvie-Thompson was a direct descendant of Rhodes.

Amidst evocative recollections of Oxford life, Ogilvie-Thompson's speech praised Rhodes as a visionary, one who wanted to use the wealth and political influ-ence of the mining companies to industrialize Southern Africa and beyond.[121] Although Rhodes's dream of a 'great African Federation' had not materialized, industrialization had transformed South Africa; black people's share of the economy was growing and economic change was forcing political reform and a 'turning away from the laager' by Afrikaners. Ogilvie-Thompson went on to urge that 'con-structive engagement' with South Africa—the current policies of the American and British governments—should be supported as the best means of encouraging urgent change in South Africa. If this statement was not without political controversy, neither was one of his concluding remarks: 'Rhodes, naturally, wanted the best students—by his definition—the better to fulfil his ideals and aims, and so the scholarships are an unashamed exercise in elitism. He was well aware, of course, that privilege confers obligations.'

It was not the pronouncement of elitism itself which was controversial at a dinner where most would have agreed with Ogilvie-Thompson's sentiments. Indeed, *Time Magazine* quoted the American General Secretary, David Alexander, saying at the time of the reunion: 'The Rhodes competition is a talent hunt for an elite that will lead.'[122] Controversy attached itself to Ogilvie-Thompson's praise for Rhodes, amidst assertions of elitism which seemingly downplayed the racially bounded nature of South Africa's elite.[123]

The second public airing of South African issues occurred during the plenary session of the reunion's 'general conference', which took place in the Sheldonian the next day. Earlier in 1983, Robin Fletcher had come to the conclusion that the 'anachronism' of the South African schools scholarships needed 're-visiting', and he had suggested to Welsh that perhaps a South African should raise the matter at the reunion.[124]

Fletcher investigated whether the schools scholars were qualitatively different from the rest. Since becoming Warden he had found that it was generally more difficult to place the schools scholars in their first-choice colleges. He compiled a table of academic per-formance for the period 1969–83 of schools scholars in comparison with South Africa-at-large ones and, interestingly, included figures for the United States. He found that a higher proportion of South African scholars (both schools (38.8 per cent) and at-large (39.2 per cent)) entered postgraduate study than did American scholars (30.5 per cent). While Fletcher's case for South Africa-at-large was strengthened by a higher proportion of undergraduate firsts (34.5 per cent) than among schools scholars (16 per cent), this

---

[121] RTF, Transcript of J. O. Thompson's speech, Rhodes Trustees reunion dinner, 28 June 1983.
[122] *Time Magazine*, 11 July 1983, 40.
[123] See e.g. RTSA 12 (1982–8), Welsh to R. W. Johnson, 30 Sept. 1983.
[124] RTSA 1 (1981–3), Flectcher to Welsh, 14 Apr. 1983.

latter figure was comparable with the proportion of US scholars obtaining firsts (19.6 per cent).[125]

In the event, the 'general conference' provided a forum for criticizing not just the schools scholarships, but all the South African ones. Leading the charge was George Keys, one of the key figures of the 1971 campaign and now an attorney in Washington. In a move which seems to have surprised Fletcher, and certainly Welsh, Keys put his points to an emotion-packed meeting.[126] Despite the reforms of the 1970s, he said, South Africa had produced just two black Rhodes scholars and only one of these was an African.[127] The four South Africa-at-large scholarships mirrored apartheid and were therefore 'unworkable' under clause 24 of the will. These four scholarships should be suspended and reallocated to other Third World countries. Welsh remained silent; he felt that the plenary was not a conducive place for a necessarily complex debate. Instead, Bremer Hofmeyr (Transvaal and University 1930) took the floor and proposed a massive increase in the Rhodes Trust scholarships and the granting of extra Rhodes scholarships to South Africa's all-black universities.

If Hofmeyr's second suggestion was a well-worn one, which Welsh had consistently rejected, Keys's criticism stung the South African General Secretary. It did so because it wrote 'failure' over the South Africa-at-large reforms for which Welsh had worked so hard. Keys had not targeted the schools scholarships, knowing that the Trust had tried, and failed, to annual these in the 1970s. He concentrated on the at-large scholarships over which the Trustees had discretion.

In his correspondence after the general conference, Welsh stressed the complexities of South Africa and its scholarships. The at-large system held out the best possible hope of combining a continuing emphasis on merit with a wider net of applicants. Exhibiting a defensiveness not seen in the 1970s, and recognizing that South Africa's worsening political turmoil threatened to suck every institution into its vortex, Welsh and his assistant secretary, Edwin Cameron, initiated a new round of deliberations amongst the scholarships' administrators. They did so amidst an impatient international discourse of human rights and anti-apartheid sanctions.

Welsh and Cameron organized the first ever national meeting, in April 1984, of regional and schools secretaries combined.[128] It was a sign of the hitherto loose nature of the organization of the South African scholarships that such a meeting happened only in this moment of crisis. Discussions were deep and wide-ranging, giving rise to fundamental questions. How should principles of merit and competition be combined with those of social representation, particularly affirmative action in favour of disadvantaged black South Africans? How far should the famous selection criteria be pliable? What was the desired image of the scholarships, and how should this image be made more attractive

---

[125] A copy of Fletcher's table can be found in RTF 3576.

[126] For details see RTSA 1 (1983), Fletcher to Welsh, 27 Sept. 1983, enclosing transcripts of the 'general conference'.

[127] The correct number of black Rhodes scholars was four, a total made up, in South Africa's racial parlance, of one African, two Indians, and one 'coloured' person.

[128] RTSA 1 (1984–5), Fletcher to Justice M. Corbett, 19 Jan. 1984; Memorandum on the meeting of representatives of the South African selection committees held on 28 Apr. 1984, Johannesburg.

to a wider pool of applicants? Were the scholarships best publicized through more public advertising or through personal networks of mentors based on university campuses? How much could be gained from tapping into the attempts of businesses such as Shell and Mobil to recruit young black managers through their 'cadet schemes'? Should there be a full-time, paid general secretary to push through change in the administration of the scholarships?

The answers signalled the limits to which the South African officials were willing to go. The high entrance requirements of Oxford forced caution, and endorsed merit and competition in scholar selections. The idea of scholarships geared especially towards black applicants was rejected. A full-time paid general secretary was neither needed nor desirable; the suggestion of such a post was perceived more as a criticism of Welsh than as a mechanism for repositioning the scholarships within South Africa's social landscape. The secretaries' meeting resolved to take positive action in two main areas. The age limit for scholarship applicants was already 27 years for whites conscripted into the armed forces; this limit should apply to all applicants in recognition of the late age at which many black children started school. Secondly, a special effort should be made to strengthen the informal networks of 'talent scouts' at the black universities. It was noted that the traditionally white universities were enrolling a rising number of black students who would need to be attracted to apply for the scholarships. It was striking that the secretaries' meeting hardly discussed questions relating to the schools scholarships.

In the event, the call of George Keys for the abolition of the South Africa-at-large scholarships did not gain momentum. While the pressure on South Africa-at-large to deliver black scholars remained, not least through periodic urgings from Rhodes House, the focus of the controversy shifted to the schools scholarships. There were two impulses in this shift. The first came from scholars resident in Oxford during 1984–5, the second from the American Association of Rhodes Scholars across the Atlantic.

With Americans prominent, but with South Africans also involved, a group of scholars in residence argued that Britain's Race Relations Act of 1976 provided a lever against the schools scholarships that had not existed during the legal proceedings of the early 1970s. Surely, too, they suggested, the Sex Discrimination Act of 1976 could be used against the schools? In meeting with the campaign leaders, Robin Fletcher had less of a hard time than had Bill Williams. The campaigners pressed their points firmly, but less confrontationally than their predecessors of the previous decade. Furthermore, they responded positively to the Warden's suggestion that scholars in residence should contribute funds to the schooling of black South Africans.

Rob Baston (South Africa-at-large and Magdalen 1982) and François van der Merwe (Paul Roos Gymnasium and University 1982) spelt out their views in a memorandum which was circulated amongst South African scholars in residence.[129] The memorandum's main point was that the vast majority of South African Rhodes scholars came from white, English-speaking families rooted in the professional or business world. The prototype

---

[129] RTSA 1 (1984–5), R. Baston and F. van der Merwe to Welsh, 14 Mar. 1984, enclosing their memorandum 'Rhodes Scholarships in South Africa'.

Rhodes scholar was, in their words, 'Anglo liberal white'. Not only were black scholars grossly underrepresented (understandable in part due to a 6 : 1 ratio of white to black university graduates), but so too were scholars from Afrikaans-speaking backgrounds. In its appeal for a general 'opening up' of the scholarships to new potential applicants this memorandum added to the general ferment of discussion at Oxford during 1984 and 1985. Baston and van der Merwe's plan of action included the redistribution of the schools scholarships 'across the country', the raising of the age limit to cater for older black graduates, an extensive marketing campaign, and a paid full-time official to implement the South African scholarships.

In March 1985, 171 scholars in residence signed a petition calling for the Trustees to 'amend the Will with respect to the South African schools Scholarships', protesting that two of the schools explicitly excluded blacks and that all four excluded women applicants.[130] The petition was strong in its condemnation of apartheid, but cautiously worded in its injunctions to the Trustees. It expressed a tone of student politics less militant than that of the early 1970s. That seventeen South African scholars in residence, including six from the schools, signed this petition signalled the general pressure on them to be seen to be making a stand on this issue, as part of a wider political campaign against apartheid at a time when widespread township rebellions were occurring at home.

The year 1985 saw the American Association of Rhodes Scholars (AARS) take a number of initiatives to become involved in the South African scholarships controversy. There were good political reasons for distancing the American Rhodes scholarships from the South African ones. As one American Rhodes scholar put it, 'The magnificent public relations job [for the scholarships] done by Frank Aydelotte and his contemporaries is threatened by potential attacks from American students who want to have nothing to do with gold, diamonds, and apartheid.'[131] Another said: 'I share the conviction that those of us who have benefitted so handsomely from the Rhodes Trust have both a special obligation and unique opportunity to help South Africa overcome the curse of apartheid.' The issue of the South African connection was canvassed widely in the American press. There was a certain irony in the *Wall Street Journal* quoting an American Rhodes scholar's reference to the 'blood money' of 'Mr Rhodes' apartheid legacy'. It was a morally stark discourse. A South African Rhodes scholar living in the United States wrote a letter to the *American Oxonian* outlining Rhodes's original desires for the schools scholarships. The journal refused to publish this letter, and this prompted Welsh to satirical exasperation:

Perhaps legislation ought to be promoted in the Parliament of the United Kingdom, or even in the Congress of the United States of America, containing a clause along the following lines: 'The funds of the Rhodes Trust shall henceforth be deemed not to have been derived from any of the business operations carried on by the late Cecil John Rhodes, Esquire, in any part of Southern Africa, or to have had any connection whatsoever with gold, diamonds or apartheid.'[132]

[130] RTSA 1 (1984–5), 'Petition Regarding the Rhodes Scholarship and South Africa', 11 Mar. 1985.
[131] This and the following quotations in this paragraph are drawn from RTF 3576, B. McClellan to Fletcher, 28 June 1985; R. E. Montgomery to Fletcher, 27 Dec. 1984; 'Rhodes Scholars Quietly Protest Founder's Rules', *Wall Street Journal*, 31 July 1985.
[132] RTSA 1 (1984–5), Welsh to Fletcher, 18 Oct. 1985.

The American activists were critical of the South African scholarships in general as a mirror of apartheid, but it was the schools scholarships which attracted special attention.[133] A number of pressing questions arose. How far should Rhodes scholars in one constituency influence the Trust's policy in another? How much say should Rhodes scholars have in the Trust's business, and how far should the Trustees be answerable to Rhodes scholar communities? How far should the Trust intervene politically in the countries from which it draws scholars? The Trustees' answers to these questions were, in general, defensive ones; and it was Robin Fletcher's task to mediate numerous awkward transatlantic conversations.[134]

The combined impact of the near-universal petition of scholars in residence and the American agitations pushed the Trustees into action. In mid-1985 the chairperson, Lord Blake, wrote to the headmasters of the four schools inviting their comments on the Trustees' view that the schools scholarships were 'anachronistic'. The Trustees decided to initiate legal proceedings against Paul Roos and SACS which, as government schools, admitted only white pupils. The Trustees' grounds for this action rehearsed those of the 1970s: the schools' racial exclusiveness contravened clause 24 of the will. But the Trust's lawyers were now able to add the argument that the continued operation of these scholarships threatened the reputation and workability of the US scholarships. Furthermore, the administrative and legal route for amending Rhodes's will was now different from that of the 1970s.

Robin Fletcher visited Cape Town in mid-1985 to inform the schools of the Trust's intentions. The headmasters invited Sir Richard Luyt, their champion of 1972, to attend. Two contrasting paradigms confronted each other. Fletcher sensed the isolation of the schools from the swirling currents of Oxford and 'the world in the later part of the twentieth century'.[135] The second paradigm was the schools' appeal to a unique tradition that was treasured by them and which had produced an array of prominent scholars. The notes of the headmasters; meeting with Fletcher, penned by a schools' scribe, stated tersely: 'It was strongly argued that the terms of the Will were of overriding importance. The Secretary [Fletcher] said that this point appeared to have lost some of its validity in recent years.'[136] The schools' request for a meeting with the Trustees was blocked. The four schools agreed in principle to stand alongside one another, even though only two were being targeted for abolition.

In practice though, as events unfolded, it was up to each school to defend its scholarship.[137] There was surely no coincidence in the fact that SACS was one of the first state

---

[133] RTF 3576, B. McClellan to Fletcher, 28 June 1985.

[134] RTF 3576, various letters and 'Notes of an informal meeting between Dr Bruce McClellan and Mr Charles Barber, President and Vice-President of the AARS, and the Chairman and Secretary of the Rhodes Trust, Rhodes House, 22 November 1985'.

[135] RTSA 1 (1984–5), Welsh's note on a meeting with Fletcher, Jan Smuts airport, 23 July 1985.

[136] RTF 3576, Notes on a meeting between the Secretary of the Rhodes Trust and representatives of the four schools named in the will of Cecil Rhodes, Diocesan College, Rondebosch, 22 July 1985.

[137] Details for this paragraph are drawn from: various articles in the *Cape Times*, Jan. and Feb. 1986; author's interview with Gordon Law, Cape Town, 7 Dec. 1998; RTF 3576, Fletcher to Peake, 7 July 1987, and Fletcher to J. P. Kent, 19 Nov. 1987.

schools in the Western Cape to mobilize an 'open schools' campaign in 1986, and to secure a majority of parents' support for the admission of black pupils. The national education department, however, remained intransigent and rapped the SACS headmaster on the knuckles. The Bishops council, nudged by Fletcher and the new headmaster, John Peake, agreed to change the rules during 1987 to make post-matrics eligible for the Bishops scholarship after just one year at the school. The existing rule was that eligibility was earned after three years. This move coincided with the admission of girls into post-matric, meaning that the Bishops scholarship was no longer strictly for boys only. During the same year Fletcher mooted the idea that St Andrew's which had shared its senior classes with girls from the neighbouring Diocesan School for Girls since the late 1970s, should open its scholarship to applicants from its sister school. This idea was implemented in 1989.

The South African scholarships controversy of the 1980s pitted two contrasting worldviews against one another: a forceful, egalitarian human rights culture, invoked most loudly in the United States and at Oxford; and a stoical legalism, invoked by the schools' defenders in South Africa and cohering around the view that Rhodes's will was inviolate. In the words of John Peake, head of Bishops, 'any tampering with a Will is illegal'. Similarly, Jack Kent (Diocesan College and Corpus Christi 1929) who was vice-chair of the Cape School Board in 1987, viewed the proceedings against SACS and Paul Roos as 'ill-advised and immoral'.[138] The 'human rights' paradigm criticized the South African scholarships in a broad assault on apartheid. The 'legalistic' paradigm defended the tradition and success of the schools scholarships. For the schools, the scholarships were integral to their identity and status as high-quality centres of education with a link to one of the world's premier universities.

Welsh, joined by Cameron, continued to hold the view that the schools scholarships should be converted into at-large ones.[139] But, with the institution of legal proceedings underway against the two schools, Welsh and Cameron tended to keep their views close to their chest. Nearing the end of his term of office, Welsh was not about to initiate a reopening of the whole schools question, although he did agree to the invitation of the American Association of Rhodes Scholars that he address them in New York in 1986. He withdrew his acceptance, however, after Fletcher and the Trustees advised him against making the visit. Perhaps sensing Welsh's cautious defensiveness—a stance quite different in tone from that of the 1970s—the schools all began sending observers to the South Africa-at-large selection meetings from the mid-1980s onwards.

The proceedings of the Trust's legal case against Paul Roos and SACS are outlined elsewhere in this book. As the case dragged into 1987 it contributed to a sense of anxiety and frustration for the schools at a time of widespread uncertainty in South Africa's national politics. Only in late 1987 did the Charity Commissioners grant a scheme for High Court action against the two schools, and the lawyers for the two sides entered a dispute over whether the Trust would continue to pay the schools' legal expenses.[140]

---

[138] RTF 3576, Peake to Fletcher, 30 Sept. 1987; Kent to Fletcher, Oct. 1987.
[139] See for example RTSA 1 (1984–5), Welsh to Fletcher, 16 Sept. 1985.
[140] The bulky correspondence can be followed in RTF 3576.

In the meantime, Edwin Cameron played an important role in assisting Welsh with the choice of selectors for the South Africa-at-large committee and for some of the provincial committees. As a politically active lawyer, connected to a number of anti-apartheid organizations, Cameron had an informed sense of the kind of image which the Rhodes scholarship administration should project. His most radical suggestion, one which Welsh successfully resisted, was that Cyril Ramaphosa should join the South Africa-at-large committee. At that time, Ramaphosa (whom Cameron knew personally) was secretary general of the militant Mine Workers' Union, engaged in a sustained stand-off with the Chamber of Mines. In the end not Ramaphosa but Don Ncube, a human resources manager at Anglo-American, was asked to fill that particular vacancy on the committee.[141] A selector about whom Cameron and Welsh agreed was Arthur Chaskalson. A Johannesburg lawyer of distinction who had founded the Legal Resources Centre, Chaskalson became chair of the Transvaal selection committee in the mid-1980s and agreed to fill Judge Corbett's shoes on the national committee in 1988. Corbett was soon to become South Africa's Chief Justice and, in 1994, Chaskalson was to become head of the country's new Constitutional Court.

In 1985, Cameron invited Elizabeth Mokoteng, a Pretoria-based social worker, to join the at-large committee as its first black woman selector. She joined Denise Ackermann, a feminist theologian in Pretoria, Libby Ardington, a Durban social scientist, and Margie Henderson (South Africa-at-large and Lincoln 1981), a researcher at the Urban Foundation, as selectors during the mid- to late 1980s. Welsh, keen to bring in some new blood among the regional secretaries, asked Henderson to take over as secretary of the Transvaal committee, and Belinda van Heerden (South Africa-at-large and Brasenose 1982) to fill Peter Sauerman's shoes in Cape Town. The first women to hold these positions, both had returned recently from Oxford.

The 1980s, then, saw conscious efforts to create selection committees that were lively and reflective of a changing South Africa. What were the effects on selection patterns? By far the majority of applications continued to come from well-qualified white students; the huge political turmoil of those years reduced the number of qualifying black applicants. Out of a possible twenty-five scholars selected by the Natal and South Africa-at-large committees between 1983 and 1987, six were women and three were black candidates. The biographies of each of the black scholars are interesting for what they reveal about the continuing hurdles faced by black South Africans in open competition. In 1984, Liyanda Lekalake became the first black woman to win a South African Rhodes scholarship. She was also the first Botswana citizen to do so. She had attended Maru a Pula, a private school in Gaberone, and then studied in Britain and Canada before applying for the Rhodes. If Welsh was impressed with Lekalake, his praise was even more effusive for Satish Keshav, a medical student from the University of the Witwatersrand: 'one of the best Scholars-Elect of my time'.[142] Keshav had grown up in Zambia and done most of his schooling there. The following year saw Kumi Naidoo selected. He was a student

---

[141] Ramaphosa later went on to become a central negotiator in the transition to democracy, and by the late 1990s had become one of South Africa's leading black business figures.

[142] RTSA 1 (1984–5), Welsh to Fletcher, 3 Dec. 1985.

leader and civic activist in Durban, and during 1987 was operating 'underground' to escape arrest by the security police. The Natal secretary, Tommy Bedford, helped to smuggle him out of the country and a special arrangement was made with Rhodes House to accommodate him in Oxford before his scheduled Michaelmas term arrival. Abnormal times, indeed.

Welsh planned to retire at the end of 1987. He wanted to ensure a smoother succession than his own abrupt induction as General Secretary. During 1986 he persuaded Laurie Ackermann (Cape Province and Worcester 1954) to succeed him from January 1988. Ackermann had practised as an advocate at the Transvaal Bar, then been appointed a Supreme Court judge. During 1987, he resigned from the bench to become the first holder of the H. F. Oppenheimer Chair of Human Rights Law at the University of Stellenbosch. Welsh termed this new post 'a very courageous new enterprise at the very heart of Afrikanerdom', and Ackermann joined other leading South Africans in talks with exiled ANC leaders during the late 1980s.[143] That an Oppenheimer Chair was created at Stellenbosch was an intriguing development in itself, given the respective histories of the English-dominated mining houses and the Afrikaner nationalist seat of learning. Times were changing fast. Adding a further twist was Ackermann's personal history: members of his family had been interned in British concentration camps during the Anglo-Boer War, his senior schooling had been in English, and his undergraduate studies at Stellenbosch had been in Afrikaans. He was fourth in an unbroken line of lawyers holding the office of South African Secretary for the Trust. Ackermann had been a Transvaal selector; he and Welsh wisely decided that he should attend the 1986 and 1987 at-large selections in order to prepare for taking over the running of the complex and sensitive South African scholarships.

The 1986 meeting was lively and the field of applicants deep, but the 1987 one was disappointing and only two scholars were selected. This was the first time in the history of the at-large scheme that the full complement of four scholars had not been selected. Whether one considers this a courageous step, or an over-cautious one, it signalled a gloomy valedictory for Welsh at the end of his twenty-one-year term. He wrote in this vein to Cameron, speculating that the 1987 experience boded ill for the future of the South African scholarships. Reflecting a wider pessimism about the country's political future in the dark days of emergency rule and ungovernability, Welsh pondered whether the scholarships would suffer a growing irrelevance amongst both white and black graduates.[144] It was a sombre moment for someone who had invested so much energy and emotion as General Secretary in 'this lonely and extraordinarily difficult constituency'.

Welsh's disillusionment was no doubt heightened by his keen appreciation of the significant impact which Rhodes scholars had made on South African life, and beyond, during the course of the twentieth century. It is to an overview of this impact that we now turn, before resuming the narrative of scholarship administration from 1988 onwards.

---

[143] RTSA 1 (1986–9), Welsh to Kenny, 11 Nov. 1987.
[144] RTSA 12 (1982–8), Welsh to Cameron, 22 Mar. 1988.

Profiles and impact of South African scholars

The years 1902 to 1999 saw 735 South African Rhodes scholars selected. The *Register of Rhodes Scholars* which was published in 1981 and again in 1995 provides a rich resource for studying the impact of these scholars on the societies in which they have worked. I have used 1985 as a cut-off date in this study, on the grounds that scholars selected after this date would not yet have had time to establish careers of significance before the publication of the 1995 *Register*. Between 1902 and 1985, 612 scholars were selected. I have characterized and quantified the careers which these scholars pursued, according to the following categories: business, higher education and research, school education, law, medicine, politics and government, agriculture, journalism, the military, and 'other professions'. Sometimes an individual's careers were pursued sequentially, for example in moving from legal practice to the business sector. Sometimes careers were pursued simultaneously, for example, when a farmer was also a member of parliament. Career changes are not always easy to track from the details in the *Register*, but in doing so I have identified a total of 815 careers pursued by the 612 scholars selected up to 1985. The details of these careers are dependent on the entries in the *Register*, and these details are sometimes incomplete. Nevertheless, there is enough material there for an overview of the different career categories. In each category, I mention a small selection, for illustrative purposes, of highly prominent and distinguished scholars. Before quantifying the dominant career patterns of South African scholars, it is necessary to outline trends in their place of residence. On the basis of details in the *Register* it is possible to gain a picture of where scholars lived in the early 1980s and the mid-1990s. This information is interesting because it shapes the extent to which South African scholars have made an impact on national life at the southern tip of Africa. Of the scholars alive in 1981, and whose address was known, some 58 per cent lived in South Africa and 42 per cent outside the country. Of those resident in the country, nearly half lived in the Transvaal and nearly a third in the Western Cape. The remaining third was made up, roughly equally, of scholars living in Natal and the Eastern Cape. Nearly two-thirds of scholars living overseas resided in the United Kingdom and just under a quarter had North American addresses.

The information recorded in the *Register* of 1995 indicates proportionately fewer South African addresses and more overseas ones than in 1981. Calculations based on living scholars selected up to 1985 indicate that 52 per cent of known addresses were in South Africa and 48 per cent were outside the country. If the places of residence of scholars selected after 1985 were included, the non-South African addresses would constitute more than half of the total. Since the 1960s a growing number of South African scholars have emigrated, and this was particularly so in the highly troubled political situation of the 1980s and early 1990s. In 1995, some 39 per cent of the pre-1986 scholars living in South Africa resided in the Transvaal, now Gauteng, but their share of the total was declining and the proportion of Western Cape-based scholars was rising. Natal retained about 15 per cent, while the Eastern Cape declined to 6 per cent of the total. Overseas, the United Kingdom remained the favoured location, accounting for 56 per cent of émigré scholars. The proportion of overseas residents based in North America had risen to 28 per cent and Australia was growing in significance as a destination.

Rhodes scholars working in universities, colleges, and research institutes account for 25 per cent of the career total. This proportion excludes academics in the fields of law and medicine, who are treated separately on the grounds that many lawyers and doctors alternated between their practices and the academy, or combined these two spheres. If legal and medical academics are added, the percentage share moves into the upper twenties.

Over the past century, Rhodes scholars have been influential in leading and shaping higher education from its small beginnings in the emergent Union of South Africa. This has been particularly so at the following universities, in a rough order of impact based on the employment of senior academics: the Witwatersrand, Cape Town, Natal, Rhodes, Stellenbosch, Pretoria, the Free State, Western Cape, and the University of South Africa. The disciplines in which Rhodes scholars have been most influential at South African universities are, in order again: English, Mathematics and Statistics, Physics, History, Economics, Classics, Chemistry, Engineering, Philosophy, Politics, and Biochemistry.

In addition to playing leading roles in these disciplines, Rhodes scholars have occupied top management posts in South African universities. Rhodes scholars have been chancellors at the universities of the Witwatersrand, Cape Town, and Pretoria. Eight scholars were, or are, university vice-chancellors, one a principal of a technical college, and another a principal of a teachers' college. Six Rhodes scholars have been deputy vice-chancellors or vice-principals. The Rhodes scholar vice-chancellors of the 1990s have been D. S. Henderson (Eastern Province and Lincoln 1949) at Rhodes University, succeeded on his retirement by D. R. Woods (Natal and University 1963); F. P. Retief (Paul Roos and University 1956) at the University of the Free State; and C. J. Bundy (Natal and Merton, 1968) at the University of the Witwatersrand.

Since the 1950s, South African scholars have been appointed to at least 120 academic posts outside the country, the majority at professorial level. This figure reflects the diaspora of South Africans during the apartheid era, as well as the burgeoning of higher education worldwide since the Second World War. The academic posts were spread across 34 British, 21 American, 8 Australasian, 6 African, and 5 Canadian universities. The largest concentrations of overseas appointments were at Oxford, where 14 scholars were selected as fellows or professors, and at the University of London, where 12 scholars found posts. The disciplines in which South African scholars have been prominent in foreign universities include English, History, Mathematics, Economics, Development Studies, Politics, and Philosophy.

South African scholars have achieved prominence at research institutes both in South Africa and abroad. In chemistry, scholars have worked at institutes in Canada, the United States, and Switzerland, as well as the Fuel Research Laboratory in South Africa. In physics, scholars have been influential in the National Physics Research Laboratory and the Atomic Energy Board in Pretoria; and in the Rutherford Appleton Laboratory in the United Kingdom. In social policy research, scholars have played leading management roles in the South African Institute of Race Relations and the Urban Foundation.

Careers in business follow closely on the higher education and research category, also making up 25 per cent of the total. This career choice became far more common after the Second World War, a reflection of the growth of a manufacturing sector in a diversifying national economy from the 1940s onwards. The expansion of the Orange Free State gold mines was also a crucial influence. Until the 1970s, scholars tended to work in the big corporations in mining, heavy industry, retail banking, and insurance. Since then, reflecting worldwide changes in the nature of business, scholars are to be found in greater numbers in financial services, management consultancies, and information technology companies.

The mining houses and their industrial subsidiaries have dominated large portions of the South African economy during the twentieth century. It is in these companies that the largest concentration of Rhodes scholars in business has occurred. The significance of this concentration is far more than a numerical one, for scholars have run these networks of vast companies. The Anglo-American Corporation is the pre-eminent example. No fewer than 19 scholars have achieved top positions there, and this cadre of leaders has criss-crossed with executive positions in De Beers, Minorco, Gold Fields, and Charter Consolidated. In the 1970s and 1980s, six of the eight divisions at Anglo-American were headed by five Rhodes scholars.[145] In addition to the 19 Anglo executives, another six scholars worked at Anglo for a period before moving elsewhere in their business careers. At least another 20 scholars gained prominence in the South African mining sector, on mines or in companies which may or may not have been linked with the Anglo-American Corporation.

After mining, the field of banking and finance has attracted the second largest cluster of Rhodes scholar business executives, with careers in these fields numbering around thirty. Rhodes scholars have reached the top of Barclays, Volkskas, and Standard banks, as well as the United Building Society. Insurance companies such as AA Mutual and Southern Life have also seen Rhodes scholars at the helm. Alongside the financial sector, engineering business has also been a popular choice, and it is worth noting that four scholars have been prominent in large-scale water engineering, including the building of the Verwoerd (now Gariep) and Kariba dams, and the Lesotho Highlands Water Project. The list of some of the other companies in which scholars have been executives ranges across South African big business: African Explosives and Chemical Industries; Scaw Metals, Union Steel, the Rembrandt group, Syfrets, OK Bazaars, Checkers, Unilever, Lonhro, Shell, the Argus group, South African Airways, and Ster Kinekor.

The impact of Rhodes scholar business leaders has extended beyond the companies they run. There is an impressive record of scholars assuming office in regional and national chambers of business, commerce, and mining, and, more recently, in structures such as the National Business Initiative. Two Rhodes scholars were business representatives on the Prime Minister's Economic Advisory Council during the 1960s and 1970s,

[145] Author's interview with Julian Ogilvie-Thompson, Johannesburg, 21 Mar. 1999.

highlighting the often controversial relationships between 'business' and 'apartheid'. It is widely recognized that business leaders have played a powerful role in the political transition beyond apartheid, and Rhodes scholars have been among them.

South African Rhodes scholars have also risen to top positions in business outside the country, most notably in the United Kingdom and the United States. This has been particularly so in the fields of merchant banking, investment finance, management consultancy, engineering, oil and petrol, food and beverages, and information technology. It is of interest to note that four scholars have risen in the ranks of Lever Brothers, another four in the World Bank, and one to head the London office of Walt Disney.

As the above account indicates, the list of business notables among South African Rhodes scholars is long and deep. For purposes of illustration, three leaders can be mentioned. First, J. Ogilvie-Thompson (Diocesan College and Worcester 1953) whose long career in Anglo-American since the 1950s has taken him to the top of that company, as well as De Beers, Minorco, and Charter Consolidated. Second, H. S. Mabin (Cape Province and Balliol 1936), who was secretary and then executive director of the Association of Chambers of Commerce in South Africa between 1949 and the mid-1970s, before becoming deputy chair of the Board of Trade and Industry. Third, W. G. Pietersen (Eastern Province and University 1961), who emigrated in the 1970s and became president of the Foods Division of Lever Brothers in the United States in 1980 and then president of Guinness America in 1987.

The legal field accounts for the third biggest career category, 16 per cent of the total number of careers. Around a third of the lawyers have worked in Caper Town; the next largest concentrations have been in Johannesburg–Pretoria and then Durban. After Durban, London was the next biggest centre, with thirteen lawyers practising there. Rhodes scholars in legal practice have commonly risen to positions of leadership in bar associations, in university councils, in non-governmental organizations such as Lawyers for Human Rights, and in the administration of the Anglican Church. A number became leading advocates of national stature.

Twenty-one Rhodes scholars have been appointed supreme court or high court judges in South Africa. Six became provincial judge presidents, one a provincial attorney general, and one has been appointed to the new Constitutional Court since 1994. One scholar was appointed chief justice in South Africa, another in Rhodesia, and another in the 'homeland' of Transkei. Three scholars have risen to prominent judicial positions in the United Kingdom.

Compared to the distinguished profile of scholars as judges, advocates, and attorneys, the number of scholars in senior academic law positions has been relatively small. Four scholars became law professors at Stellenbosch, two each at Cape Town, the Witwatersrand, and Rhodes, and one each at Pretoria, Port Elizabeth, and the University of South Africa. By contrast with the South African profile, Oxford has seen five law fellows appointed, including the Rhodes reader in Roman Dutch law, a post funded by the Rhodes Trust in the 1950s.

In the legal field special mention can be made of A. van der Sandt Centlivres (South African College School and New College 1907), who was appointed South

African Chief Justice between 1950 and 1957. During this period he clashed head-on with the Afrikaner Nationalist government over the legality of removing Coloured voters from the common roll. The three South Africans on the British bench are also worthy of remark. First, there was G. R. Thomson (South African College School and Corpus Christi 1911) who was the Lord Justice Clerk of Scotland from the 1940s to the 1960s. L. H. Hoffman (South African College School and Queen's 1954) and J. van Zyl Steyn (Cape Province and University 1955) were both appointed Lord Justices of Appeal in 1992 and have had a high public profile in British law, both now in the House of Lords.

South African Rhodes scholars have had a wide-ranging impact in the political field in South Africa, elsewhere in Africa, and to a lesser extent overseas. Careers in politics and government account for 12 per cent of the total. Scholars have been influential as civil servants in eleven national government departments, most particularly in Finance, Forestry, and Health. In Finance, one scholar was secretary, two were deputy secretaries, and one was confidential adviser to the minister during the Second World War. Similar kinds of leadership occurred in the Health Department. One scholar was Administrator of the Transvaal. Other national government bodies in which scholars have been prominent include the Social and Economic Planning Council, the South African Tourist Corporation, the Industrial Development Corporation, the South African Foundation, and the Central Statistical Service.

A striking number of South African Rhodes scholars held high administrative positions in Britain's African colonies. No doubt shaped by their experiences at Oxford—the 'university of empire'—South Africans took up posts in Botswana, Swaziland, Tanganyika, Kenya, the Sudan, Northern Rhodesia, and Lesotho between the 1930s and 1970s. A handful of scholars rose to the top in the Rhodesian civil service. Further afield in the British Empire and Commonwealth, one South African scholar was a civil servant in India in the 1920s and another the Governor of Guyana in the 1960s. In the United Kingdom one scholar has risen to the upper levels of the Foreign Office.

In the arena of South African party politics Rhodes scholars have, in relatively small numbers, been prominent across the spectrum. Three scholars have been cabinet ministers, two for the Nationalist Party and one for the United Party. Two scholars were Senators. Twelve have been members of parliament, for the most part on the opposition benches during the long decades of apartheid. Two scholars were opposition Chief Whips during the 1970s and 1980s, one for the United Party and the other for the Progressive Federal Party. In extra-parliamentary politics, a handful of scholars have been prominent. In the ranks of the African National Congress and the South African Communist Party, one scholar was politically imprisoned for life by the South African government and another was expelled from the ANC-in-exile for his Trotskyist leanings. One scholar was a founding member of the Liberal Party in the 1950s; another rose to be vice-chair in the 1960s and was banned by the government. Beyond South Africa, one scholar was an MP and then cabinet minister in Southern Rhodesia during the 1930s, and another an MP for East Edinburgh, Scotland, during the 1940s.

In various other ways South African scholars have influenced national, provincial, and local politics. Three scholars sat on provincial councils. Ten have been members of town or city councils, three of these as mayors. Rhodes scholars have been leading figures in organizations such as the Christian Institute of South Africa, the Institute for Multi-Party Democracy, and the Helen Suzman Foundation. Several scholars have played prominent roles in South Africa's political transition during the 1980s and 1990s through participation in extra-parliamentary politics and non-governmental organizations, through research and journalism, through participating in the multi-party negotiations, and through membership of the Independent Electoral Commission which organized the historic 1994 elections.

The following sample of notables illustrates varying poles of influence in South African politics. Among civil servants in national government, G. W. G. Browne (South African College School and Hertford 1936) deserves mention. Having been secretary of the Social and Economic Planning Council during the 1940s he rose quickly in the Department of Finance. He became deputy secretary in 1957 and then began a seventeen-year innings as secretary in 1960. Amongst party politicians, the brilliant career of J. H. Hofmeyr (South African College School and Hertford 1910) dominates the first half-century of scholars. In 1924, at the age of 30, he was appointed Administrator of the Transvaal. Five years later he was elected an MP for Johannesburg North, a seat he retained until his untimely death in 1948. From 1933 onwards he was a United Party minister in the cabinet of Jan Smuts, holding the position of Deputy Prime Minister from 1942. The Nationalist Party which won the landmark 1948 elections became the political home of two Rhodes scholars who became long-standing cabinet ministers during the apartheid years. H. Muller (Transvaal and University 1937) entered parliament in 1958. He was the ambassador to London in the immediate aftermath of South Africa's controversial withdrawal from the British Commonwealth in 1961. From 1964 to 1977 he was Foreign Minister. P. G. J. Koornhof (Paul Roos Gymnasium and Hertford 1948) started his political career in the civil service and then entered parliament in 1964. By 1968 he was in the cabinet and he remained there until the turbulent 1980s. The last phase of his long political life saw him appointed as ambassador to the United States between 1986 and 1991. In the ranks of parliamentary opposition B. R. Bamford (Diocesan College and University 1951) stands out. Having sat in the Cape Provincial Council from the mid-1960s to the mid-1970s, and then the South African Senate 1974–7, he was opposition Chief Whip for the Progressive Federal Party 1978–87.

Among a handful of scholars who helped lead extra-parliamentary struggles against apartheid, A. Fischer (Orange Free State and New College 1931) was especially important. He belonged to a well-connected Afrikaner family in Bloemfontein. Instead of walking through the open doors of the political establishment, he joined the South African Communist Party, becoming a leading figure from the mid-1940s. Somewhat incongruously, he did legal work for the mining houses, but became famous for his representation of the Congress treason trialists of the 1950s and particularly the Rivonia trialists of the 1960s. He and his legal team averted the death sentence for Nelson Mandela and the other Rivonia accused, securing life imprisonment instead. After this profoundly significant trial, Fischer went into disguise and lived an undercover political life. He evaded the security police for nine months before his own arrest and sentence to life imprisonment.

Around 8 per cent of scholars' careers have been in the medical field. It was common for these scholars to proceed from graduation at Oxford to hospital work in Britain, with London and Oxford the most popular venues. Some created careers in Britain, but the majority returned to practise in Johannesburg, Cape Town, and Durban. Rhodes scholar doctors worked in less well-known centres, too, ranging from Welkom to Idutywa in the Transkei.

Rhodes scholars attained senior academic positions at each of South Africa's main medical schools, and were particularly prominent at the universities of Cape Town and the Witwatersrand. A small number of Rhodes scholar medical academics have played an important role in matters of public health policy and practice. The academic pattern in overseas universities is less emphatic, with scholars spread across four medical schools in Britain, four in the United States, and one in Canada.

Two medical Rhodes scholars can be highlighted. First, E. H. Cluver (Boys' High School, Stellenbosch, and Hertford 1914) combined his academic and public roles to great effect. A founding professor of medicine at the new University of the Witwatersrand, he worked simultaneously in the national Department of Health, becoming Secretary for Public Health at the end of the 1930s. During the 1940s and 1950s he directed the South African Institute for Medical Research. Secondly, L. H. Opie (Cape Province and Lincoln 1956) of the University of Cape Town has become an internationally renowned figure in cardiac medicine.

The last significant category is school teaching, accounting for 7 per cent of the careers in the survey. Most scholars have taught in South Africa, but since the 1960s a sizeable minority has worked in England. The South African schools at which Rhodes scholar teachers have been most prominent are, in order, St Andrew's in Grahamstown, Michaelhouse near Pietermaritzburg, Diocesan College in Cape Town, Kingswood in Grahamstown, and Grey College in Bloemfontein. Rhodes scholars became headmasters at each of these schools, as well as at St John's in Johannesburg, Kearsney College near Durban, St Andrew's in Bloemfontein, and Pinelands in Cape Town. Scholars also became heads of two well-known private preparatory schools in Johannesburg. This list of schools, which ranks amongst South Africa's best, has been significant not only in educating Rhodes scholars-to-be, but in receiving grants from the Rhodes Trust during the course of the last century. It is worth noting that South African scholars have also become heads of less well-known schools, such as Maru a Pula in Botswana and the Ndamase Bantu School in Umtata. A South African scholar became principal of one of the Fairbridge schools in Australia.

The above categories cover around 93 per cent of the careers pursued by Rhodes scholars. Lesser categories include agriculture, journalism, the Church, architecture, and the military. Twenty-three careers are recorded in agriculture, and Rhodes scholars have played leading roles, for example, in the sugar industry and the South African Agricultural Union. Thirteen careers in journalism are listed, with a couple of

Rhodes scholars reaching top positions as editors and managers of both Afrikaans and English newspapers. There has been a sprinkling of other professionals, such as architects, writers, and church ministers. Only three scholars have pursued careers in the army, one of whom assumed the rank of brigadier in the 1960s. By contrast with the low number of military careers, there is a striking pattern of scholars serving in senior officer ranks during the two World Wars. By 1918, eighty-seven South African Rhodes scholars had been selected; twenty-six of these had assumed senior leadership positions during the First World War. During the Second World War, fifty-eight scholars served in this capacity.

It is appropriate to end this profile of South African scholars with a few points about sport, a theme which has loomed large in selection deliberations for much of the century. Of the 612 scholars selected up to 1985, roughly one in four played top-level sport for Oxford University. Of the 156 scholars who played at this level, 30 did so in two sports. Twenty-nine scholars made their way into national teams, playing for England or South Africa: 13 rugby players, 7 cricketers, and 5 athletes. Rugby was by far the most significant university sport for South African scholars, with 58 playing for Oxford. The other notable categories are athletics (27 scholars), swimming (24), cricket (13), boxing (12), tennis (11), and hockey (10). Beyond these traditional sports, there is an interesting array of South African representation across thirteen others, including archery, fencing, and, in the 1930s, three scholars who represented Oxford at ju-jitsu wrestling. The decade after the Second World War produced the most pronounced pattern of sporting success among South African scholars, and this helped to set the tone for scholar selections until the 1970s. The period from the 1940s to the 1970s also saw remarkable involvement of South Africans in Oxford's leading sports clubs such as Vincent's, Greyhounds, Authentics, and Occasionals.

On the basis of their sporting activities at Oxford and beyond, the following scholars deserve special mention. R. O. Lagden, selected by the Trustees as an extra scholar in 1908, played for Oxford first teams in tennis, cricket, hockey, and rugby, and he won a rugby cap for England in 1912. Lagden was killed in action in 1915. V. H. Neser (Transvaal and Brasenose 1918) played rugby and cricket for Oxford, and represented South Africa in both these sports in the mid-1920s. H. G. Owen-Smith (Diocesan College and Magdalen 1930) was a member of Oxford's cricket, rugby, and boxing teams; he then played rugby for England and, later, cricket for South Africa. C. B. van Ryneveld (Diocesan College and University 1947) played rugby for both Oxford and England; he also captained the Oxford cricket team and, a few years later, the South African team. T. P. Bedford (Natal and St Edmund Hall 1965) played rugby for Oxford and then went on to captain the South African team.

The 1980s and especially the 1990s have seen a significant decline in the significance of sporting prowess as a criterion of selection, at least in the South Africa-at-large committee. This has been part of a broader picture of change jostling with continuity in the administration of the scholarships since Laurie Ackermann became General Secretary in 1988.

Negotiating Political Change and Questions of Legitimacy:
The Ackermann Years since 1988

Two years after Laurie Ackermann took up office as South African General Secretary, the state President. F. W. de Klerk, made the surprising announcement that the government was to unban the African National Congress and other liberation organizations. The country entered a new, uncertain phase in its turbulent political history. It reached a dramatic milestone with the relatively peaceful elections of 1994 which ushered in a new, inclusive democracy. South Africa experienced an inspiring passage from bitterness and hatred to the possibilities of reconciliation and regeneration. One of the consequences was that South Africans could begin to see themselves differently.

Ackermann and the chair of the South Africa-at-large committee, Arthur Chaskalson, were well placed, politically, to lead the administration of the Rhodes scholarships into the new era. Both men were to be appointed to the new Constitutional Court. Edwin Cameron stayed on as assistant general secretary until 1992, and he continued to lend political credibility to the national secretariat. After the short tenure of Charles Carter (Diocesan College and Wolfson 1986) as Cameron's successor, Ackermann appointed Janet Kentridge (South Africa-at-large and Balliol 1986) and Isaac Shongwe (South Africa-at-large and Christ Church 1989) as joint assistants. Annette Gibson, whom Rex Welsh had recruited as his administrative secretary in 1982, provided the organizational continuity and drew on her wealth of experience in personal interactions with regional and school secretaries and with scholars-elect. When Chaskalson retired from the South Africa-at-large committee in 1993, Ackermann persuaded Dr Mamphela Ramphele to take his place. It was a highly significant move.

Mamphela Ramphele became the first black person and the first woman to chair the national committee, and the first outside the legal field. Once a student activist in the Black Consciousness Movement, and a close friend of Steve Biko, Ramphele was a rapidly rising star at the University of Cape Town where, in 1996, she was appointed Vice-Chancellor. Well aware of the potent legacy of Cecil Rhodes in Cape Town and beyond, she used her inauguration as Vice-Chancellor to urge that some of his ideals be reinterpreted in the 'new' South Africa. In her closing remarks at the 1998 South Africa-at-large selections, Ramphele said:

I willingly devote a whole weekend to the Rhodes Scholarships selection meeting at a very busy time of year because I find it such a rejuvenating experience. To meet young people of such calibre— leaders of the future—excites me and gives me hope for South Africa. It is indeed ironic that Cecil Rhodes, who epitomises imperialism in South Africa, offered a scholarship scheme that has become a hugely significant vehicle for helping to create a new kind of society at the end of the twentieth century.[146]

Ramphele expressed her optimism despite the continuing difficulties in attracting substantial numbers of high-quality black applicants for the scholarships. At the meetings of regional secretaries inaugurated by Ackermann from 1988 this matter was discussed

---

[146] The quotation is from notes made by the author at the selection meeting, 6 Dec. 1998.

extensively, and in 1993 Charles Carter and Annette Gibson undertook a detailed demographic study of selection patterns during the previous two decades. When Ackermann was petitioned from Oxford in 1995 by the Rhodes Scholars Southern Africa Forum about the continuing paucity of black scholars he was able to signal his informed awareness of the issues confronting selection committees.[147] South Africa-at-large statistics for the period from 1988 to 1998 reveal that nine of the forty-six selections were of black candidates. The Natal committee selected two black scholars out of a total of eleven. The schools committees have yet to select a person of colour as a scholar.

Throughout the 1990s South African selectors have continued to grapple with the challenges of awarding scholarships based on merit but in a highly unequal society where the racial legacies of apartheid run deep. In 1998, the South Africa-at-large committee decided that the time had come to reduce the age limit of applicants to the worldwide norm of 25 years. The age limit of 27 had first been introduced in the 1980s to cater for white applicants forced to serve two years in the military, and then been justified for black applicants whose education had been disrupted by political strife. The decision to reduce the age limit signalled the view that there are now sufficiently large numbers of young black students who are potential applicants for the Rhodes scholarships.

The period 1988–98 saw an increase in the proportion of women scholars selected. Of the 46 South Africa-at-large scholars, 19 were women. To put this another way, these scholars were made up of 22 white men, 15 white women, 5 black men, and 4 black women. In the case of Natal, 4 of the 11 successful candidates were women, 2 black and 2 white. Of 41 schools scholars, just 1 was a woman.

The last decade of the century therefore saw increasing social diversification of scholars, beyond the traditionally homogeneous constituency of white men. White the four schools scholarships were the main source of continuity, changes in regional selections forwarded to South Africa-at-large signal social 'mining' in new soil. One of the consequences has been less and less emphasis on sporting achievements—'muscularity'—as a selection criterion for the South Africa-at-large committee. The impressive record of sporting achievements by South African scholars in previous decades will be difficult to sustain. It is also unlikely that the South African constituency will maintain its remarkable pattern of family connections among its Rhodes scholars. Three sets of grandparents and grandchildren have been scholars, as have twelve sets of parents and children.[148] Furthermore, there are two instances where three siblings have won scholarships, and twenty-two instances of two siblings doing so.

The four schools scholarships remain a distinctive feature of the South African constituency. The South African College School and Paul Roos Gymnasium survived the Trust's legal action against them, not without considerable tension between these two institutions and Trust officials, both locally and at Oxford. The story of the case, which dragged on from 1987 to 1991, is outlined elsewhere in this book. In brief, the political

---

[147] RTSA 9 (1990–6), K. Dlamini to L. Ackermann, 1 Mar. 1995, and Ackermann's reply of 23 Mar. 1995.

[148] Personal communication from L. Ackermann, 14 Oct. 1998, to whom I am grateful for drawing my attention to the phenomenon of extensive family connections.

changes of 1990 brought about a relaxing of a government policy on racially organized schooling; the parents at SACS and then Paul Roos voted to admit pupils of all races. The basis for the Trust's case against the two schools—racial exclusion—fell away, and in 1991 the Trust withdrew its application for abolition of these scholarships.

My interviews with leading figures at the four schools during 1998–9 indicated varying sensitivities to the possibility of further criticisms of their scholarships.[149] In 1993 the schools proposed an arrangement that if they did not select a scholar in any year then that scholarship should be added to the South Africa-at-large ones. This proposal, a constructive counter against future criticism, was accepted by the Trustees. The school committees remain closely connected to the national secretariat, regularly sending observers to the South Africa-at-large selections. Laurie Ackermann, in turn, ensures the presence of an observer at school selections. Each of the schools remains highly attached to its scholarship, stressing the profound influences it has on the ethos of 'rounded' leadership at the school. A strong sense of tradition permeates these boys' schools, and the Rhodes scholarship is seen as integral to this. The scholarship is important for each school's claim to be a centre of excellence at a time of uncertainty in a national schooling system undergoing post-apartheid transformation. The schools' proponents emphasize excellence and roundedness, not elitism, as their defining characteristics.[150]

The gender exclusiveness of the schools remains a possible source of continuing contention. In 1998, the St Andrew's committee, which in 1989 extended eligibility for its scholarship to matriculants of the neighbouring Diocesan School for Girls, selected its first woman Rhodes scholar, Marisa Fassler. The chances of a woman being selected from graduates of the post-matriculation class at Bishops remain slim; and there is no possibility of this happening at Paul Roos and SACS.

The political changes in South Africa, and its return to the Commonwealth, enabled the Rhodes Trust to resume benefactions to the country of its origins. Several Trustees and the new Warden at Rhodes House, Anthony Kenny, were enthusiastic promoters of this resumption. A range of social projects benefited, with the biggest grants going to education. The Rhodes Trust scholarships scheme, which continues to support black schoolchildren of potential, received a significant boost. Its annual grant totalled nearly half a million rand by 1998. In other grants, Rhodes University and the University of Cape Town were the biggest single beneficiaries, receiving money for buildings and bursaries for black students. Decades-old links, which had been severed by apartheid, have been rejuvenated. Furthermore, in 1995 the Trustees created a new scholarship for applicants from Botswana, Lesotho, Namibia, and Swaziland, adding Malawi in 1997.

The beneficence of the Rhodes Trust, and not just the Rhodes scholarships, was probably in Mamphela Ramphele's mind when she made her closing remarks at the end of the selection meeting in 1998. In stressing the significance of the scholarships as a vehicle

---

[149] Author's interviews with John Gardener of Bishops, Cape Town, 4 Dec. 1998; Derek Swart of Paul Roos, Stellenbosch, 6 Dec. 1998; Gordon Law of SACS, Cape Town, 7 Dec. 1998; and Anthony Clark of St Andrew's, Grahamstown, 29 July 1999.

[150] Author's interview with John Gardener, Cape Town, 4 Dec. 1998. Gardener drew an analogy with the All Blacks rugby team, among the world's best but drawn from New Zealand's tiny population.

for creating the leaders of the future, she would also no doubt have been thinking of the prominence in South African life of present and past Rhodes scholars. In her work, both within and beyond the university world, she would have interacted with many leading scholars. Why Rhodes scholars have become so influential remains an interesting question. George Parkin wrote in 1912: 'It is characteristic, speaking generally, of the Oxford man to play a game rather than to watch one.'[151] Bram Gie wrote in 1941 that Rhodes scholars were 'a group of fortunate individuals who had obligations to a great institution, founded on a wonderful ideal'.[152] Other Rhodes scholars, in interviews, echoed these sentiments. From these statements we gain a glimpse of the impulses behind the actions and aspirations of Rhodes scholars.

Over the past century, Oxford and South Africa have both changed a great deal, as have the Rhodes scholarships, founded on the periphery of the British Empire. A century after their founding, South Africa finds itself once again a frontier society. This time it is the frontier beyond apartheid, and the leadership challenges and opportunities are immense. At the start of their second century, the South African Rhodes scholarships face these prospects.

In 1998 the Unilever Foundation launched a new Nelson Mandela scholarship scheme for black South Africans to study in Britain.[153] Newspaper advertisements posed the question: 'Do you have what it takes to become a Nelson Mandela Scholar?' The scheme, and the question, could not make sense without reference to the scholarships initiated long ago by another, very different colossus, Cecil Rhodes.

[151] Parkin, *The Rhodes Scholarships*, 197.
[152] RTSA 1, Gie to Elton, 7 Jan. 1941.
[153] *Mail and Guardian*, 5 June 1998.

5

The Rhodes Scholarships in Australia

JOHN POYNTER

Rhodes and Australia

When Cecil Rhodes wrote his will, 'Australia' consisted of six self-governing colonies within the British Empire. As a federalist, advocate of federal structures for Southern Africa, for Britain itself as an answer to the Irish Question, for the Empire in general, and for its reunification with the United States as a new world power and peace-keeper, Rhodes used Australian examples in arguing that colonial governments should be directly represented in the Westminster Parliament, and followed the debates which culminated in the federation of the six Australian colonies into the new Commonwealth of Australia in 1901.

There were many Australians sympathetic to the imperial relationships which Rhodes sought. His spectacular successes won him a place among their recognized imperial heroes, though the fiasco of the Jameson Raid dented his reputation. When war finally erupted in South Africa, Australian criticism of the tactics of Empire was muted, and each of the six still-separate colonies enthusiastically sent contingents to fight the Boers. After Federation a new Australian patriotism reinforced their imperial loyalty, and one of the government's first acts was to send a contingent of 'Australian Commonwealth Horse' to South Africa. Rhodes's unexpected death in March 1902, a few weeks before the war ended, brought public eulogies appropriate for a hero, and even his flaws were seen as heroic in scale.

Also seen as heroic, when revealed a few weeks later, was Rhodes's strange visionary scheme for scholarships to send future leaders to Oxford, 'for their instruction in life and manners' and to instil in them the value of 'the unity of the Empire'. Rhodes's list of the qualities which new societies needed to nurture in their leaders coincided well enough with Australian values of the time, and the scholarships were generally approved; 'I was myself a boy in Australia,' a Warden of Rhodes House later wrote, 'I well remember how this great imaginative scheme was on everybody's lips in a country where the name of Oxford had strange magic and where distant England was thought of . . . as "Home".'[1] Australians whose origins were in Ireland or Scotland were not so Anglocentric, and some thought the social prejudices of 'Home' all too dominant in Australian society, but the scholarships gained such immediate prestige among the majority that everywhere the

---

[1] C. K. Allen, *Forty Years of the Rhodes Scholarships* (Oxford: Oxford University Press, 1944), 3.

annual selection of the Rhodes scholar became a major event. In Queensland the state created a perpetual trophy which the Minister of Education presented each year to the school which had nurtured that year's young paragon, the Rhodes scholar.

Although the Rhodes ideal was immediately attractive, a practicable system of selecting young Australians to become future leaders was difficult to achieve. The will, drawn up before the new Commonwealth existed, gave an annual scholarship to each of the six colonies, and in 1902 the Trustees asked the 'colonial' governments to suggest mechanisms for implementing the scheme. Public discussion in Australia began with three assumptions, all easily drawn from Rhodes's will: that the scholars would be young, probably going straight from school to Oxford; that they would be elected by their 'companions and friends'; and that they were to be 'all-rounders', with excellence in sport an absolute requirement. These notions so coincided with current educational ideals in Australia that schools began to award 'Rhodes' prizes for 'general excellence in lessons, sport and conduct', and the practice of awarding 'Rhodes Ideal' prizes even spread to girls' schools, half a century before women became eligible for Cecil Rhodes's scholarships.

Paradoxically, the 'ideal' which became etched in Australian public consciousness differed significantly from that sought by Rhodes's own Trustees, who frequently remonstrated against overemphasis on sport among the qualities sought in candidates. They also decided, from the beginning, that Rhodes scholars would be chosen rather than elected, and where possible from among university students rather than schoolboys. George Parkin, the Canadian appointed to be Organizing Secretary, was aware that colonial schoolboys would be difficult to place in Oxford colleges; 'Oxford would not lick itself into shape for the Rhodes scholars', he told a meeting in Sydney, they 'would have to accommodate themselves to Oxford'.[2] Francis Wylie, the Trust's Oxford Secretary, also wanted Rhodes scholars old enough and bright enough to adapt to Oxford and do well there.

Parkin and the States of the Nation

Parkin proved pragmatic in translating Rhodes's ideal to reality. Touring the world, he found 'practically unanimous' support in North America for requiring applicants to have attended a university, but in Australia witnessed heated debates between university and school men in 'conferences' in several of the states he visited in the later months of 1903.[3] The four universities in the six Australian states sought to control selection, but it was impossible to insist that applicants in Brisbane or Perth had undergraduate experience before the University of Queensland was founded in 1909 and that of Western Australia in 1911. In every state influential headmasters of leading schools, most of them British by birth and education, demanded that their schoolboys be eligible to compete, and that they themselves participate in selection.

---

[2] Report in *Sydney Morning Herald*, 7 Oct. 1903.
[3] George R. Parkin, report in *The Times*, 13 Oct. 1904, and *The Rhodes Scholarships* (Toronto: Copp Clark Company Ltd., 1912), 134–5.

Parkin would have liked his friend Lord Tennyson, the Governor General, to have presided over 'a general conference for Australia', but found that despite Federation 'the various states had no idea of being consulted jointly'. 'The Australasian States will have to be treated in a more individual way than any of the places yet visited,' he reported, later recalling that 'the State feeling' was so 'overwhelmingly strong' that he had 'had to make various concessions to it'.[4]

Parkin's first call in Australasia should have been Tasmania, but a case of smallpox on the island placed it in quarantine. Parkin could not land, and a group of Tasmanians later met him in Melbourne, to consider its 'distinctly peculiar' situation. 'They have an embryo University', he reported, 'which they think it is a great object to encourage by such help as these scholarships.' After discussion, the university was given a majority on the selection committee, and candidates were required to have spent at least two years enrolled there, measures which helped to fend off its critics.[5]

In New South Wales Parkin had to confront the formidable Chancellor of the University of Sydney, Sir Normand MacLaurin, 'a strong-willed and dogmatic Scot', as tough a nut as any he encountered in his journey around the world. The University had 'strongly recommended' that the scholarship be restricted to its graduates, since schoolboys were unlikely to appreciate the 'special influences' Rhodes valued, and the Chancellor now insisted that the University senate, over which he presided, was 'the only possible agency' to use in selecting the student-scholar. Parkin 'had to argue for hours' to overcome his view 'that all consultation with the Governor, the Minister of Education, Professors and Headmasters was quite superfluous'. It required a 'good deal of tact and patience' to induce 'the autocratic old Chancellor' to call a conference.[6]

Before it met, Parkin forayed north. The Queenslanders, hearing that he was likely to prefer university students, persuaded Parkin to visit Brisbane; there, 'a most interesting and useful' conference on 28 September convinced him that 'the case of Queensland is quite peculiar'. The locals were 'bent on sending younger fellows', 'as they have no university, and do not wish their lads to go to Sydney or Melbourne as preliminary to Oxford', and their schools were 'already sending very good men directly to the English Universities'. He was pleased: 'fifteen hundred miles ride for a single day's work seems a good bit of distance,' he wrote, 'but I have never felt better repaid.'[7]

Parkin returned to Sydney, in time for the 'meeting of gentlemen interested in education' reluctantly summoned by Chancellor MacLaurin. Parkin spoke for an hour, leaving the questions of age, school or collegiate standing, and methods of selection remarkably open. Not so the Chancellor, presiding; he 'relentlessly squashed the school men, the most prominent of whom sat silent and seemed afraid to speak'. The schoolmasters were routed by a large majority, which resolved that candidates should have three

---

[4] Parkin to Jameson, 9 Oct. 1903 (RTF 1256); Parkin to Grigg, 24 Mar. 1920 (RTF 2500).

[5] Parkin to Hawksley, 2 Sept. and 22 Oct. 1903 (RTF 1537).

[6] Agent General to Hawksley, 7 Oct. 1902; Parkin to Hawksley, 28 Sept. 1903; Parkin to Jameson, 9 Oct. 1903 (RTF 1256).

[7] A committee including four members elected by headmasters would select from candidates nominated by schools; enrolment at any university for more than three years disqualified (Parkin to Jameson, 9 Oct. 1903; R. H. Roe to Parkin, 17 Oct. 1903; Parkin to Hawksley, 28 Sept. 1903 (RTF 1256).)

years' standing at the University of Sydney, and that selection be 'left to the Senate of the University'.[8] The ensuing discord pursued Parkin around Australia. 'May I', the formidable headmaster of Sydney Grammar pleaded, 'write what I could not say? Were not schoolboys, and not university students, the intended beneficiaries?' But Parkin was also advised that the state schools supported the resolutions passed, and accepted the senate of the University as 'the only body in which the state schools have confidence'.[9]

'The whole affair', Parkin wrote to Hawksley, 'is very characteristic of Sydney', but he found a similar contention between 'the School and the University view' in Melbourne. Staying at the grandiose Government House in the Victorian (and temporarily federal) capital, he was fêted, but found the University dignitaries 'curiously anxious' over meeting the schoolmasters, who had 'very strongly objected' to any University involvement. The professors feared that the scholarships might be limited to schools in which 'the boys are mostly from wealthy classes', 'whose personal influence in this democratic community is comparatively limited'. This time Parkin prevailed. Selection would be made by the state's Director of Education, the president of the professorial board, and one member of the teaching staff nominated by the University; enrolment at the University was not required, but would be likely, since candidates were to be at least 19. 'The Melbourne decision was good,' Parkin reported, 'a small representative Committee of selection given a free hand in their choice.'[10]

In South Australia, Parkin stayed with another old friend, the Chief Justice and Chancellor of the University, the ubiquitous and voluble Sir Samuel Way, who believed that the scholars would be 'raw boys' unless they had some university training in Australia. Parkin noted that Adelaide University was 'likely to send exceedingly good men', but South Australia also had influential secondary schools, and it was 'very necessary to straighten out differences of opinion'. In the event three simple recommendations—that candidates be aged between 19 and 24; have lived in South Australia for four of the preceding six years; and that the selection be made by the Chief Justice and four other persons appointed annually by the University of Adelaide—received 'practically unanimous' support. The University of Adelaide gave Parkin an honorary LL D before he sailed for Western Australia.[11]

Parkin's Australian tour ended in Perth, capital of a vast province but the city in the world furthest from any other city. Western Australians were conscious of isolation in a small community which had found growth elusive until gold was discovered in the 1890s; and the state had no university to contest the view that Cecil Rhodes's scholarships were manifestly intended for schoolboys. To nurture the scholarships Parkin found a young

---

[8] *Sydney Morning Herald*, 7 and 8 Oct. Parkin's 'energetic intervention' added a provision that the senate should appoint on the advice of the professorial board (Parkin to Hawksley, 13 Oct. 1903, RTF 1155).

[9] A. B. Weigall to Parkin, 8 Oct. 1903; Francis Anderson to Parkin, 2 Nov. 1903 (RTF 1155; and printed, without comment, in Parkin's Report, pp. xxxix–xli).

[10] Parkin to Jameson, 9 Oct. 1903; J. W. Gregory to Parkin, 9 Oct. 1903; Parkin to Hawksley, 22 Oct. 1903 (RTF 1160).

[11] Way to Governor Le Hunte, 6 Aug. 1903 (Adelaide University Archives, series 434, Unregistered Correspondence 1903–18); Parkin to Hawksley, 22 Oct., 2 Nov. 1903 (RTF 1537).

classicist from Oxford, Cecil Andrews, the state's new Inspector General of Schools, who after consultation happily drafted a regulation: the scholar—who must have attended a recognized school in Western Australia for at least three years (and would be disqualified if he had ever attended a university)—would be chosen by a committee consisting of the Governor, the Chief Justice, and the Inspector General of Schools himself. Andrews persuaded Parkin to set a very low minimum age; 'the most unwilling concession I ever made to local feeling', Parkin told him later, 'was when I agreed to allow you to appoint as young as 17. I knew well that it was a mistake.'[12]

In London, in the New Year, Parkin put the six state regulations in order. He gave each selection committee the highest possible status by arranging that the Governor—the King's representative, a Briton not an Australian, nominal head of the state constitution, and actual head of local 'society'—would take the chair, and the state's Chief Justice be a member ex officio. Nevertheless it had proved impossible to achieve uniform procedures in Australia; and for nearly half a century practices continued in one Australian state or another which the Trust periodically sought to amend. Procedures eventually became formally identical, and were capped with an additional nationwide selection, but each state developed a distinctive tradition in the selection of Rhodes scholars, echoes of which persist a century later.

Picking Winners

Rhodes's will left room for disagreement over the criteria he listed. His confidant W. T. Stead recalled Rhodes himself labelling, with jocular irreverence, success in sport as 'brutality', scholarship as 'smug', and 'sympathy for the weak etc.' as 'unctuous rectitude', only 'tact and leadership' remaining unridiculed.[13] The scholarship had such high prestige in the public mind precisely because it was not a purely academic award, but balancing such disparate criteria would never be easy.

In June 1904 the New South Wales selection committee accepted the recommendation of the University's professorial board that the first scholarship be awarded, from a field which included one schoolboy, to W. A. Barton, son of Australia's first Prime Minister. Barton, who went on to win the Vinerian scholarship at Oxford and became a barrister in Britain, was a strong candidate, but his selection had been delayed while the Governor argued to the Trustees that if a graduate working as a judge's associate was eligible, it was 'little less than a farce' to allow boys to apply since they could not win.[14] He sought amendments to 'prevent the Professors of the local university using our scholarships as their own preserve', but no change had been made by February 1905, when the Committee again chose a lawyer, P. Halse Rogers, a future Chancellor of the University of Sydney. Despite internal conflicts, they were making strong appointments. Parkin then revised the regulations; henceforth, in New South Wales, all candidates had to be

[12] Andrews to Parkin, 30 Nov. 1903; Parkin to Andrews, 6 May 1920 (RTF 1014).

[13] *The Last Will and Testament of Cecil John Rhodes . . .* , ed. W. T. Stead (London: *Review of Reviews* Office, 1902), 38–9.

[14] Sir Harry Rawson to Trustees, 11 July 1904; Boyd to Parkin, 5 Dec. 1904 (RTF 1155).

undergraduates or graduates of the University of Sydney, as the Chancellor had sought; the committee was listed as the Governor, the Chief Justice, and the University ('acting on the advice of the Professorial Board'), a note defining the University representatives as the Chancellor, the Vice-Chancellor, and the chairman of the board. The Chief Justice, displeased, declined 'to be party to so transparent a breach of trust and one which entirely defeats the manifest intention of the Testator'.[15]

The University of Sydney dominated the New South Wales selection for the next forty years, developing unique procedures. Parkin had urged committees to consider 'the votes of fellow students' concerning success in sport and 'manhood etc.', and all states began with some form of certification of approval by candidates' schools or universities, but only New South Wales constructed an elective system within a single institution. The professorial board made its recommendation to the selection committee only after receiving formal assessments of the applicants from the University's sports union (awarding up to twenty points for 'fondness for and success in manly outdoor sports'), the undergraduate association (up to thirty for 'qualities of manhood, truth etc.'), and the board itself (up to twenty for 'moral force of character etc.'); a further thirty were awarded for 'literary and scholastic attributes' on the basis of the candidate's academic record. The board at first followed the arithmetical marks allotted with little question, and the selection committee—which believed it could not act without a recommendation from the board—interviewed the preferred candidate only as a formality. The process favoured all-rounders, such as G. V. Portus, selected for 1907, who played rugby for England in 1908, was ordained a clergyman in 1911, and became an influential professor of history and political science in Adelaide. In 1910 the professorial board split seven votes to five (with one abstention), the majority favouring J. R. Hooton (later a successful barrister) over Carleton Kemp Allen, who had been given maximum marks for scholarship and a middling rank for character, but only two out of twenty for sport. Allen went to Oxford nevertheless, became a fellow of University College and a noted legal author, and in 1931 was appointed Warden of Rhodes House.

In Victoria, the University of Melbourne had no formal role in slection other than providing three of the six members of the committee, which included also the state Director of Education (Frank Tate, a powerful figure on the committee for the next twenty-three years). The requirement that each applicant provide a certificate from his 'School or College' that he had been selected as the candidate 'who best fulfilled the ideas of Mr Rhodes' bequest' opened the door to the three powerful—and competing—Protestant denominational residential colleges affiliated with the University (Trinity, Ormond, and Queen's). In June 1904, after interviewing nine candidates, the committee 'unanimously selected' J. C. V. Behan, a young law graduate from Trinity.

The decision raised a storm. The favoured candidate elected by Trinity's undergraduates was not Behan, a brilliant scholar, but Harvey Sutton, an athletic medical student, and Behan's lack of a 'sporting record' caused fierce complaint. His professor of law

---

[15] Barff to Parkin, 7 Nov. 1905; Parkin to Barff, 18 Dec. 1905 (RTF 1155); Parkin, 'Schemes for the Selection of the Rhodes Scholars', 27 July 1905 (RTF 2560), and 'The Rhodes Scholarships in Australia' (RTF 2557).

remarked that attempting three honours schools at once (and gaining firsts in all three) meant that he 'clearly had no time for sport'. Sporting organizations were not so easily mollified: a meeting of protest was 'crammed to the very door', and resolutions condemning the selectors and asking the Trustees to cancel the nomination were carried with 'acclaim'. Reports of the meeting filled columns in the newspapers.[16]

The selection committee submitted that 'provided the candidate shows that he possesses generally the qualifications of manhood, force of character, etc. he should be eligible for the scholarship whether he does or does not possess a distinct record in sports'. The Trustees accepted the committee's argument. Mutterings from the sporting organizations were muted a few months later when the Victorian committee chose for the 1905 scholarship the popular Harvey Sutton, though his selection raised a new problem: having already completed his medical degree, he wished to undertake research, an activity still regarded as unusual in Oxford. Parkin immediately saw that 'the kind of thing' he was aiming at would have 'great significance in the future for our Trust'; 'I shall be much interested to . . . know precisely how the University deals with such a student, and how you deal with the opportunity to prosecute original work'.[17] Sutton completed a B.Sc. in physiology (and became, as a professor in Sydney, a powerful advocate of public health, especially of children).

After the fuss of the first year, the selection of the Victorian Rhodes scholar became a peaceful and almost private process. Committee membership was very stable, and since scholars were often selected only at their second attempt, each year there were familiar faces among the candidates as well as the committee.

In Tasmania, selection of the scholar for 1904 was delayed by the Trust addressing the regulation to an outgoing Governor, the letter following him 'Home'; eventually L. N. Morrison, an arts student who had also been in residence in Trinity College Melbourne, was selected.[18] The new Governor was the able and awkward Sir Gerald Strickland, whose extraordinary career included dismissal as Governor of New South Wales and the prime ministership of Malta; as Governor of Tasmania 1904–9, Western Australia 1909–13, and New South Wales 1913–17 he chaired three Rhodes selection committees over thirteen years. The Tasmanian committee's practice was to interview two or three applicants, after excluding others (if any: there were never more than five). Since Tasmania did not have engineering or medical schools, most of the early applicants were enrolled in arts or law.

In South Australia, the other state with a university, the process of selection ran smoothly, in a stately routine: applications were received in sealed envelopes, and the committee met formally to open them, later meeting again to interview and choose. Decisions were always unanimous, and never criticized (according to one member, apparently deaf to several grumbles noted in the records).[19] Perhaps because the committee included a future Nobel Laureate in physics and another influential FRS, it developed a habit of choosing

[16] The account is Behan's own, published much later in the *Hobart Mercury*, 11 May 1928.
[17] Parkin to Sutton, 2 Nov. 1905 (RTF 1160).
[18] Sir John Dodds to Parkin, 15 July 1904 (RTF 1542).
[19] Sir George Murray to Dawson, 11 July 1922 (RTF 1531).

graduate scientists or medicos, leavened with an occasional lawyer. By coincidence, the first two South Australian scholars took the new course in forestry at Oxford, with notable success: N. W. Jolley (1904) returned to Adelaide as professor of forestry, and the illustrious R. L. Robinson (1905), later chairman of the British Forestry Commission, was the first Rhodes scholar to be knighted and the first to be made a peer.

In Queensland, a state without a university, the selection committee included four members elected by headmasters: a Prussian-born provincial businessman (president of the Hebrew Congregation); a solicitor-politician (a leading Catholic layman, said to be 'as straight as a gun barrel and as nimble as a possum'); the state's leading barrister (a prominent Anglican); and a Liverpool-born, Harrow-and-Balliol-educated barrister.[20] In July 1904 four schools each sent forward the applicant 'who best fulfils the ideas of Mr Rhodes' bequest', and the first scholar chosen was A. S. Roe, son of the headmaster who had devised the method of selection. In 1911 the establishment of the University prompted the appointment, in place of the four members elected by the headmasters, of the Chancellor, the president of the University's board of faculties and two members chosen by senate. Parkin approved, but stipulated that after 1915 the minimum age of applicants be raised from 18 to 19, and that once the new university was recognized by Oxford two years' university experience would be required of candidates.[21] After 1912 the Queensland committee's structure resembled that of New South Wales, and it also adopted Sydney's habit of consulting—though less formally—undergraduate organizations.

In Western Australia, Andrews reported in 1904 a 'very smooth' beginning for his committee of three, although 'of course' the field was very small, with only four schools capable of 'sending in candidates'.[22] J. L. Walker was chosen unanimously; 19 when he reached Oxford, Walker read law, became a judge of the Supreme Court, and a long-serving member of the selection committee. The private schools, which produced all the early Rhodes scholars in the west, 'bitterly opposed' the involvement of the secondary schools begun by the state after 1910. The argument became public in 1912, when a technical school student was ruled ineligible by the committee, and 'heated discussion' in the Perth press produced a proposal to send the excluded student to Oxford by public subscription. In July the *Sun* jubilantly reported 'A GROSS INJUSTICE REMEDIED: The disqualification of a State school boy simply because he is a State school boy will not be repeated.' The 'second scholar' left for Oxford on the same boat as the Rhodes scholar, while Parkin warned the Trustees that 'the argument that the scholarships are intended only for the use of poor men' could 'harm our representation at Oxford'.[23]

The opening of the University of Western Australia in 1913 enabled the Trustees to enlarge the committee to seven, including two representatives of the University and two members elected by the heads of secondary schools. Parkin then raised the age limit, in

---

[20] A. M. Hertzberg, the Hon. A. J. Thynne MLC, A. H. H. M. Feez, and W. A. B. Shand respectively.
[21] Parkin to Macgregor, 5 Apr. 1911 and 8 Mar. 1912; Governor to Parkin, 18 Dec. 1911 (RTF 1113); RTM 3 Apr. 1911.
[22] Andrews to Parkin, 23 Oct. 1904; Parkin to Andrews, 11 May 1905 (RTF 1014).
[23] Andrews to Parkin, 12 Mar. 1912; Parkin to Andrews, 11 Apr. 1912; Memorandum to Trustees, n.d. (RTF 1014); *Sun*, 28 July 1912.

two stages, to 19. Even that was too low for Wylie, who in 1914 told an envoy of the South Australian committee that he 'dreaded' taking responsibility for youths of 19.[24]

The First Rhodes Scholars

Most of the early Australian Rhodes scholars were drawn from the schools whose head-masters had sought to control the process of selection; naturally enough, since their schools, based on the English public school model (and usually linked with a Protestant religious denomination), provided most of the country's secondary education, sharing the task with a limited number of schools established by the states or by Roman Catholic orders. In most states certain schools (and university colleges) dominated the competition; since these institutions were fee-paying, most of their students came from relatively affluent backgrounds, but scholarships gave entry to many boys from less well-off families, including J. C. V. Behan and R. L. Robinson (who had 'kept up the study of Greek' while employed in the Golden Horseshoe Mine in Western Australia).

Again, there were differences between states. In New South Wales, which had strong state high schools, success in the University of Sydney's undergraduate environment was the main prerequisite. In Victoria, where the state entered secondary education much later, all but one of Victoria's first twenty Rhodes scholars came from church-affiliated schools and university colleges, none Roman Catholic.[25] In Tasmania the Protestant schools also dominated selection in the first decades, as they did in South Australia (though Christian Brothers' College, Adelaide, won one). In Western Australia, where all the secondary schools were 'independent' until 1911, Christian Brothers' College, Perth, produced four and distant Kalgoorlie High School one. Regional schools scored well in Queensland, the Australian state least dominated by its capital city (and unusual also in that the grammar schools, although independent in status, were state-supported); Brisbane Grammar School scored ten, but eight came from provincial schools, and three had attended the Christian Brothers' College, Nudgee.

Some diversity in social background among the first Rhodes scholars is discernible. A. Juett (Western Australia and Brasenose 1906) had left school 'to work as a miner on the Murchison Goldfield', before his father, then 'a working miner', decided to send him to Christian Brothers' College, Perth; and H. H. L. A. Brose (South Australia and Christ Church 1913), 'a scientist whose career was unusually varied and personal life unusually troubled', was the son of a hairdresser, a recent immigrant from Germany.[26] The father of G. F. E. Hall (Queensland and Lincoln 1910) was black, said to be from Tobago; he had worked as a carter and miner on the Charters Towers goldfield and married an Eng-lishwoman, and their son George won a scholarship from a state primary school to

[24] Parkin to Strickland, 9 Oct. 1911 and 6 Feb. 1912; Strickland to Parkin, 14 Nov. 1911; Parkin to Trustees, 21 Jan. 1912 (RTF 1014); G. C. Henderson to Hodge, SA Minute Book, 5 Nov. 1914.

[25] J. C. Eccles (1925), a future Nobel Laureate and probably the first Roman Catholic selected in Victoria, was a member of Newman College, opened in 1918.

[26] Andrews to Parkin, 29 June 1906 (RTF 1014); 'Jenkin, John', *Australian Dictionary of Biography* entry, and 'Henry Herman Leopold Adolph Brose: Vagaries of an Extraordinary Australian Scientist', *Historical Records of Australian Science*, 12/3 (June 1999), 287–312.

Townsville Grammar. There he excelled—in six sports, as a scholar, and as head prefect—and the whole school enthusiastically supported his application for the Rhodes scholarship. The selection committee 'had no difficulty' in selecting him 'as entitled to the appointment on his records and credentials', and, after considering Rhodes's stipulation that no student should be disqualified 'on account of his race or religious opinions', came to the conclusion that 'his paternity should not debar him'. The school's Old Boys and Charters Towers business men raised £70 for Hall's fare, but even his supporters were apprehensive lest Hall's 'colour and appearance' should tell against him in Oxford.[27] Hall was accepted by Lincoln, and Parkin became his mentor, advising him frankly on his course and career; he took a creditable second in engineering, and returned to Australia after war service to hold senior positions in Sydney.[28]

Some Australians found it hard to cope with Oxford's narrow society: Halse Rogers, son of a Sydney Methodist minister, liked England but complained of being treated as a 'colonial', and that 'in all the three years I did not get on very friendly terms with any Englishman'. Harry Thomson (South Australia and Balliol 1910), working towards a first in jurisprudence in Balliol, wrote of the common colonial experience of being at first dazzled by the fluency with which English students discussed subjects of which he knew nothing, and then disillusioned by the superficiality he found when they discussed something he knew about.[29]

There were other Rhodes scholars to meet in Oxford, as well as Englishmen. In June 1909 R. G. Waddy (New South Wales and Balliol 1908) was among more than fifty from all parts of the Empire who heard the 'imperialist and idealist' Kingsley Fairbridge (Rhodesia and Exeter 1908) address the Colonial Club on 'The Emigration of Poor Children to the Colonies'. While still a child, Fairbridge had formed a vision of peopling the 'vacant' regions of the Empire with the 'unwanted' children of Britain, and the 'colonials' were moved to form the Child Emigration Society that same evening. Child emigration as a form of 'child saving'—although vilified in the late twentieth century—had become in the nineteenth a major philanthropic cause, in which the Trust was already interested. When his first schemes for farm schools in Rhodesia and Canada fell through, Fairbridge and his wife settled on a small mixed farm at Pinjarra, Western Australia, where, in primitive conditions, they received thirty-five Poor Law 'orphan' boys from Britain in 1913, before war stopped the flow.[30]

Almost all the first Australian Rhodes scholars met Oxford's intellectual demands, and some performed spectacularly well. Behan entered in his second year for both the BCL

[27] Arthur Feez to Wylie, 5 Mar. 1910. His headmaster implored Parkin to get him into a suitable college ('as Hall is a Methodist, Keble is impossible for him'): A. F. Rowland to Parkin, 11 July 1910 (RTF 1113). The Trustees, confirming his appointment, noted the election of a 'coloured man'.

[28] 'I have urged him to do his very best to make a success of his Oxford course. If he can do this, it will mean more than anything else for any coloured men who come after. . . . There is something very pathetic in the present situation of things for able and energetic men of his race' (Parkin to Wylie, 7, 13 Sept. 1910; Parkin to Rowland, 21 Sept. 1910; RTF 1113).

[29] J. M. Bennett, 'Sir Percival Halse Rogers', *Australian Dictionary of Biography*, vol. xi; H. Thomson to 'Mr Grundy', 7 May 1911 (RTF 1537).

[30] Geoffrey Sherington and Chris Jeffery, *Fairbridge, Empire and Child Migration* (London: Woburn Press, 1999), is the best account of the Fairbridge movement; they cite the principal critics (pp. xi–xiii).

and the honour school of jurisprudence, despite two papers falling at the same time; he completed each in half the time allowed, sprinting from one examination room to the other with unwonted speed, and took firsts in both degrees, winning also the Vinerian and Eldon scholarships, and in 1909 a fellowship—the first to be won by a Rhodes scholar—at University College. When the Trust issued a printed report for 1906–7 it listed seven distinctions won by Rhodes scholars; four had been won by Australians.[31]

The academic activities of the Australian universities were more heavily directed towards professional courses than Oxford's predominant fields of scholarship. Of the first sixty Australian Rhodes scholars, selected between 1904 and 1913, over half chose courses at Oxford related to medicine (sixteen) or law (fifteen). Two read forestry, three engineering, and eight other areas of science, while six studied history and five classics. Not all the scholars made their careers in their original fields of study, but by the mid-1920s the professions of law (fifteen) and medicine (fourteen) were still their predominant occupations. A further nineteen made careers as teachers, in universities or schools, and two in business. Only three had entered politics, fewer than the public seems to have expected.

The First World War

The *Sydney Bulletin*, never sympathetic to 'the Rhodes ideal', remarked after the First World War that the Australian Rhodes scholars had pulled less than their weight in that conflict.[32] That was scarcely true of the scholars at Oxford in 1914, virtually all of whom either interrupted their courses or postponed their careers to serve in British regiments. The Trust had allowed C. T. Madigan (South Australia and Magdalen 1911) to delay taking up his scholarship to enable him to join Mawson's Antarctic Expedition; he came up to Magdalen in 1914 with a King's Polar Medal among his accoutrements, left for France after one term, and did not return until 1919. E. F. Herring (Victoria and New College 1912), beginning a notable military career, earned the rank of major and a DSO. Of the 1913 scholars, five served in the forces and the sixth, the young physicist H. H. L. A. Brose (South Australia), had an unusual war; interned while visiting Germany in 1914, he lectured fellow prisoners in mathematics and translated important German books on physics into English.[33]

The Trust permitted scholars to defer taking up their awards, and selection continued, accommodating as best it could applicants already overseas on service. Most of those selected in Australia after 1914 served in the Australian forces, in the Middle East or France; H. W. B. Cairns, later to be the first Nuffield Professor of Surgery at Oxford, was already serving with the Australian Medical Corps when selected for South Australia

---

[31] Wylie tells of the Behan coup in Lord Elton (ed.), *The First Fifty Years of the Rhodes Trust and the Rhodes Scholarships 1903–1953* (Oxford: Basil Blackwell, 1955), 85.

[32] 'Rhodes' disappointing Scholars', *Bulletin*, 24 Oct. 1928.

[33] Jenkin, 'Henry Herman Leopold Adolph Brose: Vagaries of an Extraordinary Australian Scientist', 292–3.

for 1917. Thirty-seven of the forty-one scholars selected between 1911 and 1917, and twenty-two of the thirty-six scholars selected before 1911, served in the First World War, while thirteen candidates with war service were selected after the war ended.

In March 1918 all elections were suspended until after the war. When the Trustees decided to resume selection, in May 1919, they asked that the 1918 and 1919 scholars be elected by October, and scholars for both 1920 and 1921 in October 1920, resuming the normal timetable thereafter. Each committee had to select four scholars in sixteen months; many candidates were still overseas with the forces, and some fields were small, prompting Tasmania and South Australia to seek permission to delay selecting their 1921 scholars. In Adelaide, postponement inconvenienced H. W. Florey, a boot manufacturer's son, one of only three applicants when the 1920 and 1921 scholarships were advertised together. Florey explained that his application was for the 1921 scholarship only; moreover he wished to delay entry to finish his medical degree and to avoid having 'to begin all over again'. The Committee sought and gained the Trustees' approval for deferment some months before Florey was actually selected for the scholarship. The future Nobel Laureate—and only Rhodes scholar, so far, with a memorial in Westminster Abbey—was a persistent man.

Australia-at-Large

Parkin retired in 1920. In the decades between the wars his immediate successors—Edward Grigg and Geoffrey Dawson—lacked his instinctive understanding of dominion views; the sympathies of Philip Kerr, Secretary from 1925, were broader, and C. K. Allen, who succeeded Wylie in 1931, would have been an Australian Rhodes scholar himself had the close vote in Sydney gone the other way.

Grigg toured Australia in 1920, as military secretary to the Prince of Wales—a delicate task, since the Prince was inclined to have too many late nights and (as the Governor General tactfully put it) become 'nervous'—and drew three 'initial' conclusions: that states with small populations had 'too great an advantage'; that 'old Rhodes Scholars' should be involved in selection; and that (in the view of 'real enthusiasts for the Rhodes idea') the scholars chosen were 'not at present pulling the weight expected of them'.[34] These three themes became the basis for new policies.

Grigg had instructions to devise procedures for the award of a 'special Scholarship' for 1920, in consultation with Behan, who had returned to Australia in 1918 to be Warden of Trinity, his old Melbourne college. The award, for Australia-at-Large, was the first—and for fifty-seven years the only—Rhodes scholarship awarded in Australia on a national rather than state basis. Behan devised an intricate process: the scholars in each state, meeting for the first time in committees, chose the strongest local applicant, and a special selection committee, chaired by the Governor General, met in Melbourne to make the final selection. The committee chose W. K. Hancock, a brilliant young Melbourne historian then lecturing in Western Australia. Hancock, whose illustrious career was to be

---

[34] Report, attached to Grigg to Lord Milner, 7 Oct. 1920 (RTF 2500).

divided between Oxford, Adelaide, London, and Canberra, had also been placed first in a special ballot by all Rhodes scholars.[35]

Grigg concluded from the process that the six existing Rhodes scholarships should no longer be awarded by the individual states but allocated to Australia-at-large.[36] Behan warned that such a change would 'create an outcry in the less advanced States', and a legal opinion that such radical reorganization would be 'directly contrary' to the wishes of the testator froze the matter. The major American reorganization made possible by the Rhodes Trust Act of 1929 passed Australia by.

The Trustees contemplated allotting a continuing seventh scholarship for Australia-at-large, but the local scholars said they would prefer the money used to raise stipends. Australia was distant, the Trust did not pay fares, and scholars had to maintain themselves in vacations. Behan wanted the value of Rhodes scholarships 'equalized', by giving more to those from distant constituencies, but in 1925 the Trust's emissary Dr J. M. Rendall recommended instead negotiations with the shipping lines for scholars to receive free passages (which was done). He also reported against the additional scholarship, which remained in abeyance.[37]

Measures of Reform

If Australian selection could not be centralized, it could at least be coordinated. In 1921 the state governors were told that 'Jock' Behan had been appointed 'general secretary for Rhodes scholarships in Australia'. The new Secretary would 'take no part in the selection of Rhodes scholars', but was to be 'the normal channel of communication' between the Trustees and selection committees, who would no longer write directly to Oxford.[38]

The Western Australians, prone to secessionist impulses at this time, exploded in fury against the appointment of an Australian Secretary from the distant 'east'. Melbourne, the selection committee insisted, was 2,000 miles further from England than Perth, and West Australians 'would not think that they were adequately represented' by anyone living in Melbourne. The Governor underlined the point: 'Perhaps I might be permitted to personally say that Western Australia has nothing whatever to do with the State of Victoria . . . except that both States belong to the Australian Federation. . . . It would be undesirable for any gentleman from Melbourne, however distinguished, or from any other part of Australia, to give us advice usefully as to our selection of Rhodes Scholars. It would be impossible for him to give you advice as to what we should do thereon.'[39] The Trustees backed off, allowed candidates' papers to continue to be sent direct to Oxford, and told their new General Secretary—whose happy acceptance of the post had

---

[35] Grigg to Parkin, 14 June 1920; Behan to Parkin, 2 Aug. and 14 Oct. 1920 (RTF 2500).
[36] Memorandum, 3 June 1921 (wrongly dated 1931) (RTF 2524). Grigg argued that 'pooling' would enable the central selection committee to direct scholars into 'better' fields, and proposed asking dominion prime ministers to guarantee returned scholars jobs in public service.
[37] Report, 11.
[38] Dawson to Governors, 23 Sept. 1921. The position was offered to Behan on 1 July 1921 (RTF 2554).
[39] Sir Francis Newdegate to Dawson, 8 Nov. 1921 (RTF 2554).

been clouded by the Perth protest—to delay his planned grand tour, in which he, a lawyer by instinct as well as training, had hoped to achieve 'the adoption of uniform conditions throughout the States'.[40]

In 1922 the Trustees further informed selection committees that they wished to 'associate' former Rhodes scholars 'with the work of selecting their successors'; naming two 'senior ex-Scholars' in each state', they proposed that at least one be added to the committee immediately. The change did not give Australian scholars the whole carriage of selection, which the Western Australian Rhodes scholars (but not others) continued to seek.[41]

How many Rhodes scholars should be on each committee, and who should choose them, became an issue in most states. In Tasmania the committee discerned a 'plot' to create a committee solely of Rhodes scholars, and resigned en masse; reassured and re-appointed, they agreed to add two Rhodes scholar members. In South Australia the existing committee argued that its membership was already excellent, and the Trust accepted that the two nominated Rhodes scholars sit with 'some or all' of the existing committee. The New South Wales committee, after some argument, allowed the newly formed Fellowship of Rhodes Scholars to join the student groups as an adviser to the professorial board.[42]

In 1927 a new Memorandum on the Constitution of Selection Committees introduced several provisions which remained unchanged for decades, though it took almost as long to have them all adopted. Committees should have between five and seven members, including at least two of 'public eminence', at least two Rhodes scholars ('suggested by them'), 'representatives of the legal profession and from the business world', and one member who had been in residence in Oxford in the previous ten years. No appointment should be made for more than five years, and 'fresh blood' ought to be introduced into selection committees at least every few years. In response to the document the eight members of the South Australian committee agreed they should reduce themselves to seven, and waited for someone to die or leave Adelaide. In New South Wales the *Memorandum* provoked a battle between the Rhodes scholars and the University for control of selection; the scholars did not win a majority, but—after Kerr had intervened—the committee at last took the power of decision from the professorial board, which in future would advise on academic matters only.[43]

In 1930 Behan brought from Oxford a new requirement: the Trustees had decided to end ex officio membership of committees, though Behan had won—with difficulty—agreement that governors could continue to be chairmen. Change came easily in four states, although in Adelaide the committee, after agreeing that the Chief Justice be no longer an ex officio member, promptly continued him as an ordinary member. In Sydney,

[40] Behan to Dawson, 18 Nov. 1921 (RTF 2554); RTM 17 Jan. 1922.
[41] Dawson to Behan, 18 Oct. 1921 (RTF 2500); Dawson to Chairman, 8 May 1922 and 26 July 1922 (RTF 1014).
[42] Nicholls to Dawson, 8 May 1922 (RTF 1542); Sir George Murray to Dawson, 11 July 1922 (Australian Secretary's Files), Behan to Grigg, 31 Mar. 1924; Minutes of meeting, 8 July 1924, sent to Grigg by MacCallum (RTF 1155).
[43] South Australian minutes of 9 June 1928; Behan to Kerr, 18 June 1928 (RTF 2500); Portus to Behan, 19 Mar. 1929; Kerr to Behan, 26 July 1929 (RTF 1155).

Behan retreated when the three ex officio members of the committee threatened to resign; he advised the Trust that selection by the former scholars alone 'would certainly not command the confidence of the public in New South Wales'.[44] In Queensland, when Behan reported failure, the Trustees asked Sir Francis Wylie, visiting Australia, 'to settle it'. He did so, finding the Queenslanders less 'difficult' than Behan had suggested. Even in Sydney (which was too busy opening its new Harbour Bridge to hold a committee meeting), members he saw seemed amenable, his experience confirming Oxford's suspicion that Behan increased his own difficulties by antagonizing committees.[45]

Despite these reforms, the committees changed little. Senior officers, previously ex officio members, stayed on as men of 'public eminence', and few committees enforced the principle of 'rotation', some 'eminent' members of committees serving for very long periods. But committees continued to do their tasks conscientiously, and—judging by results—well.

Who to Choose, Revisited

Grigg's concern that 'Rhodes cannot have wanted merely to manufacture new brass plates for Macquarie Street' was widely shared, though the nature of the ideal Rhodes scholar, and how to ensure he was selected, was a matter of many opinions. Grigg's own model was one more readily conceived in Balliol than in Brisbane: a scholar should take humanities at Oxford, and enter the dominion civil services ('which are at a low level everywhere'), or the teaching profession ('which is in constant need for better men'), or journalism ('where the lack of them is a danger for the whole Imperial movement'), and ('ultimately as one hopes') politics.[46]

The political views of several post-war Rhodes scholars proved hard for their predecessors to accept, although a Victorian candidate who offered a 'short address' on socialism as the 'remedy for many evils' in Australia was said by the Governor not to have prejudiced his chances: 'a definite political philosophy would with the Committee as I know it be a point in favour of the candidate.' Not with P. M. Hamilton (Victoria and Balliol 1917), principal of a Queensland school, who remarked publicly in 1926 that he regarded 'with contempt any man who would accept a Rhodes Scholarship and then preach doctrines subversive to the very principles for which those scholarships stand'. He referred to P. R. Stephensen (Queensland and Queen's 1924), who in January 1926 had been summoned before the proctors for distributing 'Communistic' propaganda among Indian students, and required by the Vice-Chancellor to give a guarantee that he would cease, or be sent down.[47]

[44] Behan to Kerr, 12 Nov. 1930; Kerr to Behan, 23 Dec. 1930 (RTF 2500).
[45] 'Report by the Late Oxford Secretary on his Tour in Australasia', Apr. 1932, esp. pp. 20–1; Wylie to Selection Committees, 12 Apr. 1932 (Australian Secretary's files); Behan to Lothian, 29 June 1932 (RTF 1160).
[46] Report attached to Grigg to Lord Milner, 7 Oct. 1920 (RTF 2500). Macquarie Street was the Harley Street of Sydney.
[47] Brisbane Courier, 20 and 26 Oct. 1926. Stephensen had to promise to 'hold no communication, direct or indirect, with any organised Communist association', and not to 'endeavour to propagate Communist views, either directly or indirectly'.

'Oxford Sensation. Communist Propaganda. Queensland Rhodes Scholar on the Carpet', the *Brisbane Courier* had trumpeted on 21 January. Stephensen gave the Vice-Chancellor his promise, but complained to Wylie that he regarded himself as a student with only 'a theoretical interest in politics while in that status'. Wylie believed that there was 'no doubt that Stephensen has been engaged in secret propaganda of a revolutionary nature on behalf of the Communist Party in Oxford', and Stephensen, writing in the *Brisbane Standard*, identified himself as a 'Communist Rhodes Scholar'. He claimed that he had offered to resign his scholarship but had been told that political considerations did not affect its tenure: Rhodes scholars were not morally bound to support 'Imperialist politics'. The scholarships were 'a public utility' open to all 'without political prejudice', and no 'Tory-minded clique' in Queensland should 'discriminate against Communist or Socialist students on political grounds'.[48] (Conservatives in Queensland were no doubt cheered by remarks attributed to the triple blue and rugby international 'Tommy' Lawton (1921) on his return from Oxford in 1925: 'I am going to be a farmer in Queensland. My B.A. will be useful when I am feeding my pigs'.[49]) 'Inky' Stephensen returned to Australia in 1931, to a literary-political career which was public enough if scarcely acceptable in all circles as always one of service.

Stephensen was not alone in finding much to deplore in post-war politics and society. A. W. Wheen (New South Wales and New College 1919), who had won an MM with two bars in France, became a prominent London pacifist and translator of Remarque's *All Quiet on the Western Front*. Hancock, enjoying a belated adolescence touring Tuscany in the early 1920s, was repelled by the early manifestations of fascism, and used his newly won All Souls fellowship to write about a nineteenth-century Italian liberal patriot. Other Australian scholars at Oxford in the 1920s usually found post-war life enjoyably relaxed. R. R. Sholl (Victoria and New College 1924), the all-rounder credited with introducing the annual Australian Rules football match between Oxford and Cambridge, happily told a Melbourne paper he was 'lost in admiration of the self-possession and sangfroid of the English "freshers", who . . . converse at the table in extempore Latin hexameters, and lightly demolish the cherished deliveries of cabinet ministers. They are a type we do not have at home.'[50]

Views from Britain

When, in 1925, the Trustees sent the opinionated, richly moustached Dr M. J. Rendall, headmaster of Winchester, on a tour of Rhodes constituencies, his brief was ill defined, but he proved happy to lecture anyone on Rhodes's ideals, English literature, 'and especially on the Ideals of English Public Schools'. He found all the Australian selection

---

[48] Wylie to the Secretary of the Queensland Selection Committee; the Trustees had discussed the incident on 26 Jan. 1926. *Brisbane Standard*, 7 Jan. 1927. On Stephensen, see Craig Munro, *Wild Man of Letters: the Story of P. R. Stephensen* (Melbourne: Melbourne University Press, 1984).

[49] *Sydney Evening News*, 19 Mar. 1925 ('T. Lawton, Rhodes scholar and famous footballer, returns'). His BA was in fact in agriculture.

[50] *Argus*, 19 Mar. 1925; *Isis*, 28 Jan. 1927.

committees 'conscientious and efficient'; privately he was convinced they were 'too academic, and that you want a kind of Public School Governing Body: a good doctor and a good general are additional possibilities.' He made a similar judgement of the Australian Secretary, as 'a nervous, fussy, academic fellow, just the sort of fellow we don't want'.[51]

Rendall would have selected schoolboys as Rhodes scholars—if only Australian schools were good enough. Australia did not have 'a different type of education', like America, merely one that lacked 'breadth and inspiration', and which faced 'one great difficulty', not felt in English public schools: 'how to reconcile culture and advanced education with democratic ideas'. Rendall's ideal Rhodes scholar would be a scholar (but not too academic), a sportsman (but a gentleman), and a man of affairs (rather than a member of a profession). Few Australian Rhodes scholars met those standards: in Brisbane he was put off by finding 'one very prominent Bolshevist among them', and in Melbourne he provoked lively discussion by remarking that 'no Victorian Rhodes scholar has yet won marked distinction outside the academic or scholastic field'. The *Bulletin* agreed: 'the RHODES system has given us many "blues", but never a statesmen or leader of note'. Rendall's further suggestion that in time women might also be awarded Rhodes scholarships was reported without comment.[52]

Rendall's concept of a Rhodes scholar was tested when, visiting Hobart, he walked into a row over the most recent selection. In January 1925 a member of the House of Commons asked Grigg to investigate why one Wilson had been chosen ahead of his nephew, and Grigg asked Rendall to investigate.[53] He reported that two very strong candidates from Hutchins School (one of them the nephew) had both been 'turned down in favour of a comparatively inconspicuous boy from a Government School', provoking complaints in the press that 'the wrong type of man'—a commerce student—had been chosen. Rendall publicly rebuked the critics; he had met the new scholar, who intended studying politics and economics at Oxford. 'There can be no better door to public life,' Rendall insisted, but his heart was not in it; privately he reported that the committee had been 'overpersuaded by the insistence and enthusiasm of the representatives of modern education and the Government Schools to make an unwise choice'.[54] He thought the new Rhodes scholar 'an attractive little fellow; but he could by no stretch of the imagination be described as a "leader of men"'. His imagination was proved insufficiently elastic: (Sir) Roland Wilson, the scholar in question, became one of Australia's most powerful public servants, serving as Secretary of the Department of Labour

[51] *Report*, 6–9; Rendall to Grigg, 18 Apr. 1925.

[52] *Report*, 6, 19; *Herald*, 20 Oct. 1925; *Bulletin*, 4 June 1925; *Herald*, 10 Mar. 1925. The 'Bolshevist' in Queensland was F. W. Paterson (1918), who 'went to Oxford a meek boy beloved of church dignitaries'— he studied theology there—'and returned an atheist and red-hot Socialist': *Bulletin*, 17 Sept. 1925. He was tried (and acquitted) for sedition after a speech in Brisbane in 1930 (*Brisbane Daily Telegraph*, 16 May 1930).

[53] R. Hamilton to Grigg, 28 Jan. 1925 (RTF 1542).

[54] The election had become 'a battle between the old learning, the humanities . . . and the so-called "Economics" School, which is mainly a training for business and is at present enjoying much popularity' (Rendall, Report, 20–1; Rendall to Grigg, 25 Mar. 1925; *Hobart Mercury*, 13 Dec. 1924 and 23 Mar. 1925).

and National Service during the war and as Secretary to the Treasury for fifteen years from 1951.[55]

When not to

Two selection committees took to heart the Trustees' pleas to maintain high standards in selection. In December 1926 the South Australian committee decided to appoint none of the applicants before it; Adelaide accepted the decision, but when the Tasmanian committee reached a similar conclusion the following year a public meeting in Hobart demanded that this slight to Tasmanian youth be reversed. The state had been 'robbed of £1,000' it could ill afford to lose. The Trustees expressed full confidence in the committee, provoking a sour complaint in the *Hobart Mercury* that the Prime Minister of Great Britain and his ilk were as usual not interested in the rights of a distant island people.[56]

Behan, peacemaking, presented to the selection committee in April a paper on selection procedures, which was then 'handed to the press for publication'. He rejected appeals to make public, as a guide to candidates, the Trustees' instructions to selection committees; too much deliberate grooming was already an 'inherent weakness of the Rhodes Scholarship system'.

Almost from the cradle every male child of unusual promise is encouraged, first by fond parents and later by ambitious schoolmasters, to fix his eagle eye upon the Rhodes Scholarships as the crowning point of his academic career . . . he is incited . . . to win his way into the good graces of his contemporaries . . . in order that . . . making him a member of numberless committees may give proof of his astounding popularity, strength of character, and qualities of leadership; to the same end he is urged to attend prayer meetings, write poetry, cultivate the art of rhetoric, edit magazines . . . and so on ad nauseam.

The publication of Rhodes's 'unusual conditions' had 'most unhappily created in the public mind the utterly erroneous notion of the "good all-round man"'. Hence 'the assiduity with which candidates compile records subtly calculated to entrap committees of selection into the delusion that they are prodigies of learning, physical prowess and moral perfection'.[57]

The statement did not please the Tasmanians, but the Trustees supported Behan strongly: 'Nothing could be worse for the Rhodes Scholarship system than that the idea should become common that the Rhodes Scholarship can be won without exceptional qualities and merit of some kind.' The Trustees 'were inclined to congratulate' the selection committee on having the courage to incur the odium which was inevitable from their decision.'[58] Arthur Smithies, rejected in 1927, was selected in 1928. His later career—

---

[55] Wylie saw no evidence the committee had been 'motivated by any improper considerations. It may have been only a faith in brains' (Wylie to Grigg, 31 Jan. 1925; RTF 1542).

[56] *Mercury*, 21 Feb., 1, 3, 20 Mar. 1928. On 7 February 1928 Behan cabled a report to the Trust, which also sought confidential advice from the Governor.

[57] *Mercury*, 10, 11, 14 May 1928; 500 copies were reprinted as a pamphlet.

[58] Behan's letter of 24 Oct. 1928 was quoted in the *Mercury*, 12 Nov. 1928.

which included a chair in economics at Harvard and senior positions with the United States government—suggests that the committee had been excessively cautious in 1927. The smallness of the Tasmanian constituency might breed disputes over selection, but the island state continued to send outstanding young men to Oxford.

Behan's allegations that schoolmasters groomed candidates to compete for Rhodes scholarships prompted protests from the Associated Public School Headmasters in Melbourne. L. A. Adamson, headmaster of Wesley College, protested that Cecil Rhodes himself was responsible for the change in boys' aspirations. His scholarships had caused 'a startling revolution': 'Clever boys no longer "kept themselves to themselves", but entered more and more fully into the general life of the school to the great good of the common life . . . Now, if a boy has brains, and has the slightest chance of winning the scholarship, he pays attention to his sports as well as to his study, and he is twice the boy for doing so.'[59]

Taking Stock

Adamson also defended Australian Rhodes scholars against accusations, frequent in these years, of 'not fulfilling the objects of Cecil Rhodes'. Most had to make their living, and the 'high character that is brought by them to any profession or calling' was 'just as valuable to the community as is a life of politics'.[60] Amery, visiting in 1927 as Colonial Secretary, thought the social class of Australian applicants 'one of the troubles of the whole system'. 'The type of men we get are obviously the keen men who have got to earn their living and tend to do it in the professions. From the point of view of public service afterwards there might be much to be said for giving our scholarships to the sons of the wealthy squatters or business men and insisting on a high means qualification on the part of parents.'[61]

Australian comments about Rhodes scholars had a different tone. In October 1928 the *Sydney Labour Daily* complained that a Rhodes scholar was chosen for sport or as a swot; 'he proceeds to Oxford, from which he returns with an Oxford accent, a considerable share of that boredom which characterises the idle rich of England, and generally, contempt for the ideals of his motherland'. He would do better to spend two years 'looking at the problems of his own country'. In December a more temperate 'Australian' asked in the *Adelaide Advertiser* whether Australia had not lost more than it had gained by the system. Too many scholars were professional men or schoolmasters, and too many remained abroad, and most were too mercenary.[62]

Kerr, distributing the results in schools of all Rhodes scholars up to 1925, observed that South Australia had the best results among single constituencies, and Australia had come second only to New Zealand among all the countries represented.[63] From the late 1920s,

---

[59] Felix Meyer (ed.), *Adamson of Wesley: The Story of a Great Headmaster* (Melbourne: Robertson & Mullins, 1932), 174–6.
[60] *Melbourne Herald*, May 1932.   [61] Amery to Kerr, 24 Nov. 1927 (RTF 2500).
[62] *Sydney Labour Daily*, 22 Oct. 1928; *Adelaide Advertiser*, 13 Dec. 1928.
[63] Memorandum to Selection Committees 1926.

opinion in their homeland seems to have turned in favour of the Australian Rhodes scholars. The senior lawyers had as yet achieved silk rather than the bench, and only three had entered a parliament, but there were many professors and headmasters among the educationists, and the appointment in 1926 of A. C. D. Rivett (Victoria and Lincoln 1907) to head the Commonwealth's new Council for Scientific and Industrial Research heralded the entry of Rhodes scholars into fields of public service never envisaged by Cecil Rhodes. In the 1930s, most judgement in the press became positive: a headline in 1938—'Scholars Satisfy'—was a change from earlier grumbles of a 'failed experiment'.[64]

The Scholars Associate

New South Wales was first to organize a formal 'Fellowship' of Rhodes scholars, in 1923, though local groups had been meeting informally for many years.[65] In 1924 Wylie proposed that Rhodes scholars all over the world dine together on same night as the Trustees dined with the departing scholars in Oxford. Proceedings at the dinner in Melbourne that June took the form which remained standard in most states for many years: the scholars present toasted the King and the Founder (with an appropriate pause for silent contemplation), and the most recently returned scholar proposed the health of the scholar-elect. (The New South Wales scholars added a ceremony with a loving cup, each scholar naming his college as he drank; and Portus, moving to Adelaide from Sydney in 1934, presented the South Australians with a silver chalice in 1937, for a similar ritual.) Dinners were usually reported in the press.

Behan, who had always been keen to form an Australian Association of Rhodes Scholars, called an 'inaugurating conference' in February 1931. The first object in the Association's constitution—'to further the aims of the Founder of the Rhodes Scholarships'—implied a commitment which was almost ideological, though no longer embracing the furthest reaches of Cecil Rhodes's imagination. 'Particular objects' included a pledge 'to promote the interests of higher education in Australia', and especially the development of residential colleges, and publication of a periodical.[66] Behan, as secretary of the new Association, ensured that business at its conferences, biennial from 1933 until the war, was reported in detail across the nation.

The Rhodes scholarships themselves were always on the agenda, but other topics ranged broadly. How far, one conference was asked, had the concept of empire changed? Should Rhodes scholars formulate definite attitudes on questions such as the appointment of governors general (a live issue after the King's reluctance in 1930 to appoint an Australian)? In 1937 the press in all capitals reported the sometimes pungent views on

---

[64] *Melbourne Herald*, 15 Oct. 1937, 2 Feb. 1938.

[65] In Perth in 1913, six Rhodes scholars—including Kingsley Fairbridge—had dined together and contemplated 'the formation of an association in the immediate future' (*Sunday Times*, 13 July 1913).

[66] Other objects were 'to promote the growth of common feeling and social intercourse among Rhodes Scholars resident in Australia', to coordinate their activities, the circulation of a record, and assistance to Rhodes scholars on election and return (Behan to Lothian, 23 Mar. 1931; RTF 2500).

education and schools of the several Rhodes scholar headmasters, and of J. A. Seitz (Victoria and Merton 1906), newly appointed Director of Education in Victoria. The conference also pursued the idea of a 'Rhodes Scholarship in Reverse', a plan linked to a proposal for a special Trust Fund, 'to which Rhodes Scholars (and others) who lack either the ability or the opportunity to undertake active public service might make contributions'. In 1938 Seitz, succeeding Behan as the Association's secretary, inaugurated a Newsletter, distributed approximately quarterly.

The Association's fourth biennial conference was planned for Adelaide in August 1940, but war forced its abandonment. The Newsletter continued to appear sporadically, but soon contained only news of Rhodes scholars on service.

The Fairbridge Cause

The Farm School at Pinjarra survived the First World War with difficulty, but local support enabled the charismatic Fairbridge to build a large new school by 1924, the year of his premature death. Although never achieving all that its founder had envisaged, the project won increasing favour among Rhodes scholars; in 1928 Behan held up Fairbridge as 'beyond all question the type of man Rhodes had in mind', and in 1931 the new Association of Rhodes Scholars included 'the stimulation of a realisation of the imperial significance of the Kingsley Fairbridge Farm School' among its 'particular' aims.[67] With economic and social conditions depressed at both ends of the colonial axis, the notion of transplanting orphans from British slums to Australia's sparsely populated acres seemed to combine humanitarian and economic benefits in fortunate conjunction, especially to those who saw imperial economic integration as the only hope for material progress in a hostile world.

At the Association's 1935 conference, each state pledged to form a committee to support Fairbridge. Negotiations to establish schools in Queensland and South Australia failed, but Victorian Rhodes scholars supported a farm school founded near Bacchus Marsh in 1937 by the Trustees of a large bequest from Lady Northcote, widow of a former Governor General. The school relied on the Fairbridge organization in Britain for its supply of children, the first twenty-eight arriving in 1937 to much trumpeting of the Fairbridge cause in the Melbourne press. Although the Fairbridge Society was not keen to compete with Barnardo's large establishment in New South Wales, the local Rhodes scholars, aided by influential supporters, forced the pace, raising more than £50,000 through a public appeal, and acquiring land at Molong. The governments of the United Kingdom and of New South Wales provided loans for building and maintenance grants for the children, and with the blessing of the Commonwealth government the school was opened by the Governor General in November 1937. The first group of twenty-eight migrant boys arrived from Britain in March 1938, and about 100 more reached Molong before war interrupted supply, as it did at Pinjarra and Bacchus Marsh. Despite objections from the organization in London, the Fairbridge Farm Schools of New South Wales became an

[67] *Hobart Mercury*, 14 May 1928; *West Australian*, 19, 25 Feb. 1936.

independent incorporated body, with Rhodes scholars represented on its council and active in its development.[68]

The three Farm Schools in Australia were well established by 1939. The regimen resembled Fairbridge's original model, but the child population had changed, partly through stricter government regulation. True orphans formed a much smaller proportion of the children sent, most being nominated by a parent or parents in difficult circumstances. Tension arose between Australia and London, partly because the Society give priority to destitute children, while the Farm Schools were increasingly concerned over the 'quality' of the children sent. They wanted only 'the best' children, unspoiled by their early deprivations and therefore readily moulded into the Farm School communities, while in reality in Britain those most needing help had already suffered damage requiring remedy.

Like many imperial schemes, Fairbridge's had been a romantic ideal ever since he conceived it in his Rhodesian adolescence. In 1938 the *Sydney Bulletin*, always prone to surges of romanticism about life in the bush, praised Fairbridge schools with unusual enthusiasm: 'The Fairbridge plan should be extended to Australian cities. There are thousands of city-bred youngsters with poor prospects in our huge wens who, trained in farm schools of the Fairbridge type, would make good as farmers.' It did not happen.[69]

The Australian Rhodes Review

Rhodes scholars at the first meeting of their Association in 1931 made a bold decision to publish a review, 'to show Australians at large what are the public questions with which their Rhodes Scholars are concerning themselves'. Twenty scholars contributed articles or reviews to the first issue of the *Australian Rhodes Review*, published by Melbourne University Press and the Association in 1934; an elegantly produced volume with an Oxford blue cover, it was bulky, expensive (3s. 6d.) and remarkably eclectic in content. 'Being a cross-section of the Australian lump', the editors explained, 'Australian Rhodes Scholars are not thinking in any specific Rhodes Scholar-ish way'; they embraced 'every shade of political opinion, from true-blue conservatism through moderate liberalism towards bright shades of red'. 'We do not even think alike about body-line bowling.'[70]

Although the *Bulletin* complained that throughout the pages of the *Review* 'the platitudinarian roams unchecked', the journal was generally well received, the *Argus* praising it as the 'equal of any of its kind produced in Australia'; and in Oxford Allen confessed that this 'most impressive' publication 'has taken me by surprise'.[71] The Trustees, who had agreed to grant £100 and to buy 250 copies to support the publication, sent free copies to universities and libraries all over the world, and to schools in South Africa.

---

[68] Sherington and Jeffery, *Fairbridge, Empire and Child Migration*, 164–72; *Melbourne Sun*, 29 June 1936; D. A. Rutherford, 'A Brief History of the Fairbridge Farm School, Molong, N. S. W.', *Molong Historian*, 2/11 (Feb. 1979).

[69] *Bulletin*, 9 Aug. 1938.

[70] Editorial, *Australian Rhodes Review* (Melbourne: Melbourne University Press, 1934).

[71] *Bulletin*, 2 May 1934; *Argus*, 7 Apr. 1934. Lothian cabled Behan his 'heartiest congratulations' (Lothian to Behan, 7 May 1934; RTF 2811).

Unfortunately the *Australian Rhodes Review* proved easier to give away than to sell. After the second number was published in 1936, Melbourne University Press withdrew as co-publisher, and the third issue, appearing in 1937, was an obviously cheaper production; it was also slight, as was its successor in 1939.

The Empire was a major theme of the journal, but the discussion would have disappointed Cecil Rhodes, since its future was much in question by the 1930s. K. H. Bailey, professor of public law in Melbourne, urged Australia to accept legal independence by adopting the Statute of Westminster; 'for most people in the Dominions "Empire" has lost its vitality', he wrote in the first number, 'but there is unhappily—as yet—no practical philosophy of "Commonwealth" to take its place'. Hancock's delightful 'A Veray and True Comyn Wele', on the origins of the word 'Commonwealth', was a beginning. In the 1937 issue the quirky Stephensen provocatively looked forward, in both the literal and the colloquial sense, to the decline and fall of the British Empire. In the following issue Bailey firmly rejected Stephensen's argument that England's weakness was Australia's opportunity to break free, while N. H. MacNeil warned that Australians could no longer rely solely on Britain for national defence. Issues of colony and race were not evaded: F. E. Williams's essay on 'Native Welfare in Papua' urged Papuans to retain their culture, but also to learn from Europeans, and in 1936 H. K. Fry's widely noticed article pleaded for a central authority to ensure 'a more just and enlightened administration of aboriginal affairs'. In the fourth issue M. R. Thwaites (Victoria and New College 1937), fresh from winning the Newdigate Prize, contributed a poem of high quality.

At the 1937 conference MacNeil complained that the *Review* did not stand for anything; it should have proclaimed 'the Rhodes Ideal'. Others did not agree, and were content that the journal gave evidence of the several skills and interests of the relatively small group of Rhodes scholars in Australia between the wars, a group disparate enough to include both conservative ministers and natural rebels like Stephensen, but sharing some sense of common obligation.

Forwards and Backs

In the 1930s a serious rift developed between the New South Wales selection committee and the Trust's secretaries in Oxford and London. Lothian was concerned that few New South Wales Rhodes scholars did well in Oxford examinations, and Allen, newly appointed Warden of Rhodes House, thought the New South Wales selection procedures—of which he had experience—'thoroughly bad in principle', based on too narrow a notion of what a Rhodes scholar ought to be.[72] Portus, one of the Sydney selectors, had put their view bluntly:

Until the Trust is varied, I cannot see what the Final Selectors can do, but prefer a mediocre all round man to a brilliant academic person . . . It seems to me that it is quite useless to talk about sending distinguished academic men, when no distinguished academic man applies who is likely to get any backing from the undergraduates . . . a first Class Honours man who does not play sport

[72] Allen to Lothian, 11 Feb. 1933 (RTF 1155).

and takes no part in the undergraduates' activities outside the classroom, will not commend himself for selection to the undergrads, and they will put him at the bottom of their list.[73]

The selection committee's stance gained support from Australia's first national universities' students' congress in 1937, which asked for more 'direct consultation with student authorities'.[74] The local Rhodes scholars, however, led by Halse Rogers, since 1936 the University's Chancellor, wanted the committee freed from University control. In 1938 Lothian offered his advice in person; visiting Australia, he described his meetings with the Rhodes scholars and the selection committee in Sydney as protracted but 'very satisfactory'—'the whole question has now been thoroughly ventilated'—but could not report explicit agreement.[75] To reinforce his message, he wrote a blunt letter to the selection committee on the eve of his departure, asking it to find 'some way of ensuring that the New South Wales Rhodes Scholars in future at least reach the level of attainment at Oxford of the scholars of the other leading states of the Commonwealth', and advising the committee to bring its method of selection 'into line with that which obtains not only in all the other Australian States but everywhere else as well, both throughout the British Empire and the United States'.[76]

Lothian, with a preference for Oxford's older disciplines and prejudice against sciences, no doubt undervalued the procession of able young engineers sent to Oxford from Sydney in the 1930s, their strengths less evident than the exceptional brilliance of some of the young men from other Australian states. In Australia, Victoria was criticized for undervaluing sport, a journalist complaining that 'the Victorian scholars are chosen almost solely on their exhibitions, and the merest pretence at sport is allowed to pass', but in Oxford in 1932 Allen drew attention to 'the remarkable record of the Victorians', with nine of the ten scholars since 1924 taking firsts. The Trustees recorded their 'deep satisfaction' and formally congratulated the Victorian committee, untroubled that one of the most brilliant of its scholars had listed 'marbles' as his sport.[77]

It was not until September 1940 that the committee approved a long reply to Lothian's letter of two years before. 'A Rhodes Scholar should be judged by his career after he leaves Oxford', not by his academic performance there. Nevertheless a comparison of the later achievements of the New South Wales Rhodes scholars from 1904 to 1930 with those of the unsuccessful applicants, and also with the holders of other travelling scholarships, had not proved reassuring. 'In the great majority of cases' the later achievements of Rhodes scholars had 'measured up fairly satisfactorily to Mr Rhodes' ideals', but 'in a large proportion of cases the Rhodes Scholar has been outdistanced either by one of the unsuccessful applicants, or by the holder of one of the other Scholarships'; and it was 'undoubtedly true' that students of 'outstanding mental ability' had 'chosen to apply for one of the other travelling Scholarships in preference to the Rhodes Scholarship'. But the

---

[73] Portus to Wylie Nov. 1925 (RTF 1155).

[74] 'Some of the selectors are old gentlemen who consider themselves God and who choose students in their own image' (*Adelaide Advertiser*, 19 Feb. 1937).

[75] Lord Lothian, 'Visit to Australia and New Zealand', 2 Nov. 1938 (RTF 2500).

[76] Lothian to W. A. Selle, 28 Sept. 1938 (Australian Secretary File).

[77] *Table Talk*, 28 July 1927; Wylie's Report, 24 Sept. 1932 (RTF 1160).

practice of consulting other bodies was not the cause, since the reports were 'regarded merely as reliable evidence' of the capabilities of the candidates.[78]

By the time this letter was written, Lord Lothian was Ambassador in Washington, and Lord Elton had succeeded him as Secretary to the Trust. When Elton replied, in February 1941, Lothian was dead, and the selection of Rhodes scholars was about to be suspended for the duration of the war. Allen briefed Elton, including a new criticism of his home state:

> To elect a candidate merely because he is either a good athlete or a virtuous young man has proved again and again to be a failure. . . . the New South Wales Committee has always been over-impressed by athletic qualifications or by a certain goody-goodness . . . It is ridiculous to elect a candidate merely because he is a prominent member of the Students' Christian Union and it is ridiculous to exclude a candidate merely because he has been known to get tight or use bad language on occasion. You can steer a middle course between these two things without getting 'plaster saints' (who are usually bad Rhodes Scholars) or bad hats (who are still worse Rhodes Scholars).

'I know from experience', he added, 'that candidates do not relish submitting themselves' to the judgement of bodies 'by no means always representative'. Moreover the committee had 'misunderstood' the principle, 'justified by nearly forty years experience', that 'the intellectual qualification . . . is the safest general criterion'. Elton's response to the New South Wales Committee incorporated all Allen's arguments, in more diplomatic prose. The committee, in abeyance for the duration of the war, did not consider his advice until it reconvened after hostilities ended.[79]

The Expatriates

During his visit in 1938, Lothian told the Australian press that 'the only real concern of the Rhodes Trust today' was 'the large proportion' of scholars who did not return to their own country, 'especially since the depression'. According to the editors of the *Rhodes Review*, there were 99 Rhodes scholars resident in 1937, 96 had not returned, and 12 were dead. If Australia did not 'take the trouble to induce' their first-class scholars to come home again, Lothian warned, 'other parts of the Empire are the gainers'.

Australian society gave opportunities in the professions and in business, but Australian universities were too poorly funded to support many high-fliers. 'Placing' returning Rhodes scholars became a constant theme at conferences, and an ironic piece by Lewis Wilcher in the *Review*, on an imaginary Rhodes scholar who could only find work teaching arithmetic in a primary school, was a tract for the 1930s. Seitz's Newsletter included notices of vacant positions suitable for Rhodes scholars, and the Association gathered information on opportunities for graduate employment in the public services, finding, as expected, that most posts were reserved for boys leaving school. (The Department of External Affairs, founded in 1937, was an exception, several Rhodes scholars making distinguished careers as diplomats.)

---

[78] Letter sent on by Behan, 4 Nov. 1940 (RTF 1155).
[79] Allen to Elton, 17 Feb. 1941; Elton to Madgwick, 27 Feb. 1941 (RTF 1155).

A few of the Australian Rhodes scholars living abroad worked in the British colonies, but most were in Britain, in medicine, engineering, or in business; among those in the civil service, Sir Roy (later Lord) Robinson became Chairman of the British Forestry Commission in 1932. Most of the academics were in Oxford, though the unusual career of H. H. L. A. Brose (South Australia and Christ Church 1913), translator of Einstein, took him to be professor of physics at Nottingham in 1931 after completing the first D.Phil. by an Australian Rhodes scholar in 1925. K. C. Wheare (Victoria and Oriel 1929) remained in Oxford, becoming in time Gladstone Professor of Government and Public Administration, a Rhodes Trustee, Rector of Exeter and the first Australian Vice-Chancellor of Oxford. W. K. Hancock, having left his All Souls fellowship to return to Australia in 1926, returned in 1934 to occupy a succession of chairs in Britain and to write, in his massive *Survey of British Commonwealth Affairs*, classic statements of those issues of empire which were as prominent in expatriate Australian minds as in the *Rhodes Review*. J. C. Eccles (Victoria and Magdalen 1925) became a fellow of Magdalen in 1937; he was later to occupy a chair in Canberra, unlike another Nobel Laureate, H. D. Florey (South Australia and Magdalen 1921), professor of pathology in Oxford from 1935, who returned to Australia only as the ANU's Chancellor. With the appointments of H. W. B. Cairns (South Australia and Balliol 1917) to be Nuffield Professor of Surgery in 1939, Hancock to the chair of economic history in 1941, and Wheare to the Gladstone Chair in 1944, the academic presence of Australian Rhodes scholars in Oxford was wide-ranging and—with four of the five Rhodes scholar professors—impressively senior.

Rumours, and War

From some time in the 1930s every young Australian Rhodes scholar expected his career to be interrupted by another European war. In May 1939 the Governor of Tasmania was so infuriated by the appearance, in a student hoax, of placards prematurely announcing the outbreak of war—'Hitler invades Poland . . . At 10 am. to-day the German troops crossed the Polish frontier . . . Great Britain and France . . . expected to declare war immediately'—that he publicly insisted that the perpetrators be gaoled. When he discovered that 'Mr R. W. Baker, the recommended Rhodes Scholar', had written one of the placards, he called a special meeting of the selection committee, intending to have Baker's Rhodes scholarship cancelled. The Minute Book of the Tasmanian selection committee contains a sealed envelope enclosing an account of the incident.

The Governor was foiled. The committee agreed only that the facts 'should be reported to the Rhodes Trustees at Oxford without comment', and although Behan forwarded the report with a tiny handwritten attachment ('strictly entre nous I hope the Trustees will take strong action') they responded mildly.[80] Formally, they resolved to suspend Baker's scholarship until a report from Allen was considered, but their intention was to make him aware of 'the seriousness of his action' and then admit him to residence. Allen interviewed Baker on 21 September, after the war he had prematurely announced had broken

---

[80] Behan to Acting Secretary, 29 June 1939 (RTF 1542).

out, and found none of the charges against him sustained. The University of Tasmania's historian is correct in stating that the scholar-elect was saved from the wrath of His Majesty's Representative 'by the good sense of the Rhodes Trustees in England'.[81]

When war was declared, in September 1939, the Trust immediately suspended all Rhodes scholarships not already taken up. In October the Trust changed its mind: selection from the dominions would continue, but scholarships awarded in wartime would be suspended until the end of the war. In Australia, the scholars for 1940 and 1941 were chosen, but in May 1941—with the phoney war all too obviously over—the selection process itself was suspended 'for the duration of hostilities'. Selection committees adjourned indefinitely.

Almost all the scholars selected for 1939–41 served, and more than thirty of the 125 Australian Rhodes scholars elected between 1918 and 1938 also enlisted. So did several who had served in the First World War, including E. F. Herring (Victoria and New College 1912), who achieved the highest rank of any Rhodes scholar from any country in the Second World War, commanding I Australian Corps and New Guinea Force before resigning in 1944 to become Chief Justice of Victoria. At least twenty of the numerous medical graduates among the Rhodes scholars held some service rank, overseas or in Australia. Seven Australian Rhodes scholars were killed.

Rhodes scholars who joined the infant Department of External Affairs found themselves practising diplomacy as an extension of war (much of it, the documents suggest, with their Allies rather than the enemy). Elsewhere in the Australian public service, Roland Wilson (Tasmania and Oriel 1925) held the most senior post, as Head of the Department of Labour and National Service, and among the Australian Rhodes scholars working abroad W. K. Hancock broke yet more new ground when appointed Supervisor of Civil Histories in the offices of the war cabinet in London in 1941. A. Smithies (Tasmania and Magdalen 1929), an economist in the Australian Treasury before he migrated to Michigan in 1938, joined the economic branch of the US Bureau of the Budget in 1943 and became its chief in 1946.

The wartime mobilization of science involved many Rhodes scholars. A sizeable number—including five young Tasmanians—were engaged in aeronautical research, and at least one Australian Rhodes scholar worked on the atomic project in the United States. In Oxford, Howard Florey, knighted in 1944, became an honorary consultant in pathology to the British Army, while contributing massively to humankind with his work on penicillin. His colleague Hugh Cairns, a consulting neurosurgeon to the British Army, cooperated in its application to the battlefield.

'Inky' Stephensen swam, as usual, against the stream. To the dismay of his friends, the enterprising publisher and injudicious publicist became a proto-fascist in the 1930s, wrote admiringly of Hitler and the Japanese, became a founder of the Australia First Movement, and was interned as a threat to Australian security after the fall of Singapore in 1942. His former Party comrade, F. W. Paterson, remained a communist, and in 1944

---

[81] R. Davis, *Open to Talent* (Hobart: University of Tasmania, 1990), 84; Allen's note of interview, 21 Sept. 1939 (RTF 1542). Baker returned to Hobart in 1947, to become a professor of law and later a member of the Tasmanian Parliament.

won for the Party the only parliamentary seat it ever held in Australia, in the Queensland Legislative Assembly.[82] H. H. L. A. Brose had the unusual experience of being
interned in Germany in the First World War and in Australia in 1940 as a German sym-
pathizer. Arrested in Sydney for having friends among the enemy, he soon found that he
had made too many enemies among his friends; when one of a succession of appeals
cleared him of any 'positive act' of disloyalty, hostile former colleagues persuaded authorities that he was 'of great potential danger to this country', and he was not released
until 1945.[83]

Revival 1945

In August 1945, with the war over in Europe, the Trustees announced the reopening of
the scholarships 'wherever it seems practicable to do so'. Two scholarships were offered
in each Australian constituency, restricted to applicants who had spent at least one year
with the armed forces or in another service approved by the Trust. For them the age limit
was extended, the minimum academic qualification reduced, and disqualification by
marriage suspended.

Elton assumed there could be no elections in Australia before the end of war with
Japan, but Behan's 'vigorous negotiations' gained the agreement of the Prime Minister
and the service chiefs to bring back to Australia by air applicants shortlisted for interview, so that 'men still fighting in the forward areas' could compete 'on a footing of
equality' with men already discharged. (Allen, impressed, minuted an account of the
preparations: 'very interesting. I think B has done a good job for us'.) In 1946 Behan sent
to Oxford a document Elton described as 'the fullest and clearest report which I have yet
seen on a large scale Rhodes Scholarship election'.[84]

The fields in 1945 were large—110 in total—and generally strong, two states asking in
vain for a third scholarship to award. Most of those selected did well at Oxford, some
exceptionally: the two Queenslanders both took firsts, while the highly original Hugh
Stretton (Victoria) was appointed a fellow of Balliol in 1948, the year he took his first in
history. An analysis of the academic results of all Rhodes scholars elected between 1903
and 1947 showed that the percentage of firsts gained by Australians, 35.36 per cent, was
more than double that for the dominions as a whole (17.16 per cent) or the United States
(15.5 per cent). Australians had gained 27 of the 94 D.Phils.[85]

In 1945 Behan foreshadowed a 'general review' to remove anomalies in the constitutions
of the State selection committees, which he drew to their attention with more severity
than tact. He toured all the states in 1946, with little success, except—unexpectedly—in
New South Wales. In 1945 the committee had insisted on its old procedures, but Allen,
in Oxford, heard 'that the New South Wales Committee was retaining its old system

---

[82] Munro, *Wild Man of Letters*, 195, 223–4.
[83] Jenkin, 'Henry Herman Leopold Adolph Brose: Vagaries of an Extraordinary Australian Scientist',
302–5. Behan made unsuccessful representations on Brose's behalf.
[84] Behan to Elton, 7 May 1945; Elton to Behan, 28 May, 11 July, 20 Aug. 1945, 9 Jan. 1946 (RTF 2500).
[85] The analysis was published in 1950.

principally out of personal antagonism to Behan', who had provoked them to be 'more inclined than they might otherwise have been to look for reasons to justify their methods'. In August 1946 Elton wrote to the new Governor, Sir John Northcott, politely informing him that the Trustees were convinced that 'it would be all to the good if the New South Wales committee were to decide to assimilate its procedure to that which is the universal practice elsewhere'. Northcott, pleased to be able 'to appear intelligent' at his first meeting, steered the committee to the desired conclusion, Rhodes scholar members moving and seconding a motion to 'dispense with formal reports from the Professorial Board, the Rhodes Fellowship, the Sports Union, and the SRC, while reserving the right to obtain such additional information as the Committee may desire'.[86]

After 1946 the procedures of the New South Wales committee resembled those in other states, though distinctive traditions remained discernible. The 'salutary interest in the Rhodes Scholarship in the University', which Lothian had conceded, did not quickly wane, and the sporting clubs continued to ensure that promising young players had a Rhodes scholarship among their goals in life. New South Wales continued to send all-rounders to Oxford, though there were no longer general complaints of shortcomings in 'mental abilities'.

Behan also moved quickly to revive the Association of Rhodes Scholars in Australia, calling a conference in February 1946 in Trinity College (where he was to retire as Warden in mid-year). Old threads were picked up: a trust fund was again approved in principle; concern was expressed over the delay in reviving the Farm Schools; and despite the doubts of some delegates the conference decided to revive the *Review*. The doubts proved well founded: the contents of the issue published in 1947 offered (as the *Argus* complained) 'no very profound thoughts, and in several cases do not even deal with questions of wide public interest'. Behan soon reported his grief over 'the end of the most praiseworthy and distinctive work of the Association of Rhodes Scholars in Australia'.[87]

Reports to the Adelaide conference in 1948 gave a picture of the post-war activities of state associations. Several groups sent parcels of food regularly to the Wylies and the Allens, and all dined together at least once a year. The conference debated whether the Association should present a formal address during the royal visit, but the idea, like the visit, lapsed.

The ACT had as yet no branch of the Association. The war had greatly increased the power of the Commonwealth at the expense of the states, and the created capital city of Canberra grew rapidly in the post-war years. In 1949 a Canberra resident, P. H. Bailey, won the Victorian Rhodes scholarship (as his father had before him), raising the question where an applicant from the Australian Capital Territory should apply if he had no right to do so in a state. Behan consulted Elton, who agreed that New South Wales was the logical constituency, citing as precedent Maryland's acceptance of candidates from the District of Columbia. In October 1950 the Trustees so determined, subject

---

[86] Allen's informant was Madgwick, formerly secretary of the committee (Allen to Elton, 7 May 1946; Elton to Madgwick, 14 May 1946; Madgwick to Elton, 24 June 1946; Elton to Northcott, 9 Aug. 1946; Northcott to Elton, 6 Sept. 1946; RTF 1155).

[87] *Argus*, 2 Mar. 1947; Behan to Elton, 14 Apr. 1948 (RTF 2811).

to Sydney's concurrence, but the New South Wales committee emphatically rejected the notion.[88]

Stability and Change

The massive immigration of the post-war years transformed Australian society, diluting its preponderantly British composition. Australia long remained overtly British in its loyalties, but looked to the United States as well as to Britain to sustain its international stance in the Cold War. When Britain committed itself to Europe, and Australia entered the war in Vietnam, each withdrew predominantly into its own hemisphere. Australians ceased to have automatic entry to Britain, although their passports identified them as British subjects as well as Australian citizens until 1973; British subjects lost special naturalization privileges in Australia in 1984. The Rhodes scholarships had to maintain their place without the buttress of empire—had, indeed, to escape the obloquy of their imperialist origins, as everywhere in the West the values of Rhodes's own era were challenged and found wanting. The process was slow, and the seeds of the revolutions in accepted attitudes which marked the end of the 1960s, convulsing the universities in particular, seem obvious only in retrospect.

There were straws in the wind of change. The selection of J. A. Gobbo in Victoria in 1952, and of Sergio Giudici in Tasmania in 1960, began a trickle of Australian Rhodes scholars whose cultural backgrounds, and in some cases birthplaces, were European but not British. Eventually, after Australia had abandoned discriminatory immigration policies, Australians of Asian background joined the stream, and by the end of the century almost two out of three Australians had ethnically mixed ancestry. Australian society became much more diverse, at the same time as Oxford became more emphatically and attractively international.

The Cold War, and related manifestations of political radicalism and reaction, for a time dominated internal as well as international politics. In 1949 Lord Elton issued a carefully worded warning that selection committees might 'occasionally find difficulty in considering the claims of the promising candidate who has embraced some political theory apparently in direct conflict with the well-known ideals of the Founder'; they should remember that 'no political or religious test of any kind has ever been admitted in the Rhodes Scholarship elections'. The presence in the chair of each Australian selection committee of the state governor, drawn from the services or the judiciary and quite probably from Britain, inevitably gave to young applicants an impression of conservatism, which the Trust's insistence on one member being young could scarcely dispel.[89] Hearsay told tales of occasional politically biased questions, but the larger than usual number of scholars selected in those years who entered politics in Australia varied greatly in their opinions. Those on the Liberal side included I. B. C. Wilson (South Australia and

[88] NSW selection committee minutes, 17 Apr., 22 Sept. 1953; Behan to Elton, 28 June 1950, 21 Aug. 1952; Elton to Behan, 18 Oct. 1950, 24 Sept. 1952 (RTF 3102).
[89] Elton feared governors might exert 'undue influence', but Behan, twice defended them (Elton to Behan, 15 Mar. 1945, 5 Apr. 1948; Behan to Elton, 18 Apr. 1945, 20 Apr. 1948; RTF 2500).

Magdalen 1955), (Sir) Max Bingham (Tasmania and Lincoln 1950), later the state's Deputy Premier) and P. D. Durack (Western Australia and Lincoln 1949), and on Labor's N. Blewett (Tasmania and Jesus 1957). In 1951 Western Australia chose J. O. Stone, who after a distinguished career in the Australian Treasury became leader of the National Party in the Senate; two years later it selected R. J. L. Hawke, whose career in the union and labor movements culminated in his election as Prime Minister in 1983. It is difficult to argue that selection committees were ideologically blinkered.

New Men

In 1952, after thirty years as the Australian Secretary to the Trust—service which earned him a knighthood in 1949—Sir John Behan gave over to Professor G. W. Paton (Victoria and Magdalen 1926). Wheare, visiting in 1949, identified Paton, then dean of law in the University of Melbourne, as 'the one for the job'; he accepted the Trustees' invitation in March 1950, but in December he was appointed Melbourne's new Vice-Chancellor, and for a time ruled himself ineligible. It was not until the end of 1952 that Behan's marvellously ordered files moved into the Vice-Chancellor's office.[90] Behan himself withdrew to a mountain retreat outside Melbourne, where in 1952 a new Warden of Rhodes House visited him. 'Jock Behan is old and melancholy', Bill Williams wrote to Elton. 'Would you be most kind and tell him how grateful we are . . . I think he'd be glad of a remembrance'.[91] Behan died suddenly in 1957, aged 75.

The new Australian Secretary inherited a system operating smoothly. State differences were diminishing, and controversy over selection had become rare. Like Behan, Paton was a lawyer, but did not share Behan's passion for procedural niceties; he had a close relationship with Elton, and agreed with him on most matters to do with selection (for example that professors were less effective on selection committees than outside members; they were too apt 'to use ordinary scholarship methods').[92] He took to heart Oxford's advice to avoid excessively formal interview procedures, and in 1956 he urged the other states to adopt the practice, introduced in Victoria, of including a social occasion involving shortlisted candidates and the members of the selection committee and their wives. New South Wales demurred, the Governor thinking it 'unfortunate if an unsuccessful candidate considered himself eliminated on the grounds that he lacked social grace', and even more if he thought he had not been selected 'because a wife of one of the members of the Selection Committee had not taken to him'.[93] But Sydney did introduce an afternoon tea at Government House, a ritual at which each member of the committee sat at a separate table for two, the candidates moving from one to the other for successive brief têtes-à-têtes, suppressing as best they could the nervous rattle of teacup en route. (Such informality would have offended the candidate who, after four failed applications in

---

[90] Wheare to Elton, 24 Nov. 1949 (RTF 2500); Paton to Elton, 6 Dec. 1950; Elton to Behan, 12 Feb. 1951; Allen to Elton, 9 Jan. 1951; Allen to Behan, 13 Jan. 1951 (RTF 2554).
[91] Williams to Elton, 11 May 1952 (RTF 2554).   [92] Paton to Elton, 1 Feb. 1956 (RTF 2500).
[93] Butchart, Memorandum to McCredie, 12 Nov. 1954 (Sydney University Archives, Rhodes Scholarships, NSW Selection Committee).

Western Australia in 1919–20, demanded that applicants be represented by counsel, who could cross-examine their clients' rivals on the veracity of their applications.[94])

From September 1952 the care of the Rhodes scholars in Oxford came under the perceptive eye of E. T. Williams, fellow of Balliol, famous for his brilliance as an intelligence officer during the War. Before taking office, Williams visited all the Australian capitals, finding 'a great fund of good will' among Rhodes scholars, and 'noticing to what a remarkable extent they are men who count in their communities'. His manner was urbane, his message positive but cautious. In Perth he discussed changes in universities, especially Oxford, and in Rhodes scholars, suggesting that 'they were less impressive as personalities and more impressive as intellectual machines'. He warned the South Australian selection committee that with new research schools (such as the ANU in Canberra), and more competing scholarships, there could be 'a tendency for the scholars to be drawn from fields less strong than hitherto'.[95] Williams and his wife took back to Rhodes House a large, sunlit Arthur Boyd painting of *The Wheat Field, Berwick, Victoria* 'presented by Rhodes Scholars in Australia 1952'. The scholars then raised £170 for a centenary gift, an equally impressive landscape by Lloyd Rees; the two paintings were welcoming images to Australian scholars entering the Warden's office for the first time.[96]

One of Williams's first tasks in Oxford was to organize the celebration of Rhodes's Centenary in June–July 1953. Some forty-four Australian scholars attended, and the one of their number chosen to receive an honorary degree in the Sheldonian was Sir Edmund Herring (Elton's 'ideal Rhodes Scholar'), replete with achievements in war and peace. The new Warden's administrative style was brisk and his communications pithy: his report on a bright but brash Australian scholar began 'I like this oaf', and went on to predict a distinguished career. A few scholars found him daunting, but most of the Australians liked and admired him.

In 1959, when Lord Elton retired, Williams became Secretary of the Trust as well as Warden of Rhodes House. The Eltons visited Australia in February–March 1958; he was perhaps surprised to receive a welcoming letter from 'Inky' Stephensen, enclosing for his former tutor's attention an article on Rhodes scholars—an informative and judicious piece—he had written for the *Australian Encyclopaedia*.

Fairbridge: New Beginnings and an End

In 1945, an ARSA circular distributed by Seitz argued that the Fairbridge scheme should be reassessed. 'Weaknesses' identified included too many unhealthy and 'problem' children received from Britain; a cottage system which 'did not simulate home conditions sufficiently'; problems caused by mixing girls and boys on the same farm; and a tendency to 'build up a separate little English community in the farm school'. In future English children should be mixed with locals, and all should be given a broad education, to uni-

---

[94] Parkin to Trustees, n.d. (RTF 1014).
[95] Western Australian minute book, 10 Apr. 1952; South Australian meeting of 7 Apr. 1952.
[96] ARSA Secretary K. L. Cooper to Williams, 21 Oct. 1952 (RTF 2811).

versity level. Gordon Green, general secretary of Fairbridge Farm Schools Inc. of London, denied the charges and sought Elton's help to 'educate' these misguided Rhodes scholars 'in the Fairbridge mission'. Elton's reply was non-committal.[97]

Most of the Rhodes scholars wanted Fairbridge to continue, and were alarmed that shipping shortages were preventing the arrival of children from Britain. The rift between the London Society and Pinjarra evident before the war had become a chasm: in Pinjarra's view London had sent too few children (some of 'poor' quality) before 1939, and was now withholding money needed in Western Australia; but Elton's enquiries in London convinced him that 'the local committees' had 'in the main, been wrong'. Behan persuaded the Western Australian Rhodes Scholars Association to undertake the 'rejuvenation' of Kingsley Fairbridge Farm School of WA Inc.; all the local scholars enrolled in the society, and Walker joined the committee.[98]

The chairman of Fairbridge Farm Schools, Sir Charles Hambro (whose attention had been diverted from their affairs during the war by being head of MI6), told Elton that Western Australia was 'a very parochial place', unwilling 'to grow with the times', but since the problem was remoteness, and not ill will, a personal visit by him should overcome it. The outcome was a major reorganization, tactfully managed by Hambro late in 1947. The London Society took direct responsibility for the management of the Farm Schools, the local committees' roles being to raise funds and negotiate with Australian governments. In New South Wales the existing organization continued to own Molong, but in the west ownership of Pinjarra passed to London, and the local committee was reconstituted to include nominees of the state government and of the Rhodes Scholars' Association. The Trustees of the Northcote School—with which the Victorian Rhodes scholars had no formal connection, though some retained an interest—resisted the new dispensation, and decided to recruit their own children.

In both Britain and Australia the concept of empire was in eclipse, and when Hambro produced a new constitution for Fairbridge Farm Schools Inc.—incidentally renaming it the Fairbridge Society Incorporated—the primary aim stated was simply 'to promote the settlement within the British Commonwealth of poor boys and girls, resident in the United Kingdom, who lack ordinary family care and protection and amenities'. The ideological shift was significant.

In 1950 H. A. Henry (New South Wales and New College 1914), chairman of the Fairbridge Society of NSW, complained gloomily that 'the standard of the children sent out appears to be steadily deteriorating', but V. S. Murphy (Western Australia and University 1921) reported no complaints from Pinjarra, where prospects were good, though only (he agreed) 'if the right type of child migrant was sent out'. Elton, asked to make representations to improve the quality of the children sent, consulted the director in London, and was told that the complaints were exaggerated. He was also reminded— and reminded Seitz—that 'the original object' was to enable children from 'inferior

---

[97] Green to Elton, 21 Aug. 1945; Sherington and Jeffery, *Fairbridge, Empire and Child Migration*, ch. 6, discuss Fairbridge after the war.

[98] Local Rhodes scholars' involvement can be traced in the minutes of the Western Australian Rhodes Scholars' Association, and the Trust's in RTF 1567.

surroundings with poor prospects' to have a chance 'to make good in a country with better prospects'.[99]

For a few post-war years the Farm Schools flourished. Pinjarra became the most innovative, with emphasis on educational opportunity rather than farm training. At Molong, F. K. S. Woods (Orange Free State and Brasenose 1929) maintained a rigidly traditional Fairbridge ethos and regimen for twenty years from 1946. Post-war child migration to Australia was busiest between 1947 and 1953—with most going to Roman Catholic institutions, and the majority of those sent by Fairbridge enrolled in the scheme by their parents—but its days were numbered. The emigration of unaccompanied children, already declining, virtually ceased after 1956, when a mission sent by the Overseas Migration Board found—under the principles of child care it now espoused, which favoured boarding out in homes and distrusted institutional care—several schools, including Molong and Pinjarra, unsuitable for approved child migration.[100]

There were soon many vacancies in the Farm Schools. At the 1958 ARSA Conference Pinjarra was said to be still in a 'sound position', but Molong was not full. The Conference decided to commend the schools to Rhodes scholars for continued support, but few of the younger scholars shared the interest of the older generation. In 1959, when asking the Trust for a donation to mark the fiftieth anniversary of Fairbridge's speech to the Colonial Club, Hambro could still claim success, but Elton's long note advising the Trustees to be moderately generous now reads like an obituary for the Fairbridge scheme as a whole. The schools improvised schemes for child residence which enabled them to continue for some time, but in 1973 Molong was closed and sold. The governing body became the Fairbridge Foundation and Trust, which distributes its income annually to institutions concerned with the welfare of children. Pinjarra lingered on until 1981.

Scholars, Colleges, Committees, and Applicants

As a national organization, the Association of Rhodes Scholars had lost momentum by 1960. General meetings were held biennially in different cities, but attended only by local scholars and a delegate from each of the other states. Such meetings could scarcely address the great issues of the day, but did conduct the Association's business, such as the 'Rhodes Scholarship in Reverse'.

In 1948 the Association had finally agreed 'to make provision for graduates of British Universities to come out to Australia for a period of one or two years'. Unfortunately Seitz, retiring and clearing out his desk, stalled proceedings by changing the object to educating former Fairbridgians, a change unwelcome to others. New efforts were made to create the Association's Trust Fund, but it was not until 1960 that the University of Melbourne accepted £2,000 and the responsibility of awarding an 'Association of Rhodes Scholars in Australia Scholarship', on the recommendation of a committee with three

---

[99] Elton to Seitz, 1 Aug. 1950 (RTF 1567).
[100] Sherington and Jeffery, *Fairbridge, Empire and Child Migration*, 228–234.

members nominated by the Association. The first scholarship, advertised as open to a United Kingdom graduate to attend an Australian university for two years, was awarded in 1967 to a scientist and (it was noted, in some quarters with unease) a woman. The second award, not made until 1977, was open to a scholar from any university in the Commonwealth.

In 1957 Menzies steered through Parliament radical measures launching a major expansion for Australian universities. The 'promotion of the interests of higher education in Australia, and especially the establishment and development of residential colleges' was a stated purpose of the Association, and 'Jock' Behan's mantle as chief champion of the collegiate ideal had fallen on 'Josh' Reynolds, Warden of St George's College, Perth, since 1940 and secretary of the Western Australian selection committee. At the Association's 1958 conference, Reynolds reminded delegates that the Australian colleges had produced all but five of the fifty-one scholars from Victoria, about forty (including twelve of the last fifteen) from NSW, twelve in Western Australia since 1931, and eleven of fifty in Tasmania. The colleges had 'provided a milieu of a character congenial to and productive of the types of men whom the founder had in mind', and 'Rhodes scholars should take practical steps to assist' them. The climate was fair; university residences, including colleges, proliferated in the early 1960s, and individual Rhodes scholars were important in that growth.

The Australian university system expanded rapidly, but the number of applicants for Rhodes scholarships did not rise in proportion. The total applying in Australia averaged only thirty-five in the years 1953–7; it then rose to exceed forty in most years, but fell again in 1968–72. Only Victoria regularly had ten or more applicants between 1962 and 1975, New South Wales fluctuating between sixteen and six. There was of course much 'pre-selection', with committee secretaries discouraging enquirers with uncompetitive records, but the lack of interest among students in the new universities was troubling.

The new universities posed problems for the traditional selection mechanisms. In 1958, when the ANU was about to merge with the Canberra University College, the status of applicants from the ACT again became an issue, resolved only in 1963, when the New South Wales committee at last conceded they could apply in Sydney. New South Wales had already become the first state in Australia to have more than one university, but the creation in 1949 of the University of Technology (later the University of New South Wales) had been bitterly opposed by the University of Sydney, and the selection committee was relieved to be advised by its secretary that the new university's students could not be eligible for Rhodes scholarships until Oxford recognized its degrees. Unfortunately, when this condition had been met, he neglected to inform potential applicants or anyone else, and in 1958 Williams was furious to discover that applications from the University of Technology were still being refused.[101] After his intervention J. P. Kennedy applied, and became the first Rhodes scholar from New South Wales who had not attended the University of Sydney. Soon, however, the states were encouraging

---

[101] Williams to Elton, 3, 5 July 1958 (RTF 1155).

applications from all 'degree-granting bodies', which in the 1960s began to include some colleges of advanced education as well as universities. The Association of Rhodes Scholars assisted by producing a small booklet on *Oxford Today and the Australian Rhodes Scholarships*, but it was out of date almost as soon as it was published in 1972, and was replaced with a semi-official supplement to the Memorandum and Application Form.

In states with smaller student populations, fluctuations in the number of applicants frequently worried selection committees. South Australia became alarmed in the 1960s, especially when candidates withdrew after winning the newly created Shell travelling scholarships, comparable in value and criteria and usually chosen a little earlier. In 1965, an attempt to give some publicity 'to the opportunities available by reason of the Scholarship' by a sober announcement in the Adelaide student newspaper *On Dit* caused alarm when the editors published it under the heading 'Cash in on Imperialism! Apply for a Rhodes!' For the rest of the century, selection committees in Australia continued to complain that the number of applicants had not increased in proportion to the student population, but only in 1970 was a Rhodes scholarship withheld because the field was weak.

Radical Changes

The late 1960s and early 1970s were marked throughout the Western university world by ideological and political turbulence among the greatly expanded student populations. In Australia the Rhodes scholarships were criticized as a relic of imperialism and spurned by some potential candidates, but they were not more than a peripheral target in campaigns aimed at local institutions. The residential colleges, which had produced so many Australian Rhodes scholars and been championed by them, suffered great if temporary damage, mainly from a decline in demand for their services, as a generation of students turned to more libertarian lifestyles.

After the election of a Labor government in 1972, the Australian government assumed sole financial responsibility for the rapidly expanding system of higher education, a development which had less impact on the Rhodes scholarship system than might have been expected. The abolition of university fees, while an unexpected boon to middle-class parents, did not greatly change the social composition of the student population, except in attracting large numbers of mature-age students, by definition ineligible for the Rhodes. The long period of expansion of higher education in Australia was in any case coming to an end; the university sector remained in a relatively stable state between 1975 and 1988, when expansion began again, in a radically reorganized 'Uniform National System'. Through all this, the most able of the younger students continued to congregate in the few institutions—between two and four in each state—which produced most of the applicants for Rhodes scholarships.

Williams was in Australia again in 1973, and after his return to Oxford the Trust announced the retirement of Sir George Paton as Australian Secretary, and the appointment of John Poynter (Victoria and Magdalen 1951), then a pro-Vice-Chancellor in the University of Melbourne. The new Secretary soon had the task of reorganizing the structure and procedures of all selection committees in Australia to accommodate two major innovations, the eligibility of women, and the creation by the Trust of a new national scholarship, both planned for the selection held in 1976.

The admission of women to eligibility for Rhodes scholarships, hotly debated in the United States and warmly elsewhere, had not been a major issue in Australia, though student organizations occasionally criticized the Trust's eligibility rules, and some applicants for other scholarships announced that their principles prevented them from applying for a 'discriminatory' award.[102] In September 1975, when the *Australian* announced that 'the 2000-year era of male dominance' was crumbling—'the keystone of sexist privilege, the Rhodes Scholarship, is to be open to women applicants'—Poynter was implementing a preparatory edict from Oxford that at least one woman be included on each selection committee. When the eligibility of women was at last formally announced in July 1976, it was welcomed in the press and received by former Rhodes scholars with varying warmth; very few among the scholars of middle age or younger thought it inappropriate or untimely. The residential colleges, most of which had recently become co-residential, also approved.

Williams told Poynter of his 'suspicion that whereas a girl might find it difficult to get a State Rhodes Scholarship because there is but one per State, the first might (therefore) make it in a Commonwealth award-at-Large when that occurs'.[103] He was proved wrong: when the new terms were advertised, women applied in all states except Tasmania, and in November and December Victoria selected a medical student from Monash, one of four women in a field of eleven, and Western Australia the only woman in a field of ten. They were not the first. On 26 October 1976 the early-meeting and frequently enterprising Queensland selection committee had chosen, from a field of seven, Elizabeth Woods to be the first woman Rhodes scholar selected in the world. Of the six Australian Rhodes scholars for 1977, three were men and three women, but the balance was not maintained: of the first hundred Rhodes scholars selected in Australia after eligibility was widened, twenty-six were women. At least one woman was selected each year, but it was not until 1997 that a majority of the awards made in a year went to women.

At-Large at Last

Arguments for another Rhodes scholarship for Australia had emerged intermittently since the 'Special' scholarship of 1920. Australian population had grown from about 4 million when the scholarships were founded to 12.8 million in 1971, and the rapid proliferation of universities after 1958 provided the general case. Increasing disparity between the states supported the argument, regularly put by the fellowship in Sydney, that if Tasmania had one scholarship, New South Wales, which even in the 1950s had three universities and eleven times the population, should have two. The alternative of merging smaller constituencies was geographically impracticable, and ruled out by the Rhodes Trust Act of

---

[102] 'I don't think it's fair to have male-only scholarships', said a Shell scholarship winner to the *Melbourne Age*, which reported him under the headline 'He Spurns the Rhodes' (*Age*, 16 Dec. 1975).

[103] Williams to Poynter, 7 Apr. 1976 (RTF 2554).

1929. New South Wales sought Victorian support by suggesting that a new scholarship might alternate between the two most populous states; Oxford listened sympathetically, but declined to act.

The growth of the ACT added a new claimant. Its undergraduate population was growing, and the concentration in Canberra of the Australian public service increased the number of Rhodes scholars living there until it outstripped all state capitals except Sydney. Territorians complained that candidates from the ACT got short shrift from the NSW selection committee, an assertion with little evidence beyond a chance remark from a committee member that Canberra applicants were simple country boys compared with their sophisticated Sydney rivals. The Association, while sympathetic to the arguments of NSW, had less time for those from Canberra (which lacked a branch of the ARSA until 1973), and the Trust rightly told the ACT that it was undesirable to create another small constituency.

In November 1975, the Trust at last approved an additional scholarship for Australia, to be awarded every third year if the first election proved successful. The new award would be made on a national basis, and called a scholarship for 'Australia-at-Large', in effect adding, three-quarters of a century after Federation, a federal layer to the state-based selection process.

Poynter, asked to devise a method for selecting the seventh Australian Rhodes scholar, set out to consult the six existing Rhodes constituencies ignorant of Dr Rendall's earlier scheme, for a 'primus inter secundos', but geography and the logic of federalism forced its reinvention. In February 1976 Poynter proposed that a central selection committee consider candidates nominated by the state committees after they had chosen the scholar for their state; but gaining agreement proved difficult, and he was forced to ask that the selection be delayed until 1977.[104] Discussion with each state committee was complicated by the Trust's decision, resented by many, to enforce a retiring age of 69 (later 65) for committee members.

All the states would have accepted an additional scholarship 'available to New South Wales and Victoria, either in turn or as a combined electorate', but there was 'almost universal concern' to avoid reducing the status of the existing scholarships by creating a 'super-Scholarship for Australia at Large'. There was also opposition to allowing direct application for the new award—even by residents of the ACT, as Poynter had suggested—though 'the logic of carrying out the actual selection' in Canberra 'was generally conceded'. A two-tiered process was eventually accepted, despite 'apprehension' (especially in New South Wales) that it would produce 'a second-class field', and that 'the Additional Rhodes Scholar would suffer the burden of inferior status'. Between the Scylla of superiority in repute and the Charybdis of inferiority in status the strait for the new award was narrow indeed.

The new process required an administrative base in Canberra. Fortunately the Vice-Chancellor of the ANU was 'glad to help', though the academic registrar—soon to

---

[104] Poynter, Report on the selection of an additional Rhodes scholar from Australia for 1978, 1 (RTF 2554).

become an excellent secretary to the committee—had initial qualms, thinking it 'a little 'infra dig' for ANU to be 'concerned with selecting a 'second best'. Concern about status continued everywhere: state committees were told in February 1977 that the term 'Australia-at-large' had been dropped in favour of the unpretentious 'Additional Rhodes Scholarship for Australia', and in August that the new scholar would be identified in Rhodes lists simply as 'Australia and (College)', to avoid any inference of superiority. The title 'Australia-at-large' nevertheless persisted in use, in both Oxford and Australia.[105]

Poynter reported 'plenty of starters' for membership of the committee—chaired by Vice-Chancellor Anthony Low—in all categories except business, underrepresented in a town well supplied with politicians, administrators, academics, and journalists.[106] In 1977 four of the six states (but not Tasmania or Western Australia) each nominated one candidate for consideration; on 8 December the committee interviewed the four, brought to Canberra for the purpose and accommodated at University House, where both a dinner and the interviews were held. The field was gratifyingly strong; after discussion the committee elected Pauline Nestor, a graduate in English from the University of Melbourne, to the additional Rhodes scholarship for Australia for 1978.

One state found fault with the process. In November 1977 the South Australian selection committee objected strongly, to the Warden and to the Australian Secretary, that the committee about to meet did not include the deputy chairmen of state committees 'as had been proposed earlier'. Poynter met the committee twice in 1978, first to explain that inclusion of deputy chairmen had been dropped as unnecessarily expensive, and because it would have made difficult the inclusion of scholars from the ACT; and later to give the welcome news that there would be another additional scholarship awarded that year. The Trustees eventually made the award annual in October 1979, when they recorded, but did not announce, that Australians had been 'the best Scholars'.

In December 1977, before the second award was made, Sir Zelman Cowen (Victoria 1941), then Vice-Chancellor of the University of Queensland, became Governor General. The Trust frowned on Rhodes scholars chairing selection committees, but Sir Zelman cited a New Zealand governor general as precedent, and Poynter added that his involvement 'would be a help in allaying State fears that the ANU might capture the Award'. Sir Zelman conducted the next selection round 'impeccably', inviting committee members and their spouses, and the candidates, to a dinner at Government House, where the Yarralumla lawns sloped down to Lake Burley Griffin, and presiding over the interviews next day with kindly tact and iron control.[107]

Festivals and Celebrations

In 1979 Dr Robin Fletcher was appointed to succeed Sir Edgar Williams as Warden and Secretary of the Trust in June 1980, and in November 1979 the Fletchers visited the

---

[105] Poynter to State Secretaries, 17 Feb. 12 Aug. 1977.
[106] Poynter to Williams, 11 July, 18 Aug. 1977 (RTF 2554).
[107] Poynter to Williams, 12 Sept. 1978, 8 Jan. 1979 (RTF 2554).

Australian constituencies. Their itinerary included that peculiar Australian festival, the Melbourne Cup; it proved just as difficult to pick the winner from among the four candidates interviewed in Canberra a few weeks later. The Canberra branch of the Association of Rhodes Scholars developed the custom of inviting the successful candidate to attend their annual dinner, held on the night of the selection.

In 1982 Sir Zelman resigned, to return to Oxford as Provost of Oriel. His successor, Sir Ninian Stephen, by coincidence a member of the Victorian selection committee, was happy to continue the Governor General's role as chairman of the committee in Canberra. In June 1983, after the ACT scholars had lobbied a visiting Trustee, applicants from Commonwealth Territories were permitted to apply directly for the additional scholarship, and a preliminary selection committee created to consider them; it had no scholarship to award, but the same power to nominate as the state committees.

At the Rhodes reunion in Oxford June 1983 the Australian honoured was Sir Zelman Cowen. Australia was preparing a celebration of its own, and in May 1987 the Governor General announced that the Rhodes Trustees would mark the bicentennial of European settlement in Australia by creating a bicentennial Rhodes scholarship. The calibre of the more than 450 Rhodes scholars selected from Australia over eighty-five years had 'brought great benefit to Oxford and much prestige to the Rhodes Trust', fulfilling Rhodes's hope that his benefaction 'would attract young people of exceptional quality'. The capital value of the gift was estimated at more than $A1 million.[108]

In February 1988, the Association of Rhodes Scholars in Australia held its own 'Endorsed Bicentennial Activity', a reunion meeting in Canberra with the theme 'Australia: Whither Next', an event on a grander scale than the ARSA's conferences of the 1930s. Ninety-five scholars attended, and from Britain Oxford's Vice-Chancellor, the Warden of Rhodes House, and—for the first time in Australia—the chairman of the Trust. Festivities included a reunion dinner and a vice-regal reception, the guests arriving across Lake Burley Griffin and disembarking at the Government House landing stage. The serious discussion of Australia's future took two days, in sessions on 'Australia in the World', 'Australian Culture and Society', and (a theme which earlier generations of Rhodes scholars could not have envisaged) 'The Environment and the Economy'.

The main continuing national activity of the ARSA was the Association's scholarship, awarded for the third time in 1985. An advertisement in 1991 attracted 298 applicants from 17 countries, but fees levied on overseas students made the award difficult to accept; and in 1994 the scholarship was replaced with travel bursaries, enabling scholars enrolled for a Ph.D. in a Commonwealth university to spend periods working in an Australian university. The new awards proved popular and effective.

The Closing Decade of a Century

When Sir Ninian Stephen retired as Governor General in 1989, his successor chose not to chair the selection committee for Australia-at-large. From 1990 until 1998 the chair-

---

[108] A bicentennial gift had first been considered by the Trustees in 1983. When approached in 1986 for a donation to a British bicentennial gift, they replied that they would prefer a scheme 'managed under their existing organisation and financed by the Trust' (RTM 7 June 1986).

man was Professor Peter Karmel, the committee's deputy chair when Vice-Chancellor of the ANU, a man of distinction and perspicacity. Candidates and committee dined together at the new Parliament House rather than Yarralumla, but the process remained a special experience for the candidates, successful or not.

(Sir) Anthony Kenny, appointed to succeed Fletcher as Warden in March 1988, visited Australia in September 1989. Observing the scene with a fresh eye, he found the selection procedures efficient and the prestige of the scholarships, like the general standard of the applications, high, though the proliferation of graduate programmes within Australia, and of alternative opportunities to study abroad, left no room for complacency. The perception that certain universities—normally the senior in each state—had a 'virtual monopoly over the scholarships' was a problem, but there was 'surprisingly little resentment' that candidates from populous states had 'a much poorer chance' of selection than candidates from small states. The odds for the candidates from the populous states had been improved by the scholarships-at-large; and in 1991, when the Australian Secretary conveyed, without optimism, a request to the Trust that a third scholarship be awarded 'at-large', the Trustees granted it, to his pleased surprise. The number of candidates each committee could nominate remained at two, but the selection committee found plenty of talented applicants for all three awards.[109] In 1996 Sir Anthony Kenny again visited Australia, primarily to consult concerning a successor to Poynter as Australian Secretary. After his return the Trust appointed Professor Graham Hutchinson (Victoria and Magdalen 1971) to take the post from August 1997.

As the twentieth century drew to a close it was difficult to argue that Rhodes scholars were not prominent in public life in Australia. When R. J. L. Hawke was Prime Minister his government included three Rhodes scholars (one of them a later leader of the opposition), and there were three more on the opposition front bench. In the state parliaments, in the 1990s, a Rhodes scholar led the opposition in Western Australia and another was a minister in Queensland. When the debate for and against an Australian republic first became serious, a Rhodes scholar led the Republicans, and another the Constitutional Monarchists, while a third was the Attorney General responsible for the conduct of the (failed) 1999 referendum on the matter. Towards the end of the century, a Rhodes scholar was Australian High Commissioner in London; another headed the Department of Foreign Affairs and Trade. A former judge was Governor of Victoria, and other Rhodes scholars in the judiciary included a judge of the High Court and two state chief justices. Rhodes scholar medicos were fewer in number than before, but distinguished, especially in research. The number of Rhodes scholars entering business was increasing; in the 1990s one was chairman of BHP, 'the Big Australian', while another headed one of Australia's two major airlines before becoming head of British Airways. Several Rhodes scholars were writers of note, but there were no full-time visual artists (or musicians, despite Poynter's occasional reminders to committees that music is one of Oxford's oldest active disciplines).

At the end of the century the prestige of the Rhodes scholarships remained extraordinarily high in Australia, though the reasons had changed over the years. When, in

---

[109] At the same time the age limit for Australian applicants was raised to 26, to allow for the different academic calendar in the southern hemisphere.

the last decade of the century, competition between Australian universities for the best students became overtly commercial in its techniques, the standing of the scholarship was both exploited and enhanced by individual universities, proudly announcing that their students had just won one, two, or even three Rhodes scholarships. At least one university began to groom potential candidates by providing professional advice, causing a minor seismic disturbance as Sir John Behan turned in his grave. Fields in the largest states grew to between thirty-five and fifty, and even in the smallest, fields of fewer than a dozen became rare. Oxford and a Rhodes scholarship seem not to be among the goals sought by the small number of Aboriginal students becoming eligible, but in other respects the diversity of backgrounds became greater, with many more applicants of Asian origin. As in earlier decades, the preponderance of certain institutions as producers of Rhodes scholars masked the changing composition of Australian elites.

In the later years of the century, sitting as a member of a Rhodes scholarship selection committee remained a special experience. 'I am amazed every year by the very high standard of the field', the ANU registrar wrote to the NSW Secretary in 1988.[110] A retiring chairman in Victoria remarked in 1992 that the fields were so even that he hated making a choice among the candidates appearing before the committee, but was always heartened for the future of a country which could produce such impressive young men and women. Latter-day candidates are not the young schoolboys Rhodes envisaged, applying for his scholarships to gain experience of the world outside their remote localities. Virtually all have travelled internationally while still at school, many have already worked in foreign countries, in a variety of roles and causes, and men and women candidates have had similar experiences. Their views of the world are international, not imperial, and their sophistication would have astonished Cecil Rhodes, though it is likely he would have recognized their qualities, and the promise they offer of significant achievement in 'the world's fight'.

[110] Ros Dubs to Stephen Harrison, 6 Dec. 1988 (ANU File 14.4.1.44D).

6

The German Rhodes Scholarships

RICHARD SHEPPARD

March 1902–Autumn 1903

In March 1899, Cecil Rhodes, clad not in court dress but informally, visited Kaiser Wilhelm II in Berlin to ask his permission for the telegraph line which was to link British possessions in northern and southern Africa to pass through German East Africa, now Tanzania.[1] He also used the occasion to encourage the Kaiser's imperial ambitions in the Middle East.[2] Unlike Leopold II of Belgium, to whom Rhodes had put a similar request, the Kaiser was so impressed by him as a person and entrepreneur that he assented. Partly as a gesture of thanks, partly because he understood (erroneously) that the Kaiser had recently made English compulsory in schools, and partly in the hope that stronger educational links and greater understanding between 'the three great powers' would 'render war impossible', Rhodes, in January 1901, added a codicil to his seventh and final will of July 1899. This created five German scholarships per annum besides those already allocated to the Empire and the USA.

Rhodes died on 26 March 1902 and his Trustees first met on 2 May, but things in

I would like to thank the DAAD for funding my preliminary research for this chapter in summer 1998 and the following people who have given me their help and support over the past year: Ms Caroline Brown (Rhodes House); Prof. Fritz Caspari; Prof. Richard Evans (Cambridge); Herr Wolfgang Fontaine; Mr Rolf James; Dr Eric de Saventhem; Dr Dietrich von Bothmer; Thomas and Sylvia Böcking; Lippold and Christine von Klencke; Dr Arnd D. Kumerloeve; Mr Simon Bailey (Oxford University Archives); Herr Christoph von Bethmann Hollweg (AA); Herr Lutz Möser (BAB); Dr Moritz Graf Strachwitz (Adelsarchiv, Marburg); Dr Jürgen Real (BAK); and Mr Stephen Walton (IWM).

The following abbreviations have been used in both footnotes and text: AA = Archiv Altenhof; AB = Archiv Böcking; AvK = Archiv von Klencke; BAA = Bundesarchiv (Aachen); BAB = Bundesarchiv (Berlin); BAK = Bundesarchiv (Koblenz); BHStA = Bayrisches Hauptstaatsarchiv (Munich); BL = Bodleian Library; GStPK = Geheimes Staatsarchiv Preussischer Kulturbesitz (Berlin); IfZ = Institut für Zeitgeschichte (Munich); IWM = Imperial War Museum (London); MUA = Munich University Archive; PAB = Politisches Archiv des Auswärtigen Amtes (Berlin); PRO = Public Records Office (Kew); NLAB = Nachlass Albrecht Graf Bernstorff (AA); NLB = Nachlass Alexander Böker (IfZ); NLF = Nachlass August Wilhelm Fehling (BAK); NLSvK = Nachlass Lutz Graf Schwerin von Krosigk (BAK); NLvLW = Nachlass Hans Erdmann von Lindeiner-Wildau (BAK); NLvM = Nachlass Karl Alexander von Müller (BHStA). In every case, the number following the abbreviation indicates the box, file, or folder in which the cited document is preserved.

[1] Werner Engelmann, *Die Cecil-Rhodes-Stipendien: Ihre Vorgeschichte und ihre Bedeutung für die deutschen Stipendiaten* (Heidelberg: Julius Gross, 1965), 25.

[2] Ibid. 31.

Germany had already begun to move. On 3 April 1902, the German Embassy in London had sent a coded telegram to the German Foreign Office informing them of the codicil and the Kaiser drafted a telegram of acceptance.[3] On 15 April a message went from Berlin to Graf Metternich, the German Ambassador in London, saying that the Kaiser wanted to be kept informed about the financial situation of the Rhodes Trust. Articles on the subject appeared in at least two leading German newspapers on 22 and 24 April, and on 28 April, Friedrich Althoff (1839–1908), the formidable Prussian Education Minister, asked the then Chancellor and Foreign Minister, Graf von Bülow, for more information on the terms of the will (BAB, R 901, 1 (38947)).

Despite the positive reactions among the Prussian bureaucratic elite and despite the fact that fifteen German students had matriculated at Oxford since 1899,[4] there was less enthusiasm about the new scholarships in Germany as a whole. This was partly due to the growing rivalry between Britain and Germany and partly because the German people, unlike the Kaiser himself, had, on the whole, been pro-Boer.[5] Nevertheless, the Kaiser's will prevailed, as it was entitled to under the terms of Rhodes's codicil, and preparations were made to send the first five scholars in autumn 1903. But because of the political situation, very little happened until late September 1902 when the Kaiser decided to take Dr Friedrich Schmidt (1860–1956), Althoff's right-hand man in the Education Ministry and known to the Kaiser since their schooldays in Kassel, with him on the two-week private visit that he was intending to make to Britain in November (ostensibly to see his uncle, Edward VII, on the occasion of his sixty-first birthday).[6] Schmidt, the Kaiser ordained, should visit Oxford and negotiate the terms of the scholarships with the help of Professor Franz Kielhorn (1840–1908), the professor of Indian philology at Göttingen since 1882 and the recipient of an Oxford D. Litt. on 24 June 1902 (BAB, R 901, 1 (38947)).[7] In preparation for this visit, Oxford University's Council appointed a standing committee on Rhodes scholarships on 3 November. Schmidt arrived in London on 8 November; reported to the German Embassy (where he was received by Graf Johann Heinrich Bernstorff (see n. 23), newly and probably not coincidentally arrived from Munich); met up with Kielhorn; and travelled with him to Oxford on 12

---

[3] PAB, R 5927 and BAB, R 901 (Auswärtiges Amt) (Cecil Rhodes-Stiftung), 1 (38947). Hereafter cited in the text.

[4] Thomas Weber, 'A Stormy Romance: Germans at Oxford between 1900 and 1938', M.St. thesis (Oxford, 1998), [68–9].

[5] See 'Die Rhodes-Stipendien', *Tägliche Rundschau* (Berlin), 22 Apr. 1902, where the German Rhodes scholarships are roundly denounced because of Rhodes's imperialism and the Boer War and 'Deutsche Studenten in Oxford', *Hamburger Nachrichten*, 24 Apr. 1902, which suggests that the German scholarships were receiving wide press coverage in Germany.

[6] GStPK, Rep. 92 Althoff B, no. 166, vol. ii (Schmidt-Althoff), Schmidt to Althoff, 28 Sept. 1902; Friedrich Schmidt-Ott, *Erlebtes und Erstrebtes 1860–1950* (Wiesbaden: Franz Steiner, 1952), 54–6 and 100–4. In 1897, Schmidt had taken over from Althoff as the director of the department which looked after art and general academic affairs (p. 47). He was the last royal Prussian Minister of Education (1917–18) and added the suffix 'Ott', his wife's maiden name, in 1920.

[7] Schmidt knew virtually no English then whereas Kielhorn, who had studied under Max Müller in Oxford and taught in Poona for fifteen years, spoke near-perfect English. The deployment of an academic from Göttingen was also a shrewd move since that University had been founded in the mid-1730s by the Hanoverian George II.

November.[8] On the same day, David Munro, the Vice-Chancellor since 1901 and Provost of Oriel, wrote to them at the Clarendon Hotel inviting them to attend the committee's first meeting on 14 November. And on 30 November, Edward Caird, the Master of Balliol, wrote to Kielhorn that they 'have resolved to leave it entirely to His Majesty the Emperor to decide for what terms the Scholars shall reside'.[9] Two weeks of diplomatic activity at the highest level had produced the conclusion that nobody really knew what practical steps to take because so much depended on the individual colleges—Francis Wylie would not be appointed as the Trust's Oxford Secretary until May 1903.

So Schmidt and Kielhorn drew up a six-page, fifteen-item questionnaire (n. 9) and sent it to twenty colleges in January 1903. It took until late March for all the answers to arrive, and Kielhorn then used these to prepare a tabular statement of the various colleges' terms and conditions for Schmidt to present to Althoff (draft in GStPK (n. 9)). The colleges may have been slow to respond and their responses very heterogeneous, but they showed a general readiness to accept German scholars despite the tense political situation—of which Schmidt had been acutely aware[10]—and on 27 March Kielhorn drafted a letter to Bourchier F. Hawksley, a Rhodes Trustee and the Trust's solicitor, saying that 'So far as I can judge, we have every reason to be satisfied with the result.'[11] Nevertheless, and much to the annoyance of people in Oxford, internal and external factors prevented the Kaiser from naming his five candidates until 13 October.[12] The Trust received the names three days later.[13] Consequently, the candidates arrived in Oxford well after the start of term, and in some cases without the necessary testimonials and/or exam certificates. This provoked Thomas Herbert Warren, the President of Magdalen, to write a furious letter of protest to Kielhorn on 10 November: Oxford was having no nonsense from the Second Reich.[14]

Autumn 1903–Autumn 1910

The German and South African scholars formed the vanguard of the larger, multinational contingent of 1904 and settled down very quickly. On 12 December 1903, the *New York Sun* could report that 'the most notable feature is the case with which [the Germans] have adapted themselves to the new conditions' (BAB, R 901, 2 (38948)). In

---

[8] GStPK, Rep. 92 Althoff B, no. 166, vol. ii, Schmidt to Althoff, 8 Nov. 1902; ibid., telegram Schmidt to Althoff, 11 Nov. 1902.

[9] GStPK, Rep. 92 Schmidt-Ott, B XXXXII (1) (Cecil Rhodes-Stiftung).

[10] See Schmidt to Althoff, 8 Nov. 1902, in which Schmidt—wrongly—anticipated that the negotiations in Oxford would be difficult because of the prevailing anti-German mood in England; cf. Schmidt-Ott, *Erlebtes und Erstrebtes*, 54.

[11] GStPK, Rep. 92 Schmidt-Ott, B XXXXII (1).

[12] See ibid., Schmidt to Kielhorn, 13 July, 21 Oct. 1903; also BAB, R 901, 2 (38948), German Embassy in London to Graf von Bülow, 24 Sept. 1903.

[13] RTF 1682, Boyd to Lord Rosebery, 16 Oct. 1903.

[14] GStPK, Rep. 92 Schmidt-Ott, B XXXXII (1). The first arrivals are described in Karl Alexander von Müller, *Aus Gärten der Vergangenheit: Erinnerungen 1882–1914* (Stuttgart: Gustav Klipper, 1951), 301–13 and Sir Francis Wylie, 'First Arrivals', in Lord Elton (ed.), *The First Fifty Years of the Rhodes Trust and the Rhodes Scholarships* (Oxford: Basil Blackwell, 1955), 78–82.

early 1904, an official of the German Embassy spent some time in Oxford and sent an entirely favourable, five-page report back to the Berlin authorities (ibid.). In November 1905, Schmidt sent Althoff transcripts of three letters from Conrad Roediger (Trinity 1905) in which he enthusiastically describes his first weeks at Oxford.[15]

Nevertheless, at least seven sizeable problems existed, some of which would persist until 1939 and even beyond. First, on the German side, it proved very hard to get permission for Rhodes scholars to interrupt their studies for two years. Consequently, two of the first batch had, with genuine reluctance, to return to Germany to complete their studies after only one year.[16] Second, there was to question of entrance qualifications. Although the Oxford authorities agreed to deem a German *Abitur* (Higher School Leaving Certificate) from a *Gymnasium* (grammar school) as the equivalent of Responsions,[17] this meant in practice that most German scholars had to have attended a *Humanistisches Gymnasium* or equivalent, where Latin and Greek were major subjects, so that candidates from other kinds of *Gymnasium* were very much the exception.[18] Combined with the fact that science and engineering at Oxford were considered low-grade at that time by German standards,[19] almost all pre-1914 German scholars came from a non-scientific background. As the *Tägliche Rundschau* article asked with some trenchancy: what exactly *could* Germans study with profit at Oxford?

Third, the BA normally took three years and Oxford's *Decrees* stipulated that German matriculands could take it in two years only if they had a German doctorate with one of the two lower grades (*rite* or *cum laude*). A fortiori, if a German matriculand wanted to read for postgraduate degrees like the B. Litt. or B. Sc. (instituted 1895), he needed a German doctorate with one of the two higher grades (*magna cum laude* or *summa cum laude*). Luckily, the Diploma in Economics had been authorized on 16 June 1903 and of the fifty-eight German scholars who matriculated before 1914, thirty-nine read for this qualification—which came formally to the notice of the German authorities only in July 1907, one year after the first German scholar had acquired one.[20] This qualification was ideal for those scholars who hoped to join the German civil service—especially the diplomatic or consular services—because of the range of papers on current affairs and modern historical topics that it offered. Ten would pass with distinction by summer 1914.

Fourth, and perhaps most prominently, there was the problem of cost. Rhodes's codicil

---

[15] GStPK, Rep. 92 Althoff B, no. 166, vol. ii.

[16] Von Müller, *Aus Gärten der Vergangenheit*, 386–8; Hans E[rdmann] von Lindeiner-Wildau, 'A Rhodes Scholar from Germany on Oxford', *Cornhill Magazine*, NS 18 (1905), 51; see also Karl Alexander von Müller to Prussian Ministry of Education, 18 June 1904, and to Dr Friedrich Schmidt, 11 July 1904 (BAB, R 901, 3 (38949)).

[17] Engelmann, *Die Cecil-Rhodes-Stipendien*, 46.

[18] See GStPK, Rep. Schmidt-Ott B, XXXXII (2) (Cecil Rhodes-Stiftung), Wylie to Schmidt, 22 Mar. 1913, concerning the problems that faced a successful candidate who had been to a *Realgymnasium*.

[19] See Schmidt to the German Foreign Office, 11 Apr. 1904, where he explains that a candidate has been turned down because he has studied engineering so that Oxford was not adequately equipped to further his education (BAB, R 901, 3 (38949)).

[20] See BAB, R 901, 6 (38952), which contains the relevant regulations and a German translation.

had awarded German scholars £50 per annum less than other scholars on the grounds that they would return home during the vacations. Now, while £250 was a relatively large sum of money, it cost more to study at Oxford than in Germany and some colleges were significantly more expensive. Magdalen, for example, one of the most expensive, expected a down payment on arrival of £47 3s. (matriculation fees, caution money, JCR fees, and Consolidated Clubs fees) plus a further £45 17s. caution money against damage to furniture, and Oriel expected only slightly less.[21] This meant that a third of the scholarship was used up before the academic year had even begun. Schmidt, realizing the problem, had tried without success to get the £250 raised to £300 when in Oxford,[22] and during the first year of the scheme's operation he had to arrange for his Ministry to lend the first five scholars a total of 5,800 M (£290). He also had one of his staff bring the problem to the attention first of the Prussian Finance Ministry and then of the Kaiser himself. In his estimation, the average German needed an extra 2,000 M (£100) per annum to live in Oxford in an appropriate style (BAB, R 901, 7 (38953)). Nothing was done and a letter from the Prussian Education Ministry to the Finance Ministry of 7 March 1908 indicates that Schmidt had by then authorized subsidies of 6,800 M (£340) to seven scholars (BAB, R 901, 7 (38953)). Whether these were ever repaid is unclear.

The financial problem was closely bound up with a fifth problem: the business of selection. According to Rhodes's codicil, the German scholars were to be 'nominated by the German Emperor for the time being'. But in practice, Schmidt did the initial, mainly proactive selection: he put out feelers, drew up a shortlist, and sent it, not necessarily under his own signature, in an annual, respectfully phrased report to the Foreign Minister/Chancellor. He then submitted it to the Kaiser's Privy Council; the Kaiser, with the occasional intervention, gave his assent; and his Imperial Majesty's wishes were made known to the German Embassy in London via the German Foreign Office, which then transmitted them to the Rhodes Trust in London. Schmidt's task was delicate for, as Graf Johann Bernstorff already realized in April 1904,[23] he had to take four considerations into account besides Rhodes's four criteria:[24] school background,[25] the ability to mix as equals

---

[21] See the extensive correspondence in BAB, R 901, 2 (38948); also von Müller, *Aus Gärten der Vergangenheit*, 313, who estimated that it cost between 7,000 M and 9,000 M (£350–£450) p.a. to study at 'top' colleges like Magdalen and Christ Church.

[22] Schmidt to Althoff, 8 Nov. 1902 (n. 8). Of the 316 students whom Weber records matriculating at Oxford 1899–1914, 138 were non-collegiate. Of these, 16 came from aristocratic and 122 from non-aristocratic backgrounds. This almost certainly reflects relative wealth in relation to the cost of college membership.

[23] Graf Johann-Heinrich Bernstorff to Graf von Bülow, 16 Apr. 1904 (BAB, R 901, 3 (38949)). Graf Johann or 'Johnny' (1862–1939) was the uncle of Albrecht Graf Bernstorff; had been born in England; worked in the German Embassy in London as a counsellor 1902–6; and was one of Schmidt's principal contacts there. Cf. Knut Hansen, *Albrecht Graf von Bernstorff: Diplomat und Bankier zwischen Kaiserreich und Nationalsozialismus* (Frankfurt am Main: Peter Lang, 1996), 22–3 *et passim*.

[24] Engelmann, *Die Cecil-Rhodes-Stipendien*, 41.

[25] See O. J. W. Rosenberger, 'A German Rhodes Scholar', *University College Record* (1970), 366; Giles MacDonough, *A Good German: Adam von Trott zu Solz*, rev. edn. (London: Quartet, 1994), 12; von Müller, *Aus Gärten der Vergangenheit*, 492; Lutz Graf Schwerin von Krosigk, *Persönliche Erinnerungen*, 3 vols. (privately printed typescript, n.d.), i. 159–60.

with the English social elite,[26] patronage, and, increasingly, family wealth. Consequently, most pre-1914 scholars came from top German *Gymnasien* and wealthy noble or upper-middle-class families. They were known either to Schmidt himself or to his friends and colleagues in the state bureaucracy.[27] And they usually had the backing of one of Germany's top headmasters, a senior civil servant, the internal envoy ('Minister') to Prussia of one of the other states which constituted the Second Reich 1871–1919, and/or the Kaiser himself. As a result, several scholars, especially during the early years, seem not to have known that they were candidates for a scholarship until they were summoned to Berlin by Schmidt. Conversely, the files in the BAB and GStPK contain an increasing number of applications for scholarships from private individuals, mainly from the upper middle classes. But as far as I can see, only one was successful: not only was he a member of the nobility, he also had the backing of the minister in Berlin who represented the kingdom of Württemberg.

Sixth, more than a few German scholars had, initially at least, an inadequate command of English. This may have contributed to a certain cliquiness among the German contingent at Oxford. As Weber's research has shown, this steadily grew from eleven non-Rhodes matriculands in 1903 to thirty-eight in 1911 before dipping to twenty-seven in 1913; it consisted mainly of men from the nobility; and it formed 'by far the biggest non-English speaking foreign community at Oxford'.[28] When the Germans did get together, it seems fairly certain, judging by various memoirs, that they would have spent considerable time complaining about the seventh major problem: the regimentation of Oxford college life in contrast to the freedom enjoyed by German students. Although von Lindeiner-Wildau conceded that college life made it easier for the newcomer to settle in and make friends,[29] German students, especially older men with military service behind them, found compulsory rising followed by roll-call or chapel, the prohibitions on dining out and drinking in pubs, the compulsory wearing of gowns on the streets after 9.10 p.m., the fixed times by which they had to be in college and bed, and the routine production of tutorial essays extremely irksome.[30] Von Lindeiner-Wildau thought that this prolongation of school life kept English undergraduates in an extended state of childish dependence;[31] von Müller described it as 'medieval nannying';[32] and the Expressionist dramatist Walter Hasenclever, who spent six months as a non-collegiate student in Oxford in 1908, bitterly regretted the absence of beer and women from Oxford student life.[33]

---

[26] The Kaiser and his Privy Council were so worried that the manners of the one pre-1914 scholar from a skilled working-class background would not be up to Oxford standards that they initially granted him a scholarship for one year only even though he had excellent qualifications and eventually stayed in Oxford for three years to read for a B.Litt. See GStPK, Rep. 92 Schmidt-Ott B, XXXXII (1), Freiherr von Hülsen to Kielhorn, 6 May 1904, and BAB, R 901, 3 (38949), Geheimes Zivilkabinett to Prussian Education Ministry, 31 Aug. 1904.

[27] Engelmann, *Die Cecil-Rhodes-Stipendien*, 83.

[28] Weber, 'A Stormy Romance', 9.   [29] 'A Rhodes Scholar', 45.

[30] Ibid. 45, 48, and 50; von Müller, *Aus Gärten der Vergangenheit*, 304.

[31] 'A Rhodes Scholar', 45.   [32] *Aus Gärten der Vergangenheit*, 304.

[33] Walter Hasenclever, 'Oxford: Erinnerungen eines deutschen Studenten', *St Petersburger Zeitung* (14 June 1914).

The second generation of German Rhodes scholars had similar, albeit less strong feelings in the more liberal 1930s.[34]

Despite these problems, the German scheme worked well up to early 1908 by which time Schmidt, following Althoff's resignation in 1907, had become an even more senior official in the Education Ministry. Scholars came and went; six applied for and were readily granted a third year of residence (during which two, both from non-aristocratic backgrounds, obtained a B.Litt.); and a third obtained a B. Litt. in two years which was subsequently turned into two substantial articles for the prestigious *English Historical Review*.[35] In November 1907, a deputation from Oxford headed by the Chancellor (Lord Curzon) and the Vice-Chancellor (Warren) went to Windsor to honour the Kaiser with a DCL; and every Christmas, a group photograph of current scholars was sent to the Kaiser via Schmidt.[36]

But in early 1908, Wylie informed Schmidt that a German scholar, one of the Kaiser's personal nominees, was doing very little work. In summer 1908, both he and another personal nominee (whom the Kaiser had actually substituted for one of Schmidt's non-aristocratic nominees) withdrew from the Diploma of Economics examination after sitting one paper only and were sent down a week early. So Wylie, while conceding in a long letter to Schmidt of 13 June 1908 that some of the best and most suitable scholars had been nobles, made it very clear that he would prefer men who, like the three-year B.Litt. candidates, 'were prepared to take the *work* seriously, and not the play only'. He therefore urged Schmidt to 'bring a[s] much pressure as you can to bear on your Scholars after their appointment, and *during their time here*, to ensure their industry'.[37]

In his previous annual report to the Kaiser (29 Apr. 1907) Schmidt had tactfully hinted at the high esteem in which 'older undergraduates and genuine students (academics)' like Dr Erbe (Merton 1903), Dr Drechsler (Worcester 1904), and Dr Stadler (Magdalen 1906)—i.e. the non-aristocratic scholars, two of whom were B.Litt. candidates—were held in Oxford (BAB, R 901, 6 (38952)). But the Kaiser had not taken the hint and Schmidt in his next annual report (28 Mar. 1909) (BAB, R 901, 2 (38954)) omitted to mention the failure of the two imperial nominees in 1908. But criticism of the scheme was growing within Germany itself. On 3 May 1906, the *Berliner Tageblatt*, Germany's leading liberal newspaper, had criticized the lack of open competition and suggested, using a letter by a rejected candidate as the occasion, that too many scholarships were going to highly placed Prussians. And on 10 July 1909, the Stuttgart *Neues Tagblatt*

[34] See Adolf Schlepegrell, 'Oxford's Glamour in a Foreign Student's Eyes', *Daily Telegraph*, 12 Sept. 1934, 10; Alexander Böker, '1934', in Brian Harrison (ed.), *Corpuscles: A History of Corpus Christi College, Oxford in the Twentieth Century* (Oxford: Alden Press, 1994), 98.

[35] Carl Brinkmann, 'England and the Hanse under Charles II', *English Historical Review*, 23 (1908), 683–708; id., 'The Relations between England and Germany, 1660–1688', *English Historical Review*, 24 (1909), 247–77 and 448–9.

[36] RTF 1682, Schmidt-Ott to Wylie, 5 Sept. 1952. See also Schmidt-Ott, *Erlebtes and Erstrebtes*, 57. Some of these are extant in Rhodes House and also, possibly, in the Kaiser's collection of 11,000 photographs in the Huis Doorn (where he lived in exile after 1918).

[37] GStPK, Rep. 92 Schmidt-Ott, B XXXXII (2), Wylie to Schmidt, 11 Feb. and 13 June 1908.

published an ironic article which pointed out that of the eleven scholars currently at Oxford, seven were from the nobility and the Prussian nobility at that—presumably because they so resembled their English counterparts.[38] But once again, in his next annual report (8 Apr. 1910), Schmidt did not draw the Kaiser's attention to this growing problem and nominated three Prussian aristocrats, one Bavarian aristocrat from a recently ennobled family whose brother had already been a Rhodes scholar, and only one non-aristocrat.[39] All were accepted by the Kaiser without demur (as had been the case since 1908 and would continue to be the case until 1914).

Autumn 1910–August 1914

The situation went critical on 20 October 1910 when Archibald Marshall, a journalist known for his anti-German views, published an article as the sixth of a series on Rhodes scholars in Lord Northcliffe's equally anti-German *Daily Mail*.[40] Here, Marshall pointed out how many German scholars were aristocrats, accused them of looking down on the British, and claimed that some of them spent their time in Oxford 'chiefly amusing themselves in the manner of aristocratic and wealthy young men elsewhere'. He also censured them for their resentment and frequent transgression of Oxford's rules, and for their poor English and poor reputation with the University authorities. The wrong type of German was coming to Oxford and Rhodes, who 'loved workers', 'would have had no sympathy with the young aristocrat who came to Oxford to amuse himself, to hunt and to play polo, and at the most to acquire a colloquial knowledge of English'. Although, given what has been said so far, there was some truth in these allegations, especially the first,[41] most of them were wildly exaggerated and probably derived from the failures of 1908.

Because of its polemical partiality, the piece caused quite a debate in the German press.[42] But the most extensive response, by Baron Wernher Melchior von Ow-

---

[38] 'Wer erhält die Cecil Rhodes-Stipendien?', *Berliner Tageblatt*, 3 May 1906; 'Das Fähnlein der sieben Adligen', *Neues Tagblatt* (Stuttgart), 10 July 1909.

[39] BAB, R 901, 9 (38955). This report was, incidentally, signed by August Graf von Trott zu Solz, the father of Adam, who had taken over as Prussian Minister of Education in 1909.

[40] Archibald Marshall, 'The Germans at Oxford', *Daily Mail*, 20 Oct. 1910, 6. The first five had concentrated on North American scholars.

[41] Of the 181 German matriculands listed by Weber, 26.5% (48) were aristocrats and 73.48% (133) non-aristocrats. But of the 40 German Rhodes scholars elected 1903–10, 67.5% (27) were aristocrats and 32.5% (13) non-aristocrats. This means that over half of Oxford's aristocratic German matriculands 1903–10 were Rhodes scholars. Moreover, when the Kaiser actively intervened in the selection process 1903–7, he did so four times on behalf of aristocratic candidates to the detriment of non-aristocratic candidates and only once on behalf of a non-aristocrat (who then went on to fail his exam). Indeed, in 1907, one of the above four imperial protégés had not even featured on Schmidt's list of reserve candidates.

[42] Georg Lüneburg, 'Die Cecil-Rhodes-Studenten', *Tägliche Rundschau*, 9 Dec. 1910; W[ilhelm] Rein, 'Die deutschen Rhodes-Stipendiaten in Oxford', *Der Tag* (Berlin), 5 Nov. 1910; H[arald] A. F. Loeffler, 'Die Rhodes-Studenten: Eine Ergänzung', *Tägliche Rundschau*, 16 Dec. 1910; Freiherr [Wilhelm] von Sell, 'Die deutschen Studenten in Oxford'; Dr Alexander Lang, 'Die deutschen Studenten in Oxford' (the last two unattributed cuttings, probably from *Der Tag*, are in the papers of Prof. Hermann Georg Fiedler, Taylor Institution, Oxford). Rein (1847–1929) was a distinguished professor of education in Jena; von Sell had been a Rhodes scholar (New 1906); and Loeffler had been a recent non-collegiate student at Oxford.

Wachendorf (Christ Church 1907), a fervent admirer of Rhodes, was published in the *Daily Mail* on 18 November.[43] Although von Ow-Wachendorf was somewhat dewy-eyed about the Oxford experience and allowed that there had been some unfortunate choices and, in one case, disciplinary problems, he effectively refuted Marshall's allegations with one major exception: the preponderance of the nobility who, he wrongly maintained, 'have never received preference'. Schmidt's next annual report (26 Mar. 1911) (PAB, R 62322) mentions Marshall's article—which implies that the Kaiser had already got wind of it—but dismisses it as involving 'inappropriate and unsubstantiated judgements', and on the surface it looks as though the case was closed.[44] But more careful analysis suggests that the controversy enabled Schmidt to use the Kaiser's non-involvement in the selection process to achieve something he had been quietly trying to bring about for years: a shift in the ratio of aristocratic to non-aristocratic candidates (though he says nothing about this in his autobiography).

Between 1903 and 1910, Schmidt had usually offered the Kaiser a list of reserve candidates, and in 1908 and 1909 he had recommended only three and four candidates respectively, leaving the Kaiser to choose the others from lists of six and eight reserves. If one takes these reserves into account, then only 56.76 per cent of the names that reached the Kaiser *in toto* were those of aristocrats and 43.24 per cent those of non-aristocrats, since 44.12 per cent of the reserves were aristocrats and 55.88 per cent non-aristocrats (cf. n. 41). Schmidt had clearly been trying to get the Kaiser used to the idea of suitable candidates who were not from the nobility. After the Marshall controversy, however, 42.31 per cent of the candidates elected 1911–14 were aristocrats and 57.69 per cent non-aristocrats—proportions which are very close to those of the reserve candidates 1903–10.[45] It is also very noticeable that the candidates elected 1911–14 were, with one notable exception, less idiosyncratically adventurous, more solid, middle-of-the-road personalities than their predecessors (who included a future Expressionist poet, a passionate devotee of Nietzsche who would become a member of the circle around the poet Stefan George (1868–1933) and introduce Claus Graf Schenck von Stauffenberg to that circle, one of Hitler's ministers, two controversial academics, one man who gave up a career in the Prussian civil service after five years to work in the slums of a British city, two (possibly three) suicides, one bohemian, one international playboy, and one outspoken anti-Nazi who would be murdered by the SS). None of the post-1911 group stayed for three years or took a B.Litt., but none of them failed the Diploma in Economics (as two more of the Kaiser's favoured candidates did after 1908) or got into trouble. In spring 1911, Schmidt had decided to play safe, and the Kaiser, with the second Morocco crisis looming, was prepared to let him do so.

In late April 1911 Wylie was visited by Professor Ernst Sieper (1863–1918), a professor of English at Munich University and a corresponding member of the Deutsche

[43] Baron W[ernher] von Ow-Wachendorf, 'Why we Go to Oxford: The Germans Reply to their Critics', *Daily Mail*, 18 Nov. 1910, 6.

[44] Engelmann, *Die Cecil-Rhodes-Stipendien*, 89.

[45] These data have been extracted from the annual reports to the Kaiser in the BAB and the PAB and include the seven candidates who were elected in 1914 but never matriculated.

Wissenschaftliche Vereinigung (Anglo-German Society), who put two points to him with some force. The German nobility was overrepresented among the German scholars and this class was not the one from which the influential men of the future would come. Prompted by this visit, Wylie wrote to ten colleges asking about their experience of the German scholars and summarized his findings in a letter to the Trust's Solicitor of 29 April 1911. 'It is worth noting', he wrote, 'that, *this year*, four "Commoners" have been elected, and only one "Aristocrat": and a German Rhodes Scholar happened to mention to me, only this morning, that remarks in the Press are supposed to have affected the policy of the German Government in this respect.' Consequently, he advised the Trustees to wait and see whether this trend continued and undertook to ask Schmidt to send Oxford 'more genuine "students", provided that they were prepared to adapt themselves to the conditions of life in an Oxford College.'[46] On 12 May and 16 June 1911 Sieper wrote to Sir George Parkin, the Organizing Secretary of the Trust outside Oxford (RTF 1682). He pressed home the points he had made to Wylie; stressed the significance of Professor Rein's intervention in the public debate (n. 42); emphasized the growing criticism of the selection procedure within the German student body as a whole; and expressed surprise that Oxford was as satisfied with its German scholars as Wylie professed it to be. Interestingly, he ended the second letter by promising to confer with prominent people about the matter when he next visited Berlin since he realized that Schmidt 'would hardly venture to criticize the present method of appointment to the most exalted place'. But as we have seen, the wily Schmidt was already at work, and to such good effect that the controversy died down. The Trustees' decided in spring 1912 to fulfil the terms of Rhodes's codicil whereby fifteen German scholars should be at Oxford at any given time by increasing the number elected to seven and eight in alternate years.[47]

The proviso at the end of Wylie's letter to Hawksley brings us to one final problem which had been identified by German academics when the scheme was first announced (n. 5) and which, although affecting only three scholars 1903–10 and none 1911–14, was none the less real for that. In the early years of this century, there seem to have been two coexisting, albeit overlapping cultures in Oxford. On the one hand, a college-based culture in which tutors sought primarily to produce (reasonably) well-read, physically fit, rounded, and well-mannered gentlemen who were imbued with team spirit, a sense of fair play, institutional loyalty, and the service ethic, and who would find their proper place in the hierarchies of the Empire at home or abroad. On the other hand, there was a more University-based culture in which University appointees, following more the Humboldtian model, saw their principal task as the advancement of 'Wissenschaft'— systematic research leading to systematized, published knowledge. Alexander von Grunelius (1890–1977) (University 1910), a German who was not a Rhodes scholar, perceived this very clearly in a talk which he gave to the Anglo-German Society on 15 May 1912. Here, he distinguished between the 'scholars' (who would become academics and senior civil servants) and various other categories of student for whom academic

[46] RTF 1682, Wylie to Bourchier Hawksley, 29 Apr. 1911.

[47] PAB, R 62322, annual report to the Kaiser, 20 Mar. 1912. This possibility had first been mooted in 1905 and raised again in 1908. As a result, seven scholars were elected in 1912 and seven in 1913.

work was of lesser importance.[48] Although the debate about the (de-)merits of the Humboldtian model had been going on in Oxford since *c.*1850 and produced tangible results by 1903,[49] the former culture would be far more visible than the latter until well into this century. Indeed, Rhodes's 'ideal qualified student' as described in clause 23 of his seventh will (in whom 'literary and scholastic attainments' would constitute only 40 per cent of his personality) was simply a larger-than-life version of the kind of person whom Oxford was already producing.

Those German scholars who were studying for a degree primarily for career reasons and had some sporting ability fitted into collegiate culture without too much difficulty (even if they had a pretty low opinion of Oxford's academic standards and intellectual life).[50] But a German scholar who saw himself primarily as an apprentice 'Wissenschaftler', had little interest in sport (by general German consensus the most important aspect of collegiate culture),[51] and found that culture somewhat juvenile had a much less congenial time at Oxford unless he could make a connection with the extra-collegiate research culture. Von Müller enjoyed his year at Oriel precisely because at this juncture he intended to take a degree in law and become a civil servant—not a professional historian. Carl Brinkmann (Queen's 1904), a budding polymath and future co-founder of the Institute for Social and Political Science in Heidelberg in 1924, clearly managed to relate to Oxford's research culture (cf. n. 35). But he asked to move out of college very early on in his stay and was generally regarded as an unsatisfactory Rhodes scholar because he was 'too much of a recluse' who 'knew practically nobody in College'.[52] Albrecht von Blumenthal (Lincoln 1907), a future professor of classics, was described by the Rector of Lincoln as 'rather a fish out of water here' because, 'if he had it all his own way, I think he would brood over Nietzsche and Schopenhauer and bask in the sunlight of his beloved Goethe'.[53] And I have shown elsewhere how Ernst Stadler, a future professor of German and comparative literature whose brilliant career was cut short by the war but who survives as Robert von Stohr in Otto Flake's novel *Horns Ring* (1916), experienced similar difficulties and negotiated them only with the help and encouragement

[48] [Alexander von Grunelius], 'Zur Einführung', in [Alexander von Grunelius and Albrecht Graf Bernstorff (eds.)], *Des Teutschen Scholaren Glossarium in Oxford* [privately printed booklet, Nov. 1912], 3. A letter from Bernstorff to his lifelong friend Elly Gräfin von Reventlow (1875–1960) (Hansen, *Bernstorff, passim*) of 20 Nov. 1912 (AA, NLAB, 1) indicates that Grunelius wrote the first essay, that Bernstorff wrote the section on public schools (pp. 53–66), and that the two of them were jointly responsible for the rest of the booklet.

[49] Marc Schalenberg, 'Die Rezeption des deutschen Universitätsmodells in Oxford 1850–1914', in Rudolf Muhs, Johannes Paulmann, and Willibald Steinmetz (eds.), *Aneignung und Abwehr: Interkultureller Transfer zwischen Deutschland und Großbritannien im 19. Jahrhundert* (Bodenheim: Philo, 1998), 200–26.

[50] See von Müller, *Aus Gärten der Vergangenheit*, 332, 371, and 379 (where the differences between Oxford and German universities are identified with extreme precision); von Lindeiner-Wildau, 'A Rhodes Scholar', 47–8; Engelmann, *Die Cecil-Rhodes-Stipendien*, 85; von Grunelius and Bernstorff, *Glossarium*, 2–3 and 6–8. Schlepegrell would make the same point in 1934 (n. 34).

[51] Hasenclever said that 'sport constitutes life for the English student'; Bernstorff's *Glossarium* described the sport cult at Oxford as 'exaggerated' (p. 4); and von Müller wondered whether Oxford students could talk about anything else (*Aus Gärten der Vergangenheit*, 307).

[52] RTF 1682, Note by Wylie, 28 Feb. 1911.

[53] GStPK, Rep. 92 Schmidt-Ott, B XXXXII (1), Rector of Lincoln to an unnamed friend of Schmidt's, 13 Nov. [1907].

of Professor Hermann Georg Fiedler (1862–1945), the (originally German) Taylor Professor of German since 1903.[54] All three were, in terms of Rhodes's will, 'merely book-worms' and should not have come to Oxford as Rhodes scholars even though all three variously acquired something from the experience. Brinkmann developed a lifelong pre-occupation with British history, a marked hostility to British imperialism and capitalism (which would culminate in his extremely critical *Der wirtschaftliche Liberalismus als System der britischen Weltanschauung* (1940)), and a determination to find a 'third way' between communism and capitalism.[55] Von Blumenthal found himself an English fiancée. Stadler produced a *Habilitation* and a major edition for the Preussische Akademie der Wissenschaften, and assimilated material for a number of poems.

Despite the difficulties, most German scholars seem to have enjoyed and gained some-thing from their time in Oxford without too much friction.[56] Von Lindeiner-Wildau, a leading politician of the nationalist Right during the Weimar Republic, came to 'admire sincerely the unlimited cultivation of athletics to be found there' and Oxford's 'pious and proud clinging to ancient tradition'.[57] Von Müller's memoirs indicate that an accumula-tion of near visionary experiences in Oxford converted him from law to history by reveal-ing to him what Germany lacked: a sense of unity such as had (allegedly) existed in the Middle Ages.[58] Wilhelm Goebel (St John's 1904) was, like some of the other Germans, so impressed by the University's missions to inner cities,[59] and so influenced by the Fabian socialism of his tutor Sidney Ball (1857–1918), that he went to work in Birmingham's Street Children Union in 1913 and died there of nephritis on 2 April 1914.[60] Roediger recorded that Oxford taught him common sense, practicality, discrimination, the value of tradition, and team-work.[61] Kurt von Kamphoevener (St John's 1907) wrote to Wylie of 'the enormous value of Oxford's subtle influence on our own somewhat rigid men-tality' (RTPF, 20 Dec. 1923). Albrecht Graf Bernstorff (Trinity 1909) always maintained that the Oxford experience was crucial in the development of his political liberalism;[62] lyricized about Oxford's 'timeless beauty' and ability to synthesize 'Greek perfection, clas-sical harmony, medieval scholarly wisdom and modern-day life';[63] and returned when-ever he could over the next thirty years. Oskar Rosenberger (University 1911), after leaving

[54] Richard Sheppard, *Ernst Stadler (1883–1914): A German Expressionist Poet at Oxford* (Oxford: Magdalen College, 1994) and 'Ernst Stadler in Oxford', in Michael Butler and Robert Evans (ed.), *The Challenge of German Culture: Essays Presented to Wilfrid van der Will* (Basingstoke; Palgrave, 2000), 59–76.

[55] See 'Germans at Oxford' (letters), *Spectator*, 1 June 1945, 502; Erwin von Beckerath, 'Carl Brinkmann', *Zeitschrift für die gesamte Staatswissenschaft*, 111/3 (1955), 389.

[56] See [Wernher Melchior von Ow-Wachendorf], 'Studium in Oxford', *Germania* (Berlin), 5 Mar. 1927, and Waldemar von Mohl, 'Erinnerungen', in Gräfin Elly von Reventlow (ed.), *Albrecht Bernstorff zum Gedächtnis* (n.p.: 1952), 21.

[57] 'A Rhodes Scholar', 45, 50.   [58] *Aus Gärten der Vergangenheit*, 318–20, 355.

[59] Cf. von Grunelius and Bernstorff, *Glossarium*, 30–2; Conrad Roediger, 'A German's Experience of England', unpublished 23-page typescript (c.1966), 11–12; Sheppard, 'Ernst Stadler', 59–76.

[60] RT PF Goebel, Goebel to Wylie, 12 Nov. 1913. The Union was based at Cathedral House (71 Newhall St, Birmingham) and had opened on 6 Dec. 1905 for the express purpose of turning slum children, par-ticularly boys, away from unemployment, hooliganism, and crime ('Opening of the Cathedral House', *Birmingham Diocesan Magazine*, 1/1 (1906), 22–4).

[61] 'A German's Experience', 22–3.   [62] Hansen, *Bernstroff*, 29, 79.

[63] AA, NLAB, 2, Bernstorff to Reventlow, 13 May [1913].

the right-wing German National People's Party (DNVP) in 1924, organized round-table discussions in conservative circles all over Germany because he believed that 'the method of the round table and the club, both taken over from England to Germany, show at the same time a mental relationship: the tendency to democracy'.[64] In 1928, Hans Boden (Worcester 1912), then on the Reparations Commission in Paris, wrote to Wylie that nearly all the members of the British delegation were Oxford men, too, and that this was 'often a great help in settling affairs'.[65] Fridolin von Senger und Etterlin (St John's 1912), the future general who would delay the Allies for eight months around Monte Cassino (Jan.–Aug. 1944), said that the experience of Oxford 'vastly broadened his world' and made him more sympathetic to democracy.[66] Wilhelm von Richthofen (Lincoln 1913), a cousin of the Red Baron, was so impressed by Oxford's federal collegiate structure and Rhodes's founding vision that he published a book in 1930. Here, citing Rhodes's codicil, he argued that the only way to prevent the coming world war and Bolshevik hegemony was to turn the British Empire into a federal state, assimilate Germany, and create a Brito-Germanic Empire.[67] And even Stadler, who had every reason to feel resentful, could, on 26 January 1910, write to Wylie about how much he was looking forward to Trinity term 'which I shall be allowed to spend at the dear old Oxford'.[68]

Had war not intervened, German Rhodes scholars would, we can be sure, have continued to play a leading role in the OU German Literary Society (founded by Fiedler on 10 November 1909 with President Warren as its patron).[69] It is also fairly certain that the Anglo-German Society would have continued with German scholars at the helm. Founded by von Ow-Wachendorf on 16 November 1908, its major aims were to improve Anglo-German relations and help English people who were intending to study in Germany.[70] In early 1909, the future diplomat Eugen Millington-Drake (1889–1972) (Magdalen 1908) and von Ow-Wachendorf went on a tour of German universities to promote the Society and improve Anglo-German relations using the argument enshrined in Rhodes's codicil that 'all Anglo-saxon and Germanic races should form a cultural federation and fight for progress shoulder to shoulder'.[71] And on 15 February 1909, at a

---

[64] RTF 1682, Rosenberger to Allied Control Commission, 10 Nov. 1945. Cf. AvK, circular from Rosenberger June 1971 in which he says that he had worked for twenty years to promote an 'authoritarian democracy' like that preserved in England and help create a new ruling class.

[65] RT PF, Boden to Wylie, 30 Dec. 1928.

[66] Ferdinand von Senger und Etterlin, 'Senger', in Correlli Barnett (ed.), *Hitler's Generals* (London: Weidenfeld & Nicolson, 1989), 376; Fridolin von Senger und Etterlin, *Neither Fear nor Hope*, trans. George Malcolm (London: Macdonald, 1963), 42 and 350.

[67] Wilhelm Freiherr von Richthofen, *Brito-Germania: Ein Weg zu Paneuropa* (Berlin: Verlag für aktuelle Politik, 1930), 131–2, 136–7, and 153–6.

[68] Ernst Stadler, *Dichtungen, Schriften, Briefe*, ed. Klaus Hurlebusch and Karl Ludwig Schneider (Munich: C. H. Beck, 1983), 474–5.

[69] See BL, GA Oxon. b. 147. Its founding members included five German Rhodes scholars; Martin Hunnius (Hertford 1909) was its secretary 1910–11 (when ten German Rhodes scholars were numbered among its members); Baron Georg von Dalwig (Brasenose 1910) was its secretary 1911–12; and its final event, a banquet in honour of the German Ambassador Prince Lichnowsky that was attended by ninety-one guests, involved twelve German Rhodes scholars.

[70] GStPK, Rep. 92 Schmidt-Ott, B XXXXII (2), document dated 12 Oct. 1908.

[71] 'Die wirtschaftlichen und kulturellen Beziehungen . . .', *Kölnische Volkszeitung*, 18 Jan. 1909.

dinner in honour of Rhodes that was held in the Lyceum Club, Piccadilly and attended by twenty-five German Rhodes scholars, von Ow-Wachendorf, to cheers, enunciated the same aims in considerably more highly coloured rhetoric using the same missionary justification as he had done in Cologne.[72]

By mid-June 1909 the Society had 370 honorary English and 566 subscribing German members.[73] With this support, the Society was able to provide 102 letters of introduction for British subjects in Germany; arrange five appointments in Germany; and, in Hilary term 1909, open a reading room on the second floor of 50 Cornmarket that was open from 9.30 a.m. to 9.30 p.m. It subscribed to four daily papers, three weeklies, four comic papers, and six monthly periodicals (all liberal-conservative). The Society also established a library of novels there and 'a series of publications of students' societies, the lecture lists of all the German Universities for the next semester and the vacation courses and other information that would be of value to those of our English Members who are thinking of going to Germany'.[74] The Society lasted until the end of Trinity term 1914, and an impression of the way it conducted its day-to-day business during the last eighteen months of its existence can be gained from its Suggestions Book, most of whose entries are by Rhodes scholars.[75] Its last major event seems to have been a debate on 28 May 1914 on the motion 'That Parliamentary Government would be advantageous for Germany'. But for the war, the Society might have developed into a more officially sanctioned institution since the largest proportion of pre-1914 German scholars, unlike those from elsewhere, was destined for state service. This would not only have allowed them to exert influence in Germany on the Society's behalf, it would also have enabled a significant number of them to fulfil Rhodes's wish that his scholars dedicate themselves to public service.[76]

August 1914–January 1933

The war killed twelve German scholars (including two who never matriculated, the son of the German Chancellor, and Cornelius Balduin Waldhausen (Exeter 1912), a promising young translator and protégé of Stefan George, to whom this poet would dedicate two poems in his collection *Das neue Reich* (1928)).[77] It also did lasting psychological damage to a thirteenth;[78] smashed at least two marriages; generated one set of angry,

---

[72] 'The German Rhodes Scholars', *The Times*, 16 Feb. 1909, 8. Von Ow-Wachendorf's enthusiasm for Rhodes was so great that he returned to London and Oxford in early 1911 to write a (never-published) book entitled *Cecil Rhodes and the Chartered Company* (PAB, PF).

[73] Letter to the *Spectator* from Beatrice Erskine, 19 June 1909, 974. The context of this letter was a protracted debate about Germany's political and military intentions.

[74] BL, GA Oxon. b. 147, letter, 25 Apr. 1910, signed by the Society's president, Gustav Adolph Jacobi (Queen's 1907).

[75] BL, MS Top. Oxon. d. 417.

[76] A *Times* leader of 7 Dec. 1922 (13) expressed surprise that 'so few scholars have as yet risen to positions of public leadership (which was Rhodes's underlying idea) except in the domain of teaching'. But for the war, Germany might well have formed the exception to this generalization.

[77] Stefan George, *Werke in Zwei Bänden*, 2 vols. (Munich: Helmut Küpper, 1958), i. 457–8; see also 'Cornelius Balduin Waldhausen', *Castrum Peregrini*, 111–15 (1974), 274–6.

[78] RTF 1682, C. K. Allen to Lord Elton, 27 Oct. 1944.

disillusioned memoirs;[79] and inspired a British author to write a (still readable) novel on the fatal hazards of marrying even the most Anglophile of German Rhodes scholars on the eve of a war.[80] At first, when it appeared that the war would be over quickly, the Rhodes Trustees were content that the German scholarships should simply be held in abeyance, and as late as 26 July 1915 the Prime Minister told Parliament that he was not prepared to initiate legislation to alter this situation.[81] But after a German academic who had accepted on Oxford DCL before the war published a particularly vicious attack on Oxford and Cambridge in general and the value of the Rhodes scholarships in particular,[82] and as the casualty lists lengthened in 1916 with no end of hostilities in sight, the Trustees reluctantly decided that the German scholarships should be abolished by an Act of Parliament which was passed towards the end of that year.

According to Weber,[83] no German students matriculated at Oxford until 1925, and for the four years after that no more than four per year did so (fourteen in all including one woman). This was due partly to the highly unstable economic situation in Germany until 1924, partly to the enduring sense of hostility between Britain and Germany, and partly to the intense sense of outrage in Germany at the extremely harsh terms of the Treaty of Versailles (1919) (which three former German scholars, seeing the dangers, attacked in print).[84] As far as the Trustees were concerned, it seems, the war meant that the German part of Rhodes's experiment was a failure and could be forgotten. Nevertheless, in June–August 1922, Wylie, who does not seem to have shared that view, sought to break the ice by contacting as many former German scholars as he could, requesting biographical data for the Rhodes House *Record*. But the war and its aftermath had done serious damage to the internationalist aspect of Rhodes's founding vision: some scholars declined to reply and some sent the information. But several of them replied with some bitterness that they were unwilling to provide such information or even have their names included in the *Record* because of the abolition of the scholarships, with one making explicit reference to the Treaty of Versailles.

Wylie reported this to the Trustees and included extracts from his respondents,[85] but

[79] Wilhelm Freiherr von Richthofen, *Zurückgehaltenes und Unterdrücktes aus vier Kriegsjahren* (Berlin: Karl Curtius, 1919).

[80] Harold Spender, *The Dividing Sword* (London: Mills & Boon, [late] 1916). Its hero, Count Rudolph von Adelhaus, is reading law at Christ Church and bears no resemblance to any real person.

[81] 'Rhodes Scholarships Held by Germans', *The Times*, 27 July 1915, 8.

[82] Eduard Meyer, *England: Seine staatliche und politische Entwicklung und der Krieg gegen Deutschland* (Stuttgart: J. G. Cotta'sche Buchhandlung Nachfolger, [c.Sept.] 1915), 38–41.

[83] 'A Stormy Romance', 22, 29.

[84] Hans Erdmann von Lindeiner-Wildau, *Wie der Gewaltfriede aussieht*, Deutschnationale Flugschrift 17 [Berlin, c.1919]; Karl Alexander von Müller, *Des deutschen Volkes Not und der Vertrag von Versailles* (Munich: Knorr & Hirth, 1922); Carl Brinkmann, *Die bewegenden Kräfte in der deutschen Volksgeschichte: Ein Beitrag zur politischen Soziologie* (Leipzig: B. G. Teubner, 1922), 76. Ironically, Philip Kerr, while exercising a moderating influence on French demands at the Versailles Conference, was responsible, as Lloyd George's right-hand man, for drafting the reply to the German delegation's challenge to that clause of the Treaty which probably caused the most outrage in Germany: clause 231 which declared that Germany was solely responsible for the war (David Lloyd George, *The Truth about the Peace Treaties*, 2 vols. (London: Victor Gollancz, 1938), i. 263–4, 397–8, and 403–4. On the other side of the table, Roediger was PPA to Graf Brockdorff-Rantzau, who headed the German delegation.

[85] RT PF, Wylie to Dawson, 7 Sept. 1922.

on 26 September (RTM 2467) the Trustees 'agreed that the time had not come to take
any action in the matter'. Although, from then on, Wylie and the Trust were continu-
ally asked by a variety of individuals and groups to reinstate the scholarships, the Trustees
would not change their mind for six years. On 22 February 1923, the Oxford Union
passed the motion (177:74) 'That the time has come when the enmities engendered by
the War should give way to a friendly attitude towards all the peoples that fought under
the Central Powers' and this was duly noted by the Trust. In June 1923, Bernstorff, a
Legationssekretär in the German Embassy in London since 20 January 1923, reported on
the first visit of a group of German students to Oxford since the war in an article in the
Deutsche Nation and expressed the hope that the German scholarships would be reinstated.[86] On 9 April 1924, Friedrich Sthamer (1856–1931), the German Ambassador in
London 1920–30, reported to the Foreign Office in Berlin that although the question of
reinstatement had not been discussed publicly during the German students' visit to
Oxford in May 1923, members of his Embassy were raising the possibility with interested
parties since there was considerable support for the move in German academic circles.
On 12 September 1924, another letter from Sthamer said that although it would be a tactical error to put direct pressure on the Trustees, everything possible was being done to
keep the issue alive among English academics (PAB, R 62322). On 12 June 1925, an Australian Scholar, Frank L. Apperly (Victoria and Lincoln 1910), now an academic, wrote
a letter to *The Times* (which was not published but passed on to Wylie, probably via
Geoffrey Dawson (1874–1944) who was its editor 1923–41 and now a Trustee). Here,
Apperly argued for reinstatement on the grounds that 'the growing menace of
Bolshevism makes such a move imperative' (RTF 1682). In 1924, the Conference of Students of the Empire had voted for reinstatement, and on 22 May 1926, the President of
Victoria University Students' Association (NZ) wrote to Philip Kerr, in support of that
resolution (RTF 1682). On 18 February 1927, Kerr, reporting on a visit to South Africa,
said that there 'was widespread feeling everywhere in favour of [the German scholarships]
being restored in the near future' (RTF 1682). On 5 March 1927, von Ow-Wachendorf
published a long, anonymous article in *Germania*, the organ of the Catholic Centre Party,
extolling the virtues of the scholarships, which was noted in the *Observer* on 13 March.[87]
On 26 March 1927, von Lindeiner-Wildau, now a prominent member of the moderate
wing of the DNVP and a Reichstag Deputy since 1924, wrote to Wylie hoping for better
relations between Germany and Oxford once more (RTPF).[88] And on 26 January 1929,
Arthur Mee published a piece in his *Children's Newspaper* in which he asked Parliament
to revoke the 1916 bill, unaware that the Trustees had voted for reinstatement on 4
December 1928.

[86] Hansen, *Bernstorff*, 130, 181. Von Ow-Wachendorf, by now a career diplomat too, had a hand in
organizing this visit (RT PF, letter to Wylie, 21 Feb. 1923).
[87] RT Press Cuttings X; see n. 56.
[88] During the 1920s, von Lindeiner-Wildau had edited the periodical *Der deutsche Führer* (1922–4) and
his political views are contained in three pamphlets published in Berlin by the DNVP: *Wir und die
Deutsche Volkspartei* (1921); *Aufgaben völkischer Politik* (1924); *Die Ziele der Deutschnationalen* (1926). See
also Erasmus Jones, *Die Volkskonservativen 1928–1933: Entwicklung, Struktur, Standort und staatspolitische
Zielsetzung* (Düsseldorf: Droste, 1965), 25–7, 58, 80, 84–5, and 144.

The Trustees decided to keep their decision secret for the time being and on 9 April 1929, Bernstorff sent a note of a conversation with Kerr to the German Foreign Office during which Kerr had allegedly said that although he had never been able to find out anything definite about this matter, an announcement could be expected in July (PAB, London 1540). Nevertheless, both von Lindeiner-Wildau and the Berlin Foreign Office had heard rumours in late summer/autumn 1928.[89] On 5 July 1929 Bernstorff wrote back to the Berlin Foreign Office recommending that as many former German scholars as possible should go to the annual Rhodes dinner (which was to take place in the newly opened Rhodes House).[90] A letter from a miffed von Ow-Wachendorf to Bernstorff of 26 October 1929 suggests that, between April and July, a few selected German scholars were encouraged to attend that dinner by being told what they might hear there.[91] Consequently, eleven made the journey (RTF 2737) and, in the presence of the Prince of Wales (who also spoke), heard Stanley Baldwin announce that two German scholarships per annum would be offered from 1930. Brinkmann gave a speech of thanks; the news was reported the next day in at least seven major German newspapers; *The Times* gave its approval to 'that wise decision' on 8 and 9 July; a copy of Baldwin's speech was procured for the German Foreign Office's files; and on 11 July, Ambassador Sthamer wrote a long letter to de Haas about the Trustees' decision and the plans for its implementation (PAB, London 1540).

Despite the technical and personal reasons for the long-delayed reinstatement, relations between Britain and Germany had been slowly improving since Ramsay MacDonald's brief term as Prime Minister and Foreign Secretary January–November 1924.[92] Bernstorff, who had kept up his contacts with the Trust ever since coming to London as a diplomat,[93] rapidly built up an excellent relationship with Kerr, and on 17 June 1926—the year when Germany was granted full membership of the League of Nations—he and the Anglophile Harald Mandt (Brasenose 1908; honorary fellow 1973) were the first Germans to attend a post-war annual Rhodes scholars' dinner in Oxford. On 25 June 1926, the Anglo-German Academic Board (AGAB) was constituted to act in cooperation with the AAD. In June 1927, a branch of the AAD, and its British counterpart the Anglo-German Academic Bureau, were opened in London.[94] And in July 1926, the Rhodes Trustees resolved to make a grant of £500 per annum to the AGAB for three years to 'assist the interchange of University students between Great Britain and Germany'. This decision was almost certainly initiated by Kerr, with the support of Wylie and Bernstorff,[95] in order to create a climate in which reinstatement would first become

---

[89] PAB, London 1540, von Lindeiner-Wildau to Berlin Foreign Office, 28 Nov. 1928; Ministerialrat Walter de Haas (1864–1931) to von Lindeiner-Wildau, 29 Nov. 1928.

[90] PAB, London 1540, Bernstorff to de Haas, 4 Dec. 1928.

[91] BAK, NLF, 93. Von Ow-Wachendorf had not been one of the privileged few and so had boycotted the July dinner.

[92] See David Marquand, *Ramsay MacDonald* (London: Richard Cohen Books, 1977), 329–56.

[93] Hansen, *Bernstorff,* 181 n. 70.

[94] *Der Deutsche Akademische Austauschdienst 1925 bis 1975* (Bonn: DAAD, 1975), 18–20; RTF 2706.

[95] Cf. BAK, NLF, 93, Bernstorff to Adolf Morsbach (AAD), 24 Aug. 1929, and Morsbach to Bernstorff, 28 Aug. 1929; also PAB, London 1540, AAD to Bernstorff, 28 Mar. 1930.

thinkable and then possible. Certainly, on 11 May 1927 Wylie wrote to Kerr (RTF 1682) that 'so far as one can see, it will be, in a couple of years, still more possible [for Germans to come here]', and proposed that the Trustees consider taking two German scholars per year. Furthermore, Kerr's report to the Trustees of 7 December 1928 clinched their decision of three days earlier by pointing out that if they could fund Anglo-German exchanges at £500 per annum, then they could fund two German scholars, thereby demolishing once and for all the economic argument which the Trustees had used as their official reason for non-reinstatement (RTF 1682). The Trustees made two further grants to the AAD £500 in 1929 and 1930 (cf. n. 95), and one final grant of £250 in the economically critical year of 1931. This meant that, for five years, the Rhodes Trust had contributed five times as much to the promotion of Anglo-German academic relations as the AGAB's next largest donor—Baron Schröder (RTF 2706). But of the twenty-two German students who came to Britain 1926–9 with the AGAB's support, none studied at Oxford—partly, I imagine, because of the cost and partly to prevent any suggestion that the German scholarships were being tacitly revived *de facto*.

On the morning of 6 July 1929, the eleven Germans who had attended the Rhodes dinner set up an Association of Former German Rhodes Scholars and were consulted about selection procedures. They 'headed by Bernstorff and Brinkmann, were strongly of [the] opinion that the State should not be brought into the selection in any way'.[96] But according to a furious reminder from von Lindeiner-Wildau to Bernstorff of 15 October 1929 (BAK, NLF, 93), they had also resolved that German scholars should form a majority on their selection committee. This is confirmed by a detailed, four-page memorandum that Bernstorff had sent to Sir Otto Beit, one of the most senior Trustees, on 15 July 1929. Here, Bernstorff reiterated the first point and proposed that the committee should include '3 [former German scholars] out of 5 or 4 out of 7 members'. He also suggested that Schmidt-Ott (see n. 6) should be its independent chairman given his ex-ministerial standing and commitment to furthering university education since 1920 via the leading role he had played in the Notgemeinschaft der deutschen Wissenschaft (NDW) (Emergency Committee for German Scholarship/Science). Bernstorff also recommended using the politically independent AAD as the clearing-house in Germany for applications given the links between it and the Trust via the AGAB, and inviting Dr Adolf Morsbach (1890–1937)—whom he had already approached on 12 July—to act as the committee's secretary.[97] Finally, he proposed inviting Dr Wilhelm Solf (1862–1936), the former German Minister for the Colonies and long-time Ambassador to Tokyo, and Professor Albrecht Mendelssohn-Bartholdy (1874–1936), the Director of Hamburg's Institute for Foreign Policy, to serve on the committee as independent members. On 8 October, the Trustees approved Bernstorff's plan 'in general',[98] but rejected the proposal

[96] RTF 1682, Kerr to Dr Abraham Flexner, 15 July 1929.
[97] *Deutsche Akademische Austauschdienst*, 18. Bernstorff omitted to mention that the AAD had rooms in the same building—the Berlin *Schloss*—as the NDW and that both Brinkmann and Schmid-Ott were on the *Kuratorium* (board of governors) of the AAD (see BAK, NLF, 93, Bernstorff to Morsbach, 12 July 1929, and Morsbach to Brinkmann, 30 July 1929).
[98] RTF 1682, Kerr to Morsbach, 9 Oct. 1929.

that former German scholars form a majority. After extensive correspondence (RTF 1682), Kerr and Beit went to Berlin from 28 to 30 October 1929 to finalize matters, and the committee, consisting of Schmidt-Ott, Mendelssohn-Bartholdy, Morsbach, Dr Walther Simons (1861–1937),[99] Brinkmann, Bernstorff, and Mandt met in Berlin's *Schloss* (n. 97) on 25 January 1930 to make its first selection. Forty-five people had expressed interest; twenty-seven serious candidates were considered; and six were interviewed. Ernst Fritz Schumacher (New), who would make the phrases 'small is beautiful' and 'intermediate technology' current in the English language and whose global impact through his work on ecological and environmental issues has probably been greater than that of any other German Rhodes scholar, was elected unanimously, and Willi Koelle (Magdalen) by six votes to one.[100] Helmuth James Graf von Moltke, who was executed on 23 January 1945 for the leading part he had played in the German Resistance movement, had wanted to apply, but was advised that he was too old.[101]

But the process had not been entirely smooth. The old problems about entrance requirements, standing, timing, and appropriate courses of study had exercised the English and German authorities throughout 1929 and would become more acute as more colleges required 'their men for an Honours degree of research' and became correspond-ingly reluctant to take 'a man for two years only who read for the Economics Diploma'.[102] The Germans had considerable difficulties drawing up an accurate memorandum for applicants and found it especially hard to translate the four selection criteria laid down by Rhodes in his will. On 9 October 1929, Kerr paraphrased them for Morsbach accord-ing to his own lights, but far from helping Morsbach, Kerr's paraphrase caused him even greater problems. So Morsbach reduced the four to three and did his best. But given what lay in store politically, there is an awful irony in his inability to translate Kerr's 'gentler moral qualities' and 'leadership' adequately: they came out as 'Persönlichkeit, Pflicht-gefühl und kameradschaftliche Gesinnung'.[103] But more seriously still and despite the scholars' intentions, German politics, as Brinkmann wrote to Wylie on 25 November 1929 (RTPF), had intervened in the shape of a fundamental antagonism between the liberal, cosmopolitan, non-partisan Bernstorff and the right-wing, nationalist von Lindeiner-Wildau that would persist throughout most of the 1930s.

File 93 of the NLF (BAK) indicates that from July 1929, Bernstorff and Morsbach had

---

[99] Dr Solf had declined membership as his son wished to apply for a scholarship (RTF 1682, Bern-storff to Kerr, 11 Sept. 1929), whereupon Bernstorff proposed five other names including Simons's. Simons would have been known to Roediger (since both were members of the German delegation to Versailles) and to several other former Rhodes scholars (since he had been Foreign Minister June 1920–May 1921). From 1922 to 1929, he was President of Germany's Supreme Court. Kerr returned to England via Hamburg, where, probably at the invitation of Mendelssohn-Bartholdy, he gave a lecture on the League of Nations during which he repudiated the idea that any one country was responsible for the war (cf. n. 84). See John Pinder and Andrea Bosco (eds.), *Pacifism is not Enough: Collected Lectures and Speeches of Lord Lothian* (London: Lothian Foundation Press, 1990), 121–45 (pp. 121–2).

[100] RTF, Bernstorff to Wylie, 26 Jan. 1930.

[101] RTF 1682, Dorothy Moltke to Kerr, 22 Dec. 1929; RTF 1682A, Prof. H. J. Paton to Wylie, 4 Jan. 1930.

[102] RTF 1682, C. K. Allen (Warden and Oxford Secretary since autumn 1931) to Lothian (formerly Kerr), 24 Oct. 1932.

[103] RTF 1682, Morsbach to Kerr, 14 Oct. 1929.

been quietly (and successfully) manœuvring to ensure that the political complexion of the selection committee was predominantly liberal.[104] They also tacitly accepted the ruling that former scholars could not form a majority. The politically astute von Lindeiner-Wildau quickly spotted this and seems to have encouraged other, more conservatively minded scholars to protest against such an unrepresentative situation—but only when it was too late.[105] Indeed, Günther von Diergardt (Christ Church 1906) thought that the reduction of scholarships to two should have caused the German scholars to boycott the scheme altogether back in July.[106] Word of this controversy reached the Trustees, and on 26 November, Beit protested to Schmidt-Ott about von Lindeiner-Wildau's 'agitation' and attempts to get onto an enlarged selection committee and stated categorically that former scholars must be in a minority on the German committee (BAK, NLF, 92). But by then, the situation in Berlin had become so heated that on 28 October, von Lindeiner-Wildau asked a very unhappy Schmidt-Ott to arbitrate.[107] A meeting of all the scholars was held in Berlin on 7 December, and on 10 December, von Ow-Wachendorf informed Kerr (RTF 1682) that Schmidt-Ott had come up with a solution. In future, the Association of Former German Rhodes Scholars (whose president was to be von Lindeiner-Wildau until 1935) should choose three of its members annually for the selection committee and submit their names to the Trustees for approval. But even this solution seems not to have been entirely acceptable to von Lindeiner-Wildau, for on 15 February 1930, T. E. Breen, an official in the British Embassy in Berlin, informed Kerr (RTF 1682) that 'some Germans seem to think that the Committee is preponderatingly representative of the Democratic Party'[108] and that von Lindeiner-Wildau still thought 'that the old Rhodes Scholars were not adequately represented' (i.e. not a majority). Breen's letter implies that the more conservative scholars particularly objected to Brinkmann's membership since he was well known at that time as a liberal whose views were tinged with a socialist anti-capitalism, as a proponent of Western-style democracy, and as a protagonist of the Weimar constitution.[109] Nevertheless, on 17 February Kerr recommended to the Trustees that they accept the Association's proposals of 10 December: one scholar should retire each year subject to re-election; one of the Association's officers should always be on the committee; and Brinkmann should be replaced in the coming round (RTF 1682).

The Trustees concurred and the Association met for its first annual dinner in December 1930 (to which Chancellor Brüning was invited and which was attended by Konstantin von Neurath (1873–1956), Germany's Foreign Minister 1932–36, Lutz Graf

---

[104]   See especially Morsbach to Bernstorff, 3 Aug. 1929.

[105]   See von Ow-Wachendorf to Bernstorff, 26 Oct. 1929; Rosenberger to Schmidt-Ott, 1929. BAB, NLF, 93; cf. AA, NLAB, 22, Bernstorff to Gräfin von Reventlow, 4 Nov. 1929, cited in Hansen, *Bernstorff*, 183–4; also RTF 1682, Kerr's Report to the Trustees, 8 Nov. 1929.

[106]   BAK, NLF, 93, von Diergardt to Schmidt-Ott, 29 Nov. 1929.

[107]   BAK, NLF, 93, von Lindeiner-Wildau to Schmidt-Ott, 28 Oct. 1929.

[108]   i.e. the DDP—which Bernstorff's Uncle Johnny had helped found in 1919, which he represented in the Reichstag 1921–8, and of which Bernstorff himself had been a member 1919–20 (see Hansen, *Bernstorff*, 22–3, 107).

[109]   See Carl Brinkmann, *Recent Theories of Citizenship and its Relation to Government* (New Haven: Yale University Press, 1927), 6–7, 61–2, 82–7, 113–14. See also Kerr to Breen, 18 Feb. 1930 (RTF 1682).

Schwerin von Krosigk (Oriel 1905), a rising star in the German Finance Ministry, and Sir Horace Rumbold (1866–1941), the British Ambassador to Berlin 1928–33.[110] Brinkmann was replaced by the non-partisan Hans Eberhard von Schweinitz (Balliol 1905), and the new committee met on 16 January 1931 to interview fourteen candidates out of seventy applicants. It selected Adolf Schlepegrell (University) and Adam von Trott zu Solz (Balliol), the nephew of von Schweinitz and the son of a minister under whom Schmidt-Ott had served (n. 39). On 20 March 1931, Brinkmann wrote a note to Wylie in which he complained, with considerable justification, at being pushed off the committee 'by what seems an absurd coalition of nationalists, to whom my Oxford speech of July 5, 1929 was too conciliatory, and pacifists like Mendelssohn-Bartholdy to whom I appear to be lacking in "international-mindedness"'. Henceforth, Brinkmann concluded, he would keep his distance from the German Rhodes Association (RTF 1682). The committee, unchanged but lacking Dr Simons, met on 21 December 1931 to interview twelve candidates out of the fifty serious applicants and, uniquely in the 1930s, selected two members of the nobility for 1932.[111] It met, again unchanged, for the last time before Hitler's seizure of power, on 19 December 1932, with C. K. Allen in attendance to interview twelve candidates. Allen sent an eyewitness account to Lothian on 28 December (RTF 1682) which is worth quoting at length since it gives a unique insight into how the committee functioned and how, by extension, the Nazis might try to exert pressure on it after January 1933:

The procedure is that an elimination of the applicants is made in the first instance by the Secretary, and those who appear to have prima facie qualifications are summoned to attend the Committee. It is evident that this preliminary selection is made judiciously, as the candidates who were summoned were by no means standardized, but represented very different types of German youth. Twenty of them appeared before the Committee. They came from widely separated parts of the Reich . . . Most of them came from professional, academic and propertied families, but one, a very interesting type, was the son of a peasant, and had a more remarkable flow of language than I have ever encountered in any human being. He was not elected, chiefly on the ground that no Oxford tutor could possibly stand the strain.

Each member of the Committee is responsible for a certain number of dossiers, which are summarized and discussed before the candidate is called in. The candidate then has an interview of about ten or fifteen minutes, answering questions from all members of the Committee. The Chairman is very adroit and kindly in putting him at his ease. . . . The selection was rapid and unanimous, and if I had been a voting member, I should have concurred entirely in the decision, with a third candidate as proxime accessit.

The first four post-war German scholars had mixed experiences at Oxford between October 1930 and January 1933. Although German scholars now received £300 per annum (not £400 like all the others), Koelle found it increasingly hard to make ends meet at an

---

[110] See Hansen, *Bernstorff*, 185 where Hansen makes the important point that this guest list gives some idea of the significance of the scholarships among the German elites.

[111] Interestingly, 8 of the 12 candidates interviewed for 1932 were from the former nobility whereas only 3 out of the 14 interviewed in the previous round came from that class, a fact which probably derives from Germany's economic situation in 1931–2. Of the 20 German scholars selected 1929–39, 6 (30%) came from the former nobility and 14 (70%) from the middle classes.

expensive college like Magdalen for the same reasons that his pre-1914 forebears had done, but with the added difficulties caused by the economic crisis in Germany after the Wall Street crash.[112] Realizing that this problem affected all German scholars, the Trustees immediately raised the German scholarship to £350 per annum on 12 January 1932 (RTM 1 Jan. 1932). Even so, most candidates throughout the 1930s would need additional funding.[113] Despite these difficulties, Koelle wrote a report for the German selection committee in August 1932 which very clearly explains why his experience of Oxford would cause him to form a lifelong attachment to the place (BAK, NLF, 101). Because of Oxford's regulations on standing, he had not been able to read for a degree in two years. So he had used his time to work on his German doctorate; thrown himself into all aspects of college life; and been warmly welcomed by his English peers (especially in Magdalen's rowing club). Although, in a report written at the end of his first term (7 Dec. 1930), Koelle had regretted a lack of interest in matters political, especially among English undergraduates from well-heeled and unproblematic backgrounds (BAK, NLF, 98), his 1932 report says that he had been in great demand to talk in all kinds of contexts about 'our political servitude under the Dictate of Versailles and our dire economic situation'.

Schumacher, who saw himself primarily as a 'Wissenschaftler' and had come to Oxford to investigate 'why the Gold Standard worked comparatively smoothly before the war and so completely failed to fulfill its purpose in recent times', experienced the same structural problem as his three pre-1914 predecessors.[114] He had already studied under Joseph Schumpeter (1883–1950) in Bonn and briefly under Keynes in Cambridge (from whom, respectively, he had learnt a diachronic approach to economics and a concern with current problems), and he had come to Oxford with high expectations. But he had to spend his first year taking the Diploma in Economics (which he found interesting, but rather elementary and superficial),[115] and he met no one teaching economics at Oxford of the stature of his two previous mentors. Consequently, he never really found his way into Oxford's research culture,[116] and on 28 December 1931 he wrote to Bernstorff (RTF 1682) asking if he could spend his third year as a Rhodes scholar at an American university (Columbia in New York, where he was much happier).[117] Schumacher was also not impressed by the intellectual quality of Oxford student life and considerably more appalled than Koelle by Oxford's lack of concern about the situation that was developing in Germany.[118] Oxford may have been moving towards the left and its Union may have begun to debate more serious topics, especially after summer 1931.[119] But, in

---

[112] RTF 1682, Koelle to Bernstorff, 5 Jan. 1932.

[113] Cf. BAK, NLF, 99, Fehling to Deutsche Kongresszentrale, 30 Sept. 1936.

[114] Barbara Wood, *Alias Papa: A life of Fritz Schumacher* (Oxford: Oxford University Press, 1985), 24–7.

[115] BAK, NLF, 101, Report of Schumacher to German Rhodes selection committee, 15 July 1932.

[116] Wood, *Alias Papa*, 35–6.

[117] Ibid. 36–7 and 47. Schumacher's request was put formally to Allen on 30 Jan. 1932 (RTF 1682) and granted by the Trustees on 1 Mar. 1932 (RTM 1008).

[118] Wood, *Alias Papa*, 25, 27–8.

[119] Brian Harrison, 'Politics', in Trevor Henry Aston et al. (eds.), *The History of the University of Oxford* 8 vols. (Oxford: Oxford University Press, 1984–2000), viii. 398–9. The minute book of the Oxford University Labour Club 1926–31 has been preserved (BL, MS Top. Oxon. d. 298), but contains only one brief mention of Germany (17 Oct. 1930) for the period that overlaps with Schumacher's first year.

Schumacher's mind, it lacked a sense of urgency and so, according to his biographer, he took every opportunity to try and explain the reasons for the rise of Hitler as well as the dangers this involved.[120] In the context of this resolve, Schumacher, with Koelle's help, revivified and enlarged the scope of the University German Club (which had existed since 1921 but was defunct by the late 1920s) almost as soon as he arrived in Oxford.[121] It was probably Schumacher, too, who persuaded Richard Crossman, the philosophy tutor at New College since autumn 1931, to get himself appointed as the Club's senior president since Crossman had shared Schumacher's political concerns ever since his first stay in Germany in October 1930.[122] During the 1930s, Crossman would become a leading writer and broadcaster on matters German, and, like Schumacher, he was deeply concerned to make Oxford aware 'that National Socialism was a formidable, even revolutionary movement with a broad base of popular support' and so, according to Howard, of making 'Oxford in general, and the Left in particular' understand 'just what it did not want to hear'.

Von Trott, who became a close friend of Schumacher's and may well have collaborated with him and others to produce an extremely insightful, anonymous article entitled 'How Nazis Think' that appeared in a short-lived periodical edited by Crossman,[123] had a much more brilliant, profitable, and happy time at Oxford than his friend. One biographer goes so far as to say that he made a significant impact on Oxford.[124] This was partly because of his more outgoing personality, partly because he found a mentor in Crossman (whom he met via the Labour Club and who helped turn him from a Hegelian into a Fabian socialist),[125] and partly because, by the time he matriculated, after the crucial summer of 1931, Oxford students were becoming more politically conscious in a way that would have been congenial to von Trott (n. 119). He, too, sent a long report to the German selection committee at the end of his first year in which he described the difficulties of being a German Rhodes scholar in the prevailing political circumstances. But he thought that German students were, on the whole, too quick to judge 'English lack of thoroughness and academic rigour' ('englische Ungründlichkeit und Unwissenschaftlichkeit') and was full of praise for the intellectual profits that Oxford offered both formally and informally to a young German—provided, of course, that he had the insight to see them and the independence of character to grasp them.[126]

Schlepegrell also profited greatly from Oxford and stayed for three years to write a

---

[120] Wood, *Alias Papa*, 28–32.

[121] See Schumacher, Report of 15 July 1932. According to Koelle's Report of 7 Dec. 1930, the Club's weekly meetings were attracting audiences of about 70, and according to Schumacher's Report, that number had risen to 150 and the Club was the best-attended club of its kind. The Club held its weekly meetings in Rhodes House and attracted guests and speakers as diverse as Albert Einstein (14 May 1932) and Leni Riefenstahl (25 Apr. 1934). It dissolved itself in summer 1936 after several attempts by the Nazis to overturn its tradition of political impartiality but seems to have had a brief renaissance in summer 1937 when pro-Nazi students made it their platform—albeit without Crossman's support (BAK, NLF, 99).

[122] See Böker, '1934', 101; Anthony Howard, *Crossman: The Pursuit of Power* (London: Jonathan Cape, 1990), 30–4.

[123] 'How Nazis Think', *New Oxford Outlook*, 1/1 (May 1933), 10–18.

[124] MacDonough, *A Good German*, 53.   [125] Ibid. 35, 50.

[126] BAK, NLF, 101, Report of von Trott to German Rhodes selection committee, summer 1932. Dr Clarita von Trott (Berlin) kindly made a copy available before I discovered the whereabouts of the original.

B.Litt. thesis on 'German Borrowings Abroad 1924–1930'. He was also probably the first German scholar to note that although sport was a crucial way of being accepted with a college it was by no means the only way.[127] His intellectual tastes were similar to von Trott's, and even if his politics were more conservative, he accompanied him on weekends at the country house of Stafford Cripps; moved in the circle around Crossman (who would procure him a job in London 1942–6); and followed Schumacher and Koelle as president of the German Club.[128] Like von Trott, he perceived that Oxford involved two cultures: it was 'clearly divided into a higher school and a university in the Continental sense' and because 'the school is so much more striking, and is so new to the foreign student . . . he is apt to overlook the university at first'. Like von Trott, too, he made a considerable impact on the University—but via the Oxford Union (where von Trott spoke twice and then unmemorably).[129] His name first occurs in the Union's archives on 20 October 1932 (when he spoke against the motion 'That this House believes that the Russian experiment is succeeding, and welcomes its success'). He subsequently spoke in at least twelve debates, mainly on motions dealing with world politics or British foreign policy. But he attracted increasing attention in the University, local, and national press after his fifth speech, delivered during the famous 'King and Country' debate of 9 February 1933 (i.e. ten days after Hitler had become Chancellor), when he spoke against the motion in eighth place.[130] He then rose through the Union's hierarchy until, in spring 1934, he was elected secretary for Trinity term by two votes. After the last debate in which he spoke, on 7 June 1934 in favour of the motion 'That the acceptance of the German claims to arms equality is essential to the preservation of European peace', the *Oxford Magazine* commented that the debate was 'chiefly remarkable for the farewell speech of Mr. Schlepegrell, the Secretary, who, if he had stayed longer, would certainly have become President of the Union'.[131] He also gained some notoriety after Churchill, at the invitation of the Conservative Club, had given a speech in the Union on 27 February 1934. When questions were invited, Schlepegrell asked: 'Does Mr. Churchill consider that Germany was solely responsible for the Great War?' When, after a silence, Schlepegrell repeated the question and Churchill answered 'yes,' Schlepegrell walked out of the hall, showing how much clause 231 still rankled with someone who was only 7 when the Treaty of Versailles was signed.

January 1933–May 1945

The government that took power in Germany was actually a coalition of the Nazis (NSDAP) and the DNVP (from which von Lindeiner-Wildau and eleven other leading members had resigned in December 1929 when Alfred Hugenberg (1865–1951), the anti-

[127] BAK, NLF, 101, Report of Schlepegrell to German Rhodes selection committee, Sept. 1932. NLF, 100 contains a report of 3 July 1934.

[128] Wood, *Alias Papa*, 35; von Trott, Report.

[129] Schlepegrell, 'Oxford's Glamour'; MacDonough, *A Good German*, 35.

[130] See Martin Ceadel, 'The "King and Country" Debate, 1933: Student Politics, Pacifism and the Dictators', *Historical Review*, 22 (1979), 397–422; 'The Union Debate', *Oxford Magazine*, 16 Feb. 1933, 441.

[131] 'The Union Debate', *Oxford Magazine*, 14 June 1934, 830.

parliamentarian industrialist turned newspaper magnate and the Party's leader since 20 October 1928, moved too close to the Nazis).[132] On 28 February, the day after the Reichstag fire, Hitler was given emergency powers, and civil liberties were suspended by decree. On 23 March, the Enabling Act (which conferred general powers on the government for four years to permit the consolidation of the so-called National Revolution) was ratified by 441 votes to 94. On 28 June, Hugenberg's Party was dissolved. And on 7 April, the first implicitly anti-Jewish law was passed, decreeing *inter alia* the suspension until further notice of Jewish civil servants, workers, and staff in the public service. A process had begun that would put the selection committee under political pressure for the rest of its existence. But these ominous developments did not, unfortunately, prevent the German Scholars' Association from inviting Dr Ernst Hanfstaengl, a long-standing intimate of Hitler's, and Goebbels himself to its annual dinner on 18 December 1933, presumably as a gesture of appeasement.[133]

Hitler's anti-Semitic policies directly affected one scholar in early 1934. One of Schlepegrell's grandmothers was Jewish, which meant that, as a 'non-Aryan', he was no longer eligible to enter state service or practice law (as he had intended). As it was possible, under exceptional circumstances, to be deemed an 'honorary Aryan', Schlepegrell tried to have his status reconsidered. But as a declared non-Nazi with a high political profile in the Oxford Union,[134] his appeal was turned down irrevocably, despite the intercession of Schwerin von Krosigk (the Finance Minister since 1932), in June 1934.[135]

On 11 May 1945, Allen published an article in the *Spectator* entitled 'Germans at Oxford' in which, on the basis of (inevitably) scant information, he painted a reasonably positive picture of how German Rhodes scholars had reacted to the Nazi regime. Since then, the immense civil courage shown by von Trott and Bernstorff (to whom Harold Nicolson devoted a complete article in the *Spectator* on 10 August 1945) has tended to obscure how other scholars responded 1933–45. Moreover, in the immediate post-war years, the eminent educationalist Kurt Hahn (1886–1974) (who had studied at Christ Church before the Great War and been forced into exile in 1933) sought to prove that 'German Rhodes Scholars were to a large extent immune to the ideologies of nazism'.[136] Furthermore, one often reads statements to the effect that the Nazis failed to penetrate the selection committee except in one, or possibly two cases.[137] Given the more extensive data now available, it is time to re-examine these questions and if, in doing so, I devote less space to von Trott and Bernstorff than might be expected, it is because several

---

[132] Von Lindeiner-Wildau then founded his short-lived, politically insignificant, but parliamentarian Conservative People's Party on 23 July 1930 and represented it in the Reichstag Sept. 1930–July 1932.

[133] IfZ, NLB, File New York B/Oxford bis 1934, circular letter, 9 Dec. 1933. As far as is known, Goebbels did not attend.

[134] See 'The Union Debate', *Oxford Magazine*, 18 May 1933, 674. In his letters to the Vice-Master and Master of University College of 16 Feb. 1935 and 11 Feb. 1936 (RTF 2326A), Allen confirms that Schlepegrell's Union activities were not looked on 'with [great] favour in Germany'.

[135] RTF 1682 *passim*, and BAK, NLF, 98.

[136] RT PF, von Senger und Etterlin to Allen, 15 Nov. 1948; RTF 1682A, Mandt to Allen, 29 Dec. 1948.

[137] See for instance Wilhelm Sternfeld, 'Die deutschen Rhodes-Studenten', *Deutsche Rundschau*, 77/5 (May 1951), 446; J. R. M. Butler, *Lord Lothian* (London: Macmillan, 1960), 138. Roediger, 'A German's Experience', 20; Böker, '1934', 101–2; Hansen, *Bernstorff*, 185, 238; MacDonough, *A Good German*, 30.

excellent books on these relatively well-known anti-Nazis and the German Resistance in general are now available.

To begin with, the records in the Documentation Center (BAB) show that of the 72 German scholars who were elected up to 1939 (a figure which excludes, of course, those who died prematurely or in the Great War), 26 became full or probationary members of the NSDAP (one while studying at Oxford); 3 applied for membership but were turned down; 1, Schwerin von Krosigk, accepted the Golden Party Badge and therefore special membership in 1937;[138] and 3 others had pro-Nazi sympathies but never became Party members. Of the 26, 1 joined in 1930; 1 in 1931; 6 in 1933; 1 in 1934; 3 in 1936; 8 in 1937; and 6 in 1940. But one of these was von Trott (who, as is now well known, joined the Party to work against the system from within) and two were turned down once and twice respectively before being accepted because of their lack of active commitment. At least four of the pro-Nazi scholars were in the SA (i.e. brownshirt storm troopers) (but here it should be remembered that *all* German students were under considerable pressure to join the SA and a report in the BAB on one of the four indicates that he was anything but an activist and had joined for reasons of professional expediency). Two were in the *Reiter-SS* (SS Cavalry) (both in the elite *Reitersturm* 1/R/7 based in Düppel (Berlin)). But the *Reiter-SS* had been formed in 1933 by the assimilation of up-market riding clubs into the *Allgemeine SS* (part-time, unpaid, and voluntary SS) in order to improve the social profile of the SS and was the one part of that organization not to be deemed criminal by the post-war Nuremberg Tribunal.[139] A third scholar was in the *Allgemeine SS* (*Motorsturm* 10/1), but the experience seems to have turned him into a convinced anti-Nazi. None of the three SS men served in the SS during the war, and the activities of the two in the *Reiter-SS* were confined to state and ceremonial occasions (e.g. interpreting at the 1936 Olympic Games).

Unlike Marxism, Nazism is not a coherent philosophy, and although their policies overlapped, there is a significant gap between even the most right-wing form of anti-parliamentarian conservative nationalism (represented by the right wing of the DNVP) and the racially based ('völkisch') nationalism of the new revolutionary Right. Thus, of the 108 DNVP Reichstag Deputies in 1926, only 25 joined the NSDAP after 1933 and 11 were actively persecuted by the Nazis. Similarly, of the 77 DNVP Deputies in 1929, only 13 joined the NSDAP after 1933 with the same number experiencing active persecution. Indeed, one was finally executed for his part in the 20 July conspiracy. Most of the older German scholars who joined or had leanings towards the NSDAP belonged to one of the parties of the old conservative Right and were moved to join or support the NSDAP by one or more of a complex of reasons: expediency (the desire for promotion or a more comfortable job); economic need (the man who joined in 1930 was all but blind, out of

---

[138] Klaus Goehrke, *In den Fesseln der Pflicht: Der Weg des Reichsfinanzministers Lutz Graf Schwerin von Krosigk* (Cologne: Verlag Wissenschaft und Politik, 1995), 35.

[139] See Ermenhild Neusüss-Hunkel, *Die SS* (Hanover: O. Goedel, 1956), 15–17; Helmut Krausnick and Martin Broszat (eds.), *Anatomy of the SS State* (London: Paladin, 1970), 260; Robert Lewis Koehl, *The Black Corps: The Structure and Power Struggles of the Nazi SS* (Madison: Wisconsin University Press, 1983), 92, 109, 112, 207; Michael Burleigh and Wolfgang Wippermann, *The Racial State: Germany 1933–1945* (Cambridge: Cambridge University Press, 1991), 62.

work, and held down a Party-financed job in one of Berlin's poorer areas); overlap of political and/or economic agendas;[140] fear (of Bolshevism at home and abroad,[141] of losing a good job, of being called up for the second time, of being sent somewhere unhealthy overseas or, during the war, to the Russian front); the desire for the 9.5 million German-speakers who now lived outside Germany (c.13 per cent of Europe's German-speaking population) to be reintegrated with the Reich;[142] the hope that the new regime would, as initially occurred, lessen the tax burden on the agricultural sector (in which several of the older generation, being landowners, had a considerable interest and about which they were writing to Wylie well before 1933); approval of Hitler's initial success in reducing unemployment; the hope that Hitler would redress the terms of the Treaty of Versailles and restore national pride; the need for a leader and authoritarian institutions after the failure of Weimar democracy;[143] and the desire to protect non-German or Jewish wives. On 29 December 1938, a non-Nazi scholar who was married to a wife of Jewish descent, who lived in a city where the synagogue had burned several months before 'Kristallnacht' of 9/10 November 1938, and who was clearly terrified of censorship, wrote to Allen: 'Life [during the past year] went on quite normally. Hardly anything was to be noticed. Nobody wishes for a war and a war with England specially would be absolutely unpopular.' Some young scholars were moved by the same reasons, together with naive political idealism, the wish to enter state service, paramilitary euphoria, and, dare one say, so trivial a factor as the lure of fancy uniforms.

But I can find no evidence that any German scholar with NSDAP leanings either wanted the kind of war that Hitler would eventually wage or was ideologically 'völkisch' in the hard-line sense. Von Müller went furthest down this road but had his limits. Schwerin von Krosigk, the most highly placed scholar, was unequivocally acquitted on the count of conspiring to wage a war of aggression at his post-war trial. And even the committed Nazi scholar whom Allen referred to in his 1945 article had come to the conclusion by mid-1937 that a war in central Europe would be 'madness' and was, according to a friend who wrote to Allen after the war, 'panic-stricken' when he realized in 1938 that such a war was inevitable. I know of only five German scholars who wrote, published, or uttered anti-Semitic remarks. One is to be found in a letter to Wylie of later 1922 where the writer, who never joined the NSDAP and may have been arrested during the war, blamed international Jewry for enriching themselves 'still more than they did during the war and by the revolution' and concluded that in his view 'they are also the real originators of this war'. Another occurs in an article by von Müller (n. 167). Goehrke,

---

[140] Brinkmann, who was more liberal than most of the older generation, never a member of the NSDAP, and certainly opposed to its racial policies, nevertheless spoke up on behalf of Nazi economics during the early period at least because he felt that they freed people from the 'automatism' and 'automatic competition' of free market capitalism (see his 'Theoretische Bemerkungen zum nationalsozialistischen Wirtschaftsprogramm', *Schmollers Jahrbuch Für Gesetzgebung, Verwaltung und Volkswirtschaft im Deutschen Reich*, 58/1 (Feb. 1934), 1–4).

[141] Goehrke, *In den Fesseln der Pflicht*, 102.   [142] Cf. Jones, *Die Volkskonservativen*, 452.

[143] Cf. von Senger und Etterlin, *Neither Fear nor Hope*, 348–9; von Richthofen, *Brito-Germania*, 6, 55–7, 61, 66–9, 74, 78, 87, 115, 117, and 150–1 (where several of these issues are discussed); Christian Jansen, *Professoren und Politik: Politisches Denken und Handeln der Heidelberger Hochschullehrer 1914–1935* (Göttingen: Vandenhoek & Rupprecht, 1992), 258–9.

who is right to say that Schwerin von Krosigk was not in general an anti-Semite ('generell gegen Juden'), nevertheless cites a speech that he gave at a family gathering in June 1933 in which he (uncharacteristically) used 'völkisch' ideas to condemn marriages between German aristocrats and Jews.[144] Such remarks are reprehensible, but they are untypical of their originators and relatively mild in comparison with the growing torrent of anti-Semitic abuse which poured from Nazi presses 1918–45 and which von Richthofen denounced, in his *Brito-Germania* (p. 122), for the damage it was doing to German's good name.

Finally, leaving aside the complex cases of von Müller and Schwerin von Krosigk, I also know of only one German scholar whose involvement with Nazism remained at all strong after the period October 1938–March 1939 (when Hitler carved up Czechoslovakia and the synagogues burned). He was so well known for his views while at Oxford that, as a senior Nazi official proudly wrote to his father after visiting him there, his English fellow-students would greet him on the street with the Hitler salute ('dem deutschen Gruße') (BAK, NLF, 98). Clearly, some English jokes are no laughing matter either. And his military record in the BAA contains reports from the later war years which commend him, uniquely among the scholars in the German armed forces, for his 'positive attitude towards Nazi ideology' and his ability to communicate it to his subordinates. Most other scholars who joined or sympathized with the NSDAP for politico-economic reasons (rather than expediency—like the six who were enrolled in 1940) had, as far as I can judge, lost much if not all of their 'positive attitude' well before that and realized that the long-term evils of Nazism were rapidly outweighing its short-term gains. The man who joined the Party in 1931 left it in 1933, was arrested briefly by the Gestapo in 1934, went into voluntary exile in England in January 1935, and published pamphlets during the war denouncing Nazi atrocities. Another who joined in 1933 at the behest of his professional superiors was openly contemptuous of the Nazi leadership throughout the entire period and narrowly escaped arrest after the failure of the 20 July conspiracy. A third, who had also joined in 1933, remained one of Bernstorff's closest Rhodes scholar friends and demonstrably heard both him and von Trott make treasonable utterances during the 1930s—but never informed on them.

Looking back, Roediger and von Senger und Etterlin stressed that many old-style civil servants stayed in post under the Nazis because they had been inculcated with the values of loyalty to the state, incorruptibility, dutifulness, and service; underestimated the Nazis' staying power and capacity for ruthless evil; and overestimated their own ability to moderate the Nazis' excesses.[145] Goehrke agrees that precisely these values typified Schwerin von Krosigk's mentality,[146] causing him to stay in office to the bitter end (when, for three weeks after Hitler's death, he was Admiral Doenitz's Foreign Minister). A deeply committed Lutheran with a brilliant financial mind, he had risen, during the 1920s, rapidly through

---

[144] *In den Fesseln der Pflicht*, 32–3, 102; Lutz Graf Schwerin von Krosigk, 'Der Adel im nationalsozialistischen Staat', 6-page unpublished typescript, BAK, NLSvK, 12.

[145] Conrad Roediger, 'Der Auswärtige Dienst im zweimaligen Umbruch', 31-page unpublished typescript (1969), 18, 31; von Senger und Etterlin, 'Senger', 376.

[146] *In den Fesseln der Pflicht*, 28–9.

the ranks of the Finance Ministry (the smaller partner of the Economics Ministry that exercised many of the functions of the British Treasury and dealt primarily with questions of taxation, allocation of expendture, customs, and excise). He represented Germany at the London Conference of early July 1931 (where the end of reparations was negotiated) and then, as the non-partisan Finance Minister under Brüning, at the Lausanne Conference of July 1932 (where reparations were formally terminated because of the German economic crisis). He continued to serve under von Papen and Schleicher and played a key role in helping Germany recover economically during the early Nazi years—mainly through work-creation schemes and a fairer taxation system.[147] The many articles that he published during the 1930s and 1940s are those of a skilled technocrat with a penchant for machine imagery and are totally free from 'völkisch' vocabulary, anti-Semitism of any kind, and sycophantic paeans to the achievement of the Führer and the Party.[148]

At his trial in Nuremberg before three North American judges, he defended his complicity with a regime about which he had allegedly had misgivings since its very earliest days[149] on the following grounds. He had never voluntarily joined the Party (pp. 22873, 22903) and had declined an honorary rank in the SS so as to keep his independence (p. 22891). He had spoken out against the anti-Semitic legislation of 1933 (pp. 22897–8, 23307). He had been able to prevent Nazis from predominating in his Ministry (p. 22903). After the Night of the Long Knives (30 June 1934), he could have found a better-paid job in the private sector but stayed on as Minister to protect his staff and exercise a moderating influence (pp. 22916–19). He had been able to help a large number of individuals, including would-be Jewish emigrants before the war (p. 23346), and the families of the 20 July conspirators (pp. 22922, 23126–7, 23346). He had never belonged to the Nazi inner circle and was never consulted on military matters or questions of foreign policy (pp. 22934, 23590). But he *had* tried to use his influence to prevent the attacks in the West and on Russia (pp. 23076–7). He had personally protested to Goering and Goebbels about the excesses of 'Kristallnacht' (p. 23286); he had persuaded Goering to have many of the thousands of Jews who had been arrested then released from concentration camps (p. 23295); and he had personally interceded with Hitler to prevent the arrest of the families of the 20 July plotters (pp. 23128–9). He genuinely thought that the Jews being 'evacuated' from Germany were being resettled in the so-called 'Paradise Ghetto' of Theresienstadt, the one camp in the east that was known to him (p. 23296), but had,

---

[147] See Graf Schwerin von Krosigk, 'Wirtschaftspolitik und sozialpolitische Grundsätze der deutschen Steuergesetzgebung', *Zeitschrift der Akademie für Deutsches Recht*, 4/19 (1 Oct. 1937), 611.

[148] On 13 May 1945, Ernst Schumacher published an (unsigned) article about Schwerin von Krosigk in the *Observer* in which he described him in just such terms and concluded that he 'represents the "fragmentary man" of the twentieth century, incomplete, misleading, immoral, a man no more, just an instrument'. Cf. Graf Schwerin von Krosigk, 'Die Bedeutung der Finanzierung für den Sieg', *Der deutsche Volkswirt* 15 (21 Mar. 1941), 10. Even the peroration of his pamphlet *Nationalsozialistische Finanzpolitik* (Jena: Gustav Fischer, 1936) consists of an appeal to the 'Volk' for more work, sacrifice, and responsibility and makes one brief reference to the government (p. 11), not to Hitler or the NSDAP.

[149] Case 11 (Ministries 23–30 Sept. 1948 and 1 Oct. 1948 in Nuremberg), p. 22893. Affidavits on behalf of von Krosigk relating to his activity on the selection committee are in Document Book 1, pp. 139–44, 152–4, and Document Book 2, pp. 40–2. Subsequent page references within the text are to the transcripts held in the IWM.

in any case, no influence over the running of the concentration camps that his Ministry had helped finance (p. 23300). And he repeatedly insisted that many of his actions were motivated by his lifelong fear of Bolshevism. Although the Presiding Judge was impressed by his person and accepted a lot of his defence (pp. 28569–70), two out of the three judges found him guilty on two out of three counts: 'Atrocities and Offences Committed against Civilian Populations' and 'Plunder and Spoliation'. In the Court's view, he had not protested loudly enough against criminal measures when he had had the chance (p. 28573). He had compromised himself by participating actively in the infamous conference chaired by Goering on 12 November 1938; assenting to the increasingly harsh measures taken against the Jews after 'Kristallnacht',[150] and taking a proactive part in the expropriation of Jewish property during the war (pp. 28575–8) even if he knew nothing concrete about the fate of its owners. He had also colluded in the systematic spoliation of Poland (pp. 28709–13). So, having spent three years already in a variety or prisons, Schwerin von Krosigk was sentenced to ten years' further imprisonment (but released on appeal in February 1951 on a full ministerial pension). 'It is', the Presiding Judge commented (p. 28570), 'one of the humane [*sic*] tragedies which are so often found in life': an essentially decent man of high private moral standards found himself in a situation where the decision to leave his post would have seemed dishonourable and the decision to stay entangled him in terrible crimes against humanity for which he must be held partly responsible, but whose enormity he either did not or chose not to see.

Then there is the even stranger case of von Müller, the Munich historian who was well known for his expertise in the areas of Bavarian, British, and German history and who became a full professor at Munich University on 18 February 1928. Von Müller was a charming, kind, and friendly man, who was passionately interested in all things Bavarian and rarely left Bavaria. His unaffected geniality and bonhomie were proverbial[151] and he was liked by nearly everyone—even some of his post-war detractors. He first met Hitler during the abortive Munich Soviet of spring 1919; appeared as a defence witness at Hitler's trial in March 1924 after his failed putsch;[152] and mixed in right-wing circles throughout the 1920s (something that, in his view, cost him several prestigious chairs in northern Germany).[153] He was made a probationary member of the NSDAP on 1 August 1933 at the express request of his former student Rudolf Hess, having allegedly had leanings in that political direction even before Hitler's seizure of power.[154] A brilliant essay-

---

[150] See Burleigh and Wippermann, *The Racial State*, 92–3.

[151] BAB, Archive Documentation Center, PF von Müller, Report on von Müller from the Gauleitung München-Oberbayern 7 Oct. 1942.

[152] Lothar Gruchmann, Reinhard Weber, and Otto Gritschneder (eds.), *Der Hitler-Prozess 1924: Wortlaut der Hauptverhandlung vor dem Volksgericht München I*, 4 vols. (Munich: K. G. Saur, 1997), ii. 596–601. After his release, Hitler allegedly presented von Müller with a hand-signed copy of *Mein Kampf* in gratitude for his support (see BHStA, File MK 44052, PF von Müller, Dozentschaft der Universität to the Rector, 4 Jan. 1936).

[153] See BHStA, NLvM, 10, von Müller to the Staatsarchivrat of the Reich Education Ministry, 28 Oct. 1935.

[154] MUA, RF von Müller, Deputy Dean of the Philosophy Faculty to the Rector, 6 Sept. 1935; BAB, Archive Documentation Center, PF von Müller, Gaupersonalamtsleiter to Reichsleitung der NSDAP, 27 Nov. 1939.

ist and charismatic teacher, his lectures provoked by far the greatest response among Munich students,[155] and of all the Munich historians, the Nazi leadership regarded him as the only one who was deeply committed to the 'grossdeutschen und volksdeutschen Gedanken' (i.e. the idea of a Greater Germany that would unite the entire German 'Volk').[156] On the basis of this conviction, he published a number of non-academic articles and popularizing books 1933–44 in which he enthusiastically supported the regime using 'völkisch' terminology.[157] He gave a lecture at the Salzburg conference organized by the *Stiftung 'Ahnenerbe'*, the cultural branch of the SS that was dedicated to the propagation of 'völkisch' mythology, from 23 August to 2 September 1939.[158] He also offered his book *Deutschland und England: Ein weltgeschichtliches Bild*, whose thesis was substantially that of the lecture, to the publishing house of the *Stiftung 'Ahnenerbe'* on the outbreak of war. Because of von Müller's academic standing, it was immediately accepted for distribution to the troops: 71,460 copies had been published by late 1939 and 200,000 copies by mid-March 1942.[159]

Von Müller's vision of German history, which went back to 1914 at least, was consistent and straightforward. Bismarck had unified Germany politically, but unlike Britain, the Second Reich was 'oppressive and full of tensions'.[160] Now, however, thanks to the Führer, the shame of defeat and the injustices of the Treaty of Versailles had been overcome and Germany was, for the first time since the Middle Ages, a socialist Reich that was unified, grounded in the community of the entire German 'Volk', and driven by the inner power of that people ('völkische Kraft').[161] In other words, although von Müller had little or no contact with the Rhodes Trust in the 1920s and 1930s, he believed that Hitler and the Party had made of Germany what he thought he had glimpsed in Oxford during those quasi-visionary experiences before the war: a society which was in thrall neither to capitalism nor to communism and which had become an organic unity once more, in touch with its deepest affective roots.

At the same time, von Müller the professional historian knew that this (by no means unusual) assessment of the contemporary German situation was highly romanticized

[155] These included Hermann Goering (who attended the occasional lecture), Ernst ('Putzi') Hanfstaengl, Baldur von Schirach, Ottokar Lorenz, Walter Frank, and Karl Richard Ganzer. See Karl Ferdinand Werner, *Das NS-Geschichtsbild und die deutsche Geschichtswissenschaft* (Stuttgart: Kohlhammer, 1967), 27.

[156] See n. 154, letter, 27 Nov. 1939; also 'Universitas Litterarum', *Münchner neueste Nachrichten*, 14 (15 Jan. 1943), 1.

[157] See Karen Schönwälder, *Historiker und Politik: Geschichtswissenschaft im Nationalsozialismus* (Frankfurt am Main: Campus, 1992), 113 and 328 n. 162, 118, 128–9, and 136.

[158] Michael H., Kater, *Das 'Ahnenerbe' der SS 1935–1945: Ein Beitrag zur Kulturpolitik des Dritten Reiches* (Munich: Oldenbourg, 1997), 117; Burleigh and Wippermann, *The Racial State*, 64.

[159] BAB, Archive Documentation Center, PF von Müller, *Ahnenerbe* to Editor of *Der schwarze Korps*, 1 Dec. 1939; BHStM, MK 44052, Bayerischer Volksbildungs-Verband to Bavarian Education Ministry, 14 Mar. 1942; Kater, *Das 'Ahnenerbe' der SS*, 199.

[160] Karl Alexander von Müller, 'Das neue Deutschland', *Süddeutsche Monatshefte*, 12/10 (Oct. 1914), 88–95; 'Deutsche Größe', *Volk und Welt* (Dec. 1943), 4.

[161] See Karl Alexander von Müller, 'Der Führer', *Deutsche Volksbildung*, 9/2 (June 1934), 23–8; 'Zum 2. August 1939', *Velhagen und Klasings Monatshefte*, 53/2 (1939), 529–32; 'Gestalt und Wandel des Reiches', in Hans Hagemeyer (ed.), *Gestalt und Wandel des Reiches* (Berlin: Propyläen-Verlag, 1944), 9–35 (which derives from 'Deutsche Größe' (see Schönwälder, *Historiker und Politik*, 263–4 and 377 n. 837)).

and that there was a much more sinister side to the new Reich—an aspect of his personality that commentators play down because of the lurid nature of his public utterances. This awareness manifests itself on the one hand in the way he edited Germany's leading historical review, the *Historische Zeitschrift* (*HZ*), from autumn 1935 to 1944 and on the other in his relationship with his former student Walter Frank (1905–45). Frank became the Director of the Institute for the History of the New Germany which opened in Berlin at exactly the same time that von Müller took over the editorship of the *HZ* from Germany's most distinguished historian Friedrich Meinecke (1862–1954). There is evidence that the two events were connected and that Frank may even have had a hand in procuring the editorship for von Müller in the hope that the *HZ* would become the mouthpiece of his Institute (of which von Müller was immediately made an honorary member).[162] At the same time, Frank also became the editor of the *Forschungen zur Judenfrage* (*Research on the Jewish Question*) (*FzJ*), the organ of that department of his Institute which was located in Munich and specially concerned with that area. Exhaustive research has shown that von Müller collaborated with Frank for a while; that Frank's influence over the *HZ* peaked in 1937; and that von Müller agreed to write three 'educational tracts' on British politics for his Institute in 1939. But it has also shown that von Müller stopped publishing reports in the *HZ* by Wilhelm Grau, Frank's deputy, on research into the 'Jewish Question' in spring 1938; that the tracts never materialized; that nothing more on the 'Jewish Question' appeared in the *HZ* until September 1940; and that contributions on the subject stopped for good in 1942 (i.e. when it must have been clear to many Bavarians that something extremely dire was happening around them).[163] The same research has shown that scholarly articles predominated in the *HZ* while von Müller was its editor and that over two-thirds of the 1942/3 volume constituted a Festschrift in honour of Meinecke, a well-known anti-Nazi whom von Müller had already defended against an attack by Frank in the *HZ*.[164] Conversely, although von Müller allowed his speech of welcome on 19 November 1936 at the first Munich conference of Grau's department to be published in volume 1 of the *FzJ* (pp. 11–12), it is phrased in the most general terms, contains not a single anti-Semitic utterance, and implies very strongly that its author hopes that the new department will not see its task as the provision of racist propaganda. Only one essay to appear in the *HZ* (25 Feb. 1937) also appeared in the *FzJ* (1937). Von Müller withdrew the foreword that he had written for the first edition of Grau's book on medieval anti-Semitism (June 1934) when its much more overtly anti-Semitic second edition appeared in 1939.[165] And Heiber maintains that von

---

[162] 'Wechsel in der Leitung der "Historischen Zeitschrift"', *Nationalsozialistische Partei-Korrespondenz*, part 233 (5 Oct. 1935), fo. b; 'Frisches Blut in der Wissenschaft', ibid.; BHStA, NLvM, 10, Walter Frank to von Müller, 12 May 1935.

[163] See Martin Gilbert, *Atlas of the Holocaust* (London: Michael Joseph, 1982), 96.

[164] Helmut Heiber, *Walter Frank und sein Reichsinstitut für Geschichte des neuen Deutschlands* (Stuttgart: Deutsche Verlags-Anstalt, 1966), 227, 308, 311–12, 1026–7, 1107, 1109; Werner, *Das NS-Geschichtsbild*, 64–6 and Schönwälder, *Historiker und Politik*, 33 and 87. See also Karl Alexander von Müller, 'Vorwort', *HZ* 163/1 (Nov. 1940), 2 and BHStA, NLvM, 457 which contains considerable material documenting von Müller's growing hostility to Frank and awareness of the political significance of his pro-Meinecke stance.

[165] Cf. Wilhelm Grau, 'Einleitung', in *Antisemitismus im späten Mittelalter* (Munich: Duncker & Humblot, 1939), 16.

Müller, who together with Frank and Grau was nominally a director of the Munich Department, had as little to do with it as possible in practice even before the war turned its theoretical concerns into the most appalling reality.[166] One can find the occasional anti-Semitic remark in von Müller's pre-war writings,[167] but he was no anti-Semite in the hard-line Nazi sense. There is also considerable evidence that von Müller, despite his pro-Nazi publications, refused to let Nazi ideology, especially its racial doctrines, affect his day-to-day teaching; that he supervised at least thirty-three doctoral dissertations during the Nazi years whose content was not compatible with Nazi ideology; that he befriended students who were Jewish and/or opposed to the regime; and that he enabled, by means of an inertia which became ever more pronounced after 1938, the Bavarian Academy of Science (whose president he had become—also in late 1935) to get on with most of its scholarly tasks despite a concerted attempt by the Nazis to assimilate it and the dismissal of its Jewish members.[168]

Probably because of his commitment to the idea of a Greater Germany, von Müller seems to have been able to accept the invasion of Poland, France, and the Low Countries and published three article justifying the war as late as 1941.[169] But after the invasion of Russia, such pieces cease: von Müller must have realized that Germany was waging a cynical war of aggression, not one of national liberation. A younger brother died in Russia in October 1941; one of his twin sons went missing in February 1943 and was never heard of again; the other was taken prisoner in Russia and did not return until summer 1948; and another brother was killed in Greece in September 1944. But the event which really made von Müller understand the true nature of the NS regime was the arrest and execution, on 13 July 1943, of his long-standing friend Professor Kurt Huber, the academic behind the 'White Rose' group at Munich University.[170] Von Müller, at some risk to himself, lent active support to Huber's family but increasingly withdrew from public life and, pleading illness, spent ever more time in rural Rottach-Egern. He was removed from his university post by the American Military Government in January 1946; spent two years eking out a living gathering medicinal herbs in the mountains around his home; was found guilty of 'Mitläufertum' (being a fellow traveller) and fined RM2,000 plus costs on 12 February 1948. Although von Müller never taught again, he was gradually reinstated both in his profession and in Bavarian public life, and by the time of his

[166] *Walter Frank*, 415, 577.

[167] See von Müller, 'Zum 2. August 1939', 531 (where he speaks of 'der jüdische Spaltpilz, der das völkische Leben selbst im Innersten anfraß' ('the Jewish bacterium which sank its teeth into the innermost being/life of our "Volk"')); also BHStA, NLvM, 10, von Müller to Staatsarchivrat Engel, 22 Nov. 1935.

[168] See the numerous affidavits to this effect in BHStA, MK 44052 and MUA, PF von Müller; also Archiv der Bayerischen Akademie der Wissenschaften (Munich), PF von Müller, 16-page letter of 29 Aug. 1945, and Monika Stoermer, 'Die Bayerische Akademie der Wissenschaften im Dritten Reich', *Acta historica Leopoldina*, 22 (1995), 89–111.

[169] Karl Alexander von Müller, 'Die deutsche Geisteswissenschaft im Kriege', *Die Bewegung: Zentralorgan des NSD-Studentenbundes* (Munich), 9/1–2 (1941), 11, 'Warum Deutschland Siegen muß', *Völkischer Beobachter* (Munich), 30 (30 Jan. 1941), 23; also as 'Gewißheit des Sieges', *Volk und Welt* (May 1941), 5–9.

[170] See Hinrich Siefken, *Die Weiße Rose und ihre Flugblätter* (Manchester: Manchester University Press, 1994).

death in late 1964 he had become a respected public figure who genuinely, I think, accepted his due measure of guilt for his political blindness and self-deluding complicity.[171] So while there is some truth in Kurt Hahn's post-war thesis and while von Müller forms its most spectacular exception, it has very clear limitations.

But the Nazis certainly wanted to get their men into Oxford. While the files of the Nationalsozialistischer Deutscher Studentenbund (NDS) in the Würzburg Staatsarchiv contain nothing on the Rhodes Trust as such, they do contain a letter from the NDS's directorate of 12 May 1933 which says that several pro-Nazi students are already in Oxford and that their main man there is in contact with the AGAB.[172] The letter's author implies that it would be desirable to get more Nazi students into Oxford and build up an organization there for propaganda purposes, but states that this will be a very expensive undertaking given the 'well-known plutocratic circumstances' which obtain. Thus, given the high status that the German scholarships already had in governmental circles (see n. 110), it would only be natural for the NSDAP to want to infiltrate it via the selection committee since this would solve the financial problem for two well-placed students per year. Consequently, the history of the German Rhodes scholarships until 1939 involves two conflicting pressures: fairly uncoordinated attempts by the Nazis to get their men into Oxford using the weak points in the selection procedure described above, and a fairly determined attempt by the Rhodes Trust on both sides of the Channel to resist such infiltration.

Again, a certain amount of background information is necessary before we can decide who won that struggle. The Nazis' seizure of power had several fairly immediate effects on the constitution and administration of the selection committee. Simons and Mendelssohn-Bartholdy were eased out of public life by mid-October 1933 (but kept their places on the committee for the 1933–4 round).[173] Bernstorff, who saw where things were going with extreme lucidity and made no secret of his conviction that the Nazis' anti-Semitism would alienate Anglo-Saxon opinion, was sent on leave from the Foreign Office in May 1933 and recalled to Berlin on 24 June (but kept his place on the committee too).[174] The hostility between him and von Lindeiner-Wildau (who had joined the NSDAP on 1 May 1933) became even more acute,[175] and as the Nazis tried to assimilate the AAD from mid-1933, so Morsbach came under increasing pressure as secretary to the selection committee. Immediately after meeting Morsbach on 16 February 1934, Allen wrote to Lothian (RTF 1628) that he felt Morsbach's position to be 'highly precarious', that he was 'a much driven man', and that 'it will not be at all easy in future to find suitable types for the German Rhodes Scholarships'. After the Night of the Long Knives, Morsbach was arrested for soliciting Ernst Röhm's help in his attempt to prevent the Nazification of the AAD.[176] He spent nearly two months in the Torgau concentration

---

[171]   See BHStA, NLvM, 3 'Meine Beziehungen zur NSDAP', 7-page unpublished typescript (mid-1945). Cf. Heinz Gollwitzer, 'Karl Alexander von Müller 1882–1964: Ein Nachruf', *HZ* 205/2 (1967), 295–322 and Peter Jahn, 'Beschönigungen', *Der Monat*, 22/233 (Feb. 1968), 90–3.

[172]   Weber's research shows that there were about fourteen German students at Oxford in May 1933 not counting the Rhodes scholars.

[173]   RTF 1682, Schmidt-Ott to Lothian, 8 Nov. 1933.   [174]   Hansen, *Bernstorff*, 193–7.

[175]   RTF 1682, Memorandum of Lothian to Trustees, 2 Jan. 1934.

[176]   *Deutsche Akademische Austauschdienst*, 23–5.

camp; was dismissed from the AAD;[177] and died prematurely three years later. So in autumn 1934, the Trust had to find a new secretary and a replacement for Mendelssohn-Bartholdy (who began at Balliol as a senior research fellow in October.[178] At Bernstorff's suggestion, Morsbach was replaced by Georg Freiherr von Fritsch (1901–1902), a Saxon state official who had had himself transferred to the AAD in Berlin immediately after Hitler's seizure of power because of trouble with the Nazis in Saxony,[179] and whom Bernstorff described as 'a reasonable and sound man'. Mendelssohn-Bartholdy was replaced by Schwerin von Krosigk, who Schmidt-Ott thought would be a 'usefull [sic] link . . . (at least it can be represented in this way) . . . with the powers that be without on the other hand accepting any Party influence'. From the same letter it transpires that Bernstorff had tried to get von Trott onto the selection committee, [180] but that von Lindeiner-Wildau had persuaded the German Association to retain von Schweinitz and to replace Bernstorff by his old friend[181] and colleague Adolf Freiherr Marschall von Bieberstein (Christ Church 1913) on the grounds that he was now (April 1934–April 1937) a *Legationssekretär* at the London Embassy and thus another useful link with the Trustees.

Given these upheavals and various rumours that had reached the Trust, the Trustees were clearly worried that the new regime would try to take over the selection committee, and although Lothian and Dawson were prominent appeasers until the *Anschluss* of Austria in March–April 1938, even they were not prepared to appease the Nazis over this particular matter.[182] On 1 August 1933, Lothian, who detested totalitarianism of any kind, had sent a memo to the Trustees from which it is clear that he opposed the Nazis' anti-Semitism and in which he implied that it would not be desirable to have someone on the selection committee 'who was known to be in reasonably friendly relations with the new regime' (RTF 1682). So in late January 1935, he went to Berlin himself to see how matters stood. He assured himself that the Nazis had not hijacked the committee; used the opportunity to meet von Ribbentrop, von Neurath, Hess, and the Defence Minister General von Blomberg; and even, through the good offices of Schwerin von

[177] RTF 1682 Bernstorff to Lothian, 25 July 1934; Frank Aydelotte to Lothian, 20 Aug. 1934; German Rhodes Committee to Lothian, 29 Aug. 1934.

[178] RTF 1682, Bernstorff to Eric Millar, 14 Oct. 1934.

[179] Ibid. Volkhard Laitenberger, *Akademischer Austausch und auswärtige Kulturpolitik 1923 bis 1945* (Göttingen: Frankfurt am Main, 1976), 71, 124–5; see also IfZ, ZS 2091 (Georg Freiherr von Fritsch), letter, 16 Jan. 1968.

[180] RTF 1682, Bernstorff to Millar, 14 Oct. 1934. Letters in RTF 1682 and the AA indicate very clearly that Bernstorff, who had first met von Trott at interview in 1930, regarded him as his protégé. His name appears more frequently than that of any other German Rhodes scholar in Bernstorff's letters to Gräfin Reventlow 1931–41, most compromisingly in that of 7 Aug. 1941 when Bernstorff, after a meal with various members of the Resistance including von Trott, wrote: 'Good conversation: No. 1 [i.e. Hitler] must disappear.'

[181] AA, NLB, 2, Bernstorff to Gräfin von Reventlow, 13 May [1913].

[182] See Butler, *Lothian*, 190–237; Martin Gilbert and Richard Gott, *The Appeasers* (London: Weidenfeld & Nicolson, 1963), 8, 14, 27, 35, 38–9, 41, 46–9, 66–7, 91–2, 217, 358, 368; Neville Thompson, *The Anti-Appeasers: Conservative Opposition to Appeasement in the 1930s* (Oxford: Clarendon Press, 1971), 40, 105, 157–8; Richard Griffiths, *Fellow Travellers of the Right: British Enthusiasts for Nazi Germany 1933–39* (Oxford: Oxford University Press, 1983), 113, 119, 154, 270–1; James Fox, *The Langhorne Sisters* (London: Granta Books, 1998), 490–501.

Krosigk, had a two-and-a-half-hour-long conversation with Hitler himself.[183] But during his visit, he made it absolutely clear to Schwerin von Krosigk and Schmidt-Ott that the Trustees would tolerate no infiltration by Party nominees. And as an extra safeguard, given the pivotal role of the secretary in the selection process, Lothian also made it clear that von Fritsch, who was not then in the Party, would 'hold the Secretaryship purely in his personal capacity and not as a member of the Austauschdienst, and if he is moved the question of his successor will have to be considered in the light of the circumstances of that time'.[184]

Lothian's suspicions had not, however, prevented him from being impressed by Hitler and his good intentions. So immediately after his return, he published a long, two-part article in *The Times* stating that although the new regime was 'harsh, brutal, and ruthless', it had come into being 'largely to end the abasement of Germany'; was 'not imperialist'; wanted 'equality, not war'; and should be allowed to rearm so that it could settle its disputes with its neighbours as an equal—and besides, it would 'take seven or eight years to restore the full efficiency of the German army'.[185] On 2 February 1935, the Berlin correspondent of *The Times* reported that 'the general lines' of Lothian's article 'obviously met with approval in Berlin' and quoted Goebbels telling a 'packed' Nazi meeting that 'influential newspapers in England, *The Times*, for instance, were publishing articles in which the German view was fairly presented'.[186] By convincing Lothian that their global intentions were peaceful and giving him the impression that they would leave the selection committee alone, the Nazis, who overestimated the real political importance of the British aristocracy outside the government, had achieved three things. They had gained a channel to the major newspaper of the British elites (since Dawson relied on Lothian for much of his information on Germany), possibly the *Observer* as well (of which Lothian was a director), and broad segments of the British public (since Lothian was much in demand as a speaker and his speeches were regularly reported in the press). They had also forged a link between Lothian and von Ribbentrop (who had entertained him in Berlin) which would produce extensive discussions on European hegemony in summer 1935 and 1936 (n. 182). As a result, Lothian, who now suffered from an acute sense of guilt over the part he had played in formulating the Treaty of Versailles (nn. 84, 99), continued to justify Germany's demands until mid-1936 at least (by which time Germany had reoccupied the demilitarized Rhineland, rearmed, and created a modern air force).[187] Lothian met Hitler again for one and a half hours on 4 May 1937 and spoke briefly to Goering on the 'general political situation'.[188] But this time there was no big follow-up in *The Times*: possibly because the brief report on the visit was printed on the same page as a long report on the bombing of Guernica. The scales were beginning to drop from the appeasers' eyes.

---

[183] IfZ, ZS 145, vol. iv (Schwerin von Krosigk on Hitler), 33; see Butler, *Lothian*, 202–5 and 330–7 for details of this conversation.

[184] RTF 1682, Report of Lothian to Trustees, 15 Feb. 1935.

[185] Lord Lothian, 'Germany and France', *The Times*, 31 Jan. 1933, 15–16; 1 Feb. 1935, 15–16.

[186] 'German Interest', *The Times*, 2 Feb. 1935, 12.

[187] Lothian's last significant speech in this vein to be reported in *The Times* is summarized in 'Future of the League', 27 June 1936, 8.　　　[188] 'Lord Lothian's Visit to Hitler', *The Times*, 6 May 1937, 15.

Schwerin von Krosigk replaced von Lindeiner-Wildau as chairman of the German Rhodes Scholars' Association at its dinner on 26 January 1935, and Lothian (who was there) implies in both his report of 15 February and a later memo to the Trustees of 30 April 1937 (RTF 1682) that the body of the scholars welcomed this move since they were becoming increasingly irritated by the politically derived friction between Bernstorff and von Lindeiner-Wildau and wanted, like Lothian, to depoliticize the selection procedure as far as possible. But this was no easy task. In November 1935, the Gestapo began to watch von Fritsch and in early 1936 he had himself moved to the War Ministry but still remained under pressure by the Nazis.[189] Hjalmar Schacht (1877–1970), the president of the Reichsbank (1933–9) and Economics Minister (1934–7), who was coming into increasing conflict with the Nazis over their policy of boosting the economy through rearmament and whom Lothian had met on 5 May 1937,[190] took over from Simons on the committee after the latter's death in mid-1937. And Dr August Wilhelm Fehling (1896–1964), a resolute anti-Nazi who had worked with Schmidt-Ott in the NDW since 1922 and helped him with the administration of the selection committee since 1930, relieved von Fritsch in March 1937.[191] But the Trustees were still so concerned about infiltration in late 1936 that Lothian broached the question with von Ribbentrop, whom he now knew well and who had become the German Ambassador to Britain on 26 October 1936.[192] Von Ribbentrop replied 'that whatever other people may think of it the overwhelming mass of young Germans to-day are National Socialists and accept its general view of life', and Lothian was forced to concede: 'I am afraid it is inevitable that the German Rhodes Scholars in future will increasingly be National Socialists in their general outlook, though I think we can rely on the Selection Committee not choosing the more militant or aggressive types.'

So were Lothian's hopes or fears fulfilled during the most fraught period of the German scholarships' existence? Overall, the answer has to be that the committee succeeded in resisting Nazi infiltration to a very significant extent. There were never more than two NSDAP members on the selection committee in any given year; these seem to have become Party members mainly for reasons of professional expediency; and all seem to have done their best to judge the candidates according to Rhodes's criteria. To take one example only: one clearly anti-Nazi scholar who was very much liked at Oxford was strongly backed by von Lindeiner-Wildau (who had, at the dinner of 26 January 1935, given a long speech in praise of 'our Leader and his ideas', the 'new Reich' and its 'leading ideas', and the 'virtues' which had brought it into existence and were now sustaining it (RTF 1682)). Of the fourteen scholars elected 1933–9,[193] only five had any serious Party affiliation, and of these, only three became Party members after they had left Oxford, two from conviction and one in order to enter state service. None of these three said

[189] See n. 179. RTF 1682, Memorandum of Millar to Trustees, 15 Jan. 1936.
[190] Butler, *Lothian*, 217.
[191] BAK, NLF, 75–84 concern Fehling's time as secretary. On Fehling himself, see the *Schleswig-Holsteinisches Biografisches Lexikon* (Neumünster: Wachholtz, 1976), iv. 65–8.
[192] RTF 1682, Lothian to Allen, 11 Dec. 1936.
[193] Two scholars—Erich Vermehren (b. 1919) and Wolfgang Fontaine (b. 1917)—were elected for 1939 but never matriculated because of the war.

anything about their political leanings in their applications; one consistently refused to talk about his politics while at Oxford and was known in his college as 'politically a dark horse'; and even the most evangelical of the three, who was a leading member of the Nazi student organization at his home university and strongly backed by its Nazi Rector,[194] was a heavy-footed, authoritarian nationalist, not a 'völkisch' ideologue. Indeed, an examination of the files in the NLF (which include those of candidates who were short-listed but not selected) suggests that von Fritsch and Fehling always invited a reasona-ble number of convinced, hard-line Nazis for interview so that they could not be accused of overt political discrimination, and then let them dig their own graves. According to an eyewitness account, one such candidate informed the committee that he wished to go to Oxford in order to convert the British people to National Socialism—whereupon Schacht drily remarked, 'I wish you much success.' According to the same source, Fehling in particular sometimes advised would-be candidates who were anti-Nazi to make sure that they joined at least one low-grade Nazi organization for form's sake so that it would be harder for the Nazi student organization, as happened in two cases respectively, to make difficulties over the visa or have the passport confiscated.[195]

Although it is clear that the Nazi authorities realized that most Rhodes scholars were not ideal spokesmen for the new Germany and knew what the selection committee was doing, they took no active steps against it for most of the 1930s. This was due partly to its distinguished membership and partly so as not to alienate Lothian (whom von Rib-bentrop allegedly described to Hitler as 'the most influential Englishman outside the Government' and who, for a while at least, was able to countenance 'Hitler's Anglo-German dream' of joint hegemony in order to keep Britain out of a European war).[196] Thus, on 31 October 1938, the *Landesgruppenleiter* of the NSDAP in London wrote a very irate and frustrated letter to the German Embassy complaining that *yet again*, the new German Rhodes scholars—unlike other exchange scholars—had failed to report to his office, and that, *as usual*, they wanted to do their own thing and did not care about 'Deutschtum' (Germanness). In response, the Embassy drafted a memo on 8 December 1938 to no one in particular in which it requested the two new scholars to report at the Embassy and the London office of the NSDAP to give an account of the situation in Oxford (PAB, London 1540). But given the political crisis that was by now unfolding, the scholars seem not to have received, let alone heeded it.

Conversely, as the above exchange suggests, it is the anti-Nazi record of the entire second generation of scholars that is the more striking. One became in turn a natural-ized Canadian and Briton and worked for British political intelligence during the war.

---

[194] BAK, NLF, 99. R. H. Crossman found him in his rooms, 'rummaging among his papers', and he was also discovered snooping around the rooms of two other German scholars. Schmidt-Ott seems to have heard about this and summoned him back to Berlin at his own expense, presumably to find out what was going on and, if necessary, to tell him to desist (PAB, London 1540). After the war, when he had undergone a major change of heart, he apologized to Allen by letter and to several other people in person whom he felt that he had wronged.

[195] Wolfgang Fontaine, 'Mein Leben und Wirken: Schulzeit und Studium während der NS-Zeit, Rhodes-Stipendium, Überleben im Krieg', unpublished 11-page typescript (1998), 7 and 10.

[196] Fox, *The Langhorne Sisters*, 500; Michael Bloch, *Ribbentrop* (London: Bantam Press, 1992), 92.

Several went into exile in Britain, the USA, Canada, or Switzerland in more or less difficult physical and psychological circumstances. On 4 April 1940, for instance, one of them wrote to Allen painting a very depressed picture of a post-war Europe that would be 'economic[ally] ruined, politically unstable and, worse [sic] of all, morally and intellectually poisoned' and concluding that 'to keep preparing oneself to return to such a place to do whatever falls to one's lot is the only role I can think of for myself at this moment'. After three months' internment, one worked for the BBC's Overseas Service throughout the war. One spent four miserable years in internment camps in this country and Canada, and then in the Pioneer Corps, living under canvas and building roads in Wales and Yorkshire, before more appropriate work could be arranged for him. One worked as a farm labourer in England and another as a cowboy in the USA. One was detained by the FBI for some time for investigation as an enemy alien after being denounced by a local patriotic organization. One, together with his wife, deserted from the German diplomatic service via Turkey in 1944 and made a highly anti-Nazi statement in which he described the regime as 'the bitterest enemies of Germany'. Allied journalists published the story and revealed his name, thereby putting two families in mortal danger because of the Nazi principle of *Sippenhaft* (collective family arrest).[197] One served with the American Army in the Pacific, was wounded, and won the Bronze Star, the Purple Heart, and the Combat Infantryman Badge. Von Trott went to the USA after the outbreak of war to establish a link between the German Resistance and the US Government—an attempt which failed. He returned to Germany and joined the Foreign Office, a major centre of resistance, to work against the regime, and try to shorten the war,—with all the risks, moral ambiguities, and misunderstandings that such a decision involved.[198] With von Moltke, he became a leading member of the Kreisau Circle and was hanged on 11 September 1944 for his part in the 20 July conspiracy. And of those who returned to Germany and were called up, one tried to limit the damage by serving in the Medical Corps and one volunteered for service on the much more dangerous eastern front so as not to have to fight against Britain. So, given the massive support for the Nazis among German youth[199] and its situation under a totalitarian regime, the selection committee's record is more than creditable. But ironically, quite a lot of that credit has to go to Schwerin von Krosigk, in whose offices on Berlin's Wilhelmsplatz the interviews had been held since the Nazification of the AAD. He used this as part of his defence (see n. 149; p. 22699), and before his trial, Roediger, Schmidt-Ott, von Kamphoevener, Fehling, and Allen all swore affidavits to that effect. Similarly, Fritz Caspari (St John's 1933; honorary fellow 1972) tells me that several Rhodes scholars complained to him about attempted Nazi interference and that he usually tried to do something about it.

---

[197] See 'German Diplomatist Disappears', *The Times*, 9 Feb. 1944, 4; 'Flight of German Diplomatist', *The Times*, 10 Feb. 1944, 4; 'A German and his "Conscience"', *The Times*, 10 Mar. 1944, 4; MacDonough, *A Good German*, 246–7, 268; Winfried Meyer (ed.), *Hans von Dohnany und die Häftlinge des 20. Juli 1944 im KZ Sachsenhausen*, Schriftenreihe der Stiftung Brandenburgische Gedenkstätten: Oranienburg 5 (Berlin: Hentrich, 1998), 365–73. According to BAK, NLF, 81 and 82, the fugitive already had the rare distinction of having been thrown out of the Hitler Jugend.
[198] MacDonough, *A Good German*, 132–59.
[199] See A. J. Nicholls, *Weimar and the Rise of Hitler* (London: Macmillan, 1977), 170–1.

Against the worsening political background 1933–9, around forty to fifty-five Germans per annum, many of them Jewish, applied for Rhodes scholarships,[200] and the fortunate few seem to have met varying degrees of political interest, indifference, or hostility in Oxford depending upon the circles in which they moved. As early as August 1934, Justus-Carl von Ruperti (Brasenose 1934) reported to the German selection committee that anti-German feeling had run particularly high throughout Britain in the previous October; that it was especially strong in Oxford; and that after a respite during the winter, it was prevalent everywhere once more (AA, NLAB; AvK). But Böker's report to von Fritsch of 5 December 1934 says nothing of this; remarks on the extent to which Oxford students are open to discussions about German culture and politics provided that these are conducted tactfully; and records how many of them seem to have spent happy summer holidays in Bavaria or Austria (BAK, NLF, 99). On the other hand, Böker recorded in retrospect that most Oxford students during his time considered Hitler and the Nazis 'rather ridiculous' and were suspicious of anyone who tried to persuade them otherwise;[201] and according to an unpublished interview with James Fox of the *Sunday Times Magazine* which he gave in the late 1960s, Dietrich von Bothmer (Wadham 1938; honorary fellow 1987) considered his English coevals 'extraordinarily uninformed about Europe' and not particularly interested in the really pressing problems of the day (RTF 1682C). Whatever, the scholars did their best to fit in, use their time well, make their mark on Oxford, and, as far as one can tell, profited from the experience. Caspari became the second interwar scholar to get a B.Litt. (in history). Erich Etienne (Wadham 1934), whose passion for meteorology would lead directly to his death in the war (BAA), took part as a meteorologist in three University expeditions to Greenland. Hans Hammelmann (Brasenose 1935) took advantage of the newly liberalized statutes on standing, and, having studied for two years at a German university, became the first German scholar to take a first-class honours degree (in law). He was also awarded a senior Hulme scholarship; played chess against Cambridge; and after the war became the first German scholar to gain an Oxford D.Phil. and be called to the English Bar (middle Temple). Karl Günther Motz (Oriel 1935) and Rolf Mühlinghaus (Exeter 1936) made it to the trial eights in 1936 and 1937 respectively, and Helge Merz (Trinity 1937) had the rare distinction of obtaining three half-blues (hockey, athletics, and skiing). Von Bothmer had wanted to become an archaeologist since the age of 12 and so thought of himself in the first place as a 'Wissenschaftler'. But unlike Schumacher, he found his way into Oxford's expanding research culture and enjoyed his time at Oxford. Here, he laid the foundations of a career as a classical archaeologist (which he would crown by becoming Distinguished Research Curator at the New York Metropolitan Museum of Art) by reading for the Diploma of Classical Archaeology under Sir John Beazley (1885–1970). Sir Maurice Bowra described Beazley as 'the greatest expert in the world on the subject', and von Bothmer would later characterize him, significantly, as 'Oxford all his life' but 'not typically Oxford' (RTF 1682C).[202] In general,

---

[200] Schmidt-Ott, *Erlebtes und Erstrebtes*, 295; BAK, NLF, 75 and 76.　　　[201] Böker, '1934', 97–8.
[202] See also D[ietrich] von B[othmer], 'Sir John Beazley', *Oxford Magazine*, 12 June 1970, 299–302. More recently, von Bothmer made the magnificent donation of a great collection of Greek vases to the Ashmolean and, together with his wife, became the first German Rhodes scholar to be made a member of the Chancellor's Court of Benefactors.

most of the second-generation scholars seem to have found that they were received positively, whatever their politics and despite the worsening international situation, provided that they were prepared to involve themselves actively in some aspect of college or University life, and there is some evidence that Oxford had a liberalizing effect on some of them. Certainly, one non-Nazi scholar who had come to Oxford with the stated intention of defending the new Germany had become much more critical by the time he left, and the most pro-Nazi scholar conceded at the end of his stay that he had, to his own surprise, become more open-minded and even something of a pacifist (BAK, NLF, 99).

Finances continued to cause difficulties—the Reichsmark stood at 11.76 to the pound in 1935 and 15 in December 1936. In late 1936, and despite initiatives by Schwerin von Krosigk,[203] a regulation came into force which prevented German scholars from getting any extra money from Germany over and above the RM10 permitted to all German citizens.[204] This, in Allen's view, was a 'sudden action . . . intended to convey displeasure',[205] so Lothian approached von Ribbentrop who 'said in effect that he hoped it would not be necessary to transfer more than say £50 in the case of any one Scholar or more than £200 altogether' (RTF 1682 Lothian to Allen 11 December 1936; see also ibid. letter Allen to Fehling 25 July 1937).[206] Nevertheless, in October 1937, the Hamburg businessman Alfred Toepfer founded the Hanseatic scholarships—which were open then to all universities of the Empire with a preference for Great Britain—as an expression of gratitude to the Rhodes Trustees. They were worth RM3,000 per annum; the British selection committee was chaired by Lothian; their patron was the German Ambassador; and Neville Chamberlain expressed his approval of them because of their ability to further 'mutual cooperation and knowledge of one another'.[207] But Schmidt-Ott was unable to persuade the Rhodes Trust to match this gesture by increasing the German scholarships to three in the following year—probably because his letter coincided with the *Anschluss*.[208] By early 1938, the Nazi authorities were threatening to withdraw the concession arranged by von Ribbentrop—possibly, as Bernstorff wrote to Lothian on 20 February 1938 (citing Fehling; RTF 1628), because the Nazis 'very much resent the Committee not being under their complete control'. But besides that consideration, British public opinion was turning against appeasement (so that there was less point in courting it via the appeasers), and the Nazis' expansionist politics were by now alienating the appeasers amongst the Trustees (of whose goodwill they had correspondingly less need).[209] Lothian's letter to *The Times* of 14 March 1938 may have advocated economic appeasement, but it also advocated 'universal national service' and is marked by a sense that war is approaching.

[203] BAK, NLF, 75, Fehling to Allen, 15 Jan. 1937.
[204] RTF 1682, Lothian to Allen, 16 Nov. 1936.   [205] RTF 1682, Allen to Lothian, 5 Dec. 1936.
[206] RTF 1682, Lothian to Allen, 11 Dec. 1936; see also RTF 1682, Allen to Fehling, 25 July 1937.
[207] See 'German "Rhodes Trust"', *The Times*, 16 Oct. 1937, 16; 'German "Rhodes" Scholarships', *The Times*, 23 Oct. 1937, 14.
[208] Schmidt-Ott, *Erlebtes und Erstrebtes*, 296; BAK, NLF, 75, Lothian to Schmidt-Ott, 29 Mar. 1938.
[209] Cf. Douglas Reed, *Insanity Fair* (London: Jonathan Cape, 1938), 373–4; Gilbert and Gott, *The Appeasers*, 92, 217, 368; Hermann Graml, 'Resistance Thinking on Foreign Policy', in Walter Schmitthenner and Hans Buchheim (eds.), *The German Resistance to Hitler* (London: Batsford, 1970), 38; Griffiths, *Fellow Travellers*, 287; MacDonough, *A Good German*, 44; Weber, 'A Stormy Romance', 137; Joachim Fest, 'Portrait Adam von Trott', *Prospect* (July 1998), 51; Fox, *The Langhorne Sisters*, 503.

But more significantly, it was immediately followed by a letter from L. S. Amery, the chairman of the Rhodes Trustees, which said that the *Anschluss* meant 'an end of all discussion for a settlement with Germany', called for rearmament, and advised the nation to keep very close to France and the Commonwealth. The concession had not been withdrawn by May 1938.[210] But within such an uncertain climate, the Trustees resolved to raise the German scholarships by £50 per annum 'so long as the existing exchange restrictions remain in force'.[211]

The Nazi regime also affected the older generation of German scholars, most of whom were more restricted by family and professional responsibilities than their younger counterparts. Several went into inner emigration and simply kept their heads down. Von Schweinitz was eased out of the Deutsche Forschungsgemeinschaft (as the NDW became known in 1934) in 1936.[212] Bernstorff, who never served in the diplomatic service again after his recall in 1933, was permanently retired on 24 March 1937.[213] Others tried to carry on with their work even though this sometimes meant complicity with a government whose true nature became increasingly and painfully apparent as the war drew nearer. In 1932, at the end of his political career, von Lindeiner-Wildau had described his main political task of the past twenty-two years as 'concern for Germany's rural population'. In order to continue his political work by other means, he joined the Board of the Preussische Zentralgenossenschaftskasse—the major source of finance for Prussia's agricultural and craft cooperatives. When the Nazis seized power, Dr Hans Helferich, the Bank's president since 1932, persuaded him to join the NSDAP on 1 May 1933 to protect the independence of a bank which looked after more than twelve billion Reichmarks belonging to several million small savers.[214] At Heidelberg University, Brinkmann, while no Party member, found himself in an even more ambivalent position after his disillusion with the Weimar regime.[215] Von Ow-Wachendorf, who had been active in the Catholic Centre Party 1930–1, was transferred from Luxembourg in May 1934; given two less salubrious postings; resigned in disgust in January 1939 after being threatened with disciplinary action on utterly fantastic charges in the previous November; and died on Java in August 1939 (PAB, PF). Something similar happened to Hans von Heinz (New College 1911) with the result that he, too, resigned from the diplomatic service in September 1938 (PAB, PF). He was subsequently called up (for the second time) at the age

---

[210] BAK, NLF, 99, Fehling to Jobst von der Groeben (New 1936), 14 May 1938.

[211] BAK, NLF, 75, Lothian to Fehling, 31 Mar. 8 Apr. 1938.

[212] Cf. Kurt Zierold, *Forschungsförderung in drei Epochen: Deutsche Forschungsgemeinschaft, Geschichte, Arbeitsweise* (Wiesbaden: Verlag Franz Steiner, 1968), 44 and 214.

[213] Hansen, *Bernstorff*, 127.

[214] BAK, NLvLW, 1, von Lindeiner-Wildau to Die Landbünde Teltow und Berkin, 12 Apr. 1932; ibid. 4, 13 Nov. 1945, to Paul Loebe (1875–1967) (SPD Reichstag Deputy 1919–33), and 18 Dec. 1946, to Gottfried Treviranus (1891–1971) (DNVP Deputy who had had to flee for his life at the end of June 1934).

[215] Cf. Carsten Klingemann, 'Das "Institut für Sozial- und Staatswissenschaften" an der Universität Heidelberg zum Ende der Weimarer Republik und während des Nationalsozialismus', *Jahrbuch für Soziologiegeschichte*, 1 (1990), 79–120 and *Soziologie im Dritten Reich* (Baden-Baden: Nomos, 1996), 137–48, 152–8, 162, 294; Jansen, *Professoren und Politik*, 57 and 278; Klaus-Rainer Brintzinger, *Die Nationalökonomie an den Universitäten Freiburg, Heidelberg und Tübingen 1918–1945* (Frankfurt am Main: Peter Lang, 1996), 209–17, 238–40.

of 46 and died on the Russian front.[216] Georg Rosen (Oriel 1913), an outstanding linguist, had two Jewish grandmothers and so was officially a 'non-Aryan'. But because he had fought at the front in the Great War, he was not affected by the Law of 7 April 1933 but given increasingly hazardous postings in war-torn China (whence he returned in 1938). Nevertheless, the Reich Citizenship Law of 14 November 1935 (which revoked the 1933 concession)[217] caught up with him in China in December 1936[218] and he was suspended from duty in May 1938. With the connivance of his superiors he came to England in 1938 (i.e. soon after 'Kristallnacht'), ostensibly to visit his British mother in London. He then contrived to miss the transports back to Germany in September 1939 and be interned so that the German government would continue to pay a salary to his family (whom he had had to leave in Berlin). Sadly, his wife was killed there by an Allied bomb on 6 March 1944 while he was teaching as a refugee in the USA (PAB, PF). In October 1944, Drechsler was suspended from his consular job in the Foreign Office under the terms of Hitler's directive of 19 May 1943 because he had a non-German wife (PAB, PF). Two others spent the war as internees outside Germany.

Others opted for damage limitation. Boden, a senior member of Germany's largest electricity company since 1929, did his best (unsuccessfully) to ensure that it made no use of forced labour from concentration camps; was dismissed by the Nazis in spring 1944; and was responsible for ensuring that the AEG paid out four million marks compensation to bona fide claimants after the war.[219] From September 1942 to late 1944, Roediger, who headed the Legal Department of the Foreign Office in Berlin, worked with the Red Cross to bring food relief to Belgium and Greece.[220] In March 1934, Bernstorff began working with the Bank of A. E. Wassermann in Berlin whose owners were Jewish and whose clients were overwhelmingly Jewish. Here, until autumn 1937, when the regime began to persecute Jewish communities even more severely, he was primarily engaged in the legal transfer of Jewish capital abroad. Thereafter, there are indications that he actively assisted people to flee to Switzerland and even used his own money to purchase their passports. Although never a member of the organized Resistance despite his friendship with von Trott, Bernstorff sent a stream of information to his old friend Harold Nicolson, one of the few British MPs who was opposed to appeasement, and kept in contact with the British Foreign Office.[221] In February 1937, he warned a representative of the impending threat to Czechoslovakia; foresaw the possibility of a German–Soviet pact; and advised getting tough with Hitler. In June 1937, he voiced his extreme disquiet at the worsening treatment of Germany's Jews. In November 1937, he said how distressed he was 'to find how frankly people admitted that England was not really interested in the fate of Austria and Czecho-Slovakia' and expressed his fear 'that

---

[216] In a letter to Allen of 21 June 1946 (BAK, NLF, 82), Fehling described von Heinz as 'one of the most courageous men I know of, in helping the displaced of the first years after 33'.

[217] Burleigh and Wippermann, *The Racial State*, 78, 82.

[218] RTF 2747, Rosen to Wylie, 7 Dec. 1936.

[219] Benjamin B. Ferencz, *Lohn des Grauens* (Frankfurt am Main: Campus, 1986), 149–52.

[220] Conrad Roediger, 'Die internationale Hilfaktion für die Bevölkerung Griechenlands im Zweiten Weltkrieg', *Vierteljahreshefte für Zeitgeschichte*, 11/1 (Jan. 1963), 49–71.

[221] Hansen, *Bernstorff*, 212–17, 227, 230, 255, 264–5, 276.

this attitude would encourage the German Government in their eastward expansion schemes'.[222] And on 15 February 1940, a letter was sent to Viscount Halifax from the British Legation in Copenhagen containing a memo from an informant who had spoken to Bernstorff in Germany. Bernstorff had warned that the Germans would attack through Holland or Belgium in the spring 'because they . . . could do nothing against the Maginot Line' and reported on 'mass executions and other atrocities of many kinds' that were happening in the east.[223] Bravery or recklessness born of despair? Whichever, Bernstorff's character cost him five months in Dachau May–September 1940 and his life a few days before the end of the war in Europe. He refused the chance to stay in Switzerland, was arrested on 30 July 1943, tortured, maltreated, never brought to trial, and summarily murdered in Berlin by the SS. His body was never found, but he is commemorated in Enid Bagnold's novel *The Loved and the Envied* (1951).[224]

Displaying a different kind of defiance, General von Senger und Etterlin, a professional soldier and committed Catholic who, from the outset, was under no illusions about the heavy moral responsibility incurred by serving an evil regime, refused, contrary to Hitler's orders, to cling to hopeless military positions with the attendant loss of life. While organizing the evacuation of Corsica in autumn 1943, he refused outright to obey the directive from the German High Command that all Italian officers who were captured after 10 September and had fought after that date should be shot as guerrillas, thereby saving the lives of over 200 men. He also arranged for the treasures in the Monastery of Monte Cassino to be removed to a place of safety before the Allies bombed it flat on 15 February 1944. Together with his superior, Field Marshal Kesselring, he ensured that the Italian cities of Bologna, Pisa, Lucca, and Florence would not be included in the Germans' defensive plan. Contrary to the wishes of the Nazi leadership, he refused to show any public jubilation before his troops that Hitler had survived the 20 July bomb and even took the son of General Oster, one of the leading conspirators, onto his staff.[225] Finally, Paul Gerhardt Feine (1894–1959), one of the seven scholars who was elected in 1914 but never matriculated, was a career diplomat. But he was also a member of the oppositional Confessing Church whose uncompromising anti-Nazi stance caused that career to come to a halt in 1933. Nevertheless, while working in the German Embassy in Budapest spring–autumn 1944 he both collaborated with the Red Cross to facilitate the transfer of Hungarian Jews to Palestine after Hungary was taken over by the Germans on 19 March 1944, and, after the collapse of Admiral Horthy's fascist regime in autumn 1944, he negotiated on its behalf with the new, more pro-Nazi government to ensure that 50,000 Budapest Jews were not 'evacuated' (i.e. sent to Auschwitz).[226]

---

[222] PRO, FO 371, File 20734, Memorandum of 2 Feb. 1937; File 20733, Memorandum of 15 June 1937; File 20712, Memorandum of 22 Nov. 1937—all on conversations with Bernstorff.

[223] PRO, FO 371, File 24388. The comment on this memo exhorts its readers to treat Bernstorff's views 'with great reserve' and concludes, ambiguously, 'but there is nothing much new in this'.

[224] Hansen, *Bernstorff*, 208, 260–72.

[225] von Senger und Etterlin, *Neither Fear nor Hope*, 163–4, 274, 202; von Senger und Etterlin, 'Senger', 381, 385–7.

[226] PAB, PF. See especially the affidavits by the Swiss Consul in Budapest, Charles Lutz, of 26 Feb. 1947 and 12 Nov. 1952.

May 1945–December 1969

During the confusion of the early post-war years, wild rumours about the deeds and feats of the German scholars regularly reached Wylie and Allen. As far as I can judge after extensive checks, five German scholars had died in action; two (probably three) had committed suicide out of a sense of despair at the situation in Germany; two had died at the hands of the Nazis; and another, Hans Rehmke (Brasenose 1911), a lawyer who was manager of Hamburg's Shipping Association and an anti-Nazi, had spent three and a half years in prison on charges that were almost certainly trumped up.[227] One member of the diplomatic corps stayed at his post in the Berlin Foreign Office to the bitter end, was captured by the Russians, and probably died in the Lubyanka in September 1946. Another, who happened to have the same surname as Alfred Rosenberg's deputy, was arrested in error and spent *circa* three years in the harsh conditions of a Russian internment camp. After the war, another was accidentally shot by a drunken Russian soldier in a POW camp. At least three, whose family estates were mainly in the east, were dispossessed. Two died prematurely because of malnutrition or maltreatment during the war. One was arrested in late 1945 in Pomerania (where he had gone on a business trip) and spent nearly eleven years in a labour camp. About three lost their jobs because of their (nominal) Party membership. But as early as March 1946, Merz was trying to locate all the surviving scholars.[228] By summer 1947, Mandt was trying to re-establish the Association of Former German Rhodes Scholars,[229] and its first reunion took place in July 1952 when about eighteen scholars met in Boden's office in Frankfurt am Main.

After 1945, about ten German scholars decided to emigrate or to continue to live outside Germany, three with changed names and about seven with changed nationalities, and several simply retired. But a significant number decided that, in accordance with the expectations Rhodes had of his scholars, they had something to contribute to what Böker described as 'the job of moral, economic and political reconstruction' of Germany and its rehabilitation in the West.[230] Seven sought to further democracy through education (Brinkmann, Drechsler, Roediger, Ries, von Senger und Etterlin (with Kurt Hahn at Salem),[231] Koelle, and Merz (who ran his own school in Stuttgart)). Walther von Chappuis (University 1913) was a senior judge in Berlin 1945–66. Schumacher acted as economic adviser to the British Control Commission in Germany 1945–50. Motz helped revivify Germany's coal industry 1946–54. After his release, Schwerin von Krosigk worked anonymously for the Federal Finance Ministry and wrote extensively for the government on economic matters for at least fifteen years.[232] Von Kamphoevener, Carl von Campe

---

[227] Rehmke was arrested on 2 Mar. 1940, sentenced to five years' imprisonment on 8 Aug. 1942, and released on health grounds on 4 Aug. 1943 (letter from Hamburg Staatsarchiv of 15 Oct. 1998). The records of his trial were destroyed in the war.

[228] BAK, NLF, 82, Fehling to Allied Information Service, 6 May 1946.

[229] RTF 1682, Theodor Ries to Allen, *c*. Aug. 1947.

[230] Harold Nicolson, 'Marginal Comment', *Spectator*, 26 Apr. 1946, 426.

[231] General F[ridolin] von Senger und Etterlin, 'Education for Leadership in Germany', *Listener*, 17 June 1954, 1042–3.

[232] Goehrke, *In den Fesseln der Pflicht*, 92–3.

(Brasenose 1912), Rosen, Feine, Caspari, Böker, and Motz worked in the consular or diplomatic service for various periods of time, with four attaining ambassadorial rank. In 1948, von Campe was elected to the German Economic Council in Frankfurt am Main. In 1949, Böker became an essential part of the nucleus around Konrad Adenauer, West Germany's first Chancellor, with special responsibility for liaising with the three High Commissioners who governed the country until 1955, and from 1958 to 1963 he was senior political adviser to the Secretary General of NATO. Caspari was invited by Adenauer to join the German Foreign Office in Bonn. He returned from the USA and, from 1954, worked briefly in the North American section and then for eight years in the field of Anglo-German relations—first as head of the British, Commonwealth, and Irish section and then, from 1958 to 1963, as political counsellor and chargé d'affaires in London with special responsibility for Anglo-German relations. In these capacities, he organized, in 1955, the first official visit of a German Foreign Minister since the war; in 1958, the political side of the first state visit of a German head of state (President Heuss) to Britain since before the Great War; and, in 1972, the state visit of President Heinemann. From July 1969 to June 1974, he was deputy head of the Presidential Office under Heinemann.[233] In all of this, Caspari tells me, Rhodes's founding ideas and the experience of Oxford were a major source of inspiration to both himself and Böker. Roediger led the German delegation to Paris February–July 1951 in order to work out the first stages of the European Defence Treaty. Schlepegrell worked with Schumacher after the war and finally became a senior executive of the OECD. But the individual who probably did most to restore Germany's economic health within a unifying Europe was Boden. He returned to the shattered AEG as soon as peace was declared, reorganized its administration, and played a major role in increasing its yearly turnover from DM432 million to DM2 billion in a decade. Boden also served on the boards of several major German companies; took part in the delegation which evolved the Schumann plan in 1950; was an influential member of the German CBI; and, in 1961, became the president of Germany's International Chamber of Commerce.[234]

After the First World War, individual initiatives to reinstate the German scholarships began quite soon, but nothing happened for a decade and then without any governmental intervention. The devastation of Germany after the Second World War meant that the surviving German scholars had other, more fundamental preoccupations for a good five years, and the memories of industrialized genocide, the Blitz, and the V-weapons probably meant that grass-roots opinion in Britain was even more anti-German than had been the case twenty-five years earlier. L. S. Amery, who had been a member of Churchill's cabinet, must have felt particularly hostile towards the Germans during the last decade of his life. For it was they who had suborned his elder son John during the war, persuading him to speak and broadcast on behalf of the Nazi regime and found

---

[233] Fritz Caspari, 'Erlebnisse eines Botschafters in Portugal: 1974–1979', in Lothar Bossle (ed.), *Pforten zur Freiheit: Festschrift für Alexander Böker zum 85. Geburtstag* (Paderborn: Bonifatius Verlag, 1997), 243–61.

[234] Hans Georg Bröckerhoff, 'Mehr Diplomat als Herrscher: Hans Constantin Boden 70 Jahre alt', *Deutsche Zeitung*, 171 (27–8 July 1963), 2; Kr., 'Hans C. Boden 70 Jahre alt', *FAZ* 171 (27 July 1963), 8.

the abortive Legion of St George, the minuscule British unit of the *Waffen-SS*. John Amery was brought back to England in 1945, tried for high treason, and executed on 19 December.[235] Allen's attitude to reinstatement was demonstrably not helped by the letters he received from German scholars during the immediate post-war years in which they complained about the hardships being endured by their countrymen but failed to say anything whatsoever about the political cause of those hardships (let alone about the Final Solution). In this connection, it is worth quoting an almost unique letter from one of the younger scholars, a devotee of Kant, that was sent to Allen on 18 March 1947:

It is a very sad experience to see that men especially here in this country are not willing to learn from the past. All these terrible things that happened and all these cruelties that were done by us Germans are so quickly forgotten by most of my countrymen. The reason for the disaster—in their mind—lies always somewhere else. It is either the 'cold winter' or the Americans or the French etc. but it is never ourselves. In my idea there is only one alternative for us Germans and that is either to fall back into a kind of resentment and dream of Hitler, Bismarck, Fredric [*sic*] the Great or to realize that this policy of 'Wille zur Macht' was a fallacy which was on the way to turn this people into a nation of wild beasts.

But in order not to repeat the revanchism of 1919 in the context of the Cold War, the British Foreign Office began urging the Rhodes Trustees to renew the scholarships as early as October 1950[236] on the grounds that this would help 'bring to an end the state of war with Germany' and 're-integrate Germany into Western Europe'—a suggestion that was turned down flat on 26 October (RTM 26 Oct. 1950). In late autumn 1951, a number of people organized a visit to Oxford by Adenauer for the 'express purpose of promoting the reinstatement of Rhodes Scholarships for Germans'.[237] These initiatives were followed in August 1952 by an approach from the financier Eric Warburg. And when thirteen German scholars attended the Rhodes Golden Jubilee in Oxford 29 June–2 July 1953, an event that was reported in the German press,[238] a New Zealand scholar asked John Lowe, the Dean of Christ Church, himself a Canadian scholar and Trustee who was chairing the plenary session on 2 July, when the German scholarships would be reinstated. A delighted Mandt, who had been present, sent a report on the event to all other German scholars. In it, he remarked that the German Foreign Office had actively encouraged participation, that Commonwealth and American scholars were positive about reinstatement, and that the resistance was coming from the Trustees (notably Amery) and the new Warden, Williams.[239] On 15 January 1957, Caspari, working from the German Foreign Office, sent Mandt a confidential memo on a conversation he had had with the

---

[235] See 'John Amery for Trial', *The Times*, 31 July 1945, 2; 'Amery Sentenced to Death', *The Times*, 29 November 1945, 2; Ronald Seth, *Jackals of the Reich: The Story of the British Free Corps* (London: New English Library, 1972), 17–32, 157–9.

[236] RTF 1682, Lord Henderson to Elton, 4 Oct. 1950.

[237] John Faulder, 'Alice and Adenauer', *Christ Church Matters*, 2 (Michaelmas 1998), 6.

[238] Alex Natan, 'Ehemalige Rhodes-Stipendiaten feiern Wiedersehen in Oxford', *Neue Zeitung* (Bremen), 18 July 1953.

[239] IfZ, NLB, File New York B/Oxford bis 1994.

British cultural attaché, Professor Potter, on the previous day. Potter confirmed that both
Foreign Offices and the British Ambassador to Germany, Sir Frederick Hoyer Millar, had
been pressing for reinstatement for two years; that Williams was now not against it but
had limited influence over the Trustees; that Amery's family history had indeed been a
major obstacle; that the major opponent was now Lord Elton; and that the financial
reasons being given for non-reinstatement were not the real ones ('maßgebend') (AvK).[240]
Replying to Caspari on 18 January, Mandt said with some fervour that he found this anti-
German attitude incomprehensible in the current political climate (AvK). When, on 9
April 1957, the Foreign Office put out another feeler to Elton via Sir David Ormsby-
Gore (RTF 1682), the Trustees remained equally obdurate even though the offer of funds
was still on the table.[241] They displayed the same obduracy on 5 February 1959 (RTM
3100) after Diana Hopkinson, a close friend of von Trott during the 1930s, had published
a letter in *The Times* advocating reinstatement.[242] Elton advised: 'I do not feel that, susceptibilities or no susceptibilities, in view of its Black Record the German nation has a
claim to be given a third chance.' The Trustees agreed with him and minuted: 'these
Scholarships cannot at present be revived, since the first obligation of the Rhodes Trust
is to the British Commonwealth.'

The pressure continued to build up in 1960: from M. Antonin Besse, the son of the
founder of St Antony's College, who wrote that the necessary funds could be found if
money were the problem; from Mandt in person (now an honorary OBE); and from
the Canadian and Australian ambassadors in Bonn (both Rhodes scholars and friends
of Caspari's). So, on 23 July the Trustees discussed the matter yet again and resolved
'to reach a decision . . . before the end of the present year'. But even after the Prime
Minister, Harold Macmillan, who became Chancellor of Oxford University in autumn
1960, sounded out Vice-Chancellor Norrington and three heads of houses (Balliol, Magdalen, and Worcester), and found them all in favour of reinstatement (RTF 1628), the
Trustees refused to budge. For their meeting of 19 January 1961 Williams prepared a report
(dated 18 Nov. 1960) in which he set out the arguments for and against. But despite an
indirect appeal from the Prime Minister,[243] the Trustees were adamant (RTM 19 Jan.
1961): 'the growing needs of the developing Commonwealth have the prior claim upon
the resources of the Rhodes Trust.' The creation of the second Indian scholarship later
in 1961 made the exclusion of the Germans even more pointed since some believed the
first Indian scholarship had been financed after the Great War with moneys formerly
allocated to the Germans.

In 1963, Edward Heath, Lord Privy Seal with Foreign Office responsibilities since 1960,
renewed the Foreign Office assault in a letter of 11 July to Lord Franks (which was duly
passed on to Williams and the Trustees):

[240] In July 1953, the Foreign Office had prompted Robert Birley (RTF 1682) to write to Williams saying
that they were so 'keen' to reinstate that they 'would very probably be ready to make a grant to the Rhodes
Trustees to cover the cost of, say two Rhodes Scholars from Germany'.
[241] See n. 240. Report to Trustees, 4 May 1957; RTM 4 May 1957.
[242] Diana Hopkinson, 'Beyond Rhodes', *The Times*, 12 Jan. 1959, 9. This again provoked a reaction in
the German press (Alex Natan, 'Feme gegen deutsche Studenten', *Bremer Nachrichten*, 15 Jan. 1959).
[243] RTF 1682, David Stephens (FO) to Williams, 1 Dec. 1960.

I hardly need emphasize that the reinstitution of the scholarships would be a gesture of very great political value in our relations with Europe. The Germans have not raised the matter since 1960, but we have reason to know th[at] they feel very keenly their exclusion from a scheme in which they formerly shared, and which, if they were re-admitted, could play a full and useful part in strengthening the bonds of Atlantic union. (RTF 1682).

Heath's *démarche* was leaked to Peterborough of the *Daily Telegraph* who, to the Trustees' great annoyance, backed reinstatement before they had had the opportunity of discussing Heath's letter. Indeed, Peterborough's piece and Heath's intervention seem to have made them all the more determined not to yield[244]—a decision which produced a strongly worded leader in, and nine out of ten letters to, *The Times* in favour of reinstatement (plus milder leaders in two other British broadsheets and a front-page article in Germany's major weekly broadsheet).[245]

Heath expressed his disappointment at the result and Viscount Amory, a Trustee since 1961, wrote to Williams that up to a month ago his morning mail had been full of the subject, and 'sometimes not very agreeably presented'.[246] Although the matter would not be raised again formally until 1969, the context of the debate changed significantly over the next four and a half years. In early 1964, the Wills family offered to fund three scholarships to bring Germans to Oxford, a gesture that in the view of the President of Magdalen 'undoubtedly [arose] from the correspondence in *The Times* regretting that the Rhodes Scholarships to Germany had not been renewed'.[247] In spring 1965, the Queen paid an official visit to Germany. By April 1965, eleven scholarships were in place enabling Germans to study in Oxford,[248] and in June 1965, Günther Gillessen (b. 1928), an editor of one of Germany's most influential conservative newspapers who had himself studied at St Antony's College in the late 1950s, wrote a fierce article pointing this out and condemning the Trustees' 1963 decision as 'absurd'.[249] More importantly, Britain was moving closer to Europe (even though de Gaulle had vetoed its application to join the Common Market in 1963 and 1967); General Sir Archibald Nye, who had been vice-chief of the Imperial General Staff 1941–6 and a firm opponent of reinstatement, died in 1967; Christopher Sykes's controversial but well-received biography of von Trott (1968) drew forcible attention to a hero of the German Resistance who had also been a Rhodes scholar; the ideas of another German scholar, Schumacher, gained worldwide currency; and in early 1969, Sir George Abell, who had been sympathetic to reinstatement all along, became the Trustees' chairman. Accordingly, Williams placed the question on the Trustees' agenda for 6 February 1969 in a terse note:

[244] RTF 3150, Sir Archibald Nye to Williams, 5 Oct. 1963; RTM 5 Oct. 1963.
[245] Peterborough, 'Admitting Germans', *Daily Telegraph*, 30 Sept. 1963, 14; 'Don't be Mean', *The Times*, 5 Oct. 1963, 9; the letters appeared there between 8 and 16 Oct. See also 'Rhodes's Big Idea', *Observer*, 6 Oct. 1963, 10; 'Priorities', *Sunday Telegraph*, 6 Oct. 1963, 14; [Marion Gräfin] D[önho]ff, 'Nicht für Deutsche', *Die Zeit*, 25 Oct. 1963, 1. Dr Dönhoff, one of Germany's leading journalists, had been a friend of Bernstorff's.
[246] RTF 1682, Amory to Williams, 19 June 1964; RTF 3189, Amory to Williams, 26 June 1964.
[247] IfZ, NLB, Ordner New York B/Oxford bis 1994, T. S. R. Boase to Böker, 5 Feb. 1964.
[248] Ibid., Mandt to Böker, 20 Apr. 1965.
[249] Günther Gillessen, 'Ersatz für die Cecil-Rhodes-Stipendien', *FAZ* 15 June 1965, 9.

Lord Amory would like the Trustees to begin discussing the question of creating Rhodes Scholarships for Germans. Counsels' opinion in 1963 was that this would be permissible from the Public
Purposes Fund. It may not be done from the Scholarship Fund.

So, at last, the Trustees resolved 'to create two annual Scholarships for men chosen from
the Universities of the Federal German Republic, the first elections to be held in 1969'
(RTM 6 Mar. 1969). One political commentator felt that the Trustees had taken this decision to procure West German support for Britain's next application to join the Common
Market.[250] Although there is no hard evidence for this, de Gaulle's position was becoming
increasingly precarious at the time and his resignation as President in the very next month
certainly opened the way for Britain's eventual entry into Europe. The surviving Rhodes
scholars were naturally delighted and Alfred Toepfer immediately reciprocated by rein-
stating the Hanseatic scholarships, this time exclusively for Oxford students.[251]

The politicking surrounding the creation of the 1929 selection committee was almost
totally absent in 1969, and just to make the point completely clear, it was decided to
interview candidates in Mandt's office in the Albingia Insurance Company in Hamburg
(where, incidentally, the interviews still take place) rather than Bonn or Berlin. The committee, consisting of Mandt (chairman),[252] Koelle (secretary), Caspari (the one scholar
to have served on a pre-war committee (1938–9) and who would be replaced by his friend
Böker in 1974), Merz, Gillessen, Professor Willibald Jentschke (a distinguished physicist
at Hamburg University) and Dr (now Professor) Hartmut Pogge von Strandmann, then
a junior research fellow at Balliol who was known to Mandt. Fifteen people applied; eight
were shortlisted; and Thomas Böcking and Lippold von Klencke, who knew of the scholarships because of their respective stepfather (Schlepegrell) and uncle (von Ruperti),
were elected. Williams attended the interview and found the candidates impressive
despite the smallness of the field: 'All eight men were electable,' he wrote, 'and certainly
four of them would have been admirable. It was a very useful visit, free from tension and
most enthusiastic.'

1970–1999

Because of Germany's chequered history, no 'Rhodes legend' had grown up in Germany
as it had elsewhere, and for the first few years, the number of applications was low: 1970–1—
6; 1971–2—21; 1972–3—15; 1973–4—16; 1974–5—15; 1975–6—11; 1976–7—13 (including 5
from women for the first time thanks to the Equal Opportunities Act,[253] one of whom,
Erika Kress (Wolfson 1977), was elected); and 1977–8—17. Numbers began gradually to
rise after Böcking took over from Koelle (now aged 67) on 1 July 1979 and the scholarships
became more widely publicized with the help of the DAAD. Consequently, by the 1990s,
the numbers of applications are as follows: 1991–2—48; 1993–4—57; 1994–5—61; 1995–6—

---

[250] Karl E. Meyer, 'Rhodes Trustees Vote on Germans', *International Herald Tribune*, 1–2 Mar. 1969.
[251] RTF 1682, Mandt to Williams, 21 Mar. 1969.
[252] Mandt retired on his 85th birthday (13 Apr. 1973), since when, as elsewhere, the chairman has been
a non-Rhodes scholar.
[253] Cf. 'Rhodes-Stipendien jetzt auch für Frauen', *FAZ* 25 June 1976, 4.

49; 1996–7—64; 1997–8—45 (AB). Furthermore, during that same decade, the lowest number of enquiries in any given year was 234 (compared with *c.*86 in 1976/7 and 166 in 1979/80),[254] and the highest 419, with the average being 305 per annum. In 1990, the number of scholarships was raised to three per annum and, as a result of a suggestion by the scholars already at Oxford which was positively received by the Warden,[255] one of these was earmarked for a candidate from the (then vanishing) GDR. The proposal was received 'with enthusiasm' by the German selection committee[256] and agreed to by the Trustees in March. Consequently, a separate ad hoc meeting was held in Halle in December—the first extension eastwards of any Western scholarship programme after the collapse of the Soviet empire. In 1993, the number was raised to four per annum—though for various reasons, the full number has not always been taken up. In 1991–2, more women than men were selected for the first (but not the last) time.

By the time of the second reinstatement, virtually all the problems that had bedevilled the first two periods had vanished. By 1970, Oxford's university-based research culture had become as important as if not more important than the more traditional collegiate culture of earlier days. It was, I suspect, no accident that this shift took place during precisely that period when Britain was losing an empire, looking more towards Europe, and having to redefine both its own role in the world and that of the two universities which had, since the mid-nineteenth century at least, provided its imperial elite. The same shift explains both why Oxford became more attractive for German students and why relatively few of the third generation of Rhodes scholars have had major problems on the academic front. Of the 72 German scholars who have matriculated between 1970 and 1999, 11 have studied at the newer graduate colleges; 2 have read for the M.Sc.; 1 for the M.Jur.; 16 for the B.Phil. or (since 1979) the M.Phil.; 5 for the B.Litt. or (since 1979) the M.Litt.; 36 for the D.Phil.; and in 1999 5 were probationer research students. Between 1990 and 1999 only 6 read for a BA and only 6 left Oxford with no qualification at all. This has meant that, on graduation, most German scholars could return to Germany with a Doctorate or a degree that is regarded as the equivalent of a German *Magister* and continue their studies there with relative ease. Others, given the increasing unification of Europe and the emergence of English as the dominant world language, have been able to work either inside or outside Academe in an English-speaking country. It is within this context that at least five post-1970 German scholars have entered government service, especially the diplomatic service, and risen to important positions there. At least eight more work outside Germany or in posts with an international orientation. And another five, beginning with Ute Wartenberg (Corpus Christi 1987), have obtained junior research fellowships in Oxford itself. Furthermore, in contrast to the first two periods, the German scholars have studied a much broader range of subjects (including mathematics, natural sciences, biological sciences, and even medicine), with Alexander Straub (St John's 1996) and Rouzbeh Pirouz (Canada and Corpus Christi 1996) winning £1 million of backing in the 1999 3 i Technology Catapult Competition for the Internet company Mundus.com

---

[254] IfZ, NLB, Ordner New York B/Oxford bis 1994. [255] AB, Kenny to Böcking, 24 Jan. 1990.
[256] AB, Prof. C. von Campenhausen (chairman) to Kenny, 19 Feb. 1990.

which they had set up in 1997. Correspondence with post-1970 German Scholars confirms this picture. A significant number have told me that they specifically wanted to come to Oxford either to study with world-class scholars or scientists; or to escape the post-1968 turmoil in German universities (which impeded serious study); or to work in a more liberal academic atmosphere. Nowadays, Stadler, Brinkmann, von Blumenthal, and Schumacher would find Oxford's atmosphere more congenial and less like a glorified boarding school.

The same correspondence reveals how much the post-1970 generation has appreciated the greater closeness between Oxford's teachers and students than is the norm in German universities; the informal contact that is possible with world-class academics even when they are not one's supervisor; the speed with which it is possible to complete a post-graduate degree in Oxford; and the 'intellectual discipline', 'ability to formulate', 'level-headedness', 'moral independence', 'openness', and 'humaneness' which they have learnt there. It also seems that the pressure to be 'a good college man' has all but disappeared and that college life is nowadays most appreciated for the opportunities it affords for meeting people from all over the world—especially in Oxford's increasingly multicultural MCRs.

On the other hand, the experiences of the third generation have not been entirely positive. More than a few have commented on the hermetic, 'monastic', 'museumlike' unreality of Oxford life; its lack of transparency; its numerous petty restrictions; the unjustified intellectual arrogance displayed by some senior and junior members of a body that considers itself an elite; the poor quality of some of its graduate accommodation and cramped laboratory facilities; its bleak Sunday afternoons; and some occasional (but residual) anti-German feeling. But such comments are made with greater force by scholars who were here before the mid-1980s, and overall, it would seem that the relationship which Thomas Weber characterized as a 'stormy romance' has become considerably less stormy—and also less romantic—over the past twenty-nine years. Because of the fragmented history of the German scholarships, they do not have the same cachet as they do in, say, Australia or the USA, and they are certainly not an automatic passport to power and prestige in the German worlds of politics and business. Moreover, because the relationship between modern German students and their universities tends to be more functionally academic than is the case in a collegiate university in the English-speaking world, the post-1970 German scholars seem to be less fixated on Oxford's 'dreaming spires' (and all that that metaphor stands for) than more than a few of their forebears. But this does not prevent them from appreciating in a more pragmatic sense that they have been able to obtain an academic training in Oxford which will take them into, and even help them rise, eventually, to the top of their chosen professions—albeit within a world order that is very different from the one envisaged by Rhodes. Equally, because that generation has known less turmoil at home and fewer personal conflicts at Oxford because of that turmoil, it can look back on Oxford and the Rhodes Trust with a quieter, less complex (but none the less genuine) attachment than its predecessors. It is surely no bad thing that none of the post-1970 scholars has had to say what one of the inter-war scholars said to me: 'Oxford and the Rhodes Trust saved my life.'

7

Zimbabwean Rhodes Scholarships

DAVID MORGAN

The will provided three scholarships per year for Rhodesia. In the context of a scheme to bring together each year, at a central place of learning, fifty-seven young potential leaders from the British Empire, the USA, and Germany, in the hope that their shared relationships might secure world peace, the benefaction to Rhodesia was remarkable. After all the total allocation to the British Empire was only twenty. More remarkable still was the provision that if the resources to fund the scholarship proved inadequate and scholarships had to be sacrificed the last to go should be the Rhodesian ones. What was this country, Rhodesia, that in 1902 it should be so favoured?

Rhodes, from early on in his diamond mining career in Kimberley, had nurtured the view that Africa would be best served under British influence. It was his dream to extend that influence from the Cape, where he became Prime Minister in 1890 at age 37, northwards via Central Africa. To that end he obtained from King Lobengula, who claimed sovereignty over much of present-day Zimbabwe, a concession in 1888 to dig for minerals in his kingdom. This same area fell within Britain's proclaimed exclusive sphere of influence and in 1889 Rhodes obtained from Queen Victoria a royal charter to establish the British South Africa Company entitling it to operate, subject to such grants and concessions as it might obtain, anywhere in the region of South Africa lying immediately to the north of British Bechuanaland, to the north and west of the Transvaal, and to the west of the Portuguese dominions (present-day Mozambique). By 1891 the British government had accepted that the territories comprising modern Zimbabwe and Zambia fell under the BSA Company's charter and by 1894 the administration of both territories was placed under the control of the Company by the British government with certain reserved powers. Within a year the former territory had adopted the name Southern Rhodesia and the latter territory the name Northern Rhodesia. In 1923 Southern Rhodesia passed from chartered company rule to settler self-government as a British colony whilst Northern Rhodesia passed from company control to the status of a British protectorate. The two countries came together briefly as part of the Central African Federation between 1953 and 1963 whereafter Northern Rhodesia became independent as Zambia in 1964 and Southern Rhodesia followed suit as Zimbabwe in 1980. The 'Rhodesia' to which Rhodes gave his scholarships was therefore Southern Rhodesia and Northern Rhodesia and the scholarships were awarded initially by the Trustees in England but by 1923 by a single selection committee drawn from both countries (subject to approval by the Trustees), until 1973, when political developments in Southern Rhodesia resulted in the scholarships being divided between the two countries with separate selection committees. Initially one scholarship went to each country with the third switching between them in alternate years until the 1980s, when the floating scholarship was left with Zimbabwe. In this connection the names Southern and Northern Rhodesia will be used for those countries until their independence and the word 'Rhodesia' for the two together whereafter they will be referred to under their present names.

At the time of Rhodes's arrival in Southern Rhodesia in 1890 the indigenous population was estimated to number something under 500,000 people in a land of 150,500 square miles, or a little over 3 people per square mile. The people practised a subsistence agriculture, living in scattered villages across the country. There was no formal schooling and no written language. The chartered company moved quickly to open up the country and within fourteen years had constructed a basic railway system for it linking Kimberley in the Cape to the newly established towns of Bulawayo in the southwest and Harare (Salisbury) in the north-east of the country with extension lines to Beira on the Mozambique coast and to the Victoria Falls on the north-western border with Northern Rhodesia. Telegraph lines had preceded the railways and Harare was linked to the Cape by 1894. Despite these developments the settler population, attracted by gold and farmland, grew slowly. By 1902 the settler population was only some 10,000 people. In Northern Rhodesia the settler population was much smaller, only reaching 1,500 in 1910.

The grant of three Rhodes scholarships per annum from 1903 was a feast to which Southern Rhodesia's then academic resources could hardly do justice. Missionary societies assumed responsibility for the education of the indigenous population from the outset of the settler arrival and have played an important role in the educational system ever since, and to that end were given extensive land grants by the chartered company. As the economy and the educational system developed, the government provided financial assistance to the mission schools, controlled the syllabus, and made periodic inspections; the missions supervised and managed the schools and the parents contributed the buildings and books. It was a system geared largely to religious, agricultural, and industrial training and instruction. Academic standards were elementary. It was not until 1944 and the growing influx of Africans into the towns, where mission schools did not by and large operate, that government began to assume a responsibility for African education, which remained separated from its non-African counterparts until 1980 (save for a few private schools which admitted all races). Only after the Second World War were the first secondary schools for Africans established by the government and the missions (save for one mission secondary school established in 1939) and not until many years later did such schools attain upper sixth level (thirteen years of schooling) and thereby provide a generally recognized springboard to university.

The chartered company until 1923 and thereafter the government provided for the educational needs of the settler population in Southern Rhodesia at primary and secondary school level, aided by religious bodies and private organizations. The European population in Southern Rhodesia was only 27,000 in 1914 and 69,000 in 1941, growing to 138,000 in 1951 and 274,000 in 1974 (its largest ever figure). The number of schools required to serve their needs, particularly in the earlier years, was very few and academic standards in these earlier pioneering years were not high. Greek and Latin qualifications were required for Oxford until 1919 and only one school, St George's (a Catholic private school), taught Greek. Not surprisingly therefore finding home-grown candidates of a suitable quality in the early years of the scholarships proved difficult. This problem was even more acute in respect of potential candidates from Northern Rhodesia, where there were no senior schools until 1927 and where the settler population was only 3,000 in 1919. In consequence in the first ten years of the scholarships the selectors had to pass over the opportunity to make eleven awards, selected six scholars who, being sons of senior BSA Company officials, had grown up and been educated in Britain, chose another three who had been educated at South African schools, leaving ten out of a possible thirty as 'home growns', all from St George's, three of whom did not take up or complete their scholarships.[1] Such were the early standards that Rhodesia had to wait until 1924 to produce its first scholar to take a first and, with one exception, until 1953 for its first scholar to read for a doctorate. Confronted with these difficulties the Rhodes Trust's Organizing Secretary suggested that local candidates from Rhodesia would profit by attending university in South Africa before applying for scholarships and going on to Oxford. This pattern began to develop from 1913 and was well established by 1923. To assist parents in keeping children at primary and secondary schools and to enable them to attend university, scholarships were provided from a £200,000 bequest under the will of Sir Alfred Beit, Rhodes's close mining associate on the Kimberley diamond and Transvaal gold fields, a director of the BSA Company and an original Trustee of the Rhodes Trust. So imbued was he with Rhodes's dream of extending the British way of life northwards in Africa that on his death in 1906 Beit left a further £1,200,000 to a trust, the Beit Trust, for the development of communications in Rhodesia and thereafter for charitable, educational, and other public purposes. This sum financed new railways, large bridges, rolling stock, numerous school buildings, hospitals, and contributed greatly to the development of the country.

The selection procedure for Rhodes scholars in Rhodesia was initially haphazard. Credentials were forwarded by the Southern Rhodesian Director of Education to the Trustees with his recommendations but not always with the benefit of an interview. On this basis it was possible for the Trustees in 1916 to award a scholarship to an impostor whose award was based on qualifications he did not possess (RTM 11 Dec. 1916). Fortunately this came to light before he went into residence and his scholarship was withdrawn. The incident led by 1920 to the appointment of a local selection committee which by 1923 had almost sole responsibility for the choice of Rhodesian scholars. It was a development which brought to an end protracted exchanges with the Trustees over eligibility and in

[1] See R. J. Challiss, *Vicarious Rhodesians: Problems Affecting the Selection of Rhodesian Rhodes Scholars, 1904–1923* (Salisbury: Central Africa Historical Association, 1977). Also RTM 20 Feb. 1903, 30 Sept. 1904, 5 Dec. 1905, 3 July 1911, 7 Oct. 1912.

particular a residential basis in Rhodesia for applicants (RTM 10 May 1920, 4 Oct. 1920, 8 Nov. 1920).

Notwithstanding the limited field of possible candidates for Rhodesian scholarships Rhodesia provided two of the twelve Rhodes scholars to reach Oxford in 1903, the other ten coming from Germany and South Africa. This unusual situation arose because the German scholars were the choice of the Kaiser, the South Africa scholars were the choice of four schools and the nomination from Natal of its Director of Education, and the Rhodesian scholars were likewise the nomination of its Director of Education. Selection committees for the remaining forty-five scholarships were not in place until 1904.

For determination to surmount limited academic opportunities Southern Rhodesia's Kingsley Fairbridge was a fine example. In 1896, aged 11 years, he left school in South Africa to help his father in his land survey business in the eastern districts of Southern Rhodesia. This often entailed his moving by ox-wagon as a young lad to remote parts of the country with a couple of retainers to set up camp for his father and with only the land to live off. He fell in love with the vast open spaces and the thought came to him that if he could bring underprivileged children from overcrowded England and give them an opportunity to develop in the healthy outdoor climate of Southern Rhodesia he would benefit them and the country of his adoption. He determined to get to England to advance the idea. He worked, with some tutoring in Mutare (Umtali), for his South African matriculation examination and then, with a promise from the Rhodes Trustees of a scholarship if he could pass the Oxford entrance examination, he went to England and at the fourth attempt at the examinations passed and at 23 years of age entered Exeter College in 1908 (RTM 3 Feb. 1908). He opted for a diploma in forestry, thereby by passing the need for Greek and Latin. He won a boxing blue and in 1909 founded the 'Child Protection Society'. However, the chartered company did not consider Southern Rhodesia's then state of development a suitable environment for his experiment. In 1912 therefore he established the first Fairbridge Farm School in Western Australia. Further schools followed later in Queensland, New Zealand, and Canada and eventually in 1946 in Southern Rhodesia. Dogged by malaria, Fairbridge died at the age of 39. His name survived in the Farm Schools called after him. He was the first Rhodes scholar worldwide to appear in the *Dictionary of National Biography* and his painting is one of the very few to hang in the main hall of Rhodes House. Sir Carleton Allen, the Warden of Rhodes House, in reviewing Rhodes scholarships in 1944 described Fairbridge as 'perhaps the most remarkable and certainly the most original of all Rhodes Scholars'.

If finding suitable candidates posed a problem in the selection of Rhodesian scholars in the early years of the awards, the First World War robbed the country of many of those who were selected. Some 5,500 of its residents, out of a European population of 27,000 (one person in five), volunteered to fight for Britain and the Empire, and of those nine of the country's first thirty scholars were killed in action or died as a result. Four of those scholars were awarded the Military Cross, one of them with bar. All six of the 1918 and 1919 Rhodes scholars had served in the war. The call to arms for Britain was similarly answered in 1939 by Rhodesians of all races. Fortunately in this war only three scholars lost their lives, one of them being the first Rhodes scholar to be killed in the Second

World War. To spread the risk the Southern Rhodesian Minister of Defence in the Second World War, Sir Robert Tredgold, who was himself a Rhodesian Rhodes scholar, had made it clear that Southern Rhodesia's limited manpower should not be concentrated in a national force which might be destroyed in a single engagement. It was in the air and through the eleven air training schools for Empire pilots established in the country that Southern Rhodesia made its special contribution to Britain in the Second World War. One of the country's highest decorated airmen to emerge at war's end as a wing commander was scholar Hardwicke Holderness with a DSO, DFC, and AFC. (In this connection only 9 DSOs, 17 DFCs, and 69 MCs were awarded to Rhodes scholars in both world wars).

In so far as the award of a double first in law to 1924 scholar Charles Cummings (later to be knighted) was a landmark for Rhodesian scholars it also highlighted the contributions in the field of law which early Rhodesian scholars would make to the country. Between 1936 and 1998 there was, with the exception of the years 1981–90, at least one Rhodes scholar judge and sometimes as many as three or four on the small Southern Rhodesian/Zimbabwean High Court bench: judges C. T. Blakeway 1938–44, W. E. Thomas 1944, V. A. Lewis 1936–50, R. C. Tredgold 1943–55, T. H. W. Beadle 1950–77, C. L. Beck 1970–81, J. M. Greenfield 1968–74, W. H. G. Newham 1974–80, and D. A. B. Robinson 1991–8. Of these judges Lewis, Tredgold, and Beadle became chief justices of Rhodesia and were knighted and Sir Robert Tredgold (whose older brother was also a Rhodes scholar, who was killed in the First World War) served later as Chief Justice of the short-lived Federation of Rhodesia and Nyasaland 1955–9. Judge Beck was the senior puisne judge and a judge of appeal at his retirement in 1981, later to serve as Chief Justice of the Transkei. He and Judge Lewis were not Southern Rhodesian but South African Rhodes scholars who made their homes in Rhodesia. Indeed Southern Rhodesia was to benefit from a number of scholars from other countries in the years between 1928 and 1981, one of the most distinguished of whom was Baron Robins of Rhodesia and Chelsea who was in the first wave of American Rhodes scholars to reach Oxford in 1904, becoming the resident director of Rhodes's chartered company in Southern Rhodesia in 1928 and its president in 1957. He was knighted in 1954 and created a baron in 1958, one of only two Southern Rhodesians ever to have been raised to the peerage.

Chief justices Tredgold and Beadle were men destined to play significant roles in the history of Rhodesia. Tredgold came from an interesting lineage. Born in Bulawayo in 1899, he was the son of Sir Clarkson Tredgold, a confidant of Rhodes and Attorney General of Southern Rhodesia under chartered company rule and later a judge. His mother was a granddaughter of Robert Moffat, the celebrated missionary in Central Africa, and a niece of the explorer David Livingstone. His uncle was the second Prime Minister of Southern Rhodesia. He was appointed as an acting judge in Northern Rhodesia at age 32, entered politics in 1934, and in 1937, at age 37, became the first man born in Rhodesia to become a cabinet minister. He variously held the portfolios of Justice, Defence, Native Affairs, and Air, made more than one trip to Britain in the war years to confer with the war cabinet, and handled the merging of the Southern Rhodesian forces into the Southern Command under General Smuts. In 1943 he became the first

Rhodesian-born Rhodes scholar to become a judge in the country and eventually Chief Justice of Southern Rhodesia and of the Federation and President of the Rhodesia and Nyasaland Court of Appeal. He was made a Privy Counsellor and on occasion acted as Governor General of the Federation. In 1960 with restlessness brewing over the limited constitutional rights of the bulk of the population and the consequent introduction of Law and Order Maintenance legislation, which he considered an unwarranted invasion by the executive in the sphere of the courts and an outrage to every basic human right, he resigned. He opposed the country's 1961 constitution as unacceptable in its franchise arrangements. A right-wing government came into power, and a unilateral declaration of independence followed in 1965, followed in turn by a conflict which was only resolved in 1980 with a new government elected under a universal franchise. Like Rhodes he loved the Matopos, the majestic granite hills in which Rhodes and Jameson are buried. He was always at pains to point out that Rhodes was not buried at 'World's View', as many thought, indeed the views from his burial site are not ever the best in the Matopos, but at what Rhodes called 'The View of the World', by which he meant that sitting there he could see all over the world in his thoughts.

Unlike Sir Robert Tredgold, who had gone straight from school to Oxford after service at the tail end of the First World War, Sir Hugh Beadle followed the accepted post-First World War practice of doing an initial degree or degrees at a South African university. His first acquaintance with Oxford was as captain of the combined South African universities boxing team against an Oxford and Cambridge boxing team touring South Africa in 1926. The following year he was at Oxford and boxing for his new university. He qualified as a pilot at Oxford but when the Second World War broke out he served at the outset as a major in the army. When the war was over he became Minister of Justice and Internal Affairs and then of Education and Health in Southern Rhodesia before being appointed to the bench in 1950, where he served for a record twenty-six years, sixteen as Chief Justice. He too was knighted and made a Privy Counsellor. It fell to his lot in 1968 to decide on the legal status of the government and the new constitution it had introduced following the Unilateral Declaration of Independence in 1965. Two years and nine months had passed since the Declaration. He and his Court held that the *de facto* government was firmly in control of the country and that it had attained *de jure* status. In passing judgement the judges held that they had either to preside as judges under the new constitution in the interests of protecting the fabric of society or to resign and create a chaotic situation. They opted to preside under the new constitution.

Apart from the judiciary there were many other Rhodes scholar lawyers making a contribution to the country as advocates and attorneys and on the Government side of the law Sir Victor Robinson became the country's Federal Attorney General 1954–9 and was chairman of the Constitutional Council of Southern Rhodesia in 1962. Southern Rhodesia's legal gain from imported scholars was not a one-way trade: 1920 scholar Vair Turnbull became Solicitor General of the Sudan and 1925 scholar Sir Charles Cummings became Chief Justice of the Sudan and, on his retirement, general manager of the chartered company in Rhodesia. The 1973 scholar Michael

Tselentis has served as chairman of the Johannesburg Bar Council and as an acting judge in the Transvaal.

Rhodes scholar lawyers in Zimbabwe have produced two three-generation Rhodes scholarship families. Chief Justice Vernon Lewis was succeeded as a Rhodes scholar by his son C. P. J. Lewis, the senior partner in a large attorney's practice in Harare and grand-nephew of Jameson, and the Chief Justice's great-grandson, Simon Lewis, was a Zimbabwe Rhodes scholar for 1998. Sir Victor Robinson was followed as a Rhodesian Rhodes scholar by his son D. A. B. Robinson, a judge of the Zimbabwe High Court, and he in turn by his son, J. V. Robinson, who subsequently emigrated to the United States of America where he is a practising lawyer.

Legal and political careers have been somewhat intertwined in Southern Rhodesia. Apart from the involvement of Sir Robert Tredgold and Sir Hugh Beadle, Chief Justice Vernon Lewis was, before going on to the bench, Minister of Justice in Southern Rhodesia in 1936 and Judge Greenfield before taking judicial appointment spent the years 1950–4 as Southern Rhodesian Minister of Justice and the years 1954 to 1963 as Federal Minister of Home Affairs and of Law and Education, becoming leader of the House in 1957. B. V. Ewing, who had taken a first in mining engineering at Witwatersrand University followed by a first in jurisprudence at Oxford, became Southern Rhodesia's youngest cabinet minister in 1962 at the age of 34 before following a highly successful business career in South Africa.

Since 1963 no Rhodes scholar has been a member of Parliament. Those opting for the civil service as a career have also declined in the last forty years. Early scholars to achieve distinction in this area were 1912 scholars Sir Stanley Howard, who became Inspector General of Forests in India, and L. Powys Jones, who became Chief Native Commissioner of Southern Rhodesia, a department of government which was almost a state within a state. 1932 scholar Sir Evelyn Hone became the Governor of Zambia and 1946 scholar I. McDonald became the director of the Tobacco Research Board.

Academic life and research has had increasing appeal for Southern Rhodesian/Zimbabwean scholars over the past forty-five years although this has increasingly led to their departure from the country. Thus at the time of writing 1953 scholar M. A. Denborough is a highly honoured professor of medicine at the Australian National University; 1957 scholar H. C. Hummel was a professor of history at Rhodes University in South Africa; 1958 scholar F. K. J. Pichanick is a professor of physics at the University of Massachusetts; 1959 scholar R. C. Barrett is a nuclear physicist in the United Kingdom; 1961 scholar A. G. Bishop is a professor of English at McMaster University, Canada; 1961 scholar B. R. Tulloch is a professor of medicine at the University of Texas; 1963 scholar J. M. Eekelaar, with a first in the BCL, is a fellow of Pembroke; and his co-1963 scholar J. H. McDowell, with a first in Literae Humaniores, a professor of philosophy and emeritus fellow of University College, Oxford; 1964 scholar D. M. Schreuder is a professor and Vice-Chancellor of the University of West Sydney; 1965 scholar P. D. V. Bourdillon is a professor of medicine at the University of Indiana; 1966 scholar B. J. Gersh is a professor of medicine at Mayo Clinic; 1968 scholar L. H. Johnston is the head of laboratory genetics at the National Institute of Medical Research in London;

1972 scholar R. B. Tait is a Professor of Mechanical Engineering in Cape Town; 1974 scholar P. F. Woodall is a senior lecturer in Australia; 1975 scholar L. W. Wright is Director and professor at the Institute for the Study of English in Africa in Grahamstown; 1991 scholar A. G. O. Mutambara is a professor at Florida State University; 1991 scholar S. W. Utete has a research fellowship at St Hilda's; 1992 scholar M. A. H. Kachingwe has a junior fellowship at Nuffield; 1992 scholar C. Ruwende has a junior fellowship at St Cross. These scholars certainly constitute a major brain drain from Zimbabwe. Only 1960 scholar A. M. Hawkins, the professor and head of business studies at the University of Zimbabwe, and 1985 scholar P. M. Nherere, lecturer in law at the University of Zimbabwe, remain as academics in Zimbabwe though there has been steady support for medicine and engineering as a career over the years not only for research but also for general practice. The fastest growing of the career choices have, however, been those leading on to careers in business. The lure of a larger business climate than Zimbabwe has to offer has meant a haemorrhage of talent from the country.

The level of degrees taken over the years has also been changing. With the exception of the BCL the degrees taken until the mid-1950s were largely undergraduate degrees. Since then advanced degrees have increasingly found favour (twenty-nine since 1972 out of forty-nine scholars). The quality of the classes for undergraduate and BCL degrees has also improved steadily: between 1960 and 1992 there were seven firsts (three in one year (1973) and two in another (1963)), twenty-one seconds, and seven others.

With the improved access to education for all races in Zimbabwe black Zimbabwe scholars have, since 1989, formed the majority of those selected. Early amongst them was a blind scholar, P. M. Nherere, who after taking an LL M. at Cambridge obtained a second for his BCL and is lecturing in law at the University of Zimbabwe. J. M. Manyika, who was awarded a D.Phil. in engineering science in 1993, won a basketball blue, was given a junior research fellowship at Balliol, was a junior research scientist at NASA, and was an exchange fellow at Massachusetts Institute of Technology. He is now a management consultant in California.

The opening of the scholarships to women for election in 1977 has resulted in awards to them after 1989 of some 30 per cent of the available scholarships. The first woman scholar from Southern Rhodesia, D. J. Saunder, elected in 1977, did a Bachelor of Fine Arts degree at Oxford, held an exhibition of her art at Oxford, won a blue for hockey, was awarded a Knox fellowship to Harvard, has held exhibitions of her sculpture and paintings in Washington and New York, and has had public sculptures erected in Washington, Rockville, and Virginia. The 1989 woman scholar H. S. Fearnhead in her final year of medicine won the Peter Tizzard Prize for paediatrics, the British Paediatrics Association student prize, the John Pearce Memorial Prize for surgery, and the Radcliffe Prize for her performance in her final examinations and throughout her clinical training at Oxford.

On the sporting front Southern Rhodesia/Zimbabwe scholars have won some 50 blues (excluding repeat awards) in 16 sports, the major sports being rugby (8), water polo (8), cricket (7), athletics (6), hockey (5), boxing (4), swimming (4), and squash (3). Between 1965 and 1973 there were 6 cricket blues and, remarkably, 5 Oxford cricket captains, namely G. N. S. Ridley (1967), F. S. Goldstein (1968), M. St J. W. Burton (1970), B. May (1971), P. C. H. Jones (1972). D. B. Pithey who won a cricket blue in 1959 also played cricket for South Africa. In the same period between 1965 and 1971 there were 3 hockey blues and an Oxford hockey captain, P. R. B. Wilson (1969), who also played cricket for Oxford, a squash captain, R. M. Zachs (1970), a sailing blue and vice commodore, H. Ashton (1973), 3 water polo blues, and pentathlon, swimming, athletics, rugby, and skiing blues. It was certainly a golden sporting era for the country's scholars. There was a further squash captain, G. C. G. Light (1984), and much earlier there was a boxing captain. S. A. Richardson (1928). One scholar, C. W. Adams (1969–71), earned triple blues in pentathlon, water polo, and skiing; a number won double blues, B. C. D. Mundy for water polo and swimming (1949), D. B. Pithey (1960–2) and B. May (1970–2) both for cricket and hockey, C. W. Sherwell (1969–71), J. G. Rex-Walker (1976–8), and M. J. Addison (1981–3) for swimming and water polo, and R. B. Tait (1973–4) for athletics and rugby. L. P. Maclachlan who won a blue for rugby in 1953 also played rugby for Rhodesia, Scotland, and the Barbarians, and D. A. B. Robinson who won a blue for rugby in 1952–4 went on to play rugby for Rhodesia. Only one of the women scholars has won a blue, D. J. Saunder for hockey, and with basketball a favourite with black Zimbabweans three basketball blues have been won since 1989. On the administrative side of sport 1930 scholar N. Jacobson subsequently served as president of the Rhodesian Bowls Association, 1952 scholar D. A. B. Robinson served as the convenor of the Zimbabwean National Rugby Selectors for some years, and 1958 scholar D. L. L. Morgan served as president of the Zimbabwe Rugby Union over the years 1980–3 and 1986–9 and on the Zimbabwe Sports Council and its successor the Zimbabwe Sports and Recreation Commission.

Whilst the appointment of a local selection committee for Rhodesia in 1920 and the grant of almost sole responsibility to it for Rhodesian selections in 1923 brought to an end a protracted correspondence with the Trustees over the need for candidates to have well-based residential qualifications in Rhodesia, refinements to the conditions of eligibility, selection processes, and the composition of the committee continued to be made over the years. The committee, comprising eight, now seven, members on five-year tenures, of whom three were normally former scholars, was chaired until 1946 by the Governor of Southern Rhodesia and had as its secretary until 1959 the Southern Rhodesian Director of Education, and it included, until the split with Northern Rhodesia in 1973, a representative from that country. With the eligibility of women as scholars in 1977 the previously all-male panel has since 1978 included women selectors. Appearance for interview before the Rhodesian selection panel became a sine qua non for consideration although on a few occasions in the earlier years a subcommittee to interview applicants in England was permitted. The 1959 scholar D. B. Pithey had to miss the first match of a Springbok cricket tour for which he was selected in order to meet the interview requirement.

One of the more contentious conditions of eligibility has been whether or not awards could be made straight from school. Awards from school were standard until 1912, at which stage applicants were required to have passed the first-year intermediate examination at a South African university. After the First World War this requirement was changed to the completion of two years at a South African university and most applicants, having progressed that far, completed their degrees before going up to Oxford. In 1934, however, the selectors were empowered to choose one schoolboy per year, if suitable, with a Higher School Certificate qualification, a ruling which was rescinded in 1945. In 1961 the schoolboy concession was once again allowed provided that the applicant had an acceptance from an Oxford college, only to be revoked in 1988. Very few such awards were made.

Another of the eligibility conditions which has created problems is that of residence. Until 1946 an applicant for a Rhodesian scholarship could satisfy the residence qualification with residence in South Africa; for many years he could satisfy the residence qualification through his parents; the period of residence has also varied. The period is at present five years' residence in Zimbabwe in the ten years prior to application, a qualification which can be met by schooling in Zimbabwe for five years even if the applicant's home is elsewhere.

The requirement of two years at a South African university was not immediately extended to the University of Rhodesia and Nyasaland. Nor was it, until comparatively recently, that a degree from a university outside Southern Africa met the conditions of eligibility. Perhaps it is thought that a student who had spent three years outside Africa at university followed by a further two or three at Oxford might not return home. At various times it has been suggested that an obligation to return home should be made a condition but it has always been recognized as impractical. Rhodesia/Zimbabwe has lost many of its bright young scholars but it has also benefited greatly in earlier years from scholars from other countries. The country would dearly like the tide to turn.

Rhodesia struggled in its early years, with its small eligible population base, to produce consistently high-quality scholars. But the widening of that base after the Second World War, and particularly after 1980, has resulted in scholars able to hold their own with the best. As Sir Anthony Kenny commented in the early 1990s, after a particularly good run of Zimbabwe scholars, 'Zimbabwe Scholars coming up to Oxford rank in the top 20% of all current Rhodes Scholars.'

8

The Smaller Constituencies

ANTHONY KENNY

New Zealand

New Zealand was one of Parkin's ports of call on his world tour to set up the scholarships. By the time he got there, he already had experience of the debates in the United States, Canada, and Australia between those who wanted Rhodes scholars to be chosen straight from school and those who wanted them to have a university degree before election. In Canada and the States, he told a conference in September 1903, it had been decided that a period at university was essential; but New Zealand was the most English of all the colonies, and a New Zealander would fit easily into Oxford life. If you limited the scholarship to those who had attended university, you would cut out some good candidates. The conference, however, was of a different mind, and decided that the scholarships should be awarded to candidates between 19 and 22, graduates or undergraduates of two years' standing. The selection committee, it suggested, should consist of the Chancellor of the University of New Zealand, with four electors appointed by the professorial board of the University's four constituent colleges.[1]

The Governor General, Lord Ranfurly, urged that the upper age limit be raised to 30, and represented to the Trustees that the selection committee should include the Governor in his private capacity. No notice was taken of his first suggestion but it became, and remains, the practice for the New Zealand selection committee to be presided over by the Governor General and for the elections to take place in Government House. The first scholar elected was James Allan Thomson, a geologist from Otago.

Difficulties were caused in New Zealand as elsewhere by Oxford's requirement for qualification in Greek. Canterbury College eliminated from the outset candidates who had no Greek, and their elector, Haslam, wrote in protest when a Greekless candidate from another college was elected to the scholarship. In September 1906 the Trustees decided that they would accept candidates nominated by approved universities even if they had no Greek, though of course they would have to have acquired enough of the language to pass Responsions when they reached Oxford.[2]

---

[1] A verbatim record of the conference is preserved in RTF 1628. It was presided over by the Chief Justice, and Hogben, the Secretary for Education, took a prominent part in the debate. Documents cited in this section, unless otherwise indicated, are preserved in RT 1628.

[2] RTM 20 Sept. 1906.

The Rhodes Scholars elected from New Zealand set a high standard from the start. The first two elected both obtained firsts in Schools, and Parkin wrote to the Chief Justice in 1906, 'I often wish we had an extra scholarship to give you in New Zealand, as I can see that you have plenty of excellent material.'[3] The election of the scholar of 1908, Solomon Ziman, a first-class mathematician, drew a protest from New Zealand; Hogben, in somewhat equivocal terms, urged Parkin to dismiss the protest as mere anti-Semitism. Ziman's father was a merchant in good standing, 'decidedly pleasant to speak to, without any specially Jewish characteristics of thought or manner'.[4]

Some in New Zealand were discontented with the preference shown to candidates from university, and from time to time attempts were made to ensure that it was possible for scholars to be elected straight from school. In 1911 the New Zealand Press Agency told Lord Rosebery that people in Wellington thought that Cecil Rhodes had wanted his scholars to be of the same age as the typical Oxford fresher. Haslam, whose college, Canterbury, had not yet won a scholarship, joined the protest, and his students complained that the selectors were paying too much attention to purely academic criteria. But Stout, the Chancellor of the University, defended the committee's practices, while Parkin told the New Zealand press that in most cases a man of 22 stood the transplantation better than a boy straight from school.

When war broke out New Zealand Rhodes scholars hastened to enlist. The scholar-elect for 1916, Athol Hudson, was killed in France before he could come into residence. By this time, of the twelve scholars who had hitherto been elected, eight were serving in the forces on a variety of fronts. The New Zealand committee were allowed to elect an extra scholar for 1917. In a very short time both the year's scholars were at the front and wounded. By 1918 four New Zealand scholars had lost their lives.

At the end of the war there was great confusion about the election to the New Zealand scholarship. The Trustees cancelled the elections for 1918 worldwide. The New Zealand committee, under the Governor General Lord Liverpool, went ahead and chose a scholar. The Trustees cancelled the election, and then reinstated it; but in the meantime the successful candidate accepted a different scholarship to the Sorbonne. Exceptionally, the selection committee was allowed to appoint a substitute.[5]

Though the New Zealand scholars consistently acquitted themselves well in England, there were discontents both in Oxford and in New Zealand about the method of election. In June 1920 the senate of the University of New Zealand proposed that professorial boards should be allowed to nominate candidates. Wylie, however, believed that members of committees should not be institutional representatives, and the board of final selection must have a choice between more than one candidate from each institution. As soon as possible, Rhodes scholars should be brought onto the selection committee,

---

[3] Parkin to Chief Justice, 16 May 1906.   [4] Hogben to [Parkin?], 20 Aug. 1908.
[5] The cables and correspondence are in RT 1628. Correspondence between Britain and New Zealand was in wartime slow and erratic; it was often found convenient to route it through the Colonial Office at this time, since Milner was both a Trustee and Colonial Secretary (1918–21).

though for the time being it should continue to be serviced by the registrar of the University of New Zealand.[6]

In 1920 Grigg visited New Zealand in the entourage of the Prince of Wales, and planned to discuss with the Governor General, Lord Jellicoe, the constitution of the selection committee. However, he was kept too busy by the Prince, and it was not until 1922 that his successor as Secretary, Dawson, informed Jellicoe that the Trustees had adopted the principle of excluding from selection committees representatives of competing institutions. After a long and sometimes testy correspondence Jellicoe reconstituted the board in the manner preferred by the Trustees, and dealt vigorously with ensuing letters of protest from Wellington, Canterbury, and Auckland.[7] The last scholar elected under the old arrangment was Arthur Porritt, who was to enter the House of Lords, and later to return home as Governor General himself.

Montague Rendall, the headmaster of Winchester, visited New Zealand on behalf of the Trustees in 1925, accompanied by two young Balliol graduates.[8] He found the committee sound and well balanced and generally happy with the reconstitution; but it was still unsatisfactory that each institution sent only one candidate. Everyone who wished to do so should be allowed to send his own dossier to the central committee. The main problem for New Zealand Rhodes scholars was the expense of travel: could anything be added to the stipend of scholars who came from very distant constituencies?[9]

Rendall was approached with requests for a second scholarship, and recommended that the Trustees should agree. Kerr, now Secretary, agreed with the recommendation.

After discussions with Rendall, Aydelotte & MacDonnell I have come to the conclusion, a conclusion with which they concur, that if the Trustees are to add to the number of Scholarships at all, the most urgent case is New Zealand . . . It has had an extraordinarily high record in the achievements of its Rhodes Scholars, and provided they go back to New Zealand, they can probably exercise more infuence on the thought and education of New Zealand than any other Dominion.[10]

Wylie concurred. He calculated that New Zealand had one scholarship for its population of 1,320,000, while Australia had one scholarship per 925,000 and Canada one per 976,000, so that New Zealand had the strongest claim. The Trustees decided, therefore, to allow two annual scholarships to New Zealand, commencing with the election for 1926. In communicating the decision, they stated: 'New Zealand stands at the head of the record of Rhodes Scholars from the Dominions' (RTM 13 Oct. 1925).

---

[6] Wylie to Dawson, 8 Mar. 1922. Norris, the registrar, who had serviced the committee since 1915, in fact continued to do so until his retirement as registrar in 1936.

[7] Dawson to Jellicoe, 8 Mar. 1922; Jellicoe to Dawson, 22 May 1922; Grigg to Jellicoe, 24 Apr. 1923; Jellicoe to Boyd Wilson, 13 July 1923.

[8] 'Balliol', Rendall wrote, 'has perhaps more than any other college entered into the ideas of Cecil Rhodes and done its best to help Rhodes Scholars.'

[9] RTA, Rendall's report to the Trustees, 24 Sept. 1925. It seems that it was not until 1945 that the Trustees began regularly to reimburse ocean fares from New Zealand.

[10] Kerr to Wylie, 15 Sept. 1925.

Rendall brought back from New Zealand a number of complaints that the Rhodes scholarships took the best men away from the country and that few returned. This was to be a recurrent theme in the 1930s. Wylie, reporting on a visit to Australasia in early 1932, placed the blame on New Zealand employment practices.

No encouragement is given to men who continue their education overseas to return. On the contrary, in the government service, administrative and educational, these men are obliged to start at the bottom, alongside of men many years their juniors.

This was confirmed by Norris, the secretary of the New Zealand selection committee, in a memorandum of July 1932. Of the thirty-eight who had been elected to Rhodes scholarships only twelve were now in New Zealand, almost all teachers by profession.[11] Business and the civil service did not attract or welcome them; so they joined the civil service of other countries, or international business firms.[12]

By 1933 the selection committee had begun to demand from candidates a promise to return to New Zealand, and in some cases to follow a particular profession. Before this, in 1926, the committee had resolved that they would not normally consider any candidate who would be 22 on reaching Oxford. Partly as a result of these restrictions imposed by the committee—both unauthorized by the Trust, and the second actually overruled—no election was made for the year 1933. There was great public outcry, which was made worse by the Governor General, Lord Bledisloe, who in one public speech said that all the candidates were worthless, and in another that an excellent candidate had been excluded by the 22-year age rule. The mother of this candidate lodged a complaint, and concerned citizens in Auckland and embattled barristers in Wellington petitioned Bledisloe to allow a second round of nominations. Allen, from Oxford, had made his own enquiries and believed that the failure to elect was not due to a real lack of suitable candidates, but to the arbitrary and mechanical system of voting in the colleges, and to partisan dissension on the selection committee. But Bledisloe was adamant, and despite the protests he declined Lothian's invitation to reopen the issue.[13]

Public anger over the 1933 debacle was exacerbated by special features of the election procedure, which had become more contentious in New Zealand than in any other constituency. In each college the student representatives made nominations to the professorial board, and in two colleges the presidents of the students' associations attended the board's meetings. The professorial board passed on the names to the Governor General's committee in Wellington. Proceedings were public and often acrimonious. In this particular year one of those passed over was a well-known and controversial figure, F. X. Mulgan, a left-wing student at Auckland who had been involved in campus debates about free speech. Mulgan had been runner-up in the election for 1932 and it was widely

[11] By 1936, of the scholars elected since 1920, sixteen were abroad and only four in New Zealand.
[12] The Governor General, Lord Bledisloe, contradicted this report in a letter to Lothian, 22 May 1933. Returning Rhodes scholars were not unwelcome, he said, 'but only the lower class enter Parliament here and naturally they favour their own kind in public appointments'.
[13] Norris to Lothian, 6 Feb. 1933; Allen to Lothian, 11 Feb. 1933; 28 Feb. 1933; Mrs Strang to Trustees, 16 July 1933 and 26 July 1933.

believed that he had been excluded in 1933 as a result of tactical voting by the Auckland professors.[14]

The Trustees did their best to repair the damage. New Zealand was offered three scholarships in the two succeeding years. Allen told Lothian that the student vote should be reviewed, that the professoriate should delegate its nomination to a committee which should send on more than two names, and that the number of ex officio members on the central committee should be reduced. Finally, he questioned whether the Governor General should continue to chair the committee.[15]

Lord Galway, however, who succeeded Bledisloe in 1935, proved to be a helpful member of the selection committee, and the Trustees concentrated rather on eliminating the other ex officio members from the committee.[16] The new registrar, McKenzie, described by one who knew him as a man of 'dour strength and fanatical persnicketiness', was no supporter of hasty changes; rather than eliminate the ex officio members he agreed to add a further Rhodes scholar to the committee. In 1938, after attending a Commonwealth conference in Sydney, Lothian went on to New Zealand and stayed with Galway, meeting the selection committee in October. In spite of the recurring problems with the election procedures, he was able to report on the high standard of the scholars selected. Of the thirty-eight Rhodes scholars from the dominion, ten had achieved firsts, and sixteen had had blues awarded—only one less than the whole of Australia.[17]

Lothian was seriously concerned about the failure of Rhodes scholars to return to New Zealand. He suggested that scholars-elect should be interviewed by the Public Services Commission before they left for Oxford; and he wrote personally to the Governor General and cabinet ministers to secure a placement for one scholar who did want to return. After his visit, an Association of Rhodes Scholars was formed; but because of the absences overseas it was small in number and its secretary was an Australian, C. M. Focken, the Victoria scholar of 1923.

In the Second World War the New Zealand Rhodes scholars of the 1930s, like their predecessors, served with distinction on several fronts. Of the four elected during the war years one died of wounds in Italy in 1945, and the other three served in the Royal New Zealand Navy volunteer reserve. In 1945 three scholars were elected, even though not all candidates could be interviewed because they were still on active service.

In 1948 McKenzie visited England, which gave Elton and Allen an opportunity to discuss with him their continuing worries about the selection procedures. Recommendations were still made by the student body to the professorial board, and the Trustees,

[14] Allen was told that there was hysterical anti-Bolshevism in official circles in New Zealand. Sisam to Allen, 16 Nov. 1933. His account is confirmed by Gillray to Wylie, 31 Mar. 1934.
[15] Allen to Lothian, 10 July 1934. Bledisloe had made himself unpopular with the Trust in several ways: he was a poor correspondent, and he had interfered in candidates' choice of colleges. In private correspondence Allen referred to him as 'Lord Bloody Slow'.
[16] In 1945 Elton raised once again the question whether the Governor General should continue to chair the selection. Opinion in New Zealand was in favour. Elton to McKenzie, 15 Mar. 1945.
[17] Lothian's report to Trustees, 2 Nov. 1938. Galway later sent him a lively account of the selection meeting on 20 Dec. 1938.

though as satisfied as ever with the standard of scholars chosen, were worried about the part played in their election by undergraduates.[18]

The person who took the initiative in reforming the selection procedure was Robert Aitken, who, after a distinguished medical career in England and Scotland, returned to New Zealand as Vice-Chancellor of Otago University in 1948. From 1950 the professoriates ceased to invite nominations from the student body, but instead made confidential enquiries about applicants. They still, however, in the view of E. T. Williams, who visited New Zealand in 1952, paid too much attention to academic criteria. So in 1953 the professorial boards were replaced by small local committees, appointed by the central committee, consisting of three or five persons, including Rhodes scholars and local non-academics in addition to the respective college heads. On the central committee the number of ex officio members was reduced. Aitken, who had himself been an ex officio member as chairman of the University's academic board, was re-elected in a personal capacity, and when he left in 1953 to become Vice-Chancellor of Birmingham he was replaced by another Rhodes scholar.[19]

The central committee continued to contain, however, three ex officio members, the Governor General, the Chief Justice, and the Chancellor of the University. It was a recurrent complaint by Rhodes scholars that the ex officio members paid too much attention to academic talent and not enough to the other qualities specified in Rhodes's will. The election of the 1958 scholar, David Vere-Jones, brought the issue to a head, and caused acute public controversy. The Trustees were not made aware of this until Elton visited New Zealand some months after the election. Was it true, he asked the Governor General, Lord Cobham, that Vere-Jones was a mere scholar? Cobham rushed to defend his committee's chosen candidate: 'an amalgam of the poetry inherent in the Welsh blood combined with mathematical genius', and indeed a potential Einstein. It was in any case difficult, he said, to find candidates in New Zealand who had real political ambition; the country was one huge farm and market garden. But he was willing to do his best for the Rhodes scholarship, since his grandfather had been an associate of Cecil Rhodes, and he offered to entertain candidates for a week in Government House.[20]

In his report to the Trustees on his return Elton took up a theme familiar from the 1930s.

The most distinguished of our New Zealanders have made their careers in this country. Thus Robert Aitken is Vice-Chancellor of Birmingham, Sir Arthur Porritt, once an Oxford & Olympic sprinter, is a leading surgeon in England, the late Jack Lovelock, who held the world record for the mile, distinguished himself as a physician in England and America, and Geoffrey Cox, formerly Political Correspondent of the News Chronicle is now Editor of Independent Television News, while

---

[18] Elton to Mckenzie, 31 Dec. 1948. When, a little later, Elton asked Allen about the quality of post-war New Zealand scholars, he was told 'they continue to be, on the whole, among our most successful Rhodes Scholars' (Elton to Allen, 14 Sept. 1951).

[19] Williams to Elton, 25 Mar. 1952; McKenzie to Elton, 8 May 1952; Aitken to Elton, 12 June 1952. Otago, Canterbury, and Auckland agreed to the new arrangements with good grace; Victoria fought a delaying action, but a committee was in place by June 1953 (McKenzie to Elton, 18 June 1953), and the new committees were confirmed by the Trustees in July 1953.

[20] Elton to Trustees, 17 May 1958.

J. F. Platts-Mills is one of the two Rhodes Scholars who have been elected to the British House of Commons.

Oxford University, both before and after the war, was to be one of the gainers from New Zealand's loss. Rhodes scholars became long-serving tutors, such as S. McCallum (1920), physics fellow and later bursar of New College 1926–40, or G. Cawkwell (1946), praelector in classics at University College 1949–87. Others became professors, such as N. Davis (1934), Merton Professor of English 1959–80, or L. C. Woods (1948), a long-time fellow of Balliol who became the first professor of plasma physics at Oxford. Most remarkable of all was the New Zealand connection at Oxford University Press. Kenneth Sisam, the 1910 scholar, was employed by the Press 1923–48 and during the 1940s was its chief executive. Just before retiring he appointed Dan Davin (1936) as deputy secretary to the Delegates of the Press, a post which he held until 1978. R. W. Burchfield (1949) was chief editor of the Oxford English dictionaries from 1971 and was responsible for the successive supplements which were incorporated into the second edition of the *OED*.

One of the most energetic of the Rhodes scholars who had returned to New Zealand was the 1932 scholar, James Bertram. From 1937 to 1940 he had been a newspaper correspondent in China; during the war he had served in Hong Kong and been taken prisoner by the Japanese. After his release he joined the English department of Victoria College. By 1954 he was a member of both the Victoria and the central selection committees, and kept up a correspondence with Elton in which he made clear his distaste for the ex officio members. The Chancellor of the University, he thought, paid insufficient attention to matters of character. The Chancellor, on the other hand, thought Bertram a dangerous radical. McKenzie, too, clearly regarded him as a meddler.

After McKenzie's retirement as secretary to the committee he was replaced by his successor as registrar, Kedgley. Bertram campaigned for the job to be given to a Rhodes scholar. A suitable person would be Alec Haslam, recently appointed to the Supreme Court: Kedgley would find it easier to make way for a judge. In response Elton told Bertram, as he was no doubt intended to, 'You are the right Secretary for the Central Committee, if you are willing to take on the job.'[21]

Elton must have regretted writing this letter when Bertram took it as his cue to urge Haslam to step down from the committee. Elton had to apologize to both Haslam and Kedgley, and confirm them both in office until 1961. Bertram had to agree that it would be a few years before there could be a Rhodes scholar secretary. But he had not quite given up hopes of getting his own foot in the door. 'There is a feeling among the younger Scholars', he wrote to Elton, 'that Haslam might be the official secretary, with someone junior to stand in for him and do the donkey work.'[22]

When Williams took over in Oxford as General Secretary in 1959, Bertram hastened to congratulate him. It would be a relief, he said, not to have any more four-page letters from Elton full of goodwill and vagueness. But Williams, having taken the advice of the

[21] Bertram to Elton, 29 Nov. 1958. Elton to Bertram, 23 Dec. 1958.
[22] Bertram to Elton, 2 May 1958.

Vice-Chancellor of Canterbury University, very quickly decided that Haslam was the right person to be the secretary, and wrote to tell him so. The problem would be to get rid of Kedgley without offence.[23]

Haslam accepted the job, but proposed to delay taking it up until the appearance of the Hughes–Parry report on New Zealand Higher Education. Now that the separate colleges had been made autonomous universities, it was not clear what role remained for the University of New Zealand. The University was indeed dissolved at the end of 1961, but Williams did not wait for this to suggest to Kedgley that he might 'slip out leaving a Rhodes Scholar in charge'. Kedgley initially took the suggestion with good grace, but took offence when he realized that Haslam was proposing to use the University staff to do the paperwork. Williams admitted he had not handled the matter very tactfully. 'Blame me', he wrote to Haslam, 'as the worst example of Mr Mother Country.' It was agreed that after 1961 Haslam would take up the secretaryship and the University Grants Committee would service the committee. The secretary of the new UGC turned out to be none other than Kedgley.[24]

One thing on which Bertram, Haslam, and Kedgley agreed was in praising the Governor General, Lord Cobham. 'Our present chairman', Haslam had written to Elton, 'is the only incumbent of that high office who has been of any practical benefit to us.' Cobham wrote to Williams to ask whether the committees were producing the right kind of fellow. Before the war, Wiliams responded, New Zealand sent good eccentrics; nowadays Oxford seemed to be getting the orthodox and often the unexciting orthodox. Perhaps there were too many judges on the selection committee.

The Rhodes Scholarship is not for academics. . . . So long as a chap can get a decent second the academic side is adequate. . . . New Zealand life with its mountains, its bush and its sailing, surely can provide evidence of unselfseeking leadership once a year?

Cobham, in response, lamented that the committee seemed to be getting the candidates who had given their schoolmasters the least trouble.[25]

Initially Haslam had some difficulty in getting his authority accepted in all the four universities. But after a brief period selection arrangements in New Zealand settled into the pattern which has continued to the present day. It was agreed that he could sit in on pre-selection committees, and he acted as secretary of the committee of final award under the chairmanship of the Governor General.[26] In 1963 a new Governor General arrived, Bernard Ferguson. He too took a keen interest in the scholarship, being the son of a previous Governor General who had chosen Rhodes scholars in the 1920s,

[23] Bertram to Williams, 3 Nov. 1959. Williams to Haslam, 12 Nov. 1959.

[24] Williams to Kedgley, 31 Oct. 1960; Kedgley to Williams, 8 Nov., 5 Dec. 1960. Williams to Haslam, 1 Mar. 1961: 'We mustn't seem to kick Kedgley out & then use his staff.'

[25] Cobham to Williams, 12 Jan. 1961; Williams to Cobham, 1 Mar. 1961. Haslam, too, worried that the scholarships were not getting the best talent available from New Zealand universities: Oxford, he said, was no longer the draw it once was (Haslam to Williams, 15 Dec. 1960).

[26] Kedgley continued as the administrative secretary until he left to become registrar of the new University of Papua New Guinea in 1966, when he was succeeded by W. O. Broad. Williams to Kedgley, 12 May 1966.

including Haslam himself. One of the first selections of the new committee was David Baragwanath, who was in due course to succeed Haslam as the New Zealand secretary of the Trust.[27]

Ferguson's governorship coincided with a period of student unrest in New Zealand, as elsewhere in the world. He enquired of Williams how discipline was enforced in Oxford. Williams sent him, for communication to the Minster of Education, the report on discipline of an Oxford committee he had recently himself chaired; but he opined that the age-old collaboration between college deans, university proctors, and city police would be hard to create from scratch in New Zealand.[28]

Wiliams was generally content with the standard of candidate sent to Oxford. 'New Zealanders rarely create any complications,' he said. But he added, 'they also don't set many rivers on fire'. Haslam worried about the non-academic qualifications of some of the candidates. In December 1965, he wrote, 'we were faced with a candidate whose only sport of any consequences was chess. We were inclined to think it worthy but not 'manly' within the meaning of the definition.' Two years later there was no lack of sporting candidates: the winner was Chris Laidlaw, who played rugby for New Zealand every year from 1962 to 1970 and was given a special interview in October so that he could tour with the All Blacks.

In 1967 Arthur Porritt returned to New Zealand as the first Rhodes scholar Governor General. His appointment was a fitting symbol of a new era when most Rhodes scholars after completing their course made their lives in New Zealand rather than spending them in the service of other countries.[29]

New Zealand selection committees began to worry about a rather different problem. In all the history of the New Zealand scholarships there had never been a Maori scholar. Indeed, a new administrative secretary on taking office in 1969 innocently inquired of the Trustees whether Maoris were eligible. The answer of course was yes, on the basis of the will. In 1958 a half-Maori candidate, Winiata, had been nominated by a pre-selection committee, but he turned out to be two months over age.[30] But it was not until 1986 that a Maori was appointed to the selection committee: Robert Mahtua, the head of Maori studies at Waikato, a half-brother of a Maori queen. The first Maori scholar elected was Marama Findlay, who came up to Balliol to read PPE in 1989.

In 1972 Haslam began to talk of stepping down as secretary. He recommended as his successor David Baragwanath, who had not long turned 30. Williams had no objection on grounds of age; he had recently appointed a similarly youthful secretary in Canada. Baragwanath took office for the elections of 1975 and remained in post until the end of the century, by which time he was a High Court judge and head of the New Zealand Law Commission.

[27] Haslam to Williams, 30 Apr. 1963; Ferguson to Williams, 27 May 1963. Haslam to Williams, 2 Dec. 1963.
[28] Ferguson to Williams, 24 Apr. 1967; Williams to Ferguson, 27 Apr. 1967.
[29] According to the 1995 *Register*, whereas only 7 out of 17 scholars elected in the 1950s had returned home, 13 out of 19 elected in the 1960s were living in New Zealand.
[30] Bertram to Elton, 2 May 1958. For years, Bertram wrote, the New Zealand committee had been looking for a suitably qualified Maori.

An unusual problem was presented by the election held in 1980. One of the successful candidates was Simon Upton. On election he asked to postpone a decision on
accepting the scholarship because he was a contender for a parliamentary nomination.
He was told by Fletcher to proceed with his application and withdraw if he was
nominated. Accordingly, he applied for the BCL and was accepted by Pembroke. In
June of 1981 he was selected, and later elected to the Raglan constituency, and withdrew
from his scholarship. Fletcher refused to allow the committee to choose an alternative,
and in 1988 Upton secured permission to take up his scholarship and undertook
research—an M.Litt. in politics at Wolfson from 1988 to 1990. In 1993, having by then
been Minister of Health for two years in the New Zealand government, he completed
his M.Litt.

In 1986 Duncan Stewart, one of the scholars for 1953 and now the first male Principal
of Lady Margaret Hall, became a Rhodes Trustee: the first and so far the only New
Zealand scholar to have served.

In 1990 New Zealand celebrated the sesquicentenary of the Treaty of Waitangi, which
regulated regulations between Maoris and whites (Pakeha). A conference was held in
Rhodes House to review the history of race relations in New Zealand. In celebration of
the occasion, the Trustees allotted New Zealand a third scholarship. It was a suitable
award to mark the consistently satisfactory performance of New Zealand Rhodes scholars through the century.[31]

Bermuda

It was something of a mystery why Cecil Rhodes in his will had assigned an annual scholarship to Bermuda, a small island with a population of only 20,000, including no more
than 5,000 colonists, and with a very inadequate school system. The best guess made by
local inhabitants was that his brother had once been stationed there and had taken a
liking to the place. But no one really knew, and the Trustees sometimes wondered if the
Founder, when he inserted its name in his schedule, had had any clear picture of the
colony in his mind.

Nowhere else in the world did the announcement of the scholarship make such an
impact. In 1902 Joseph Chamberlain, the Secretary of State for the Colonies, sent a copy
of the will to the Governor, whose Colonial Secretary consulted sixty prominent citizens
about the conditions of eligibility and method of award of the scholarship. The principal questions to be addressed were whether any school in the island was good enough to
provide candidates, and whether boys educated overseas should be allowed to compete.
The citizenry rose impressively to the challenge. Before 1902 was over £1,100 per annum
for six years had been raised by subscription to improve the quality of the only good
school, Saltus School, and in 1905 the legislature passed an act founding two Bermuda
scholarships 'with the object of encouraging competitors for the Rhodes Scholarships'.
These were to be offered to 17-year-olds to enable them to complete their schooling in

---

[31] A conference was also held in Rhodes House to review the history of race relations in New Zealand.

Canada so that they could compete, two years later, with boys who had been educated in England.[32]

It was agreed that to compete a boy must be a British subject born in Bermuda, one of whose parents had been resident for the five years prior to the competition, and who must have been educated for five years in Bermuda between the ages of 12 and 20. The scholar should be chosen by a committee of British administrators, the Governor, the Chief Justice, and the Colonial Secretary. In the first year, however, the choice was made by the Trustees. Three Bermudan public schoolboys in England were interviewed by Parkin and Wylie, and Henry Conyers Cox was chosen as the scholar for 1904.

Normal selection procedure by local interview was difficult, since candidates might be in Bermuda, Canada, or England. The successful candidate for 1905, for instance, was interviewed by Parkin in New Brunswick. When the scholarship was advertised in Bermuda for 1906 no candidate applied; of the two schoolboys who applied in England, one did not fulfil the Bermudan educational qualification, and the other was too young.[33]

From 1907 holders of the Bermuda scholarship to Canada came on stream as applicants. Each year's Bermuda scholar secured virtually automatic election to the Rhodes scholarship. This was the case with the 1907 scholar, Joseph Gilbert, a future Chief Justice, the 1908 scholar, Thomas Waddington, son of the headmaster of Saltus, and the 1909 scholar, his brother John Waddington, a future Colonial Secretary.[34]

Throughout the next decade it remained common practice to elect to the Rhodes scholarship the holder of the Bermudan scholarship of two years earlier. In 1915 Parkin told the Trustees that the scholarship was out of all proportion to the population of the island; he recommended that an election should be made only two years out of three, and the scholarship in the third year should be awarded in the Bahamas. But no action was taken, and nobody could make any complaint about the Bermudans' war record. Eight out of the first twelve scholars volunteered to serve. Three were awarded the MC. The scholars of 1905, 1915, and 1916 were killed in action. Harry Butterfield was awarded the 1917 scholarship while he was a sergeant on the western front serving with a Canadian siege battery.[35]

Because of the small size of the colony, Bermudan scholars tended to be drawn from a small group of families.[36] For this reason the Colonial Secretary in 1921 resisted a suggestion from the Trustees that Rhodes scholars should be added to the selection committee. A committee of selection entirely independent of local influence, he advised, would command more confidence. The selection committee's role, in fact, was minimal,

[32] Governor to Chamberlain, 20 Dec. 1902; Parkin to Boyd, 15 Apr. 1904, to Trustees, 19 Apr. 1904. 'Every body here', Parkin wrote, 'wonders how Mr Rhodes came to assign so small a population so great a prize.' All documents quoted in this section, unless otherwise indicated, come from RTF 1546 (1).

[33] In the end, against the wishes of the local committee, the Trustees gave the scholarship to F. Eardley-Smith, though he did not meet the educational qualification and had already twice failed to get into Oxford. He was accepted by Worcester and obtained a second class in law in 1909.

[34] RTF 1546 (1).

[35] RTA Parkin, Report 149 to Trustees, 8 Dec. 1915. The Governor asked the Trustees to award an extra scholarship to replace a scholar killed in action, but his request was refused.

[36] By 1925, for instance, several pairs of brothers had been elected, and five members of the Smith family.

since scholars from Bermuda were exempted from normal interview requirements and there was rarely more than one candidate. In effect, the significant choice was made by the Governor when he appointed the Bermuda scholar at the age of 17. In some years it was difficult to find a Rhodes candidate at all. No scholars were elected for 1919 or 1920 and in 1925 the committee made no election because the sole candidate had not passed Responsions. Supported by Wylie, the candidate appealed, saying that according to precedent he should have been elected on condition he passed later. The committee had second thoughts, and the Trustees confirmed the election.[37]

Montague Rendall, the headmaster of Winchester, took in Bermuda on his world tour for the Trustees in 1926. He reported that Rhodes scholars in the colony had been chosen

entirely from the Anglo-Saxons, a pure and homogeneous race, containing a large number of old families, who are proud of their ancestry, their Island and their connection with Great Britain; owing no doubt partly to their climate, they produce few men of much distinction or energy.

He was unexpectedly impressed by the nine ex-scholars he met; but found them disappointingly ill informed about what he called the Rhodes 'movement'. Life on the island had recently been enlivened, he reported, by the arrival of New Yorkers fleeing from Prohibition.[38]

After Rendall's visit Kerr told the Colonial Secretary that a number of changes were necessary. He admitted that the Bermudan scholars' results at Oxford had not been unsatisfactory, taking into account that they were some years younger than the typical American or dominion scholar. But the Schools in Bermuda, though they had able headmasters, were incapable of producing scholars at the age of 18 or 19; Saltus School had no library or scientific equipment. The period during which candidates could acquire their five years of Bermudan education should be increased to the years of age between 9 and 20. Bermuda scholars should be elected at 15 not 17, so that they would have the chance of being prefects before competing for a Rhodes scholarship, and it should no longer be a matter of course that the Bermuda scholar became the Rhodes scholar. Finally, four Rhodes scholars should be added to the selection committee, elected by the scholars resident in Bermuda.[39]

The Colonial Secretary agreed to the changes in the selection procedure, and the Bermuda scholarship was extended from two years to three. He objected to an alteration which the Trustees were making worldwide, replacing in the memorandum the words 'fondness of and success in manly outdoor sports' with 'physical activity as evidenced by fondness for manly outdoor sports'.[40]

Kerr assured the Bermudan authorities that he did not wish to reduce the frequency of their scholarships. On the contrary, they had an important role in assisting Bermuda

[37] Kerr to Rendall, 25 Nov. 1925. The scholar, a Smith, passed the examination and was admitted to St John's, but he failed law prelims twice, was rusticated, and resigned his scholarship.

[38] Rendall to Trustees, 5 Mar. 1926.   [39] Kerr to Colonial Secretary, 12 Aug. 1926.

[40] Others elsewhere disliked this alteration, which was seen as a weakening of the sporting element of the scholarship. But the objection came rather oddly from Bermuda, which produced only one blue in the first twenty-five years of the scholarship.

to resist American penetration. Everything possible must be done to 'maintain & advance English standards of refinement & civilisation'. The influx of scholars, he thought, might 'overcome the strange drowsiness of the island'. Two years later, however, he had changed his mind. The Bermudan scholarships, he decided, did nothing to promote the unity of the Empire as Rhodes had wished, and accordingly they should be abolished.[41]

An opportunity presented itself when in July 1928 the Trustees decided to promote a private bill to permit them to reorganize the United States scholarships on the lines proposed by Aydelotte.[42] The bill enabled the Trustees to make such changes in the number and tenure of the scholarships as would in their judgement best fulfil the testator's purpose; but they were not to make any change in the total number of scholarships allotted to particular countries listed in the bill. The list in the bill as at first prepared did not include Bermuda or Jamaica, and the Trustees had in mind to replace these scholarships with scholarships to be competed for more widely throughout the Caribbean.

The omission of Bermuda from the list of protected scholarships was quickly noticed, and the Governor sent a dispatch to the Colonial Secretary in November asking him to resist power being given to the Trustees to deprive the colony of its scholarship. The Bermudan Parliament also passed a motion of protest. Cecil Rhodes, it claimed, had been well aware of the island's small size and population, which had since increased. The colony had spent £7,000 on Bermuda scholarships in support of the Rhodes scheme. The Trustees were preserving the US scholarships and removing colonial ones, reversing Rhodes's sense of priorities. The recent alteration in the wording of the clause on manly sports was cited as an example of the Trustees' wanton habit of tampering with the very plain words and meaning of the will.[43]

In March 1929 Kerr presented the Trust's proposals to the House of Lords committee on private bills, chaired by Lord Chelmsford. On the issue of reducing the Bermudan and Jamaican scholarships, Montague Rendall gave evidence in support of the Trust.

When I visited [the islands] three years ago I was inclined to recommend some small tinkering measures . . . but I am inclined to think that more fundamental measures will be more effective, and I like the suggestion put forward by Mr Kerr.

Extending the competition to include Caribbean countries would be good for both Bermuda and Jamaica, he said. In their own submissions, the Trustees insisted that it would not be possible simply to add extra scholarships for Trinidad, Barbados, and other countries. Oxford was 'saturated' with Rhodes scholars, and admissions criteria had recently been tightened up. In any case 6 out of a total of 196 scholarships was a fair proportion for the entire west Atlantic area.

The Bermudan Colonial Secretary, Henniker Heaton, had travelled over to give evidence to the House of Lords. He said that Bermudans would regard the throwing open to general competition as an injustice, and might refuse to compete in any future

---

[41] Memorandum of 6 Feb. 1929.   [42] See pp. 29–30 above.
[43] Gilbert to Wylie, 28 Dec. 1928; Amery to Colonial Secretary, 1 Mar. 1929; Governor of Bermuda to Secretary of State for Colonies, 29 Nov. 1923.

election. The Trustees quickly gave in, and agreed to amend the bill so as to leave the legal position of Bermuda and Jamaica unchanged. They did this, H. A. L. Fisher told the Lords, 'in view of that fact that Mr Henniker Heaton had stated that if Bermuda had been consulted beforehand it might have been possible to have arrived by agreement at some such solution as was now proposed in the Bill'.

If this was a genuine hope of the Trustees, rather than a fig-leaf to cover capitulation, it was quickly disappointed. When a meeting between the Trustees and the Bermudan representatives took place at the Colonial Office on 12 April 1929 it concentrated on the raising of educational standards in Bermuda, and there was no mention of any dilution of the scheme of annual scholarships. Amery, who was Colonial Secretary, took the chair; Beit, Dawson, and Peacock appeared for the Trustees, with Kerr and Wylie in attendance; Henniker Heaton and the Attorney General appeared for Bermuda, with a representative of Jamaica. Beit claimed that the least that could be expected from Bermudan scholars was a Higher Certificate. The Trustees, advised by Rendall, were of the opinion that if only Bermudans would be willing to pay income tax, they could much improve the standard of education, and perhaps even found a proper public school there. The Bermudan representative countered that the record of Bermudan scholars was highly creditable: two failures in twenty-five years was not a catastrophe. What village in England could produce scholars year after year, more than a quarter of whom obtained second-class honours at Oxford? Bermuda should not be held to the standard of sixth-form boys in English public schools. The most that could reasonably be required was that a candidate should pass school certificate, and qualify for exemption from Responsions.[44]

In the end the Trustees accepted Henniker Heaton's proposals, but only (they said) for an intermediate period. They even agreed to pay the travel expenses of the Bermudan delegation that had come to block their bill. Communicating this decision to Henniker Heaton, Kerr, never a good loser, remonstrated about the 'prodigious' scale of the expenses. Why should heavy subsistence be paid to delegates on luxury liners? 'Do not press the Trustees too far!'[45]

For a while it looked as if the Trustees' initiative, though thwarted in the House of Lords, would have a real effect on educational standards in Bermuda. The Governor printed the Trustees' memorandum and circularized parents, asking how many would be willing to pay £100 a year to support a public school. It was reckoned that £25,000 would be needed to build such a school, and £7,000 per annum to maintain it. But the proposal was still stalled in the legislature eighteen months later.[46]

Bermudan scholars continued to worry the Oxford authorities. Wylie complained of the academic record of the scholars for 1926–9; one of them had achieved a record by failing every single paper in history Schools. No election was made in 1930. In 1932 the selection committee at last agreed that possession of a Higher School Certificate should be made a condition of election. No election was made in 1935 because the most promis-

[44] The minutes of the meeting and the supporting memoranda are in RTF 1546.
[45] Kerr to Henniker Heaton, 26 Apr. 1929, 27 May 1929. The Trustees agreed to refund the entire Bermudan expenses, estimated at £1,355. The sum of £259 was later returned from Bermuda.
[46] Lothian to Colonial Secretary, Dec. 1930.

ing candidate, a Haileybury boy, Henry Marriott, had not passed the HSC. Lothian said that this requirement could not be waived. It was pointed out that he had already won an exhibition to Brasenose. But according to malicious rumours in the University, Allen told Lothian, 'Brasenose is not averse from giving scholarships and exhibitions to good bowlers & powerful heelers in the scrum.' None the less, an exhibition might be held to outweigh the lack of a Higher. The Principal of Brasenose added his voice in support of Marriott. Finally, the Master of Haileybury pointed out that, by an oversight, no mention had been made of the requirement of a Higher when printing the Bermuda memorandum in 1935. Lothian and Allen had to admit they had been caught out; the Bermudan committee was allowed to elect Marriott and his scholarship was confirmed for 1936.[47]

Right up to the Second World War the Bermuda scholarship continued to be an anomaly: it seems that up to 1939 only a single scholar had attended a university before coming to Oxford. When the Trustees decided to suspend scholarships during the war, Bermuda again presented a problem. In April 1941 Elton notified the Colonial Secretary that the Trustees had decided not to hold elections for 1942, because of the backlog of scholars-elect which had built up worldwide. In reply, the Colonial Secretary enquired whether there was anything in the will or in the 1929 Act empowering the Trustee to cancel elections. Elton consulted the Trust's lawyers, who were not very helpful: the Trustees, they said, could consult the Attorney General, or apply to the court, or promote a private bill. Having had their fingers burnt so badly in 1928, the Trustees decided not to put the issue to the test. They told the Bermudan committee that if the suspension of the 1942 scholarship was seen as a hardship they would authorize the holding of an election. The committee put forward a law student already resident at St Edmund Hall, whose scholarship was confirmed after an interview by an Oxford committee.[48]

The Trustees again suspended elections for 1943, throughout all constituencies, and this time there was no protest. When, however, it was decided not to hold an election for 1944 Bermuda protested again, this time to the Colonial Office. Elton urged the Office to persuade the Bermudans to fall in line; elections there, he said, would cause resentment worldwide, since it would be felt that this was a provision of special facilites for shirkers and pacifists. He secured the support of Sir John Waddington, the scholar of 1909, who was visiting London as Governor of Northern Rhodesia. The Colonial Office, however, took the Bermudan side: Christopher Cox, at a meeting with Elton in May 1944, urged that Bermuda differed from all other consituencies, since its scholarships were awarded to boys of 19 who had just left school, and the Rhodes scholarships were in effect the only university scholarships for Bermudans.[49]

Allen was unconvinced by Cox, but he was overruled by the Trustees, who were afraid that insistence on the suspension might trigger Bermudan opposition to the new bill they were drafting which would give them increased powers in a variety of areas. The Bermudans were allowed to hold elections in 1944 and 1945, and to choose two scholars

---

[47] RTM 18 Feb. 1936.
[48] RTM SF 1995. The scholar was another member of the Smith family, the sixth to date.
[49] Sir George Gater to Elton, 26 May 1944; Report no. 361 to Trustees.

for 1946. One of these was a student at a Canadian university. This set a precedent which later became a regular pattern.[50]

No election was held for 1947. Henniker Heaton, now retired, wrote to the *Royal Gazette* in Bermuda denouncing the selection committee for dereliction of duty. His successor as Colonial Secretary wrote to remind the Trustees that passing an election was no novelty: it had been done in no less than seven previous years. Allen travelled out to Bermuda and defended the selection committee's action; but his report to the Trustees on his return was a gloomy one. The selection committee was not very satisfactory; it would be better to have a Rhodes scholar as secretary rather than the Colonial Secretary, but no suitable candidate could be found. The island was fearful of transfer of sovereignty to the USA, he reported, and immigrant agitators were playing on the racial issue.[51]

Throughout the 1950s Elton made a series of efforts to reduce the number of ex officio members on the committee, to find a Rhodes scholar as secretary, and to increase the academic qualification of scholars. He had an uphill task. While scholars from elsewhere in the world came to Oxford with two years of university education behind them, in all Bermuda there might be no more than two schoolboys in a year who passed Higher School Certificate. Of the first four scholars of the 1950s, two failed prelims twice on arrival in Oxford.

The Bermudan response was set out in a long letter from J. T. Gilbert, the 1907 scholar, who was now Chief Justice and an ex officio member of the selection committee. The Bermuda scholarship to prepare Rhodes candidates could be held either at school or at university: but schoolboy candidates were preferable because they would fit better into colleges. It was important to retain the Governor and non-Rhodes selectors not for the sake of prestige, but to secure impartiality. The only change which should be contemplated was to appoint a Rhodes scholar as an unofficial correspondent with the Trust, while the Colonial Secretary remained officially in charge.[52]

The new Warden, Williams, agreed with Elton that the situation was unsatisfactory. The Bermuda scholarship amounted to prejudicial pre-selection, and the results were unimpressive academically.

we like Rhodes Scholars to get Blues but we expect them to be sufficiently sensible to know that the proper price of a Blue is to pass the necessary examinations at the first attempt and to proceed on to at least a reasonable Second or the sort of Third that the College grumbles about as unfair to the man's real ability.[53]

Things took a turn for the better when in 1955 a Rhodes Scholar Association was formed in Bermuda with Harry Butterfield, the 1917 scholar, in the chair. His son Chester, the 1949 scholar, shortly afterward became secretary to the selection committee. When

---

[50] Elton to Peacock, 19 June 1944. RTM SF 2162.   [51] Report no. 379.
[52] Elton to Gilbert, 15 July 1954, Gilbert to Elton, 28 Aug. 1954. Elton had complained that it was not easy to deal with 'a correspondent who addresses me as "My Lord", is "my obedient servant", "is directed to inform me" and numbers the paragraphs of his letters'.
[53] Williams to Elton, 1 Sept. 1954.

the Eltons visited Bermuda in November 1956 they could report that goodwill had been restored between the Rhodes scholar community and the Trust.

A new problem, however, raised its head. Hitherto all Rhodes scholars had been elected from the white population of the island—the buccaneer families, as Elton called them. Two delegations visited him to complain. The colour bar, he reported to the Trustees, was very strict, though the coloured folk were prosperous. The whites told him that without a colour bar the island would lose the American tourists on which its prosperity depended; but he was disinclined to believe this, since Americans came to Jamaica where there was no colour bar. Coloured candidates had not been excluded: two had come forward in the 1920s, but neither had been successful. The local committee was very resistant to any suggestion of affirmative action. Chester Butterfield complained that the Colonial Office in London had been bringing pressure on civil servants involved in the selection 'to select or appoint negroes with only secondary regard being given to the actual qualifications of the applicant concerned'.[54] The first black scholar from Bermuda was elected in 1964.[55]

Butterfield remained secretary of the selection committee for twenty-eight years until his death in 1987. When he died he was succeeded by John Collis, the scholar of 1979, a Hamilton barrister. Collis was the son of the scholar of 1953. Thus a Rhodes scholar son of a Rhodes scholar succeeded a Rhodes scholar son of a Rhodes scholar.

In the last decades of the century the Bermudan scholarship grew to resemble the scholarships in the larger constituencies, with most scholars being elected as graduates and performing creditably in Oxford. In the ten years between 1984 and 1993, for instance, of the ten scholars three were awarded firsts in honour schools, two got good seconds in law degrees, one obtained a BM, and three took Master's degrees; only one left Oxford without a degree. At the end of the century the Bermuda scholars amply fulfilled the boast of the Bermudan representatives to the House of Lords in 1929 that they had a record which could not be equalled by any community of similar size in England.

Jamaica

Jamaica was the last colony to be named in the schedule of colonial scholarships in Cecil Rhodes's will. Parkin had difficulty in visiting it during his initial world tour to establish the scholarships, and the Governor asked the Archbishop of the West Indies (who was also chair of the Board of Education) to preside over a committee to organize the selection of scholars. As in Bermuda, the foundation of the Rhodes scholarship had an impact on the local system of secondary education. As in several other colonies, the most

---

[54] Elton, in Report no. 666. Chester Butterfield to Elton, 14 Apr. 1959; Elton to Butterfield, 21 Apr. 1959.

[55] His academic record was not strong, and it took Williams a while to place him in a college. The Bermudan committee worried that they had elected a 'hot potato', but Williams replied, 'The hotness of the potato was not because of its skin, but because of the inadequacy of its cooking' (Williams to Butterfield, 6 June 1964).

contentious issue in the arrangements for the competition was whether boys educated abroad should be allowed to compete. In Jamaica the question had a particular edge to it, because there was no colour bar and all the local schools were mixed.

According to Nero Capper, the Inspector of Schools for Jamaica, the schools and colleges of Jamaica were quite unfit to produce Rhodes's ideal student. 'Parents send their children away,' Parkin was informed, 'not merely to get better schools for them, but to arrest by residence in a colder climate the physical development which turns boys & girls into men & women years before this occurs further North.' Capper insisted that it was important not to exclude boys at school in England. Representatives of the local schools, on the other hand, believed that no one who was educated outside the island should be allowed to compete for the scholarship.[56]

A compromise was reached. The first national memorandum provided that candidates should be between 17 and 20, have spent five years of their life in Jamaica, and should not have left it finally before the age of 11. Candidates should have taken the Cambridge senior local examination, and should declare their intention to return to Jamaica after the scholarship. In every third year the selection was to be made from candidates who had lived in Jamaica for the whole seven years before the exam. The selection committee was to consist of the Governor, the Chief Justice, the Chief Inspector of Schools, and the chair of the schools commission, with a co-opted member.

The first scholar, Reginald Murray, was a product of Jamaica High School: later in life he was to be headmaster of one of the other principal schools in Kingston, Wolmer's. The 1905 scholar was from Exeter School in England, and the 1906 one from Jamaica College. The 1907 award again went to a local candidate, Oliver Calder, from Munro College. However, it caused a protest from the Wolmer's Old Boys' Association who believed that the award should have gone to a black Wolmer's boy, Mercier, whose home had just been destroyed in an earthquake. Calder might have been the better scholar, they said, but Mercier had more of the other qualities specified in the will.[57] Despite this controversy, it could not be said that under the compromise memorandum local institutions had fared badly.

There was soon pressure, however, to exclude overseas candidates not just every third year, but every other year, or indeed every year. The election for 1908 of Theodore Williams, a schoolboy at Bath, caused an uproar. The authorities at Wolmer's, the school of the defeated candidate Stephenson, alleged that Capper had improperly changed the date of the competition to allow Williams to return from England. Impassioned and potentially libellous letters were published in the local paper, the *Gleaner*, and the mayor and council of Kingston (who were responsible for the running of Wolmer's) passed a motion of protest. On the other side it was alleged that Stephenson was the adopted son of the headmaster of Wolmer's and had been improperly put forward as a candidate. The Governor referred the matter to his Privy Council, who gave a unani-

---

[56] The report of the Archbishop's committee is in RTF 1346, from which, unless otherwise indicated, other documents cited in this section are drawn. See also Parkin to Trustees, 17 May 1904.

[57] The Trustees did not interfere with the selection committee's choice; they merely noted that they had received a protest 'on the Negro question'. RTM 4 June 1907.

mous vote of confidence to the selection committee. On the general issue, the council-lors voted by 6 to 2 that boys from England should be allowed to compete at least every other year.[58]

At Parkin's request, the Governor consulted local headmasters and members of the education committee about the restriction to Jamaican schools in particular years. The two dozen replies received were fairly evenly divided. Capper, however, wanted the scholarship thrown open to overseas candidates every year. Education in Jamaica, he said, was injurious to the moral fibre.

In an island in the population of which a morbid unnatural sexual precocity is common, in which nearly three fourths of the births are illegitimate and many black or coloured girls think that it ele-vates them in the social scale to have a bastard child for a father of lighter colour than themselves this is inevitable.

Canon Simms, the headmaster of Jamaica College, had long argued on the other side. How could the opponents of the restriction say simultaneously that education in England gave an overwhelmingly superior moral advantage and that in an unrestricted com-petition Jamaican-educated schoolboys would have an equal chance? The Governor, having completed his enquiries, came down in favour of the existing system of protect-ing Jamaican schools for one year in three.[59]

In London, Michell and Parkin studied the correspondence. They decided to recom-mend to the Trustees that the scholarship should be restricted to Jamaican schools every other year. But then the West Indian committee of the House of Commons weighed in. To the extent that the prize was reserved for Jamaican-educated candidates, the com-mittee argued, fewer boys would be sent to England for education, and that would be bad for them and bad for the colony. Parkin changed his mind, and in November the Trustees reaffirmed the one-year-in-three rule.[60]

In fact, all the scholars elected between 1909 and the outbreak of war had received their schooling in Jamaica. In 1909 a candidate who had been educated at Brown Uni-versity in the USA was discouraged. At the end of the decade Parkin could write to Capper, 'On the whole your Jamaica men have done very creditably at Oxford.' The scholar for 1914 was Norman Manley, later to be the first Prime Minister of an inde-pendent Jamaica.[61]

Eleven Jamaican Rhodes scholars served in the war. The scholars of 1911 and 1912 were both killed in 1915. In 1916 the committee elected, without interview or examination, a Lieutenant Mulholland who was on active service in France and had been awarded an exhibition to Balliol. The committee's action was warmly commended from London; but

---

[58] The Council resolution of 20 May 1908 is in RTF 1346. Parkin, Report no. 62. Capper to Parkin, 18 May 1908; Williams senior to Parkin, 30 June 1908; Governor's minute of Sept. 1908.

[59] Capper to Governor, 29 Aug. 1908; Canon Simms in the *Daily Telegraph*, 16 May 1904, transmitted to Parkin in 1908. One suggestion which the Governor forwarded to London, but which the Trustees declined to accept, was that a special committee should be set up to watch the athletic performance of candidates.

[60] West India Committee Circular, 29 Sept. 1908; RTM 2 Nov. 1909.

[61] Parkin, memorandum of 27 May 1909; Parkin to Capper, 28 July 1909.

Mulholland was never able to take up his exhibition or his scholarship, because he died of wounds in 1918.[62]

In 1916 there was a disagreement between the Governor of Jamaica and his law officer whether 'Jamaica' in the scholarship regulations could be taken to mean 'Jamaica and its Dependencies' and thus include the Cayman islands and the Turks and Caicos. Parkin and the Trustees were in favour of so interpreting it, but thought it was a matter for the selection committee to decide. In the aftermath of the abolition of the German scholarships, Parkin told the Jamaicans that he had some hopes 'that we may be able to assign a scholarship to the parts of the West Indies which lie between Demarara & you'. But the hopes did not see fruition until after the Second World War.[63]

Until 1919 Jamaican candidates had to take a qualifying examination, usually in Jamaica itself. When, in 1919, the Trustees abolished the special examination in the USA they decided that no examination was needed in Jamaica either. Instead, the Jamaican committee adopted the Higher School Certificate as the qualifying condition. By this time, in almost all constituencies candidates had to have two years of university education in order to apply. Parkin suggested that Jamaican candidates might be given some university experience in Canada; but the committee thought that it would be impossible in Jamaica to get graduate candidates.[64]

In 1926 Montague Rendall included Jamaica in his world tour. The population of the island, he reported, was 942,000, of whom only 14,500 were white. 'There is no sharp discrimination, social or other,' he noted, 'between the white and the coloured element (always excepting the negroes).' All the elected members of the legislative council were coloured. Schools were mixed, and all the children sat at the same benches. Educational standards were quite impressive, and the schools in Jamaica were quite adequate to produce Rhodes scholars.[65]

Twenty-two scholars had been elected to date. Seven had come from Jamaica College, 6 from Munro College, 4 from Wolmer's, 4 from English schools, and one from another school in Jamaica. More than half of them had been 'coloured', and those who had spoken to Rendall had told him they had not found colour a problem in Oxford.[66] The academic performance of the scholars at the University had been fair but not brilliant. Of the Rhodes scholars who had completed their courses and survived the war, six were now working in England, five in Jamaica, and three in other countries. Of those in Jamaica, Rendall singled out for praise Murray, the headmaster of Wolmer's, Morales, the Schools Inspector, and Manley, now a flourishing barrister.[67]

Rendall recommended that the Trustees should retain the Jamaican scholarship as pro-

[62] Cundall [the secretary of the committee] to Parkin, 15 Feb. 1916.

[63] Parkin to Cundall, 31 Oct. 1916.

[64] Parkin to Cundall, 13 Jan. 1999. Cundall to Parkin, 24 Nov. 1919. Cundall to Parkin, 28 Apr. 1919.

[65] Rendall's report to the Trustees, 20 Apr. 1926, and subsequent memorandum for the House of Lords private bill committee.

[66] In 1938 a Warden could write from Oxford, '[W]e never quite know until our Jamaica Rhodes Scholars arrive exactly what nuance of colour they are going to be!' Allen to Crofton, 6 June 1938.

[67] According to Rendall, Manley told him 'that it would be very undesirable for him, as a barrister, to enter the unseemly scuffles of politics, where divisions are sharp and feeling bitter'.

vided in the will—partly in order to offset American influence on the island. Boys educated in England should no longer be allowed to compete against those from the Jamaican
schools. Two Rhodes scholars should be added to the selection committee, and in due
course one of them should become secretary.

Rendall's report was not what Kerr had hoped to read. In view of the small and diminishing number of whites in Jamaica, and the indifferent performance of Jamaicans in
Schools, he had favoured abolishing the scholarship or reducing its frequency. However,
he wrote to the selection committee setting out a number of recommendations based on
Rendall's report.[68]

The Governor and his committee were aghast at the idea of adding Rhodes scholars
to the committee. They eventually agreed, but only on condition that the scholar member
was co-opted, not elected. Wylie, in Oxford, suspected that this was because they wanted
to exclude coloured men from the committee.[69] In 1928 the 1908 scholar, Theodore
Williams, a white farmer, was co-opted as a selector.

Meanwhile the Trustees were preparing the bill which would give them power to
reorganize the scholarships. Jamaica, like Bermuda, did not appear in the list of constituencies to be preserved. In arguing the case before Parliament, Kerr used the committee's opinion about the unsuitability of scholars as selectors as an argument for curtailing
the scholarship. The Higher School Certificate which most Jamaican candidates held, he
said, was an insufficient qualification for a scholarship. In a memorandum Rendall suggested that one of the Jamaican schools, perhaps Munro College on its mountain site,
should be brought up to the standard of an English public school, with a library and laboratories, and a good sixth form including prefects, and with a staff pension fund, all to
be paid for out of high fees. This could easily be done if Munro could get a great man
as a headmaster.

In two memoranda dispatched to England the selection committee defended the
Jamaican scholarship. It had contributed to the progressive spirit in education on the
island for twenty-five years. The payment of fees at an English level would be quite
impractical in Jamaica. If required, the schools were quite capable of producing candidates with distinctions in the Higher School Certificate. The record of Rhodes scholars
after completing their course had been highly creditable.[70]

Sir Algernon Aspinall, the secretary of the Commons West Indian committee, held a
watching brief for the Jamaican scholarship as the Rhodes bill came before the private
bill committee. Though it was the Bermudans who made the running in the parliamentary proceedings, when the bill became the Rhodes Trust Act of 1929, the Jamaican
as well as the Bermudan scholarship was entrenched.[71]

In the 1930s Jamaican Rhodes scholars were generally popular in Rhodes House
and in Oxford, but from time to time complaints were made about poor academic

---

[68] Kerr to Mitchell [the secretary of the committee], 16 Aug. 1926.
[69] Mitchell to Kerr, 4 Apr. 1927. Wylie to Millar, 5 Oct. 1927. The committee's arguments gave several
grounds for suspicion of bias: for instance, they described Manley as 'an articled clerk'.
[70] Manley was now described as 'a very able & influential advocate'.
[71] Kerr to Aspinall, 7 Nov. 1928.

performance and failures in Schools. In 1937 Lothian rebuked the selection committee for two recent elections, and told them they should make no election if candidates were not up to standard. One of the scholars, it was complained, did little work and spent all his time in the Labour Club and distributing pacifist propaganda.[72]

There were particular difficulties in placing scholars who wished to read medicine, because of the inadequacy of laboratories in Jamaican schools. The Governor expressed pleasure when Lothian wrote to complain of this, because the letter gave him ammunition in his own campaign to improve scientific schooling. He went out of his way to secure a grant from the Jamaican government to obtain special tuition in London for the 1938 scholar, Roy Levy, prior to his taking up his Oxford studies.[73]

During the Second World War Jamaica, unlike Bermuda, did not insist on the continuation of elections after 1941; indeed the Governor rejected an offer of a scholarship for 1942 for fear that it would compete with enlistment for the RAF. The scholar for 1941, William Burrowes, a government botanist, wished to come up to read for agriculture; he was thwarted by the closure of the rural economy department in Oxford.[74] He eventually came up, in the huge 1946 contingent of post-war scholars, along with two other Jamaican scholars, who, through a misunderstanding, had been elected very late in the season.[75]

At the end of the war Jamaica received a new constitution. Elton wrote confidentially to Manley to ask, whether, in these circumstances, it was still appropriate for the Governor General to chair the selection committee. Manley recommended that the Governor be retained as chairman, but that the secretaryship should be held by a Rhodes scholar rather than as hitherto by a government official, the secretary of the schools commission. The Governor has continued to chair the committee until the present day, and it was to be some time yet before a Rhodes scholar would become secretary.[76]

In the post-war period the character of the Jamaican Rhodes scholarship was changed substantially by the foundation of the University College of the West Indies. During the 1950s the typical Jamaican Rhodes scholar had spent three years at UCWI and taken an external degree from London University. The last two scholars to be elected in Jamaica straight from school, Stuart Hall in 1951 and Desmond Costa in 1954, both went on to

[72] Allen to Lothian, 8 Nov. 1937. Lothian to Selection Committee, 17 Nov. 1937. Of the two scholars complained about, one was killed in the war and the other went on to a distinguished teaching career.

[73] Governor to Lothian, 22 Jan. 1938. Allen secured a place for Levy to reside at London House. He had been told that it operated a strict colour bar, so he wrote to Crofton, the comptroller, 'I am glad to be able to tell you that Levy appears to be entirely fair-skinned! He is, of course, Jewish, but that, I presume, is not so relevant as the other question.' Allen to Crofton, 6 June 1938. Levy, after a medical course curtailed by war and after distinguished military service, held many medical posts in Jamaica and Canada.

[74] There is considerable correspondence in RTF 1346, eventually involving the Colonial Office, as to whether he should be funded to study elsewhere, in Trinidad or Canada.

[75] Allen had difficulty in placing the unprecedented number of scholars in 1946. 'I am a little apprehensive', he wrote in February, 'that unless they can find good men it will be exceedingly difficult to get two Jamaicans placed next term, when the Colleges will have completed their lists. My only hope is that black men are now so popular in Oxford that, possibly, if the Jamaicans are dark skinned that will be their chief attraction.' Allen to Elton, 26 Feb. 1946.

[76] Elton to Manley, 28 Mar. 1945. Manley to Elton, 16 Apr. 1945.

a lifetime of notable academic success in England; but with the foundation of the University College, and its eventual transformation into a university, the way was open for Jamaican scholars to pursue an academic career in their own country. This several of the scholars of the 1950s did, often combining a university post with some form of public service.

By now the selection committee had three official members and four Rhodes scholars, of whom Manley was the most influential. At a gathering of the selection committee in 1950 to greet Harlow, the Beit Professor, visiting from Oxford, Manley put the question: should not an intellectual with middling athletic ability be preferred to a first-rate athlete of mediocre intelligence? Harlow was quite sure he had the backing of the Trustees in answering 'Yes'.[77]

The Governor General of Jamaica between 1951 and 1957 was Sir Hugh Foot. He invited Elton to visit the island in November 1955, dealt patiently with his fussy queries about weather and wardrobe, and entertained him warmly in spite of being confined to bed for part of the visit. He encouraged him to hold forth in the pulpit and on the radio. On his return Elton reported enthusiastically to the Trustees: he liked the climate, the lack of colour bar, the university college. The selection committee, he considered, was superior to two New England committees which he had visited on the same trip. The twenty-two Rhodes scholars living on the island, he reported, included the Prime Minister ('a charmer'), the Finance Minister, two university teachers, three schoolteachers, and five doctors. Whereas before the war no scholar had been, by Jamaican reckoning, black, the committee, though still all white, had now elected two fully black scholars.[78]

In 1956 a Jamaican Rhodes Scholar Association was set up, at the initiative of Roy Levy, the 1938 scholar. The members of the Association voted that the secretary of the selection committee should be a Rhodes scholar and elected Hector Wynter to the post. The Governor and the existing secretary concurred, and the Trustees confirmed the appointment in May 1957. One of the earliest functions of the Association was a dinner to celebrate the election of Norman Manley to an honorary fellowship at his college, Jesus.[79]

In 1958 the Colonial Office set up the Federation of the West Indies, consisting of a dozen different colonies. Wynter asked for an extra scholarship for the federation, for graduates of the University of the West Indies, which had campuses in Trinidad and Barbados as well as in Jamaica. By the time the Trustees had agreed and set up the appropriate administrative arrangements, the Federation was no more: in 1961 Jamaica voted in a referendum to depart from it and seek separate independence. Trinidad and Barbados and the smaller islands soon followed suit. However, the scholarship survived the

---

[77] Harlow to Elton, 6 Apr. 1950.

[78] Elton to Foot, 10 Jan. 1956; Elton to Ogle (10 Jan. 1956); RTR 421. During their trip the Eltons visited the home of Tenn, a scholar-elect currently at Princeton. They also tried to visit the home of Everard Nelson, the first black Jamaican scholar, but the visit aborted because a telegram reading 'Lord Elton will call on you on Thursday' was transmitted as 'Lord will call on you on Thursday'.

[79] Levy to Elton, 21 Sept. 1956; Levy to Foot, 29 Jan. 1957; Elton to Foot, 17 May 1957. Mrs Manley was unable to attend the dinner as she was in Havana celebrating the victory of Fidel Castro.

break-up of the federation for which it was designed, and the first British Caribbean scholar was elected for 1962, Robert Ogilvie from Grenada.

The Caribbean scholarship was at first only triennial, and it took some time for it to establish a record comparable to that of the Jamaican scholars. It was not until 1974 that the first Caribbean scholar obtained an Oxford degree. But from the outset the scholarship did attract candidates from many parts of the constituency: of the first ten scholars, two were from Guyana, two from Trinidad, and one each from Grenada, Belize, St Vincent, Barbados, St Kitts, and Nevis. In 1985 the scholarship was made an annual one, and a further Caribbean scholarship (open also to Jamaicans) was created in the 1990s.

Wynter, when appointed secretary, tried to encourage schoolboys to compete, as of old, against graduates; but he quickly had to admit defeat. From 1957 to 1977 every single scholar had attended the University of the West Indies before election. The line was broken in 1978 with the election of the first female Jamaican scholar, Evelyn O'Callaghan, who was a graduate of Cork University in Ireland. From that time UWI graduates alternated with scholars who attended universities overseas, usually in the USA.

Among the disciplines favoured by scholars, medicine and law predominated; following the example of Norman Manley a number went into public service or politics. Delroy Chuck, for instance, the scholar of 1973, took a BA and BCL in law in Oxford and went on to a career at the Bar in Jamaica; he succeeded Wynter as secretary of the selection committee, and served until he retired in 1998 to take up a political career. Others distinguished themselves in academic, literary, and artistic pursuits. Rex Nettleford, of 1957, combined an academic career leading to the pro-vice-chancellorship of UWI with a series of books on Jamaican culture and a directing role in the National Dance Theatre.

Intended originally for members of a tiny group of white colonist schoolboys, the Jamaican scholarship blossomed over the years into one of the most successful multiracial awards, and Jamaican scholars can look back with pride on the contribution which they and their forebears have made to the academic, cultural, and political life of an independent nation.

Malta

Malta was the first constituency not mentioned in the will to be awarded a scholarship. At the request of Leo Amery, newly elected as a Trustee while he was holding office as Under-Secretary for the Colonies, the Trustees put Malta on the agenda of their meeting of 6 October 1919. They postponed consideration while Parkin was consulted. Parkin would have preferred a scholarship rotating between a number of small colonies, such as Gibraltar, Trinidad, and Hong Kong as well as Malta. But Malta was a special case, Amery insisted. The Maltese should be treated like the French Canadians or the South African Dutch: they needed special attention so that they would stick to British ideals and not be attracted to a spurious Italian nationalism. His arguments carried the day with the

Trustees, and at their next meeting they approved an annual scholarship in principle, but asked Dawson to travel to Malta to investigate educational standards there.[80]

In Malta people wanted to know what life was like for Catholics in Oxford. Briefed by Wylie, Dawson could report that there were about 110 Roman Catholics in residence, and that there had been 33 Catholic Rhodes scholars to date. He also reported on the wide influence exerted by the Catholic Balliol don F. F. Urquhart. He discovered that the University of Malta provided a three-year course of preliminary instruction, which was offered only once every three years. The current one was to terminate in 1921, so that if there was to be a scholarship the first scholar would have to be elected in 1920 to take up his place in the following year. The Governor, Field Marshal Lord Plumer, agreed to chair a selection committee which would include the chief secretary to the government, the Archbishop, the Rector of the university, and two members of the learned professions. He announced the foundation of the scholarship at the University in April 1920, and the first scholar, the chemist Harold Cassar, came into residence at Exeter College in autumn 1921.[81]

Amery had clearly envisaged an annual scholarship, but because the University in Valetta ran a course only once every three years, the Maltese scholarship was from the outset triennial. Indeed Grigg, when he succeeded Dawson as Secretary, raised the question whether the Trustees had made a settled grant, or had merely given a single scholarship as an experiment. Wylie was clearly unenthusiastic about the scholarship, and Cassar did not have an easy passage, failing his divinity examination at the third attempt. But Dawson was clear that the scholarship was meant to be permanent, and an election was held in 1923 at which Edward Scicluna was elected.[82]

The next election was due for 1927. In that year Malta achieved self-government and Sir Gerald (soon to be Lord) Strickland, who had helped Amery frame the Maltese constitution in 1921, became Prime Minister of a coalition government. He wrote to ask whether a second scholarship could be given to celebrate self-government, but was rebuffed by the Trustees. The scholar for 1927, J. P. Vassallo, did not get on with his tutors at Queen's and failed pass Moderations more than once; he resigned his scholarship in May 1929. Thereupon Strickland's niece Mabel proposed that the remaining portion of the scholarship should pass to her brother George, also at Queen's, who had been the runner-up in the election for 1927. Queen's College and the Maltese selection committee supported her proposal. The Maltese secretary added a hand-written note:

In the memorandum on his nephew's claims to be allowed to succeed to the Malta Rhodes scholarship for the year, Lord Strickland adds to the points mentioned in my official letter that it

[80] RTM 6 Oct., 1 Dec. 1919. Parkin to Amery, 10 Oct. 1919; Amery to Parkin, 13 Oct. 1919. Amery gives his own account of his part in the creation of the scholarship in his autobiography, *My Political Life* (London: Hutchinson 1953), ii. 191. Documents cited in this section are, unless otherwise indicated, filed in RTF 2461.

[81] Dawson to Plumer, 19 Apr. 1920; Plumer to Dawson, 21 Apr. 1920.

[82] Grigg to Dawson, 22 June 1923. Wylie to Grigg, 4 July 1923. Scicluna was the son of Sir Hannibal Scicluna, Director of the Malta Public Library, who later presented a fine collection of Melitensia to the Rhodes House Library.

was rumoured in Malta that George Strickland would have been recommended for the 1927 scholarship had he not been the nephew of Lord Strickland, who was then (as now) engaged in fighting the Nationalist party in politics, and goes on to say that he represented the British and Imperial side which Mr Rhodes would have approved. This is correct, but such considerations were never before the selection Committee and had no weight in their decision to recommend Vassallo.

Kerr told the Governor, Sir John Ducane, that it was the universal practice of the Trustees not to reallocate the unused portion of the scholarships. Sir John did not insist on the selection committee's point, and the scholarship was allowed to lapse.[83]

Scholars were elected for 1930, 1933, and 1936 without controversy. Malta University was oriented to providing candidates for the professions of law, theology, medicine, or architecture. It was lawyers who found themselves most comfortable in Oxford; but the scholar elected for 1939 was a third-year student in architecture, Don Mintoff. He joined Hertford College, and read for engineering, in which he obtained a third class in 1941.[84]

During the Second World War Malta played a key role in the Mediterranean theatre, and suffered continual attack by the Axis powers. The fortitude of the inhabitants was much admired in Britain, and the island was awarded the George Cross in 1942. In that year the Trustees decided to grant a yearly scholarship in place of the triennial one, 'in admiration of the gallant role played by Malta in the present war'. Moreover, Malta was exempted from the wartime suspension of scholarships. Between 1942 and 1945 only eight scholarships were awarded worldwide: four of these went to Malta.[85]

Besides their wartime travails, the Maltese, with 2,000 people to the square mile, were also worrying about overpopulation. Edward Scicluna asked the Trust to fund a scheme for young men to travel around the Empire to promote Maltese emigration. The Trustees were sceptical. 'The Dominions', said Amery, himself a great admirer of the Maltese, 'are inclined to regard the Maltese as a sinister type of Asiatic.' Elton sought advice from Attlee, the Secretary of State for the Dominions, and from Harold Macmillan in the Colonial Office. Macmillan, like Amery, thought Scicluna's proposal would not work; but he recognized the problem as a serious one which the government would have to tackle. The Trustees, however, were not further involved.[86]

The Maltese scholars elected during the war came into residence in 1945. Three of them were medics, and found difficulty in slotting into Oxford. Allen wrote to Malta explaining that medical graduates from Valetta either had to read for a BA in physiology, which was retracing their steps, or start research, for which they were not qualified. Professor Seddon, the Nuffield Professor of Orthopaedic Surgery, asked the Trustees to

[83] Sir Gerald Strickland to Amery, 25 Feb. 1927; Wylie to Kerr, 2 May 1929; Mabel Strickland to Kerr, 2 June 1929; Best to Kerr, 22 July 1929. Kerr to Ducane, 29 Aug. 1929. Strickland had already been involved with Rhodes scholarships as Governor of three Australian states; see p. 321 above.

[84] Scicluna to Lothian, 8 Sept. 1932; Governor to Lothian, 26 Nov. 1938.

[85] RTM 13 June 1942. In response to congratulations from the Colonial Office, Elton wrote, 'the Maltese scholars have not been of a high academic level, but they have been men of excellent character and personality and therefore may be said to have held their own at Oxford' (Elton to Cox, 21 Oct. 1942).

[86] Elton to Macmillan, 14 Dec. 1942. Elton to Scicluna, 18 Dec. 1942; Macmillan to Elton, Dec. 1942.

support the reconstruction of Malta University and to endow a medical professorship there. But the Trustees felt they had been generous enough to Malta. They ruled that medical scholars would be accepted henceforth only on the understanding that they would read for the physiology final honour school.[87]

In the immediate post-war period the rule against the marriage of Rhodes scholars was relaxed for those who had been on active service. E. J. Borg-Costanzi, the scholar for 1945 who was later to become Rector of the University, was given permission to marry while on stipend, even though he had not served in the forces. The Trustees accepted the argument that during the war everyone living in Malta had been in the front line. In 1946 the Malta selection committee broke new ground by interviewing a woman candidate. They did not, however, elect her, and were told by the Trustees that if they had done so the election would not have been confirmed.[88]

In February 1950 Elton visited Malta, staying three days at Government House and then moving to the Phoenicia Hotel. He was entertained in style by the Governor and the Admiral commanding the Mediterranean Fleet, and gave tea parties for all the Rhodes scholars on the island. He was most surprised to be given supper by Don Mintoff, whom he described as the leader of the 'extreme left splinter group in the Maltese Parliament', who had refused to attend the Governor's official dinner in his honour.

Mintoff, after graduating, had worked with a firm of civil engineers, and had become civilian garrison engineer in the South Midland district. He had been anxious to return to Malta, but difficulties had been placed in his way; Elton had interceded with the Governor to get him a passage back in 1943. Already before taking up his scholarship Mintoff had been general secretary of the Malta Labour Party, and by the time of Elton's visit he had had two years of office as Deputy Prime Minister and Minister of Works. In 1947 he had married Moyra Cavendish-Bentinck whom he had originally met in 1941 while being entertained by her family under Lady Frances Ryder's hospitality scheme for Rhodes scholars. 'He is', Elton reported to the Trustees 'by far the ablest man in Maltese politics (the standards of which are not high); [he] is reputed to be a Communist and avoids all contact with society.' But after an initially prickly meeting, the two parted on the best of terms.[89]

The Royal University continued to admit freshmen only once every three years, and this presented difficulties for an annual scholarship. The scholar elected in 1952, the medic Edward de Bono, had to obtain the Trustees' permission to postpone for two years his coming into residence at Christ Church to read for philosophy, psychology, and physiology. He came up in the same year as Peter Serracino-Inglott, later to be another Rhodes scholar Rector of Malta University. Once the wartime enthusiasm had worn off, the Trust's officers were obviously unhappy with the annual scholarship. Elton, as he explained to Sir Richard Laycock when he became Governor in 1953, did not like either

---

[87] Allen to Scicluna, 26 Apr. 1944; Allen to Elton, 20 Sept. 1949.
[88] Allen to Elton, 3 Feb. 1950.
[89] The full programme of Elton's visit is given in RT 2461, including the notes for his speeches; he presented a report to the Trustees on 14 Mar. 1950.

alternative of offering three scholarships every third year, or of allowing the committee to accumulate scholars-elect. But it was not until 1975 that the Trustees reverted to a three-year cycle for elections.

During the 1960s there were a number of minor crises in connection with elections. In one year the selection committee wished to elect a candidate three days over age; Warden Williams wisely refused permission. The Student Representative Council wrote to Oxford to protest against the choice of the scholar of 1963 on the grounds that he was not a British subject; the Trustees ruled him eligible.

It was the normal practice for the Rector Magnificus of the University to act as secretary to the selection committee. Thus Joseph Borg Costanzi, the 1945 scholar, took over in 1964 when he succeeded Rector Manché. But the University was soon in deep trouble. In 1964 Malta was granted full independence from Britain and in 1971 Mintoff, who had been the leader of the Malta Liberation Movement since 1958, became Prime Minister. He turned Malta into a republic and instituted a number of educational reforms which completely changed the nature of the university. Students now took five-year courses, with six months of each year spent in study and six months in work experience. The reforms led in 1978 to the dismissal or resignation of many of the staff (such as William Bannister, the 1959 scholar, a distinguished clinical biochemist) and there was constant government interference in appointments and scholarships. In 1979 Williams told the committee not to advertise the scholarship, because of the overseas fees crisis in Oxford; but when, at the beginning of Fletcher's wardenship, that crisis was resolved, the Malta scholarship was not renewed.[90]

In 1983 requests were received from Malta for the renewal of the scholarship, but the Trustees responded that 'they would like to allow more time for the University to settle down in its reconstituted form'. Mintoff ceased to be Prime Minister in 1984 and in 1986 A. S. Trigona, the scholar of 1973, now Minister of Foreign Affairs, visited Fletcher and pleaded for a restoration of the scholarship. The Trustees asked for advice from the British Council and were told that while 'there are signs of a mood in Malta to put aside the educational excesses of the Mintoff past' there were unlikely to be suitable scholarship candidates at the present time. At the end of the 1980s the government restored autonomy to the University, and some of those dismissed in 1978 were reinstated. Ugo Bonnici, the Minister of Education, visited Rhodes House in 1988 to describe the reforms. Borg-Costanzi, however, advised Fletcher to wait a year or two before restoring the scholarship. The year 1992 was the fiftieth anniversary of the award of the George Cross. By this time, after a strategic plan for the University had been drawn up by the registrar of Warwick University, academic life had returned to normal. To mark the anniversary an election was held in Malta in 1992 for a scholar to come into residence in 1993. However, since the 1993 scholar completed his course in Oxford no further award has been made.[91]

---

[90] Williams to Borg Costanzi, 22 Aug. 1979. In 1970 the Fletchers visited Malta and lunched with Mintoff, but were able to make only vague allusions to the problems of the University.

[91] Trigona to Fletcher, 28 Nov. 1985; Borg-Costanzi to Fletcher, 18 Mar. 1988; Kenny to Serracino-Inglott, 13 Mar. 1992.

The Indian Subcontinent

During the first decade after the Founder's death, Rhodes scholars stood out in Oxford among an overwhelmingly British undergraduate body. However, students began to come to Oxford from parts of the Empire not provided for in the will, most notably India. By Trinity term 1914 Oxford was housing seventy Indian students in Oxford, and had set up a delegacy devoted to their welfare.[92] Shortly after the outbreak of war the delegacy wrote to the India Office proposing that the Rhodes scholarships vacated by the Germans should be used for Indians. '[Rhodes] evidently did not mean to exclude all who were not of white race,' the writer said, 'for the conferment of scholarships on Jamaica and Barbadoes has opened the door to other races, and the open door has been used.'[93]

The India Office sent the letter on to Rosebery, who thought poorly of the proposal and did not trouble his fellow Trustees with it. The idea did not, however, go away; and when in 1916 it was proposed to abolish the German scholarships by Act of Parliament many distinguished persons urged that they should be transferred to Indians. Enthusiasts included the Secretary of State for India, Austen Chamberlain, and the Vice-Chancellor of Oxford, Dean Strong of Christ Church. Chamberlain received a holding reply from Milner in encouraging terms. Not all the petitioners thought that the new Indian scholarships should be wide open to all residents of the subcontinent: some, including the bishops of Calcutta and Oxford, thought that they should be offered to 'the domiciled community' of English and Eurasians in India.[94] Lord Curzon, solicited for his support, wrote with characteristic disdain, 'I cannot believe myself that the Eurasian community in India are at all fitted for participation in Rhodes Scholarships. I am afraid they would lower the standard (even if they were ever selected) and not add to the credit of the community. I did all that I could for them in India but I am afraid that I left with a poor opinion of their capacity for anything but complaint.'[95]

The reallocation of the German scholarships was considered by a full meeting of the Trustees on 10 September 1917, the first meeting attended by Rudyard Kipling. India was not awarded a scholarship, but the proposal to give one to the domiciled community was adjourned (RTM 10 Sept. 1917). No further consideration seems to have been given to the Indian scholarship project until 1920 when Colonel Lascelles, the director of military education in Delhi, urged that it would be appropriate to allocate Rhodes scholarships now that the subcontinent's first residential teaching university had been set up at Dacca.[96]

Once again, the Trustees hesitated. Wylie was asked to take soundings in Oxford. He consulted heads of houses and the Indian delegacy, and reported that the balance of

[92] J. G. Darwin, 'A World University', in B. Harrison (ed.), *The History of the University of Oxford*, viii (Oxford: Clarendon Press, 1994), 609.

[93] Letter of Dr Burrows, Principal of King's College London, 3 Nov. 1914, RTF 2361.

[94] Memorandum of Parkin, 20 Mar. 1916, RTF 2361.

[95] Curzon to Robertson, 24 Nov. 1916; communicated to the Trust by Mr Kenneth Rose in 1970.

[96] RTR 175, quoting a letter of 15 Jan. 1920 to Amery, since 1919 a Rhodes Trustee and Under-Secretary in the Colonial Office.

opinion was against the establishment of ordinary Rhodes scholarships for Indians. Colleges on the whole were not enthusiastic about Indian students. The delegacy thought that Oxford had as many as it could digest, though carefully selected Rhodes scholars might be better than the haphazard group of Indians at present in Oxford. As for the community of Rhodes scholars, Wylie feared that 'the introduction of the Oriental element will be a somewhat disturbing complication'.[97]

A year later, when the Indian Council of State was in session at Simla, Phiroze C. Sethna proposed a motion asking that the discontinued German scholarships should be transferred to Indian students. 'Were [Rhodes] alive today he would assuredly have made a second codicil by which he would have given to India not five, but twice or three times as many scholarships.' The motion was opposed by some such as Jogendra Singh and Zulfikar Ali Khan who thought it was undignified to petition: the Trustees should be left to volunteer. Sethna responded that even a mother would not give milk to her child unless he cried for it, and the resolution was adopted.[98]

The government of India wrote in support of the motion, and the India Office passed on the correspondence to the Trustees. Dawson told the Office that they should have known that the German scholarships had all been reallocated long since, and that the Trustees were not in a position to create new scholarships.[99] There the matter rested for twelve years.

In 1931–2 Lothian combined the secretaryship of the Rhodes Trust with the office of Under-Secretary of state for India. It was not he, however, but his successor in the India Office, R. A. Butler, who urged the Trustees to think again about the scholarships, emphasizing the political value their foundation would have. 'It would mark a further field in which Indians were being offered the same opportunities as the inhabitants of the Dominions.'[100] Lothian replied that the Trust had no money to spare; but he drew attention to the Trustees' attempts to bring Indian lecturers to Oxford.[101]

During the 1930s Lothian persuaded the Trust to finance three visits to India by Edward Thompson: a cultural tour in 1932, a historical one in 1935, and a political one in 1939.[102] The report of the first visit largely concerned literature in Bengal, and included a report of a brief meeting with Rabindranath Tagore. In the course of the second, undertaken while writing a biography of Lord Metcalfe, Thompson established a good rela-

---

[97] Wylie to Dawson, 13 May. 1920; RTF 2361.

[98] Proceedings of the Council of State, in RT 2361.

[99] Dawson to India Office, 5 Oct. 1921. His letter drew a tart response, which recalled Milner's encouraging letter of 1916. 'One might have supposed that when the Trustees decided to reject Mr Chamberlain's request, which the Act would have enabled them to meet had they thought fit, some communication would be made to the India Office. Your tone of indignation . . . would perhaps have impressed us more if the fact that the scholarships had "long since" been allotted elsewhere had not been left to us to discover.' India Office to Dawson, 29 Dec. 1921. RTF 2361.

[100] Butler to Lothian, 28 June 1933, RTF 2361.

[101] Srinavasa Sastri and Muhammad Iqbal were both invited to give Rhodes memorial lectures but declined on health grounds; see Darwin, p. 513 below. The Trust also offered in 1932 to set up a special visiting lectureship on Indian history, literature, and art, but nothing came of the scheme; see R. Symonds, *Oxford and Empire* (Oxford: OUP, 1986), 117.

[102] These are described more fully by Darwin, pp. 514–15 below.

tionship with Nehru, whose daughter Indira was then at Somerville. Lothian entertained Nehru at Blickling during his visit to England in 1938,[103] and later proposed him as Rhodes Memorial Lecturer. When war broke out Lothian, with the approval of the Viceroy and the Foreign Secretary, arranged for Thompson to visit the Congress leaders so as to enlist their support for the war effort. The mission achieved little, but Thomson's report to the Trustees (RTF 2844) makes interesting reading.

A few weeks before the outbreak of war the Indian High Commissioner in London, Firozkhan Noon, wrote to Lothian asking whether the reversion of the Dalham estate would at last make it possible for Indian Rhodes scholarships to be established. The Trustees responded that the estate had not yet come in; but in the meantime they consulted the Viceroy (the Marquess of Zetland) and the Foreign Secretary (Lord Halifax) about the desirability of Indian scholarships. They received a mixed response. Halifax thought that the creation of a few Rhodes scholarships for young Indians would really cut no ice at all. He was much more enthusiastic about a proposal to offer the Rhodes Memorial Lecture to Nehru. Zetland, on the other hand, gave the scholarships a warm welcome on his own behalf and on that of the Secretary of State for India; but he cautioned against inviting Nehru. 'The coming year is bound to be a critical period in the political life of India and we hesitate to support a proposal which would involve the absence from India for a substantial period of one of her prominent political leaders.'

In Oxford, the idea of Indian Rhodes scholarships was supported by the Vice-Chancellor. C. K. Allen did not want any overall increase in the number of scholars; but perhaps Indians could take up scholarships vacated because of the war.

If I may volunteer a personal opinon, I should be glad to see Indian Rhodes Scholars at Oxford. I see no reason why they should not be successful, if they were carefully selected. Some of the Indian-born civil service probationers who have been to Oxford in recent years have been excellent persons and I believe, have got on very well in Oxford. The prejudice which has undoubtedly existed in the past in Oxford against Indians has not, in my opinion, been on account of their race, but because a good many of the Indian students who come over here, either to Oxford or Cambridge or London, are not really representatives of the best types of young Indians.

Wylie had worried that social relations between Indians and other Rhodes scholars might be difficult; but now, Allen felt, opinion about the colour bar had been changing. The principal opposition to the proposal came, surprisingly, from Lothian who was now in Washington. His warning against straining the finances of the Trust was countered by the argument that, at least in the short term, the cost could be met by savings from the German scholarships.[104]

It was on 27 February 1940 that the Trustees voted to found Indian Rhodes scholarships, but it was not to be until 1947 that the first Indian scholar came into residence.

---

[103] This horrified Indira, who vainly urged her father to decline Lothian's invitation. 'He is a thorough Fascist and doesnt make any bones about it. Your staying with him would amount to the same as if you spent a weekend with Hitler or Mussolini.' *Oxford Today* (Michaelmas 1999), 51.
[104] Allen to Elton, 26 Jan. 1940, RT; RTF 2361.

From the outset, the Trustees had decided that no election was to take place until after the war; and they held to that decision even though one of their number, Leo Amery, became Secretary of State for India later in the year, and urged that elections should take place during wartime with a view to scholars taking up residence later.[105] The war years were spent in exploring different methods of selection, in choosing a selection committee with its chairman and secretary, and in deciding questions of principle about eligibility for the scholarship.

The Trustees' decision was announced with a fanfare, with leading slots in BBC news bulletins and a laudatory leader in *The Times*, which hailed the scholarship as 'recognition of the assured progress of India towards the status of a Dominion'. The Secretary of State was asked to give advance notice to the the Viceroy. Congress newspapers were not impressed. 'The award may constitute a compliment to Hitler but it is certainly no better than a cheap ironical gesture to India,' said the *Bombay Chronicle*. In Calcutta a Congress leader writer advised, 'Indians with a grain of self-respect should think twice before accepting the crumbs thrown out from that arch-imperialist's table.' Despite this, many premature applications were received from Indian students. From Washington, Lothian recorded his disapproval. 'I have long doubted whether it is a good plan to bring Indian adolescents to spend three years in Oxford. If they don't fit in they become embittered; if they do, they never feel at home when they get back to India.'

At the suggestion of Edward Thompson the Trustees invited Sir Maurice Gwyer to become chairman of the future selection committee. Gwyer was the Chief Justice of India and also the Vice-Chancellor of Delhi University. He was asked to set up a committee with two Europeans, two Hindus, and two Muslims; much correspondence ensued about the best method of choosing the Hindu and Muslim members. At Gwyer's suggestion a Cambridge man, F. C. Edmonds, the secretary to the federal Public Services Commitee, was invited to become secretary.[106]

The contents of the memorandum of selection were debated in snail-like exchanges between Elton, Gwyer, and Edmonds. Should Eurasians and British residents in India be eligible? Yes, but committees should be discouraged from choosing Englishmen, at least in the early years. Should Indian vice-chancellors sit on the selection committee, or should they nominate candidates? No, but they should weed out poor applicants. Should scholars have to be qualified for senior status at Oxford? Yes, said Elton at first. But if so, they would have to come from institutions listed on Oxford's official but private table of approved universities. The table would soon become known, and 'for my part', Gwyer wrote, 'I can think of nothing more likely to excite feelings of hatred, malice and all uncharitableness in the Indian University world than that knowledge.' A compromise was reached, and endorsed by Oxford University: candidates from any university would be acceptable provided they had a first-class BA or B.Sc., and the selection committee was empowered, for a period of five years, to confer senior status on the candidates elected.[107]

---

[105] Amery to Elton, 30 July 1940, RTF 2361.
[106] Elton's invitation to Gwyer was dated 22 May. It travelled by sea mail and did not arrive until the end of July; Gwyer's acceptance was not cabled until late Sept.
[107] Gwyer to Elton, 11 May 1941; Elton to Gwyer, 29 Aug. 1941; RTF 2361.

The war dragged on and in 1943 Gwyer reached retiring age. He agreed to continue, though enquiring plaintively if there was any chance of Indian scholars being appointed before the end of the war. To this, and to similar representations, Elton insisted that it was best if the Indian scholars came up with the mainstream of post-war elections. Some members of the selection committee, appointed after lengthy discussions, retired without ever having taken part in an election. When the memorandum for the first election was distributed in 1946 the committee consisted entirely of Europeans except for G. D. Birla, a Zemindar friend of Gandhi, and Sir Akbar Hydari, a Muslim member of the Governor General's executive council. Two hundred and fifteen applications were received, 85 of which were ineligible for various reasons; all of the 130 eligible candidates had first-class degrees. A subcommittee produced a short list, and 18 candidates were interviewed in Delhi in December 1946. Neither Birla nor Hydari was able in the event to attend the interviews.[108] The chosen candidates were A. K. Datta (later dean and Principal of the College of Arts at Jadavpur University in Calcutta) and Lovraj Kumar (who was for years secretary to the Ministry of Steel and Mines). Edmonds, having organized his first and only election to the scholarships, handed over to another Cambridge man, H. W. M. Sadleir.

The earliest Indian Rhodes scholars had not started their first term in Oxford when India was partitioned and the state of Pakistan came into existence, on 15 August 1947. Should there now be one scholar a year for India and one for Pakistan, Allen and Elton wondered? Gwyer wrote:

I do not think that it would be possible to allow one scholarship this year to Hindustan and the other to Pakistan, for that would be unjust to Hindustan with its immense preponderance of inhabitants. Also, until the border question is settled, a large number of people in the Punjab will not know whether they are Hindustanis or Pakistanis.[109]

The ideal solution, he thought, would be for the Trustees to give three scholarships to the subcontinent, two for India and one for Pakistan; but Allen was opposed to this, and the Trustees decided that there should be just one for each nation.

There was much discussion about methods of selection. Allen quickly realized that there would have to be two quite separate selection committees; but Elton persisted in arguing in favour of a single committee.[110] Gywer thought that this would work only if the committee consisted entirely of Europeans and met on two separate occasions.

Sixteen candidates were interviewed in Delhi in December 1947 in conditions of great difficulty. Gwyer was crippled with arthritis, and desolated by the loss of the Muslim staff of Delhi University, of which he was still Vice-Chancellor. The one Muslim candidate travelled by train from Aligarh under police protection and had to be met at the station by Gwyer's official car. The secretary Sadleir was due to take up a new post

---

[108] Hydari's place was taken by Zakir Hussain, later to be Vice-President of India.

[109] Gwyer to Elton, 2 July 1947.

[110] In November Allen wrote to Elton, 'Gwyer or somebody will have to get on pretty quickly with finding two Selection Committees and two secretaries. Let us hope that they will not all be assassinated before the elections take place' (10 Nov. 1947; RTF 2361).

in Tasmania, but having muddled the selection committee's accounts, he committed suicide on 26 December immediately after handing over to his successor C. Eyre Walker, an Exeter College graduate on the staff of St Stephen's College. Gloom was everywhere.[111]

The two scholars elected for 1948 were both Indian: Eric Philip, later Prabakhar, an Olympic runner from Madras, and Caithra Warrior from Simla. Elton was still hoping that a single chair and a single secretariat would handle elections in both countries, and when a special memorandum was drawn up for Pakistan for the following year, it was to be distributed by Eyre Walker from Delhi. But the Lambeth conference of 1948 provided a new opportunity. One of the secretaries of that conference was Bishop Barne of Lahore, whose diocese included both East and West Punjab, and who had been a member of the Indian committee before partition. Elton saw him in England, and offered him the chair of the Pakistan committee.[112]

By September 1948 two committees had been set up, both still serviced by Walker. Neither committee was able to make a normal election in December. Bishop Barne suffered a coronary, and the Indian committee could not reach agreement on which of their five candidates to select. The secretary tried, in vain, to get the Trustees to make the decision. Both committees reconvened in January, by which time Bishop Barne had recovered. In Delhi the physicist B. S. Chandrasekar was elected by a majority. The Pakistan committee, of four Oxford expatriates and three Pakistanis, chose a candidate who was difficult to place.[113] The Bishop was dissatisfied with the candidates who presented themselves, and asked the Trustees to modify the rule requiring a first class. 'In this part of India we produce a fine, manly, robust type which Cecil Rhodes would have approved of. The Punjabi Mussulman is not overbrainy but he is a man of character and action.' The Trustees refused to alter the rule: but they yielded to Barne's insistence, endorsed by Walker, that Pakistan needed a wholly separate commitee. This was set up in 1949 under the chairmanship of Archdeacon Woolner, shortly to succeed Barnes as Bishop of Lahore, with Gwyn, the Principal of Aitchison College, as secretary.[114]

In April 1950 Gwyer retired as Vice-Chancellor of Delhi and left India for good: on the morning of his departure an honorary doctorate was conferred on him by the President of the newly constituted Republic of India. At Gwyer's suggestion, the Trustees appointed a highly respected civil servant, Sir Penderel Moon, to succeed him as chair of the selection committee.[115]

---

[111] Early in the New Year, Allen wrote to Elton 'It is my own private hope that after an experimental period of, say, five years, the Indian scholarships will prove to be unworkable, and I shall see them go without regret' (21 Jan. 1948).

[112] Elton to Bp. Barne, 23 July 1948. Barne was in fact invited to chair both committees, since Gwyer had returned to England; but Gwyer later decided to return to India and resumed the chair of the Indian committee.

[113] His first degree was a third class, and no references had been taken up. The irregularities in his election seem to have been due to Walker's difficulty in communicating with the committee. Barnes to Elton, 23 Mar. 1949.

[114] Barnes to Elton, 23 Mar. 1949 and 30 May 1949.

[115] Gwyer to Elton, 3 May 1950, Elton to Moon, 8 May 1950.

When the time came for the Trustees to review the Indian Rhodes scholarships five years after their foundation, Allen could report that the scheme had fully justified itself: none of the scholars had obtained less than a second, and several of them had been quite outstanding. The story was rather different in Pakistan, where a scholar had recently got into trouble with the police, and had had to be flown home by the Trust (RTM 28 Apr., 21 July 1951). None the less the Trustees decided to renew both scholarships on a permanent basis. (RT SF min. 2593) Their principal concern now was the great expense of the Indian selection procedure. Moon thought that in his predecessor's day too many candidates had been brought for interview and too generous honoraria had been paid. At the beginning of 1953 Walker could report to Elton that between 1946 and 1952 the cost of the scholarship selection had been brought down from 6,000 rupees to 1,500 rupees.[116]

By the mid-1950s the first two Indian Rhodes scholars had joined the selection committee, and Raghavan Iyer, the scholar of 1950, had become president of the Oxford Union. Ved Mehta, the blind writer, applied in 1955 for the 1956 scholarship, supported by a sheaf of glowing testimonials; but he was disqualified because he had received his higher education in the USA and had not attended an Indian university. If he were allowed to compete, Elton wrote, 'the Indians of India, which has only one scholarship for its teeming millions, might well have a legitimate grievance'.

The candidate who was elected for 1996 caused problems to the Trustees. A. M. L. Sondhi, after election, came first in the examinations for the Indian civil service and chose to join the foreign service. He asked the Indian government for two years' leave to take up his scholarship, but was refused. Moon asked Elton to accept in his stead the runner-up, Virendra Dayal, but the Trustees were unwilling to set such a precedent, which would cause problems of college placement. It would be much better, they thought, to bring pressure on the Indian government to change its mind. Sir George Abell wrote to the Secretary General of the Indian foreign service, and Elton composed a letter to Nehru, who had sent civil servants to Balliol for training after the war, asking him to step in and rule that Sondhi be given leave. He sent the letter to Malcolm MacDonald, a Trustee who was now High Commissioner in India. MacDonald in a sharp note refused to pass the letter on; the Indian government could not be expected to rewrite the rules of its training system to satisfy the deadlines of Oxford.[117] Eventually the Trustees gave in and a place was found, late in the season, for Dayal.[118]

Elton and the new Warden, Williams, worried about the future. Moon, Walker, and the Revd W. A. Jarvis of St Stephen's, Delhi, who had succeeded him as secretary, attended a conference in Oxford in June 1956. Moon said that the problem was likely to recur, now that government service had resumed its attraction for bright young men. If successful ICS candidates could not pass on their scholarships to alternatives, selection committees were not likely to consider civil service candidates seriously at all. Elton persisted in asking MacDonald to press Nehru to allow two years' leave for successful Rhodes

---

[116] Walker to Elton, 5 Feb. 1953.   [117] Elton, Report to Trustees 422.
[118] In 1957 Sondhi came to Oxford, for a year's study at Balliol.

candidates, but Moon joined MacDonald in opposing this. The real solution, in Mac-Donald's view, was for the Trustees to set up more scholarships. But Elton claimed that this was impossible because the British baby boom and the end of compulsory national service were cramming the colleges with home students.[119]

In 1961, however, the Trustees approved a second Indian scholarship, timing the announcement to coincide with a visit to India by Queen Elizabeth II.[120] In the same year, on the retirement of Moon, the selection committee received its first Indian chairman, Krishna Prasada, a New College graduate and tennis blue. In April of the following year Jarvis handed over the secretaryship to Ranjit Bhatia, the Rhodes scholar of 1957, and Indian Olympic runner in 1960, recently returned from Jesus and a mathematics lecturer at St Stephen's. Bhatia continued as secretary until 1998. For some years yet the committee was still not wholly Indian, often containing a Rhodes scholar diplomat temporarily in the country, such as Roland Michener who was Canadian High Commissioner in 1965. In 1968 the elections were attended by Warden Williams, who had recently rebuffed, with characteristic vigour, an attempt by the Indian government to take over the administration of the scholarships.[121]

Up to 1968 all interviews for Rhodes scholarships had taken place in Delhi. It was now proposed that the selection procedures should rotate between different centres of population. The 1969 interviews were arranged for Bangalore; however, the Vice-Chancellor who was to have acted as host had to resign as a result of student unrest, and the plan was cancelled. The first interviews to be held outside Delhi were held in Elphinstone College, Bombay, in 1969, under the chairmanship of Lt. Gen. Dunn. Since that time it has been customary to hold interviews in Delhi, Bombay, and Calcutta in a triennial cycle.

In recent decades other scholarships, such as the Inlaks, Felix, and Radhakrishnan scholarships, have joined the Rhodes scholarships as vehicles for bringing Indian students to Oxford, often administered by committees with overlapping memberships and serviced by Ranjit Bhatia.[122] In 1985 the Trustees added a third annual Indian scholarship, and during the 1990s the number of scholarships was increased to its present total of six per annum. The increase in the number of scholarships available for India permitted the Trustees to secure the agreement of the Indian selection committee to consider candidates studying in universities outside India.[123]

One of the scholars for 1988 was Mridula Shastri, who had represented India as a swimmer at the Asian games and who captained the Indian water polo team. At the

[119] Elton to MacDonald, 29 June 1956. MacDonald to Elton, 9 Nov. 1956. A similar set of events took place in the case of the scholar for 1959; this time it was Williams who urged MacDonald in vain to take the case to Nehru (letter of 26 May 1959).

[120] They had hoped the Queen would make the announcement herself, but the Palace declined (Charteris to Williams, 27 Jan. 1961).

[121] In 1968, however, the chair was taken by M. C. Chagla, a former Minister of Education in the Indian government.

[122] However, the Trustees declined a suggestion, made by Sir David Goodall in a letter of 8 Sept. 1987, for a new scholarship programme to be jointly funded by the Trust and the FCO.

[123] This issue was the topic of correspondence with several US university officials during the 1970s and 1980s. See Bhatia to Fletcher, 16 Jan. 1981, and RTM 30 Mar. 1981.

beginning of an Oxford career of great promise she was killed in the air crash at Locker-bie in December 1988. A scholarship trust was set up in Bombay in her memory.

By 1996, when the one hundredth Indian Rhodes scholar was elected in Bombay, the scheme could fairly consider itself to have come of age. Indian scholars have distinguished themselves in Oxford in both academic and sporting activities, and India has taken its place as one of the most vigorous of the Rhodes constituencies.

Meanwhile, the Pakistani committee had gone its separate way. For many years the Bishop of Lahore chaired the committee, its official secretary being Mr Justice Ortche-son, while the paperwork was handled by a clerk, M. D. Khalid. After its initial difficult start the committee during the 1950s and early 1960s sent to Oxford a series of solid scholars who went on to distinguished careers, very often in medicine abroad but also in a few cases in government service in Pakistan. The scholar elected for 1964 was Wasim Sajjad, who was to become the secretary of the Trust in Pakistan and the chairman of the Senate.

In 1962, however, a delegation of Pakistani students in Oxford complained to Warden Williams that the scholarships were not sufficiently well known or advertised. In particular there had been a shortage of candidates from East Pakistan. In 1965 a candidate from East Pakistan did present himself, but was not elected. The Bishop wrote to Williams:

The candidate from E. Pakistan was a likeable man but plainly not of the calibre required. This was the first time for several years that we had called a man over from the other wing of Pakistan. During my 16 years as chairman of this selection committee we have only twice chosen East Pakistanis, and my estimate of Bengali candidates is not encouraging.[124]

Pakistan scholars continued to be drawn from the west (and usually from Lahore) throughout the 1960s. But at the beginning of the 1970s, two were elected in succession from Chittagong and Dacca. The war which turned East Pakistan into the separate state of Bangladesh broke out while the second of these, Gowher Rizvi, was being elected. He was detained for a period and released only after Williams had written personally to the President, Z. A. Bhutto. By the time he took up his scholarship in 1972 he was no longer a Pakistani.[125]

In Pakistan more than in other constituencies the parents of disappointed candidates were inclined to complain vociferously, usually on very slender evidence, of bias and family favouritism in the selection procedures. The Revd Norman Green of the Cathe-dral School at Lahore, who had succeeded Ortcheson as secretary in 1965, dismissed the 'wild charges' and described to Williams the disagreeable amount of lobbying and pes-tering which he received from the families of candidates in the course of the selection procedure. Williams was sufficiently concerned to fly out to monitor the selection pro-cedure in 1968.[126] From 1971 Bhutto's government made attempts to take over the

---

[124] Woolner to Williams, 16 Dec. 1964; RTF 3090.

[125] He had a successful career as a scholar and historian, and assisted E. T. Williams in editing the Rhodes Scholar *Register* in 1981.

[126] Green to Williams, 25 Jan. 1968; RTF 3090.

management of the scholarship, the Minister of Education writing that 'all foreign organ-isations are expected to offer scholarships through the government of Pakistan'. Writing through the diplomatic bag Peter Wilson, another member of the Cathedral School staff who had succeeded Green, said that government intervention would open the door to corruption; but he and his family had to be evacuated from Islamabad by the RAF in 1972. He was succeeded by Christopher Lamb of the Church Missionary Society.

The Trustees decided that the 1973 election, for 1974, should be for Pakistan alone. The successful candidate was M. A. Tahir, later to be High Commissioner in London. In the following year it was proposed to offer a scholarship only in Bangladesh. Lamb wrote (bypassing the censor) to say that this would be seen in Pakistan as a provocation and used as a pretext for intervening in the Rhodes selection.[127]

The Trustees cancelled the scholarship and in the event no Rhodes scholar was elected from Bangladesh until 1997. None the less the *Pakistan Times* announced that the schol-arship was to go to Bangladesh in 1975, which caused complaints that the Trust were not treating Pakistan and Bangladesh as two independent sovereign states and led the FCO to protest to the Trustees.

In 1974 Pakistan left the Commonwealth. Williams at first proposed that its scholar-ship be withdrawn. However, he was angered by the decision of Oxford's Congregation to refuse to Prime Minister Bhutto the honorary degree which was proposed for him in 1975, and he persuaded the Trustees to continue the scholarship for 1976, and for every third year thereafter.[128] Oddly, the question does not seem to have been raised whether the Trustees were within their rights in funding a scholarship to a non-Commonwealth country not mentioned in the will. The payment of the German scholarships from the Public Purposes Fund since 1969 (RTR 467) must have been thought a sufficient precedent.

In 1981 Fletcher invited Wasim Sajjad to take over the running of the selection committee in Pakistan, with Mr Khalid continuing as clerk. In 1984 the triennial scholarship was replaced by an annual one, and in 1996 a second annual scholarship was added.

Africa and the New Commonwealth

For the first thirty years of the Trust's existence there were no scholarships in Africa outside Rhodesia and South Africa. In February 1924 Sir Robert Coryndon, a former sec-retary to Cecil Rhodes, asked for a Rhodes scholarship to be given to Kenya, of which he was now Governor. In December he was told by Edward Grigg, then Secretary of the Trust, that the Trustees had refused the request 'on the ground that the size of the edu-cated population was not at present sufficient to justify the grant' (RTM 26 Feb., 16 Dec. 1924). Six months later Coryndon was dead and had been succeeded as Governor of Kenya by Grigg.

---

[127] Lamb to Williams, 9 Feb. 1974; RTF 3090.
[128] RTR 490; Williams to Mrs Rogers, 29 Aug. 1975, 7 Jan. 1976.

During his term as Governor Grigg tried to persuade the Trustees to reverse their decision (RTM 23 July 1929), but in the short term he was unsuccessful. In 1929, however, the Trustees agreed to set up a two-year scholarship of £200 per annum for an East African to study at Rhodes University College at Grahamstown in South Africa, with a view to him being a candidate for a Rhodes scholarship if, at the end of his term, the senate of Rhodes University College found him suitable (RTM 8 Oct. 1929). This scholarship, the Trustees decided, since it was not a Rhodes scholarship comparable to those specified in the original bequest, was not tied by the will's prohibition on racial discrimination; accordingly, they restricted it to candidates of European origin.[129] In 1932, Grigg having returned to England, a committee was set up to elect to a triennial Rhodes scholarship for East Africa (RTM 19 July 1932), and William McEwan, the holder of the scholarship to Grahamstown, was elected as the first scholar, for 1933.[130]

The East African Rhodes scholarship was open to candidates from Kenya, Uganda, and Tanganyika. Elections were made for 1936, 1939, 1942, 1947, and 1950. All those elected were white: in response to a query from the Principal of Makerere in 1939, Allen opined that Ugandan and Zanzibar and Tanganyika 'natives' were not British subjects, and therefore were ineligible.[131] Of the six scholars elected, four returned to make a career in East Africa, one in the Department of Agriculture in Tanganyika, another in the Government Chemist's Department in the same country, one to practise law in Kampala and one to practise law in Nairobi.

After the election for 1950, however, the Trustees decided to suspend the scholarship, on the grounds that too few candidates of the right quality could be found in East Africa, Makerere being the only institution of university standard. At the end of 1951 the Director of Education asked for the scholarship to be restored since there was a very able candidate for 1953. The Trustees refused. They persisted in their refusal in the following spring, in spite of remonstrance from Grigg, now Lord Altrincham. Letters of petition poured in from noble supporters of the candidate. Altrincham wrote emotionally, appealing to the memories of Milner, Jameson, and Kipling, and threatening to write to *The Times*. Elton continued to stand out against renewal, backed by Wheare, but Amery and Peacock began to waver. Meanwhile, the favoured schoolboy, John Silvester, had secured himself a place at Jesus College, and the Principal, Christie, joined the Governor of

---

[129] An application in August 1930 by a black Ugandan, Mukasa, led to a long correspondence with Scott, the Director of Education in Kenya. It was decided that Mukasa was not eligible for the Grahamstown scholarship, but would—if only he were not over age—be eligible for the eventual East African Rhodes scholarship, which was not to be confined to Grahamstown scholars. The Trustees considered making Mukasa an independent grant, but this was pre-empted by his receiving a four-year scholarship to the USA funded by the Principal of Morehead College in Atlanta. (See RTR 257, and Lothian to Scott 13 Mar. 1930; Scott to Lothian, 6 Dec. 1930; RTF 2785.)

[130] McEwen was elected rather late in the year and Warden Allen, who apparently had not been told of the racial requirement on the Grahamstown scholarship, wrote anxiously in April to ask what colour he was. 'It will be by no means easy to place another so late in the year, especially if he is not white' (RTF 2785).

[131] From 1939 on, however, a number of special grants were made to Africans for study and research: Eliud Mathu of Kenya was supported at Balliol, and W. J. Mseleku of Kenya and K. A. Abayomi and W. A. M. Akiyemi of Nigeria were given grants to study or complete courses in the UK; Kofi Busia was given a grant to research Ashanti politics.

Kenya, Sir Evelyn Baring, in bringing pressure to bear on individual Trustees. Finally Elton gave in and recommended an election; the Trustees agreed to revive the scholarship for one last time. After the usual competition, Silvester was elected, the last East African scholar. Having taken his BA and been admitted to the English Bar he returned to the practice of law in Nairobi in 1959.[132]

Lord Altrincham had died in 1955, and there were no more scholarships for East Africa for another thirty years. The Trustees' attention shifted rather to the west coast, where in 1957 Ghana was the first African colony to become independent. In the same year independence was granted to the Federation of Malaya, and soon other colonies were given their freedom. Elton came round to the view that the Trust should make some provision for the rapidly emerging self-governing Commonwealth. 'The civilisation which we are handing on', he told the Trustees (RTR 429, 27), 'may collapse before it has been able to take root.' To prevent the Commonwealth fragmenting, leadership in the new nations, such as Ghana and Malaya, was desparately needed, and Rhodes scholarships provided a method of selecting and training young men with the appropriate qualities.

Elton reached this view after considerable discussion with the Colonial Office. He had at first had some hesitation about proposing a scholarship for Ghana, for fear Oxford might turn the scholar into a communist.[133] But he soon became an enthusiast for expanding the scholarships. In August Christopher Cox of the Colonial Office discussed with Warden Williams a proposal for five scholarships each year for each of five new constituencies: Malaya, Ghana, Nigeria, Ceylon, and the Caribbean area. The Office was willing to raise the extra funds which would be necessary for the new scholarships, possibly from the Ford Foundation. Williams was much less enthusiastic about the scheme than Elton, and stressed that Oxford was already overcrowded and that there was difficulty in placing Rhodes scholars.[134]

Before approaching the Trustees, Elton made enquiries about educational opportunities in the new Commonwealth, and consulted the secretaries of the traditional Rhodes constituencies. Douglas Veale, Oxford's registrar, knew several African universities at first hand; he thought that in Ghana, where there were professional families going back three generations, there would be no difficulty in finding a satisfactory candidate annually; in East Africa, however, Makerere was not likely to produce a scholar more than one year in three, and there would be difficulty in finding a selection committee in Uganda. He told Elton that if the Trust gave scholarships to one newly independent country, it would have to do the same for all of them, with perhaps three for Nigeria, given its size. This was not to the liking of Williams, who wrote, 'In other words, the Government will be choosing our Rhodes Scholarships for us, and not necessarily choosing them wisely; we

---

[132] RTR 2785 contains letters of Lady Eleonor Cole, Lady Eve Balfour, Lord Sempill, Sir Philip Mitchell, as well as those from Altrincham, Amery, Peacock, Baring, and members of the Silvester family.
[133] A former pupil of his in the Colonial Office reassured him. 'I do not think we need worry about Oxford converting the Scholar to communism any more than to any of its other lost causes' (Cockram to Elton, 25 July 1957; RTF 3143).
[134] Williams to Elton, 15 Aug. 1957; RTF 3143.

shall have jumped on to the Government bandwagon in the course of its somewhat Gadarene progress.' Williams was not in favour of scholarships for Ceylon or Malaysia; if there were to be new ones they should go to India and the Caribbean.[135]

With one exception, the secretaries of the old constituencies were in favour of extending the scholarship scheme into the new Commonwealth. But from South Africa Bram Gie telegraphed, 'Unanimous opinion against awards.' He followed it up with a letter arguing that the extension of the scheme would harm the prestige of the scholarships in South Africa, would offend Afrikaners, and would be unfaithful to the intentions of the Founder. There could not be natural friendships, he said, between the new scholars and the old; and it was a mistake to think that Africans who studied in Oxford would go home with an affection for Britain. They would not stand by the mother country in a war, as the scholars from the old dominions had done. Only one scholar in South Africa dissented from Gie's view, R. F. Currey, the headmaster of Grahamstown. Rhodes, he argued, was no narrow imperialist, as the American and German awards proved; he would have been glad to see the development of the scholarship in a multiracial Commonwealth. But the scholarships should not be given on a plate to Nkrumah and Bandaranaike; they should have to ask for them. No one wanted to train up young Mintoff Rhodes scholars.[136]

In the autumn there were lengthy discussions with the Colonial Office. Cox had now dropped the request for twenty-five new scholarships in five countries, and was indeed willing to settle for one triennial scholarship in each country. Elton, however, was ready to fight for annual scholarships. Cox rejected the idea that each new independent territory should necessarily get a scholarship: indeed, the CO placed the highest priority on Nigeria, which was not yet independent. He urged that the East African scholarship should not be allowed to lapse, in spite of problems created by the independence of Uganda. Sierra Leone, Gambia, and Hong Kong were briefly considered for scholarships, but passed over. The constant emphasis of the CO was on 'strengthening the new leadership in those parts of the new Commonwealth where the future was in the balance'.[137]

The proposal that was put to the Trustees at their meeting on the last day of October in 1957 was for one scholarship each for Ceylon, Ghana, Nigeria, the Malayan region, and the Caribbean region, plus a revival of the East African scholarship. Elton and Williams did not disguise their differences. Elton argued that the scholarships should be annual rather than triennial, so as to make it easier to satisfy 'the aspirations of sensitive rival nationalities or religions'. He was optimistic that in spite of local tensions it would be possible to set up in each constituency appropriate committees of selection. The Colonial Office, he said, believed that they could find an extra £10,000 per annum 'from benefactors interested in the various regions concerned'. Williams, on the other hand, stressed the difficulties of placing Rhodes scholars in colleges.

---

[135] Elton, Memorandum of 9 Sept. 1957 (RTF 3143).
[136] Gie to Elton, 26 Oct. 1957; Currey to Elton, 2 Oct. 1957; RTF 3143.
[137] Memoranda by Elton and Cox of meeting on 11 Sept. 1997 and of meeting with Sir John Martin on 28 Sept. 1957 in RTF 3143.

whereas the Governing Bodies of most Colleges are prepared to lean over backwards to admit an African, so that there would probably be little difficulty in obtaining admissions for the five additional scholars, Colleges are accustomed to a certain familiar quota of our scholars, and there would thus be a risk that the new men would squeeze out some of the weaker elections from our present flock, e.g. the Bermudans or Maltese.

Elton's own paper concluded with these words

By its very nature the Rhodes trust has a duty to the Commonwealth; the multiracial Commonwealth, if it establishes itself, may prove to be of incalculable benefit to the world; by providing the five new constituencies which are proposed with a small but steady stream of young men with qualities of leadership and well disposed to Britian we might render invaluable service to the new experiment.

The Trustees' response was cautious. They minuted that while the proposal to establish these scholarships was in itself desirable, they did not wish to accept gifts of money from outside sources in order to make it possible, and they would not be justified at present in spending the sum required from their own resources.

In July Elton returned to the charge with a more modest proposal for triennial rather than annual scholarships. Once more, Williams expressed himself worried about the placement of scholars. 'From the point of view of our public relations with Colleges there could hardly be a less opportune time to tell them that we propose to offer them more scholars.' He suggested that if there were to be triennial scholarships, elections should be staggered so that there was no great influx in any one year.[138]

The Trustees accepted Elton's revised proposal, and took Williams's point about staggering. In November they decided that there should be a 1959 scholarship for Ceylon, a 1960 scholarship for Ghana, and one in 1961 for the Malayan region. The Colonial Office, disappointed at the news that the elections were to be staggered, none the less produced an effusive letter of thanks from the Colonial Secretary. Elton proceeded with the task—sometimes involving complicated issues of diplomatic protocol—of setting up the appropriate selection committes. He consulted high commissioners and governors general and received warm approval from President Nkrumah of Ghana. His main problem, he told Cox, was that the prime ministers of the new countries seemed to think that their governments would have the appontment of the selection committees. The press was well briefed for the official announcement on 1 January 1959, and the *Telegraph* carried a sympathetic leader under the headline 'New Men for the World's Fight.'

The setting up of these Commonwealth scholarships was Elton's last act as Secretary: it was left to his successor, Williams, to welcome the new scholars. Williams had been lukewarm about this scheme from the start, and its operation in its early years did little to allay his misgivings. True, Ceylon had no difficulty in electing, every three years from 1959, scholars who found places in colleges and successfully completed graduate courses. But the committee in Ghana failed to make an election in 1962 and of the two scholars

---

[138] Williams to Elton, 7 July 1958.

it did elect in the 1960s, one obtained a third in PPE and the other was sent home without a degree. After the second election President Nkrumah informed the selection committee that their choices in future should be submitted to his cabinet committee for approval. Williams's response was robust: 'we have managed over the sixty odd years of the RT's history to keep free from governmental influence most deliberately, and I want to make it quite clear that we could not have the selection of our Scholars taken out of the hands of the Trust.' The first Nigerian scholar found life in Oxford very difficult, but overcame the difficulties to obtain a doctorate; his successor, elected after a year in which no suitable candidate could be found, had to leave Oxford to complete his degree elsewhere. From 1961 the Malaysian region sent a series of solid scholars, though there too the committee was unable to make an election in 1965. None of the first three scholars elected in the new Caribbean constituency obtained Oxford degrees, though they went on to distinguished careers with qualifications from elsewhere. By the end of the decade only a dozen scholars had been elected to any of the new Commonwealth scholarships. It was very different from Elton's vision of a generation of Oxford-trained leaders of the multiracial Commonwealth.

In the 1970s elections were held in the British Caribbean and Ceylon for scholars for 1971 and 1974, for Nigeria and Ghana for 1972 and 1975, and for Malaya/Singapore in 1973 and 1976. For the rest of the decade, however, there were no further elections from Nigeria, Ghana, or Sri Lanka, and there were no suggestions of extension to new constituencies while Williams remained Secretary. In the 1980s, however, under his successor Fletcher, the Trustees began to consider further expansion. 'The present financial climate', Fletcher said in 1981, 'cannot permit much enlargement of scholarship numbers, but the Trustees might like to consider whether one of the present triennial scholarships might be tried out on an annual basis' (RTR 514, 22). By June 1982 he felt confident enough of the financial position to suggest that further scholarships might be given to African and Far Eastern countries. The Trustees gave this paper a cautious welcome; some of them were anxious to attract scholars to England from the Middle East as well. The Secretary was instructed to explore the possibilities.

In a report in November Fletcher ruled out Middle Eastern scholarships as excluded by the terms of the 1946 Act. Having taken advice from the British Council he reported that, in Africa, only Nigeria and Kenya looked like providing qualified Rhodes scholars on a regular basis. Rather than add to the existing Rhodes scholarships, a scheme of postdoctoral awards for Third World countries might be created. These might well replace the existing Nigerian, Malayan, and Caribbean scholarships (RTR 518, 27).

The Trustees disliked the proposal for postdoctoral fellowships, and thought colleges would not welcome fellowships restricted to underdeveloped countries (RTM 16 Mar. 1984; RTR 524, 30). It took several meetings, however, before they agreed on an alternative. At the meeting of June 1984 Fletcher expressed the opinion that 'a traditional Rhodes Scholarship programme aiming to make an appreciable impact in third world Africa would require a very large scheme involving a great deal of money'; and even if the funds were available he doubted if it would be possible to make a success of such a scheme in traditional Rhodes scholar terms at Oxford. It might be preferable to fund a large scheme

of a different kind, focusing on professional and technical education elsewhere than in
Oxford; but the Trustees had no obligation to do anything of the kind.

The Secretary sees no logic in the argument that the Trust has a special obligation to African countries other than those particularly associated with Cecil Rhodes, for which ample provision is already
made by the Act. The choice between countries of the commonwealth should, in his opinion, rather
be made on grounds of benefits to the individual award holders of an Oxford education (and, to
some extent, vice-versa) and to the concept of the union of English-speaking peoples, and to
strength of competition. (RTR 524, 29)

On these criteria, Malta, Malaysia, Singapore, and India would have greater claims than
Africa.

At this meeting the Trustees resolved on a substantial increase in the traditional Rhodes
scholarship scheme. It was decided to offer an annual scholarship to Kenya in place of
the old East African scholarship abolished in the 1950s; the last East African scholar, John
Silvester, became the first secretary of the new Kenya selection commitee. The triennial
scholarships for Nigeria, Pakistan, and the British Caribbean were converted into annual
scholarships. The Ghanaian scholarship was not revived. New annual scholarships were
to be offered to Malaysia and Singapore in place of the triennial Malay region scholarship, and a new annual scholarship was offered to Hong Kong.[139]

Fletcher authorized elections in Nigeria, Singapore, Malaysia, and the British
Caribbean for November 1984, and made arrangements in Kenya and Hong Kong for
elections in 1985. Thenceforth scholarships were offered annually in these constituencies
throughout the rest of the 1980s and the 1990s, except in Nigeria where after 1992 it
proved impossible to carry out normal selection procedures. Kenya was given a second
annual scholarship in 1991, and in 1995 a new scholarship was founded in Uganda.[140]

[139] The selection committee in Kenya consisted of an independent chairman, a representative from
the Nairobi office of the British Council, a representative nominated by the Ministry of Education,
and four others, including three women and at least one former Rhodes scholar. Elections in Malaysia
were carried out by the British Council; in Singapore and Hong Kong the arrangements were made
by local universities, with (in the former case) a Rhodes scholar secretary and (in the latter) a Rhodes
scholar chair.
[140] The elections to Rhodes scholarships from the African constituencies are catalogued in A. Kirk-
Greene, 'Doubly Elite: African Rhodes Scholars, 1960-90', *Immigrants and Minorities*, 12/3 (Nov. 1993),
220–36.

9

The Rhodes Trust in the Age of Empire

JOHN DARWIN

The history of the Rhodes Trust, like that of most long-lived institutions, is as much a record of lost visions, forgotten purposes, and failed projects as of purposeful growth towards a planned objective. Today the Rhodes Trust is an educational charity dedicated mainly to funding and administering the Rhodes scholarships which bring students from Commonwealth countries, Europe, and the United States to Oxford University. It supports certain academic activities in Oxford itself, where Rhodes House serves as its headquarters. But for much of its existence from 1902 the Trust was neither so purely academic in its functions nor so single-mindedly focused upon Oxford. The Trustees saw their task as promoting Cecil Rhodes's wider objectives and sustaining the causes they thought close to his heart. Until the 1950s—perhaps later—its leading figures shared a deep faith in the idea of the British Empire as a global community bound together by common loyalties and racial sympathy. They saw themselves as unofficial agents of empire, promoting the imperial interest in spheres where the formal apparatus of government in Whitehall was too clumsy or too parsimonious to intervene. They believed that they stood for a modern and enlightened imperialism, best disseminated through teaching, research, and other forms of 'public education'. They feared the absence, or decline, of a sufficient imperial faith in Britain itself and tried spasmodically to promote it.

In all these endeavours they were part of a wider network of 'imperialists' active in British society and politics. This included the circle around the influential monthly the *Round Table*, founded in 1910 with financial help from the Rhodes Trust and with (later) a significant overlap in personnel; ardent followers of Joseph Chamberlain's great scheme for tariff reform and imperial unity, including Lord Milner (a Trustee until his death in 1925) and Edward Grigg, briefly Secretary in the early 1920s; leading educationalists including Herbert Fisher, a cabinet minister under Lloyd George, Warden of New College, and a Trustee 1925–1940, Montague Rendall, headmaster of Winchester, and Michael Sadler, sometime Master of University College, Oxford; the phalanx of Tory protectionists in the inter-war years; and the legion of ex-colonial and ex-Indian officials, among whom Lord Hailey (a Trustee 1941–64) was pre-eminent. In this stage army of empire, the Trustees and those close to them aspired to be (discreetly and often

I would like to thank Caroline Brown whose close knowledge of the Rhodes Trust Archive was invaluable, and Professor David Torrance for helpful advice about the Trust's finances.

anonymously) a 'ginger group', encouraging a thoughtful and rational imperial-minded-ness, far removed (or so they thought) from the antiquated prejudices behind Winston Churchill's attack on Indian self-government in the 1930s. It was no coincidence that Stanley Baldwin, the target of much Churchillian abuse, and the key parliamentary cham-pion of Indian reform, was a Rhodes Trustee (1925–47).

This is the context in which the pattern of the Trust's activity and expenditure between 1902 and the 1960s must be set. It was not a free-standing educational enterprise but, in many ways, a revealing epiphenomenon of the last phase of British world power. The reach of its influence suggests some of the ways in which politics and academic life—in Oxford and elsewhere—were interpenetrated. In Oxford, the Trust saw itself as a modernizing force, bringing new ideas and institutions to revitalize an introverted classical tradition. Its obligations as manager of the scholarship scheme made it anxious that Oxford should keep pace with the leading universities of the English-speaking world, particularly in America. At the same time it remained deeply conscious of its other duty—exemplified in the scholarships themselves—to promote solidarity especially between the 'white dominions' and Britain. To a marked degree, and perhaps for reasons connected with its own origins, much of that concern was focused upon South Africa, 'the weak link in the imperial chain', and overwhelmingly the most important recipient of the Trust's non-scholarship expenditure. Indeed, the first sixty years of the Trust's existence coincided with what might be called the 'South African moment' in British imperial history: when South Africa produced a class of super-rich 'Randlords', as profligate as the 'nabobs' of eighteenth-century England, when it exerted a major influ-ence on the English literary imagination through writers like Rider Haggard, Kipling, and John Buchan;[1] and when it seemed to exemplify some of the highest hopes of the imperial mission (in the person of Smuts) as well as some of the deepest moral dilem-mas of colonialism. Figuratively and physically (in the architecture of Rhodes Houses) the Trust could almost be seen as a magnificent relic of the lost cause of 'British South Africa', come to rest in the great home of lost causes. By contrast, the American con-nection, so important to the scholarships and a constant, subtle influence on the Trust's activity in Oxford, was understated and largely devolved to an American Organizing Sec-retary after 1920. From all this we can see that the Trust was an important and intrigu-ing institution in its own right; but that it can also serve as a lens through which to peer at the vanished political and academic culture of a Britain that has itself been decolo-nized. In the chapter which follows, the opening sections offer a panoptic view of the Trust's development between 1902 and 1960 and the rest a more detailed account of its activities in South Africa, Oxford, and elsewhere.

'So Much to Do': Rhodes's Unfinished Business

The Rhodes Trust was the product of Cecil Rhodes's vast fortune and fertile imagina-tion. The scale of Rhodes's wealth was legendary though not remotely on the same scale

[1] Bill Schwarz, 'The Romance of the Veld', in A. Bosco and A. May (eds.), *The Round Table, the Empire/Commonwealth and British Foreign Policy* (London, 1997), 65–125.

as the colossal sums distributed by Carnegie, Ford, or Rockefeller. On his death in March 1902, Rhodes left something over £4 million, quickly reduced by debts and death duties to £3.3 million. Much of this came to the Trustees in the form of shares in the De Beers Consolidated Mines Company, the great combine Rhodes had formed with Alfred Beit and others to control the production and sale of diamonds from Kimberley.[2] Though often impatient of detail, Rhodes's great talent in business, as in all his activities, lay in mobilizing the enthusiasm, expertise, and energy of others and driving it towards the goals he conjured up with astonishing facility. He displayed a genius for company promotion, not least in his sharp eye for decorating the boards of his companies with sprigs of the landed aristocracy, then in the throes of agrarian depression. But his seductive vision of a South African eldorado would have had little appeal in Britain had it not been for the frenzied mood of speculation set off by the gold rush on the Witwatersrand after 1886.

Famously, Rhodes combined his business ventures in South Africa with the urge, bordering on megalomania, to use his newfound wealth to promote a worldwide hegemony of 'Anglo-Saxondom'—the ultimate object behind the scholarship scheme that dominated his will. Equally notorious is his passionate belief in an Africa united from Cape to Cairo under the British flag. But Rhodes was not simply a ruthless tycoon with fantastic unrealized dreams of global domination.[3] Nor was he straightforwardly 'imperialist' in outlook—a fact of considerable importance for the later purposes of the Trust. From his early days in Kimberley, Rhodes had grasped that his commercial and political ambitions were inseparable. If the diamond fields and the oligarchy that controlled them were to escape interference and taxation, their interests had to be defended forcefully in the local politics of the Cape Colony. Secondly, as Rhodes saw more clearly than any of his colleagues, if the 'mineral revolution' (based on a diminishing resource of precious stones) was to have lasting effects on the previously stagnant South African economy, the profits it generated had to be ploughed into the development of the Cape and its vast hinterland. That demanded schemes for railways, scientific (and intensive) farming, and, above all, the purchase of the northern interior in Bechuanaland (now Botswana), Zambezia (today's Zimbabwe and Zambia), and beyond for mining and settlement. None of this meant, however, that Rhodes saw himself as the tool of imperial interests in London, let alone of the British government. Still less that he wished to rivet Whitehall's or the City's control more firmly over the whole of Southern Africa.

Rhodes's aim was to create under his control and that of his associates a political and financial octopus strong enough pull the whole subcontinent into a single polity—a 'British South Africa'. Like Canada or the Australian colonies, it would be a self-governing 'white man's country'. It would be British in its forms of government; because its development would suck in a stream of British migrants; and because it would form part of the invisible empire of trade, industry, and finance centred in the Home Islands. From the first, Rhodes was determined (though with only limited success) to channel

---

[2] The authoritative study is C. W. Newbury, *The Diamond Ring* (Oxford, 1989).
[3] The authoritative biography is now Robert Rotberg, *The Founder* (Oxford, 1988).

the profits of De Beers (which he envisaged as a great holding company for sub-imperial development) into these projects. De Beers money did indeed pay for his conquest of Zimbabwe in 1890.[4] He also set out to build an Anglo-Afrikaner political coalition in Cape Colony[5] partly as a vehicle for his influence in the two autonomous Afrikaner republics of the Transvaal and Orange Free State. But there he was blocked by the tenacious cunning of Kruger, the Transvaal President, who used the explosion of gold wealth on the Rand (which Rhodes had failed to capture commercially) to fashion an Afrikaner state more and more resistant to British influence. After the catastrophe of the Jameson Raid in 1896, Rhodes could no longer act openly in South African politics. But his determination to achieve a unified British South Africa remained stronger than ever. Indeed, the outbreak of the Boer War in 1899 made it seem more urgent, and more achievable, than ever before.

It was the scale of Rhodes's vision, the ruthless energy with which he sought to realize it (exemplified in the occupation of Zambezia), and the seemingly limitless resources at his disposal which made him so widely attractive, especially among the gilded circles in Britain for whom a mere colonial politician (let alone businessman) was an object of ignorant contempt. They explain why Rhodes chose some of the Trustees that he did, and why they were willing to serve. Of course, most of them were his old associates, his colleagues in the grand enterprise. Bourchier Hawksley had been the company lawyer for De Beers and Rhodes's principal legal adviser in London. Given Rhodes's propensity for sailing close to the wind, he had been an indispensable navigation officer. Alfred Beit had been his closest business partner, a fellow 'life governor' of De Beers, and a loyal supporter of his political schemes. Wernher Beit, Beit's partnership with Julius Wernher—also a life governor of De Beers—was one of the largest mining houses on the Rand, the financial and industrial powerhouse from which the achievement of 'British South Africa' would have to be directed. Lewis Michell was Rhodes's banker. As general manager of the Standard Bank of South Africa (where Rhodes's account was held) his knowledge and influence were an obvious asset. He was also chairman of De Beers. Leander Starr (soon to be Sir Starr) Jameson had been Rhodes's doctor and boon companion, combining charm, recklessness, and derring-do with a pronounced streak of cynicism and ruthlessness. Jameson had nearly destroyed Rhodes with his disastrous raid. But as administrator of Rhodesia (1891–5) he had organized the conquest of Rhodes's private empire. The outbreak of the Boer War refurbished his laurels as a hero and made him heir apparent to Rhodes's political influence and machine. If anyone was to unite the fractured British communities in South Africa and further Rhodes's political project, it was he. Earl Grey, the scion of a great political family, had been one of Rhodes's aristocratic recruits. A former Liberal MP, he had become a director of Rhodes's chartered company, the British South Africa Company, and Administrator of Rhodesia after Jameson. He was an ardent champion of imperial unity (meaning the 'white' parts of the British Empire) and was appointed Governor General of Canada in 1904.

[4] Newbury, *Diamond Ring*, 150.
[5] See M. Tamarkin, *Cecil Rhodes and the Cape Afrikaners* (London, 1996).

Two Trustees were not drawn from Rhodes's close circle of partners and protégés. Lord Rosebery, the senior Trustee and chairman until his retirement in 1917, was a former Liberal Prime Minister. His trusteeship conferred significant political and social cachet. In the 1890s he had been closely identified with Britain's imperial self-assertion in Africa and his diplomatic efforts to strengthen British influence in Central Africa had made him an ally of Rhodes. Like almost all the Trustees, he was by 1902 a director of the British South Africa Company. The exception was Milner, whose active participation in the Trust's affairs was deferred until his (unexpectedly sudden) return from South Africa in 1905. Milner had had considerable reservations about Rhodes's political and financial clique in South Africa. But as High Commissioner in South Africa from 1897 he had depended on Rhodes's political support in the struggle with Kruger and shared his vision of a united British South Africa. After Rhodes's death, Milner more than any other political figure in Britain identified himself with Rhodes's South African objectives, as well as the grand design—into which the scholarships fitted so well—for a closer union between Britain and what came to be called the 'white dominions'. Though Milner's wider political influence fell under a cloud in Britain after 1905, and he lacked the skills to be an effective parliamentary politician, he was a formidably effective administrator and the focus of a devoted band of imperial-minded acolytes, mostly former members of his South African 'Kindergarten'. Much of the later character of the Rhodes Trust sprang from the fusion of two remarkable camp followings: Rhodes's own with that of Milner.

These were the first Trustees. The legacy they had to administer was complex. There was Rhodes's property in shares and real estate, some of it in unexpected pockets. There was his will with its elaborate schedule of scholarships. There was his political 'estate'—a far-reaching network of friends, associates, admirers, clients, protégés, depend-ants, and debtors. And there was his myth: a seductive amalgam of political prophecy, pedagogic dogma, and cultural symbolism (potently expressed in Rhodes's architectural passions), catalysed by the masculine camaraderie of his inner circle. The Trust long regarded itself as the guardian of his memory and reputation. Rhodes himself was pre-occupied with memorials and monuments—his own and that of the whites who died at Shangani were provided for in his will—and grasped instinctively their power over the imagination.

It was clear that the Trustees' first task was to set up the scholarships without delay. The full story of the Rhodes scholarships is told elsewhere in this volume. Here it is enough to say that they were assumed from the beginning to be the largest single item of expenditure, leaving a 'residue' (in Milner's phrase) of uncertain size for other objects. On a conservative estimate, they might have been expected to consume something over half the income derived from Rhodes's estate.[6] There is nothing to show from their minutes how the Trustees regarded Rhodes's big idea although the generous provision for Rhodesia and South Africa at a time when higher education in the subcontinent was in

---

[6] Rhodes thought they would cost some £60,000. An annual return of 3.5% on his estate as proved would have been approximately £115,000.

its infancy might well have struck them as a logical part of Rhodes's desire to create a progressive ruling elite in his own image. The remaining 'colonial' scholarships extended this to the other colonies of white settlement in order (in Rhodes's words) 'to give breadth to their views for their instruction in life and manners and for instilling . . . the advantage to the Colonies as well as to the United Kingdom of the retention of the unity of the Empire'.[7] An enlightened colonial elite would promote the interdependence between the different parts of a self-governing imperial community. The extension of this formula to the United States was, perhaps, the most surprising part of Rhodes's will, especially since the American scholarships formed over half the total. To Milner, certainly,[8] and perhaps to other Trustees, Rhodes's transatlantic generosity had been a little obtuse, given the pressing needs of the Empire. But Rhodes's belief in the 'unity of the English-speaking peoples' was not eccentric. In the later nineteenth century, a social and cultural rapprochement between the propertied classes on both sides of the Atlantic was well under way, registered in marriage treaties and reflected in literary taste.[9] Diplomatic sympathy followed in its wake. Imperialists as different as Joseph Chamberlain, George Nathaniel Curzon, and Rudyard Kipling married American wives. Americans, especially mining engineers, were familiar in South Africa, and like other colonial leaders, Rhodes could hardly have overlooked the greatest 'white man's country' of all (as the United States was still regarded), nor its model of federal unity. The real daring of Rhodes's plan was his assumption that American students, with their own well-developed academic system, would come willingly to collegiate Oxford, then at the height of its love affair with the classics.

But how else were the Trustees to carry out Rhodes's wishes and carry forward the 'Rhodes-ian' programme? Partly by continuing his practice of subsidizing his political allies and the Progressive Party in Cape Colony. At their first meeting, the Trustees agreed that Jameson should make payments for political purposes 'in continuance and on the same scale as Mr Rhodes'.[10] From South Africa, Milner argued (as well he might) that 'there are certain objects—political—over here which will be seriously imperilled if Rhodes' support is suddenly withdrawn' and urged that Jameson and Michell should have a fund at their discretion. Rhodes himself had made some 'suggestions' in a letter to Grey in 1901. There should be a reserve fund for the scholarships 'as the Diamond Mines cannot last for ever'. There should be help for the most promising scholars setting up in professions. 'If deemed advisable', the Trustees should help to form a parliamentary party who 'without any desire for office will always give their vote to Imperial purposes'. (Here Rhodes was venting the common grievance of settler politicians at the introverted nature of British party politics.) But then Rhodes turned to what had become a favourite theme. 'The most dangerous portion of the Empire being [South] Africa, the steady encouragement of Emigration, especially women, and getting people on the land . . . We shall never be safe in Africa unless we occupy the soil equally with

[7] Clause 16 of Rhodes's will.
[8] Milner to J. A. R. Marriott, 2 Feb. 1915; Milner Papers 469, Bodleian Library.
[9] Mark Twain received a doctorate of letters in Oxford in 1907.   [10] RTM 10 May 1902.

the Dutch.'[11] Jameson reminded the others that he had discussed precisely this topic with Rhodes before his death. He and Michell were promptly authorized to investigate a scheme for female emigration and two months later an initial grant (of £1,000) was made.

In fact, between 1902 and the outbreak of war in 1914, the Trustees' attention was divided between the scholarships and the management of what might be called the Rhodes 'interest' in South Africa. The prominence of South African concerns was not, perhaps, entirely uncontested. Rosebery won agreement in 1904 to a statement of principles recognizing that Rhodes had meant his benefactions to be 'applicable to the Empire at large', and not just South Africa,[12] although Rhodes's 'strong intention and wish' to further British settlement in South Africa was conceded to be the second object of the Trust after the scholarships. The appointment of the Canadian George Parkin as Organizing Secretary for the scholarship scheme, enthusiastically recommended by Grey and Milner, was more than just a tribute to his educational expertise as Principal of Upper Canada College, the premier private school in Ontario. Parkin was an enthusiastic protagonist of imperial federation and a key figure among those in Canada who saw the path to Canadian greatness lying through 'closer union' with the rest of the Empire.[13] Parkin had met Milner in Oxford in the 1870s. He was also a keen proponent of Anglo-American friendship and of America's share in the Anglo-Saxon imperial mission. His influence might have been expected to counteract the South African magnet, for Parkin, as Milner sharply pointed out, took a more relaxed view of what was needed to achieve the Rhodes-ian project there than some of the Trustees.[14] But perhaps his energies were fully consumed by managing the scholarships, especially in the United States where no Trustee had expert knowledge. There is certainly little evidence that the Trust responded with overmuch enthusiasm to wider imperial concerns despite the presence of Rosebery and Milner, and despite the ferocity with which tariff reform and imperial unity were debated politically between 1903 and 1911. Sponsorship of Stephen Leacock's 'imperial missionary work' around the Empire in 1907—Leacock was a Canadian protégé of Grey and Parkin—was not repeated and Leacock himself became something of an embarrassment.[15] There were small payments to the Victoria League to promote imperial-mindedness at home, and to encourage imperial studies at King's College London. But it was South Africa which preoccupied the Trustees and swallowed most of their 'residue'.

Of course, given the source of their income and their feeling about Rhodes's legacy (in its broad sense) it is easy to see why. But this pattern also showed the impress of two powerful personalities. After 1905 the most influential Trustees were Milner, usually in London, and Jameson, usually at the Cape until 1912. As leader of the Cape Progressive

[11] Rhodes to Grey, 25 Aug. 1901; Milner Papers 467.   [12] RTM 10 Sept. 1904.

[13] Carl Berger, *The Sense of Power: Studies in the Ideas of Canadian Imperialism 1867–1914* (Toronto: University of Toronto Press, 1970), 35–6.

[14] Milner to Parkin, 21 June 1912; RTF 2109.

[15] *The Social Criticism of Stephen Leacock*, ed. A. Bowker (Toronto, 1973), pp. xiii–xiv.

Party from 1903, and Cape Prime Minister between 1904 and 1908, Jameson's claims on the Trust were hard to resist. This was widely seen as the critical period when, with the advent of self-rule in the ex-republics and the momentum towards union, the fate of the British connection would be sealed. The Trust had already sanctioned a political fund at its first meeting. After the death of Alfred Beit in 1906 the proceeds of his joint venture with Rhodes, known as the Rhodes-Beit Share Fund, were kept separate from the Trust's main investment and placed under a subcommittee of Milner, Jameson, and Michell. Much of its income was used to meet the election expenses of the Progressives (later renamed 'Unionists')[16] and subvent its leading spokesmen, Percy Fitzpatrick and, after Jameson's retirement, Thomas Smartt.[17] Fitzpatrick's arrangement, much disliked by Michell, brought him the princely allowance of £4,500 per annum. Milner, who had returned from South Africa following the scandal over 'Chinese slavery', immediately became the most regular and authoritative of the London-based Trustees, taking the chair in Rosebery's absence. He was fiercely critical of what he saw as the premature concession of self-government in the Transvaal and Orange Free State before full-scale 'reconstruction'—by which he meant a large in-migration of British settlers and the diffusion of an Anglicized culture—could be completed. For him, as for Jameson and his party henchmen, it was vital, if a revived Afrikanerdom was not to triumph by default, to consolidate the British communities in South Africa and swell their numbers. For him, as for Jameson, the priorities, apart from party subsidies, were land settlement and education.

From 1902 until 1914, the Trustees authorized a steady trickle of grants to hostels (to accommodate arriving migrants) and settlement schemes in the Transvaal, Free State, and Rhodesia. But much their heaviest expense was the large and growing investment in the 'Smartt Syndicate', to which £100,000 had been committed as early as February 1903. Thomas Smartt was an Irish-born doctor turned politician (a common genus in Southern Africa) who had attached himself to Rhodes in the bitter aftermath of the Jameson Raid when the racial gulf between British and Afrikaners had widened sharply. Like many of Rhodes's followers he became a shareholder in De Beers. After Rhodes's death, he served Jameson as his right-hand man in Cape politics. If Jameson had been Rhodes's boon companion, Smartt was Jameson's.[18] The idea behind his syndicate was to irrigate a large tract of semi-arid land and open it for intensive cultivation by new settlers. Smartt's scheme was based at Britstown in the Northern Cape, where, coincidentally, he had first arrived as a medical officer of health, becoming later a substantial landowner with a reputation for progressive sheep-raising.[19] Britstown was not far from De Aar, the main railway junction in Cape Colony, and the main line to Kimberley and the Rand.

[16] Together with Wernher Beit, Consolidated Gold Fields, and others, the Trust was expected to meet party expenses. Lionel Phillips to Julius Wernher, 24 Oct. 1910. *All That Glitters: Selected Correspondence of Lionel Pillips 1890–1924*, ed. A. Jeeves and M. Fraser (Cape Town, 1977), 230.

[17] Otto Beit to Milner, 6 Mar. 1918; Milner Papers 475.

[18] Ian Colvin, *The Life of Jameson* (London, 1922), ii. 313.

[19] L. E. Neame, *Some South African Politicians* (Cape Town, 1929), 87–91. For Smartt's farming reputation, see *Journal of the Agricultural Society of the Cape of Good Hope*, 36/3 (1910) in RTF 1854 (1).

Smartt was not the first (or the last) to dream of the profits (financial and political) to be made from irrigation and intensive farming. At almost the same time, Percy Fitz-patrick launched his 'Sunday's River Settlement' in the Eastern Cape. Rhodes himself had been involved in similar ventures in the Vaal-Harts valley north of Kimberley in the 1880s and 1890s.[20] It was generally assumed in South Africa, far beyond Rhodes's circle, that agriculture, the Cinderella of the colonial economy, would have to be the vehicle of growth when the mines were worked out—an assumption that only began to fade with the second gold boom of the 1930s and 1940s. Agricultural progress seemed to depend above all on substituting close settlement for the casual and inefficient methods of large-scale landowners. Higher productivity and a larger population would justify further investment, especially in railways and roads: the virtuous circle of growth would be set in motion.

But of course it was not just the benefits of economic progress which interested Smartt, Jameson, and Milner. Close rural settlement had a number of advantages. It would serve as a conduit through which British migrants with limited capital could enter South Africa and 'swamp' the Afrikaner population—the only ultimate security in Milner's view against the revival of Krugerite nationalism. In the decade before 1914 when emigration from the British Isles was at record levels (net emigration from the UK in 1900–14 was 2.4 million) only a small share of this vast stream would have been enough to tip the South African balance. A scheme such as Smartt's had a second attraction. Milner, like Rhodes, laid huge emphasis on *rural* settlement (immigration on the land was 'the real point', he insisted[21]). This revealed a suspicion that urban migrants, like those who had rushed to Kimberley or the Rand, were birds of passage who would move on when the mining economy declined. They were volatile and unpatriotic. The landed settler was a fixture. He was also a vital means of penetrating the rural fastnesses of the Afrikaners, a source of intelligence as well as a missionary of progress. The north and north-western Cape, Milner told his successor Selborne, was a tract of 'unbroken Boerdom': it was a Kamchatka of imperial ignorance.[22] For Smartt and Jameson, a bloc of British voters in this heartland of Afrikaner dissidence would be a political dividend to sweeten any commercial profit.

These arguments help to explain why, despite some unease at the sums committed and the methods of the syndicate, the Trust steadily increased its investment. Milner himself had doubts, but he could not prevail over Jameson and Michell (also a periodic sceptic).[23] Nor could Jameson easily disavow his closest comrade in arms in South Africa. In fact, Jameson (who sat on the Smartt board as the Trust's representative) took a bullish view of the scheme's prospects.[24] Smartt himself, warned Michell in 1914, held a written promise of the Trust's support from Hawksley.[25] In any event, close settlement had

[20] K. Shillington, 'Irrigation, Agriculture and the State: The Harts Valley in Historical Perspective', in W. Beinart, P. Delius, and S. Trapido (eds.), *Putting the Plough to the Ground* (Johannesburg, 1986), 311–35.

[21] Milner to Patrick Duncan; Patrick Duncan Papers D 1.28.2, Jagger Library, University of Cape Town.

[22] Milner to Selborne, 14 Apr. 1905; Selborne Papers 12, Bodleian Library.

[23] Milner to Lewis Michell, 24 Aug. 1909; Michell to Milner, 27 Sept. 1909; Milner Papers 468.

[24] Jameson to Hawksley, 13 Apr. 1910; RTF 1854 (1).

[25] Michell to Milner, 9 Sept. 1914; Milner Papers 469.

become a key plank in the platform of the reorganized Unionist Party (formerly the Progressives) after Union in 1910.[26] It was also a highly sensitive issue. To some Unionists like Patrick Duncan (a former official under Milner and later one of the Trust's main South African advisers) the real priority was to secure South Africa as a 'white man's country' by a large influx of Europeans. That meant excluding migrant black labour, and progressively whitening the labour force. But such a policy, with its implications for their wage costs, was intolerable to the mining interests on whose financial backing the party depended.[27] Rural white settlement was a compromise on which all could agree: the acceptable (if not the most plausible) means of reinforcing the imperial connection.

Much smaller sums were granted by the Trust towards education. The main exception (to be discussed later) was the £50,000 promised in 1904 towards the establishment of Rhodes University College at Grahamstown. (Since Jameson had recently moved his parliamentary seat to the city, it was unlikely that this splendid display of patronage in the Eastern Cape lacked his support). Even so, well before 1914, the Trust had embarked upon its long commitment to independent English-speaking schools. The peculiar organization of the Rhodes scholarships in the Cape, confining election to four schools, encouraged perhaps a reciprocal sense of claim and obligation. Michell became the channel for a steady stream of requests, and Jameson their arbiter. But Milner was also acutely conscious of the value of education as a solvent of 'Krugerism' and had insisted upon English as the medium of instruction in the ex-republics. In the early years of the Trust, English-language education seemed safe enough in the hands of the new colonial governments set up after the defeat of the Boers. By 1912, however, the Afrikaner 'Christian National' counter-offensive was well under way. The schools crisis in the Orange Free State, complained Milner, revealed the 'extreme weakness' of the British minority in the province.[28] Now it was a question not of acculturating Afrikaners but of how to safeguard English education where anglophones were outnumbered. Higher school education in South Africa, Milner told another former official, Richard Feetham in 1912, was now the Trust's first priority after the scholarships.[29] But the question (as we shall see) was how the Trust's limited resources could be used to best effect.

Thus despite a somewhat haphazard organization (or perhaps because of it), periodic financial alarms, and some disagreement (notably from Michell[30]) over how far Rhodes's wishes were being honoured, the broad pattern of the Trust's future preoccupations had emerged by 1914. Of course, much of its time and energy was consumed by relatively trivial questions arising from the management of so much far-flung property, the particularities of the scholarships, and the personal guarantees and subventions so characteristic of Rhodes's methods of clientelism. There was little sense of overall direction and

---

[26] A. T. Hennessy to Sir E. Walton, 14 Mar. 1910; Walton Papers MS 17 142, Cory Library, Rhodes University. A copy of the Unionist manifesto of 1912 is in the Charles Crewe Papers, also in the Cory Library.

[27] L. S. Amery to Duncan, 22 Mar. 1910; Duncan Papers D 1.1.1.

[28] Milner to Duncan, 27 July 1912; Duncan Papers D 15.1.43.

[29] Milner to Richard Feetham, 6 Sept. 1912; Milner Papers 468.

[30] Michell to Milner, 26 Sept. 1909; Milner Papers 468.

no evidence from the Trustees' minutes of any real discussion of policy after Rosebery's 'principles' of 1904. To Milner, we may suspect, this was anathema. But Milner, forceful and energetic as he was, could not alter the habits of the Trustees who were as much Rhodes's appointees as he was. The dispersal of the Trustees also militated against central direction. Once Jameson withdrew from South African politics (he retired as leader of the Unionist Party in April 1912 and gave up his parliamentary seat in October) and spent more time in Britain, a more effective management of the Trust's business seemed possible.

It was the war which was the real instigator of change. Indeed, the war years produced something of a crisis in the Trust's affairs. The first and greatest impact was on its finances. Something over a third of the Trust's capital (£3.3 million in 1913) was still vested in De Beers' shares despite the Trustees' efforts to diversify their portfolio into consols and overseas stocks, including a substantial holding in American, Canadian and Argentinian railways. It was slow work getting out of De Beers, complained Milner.[31] But the impact of the war on De Beers was particularly devastating. Production and profits slumped alarmingly in 1915 and 1916 as the diamond trade with Holland and Germany dried up under blockade.[32] The Trust felt the effects immediately. There was only enough revenue to meet the costs of the scholarships and nothing else, Milner told Otto Beit in September 1914;[33] three months earlier, in more cheerful mood, the Trustees had given £1,000 to the Boy Scout movement. By February 1915, Milner was telling a confidant that there were no spare funds, but nothing was being said to avoid a scare.[34] Even the voracious demands of the Smartt Syndicate were checked, and Otto Beit, fearing that the Trust might withdraw altogether, assumed part of its liability for Smartt's capital needs.[35]

Declining revenues were only part of the problem. With the death of Bourchier Hawksley (the second Trustee to die) at the end of 1915, the disadvantage of the Trust's peculiar structure became obvious. In effect, each Trustee was deemed in law to be a co-owner of Rhodes's estate, so that death duties were payable on his notional share. Soon after Hawksley's death, Milner sought legal advice on how to avoid this potentially crippling burden. Neither recommendation—to become a charity under the supervision of the Charity Commissioners, or a public company with a board of directors—was attractive. Already, under the stress of financial uncertainty, some progress had been made towards more regular oversight of the Trust's income—almost certainly at Milner's prompting. In October 1915 it was agreed that receipts and expenditure should be tabled monthly.[36] Milner urged that there should be an annual audit—a very proper recommendation from a former chairman of the Inland Revenue.[37] In April 1916, a finance committee was established comprising Milner, Jameson, and Michell—the real triumvirate in the dwindling

[31] Milner to Marriott, 2 Feb. 1915; Milner Papers 469.
[32] See Newbury, *Diamond Ring*, tables A1 and A2.
[33] Milner to Otto Beit, 9 Sept. 1914; Milner Papers 469.   [34] See n. 31.
[35] Otto Beit to Percy Fitzpatrick, 30 May 1916; Percy Fitzpatrick Papers B/A VI 1068/101, National English Literary Museum, Grahamstown. I am grateful for this reference to Dr Kent Fedorowich.
[36] RTM 4 Oct. 1915.   [37] Milner to Michell, 31 Dec. 1915; Milner Papers 470.

company of extant Trustees. But with Jameson and Michell often abroad, even the mundane task of signing cheques could become ludicrously burdensome. To add to the Trust's difficulties, the delicate question of abolishing the German scholarships (which meant varying Rhodes's will by private Act of Parliament) risked unwelcome scrutiny of the Trust's convoluted (not to say controversial) activities. Reallocating the scholarships threatened to become a serious bone of contention between Michell and the other Trustees.[38]

Behind these wartime shifts and squalls we can glimpse a deeper question: in what form was the Trust to continue? Death, age, and infirmity were reducing the original Trustees. The scale and scope of its commitments had become financially and administratively taxing. One solution was to shed the burdens the Trustees seemed least fitted to discharge. Michell was eager to sell off the Rhodes Fruit Farms, and both he and Jameson favoured handing over Rhodes's two estates in Southern Rhodesia (Zimbabwe) at Matopos and Inyanga to the British South Africa Company administration in Salisbury (now Harare).[39] The transfer was presented as a way of meeting Rhodes's supposed wish that 'the people of the territory' should control both properties as a public domain.[40] But, as Milner admitted to J. G. McDonald, the Trust's Rhodesian agent, 'we have adopted a policy more or less imposed on us by circumstances since . . . a number of Trustees living in this country could not permanently supervise the work in Rhodesia'.[41]

Michell's other suggestion was much more radical. Had he considered, he asked Milner, giving Oxford the money to administer the Rhodes scholarships? 'I cannot feel so sure that our coopted successors—nor any ordinary lay statutory body—could be similarly relied on' to administer them on educational lines.[42] Michell seems to have envisaged the Trust's reverting to an almost passive role, merely managing the investment income to support the scholarships. Perhaps he also assumed that the sub-trust set up in 1907 to manage the Rhodes-Beit Share Fund (and on which he sat with Jameson and Milner) would become all but independent: certainly he believed that only he and Jameson were empowered to make decisions on the Trust's South African assets.[43] Nor was it impossible that the other Trustees would have found a solution along these lines the best way of reconciling Rhodes's wishes with the mounting practical difficulties they faced. By 1916, Grey was ill and inactive. Jameson, whose health was uncertain and who had a major operation in 1916, was immersed in the wartime problems of the two Rhodesias which the chartered company was anxious to amalgamate.[44] Rosebery, whose indolence was legendary, seems to have felt increasingly detached from the Trust's South

[38]   Michell to Milner, 20 Mar. 1916; Milner Papers 470.
[39]   Michell to Milner, 12 Jan. 1916; Milner Papers 470.
[40]   Drummond Chaplin (Administrator of Southern Rhodesia) to Michell, 14 Nov. 1916; RTF 1855 (4).
[41]   Milner to J. G. McDonald, 17 July 1917; RTF 1855 (5).
[42]   Michell to Milner, 7 Dec. 1915; Milner Papers 470.
[43]   Michell to Jameson, 12 Jan. 1917; RTF 1855 (4).
[44]   Jameson had been president of the British South Africa Co. since 1913. For the war period, L. H. Gann, *The History of Southern Rhodesia: Early Days to 1934* (London, 1965), 218–31.

African preoccupations. When he resigned in 1917, he told Milner that he knew very little about South Africa and felt he had been of little use.[45] Rosebery's real concern was with the scholarships, and it was with his strong support that Milner was able to push through what turned out to be the most important organizational change of the war years: the creation of a dedicated Scholarship Trust with its own endowment. 'At last the Scholarship Fund has been constituted,' Gilmour, the Trust's London Secretary, told George Parkin, then in Canada. 'The securities for the necessary amount have been . . . earmarked for that Fund.'[46] At the same meeting of the Trustees, the final decision to transfer the Rhodesian estates had been made. Hyperbolically Gilmour added: 'in future the Trustees will have no connection with South Africa, except of course as holders of South African securities apart from the question of the Scholarships.'[47]

Gilmour was wrong: the Trust did not abandon its South African concerns. Nor did it cede control over the scholarships to a committee of Oxford dons. Instead the holocaust of original Trustees in 1917—Grey and Jameson died; Rosebery and Michell retired—left Milner in full control as the last of Rhodes's appointees. By December 1917, when Jameson died, Milner had been in the war cabinet for a year and directly responsible for Britain's global war effort. But his determination to reconstruct the Trust and use it to promote imperial unity was stronger than ever. In December 1915 he had vehemently rejected Michell's suggestion about the scholarships. He was 'dead against' handing over the scholarships to be run by 'Dons with Donnish ideas'. The Rhodes Trust 'had done invaluable service to Oxford by letting in a fresh stream of influence': no body of dons could have done this.[48] But he conceded that this 'educational work' needed one or two Trustees to look after it. Milner favoured recruiting several new Trustees: '(a) A man—if there is still a man—of what you might call the Rhodes group and even the Rhodes tradition [Milner's choice was Otto Beit] . . . (b) A man of good position who has first rate legal training and regal mind . . .' and '(c) a man of high educational standing.' Milner suggested Herbert Fisher, Montague Burrows, or Michael Sadler, arguing that the 'new universities' were more likely than Oxford to provide a Trustee sympathetic to America and the dominions.[49]

Otto Beit, on whose financial acumen Milner had already come to rely, became a Trustee in 1917. With Grey ill and the impending resignations of Rosebery and Michell, Milner was able to secure the appointment of Lord Lovat. Lovat had helped found the *Round Table*, house journal of the Milnerite Kindergarten and the trumpet of imperial unity. Like Milner, Lovat had played a leading role in the pre-war campaign for conscription. It was to him that Milner revealed his ambitions for the Trust. 'Hitherto', he wrote, 'we have done little besides managing the scholarships at Oxford . . . but in future we shall, as I believe, have the opportunity of much more extended usefulness.'[50]

[45] Rosebery to Milner, 17 May 1917; Milner Papers 471.
[46] T. L. Gilmour to Parkin, 18 July 1917; RTF 666.   [47] Ibid.
[48] Milner to Michell, 31 Dec. 1915; Milner Papers 470.   [49] Ibid.
[50] Milner to Lord Lovat, 6 July 1917; Milner Papers 471.

Previous caution had been necessary because of the heavy dependence on the income from volatile diamond shares. But with the scholarships now protected by an adequate fund of gilt-edged securities, the Trustees would be free to spend a residue of £40,000 or £50,000 a year—a sign of how well the Trust had recovered from the dark days earlier in the war. But 'it was a matter of the greatest importance that the disposition of this large sum should be exclusively in the hands of people who sympathise with the aims of Rhodes' and who had 'a broad imperial spirit'. Thus far, the Trust had supported the Imperial Forestry School in Oxford and agricultural development in South Africa. But after the war, he added portentously, 'we shall be able to do bigger things'.[51]

Milner was the true architect of the modern Rhodes Trust as it functioned up to the 1960s: in his determination to secure the scholarships financially; in his insistence upon the wider imperial outlook Rosebery had urged in 1904; and in his belief that the Trust could use its presence in Oxford to help modernize the university. With the end of the war, he was impatient to leave office and concentrate upon his grand design, the close political and economic integration of Britain and the 'white dominions'.[52] 'I much prefer my independence' he told Otto Beit.[53] But he accepted appointment as Colonial Secretary in Lloyd George's post-war coalition government and was embroiled in the Peace Conference squabbles over colonial war gains. At the end of 1919 he set off for Egypt, which had exploded into nationalist revolt in March, charged with framing a political settlement for a British protectorate whose strategic importance seemed greater than ever. But Egypt was a bed of nails: Milner's proposals were resisted by local nationalists and savaged by cabinet colleagues (like Churchill) who opposed what they saw as a dangerous policy of appeasement. Failure in Egypt, the reversal of his wartime agricultural policy, and minimal progress towards tariff reform and dominion unity made up a bitter ministerial swansong. In early 1921 Milner eventually left office, exhausted, frustrated, but at least happily married.

The toll of these bruising post-war defeats may help to explain why the breezy confidence of Milner's letter to Lovat was only modestly reflected in the Trust's activity under his stewardship up to his unexpected death in 1925. There was no doubt of Milner's ambition. He was determined to give the Trust a suitably vigorous and empire-minded leadership. Parkin, he told Beit, should be pensioned off and his post as Organizing Secretary merged into a general secretaryship. It was important to get 'a thoroughly able man of progressive ideas'.[54] To reinforce the band of Trustees (Kipling had also been elected in 1917), Milner wanted his close political disciple L. S. Amery, 'the best man we could get as a Trustee'; or, since Amery was likely to be too busy (as Milner's deputy at the Colonial Office), Sir Halford Mackinder, 'a progressive educationalist of great ability and sound imperialism'.[55] Mackinder was a major academic figure whose writings commanded wide influence, as well as a politician deeply committed to the Milnerite programme. To replace Parkin, Milner chose Edward Grigg who had had been colonial editor

[51] Milner to Lord Lovat, 6 July 1917; Milner Papers 471.
[52] The best introduction to Milner's ideas is in his *Questions of the Hour*, new end. (London, 1925).
[53] Milner to Otto Beit, 18 Feb. 1919; Milner Papers 472.
[54] Milner to Otto Beit, 11 Jan 1919; Milner Papers 472.   [55] Ibid.

at *The Times* before the war, had served as joint editor of the *Round Table*, and was now military secretary to the Prince of Wales. Choosing him and Amery (who was eventually preferred over Mackinder) hints at the way Milner intended to raise the profile of the Trust and pull it away simultaneously from excessive preoccupation with funding the scholarships and an unwholesome association with the chartered company and the Randlords. The Trust was to be authentically imperial in outlook, no longer parochially South African.

By 1919 there seemed to be adequate means for these imperial ends. 'Our finances are straightened out', chortled Beit, who supervised the Trust's portfolio, 'and we shall be able to dispose of an ample income'.[56] After meeting the cost of the scholarships, the Trust in 1919 had nearly £70,000 to spend,[57] excluding the South African income of the Rhodes-Beit Share Fund. The figure for 1920 was £62,000. The Trust's purse strings were loosened. In 1919 £1,000 was given to the Royal Colonial Institute (the main publicity engine for empire in Britain) and £5,000 to Imperial College in London—for Milner was a firm believer in the imperial value of scientific progress. 'The discoveries of science', he wrote in 1923, 'are tantamount to the opening up of a new continent.'[58] In 1920, he extracted £5,000 for Victoria College in Alexandria, 'as the most important centre of British educational influence in Egypt'.[59] Five hundred pounds was given to the Imperial Forestry Conference. In 1923, a £5,000 grant went towards establishing a college of tropical agriculture (another Milner enthusiasm) in Trinidad[60] and a smaller sum to the Kitchener Memorial College in Khartoum.[61]

These grants were signposts along the Trust's new imperial path. But their comparative modesty suggests that, for all Milner's zeal, it was curiously difficult to find deserving objects of imperialist charity. Sometimes likely beneficiaries were too small, or disorganized, to justify more than a trifling grant. Perhaps a deeper problem was the underdevelopment of the structures, networks, and lobbies that Milner had in mind, or the Trust's difficulty in making contact with those that existed. The Trust itself lacked the apparatus, and ultimately the means, to create an imperial organization of its own. Nor could it have done so without jeopardizing its non-political status and with it the reputation of the scholarships—especially in the United States. It may have been this conundrum that drove Milner and the Trust back to Oxford.

As we have seen, Milner believed that the Trust and its scholarships had already brought a new influence to bear in a deeply conservative university. Milner took an irreverent view of his alma mater, seeing it as a fountainhead of the social and academic orthodoxies against which he had railed for much of his political life. The Trust's support for a chair of forestry had been an early expression of support for an academic cause which would be imperially useful (the Forestry School in Oxford trained scientific personnel for the Indian and other colonial forestry departments). The main endowment the Trust

---

[56] Otto Beit to Milner, 26 Mar. 1919; Milner Papers 472.
[57] Trust Estimates, 31 May 1919. Copy in Milner Papers 472.
[58] 'Notes written in 1923–24' in Milner, *Questions*.   [59] RTM 20 June 1920.
[60] RTM 10 July 1923.   [61] RTM 16 Oct. 1923.

made in Milner's period was towards a chair of Roman Dutch law—the prevailing legal code in South Africa and Southern Rhodesia. More significant, perhaps, were the signs that the Trust was to establish itself physically in Oxford as a bridgehead of Milnerian modernity. In 1919 the first move was made towards buying a portion of the Wadham College garden.[62] The negotiations lapsed. But in 1924, the Trust seemed poised to burst upon the Oxford scene. The idea of a local centre was revived, and the Trustees debated whether to buy a large site in Broad St. not for their own needs but to resell to the University whose mortgage would be subsidized. Here the University could build 'for common purposes', provided that it allowed Herbert Baker, Rhodes's architect and the doyen of imperial architecture, to oversee the design. Grigg was an ardent supporter of this scheme. It would be a 'million pities', he urged Milner (then returning from South Africa), to miss the chance of putting the University for ever in the Trust's debt.[63] This grand project fell through. But Grigg's plan for an archipelago of new buildings (including a 'Rhodes House') to form a central focus for the University, and to reflect an imperial motif, hints at the scale of the Trust's ambitions in Oxford.

Ironically, the years between 1918 and 1925 were marked as much by enlarged commitments in South Africa as by any wider vision of the Trust's aims. For Milner, South Africa remained an obsession, not just because of his acute sense of an unfinished proconsular mission, but because South African participation was vital to the larger project of reorganizing the Empire as a 'Britannic Alliance', a confederacy of 'British' nations. Any complacency about Afrikaner loyalty under Louis Botha (South African premier 1910–19) was dispelled by the backveld rebellion of 1914–15 against involvement in an imperial war, and by the revival of republicanism at the war's end.[64] Through the Rhodes-Beit Share Fund, the Trust continued to support Jameson's old party and its leader Smartt. But the political dilemma of the Unionists was acute. During the war they had not dared oppose Botha openly for fear of provoking *toenadering*, reconciliation with the more extreme nationalists under Hertzog and D. F. Malan. After the war, and Botha's death, the same motive led to a reluctant merger with the South African Party, now led by Smuts. The danger lay in the progressive erosion of 'English' political identity, and the triumph by default of Afrikaner influence over the white 'nation'.

Here was Milner's old struggle in a new guise. Once more South Africa had to be saved for the Empire. As before, the weapons were to be settlement and education: a new stream of British migrants and the systematic reinforcement of secondary and higher education in English. The Trust's own joint venture in land settlement through the Smartt Syndicate had proved a financial albatross ('I have always *hated* that enterprise,' Milner exclaimed in 1916[65]). By 1919 even Otto Beit admitted its failings. 'We shall never see all

[62] RTM 1 Dec. 1919.   [63] Edward Grigg to Milner, 19 Feb. 1925; Milner Papers 473.
[64] See Kent Fedorowich, 'The Weak Link in the Imperial Chain', in Bosco and May (eds.), *Round Table*, 137–58.
[65] Milner to Gilmour, 9 Nov. 1916; RTF 1854 (4).

our money back', he grumbled.[66] Instead the Trust jumped at the suggestion put forward by Charles Crewe, an old political ally of Rhodes and Jameson, that it should help sub-sidize British migrants hoping to take up farming (see above p. 470). But it was aid for schools and universities which took the largest share of the Trust's greatly increased South African spending after 1919. The legacy of Milner's final visit to South African in 1924–5 was an expensive programme of educational support that the remaining Trustees felt honour bound to implement.

But if Milner's period of leadership was marked by an opening out of the Trust's inter-ests and a new conception of its role and influence, it was also the moment when its underlying financial weakness began to be exposed. The Trust's original capital had been £3.3 million. By 1917 it had fallen to £2.7 million. Under Milner it fell to its lowest point of £2.2 million in 1924. Partly this was caused by the onset of a severe depression in 1921. But the effect was magnified by the problem of death duties which struck the Trust with cumulative force. The duty payable on Hawksley, Grey, and Jameson had to be met. Belatedly, Milner had seen the urgency of gathering as much as possible of the Trust's capital into a second charitable fund, eventually set up in 1921 as the Public Purposes Trust.[67] But if the liability for duties 'were to continue unchecked', he warned, 'the result would be the gradual dissolution of the Estate'.[68] By 1924, the Trust had had to find over £360,000 out of its diminishing capital and strict economy had to be ordained.[69] Perhaps it was this more than anything else which dictated that the Trust shelter its wealth in publicly accountable charitable funds: the freedom to deploy it without scrutiny—conceivably for political ends—which Milner had been anxious to preserve proved much too costly.

Milner died at a pregnant moment in the Trust's history, with his projects unfinished and its finances embarrassed. Nevertheless, he had imparted a lasting sense of direction, helped to establish its vital trust funds, and created a strong executive secretaryship. 'He was everything to the Rhodes Trust and I was devoted to him,' wrote Grigg sadly. 'His going represents a breach in the direct relation . . . with Rhodes'.[70] Indeed, Milner's passing marked a real changing of the guard. Within a few months, Grigg himself had gone to be Governor of Kenya, Philip Kerr had replaced him as secretary, and a phalanx of new Trustees arrived to make more clearly than ever 'the end of the direct relation . . . with Rhodes'.

Between Oxford and Empire

If the years between 1917 and 1925 were the Trust's Milner period, then 1925 to 1939 was the age of Philip Kerr. Kerr, who succeeded his cousin as Marquess of Lothian in 1930, was born in 1882. He was a Catholic turned Christian Scientist, and a Liberal in

---

[66] Otto Beit to F. Hirschorn, 5 May 1919; RTF 1854 (5).
[67] Milner to E. Hawksley, ? Feb., 27 Oct. 1921; Milner Papers 472.
[68] Ibid.   [69] RTM 22 Jan. 1924.
[70] Grigg to Abe Bailey, 20 May 1925; Grigg Papers, MS Film 1001, Bodleian Library.

politics. As a very young man, he joined the Milner Kindergarten in South Africa and became editor of the *State*, the periodical through which the Kindergarten tried to promote South African unification. Kerr became a close friend of Lionel Curtis, with whom he visited Canada in 1909 as part of the campaign to make contact with those circles in the 'white dominions' sympathetic to 'closer union' with Britain, but, unlike Curtis, Kerr was unconvinced that imperial federation was politically feasible.[71] From 1910 to 1916 he was editor of the *Round Table*, and established himself as a central figure in the group of Milnerite imperialists. When Lloyd George broke the Asquith regime in December 1916 and formed a new coalition government which included Milner, his followers entered in force. Kerr became Lloyd George's private secretary with responsibility for foreign and imperial affairs, a post he retained until 1921. He was then briefly editor of the *News Chronicle*, a Liberal daily from 1921 to 1922, when the Lloyd George coalition broke up.

Kerr was not an intellectual but he took ideas seriously. Together with Curtis he helped launch the (later Royal) Institute for International Affairs in 1920. He remained a key figure in the 'Moot' as the discussion group organized around the *Round Table* called itself. He was deeply committed to the Milnerite project of building a pan-British community in which the dominions would be self-governing, willing, members and regarded as vital the 'education' of Dominion opinion in the responsibilities of an international role. The success of this enterprise depended heavily upon nurturing outward-looking and 'progressive' ideas abroad, but equally a sympathetic and responsive attitude in Britain towards dominion aspirations. This was a far cry from the kind of imperialism in which power and authority was reserved to a government in London. Indeed, Kerr, like others connected with the *Round Table*, became increasingly convinced that British foreign policy, especially in Europe, had to be adapted to the prejudices of dominion leaders, and to their instinctive dislike for continental commitments that conflicted with Britain's global burden of imperial defence.

Kerr also developed strong opinions about the United States and the future of British rule in India. Unlike many imperialists, he was keenly interested in American history and politics and lectured there (on world politics) on several occasions in the 1920s and 1930s. He was an ardent 'Atlanticist' who believed that close Anglo-American cooperation was the key to international stability and peace. 'The greatest problem that confronts us now', he wrote in 1921, 'is not Europe but our relations with the English-speaking world' . . . the American question is the great question that is looming up before us.'[72] But like the dominions, the United States had to be educated into its responsibilities, with the ultimate aim of a grand reconciliation between it and the other English-speaking nations.[73] This, rather than reliance upon the League of Nations, or the European balance of power, was the proper foundation of British policy, a conviction that led Kerr eventually to

---

[71] Bosco and May (eds.), *Round Table*, p. xiii.

[72] S. Schieren, 'Philip Kerr and Anglo-American Relations after the Great War', in Bosco and May (eds.), *Round Table*, 455.

[73] Philip Kerr to Lionel Curtis, 2 Sept. 1927; Bosco and May (eds.), *Round Table*, p. xxii. For convenience Kerr is referred to throughout this chapter by his family name and not his title of Lord Lothian.

embrace the idea of a 'federal union' between the United States and the countries of the British Empire. On India, which was the most divisive imperial issue in British politics between the wars, Kerr had equally firm opinions. Like his friends Curtis[74] and Geoffrey Dawson (a Rhodes Trustee), both also key figures in the *Round Table* circle, he saw wider self-government for Indians, especially at the provincial level, as irresistible. The survival of British influence in India depended upon building up a powerful group of Indian 'moderates'—politicians who would reject the siren call of Gandhi's anti-Western crusade in favour of a modern parliamentary state tied to Britain by bonds of friendship and mutual dependence. As we will see, Kerr groped for ways of promoting this cause through the resources of the Trust.

Kerr's relationship with the Trustees was quite different from that of his predecessors in the secretaryship. Grigg had been the first to play a more executive role, but his tenure had been brief and Milner's authority had been paramount. Kerr was a figure of wide experience at the highest levels of government (though as an official). He was fluent and self-confident in his opinions. As one of Milner's most successful protégés, he could count on the loyalty of the other Milnerites among the Trustees, Lovat, Amery, and Dawson. Kipling, who disliked him, resigned in disgust at his appointment.[75] As a member of the House of Lords from 1930, a wealthy landowner, and (briefly) a minister, it could be said that he conferred as much prestige on the Trust as it on him. Moreover, with Milner's death, no Trustee enjoyed the status of a 'founding father', and none enjoyed the personal authority that Milner had wielded. The 'new wave' of 1925 diluted the membership and made it (though not on all issues) more receptive to a firm 'steer' from a forceful Secretary. Otto Beit, the senior Trustee until his death in 1930, represented the old 'Rhodes-ian' world: he did not find relations with Kerr easy. Amery, who saw himself as Milner's political heir—'he was like a father to me,' he lamented on Milner's death[76]— was Colonial Secretary in the Baldwin government of 1925–9. He was a passionate believer in 'empire settlement'—peopling the dominions with British migrants—and embarked on an Empire tour in 1927–8 to promote their solidarity with Britain. Like Milner after 1905, Amery found himself in the political wilderness in the 1930s, but he never enjoyed the personal and intellectual prestige that had sustained Milner's influence. Lovat, whose health broke down in 1929, had worked under Amery to promote Empire settlement. Of the new appointees of 1925, Baldwin was almost continuously in high office until 1937. Lord Hailsham, a Conservative Lord Chancellor 1927–9, resigned over the revival of the German scholarships in 1929. Geoffrey Dawson, editor of *The Times* 1912–19 and 1923–41, shared much of Kerr's outlook. Herbert Fisher, the Trust's 'academic' member, was Warden of New College, Oxford, and a former Minister of Education. Edward Peacock, once a schoolmaster under Parkin at Upper Canada College, had become the European representative of a Toronto finance house and then a director of Barings and of the Bank

---

[74] For an excellent study of Curtis's ideas, D. Lavin, *From Empire to International Commonwealth: A Biography of Lionel Curtis* (Oxford, 1995).

[75] Amery's diary, 30 June 1925. *The Leo Amery Diaries 1896–1929*, ed. J. Barnes and D. Nicholson (London, 1980), 415.

[76] Ibid. 411 (13 May 1925).

of England (from 1929 to 1946). He was a key figure in Anglo-Canadian financial relations. Recruited by Milner, he was the Trust's principal investment expert. In 1932, Beit's
place as a Trustee with close South African connections was taken by Sir Reginald Sothern
Holland, a director of the Central Mining and Investment Corporation (into which the
old Wernher Beit partnership had mutated) and a former private secretary to Jameson
in his days as Cape premier. This was not a board touched by Rhodes's personal influence: but of its 'imperial' outlook there was little doubt.

For almost the whole period of Kerr's secretaryship, however, the Trust's main preoccupation was finance. Kerr's first task was to confront the implications of a declining
capital and sharply rising costs. In common with many other investors, the Trust found
that safe pre-war investments, especially railways which had then formed some 40 per
cent of British overseas holdings, fared very badly after 1921. Once the fall of prices and
profits set in, the gradual erosion of the Trust's capital base since 1902 could no longer
be ignored. As we have seen, the most painful symptom of financial difficulty was the
huge burden of death duties. But there were other pressures on the balance sheet. Wartime
inflation meant that the cost of the scholarships was driven up: the Trustees had to raise
the stipend because, most obviously in the case of the American scholarships, they had
to compete in an academic 'market'. Indeed, for much of the inter-war period, fear that
the funds put aside in 1917 would be insufficient to maintain the scholarship programme
was the magnetic pole of the Trust's financial strategy. The other great load on the
Trustees' back was the undertaking, to which they were already committed before Kerr's
arrival, to build Rhodes House.

Kerr sounded the alarm immediately. In his budget memorandum of 11 December
1925,[77] he warned the Trustees of a steadily falling investment income. The Trust had
drawn down its capital by £100,000 to build Rhodes House. At the same time, the cost
of the scholarships, which had been some £56,000 in 1913, was expected to reach almost
£100,000 a year by 1930. 'I do not think it is open to dispute', Kerr remarked a little sen-
tentiously, 'that the primary function of the Rhodes Trust today is to maintain at a
maximum efficiency the scholarship system associated with Mr Rhodes' name.' But if
the Trust did not increase its income to meet the scholarships' rising cost, the number
of scholarships would gradually fall. The circle could only be squared (since a more speculative investment policy was too risky) by cutting back on the spending Milner had initiated, particularly in South Africa.[78] A month later, Kerr rubbed in the implications.
With a surplus over scholarship expenditure of only £20,000, the Trustees would have
to be careful not to make any long-term commitments, in case scholarship costs rose
unexpectedly. And the Trustees, Kerr suggested, should follow a careful set of priorities.
First, expenditure in Oxford to maintain 'its pre-eminence as a world university'. Second,
help towards education in South Africa where 'the Trustees have a continuing obligation'.
Third 'general imperial purposes', including emigration to South Africa and supporting
imperial organizations at home. Lastly, personal grants 'arising out of the Scholarship
System and Mr Rhodes' Will'.

[77] RTF 2709.   [78] Ibid.

By the middle of 1928, Kerr believed that the storm had been weathered. 'The financial position of the Trust is . . . thoroughly sound', he pronounced.[79] With Rhodes House almost complete and a capital reserve fund in place, the outlook was more settled. Kerr now urged, reversing his previous priority, more generous spending in South Africa. Otherwise there might be criticism from there at the high cost of building Rhodes House. 'I think it is very important', he went on, in a tone which suggested a major discovery, 'that the connection of the Rhodes Trust with South Africa should not be broken. Mr Rhodes derived his fortune from South Africa. He was tremendously interested in the development of South Africa.'[80] The Trustees duly laid down that after the completion of Rhodes House, education in South Africa would have priority.[81] But within a year, the Trust was back on the rollercoaster. Investments were lost or had to be written down. There were sharp disagreements over whether to invest in safe but low-yielding gilts (favoured by Peacock and Sothern Holland) or land and equities.[82] And what was left of the Trust's help towards South African schools, Kerr told Sir Charles Crewe, could only be loans drawn on a small capital fund.[83]

From this low point, there was a steady recovery up to the end of Kerr's secretaryship. By 1935, Kerr was forecasting that both revenue and capital would be strong by 1939. The Trust would have between £10,000 and £15,000 to spend after meeting the scholarships. He recommended more help for South African schools.[84] The Scholarship Fund was adequate and the Scholarship Capital Reserve Fund was accruing rapidly.[85] But all this was relative. The Trust never recovered in the inter-war years the mood of ambition Milner had expressed. Even in 1939, its capital remained substantially lower (at £2.5 million) than its original endowment. And its 'free' income was hardly a fifth of what Milner had hoped to spend on the Trust's imperial mission.

Financial stress had forced the Trust to think seriously about its commitments in South Africa. But there was never any question of their importance. With Otto Beit, Lovat, Amery, Dawson, and later Sothern Holland as Trustees, preserving the imperial connection there was the essence of the Trust's being. Beit was deeply committed to the old leaders of the Unionist Party, now allied with Smuts. Amery, who had visited South Africa during his Empire tour in 1927, when the controversy over a new national flag was at its height, was as anxious as Milner had been to slay the serpent of Afrikaner republicanism which would take South Africa out of the Empire. Hence, perhaps, Kerr's emphatic restatement of the Trust's loyalty to the Founder's aims in 1928. It was more a question of the form that the Trust's help should take, and on that there was a sharp disagreement between Kerr and the senior Trustee, Otto Beit.

As part of his financial reconstruction, Kerr was determined to bring the Rhodes–Beit Share Fund fully under the Trust's control, not least because its legal and tax status as a 'sub-trust' was at best obscure.[86] Beit, who had run the fund since Milner's death, was anxious to regularize the position, but not if that meant giving up the Fund's

[79] Report 241, 6 July 1928; RTF 2709.   [80] Ibid.   [81] RTM 10 July 1928.
[82] RTM 3 Mar., 19 July, and 26 Sept. 1932.   [83] Kerr to Crewe, 5 Apr. 1933; RTF 2662 (2).
[84] Report 295, 14 June 1935; RTF 2709.   [85] RTM 22 June 1937.
[86] The fund's murky origins are set out in a memorandum of 24 Nov. 1925, RTF 2773 (1).

long-standing subsidy to the South African Party into which the Unionists had moved.[87] 'I am concerned', he told Kerr, 'with the purposes for which the fund was primarily established and which I gather are such as the Rhodes Trust would clearly under no circumstances desire to carry out.'[88] Kerr's views were clear. The year before he had set out the Trust's mission in South Africa. 'The future of Africa depends . . . on the character of education to be given to the younger generation. That generation is . . . being handicapped by the excessive zeal for bi-lingualism [and] the British element . . . has . . . failed to produce its share of political leadership.' The solution lay in 'judicious' help to independent schools run 'on the best British models'.[89] Through a highly educated anglophone elite, exerting its influence over white society, lay the best chance of holding South Africa to the Empire. But the Trust should not be seen to be using its money 'for ordinary political purposes': there were 'other and better ways . . . far more likely to promote the Testator's ultimate purposes of imperial and English-speaking unity'.[90]

Kerr's position was probably that of most of the Trustees. But Beit was obstinate. Milner would have supported his position, not Kerr's, he argued. If no help from outside reached the party 'whom we support . . . they could put up no fight'.[91] There was already a commitment of £3,000 a year for ten years 'in support of a political party'.[92] The outcome was a compromise. Part of the fund was handed over, but the bulk was to remain under discreet local management in South Africa until 1939 when it was to revert to the Trust. Nevertheless, if the Trustees were now anxious to disclaim any interference in South African politics, they were more than ever committed to Smuts as the *deus ex machina* of Anglo-Afrikaner unity. They continued, as might have been expected of a body that included Amery and Lovat, to subvent the cause of British emigration and rural settlement through the '1820 Memorial Settlers' Association'. So far as the black majority was concerned, their subaltern status for an indefinite time was taken, quite simply, for granted.

The wrangle between Otto Beit and Kerr had owed some of its vehemence to Kerr's efforts to find extra money for Rhodes House in 1929. Although (as he was quick to remind a sceptical Geoffrey Dawson) the decision to build Rhodes House had been taken before he had become Secretary, Kerr was an enthusiast for it. Grigg had warned him against allowing Rhodes House to be seen as a Trojan horse of imperialism in the University, or as a rival for the collegial affections of the scholars.[93] But Kerr envisaged something more than a set of useful public rooms or an out-station for the Bodleian Library. His grim warning to the Trustees in 1926 about the need to cut their South African commitments laid down a new priority for the Trust. 'The whole efficacy of the Rhodes Scholarship system', he claimed, 'depends upon the University of Oxford retaining its special eminence among the universities of the world and its capacity to draw to itself the best of the rising generation in the Dominions and the United States.' The Trust should spend

---

[87] Otto Beit to Kerr, 10 Mar. 1929; RTF 2773 (1).
[88] Otto Beit to Kerr, 2 May 1929; RTF 2773 (1).
[89] Report 241, 6 July 1928; RTF 2709.   [90] Kerr to Otto Beit, 30 May 1929; RTF 2773 (1).
[91] Otto Beit to Kerr, 1 June 1929; RTF 2773 (1).   [92] ? to Kerr, 12 June ?1930; RTF 2773 (1).
[93] Grigg to Kerr, 28 Aug. 1925; RTF 2637 (1).

a 'considerable proportion' of its resources helping the University to 'maintain its position' and Rhodes House should be organized with this objective.[94] The risk was, said
Kerr, perhaps unconsciously echoing Milner, that Oxford 'will fail to adapt itself continuously to the progress and development of the new world'. Kerr was eager to see
Rhodes House as a home for teaching and research in politics and economics or for an
institute that would study the political and economic problems of the Empire, believing, perhaps, that this would attract the increasing proportion of Rhodes scholars wanting
to pursue a higher degree. But it was the scheme to make Rhodes House a centre for the
study of Africa, floated by the Trustees' favourite statesman, Jan Smuts, and warmly
endorsed by Amery, which was the closet the Trust came to a direct intervention in
Oxford's structure and curriculum.

Without a grant from the Rockefeller Foundation (an ironic confirmation of Kerr's
theory of Anglo-American interdependence), and with the Trust's finances lurching once
more towards a crisis, the project for a centre fizzled out and the Trustees' Oxford ambitions became much more modest. But Kerr's warning about Oxford's international reputation had sunk in and the Trust responded generously in 1936 to the University's request
for research money—though it wanted it used for subjects of broadly imperial relevance.
In other smaller ways, the Trustees sponsored projects 'for general imperial purposes'
(Kerr's category), including Lord Hailey's *African Survey*, a library of imperial history at
the new Institute of Historical Research in London, and hostel accommodation for
dominion and other overseas students at London University.[95] But for all Kerr's energy
and zest, the fourteen years of his secretaryship were marked less by new beginnings or
the triumphant realization of Milner's plans than by the sometimes painful struggle to
sustain the commitments made in the most buoyant phase of the Trust's history before
1925. The Trustees had neither given up the larger imperial aspirations to which their
most forceful members were wedded nor found ways of expressing them. Like many colonial regimes in the inter-war years, they found themselves not building but caretaking.
Indeed, in retrospect, Kerr's period might be seen as marking a gradual sea-change when
the financial burden of the Rhodes scholarships, and the physical possession of Rhodes
House, began, insidiously, to narrow the Trustees' conception of their role and obligations. Oxford, rather than empire, grew, almost imperceptibly, into the prime object of
their loyalty. But before this gradual introversion could proceed very far, the Trust,
Oxford, and empire were thrown into a new age of uncertainty.

In the autumn of 1939, Kerr resigned the secretaryship to become Ambassador in Washington, to practise at a critical time twenty years of theory about Anglo-American relations.[96] His successor was another peer, Lord Elton (1892–1973), who held the office until
1959. Elton's appointment marked a break with the Milnerite tradition of Parkin, Grigg,

[94] Memorandum by Secretary, 'Rhodes House and General Financial Policy', 30 Apr. 1926; RTF
2637 (2).
[95] RTM 18 June 1935.
[96] See David Reynolds, 'Lothian, Roosevelt and Churchill and the Origins of Lend-Lease', in J. Turner
(ed.), *The Larger Idea: Lord Lothian and the Problem of National Sovereignty* (London, 1988).

and Kerr. Unlike his two predecessors and a number of the Trustees, Elton was not connected with the *Round Table* or the 'Moot'. From a landed family, he had served as a
young officer in the First World War, and had been a prisoner of war in Turkey after the
infamous surrender of Kut in 1916. In 1919, he became a fellow of Queen's, Oxford, and
taught history there for twenty years. He was an unsuccessful Labour candidate in 1927
and 1929, but his real loyalty seems to have been towards Ramsay MacDonald (whose
biographer he became), and he was expelled from the party as a supporter of MacDonald's national government in 1931. Elton was made a peer in 1934. He was interested in
broadcasting, and was an active broadcaster. His appointment as General Secretary may
have owed something to the fact that he was professionally knowledgeable about higher
education, and Oxford, as well as enjoying a wider network of contacts in public life. He
was an enthusiastic Anglican, eager to reclaim young people for religion. By the time he
became the Trust's General Secretary, his view of empire was indistinguishable from the
'progressive imperialism' of Kerr or Lionel Curtis and his popular history *Imperial Commonwealth*, published in 1945, offered a celebration of the British Empire as the bringer
of freedom and civilization. Elton had one other qualification: he was the friend and
former tutor of Malcolm MacDonald, Ramsay's son, who had spent most of the 1930s
at the Dominions Office, dealing with the 'white dominions', and had been Colonial
Secretary since 1938.

For most of Elton's period of office Leo Amery remained chairman of the Trustees
until his death in 1955. Amery was Secretary of State for India 1940–5. Herbert Fisher
(1940) and Dawson (1944) died during the war and Baldwin (1947) and Sothern Holland
(1948) soon after. Two local Oxford stopgaps (both from Christ Church) were appointed
in 1940. But the most significant addition to the Trustees was the selection of Lord Hailey
in 1941. Hailey had already enjoyed a gilded career as an Indian administrator.[97] He had
been Governor successively of both the United Provinces and the Punjab (a rare if not
unique distinction). He was the indispensable expert on whom viceroys and the British
government leant heavily throughout the tortuous process of constitutional reform for
India between 1930 and 1935. He was closely identified with the view that the extension
of Indian political participation and the attainment of self-government as a dominion
was compatible with India's loyalty to a British 'empire-commonwealth'. He became a
member of the 'Moot' from 1936 and the senior proconsul-statesman of the *Round Table*
outlook. In the later 1930s, he embarked upon an astonishing second career as director
of the demi-official *African Survey*, a vast compendium of administrative, ethnographic,
and scientific information which became, on its publication in 1938, the bible of British
colonial policy in Africa but one (like the original) whose advice was often treated as
useful rather than mandatory. The *Survey* established Hailey as the leading expert on
colonial governance in tropical Africa. During the Second World War he became the
main official exponent of African political advance, and was deployed publicly as the
acceptable face of British imperialism in which empire was partnership and colonial rule
a lesson in freedom. As we shall see, Hailey's election as a Trustee reflected the Trust's

---

[97] J. Cell *Hailey: A Study in British Imperialism 1872–1969* (Cambridge, 1992).

wartime rediscovery of its imperial mission in Oxford. After the war, the importance he and others attached to bridging the chasm between the 'white man's countries' and the 'black man's countries' of British Commonwealth Africa helped to prolong the Trust's sense of its old imperial task in South Africa.

In the early part of the war, and while fear of invasion remained acute, there was little for the Trust to do except arrange for the suspension of the scholarships and the wartime use of Rhodes House as a hospitality centre in Oxford. But after the middle of 1941, when Hitler's attack on Russia offered a psychological breathing space, there were signs that the old project for making Rhodes House an imperial 'think-tank' had taken on new life. Elton urged on the Trustees an ambitious scheme to make Rhodes House 'a real cultural centre for the Empire'.[98] It should be the home of 'planned research' into imperial problems, offering perhaps half a dozen research grants a year. With the encouragement of Vincent Harlow, an imperial historian from London and the Rhodes House Library adviser, and of Carleton Allen (Warden and Oxford Secretary since 1931), Elton clung to this vision of Rhodes House as an imperial 'laboratory' at the centre of the new concern with colonial research that the war had triggered. By early 1945, his ideas had become not just imperial but global. The partnership of the United States and the British Empire, a mere dream in Kerr's day, seemed likely to be the main factor in post-war world politics, and Rhodes House, with its American and imperial library, an obvious focus for its study. The stumbling-block, as before, was to be money.

Elton's other main preoccupation during the war was with the education of domestic opinion. Like many imperialists, not least Lord Milner, he was infuriated by the apathy and ignorance displayed by the British at home towards the empire they had inherited and the obtuseness with which its grand possibilities had been overlooked. And like many imperialists, he was alarmed that the populist mood of social reform at home (signalled by the hugely enthusiastic reception of the Beveridge Report in 1942) would combine with the democratic rhetoric made necessary by partnership with the Soviet Union and the United States to destroy the ideological credibility of empire. With comparatively modest resources, Elton used the Trust to help counter this new menace. He urged on a receptive Minister of Education the importance of imperial history.[99] With Harlow, he promoted the publication of booklets and pamphlets in which a sanitized version of British rule in different parts of the world was offered to a mass readership, especially in the armed forces. He secured a subsidy from the Trust to distribute books on the Empire through the social centres of the Young Men's (and Women's) Christian Associations. Money was given to the Imperial Institute for films and lectures that met the popular hunger in the war for serious entertainment.

This genteel imperial propaganda seems to have largely ended with the war. Harlow, Elton's main ally, returned to full-time academic life. Elton himself was disillusioned by the timidity shown by the YWCA on imperial questions.[100] Many well-intentioned

---

[98] Memorandum by Lord Elton, 7 Oct. 1941; RTF 2637 (15).
[99] Elton to R. A. Butler, 16 May 1942; RTF 2676 (1).
[100] Report 367, 16 June 1945; RTF 3012 (3).

people wanted to help the Empire, Harlow remarked, but their ideas were 'vague'.[101] The grants to the Imperial Institute ended in 1947. Perhaps the underlying factor was money. In April 1945, Elton had warned Harlow that their plans for Rhodes House would be blocked by the post-war increase in the cost of the scholarships. Certainly, by 1947, although the Trust's capital at some £3.6 million had increased considerably over the 1939 figure of £2.5 million, prices had almost doubled. The scholars' stipend rose to £500 in 1946, £600 in 1954, and £750 in 1958. The Trust's financial policy after 1945 was marked by a steady transfer of surpluses from the Public Purposes Trust to the Scholarship Capital Reserve Fund. Looking back from the late 1950s, Elton commented that in recent years the Trust had limited its (non-scholarship) grants to around £6,000 a year. 'We are not in the position', he remarked philosophically, 'to go out . . . to look for our beneficiaries, and impose a clear-cut prefabricated pattern of our own on all our grants'.[102] In its own microcosmic way, the Trust found that maintaining an empire was an expensive business.

Yet the post-war years also saw a striking reassertion of the Trust's duty to sustain 'English' education in South Africa laid down by Milner in 1925. The old suspicions of Afrikaner nationalism, dormant since the era of cooperation between Hertzog and Smuts in the 1930s, revived strongly with the political revolution of 1948 when, for the first time, an Afrikaner nationalist government was in power, unconstrained by partnership with 'English' politicians. From 1945 until the later 1950s, most of what little the Trust spent outside the scholarships went towards helping independent English-language schools in South Africa and Rhodes University, though much of this came from a remarkable local windfall (see below, p. 501). Both Elton and Hailey were deeply committed to what they saw as the struggle to preserved an enlightened British influence in a darkening landscape.[103] The Trust continued to support British immigration through the '1820 Memorial Settlers' Association'. Its concern for reconciling white and black aspirations in a (vaguely conceived) form of partnership—a key part of British imperial thinking throughout the 1950s—was reflected in a substantial loan to a (white-owned) publishing house directed at an African audience.

By the later 1950s, however, the Trust's commitment, like the British tradition in South African politics, was near its last gasp. Amery was the last chairman to embody a direct association with Rhodes and Milner. None of the three new Trustees appointed in 1957 had a particular connection with South Africa. When South Africa left the Commonwealth in 1961, the legal status of charitable spending there became invalid under the terms of the Rhodes Estate Acts (by which it was confined to Commonwealth countries and the United States). Even before this formal break, the Trust had begun to direct increasing sums to causes on its doorstep. The difference was that, far from seeking like Milner or Kerr to refashion the University, or assert a distinctive role for Rhodes House, the Trust contributed to college endowments, beginning with Oriel in 1956, and, in a gesture of exquisite symbolism, gave £50,000 (and ultimately £100,000) to the Oxford

---

[101] Harlow to Elton, 30 Jan. 1946; RTF 3012 (3).
[102] Elton to Nye 23 July 1958; RTF 3150.   [103] Elton to Koch, 8 Dec. 1953; RTF 2662 (13).

Historic Buildings Appeal the following year.[104] The pattern for the 1960s and 1970s had been set. The Empire disappeared. The Commonwealth, as a political idea, withered. South Africa (except for the increasingly divisive issue of its scholarships) ceased to be part of the Trust's charitable remit. But the needs of Oxford, in an era of rapid university expansion, pressed more and more on the Trustees, limited only by the demands of the scholarships. Not until the 1990s, with the political transition in South Africa, and its re-entry into the Commonwealth—itself undergoing a modest rehabilitation—did this trend become less pronounced. Once again, though in very different circumstances, the Trustees felt the ghostly touch of the 'Founder', and the duty, reiterated by successive secretaries, 'to concentrate a considerable proportion of our grants in South Africa . . . because this was the Founder's country, and the country from which his fortune was derived'.[105]

The Trust in South Africa

It was an irony that Rhodes might not have relished that control over his legacy had been fully repatriated to Britain by 1939 and by the 1950s was exercised by Trustees whose personal connection with South Africa was slight. Rhodes's own method of operation had been to mobilize resources and influence in Britain for his South African activities but to keep their management firmly in local hands—mainly his own. So far as his estate was concerned, the choice of Trustees suggests a similar conception. Only Rosebery, and belatedly Milner, were unequivocally based in Britain. Grey was an ex-Administrator of Rhodesia; Hawksley the chartered company's legal technician. Beit, Jameson, and Michell were 'South African' in their outlook, interests, and priorities. We might even speculate that Rhodes's motive in choosing Rosebery and Milner was to guard his grandiose scholarship scheme against the indifference or neglect of his South Africa-based Trustees, who were likely to be most active in managing the Trust's resources.

In any event, the early deaths of Beit and Jameson and the retirement of Michell had shifted the balance decisively by the 1920s. Sothern Holland was the only South African-born Trustee (though resident by this time in Britain). The proposal to elect a South African Trustee in 1955 was rejected. Nevertheless, as we have seen, the bulk of the Trust's spending, apart from the scholarships and on Rhodes House, was directed to South Africa. Part of the explanation lay in the loyalty of the early Trustees to what was known of Rhodes's wishes. Part lay in the powerful reinforcement brought by Milner, whose posthumous report on South African schools in 1925 had almost the force of a codicil. But it is unlikely that the Trust's activities would have been as extensive or as lasting had it not been for the local South African network through whom its funds were distributed.

At Rhodes's death, his 'empire' seemed to be the dominant interest in Southern Africa. His vast holding in De Beers was a fountain of wealth. His interests on the Rand were

---

[104] RTM 21 July 1956, 27 July 1957.   [105] As n. 102.

represented in the Consolidated Gold Fields Company and through an alliance with Wernher Beit—the 'Corner House', with which Percy Fitzpatrick and Lionel Philips (the leaders of British opinion in Johannesburg) were associated. A huge proportion of the business and professional elite in South Africa were British migrants, and many of its leading figures were part of the extended network of Rhodes's clients and partners. North of the Limpopo lay Rhodes' 'real' empire, the enormous expanse of Rhodesia, extending over modern Zambia and Zimbabwe and administered by his British South Africa Company, of which all the first Trustees except Milner were directors. Finally, in Cape Colony Rhodes bequeathed a political machine, the Progressive Party, funded by his Kimberley wealth and led after 1902 by his political heir, Jameson. The Progressive Party was the vehicle of loyalist sentiment during and after the Boer War, and formed the Cape government between 1904 and 1908. With South African unification, the Cape Progressives and their Transvaal allies seemed likely to command the 'British' vote and exert a large, if not decisive, influence in South African politics.

In this scenario, the Trust would have been part of a larger 'Rhodes-ian' jigsaw. It would have promoted Rhodes's dream of imperial and English-speaking unity through the scholarships. The rest of its income would have been available to support the projects of Rhodes's legatees in South Africa—the blend of business and politics aptly represented by the Smartt Syndicate. The Trust would have been the imperial jewel in a South African crown, injecting back into the mother country the ideals and some of the resources of a great colonial. But if this had been Rhodes's aspiration, by the 1920s almost nothing had gone to plan. The company had been forced to abandon his private empire in the Rhodesias, and the white settlers there elected to stay out of South Africa. The Progressives were too identified with mine-owning interests to unify the British vote and were forced with Union in 1910 to acknowledge the primacy of the Afrikaner 'generaals' Botha and Smuts. Worse still, the anxieties of wartime politics drove the leading Unionists (as they had become) to recognize that they were a permanent minority in the white 'nation' whose main hope of preserving their British links and identity lay in an accommodation with those Afrikaners who rejected secession from the Empire as a step back into introverted Krugerism.

This was the defensive mood of Rhodes's heirs in South Africa at the end of the First World War as the Trust's modern form took shape. Although Milner and Amery were determined to bolster the imperial connection in South Africa, in practice the Trust's intervention was largely shaped by the action of its local allies and associates there. By the early 1920s, direct political subsidy of the 'British' party along pre-war lines had lost much of its point with the decision of the Unionist leaders to throw in their lot with Smuts's South Africa Party. Smuts himself had made the dramatic transition from Boer leader to imperial statesman since 1917 (when he had been in the imperial war cabinet). To Milner and Amery it was he rather than any 'English' politician in South Africa who was the white hope of the imperial bond. Nevertheless, within the smaller world of the English community, the old Unionist leadership exerted considerable influence and patronage. They were anxious to maintain English solidarity and (tactfully) imperial loyalty. It was natural that they should try to exploit their connections with the Trust to reinforce the social and cultural defences of an embattled 'British South Africa'.

The extent to which the Trust could be manipulated by the 'men on the spot' in South Africa has already been seen in its pre-war commitments to the Smartt Syndicate. Even after the war, despite the growing doubts about its commercial viability, the Trust continued to invest to the point where some 10 per cent of its diminishing capital was sunk (in several senses of the word) into Smartt's network of dams and ditches in the northern Karoo. The short-lived boom of 1919–20 may have strengthened the Trustees' nerve. But the real explanation for their financial boldness lay in the extent to which they (especially Otto Beit, their South African business expert) were committed personally and politically to Sir Thomas Smartt as the leader of 'British South Africa' and thus, through Jameson, the political legatee of Rhodes. After 1920, the year of the Unionists' fusion with Smuts' South African Party, Smartt as leader of the English section became Minister of Agriculture. If anything, his leverage over the Trust increased. At Otto Beit's prompting, he deftly exploited Milner's and Amery's obsession with post-war British emigration to South Africa. A plan was drawn up to place 200 settlers on the syndicate's property.[106] 'We are all impressed with the necessity of closer settlement,' Smartt told Otto Beit, 'only settlers will save the Country as Nationalist feeling is intense and can only effectively be countered by new blood'.[107] With this persuasive argument from so well placed an ally, Beit easily obtained the approval of Milner and Amery for a further substantial investment.[108]

The syndicate's venture in close settlement was a disaster. Those who came complained bitterly that water charges were too high, their plots too small, and commercial outlets too narrow to make farming viable.[109] Amid recriminations, most left. When Philip Kerr visited in 1926–7, he found less than ten settlers and little evidence that the syndicate would ever be profitable. But Smartt could not be abandoned, as much for political as for financial reasons. All that could be done was to wait until he had left the scene and then try to sell. In fact Smartt died in 1929. But depression and defects in the syndicate's irrigation system delayed its sale until 1939 when the Trust finally recovered about a third of its original investment.

The roots of the Trust's entanglement with Smartt lay, of course, in the incestuously close relationships within Rhodes's political and business circle and in the difficulty in dealing with, or even seeking advice from, those outside the ring of Rhodes's old associates. The Trust's long involvement with the 1820 Memorial Settlers' Association, while much less unprofitable, showed a similar affinity for influential members of Rhodes's old following. The Association was founded to commemorate British settlement in the Eastern Cape. One idea had been to endow scholarships for 'Eastern Province lads.'[110] But this quickly mutated into a scheme to promote white immigration—a long-

---

[106] Report by General Byron, 6 May 1920; RTF 1954 (50).
[107] Smartt to Otto Beit, 20 Jan. 1921; RTF 1584 (5).
[108] Secretary to Otto Beit, 12 May 1921; RTF 1584 (5).
[109] Fuller to Crewe, 15 Apr. 1925; RTF 1584 (7).
[110] W. E. Stanford to Michell, 19 Dec. 1919; RTF 2478 (1).

standing plank in the Unionist party platform—by offering advice, training, and cash advances to those wanting to settle on the land. The moving spirit was Colonel Charles Crewe. Crewe had come to South Africa in the 1870s. He had served in the Cape Mounted Rifles (a border gendarmerie) and tried his hand as a bank clerk, prospector, and mine manager before settling as a farmer in the Eastern Cape. By the late 1890s he was a Cape MP, a leading figure in the loyalist South Africa League, and the main organizer of Rhodes's Progressives in the Eastern Cape.[111] After serving in the Boer War he became part-owner of the East London *Daily Despatch*, one of two leading Eastern Cape dailies, and served in Jameson's Cape ministry. In the First World War he was director of war recruitment and later commanded a formation under Smuts in East Africa. As an energetic and well-connected politician whose friendship with Milner stretched back over twenty years, Crewe was perfectly placed to channel the Trust's sympathy for settlement schemes into his organization.

The public manifesto of the Association was carefully designed to be inoffensive to moderate Afrikaner opinion, and Crewe adorned his committee with honorary members drawn from Smuts's cabinet as well as with notables from the English section. The aim, he announced, was to attract settlers with capital and 'to restore the great loss of South African manhood during the recent war'.[112] Privately, Crewe was much more candid. The objects of the Association, he told Geoffrey Dawson, then Acting Secretary of the Trust, are '(1) to provide for the settlement of persons of the British race and (2) to erect suitable monuments to the arrival of the settlers of 1820'.[113] The Trustees were enthusiastic and promised a staged contribution of £20,000 to match the £100,000 Crewe was confident of raising. With political fusion between the Unionists and Smuts on the cards, and a prominent Unionist politician, Sir Edgar Walton, as High Commissioner in London, the South African government was sympathetic.[114] Dawson himself became chairman of the British committee and its London office was conveniently (not to say symbolically) housed at the *Round Table*'s address at 175 Piccadilly. By 1925 the Association claimed to have brought to South Africa over 1,000 settlers, 600 dependants, and £3 million in capital.

But 1925 was a turning point. By then Smuts had been defeated and Hertzog's 'Pact' government was in power. It had little sympathy with immigration, still less immigration from Britain. The chronic problem of unskilled, usually Afrikaner, 'poor whites' was its main priority. In 1925, Crewe's old political ally Walton had resigned as High Commissioner. In a much harsher political climate, the Association found it was far short of its financial target and faced a dwindling supply of settlers. To make matters worse, violent political controversy broke out over the design of a new national flag, inflaming racial feeling and discouraging British immigration still more.[115] But the Association kept

---

[111] Crewe's unfinished diary, Crewe Papers, Mic. 179/III, Cory Library.
[112] Association pamphlet, 1920. RTF 2478 (1).
[113] Crewe to Geoffrey Dawson, 18 July 1920; RTF 2478 (1).
[114] K. Fedorowich, 'Anglicization and the Politicization of British Immigration to South Africa, 1899–1929', *Journal of Imperial and Commonwealth History*, 19/2 (1991), 231–40.
[115] Ibid. 237.

afloat. Crewe persuaded the Trustees to hand over the balance of their original grant unconditionally. However, his real coup was to obtain for the Association a capital fund of £100,000—part of the Rhodes-Beit Share Fund—the income from which was to supply almost 80 per cent of its operating income in South Africa.[116] The Trust's files are silent on the reasons for this sudden escalation in its support. But the circumstances are suggestive. The year 1925 was one of growing alarm at nationalist self-assertion in South Africa. It was also the year of Milner's extended tour[117] in the course of which he stayed for some days with Crewe. 'He is not popular,' Milner noted in his diary, 'but his persistence tells.' Everyone recognized his gift for organization and he was the head, life, and soul of the 1820 Association.[118] Milner's race-patriotism was already at fever pitch as he mused on the ubiquity of war memorials. 'In proportion to their numbers', he noted, 'there are no people under the British flag who made a larger contribution in manpower or who suffered heavier losses than the South Africans of British race.'[119] It seems likely that the Trust's deepening commitment to the '1820' sprang from Milner's eager response to the old proven champions of the imperial cause. Whatever its limitations, the '1820' was the only means left (with the failure of Smartt and Percy Fitzpatrick's Sunday's River settlement) of encouraging the British migration on which Rhodes and Milner had both laid such emphasis.

The capital grant of 1925, and the active sympathy of Amery, was enough to protect the '1820' from the rigours of Kerr's squeeze in 1927 and the Trust continued to subsidize the Association's London office. The '1820'—in Rhodes-ian fashion—had a London 'council' densely packed with the great and good: in the 1930s it included the dukes of Abercorn and Montrose; Lords Selborne, Bledisloe, Derby, Tweedsmuir (the former John Buchan), and Halifax; Neville Chamberlain and David Lloyd George; Peacock, Sothern Holland, and Amery among the Trustees, as well as Philip Kerr and Lady Milner, who agreed about little else. In the late 1920s, Amery as Colonial Secretary picked up the cue from the '1820's' South African leadership and was careful publicly to rest the case for immigration on the reinforcement not of the British but of the white population. 'When one looks to the future', he declaimed in 1929, 'the racial problem is how South Africa is to be kept white . . . it is essential that [it] should not be swamped'.[120] Lady Milner emphasized the social paradise that awaited the discriminating migrant. 'It is a country where there is no domestic question,' she enthused. 'If you want a cook you can get twenty, if you want a kitchen-maid . . . there are thousands of them. There is no such thing as a white woman in South Africa, however poor, who scrubs her own floor.'[121] On this account, the '1820' was not an arm of empire, but a helping hand for drones. But these imperialists protested too much. It was left to Robert Struben, Crewe's successor as chairman (1932–6), to rehearse its imperial credentials. Struben was MP for Albany, Jameson's old seat in the Eastern Cape, and had served the imperial cause in both the

---

[116] Amery to Kerr, 26 Mar. 1934; RTF 2478 (1); memorandum, n.d. but 1962; RTF 2478 (8).
[117] For Milner's 'depression' at the state of South African politics and his belief that the Hertzog government was 'untrustworthy', Duncan to Lady Selborne, 13 Dec. 1924; Duncan Papers D 5.18.13.
[118] Milner's special diary, Milner Papers 103.   [119] Ibid.
[120] Annual meeting, 3 July 1929; RTF 2478 (1).   [121] Ibid.

Boer and the Great War. 'The Empire needs bonds—intangible but close,' he told its annual meeting in 1933. The Association had always worked to increase the white population 'and to strengthen the bonds between this mother-country of the Empire and the Dominions, and South Africa'.[122]

In the 1930s some of the tensions which had surrounded the '1820' in the previous decade were lifted by the political alliance of Hertzog and Smuts after 1933 and the 'fusion' which created a United Party of English and 'moderate' Afrikaners in opposition to Malan's 'purified' Nationalists. The '1820's' efforts to promote settlement had languished—'farming settlers are for the moment hopeless', remarked the London chairman, Lord Leven, in 1938[123]—but South Africa's gold boom was now sucking in not would-be gentlemen-farmers but skilled artisans and those with capital or on pensions for whom the fiscal and the physical climate were equally attractive: over 1,000 arrived under the '1820's' auspices in 1938.[124] Even under a United Party government, however, the watchword was caution. 'We should get into political trouble if "big licks" of British settlement were to be advertised in any way,' Leven was warned in 1938,[125] especially if there were a split between Hertzog and Smuts. Malcolm's warning neatly captures the ambivalence among some of the Association's firmer friends in Britain: their eagerness on the one hand to strengthen the imperial link by encouraging economic development and British immigration; but their anxiety on the other to avoid any hint of interference in South African politics lest it throw petrol on the embers of Afrikaner nationalism. Among the *Round Table* group, which included Malcolm, Curtis, and Kerr, the importance of pacifying Afrikanerdom while the forces of modernity drew South Africa gradually into Britain's economic and cultural orbit was deemed paramount. Kerr himself had wondered in 1937 whether the '1820' was not too closely associated with 'Crewe, Smartt and the ultra-British imperialist party'.[126]

Ironically, the '1820' was given a ringing endorsement by the leader the Round Tablers and the Trust had come to regard as Rhodes's true political heir, Jan Smuts. Perhaps because of division among the Trustees, and lingering doubts about the efficiency of the '1820' in South Africa (its training farm was judged a white elephant by Kerr), the Trust had decided to investigate before agreeing to renew the income from the 1925 capital grant. John Martin, a Scots-born former president of the Chamber of Mines and a senior director of Central Mining (Sothern Holland's firm), was asked to report. His conclusions were trenchant. Only 34 per cent of the white population was of British origin, he warned. 'It is held to be essential in the interest of the Commonwealth that there should be a continuous reinforcement from Great Britain of the British section . . . to consolidate the attachment of the Union, strengthen the sense of cultural affinity and preserve the English-speaking minority from submergence.'[127] Nor, he said reassuringly, was there any longer much antipathy among Afrikaners to British immigration. But it was almost

---

[122] RTF 2478 (1).   [123] Leven to D. O. Malcolm, 17 Sept. 1938; RTF 2478 (2).
[124] Central executive report, 1943–5, 13 Oct. 1945; RTF 2478 (4).
[125] Malcolm to Leven, 17 Sept. 1938; RTF 2478 (2).
[126] Secretary's note, 23 July 1937; RTF 2478 (2).
[127] Martin's report, Apr. 1939; RTF 2478 (2).

certainly the views of Smuts, circulated confidentially to the Trustees, which carried most weight with them. 'Now that the English people have stopped migrating of their own volition', said Smuts, the Association's work was needed to reinforce the English section. Government help was out of the question—'the mere proposal would immediately become the subject of racial cries damaging to the Association and to the interest of the English section'. Smuts remarked caustically that much of Rhodes's money had been wasted, 'e.g. on the Rhodes Scholarships in America'; but no cause was more worthy of the Trust's support than the '1820'. In a prophecy that Martin underscored, Smuts warned the Trustees that 'the English section in South Africa were tending to adopt a defeatist attitude about their position'. This malaise would worsen if the Trustees withdrew their backing from the '1820' whose collapse would be inevitable.[128] In the face of so dire a warning from so powerful an ally, the Trust hastily reaffirmed its loyalty. After 1939, and up until South Africa's departure from the Commonwealth in 1961, the Trust's support for the Association was never again in question.

Far from fading away, the '1820' was to have its finest hour in the decade after the Martin report. With Smuts in the premiership after September 1939, it was assured of more sympathy in high places. Economic prosperity and the stream of British service-men passing through under the Air Training Scheme brightened South Africa's image as a post-war emigrant destination. The '1820' was being deluged with applications, reported its chairman in December 1945.[129] South Africa could support unlimited numbers of pensioners and the gold discoveries of the Orange Free State promised a second Rand. But it was Smuts who opened the floodgates. In a widely reported speech in August 1946, he projected a vision of South Africa which Rhodes might have drafted. 'We want to see a European influx into South Africa that will recreate the country,' he proclaimed. 'Let them come to our industry which is clamouring for them. I look on this as a God-given chance.'[130] In the following year, the '1820' brought out 4,000 set-tlers. A year later the post-war total reached 10,000. The second gold boom and Britain's post-war austerity promised at long last to reverse the gradual attrition of English influ-ence since 1910. It was a false dawn. By the end of 1949, the rush was 'spent completely'.[131] The new political climate after 1948 was a deterrent. Of those who came, many moved on to Southern Rhodesia, which by the 1950s was the main focus of the Association's activities.

By that time, the Trust's long partnership with the '1820' was almost at an end. The death throes of the Rhodesian Federation and the horror of Sharpeville finally shattered the dream to which Rhodes, Milner, and Smuts had all been so committed: a great white dominion from the Cape to the Zambezi, British in its institutions, if not in its culture; an outward-looking member of a British-led international association; and Britain's partner in the development of Black Africa. After May 1961, the Association lived on as an agency of the South African government; its days as an instrument of the Rhodes-ian vision were over.

---

[128] Ibid.   [129] *Outspan*, 28 Dec. 1945; RTF 2478 (4).
[130] *The Times*, 15 Aug. 1946, RTF 2478.   [131] Report of London office, 1948–9; RTF 2478 (5).

In education as much as in land settlement, the Trustees found themselves heavily dependent upon local advice and, for much of the period, closely constrained by the limited
resources at their disposal. It was inevitable that they should have regarded education in
South Africa as one of their main obligations. The peculiar structure of Rhodes's scholarship scheme in South Africa made the performance of the Cape schools essential to the
standard of the scholars they sent to Oxford, and to the wider reputation of the scholarships. But this 'parochial' consideration was quickly supplemented by a wider imperative which Milner especially, among the Trustees, regarded as of overriding importance.
The end of the Boer War in May 1902, shortly after Rhodes's death, marked the beginning of Milner's 'reconstruction' programme: a drive to expunge the remaining traces of
'Krugerism' in the ex-republics by a thoroughgoing policy of Anglicization. The spread
of 'English' education was (together with British immigration) to be the spearhead of his
policy. At the same time, Milner, Jameson, and Lewis Michell were keenly aware that
even in the Cape the influence of English education could not be taken for granted and
they viewed the Afrikaner cultural revival in the Western Cape, as, if anything, a greater
threat to the future 'British South Africa' than the defeated Boer communities in the
north.

It was perhaps for this reason that up until the end of the First World War, while the
Trustees gave some help to the 'Rhodes' schools in the Cape and to St John's College in
Johannesburg, their resources were heavily concentrated on the establishment of Rhodes
University College in Grahamstown. The seed had been sown by Parkin who had arrived
in 1903 to organize the scholarship scheme. Parkin was not impressed by the Cape schools
from which the scholars were to be drawn and urged the creation of a college which
would help prepare would-be scholars for Oxford.[132] Such a college in Grahamstown, he
added, 'would create for the Eastern Province and under very strong British influence
what is now being very energetically developed in the Western' (he meant at Stellenbosch).[133] Michell, Jameson, and Milner were enthusiastic. The Trust set aside a fund of
£50,000 to endow the College, which was opened in 1904. The College's cultural and
political role was unambiguous: it was designed to reward and consolidate the proverbial
loyalty of the Eastern Province. But it was also meant to be the engine room of English
cultural ascendancy in South Africa, as much as Trinity College, Dublin, had been in
Ireland. 'The Rhodes University College', wrote Charles Boyd, the Trust's Secretary, 'is
designed to contribute . . . to extend and strengthen the Imperial idea in South Africa.'[134]
The launching pad for this cultural and ideological enterprise could hardly be other than
the Eastern Cape, the political base of Jameson, Crewe, and Walton, the centre of Cape
loyalism between 1899 and 1902, and the home of a scholastic imperialism as fanatical
in its own way as the scholastic nationalism of the Afrikaner clerics. 'I take it', wrote the
headmaster of Kingswood, the Methodist school in Grahamstown, 'the Rhodes College
is to imply Higher Education under the best of Imperial influences'.[135] 'It is in the East',
urged one of the new college professors, '. . . that there is this stronghold of English ideas,

---

[132] Parkin to Michell, 7 Aug. 1903; RTF 1027 (1).   [133] Ibid.
[134] C. W. Boyd to Under-Secretary for War, 15 Aug. 1904; RTF 1027 (1).
[135] E. C. Gane to Boyd, 25 July 1904; RTF 1027 (1).

customs and so forth which . . . are wanted to counterbalance the overwhelming predominance of other ideals elsewhere.'[136]

At the end of the First World War, the Trustees' conception of their educational task widened considerably. Rhodes University College received the lion's share of their spending: making it a residential institution was vital if it was to recruit widely across Southern Africa. But now, in a climate of growing Afrikaner consciousness, the Trustees were deluged with requests for help from private schools struggling to maintain an English-type education in places where the public provision was controlled by an Afrikaner majority. Milner and Otto Beit were strongly sympathetic, and a stream of benefactions followed Beit's and Wylie's visit to South Africa in 1920. But it was clear, as Wylie argued, that the demand was so large that the Trust could only meet a small proportion of the requests that reached it. Many schools, including the Western Province Preparatory School, a nursery of the best if not the brightest, were sent empty away. The question was: what should the Trust's priorities be?

Milner's visit to South Africa in 1924–5, soon after the arrival in power of Hertzog's 'Pact' government, was the occasion of a careful review of the Trust's policy. As we have seen, Milner had become increasingly alarmed at what he saw as the virulence of anti-British nationalism and the danger that Hertzog might subvert South African membership of the British Empire. Milner visited a large number of schools. The plight of English people far from the main educational centres, said his widow, 'appealed to him with great force'[137]—a residue of his old obsession with planting British settlers in the Afrikaans-speaking *platteland*. But, ultimately, even Milner acknowledged that the Trust could only help those best able to help themselves. Its task was to back up the only institutions able to withstand the influences he dreaded. 'In his notes', said Lady Milner, 'he refers again and again to the way in which the English Church and Non-conformist schools kept the flag of sane and character-building education flying amid an orgy of . . . nationalist educational propaganda.'[138] Anglican bishops and diocesan schools were, *faute de mieux*, the building blocks of Milner's counter-offensive: it was the English-speaking clergy (like the Afrikaner *predikants*) who were to be the warriors in the new *Kulturkampf*. The Anglican public school model of education, with its emphasis on 'character'—an amalgam of public service, sporting prowess and gentlemanly values—catering for the English elite, but reaching perhaps beyond it, would be the sheet anchor of the imperial connection. 'Schools like St Andrew's [College, Grahamstown]', said Milner, 'are a Bulwark, the strongest that is still left, against [Afrikaner] Racialism and the extinction of British ideals. But they will have a hard struggle to hold their own.'[139] 'The last thing Milner said to me', recalled the headmaster of St Andrew's a few months later, '. . . was "we shall always be a minority in this country: we have got to be an aristocracy".'[140] Almost equal in importance, Milner added, in an interesting gloss on the pre-war priorities of the Trust, was Rhodes University College. Indeed, the development

---

[136] E. Schwarz to B. Hawksley, 3 Jan. 1911; RTF 1027 (1).
[137] Memorandum by Lady Milner, 28 May 1925; RTF 2662 (1).   [138] Ibid.
[139] Milner's diary, 16–18 Jan. 1925, quoted in Lady Milner's memorandum.
[140] Canon Kettlewell to L. Carter, 20 Dec. 1925; RTF 2676 (1).

of Grahamstown as the great centre of British and imperial influence depended on the
success of the 'various educational establishments which contribute most to . . . its distinctive character'.

The Trustees made pious haste to implement Milner's posthumous recommendations.
Almost immediately, however, they were overtaken by the dire warnings of financial crisis
voiced by Philip Kerr. Kerr was determined to bring what he saw as the Trust's era of
profligacy in South Africa to an end. The 'period had passed', he told the Trustees, when
they 'could or should continue to make the large and varied payments towards all kinds
of local purposes in South Africa they made in the past'. The cost of the scholarships, of
Rhodes House, and of the expenditure needed to make Oxford more attractive academically made this impossible.[141] At the same time, he carefully endorsed Milner's policy,
which he defined as assisting 'the leading independent schools in South Africa to develop
into first class schools of the English public school type',[142] though, unlike Milner, he
placed the Trust's obligation to Rhodes University College first. But Kerr also subtly
shifted the justification for the Trust's support away from Milner's blunt emphasis on
imperial loyalism. Like the younger ex-Milnerites, including his close friend Curtis, Kerr
was anxious to rebuild the imperial association on a voluntaristic basis that recognized
the white dominions' 'nationality'. It was a mistake, he said, 'to try and educate young
South Africans of British origin into being Englishmen rather that South Africans'. The
case for helping the independent English schools rested on the educational as much as
political damage wrought by bad teaching in government schools, and on the dangers
of allowing a government monopoly over education. Moreover, the terms on which
Rhodes scholars were selected, with the stress on 'character' rather than purely academic
attainment, meant that the independent schools would continue to be the main source
of candidates.

Kerr's prescription was avowedly elitist. The Trust's limited funds, and the political
objections to defending loyalism openly, had thrown it back upon the handful of independent boys' schools, whose pupils would have to supply the political, business, professional, and clerical leadership hitherto drawn (among the English) largely from those
who had emigrated from Britain before 1914. Even one or two schools 'of first-rate public
school quality' enjoying the same prestige as their counterparts in England would make
a difference, he argued. The key lay in the teaching, and the Trust's priority was to help
schools recruit the able young graduates upon whom English public schools depended.[143]
Kerr and the Trustees were keen to encourage young public school teachers in England
to work in Empire countries and South African private schools remained a frontier of
opportunity for British teachers at least until the 1950s.

But Kerr's iron logic was easier to preach than to practise. In reality the Trustees were
all too easily swayed by lobbying from the close network of politicians, clerics, and educationalists whom they treated as representative of the English interest in South Africa.
A vigorous campaign by Charles Crewe and the Anglican Bishop of George enlisted the

---

[141] Report on visit to South Africa, 18 Feb. 1927; RTF 2662 (1).
[142] Report 231, 1 Apr. 1927; RTF 2662 (1).
[143] Kerr's memorandum, 11 Dec. 1928; RTF 2662 (1).

support of Sir Valentine Chirol, former foreign editor of *The Times*, and of Leo Amery, then Colonial Secretary, for starting a boys' school in this small country town in the south-east Cape.[144] If the Trust realized 'the magnitude of the issues at stake', the Bishop had told Michell in 1925, 'they will feel the need of helping us maintain our British ideals'.[145] George and Knysna (which was close by) had been recommended for families sent out by the '1820', Crewe reminded Kerr.[146] Milner had promised to do something. Amery, then on his ministerial visit to South Africa, told Kerr that 'if George were not such a key position politically as a present and future centre of Englishry . . . I should vote in favour of letting it go.' Kerr caved in. With the easing of the Trust's finances, George received its grant in 1930. 'The Trustees . . . feel', Kerr told Lord Selborne (chairman of the '1820' in Britain), that 'the funds at their disposal . . . can be more usefully expended in areas where the British population is thinly distributed',[147] a cool reversal of his earlier dogma. Fear of adverse publicity over the lavish expenditure on Rhodes House led the Trustees into a similar U-turn over help for the new University of Cape Town. With a tax windfall in 1929, Kerr invited Crewe and Patrick Duncan to suggest ways of spending some £15,000.[148] Nor could the Trustees overlook the needs of Rhodes University College, which was their foundation and bore the Founder's name. Even Kerr conceded that it had first claim on the Trust's resources.

Kerr's real achievement was not to impose consistency on the Trust's policy but to exploit the financial crisis of 1931–2 (when the Scholarship Fund lurched into deficit) to scale down its educational spending in South Africa to a fraction of the levels it had reached under Milner and Otto Beit in the roaring 'twenties. Except for the freak year of 1935, when the Trust gave £10,000 to Rhodes University College, its spending on *all* external purposes unrelated to the scholarships averaged just over £8,000 a year.[149] Crewe's retirement as the Trust's main adviser in 1933 allowed Kerr to lay down a new policy for 'what is left of the Rhodes Trust's interests in education': there was to be a 'small but by no means negligible fund' comprising the loans advanced to South African schools; the slump prevented the Trustees doing more.[150] But if Kerr's economies evoked little protest from South Africa, or among the Trustees themselves, this was only partly because of a sense of financial stringency. The Jagger bequest,[151] South African prosperity in the 1930s, and the more benign political climate brought by 'Fusion' after 1934 eased the local pressures and encouraged the Trustees to think that the worst was over for the English schools.

Smuts's wartime premiership, his enhanced prestige as a world statesman, and South Africa's overwhelmingly loyal support for the Commonwealth war effort helped to

[144] Sir V. Chirol to H. A. L. Fisher, 12 Apr. 1928; Amery to Kerr, 18 Sept. 1927; RTF 2663 (1).
[145] Bishop of George to Michell, 18 Mar. 1925; RTF 2663 (1).
[146] Crewe to Kerr, 5 May 1928; RTF 2663 (1).
[147] Kerr to Selborne, 26 June 1930; RTF 2127.
[148] Report 245, 15 Feb. 1929; RTF 2662 (2).
[149] See Public Purposes Trust balance sheets; RTF 1504C (1).
[150] Kerr to Crewe, 5 Apr. 1933; RTF 2662 (2).
[151] J. W. Jagger, a Cape politician and businessman, left a large bequest for English education in South Africa.

prolong the complacency about the country's political and cultural orientation. The electoral earthquake which swept away Smuts and the United Party in 1948 was a stunning shock. The National Party overthrew Smuts's seemingly impregnable majority in parliament and D. F. Malan formed a cabinet conspicuously lacking any member drawn from the English section. To make the defeat more galling, the United Party won a majority of ballots but was defeated by the overrepresentation of the country districts. The worst-case scenario imagined by Milner and freshly evoked in Arthur Keppel-Jones's satirical prophecy *When Smuts Goes*, published in 1947, had become the grim reality. The great experiment in Anglo-Afrikaner cooperation, on which the Trust had pinned its faith, was over.

As it turned out, the National Party leaders were much more cautious than their rhetoric suggested and it was not until 1961 (and in very different circumstances) that they declared a republic and left the Commonwealth. But the alarm had been sounded and the old fears revived. Indeed, even before Smuts's defeat, Elton had listened receptively to warnings that 'the Afrikaner, more politically conscious and armed with this weapon of bilingualism, is extending his control over all forms of public activity'.[152] Elton himself was eager to reinforce the independent schools and discourage their dependence upon government help.[153] His report on his South African tour in 1947–8 invoked the spirit of Milner and Philip Kerr. 'The great independent Church Secondary Schools', he pronounced, 'are . . . the focus and nursery of what must be called the British tradition in South Africa.' They were 'the most promising product of South Africa civilisation to date . . . it is of crucial importance that they should survive'.[154] And with the flood of post-war immigration, they had a unique opportunity to consolidate their influence.

At Elton's instigation the Trustees embarked on an extensive programme of grants and loans, including the promise in 1949 of £10,000 towards a new church school foundation promoted by Richard Feetham, an old Round Tabler, long resident in South Africa. As a devout Anglican, with strong views about religious education, Elton was deeply attracted to what he saw as the exemplary Christian emphasis of a school like Michaelhouse in Natal. His initial reaction to an appeal from Rhodes University College in 1948 was correspondingly cool. The Trust's main concern, he said, must be with schools. But the severity of the College's financial crisis and the consequences of its contraction or collapse were so alarming that the Trustees eventually gave £20,000—much their largest post-war grant in South Africa—to restore a precarious financial equilibrium. It was Ronald Currey, headmaster of St Andrew's, who spelt out the dangers. Currey was an ex-Rhodes scholar and the son of an old henchman of Rhodes. In 1930, he had contributed to *Coming of Age*, a volume of essays calling for national unity between English and Afrikaner, and opposing Hertzog's 'two streams' thesis, stigmatized as Afrikaner 'segre-

---

[152] G. Orpen to Elton, 24 Sept. 1945; RTF 2662 (3). Orpen was a partner at Syfrets, which handled the Trust's South African account, and a leading figure in South African educational charities.
[153] Elton to Sothern Holland, 23 May 1948; RTF 2662 (3).
[154] Report by Elton, 27 Apr. 1948; RTF 2662 (3).

gation'.[155] Then Currey had warned that the English were being turned into *uitlanders*. In 1949 he was apocalyptic. The Malanite government, he told Elton, 'believe, and I fear are justified in believing, that the commercial and industrial British South Africans, and powerful gold interests too, will swallow anything, provided the dividends and profits are left untouched'. They regarded 'the Church Schools *and Rhodes* [as] the breeding pens and nurseries of the spirit they want to destroy'. Rhodes 'is today one of the centres and fortresses of the "English way of life" . . . and . . . one of the most critically important'.[156] Orpen and Sir Herbert Stanley, the British High Commissioner (i.e. ambassador) in South Africa, joined in the chorus of gloom.

Explicit in Currey's letter, and almost equally so in an address by the Archbishop of Cape Town in 1950 (passed to Elton by Abell, a Trustee), was the assumption that with the failure of its political leaders, and the indifference of its business class, the English section must rely on academics and clerics to defend its true interests. This was a far cry from the pre-war world in which the Trust had seen its task as helping to nurture a progressive English elite *within* South Africa's ruling class. It signalled a brutal narrowing of the base from which the Trust's influence could be exerted to a cluster of 'liberal' enclaves, increasingly regarded as marginal or even subversive as much by English-speaking whites as by Afrikaners. The instinct of the Trustees was to go on spending their local South African resources to support the existing independent schools, and even add to their number. These were, after all, still the main source of South Africa's Rhodes scholars. But the Indian summer of their generosity in South Africa after 1945 was an accident of fortune. The 'Rhodes Trust, South Africa' was a small trust fund, left for local expenses after the repatriation of the Rhodes–Beit Share Fund in 1939, with an annual income of less than £200. Among its assets was the 'East Rietfontein Syndicate', which paid nothing. By 1943 it was paying over £2,000 a year; at its peak in 1949–51, it was paying annually nearly £40,000. The capital value of the fund soared from £22,000 to nearly £200,000 by 1953. It was from this source that the urgent needs of Rhodes University were met and other donations made. From 1951 onwards, however, the Trustees steadily diverted this stream of wealth to meet the costs of the South African Rhodes scholarships, and relieve their budget at home. When local income contracted with the end of the brief bonanza, they took almost all for the scholarships and reduced their donations to a pittance.[157] From the mid-1950s this financial strategy signalled an almost tangible sense of disengagement. The feeling was mutual. English opinion in South Africa became more and more alarmed at the S-bends and U-turns of Britain's colonial policy north of the Zambezi. Harold Macmillan's 'winds of change' speech at Cape Town in 1960 was widely seen as the onset of a shameful betrayal. When South Africa's departure from the Commonwealth rang down the curtain on the Trust's self-appointed role as the guardian of English education, the 'British tradition in South Africa' (though not radical dissent among the English-speaking) had all but disappeared.

[155] See Alan Paton, *Hofmeyr*, abridged edn. (Cape Town, 1971), 128–9.
[156] Currey to Elton, 25 June 1949; RTF 1027 (4).
[157] Derived from balance sheets of the Rhodes Trust South Africa; RTF 1504E.

Although they were preoccupied with the relationship between English and Afrikaner, the Trustees were not completely oblivious of the social and educational needs of the black majority. But it was true that between 1902 and 1960 their benefactions, by comparison with those flowing towards the English minority-within-a-minority, were extremely modest. There were three reasons for this. First, even after 1945, and certainly before, the Trustees and their secretaries tended to share a conservative assumption that the pace of black advance was bound to be slow; that white rule would continue indefinitely; and that few blacks could benefit from the carefully targeted aid that the Trust had to offer. Secondly, by contrast with the elaborate network of lobbies and contacts through which help to English whites was distributed, blacks had no direct access to the Trust and virtually no means of influencing its views. Thirdly, the Trustees, as we have seen, were nervous of patronizing causes which could expose them to the charge of interfering in South African politics (a 'crime' whose scope was almost boundless). Any charitable enterprise which smacked of 'Exeter Hall'—the generic term for the missionary or humanitarian tradition in Britain since slave abolition—would have outraged not only Afrikaner but even 'loyal' English opinion.

Yet even within this timid conservative ethos, there was room for some anxiety about black interests. British opinion drew a distinction between colonial rule based on trusteeship (an imperial orthodoxy in the 1920s and 1930s) and the unfettered domination of whites over blacks. Even Lionel Curtis, who functioned intermittently as the Trust's imperial conscience, but who favoured handing over the British protectorates in Southern Africa (today's Botswana, Lesotho, and Swaziland) to the Union government, conceded the 'intensity of feeling in intellectual quarters' aroused by South Africa's 'native' policy.[158] By sponsoring Margery Perham as a travelling research fellow, and helping to publish Hailey's *African Survey*, the Trustees were acknowledging that that there was much to be learnt about African needs and welfare right across the continent. The pattern of their expenditure reveals a wary, paternalistic benevolence. Prompted by Parkin (to whom nothing was worse than an American education for South African blacks) they gave modestly to the foundation of the South African Native College at Fort Hare in 1916. At Duncan's suggestion, they supported courses in basic health care taught at the College. In 1945, they gave it £5,000 for new buildings.[159] They helped to fund a school for 'native leaders' at Modderpoort. After seeking Smuts's approval, they made a grant to the fledgling South African Institute for Race Relations in 1934.[160] After 1945, when Elton became fixated by the 'promiscuous urbanisation' of South Africa's black majority, and fearful of its consequences, the Trust made its biggest and boldest gesture. It gave £5,000 and lent a further £15,000 to the white-owned Bantu Press—a publishing company with a string of newspapers serving black readers across Southern Africa; but only after careful soundings had confirmed the approval of the Malan government. Indeed, the Bantu Press was viewed by its white ownership as a tool of education rather than information (let alone sensation). It was 'not primarily a fighting press', as the report commissioned by the Trust

---

[158] Curtis to Duncan, 16 Apr. 1935; Lionel Curtis Papers 91, Bodleian Library.
[159] Details in RTF 1156.   [160] See RTF 2881.

from a young black academic drily put it. Black readers preferred the antigovern-ment English-language newspapers.[161] It was 'performing an exceedingly valuable func-tion', said Lord Hailey, supplying unwitting proconsular confirmation of Budaza's verdict.[162]

To have expected the Trust to display more overt sympathy for black political griev-ances, or to have tried harder to meet the famine in black education, would be to mis-understand the mechanics of its role in South Africa—it was bound to work through the agency of its white English 'collaborators'—and also the Trustees' own view of political realities—that the promotion of an enlightened English culture amongst whites was the precondition for any improvement in black conditions. In the last resort, the Trust had neither the means nor the influence to do more than offer the most modest support to the most respectable causes: a mission school here, a hostel there. It was kindly: but it was not enough.

The Imperial Laboratory: Rhodes House and Oxford

In the sixty years since the Founder's death there had been a withering away of his estate in South Africa and the gradual collapse of Rhodes-ian influence in political life. In Oxford, by contrast, the Trust expanded its presence, increased its spending, widened its sphere of activity and found a new auxiliary role in the modernization of the University. This great redeployment of assets and interests forms the central fact in the Trust's history up until recent times.

In the early days of the Trust it had seemed unlikely that Oxford could ever monopo-lize its attention. Its headquarters were in London. Beit, Jameson, Hawksley, and Michell among the Trustees had no personal connection with Oxford. For nearly twenty years, the Trustees were content with a rented property in South Parks Rd from which their 'Oxford Secretary' could supervise the scholarship scheme. The deliberate integration of the scholars into college life seemed to obviate any larger institutional presence. Even the annual scholars' dinner could be accommodated in a borrowed college hall or, at a pinch, in the vulgar pomp of the Oxford Town Hall. The decision to transform this modest bridgehead into a grand imperial monument, part office, part residence, part library, part great hall, part memorial, to be designed by Herbert Baker, the doyen of imperial archi-tects and Rhodes's own, is all the more remarkable.

The impetus almost certainly came from Milner's determination to challenge Oxford's donnish introversion and make a reality of its claim to be a 'great imperial university'.[163] The Trustees had toyed with the idea of a building in Oxford before the war, and had attempted vainly to buy a piece of the Wadham College garden in 1919. But it was not until 1924 that they showed a real sense of urgency. The delay may have been caused by

[161] Report by G. Budaza, 6 Sept. 1951; RTF 3070.
[162] Hailey to Elton, 25 Apr. 1951; RTF 3070.
[163] For Oxford's imperial connections, see two excellent studies; R. Symonds, *Oxford and Empire: The Last Lost Cause?* (Oxford, 1986) and A. F. Madden and D. K. Fieldhouse (eds.), *Oxford and the Idea of Commonwealth* (London: 1982).

Milner's desire to await the outcome of the Asquith Commission report into Oxford and Cambridge, and his hope that it would recommend a radical reform in Oxford's government. The Commission did indeed propose a centralized secretariat and (less successfully) a permanent executive head.[164] It was perhaps no coincidence that Milner's acolytes were later to publish a plan for a centralized university regime in *The Government of Oxford* (1931).[165] The year 1924 was thus the moment at which the Trust could hope to exploit a new fluidity in Oxford and make its influence felt. When Milner was elected unopposed to the chancellorship of the University in April 1925, that influence might have been expected to grow.

Milner's death in May 1925 closed that prospect and deprived him of an intriguing finale to a controversial career. But the main plans for Rhodes House had been laid down in October 1924, before his ill-fated trip to South Africa. The Trustees approved proposals to build a library, offices, a common room for the scholars, accommodation for the Oxford Secretary, and a 'Rhodes Hall' to seat 200.[166] From the beginning, the library had pride of place in the Trustees' thinking. Grigg, who was anxious to represent the Trustees' plans as a gift to the University, told the Vice-Chancellor that they wanted to help the Bodleian: 'I believe there is no adequate library on Imperial subjects anywhere in the United Kingdom or in any other part of the Empire.'[167] Whether this fact impressed Dr Wells is not recorded, but the importance which Milner, Grigg, and later Philip Kerr attached to the library accurately reflected their faith that the dissemination of expert knowledge would eventually mobilize public opinion behind the imperial cause. The library, said the Trustees, would 'for the first time make a complete collection of official records and documents from all parts of the Empire'.[168] The utilitarian note is unmistakable.

But it was not the library that caused unease. Even within the Trust's own circle the scale of Baker's plans and the clear hint that what he had at first called 'Rhodes College'[169] was to be a distinct community with its own ethos alarmed those, like Geoffrey Dawson, who knew collegiate Oxford from the inside. Reginald Coupland, a *Round Table* member and Beit Professor of Colonial History since 1920, warned Grigg that encouraging the Rhodes scholars to 'herd together' would negate Rhodes's own wishes and arouse resentment in the University. The hall and common room were 'undesirable': they would emphasize the separateness of Rhodes House, not its place in the wider academic life of the University.[170] What Coupland wanted was a 'Rhodes Library': a research institute with rooms for postgraduate students arranged around 'a really big and exhaustive library' and an endowment for staff and visitors. When Kerr replaced Grigg as Secretary in 1925, his draft statement of purpose for Rhodes House, intended for *The Times*, encountered similar sharp criticism from Grigg who had taken Coupland's warnings to heart. Kerr's

[164] Brian Harrison, *The History of the University of Oxford*, viii: *The Twentieth Century* (Oxford: 1994), 689.

[165] Lavin, *Empire to International Commonwealth*, 262.   [166] RTM 14 Oct. 1924.

[167] Grigg to J. Wells, 12 Dec. 1924; RTF 2637 (1).   [168] RTM 16 Dec. 1924.

[169] Herbert Baker to Grigg, 5 Dec. 1924; RTF 2637 (1).

[170] Coupland to Grigg, 23 Dec. 1924; RTF 2637 (1).

draft would arouse suspicion that he meant to withdraw the Rhodes scholars into a 'separate community in a forcing house of imperialist ideas . . . You must make it clear as noonday sun that Rhodes House will tolerate and harbour no propaganda nor interfere in the college life of Rhodes men.'[171] Herbert Fisher, Warden of New College, told his fellow Trustees that what Oxford wanted was a library and seminar rooms, public lectures, and travelling fellowships.[172]

It was not, perhaps, surprising that, from a functional point of view, the eventual shape of Rhodes House exemplified the old adage about committees and camels. There was a hall, but no common room; a library, but no postgraduate offices; and two grand reception rooms (named for Beit and Jameson) whose splendour was ill suited to the needs of workaday academic life. And not for the first time, perhaps, the irresistible force of the clients' wishes had met the immovable object of the architect's ambition. Kerr, too, had watered down his prose, but not his enthusiasm for promoting the study of the 'English-speaking theory of government'.[173] In April 1926, in his memorandum for the Trustees on Rhodes House and 'general financial policy', he set out in detail his plans for the building's use. Kerr's scheme skilfully fused the argument that Oxford had to be modernized if it was to attract the ablest students from overseas (a key concern for the Trust) with his own 'Atlanticist' passion for combining American and imperial studies. It seems likely that Kerr's exposure to American academic expertise at the Paris Peace Conference, and his experience of lecturing at a research institute in the United States, reinforced the appeal of group research into contemporary problems, to which his close friend Lionel Curtis was also powerfully attracted. Kerr's library for the study of 'the past and current achievements of the English-speaking world' was to be backed up by provision for seminars and professorial offices, and by programmes of study into the training of 'backward peoples' for self-government, and the impact of 'large-scale economic organisation on primitive races'. The Trust should also fund travelling fellowships and a prestigious public lecture.[174]

It was clear from all this that Kerr was fully committed to the Milnerian project for injecting a powerful new academic influence into Oxford, while adding (somewhat to the displeasure of Grigg and Dawson) a strong Anglo-American flavour to his imperial cocktail. But for some three years, his plans hung fire, perhaps because of the financial stresses which he himself had emphasized to the trustees. Then in 1929 the moment for action arrived. The occasion was Smuts's visit to give the Trust's 'Rhodes Memorial Lecture'. Though out of office, Smuts was near the height of his fame as a world statesman, acquired in the war years and their diplomatic aftermath. His choice of Africa as a subject was the perfect launching pad, or so Kerr and Coupland came to think, to blast the newly finished Rhodes House into academic orbit. The problems of Africa, subjected to ordered scientific research, would be its *raison d'être*, its prime claim on the attention

[171] Grigg to Kerr, 28 Aug. 1925; RTF 2637 (1).
[172] Report by Fisher on discussions in Oxford, 9 Mar. 1926; RTF 2637 (1).
[173] Kerr to Fisher, 24 Feb. 1926; RTF 2637 (1).
[174] Memorandum by Secretary, 30 Apr. 1926; RTF 2637 (2).

of Oxford and a wider academic public. Africa would be the centrepiece of an institute devoted to contemporary world problems.

Before Smuts arrived in the autumn, Kerr and Coupland had already drafted their scheme for an 'institute of government'. There was no need for professors, said Coupland with professorial certainty, and formal teaching was a 'waste of a good man's time'.[175] What was needed was a set of research fellows and a travel fund to concentrate on law, 'native languages', comparative government, and applied economics. 'The most interesting experiment in government in the history of the world is now being made in the British Empire', but there was no one to record or observe it.[176] Nor were international relations to be neglected: the 'peace and prosperity of the white race', said Kerr and Coupland, was inseparable from that of 'other races'.[177] But Smuts's coming made it clear that this broad-based conception would have to have a much more Afrocentric bias if his prestige was to be exploited to raise money in America and enthusiasm at home. The conference on Africa, held in Oxford on 10–11 November 1929, attracted a crowd of notables from public as well as academic life. It was opened by Fisher who declared that 'the time had come to substitute fundamental thinking for aimlessness and drift in the management of the Empire'. But it was Smuts who set the tone. If fifty years, he threatened, Africa's problems might bulk as large as India's (whose constitutional advance was currently a source of bitter division in Britain). Their purpose 'should be to get the African problem out of the political atmosphere and away from sentimentalists and let science speak'. If African questions were wrenched away newspapers and 'faddists'—code for humanitarians and missionary busybodies—and subjected to rational enquiry, the conflict between the interests of black and white would be seen as irrelevant. In this great task Oxford's role was crucial: 'If Oxford would . . . turn from the Greeks to the Negroes it would help as nothing else would'[178]—a touching but implausible tribute. In his inimitable style, Leo Amery followed Smuts's lofty appeal with a bathos all his own. 'The frigidaire', he told the conference, 'would in future greatly add to the areas classed as habitable.'[179]

Kerr was delighted with the conference, which had recommended the creation of a centre for African Studies based at Rhodes House. In December he won the Trustees' approval for an extension to house what was to be their new academic engine-room. The idea of an institute of government, he told Curtis, had received 'immense impetus' from Smuts's visit.[180] Lord Lugard (then the greatest international authority on African affairs), Lord Passfield (the Colonial Secretary) and Joseph Oldham (the most influential figure in the missionary movement) had all been consulted. Smuts was going to lobby leading foundations in the United States, whose support was vital to meet the centre's running costs. Kerr and Coupland prepared an elaborate booklet for the Rockefeller Foundation. But from this high-point the project raced downhill to oblivion. There was difficulty

[175] Coupland to Curtis, 6 Apr. 1929; RTF 2792 (1).
[176] Note by Coupland, 19 Apr. 1929; RTF 2792 (1).
[177] 'Suggestions for an Institute of Government at Oxford', n.d.; RTF 2792 (1).
[178] Proceedings of Conference on Africa, 9 Nov. 1929; RTF 2792 (10).
[179] Ibid.   [180] Kerr to Curtis, 28 Feb. 1930; RTF 2792 (1).

finding a director; the new institute would compete with the existing International Institute for African Languages and Culture; and the Rockefeller Foundation had bigger fish to fry in Oxford. In May 1931 it promised over £600,000 towards building the New Bodleian.[181] In the same month it turned down the African centre: the institute was dead.

Perhaps Kerr and Coupland had been unlucky in their timing. Many bright hopes were caught by the big freeze of 1930–2 and never recovered. But the fiasco of the institute scheme seemed to show that the Trust simply lacked the resources in both manpower and money to become a significant new player on the Oxford academic scene. If the Trust were going to contribute, as Kerr insisted it must, to improving the University's standing as a centre for research (the endowment of research at Oxford was quite inadequate, Kerr told Francis Keppel of the Carnegie Foundation[182]), then it would have to do so through financial donation not institutional innovation. From 1931 onwards the idea of a University appeal for research funds had been mooted by Lionel Curtis and Fisher, the Trust's senior Oxford member. By 1935, after an unusually short delay by Oxford standards, it had reached the stage of advanced planning. Kerr, no doubt with Fisher's blessing, urged the Trustees to give £100,000 even if it meant reducing all their remaining grants to £5,000 a year.[183] The Trust agreed. The gift was made on the understanding that the University would set aside an equivalent sum for research in history, economics, and public administration.[184]

Thus, by the eve of the Second World War, urged on by financial stringency, the pressing needs of the Rhodes scholars—one-quarter of whom were postgraduates[185]—and Kerr's own stress on the importance of research into contemporary problems, the instinct of the Trustees was to submerge their purposes in those of the collegiate university and its underdeveloped common institutions. The war postponed this process and briefly seemed to offer scope for the distinctive role the Trustees had envisaged a decade earlier. Kerr's successor Lord Elton was irked by the way in which the Trust's gift to the University had been siphoned off to support the new 'colonial research programme' directed by Margery Perham from Nuffield College, two years old and as yet unbuilt. Its dependence on Rhodes House for books and the lack of any college provision was an additional grievance. 'So far as the future of imperial studies is concerned', he raged, 'this is another instance of lack of coordination.' A fraction of the money spent establishing Nuffield would have enabled the Trust to make Rhodes House 'a real cultural centre for the Empire . . . this is the true future for Rhodes House'.[186]

But what really fuelled Elton's jealousy and fired his ambition was the prospect of a large new government grant for colonial research becoming available in Oxford. The old

---

[181] Harrison (ed.), *History of the University of Oxford*, viii. 646.
[182] Kerr to F. Keppel, 2 Dec. 1936; RTF 2935B.
[183] Report 305, 13 Nov. 1936; RTF 2935 (1).
[184] Kerr to Veale (University Registrar), 11 May 1937; RTF 2935 (1).
[185] C. K. Allen to Fisher, 13 Nov. 1936; RTF 2935 (1).
[186] Elton's memorandum, 7 Oct. 1941; RTF 2637 (15).

blueprints of Kerr and Coupland were taken out and dusted down. The library could be expanded, research grants provided, distinguished visitors accommodated. Nuffield could look after the backward colonies: Rhodes House would deal with the dominions and India, which really mattered. Perhaps surprisingly, the Trustees, now without the ballast of Fisher (who had died in 1940), expressed provisional agreement. Carleton Allen, the Warden of Rhodes House, whose imperialism was as ardent as Elton's, dreamt of a post-war 'Fourth British Empire' in which the Rhodes scholars would take up the white man's burden of colonial service.[187] As the war in Europe ground to a close, Allen produced a more elaborate statement looking forward to Rhodes House's becoming 'a real centre of study'.[188] Vincent Harlow pointed out that this would require building an extension, and in a flush of enthusiasm the Trustees decided in June 1945 to approach an architect for advice.

It is hard to resist the impression that Elton, Allen, and even the Trustees were living in a wartime never-never land where the normal laws of institutional gravity had been suspended. Without the usual burden of the scholars—financial and administrative—it was easy to exaggerate the time, energy, and resources available for new academic projects. As we saw earlier, both Elton and Harlow were deeply committed during the war to countering what they saw as the blanket of public apathy towards the Empire and the scope that this gave to its domestic critics. The climax of this effort was a conference held at Rhodes House in September 1943 when Elton, Coupland, Harlow, and Hailey addressed lecturers from the Young Men and Young Women's Christian Organization—though their efforts were not helped by the appearance, uninvited, of Lionel Curtis who was riding his own hobbyhorse of Atlantic Union and denounced them as propagandists.[189] The end of the war brought a rapid deflation. Harlow went back to London. Financial realities punctured the dreams of a grander Rhodes House. Neither Elton nor Allen had the time or expertise to compete for control of the new money for colonial research. When it did come, the new Institute for Colonial (later Commonwealth) Studies emerged as a separate academic entity in 1946.

There was one residue of the spacious imperial vision Kerr had laid out for Rhodes House in 1926: the Rhodes Memorial Lectures. The Trustees resisted an early application to lecture on the scrub-cattle surplus in South Africa. As well as Smuts, an impressive cast had included Sir Robert Borden, Canadian Prime Minister during the First World War, who was the first lecturer in 1926-7, Abraham Flexner, a leading American educationalist (1927–8), Élie Halévy (1928–9), Einstein (1930–1), Gustav Cassel (1931–2), and the astronomer Hubble (1936). Performance had been mixed. Cassel had been 'almost unintelligible in public utterance'.[190] Einstein repudiated his own arguments almost immediately. Borden's account of Canadian history was dismissed (privately) by Coupland as 'inadequate and unhistorical [although] Canadian historians won't find much

---

[187] Allen's note for Elton, 10 Aug. 1943; RTF 2935 (2).
[188] Memorandum by Allen, 4 Apr. 1945; RTF 2637 (16).
[189] For Harlow's furious reaction to Curtis's intervention, Harlow to Curtis, 30 Sept. 1943; RTF 3012 (2).
[190] Undated note, RTF 2694.

fault with it'.[191] The series petered out with the failure to recruit a distinguished Indian in the later 1930s; there were no post-war lectures, although Walter Lippman was invited for 1947, and the scheme and was abandoned finally in 1954. The really lasting legacy of Kerr's grand design was Rhodes House Library, for so long at the centre of wider and wilder schemes for imperial research. With the rapid post-war growth of interest in both American and Commonwealth-colonial history for which it catered in both books and archives, its academic importance rose steadily, and with it its cost. By the early 1950s, the Trustees were spending more than twice as much on Rhodes House and the library as before the war, and twice as much as on their external grants and donations.

Of course, as we have seen already, once the interlude of war was over and the scholarship programme was resumed, its heavy financial pressure dominated every aspect of the Trust's activity. Before the war, the annual cost of the scholarships had been approximately £85,000. By 1953, when the abnormal burden of the immediate post-war years had passed, it was £100,000. By 1959, with a rising stipend, it was nearly £150,000. The result was a continuous heavy deficit in the Scholarship Fund which had to be met by regular transfers from the Public Purposes Trust into the scholarship's capital reserves. In the climate of post-war austerity which this bred, the last shreds of pre-war ambition vanished completely. When the financial situation began to ease in the mid-1950s, with regular surpluses of £50,000 in the Public Purposes Fund, the mood of the Trustees was very different from that of their pre-war counterparts. In Kenneth Wheare, Lord Franks, and Dean Lowe, the Trust had three college heads acutely aware of the pressure imposed by post-war expansion on the University's brittle infrastructure. Wheare was a key figure in the informal group who shaped many of the University's decisions in the 1950s and 1960s.[192] As the imperial horizon receded, physically and mentally, the claims of Oxford on the Trust became irresistible: especially the preservation of its aesthetic beauty (a concern of the Trustees since the 1920s) and the need for new college building to cope with rising student numbers.[193] From 1954 onwards, contributing to college endowments and (on a grand scale) to the Historic Buildings Appeal became the Trust's main concern apart from the scholarships. By degrees it had become not the progenitor of new academic causes but a hardship fund for the collegiate University. When in 1961 the Trustees offered up Rhodes House itself as an administrative office for the University, a richly symbolic gesture had been made. Milner's imperial mission among the sullen dons had finally gone native.

Imperial Work: Child Emigration and India

Up until the sea-change of the 1950s, the Trust had not been entirely forgetful of the principle laid down by Lord Rosebery in 1904, that it should not confine its imperial benefactions to South Africa. The Trust supported a variety of domestic pressure groups

---

[191] Coupland to Kerr, 13 June 1928; RTF 2694 (1).
[192] Harrison (ed.), *History of the University of Oxford*, viii. 712.   [193] Ibid. 677.

and organizations which propagated the imperial idea, including the Victoria League and the Imperial Institute. Between 1903 and 1925 the League was given nearly £10,000[194] and in both world wars its main role lay in providing hospitality for overseas troops in Britain. Apart from its own library in Rhodes House, the Trust gave money towards the teaching of 'imperial studies' at London University, and, for a number of years, helped maintain the post of 'Rhodes Professor' in imperial history at King's College. But outside Britain, the Trust's relations with the other Empire countries to which Rhodes's will had linked them through the scholarships lacked both the sense of obligation felt towards South Africa and the network of agents and claimants who channelled its funds into local causes. Nor elsewhere did the Trustees feel the same sense of political urgency. Nevertheless, on occasions they did sprinkle their aid more widely, even if with a sparing hand. The exchange of schoolmasters between independent schools in Britain and the 'white dominions', vigorously promoted by Montague Rendall, a former headmaster of Winchester, began in the 1920s and was supported by the Trust for over twenty years, though it would not, Kerr remarked drily, ' show immediate results to impatient imperialists'.[195] One of the most intriguing, and durable, of these wider commitments was the Trust's support for child emigration.

In post-imperial times, 'child emigration' has a sinister ring. Even in 1929 it struck Philip Kerr as a phrase which 'posterity might misunderstand'.[196] But the Child Emigration Society sprang from the same philanthropic impulse that had led idealistic young graduates of Oxford (like Clement Attlee) to work in the 'settlements' (the colonial analogy is striking) of the East End of London to reclaim the poor spiritually as much as physically. Its founder was Kingsley Fairbridge, a Rhodes scholar from Rhodesia, whose charismatic personality and singleness of purpose more than compensated for his modest academic attainments. Fairbridge was born in Grahamstown but went as a boy to Rhodesia in 1896. As a young man he worked in a bank and for the 'Native Labour Bureau' which recruited black workers for the farms and mines of white Rhodesia. From an early age he seems to have shared the obsession with transforming Southern Africa into a 'white man's country' by British immigration—a key element in the ideological complex of 'British South Africa'. By his own account,[197] it was the shock of seeing child poverty in the East End while on a visit to Britain in 1903 which convinced him that 'children's lives [were] wasting while the Empire cried aloud for men. There were . . . orphanages full—and no farmers.'[198] Fairbridge was determined to come back to Britain to mobilize support for his idea: the Rhodes scholarship (academic competition for which in Rhodesia then hardly existed) which brought him (after four attempts at the entry test) to Exeter College was, as he candidly admitted to the sceptical Parkin, merely a vehicle for his larger aim.[199]

The Society was founded in Oxford in October 1909 at a meeting attended by some

---

[194] Note in RTF 1203 (3).   [195] Kerr to Rendall, 3 Sept. 1933; RTF 2676 (1).
[196] His view is noted in Sir A. Lawley to Kerr, 17 Jan 1929; RTF 1567 (3).
[197] *The Story of Kingsley Fairbridge by Himself* (Oxford, 1927).
[198] Ibid. 142.   [199] Fairbridge to Parkin, 12 Jan. 1910; RTF 1567 (1).

fifty 'colonials' (Fairbridge's phrase). From the beginning Fairbridge had enjoyed the patronage of Earl Grey and the Trust supported him with a small stipend after the end of his scholarship. His movement was publicized in the *Morning Post* and quickly acquired an impressive body of patrons, including, within a few years, the bishops of London and Winchester, the Dean of Christ Church, the scientist Sir Ray Lankester, Lord Devonport, and the immensely grand Herbert Warren, President of Magdalen. Fairbridge set off to establish the first of his 'Farm Schools' in Western Australia to which thirty-five children had been dispatched before the outbreak of the First World War.

The appeal of his idea reached far beyond the circle of imperial activists like those clustered round Milner for whom empire settlement and the imperial unity of the 'British nations' were axiomatically desirable. Fairbridge's evocation of an empire-wide British identity struck a chord of race patriotism whose influence was widely diffused in Edwardian Britain. His stress on the urgency of moral and physical salvation for pauperized, abandoned, or orphaned children and the transforming effects of his 'Farm School' as a nursery of young colonial yeomen was perfectly tuned to the contemporary social conscience and to the belief, heavily canvassed since the later nineteenth century, that Britain's temperate colonies of settlement offered an Arcadian refuge from the dehumanizing squalor of its industrial cities. It was an added bonus that overseas migration evaded awkward issues of social justice and could be represented as furthering both the progress of the colony and the strength of the Empire.

For the Trustees there were added reasons why Fairbridge's appeal could not be ignored. As a pioneer Rhodesian, an accomplished athlete, and a missionary of empire, he was a scholar who exemplified Rhodes's ideal. He had mobilized the sympathy of other Rhodes scholars in Oxford and it was Australian Rhodes scholars who later provided a considerable part of the Society's funds. Thirdly, Fairbridge's insistence upon agricultural training and settlement chimed exactly with Rhodes's own injunction to the Trustees. When Fairbridge returned to Britain in 1919 to raise more money with his message of blood and soil imperial patriotism—'We should waste nothing of our British blood nor of the Imperial soil from which we spring'—his claim was irresistible. With further support from the Trust and other funds raised in Britain the Child Emigration Society had sent out over 700 children by 1931, and the original farm settlement in Western Australia boasted a church designed by Herbert Baker and a Milner Road. When he died prematurely in 1924 at the age of 39, the Trustees paid for the publication of his autobiography (reprinted eleven times by 1945) and a memorial tablet was placed in the new Rhodes House in 1929. This deliberate celebration of Fairbridge as a young, idealistic (white) hero of empire expressed as vividly as any of its other benefactions the Trust's conception of its imperial purpose in the 1920s and 1930s. It remained, especially, perhaps, in Elton, a strand in its post-war thinking. As late as 1959, by which time the old emphasis on child migration had been modified, the Trust promised £5,000 to the jubilee fund of the renamed 'Fairbridge Society' with its anodyne motto 'sailing to a new life in the Commonwealth'.[200]

---

[200] Elton to Sir Charles Hambro, 28 July 1959; RTF 1567 (4).

It was only very gradually that the Trustees' sense of catering almost exclusively for a white man's club—'No doubt we must expect the occasional coloured man from Barbados or Trinidad,' wrote Sir Francis Wylie, the Trust's Oxford Secretary in 1916, 'but that can't be helped'[201]—gave way to a broader sense of the imperial association. For them, as for British opinion at large, the change was prompted by the intense controversy over Britain's relations with India which reached its climax between 1930 and 1935. By then British policy had modulated from the avowedly authoritarian ethos of the Victorian Raj into the promise of a staged extension of self-government beginning in 1919 with the partial transfer of provincial affairs to elected Indians under 'dyarchy'. By 1930, however, it was generally agreed, by British as well as Indians, that this experiment in limited devolution had broken down. But a further measure of self-rule, especially one that gave Indians more control over the central government in New Delhi, aroused fierce opposition in Britain. It was stigmatized as the appeasement of Gandhian nationalism which, unlike other and older varieties of Indian political consciousness, called for the repudiation of Western modernity and the imperial connection. And it also seemed likely to threaten Britain's ability to exploit India for the strategic defence of the Empire as a whole. One third of the British Army was stationed in India at local expense and the Indian Army—the only other regular army in the Empire—made up one-third of its military strength on land. A self-governing India which threw off this burdensome obligation would tear up the foundations of British world power.

India had originally been of little interest to the Trustees. Even Milner, whose imperial concerns extended far beyond South Africa, rarely spoke about the subcontinent, perhaps because in his own day discussion of its affairs was largely monopolized in Britain by a specialized fraternity of 'Old India Hands' headed by the Jupiter-like figure of Lord Curzon. Amongst the Trust's South African clientele, especially Patrick Duncan, fierce anti-Indian prejudice was the corollary of their enthusiasm for more white settlement. Indians were omitted from the Founder's will, despite the fact (or perhaps because of it) that Indian students were already coming regularly to Oxford.[202] Indian studies existed in Oxford, but they were regarded mainly as the province of probationer British officials on their way to India, picking up a smattering of language (usually, it was said, in the imperative mood) and history before they went. In fact, the early years of the Trust coincided with a time when the conventional distinction between the self-governing empire of the 'white dominions' and the 'dependent' empire of despotic rule, headed by India, was at its height.

By 1930, however, within both the Trust and the *Round Table* circle to which it was closely connected, this older view had broken down. Like his mentor Lionel Curtis, Kerr had been sympathetic to the gradual assimilation of India's authoritarian system to the tradition of self-government in the white colonies. Among the Trustees, Geoffrey Dawson had visited India in 1927–8 as editor of *The Times* and returned to urge the case for a

---

[201] Quoted in C. W. Newbury, 'Cecil Rhodes and the South African Connection: "A Great Imperial University?"', in Madden and Fieldhouse (eds.), *Oxford and the Idea of Commonwealth*, 91.

[202] John Darwin, 'A World University', in Harrison, (ed.), *History of the University of Oxford*, viii. 609 n. 5: there were seventy Indian students at Oxford in 1914.

forward movement to meet Indian political aspirations. When a commission under Sir John Simon recommended full self-government in the provinces, but much more cautious advance at the centre, Kerr wrote an article in the *Round Table* to support him.[203] Kerr, by this time a member of the House of Lords, became a Liberal Party delegate to the all-party conference held in London in 1930 to thrash out a new constitution with representatives from India. As a junior minister at the India Office in 1931–2 he was closely involved in drawing up the plan for an Indian federation under which limited powers would be transferred to a federal assembly where Gandhian nationalism would be safely neutered by the conservatism of the princely states. The princes would control one-third of the legislature, Amery recorded him as saying, 'but have no difficulty whatever in buying up the rest'.[204] In 1932 Kerr went to India as chairman of the commission sent to drawn up the franchise for the new electoral system.

Kerr's essential conservatism (like most reformers he regarded the day of full Indian self-rule as infinitely remote) was far removed from simple die-hard prejudice. In common with the other champions of the federal 'solution', he thought that the careful cultivation of sympathy between Britain and India would be a key ingredient in making the new relationship work and steadily deflating the windy rhetoric of Gandhianism with its demand for civil disobedience and its rejection of all advance that fell short of *purna swaraj*—complete independence. Kerr's part in constitution-making between 1930 and 1932 had exposed him to a far wider range of Indian interests and personalities than was usual, even in the official realm of policy-making for India. Within the narrow compass of the Trust's resources, at their most straitened in the early 1930s, he became anxious to build bridges between cultural and intellectual circles in Britain and those he saw as the leaders of educated Indian opinion. The first vehicle for this enterprise was the Rhodes Memorial Lecture.

Between 1932 and 1935 Kerr made a series of attempts to bring an eminent Indian to Oxford, hoping perhaps that it might spark the kind of intellectual enthusiasm that accompanied Smuts's lectures. His choices were significant. The first was Srinavasa Sastri, the leading political 'moderate' in India, and a former member of the Viceroy's government. Like the other Indian Liberals, he was an important link between the British and more amenable sections of the congress. There was no better person, Kerr told the Vice-Chancellor, 'to interpret India to England at the present time'[205]—perhaps a guarded reference to the growing political backlash led by Churchill against the federal scheme. Sastri declined on grounds of health. Kerr's next choice was Sir Muhammad Iqbal, a lawyer, former president of the Muslim League and the leading Muslim intellectual in India, selected 'on general political grounds'.[206] It would please Indian Muslims, he told the Trustees. He urged Iqbal to lecture on Islam: English opinion was saturated with missionary prejudice. But Iqbal preferred to lecture on 'space and time', would only come in 1935, and then caught flu. By that time, the Government of India Act was safely passed

---

[203] A. C. May, 'The Round Table 1910–1966', unpublished D. Phil. thesis (Oxford, 1995), 267–77.
[204] Amery's diary, 16 June 1933, quoted in May, 'Round Table', 274.
[205] Kerr to Vice-Chancellor, 4 Aug. 1932; RTF 2694 (2).
[206] Kerr to Fisher, 31 Oct. 1933; RTF 2694 (2).

and Kerr's attention switched to Germany and European peace. The idea of an Indian lecturer lapsed until the outbreak of the Second World War and the threat of non-cooperation in the war effort by the Indian National Congress. Kerr's successor, Lord Elton, was eager to invite Jawaharlal Nehru, for practical purposes the political leader of the Congress, to deliver the Rhodes Memorial Lecture in 1940. It was necessary to do something, he told the Trustees, 'to strengthen this weak link in the British Commonwealth'.[207]

The suggestion was vetoed by the Viceroy. But Elton's anxiety for a gesture towards 'closer intellectual contacts between India and ourselves' led eventually to the Indian Rhodes scholarships. Elton's views were deeply influenced by Edward Thompson, with whom Kerr had corresponded regularly since 1931. When Elton told the Trustees that 'our contacts with India are restricted with dangerous narrowness to administration, business and big-game hunting', he was quoting directly from Thompson's diagnosis of Anglo-Indian alienation. Thompson's wide knowledge of Indian intellectual life, forceful views, and often intemperate language make his letters extraordinarily compelling, now and doubtless then. Thompson's father had been a Wesleyan missionary in south India. He himself was ordained and went in 1910 to teach at Bankura College in Bengal where his literary and poetic interests brought him into contact with leading figures in the Bengali cultural movement, including Rabindranath Tagore. After war service (as a chaplain) in the Middle East, he returned to Bankura in 1920 but came back to Britain three years later. There he published a series of novels and poems but earned his living by lecturing on Bengali to probationer British officials in Oxford, a post he held from 1923 to 1933.

Thompson had revisited India in 1931 on a Rhodes travelling fellowship. His report in April 1932[208] gave Kerr exactly what he was looking for: a strategy for promoting cultural sympathy to underpin the new and experimental phase in Anglo-Indian relations. Thompson denounced the failure of the British administration to make contact with the modern school among Indian writers who looked towards Europe. 'Immense good could be done even politically if their self respect could be helped by the feeling that their intellectual effort was . . . recognised as part of the Empire's life.'[209] Thompson urged a series of ways in which Indian art and literature could be given greater recognition in Britain. His conclusion was blunt. 'It seems to me pikestaff plain that relations that exist solely on the administrative and political plane, except for the interests of the big-game hunters and our commercial houses, are far too narrow to be safe. We can mobilise incalculable reserves of goodwill by a trivial expenditure of money and attention.'[210]

Thompson became Kerr's *éminence grise* on cultural relations with India. He was fiercely critical of the Indian studies taught in Oxford as 'solely utilitarian and governmental', and dismissed what passed for Indian history in Britain as mere official compilations. The Indian Institute (in Oxford) was 'damned beyond redemption . . . so wipe

---

[207] Report 329, 7 Dec. 1939; RTF 2694 (2).   [208] See RTF 2844 (1).
[209] Ibid.   [210] Ibid.

out the Indian Institute and all its works'.[211] No Indian, he told Kerr, 'would ever regard this jail-like structure with anything but horror and aversion'.[212] What was needed was a fund to bring over a series of visiting lecturers from India, and 'a building near Rhodes House . . . so that . . . after ten years of progressive dying down of anti-Indian prejudice, it could work as a sort of sister institution'.[213] Thompson occupied himself with histori-cal research. His study of British rule (co-written with G. T. Garratt) was admired by Coupland: 'more Indian history from his pen', he told Kerr, 'would help substantially to a better understanding between educated Indians and Englishmen.'[214] But Irwin House was never built; the scheme for visiting lecturers from India lapsed, perhaps because Kerr had 'too many irons in the fire',[215] and Kerr's attempt to get Thompson appointed to the readership in Indian history came to nothing.

But the Trust's involvement in Indian politics had a dramatic finale. In September 1939, Kerr and Tom Jones (by then chairman of the Pilgrim Trust) devised a plan to send Thompson as an unofficial emissary to the Congress leadership. In a whirlwind tour, Thompson met British officials, the Congress leadership, and Jinnah, the leader of the Muslim League. He castigated the failure of British officialdom to maintain contact with Indian politicians, even Gandhi: one governor had told him that he wanted to meet Gandhi but could not, because 'Gandhi, like the tiger, is royal game; only a viceroy can shoot him'.[216] His main conclusion was that the Congress was so committed to the inde-pendence struggle that only an immediate advance to 'dominion status' (like that enjoyed by Canada and the other 'white dominions') with control of foreign policy at the end of the war would stave off non-cooperation. Much of the interest of Thompson's report lies in its record of Indian opinions (including Iqbal's private denunciation of 'Pakistan' as 'disastrous') and his own deep commitment to close Anglo-Indian partnership within a reformed imperial association: like many critics of empire, he wanted a better empire not no empire at all. His recommendations were passed to Whitehall, but to no avail. No agreement was reached with the Congress and by the middle of 1940 the breakdown of relations marked the first step down the road towards the Quit India movement, mass gaoling, and independence though partition. Thompson, whose health had long been fragile—he had had, he told Kerr in 1935, 'a life of every kind of strain and hardship and overwork, shell shock in the war old malarias and other tropical and war diseases'[217]— died in 1946.

Towards India, as towards South Africa, we can see the Trust acting self-consciously as an informal agency of empire. In both cases its initiatives were born out of the con-viction that official policy was either too maladroit or too complacent to respond flex-ibly to the new political conditions obtaining between Britain and some of the key components of its world-system. By the inter-war years, the imperialists clustered round

---

[211] Thompson to Kerr, 14 July 1932; RTF 2844 (1).
[212] Thompson to Kerr, 27 May 1933; RTF 2844 (1).   [213] Ibid.
[214] Coupland to Kerr, 16 July 1935; RTF 2844 (1).
[215] Curtis to Elton, 22 Nov. 1939; RTF 2844 (1).
[216] Thompson's report, Dec. 1939; RTF 2844 (1).
[217] Thompson to Kerr, 17 Oct. 1935; RTF 2844 (1).

the *Round Table*, whose political views were often indistinguishable from those informing the Trustees, had come to lay greatest emphasis upon cultural and ideological sympathy as the most powerful adhesive between the mother country and its self-governing
daughter-states, even when (as in South Africa) that meant reconciling non-British communities to British values and institutions. The confidence with which these solutions
were propounded suggests that even in this autumn of empire, the end of British world
power seemed no more likely than the end of the world. Yet the Trust's engagement with
India, except through the Rhodes scholarships begun in 1946, was strangely vacuous.
Without the infrastructure to hand in South Africa, it depended largely upon Thompson. But in Oxford, Thompson was an outsider and the Trust lacked the influence to
back him effectively. With the 'criminal tribes' (Thompson's phrase) of the Oriental
Studies Faculty, as elsewhere in Oxford, the Trustees found academic discretion the better
part of imperial valour.

Doing Rhodes's Will

In the first sixty years of its existence, the Rhodes Trust lay in the shadow of the world's
largest empire, inhabited a culture suffused with imperial imagery, and looked out upon
a world much of which was organized into empires rather than nations. It was at the
centre of what the Trustees perceived as a 'British world', and what some of them would
have regarded as a distinct civilization, coeval with that of contemporary Europe. It was
natural that they should think of the scholarships, and all their activity, as contributing
to the strength and power of the British 'system', not least because they had such faith
in its institutional and ethical foundations. Even the large commitment to the American
scholarships could be recognized as an investment in the friendship of the other great
Anglo-Saxon power, whose naval strength rivalled Britain's after 1920 but who was also
its natural ally against imperialist predators in Europe and Asia. The Trustees, however,
were not simple reactionaries content to hold what Britain had. In the 1920s and 1930s
they were part of a larger group of 'modernizing imperialists' for whom the survival of
British power meant constant adaptation. They were alert to the importance of cultural
influences, and longed to make British opinion at home more receptive to the interests
and aspirations of both the 'white dominions' and India. Circumstances dictated that in
this enterprise their success was at best somewhat modest.

Ultimately, the most powerful influences upon the Trust's development between 1902
and 1960 were money and the inflexible terms in which the will provided for the scholarship programme. Rhodes's bequest turned out to be solid but not spectacular. Its limited
scale meant that the Trustees could influence the political and academic landscape around
them, but not transform it. They could support initiatives, encourage enthusiasms, and
reinforce structures—even old and battered ones. With rare exceptions (Rhodes House
and Rhodes University) they could not build their own. Everywhere they needed allies
and collaborators to supply the infrastructure their benefactions needed. For much of the
period we have traced, the Trustees were also chronically anxious that the costs of the
scholarships would outstrip their resources: good reason for their insistence upon con-

ditional gifts and time-limited grants. It is all the more striking that they were willing to tie up such large fractions of their capital in the Smartt Syndicate, Rhodes University College, and the 1820 Memorial Settlers' Association—though they did so before the fine balance between their fixed obligations and Rhodes's diminished legacy was fully recognized. In retrospect, however, we can see that the years between 1925 and 1939 were a watershed in the Trust's evolution towards an Oxford-based educational charity. It was then that the Trustees realized how burdensome the scholarships were and how difficult it would be to expand the Trust's own role in Oxford or beyond. It was then that they realised how far the terms of the will made them dependent upon the successful modernization not of the Empire, but of the University. After 1945 this movement towards Oxford coincided with the gradual atrophy of their links with the English section in South Africa, and the mounting influence within the Trust itself of 'dons with donnish ideas'. In the 1960s, with the end of empire, the Trust, like many British institutions, seemed to become more inward-looking, and its internal affairs were temporarily dominated by the racial aftermath of the colonial age. With a new century, and in a fully post-colonial world, the pattern of its activity may shift again.

Afterword

ANTHONY KENNY

In the century since Rhodes's death, have the scholarships he founded achieved his ambitions for them?

To answer this question we need to know what his ambitions were. In his fourth will of 1888 Rhodes left most of his fortune to Lord Rothschild and urged him to use it to found a secret society with a constitution modelled on that of the Jesuits but with the words 'English Empire' substituted for every occurrence of the words 'Roman Catholic Church'. Some have seen the foundation of the scholarships, in Rhodes' final will, as an execution of this fantasy: the creation of an international band of dedicated imperial missionaries. If this was his aim, then clearly it failed disastrously, and deserved to do so.

Generations of his Trustees, however, have been grateful that Rhodes's final will set out no such goal for the scholarships. It sets out in detail what kind of man is to be chosen as a scholar; it does not tell him what he is to do with his life, except that he is to 'esteem the performance of public duties as his highest aim'. The clearest statement of an object for the scholarships is contained in the German codicil of 1901: understanding between the world's great powers will keep international peace, and educational relations between their citizens will tie the nations together.

Of course, Rhodes hoped, as he said, that the education of colonists in the United Kingdom would impress upon them 'the advantage to the Colonies as well as to the United Kingdom of the retention of the unity of the Empire'. But he was not a Disraelian imperialist, glorying that vast territories marked pink on the map were ruled from Westminster. The Empire of his dreams was rather a federation of interdependent self-governing nations. That he had no narrow imperialist aim in the foundation of the scholarships is shown by the fact that of the 156 scholarships assigned in the will, 96 were to go to citizens of the United States. Rhodes believed that union between the English-speaking peoples of the world was a great good: but the attachment to England which he hoped American Rhodes scholars would feel was not, he insisted, to 'withdraw them or their sympathies from the land of their adoption or birth'.

The scholarship system, as it operated through the twentieth century, was as much a creation of Parkin as of Rhodes. A brilliant organizer and an indefatigable traveller, Parkin devised the mechanisms of selection and determined the interpretation of Rhodes's criteria for qualification. An even more ardent devotee of imperial federalism than the Founder, Parkin began his missionary activity by persuading the Trustees to quadruple the number of Canadian scholarships. This act set in motion a long process of reversing the proportions between American and colonial scholarships. From the outset some of the Trustees, particularly Milner, believed that Rhodes had made a mistake in appropriating so many scholarships to the United States. Throughout the century, as funds became available, the Trustees added to the scholarships from the Empire and then from the Commonwealth; they left the number of American scholarships untouched.

The issues that Parkin had to address were very similar in different constituencies. Domiciliary requirements were a problem everywhere, whether it was a question of the eligibility of the children of transient settlers and officials in the colonies, or, in the States, whether one could enter the competition in the state of one's education or of one's parents' home. The age qualification was a contentious issue in many places, with school headmasters and university officials pursuing divergent and ill-hidden agenda. It was Parkin who determined that, wherever possible, scholars came to Oxford not as schoolboys but as graduates.

Throughout his life, Parkin had much more influence on the history of the scholarships than any of the Trustees. The early Trustees were more interested in the political aspects of Rhodes's legacy, and for many decades after his death continued to spend money on non-educational imperial, and particularly South African, causes. But the Trust's political activities were kept strictly separate from the educational functions of the scholarship. In this the Trustees were, no doubt unwittingly, following the example of the Jesuits whose methods Rhodes had admired. In the sixteenth and seventeenth centuries Robert Persons, the arch-plotter of the British Counter-Reformation, had kept his conspiratorial activities rigorously separated from his educational role as rector of the seminary in Rome which trained priests for the English mission.

On major issues of policy, Parkin often showed himself more enlightened than some of the Trustees. When the question arose whether blacks were eligible for scholarships, he was a partisan of the liberal interpretation of the will's ambiguous remarks on 'race'. He was uncomfortable with the Trustees' decision, at the height of war fever, to abolish the German scholarships by Act of Parliament. In the early days of the Trust there was no serious consideration of allowing scholars to marry or of admitting women scholars, as much because of the ethos of Oxford as because of any expressed wish of the Founder.

As befitted the guardians of a will, the Trustees throughout the century showed themselves conservative in their interpretation of the scholarship's nature. Almost every significant change in the conditions of tenure took place after a period of outside pressure, whether it was national pressure for the termination of the German scholarships in 1916 or international pressure for the admission of women in the 1970s. For a period after the first war the Trustees showed themselves unwilling even to take account of inflation in fixing a scholar's stipend. The most significant change in the geographical distribution of the scholarships—the extension into the New Commonwealth in the 1960s—was initiated by suggestions from the Colonial Office, however enthusiastically it was eventually championed by Lord Elton. But where deep-seated feelings were involved, the Trustees were capable of resisting sustained outside pressure, as they showed in their refusal to restore the German scholarships for twenty-five years after the Second World

War. In general, their interpretation of Rhodes's vision of the ideal scholar, and of the type of international unity that the scholarship should promote, followed, after a time-lag of varying length, liberal opinion in Western society.

Over the century, what did the chosen scholars gain from their scholarship? The most accurate answer is the banal one: an Oxford education. But the value placed on that education has varied in different times and in different places. Like most Oxford graduates, most Rhodes scholars have looked back with affection on their time at the university and retain a loyalty to their college. But if we are to assess the particular debts they would acknowledge, we need to make distinctions between different periods of Oxford's history and different constituencies from which scholars have been drawn.

For candidates from Australia, Canada, South Africa, New Zealand, and the smaller constituencies, a scholarship to Oxford, throughout the century, presented an unquestioned academic opportunity. What Oxford had to offer was as good as, if not better than, the best education available in the home country. This has not always been true in the case of scholars from Germany and the United States. Early in the century, in the heyday of the great German universities, many Germans thought of Oxford colleges as little more than elegant finishing schools, and did not regard the university as a serious research institution. At that time American scholars, even from the most famous universities, stood in awe of Oxford, and regarded its classical entry requirements as a serious academic hurdle. At the end of the century, the positions were reversed. German students now flocked to Oxford in large numbers—of which Rhodes scholars were only a tiny proportion—prizing a personalized style of education which many had found hard to obtain at home. Academically ambitious Americans, on the other hand, might well feel that an Oxford training would do less to further their career than would a doctorate from one of the more prestigious universities in the USA. Those, on the other hand, who aimed at professional or public career might value their Oxford course less for its strictly academic content than for the opportunity which it provided for cultural expansion—as much, perhaps, through vacation travel as through term-time study.

Officials of the Rhodes Trust were well placed to observe the way in which during the course of the century the most celebrated American universities overtook Oxford in terms of academic prestige. Already in the 1930s Lothian warned that Oxford would have to develop its research capacity if it were to retain a position of international leadership. In the 1950s Williams told the Trustees that, if they wanted the scholarships to continue to be prized, they had to help ensure that Oxford remained good enough for Harvard men to want to come to. It was on this basis that he persuaded the Trustees to overcome their past hesitations and undertake a programme of regular benefactions to the university and the colleges.

If we ask not what Oxford has done for Rhodes scholars, but what the Rhodes scholarships have done for Oxford, the truest answer is again the most obvious one: they turned it into an international institution. At the turn of the millennium, when Rhodes scholars made up less than 10 per cent of the overseas students in the university, it was difficult to recall that when the first scholars arrived at the beginning of the century, the population of Oxford was almost exclusively British. It was Rhodes's bequest that began the process which led to Oxford's acceptance today that a regular inflow of students and scholars from abroad is a vital element in the health of a university in both education and research.

It is sometimes claimed that the requirements of Rhodes scholars led to important changes in Oxford's educational system, such as the abolition of classical entrance examinations, the introduction first of the doctorate and later of taught master's courses, and the establishment of the honour school of Politics, Philosophy, and Economics. The direct evidence for this is slight, and certainly there were other factors too pushing the university in the direction of these changes. But it is undoubtedly true that an important part in the development of Oxford syllabuses and structure has been played by the internationalization of the university which the Rhodes system inaugurated.

The emphasis which Rhodes placed on sporting ability in his blueprint for his scholars has naturally meant that Rhodes scholars have consistently been expected to make a significant contribution to Oxford sport. They have indeed done so; but the nature of their contribution has varied from constituency to constituency. Australians, New Zealanders, and South Africans have arrived with long existing experience in rugby which has enabled them to take their places without difficulty in college and university XVs. But Americans and Canadians have had to create for themselves an environment in which they could display their skills in their own national sports. The importation of baseball and ice hockey to Oxford can fairly be credited to past generations of homesick Rhodies. Scholars from all constituencies, however, quickly took to the river on arrival in Oxford and earned their place in a number of historic VIIIs.

Did the scholars take away from Oxford anything which derived specifically from their having been Rhodes scholars? In his will the Founder prescribed that scholars should be distributed among the colleges and should not 'resort in undue numbers to one or more Colleges only'. The Oxford secretaries and the wardens of Rhodes House took to heart this warning against the establishment of a Rhodes clique, and were anxious not to set up any rival loyalty to compete with scholars' loyalty to their individual colleges, or to deflect scholars from making friends with their British hosts. None the less, it was inevitable that common exile would bring together Rhodes compatriots, and that successive wardens' hospitality would bring together Rhodes scholars from different countries. Moreover, though colleges were principally responsible for the pastoral as well as academic care of the scholars who belonged to them, wardens were called on to provide a secondary pastoral care, particularly in those areas where British students with problems would expect to call upon their nearby families.

It was Wylie who set the pattern for the tutelage of Rhodes scholars in Oxford as Parkin had set it for their selection overseas. When he became Oxford secretary to the Trust he had been ten years a classics don at Brasenose and he saw his duties as similar to those of a college moral tutor or public school housemaster. Long before the opening of Rhodes House he and his wife entertained on a generous scale, and long after leaving it they kept open house for returning scholars to visit them on Boars Hill. For many years Wylie sent a birthday card to each of his former charges, and many of them treasured the portrait of him which the Trustees distributed on his retirement.

If Wylie was an archetypal college don of the old avuncular school, his successor C. K. Allen was more typical of a university which was becoming more international and more professionalized. Himself an Australian Rhodes scholar reject, he was, at the time of his appointment in 1931, professor of jurisprudence with a distinguished textbook of legal philosophy to his credit. Military in aspect, and meticulous in matters of detail, he did not allow the business of the Trust to occupy as large a part of his life as his predecessor had done. He continued to write authoritatively on administrative law, and for many years wrote pseudonymous columns in the weeklies; he was content to leave much of the management of Rhodes House in the capable hands of his wife. But according to his successor Williams he always showed the Rhodes scholars 'an imaginative fair-mindedness allied to a shrewdly dispassionate common sense'.

It was Williams who, first as Warden and then as Secretary also to the Trustees, gave the Rhodes system the shape which it maintained for the latter part of the century. Anything but tame himself in personality, he domesticated the Trust as an institution. Under his guidance the Trustees gradually gave up their more visionary imperial and internationalist aspirations and focused their attention on Oxford. During his period the number of scholarships remained stable, and the scholarships for the New Commonwealth were held to the minimum; when he pressed changes on the Trustees it was in the direction of contraction, not expansion. Like Allen before him, he kept up many interests outside Rhodes House. He was the first Warden to be a significant figure in academic administration, and Oxford is in his debt for persuading the Trustees that benefactions to the collegiate university should be a normal part of their activities. As editor of the *Dictionary of National Biography* he did much to shape his generation's picture of the preceding one. It is sad that he published little, for every paragraph he wrote grips the reader. Among the scholars he demolished with devastating effect any self-indulgence or self-importance; but for those in real trouble he was capable of taking exquisite pains. It could be said of him, as he once said of his predecessor, that he had 'a quite exceptional gift for staying outside his own firm prejudices'. To most scholars alive today, he remains the epitome of a Warden of Rhodes House.

Williams's successors were, in the main, content to walk along the paths he had laid out. Warden Fletcher, however, carried out without fuss a number of important but unobtrusive reforms, such as the repatriation of the Trust's South African funds. He improved the conditions of the scholars in several ways and he persuaded the Trustees that they could afford to resume the expansion of the scholarship system in the New Commonwealth. In the 1990s the favourable economic climate and the ending of apartheid enabled the Trustees to remember the Trust's origins and early history and to play a small but not negligible part in the rebuilding of the new South Africa.

The several chapters of this book have attempted to describe the contributions made by Rhodes scholars on their return to their own countries. In some countries the scholarships had an impact before the first scholar had returned from Oxford: small colonies like Bermuda and Rhodesia, in order to make themselves worthy of Rhodes's exceptional gift, invested in improving the educational opportunities they offered at home. Because the educational systems in the larger colonies were modelled on the English system, it was easier for scholars from those countries to adapt to Oxford's academic ways. It was much harder for scholars from the United States and Germany to make a seamless transition between their earlier education and their Oxford course. This has been, throughout the century, reflected in the academic performance of scholars once in Oxford: the examination record of Australians, for instance, has been consistently superior to that of Americans. But the ease with which the 'colonial' scholars fitted in academically brought with it a compensating disadvantage. The most talented among them, having come to the end of their scholarship, might opt to remain in Britain or elsewhere rather than returning to their own countries. The contribution of New Zealand Rhodes scholars to the study of the English language in Oxford has often been remarked on. It is no coincidence that the best-known Rhodes scholar scientist, Howard Florey, was an Australian who was working in Oxford when he discovered the therapeutic value of penicillin. By compensation, the other Rhodes Nobel laureate, Wilder Penfield, though elected from New Jersey, made his massive contributions to our knowledge of the brain while working in Canada.

During the century most of the Rhodes constituencies except the United States experienced a brain drain at some time or other. Very often the emigrations were due to political rather than academic considerations: as with German scholars in the 1930s, with South Africans under apartheid, and with Zimbabweans in recent years. At time of stress as many as half a constituency's scholars may fail to return home Given the international nature of the Rhodes scholarship ideal, and the contribution that many scholar expatriates have made to organizations working for world harmony, the patterns of migration cannot be counted as a significant defect in the scholarship system.

The United States was able to welcome back most of its scholars. Some of them brought with them educational ideals which they had learnt in Oxford. Frank Aydelotte introduced in his own college, and encouraged others to introduce elsewhere, an honours system based on Oxford tutorials. William Fulbright was inspired by the Rhodes scholarships to set up the much larger scheme of international scholarly exchange which bears his name. If the Rhodes scholarships taught Oxford that a good university in Britain needed a significant leaven of overseas students, it also taught American institutions that a good university education should make provision for a period of study abroad.

No doubt over the century the scholarships have produced a higher proportion of academics than Rhodes and his first Trustees would have liked. But Rhodes scholars have also been prominent in the more conspicuous forms of public service. The United States, Canada, Australia, New Zealand, Jamaica, and Malta have all had scholars as heads of government, or heads of state, or governors general. The history of South Africa would have been happier if a Rhodes scholar, Jan Hofmeyr, had, as he was expected to do, succeeded Field Marshal Smuts as head of its government in 1948; for much of the time since then scholars in that country have had to show their commitment to public service by working to bring about change in government rather than participating in it. In the United States Rhodes scholars were prominent in the Kennedy and Clinton administrations and have held many of the highest offices of state. The popularity of political careers in other constituencies is subject to variations not easily explained. Scholars were prominent in public life in Canada in the 1970s, but hardly in the 1990s; in Australia the pattern has been quite the opposite. In the constituencies of the New Commonwealth, in general, scholars have yet to make a public mark: but in Pakistan a Rhodes scholar has been chairman of Senate and from time to time acted as head of state.

Scholars returning to their home countries have never acted as a coherent group acting for a common purpose, whether or not this was what Rhodes expected of them. They have, indeed, retained links with each other to an extent unparalleled among the beneficiaries of other scholarship programmes; but these links have been almost entirely social, and never political. Only rarely, even in the affairs of the Trust itself, have they acted as pressure groups, as the American Association did in the case of the South African schools scholarships.

Throughout the history of the scholarship, selection committees have sought out not candidates with a particular political programme, but candidates with particular personal characteristics. With the exception of the restriction to the male sex, the qualities which Rhodes required in his scholars are qualities which are valuable in any part of the world and in any particular system. Academic competence, the healthy vigour needed for an active life, a care for the weak, and an ability to show leadership: the value of these characteristics has not dated in the years during which Rhodes's imperialist dreams have faded into oblivion.

It is a striking feature of Rhodes's specification for his scholars that the qualities which he sought were not, with the exception of leadership ability, ones which he possessed himself. His academic performance was miserable: he took seven years to obtain a pass degree. He was an indifferent sportsman, and, while capable of astonishing endurance, he was constantly dogged by ill health. And while he was capable of great kindness to individuals in trouble, he was in general prepared to sacrifice the interests of the weakest members of the community to his grander political ambitions. One thing can certainly be said to his credit: whatever his faults, he was not the kind of person who wants everyone else to be just like himself.

In the aftermath of the Jameson Raid, Rhodes was forced to resign his directorship of the British South Africa Company which governed Rhodesia. During the parliamentary inquiry into the Raid, he feared that the country it governed might lose his name. 'They can't change the name of the country, can they?' he pleaded. The inquiry left the name of Rhodes's colony unchanged; but a hundred years later the areas once known by his name are called Zimbabwe and Zambia. Worldwide, his name is now perpetuated only by the scholarships whose foundation was the best of all the things he did in his full tumultuous life.

APPENDIX I
The Rhodes Trust Archives
CAROLINE BROWN

The death of Mr Rhodes on 26th March 1902 at Muizenberg Cape Colony, South Africa was recorded.[1]

With these words the first minute book of the Rhodes Trust begins. This acknowledgement of Rhodes's death is one of the earliest records in what has grown to be a large and comprehensive collection of archives. The collection documents, in hundreds of files and volumes, the history and development of the Trust.

At that original meeting in Berkeley Square on 5 May, barely ten days after Rhodes's death, the Trustees began the process of putting into practical effect the wishes outlined in Rhodes's will. Those first minutes record the pressing issues of the day: Rhodes's last will and codicils were produced; arrangements were put in place for the funeral and a memorial service; and bankers, solicitors, and accountants were appointed. It is also possible to see, even from these early records, something of how the Trust was to develop, and something of what it has become. There were discussions on improvements to be made on Rhodes's estates, the settlement of farmers, the emigration of women, and political payments. More general obligations were recognized under 'Subscriptions and Donations', which records that it was decided to present medals to those who had helped with arrangements after Rhodes's death. At the same meeting it was agreed to continue Rhodes's 'periodical payments' to his relatives, and to honour various donations, loans, and guarantees already promised. Finally, in the last four items of the day, the Trustees turned to Rhodes's provisions to bring scholars to Oxford. The first record of the Rhodes scholarships, which were to spread to over thirty countries and have involved more than 6,000 scholars, is rather understated: 'It was decided to arrange that the Scholarships directed by Mr Rhodes to be established for the Colonies, the United States of America and Germany, commence from 1903.'[2]

The archives span the century that has passed since Rhodes died, from the creation of the Trust in 1902 to the present day.[3] Since that first meeting of the Trustees, in fact since Rhodes's death, nearly a century of activity has produced a large collection of various media, files, plans, photographs, sound recordings, and videos, which, with various related artefacts, paintings, busts, and statues, form the Trust's archive. The collection provides a fairly balanced record of the history of the Trust, its organization and structure, the significant developments and decisions, and financial policy. It also gives an insight into its daily working and the individuals involved. Some periods and subjects are more effectively covered than others, but few records appear to have been lost, there is little that is not recorded, and there is little duplication or redundancy. This chapter does not attempt to provide a list of the archives; a separate detailed catalogue is available. It does aim to give an impression of the nature and scope of the material,

---

[1] RTM 5 May 1902.   [2] Ibid.
[3] There is also a small amount of earlier material, connected in particular with reminiscences about Rhodes and with his estate.

of the types of records and different media that constitute the collection, and of the strengths and weaknesses of the archive, particularly what it reveals of the development of the Trust and its interaction with, and impact on, the wider world in which it operates.

Types of Records: Minute Books and Reports

The minute books of the Rhodes Trust record the decisions taken at each meeting of the Trustees. These meetings were originally held monthly, but once the initial pressure of business decreased it became unnecessary to meet that often. In 1947 there were full meetings around six times a year, but in 1963 the Trustees decided to reduce this to quarterly meetings and at present they meet three times a year. Decisions were taken on all aspects of the Trust's business: financial policy and investments, the management of property and other assets, appeals and donations, and the administration of the scholarships in Oxford and overseas. Particularly in the early years the Trustees also considered requests from individual scholars such as for loans or to postpone residence. These were recorded either in the general Rhodes Trust minute books or in the separate minute books which were sometimes used for each fund. The minute books are well indexed although, with the use of separate books for each fund, the numbering system became rather confused, and minute numbers are not necessarily in the correct sequence. In fact the minute books are of limited value to the researcher. Beyond confirming the decisions that were reached, and identifying which Trustees attended particular meetings, they reveal very little. There is nothing of the reasoning behind certain decisions or of the context in which they were reached. To get a broader view, and to have more of an understanding of the development of the Trust, it is necessary to look elsewhere.

The Trustees were very busy men, frequently busy outside London and often outside England. Three of them, Milner, Jameson, and Michell, spent most of their time in South Africa during the first few years after Rhodes's death and Grey was Governor General of Canada from 1904 until 1911. At their first meeting the Trustees appointed a Secretary, to be based in London, who would be in charge of the daily running of the Trust and who would act as a point of contact for the scattered Trustees. These secretaries gathered together the most significant documents and correspondence to present to the Trustees at their meetings. At first material consisted of monthly reports and correspondence from the Trustees or their representatives in Southern Africa concerning the Trust's property and Rhodes's estates. In the early years Hawksley dealt with much of the business in England and presumably he reported developments orally to the other Trustees.[4] From 1908 however, with Mrs Mavor as Acting Secretary, the reports begin to include a separate section on the scholarships and to refer to appeals and donations, and non-South African issues, such as property or grants in England. Soon all the topics that the Trustees were to discuss in their meetings were included; with extracts from letters or reports giving the Trustees the information on which to base their decisions. With so much to cover in the reports it was necessary for the Secretary to be selective and include only the most relevant correspondence.

---

[4] The archives reveal that the Trust tried on several occasions to trace Hawksley's papers, either through his firm Coward Chance (later Clifford Chance) or through his son who continued in the business. Kerr hoped that the records would come to light as Hawksley had conducted practically all of the early business of the Trust and had been responsible for drawing up Rhodes's will. The Trustees were especially keen to learn all they could about the phrasing of the will and Rhodes's intentions, the Rhodes–Beit Fund, and the position with regard to duties and tax charged on the estate (see RTF 2524, Jan. 1928, for example). Unfortunately none of the papers came to light.

The style of the reports changed further with Kerr as Secretary. He frequently summarized correspondence and included a recommendation as to what the Trustees' action should be. In this way the reports reflect the added weight given to the role of the Secretary that had begun with the death of Milner and the appointment of Kerr.

The reports have continued to the present day: at the time of writing the Warden will soon present the 600th report to the Trustees. They have remained broadly similar to those first presented by Kerr in 1925, although the style and content has changed somewhat with each Secretary or Warden. Elton's reports, for example, were sometimes rather lengthy assimilations of all available sources, in which he thoroughly examined each point of view. Those of Williams were much briefer, with the essential information given succinctly as a preamble to the discussion at the meetings. The reports can be a useful source but, because of their selective nature, they do not tell the whole story and they are not indexed, so it is often difficult to identify a particular subject or to trace certain decisions. A balanced and comprehensive view of the history of the Trust and the matters in which it has been involved can only be achieved by going back to the original source, the Rhodes Trust Files.

Types of Records: Rhodes Trust Files

The vast majority of the archive consists of files which can be broadly divided into two groups: scholars' files and subject files. Files on scholars (over 6,000 to date) have been kept by successive Oxford secretaries and wardens and will be described more fully later. A file has also been opened for every subject with which the Trust has dealt. Over the years this has meant more than 2,000 files on different topics have been opened. Since 1959 the provenance of these latter has been the office of the Rhodes Trust in Rhodes House, Oxford, but the earlier files have a slightly more complex origin.

Administrative changes, described in other chapters, have had an effect on the organization of the records so that the Rhodes Trust archive is an amalgamation of three different collections of records, not including the files generated by overseas secretaries which will be described later. The office in London was for many years the main centre of the Trust and its files form the basis of the Rhodes Trust archives. They cover a wide range of subjects including the scholarships, finance and property, appeals and donations, and administration. When opened each was given a running number, beginning with 1000[5]: RTF 1000 is Natal Scholarships, RTF 1003 is the National Museum and Library, Salisbury, and RTF 1004 is Princess Radziwill. In general, the higher the number the later a file was opened, although this is not always true. Changes in office procedure, poor filing practices, or misplaced material have meant that some earlier files were added to the numbering system at a relatively late stage. Not all the files have survived: there is, for example, no RTF 1002. In general, however, it seems that only very routine files were destroyed, although files on unsuccessful appeals have not usually been kept. The file numbering system has survived the evacuation of the London office to Rhodes House during the war, the later move to Beaumont St., Oxford, and the final amalgamation of the two offices in 1959: the file numbers have now reached more than 3,700.

Until 1906 the Trust also had an office at the Rhodes Building in Cape Town. When this was

---

[5] Earlier numbers may have been for working files, or could possibly have been used by Parkin: his official correspondence is filed with the London files, as he shared the office and facilities, but if he had his own personal filing system it has not survived.

closed Michell continued to pay for clerical assistance from the staff of the British South Africa Company but the files he had generated were closed. He kept them in storage until 1910 when Hawksley, at the time of the handover of Groote Schuur to the new Union government, declared that all the Trust's records should be sent to England. Hawksley's main concern was probably to ensure the removal of any of Rhodes's papers that had survived at Groote Schuur during its occupancy by Jameson: he was, after all, the man who was said to have destroyed some of the documents on the Jameson Raid. There is no record of whether any Cape Town office files were destroyed at this time but several were sent to the London office. Some of these were combined with London files, with all correspondence being refiled in chronological order. Other files, mainly the larger ones, were kept as separate supplementary files, and given the same number as their London counterparts, but with the addition of a suffix such as A. RTF 1086 on the South African Colonization Society, for example, contains material from both the London and Cape Town offices, while the four files about Inyanga opened in Cape Town (RTF 1815A) have been kept as separate files.

Meanwhile Wylie was producing his own records in Oxford. Originally based in a house in South Parks Rd, he had little room for voluminous records and regarded some of his correspondence, particularly with departed scholars, as personal. Very much a man of the early twentieth century, he favoured letter books and filed his official incoming and outgoing correspondence as separate series, in chronological order. Some of these letter books and correspondence files have survived in the archives.[6] By the time C. K. Allen took over, however, the number of scholars and range of the scholarships had expanded, with a parallel increase in the amount of records. An Australian lawyer with an organized turn of mind, Allen began to file his records by subject, but without a number referencing system. On the merger of the London and Oxford offices, when Williams took over Elton's role in 1959, some of the Oxford material was probably destroyed as it duplicated the London material.[7] The remainder of the files were treated as the Cape Town files had been fifty years earlier: some were merged with London files and others kept as supplements to the existing files.

The London files cover a huge range of subjects, both scholarships and general issues, those from the Cape Town office deal with South Africa and what was then Rhodesia, while the Oxford files are mainly concerned with the scholarships and scholars, with some reference to appeals related to Oxford. Some files contain series such as Statements for the Academic Year, Oxford Secretaries' Reports to the Trustees, the Christmas Letter, Newsletters, the *American Oxonian*, Balance Sheets and Accounts, and other publications. The bulk of the material in the files, however, is correspondence, either with contacts overseas, with Trustees, or between the Trust offices. The separation of the post of General Secretary from that of Warden until 1959 generated correspondence that continued even during the war when both offices were in Rhodes House and this has added to the richness of the archives. The files may also contain reports, newspaper cuttings, pamphlets or brochures, short articles, and photographs. Sometimes records of different media have been stored separately, particularly photographs, press cuttings, plans, and the few videos and sound recordings. However, for most of the century, all material relating to a subject was added to the file, including copies of correspondence, copies of reports to

---

[6] See files RTF 3076 and RTF 3076A–D.

[7] The term 'London files' has been used even though the office moved to Oxford in 1939. Similarly the Oxford files are referred to as Oxford Secretary files although from 1932 the title of Warden was increasingly used.

the Trustees, and copies of minutes. It is for this reason, because they contain a complete archival record, that the files are such a rich source for the researcher.

Although the files were opened and stored in chronological order it is possible to identify themes and subjects to which the archives relate. It is through an examination of these subjects that the significance and value of the archives can be understood. The rest of this chapter will look briefly at the content of the records, to give an overview of what they can reveal to the researcher about the Rhodes Trust, and the organizations and individuals with which it came into contact, and about the century in which it has operated.

Scholarship Files

When Rhodes's will was published his scheme to establish scholarships at Oxford seized the imagination of the public and is still the best-known aspect of the Trust's work. In fact the £1,100,000 required to fund the original 171 scholarships accounted for only around a quarter of the original value of the estate (just over £4,000,000 before duties and loss on investments). For some of the early Trustees the scholarships were only part of a broader plan that Rhodes had wanted his legatees to follow. Hawksley, for example, frequently reminded his fellow Trustees of the importance of Rhodes's Confession of Faith. As he explained to Michell: 'I know—perhaps no one better—how much store Rhodes put upon the long document and his wishes therein indicated. I think when you read the paper you will understand what I meant when I said I did not regard the Will as an Educational one in quite the sense you did.'[8] Even allowing for this wider picture, however, the scholarships were, and have remained, the central focus of the Trust's activities and this is reflected in the archives.

The Oxford Secretary or Warden was most immediately concerned with the scholars and scholarships but the London office (initially Parkin and, after his retirement, the General Secretary) was also closely involved. London was responsible for the general administration of the scheme, for dealing with the centres overseas, and for bringing policy decisions before the Trustees. Elton believed that the scholarships were central to his responsibilities: he described the landmarks of his time in office as 'the war, the Reunion, the Jubilee History, the Rhodes Trust Act of 1946, the creation, in 1940 and 1958, of seven additional Rhodes Scholarship for seven new countries, and particularly the birth of nine of the eleven existing Rhodes Scholar associations'.[9] The scholarships are therefore well documented by the subject files of the London office, as well as by the Oxford files.

Scholars

The Rhodes Trust has over 6,000 scholars' files, one for each scholar elected. The contents of the files vary considerably, depending on the date the scholar came up, but may include applications, correspondence with scholars, photographs, or published articles.

The practice of keeping files on scholars began with Wylie, probably in 1921 when he wrote to all scholars, enclosing a form and asking them to send him information about themselves. Wylie had always kept in touch with the scholars he had known; he sent many of them a private birthday greeting, a habit that was continued by his wife after his death. Some of the pre-1921 correspondence had survived and was put on the newly opened scholars' files but some, and

<hr />

[8] Letter from Hawksley to Michell, 9 Jan. 1904; a copy is in RTF 2180, filed 1935.

[9] RTF 2978, Elton to K. L. Cooper (Western Australia and Hertford 1927), 22 July 1959.

some of the more personal later letters, he kept amongst his own papers.[10] From 1921, however, Wylie regularly filed correspondence on the scholars' files. This included letters about a scholar's election, about finding a college, about their progress and activities while at Oxford, and also about their careers and lives after going down. After Wylie retired he continued this correspondence and informed his successors of anything significant that he heard. His close contact with scholars was particularly appreciated during and after the Second World War when it became difficult for the Oxford office to keep up to date with the movements and actions of some scholars. In April of 1949, for example, Wylie wrote from Boars Hill to Allen about Count Schwerin von Krosigk (Germany and Oriel 1905), due to be tried at Nuremberg: 'You may be interested to know that I heard from von Krosigk 2 days ago. He expects the sentence to come sometime this month. He was given leave in November to pay his family a visit. He continues to be hopeful.' Later in the same month, he commented on the award of an honorary fellowship to J. W. Fulbright (Arkansas and Pembroke 1925): 'He is having a rapid success that young man, isn't he? Of course, his connection with a state like Arkansas helped him to get a start in politics . . . Canham [Maine and Oriel 1926] . . . said that Fulbright seemed to him to be the one Rh-Scholar who might be regarded as perhaps of Presidential timber [sic].'[11] These references indicate that scholars felt an intense loyalty towards the Wylies and for many it became part of their lives to keep them informed of what they were doing.

Fortunately for the archives, Allen and subsequent wardens proved as determined to keep in touch with scholars as Wylie, even if this contact became, of necessity, less personal. Wylie himself had become overwhelmed by the scale of correspondence in the few years before he retired. From November 1923 he sent all scholars a circular letter, including with it the information slip for scholars to fill in. However, he continued to send each scholar a personal Christmas greeting until 1927, when he finally admitted: 'It has been borne in upon us . . . that the march of events is fast making this impossible.' With between 1,100 and 1,200 scholars, 'a separate Christmas letter must go, and . . . we must content ourselves with a general one'.[12] The circular letter, begun in 1923, was expanded and became the Christmas Letter which, with the information slips, has continued to be sent to scholars to this day. The slips form the basis of the biographical details that Rhodes House holds about scholars on which the published *Registers* are based. Allen filed all the regular correspondence he had with and about scholars on their files. A range of issues is covered by this correspondence including the scholar's qualifications, choice of subject, progress, or requests such as for extra funding or for a third year. Correspondence was usually with the scholar, overseas secretaries or committees, the London office, or Oxford colleges. As with Wylie, correspondence with the scholar often continued after he had left Oxford: Allen or future wardens were called upon to give advice on a certain career or project, or the scholar simply enjoyed keeping in touch on both a personal and professional level. Senator Fulbright, for example, returning his information slip in 1983, fell to discussing the state of his and the Warden's teeth: 'After each visit to my dentist I have a feeling of relief and gratitude that I have any teeth left.'[13] Wilder Penfield (New Jersey and Merton 1914), the world's leading neurosurgeon in the

---

[10] RTF 3676B. Wylie's letter books also contain copies of letters sent by Wylie to scholars. They are fully indexed and may provide additional information about a scholar while he was at Oxford. The only surviving letter books cover the period 1908–29.

[11] RTF 2044A, Wylie to Allen, 15 Apr. 1949. This file contains some of Allen and Wylie's correspondence once Wylie had retired and includes some references to scholars. Other comments by Wylie about news he has received can be found on country files which are explained in more detail below.

[12] RTF 3511A, Wylie, Nov. 1927.   [13] J. W. Fulbright, PF, Fulbright to Fletcher, 4 Feb. 1983.

1950s and 1960s and the first Commonwealth academic figure to receive the Order of Merit, kept up a regular correspondence with Wylie, Allen, and Williams and returned his information slip for 1968 stating under 'Present Occupation': 'Writer, with no academic title, no duties and very little income.'[14]

Wylie did not keep copies of the scholars' applications or dossiers: these were sent to their colleges. It was not until the 1930s that the American office began regularly to send two copies of the applications, one of which was filed at Rhodes House. Allen did not encourage other countries to copy this practice as he was afraid that the dossiers would take up too much filing space. Sometimes all or part of an application appears on the files of a non-American scholar, either because a duplicate was sent or because Allen did not send the whole application to the college. However, it was only in the late 1960s and early 1970s that copies of the scholars' applications, whatever their nationality, began to be kept on their files as a matter of course.

When asked, Wylie would provide reports on the progress of the scholars while at Oxford. From around 1920 he began to send regular reports to Aydelotte and from 1923 to most of the other countries. These were meant to inform selection committees how the scholars that they had chosen were faring at Oxford, the rationale being that they would be better informed as to the kind of person who did well at Oxford or who would make the most of the opportunity afforded by the scholarship. From the 1920s these reports sometimes appear on scholars' files. Allen also began filing reports from tutors and colleges on scholars' files, although these are more often than not rather too brief to be particularly revealing.

The scholars' files are a potentially useful source for the researcher or family historian: they often give an impression of a scholar's attitudes to Oxford and ambitions. The correspondence can be particularly revealing if a scholar applied to the Secretary or Trustees for a special reason such as to change course, to postpone coming into residence, or to stay a third year or for an additional grant. If the scholars were granted extra money or third years their files may also include reports or memoranda detailing how this was spent. The file on Adam von Trott zu Solz (Germany and Balliol 1931), for example, reveals that he applied and was granted a postponed third year in 1933. He wished to go back to Germany to continue his legal career but hoped to return to Oxford at some point to write a thesis on 'some aspect of the "Political Doctrines of Modern Europe"'.[15] In November 1936, however, he called to see Allen enquiring as to whether the Trustees would agree to him taking the third year teaching international law in China. According to Allen's notes on the meeting von Trott was 'very uncomfortable in Germany—difficulties about obtaining a job in academic world or industry—but wants to return to Germany to teach International Law. No further details at present, except the predominant motive is admittedly to get out of Germany.'[16] The third year was granted and in July 1938 von Trott sent Lothian a sixteen-page memorandum 'The main point of . . . [which] is the suggestion that a constructive way out of the mess in which China, Japan, England and Germany are finding themselves in the Far East could be found in Anglo-German political cooperation and possibly a joint move for peace.'[17]

Other material likely to be on the scholars' files includes press cuttings and published articles. The Trust does not, however, have a library of scholars' works. This was suggested on occasion but plans to create one never succeeded, mainly because of problems of size (Aydelotte once

---

[14] W. Penfield, PF, Information Slip, 1968.
[15] A. von Trott zu Solz, PF, von Trott to Allen, 22 May 1933.
[16] Ibid., Allen, Nov. 1936.   [17] Ibid., von Trott to Lothian, July 1938.

reported having over 600 volumes). Occasionally there may also be photographs on the files but the main sources for photographs of scholars are the annual photograph albums and the annual freshers' photograph. The former were begun in 1917 by Gilmour, the new Secretary eager to introduce some new practices, and all scholars, new and old, were asked to supply a photograph. The early albums of scholars create the disturbing impression that some of the scholars were approaching middle age when they were elected, until it is remembered that the photographs were not received until at least fifteen years after some of them had matriculated. There is not a photograph for every early scholar—some had died or did not respond when the request went out—but the albums form a complete series until the present day. The freshers' photographs are group photographs, the first of which was taken in 1906. Very few of these have survived in the archives for the early years but there is one for nearly every year from the 1960s.

Other sources of information about scholars, apart from the scholars' files, include index cards (now a database) and notebooks recording biographical information. Individuals may be mentioned in the Statement for the Academic Year or the Oxford Secretary's Reports to the Trustees. The subject files that originated in the London office also contain references. The Warden often had to write to the London office to confirm a ruling or to obtain approval for a particular course of action. Subject files were created for this correspondence on issues such as the postponement of scholarships, on scholars and marriage, on scholars' careers after leaving Oxford, or on third years. Much of this material is duplicated on the scholars' personal files as it originated in the Oxford secretaries' office, but sometimes, especially during the time of Lothian, scholars wrote or reported to the London office directly. RTF 2747 Third Years, for example, has reports and letters from von Trott that are not filed on his personal file as well as a fascinating series of letters and photographs from J. M. Bertram (New Zealand and New College 1932), who had also been granted a third year in China. The subject files that provide the most detail about scholars, as well as about the organization of scholarships, are those on individual countries. They contain information about elections, and sometimes applications if the Trustees were asked to decide between candidates, as with early elections in Prince Edward Island and Rhodesia. Overseas secretaries and the London office frequently corresponded about scholars at Oxford, especially if there was a notable achievement or problem. The Indiana file, for example, contains an early reference to a scholar who was later to play one of the most important parts in the history of the Trust. Michell relating his first meeting with Aydelotte found him 'an exceptionally engaging young fellow and likely, I think, to do us credit. The trustees will, I am sure, watch his career with interest.'[18]

Country and Other Scholarship Files

The files on individual countries document far more than just the scholars; they are the main source for understanding the development of the scholarship system itself. They cover such issues as the setting up of the selection procedures and criteria in each country; the mechanics of getting scholars to Oxford and placing them into colleges; the requirements of and subjects offered by Oxford; the disruptions caused by war; the allocation of new or additional scholarships; and, occasionally, the withdrawal of scholarships. Opened by the London office and later supplemented by the Oxford secretaries' material they include copies of the memoranda of regulations issued by each country to applicants, instructions sent from the Trust to selection committees about qualifications and qualities to look for in scholars, reports from secretaries and others who

[18] RTF 1265, Michell, 6 Oct. 1907.

visited the countries, and extracts from reports to the Trustees and minutes of meetings. Much of the material, however, is correspondence, either between the Trust and overseas or between the general and Oxford secretaries.

Many of the files date from 1902 and begin with letters commenting on Rhodes's will and offering suggestions as to how the scholarships could be organized. Thirty-three files were opened straight away for America alone, one for each state allocated a scholarship and one as a general file. There were nineteen other countries, states, provinces, or institutions mentioned in the will and six other provinces in Canada were immediately awarded scholarships by the Trustees. The sheer amount of material gives a sense of just how daunting it was to try to arrange for the initial sixty-three scholars a year to be selected, and then to find them places at Oxford. The files contain correspondence from Parkin as he travelled around the world setting up a selection process in each country. There are extracts from his reports to the Trustees, such as those describing his 17,000 miles of railway travel in America and Canada and 35,000 miles of land and sea travel to South Africa, Australia, and New Zealand in 1902 and 1903.[19]

Once a workable system had been put in place letters continued to reach the Trust from overseas describing changes in the committees or in the regulations, seeking help on problems encountered, and asking for rulings on issues of eligibility. Changes in educational systems in the countries concerned and visits by Trustees or secretaries, in particular, prompted much correspondence. One important change affected the nature of the archives. Parkin retired in 1921 and in the larger scholarship countries (America in 1918, and Canada, Australia, and South Africa in 1921) secretaries were appointed to act as a point of contact between the selection committees and the Trust. This meant that the Trust had much less direct contact with states or provinces, to the extent in America that many of the state files end at this point. The nature and comprehensiveness of the records depended to a large extent on the efficiency and procedures of these secretaries. Some regularly sent minutes or kept the Trustees informed of the composition of committees; others were not quite so forthcoming. Some countries developed a certain amount of independence but all continued to consult the Trust on matters of major policy, even when dealing with the mechanics of the selection process themselves. An example of the independence that had developed in America can be seen from the following incident from 1946. Elton, writing to Aydelotte about dealing with candidates after the war, expressed concern that committees outside the USA might have to interview candidates, but Aydelotte replied, somewhat to the former's surprise, 'these interviews in absence have been a regular feature of our America selection for something like twenty years'.[20]

From around the 1930s the material in the files includes more material of a different type, particularly statistics and analyses of the scholars as a group. There was an increasing interest in judging the success of the system by looking at the careers of the scholars themselves. Sarah Gertrude Millin's book on Rhodes had caused some consternation, particularly with Allen, by claiming that the scholars were merely 'decent fellows . . . They are to-day creditably following their professions, they are good citizens. But that, as Rhodes expected, they have had any influence on the world at large is not apparent. Few of them, proportionally speaking, have even gone into public life—hardly more than would have done so, Rhodes Scholarship or not.'[21] This

---

[19] See RTF 3675. The reports of Parkin and later secretaries on their visits overseas were usually copied onto the relevant country files. This file contains most of the reports that they produced.
[20] RTF 1233, Aydelotte to Elton, 12 Sept. 1946.
[21] Sarah Gertrude Millin, *Rhodes* (London: Chatto & Windus, 1933), 332.

prompted others to try to gauge the influence for themselves. Aydelotte, in particular, was keen on statistics, which he regularly sent to London and Oxford, although not always to good effect, as Allen revealed to Lothian: 'I am afraid I do not understand Aydelotte's figures, and, as a matter of fact, I never do. According to our figures they are never quite accurate.'[22] This production of statistics, lists, and registers increasingly appears on the files of all countries, particularly during the war when the usual routine of the scholarships was interrupted, and on occasions afterwards such as around the time of the fiftieth anniversary.

Millin's criticisms also revived the recurring debate about the type of scholar that Rhodes had envisaged. Michell, writing to Parkin in 1908, believed that although the mechanism of choosing a scholar was difficult to arrange at least it was fairly clear what type of man Rhodes would have wanted. He 'did not desire to bring over the purely intellectual students . . . He wanted to give the all round men an opportunity of acquiring the culture of our senior University. His method of ascertaining who are those all round men, may be open to revision, but those are the men the Will seeks to benefit and not the mere scholar.'[23] Dawson agreed that 'all-rounders' should be chosen while Kerr felt that the emphasis had shifted too far from intellect. Elton, characteristically, believed that Rhodes would have wanted the balance 'which comes from intellect based on character'[24] but still felt that the scholar should be distinguished in some way. Williams agreed but cautioned, 'For myself I'm sure that what makes the scheme unique, apart from its distribution, is the emphasis on character as well as ability. I like the stress on distinction but it may just be that attempts are made to find the unusual (which tends to mean the academically unusual?) without that solid note of character which makes that unusualness effective.'[25] From the 1920s the Trust issued a regular Memorandum to Selection Committees which gave guidance on choosing scholars as well as, until the 1950s, including statistics on scholars' performance. These are often filed and discussed in the country files.[26] The difficulties that arose when trying to define the 'ideal' scholar can be seen elsewhere in the archives. After inscribing the name of Kingsley Fairbridge (Rhodesia and Exeter 1908) in the rotunda at Rhodes House, it proved impossible to decide which other scholars were worthy of joining him on the panels. In the end Fairbridge's name was removed and he was commemorated with a portrait. This decision generated further correspondence as the secretaries and Trustees tried to choose which other scholars should have their portraits hung in the Milner Hall.[27]

Attempts to measure the success of the scholarships or define an ideal type of scholar were paralleled in some countries by a growing sense of the scholars as part of, if not a worldwide, then at least a national body. The files reveal that this self-awareness led, in some cases, to the formation of associations. The process began early for the Americans, with Aydelotte, as usual, providing the impetus. In the archives there are separate files for the *American Oxonian* which were opened as early as 1912, and files on the American Association of Rhodes Scholars which began in 1928. As the activities of the American scholars increased so did the files that were needed to keep up with them: the American Trust for Oxford University, the Eastman Professor, and Eastman House all generated so much material that they needed files of their own. Other countries in time formed associations, some of which gave support to projects which are documented separately, such as the Canadian scholarship in reverse. This trend to encourage Rhodes scholars to act as a body and to develop a kind of corporate spirit often owed as much

---

[22] RTF 1233, Allen to Lothian, 2 May 1939.   [23] Ibid., Michell to Parkin, 2 Jan. 1908.
[24] Ibid., Elton to Aydelotte, 29 Apr. 1940.   [25] RTF 2696, Williams to Elton, 25 Jan. 1954.
[26] See also RTF 2696.   [27] See RTF 2637 and RTF 3000.

to the encouragement of Elton as to the impetus of the scholars. In his final report to the Trustees he admitted: 'what gave me the deepest satisfaction was what may be called the oecumenical aspect of the work, and particularly the attempt, from the end of the late war onwards, to foster among Rhodes Scholars everywhere a sense of belonging to a world wide brotherhood—through the founding of the Rhodes Scholars' Associations, the centenary Reunion, the launching of the annual News Letter and our overseas journeys.'[28] Elton perhaps rather misjudged the desire or ability of scholars to join together in this way. In some countries associations were short-lived, or, although remaining active, did not generate enough material for a separate file. The files on the associations in Malta, Bermuda, and Jamaica, for example, were all opened in the 1950s, but had closed by the end of the 1960s. Williams himself saw little point in trying to take measures in Oxford to prolong the life of or increase the activities of these bodies, if the scholars themselves did not want it. He admitted: 'Old Boy dinners rather run against the grain. Besides, I think Rhodes Scholars should be yeast in their own countries rather than trying to make themselves a compact dough.'[29]

The Newsletter that Elton referred to in his report is one of several other types of records that give information on the scholarships. From 1906 to the present day the Trust has produced a Statement for the Academic Year which has listed (the exact content depends on the year) the results of scholars in examinations, blues, notable achievements at Oxford and elsewhere, and publications and careers. These were supplemented, until 1945, by an annual report by the Oxford Secretary to the Trustees, which contained much the same information plus a summary of how the system had worked in that particular year. Elton's Newsletter was an attempt to produce a similar kind of annual summary but one that would develop a mutual awareness amongst scholars worldwide, containing not only statistics, but articles about scholars and reports from associations around the world. The Newsletter was only issued from 1956 to 1959 as once the two offices were merged there was not enough time to produce both this and the Christmas Letter. Individual countries published their own newsletters, registers, address lists, or guidance for scholars. The Trust has periodically issued a record or register of Rhodes scholars, and occasionally scholars, while at Oxford, have published pamphlets or magazines. All of these, along with books and articles on the scholarships and the Trust in general, can be found in the archives. Sometimes these are filed in the country files but often they also have their own subject file and number: the Newsletter, for example, is RTF 3128.

These and other subject files dealing with the scholarships provide an opportunity to evaluate how an issue affected several different countries or how it changed or was dealt with over the years. RTF 1432 Scholars and Marriage, for example, begins in 1907 with Aydelotte again breaking fresh ground by marrying at the end of his second year. The files go on to cover special regulations during the war and the gradual relaxation of the marriage rule until all scholars were allowed to marry in 1995. RTF 1066 on the age limit has references to individual scholars and to general rules, as well as correspondence about conditions in individual countries such as South Africa. Not all files are added to as consistently as one might wish. RTF 1122 Colour Question, begin, perhaps surprisingly early, in 1902 but is all but closed by 1911. Others close once the issues begin to occur less frequently: RTF 1066 ends, for example, in 1956.

Taken together with the country files, and with Wylie's correspondence files and letter books, these subject files are an informative and comprehensive source for the history of the

---

[28] RTF 2978, Elton's Report to Trustees no. 438, 11 Feb. 1960.
[29] RTF 3148, Williams to J. C. Dakin, 6 June 1963.

scholarships. They are also interesting in what they reveal about Oxford and about the countries in which the system operated. At Oxford the arrival of up to a hundred additional scholars a year from overseas cannot have failed to have some impact. Issues such as the Greek requirement and the standing of overseas universities can be traced in the files. The file on third years includes discussions about the length of the scholarship and the types of courses that scholars should take. These debates were part of the wider context of attitudes to research at Oxford. Allen, for example, saw the whole question of whether scholars should read for a second BA or do a research-oriented course as fundamental to the nature of the scholarships. He warned, 'Oxford is, I believe, right in maintaining an attitude of caution, not to say scepticism, towards Research, with a capital R . . . a great deal of work which passes under this imposing title amounts only to spinning ropes of sand.'[30] This view was echoed much later by Elton at a point when the Trust was considering potential American funding for the scholarships. Aware that money would be more forthcoming if for research, Elton argued: 'We all know that research is essential, but we also most of us know that a certain proportion of it at any rate consists of "extracting bits out of books which nobody has ever read and putting them into books which nobody will ever read" . . . the real object of the Rhodes Foundation after all is to turn out men, rather than to add to our knowledge of bitumen, steel stresses or the Byzantine Empire.'[31]

There is, however, disappointingly little about the colleges' attitudes to scholars. Wylie's letter books and correspondence have some early letters to and from colleges as do the scholars' personal files. RTF 2326 Distribution of Scholars in Colleges includes some similar correspondence and has the following from Dean Lowe, writing to Allen about whether Christ Church or Brasenose would take a scholar: 'Between ourselves, sending another athlete to B.N.C. is sending coals to Newcastle and sending a Christian there is almost cruelty.'[32] Throughout the century the files reveal attempts by successive wardens to get all scholars placed in colleges. This was never easy and sometimes generated such comments as this from the Principal of Jesus in 1937:

I share your view that the present system of distribution is not satisfactory, but I remember the meeting at Rhodes House at which there was a discussion of possible alterations and I remember also the selfish attitude taken up by the larger and more fashionable Colleges. I do not set it up as a virtue or as any ground for favours, but it is a fact that on at least two occasions in the latter part of Wylie's time, this College took a Rhodes Scholar, whom we wished to decline, simply because we were told that unless we did so there would be no place for him.'[33]

Scholars' opinions of Oxford are documented either in their own files or on country and subject files. This early scholar from British Colombia wrote home with his first impressions, and the letter was sent on to Parkin for comment: 'I have never undergone such an overhauling as I have had at Oxford . . . I don't want to say too much yet about the drunkenness and vice in Oxford. It is likely more apparent than real, but certainly there is more than there should be.[34]

The files can also reveal something about education, and occasionally the broader political context in the scholarship countries. The difficulties experienced by some countries in meeting eligibility requirements were sometimes due to their educational systems, and the correspondence about this, often with senior figures in universities or the government, can be found on

[30] RTF 2747, extract from Oxford Secretary's Report to Trustees, 1933–4.
[31] RTF 3095, Elton to Aydelotte, 14 Aug. 1951.   [32] RTF 2326, Lowe to Allen, 16 Jan. 1948.
[33] Ibid., A. E. W. Hazel to Allen, 1 Mar. 1937.
[34] RTF 1269, T. M. Papineau (Quebec and Brasenose 1905), 4 Feb. 1906.

the files. In Rhodesia, where there were no universities, the files contain discussions on the options available for further education, possible funding for education in South Africa and the expansion of secondary education. Parkin never lost his devotion to the advancement of education in Canada and most of his correspondence with Canadians has references to wider issues. File RTF 2106 British Colombia, for example, refers to the establishment of a university, to its first president, and to the difficulties it experienced during the war. Parkin was also asked to recommend a new president for the university. Later in Jamaica, after the Trust had expressed concern in 1937 about the quality of scholars, the Governor responded by promising to put more money into education, in particular into science laboratories and scholarships to improve the education of potential scholars. Debate over the composition of the selection committees sometimes reflected not only local educational rivalries but also religious or political divides, as other chapters have shown. The chapter on Germany, for example, has examined the German selection committee of the 1930s in the wider context of political affiliation. Political changes sometimes forced the Trustees to rethink, as in India where the newly formed committee had just one year to function before it was forced to re-form after the creation of Pakistan.

Those involved with the scholarships overseas, whether on committees or as advisers, have often been fairly prominent people. In Rhodesia G. M. Huggins, Sir Drummond Chaplin, Sir Herbert Stanley, Cecil Rodwell, and Sir J. R. Chancellor were all consulted. In some countries the Governor General was often the committee's chairman. Correspondence with these can appear on the files, occasionally touching on general topics and often revealing the broader interests of the secretaries. Parkin quickly built up contacts in most of the countries he visited: his letters to America, for example, often contain educational advice of a general nature. His tour of the United States and Canada during 1917 was partly funded by the Foreign Office as an opportunity to convince American public opinion about the war. But Parkin had been conducting his own propaganda exercise before that, using every opportunity to include in his letters his thoughts about the war and the justification for it. The President of Delaware, for example, received several letters along these lines. The following is typical of Parkin's style:

We are now waiting to learn the decision Washington has come to about submarine warfare . . . All the Allies feel that prodigious sacrifices are yet to be made. How great they are you can scarcely imagine on your side of the Atlantic. On the casualty list yesterday we had nearly 200 officers and a small army of privates, and this is not at all unusual. There are very few homes that escape. I have a great sense of personal relief to-day in the fact that our only son has got back safely last night from a month at the front.[35]

The letters of Parkin, Wylie, and Aydelotte during the first war and Allen, Elton, and Aydelotte during the second often refer to the events around them, about which they were deeply concerned. This was not only because of the loss of life, which was brought home forcibly when so many scholars died, but also because of the effect on their ideas of imperial federation or the union of English-speaking peoples or the place of the Empire in the new world order. The American files, particularly while Aydelotte was Secretary, deal with these and other general themes. As the chapter on America has shown, Aydelotte himself had many interests and much influence outside the Rhodes Trust. The files reveal something of this, particularly his connection with other scholarship schemes. When discussing the content of the book on the fiftieth anniversary of the Trust he told Elton that he wished to include something on the scholarships'

---

[35] RTF 1225, Parkin to President S. C. Mitchell, 18 Apr. 1916.

contribution to 'international good will'. He submitted a series of notes on the genesis of the Commonwealth and Guggenheim fellowships, the Eastman professorship, and the Marshall scholarships, with all of which he was 'intimately connected'.[36]

The distribution of scholarships and the Trustees' reaction to requests for new and additional scholarships reveal something of their views of the changes that were taking place in the world around them and of their interpretation of Rhodes's wishes. If 'educational relations make the strongest tie',[37] given the changing political environment, between which countries were these relations to be? Early requests for an extra scholarship for Ontario were treated seriously as Canada was seen as becoming less colonial and more nationally minded. The allocation of scholarships in South Africa was influenced by changing political circumstance and the relative importance of certain areas. Michell, who had always argued that South Africa should have the first claim to extra scholarships, objected to the idea of giving Transvaal a scholarship for political reasons, as he wrote to Parkin in July 1916: 'As to the Transvaal, I am opposed to doing *anything* even though Botha & Smuts have kept faith with us in standing by the "Act of Union". But their ideal, though less crudely expressed than by Hertzog and "de Burger" is for a *Dutch* S. Africa i.e. for S. Africa so long as the Dutch remain in office *but no longer*.'[38] The other Trustees did not agree and both Transvaal and the Orange Free State received scholarships after the First World War. The allocation and removal of scholarships from other countries was subject to similar reasoning: the history of the scholarships in Germany reflects changing attitudes to Germany, its relationship with Britain, and its political system. The first application for a scholarship for Kenya was turned down as the population (that is the white population) was seen to be too small to benefit. India was finally given a scholarship in 1940 after correspondence spanning several years as to whether such a scholarship should go to Europeans in India, or whether Indians themselves would benefit. Elton, supporter of empire and author of *Imperial Commonwealth*, summed up the reasoning behind the award of scholarships to Ghana, Nigeria, Ceylon, the Malayan region, and the Caribbean in a letter to the *Daily Telegraph*: 'Mr. Rhodes' original foundation was based upon his belief in the Anglo-Saxon peoples, the extension of whose influence, he considered, must be salutary for the world as a whole. Now, however, that the British Commonwealth has embarked on the hopeful yet hazardous experiment of a multi-racial Commonwealth, the Trustees believe that Mr. Rhodes would have wished his Scholarships to make what contribution they can to the success of this great venture.'[39] More recently the Trustees acknowledged further changes in the ties between nations by experimenting with scholarships for European countries.

These examples have shown that the files relating to the scholarships reveal more than just the administration of the system; they document wider issues of education, political change, and the role of Britain within the Empire and Commonwealth. Moreover, these scholarship files form only part of the Rhodes Trust archives; the remainder have a wider relevance, and document some of the important organizations, issues, and developments of the last century.

Records of the Overseas Secretaries

Shortly after the First World War, around the time of Parkin's retirement, the Trust appointed old Rhodes scholars to act as secretaries in the major scholarship countries: America, Canada, Australia, and South Africa. They were to act as a single point of contact between the Trust and

---

[36] RTF 3121, Aydelotte to Elton, 17 June 1954.   [37] Rhodes's will, German codicil, n.d.
[38] RTF 1682, Michell to Parkin, 10 July 1916.
[39] RTF 3143, Elton to *Daily Telegraph*, 23 Dec. 1958.

the overseas selection committees, to deal with the routine administration of the scholarships in their countries, and to refer to the Trustees any problems with policy or eligibility. As the systems for the organization of the scholarships settled down these secretaries developed a certain amount of administrative autonomy, with their own routines for handling the process of electing scholars. Gradually, in the smaller constituencies, the secretary of the individual selection committee took on the role of administrator, often performing the function for a number of years. These secretaries handled enquiries from applicants, suggested the names of new committee members to the Trustees, organized the selection process by which a candidate was chosen, gathered together the applications and other material from scholars-elect, and ensured that it was sent to England. As has been seen, in many countries the sense of belonging to a special group, if not a formal association, remained with many scholars and some kept in touch with the local Secretary after they had left Oxford.

This activity generated a body of records much of which was routine or which duplicated what was being produced in England. The offices in London and Oxford were very careful to file both sides of the correspondence with the overseas secretaries but some of the material, particularly correspondence between the local Secretary and committee members, never reached the eyes of the Trust's officials in England. Sometimes records such as publicity material, minutes, or local memoranda were not copied and passed on to England so do not appear on Trust files. Many countries kept their own files on scholars and some continued to add news of scholars' activities even after they had left Oxford. The nature and amount of material that was produced and filed and which has survived depended very much on the individual Secretary. The largest surviving body of records belongs, not surprisingly, to the American office. Despite shifting location from coast to coast and contending with floods and periods of microfilming, the archive is fairly substantial and, with the microfilm, quite comprehensive in its coverage of the period from Aydelotte's appointment to the present day. The records of the Canadian and Australian office cover a similar period but fewer of the South African records have survived. Many of the earlier records of the South African office seem to have been destroyed during changes of Secretary.

The older records of the Canadian, American, and South African secretaries have been transferred to Rhodes House to ensure their survival and can be consulted under the same terms as the Trust archives. The records of the Australian Secretary are, at the time of writing, held in the University of Melbourne archives. Australia is unique in the amount of regional material that has survived: records relating to the state committees can be found in some of the state university archives. This reflects to some extent the traditional association between the universities and the administration of the selection procedure in each state. Records can also be found in some state archives as a result of the involvement of the government officials. Elsewhere, in the smaller constituencies, little material that is not already in the Trust records has survived but, as in Australia, there may be material in university, state, or national archives. In Bermuda, for example, where the administration of the scholarships was handled by the government until 1956, the Bermudan National Archives hold files of correspondence and other material relating to the scholarships. Papers of individuals may also contain references to the Trust: in Germany the Fehling Papers in the Bundesarchiv in Koblenz include the records of his time as German Secretary.

General Files

Files on the scholarships form the bulk of the Rhodes Trust archive because of the number of files on individual scholars. However, if these are not included, many, perhaps the majority, of the subject files do not directly relate to the scholarships. It is these files that contain material that will be of interest to researchers in many fields. As with the scholarship files, most were opened by the London office, many date from the early years of the Trust, and several have continued to the present day. They cover a surprising variety of issues: there are files on Rhodes's estates and property and the Trust's own property in Oxford and elsewhere; on finance and administration; on the Trust's involvement with education in Britain and overseas, particularly in Oxford and South Africa; on emigration; and on the promotion of the Empire. There are files on individual Trustees and secretaries, and on grants given to individuals, many of whom knew Rhodes. Some of the files contain just general correspondence but many also include appeals and educational or charitable grants given to organizations or individuals. Most are extremely comprehensive and contain, at least until the 1960s, all correspondence, copies of reports, and minutes relating to a particular subject. The files on appeals are particularly useful in that they may contain reports, financial statements, brochures, minutes, press cuttings, or photographs from the applicant and thus form an archival record of the organization itself.

Estate and Property

When Rhodes died he left the control of most of his property and investments in the hands of his Trustees. He described in some detail how he wished this property to be managed and these instructions and the details of the payment of some legacies take up over half of the will. Rhodes did not view his properties and investments in purely monetary terms but believed in active management and expected his Trustees to continue to aim for the same goals. The Trust's archives contain files that detail how the Trustees tried to manage the estate in South Africa, Rhodesia, and England in line with Rhodes's wishes, while at the same time trying to avoid running the enterprises at a loss, and having to take account of political and social change.

Rhodes had characteristically ambitious plans for his properties in Rhodesia. He urged the Trustees to concentrate on the irrigation and cultivation of his farms at Inyanga, and added that by cultivation he meant 'such things as experimental farming forestry market and other gardening and fruit farming irrigation and the teaching of any of those things and establishing and maintaining an Agricultural College'.[40] This was not all; the area around his burial place in the Matopos was to be transformed. Rhodes had already begun building a dam which the Trustees were to finish, they were to maintain the area as a public park, plant 'every possible tree', erect a monument to the men who fell in the Matabele War, and build a railway from Bulawayo to the dam so that day trippers could visit the park. For Rhodes, who had dreams of a Cape to Cairo railway, the short nine miles from Bulawayo to Westacre in the Matopos undoubtedly seemed perfectly feasible, but the Rhodes Trust archives reveal that his plans were rather more difficult to put into practice than perhaps he would have realized.

There are files for each property in Rhodesia, and for the few farms owned by Rhodes in South Africa; some were opened by the Cape Town, office and transferred to London, but the majority were generated by the London office. The files contain correspondence with Sir James McDonald, the Trust's agent in Rhodesia, Michell in Cape Town, and the managers of the farms. They reveal the constant struggle by the Trustees to make the various schemes profitable, as it became clear very quickly that the £6,000 a year set aside in Rhodes's will for investment in the farms would be woefully inadequate. There are frequent letters from London requiring McDonald to try to curtail his spending. In 1904 McDonald reluctantly agreed not to spend any

---

[40] Rhodes's will, clause 10, 1 July 1899.

more on the zoo at Matopos, but warned that it would take some time for the hunter van Rooyen to receive instructions to capture no more game 'as he is hunting game a good distance to the West of Victoria Falls'.[41] There are files on the railway itself, on which the Trust had, by 1905, spent nearly £19,000, with correspondence about timetables and fares. There are also files on the hotels built in the park, which ran frequently at a loss despite attempts made to improve their efficiency. McDonald felt that the London Trustees were not wholly committed to investing the resources necessary to make the experimental farms and parks a success. He was determined that the Trustees should know of and understand the effort that he and the farm managers were making. The files are full of regular, sometimes monthly, reports detailing the state of livestock and crops, problems with disease, the success of experimentation with new breeds, afforestation and irrigation projects, and the weather conditions, particularly the effects of periods of drought. McDonald felt it was important that the results of the experiments were shared with others in the farming community and he and others produced reports such as *Report on Certain Work and Experiments Carried out on Behalf of the Rhodes Trustees in the Matopo and Inyanga Estates* (1908) which can be found on the files.[42] There are also details of tenants and the labour market, and comments on the latter in particular reveal the very different attitudes of this period. E. A. Hull at Westacre Farm, for example, submitted an extremely indignant report about the state of the 'native' labour market, beginning: 'A great shortage of labour has been experienced and also great difficulty in obtaining what we have had. Young boys are practically unprocurable, as they prefer to work in towns and mines, where the rate of wages is higher . . . most drastic reforms are necessary to show the natives that they are not living on their own land.'[43] The reports continued to be sent regularly until 1917 when the Trustees transferred the properties to the Southern Rhodesian government, claiming, 'we have for some time felt that a number of Trustees living in this country could not permanently supervise the work in Rhodesia as efficiently as could those charged with the government of the country'.[44] The Trust kept hold of some farms; Majindan Farm in South Africa, for example (which came to the Trust in 1906), was not sold until 1951. This file, although smaller than those relating to the Trust's original property, has some details on agricultural conditions as well as the effect of the setting up of reserves for 'natives' on rents and the labour supply.[45] Despite the transfer of the property, the files on Inyanga and Matopos do not finish in 1917 as the Trustees continued to be consulted about developments such as housing proposals, possible wildlife parks, and the condition of Rhodes's grave.[46]

By the time the Trustees handed over the Rhodesian estates they had also relieved themselves of responsibility for another of Rhodes's properties, Groote Schuur. Rhodes's residence in Cape Town had been passed to the Union government in 1910, as instructed by Rhodes's will. Until then the files are fairly similar in content to those relating to Rhodesia, detailing schemes for afforestation, progress on the park around the house, and including updates on the condition of the wild animals. There were also the usual problems with expenditure on upkeep, although in this case it was rather more complicated, as Michell commented: 'I am of course in a delicate position criticising Groote Schuur expenditure, but it must be done.'[47] The delicate position was

---

[41] RTF 1853A, McDonald to Michell, 16 Mar. 1904. [42] RTF 1853, 1908.
[43] RTF 1332, E. A. Hull Annual Report, 1909.
[44] RTF 2224, Milner to McDonald, 17 July 1917 (draft). [45] RTF 2150.
[46] RTF 1855 covers the period 1902–64 and RTF 1815 covers 1902–58.
[47] RTF 1772A, Michell to Woods, 17 July 1905. Michell wrote this letter while he was in London to his assistant in Cape Town, Bertram Woods. The letters between Michell and his assistant which sometimes appear on the Cape Town files are useful in that they give a perspective on events not found on the other files.

caused by the fact that at that time the house was occupied by the Prime Minister of the Cape, and Michell's fellow Trustee, Jameson. The files refer to changes in the area around Table Mountain, such as the controversy over the construction of the road from Kirstenbosch to Hout Bay. The Trust continued to be informed, consulted, or called upon to act even after they had passed Groote Schuur to the government. There are reports and correspondence on the building of the hospital and university and debates as to the Trustees' rights or responsibilities with regard to controlling the types of buildings erected. The Groote Schuur file, opened in 1902, is not yet closed.

Rhodes had several other properties with which the Trust were involved and which are documented in the archives. In England, Dalham Hall in Newmarket was occupied by members of Rhodes's family, while the Dalston estate was a large residential and commercial area in Hackney, London. The Trust was later to acquire other properties: Hildersham Hall in Cambridgeshire replaced Dalham as the residence of Rhodes's closest surviving relatives and investments were made in commercial and residential properties in towns including Colchester, Brighton, and Leamington Spa. In contrast to the farms and parks in Rhodesia these properties presented the Trustees with more conventional problems. For the Dalston estate, for example, there are fifteen files in total, dating from 1908 to 1961. They include correspondence with tenants, reports on damage caused by bombing during the war, negotiations with Hackney Council, and donations to local charities, the hospital, and the church.[48]

Before Rhodes died he had invested in or given guarantees to projects that were as important to his general scheme of things as his experimental farms in Rhodesia. The investments were mainly in irrigation and land settlement schemes in South Africa. The Trustees were left to manage these and, as with the Rhodesian properties, they struggled to equate principle with profitability. There are thirteen files on the Smartt Syndicate, an irrigation and settlement scheme in the Karoo, that reveal through minutes, reports, and correspondence the attempts to ensure the success of the irrigation, to attract settlers, and, ultimately, to realise a profit. The files on the Klippoortje estate in the Transvaal describe a similar development and include issues such as claims to water and mineral rights and the development of townships. The material continues until the mid-1960s; in fact, the Trust did not sell the last of its holdings until the 1980s. Many of the schemes to which the Trust contributed involved the same individuals: Sir Thomas Smartt, Sir Abe Bailey, Sir Julius Wernher, and directors of De Beers. The files are an important record of the attempts of these groups of wealthy, influential individuals to have an effect on the kind of society that was developing in South Africa.

One of the problems that the Trustees faced was that frequently these ventures were not profitable. Michell complained to Jameson in 1906 that the Rhodes Fruit Farms 'are going to be a drain on us for an indefinite period' and suggested selling them, but only if the purchasers could be persuaded to continue to promote Rhodes's belief that, according to Michell, 'the establishment of a fruit industry, controlled by European supervision, makes for the benefit of the Colony, materially and politically'.[49] As with the other ventures and properties, the wealth of detail in the files shows how complex this vision was in practice. The files describe attempts to grow the right sort of fruit, with plans to market the produce in England, and include discussions about the potential of the market in wine. The kind of detail that may be found in the files is illustrated by a nine-page report written by Gerald Orpen in 1907 on the wine trade. It begins 'The Wine Industry is at present in a rather unfortunate position' and details the number

---

[48] RTF 1620.   [49] RTF 1085, Michell to Jameson, 6 May 1906.

of wines in the districts around the Cape, the average prices of wine, and the prospects for the future. We learn, for example, that Hermitage from the Wellington district was sold to the wine merchants J. Sedgwick & Co. at £4 10s. per leaguer in 1906.[50] Orpen was pessimistic about the market for wine, particularly in the face of French competition.

Early Grants and Political Expenditure

Whatever his biographers may make of him there is no doubt that Rhodes inspired great loyalty. He may have been a difficult man for some to get to know, but some of the Trustees, particularly Michell, Jameson, and Hawksley, could claim to be amongst his closest acquaintances, while others like Milner and Grey probably felt that they knew and understood, to some extent, his political and economic ambitions. Parkin, who never met Rhodes, described something of this loyalty in a letter to Grey referring to a conversation they had had the year before Rhodes died: 'The perfect confidence you felt that if I could talk with him I would be convinced about not only the greatness, but the nobility of his views seemed to make me understand the man more than anything I had ever heard of him.'[51] When Rhodes left the residue of his estate to the original Trustees they were all determined, and confident, that they would be able to invest and use this residue to good effect, and as Rhodes would have wished. The files that show how they decided to interpret his wishes often say more about the character and ambitions of the Trustees than they reveal about Rhodes himself. Moreover, there were others in Southern Africa and elsewhere who had known Rhodes and who were willing to offer their opinions. This group of potential advisers included Rhodes's architect Herbert Baker, his land agent James McDonald, his private secretary Philip Jourdan, his business associates at De Beers and the British South Africa Company, and fellow land settlement enthusiasts such as Sir Charles Crewe and Sir Thomas Smartt. Letters from these and others urging upon the Trustees the schemes that they felt would put Rhodes's money to best use appear frequently in the archives. Although by 1925 the value of the assets of the Trust had shrunk since Rhodes's death by nearly £1.5 million[52] there was still enough money available to make fairly substantial contributions to some schemes. From 1925 this increased as, despite some periods of uncertainty, the value of the estate began to grow. The files which document the use to which the residue was put are amongst the most interesting in the archives.

Initially it was unclear exactly how much money was available; it was not until December 1905 that Boyd was able to write that there was finally a budget worked out, detailing how much could be spent beyond regular payments.[53] Rhodes had already promised money or assistance to some organizations or schemes, particularly to local efforts in Rhodesia, so payments were made for example for Merino sheep to be sent to farmers in Melsetter, Rhodesia, and to the Masonic Education fund.[54] The Trustees based in South Africa seem to have felt that they could continue Rhodes's distribution of, often generous, gifts and donations. McDonald reported in 1902 that Beit and Jameson had both promised 'considerable sums' to people in Rhodesia but Jameson's memory was rather poor and he could not remember exactly what these were.[55] Correspondence

---

[50] RTF 1085, Report by Gerald Orpen, 9 Oct. 1907.   [51] RTF 2109, Parkin to Grey, 19 May 1913.

[52] See RTF 2709, Kerr to Peacock, 14 Aug. 1925. According to Elton, 'a substantial proportion of the loss on investments was due to the fact that Rhodes held a certain amount of stock for other than financial reasons, and these subsequently proved valueless'. RTF 1294, Elton to Aydelotte, 14 Feb. 1944.

[53] RTF 1679, Boyd to Grey, 12 Dec. 1905. The balance sheets and accounts of the Trust are described more fully below.

[54] See RTF 1320 and RTF 1308.   [55] RTF 1419, McDonald to Gordon Le Sueur, 21 Oct. 1902.

between Hawksley and Michell reveals early tensions between the two as to whether minuted payments could be met, whether shares should be sold, and what Rhodes's priorities would have been.[56] Hawksley's anxiety was partly due to his belief that Rhodes would have wished a substantial proportion of the residue to have been devoted to political expenditure. In a letter to Grey written in 1901, Rhodes had made suggestions for the disposal of the residue of his estate. These were: to create a reserve fund for the scholarships; to assist scholars in their later life; to encourage emigration; and 'If deemed advisable the assistance of the promotion of a Parliamentary Party who without any desire for office, would always give their vote for Imperial purposes.'[57] Partly because the payments were made in South Africa, sometimes after direct consultation with Hawksley, and were not controlled by the London office, the archives do not give a very clear picture of the expenditure. Hawksley's own files have not survived but amongst the Trust's records files such as RTF 1038 Political Expenditure, RTF 1961 Politics and Day, and RTF 1850A Cape Town Office, Confidential File do give some details. RTF 1210 South African Federation is particularly clear on the Trust's funding of the Selborne Memorandum, as is RTF 2220 Paarl Property on their loan of £1,500 to a Dutch paper, *De Patriot*, which was clearly seen as a political action. It is also possible to find references to payments amongst other correspondence: in RTF 1256, for example, in a letter to Michell, Hawksley writes, 'Now that you are in the thick of the General Election I suppose political payments are likely to increase. Will £20,000 from 1st January 1903, to the close of the General Election Campaign be sufficient?'[58]

Some of these files were identified at one stage or another as confidential by the Trust. The Cape Town Confidential file refers to various matters including payments, legacies, investments, and shares, and a proposed customs union.[59] There are also references to W. T. Stead, who had been named by Rhodes as a Trustee but whose appointment was later revoked because of his 'extraordinary eccentricity'.[60] It seems that Stead suggested that, because of the phrasing of the will, he could still qualify as a residuary legatee. Perhaps because of this RTF 1850A, and other files such as RTF 2118 W. T. Stead, reveal how the Trust put aside a fund of £15,000 for Stead and his *Daily Paper*.

However obscure some of the early confidential payments may be, they were at least noted in the balance sheets as political expenditure by the residuary legatees until around the time that

[56] RTF 1850A, Hawksley to Michell, 18 Oct. 1902. Michell wrote his own notes beside Hawksley's comments throughout this letter. He pencilled question marks, for example, over: 'It is clear he [Rhodes] didn't contemplate that we should before doing anything else set aside a sufficient capital sum to meet the scholarships.'

[57] Letter from Rhodes to Grey, 25 Aug. 1901; a copy is in RTF 2180 (filed 1935). The original is in Rhodes House Library (MSS Afr.t.5). Hawksley was aware of this letter despite his comments about setting aside funds for the scholarships, although perhaps not until after he had written to Michell (n. 56). He sent copies to Rosebery in Nov. 1903 (see Rosebery Papers in the National Library of Scotland, MS 10175) and Michell in Jan. 1904 (see RTF 2180) and a copy of the latter to Milner (see Milner Papers in the Bodleian, Oxford, MS Milner Dep. 468).

[58] RTF 1038, Hawksley to Michell, 17 Oct. 1903. This is part of an extract copied from the original letter which is on RTF 1256. Michell and Hawksley's early correspondence covered many topics in each letter but in general the relevant sections were copied onto other files.

[59] RTF 1850A. There are letters from Hawksley to Michell, for example, in which he warns: 'Of course I know the argument that Rhodes, if he had been alive would have agreed to almost anything to aid Federation. But we must have regards for the immediate interests of the English in Rhodesia, who have to bear the brunt of taxation and the shareholders of the Company must not be forgotten,' and: 'It is not enough to say that we should come in in order to placate Lord Milner in view of favours to come' (30 May 1903).

[60] Rhodes's codicil, Jan. 1901.

the Rhodes–Beit Fund was established as a separate fund, with its own Trustees. From this point political payments were made by the fund and become more difficult to trace. The archives have several files on the Rhodes–Beit Fund (RTF 2773) but these are largely composed of material from the 1920s and later when the Trustees were attempting to discover the nature and history of the fund. They do reveal, however, how the Trust's attitudes had changed. The last Trustee to have known Rhodes, Leopold Amery, did not leave the Trust until his death in 1955, but by the 1920s the Trustees were becoming wary of second guessing Rhodes's wishes. The world had already changed so much since his death that the causes that Rhodes had supported at the turn of the century were not necessarily the ones that his Trustees should or could support twenty or thirty years later. By the 1920s only Milner of the original Trustees remained; few of the new ones had any idea of the nature of the Rhodes–Beit Fund. Two Trustees, Otto Beit and Sothern Holland, continued to be involved but their activities were kept quite separate from those of the Trust. From the late 1920s the fund was gradually absorbed back into the Rhodes Trust proper to be used for general purposes. In fact Kerr was keen to use the money on extensions to Rhodes House, which prompted Beit to write grimly: 'You may be quite justified in suggesting that it is your business to give advice to the Trustees but permit me to say that that advice is based on the assumption on your part that what Rhodes thought in 1898 need not be the proper line to pursue today. . . . I am perhaps more correctly and more closely informed as to the political party complications in South Africa which continue to urgently need the support of outside assistance.'[61] However well informed Beit was, the absence from the files of any mention of funding for political purposes for several of the preceding years indicates that the Trustees now felt that there were more suitable ways to invest Rhodes's legacy. In South Africa the vast majority of the Trust's activities were now concerned with education.

Southern African Education

The use that the Trustees made of the residue, apart from the expenditure on the scholarships or on property, is documented mainly through appeals files. Created by the London office, allocated a number and filed with the other files they contain applications for grants or loans from individuals and organizations. A large proportion of these files relates to the funding of education in Southern Africa. Most of the individual schools or colleges that were helped by the Trustees have a file, many spanning several decades: those on the University of Cape Town and Rhodes University, for example, were opened in 1902 and continue to the present day. This breadth of material can sometimes provide an overview of the evolution of an institution. Applications were often sent with plans, reports, and accounts, and supplemented by correspondence with the Trust's advisers in South Africa. RTF 2510, just one example, has a sketch of the proposed University of Johannesburg included with an appeal from J. H. Hofmeyr.[62] If money was awarded the Trust was often kept up to date with information on how the grant was being spent, or with press cuttings and photographs. Even if there were no appeals some schools and colleges continued to correspond with the Trust. They were sometimes visited by Trustees or secretaries who would add their own reports to the files. St John's College, Johannesburg, for example, was visited between 1920 and 1958 by Beit, Wylie, Kerr, and Elton. The reports and correspondence tended to be fairly detailed because the Trustees wanted to be sure that a grant would produce real benefits. They were wary of supporting very new ventures and sometimes unwilling to contribute if they felt funds could easily be raised elsewhere. In file RTF 2663, for

---

[61] RTF 2773, Beit to Kerr, 1 June 1929.   [62] RTF 2510, Sept. 1920.

example, Sir Charles Crewe tried to persuade the Trust to contribute to the establishment of a school at George but was told that the school would have to prove itself a going concern first. Crewe complained, 'if the Trustees merely mean to assist those Schools that are in a substantial financial position much of what I hoped might be done will not be carried out'.[63] The number and range of files in the archives indicate that Crewe's protest was not completely justified: the Trust did assist a wide variety of schools and colleges at various stages in their development.

The files document the attitudes of the Trustees and of those living in South Africa. The material on Rhodes University and the University of Cape Town, for example, begins with opinions about the establishment of a university and arguments over the best potential centre, particularly from an English point of view. The archives reveal that Milner went so far as to oppose the idea of a South African university altogether, as he felt that it would be used for a purely political object: the artificial stimulation of the Dutch language.[64] In fact the earliest of the Trust's own grants were largely politically oriented: this partly underlay their decision to support Grahamstown rather than Cape Town as a university centre. Michell especially was vociferous in his support of investing in English education; this is revealed more than his backing of money for political candidates. As early as February 1903 he was writing to Hawksley that 'the educational needs of South Africa are very extensive. The late war was caused in part by ignorance. The rural population are, even now, growing up under circumstances that do not make for peace or loyalty.'[65] By 1912 Milner, who most certainly did not approve of the political climate in South Africa, could write, 'On the whole we are inclined to think that Higher School Education in South Africa, especially of the English public school type, has one of the first claims upon us after the scholarships themselves.'[66]

Visits by Beit, Milner, and Wylie in the 1920s and early 1930s provided the real impetus for donations to education in South Africa. Grants and loans were given to several of the larger public schools and some smaller ones: the emphasis continued to be on an English education. RTF 2655 St Mark's School, Swaziland provides an example of the kind of context in which the Trustees made their decisions. The first appeal in 1925 was refused as the Trust had commitments elsewhere, mainly within South Africa itself. Some of the Trustees felt that the school should try harder to secure government or local support and others were worried that Swaziland was on the point of being taken over by the Transvaal. By 1929, however, they had reconsidered and awarded the school a loan, the interest on which, from 1934, was used to repay the debt. Further grants and loans were agreed during Elton's time as Secretary: St Mark's was the kind of independent church school that he was keen to support and there were predictions in the 1940s that the introduction of compulsory bilingual education in the Transvaal would drive parents to send their children to schools in Swaziland. The preservation of the independence of these type of schools became more significant as the nationalist government extended its power and for Elton, a committed Christian, these schools had an added advantage as 'the centres of an education which is far more liberal, more English and more soundly based upon religion than is to be obtained anywhere else in SA'.[67] Elton was even able to persuade his Trustees to promise £10,000 towards a proposed New Church School at Vereeniging by arguing, after a visit to South Africa in 1948, that the independent schools 'are just about the most promising product of South African

[63] RTF 2663, Crewe [to Kerr], 16 Sept. 1927.   [64] See RTF 2109, Milner to Parkin, 21 June 1912.
[65] RTF 1247, Michell to Hawksley, 23 Feb. 1903.
[66] RTF 2119, Milner to R. Feetham, 6 Sept. 1912.
[67] RTF 1732, Elton's Report to Trustees, 14 Oct. 1948. This file, which covers the period 1902–63, provides a useful overview of the Trustees' view of the importance of these schools.

civilisation to date'.[68] The Trustees also had to take into account the debate amongst these schools about the wisdom of accepting government grants and the possible effects on their independence and correspondence about this also appears on some of the files from the 1940s. By the 1960s many of the files on these schools had closed. Among other things, South Africa's withdrawal from the Commonwealth had made it difficult to give grants in South Africa and the Trust was concentrating its efforts closer to home. However, in the 1970s, the Trustees began to fund bursaries for non-white schoolchildren in South Africa. This generated new files which were soon joined by others opened in the 1980s, and particularly the 1990s: as South Africa returned to the Commonwealth and the system of apartheid began to be replaced, the Trust began once more to make significant contributions to education and to other causes.

As has been described elsewhere, the Trust did not confine its support, even in the early years, to education for white South Africans. The first file dealing with what was then referred to as 'native education', RTF 1156 Interstate Native College Scheme/Fort Hare, was opened in 1905. It documents the early stages of attempts by the Intercolonial Native Affairs Commission and others to set up systems of training and education. The Trust promised £1,000 towards a proposed college in 1911, but it was not until later that they became more significantly involved in such funding. The files, like other appeals files, contain correspondence, reports, financial details, and sometimes photographs and brochures. They reflect with some clarity developments in education and training and the changing attitudes of the Trustees and secretaries, as well as those of others in Britain and South Africa. RTF 1156 itself covers the period 1905 to 1956 and includes a *Report of the Native Convention Held at Lovedale* (1905); reports and a constitution dating from the establishment of Fort Hare with some twenty students (1916); an appeal, graduation prospectus, and minutes, referring to over 100 students enrolled on a variety of courses (1929); and newspaper cuttings and correspondence about the closure of the college after unrest (1955).

The records show that Parkin supported the idea of some kind of 'native training' in South Africa; he felt that it would stop students having to enrol on courses in America where they might be open to unwholesome influences.[69] It was Kerr, however, who really persuaded the Trustees of the value of supporting such schools and colleges. He put the case for assistance early on in his secretaryship, arguing that 'Mr. Rhodes was very active in protecting and helping the progress of the native'[70] and 'criticism has been made of the Trustees from time to time that they devote their resources to the education of the white man both in Africa and elsewhere but that they spend little or nothing on the education of the native population in which Mr. Rhodes always took so active an interest and without whose labours he could never have amassed his fortune'.[71] He was echoing Parkin to some extent when he argued that the Trust should support schools and colleges which would 'train a number of the best of the young generation of educated natives in the public school tradition of leadership as a make-weight to the communistic type of leader which is now being produced by propaganda in all parts of the country'.[72] This conviction that the British type of education was to be preferred was not Lothian's only motivation in recommending such grants. Before he had left the Trust, the files had begun to contain appeals that referred to education for all 'Africans', not just potential leaders. The appeals in file RTF 2957 Native Schools in Johannesburg centre on campaigns for schools for children in

[68] RTF 3050, Elton's Report on visit to South Africa, 27 Apr. 1948.
[69] RTF 1156, Parkin to K. A. Hobart-Houghton, 3 Jan. 1911.
[70] RTF 2552, Kerr's Memorandum on British schools in South Africa, 23 Sept. 1925.
[71] Ibid., Lothian's Report to Trustees, 22 Jan. 1926.
[72] RTF 2817, Lothian's Report to Trustees, 3 Oct. 1930.

townships and describe the poor living conditions in these areas. Again it seems to be Lothian who was one of the main supporters. In 1939 he wrote to Nancy Astor warning that he might have problems persuading the Trustees to agree to more grants for these schools as 'they have recently jibbed at the amount of money I have asked them to spend on native education in South Africa'.[73]

As with the other archives, it is the amount of detail, the wide-ranging correspondence, and the variety of material that gives these files their value. RTF 2957 for example also contains correspondence with J. H. Hofmeyr about the relative values of assistance to primary, secondary, and higher 'native' education and RTF 2977 Gore-Browne Native Training College, Kimberley has an appeal by General Smuts as well as a discussion of the effects of the Bantu Education Act. All of the files contain letters from individuals asking the Trustees to support various schemes, but from the late 1940s these take on a more urgent and arguably less patronizing tone. Trevor Huddleston often supported appeals throughout the 1940s and 1950s and there were a number of new files opened during these decades which mirror, to some extent, developments in South Africa at this time. To take four as an example, RTF 3068, RTF 3097, RTF 3141, and RTF 3162 include Huddleston's views on education; Amery's opinion of Huddleston: 'He is really a fine man and doing admirable work, although I think he is mistaken in appealing to the public opinion in England against the Union Government. He gives a very depressing account of the way in which that Government is driving all educated native opinion into bitter anti-white hostility';[74] Huddleston's comments on the Eiselen report (1952); the Bishop of Zululand's appeal for a school in Swaziland which was submitted because, under the terms of the Bantu Education Act, his mission was not able to help African schools in South Africa itself; and an appeal from Ronald Currey for money for Basutoland schools: 'whether or no Basutoland is to be absorbed in to the Union, it is oh so important that the things Britain stand for should be well established, with the pulses beating firmly, and be able to withstand the horrible pressure of "Apartheid".'[75]

Education was not the only thing which concerned the Trust in South Africa, nor was their support of education solely confined to the Union. In what was then Rhodesia the Beit Trust was the main source of funds, but the Rhodes Trust still gave donations to some schools at various times. For nearly seventy years they funded an essay competition which was to illustrate and improve standards of English: in 1956 there were ninety-six schools taking part. There are also files on Makerere College, Uganda; the Victoria College, Alexandria, Egypt; and the Kitchener Memorial Medical School and Gordon Memorial College, Khartoum, Sudan. Further afield the Trustees supported Chinese students at the University of Hong Kong during the Second World War. These files sometimes contain references to the context in which the grants were given: to Italian propaganda and Milner's influence in Egypt, British influence in the Sudan, and protests in Khartoum. The range of other causes assisted in Southern Africa was diverse; consequently there are files, and therefore often detailed information, on a wide range of subjects. The Trust contributed to hospitals, libraries, and museums, to churches and hostels, and they even paid for a bell for City Hall in Cape Town. They supported societies and clubs for settlers and war veterans, gave grants to charitable organizations including the Salvation Army and to boy scouts,

---

[73] RTF 2957, Lothian to Nancy Astor, 4 Apr. 1939. In spite of his pessimism Lothian was able to secure another £500 grant.

[74] RTF 3068, Amery Report on visit to South Africa, 22 Sept. 1953.

[75] RTF 3097, RTF 3141, and RTF 3162, Currey to Elton, 8 May 1959.

and they assisted many organizations dedicated to helping the non-white sections of the population such as the Bantu Mines Social Centre, the Institute of Race Relations, the African Music Society, the Kabulonga Club, Lusaka, and the Bantu Press. Much of their support, particularly in the early years, went to organizations that, in one way or the other were involved in promoting emigration or the concept of empire.

Emigration

Rhodes's letter to Grey of 1901 about the residue of the estate did not mention education in South Africa but it did refer to emigration. He suggested a portion of the residue be used for the latter as 'the most dangerous portion of the Empire being, Africa, the steady encouragement of Emigration especially women, and getting *our* people on the land—we shall never be safe in Africa until we occupy the soil equally with the Dutch'.[76] The Trust's investment in land, irrigation, and settlement syndicates has already been described and from the outset they assisted other emigration and colonization schemes, initially in South Africa, but also further afield. Whether this was prompted by Parkin's belief in imperial federation, Milner's dissatisfaction with the political solution in South Africa, Michell's fervent support of all things English as opposed to Afrikaner, Lothian's interest in the union of English-speaking nations, Elton's belief in empire and Commonwealth, or because Rhodes himself had settled overseas, a large part of the Trust's files are concerned with emigration. The contributions, and the files, continued for several years; the records mainly concern appeals and funding but also document something of the wider context in which the Trust was operating.

The Trustees took Rhodes's wishes in this case to heart and early on supported many of the hostels set up to cater for women arriving and working in Southern Africa. There are several files on organizations such as the Society for the Oversea Settlement of British Women and the South African Immigration Association. Some of these contain very detailed reports describing the success or otherwise of the hostels and other schemes, as well as often including annual reports, minutes, balance sheets, and correspondence. The largest organization that the Trust supported in South Africa was Sir Charles Crewe's 1820 Memorial Settlers' Association. Frequent appeals for money, justification of expenditure, and analyses of the success of schemes generated nine extremely comprehensive files covering the history of the Association well into the 1960s. The detail in the files on emigration is such that it is not difficult to forget the political context. In RTF 1402 Society for the Oversea Settlement of British Women, Transvaal Committee, for example, the Committee approached the Trustees in 1907 because the government had discontinued their grant: Botha had been sympathetic but the cabinet was hostile, so the funding was withdrawn. The Trustees were keen to ensure that the money they gave would not be wasted and they funded several projects whose aims were to research the feasibility of proposed schemes and to judge the success of existing ones. They twice supported Henry Rider Haggard's investigations and between 1913 and 1931 gave money to Thomas Sedgwick to investigate and promote migration schemes in Australia and New Zealand. Although a supporter of emigration, the latter was not uncritical of some of the things he uncovered. He reported, for example: 'The question of aftercare is most pressing throughout Australia. I told the Under Secretary for Labour in N.S.W. that the neglect of the boys after placing was heartbreaking.'[77]

By the time of Sedgwick's final grant, the Trustees were becoming rather less supportive of emigration. Many of the files dealing with emigration to Australia and elsewhere cease in the

---

[76] See n. 57.   [77] RTF 2423, Sedgwick to Kerr, 6 Mar. 1929.

1920s, although Elton did manage to persuade later Trustees to support the Big Brother Movement until the 1950s. In 1924 one of the Trust's ties to the emigration movement outside South
Africa had been broken on the death of Kingsley Fairbridge. Fairbridge's importance to the Trust
can be illustrated by the fact that eight different subject files have been opened relating to him
or his projects, giving around seventeen files in total, not including the many references in the
country files. After his death financial and other support for the farms continued from the Trust
and scholars. In 1934, for example, Lothian, Peacock, and Amery were all patrons of the Child
Emigration Society; the Allens were prominent in the Oxford Branch for several years; and in
1949 the Trust supported a former farm pupil at Oxford. The archives reveal, however, that even
at this point there was some sensitivity around issues of emigration. As Lothian explained about
the inscription to Fairbridge at Rhodes House: 'The original idea was to phrase it "Founder of
Child Emigration" but we felt that "emigration" was rather a frigid word to apply to children,
and that posterity might misunderstand it,' so 'colonization' was used instead.[78] Overall the
declining number of files on emigration indicates that it was beginning to be seen as an unsuccessful way to use the Trust's funds. The parallel increase of files on empire movements perhaps
shows that the Trust, and Elton in particular, felt that the dominions and Commonwealth could
be best preserved, not by the promotion of emigration, but by education.

Empire and Commonwealth

It should be no surprise that the archives contain a large amount of material on the Empire and
Commonwealth, given the views of those connected with the Trust. Of the early Trustees and
secretaries, for example, Parkin, Rosebery, and Milner were all closely connected with the
imperial federation movement at the end of the last century. Parkin himself had spent several
years before working for the Trust travelling through England and the Empire promoting the
imperial cause (in fact the Trust was later to sponsor a young Canadian, Dr Stephen Leacock,
to undertake a similar project).[79] Many of the Trustees were involved with organizations that
promoted ties between countries of the Empire and Commonwealth and several held related
positions in the government. Both Milner and Amery were Colonial Secretaries, Grey was
Governor General in Canada, Lovat was Under-Secretary of State for the Dominions, Nye was
Governor of Madras and High Commissioner for Canada, MacDonald held various posts
as Governor or High Commissioner in Canada, India, the Malayan Union and Singapore,
and Kenya, and Hailey was governor of a number of provinces in India. Of the secretaries, Kerr
was for a time Under-Secretary of State for India and Williams was a member of the Devlin
Nyasaland Commission and observer on Rhodesian elections.

The files take the usual form: concentrating on appeals and grants but containing a range of
information about different organizations including correspondence, reports, accounts, photographs, and pamphlets. Many document grants given to promoting educational links between
countries in the Empire or Commonwealth. This was a cause that was strongly supported by
Parkin but the Trust has continued to this day to support schemes such as educational exchanges
or Commonwealth university conferences. RTF 1079 League of Empire includes correspondence
about a range of projects of this nature, including school linking schemes, educational conferences, the Imperial Union of Teachers, the migration and exchange of teachers, and bursaries for
school exchanges. A later file, RTF 2676 Interchange of Schoolmasters, includes correspondence
with the Headmasters' Conference, R. A. B. Butler, and the Board of Education.

[78] RTF 1567, Lothian to Sir Arthur Lawley, 16 Jan. 1929.   [79] RTF 2031.

The Trust also supported organizations that were more general in their promotion of Empire. RTF 1203 Victoria League covers the period 1901 to 1987 in seven files; from the time when it was little more than a group of committees run largely by ladies promoting good causes through funds such as the Refugees' Fund and the South African Graves' Fund. The file traces the growth of the League and the support it received from the Trust, with many Trustees and secretaries being committee members, and reports and correspondence document its activities in Britain and abroad until the closure of the Oxford branch and founding of HOST (Hosting for Overseas Students) in 1987. This type of material exists for many similar British organizations including Lady Frances Ryder's Dominions Fellowship Trust, the Over-Seas League, the Royal Colonial Institute, and for some based overseas, such as the National Council of Education of Canada.

From the time of Elton's appointment as Secretary the theme of empire and Commonwealth in the files becomes more pronounced. This was due to some extent to the war but also to Elton's personal beliefs and his fear that the Empire was in danger of disintegrating. When Nye, who had become a Trustee in 1957, enquired if the Trust had any definite policy on giving grants apart from that detailed in the Rhodes Trust Act 1946, Elton admitted; 'No tests or principles as to grants have ever been written down, although to some extent, like the British Constitution, we can perhaps claim to have evolved certain (rather vague) precedents and traditions.' He went on to try to identify patterns which had occurred during his previous twenty or so years as Secretary. Nye was told of the Trust's permanent commitments such as pensions, and of grants to the Dominions Fellowship Trust, the Oxford branch of the Victoria League, South African independent schools, and Rhodes University College. Elton also explained that, during the war, the Trust had spread the knowledge of the Commonwealth amongst the services and through organizations such as the YMCA. He then summarized: 'the clearest recurrent pattern is the giving of assistance to an organisation which seems to be trying to do valuable work for the Commonwealth or Commonwealth relations, in its early stages, when it may be having to face something of a struggle to survive.'[80] Elton was fairly clear what organizations these should be. The files contain references to the Empire Day Movement, Empire Youth Sunday, the YWCA and YMCA, and various Commonwealth clubs and societies. Many of these have their own files and many are also referred to in RTF 3012 Empire Education. This file centres on Elton's attempts, with Vincent Harlow at the Ministry of Information, to coordinate the various bodies, as the Trustees felt 'that this is the psychological moment at which much can be done to repair the very dangerous and discreditable ignorance of the British Commonwealth which we have allowed to grow up in this country'.[81] Because much of this effort was concentrated during the war the files are a useful source of information not only on the efforts to spread confidence in the Empire but also on the practical measures being taken by these bodies to provide support—hospitality, food, shelter, or recreation—for forces and civilians at home and overseas. RTF 2992 The Church Army, for example, contains photographs of mobile canteens paid for by the Trust with regular reports of their progress across Italy and France and letters that begin 'I am happy to advise you that the Rhodes Trust Mobile Canteen on the Western Front is now somewhat deep into Germany.'[82] Elton, in fact, proposed this grant to the Trustees without first being approached by the Church Army. Like many of the organizations he supported, it had a strong Christian

---

[80] RTF 3150, Elton to Nye, 23 July 1958.
[81] RTF 3012, Elton to G. Barnes at the BBC, 30 Mar. 1943.
[82] RTF 2992, letter to Elton, 23 Apr. 1945.

element. Elton liked to justify his support for such bodies as the Student Christian Movement of India by reminding the Trustees that Rhodes had been the son of a parson. The Trust's interest in ways of bringing the Commonwealth nations closer together did not end with Elton. Support for Commonwealth and international organizations, particularly those concerned with youth and promoting educational ties, has continued and there are later files on, for example, the Commonwealth Youth Exchange and the International Students Trust.

The files in fact reveal a more complex history than this seemingly linear development from Imperial Federation, through Empire and new Commonwealth, to international movements. Elton sometimes stretched the idea of empire too far for some of the Trustees. He described to Nye how he had supported an appeal by 'the Folk Song people' which he thought 'at first sight faintly ridiculous' but then felt had a strong claim as ties of sentiment could grow from these 'somewhat arty-crafty activities', but the majority of Trustees disagreed.[83] Stronger opposition to Elton's aims came from other quarters, as is demonstrated in RTF 3012, for example. The correspondence documents a rather violent disagreement between Elton, Harlow, and Lionel Curtis after the latter had 'gatecrashed' a conference at Rhodes House. This intrusion prompted Harlow to write to Curtis: 'Obsessed with your own doctrine, you weighed in and labelled the Conference as Government propaganda. It would have been difficult to make a more poisonous or more destructive comment . . . what you unwittingly did was to confirm a lurking suspicion in some minds at any rate that Elton, Coupland and I had been busily whitewashing "imperialism".'[84] Files such as RTF 3039 Empire Youth Federation show how others were uneasy with the idea of identifying with the Empire so vigorously rather than concentrating on the promotion of international movements. Lothian probably felt this to some degree; he was certainly sceptical about the amount of good some of the organizations actually did, despite having support from the powerful and influential.[85] The Trust gave grants to the Empire Day Movement while he was Secretary, but he was wary, as he wrote to Evelyn Wrench in 1930, as 'Flag wagging societies of all kinds tend to degenerate after the initial impulse has died away,' and in his June report to the Trustees in 1931 he warned: 'I am not sure that this is money which brings in much return. If we could find some better way of arousing an intelligent interest in Empire it would be all right, but I doubt if the modern Empire is much strengthened by circulating messages like Lord Jellicoe's. I am inclined to think that Rhodes' view that "educational relations make the strongest tie" is sounder.'[86] He did his best to devise schemes that would do just this, and many of these projects were centred on Oxford.

Oxford University

'I am personally strongly opposed to the Rhodes Trust making any more grants out of the funds at its disposal, towards University requirements, and hope that if it is the case that the house of the university should be set in order, to enable it to make the most possible out of Rhodes' Will, a full statement will be made and other people asked to supply the necessary funds,' wrote Grey to Wylie from Canada in 1905.[87] Letters had appeared in the Canadian press saying that Oxford would not derive the benefit from the scholarships that Rhodes had intended until 'the University has organised proper equipment for the instruction and research work of Post Graduates'.[88]

---

[83] RTF 3150, Elton to Nye, 23 July 1958.   [84] RTF 3012, Harlow to Curtis, 30 Sept. 1943.
[85] See, for example, RTF 2645.
[86] RTF 2208, Kerr to Wrench, 26 Mar. 1930, and Kerr's Report to the Trustees, 2 June 1931.
[87] RTF 3676, Grey to Wylie, 18 Jan. 1905.   [88] Ibid.

Wylie later explained that it was mainly Grey who objected to giving money to Oxford,[89] but others of the Trustees may have felt that Oxford, which had already benefited under Rhodes's will, in the form of the scholarships and the legacy to Oriel, should come fairly low down the Trustees' list of priorities. Wylie, when reporting Grey's attitude to Boyd, added: 'I can't help hoping that that may perhaps soften with time.'[90] Perhaps he felt that the influx of scholars would put pressure on the University which it was arguably the responsibility of the Trustees to relieve. More significantly, if Oxford was to attract and train the best scholars it would have to ensure that it remained one of the top universities in the world.

By this time the Trust had already begun a series of grants to the Oxford University Medical School specifically for readerships and lectureships in pathology and pharmacology,[91] no doubt prompted by Rhodes's suggestion that Oxford 'should try and extend its scope so as if possible to make its medical school as least as good as that at the University of Edinburgh'.[92] Here was Rhodes stating explicitly that if Oxford did not change some of the best overseas students would be attracted elsewhere. The will, however, did not direct his Trustees to pay for that change, yet their grant to the Medical School shows that some of the early Trustees at least were willing to give assistance to Oxford. Indeed there are several Oxford appeals files from this early period, all of which provide an insight, through correspondence and reports, into the circumstances of the particular department or body appealing for funds. For the period before the Second World War these include files on the Taylor Institution, a readership in English law, lectures on American history, University sports clubs, the School of Engineering, and the Imperial Forestry Institute. Most of these received grants, in some cases substantial ones. RTF 2421 Readers in Roman Dutch Law, for example, reveals that the Trust donated £20,000 for a professorship in 1919, £500 towards the library in 1920, and annual grants of £100 each for the teaching of elementary Dutch 1924–7. This series of grants was a direct result of their wish to ensure that the best students, including Afrikaners, would be attracted from South Africa. The file contains much on the context and history of the grants and continues, until 1971, with negotiations over the salary of the professors, correspondence about the reduction of the professorship to a readership, the election of a Rhodes scholar, A. M. Honoré (Diocesan College and New College 1940), and the change of the readership to one in Commonwealth or United States law. In addition to these academic grants there are also appeals files on other University bodies such as the British American Club, the University Club, and the Oxford Union.

The Trust, of course, was not purely a grant-giving body. It was operating within Oxford, many of its Trustees including H. A. L. Fisher, John Lowe, and Kenneth Wheare (to name just three before 1960), were and are Oxford men, and its secretaries and wardens have frequently been prominent in University academic and administrative circles and have sat on committees of other Oxford-based bodies. In the archives there are general files that reflect these interests. Material on the Beit Fund and professorship of colonial history, for example, stretches with some gaps from 1904 to the present day, and there are files on the Harmsworth Professor, clubs such as the Ralegh Club, the Oxford Provident Association, and Oxford roads. Although this close involvement with Oxford life can be seen in files throughout the history of the Trust, it is most pronounced during the time that Lothian was Secretary and from the late 1950s when Williams

[89] Lord Elton (ed.) *The First Fifty Years of the Rhodes Trust and the Rhodes Scholarships, 1903–1953* (Oxford: Basil Blackwell, 1955), Wylie, 92.
[90] RTF 1131, Wylie to Boyd, 30 Jan. 1905.
[91] See RTF 1131.   [92] Rhodes's will, clause 16, 1 July 1899.

became Warden. File RTF 2680 Oxford Preservation Trust, for example, documents grants but also reveals Lothian's close involvement with the formation of the Trust and includes some memoranda and appeal literature written by him. The Preservation Trust's first secretary was Millar, who was Lothian's assistant. RTF 2935 Oxford University Higher Studies Fund demonstrates that Lothian, Allen, and Aydelotte were all involved in raising money and negotiating with the University over the administration of the fund. The file includes discussions on the needs of the University and the targeting of the appeal. The Trust gave a donation of £100,000 because 'no University can keep in the first rank unless a considerable proportion of its leading figures are actively engaged in extending the limits of human knowledge rather than in imparting to successive generations of students the body of learning which they themselves have inherited from their predecessors'.[93] After considerable discussion of the relative merits of supporting various branches of research, from the point of view both of the scholarships and of Oxford, the Trustees accepted Lothian's suggestion of using the grant for social studies, with special reference to politics, by which he meant research into the problems of modern government, in particular the Commonwealth, American, and international bodies, 'the field in which Mr Rhodes was most interested'.[94] There are many other examples of this involvement in the University and in Oxford life and not just confined to the period of Lothian or Williams. File RTF 2844 Indian Lectures, for example, continues until 1953 and contains correspondence about Indian culture and studies and ways to promote the subject at Oxford.

These files all include references to the obligations of the Trust towards the scholarships, to the causes it should support, and to the role of the Trust in Oxford, but the most informative source relating to these issues is the files on Rhodes House, Rhodes House Library, and the related files on the use of Rhodes House. The archives document the genesis and role of Rhodes House and the Trustees' view of the building, as something more than a memorial to Rhodes or an office for the scholarships and scholars. It was to be a gift to the University and centre for research, or, as Kerr wrote to Aydelotte, 'not merely a new building in Oxford but a real contribution both to the future status of the University and to English-speaking relations'.[95] Throughout the Rhodes House files there are references to the best uses for the building. Elton's ambitions, for example, can be seen from the files on Rhodes House (RTF 2637) and Rhodes House Library (RTF 2660), particularly during the Second World War. Nuffield was establishing itself, with quite a lot of help from the Trust, as a centre for colonial studies, but he still felt that there was a role for Rhodes House as a centre of research for the dominions, perhaps with research grants and residential accommodation. Other files clearly reveal the Trust's regular attempts to expand the role of Rhodes House. RTF 2722 Rhodes House and African Civil Service Probationers (1926–36), RTF 3176 Rhodes House, Gift to the University (1961–4), and RTF 3621 Halifax House/Rhodes Society (1990s) document just three examples of schemes which, for various reasons, have failed to come to fruition. These and other Rhodes House files frequently reveal as much about Oxford and the outside world as they do about Rhodes House and the scholarships. RTF 2792 Oxford University Institute of Government, for example, concentrates on a proposal to use Rhodes House as a centre for government or African studies. The material includes reports of meetings and conferences with Smuts on African studies in Oxford, a concrete proposal for an institute (the Trust agreed to add a seminar wing to Rhodes House if additional money could be raised elsewhere), negotiations with the International Institute of African

[93] RTF 2935, Lothian Report to the Trustees, 13 Nov. 1936.   [94] Ibid.
[95] RTF 1702, Kerr to Aydelotte, 24 May 1928.

Languages and Cultures, an application to the Rockefeller Foundation for funds, and early proposals for an African Survey.

The Rhodes House and Rhodes House Library files also contain much of a more day-to-day nature. For those interested in the architect, Sir Herbert Baker, there is plenty of detail on the design and building of Rhodes House: his attention to detail and love of symbolism produced files of correspondence, which provoked reactions ranging from amusement to frustration. Kerr was probably being less than serious when he commented on a new edition of the booklet on Rhodes House: 'I would also leave in Baker's explanation of his somewhat extravagant symbolism even including the reference to the devastation of Northern England by factory smoke.'[96] There is material about gifts and items purchased for Rhodes House ranging from busts and paintings to the more unusual like antelope and buffalo heads. The archives reveal that these were not always appreciated, as Kerr commented on the busts in the rotunda and vestibule of Rhodes House: 'Our experience hitherto with busts has not always been very happy. Milner is excessively grim, Parkin is rather formless and Rhodes himself had to be skied out of sight.'[97] The Trust's close connections with the library has meant that the latter's development and expansion, and relations with the rest of the Bodleian, have been recorded in great detail: from the number of books and acquisitions to the development of the manuscript section, and policies on appeals and funding. Whatever the success of the Trust's more ambitious plans, Rhodes House has been used for a variety of functions and events during its history. Some of these are documented and generated correspondence, most notably if complaints were made. There were protests, for example, about the communist tendencies at a meeting of the Atomic Scientists' Association in 1948[98] and about the acoustics in the Milner Hall during a meeting of the Royal Empire Society which prompted Lothian to comfort Allen (who had had to deal with the complaints) with: 'These diehard Imperialists think that they own not only the Empire but everything else they can lay their hands on.'[99] The records produced during the war years are particularly interesting: Rhodes House was used to house evacuees, entertain and provide courses for the forces, as an air raid and fire warning post, and the basements were very nearly requisitioned for use by the Council. The archives give some impression of how Oxford, and of course the University, operated during the war.

Few appeals files, or other files relating to Oxford, exist for the period immediately following the war. The Trust was concerned with the resumption of the scholarships and was worried about the amount of spare funds after an increase in the stipend. The Trustees had also promised a substantial amount for an extension of the Rhodes House Library stack. In the late 1950s, however, a series of grants were approved which led to the opening of several new files and heralded something of a change in the nature of the Trust's attitude to donations, and to some extent a change in the nature of the archives. Sir Edgar Williams, more so even than Lothian who was based in London, was closely involved in many aspects of Oxford. He argued more strongly than previous wardens for the necessity of contributing to Oxford, particularly at a time when less money was available from the government. It was vital, Williams urged, to ensure that Oxford retained its status as one of the top universities and so continued to attract and benefit the best scholars. Once Elton retired and with the death of two of the most prominent London Trustees (Amery in 1955 and Peacock in 1962) and with the chairmanship of Wheare, circumstances were such that the cause of the University was likely to be strongly supported. The process

---

[96] RTF 2637, Lothian to Allen, 30 Oct. 1935.   [97] Ibid., Lothian to Allen, 25 Feb. 1936.
[98] Ibid. 1948.   [99] Ibid., Lothian to Allen, 27 Mar. 1934.

had, in fact, begun with a donation of £5,000 to Oriel (Rhodes's old college) in 1956 and an initial grant in 1957 of £50,000 to the Oxford Historic Buildings Appeal,[100] but the change really came just before Elton retired, when the Trustees agreed to a grant of £5,000 for Exeter. Peacock, explaining the reason for his support to Elton, admitted that it was 'a dangerous subject, for all the Colleges at Oxford could make claims. Nevertheless, I should be inclined to take that risk, for Wheare's arguments in favour are strong, and I feel that there is another very strong one. Wheare's own development as a Trustee has struck me as very remarkable indeed . . . he is to-day of particular importance in Oxford.'[101] From the 1960s the files contain details of regular and often substantial grants to the University, including for example to the Independence Fund, to clinical pharmacology, to the Bodleian, to new student accommodation, and to University sports. These grants have continued to the present day and the Trust is now one of the University's major benefactors. Appeals files have also continued but have changed slightly inasmuch as they contain less detailed correspondence. Once the post of Secretary and Warden had merged the correspondence between the two offices ceased. Williams also tended to rely less on lengthy written reports from those asking for funds, partly because the causes were more familiar to the Trustees.

From the late 1960s the Trust provided grants to enable women from scholarship countries to come to Oxford for a period as fellows in the women's colleges.[102] This was in part an attempt to compensate for the Trust's inability to open the scholarships to women but also continued a tradition of supporting individuals from abroad while at Oxford or supporting Oxford academics researching overseas. Two such schemes were initiated by Lothian, schemes which, unlike others that were perhaps too visionary, produced substantial practical results. The Rhodes Memorial Lectures[103] attracted to Oxford and Rhodes House such names as Einstein, Smuts, Hubble, and Flexner and correspondence with these, and details about the lectures, appear on the files. There is also correspondence with or about others who failed to accept invitations to speak, such as Muhammad Iqbal, Walter Lippman, Jawaharlal Nehru, and Dr Antonio de Oliveira Salazar. Some of these individuals are documented in several other of the Trust's files: Flexner, for example, was involved with the Eastman professorship and was suggested by Aydelotte as a possible successor to Wylie as Oxford Secretary. The second scheme, which began around the same time, was the Rhodes travelling fellowships. The Trust funded research trips for University men and women in the dominions and the United States. The files contain applications from potential fellows and reports from the successful candidates while overseas. These vary in quality and length; some were so poor that they caused the Trustees to worry that they were funding 'joy-rides'. Others are detailed documents which can be revealing about the country visited, topics covered, and the fellows themselves. One of the most notable fellows was Margery Perham who was awarded a fellowship in 1929 and whose travels through Africa are well documented by her reports to the Trustees and her correspondence with Lothian. She struck up an amiable relationship with Lothian with whom she shared common interests, but with whom she did not always agree. Their correspondence frequently refers to the 'native question' with Kerr, for example, arguing that, however valuable African traditions might be, economic changes would have an inevitable impact on Africans. He urged Perham to look at these questions while in Africa as 'our problem is not to devise safeguards for the native on the subconscious assumption that this transformation can be delayed or curbed, but safeguards which will

---

[100] RTF 3131 and RTF 3139.   [101] RTF 3158, Peacock to Elton, 14 Jan. 1959.
[102] RTF 3223.   [103] RTF 2694.

help him to get the best out of the new civilisation and to protect himself from the evils which are implicit in it'.[104]

Similarly detailed reports and correspondence were received from another fellow, Edward Thompson, and in fact correspondence from both Thompson and Perham appears in several other of the Trust's files. Thompson is well documented in the file on Indian Lectures mentioned above. This records that he was given further grants from the Trust to visit India, his last trip being in 1939 when he produced a report which was fairly critical of the actions of the government in India. This provoked varying reactions from the Trustees, several of whom had had first-hand knowledge of the Indian problem. Amery wrote to Elton, for example: 'We may have been clumsy: I believe it might well have been a good thing for the Viceroy to have convened the Council and Assembly and asked for a resolution committing India to the War.'[105] Malcolm MacDonald at the colonial office, not yet a Trustee but a close friend of Elton, wrote to the latter to take issue with Thompson's assertion that none of the cabinet was interested in India, but agreed that there was some truth in his claim 'that he personally was able to persuade the Leaders to postpone Civil Disobedience'.[106] Perham is referred to by others in several files and presented various appeals to the Trustees, either on behalf of others or for her own projects. She was often asked for her opinion on other appeals (as were others in Oxford such as Reginald Coupland) and corresponded with Elton and others about Oxford, particularly about colonial research. She felt such a debt to the Trust, particularly to Lothian, that she wrote to him after the Trustees had approved a grant to the Sudan Cultural Centre in Khartoum: 'I hope I shall find equally sympathetic access to your successor. I am inclined to look upon you as a fairy god-father.' His cable offering her a second year's fellowship 'changed my life . . . & started a rather precarious but enthralling career in the study of Africa'.[107]

Grants to Individuals and Others

The Trust has changed the course of many people's lives by giving grants to different individuals to pursue research both in the United Kingdom and abroad. There are files that document these grants containing applications for assistance, reports on the progress and outcome of the project, press cuttings and articles, and correspondence. Grants were given towards research in Africa, such as to L. S. B. Leakey in 1929 and from 1936 to 1938[108] or to Audrey Richards whose visit to Rhodesia prompted headlines such as 'Woman Learns the Secrets of Natives' and 'Songs Sung to Her for Three Weeks!' The newspaper article concludes, 'Dr Richards wore shorts in the jungle, and often had to shoot or fish for her own food,' but her application reveals that her research was more complex than that.[109] Other grants were given to those doing research or working in the fields of history or empire or on specific areas such as Bantu studies. The individuals assisted were sometimes, but by no means always, Rhodes scholars. We have already seen how the Trustees assisted scholars while at Oxford or for research projects in their third year. Rhodes in his letter to Grey about the residue went further than this. He suggested that his Trustees 'assist after college the most promising of your youths in their professions in after life, especially if they show indication of higher ideas, and a desire to undertake public duties'.[110] As just one example, Professor W. M. Macmillan (Stellenbosch and Merton 1903) at

---

[104] RTF 2695, Kerr to Perham, 11 Feb. 1930.
[106] Ibid., MacDonald to Elton, 8 Dec. 1939.
[107] RTF 2981, Perham to Lothian, 5 May 1939.
[109] RTF 2791 (*Daily Mirror*, 9 Nov. 1931).

[105] RTF 2844, Amery to Elton, Dec. 1939.

[108] See RTF 2653 and RTF 2911.
[110] See n. 57.

Witwatersrand University was given grants between 1930 and 1940 for research in Africa and towards the publication of books on Africa and the colonial Empire.

Assistance to Rhodes scholars was not given automatically. The Trustees were wary of giving grants to individuals and would only do so when they felt their assistance would be absolutely justified. This was particularly the case when giving grants to people coming to Oxford. They did not wish to fall into the habit of giving a scholarship without competition and when they did help individuals to study at Oxford such grants usually amounted to less than a Rhodes scholarship. Despite their caution there are over thirty files on men and women who were helped by the Trustees in this way. Some had shown special promise but were not eligible for a scholarship, others came from families to whom the Trust felt they (or Africa) owed a good deal (such as the sons of Paul Roos and Sir Godfrey Lagden), and some were Africans who were supported by the Trust at Oxford or Cambridge. These latter included Peter Koinange, son of a Kikuyu chief, whose case was supported by Leakey, and E. W. Mathu from Kenya who was supported by both Perham and Coupland and who went on to become prominent in the UN and private secretary to Kenyatta. Elton and Lothian were both keen to assist such individuals as long they were sure that the grant would be well used. Lothian felt that the recipient 'must be a person who can stand an education at a high class white university without becoming spoiled, who can meet colour prejudice not so much at Oxford but later on without becoming embittered and who can go back to his own country where he will have to take his place as part of the subordinate race without going "red" '.[111]

These are not the only files on individuals in the archives. Many of the early files concern people who received legacies from Rhodes, who were either mentioned in his will or whom the Trustees identified as having a justifiable claim. These included his secretaries, Gordon Le Sueur and Philip Jourdan, people who worked or lived on his estates such as John Grimmer and John Morris, servants such as Mary M'Lamla, and members of his family. The number of these appeals increase during the years after Rhodes's death and there are several new files around the 1920s and later. The new appeals were often from pioneers and others who had known Rhodes, sometimes prominent individuals, who were getting old or had fallen on hard times. The Trust was frequently generous, giving grants for their children's education, pensions for themselves or their wives, paying for medical bills, or finding them jobs. File RTF 2183, for example, documents the case of E. A. Maund, an ex-managing director of the Exploring Company, the parent company of the British South Africa Company, who helped Rhodes secure the concession from Lobengula. He was given money to educate his children and during the 1920s, as he got older, was given personal grants. A similar file exists on Benjamin 'Matabele' Wilson. For many individuals who often had nowhere else to turn, the Trust was one of the few links they had with a past they felt they could be proud of. Consequently the files frequently contain reminiscences about their time in Southern Africa or references to archives or artefacts that they collected while they were there.

Some of the files span several decades. Blanche Jourdan, the wife of Rhodes's secretary, was still writing to the Trust in the 1970s. By the 1950s and 1960s, however, the majority of these pioneers, colleagues of Rhodes, or family members had died and their files had closed. As we have seen, there are also fewer files documenting South Africa in general from the 1960s and there was a further change in the archives during this period. Elton's Empire was disintegrating, a fact he himself had acknowledged with the introduction of scholarships for the new

---

[111] RTF 2984, Lothian to Elton, 23 June 1939.

Commonwealth, and the Trust, although continuing to promote ties between nations and within the Commonwealth, was no longer called upon to give funds to promote traditional flag-waving imperial causes. The Oxford appeals files show that the Trustees were concerned that they should contribute to the survival of Oxford as one of the foremost universities and began to give substantial grants to try to ensure this. There are also a number of new files in the archives, from the 1960s, which document grants given to new bodies, most of which were based in the United Kingdom. This was not a radical change in policy; throughout its history the Trust had given money to British charities or institutions, many of which have already been described. Grants had been targeted at education in Britain, in particular at the University of London, with donations to law, imperial studies, Dutch studies, and historical studies at various times. Many of the later national donations, in the 1960s and 1970s, had a familiar feel: there were grants to the Library of Political and Economic Science at the LSE, to the ODI and VSO, and to the Florey Memorial Fund for fellowships between Australia and the United Kingdom. Other donations of this period do represent something of a change. From the 1960s and 1970s single grants were given to large national appeals such as by those of the National Trust, York Minster, Canterbury Cathedral, and the RNLI. However, in general, most of the appeals files of the latter part of the twentieth century would have been familiar to the Trustees of fifty, if not ninety, years earlier. A glance at the donations and files of the last decade of the century, with South Africa back in the Commonwealth, shows that the largest grants have been given to Oxford and its colleges, followed closely by South African and Commonwealth charities with a smaller amount going to UK and European charities, many of which had a Commonwealth or educational theme.

Financial Records

It is tempting to generalize about patterns in grant-giving that may be revealed by the archives, and about the motives of the Trustees and secretaries who made these decisions. It is, however, dangerous to assume that a full file meant a close relationship with a body or that an increase of new files meant a change in donation policy. A lot of correspondence is more likely to indicate a difficult decision and may distract from those cases where the decision did not need as much justification or information, or where payments were made regularly over the years without the need for much deliberation. With so many files it is easy to lose track of the context in which grants were being given. Fortunately the Trust's archives contain records which allow the researcher to trace the patterns of Trust spending and the balance that existed between and within the separate funds.

Traditionally the Trustees have not gone out of their way to publicize donations. When asked whether a grant to the Victoria League could be reported Milner stated: 'I am *against* communication to Press, as it will only call attention to the fact that we do give grants & bring 100.000 Beggars down upon our heads.'[112] During the Second World War Elton produced a memorandum in which he proposed that the Trustees should consider publishing some kind of annual report. At present, he argued, 'hardly any one is aware that the Rhodes Trust does anything besides running the scholarships'. An annual report would promote coordination between the bodies that received Trust support and other similar organizations; it could increase the number of applications to the Trustees, but these might include some deserving causes which otherwise would not come into contact with the Trust. On the other hand he admitted that 'at some time

---

[112] RTF 1203, Milner to Boyd, Jan. 1903.

or other political considerations might be involved' but could not think of any recent grants which the Trustees would have hesitated to include in a published report. A stronger argument against a publication 'is the present well marked tradition of reticence, and the fact that, without publicity, the Trustees remain freer to deliberate, and act, uninfluenced by any extraneous considerations'. Elton was in favour of the publication of a report, but could see the disadvantages and concluded, with a characteristic flourish of metaphor: 'I shall have no regrets if they decide to continue to hide this particular light under a bushel.'[113] The file closes with the copy of a resolution by the Trustees in January 1942 to produce such a report at the end of the war, but, after over three more years of conflict, the Trust had more pressing issues to deal with and it never materialized. Despite this, the Trust has been producing, since its conception, annual balance sheets and accounts which serve the same purpose. From these it is possible to see at a glance how much money was available and what proportion was spent on administration, the scholarships, and public purposes, even to the level of individual grants.

The first drafts of the balance sheets, with their many alterations and corrections, indicate how complex the process of settling Rhodes's estate was. It took some years for all assets and liabilities to be confirmed, an extreme example being the repayment of a debt of £13 4s. 6d. in 1946. The first balance sheet, as could be ascertained for 1 August 1902, lists debts due and other liabilities and securities, shares, and other assets. We learn that Rhodes owned livestock which was worth £6,632 of which there were 109 wild animals on his estate in Cape Town. The balance sheet of December 1903 notes political expenditure by the residuary legatees of £9,383 16s. 2d., records the purchase of a motor car in South Africa and includes a list of subscriptions and donations of £15,000 in London and South Africa. The entries for political expenditure cease after 1906, presumably because of the formation of the Rhodes–Beit Fund, but other entries continue. There are lists of amounts spent on scholarships, on administration, of debtors, of shares and investments including those in syndicates, of payments to individuals and pensions, and of subscriptions and donations. By 1920 these latter had risen to £51,000 and are all listed. This amount of detail continues to the present day, so it is possible, for example, to trace a small annual grant to the Salvation Army in South Africa that began in 1910 and was only discontinued in 1985.

There are other sources which relate to the financial policy of the Trust including a number of subject files. There are files on death duties, on income tax, on investments, on each of the various funds and on expenditure in South Africa. Correspondence files exist for the Trust's bankers, auditors, solicitors, and property agents. Three of the most useful files are perhaps RTF 2709 Financial Policy, RTF 2524 Rhodes Trust Act 1929, and RTF 3016 Rhodes Trust Act 1946. RTF 2709 deals with financial policy in general and the effect of outside pressures on the Trust's decisions; it also includes some lists of assets and liabilities and a comparison of the use of various funds. The file does not begin until 1925, when Peacock and Kerr joined the Trust; one of the earliest records is a detailed explanation of 'how the assets of the Rhodes Trust have come to shrink by about £1,400,00 since Mr Rhodes' death'.[114] RTF 2524 deals, among other things, with the setting up of the Capital Reserve Fund, but also goes into some detail about income tax, charitable purposes, and funds for Rhodes House. A memorandum prepared in 1929 lists the main outlay from the residue up to 1929, namely: death duties (£350,000), Groote Schuur (£95,000), Rhodesia (£198,000), Jameson Hall, Cape Town (£10,000), 1820 Memorial Settlers' Association (£20,000), Imperial Forestry Institute, Oxford (£5,000), School of Tropical

---

[113] RTF 3005, Elton Report to Trustees, 6 Dec. 1941.
[114] RTF 2709, Kerr to Peacock, 14 Aug. 1925. This file only continues to 1963.

Agriculture, Trinidad (£5,000), Rhodes University College (£85,000), and Rhodes House (estimated £108,000).[115] RTF 3016 shows how the Trustees reassessed their financial position in preparation for the 1946 Act, particularly with regard to what they could legally do with the various funds, under what terms they could give money outside the Commonwealth, and whether they could invest in land. The file includes several memoranda on policy and summaries and explanations of grants. Edward Peacock, for example, produced a memorandum on 'the Policy of the Trust in regard to investment in Real Estate' which described how 'The world financial crisis of 1929, the debacle in capital values which followed, and the conversions in 1932 of 5% War Loan to a lower interest basis' led the Trust to invest in property.[116] Peacock himself was well qualified to produce such a memorandum: as a director of Baring Brothers he was one of several Trustees who had financial expertise and served on the financial committee which met to discuss Trust policy.

Trustees and Secretaries

The Trustees have all been men and women of distinction, each carefully chosen with their own areas of expertise. Some have been better known than others; names such as Jameson, Kipling, and Baldwin are more readily recognizable than Millis or Hutchinson. Some only served for short periods; Alfred Beit died in 1906 and Lord Hailsham and Sir Edward Boyle both retired after four years. Others stayed with the Trust for a considerable period, the longest serving being Sir Edward Peacock who was a Trustee for thirty-seven years. Some have had more of an impact on the Trust's policy and business than others, but all have had an impact on the world in their own fields. The archives give an impression of this significance and of the personalities and opinions of some of the Trustees.

Many, but not all, of the Trustees were allocated a file. The contents of these files vary, but in general they contain little that is new or particularly startling. There may be correspondence about attendance at meetings, retirement from the Trust, and occasionally about issues or subjects raised at meetings; often there are details of memorials, obituaries, or tributes. On Jameson's file, for example, Gerald Orpen wrote after the former's death: 'I found it difficult to believe that he could have been guilty of such a really tragic mistake as the Jameson Raid. He never attached any value to money . . . He used to give money to any deserving person he considered to be in need of assistance.'[117] Jameson's most significant documented contribution to the Trust's early policy occurs elsewhere with his support of a grant to Rhodes University College.[118] The filing system until 1959 was such that most correspondence with Trustees was filed on the subject files to which it referred rather than on the individual Trustees' files. By looking at a subject file it is possible to identify some of the opinions expressed by Trustees on a particular subject, but until the 1960s it is not so easy to trace an individual's views on a range of issues from their own file. With the merger of the two offices under Williams more correspondence began to be filed on the Trustees' files, and they are, in some respects, a more useful source from this point.

The Trustees who were most involved in the business of the Trust are likely to be better documented, either because they acted as chairmen, like Milner, Amery, Peacock, and Wheare, or

---

[115] RTF 2524, Memorandum [by Millar and Kerr], 14 Mar. 1929.
[116] RTF 3016, Sir Edward Peacock, 14 Mar. 1946.
[117] RTF 1832, Orpen to Elton, 12 Jan. 1956. This is a copy; the original is filed on RTF 3121.
[118] See for example RTF 1027, Jameson to Boyd, [Aug.] 1903.

because they were frequently consulted by the secretaries. H. A. L. Fisher and other Trustees in Oxford were often consulted over policy to do with Oxford and the scholarships, and this is recorded in the files. Dawson, as editor of *The Times*, was often asked to publish editorials and articles about the Trust, particularly around the time that Rhodes House was built. Amery also appears in many of the files. When he died Elton calculated that he had missed only one Trustees' meeting during the sixteen years that Elton had been Secretary. Moreover, Amery's role at the Colonial Office meant that he frequently received appeals, some of which he passed onto the Trustees for consideration, although without always supporting them.[119] His time at the India Office had left him interested in India and correspondence with him can also be found on these files. If other Trustees were involved in causes supported by the Trust they are sometimes documented as proposing or backing a grant to a particular body. Lord Lovat, for example, was largely responsible for obtaining a grant of £5,000 for the Imperial Forestry Institute in Oxford at a time when he was the first chairman of the Forestry Commission, and several grants were given to the Institute of International Languages and Cultures because of Hailey's involvement.

Some Trustees, on the other hand, are hardly documented at all. There is very little on Baldwin in the archives. The most notable reference to him occurs when there was some discussion of portraits of the Trustees for Rhodes House and Amery wrote to Elton: 'By the way I don't believe in any of our talks about securing portraits of the present trustees we remembered a certain Lord Baldwin. You may have heard of him, though possibly not seen him, since your appointment, both as a trustee and active (or should I say inactive?) in politics.'[120] A portrait of Baldwin was commissioned and is now in Rhodes House. This commissioning of portraits of certain living Trustees provoked a storm of outrage from Sothern Holland who tendered his resignation in a seven-page letter to Elton objecting that 'there is to be discrimination (an upper and lower sixth)! Could anything be more invidious than colleagues sitting round a table going through a process of selection and voting one another to an Artists Chair. Has it ever happened that a Body of living men have embarked on a Picture Gallery with themselves as the subjects.'[121] Sothern Holland was persuaded to reconsider: he was, as were most of the Trustees, one of the 'upper sixth' in terms of commitment to the Trust.

The material on the Trustees becomes more interesting when viewed in the context of their backgrounds and their connections outside the Trust and there are occasional items in the archives that serve as a reminder of this. An appeal from Diocesan College, South Africa, is given an added dimension when it is remembered that one of the Trustees was the Prime Minister of the Cape. As Michell noted, writing on the possibility of a donation: 'Dr Jameson will probably require the acquiescence of the Dio. Coll. Rondebosch Council, in the scheme of his Government regarding a Conference to settle the lines of University Reform.'[122] Many of the Trustees had been in South Africa around the turn of the century, some being associated with Milner's Kindergarten, and these connections were later identified by some as proof of the existence of Rhodes's 'Secret Society'. The files contain a letter from Amery disputing this: 'I don't suppose any of us knew of a secret society, nor do I imagine that it even entered to any extent into Milner's own mind.'[123] There was no formal society, but correspondence in the archives

---

[119] See for example RTF 2675.   [120] RTF 3000, Amery to Elton, 10 Nov. 1941.
[121] Ibid., Sothern Holland to Elton, 30 Jan. 1942.   [122] RTF 1490, Michell to Boyd, 11 July 1907.
[123] RTF 1294, Amery to Elton, 20 Apr. 1954. Amery explores the idea of a society, mentioning connections between Milner, Parkin, Curtis, and others, in the context of his own career.

frequently serves as a reminder of the external associations which provided an undercurrent to the business of the Trust. When Otto Beit was visiting Southern Africa in 1920, partly on Trust business, he wrote to Dawson, one of the original Kindergarten, who was at that point standing in for Edward Grigg as Trust Secretary and who was later to become a Trustee. Beit had been discussing the Rhodesian elections with Sir John Chancellor and was keen to relate the latter's views to Dawson. According to Beit, Chancellor believed that 'before very long a request may be made to the Colonial Office for some form of Crown Colony Government, which Milner won't want to agree to and which the people of Rhodesia will hate when they have got it'.[124] Milner was, at that time, the senior Rhodes Trustee but also Colonial Secretary. The man he had just chosen to be his parliamentary under-secretary was the man who was to deny the secret society allegations twenty years later: Leopold Amery. Comments like the one made by Beit are, however, frequently scattered and incidental to the main subject of a file, and, for those Trustees who did not play a very great role in the Trust's affairs, very rare.

Like the Trustees the secretaries had lives, connections, and interests outside the Trust. There are individual files on most of the English secretaries, and on some of the overseas secretaries, which detail their appointments, sometimes include personal correspondence, articles, and newspaper cuttings, and often refer to their retirement and death. However, the major role that they played in the business of the Trust means that correspondence and other material relating to the secretaries occurs in most of the files. The records of the 1920s and 1930s, for example, bear witness to Lothian's extraordinary range of connections. He too had been a member of the Kindergarten and described his relationship with Milner and the 'Moot' in a letter to Basil Williams.[125] When appointed he was not in the government, but his conviction that he was perfectly qualified to advise those who were is well documented. He wrote to Amery, the Colonial Secretary, trying to persuade him not to make an official visit to South Africa as 'the really excellent result . . . of the last Imperial Conference may be imperilled if you pay an official visit at a moment when the whole country is inflamed about the Union Jack issue'.[126] Something of an impression of Lothian's beliefs and personality can be formed from those files recording the appeals and projects with which he was involved in Oxford and South Africa, and from some of the country files. A previous chapter has shown how his involvement in the German scholarships is particularly interesting in the light of his attitude to appeasement. Kerr referred explicitly to the rumours that grew to surround the so-called Cliveden Set when writing to Aydelotte, perhaps a little prematurely in 1938, that the story was now 'dead': 'It was originally started by the Communist Party . . . to arouse class consciousness and to mobilise opinion for their favourite thesis of anti-Fascist war.'[127] In his correspondence with Aydelotte, with whom he obviously had a close relationship, Lothian sometimes explored some of his political ideas or reactions to world events. Writing to Aydelotte in 1933 and referring to recent events in Japan and China he put forward a thesis whereby he compared Rhodes's views that 'the spread of civilisation and the prevention of war depended upon the association, or even the union, of those peoples who in his view had proved their capacity both for democracy and for ordered government' with those of 'liberal idealists of the war period with Woodrow Wilson at their head' and suggested that in 'the question of Wilson versus Rhodes' the Rhodes thesis was becoming more appropriate: 'the first step towards stable world peace is the re-constitution of some form of war

---

[124] RTF 1219, Beit to Acting Secretary, 10 May 1920.
[125] RTF 2286, Lothian to Williams, 16 Nov. 1934.
[126] RTF 2422, Lothian to Amery, 30 May 1927.
[127] RTF 1702, Lothian to Aydelotte, 13 June 1938.

time association of the English-speaking nations and also France (in place of Germany) as a genuinely liberal power.'[128]

This tendency of Lothian to attribute to Rhodes a belief in a kind of English-speaking internationalism was not always shared by others connected with the Trust.[129] The files show that Lothian's successor also held rather different beliefs: Elton's commitment to the Empire is clear from many of the files. The contrast with Lothian is demonstrated clearly in a letter to P. Green in RTF 3039: 'I am a little alarmed at your suggestion of beginning to stress the international rather than the imperial note. You might well find yourself flooded by UNO enthusiasts of the old League of Nations brand.' Elton urged Green not to short-circuit 'the only League of Nations which has ever yet worked in practice', by which he meant the Empire. Elton's lengthy reports and correspondence provide many examples of the causes he supported, in particular his commitment to Christian and youth organizations. Like Lothian, he shared connections and interests with some of the Trustees but his correspondence reveals he did not share the intimacy. He did, however, have a close friendship with Malcolm MacDonald and some of their correspondence is preserved in the archives.

The predecessors and successors of Lothian and Elton, and their colleagues overseas, are documented in much the same way. The correspondence of an earlier Secretary, Sir George Parkin, reveals his views on a variety of issues, in particular the value of education, and the nature and effect of the First World War. The archives also demonstrate the extraordinary effect he had on the people he met during his visits abroad. S. C. Mitchell, President of the University of South Carolina, wrote to him after his visit in 1909: 'Your address at the university of S.C. marked an epoch in our history. I am unable to thank you for the impulses you quickened in both faculty and students. You rendered us a service far greater than you yourself realise.'[130] Aydelotte's contribution to a wide variety of educational projects has already been discussed and Michener's political career has been referred to in a previous chapter. Wylie, Allen, and Williams in particular were connected with many bodies and supported many proposals in Oxford not directly related to the Trust which are sometimes mentioned in the records. For the most recent period of the Trust there exists the same complex relationship between Trustees, secretaries, and beneficiaries that can be found throughout its history, with only a slight shift away from government and South Africa towards Oxford.

Cecil Rhodes

The Rhodes Trust archives do not include the papers of Cecil Rhodes: his letters and other manuscripts are in repositories around the world, including Rhodes House Library in Oxford. The Trust's records are unique. They detail exactly what Rhodes had when he died and what happened to his legacy. The history of the Trust is the history of how the Trustees have managed his property and other assets, how they have invested and spent his residue and how they have tried to make a success of the various projects and schemes that he mentioned in his will or intended to support. The archives document what happened after Rhodes died but they also contribute something to our understanding of Rhodes himself.

[128] RTF 1233, Lothian to Aydelotte, 12 May 1933.
[129] See for example letter from Lady Milner in RTF 2021, 5 Apr. 1933 and RTF 2637, Dawson to Kerr, 29 Aug. 1925 where the former warned: 'I think you must beware of over-stating CJR's deliberate allocation of scholarships (which I believe to have been largely due to ignorance of geography) & of attributing to him too much of your own "English-speaking" ideal.'
[130] RTF 1280, Michell to Parkin, 13 Dec. 1909.

As we have already seen, throughout the archives there are references to Rhodes and to his actions and intentions. Often interpretations of Rhodes's wishes were based on fact. McDonald, for example, was usually able to confirm if Rhodes had promised support to a Rhodesian pioneer or farmer. The Trustees had Rhodes's letter to Grey with suggestions on how to spend the residue and copies of other similar letters from Rhodes to his Trustees about the legacy exist in the archives.[131] Several files contain correspondence about the genesis and purpose of the scholarships or with individuals claiming to have suggested the idea to Rhodes. J. Astley Cooper, for example, published a similar scheme in *Greater Empire* in 1891 and claimed to have asked Rhodes to finance it: 'When I put the matter before Mr. Rhodes, after Sir Henry Loch had seen him, I only asked him to finance the Scholars who would come from South Africa, hoping to find some other wealthy colonials, who would finance Australia, Canada, etc.'[132] Astley Cooper produced evidence to substantiate his claims. He sent Grey a copy of a letter he had received from Rhodes, he thought in 1892, in which Rhodes had written: 'In the Scholarships you have evolved a great idea of Imperial Union, but it will require a lot of money.'[133]

At other times the Trustees relied on their personal knowledge of Rhodes. Michell's occasional clashes with the other Trustees over policy were based on what he thought Rhodes would have wanted. He was against transferring the Rhodesian properties on the terms suggested by Jameson and convinced that the German scholarships should not be annulled by an Act of Parliament. As he wrote to Parkin: 'I am not so sure as you are that Rhodes, after what has happened, would have altered his Will. He was very farsighted and liked to plan his work over long periods.'[134] We have already seen how Lothian was warned about attributing his ideas on internationalism to Rhodes. Milner, too, occasionally ascribed his own political beliefs to Rhodes as can be seen from a letter he wrote to Parkin in 1912. He believed that Rhodes would have found little to rejoice at in the Union, despite it being under the British flag: 'all his efforts would be concentrated in keeping Rhodesia out of the Union as long as possible, in order to realise his ideal of making it a land of "more homes" for his own fellow countrymen and not a dumping ground for "bywoners" . . . let us beware of identifying him too much with the political development of South Africa since his death. I dare say he would not mind Groote Schuur being occupied by Botha . . . But I think he will turn in his grave when it is presently occupied by Hertzog or Sauer, and so on for ever and ever.'[135]

The Trustees were aware of the drawbacks in trying to second guess what Rhodes would have done. Files such as RTF 1294 Rhodes' Will, RTF 1905 Rhodes General, RTF 1181 Rhodes, Biographies and Reminiscences, RTF 2660 Rhodes House Library, and RTF 2180 Rhodes, Papers and Letters document attempts, not only to interpret Rhodes's wishes, but also to produce evidence on which to base these interpretations. The archives contain details of how the Trustees arranged

[131] See the files mentioned below and also RTF 2757. These letters did not, in fact, seem to make the Trustees any clearer or more likely to agree about Rhodes's intentions, see for example the letter referred to in n. 56.

[132] RTF 1294, Astley Cooper's letter to the Trust (1925) was quoted by Elton in a letter to Aydelotte, 24 Oct. 1955.

[133] RTF 1682, copy of a letter from Rhodes to Astley Cooper [1892], included with a letter from Astley Cooper to Beit, 16 Apr. 1927.

[134] RTF 1682, Michell to Parkin, 15 Mar. 1916. See RTF 1855 for correspondence about the transfer of the estates to the Southern Rhodesian government. The Milner Papers in the Bodleian Library, Oxford (MS Milner Dep. 468), include correspondence between Michell and Milner about Germany and the Rhodesian property.

[135] RTF 2109, Milner to Parkin, 21 June 1912.

the identification, collection, and cataloguing of papers and manuscripts relating to Rhodes. The provenance of many of the collections in Rhodes House Library can be traced through the Trust files. This process began fairly early: RTF 1181, for example, reveals how Michell removed many relevant papers from Groote Schuur while writing his biography of Rhodes. Once the early Trustees who had known Rhodes began to die, the urgency of preserving such records became more obvious. Lothian tried to gather together papers from as many sources as he could including from the Trust's own offices, from Michell's papers, and from sources in South Africa such as the Central Mining Company. After the war Elton set about trying to trace people who had know Rhodes, identifying private collections and collecting reminiscences and recollections. Many of the letters and papers he received were passed to Rhodes House Library but copies and the correspondence which generated the documents remain on the Rhodes Trust files.

Elton was not only keen to preserve paper documentation of the Founder. He also began trying to trace all the known portraits, busts, and statues of Rhodes. The Trust had already provided funds for many of the statues and memorials to Rhodes in Oxford and South Africa and there are files in the archives on many of these. RTF 2174 Rhodes Memorial Table Mountain, for example, includes correspondence with Sir Herbert Baker who designed the statue, plans and records of the construction, pamphlets and details of the unveiling, and photographs and press cuttings from the annual Rhodes Day ceremonies that were held at the memorial. References to these statues may also appear in other files; as usual Baker did not miss the opportunity to make a personal comment when writing to Kerr in 1925 over twenty years after the Bulawayo statue was built by Tweed: 'Tweed . . . continues to hate Rhodes . . . I never liked the Bulawayo Statue. I always though it had something suggestive of the sneer that he has put into his Clive.'[136] Elton energetically set about tracking down these various items, portraits, and references. Files such as RTF 2637 Rhodes House, RTF 2025 Rhodes, Busts, and RTF 2021 Portraits and Photographs of Rhodes document the location and background of many of the items that were identified. Finally, the Trustees commissioned Anita Brookner to collate all this information and in 1956 she produced a comprehensive *Iconography*.[137]

Michell was not the only acquaintance of Rhodes to believe that one way to preserve the memory of the Founder was to write his biography. The archives, in particular RTF 1181 Rhodes, Biographies and Reminiscences, contain details of other biographies and articles. In general the Trustees were supportive although, soon after Rhodes's death, they purchased some papers from his secretary, Gordon Le Sueur, in an attempt to stop him from publishing his memoirs.[138] This appears to have been an unusual action and on occasion the Trust gave grants to biographers or commissioned articles and biographies themselves. They were often asked for information about Rhodes, or for their opinions of the biographies. We have already seen the reaction to Millin's biography, but the files also include responses to others such as Kipling's views on McDonald's life of Rhodes. This correspondence and material continues throughout the century. In 1948, for example, Allen wrote to Elton saying that he wanted to keep Stead's book on Rhodes out of scholars' hands as 'it represents Rhodes as little better than a Nazi Racialist'.[139] The correspondence of more recent years has included comments on broadcasts and films about Rhodes as well as on more traditional publications.

The Trust's final direct link with Rhodes was not broken until 1978 with the death of the last of his nieces, Georgia Rhodes. It is only at that point that the files cease to contain

---

[136] RTF 2637, Baker to Kerr, 30 July 1925.   [137] See RTF 3125.
[138] See RTF 1056.   [139] RTF 2637, Allen to Elton, 25 May 1948.

correspondence with someone who had personally known Rhodes. Her death released another collection of Rhodes papers, pictures, and other heirlooms, most of which are documented in the files. Many of these items had been at Groote Schuur nearly a hundred years earlier and had been passed through the family, moving from property to property as family members died or moved on. There are items which are mentioned in the files on Groote Schuur around 1902 and 1905 which reappear in the files on Dalham and Hildersham Hall and are finally listed in the inventory made of Georgia Rhodes's property after she died.[140] These property files contain correspondence with other members of the Rhodes family, but many of the immediate relations have their own files. Files such as RTF 1174 Louisa S. M. Rhodes and RTF 2010 Captain Ernest Rhodes mainly deal with claims against the estate and with payments, but may also contain references to Rhodes himself. RTF 1189 Major Elmhurst Rhodes, for example, includes correspondence about Rhodes's will, his last wishes, and his death. More distant family members sometimes approached the Trust for funds; if so there is likely to be an individual appeal file referring to the application. Other files related to the Rhodes family are concerned with the Rhodes family tomb, appeals from Bishop's Stortford, the town in which Rhodes was born, and the granting of arms to Arthur Rhodes. The Trust did not feel obliged to help every relative or to support all the causes and organizations with which Rhodes or his family were connected but the correspondence and other material in the files provides something of a record of many of these.

The Rhodes Trust Archives and Access

The archives document the administration of Rhodes's legacy, the organization of the Rhodes scholarships, and the appeals received and benefactions given by the Trust. Many of the series which were opened in 1902 are still being added to today and, as such, form part of the working records of the Trust: it is difficult to distinguish 'current' from 'archives'. With the permission of the Warden it is possible to consult some, but not all, of these records: some are closed, either for reasons of confidentiality or because they are still in use by the Trust's office. This chapter has concentrated on the earlier records as most of the material relating to the scholarships after 1959 and to appeals from around the 1970s is closed, although there are some exceptions, particularly for items that are already in the public domain. The collection includes some of the records of overseas secretaries which have been transferred to Rhodes House as well as photographs, microfilm, film and sound recordings, volumes of press cuttings, and lantern slides. A detailed, indexed, catalogue of the archives is available which also gives information about other published and manuscript sources that relate to the Rhodes Trust. The other chapters in this book, which have drawn heavily on the archives at Rhodes House, demonstrate the value of the collection for those interested, not only in the Rhodes scholarships, but also in one of the many individuals, organizations, projects, or developments to which the Trust contributed during the twentieth century.

[140] See RTF 1771, RTF 1772, RTF 1772A, RTF 1246, and RTF 3180.

The Will of Cecil Rhodes

𝕴 THE RIGHT HONOURABLE CECIL JOHN RHODES of Cape Town in the Colony of the Cape of Good Hope hereby revoke all testamentary dispositions heretofore made by me and declare this to be my last Will which I make this 1st day of July 1899.

1. I am a natural-born British subject and I now declare that I have adopted and acquired and hereby adopt and acquire and intend to retain Rhodesia as my domicile.

2. I appoint the Right Honourable Archibald Philip Earl of Rosebery K. G. K. T. the Right Honourable Albert Henry George Earl Grey Alfred Beit of 26 Park Lane London William Thomas Stead of Mowbray House Norfolk Street Strand in the County of London Lewis Loyd Michell of Cape Town in the Colony of the Cape of Good Hope Banker and Bourchier Francis Hawksley of Mincing Lane in the City of London to be the Executors and Trustees of my Will and they and the survivors of them or other the Trustees for the time being of my Will are hereinafter called 'my Trustees.'

3. I admire the grandeur and loneliness of the Matoppos in Rhodesia and therefore I desire to be buried in the Matoppos on the hill which I used to visit and which I called the 'View of the World' in a square to be cut in the rock on the top of the hill covered with a plain brass plate with these words thereon—'Here lie the remains of Cecil John Rhodes' and accordingly I direct my Executors at the expense of my estate to take all steps and do all things necessary or proper to give effect to this my desire and afterwards to keep my grave in order at the expense of the Matoppos and Bulawayo Fund hereinafter mentioned.

4. I give the sum of £6,000 to   Kahn of Paris and I direct this legacy to be paid free of all duty whatsoever.

5. I give an annuity of £100 to each of my servants Norris and the one called Tony during his life free of all duty whatsoever and in addition to any wages due at my death.

6. I direct my Trustees on the hill aforesaid to erect or complete the monument to the men who fell in the first Matabele War at Shangani in Rhodesia the bas-reliefs for which are being made by Mr. John Tweed and I desire the said hill to be preserved as a burial-place but no person is to be buried there unless the Government for the time being of Rhodesia until the various states of South Africa or any of them shall have been federated and after such federation the Federal Government by a vote of two-thirds of its governing body says that he or she has deserved well of his or her country.

7. I give free of all duty whatsoever my landed property near Bulawayo in Matabeleland Rhodesia and my landed property at or near Inyanga near Salisbury in Mashonaland Rhodesia

to my Trustees hereinbefore named Upon trust that my Trustees shall in such manner as in their uncontrolled discretion they shall think fit cultivate the same respectively for the instruction of the people of Rhodesia.

8. I give free of all duty whatsoever to my Trustees hereinbefore named such a sum of money as they shall carefully ascertain and in their uncontrolled discretion consider ample and sufficient by its investments to yield income amounting to the sum of £4,000 sterling per annum and not less and I direct my Trustees to invest the same sum and the said sum and the investments for the time being representing it I hereinafter refer to as 'the Matoppos and Bulawayo Fund' And I direct that my Trustees shall for ever apply in such manner as in their uncontrolled discretion they shall think fit the income of the Matoppos and Bulawayo Fund in preserving protecting maintaining adorning and beautifying the said burial-place and hill and their surroundings and shall for ever apply in such manner as in their uncontrolled discretion they shall think fit the balance of the income of the Matoppos and Bulawayo Fund and any rents and profits of my said landed properties near Bulawayo in the cultivation as aforesaid of such property And in particular I direct my Trustees that a portion of my Sauerdale property a part of my said landed property near Bulawayo be planted with every possible tree and be made and preserved and maintained as a Park for the people of Bulawayo and that they complete the dam at my Westacre property if it is not completed at my death and make a short railway line from Bulawayo to Westacre so that the people of Bulawayo may enjoy the glory of the Matoppos from Saturday to Monday.

9. I give free of all duty whatsoever to my Trustees hereinbefore named such a sum of money as they shall carefully ascertain and in their uncontrolled discretion consider ample and sufficient by its investments to yield income amounting to the sum of £2,000 sterling per annum and not less and I direct my Trustees to invest the same sum and the said sum and the investments for the time being representing it I hereinafter refer to as 'the Inyanga Fund' And I direct that my Trustees shall for ever apply in such manner as in their absolute discretion they shall think fit the income of the Inyanga Fund and any rents and profits of my said landed property at or near Inyanga in the cultivation of such property and in particular I direct that with regard to such property irrigation should be the first object of my Trustees.

10. For the guidance of my Trustees I wish to record that in the cultivation of my said landed properties I include such things as experimental farming forestry market and other gardening and fruit farming irrigation and the teaching of any of those things and establishing and maintaining an Agricultural College.

11. I give all the interest to which I may at my death be entitled in any freehold copyhold or leasehold hereditaments in Dalston or elsewhere in the County of London to my Trustees hereinbefore named Upon trust that my Trustees shall lease or let and generally manage but not sell the same and pay all requisite outgoings usually paid by me in respect thereof and maintain the same in proper repair and insured against fire And upon trust that my Trustees shall so long as any one or more of my own brothers and sisters (which does not include my sister of the half blood) shall be living pay the net income derived from the said hereditaments to such of my own brothers and sisters aforesaid as shall for the time being be living and while more than one to be divided between them in equal shares And shall after the death of the survivor

of them such brothers and sisters hold my interest in the said estate and the rents and profits thereof Upon the trusts hereinafter contained concerning the same and inasmuch as those trusts are educational trusts for the benefit of the Empire I hope the means will be found for enabling my Trustees to retain my interest in the said estate unsold and with that object I authorize and require them to endeavour to obtain at the expense of my estate a private or other Act of Parliament or other sufficient authority enabling and requiring them to retain the same unsold.

12. I give the sum of £100,000 free of all duty whatsoever to my old College Oriel College in the University of Oxford and I direct that the receipt of the Bursar or other proper officer of the College shall be a complete discharge for that legacy and inasmuch as I gather that the erection of an extension to High Street of the College buildings would cost about £22,500 and that the loss to the College revenue caused by pulling down of houses to make room for the said new College buildings would be about £250 per annum I direct that the sum of £40,000 part of the said sum of £100,000 shall be applied in the first place in the erection of the said new College buildings and that the remainder of such sum of £40,000 shall be held as a fund by the income whereof the aforesaid loss to the College revenue shall so far as possible be made good And inasmuch as I gather that there is a deficiency in the College revenue of some £1,500 per annum whereby the Fellowships are impoverished and the status of the College is lowered I direct that the sum of £40,000 further part of the said sum of £100,000 shall be held as a fund by the income whereof the income of such of the resident Fellows of the College as work for the honour and dignity of the College shall be increased And I further direct that the sum of £10,000 further part of the said sum of £100,000 shall be held as a fund by the income whereof the dignity and comfort of the High Table may be maintained by which means the dignity and comfort of the resident Fellows may be increased And I further direct that the sum of £10,000 the remainder of the said sum of £100,000 shall be held as a repair fund the income whereof shall be expended in maintaining and repairing the College buildings And finally as the College authorities live secluded from the world and so are like children as to commercial matters I would advise them to consult my Trustees as to the investment of these various funds for they would receive great help and assistance from the advice of my Trustees in such matters and I direct that any investment made pursuant to such advice shall whatsoever it may be be an authorized investment for the money applied in making it.

13. I give my property following that is to say my residence known as 'De Groote Schuur' situate near Mowbray in the Cape Division in the said Colony together with all furniture plate and other articles contained therein at the time of my death and all other land belonging to me situated under Table Mountain including my property known as 'Mosterts' to my Trustees hereinbefore named upon and subject to the conditions following that is to say—

(i.) The said property (excepting any furniture or like articles which have become useless) shall not nor shall any portion thereof at any time be sold let or otherwise alienated.

(ii.) No buildings for suburban residences shall at any time be erected on the said property and any buildings which may be erected thereon shall be used exclusively for public purposes and shall be in a style of architecture similar to or in harmony with my said residence.

(iii.) The said residence and its gardens and grounds shall be retained for a residence for the Prime Minister for the time being of the said Federal Government of the States of South Africa to which I have referred in clause 6 hereof my intention being to provide a suitable official residence for the First Minister in that Government befitting the dignity of his position and until there shall be such a Federal Government may be used as a park for the people.

(iv.) The grave of the late Jan Hendrik Hofmeyr upon the said property shall be protected and access be permitted thereto at all reasonable times by any member of the Hofmeyr family for the purpose of inspection or maintenance.

14. I give to my Trustees hereinbefore named such a sum of money as they shall carefully ascertain and in their uncontrolled discretion consider to be ample and sufficient to yield income amounting to the sum of one thousand pounds sterling per annum and not less upon trust that such income shall be applied and expended for the purposes following (that is to say)—

(i.) On and for keeping and maintaining for the use of the Prime Minister for the time being of the said Federal Government of at least two carriage horses one or more carriages and sufficient stable servants.

(ii.) On and for keeping and maintaining in good order the flower and kitchen gardens appertaining to the said residence.

(iii.) On and for the payment of the wages or earnings including board and lodging of two competent men servants to be housed kept and employed in domestic service in the said residence.

(iv.) On and for the improvement repair renewal and insurance of the said residence furniture plate and other articles.

15. I direct that subject to the conditions and trusts hereinbefore contained the said Federal Government shall from the time it shall be constituted have the management administration and control of the said devise and legacy and that my Trustees shall as soon as may be thereafter vest and pay the devise and legacy given by the two last preceding clauses hereof in and to such Government if a corporate body capable of accepting and holding the same or if not then in some suitable corporate body so capable named by such Government and that in the meantime my Trustees shall in their uncontrolled discretion manage administer and control the said devise and legacy.

16. Whereas I consider that the education of young Colonists at one of the Universities in the United Kingdom is of great advantage to them for giving breadth to their views for their instruction in life and manners and for instilling into their minds the advantage to the Colonies as well as to the United Kingdom of the retention of the unity of the Empire And whereas in the case of young Colonists studying at a University in the United Kingdom I attach very great importance to the University having a residential system such as is in force at the Universities of Oxford and Cambridge for without it those students are at the most critical period of their lives left without any supervision And whereas there are at the present time 50 or more students from South Africa studying at the University of Edinburgh many of whom are attracted there

by its excellent medical school and I should like to establish some of the Scholarships hereinafter mentioned in that University but owing to its not having such a residential system as aforesaid I feel obliged to refrain from doing so And whereas my own University the University of Oxford has such a system and I suggest that it should try and extend its scope so as if possible to make its medical school at least as good as that at the University of Edinburgh And whereas I also desire to encourage and foster an appreciation of the advantages which I implicitly believe will result from the union of the English-speaking peoples throughout the world and to encourage in the students from the United States of North America who will benefit from the American Scholarships to be established for the reason above given at the University of Oxford under this my Will an attachment to the country from which they have sprung but without I hope withdrawing them or their sympathies from the land of their adoption or birth Now therefore I direct my Trustees as soon as may be after my death and either simultaneously or gradually as they shall find convenient and if gradually then in such order as they shall think fit to establish for male students the Scholarships hereinafter directed to be established each of which shall be of the yearly value of £300 and be tenable at any College in the University of Oxford for three consecutive academical years.

17. I direct my Trustees to establish certain Scholarships and these Scholarships I sometimes hereinafter refer to as 'the Colonial Scholarships.'

18. The appropriation of the Colonial Scholarships and the numbers to be annually filled up shall be in accordance with the following table:—

Total No. appropriated.	To be tenable by Students of or from	No. of Scholarships to be filled up in each year.
9	Rhodesia	3 and no more.
3	The South African College School in the Colony of the Cape of Good Hope	1 and no more.
3	The Stellenbosch College School in the same Colony	1 and no more.
3	The Diocesan College School of Rondebosch in the same Colony	1 and no more.
3	St. Andrews College School Grahamstown in the same Colony ..	1 and no more.
3	The Colony of Natal	1 and no more.
3	The Colony of New South Wales	1 and no more.
3	The Colony of Victoria	1 and no more.
3	The Colony of South Australia	1 and no more.
3	The Colony of Queensland	1 and no more.
3	The Colony of Western Australia	1 and no more.
3	The Colony of Tasmania	1 and no more.
3	The Colony of New Zealand	1 and no more.
3	The Province of Ontario in the Dominion of Canada	1 and no more.
3	The Province of Quebec in the Dominion of Canada	1 and no more.
3	The Colony or Island of Newfoundland and its Dependencies ..	1 and no more.
3	The Colony or Islands of the Bermudas	1 and no more.
3	The Colony or Island of Jamaica	1 and no more.

19. I further direct my Trustees to establish additional Scholarships sufficient in number for the appropriation in the next following clause hereof directed and those Scholarships I sometimes hereinafter refer to as 'the American Scholarships.'

20. I appropriate two of the American Scholarships to each of the present States and Territories of the United States of North America Provided that if any of the said Territories shall in my lifetime be admitted as a State the Scholarships appropriated to such Territory shall be appropriated to such State and that my Trustees may in their uncontrolled discretion withhold for such time as they shall think fit the appropriation of Scholarships to any Territory.

21. I direct that of the two Scholarships appropriated to a State or Territory not more than one shall be filled up in any year so that at no time shall more than two Scholarships be held for the same State or Territory.

22. The Scholarships shall be paid only out of income and in the event at any time of income being insufficient for payment in full of all the Scholarships for the time being payable I direct that (without prejudice to the vested interests of holders for the time being of Scholarships) the following order of priority shall regulate the payment of the Scholarships.

(i) First the Scholarships of students of or from Rhodesia shall be paid.

(ii) Secondly the Scholarships of students from the said South African Stellenbosch Rondebosch and St. Andrews Schools shall be paid.

(iii) Thirdly the remainder of the Colonial Scholarships shall be paid and if there shall not be sufficient income for the purpose such Scholarships shall abate proportionately; and

(iv) Fourthly the American Scholarships shall be paid and if there shall not be sufficient income for the purpose such Scholarships shall abate proportionately.

23. My desire being that the students who shall be elected to the Scholarships shall not be merely bookworms I direct that in the election of a student to a Scholarship regard shall be had to (i) his literary and scholastic attainments (ii) his fondness of and success in manly outdoor sports such as cricket football and the like (iii) his qualities of manhood truth courage devotion to duty sympathy for and protection of the weak kindliness unselfishness and fellowship and (iv) his exhibition during school days of moral force of character and of instincts to lead and to take an interest in his schoolmates for those latter attributes will be likely in afterlife to guide him to esteem the performance of public duties as his highest aim As mere suggestions for the guidance of those who will have the choice of students for the Scholarships I record that—

(i) My ideal qualified student would combine these four qualifications in the proportions of 4/10ths for the first 2/10ths for the second 2/10ths for the third and 2/10ths for the fourth qualification so that according to my ideas if the maximum number of marks for any Scholarship were 100 they would be apportioned as follows:—40 to the first qualification and 20 to each of the second third and fourth qualifications.

(ii) The marks for first qualification would be awarded by examination for the second and third qualifications by ballot by the fellow-students of the candidates and for the fourth qualification by the head master of the candidate's school; and

(iii) The results of the awards would be sent simultaneously to my Trustees or some one appointed to receive the same. I say simultaneously so that no awarding party should know the result of the award of any other awarding party.

24. No student shall be qualified or disqualified for election to a Scholarship on account of his race or religious opinions.

25. The election to Scholarships shall be by the Trustees after consultation with the minister having the control of education in such colony province state or territory except in the cases of the four schools hereinbefore mentioned.

26. A qualified student who has been elected as aforesaid shall within six calendar months after his election or as soon thereafter as he can be admitted into residence or within such extended time as my Trustees shall allow commence residence as an undergraduate at some college in the University of Oxford.

27. The scholarships shall be payable to him from the time when he shall commence such residence.

28. I desire that the Scholars holding the scholarships shall be distributed amongst the Colleges of the University of Oxford and not resort in undue numbers to one or more Colleges only.

29. Notwithstanding anything hereinbefore contained my Trustees may in their uncontrolled discretion suspend for such time as they shall think fit or remove any Scholar from his scholarship.

30. My Trustees may from time to time make vary and repeal regulations either general or affecting specified Scholarships only with regard to all or any of the following matters that is to say:—

(i) The election whether after examination or otherwise of qualified Students to the Scholarships or any of them and the method whether by examination or otherwise in which their qualifications are to be ascertained.

(ii) The tenure of the Scholarships by scholars.

(iii) The suspension and removal of scholars from their Scholarships.

(iv) The method and times of payment of the Scholarships.

(v) The method of giving effect to my wish expressed in clause 28 hereof and

(vi) Any and every other matter with regard to the Scholarships or any of them with regard to which they shall consider regulations necessary or desirable.

31. My Trustees may from time to time authorize regulations with regard to the election whether after examination or otherwise of qualified students for Scholarships and to the method

whether by examination or otherwise in which their qualifications are to be ascertained to be made—

(i) By a school in respect of the scholarships tenable by its students and—

(ii) By the Minister aforesaid of a Colony Province State or Territory in respect of the Scholarships tenable by students from such Colony Province State or Territory.

32. Regulations made under the last preceding clause hereof if and when approved of and not before by my Trustees shall be equivalent in all respects to regulations made by my Trustees.

33. No regulations made under clause 30 or made and approved of under clauses 31 and 32 hereof shall be inconsistent with any of the provisions herein contained.

34. In order that the scholars past and present may have opportunities of meeting and discussing their experiences and prospects I desire that my Trustees shall annually give a dinner to the past and present scholars able and willing to attend at which I hope my Trustees or some of them will be able to be present and to which they will I hope from time to time invite as guests persons who have shown sympathy with the views expressed by me in this my Will.

35. My Trustees hereinbefore named shall free of all duty whatsoever at such time as they shall think fit set apart out of my estate such a Scholarship fund (either by appropriation of existing investments or by making other investments or partly in one way and partly in the other) as they shall consider sufficient by its income to pay the Scholarships and in addition a yearly sum of £1,000.

36. My Trustees shall invest the Scholarship fund and the other funds hereinbefore established or any part thereof respectively in such investments in any part of the world as they shall in their uncontrolled discretion think fit and that without regard to any rules of equity governing investments by trustees and without any responsibility or liability should they committ any breach of any such rule with power to vary and such investments for others of a like nature.

37. Investments to bearer held as an investment may be deposited by my Trustees for safe custody in their names with any banker or banking company or with any company whose business it is to take charge of investments of that nature and my Trustees shall not be responsible for any loss incurred in consequence of such deposit.

38. My Trustees shall after the death of the survivor of my said brothers and sisters hold my said interest in the said Dalston estate as an accretion to the capital of the Scholarship fund and the net rents and profits thereof as an accretion to the income of the Scholarship fund and shall by means of the increase of income of the Scholarship fund so arising establish such number of further Scholarships of the yearly value of £300 each as such increase shall be sufficient to establish. Such further Scholarships shall be for students of such British Colony or Colonies or Dependency or Dependencies whether hereinbefore mentioned or not as my Trustees shall in their uncontrolled discretion think fit And I direct that every such further Scholarship shall correspond in all respects with the Scholarships hereinbefore directed to be established and that the preceding provisions of this my Will which apply to the Scholarships hereinbefore directed to be established or any of them shall where applicable apply to such further Scholarships.

39. Until the Scholarship fund shall have been set apart as aforesaid I charge the same and the Scholarships upon the residue of my real and personal estate.

40. I give the residue of my real and personal estate unto such of them the said Earl of Rosebery Earl Grey Alfred Beit William Thomas Stead Lewis Loyd Michell and Bourchier Francis Hawksley as shall be living at my death absolutely and if more than one as joint tenants.

41. My Trustees in the administration of the trust business may instead of acting personally employ and pay a Secretary or Agent to transact all business and do all acts required to be done in the trust including the receipt and payment of money.

42. My intention is that there shall be always at least three Trustees of my Will so far as it relates to the Scholarship Trusts and therefore I direct that whenever there shall be less than three Trustees a new Trustee or new Trustees shall be forthwith appointed.

In witness whereof I have hereunto set my hand the day and year first above written.

Signed by the said Testator The Right Honourable Cecil John Rhodes as and for his last Will and Testament in the presence of us both present at the same time who at his request in his presence and in the presence of each other have hereunto subscribed our names as witnesses } C. J. RHODES.

CHARLES T. METCALFE,
P. JOURDAN,
ARTHUR SAWYER.

Jan/1990
Really January 1901.

On account of the extraordinary eccentricity of Mr. Stead though having always a great respect for him but feeling the objects of my Will would be embarrassed by his views I hereby revoke his appointment as one of my executors.

C. J. RHODES.

Witnesses
LEWIS L. MICHELL,
H. GODDEN.

This is a further Codicil to my Will I note the German Emperor has made instruction in English compulsory in German schools I leave five yearly scholarships at Oxford of £250 per ann. to students of German birth the scholars to be nominated by the German Emperor for the time being Each scholarship to continue for three years so that each year after the first three there will be fifteen scholars The object is that an understanding between the three great powers will render war impossible and educational relations make the strongest tie.

C. J. RHODES.

Witnesses
G. V. WEBB,
W. G. V. CARTER.

America has already been provided for. C. J. R.

A yearly amount should be put in British Consols to provide for the bequests in my Will when the diamond mines work out: the above is an instruction to the Trustees of my Will.

C. J. R.

Jan/1901.

As a further Codicil to my Will I leave J. Grimmer ten thousand pounds and the use of my Inyanga farms for his life This bequest takes the place of the previous written paper given to him.

C. J. RHODES.

Witness
    W. G. V. CARTER.
    H. GODDEN.

This is a Codicil to the last Will and Testament of me THE RIGHT HONOURABLE CECIL JOHN RHODES of Cape Town in the Colony of the Cape of Good Hope which Will is dated the First day of July One thousand eight hundred and ninety-nine I appoint the Right Honourable Alfred Lord Milner to be an Executor and Trustee of my said Will jointly with those named in my said Will as my Executors and Trustees and in all respects as though he had been originally appointed one of my Executors and Trustees by my said Will And I associate him with my residuary legatees and devisees named in clause 40 of my said Will desiring and declaring that they and he are my residuary legatees and devisees in joint tenancy I revoke clauses 23, 24 and 25 in my said Will and in lieu thereof substitute the three following clauses which I direct shall be read as though originally clauses 23, 24 and 25 of my said Will:—

23. My desire being that the students who shall be elected to the Scholarships shall not be merely bookworms I direct that in the election of a student to a Scholarship regard shall be had to (i) his literary and scholastic attainments (ii) his fondness of and success in manly outdoor sports such as cricket football and the like (iii) his qualities of manhood truth courage devotion to duty sympathy for the protection of the weak kindliness unselfishness and fellow-ship and (iv) his exhibition during school days of moral force of character and of instincts to lead and to take an interest in his schoolmates for those latter attributes will be likely in after-life to guide him to esteem the performance of public duties as his highest aim As mere suggestions for the guidance of those who will have the choice of students for the Scholarships I record that (i) my ideal qualified student would combine these four qualifications in the proportions of 3/10ths for the first 2/10ths for the second 3/10ths for the third and 2/10ths for the fourth qualification so that according to my ideas if the maximum number of marks for any Scholarship were 200 they would be apportioned as follows—60 to each of the first and third qualifications and 40 to each of the second and fourth qualifications (ii) the marks for the several qualifications would be awarded independently as follows (that is to say) the marks for the first qualification by examination for the second and third qualifications respectively by ballot by the fellow-students of the candidates and for the fourth qualification by the head master of the

candidate's school and (iii) the results of the awards (that is to say the marks obtained by each candidate for each qualification) would be sent as soon as possible for consideration to the Trustees or to some person or persons appointed to receive the same and the person or persons so appointed would ascertain by averaging the marks in blocks of 20 marks each of all candidates the best ideal qualified students.

24. No student shall be qualified or disqualified for election to a Scholarship on account of his race or religious opinions.

25. Except in the cases of the four schools hereinbefore mentioned the election to Scholarships shall be by the Trustees after such (if any) consultation as they shall think fit with the Minister having the control of education in such Colony Province State or Territory.

In witness whereof I have hereunto set my hand this Eleventh day of October One thousand nine hundred and one.

Signed by the said Cecil John Rhodes as and for a Codicil to
    his last Will and Testament in the presence of us all
    present at the same time who in his presence at his   } C. J. RHODES.
    request and in the presence of each other have
    hereunto subscribed our names as witnesses.

    GEORGE FROST,
    FRANK BROWN,
        Servants to Mr. BEIT,
            26, Park Lane,
                London.

Trustees and Principal Officers
of the Rhodes Trust

Trustees

The Earl of Rosebery (1847–1929) 1902–17 (chair)
Earl Grey (1851–1917) 1902–17
Alfred Beit (1853–1906) 1902–6
Sir Lewis Michell (1842–1928) 1902–17
Bouchier Francis Hawksley (d. 1915) 1902–15
Viscount Milner (1854–1925) 1902–25 (chair 1917–25)
Sir Leander Starr Jameson (1853–1917) 1902–17
Sir Otto Beit (1865–1930) 1917–30 (chair 1925–30)
Lord Lovat (1871–1933) 1917–33 (chair 1930–3)
Rudyard Kipling (1865–1936) 1917–25
The Rt. Hon. L. S. Amery (1873–1955) 1919–55 (chair 1933–55)
Earl Baldwin of Bewdley (1867–1947) 1925–47
Sir Edward Peacock (1871–1962) 1925–62 (chair 1955–62)
Geoffrey Dawson (1874–1944) 1925–44
Sir Douglas Hogg (Viscount Hailsham) (1872–1950) 1925–9
The Rt. Hon. H. A. L. Fisher (1865–1940) 1925–40
Sir Reginald Sothern Holland (1876–1948) 1932–48
The Very Revd John Lowe (1899–1960) 1940–60
Capt G. T. Hutchinson (1880–1948) 1940–8
Lord Hailey (1872–1969) 1941–64
The Rt. Hon. Malcolm MacDonald (1901–81) 1948–57
Charles H. G. Millis (1894–1984) 1948–61
Sir Kenneth Wheare (1907–79) 1948–77 (chair 1962–9)
Sir George Abell (1904–89) 1949–74 (chair 1969–74)
Lt. Gen. Sir Archibald Nye (1895–1967) 1957–67
Sir Oliver Franks (Lord Franks) (1905–92) 1957–73
Viscount Harcourt (1908–79) 1957–79 (chair 1974–9)
Viscount Amory (1899–1981) 1961–9
John G. Phillimore (1908–   ) 1961–74
Sir Edward Boyle (Lord Boyle of Handsworth) (1923–81) 1965–9
Professor Don K. Price (1910–95) 1968–78
Sir William Paton (1917–93) 1968–87 (chair 1979–82)
Sir John Baring (Lord Ashburton (1928–   ) 1970–99 (chair 1987–99)
Lord Blake (1916–   ) 1971–87 (chair 1983–7)

Marmaduke Hussey (1923–) 1972–92
W. Greig Barr (1917–) 1975–87
Sir Robert Armstrong (Lord Armstrong of Ilminster) (1927–) 1975–97
Sir John Habbakuk (1915–) 1977–85
Mrs Mary Moore (1930–) 1984–96
Sir John Sainsbury (Lord Sainsbury of Preston Candover) (1927–) 1984–98
Sir Richard Southwood (1931–) 1986– (chair from 1999)
Duncan Stewart (1930–96) 1986–96
Dr J. M. Roberts (1928–) 1987–95
The Rt. Hon. William Waldegrave (Lord Waldegrave) (1946–) 1992–
Dr Colin Lucas (1940–) 1995–
Professor Robert O'Neill (1936–) 1995–
Mrs R. L. Deech (1943–) 1996–
Sir John Kerr (1942–) 1997–
Rosalind Hedley Miller (1966–) 1999–

Secretaries of the Trust

Organizing Secretary of the Scholarships
Sir George Parkin (1846–1922) 1902–20

London Secretaries
Douglas Brodie and Charles Boyd 1902–5
Charles Boyd (1869–1919) 1905–8
Mrs Dorothea Mavor (Lady Butterworth) 1908–16
Thomas L. Gilmour (1859–36) 1916–19

General Secretaries
Sir Edward Grigg (Lord Altrincham) (1879–1955) 1919–21, 1923–5
Geoffrey Dawson 1921–3
Philip Kerr (Marquess of Lothian) (1882–1940) 1925–39
Lord Elton (1892–1973) 1939–59

Oxford Secretaries (Wardens of Rhodes House)
Sir Francis Wylie (1865–1952) 1903–31
Sir Carleton Allen (1887–1966) 1931–52
Sir Edgar Williams (1912–98) 1952–9

Secretaries to the Trust and Wardens of Rhodes House
Sir Edgar Williams (1912–98) 1959–80
Dr Robin Fletcher (1922–) 1980–9
Sir Anthony Kenny (1931–) 1989–99

Principal Overseas Secretaries

American Secretaries
Frank Aydelotte (1880–56) 1918–52
Courtney Smith (1916–69) 1953–69

Index